SOMETHING ABOUT THE AUTHOR®

Something about
the Author *was named
an "Outstanding
Reference Source,"
the highest honor given
by the American
Library Association
Reference and Adult
Services Division.*

ISSN 0276-816X

SOMETHING ABOUT THE AUTHOR®

**Facts and Pictures about Authors
and Illustrators of Books for Young People**

volume 211

GALE
CENGAGE Learning™

Detroit • New York • San Francisco • New Haven, Conn • Waterville, Maine • London

GALE
CENGAGE Learning™

Something about the Author, Volume 211

Project Editor: Lisa Kumar

Editorial: Laura Avery, Pamela Bow, Jim Craddock, Amy Fuller, Andrea Henderson, Margaret Mazurkiewicz, Tracie Moy, Jeff Muhr, Kathy Nemeh, Mary Ruby, Mike Tyrkus

Permissions: Sara Crane, Sue Rudolph, Jhanay Williams

Imaging and Multimedia: Savannah Gignac, John Watkins

Composition and Electronic Capture: Amy Darga

Manufacturing: Drew Kalasky

Product Manager: Janet Witalec

For product information and technology assistance, contact us at
Gale Customer Support, 1-800-877-4253.
For permission to use material from this text or product,
submit all requests online at **www.cengage.com/permissions.**
Further permissions questions can be emailed to
permissionrequest@cengage.com

Gale
27500 Drake Rd.
Farmington Hills, MI, 48331-3535

LIBRARY OF CONGRESS CATALOG CARD NUMBER 62-52046

ISBN-13: 978-1-4144-4224-2
ISBN-10: 1-4144-4224-6

ISSN 0276-816X

This title is also available as an e-book.
ISBN-13: 978-1-4144-6443-5
ISBN-10: 1-4144-6443-6
Contact your Gale, Cengage Learning sales representative for ordering information.

Printed in the United States of America
1 2 3 4 5 6 7 14 13 12 11 10

Contents

Authors in Forthcoming Volumes ix

Introduction xi

SATA Product Advisory Board xiii

Illustrations Index 231

Author Index 265

A

Alley, Robert W.
    See Alley, R.W. 1

Alley, R.W. 1955- 1

Anderson, Brian 1974- 8

B

Bai, Durga 10

Banks, Erin Bennett 1978- 11

Barlow, Steve 1952- 13

Béha, Philippe 15

Bennett, Erin Susanne
    See Banks, Erin Bennett 11

Bergstein, Rita M. 18

Blake, Quentin 1932- 20

Booraem, Ellen 31

C

Calder, Lyn
    See Calmenson, Stephanie 33

Calmenson, Stephanie 1952- 33

Casilla, Robert 1959- 40

Chodos-Irvine, Margaret 43

D

DeLange, Alex Pardo
    See Pardo DeLange, Alex 135

Dillon, Anna
    See Scott, Michael 157

Dogar, Sharon 1962- 46

Doran, Colleen 1963- 47

Drake, Salamanda
    See Barlow, Steve 13

Dunbar, Polly 1980- 50

E

Edgson, Alison 54

Evans, Freddi Williams 1957- 55

F

Fox, Mem 1946- 57

Fox, Merrion Frances
    See Fox, Mem 57

G

Gibson, Sarah P. 1962- 63

Goodman Koz, Paula 63

Grant, Judyann Ackerman 64

Green, Jessica 64

Greenberg, Jan 1942- 65

Guiberson, Brenda Z. 1946- 70

H

Herlong, Madaline
    See Herlong, M.H. 76

Herlong, M.H. 76

Hoffman, Mary 1945- 77

Hoffman, Mary Margaret
    See Hoffman, Mary 77

Horacek, Judy 1961- 85

J

Jennings, Linda 1937- 87

Jennings, Linda M.
    See Jennings, Linda 87

K

Kelley, Marty 1971- 90

Kimmelman, Leslie 1958- 91

Kirsch, Vincent X. 94

Klein, Lisa 1958- 95

Klein, Lisa M.
    See Klein, Lisa 95

Koz, Paula G.
    See Goodman Koz, Paula 63

L

Landowne, Youme 1970- 97

Lassiter, Mary
    See Hoffman, Mary 77

Layson, Annelex Hofstra 1938(?)- 98

Leszczynski, Diana 99

Levert, Mireille 1956- 99

Levinson, Nancy Smiler 1938- 102

Lewis, Earl Bradley
    See Lewis, E.B. 107

Lewis, E.B. 1956- 107

Littlewood, Karin 111

Lowe, Steve
    See Barlow, Steve 13

M

MacLean, Jill 1941- 114

Manning, Maurie
    See Manning, Maurie J. 115

Manning, Maurie J. 115

Manning, Maurie Jo
    See Manning, Maurie J. 115

Marklew, Gilly 117

Maxwell, B.E. 1957- 118

Maxwell, Bruce E.
    See Maxwell, B.E. 118

McNaughton, Colin 1951- 119

Meserve, Jessica 126

Metaxas, Eric 1963- 127

Morden, Simon 1966(?)- 130

Morton, Christine
    See Morton-Shaw, Christine 131

Morton-Shaw, Christine 1957- 131

O

Offill, Jenny 1968- 133

P

Pardo DeLange, Alex 135

Pearson, Mary E. 1955- 137

Polcovar, Jane 1948- 139

R

Rappaport, Doreen 1939- 141

Reed, Mike 1951- 146

Reibstein, Mark 148

Renaud, Anne 1957- 149

Rogers, Gregory 1957- 151

Rouss, Sylvia 154

S

Sand-Eveland, Cyndi 156

Sandemose, Iben 1950- 156

Scott, Michael 1959- 157

Scott, Mike
    See Scott, Michael 157

Sederman, Marty 160

Seskin, Steve 1953- 161

Sheinmel, Courtney 1977- 163

Sigsawa, Keiichi 1972- 165

Sobol, Richard 165

Stein, David Ezra 168

Stewart, Joel 169

Sweet, Melissa 1956- 172

T

Tillman, Nancy 177

Turner, Pamela S. 1957- 178

U

Uegaki, Chieri 1969- 181

Urbain, Cat 1956- 182

Urbain, Catherine
    See Urbain, Cat 182

V

Vande Velde, Vivian 1951- 184

Van Leeuwen, Jean 1937- 191

W

Watson, Richard Jesse 1951- 200

Watson, Sasha 203

Winget, Susan 205

Winnick, Karen B. 1946- 206

Wood, Jacqueline
    See Wood, Jakki 207

Authors in Forthcoming Volumes

Below are some of the authors and illustrators that will be featured in upcoming volumes of *SATA*. These include new entries on the swiftly rising stars of the field, as well as completely revised and updated entries (indicated with *) on some of the most notable and best-loved creators of books for children.

*Ron Brooks ▌ One of the first illustrators in his native Australia to see his books published in other countries, Brooks has collaborated with noted Australian authors that include Margaret Wild, Walter McVitty, and Margaret Perversi. In addition to working as an illustrator, the award-winning Brooks has also created the original, self-illustrated picture books *Annie's Rainbow* and *Timothy and Gramps,* and works as a sculptor and educator.

*Roz Chast ▌ Chast, a cartoonist, creates humorous, offbeat drawings about the absurdities of everyday life that have made her popular with readers of the *New Yorker,* where she serves as a staff cartoonist. Her work has been collected in books such as *Unscientific Americans, Proof of Life on Earth,* and *Childproof: Cartoons about Parents and Children.* In addition to cartooning, Chast has also provided illustrations for picture books, among them Erin McKean's *Weird and Wonderful Words.*

Sarah Dyer ▌ In addition to working as a teacher at the college level, Dyer is a British illustrator and children's book writer whose self-illustrated picture books include *Five Little Fiends, Mrs. Muffly's Monster,* and *The Girl with the Bird's-Nest Hair,* as well as the "Clementine and Mungo" series. Her debut picture book *Five Little Fiends* was honored with both a Bronze Smarties' prize and a United Kingdom reading award.

Alan Gratz ▌ Based in North Carolina, Gratz boasts a writing resume that includes plays, television scripts, a popular Web log, and radio advertising. He is best known to teen readers for his novels *Samurai Shortstop, The Brooklyn Nine: A Novel in Nine Innings,* and his "Horatio Wilkes" mysteries, which are set in Elizabethan England and are based on the plays of Shakespeare.

*Kathleen Karr ▌ Karr's award-winning historical novels for young teens, which include *The Cave, In the Kaiser's Clutch, The 7th Knot,* and *Bone Dry,* are noted for their humor, high-action plots, and boldly drawn characters. Transporting readers to settings that range from the streets of New York City to the "Wild West" of the late 1800s to even more exotic locales around the world, her works also feature compelling portrayals of young people confronting adult-sized challenges and dealing with these difficulties in an optimistic fashion.

Anna Levine ▌ A Canadian-born writer and educator who now makes her home in Israel, Levine is the author of *Running on Eggs* and *Freefall,* a pair of award-winning young adult novels. Levine's picture book *Jodie's Hanukkah Dig* conveys her passion for archeology in its story of a girl who assists in her father's excavation of an ancient Middle-Eastern battlefield.

*Lisa McCue ▌ In her prolific career, McCue has illustrated many children's books, among them Mary Blount Christian's canine detective series "Sebastian (Super Sleuth)" and new editions of Don Freeman's popular "Corduroy" series about a lovable bear, as well as stories by Leslie Kimmelman, Judy Delton, and Dori Chaconas, among others. When she has the time, McCue also creates original, self-illustrated tales for very young children, several coauthored with her father, Dick McCue.

Bernadette Peters ▌ An award-winning actress and singer who is known for her curly red hair and upbeat attitude, Peters is one of the most beloved stars on Broadway. In addition to her work on Broadway and in concert, she has appeared in films and on television where she even performed alongside Jim Henson's Muppets. Inspired by her concern for stray animals in her native New York City, Peters wrote the picture books *Broadway Barks* and *Stella Is a Star,* both of which include a CD featuring her singing. Portions of the proceeds of both books benefit the Broadway Barks charity.

David Michael Slater ▌ A teacher and writer, Slater creates humorous stories that border on the nonsensical and include *Missy Swiss, Cheese Louise!, Flour Girl: A Recipe for Disaster,* and *A Wrench in the Works.* In *Missy Swiss* Slater exposes the secret world inside the average refrigerator after the door closes, while older readers will thrill to his "Sacred Books" novels, in which brave siblings Daphna and Dexter Wax are destined to save the entire world.

*David Wood ▌ Honored by Queen Elizabeth for his work in children's theatre, Wood is a writer, director, actor, and playwright whose touring company, Whirligig Theatre, is devoted entirely to sharing his love of drama with children. His plays *The Gingerbread Man* and *The Owl and the Pussycat Went to See . . .* revisit traditional tales, while *Flibberty and the Penguin* and *The See-Saw Tree* introduce original stories to young audiences. Wood has also contributed to the growth of children's theatre in both the United Kingdom and the United States through his influential book *Theatre for Children: A Guide to Writing, Adapting, Directing, and Directing.*

Introduction

Something about the Author (*SATA*) is an ongoing reference series that examines the lives and works of authors and illustrators of books for children. *SATA* includes not only well-known writers and artists but also less prominent individuals whose works are just coming to be recognized. This series is often the only readily available information source on emerging authors and illustrators. You'll find *SATA* informative and entertaining, whether you are a student, a librarian, an English teacher, a parent, or simply an adult who enjoys children's literature.

What's Inside *SATA*

SATA provides detailed information about authors and illustrators who span the full time range of children's literature, from early figures like John Newbery and L. Frank Baum to contemporary figures like Judy Blume and Richard Peck. Authors in the series represent primarily English-speaking countries, particularly the United States, Canada, and the United Kingdom. Also included, however, are authors from around the world whose works are available in English translation. The writings represented in *SATA* include those created intentionally for children and young adults as well as those written for a general audience and known to interest younger readers. These writings cover the entire spectrum of children's literature, including picture books, humor, folk and fairy tales, animal stories, mystery and adventure, science fiction and fantasy, historical fiction, poetry and nonsense verse, drama, biography, and nonfiction. Obituaries are also included in *SATA* and are intended not only as death notices but also as concise overviews of people's lives and work. Additionally, each edition features newly revised and updated entries for a selection of *SATA* listees who remain of interest to today's readers and who have been active enough to require extensive revisions of their earlier biographies.

Autobiography Feature

Beginning with Volume 103, many volumes of *SATA* feature one or more specially commissioned autobiographical essays. These unique essays, averaging about ten thousand words in length and illustrated with an abundance of personal photos, present an entertaining and informative first-person perspective on the lives and careers of prominent authors and illustrators profiled in *SATA*.

Two Convenient Indexes

In response to suggestions from librarians, *SATA* indexes no longer appear in every volume but are included in alternate (odd-numbered) volumes of the series, beginning with Volume 57.

SATA continues to include two indexes that cumulate with each alternate volume: the Illustrations Index, arranged by the name of the illustrator, gives the number of the volume and page where the illustrator's work appears in the current volume as well as all preceding volumes in the series; the Author Index gives the number of the volume in which a person's biographical sketch, autobiographical essay, or obituary appears in the current volume as well as all preceding volumes in the series.

These indexes also include references to authors and illustrators who appear in *Gale's Yesterday's Authors of Books for Children, Children's Literature Review,* and *Something about the Author Autobiography Series.*

Easy-to-Use Entry Format

Whether you're already familiar with the *SATA* series or just getting acquainted, you will want to be aware of the kind of information that an entry provides. In every *SATA* entry the editors attempt to give as complete a picture of the person's life and work as possible. A typical entry in *SATA* includes the following clearly labeled information sections:

PERSONAL: date and place of birth and death, parents' names and occupations, name of spouse, date of marriage, names of children, educational institutions attended, degrees received, religious and political affiliations, hobbies and other interests.

ADDRESSES: complete home, office, electronic mail, and agent addresses, whenever available.

CAREER: name of employer, position, and dates for each career post; art exhibitions; military service; memberships and offices held in professional and civic organizations.

MEMBER: professional, civic, and other association memberships and any official posts held.

AWARDS, HONORS: literary and professional awards received.

WRITINGS: title-by-title chronological bibliography of books written and/or illustrated, listed by genre when known; lists of other notable publications, such as plays, screenplays, and periodical contributions.

ADAPTATIONS: a list of films, television programs, plays, CD-ROMs, recordings, and other media presentations that have been adapted from the author's work.

WORK IN PROGRESS: description of projects in progress.

SIDELIGHTS: a biographical portrait of the author or illustrator's development, either directly from the biographee— and often written specifically for the *SATA* entry—or gathered from diaries, letters, interviews, or other published sources.

BIOGRAPHICAL AND CRITICAL SOURCES: cites sources quoted in "Sidelights" along with references for further reading.

EXTENSIVE ILLUSTRATIONS: photographs, movie stills, book illustrations, and other interesting visual materials supplement the text.

How a *SATA* Entry Is Compiled

SATA editors examine a wide variety of published sources to gather information for an entry. Biographical and bibliographic sources are consulted, as are book reviews, feature articles, published interviews, and material sometimes obtained from the biographee's family, publishers, agent, or other associates. Whenever possible, the author or illustrator is sent a copy of the entry to check for accuracy and completeness.

Entries that have not been verified by the biographees or their representatives are marked with an asterisk (*).

Contact the Editor

We encourage our readers to examine the entire *SATA* series. Please write and tell us if we can make *SATA* even more helpful to you. Give your comments and suggestions to the editor:

Editor
Something about the Author
Gale, Cengage Learning
27500 Drake Rd.
Farmington Hills MI 48331-3535

Toll-free: 800-877-GALE
Fax: 248-699-8070

Something about the Author Product Advisory Board

The editors of *Something about the Author* are dedicated to maintaining a high standard of excellence by publishing comprehensive, accurate, and highly readable entries on a wide array of writers for children and young adults. In addition to the quality of the content, the editors take pride in the graphic design of the series, which is intended to be orderly yet inviting, allowing readers to utilize the pages of *SATA* easily and with efficiency. Despite the longevity of the *SATA* print series, and the success of its format, we are mindful that the vitality of a literary reference product is dependent on its ability to serve its users over time. As literature, and attitudes about literature, constantly evolve, so do the reference needs of students, teachers, scholars, journalists, researchers, and book club members. To be certain that we continue to keep pace with the expectations of our customers, the editors of *SATA* listen carefully to their comments regarding the value, utility, and quality of the series. Librarians, who have firsthand knowledge of the needs of library users, are a valuable resource for us. The *Something about the Author* Product Advisory Board, made up of school, public, and academic librarians, is a forum to promote focused feedback about *SATA* on a regular basis. The nine-member advisory board includes the following individuals, whom the editors wish to thank for sharing their expertise:

SOMETHING ABOUT THE AUTHOR

ALLEY, Robert W.
　　See ALLEY, R.W.

*　　*　　*

ALLEY, R.W. 1955-
　　(Robert W. Alley)

Personal

Born 1955, in Lexington, VA; married; wife's name Zoë; children: Cassie, Max. *Education:* Graduated from Haverford College.

Addresses

Home—Barrington, RI. *Agent*—Jane Feder, 305 E. 24th St., New York, NY 10010. *E-mail*—rwalleymail@aol.com.

Career

Illustrator and graphic artist.

Member

Picturebook Artists Association, Authors Guild, Author League of America.

Awards, Honors

Smithsonian magazine Notable Book designation, 1998, for *Paddington Bear* by Michael Bond; Capitol Choices Master List inclusion, 2005, for *Pearl and Wagner:* *Three Secrets* by Kate McMullan; New Jersey Garden State Children's Book Award nomination, 2006, for *Pearl and Wagner: Two Good Friends* by McMullan; *Washington Post* Best Children's Book designation, and Cybils Awards finalist, both 2008, and Notable Children's Book in the Language Arts designation, 2009, all for *There's a Wolf at the Door* by Zoë B. Alley; Theodor Geisel Award Honor Book designation, 2010, for *Pearl and Wagner: One Funny Day* by McMullan.

Writings

SELF-ILLUSTRATED

The Ghost in Dobb's Diner, Parents Magazine Press (New York, NY), 1981.
The Silly Riddle Book, Golden (New York, NY), 1981.
Busy Farm Trucks, Grosset & Dunlap (New York, NY), 1986.
(Reteller) *Seven Fables from Aesop,* Dodd, Mead (New York, NY), 1986.
Busy People All around Town, Western Publishing (New York, NY), 1988.
Busy Things That Go, Western Publishing (New York, NY), 1988.
The Clever Carpenter, Random House (New York, NY), 1988.
Watch out, Cyrus!: A Wacky Adventure on Land, on Sea, and in the Air; or, How to Get from Here to There, Grosset & Dunlap (New York, NY), 1990.

Wee Wheels, Grosset & Dunlap (New York, NY), 1990.

The Wheels on the Bus, Western Publishing (Racine, WI), 1992.

One Little Duck, HarperFestival (New York, NY), 1995.

There Once Was a Witch, HarperFestival (New York, NY), 2003.

Making a Boring Day Better: A Kid's Guide to Battling the Blahs, One Caring Place/Abbey Press (St. Meinrad, IN), 2006.

Bratty Brothers and Selfish Sisters: All about Sibling Rivalry, One Caring Place/Abbey Press (St. Meinrad, IN), 2007.

Some of Alley's titles have been translated into French.

ILLUSTRATOR

David Lyon, *The Brave Little Computer,* Simon & Schuster (New York, NY), 1984.

Ross Robert Olney and Patricia Olney, *How Long?: To Go, to Grow, to Know,* Morrow (New York, NY), 1984.

Jane O'Connor, *The Teeny Tiny Woman,* Random House (New York, NY), 1986.

Amy Ehrlich, *Buck-buck the Chicken,* Random House (New York, NY), 1987.

Charlotte Pomerantz, *How Many Trucks Can a Tow Truck Tow?,* Random House (New York, NY), 1987.

Dinah L. Moché, *Amazing Space Facts,* Western Publishing (Racine, WI), 1988.

ABC Rhymes, D.C. Heath (Lexington, MA), 1989.

Patricia Baehr, *School Isn't Fair!,* Four Winds (New York, NY), 1989.

Stephanie Calmenson, *The Little Witch Sisters,* Parents Magazine Press (New York, NY), 1989.

Joanna Cole, *Who Put the Pepper in the Pot?,* Parents Magazine Press (New York, NY), 1989.

Harriet Ziefert, *The Prince Has a Boo-boo!,* Random House (New York, NY), 1989.

Gail Herman, *Ice Cream Soup* (based on a story by Jack Kent), Random House (New York, NY), 1990.

Robin Pulver, *Mrs. Toggle's Zipper,* Four Winds (New York, NY), 1990.

Harriet Ziefert, *The Prince's Tooth Is Loose,* Random House (New York, NY), 1990, reprinted, Sterling (New York, NY), 2005.

Old MacDonald Had a Farm, Grosset & Dunlap (New York, NY), 1991.

William H. Hooks, *Where's Lulu?,* Bantam (New York, NY), 1991.

Brian Mangas, *Follow That Puppy!,* Simon & Schuster (New York, NY), 1991.

Robin Pulver, *Mrs. Toggle and the Dinosaur,* Four Winds (New York, NY), 1991.

Teddy Slater, *Listening with Zachary,* Silver Press (Englewood Cliffs, NJ), 1991.

Teddy Slater, *Looking for Lewis,* Silver Press (Englewood Cliffs, NJ), 1991.

Sue Brownlee, *Best Kids Cookbook,* photographs by Tom Wyatt, Sunset (Menlo Park, CA), 1992.

Steven Krensky, *The Pizza Book,* Scholastic, Inc. (New York, NY), 1992.

Charlotte Pomerantz, *Serena Katz,* Macmillan (New York, NY), 1992.

Victoria Hartman, *The Silliest Joke Book Ever,* Lothrop, Lee & Shepard (New York, NY), 1993.

Fran Manushkin, *My Christmas Safari,* Dial (New York, NY), 1993.

David Packard, *The Ball Game,* Scholastic, Inc. (New York, NY), 1993.

Molly Kates, *The Little Firehouse,* Random House (New York, NY), 1994.

Marcia Leonard, *When the Giants Came to Town,* Scholastic, Inc. (New York, NY), 1994.

Robin Pulver, *Mrs. Toggle's Beautiful Blue Shoe,* Four Winds (New York, NY), 1994.

Richard Schotter, *There's a Dragon About: A Winter's Revel,* Orchard (New York, NY), 1994.

Alan Sincic, *Edward Is Only a Fish,* Holt (New York, NY), 1994.

Marilyn Singer, *Family Reunion,* Macmillan (New York, NY), 1994.

Nancy White Carlstrom, *Who Said Boo?: Halloween Poems for the Very Young,* Simon & Schuster (New York, NY), 1995.

Michele Sobel Spirn, *The Know-Nothings,* HarperCollins (New York, NY), 1995.

Robin Dexter, *Young Arthur Ashe,* Troll (Mahwah, NJ), 1996.

Katy Hall and Lisa Eisenberg, *Sheepish Riddles,* Dial (New York, NY), 1996.

Katy Hall and Lisa Eisenberg, *Trick or Eeek!, and Other Ha Ha Halloween Riddles,* HarperFestival (New York, NY), 1996.

Tony Johnston, *The Bull and the Fire Truck,* Scholastic, Inc. (New York, NY), 1996.

Elizabeth Koehler-Pentacoff, *Louise the One and Only,* Troll (Mahwah, NJ), 1996.

Judith Benét Richardson, *Old Winter,* Orchard (New York, NY), 1996.

James Skofield, *Detective Dinosaur,* HarperCollins (New York, NY), 1996.

Cindy Wheeler, *The Emperor's Birthday Suit,* Random House (New York, NY), 1996.

Katy Hall and Lisa Eisenberg, *Easter Yolks: Egg-cellent Riddles to Crack You Up,* HarperFestival (New York, NY), 1997.

Katy Hall and Lisa Eisenberg, *Hearty Har Har: Valentine Riddles You'll Love,* HarperFestival (New York, NY), 1997.

Barbara Shook Hazen, *The New Dog,* Dial (New York, NY), 1997.

Michele Sobel Spirin, *A Know-Nothing Birthday,* HarperCollins (New York, NY), 1997.

Stuart J. Murphy, *Animals on Board,* HarperCollins (New York, NY), 1998.

James Preller, *The Case of the Missing Hamster* ("Jigsaw Jones" series), Scholastic, Inc. (New York, NY), 1998.

James Preller, *The Case of the Christmas Snowman* ("Jigsaw Jones" series), Scholastic, Inc. (New York, NY), 1998.

James Skofield, *Detective Dinosaur: Lost and Found,* HarperCollins (New York, NY), 1998.

Nola Buck, *Hey, Little Baby!*, HarperFestival (New York, NY), 1999.

Nancy White Carlstrom, *Thanksgiving Day at Our House: Thanksgiving Poems for the Very Young*, Simon & Schuster (New York, NY), 1999.

Katy Hall and Lisa Eisenberg, *Kitty Riddles*, Dial (New York, NY), 2000.

Robin Pulver, *Mrs. Toggle's Class Picture Day*, Scholastic, Inc. (New York, NY), 2000.

Michele Sobel Spirn, *A Know-Nothing Halloween*, Harper-Collins (New York, NY), 2000.

Michele Sobel Spirn, *The Know-Nothings Talk Turkey*, HarperCollins (New York, NY), 2000.

Cynthia C. DeFelice, *The Real True Dulcie Campbell*, Farrar, Straus (New York, NY), 2002.

Susan Katz, *Mrs. Brown on Exhibit, And Other Museum Poems*, Simon & Schuster (New York, NY), 2002.

Dandi Daley Mackall, *Off to Bethlehem!*, HarperFestival (New York, NY), 2002.

Gloria Rand, *Little Flower*, Holt (New York, NY), 2002.

Kate Laing, *Best Kind of Baby*, Dial (New York, NY), 2003.

Kate McMullan, *Pearl and Wagner: Two Good Friends*, Dial (New York, NY), 2003.

Jane O'Connor, *The Teeny Tiny Woman*, Random House (New York, NY), 2003.

Jean Van Leeuwen, *The Great Googlestein Museum Mystery*, Phyllis Fogelman (New York, NY), 2003.

Bethany Roberts, *Cat Skidoo*, Holt (New York, NY), 2004.

Susan Katz, *A Revolutionary Field Trip: Poems of Colonial America*, Simon & Schuster (New York, NY), 2004.

Kate McMullan, *Pearl and Wagner: Three Secrets*, Dial (New York, NY), 2004.

Teri Sloat, *This Is the House That Was Tidy and Neat*, Holt (New York, NY), 2005.

Claudia Mills, *Ziggy's Blue-Ribbon Day*, Farrar, Straus (New York, NY), 2005.

Richard Krieb, *We're off to Find the Witch's House*, Dutton (New York, NY), 2005.

Bill Harley, *Dear Santa: The Letters of James B. Dobbins*, HarperCollins (New York, NY), 2005.

Andrew Clements, *Because Your Daddy Loves You*, Clarion (New York, NY), 2005.

Larry Dane Brimner, *Spring Sail*, Child's World (Chanhassen, MN), 2005.

Cindy Trumbore, *The Genie in the Book*, Handprint Books (New York, NY), 2005.

Harriet Ziefert, *A Bowlful of Rain*, Sterling (New York, NY), 2006.

Ann Heinrichs, *Mother's Day*, Child's World (Chanhassen, MN), 2006.

Ann Heinrichs, *Father's Day*, Child's World (Chanhassen, MN), 2006.

S.J. Fore, *Tiger Can't Sleep*, Viking (New York, NY), 2006.

Larry Dane Brimner, *Winter Blanket*, Child's World (Chanhassen, MN), 2006.

Larry Dane Brimner, *One Summery Day*, Child's World (Chanhassen, MN), 2006.

Larry Dane Brimner, *In the Fall*, Child's World (Chanhassen, MN), 2006.

Kimberly Brubaker Bradley, *Ballerino Nate*, Dial (New York, NY), 2006.

Larry Dale Brimner, *Spring Sail*, Child's World (Chanhassen, Minn.), 2006.

Claudia Mills, *Being Teddy Roosevelt*, Farrar, Straus & Giroux (New York, NY), 2007.

Nancy Markham Alberts, *Joselina Piggy Goes Out*, Sterling (New York, NY), 2007.

Rebecca Kai Dotlich, *Peanut and Pearl's Picnic Adventure*, HarperCollins (New York, NY), 2007.

Elizabeth Claire Alberts, *Joselina Piggy Cleans Her Room*, Sterling Pub. (New York, NY), 2008.

Zoë B. Alley, *There's a Wolf at the Door*, Roaring Brook Press (New York, NY), 2008.

Corinne Demas, *Valentine Surprise*, Walker & Co. (New York, NY), 2008.

Kate McMullan, *Pearl and Wagner: One Funny Day*, Dial Books for Young Readers (New York, NY), 2009.

Kersten Hamilton, *Police Officers on Patrol*, Viking Childrens Books (New York, NY), 2009.

John Grandits, *The Travel Game*, Clarion Books (New York, NY), 2009.

Simon Cheshire, *Saxby Smart: Curse of the Ancient Mask, and Other Case Files*, Roaring Book Press (New York, NY), 2009.

Kate McMullan, *Pearl and Wagner: Four Eyes*, Dial Books for Young Readers (New York, NY), 2010.

Simon Cheshire, *Saxby Smart: Treasure of Dead Man's Lane, and Other Cases*, Roaring Brook Press (New York, NY), 2010.

James Skofield, *Detective Dinosaur Undercover*, HarperCollins (New York, NY), 2010.

Zoë B. Alley, *There's a Princess at the Door*, Roaring Brook Press (New York, NY), 2010.

ILLUSTRATOR; "ELF HELP" SERIES; FOR ADULTS

Cherry Hartman, *Be-Good-to-Yourself Therapy*, Abbey Press (St. Meinrad, IN), 1987.

Michael Joseph, *Play Therapy*, Abbey Press (St. Meinrad, IN), 1990.

Lisa Engelhardt, *Happy Birthday Therapy*, Abbey Press (St. Meinrad, IN), 1993.

Karen Katafiasz, *Christmas Therapy*, Abbey Press (St. Meinrad, IN), 1994.

Daniel Grippo, *Work Therapy*, Abbey Press (St. Meinrad, IN), 1995.

Linus Mundy, *Everyday-Courage Therapy*, Abbey Press (St. Meinrad, IN), 1995.

Clair Bradshaw, *Get-Well Therapy*, One Caring Place (St. Meinrad, IN), 1996.

Karen Katafiasz, *Living from Your Soul*, Abbey Press (St. Meinrad, IN), 1997.

Kass P. Dotterweich, *Be-Good-to-Your-Family Therapy*, One Caring Place (St. Meinrad, IN), 1997.

Karen Katafiasz, *Teacher Therapy*, One Caring Place (St. Meinrad, IN), 1997.

Carol Ann Morrow, *Trust-in-God Therapy*, One Caring Place (St. Meinrad, IN), 1998.

Linus Mundy, *Elf-Help for Overcoming Depression*, One Caring Place (St. Meinrad, IN), 1998.

Jim Auer, *Elf-Help for Raising a Teen,* Abbey Press (St. Meinrad, IN), 2000.

Janet Getsz, *Elf-Help for Being a Good Parent,* Abbey Press (St. Meinrad, IN), 2000.

Daniel Grippo, *Worry Therapy,* Abbey Press (St. Meinrad, IN), 2000.

Rosemary Purdy, *'Tis a Blessing to Be Irish,* Abbey Press (St. Meinrad, IN), 2001.

Linus Mundy, *On the Anniversary of Your Loss,* One Caring Place/Abbey Press (St. Meinrad, IN), 2007.

Tom McGrath, *Thirty Days of Grief Prayers,* One Caring Place (St. Meinrad, IN), 2008.

Also illustrator of *Believe-in-Yourself Therapy, Healing Thoughts for Troubled Times,* and *Loneliness Therapy,* all by Daniel Grippo; *Grieving at Christmastime,* by Dwight Daniels; *Elf-Help for Giving the Gift of You!* and *Elf-Help for Coping with Pain,* both by Anne Calodich Fone; *Take Charge of Your Eating,* by Laura Pirott; *Elf-Help for Dealing with Difficult People, New Baby Therapy,* and *Acceptance Therapy,* all by Lisa Engelhardt; *Nature Therapy* and *Elf-Help for a Happy Retirement,* both by Ted O'Neal; *Gratitude Therapy* and *One-Day-at-a-Time Therapy,* by Christine A. Adams; *Elf-Help for Busy Moms,* by Molly Wigand; *Stress Therapy,* by Tom McGrath; *Making-Sense-out-of-Suffering Therapy,* by Jack Wintz; *Anger Therapy,* by Engelhardt and Karen Katafiasz; *Caregiver Therapy,* by Julie Kuebelbeck and Victoria O'Connor; *Self Esteem Therapy, Grief Therapy,* and *Celebrate-Your-Womanhood Therapy,* all by Katafiasz; *Peace Therapy,* by Carol Ann Morrow; *Take-Charge-of-Your-Life Therapy; Friendship Therapy,* by Kass P. Dotterweich and John D. Perry; *Be-Good-to-Your-Marriage Therapy,* by Dotterweich; *Forgiveness Therapy,* by David Schell; *Keep-Life-Simple Therapy* and *Slow-down Therapy,* both by Linus Mundy; *Be-Good-to-Your-Body Therapy,* by Steve Ilg; *Keeping-up-Your-Spirits Therapy,* by Linda Allison-Lewis; *Prayer Therapy,* by Keith McClellan; and *More Be-Good-to-Yourself Therapy,* by Cherry Hartman; all for Abbey Press (St. Meinrad, IN).

ILLUSTRATOR; "ELF HELP" SERIES; FOR CHILDREN

Michaelene Mundy, *Sad Isn't Bad: A Good-Grief Guidebook for Kids Dealing with Loss,* One Caring Place (St. Meinrad, IN), 1998.

Emily Menendez-Aponte, *When Mom and Dad Divorce: A Kid's Resource,* Abbey Press (St. Meinrad, IN), 1999.

Michaelene Mundy, *Mad Isn't Bad: A Child's Book about Anger,* One Caring Place (St. Meinrad, IN), 1999.

Molly Wigand, *Help Is Here for Facing Fear,* One Caring Place (St. Meinrad, IN), 2000.

Michaelene Mundy, *Getting out of a Stress Mess!: A Guide for Kids,* One Caring Place (St. Meinrad, IN), 2000.

Tom McGrath, *When You're Sick or in the Hospital: Healing Help for Kids,* Abbey Press (St. Meinrad, IN), 2002.

Michaelene Mundy, *Keeping School Cool!: A Kid's Guide to Handling School Problems,* Abbey Press (St. Meinrad, IN), 2002.

Victoria Ryan, *When Your Grandparent Dies: A Child's Guide to Good Grief,* One Caring Place (St. Meinrad, IN), 2002.

Jim Auer, *Standing up to Peer Pressure: A Guide to Being True to You,* Abbey Press (St. Meinrad, IN), 2003.

J.S. Jackson, *Bye-bye, Bully!: A Kid's Guide for Dealing with Bullies,* Abbey Press (St. Meinrad, IN), 2003.

Carol Ann Morrow, *Forgiving Is Smart for Your Heart,* One Caring Place (St. Meinrad, IN), 2003.

Ted O'Neal, *When Bad Things Happen: A Guide to Help Kids Cope,* One Caring Place (St. Meinrad, IN), 2003.

Victoria Ryan, *When Your Pet Dies: A Healing Handbook for Kids,* One Caring Place (St. Meinrad, IN), 2003.

Susan Heyboer O'Keefe, *Be the Star That You Are!: A Book for Kids Who Feel Different,* One Caring Press (St. Meinrad, IN), 2005.

Michaelene Mundy, *Saying Good-bye, Saying Hello: When Your Family Is Moving,* One Caring Place (St. Meinrad, IN), 2005.

Cynthia Geisen, *My Body Is Special: A Family Book about Sexual Abuse,* One Caring Place/Abbey Press (St. Meinrad, IN), 2006.

J.S. Jackson, *Shyness Isn't a Minus: How to Turn Bashfulness into a Plus!,* One Caring Place/Abbey Press (St. Meinrad, IN), 2006.

Ted O'Neal, *Making Christmas Count!: A Kid's Guide to Keeping the Season Sacred,* One Caring Place/Abbey Press (St. Meinrad, IN), 2006.

Molly Wigand, *Jealousy Is Not for Me: A Guide for Freeing Yourself from Envy,* One Caring Place/Abbey Press (St. Meinrad, IN), 2007.

Jim Auer, *Know How to Say No to Drugs and Alcohol: A Kid's Guide,* One Caring Place/Abbey Press (St. Meinrad, IN), 2007.

Daniel Grippo, *When Mom or Dad Dies: A Book of Comfort for Kids,* One Caring Place/Abbey Press (St. Meinrad, IN), 2008.

Daniel Fitzgerald, *When Your Parent Dies,* Abbey Press (St. Meinrad, IN), 2009.

Also illustrator of *A New Baby Is Coming!: A Guide for a Big Brother or Sister,* by Emily Menendez Aponte; *When Someone You Love Has Cancer: A Guide to Help Kids Cope,* by Alaric Lewis; *A Kid's Guide to Keeping Family First,* by J.S. Jackson; *Learning to Be a Good Friend: A Guidebook for Kids,* by Christine A. Adams; *Playing Fair, Having Fun: A Kid's Guide to Sports and Games,* by Daniel Grippo; and *A Book of Prayers for All Your Cares,* by Michaelene Mundy, all for Abbey Press (St. Meinrad, IN).

ILLUSTRATOR; "PADDINGTON BEAR" SERIES BY MICHAEL BOND

Paddington Bear and the Christmas Surprise, HarperCollins (New York, NY), 1997.

Paddington Bear All Day, HarperFestival (New York, NY), 1998.

Paddington the Artist, Collins (London, England), 1998.

Paddington at the Fair, Collins (London, England), 1998.

Paddington and the Tutti Frutti Rainbow, Collins (London, England), 1998.

Paddington at the Zoo, Collins (London, England), 1998.

Paddington Bear and the Busy Bee Carnival, HarperCollins (New York, NY), 1998.

Paddington Bear Goes to Market, HarperFestival (New York, NY), 1998.

Paddington Bear, new edition, HarperCollins (New York, NY), 1998.

Paddington at the Palace, Collins (London, England), 1999.

Paddington and the Marmalade Maze, Collins (London, England), 1999.

Paddington Minds the House, Collins (London, England), 1999.

Paddington's Busy Day, Collins (London, England), 1999.

Paddington's Party Tricks, Collins (London, England), 2000.

Paddington in Hot Water, Collins (London, England), 2000.

Paddington Bear at the Circus, HarperCollins (New York, NY), 2000.

Paddington Bear Goes to the Hospital, HarperCollins (New York, NY), 2001.

Paddington Bear in the Garden, HarperCollins (New York, NY), 2002.

Paddington Here and Now, HarperCollins (New York, NY), 2008.

Paddington at the Beach, HarperCollins (New York, NY), 2009.

Illustrator of new editions of earlier "Paddington Bear" picture books.

ILLUSTRATOR; "ALPHABET ANIMALS" SERIES BY BARBARA DERUBERTIS

Alexander Anteater's Amazing Act, Kane Press (New York, NY), 2010.

Bobby Baboon's Banana Be-bop, Kane Press (New York, NY), 2010.

Corky Cub's Crazy Caps, Kane Press (New York, NY), 2010.

Dilly Dog's Dizzy Dancing, Kane Press (New York, NY), 2010.

Sidelights

An author and illustrator of books for children, R.W. Alley received a special honor in 1997 when he was given the opportunity to illustrate Michael Bond's popular "Paddington Bear" picture-book stories. Based on Bond's 1958 children's book classic *A Bear Called Paddington,* the new books have earned Alley recognition throughout the world. In addition to his original self-illustrated books, which include *The Clever Carpenter* and *There Once Was a Witch,* Alley has also created illustrations for numerous writers besidess Bond and has worked with Abbey Press to illustrate the multivolume "Elf Help" series, which helps both children and adults cope with the troubling times in life.

Although Alley had intended to be a serious scholar of art history, during college he found himself "doodling in the margins and dreaming up stories," as he explained

on his home page. After graduating from college, he sold his first self-illustrated book, *The Ghost in Dobb's Diner.* After a brief, four-year career as an in-house greeting card artist and writer and editor, first with Hallmark Cards in Kansas City, Missouri, and then with Paramount Cards in Pawtucket, Rhode Island, he moved to writing and illustrating picture books, chapter books, and easy readers for children, all from his home studio while wearing his slippers.

Although Alley has written several self-illustrated titles, he is better known for the illustrations he creates for other writers. Of his work for Richard and Roni Schotter's picture book *There's a Dragon About: A Winter's Revel,* Linda Callaghan wrote in *Booklist* that "Alley's pen-and-ink drawings with bright watercolors capture the enthusiasm" of the tale. Reviewing *Old Winter,* written by Judith Benét Richardson, Carolyn Phelan commented in *Booklist* that "children will delight in the details of Alley's lively ink-and-watercolor illustrations." Tony Johnston's *The Bull and the Fire Truck* caused Phelan to write in a subsequent *Booklist* review that "Alley's line-and-watercolor artwork brims with action and humorous details." As a *Publishers Weekly* critic commented of Alley's illustrations for *Little Flower,* written by Gloria Rand: "Alley's kicky ink-and-watercolor artwork captures the warmth of the bond" displayed between the young pet owner heroine and her pet pig. In a review of the same title for *School Library Journal,* Jody McCoy wrote that "Alley's colorful cartoon illustrations . . . suit the text delightfully" and "flow from page to page with variety and verve."

The story of a farm girl who longs to be a princess, is told in *The Real, True Dulcie Campbell,* written by Cynthia C. DeFelice. Phelan, in her *Booklist* review, considered Alley's work for this book to be both "lively" and "appealing," while Ruth Semrau noted in *School Library Journal* that the illustrator's "pastel watercolors are light and cheerful, never too scary, even in the creepy parts." About Kate Laing's *Best Kind of Baby,* in which Sophie does not want to acknowledge that she is going to be a big sister, Connie Fletcher wrote in *Booklist:* "Alley's warmly humorous watercolors underscore Sophie's troubled state." Another picture book, Teri Sloat's *This Is the House That Was Tidy and Neat,* benefits from the artist's "endearing" tinted pen-and-ink drawings, which "make . . . the ensuing havoc" in Stoat's rhyming cumulative tale "all the more comical," according to Phelan.

Alley's illustrations tackle such subjects as fear of the dark in S.J. Fore's *Tiger Can't Sleep* and feeling out of place in both *Ballerino Nate* by Claudia Mills and *Ziggy's Blue Ribbon Day* by Kimberly Brubaker Bradley. In *Tiger Can't Sleep* a little boy deals with the dreamtime tiger hiding in his bedroom closet, and Alley's ability to capture the young hero's "delightfully expressive body language continues the comic relief," according to *School Library Journal* contributor Kirsten Cutler. Reviewing Mills' work in *Publishers Weekly,* the

contributor noted of *Ballerino Nate* that the story of a boy who prefers dancing to playing baseball is enhanced "true-to-life ink-and-watercolor illustrations" in which Alley "adroitly capture[s] the youngsters' home life" as well as the "comically realistic" emotions of young Nate and his mother.

In his work as illustrator, Alley divides his time between picture books and chapter books. In *The Great Googlestein Museum Mystery,* a chapter book featuring adventurous mice in a story written by Jean Van Leeuwen, "Alley's black-and-white sketches add to the fun and help to clarify some of the story's details," according to Kay Weisman in *Booklist.* Shara Alpern, reviewing the same title for *School Library Journal,* wrote that "the small, amusing black-and-white drawings scattered throughout further enhance the reading experience."

The award-winning "Pearl and Wagner" stories, written by Kate McMullan, are easy-to-read chapter books about a rabbit and a mouse that are the closest of friends. "Alley's expressive art captures the emotions and high jinks with winsome detail," wrote Gillian Engberg in a *Booklist* review of *Pearl and Wagner: Two Good Friends.* Laura Scott, reviewing the same title in *School Library Journal,* commented that the "cheerful illustrations enhance the text with appealing animal characters rendered with extraordinary expression." Aiding readers comprehension of McMullen's story in *Pearl and Wagner: One Funny Day,* "Alley's pen-and-ink and watercolor illustrations . . . help youngsters through any rough parts," according to *Horn Book* contributor Betty Carter. Commenting that readers will feel as though they, along with Pearl and Wagner, are members of Ms. Star's class, a *Publishers Weekly* critic wrote that "Alley's illustrations enhance this effect with their knee-level or just-at-the-next-desk perspective."

Alley's collaboration with his wife, writer, Zoë B. Alley, has resulted in *There's a Wolf at the Door,* a graphic novel that follows the rounds of the storybook wolf and the events that inspired five well-known stories that include "The Three Little Pigs," "The Boys Who Cried Wolf," and "The Wolf in Sheep's Clothing." In this story, the little pigs—Alan, Blake, and Gordon by name—successfully repulse the wolf, as do a flock of sassy sheep in the field and a little girl in a red riding hood and her granny. A follow-up picture book, *There's a Princess at the Door,* describes the adventures of five well-known fairy-tale princesses in the same comic manner. Noting the effective integration of the stories in *There's a Wolf at the Door* into a text that "is full of puns, alliteration, and occasional rhymes," Mary Jean Smith also noted Alley's "softly colored pen-and-ink drawings" in her *School Library Journal* review of *There's a Wolf at the Door,* while a *Kirkus Reviews* writer cited the book's "animated" cartoon art and "snappy dialogue."

Along with his work on picture books and chapter books, Alley has also illustrated several poetry collec-

tions. *Mrs. Brown on Exhibit, and Other Museum Poems* features twenty-one poems by Susan Katz about students and their eccentric teacher as they travel through a museum on a field trip. "Full of intriguing details and humorous touches, Alley's cheerful watercolor illustrations give young children plenty to look at," Phelan wrote in *Booklist.* Commenting on the same title for *Publishers Weekly,* a critic cited Alley's "sprightly, realistic" art. "Alley's delightful cartoon-like illustrations emphasize the fun and the action" in the poetry, according to a *Kirkus Reviews* contributor.

When HarperCollins asked Alley to illustrate Bond's "Paddington Bear" picture-book stories, they were so impressed with his work that they also hired him to re-illustrate the earlier "Paddington" picture books, which are beloved throughout the world. *Paddington Bear,* a picture book in which Bond retells his original story of how the Brown family first met the traveling bear at Paddington Station in London, was released to celebrate Paddington's fortieth anniversary. "Alley's lively ink-and-watercolor-wash illustrations capture the winsome charm and gentle humor of this unassuming bear," wrote Phelan in her *Booklist* review of the book. Discussing Alley's more recent work, *Paddington Bear in the Garden,* Phelan wrote that the artist's "endearing ink-and-watercolor illustrations offer expressive drawings in pleasing colors," while *Horn Book* contributor Sarah Ellis wrote that in *Paddington Here and Now* Alley depicts the beloved bear as "gracious, deeply engaged with life, and nobody's teddy bear."

Alley wrote on his home page: "I have been making up stories and drawing pictures to illustrate them for about as long as I can remember. In many ways, I still spend my days the same way I did when I was ten. This is somewhat confusing to my wife and children, but I don't seem to be able to help myself."

"I have never wanted to be the sort of visual artist who creates images to hang on the wall or set on a pedestal," Alley once told *SATA:* "I've always enjoyed looking at these things, thinking about them, visiting galleries and museums full of them and, of course, studying their history. But, making them . . . no, that wasn't me. Making art for me has always been about telling stories and sharing those stories with as many people as possible. I figured out early on that books were the way to do this. I like writing my own stories because I have complete control over what part of the story is told with words and what is told with pictures. In illustrating another author's words, my focus changes; I have to find ways into the story that will allow me to add to the words, without changing their tone and meaning. In both cases, the key to being a good illustrator is, I think, to be able to first present the narrative of the story in a clear and inviting format and then to enlarge the narrative with strong character drawing and scene-setting. I know I've been successful when I go to a library and find copies of my books that have been truly worn and torn."

"Artistically, I find that I am concentrating much more on pen and ink work with a splash of color here and there," Alley more recently observed to *SATA*. "Over the years I gravitated to this style as my strongest story-telling method. The ink line is what it's all about. The color? Well, that seems to come from just about anything at hand. Water colors, pencils, acrylic paints, gouache paints and the occasional coffee spill all play a part. Accidents are very useful. I would like to think of them as a reflection of the enthusiasm with which the art is created.

"I also should note that I am very excited about the wave of comic panel books being published for American children these days. This is not a new format in the rest of the world—especially in Europe—but, it is here and I think U.S. publishers are taking full advantage of the homegrown talent of authors and illustrators to make very strong books in this format. The best thing about illustrating these books for me is that I can draw so very many pictures and really set the characters in motion."

Biographical and Critical Sources

PERIODICALS

Booklist, November 1, 1994, Linda Callaghan, review of *There's a Dragon About: A Winter's Revel,* p. 509; July, 1995, Stephanie Zvirin, review of *The Know-Nothings,* p. 1885; September 15, 1995, Hazel Rochman, review of *Who Said Boo?: Halloween Poems for the Very Young,* p. 168; February 15, 1996, Carolyn Phelan, review of *Young Arthur Ashe: Brave Champion,* p. 1011; October 1, 1996, Carolyn Phelan, review of *Old Winter,* p. 359; February 1, 1997, Carolyn Phelan, review of *The Bull and the Fire Truck,* p. 949; August, 1997, Stephanie Zvirin, review of *The New Dog,* p. 1906; February 1, 1998, Ilene Cooper, review of *Detective Dinosaur: Lost and Found,* p. 928; April, 1998, Carolyn Phelan, review of *Paddington Bear All Day,* p. 1329; November 1, 1998, Kathy Broderick, review of *Animals on Board,* p. 504; January 1, 1999, Carolyn Phelan, review of *Paddington Bear,* p. 886; February 1, 1999, Hazel Rochman, review of *Hey, Little Baby!,* p. 978; February 15, 2000, Hazel Rochman, review of *Kitty Riddles,* p. 1123; April 15, 2002, Carolyn Phelan, review of *Paddington Bear in the Garden,* p. 1405; June 1, 2002, Carolyn Phelan, review of *Mrs. Brown on Exhibit, and Other Museum Poems,* p. 1714; August, 2002, Carolyn Phelan, review of *The Real, True Dulcie Campbell,* p. 1969; February 1, 2003, Kay Weisman, review of *The Great Googlestein Museum Mystery,* p. 996; July, 2003, Gillian Engberg, review of *Pearl and Wagner: Two Good Friends,* p. 1899; August, 2003, Connie Fletcher, review of *Best Kind of Baby,* p. 1989; March 1, 2005, Ilene Cooper, review of *Because Your Daddy Loves You,* p. 1202; May 1, 2005, Carolyn Phelan, review of *This Is the House That Was Tidy and Neat,* p. 1593; September 15, 2005, Carolyn Phelan, review of *We're Off to Find the Witch's House,* p. 73; October 1, 2005, Jennifer Mattson, review of *Dear Santa: The Letters of James B. Dobbins,* p. 62; February 1, 2006, review of Jennifer Mattson, review of *Ballerino Nate,* p. 53; May 1, 2007, Ilene Cooper, review of *Peanut and Pearl's Picnic Adventure,* p. 97; November 15, 2008, Carolyn Phelan, review of *Pearl and Wagner: One Funny Day,* p. 51; January 1, 2008, Krista Hutley, review of *Valentine Surprise,* p. 96; May 1, 2009, Carolyn Phelan, review of *The Curse of the Ancient Mask and Other Case Files,* p. 42.

East Bay Newspapers (Barrington, RI), October 28, 2003, Amy Myrick, "Drawing Flights of Fancy in Barrington."

Horn Book, September-October, 2004, Martha V. Parravano, review of *Pear and Wagner: Three Secrets,* p. 593; September-October, 2008, Sarah Ellis, review of *Paddington Here and now,* p. 577; March-April, 2009, Betty Carter, review of *Pearl and Wagner: One Funny Day,* p. 199.

Kirkus Reviews, March 1, 2002, review of *Little Flower,* p. 344; June 15, 2002, review of *Mrs. Brown on Exhibit, and Other Museum Poems,* p. 883; March 15, 2003, review of *The Great Googlestein Museum Mystery,* p. 480; August 1, 2003, review of *Pearl and Wagner: Two Good Friends,* p. 1020; May 1, 2004, review of *Pearl and Wagner: Three Secrets,* p. 445; May 1, 2005, review of *Because Your Daddy Loves You,* p. 536; July 1, 2005, review of *We're Off to Find the Witch's House,* p. 737; June 15, 2007, review of *Peanut and Pearl's Picnic Adventure;* September 1, 2008, review of *There's a Wolf at the Door.*

People, November 4, 1996, Kristin McMurran, review of *Trick or Eeek!,* p. 43.

Publishers Weekly, February 18, 2002, review of *Little Flower,* p. 95; June 3, 2002, review of *Mrs. Brown on Exhibit, and Other Museum Poems,* p. 88; July 15, 2002, review of *The Real, True Dulcie Campbell,* p. 73; May 26, 2003, review of *Best Kind of Baby,* p. 70; September 26, 2005, review of *Dear Santa,* p. 86; January 2, 2006, review of *Tiger Can't Sleep,* p. 60; March 13, 2006, review of *Ballerino Nate,* p. 65; February 26, 2007, review of *Being Teddy Roosevelt,* p. 90.

School Library Journal, August, 2002, Susan Scheps, review of *Mrs. Brown on Exhibit, and Other Museum Poems,* p. 177; August, 2002, Jody McCoy, review of *Little Flower,* p. 165; September, 2002, Ruth Semrau, review of *The Real, True Dulcie Campbell,* p. 183; May, 2003, Shara Alpern, review of *The Great Googlestein Museum Mystery,* p. 131; July, 2003, Martha Topol, review of *Best Kind of Baby,* p. 100; September, 2003, Laura Scott, review of *Pearl and Wagner: Two Good Friends,* p. 184; January, 2005, Alison Grant, review of *The Genie in the Book,* p. 98; February, 2006, Kirsten Cutler, review of *Tiger Can't Sleep,* p. 97; March, 2008, Kelly Roth, review of *Valentine Surprise,* p. 156; September, 2008, Mary Jean Smith, review of *There's a Wolf at the Door,* p. 162.

ONLINE

R.W. Alley Home Page, http://www.rwalley.com (December 15, 2009).

ANDERSON, Brian 1974-

Personal

Born 1974; married 2003; wife's name Tammy; children: Liam. *Education:* Graduated from College of the Holy Cross, 1996. *Hobbies and other interests:* Movies, cartooning, magic, martial arts.

Addresses

Home—Natick, MA. *Agent*—c/o Rosemary Stimola, Stimola Literary Studio LLC, 306 Chase Court, Edgewater, NJ 07020. *E-mail*—brian@dogeatdoug.com.

Career

Cartoonist, author, screenwriter, and graphic designer. Creator of syndicated comic "Dog Eat Doug," beginning 2005; creator of web-comic "The Conjurers."

Writings

Nighty Nights, Sleepy Sleeps (picture book), Roaring Brook Press (New York, NY), 2008.
Dog Eat Doug: It's a Good Thing They're Cute (comics collection), Andrews McMeel (Kansas City, MO), 2008.

Author of story for graphic novel *Harbor Moon*, Arcana Studio, 2010.

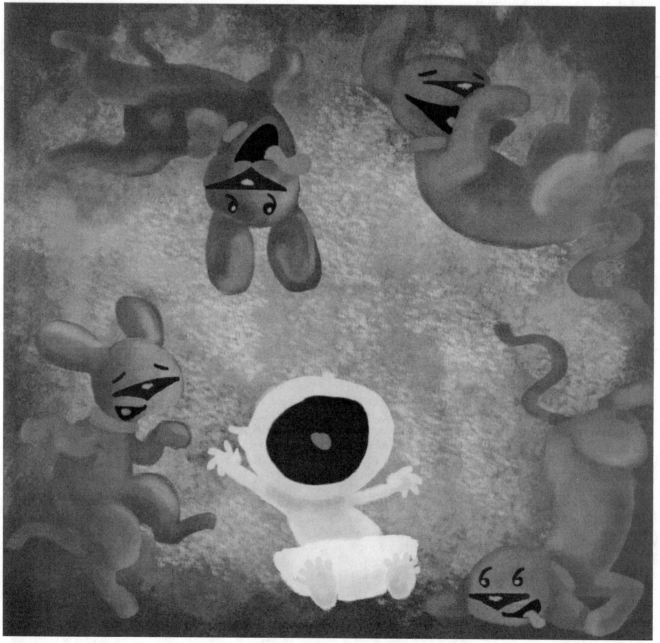

Brian Anderson tells the story of several perplexed babysitters in his self-illustrated picture book Nighty Nights, Sleepy Sleeps. (Copyright © 2008 by Brian Anderson. Reprinted by arrangement with Henry Holt & Company, LLC.)

Sidelights

Author and illustrator Brian Anderson has been drawing comics ever since he was a young boy. He published cartoons in high school and college campus newspapers and hoped some day to draw for Marvel Comics. After college, Anderson worked as a graphic artist until he developed a new idea for a comic strip, inspired by the chocolate Labrador puppy he and his wife had adopted. "One day sitting around on the couch with my dog, the whole 'Dog Eat Doug' thing hit me," the cartoonist told *Collective Inkwell* online interviewer David Wright. "The title, the characters and the first dozen or so strips materialized in a flash." In the strip, a puppy named Sophie is disturbed when baby Doug joins the household. The two sometimes battle, but more often join forces against the resident adults. The strip debuted as a Web comic in 2004, and by the end of the year Anderson had signed a seven-year deal with Creators Syndicate. By 2010 "Dog Eat Doug" ran in over forty daily newspapers in North America, and was also anthologized in *Dog Eat Doug: It's a Good Thing They're Cute.*

Anderson introduces Sophie and Doug to a new audience in his first picture book, *Nighty Nights, Sleepy Sleeps.* Although it is supposed to be their bedtime, baby Doug and dog Sophie roam the house, causing trouble before finally falling asleep on the bedroom floor. *School Library Journal* contributor Catherine Callegari called the book "a fun and quirky bedtime story" and added that Anderson's text "sometimes misses its mark but is always full of energy." "The skewed perspectives of the heavily pigmented illustrations nicely complement the rambunctious verses," a *Kirkus Reviews* writer noted, concluding that *Nighty Nights, Sleepy Sleeps* is "pure good fun."

Although Anderson has worked on novels, screenplays, and graphic novels, he plans to continue with "Dog Eat Doug" for some time. "You have to love your characters because you have to live with them for so long," Anderson explained in an interview for the *Atlanta Journal-Constitution.* "Every morning you get two seconds to make someone smile. That's all I'm shooting for, that readers can count on it being there. That's a great job."

Biographical and Critical Sources

PERIODICALS

Atlanta Journal-Constitution, November 14, 2005, Frank C. Rizzo, "Two New Comics Debut Today," p. E1.
Kirkus Reviews, October 1, 2008, review of *Nighty Nights, Sleepy Sleeps.*
School Library Journal, October, 2008, Catherine Callegari, review of *Nighty Nights, Sleepy Sleeps,* p. 100.

ONLINE

Collective Inkwell Web site, http://collectiveinkwell.com/ (May 6, 2009), David Wright, "The Collective Inkwell Interview: Brian Anderson of Dog Eat Doug."*

B

BAI, Durga

Personal

Born in Burbaspur, Madhya Pradesh, India; married Subhash Vyam (an artist and toymaker); children: Mansingh (son), two daughters.

Addresses

Home—Madhya Pradesh, India.

Career

Artist and illustrator. *Exhibitions:* Paintings exhibited in Indian cities, including Bhopal, Chennai, Delhi, Indore, Raipur, and Mumbai, as well as in an exhibition of Gond art that toured U.S. museums.

Awards, Honors

Handicraft Development Council award; Indian State Award; Indira Gandhi National Centre for the Arts scholarship award, 2006-07; Ragazzi Award (with others), Bologna Book Festival, 2008, for *The Night Life of Trees.*

Illustrator

Anushka Ravishankar and Sirish Rao, *One, Two, Tree!,* Tara Pub. (New Delhi, India), 2003.

(With Bhajju Shyam and Ram Singh Urveti) Gita Wolf and Sirish Rao, adaptors, *The Night Life of Trees* (based on Hindi narratives), Tara Pub. (Chennai, India), 2006.

Sirish Rao, *The Old Animals' Forest Band,* Tara Pub. (Chennai, India), 2008.

Sidelights

Durga Bai is a Gond artist from Madhya Pradesh in central India. In her detailed paintings, with their stylized, patterned images and brilliant colors, she captures the history and traditions of her tribe and the techniques that she inherited from her grandmother.

As a child, Bai exhibited a talent for decorating the clay walls of homes during special festivals and other occasions. Called *digna,* the technique involves reproducing traditional patterns using a tinted mixture of clay and cow dung. Beginning to paint soon after her marriage, at age twelve, Bai raised her three children while also helping her husband, a screen painter and toy maker. After she learned the brush technique of her brother-in-law, noted Adivasi artist Jangarh Singh, painting became a major part of Bai's life. Her paintings and ink drawings, which feature intricate images that evoke traditional Gond stories, are popular her native India and have also appeared in several picture books coauthored by writer Sirish Rao.

In bringing to life *One, Two, Tree!,* a counting story written by Rao and Anushka Ravishankar, Bai created a sequence of pictures in which an increasing succession of new animals—from one ant to ten elephants—take their places in the branches of a growing tree with each turn of the page. As new animals are introduced, those from previous pages begin to disappear into the tree's detailed foliage, transforming *One, Two, Tree!* "into a game to find them" as well as "a showpiece for the artist's skillful work," according to *School Library Journal* reviewer Margaret R. Tassia. In Rao's *The Old Animals' Forest Band,* which retells the Grimm Brothers' story of "The Bremen Town Musicians," Bai contributes detailed illustrations that possess what a *Kirkus Revews* writer described as "subcontinental flair" due to their one-dimensional images rendered using "repetitive shapes and cross-hatching in delicate ink lines."

Described by a *Publishers Weekly* contributor as "a glowingly mysterious and charming" picture book, *The Night Life of Trees* collects Gond legends and illuminates them with paintings by Bai as well as fellow artists Bhajju Shyam and Ram Singh Urveti. Several of the stories feature traditional Hindu characters and focus on the melding of the spirit world and nature. Describing the book as a "mingling of the mythic, mundane, and poetic," the critic added that *The Night Life of Trees* provides readers with "an alluring glimpse" into a fascinating culture.

Respected for her ability to generate new interest in a traditional art form, Bai continues to paint, and she has now been joined by her three children, all of whom are interested in preserving the traditional Gond stories and arts. "If I was educated, I could have written books about my stories and illustrated them," the artist told *Hindu* online contributor Madhu Gurung. "I am educating my children. They should do what I could not."

Biographical and Critical Sources

PERIODICALS

Kirkus Reviews, October 1, 2008, review of *The Old Animals' Forest Band.*

Publishers Weekly, May 22, 2006, review of *The Night Life of Trees,* p. 47.

School Library Journal, October, 2004, Margaret R. Tassia, review of *One, Two, Tree!,* p. 128.

ONLINE

Hindu Online, http://www.thehindu.com/ (July 30, 2006), Madhu Gurung, "Tears and Triumphs."

Indira Gandhi National Centre for the Arts Web site, http://www.ignca.nic.in/ (December 15, 2009), "Durga Bai."*

                              *   *   *

BANKS, Erin Bennett 1978-
(Erin Susanne Bennett)

Personal

Born 1978; married Timothy Banks (an artist and illustrator). *Education:* Houghton College (Houghton, NY), B.A. (studio art and graphic design); Savannah College of Art and Design, M.F.A. (illustration).

Addresses

Home—Charleston, SC. *E-mail*—erin@erinbanks.com.

Career

Artist specializing in children's book illustration. Illustrator for editorial markets. Artwork has been licensed to vendors such as J.C. Penney, Bed Bath & Beyond, and Art & Artifacts.

Illustrator

(As Erin Susanne Bennett) Bettye Stroud, *The Patchwork Path: A Quilt Map to Freedom,* Candlewick Press (Cambridge, MA), 2005.

Dylan Pritchett, *The First Music,* August House/Little Folk (Little Rock, AR), 2006.

Erin Bennett Banks (Reproduced by permission.)

Freddi Williams Evans, *Hush Harbor: Praying in Secret,* Carolrhoda Books (Minneapolis, MN), 2008.

Sidelights

Erin Bennett Banks was raised in upstate New York and studied art at Houghton College in New York as well as at the Savannah College of Art and Design. She has worked as an illustrator for magazines and newspapers, and has had her Art Nouveau-style paintings licensed as prints for vendors such as J.C. Penney. Banks has a particular affinity for multicultural subjects, as can be seen in her illustrations for children's books such as Bettye Stroud's *The Patchwork Path: A Quilt Map to Freedom* and Dylan Pritchett's *The First Music.*

The Patchwork Path (which Banks illustrated under her maiden name, Erin Susanne Bennett) was inspired by the actual use of quilts by slaves escaping on the Underground Railroad. In the story, a slave girl and her father follow the instructions coded in a patchwork quilt in order to move north to freedom. Banks' "bright oil paintings make dramatic use of collage to show the quilt code and the brave fugitives," as Hazel Rochman observed in her review for *Booklist.* A *Publishers Weekly* contributor found the geometric style to be "ideally

Banks contributes folk-style art to Freddi William Evans' slave story
Hush Harbor. (Illustration copyright © 2008 by Erin Bennett Banks. Reprinted with
the permission of Carolrhoda Books, a division of Lerner Publishing Group, Inc. Pack-
aged by Design Press, a division of the Savannah College of Arts and Design. All rights
reserved. No part of this excerpt may be used or reproduced in any manner whatsoever
without the prior written permission of Lerner Publishing Group, Inc.)

suited to the full-spread compositions and the quilt patterns themselves," and *School Library Journal* contributor Lauralyn Persson observed that the book's
"vivid oil paintings are skillfully done, with the characters' expressive faces reflecting their fear and courage,
and angular lines echoing the quilt squares."

Banks again uses oils to illustrate Pritchett's *The First
Music.* This tale relates how music was born from the
animals of Africa, and its accompanying "stylized oil
paintings give the African forest a rich, dark beauty," a
Kirkus Reviews critic noted. In *School Library Journal*
Miriam Lang Budin similarly praised the book's art,
writing that Banks' "stylized earth-toned illustrations
employ patterns found in African carvings and fabrics
to good effect." While dubbing Pritchett's text entertaining, Julie Cummins added in *Booklist* that it is
Banks's paintings "that really rock and roll, evoking the
synergy of the forest animals."

Banks returns to the subject of slavery in her illustrations for Freddi Williams Evans' picture book *Hush
Harbor: Praying in Secret.* This story relates how slaves
would break rules that forbade gatherings so that they
could pray together in a secret "hush harbor." A young
boy serves as lookout at one of these meetings, at which
the joy of prayer and singing combines with the fear of

being caught. Banks's "extremely stylized pictures . . .
don't prettify their subjects," Ilene Cooper asserted in
Booklist. The book's "oversized, almost muralistic figures reflect the strength of the Africans' spirits and their
tremendous physicality," a *Kirkus Reviews* critic maintained, and Banks's use of red outlines "evoke both
warmth and danger." *School Library Journal* contributor Grace Oliff praised the way the artist employs yellow tones to create moonlight scenes that are not too
dim, and concluded in her review of *Hush Harbor* that
"Banks's highly stylized paintings are wonderfully expressive and amplify the deep emotion of the situation."

Biographical and Critical Sources

PERIODICALS

Booklist, February 1, 2005, Hazel Rochman, review of
The Patchwork Path: A Quilt Map to Freedom, p.
978; November 15, 2006, Julie Cummins, review of
The First Music, p. 54; October 1, 2008, Ilene Cooper, review of *Hush Harbor: Praying in Secret,* p. 51.

"Harmony," an oil painting by Banks. (Reproduced by permission.)

Kirkus Reviews, November 1, 2006, review of *The First Music,* p. 1124; October 1, 2008, review of *Hush Harbor.*

Publishers Weekly, The January 3, 2005, review of *The Patchwork Path,* p. 55.

School Library Journal, January, 2005, Lauralyn Persson, review of *The Patchwork Path,* p. 98; January, 2007, Miriam Lang Budin, review of *The First Music,* p. 107; November 2008, Grace Oliff, review of *Hush Harbor,* p. 88.

*   *   *

BARLOW, Steve 1952-
(Salamanda Drake, a joint pseudonym, Steve Lowe)

Personal

Born 1952, in Crewe, Cheshire, England; son of Charles and Mona Lowe; married; wife's name Cathy; children: Amy, Robbie. *Education:* Warwick University, B.A. (English and American literature; with honors); Nottingham University, postgraduate certificate of education in drama and English. *Hobbies and other interests:* Walking, sailing, reading, listening to music.

Addresses

Home—Somerset, England. *E-mail*—2steves@the2steves.net.

Career

Author and educator. Writer and presenter, with Steve Skidmore, under name "Two Steves." Formerly worked as an actor, puppeteer, and stage manager. Former teacher in Botswana; formerly taught drama and performing arts in Nottingham, England.

Writings

FOR CHILDREN; WITH STEVE SKIDMORE

The Monster Project Book, illustrated by Andrew Warrington, Headway, 1993.

Thingumybob, illustrated by Mark Burgess, Ginn (Aylesbury, England), 1993.

I Fell in Love with a Leather Jacket, Piccadilly Press (London, England), 1993.

The Unsolved Mysteries Project Book, Hodder & Stoughton (Sevenoaks, Kent, England), 1993.

The Adventures of B. Bookworm: Pirate Treasure, illustrated by Kevin McAleenan, Piccadilly Press (London, England), 1994.

School: The Worst Days of Your Life, illustrated by Alan Rowe, Franklin Watts (London, England), 1995.

At the Court of King Arthur, illustrated by Kevin McAleenan, Piccadilly Press (London, England), 1995.

Diary of a Megahero, illustrated by Fred Pipes, Ginn (Aylesbury, England), 1995.

Colin the Barbarian, illustrated by Geo. Parkin, Ginn (Aylesbury, England), 1995.

The Twentieth Century: What Really Happened, illustrated by Roger Langridge, Kingfisher (London, England), 1996.

Flops and Failures, Franklin Watts (London, England), 1996.

Action Replay, illustrated by Iain Carter, Piccadilly Press (London, England), 1996.

The Monsters Guide to Good Behaviour, illustrated by John Pickering, Kingfisher (London, England), 1996.

Nev's Big Day, illustrated by Geo. Parkin, Ginn (Aylesbury, England), 1996.

Puberty Unplugged, illustrated by Stuart Harrison, Kingfisher (London, England), 1996.

Colin II: The Barbarian Returns, illustrated by Geo. Parkins, Ginn (Aylesbury, England), 1997.

The Lost Diary of Julius Caesar's Slave, Collins (London, England), 1997.

Sir Gawin and the Green Knight, illustrated by Bethan Matthews, Ginn (Aylesbury, England), 1997.

The Lost Diary of King Henry VIII's Executioner, Collins (London, England), 1997.

The Lost Diary of Erik Bloodaxe, Viking Warrior: Sometime King of Norway, King of the Hebrides, and King of the Kingdom of York, Collins (London, England), 1997.

The Lost Diary of Hercules' Personal Trainer, illustrated by George Hollingsworth, Collins (London, England), 1998.

Say What You Mean!, illustrated by Jill Newton, Ginn (Aylesbury, England), 1998.

Megahero: The Truth, illustrated by Fred Pipes, Ginn (Aylesbury, England), 1998.

Dream On!, Piccadilly Press (London, England), 1998.

(Adaptor) *The Final Battle: The Death of King Arthur* (based on *Le Morte d'Arthur* by Thomas Mallory), illustrated by Mike White, Ginn (Aylesbury, England), 1999.

Star Bores: The Novel, illustrated by Paddy Mounter, Element (Shaftsbury, England), 1999.

The Lost Diary of Shakespeare's Ghostwriter, illustrated by George Hollingsworth, Collins (London, England), 1999.

The Lost Diary of Robin Hood's Money Man, illustrated by George Hollingsworth, Collins (London, England), 1999.

The Weather Warriors, illustrated by Geo. Parkins, Ginn (Oxford, England), 1999.

(Reteller) *Twelfth Night* (based on the play by William Shakespeare), illustrated by Catherine Ward, Heinemann (Oxford, England), 2000.

(Reteller) *Romeo and Juliet* (based on the play by William Shakespeare), illustrated by Catherine Ward, Heinemann (Oxford, England), 2000.

(Editor) *Into the Unknown: A New Windmill Book of Fantasy and Science Fiction,* Heinemann (Oxford, England), 2000.

(Editor) *Taking Off!: A New Windmill Book of Fiction and Nonfiction,* Heinemann (Oxford, England), 2000.

(Reteller) *The Merchant of Venice* (based on the play by William Shakespeare), Heinemann (Oxford, England), 2001.

(Reteller) *Henry V* (based on the play by William Shakespeare), Heinemann (Oxford, England), 2001.

Star Bores: The Original Parody/The Parody Prequel (also see below), Collins (London, England), 2004.

The Doomsday Virus, illustrated by Harriet Buckley, Barrington Stoke (Edinburgh, Scotland), 2005.

Funny Business, Barrington Stoke (Edinburgh, Scotland), 2006.

The Doomsday Watchers, illustrated by Nigel Dobbyn, Barrington Stoke (Edinburgh, Scotland), 2007.

Viking Blood, illustrated by Sonia Leong, Franklin Watts (London, England), 2007.

Gorgon's Cave, illustrated by Sonia Leong, Franklin Watts (London, England), 2007.

(Writing as Salamanda Drake) *Dragonsdale,* illustrated by Gilly Marklew, Chicken House/Scholastic (Frome, England), 2007.

(Writing as Salamanda Drake) *Dragonsdale: Riding the Storm,* illustrated by Gilly Marklew, Chicken House/Scholastic (Frome, England), 2008.

Killer Clone, illustrated by Dylan Gibson, Barrington Stoke (Edinburgh, Scotland), 2009.

"MAD MYTHS" SERIES; WITH STEVE SKIDMORE

Stone Me!, illustrated by Mike Gordon, Ginn (Aylesbury, England), 1993.

Mind the Door!, illustrated by Tony Ross, Hamish Hamilton (London, England), 1996.

A Touch of Wind!, illustrated by Tony Ross, Puffin (London, England), 1998.

Must Fly!, Puffin (London, England), 1998.

Don't Look Back, illustrated by Tony Ross, Barn Owl Books (London, England), 2006.

"VERNON BRIGHT" SERIES; WITH STEVE SKIDMORE

Vernon Bright and the Magnetic Banana, illustrated by Geo. Parkin, Puffin (London, England), 2000.

Vernon Bright and Frankenstein's Hamster, illustrated by Geo. Parkin, Puffin (London, England), 2000.

Vernon Bright and the Faster-than-Light Show, illustrated by Geo. Parkin, Puffin (London, England), 2001.

Vernon Bright and the End of the World, illustrated by Geo. Parkin, Puffin (London, England), 2002.

"TALES OF THE DARK FOREST" SERIES; WITH STEVE SKIDMORE

Goodknyght!, illustrated by Fiona Land, Collins (London, England), 2001.

Whizzard!, illustrated by Fiona Land, Collins (London, England), 2002.

Trollogy!, illustrated by Fiona Land, Collins (London, England), 2002.

Knyghtmare!, illustrated by Fiona Land, Collins (London, England), 2002.

"OUTERNET" SERIES; WITH STEVE SKIDMORE

Friend or Foe?, Scholastic (London, England), 2002.

Control, Scholastic (London, England), 2002.

Odyssey, Scholastic (London, England), 2002.

Time Out, Scholastic (London, England), 2002.

The Hunt, Scholastic (London, England), 2003.

Weaver, Scholastic (London, England), 2003.

"I, HERO" SERIES; WITH STEVE SKIDMORE

Viking Blood, illustrated by Sonia Leong, Franklin Watts (London, England), 2007.

Gorgon's Cave, illustrated by Sonia Leong, Franklin Watts (London, England), 2007.

Code Mission, illustrated by Sonia Leong, Franklin Watts (London, England), 2007.

Death or Glory!, illustrated by Sonia Leong, Franklin Watts (London, England), 2007.

Save the Empire, illustrated by Sonia Leong, Franklin Watts (London, England), 2007.

Pirate Gold!, illustrated by Sonia Leong, Franklin Watts (London, England), 2007.

Strike Force!, illustrated by Sonia Leong, Franklin Watts (London, England), 2007.

Space Rescue, illustrated by Sue Mason, A. & C. Black (London, England), 2007.

PLAYS; WITH STEVE SKIDMORE

Paper Tigers, Oxford University Press (Oxford, England), 1991.

Tigers on the Prowl, Oxford University Press (Oxford, England), 1993.

(Adaptor) *The Pied Piper of Hamelin,* Ginn (Aylesbury, England), 1994.

(Adaptor) *A Tale of Two Cities* (based on the novel by Charles Dickens), Oxford University Press (Oxford, England), 1996.

Star Bores, illustrated by Geo. Parkin, Ginn (Aylesbury, England), 1997.

(Adaptor) *Nicholas Nickleby* (based on the novel by Charles Dickins), illustrated by Annabel Spenceley, Ginn (Aylesbury, England), 1997.

(Adaptor) *Jane Eyre* (based on the novel by Charlotte Brontë), Oxford University Press (Oxford, England), 1998.

Sick as a Parrot!, illustrated by Roger Langridge, Ginn (Aylesbury, England), 1999.

Have a Nice Day!, illustrated by Carlos Pino, Oxford University Press (Oxford, England), 2001.

Send in the Clones: Three Plays, Heinemann (Oxford, England), 2002.

Silly Liar: Three Plays, illustrated by Keith Page, Heinemann (Oxford, England), 2003.

Time Switch, illustrated by Sue Mason, A. & C. Black (London, England), 2007.

Contributor to books, including *New Plays,* 3 volumes, edited by Peter Terson, Oxford University Press, 1988-89. Editor, with Steve Skidmore, of "High Impact" play series, Heinemann.

OTHER

In Love with an Urban Gorilla: Recycled Confessions, Piccadilly Press (London, England), 1994.
Dramaform: A Practical Guide to Drama Techniques, Hodder & Stoughton (London, England), 1994.

Author of educational curricula for Oxford University Press; editor of "New Windmills" reading series for Heinemann.

Biographical and Critical Sources

PERIODICALS

School Library Journal, February, 2004, John Peters, review of *Whizzard!,* p. 141.

ONLINE

Steve Barlow Home Page, http://the2steves.net (January 10, 2010).

* * *

BÉHA, Philippe

Personal

Born in France. *Education:* Beaux Arts de Strasbourg, degree, 1976.

Addresses

Home—Montréal, Québec, Canada. *Agent*—iiARt Inc., infoi2iart.com. *E-mail*—beha@sympatico.ca.

Career

Illustrator and graphic designer, beginning late 1970s. Film work includes special effects for film *Le million tout-puissant.*

Member

Association de Illustrateurs et Illustratices du Québec.

Awards, Honors

Two Governor General's awards, including 1996, for *Au coeur de la tête*; Mr. Christie's Book Award; Silver Birch Award shortlist, Saskatchewan Book Award shortlist, and Diamond Willow Award nomination, all 2004, all for *The Prairie Dogs* by Glenda Goertzen; numerous other awards for illustration.

Writings

SELF-ILLUSTRATED

Musimaux, Ovale (Sillery, Québec, Canada), 1983.

L'arbre, Ovale (Sillery, Québec, Canada), 1984, translated as *The Tree,* Lorimer (Toronto, Ontario, Canada), 1984.
Combien?, Ovale (Sillery, Québec, Canada), 1984, translated as *How Many?,* Lorimer (Toronto, Ontario, Canada), 1985.
C'est à qui?, Ovale (Sillery, Québec, Canada), 1984, translated as *Whose Is It?,* Lorimer (Toronto, Ontario, Canada), 1985.
Je m'habille, Ovale (Sillery, Québec, Canada), 1984, translated as *Getting Dressed,* Lorimer (Toronto, Ontario, Canada), 1985.
Ou dors-tu?, Ovale (Sillery, Québec, Canada), 1984, translated as *Where Do You Sleep?,* Lorimer (Toronto, Ontario, Canada), 1985.
La mer, Ovale (Sillery, Québec, Canada), 1985, translated as *The Sea,* Lorimer (Toronto, Ontario, Canada), 1985.
La reine rouge, Les 400 Coups (Montréal, Québec, Canada), 2001.
Pas si bête, Hurtubise HMH (Montréal, Québec, Canada), 2005.
Ah! ha!, Hurtubise HMH (Montréal, Québec, Canada), 2007.
J'ai perdu mon chat, Imagine (Montréal, Québec, Canada), 2008.
Monsieur Leloup, Fides (Montréal, Québec, Canada), 2009.

ILLUSTRATOR

De nouvelles aventures, compiled by Colette Lussier, Raymonde Picard, and Monique Pouliot, Editions Projets (Montréal, Québec, Canada), 1978.
Grand-père Cailloux, *Lune en or,* Editions la Courte Échelle (Montréal, Québec, Canada), 1979.
Grand-père Cailloux, *Mon grand-père a un jardin,* Editions la Courte Échelle (Montréal, Québec, Canada), 1979.
Lucille Richard, *La poupee oubliee,* Mondia (Laval, Québec, Canada), 1980.
Lucille Richard, *Le chat sale,* Mondia (Laval, Québec, Canada), 1980.
Lucille Richard, *La neige,* Mondia (Laval, Québec, Canada), 1980.
Lucille Richard, *Le ballon rouge,* Mondia (Laval, Québec, Canada), 1980.
Lucille Richard, *Nicolas dans la cour de l'école,* Mondia (Laval, Québec, Canada), 1980.
Lucille Richard, *Le rêve de Mathieu,* Mondia (Laval, Québec, Canada), 1980.
Lucille Richard, *La salade de fruits,* Mondia (Laval, Québec, Canada), 1980.
Lucille Richard, *La lune,* Mondia (Laval, Québec, Canada), 1980.
Lucille Richard, *Valérie dessine,* Mondia (Laval, Québec, Canada), 1980.
Lucille Richard, *À mots découvertes,* Mondia (Laval, Québec, Canada), 1980.
Lucille Richard, *Les marionnettes,* Mondia (Laval, Québec, Canada), 1980.
Lucille Richard, *Nicolas est malade,* Mondia (Laval, Québec, Canada), 1980.

Lucille Richard, *À table,* Mondia (Laval, Québec, Canada), 1980.

Lucille Richard, *Après l'école,* Mondia (Laval, Québec, Canada), 1980.

Lucille Richard, *La chatte Mimine,* Mondia (Laval, Québec, Canada), 1980.

Lucille Richard, *Le caribou,* Mondia (Laval, Québec, Canada), 1980.

Lucille Richard, *Une idée de jeu,* Mondia (Laval, Québec, Canada), 1980.

Lucille Richard, *Le plus beau voyage,* Mondia (Laval, Québec, Canada), 1980.

Lucille Richard, *Marie-Lise,* Mondia (Laval, Québec, Canada), 1980.

Lucie Ledoux, *Le voyage à recherche du temps,* Mondia (Laval, Québec, Canada), 1981.

Malou, *La neige,* Le Sablier (Boucherville, Québec, Canada), 1981.

Malou, *Collection Moustique,* Le Sablier (Boucherville, Québec, Canada), 1981.

Malou, *Bonjour les amis!,* Le Sablier (Boucherville, Québec, Canada), 1981.

Malou, *En voyage,* Le Sablier (Boucherville, Québec, Canada), 1981.

Malou, *Un poisson pour Gédéon,* Le Sablier (Boucherville, Québec, Canada), 1981.

Malou, *Petit Radis aide Gédéon,* Le Sablier (Boucherville, Québec, Canada), 1981.

Malou, *Le jardin de Pétunia,* Le Sablier (Boucherville, Québec, Canada), 1981.

Malou, *Loup, o? es-tu?,* Publications Graficor (Varennes, Québec, Canada), 1982.

Sylvie Assathiany and Louise Pelletier, *Mes cheveux,* Ovale (Sillery, Québec, Canada), 1982, translated as *Don't Cut My Hair,* Lorimer (Toronto, Ontario, Canada), 1984.

Pierre Achim, *Un bébé,* Mondia (Laval, Québec, Canada), 1982.

Sylvie Assathiany and Louise Pelletier, *Pipi dans le pot,* Ovale (Sillery, Québec, Canada), 1982, translated as *Peepee in the Potty,* Lorimer (Toronto, Ontario, Canada), 1984.

Sylvie Assathiany and Louise Pelletier, *Dors petit ours,* Ovale (Sillery, Québec, Canada), 1982, translated as *Little Bear Can't Sleep,* Lorimer (Toronto, Ontario, Canada), 1984.

Sylvie Assathiany and Louise Pelletier, *J'aime Claire,* Ovale (Sillery, Québec, Canada), 1982, translated as *I Love My Babysitter,* Lorimer (Toronto, Ontario, Canada), 1984.

Robert Soulières, *Un été sur le Richelieu* (novel), P. Tisseyre (Montréal, Québec, Canada), 1982.

Malou, *Bonne fête, Pétunia,* Publications Graficor (Varennes, Québec, Canada), 1982.

Robert Soulières, *Seul au monde,* Québec/Amérique (Montréal, Québec, Canada), 1982.

Malou, *On part en ballon,* Publications Graficor (Varennes, Québec, Canada), 1982.

Malou, *Le soleil,* Publications Graficor (Varennes, Québec, Canada), 1982.

Malou, *Le soulier de Pétunia,* Publications Graficor (Varennes, Québec, Canada), 1982.

Pierre Achim, *Ma chatte,* Mondia (Laval, Québec, Canada), 1982.

Malou, *Gédéon a peur la nuit* Publications Graficor (Varennes, Québec, Canada), 1982.

Jean-Claude Lessard, *Marionnettes pour tous,* Mondia (Laval, Québec, Canada), 1982.

Jean-Claude Lessard, *Un mobile pour bébé,* Mondia (Laval, Québec, Canada), 1982.

Pierre Achim, *La mascarade,* Mondia (Laval, Québec, Canada), 1982.

Jean-Claude Lessard, *Les fruits,* Mondia (Laval, Québec, Canada), 1982.

Sylvie Assathiany et Louise Pelletier, *Grand-maman,* Ovale (Sillery, Québec, Canada), 1983, translated as *Grandma's Visit,* Lorimer (Toronto, Ontario, Canada), 1985.

Sylvie Assathiany et Louise Pelletier, *Quand ça va mal,* Ovale (Sillery, Québec, Canada), 1983, translated as *The Bad Day,* Lorimer (Toronto, Ontario, Canada), 1985.

Sylvie Assathiany et Louise Pelletier, *Où est ma tétine?,* Ovale (Sillery, Québec, Canada), 1983, translated as *Where Is My Dummy?,* Lorimer (Toronto, Ontario, Canada), 1985.

Louise Vanhee-Nelson, *Archibaldo, le dragon,* Éditions Paulines (Montréal, Québec, Canada), 1983.

Sylvie Assathiany and Louise Pelletier, *Mon bébé-soeur,* Ovale (Sillery, Québec, Canada), 1983, translated as *My Baby Sister,* Lorimer (Toronto, Ontario, Canada), 1985.

Chrystine Brouillet, *Un secret bien gardé,* La Courte Echelle (Montréal, Québec, Canada), 1983.

Michelyne Lortie-Paquette, *Lapala,* Éditions NHP (Victoriaville, Québec, Canada), 1984.

Danielle Marcotte, *Par la bave de mon crapaud,* Ovale (Sillery, Québec, Canada), 1984.

Robert Soulières, *Tony et Vladimir,* P. Tisseyre (Montréal, Québec, Canada), 1984.

Méli-mélo, Ovale (Sillery, Québec, Canada), 1985.

Danielle Marcotte, *Les nuits d'Arthur,* Ovale (Sillery, Québec, Canada), 1986.

(With others) Marie-Antoinette Delolme, *Intra,* Graficor (Boucherville, Québec, Canada), 1986.

(With others) Marie-Antoinette Delolme, *Inter,* Graficor (Boucherville, Québec, Canada), 1986.

(With others) Marie-Antoinette Delolme, *Extra,* Graficor (Boucherville, Québec, Canada), 1986.

Marie-Antoinette Delolme, *Les jeux de pic-mots,* Graficor (Boucherville, Québec, Canada), 1986.

Christiane Duchesne, *Mr. O's Metamorphoses,* Brault et Bouthillier (Montréal, Québec, Canada), 1987.

Christiane Duchesne, *Bébert et Cie,* Brault et Bouthillier (Montréal, Québec, Canada), 1987, translated by Sheila Burke as *We Are the Champions,* 1987.

Christiane Duchesne, *La maison sans trésor,* Brault et Bouthillier (Montréal, Québec, Canada), 1987, translated by Sheila Burke as *The House with No Treasure,* 1987.

Christiane Duchesne, *Les aventures de Carafus,* Brault et Bouthillier (Montréal, Québec, Canada), 1987, translated by Sheila Burke as *The Adventures of Cataplunk,* 1987.

Jocelyne Goyette, *Moulitou,* Éducation Québec (Québec, Canada), 1987.

Henriette Major, *Le bout du monde,* Héritage (Saint-Lambert, Québec, Canada), 1987, translated by Alan Brown as *The End of the World,* McClelland & Stewart (Toronto, Ontario, Canada), 1988.

Michel Luppens, *Mais que font les fées avec toutes ces dents?,* Éditions du Raton laveur (St. Hubert, Québec, Canada), 1989, translated by Jane Brierley as *What Do the Fairies Do with All Those Teeth?,* Scholastic Canada (Richmond Hill, Ontario, Canada), 1991.

Marie-Hélène Jarry, *Les grandes menaces,* Éditions du Raton laveur (St. Hubert, Québec, Canada), 1989.

Alain Serres, *Krocobill et Robot-Bix,* Messidor/La Farandole (Paris, France), 1990.

Raymond Plante and André Melan͵on, *Le chien saucisse et les voleurs de diamants* (novel) Boréal (Montréal, Québec, Canada), 1991.

Dominique Demers, *Valentine Picotée,* Courte échelle (Montréal, Québec, Canada), 1991.

Dominique Demers, *Toto la brute* Éditions de la Courte échelle (Montréal, Québec, Canada), 1992.

Danielle Simard, *Lia et le nu-mains,* Héritage Jeunesse (Saint-Lambert, Québec, Canada), 1994.

Danielle Simard, *Lia et les sorcières,* Héritage Jeunesse (Saint-Lambert, Québec, Canada), 1994.

Danielle Simard, *Lia et le nu-mains,* Héritage Jeunesse (Saint-Lambert, Québec, Canada), 1995.

Sylvie Nicolas, *On a perdu la tête,* Héritage Jeunesse (Saint-Lambert, Québec, Canada), 1995.

Michel Rivard and Christiane Duchesne, *Au coeur de la tête,* Le 400 Coups (Laval, Québec, Canada), 1996.

Danielle Simard, *Lia dans l'autre monde,* Héritage Jeunesse (Saint-Lambert, Québec, Canada), 1996.

Michel Luppens, *Mais ò les fées des dents vont-elles chercher tout cet argent?,* Éditions du Raton laveur (Saint-Hubert, Québec, Canada), 1996.

Barbara Nichol, *Biscuits in the Cupboard,* Stoddard Kids (Buffalo, NY), 1997.

Dominique Demers, *Marie la chipie,* Québec/Amérique (Montréal, Québec, Canada), 1997.

Dominique Demers, *Roméo Lebeau,* Québec Amérique (Montréal, Québec, Canada), 1999.

Nancy Furstinger, *Creative Crafts for Critters,* Stoddart Kids (Toronto, Ontario, Canada), 2000.

Dominique Demers, *Léon Maigrichon,* Québec Amérique (Montréal, Québec, Canada), 2000.

Henriette Major, *J'aime les poèmes,* Hurtubise HMH (Montréal, Québec, Canada), 2002.

Henriette Major, *Les devinettes d'Henriette,* Hurtubise HMH (Montréal, Québec, Canada), 2004.

Mario Brassard, *Que faire si des extraterrestres atterissent sur votre tête?: guide à l'usage des lecteurs qui ont moins de trois yeux et plus d'une oreille ou l'inverse,* Souliéres Éditeur (Saint-Lambert, Québec, Canada), 2004.

Glenda Goertzen, *The Prairie Dogs,* Fitzhenry & Whiteside (Markham, Ontario, Canada), 2005.

Dominique Demers, *Alexa Gougougaga,* Québec Amérique (Montréal, Québec, Canada), 2005.

Dominique Demers, *La plus belle histoire d'amour,* Éditions Imagine (Montréal, Québec, Canada), 2006.

Bertrand Gauthier, *D'Alex à Zoé: un abécédaire,* Québec Amérique (Montréal, Québec, Canada), 2006.

Paule Brière, *Les indésirables,* Les 400 Coups (Montréal, Québec, Canada), 2006.

Henriette Major, *Jongleries,* Hurtubise HMH (Montréal, Québec, Canada), 2006.

Jane Yolen, *Fairy Tale Feasts: A Literary Cookbook for Young Readers and Eaters,* recipes by Heidi E.Y. Stemple, Crocodile Books (Northampton, MA), 2006.

Louise Phaneuf, *Vous êtes la meilleure personne pour aider votre enfant!: comment préparer votre enfant pour l'école,* Comprendre la petite enfance (Montréal, Québec, Canada), 2006.

Louise Tondreau-Levert, *Les oreilles de grand-père,* Éditions du Renouveau pédagogique (Saint-Laurent, Québec, Canada), 2006.

Robert Souliéres, *La folie des spaghettis,* Éditions du Renouveau pédagogique (Saint-Laurent, Québec, Canada), 2006.

Andrée Poulin, *Le meilleur moment,* Éditions Imagine (Montréal, Québec, Canada), 2007.

Bertrand Gauthier, *De Mimi Petit à Tarzan Legrand: une suite de contraires,* Québec Amérique Jeunesse (Montréal, Québec, Canada), 2007.

Ghislain Bédard and Annie Pettigrew, *Les flaques d'eau: poèmes et prières du printemps,* Fides-Médiaspaul (Montréal, Québec, Canada), 2007.

Henriette Major, *Les pays inventés,* Hurtubise HMH (Montréal, Québec, Canada), 2007.

Denis Vézina, *Victor et Victor,* Souliéres (Saint-Laurent, Québec, Canada), 2007.

Philippe Mollé, *Recettes pour épater: la bonne cuisine pour petits et grands,* Fides (Montréal, Québec, Canada), 2007.

Florence Ducatteau, *Un ogre trop gourmand,* Éditions du Renouveau pédagogique (Saint-Laurent, Québec, Canada), 2008.

Andrée Poulin, *Le pire moment,* Éditions Imagine (Montréal, Québec, Canada), 2008.

Denis Vézina, *Victor, l'invincible,* Souliéres éditeur (Saint-Laurent, Québec, Canada), 2008.

Paule Brière, *The Undesirables,* Simply Read Books (Vancouver, British Columbia, Canada), 2008.

Louise Portal, *Ulysse et Pénélope,* Hurtubise HMH (Montréal, Québec, Canada), 2008.

Katarina Jovanovic, *The King Has Goat Ears,* Tradewind Books (Vancouver, British Columbia, Canada), 2008.

Dominique Demers, *Macaroni en folie,* Québec Amérique (Montréal, Québec, Canada), 2009.

Gilles Tibo, *Le dico de Tibo,* Souliéres éditeur (Saint-Laurent, Québec, Canada), 2009.

Denis Vézina, *Un chat nommé Victor,* Souliéres éditeur (Saint-Laurent, Québec, Canada), 2009.

Bertrand Gauthier, *Filou s'amuse avec Zami,* Québec Amérique jeunesse (Montréal, Québec, Canada), 2009.

Bertrand Gauthier, *Filou et Zami se déguisent. 2,* Québec Amérique Jeunesse (Montréal, Québec, Canada), 2009.

Sidelights

Born in France and educated at the Beaux Arts de Strasbourg, illustrator Philippe Béha now makes his home in his adopted Québec, Canada. The recipient of several top awards, Béha's colorful, modernistic mixed-media art is featured in over a hundred French-language books for children, as well as several works for English-speaking readers.

In Jane Yolen and Heidi E.Y. Stemple's *Fairy Tale Feasts: A Literary Cookbook for Young Readers and Eaters,* a mother-daughter project that combines traditional stories with yummy recipes, Béha contributes what a *Kirkus Reviews* writer described as "colorful, whimsical illustrations [that] hit just the right note." In *School Library Journal* Lauralyn Persson cited the artist's effective use of "bright colors and bold, simple lines," both of which are "set off by lots of white space" in the large-format book. Béha's "spare, whimsical sport illustrations" combine with the stories and recipes in *Fairy Tale Feasts* to "capture children's fancy," concluded *Booklist* critic Gillian Engberg.

In illustrating Katarina Jovanovic's folktale adaptation *The King Has Goat Ears,* Béha's collage art is enhanced by what *Resource Links* contributor Linda Ludke praised as "striking oil paintings," and a *Kirkus Reviews* critic described *The King Has Goat Ears* as a mix of photographs, "Chagall-esque, white-faced figures and waxy layers of color." Appraising the artwork featured in Denis Vézina's easy-reading *Victor et Victor,* one of several collaborations between author and artist, *Resource Links* contributor Mary Moroska wrote that Béha's pen-and-ink illustrations for this book feature "exaggerated lines [that] add to the . . . humorous mood" of Vézina's story.

Biographical and Critical Sources

PERIODICALS

Booklist, November 1, 2006, Gillian Engberg, review of *Fairy Tale Feasts: A Literary Cookbook for Young Readers and Eaters,* p. 62.
Kirkus Reviews, July 15, 2006, review of *Fairy Tale Feasts,* p. 731; September 15, 2008, review of *The King Has Goat Ears.*
School Library Journal, January, 2002, Lynda Ritterman, review of *Creative Crafts for Critters,* p. 117; August, 2005, Sharon R. Pearce, review of *The Prairie Dogs,* p. 94; November, 2006, Lauralyn Persson, review of *Fairy Tale Feasts,* p. 126.

Resource Links, April, 2005, Carolyn Cutt, review of *The Prairie Dogs,* p. 9; June, 2008, Louise Melancon, review of *Victor l'invisible,* p. 45; April, 2008, Mary Moroska, review of *Victor et Victor,* p. 62; October, 2008, Linda Ludke, review of *The King Has Goat Ears,* p. 1.

ONLINE

Association de Illustrateurs et Illustratices du Québec Web site, http://www.illustrationquebec.com/ (December 15, 2009), "Philippe Béha."*

*   *   *

BENNETT, Erin Susanne
See BANKS, Erin Bennett

*   *   *

BERGSTEIN, Rita M.

Personal

Married; children: three daughters.

Addresses

Home—North Huntingdon, PA. *E-mail*—R.Bergstein@comcast.net.

Career

Author and storyteller. Regional sales coordinator for AFLAC Insurance. Founder, National Book at Bedtime Family Night.

Awards, Honors

Best Book of the Year citation, Bank Street College of Education, 2009, for *Your Own Big Bed.*

Writings

Your Own Big Bed, illustrated by Susan Kathleen Hartung, Viking (New York, NY), 2008.

Sidelights

Rita M. Bergstein's picture book *Your Own Big Bed* grew out of her experiences as a mother to three girls. Bergstein had always enjoyed making up stories for bedtime, but her youngest daughter would not settle down for sleep because she was scared of sleeping in her new bed. Bergstein reassured the girl by explaining

Rita M. Bergstein's bedtime picture book Your Own Big Bed *features Susan Kathleen Hartug's stylized illustrations.* (Illustration copyright © 2008 by Susan Kathleen Hartung. Reproduced by permission of Viking, a division of Penguin Putnam Books for Young Readers.)

that the change from a crib to a big bed is a natural part of growing up, just like baby birds move from an egg to a nest to the open sky.

In her picture book, illustrated by Susan Kathleen Hartung, Bergstein shows various animals making the transition to new, bigger homes. Whether a chick, a baby kangaroo, or a tiger cub, all animals grow and change. The comparison between children and animals "adds both comfort and acknowledgment of a little one's movement from the familiar to the new," a *Kirkus Reviews* critic noted, while *School Library Journal* contributor Martha Simpson remarked that "the absence of the anxiety, whining, or excuses common to books of this ilk is [a] refreshing" aspect of *Your Own Big Bed.* Gillian Engberg, writing in *Booklist,* praised the "soothing sounds and rhythms in the simple words," and concluded that *Your Own Big Bed* is "a lovely, sensitive offering."

Biographical and Critical Sources

PERIODICALS

Booklist, July 1, 2008, Gillian Engberg, review of *Your Own Big Bed,* p. 75.

Kirkus Reviews, May 1, 2008, review of *Your Own Big Bed.*

School Library Journal, July, 2008, Martha Simpson, review of *Your Own Big Bed,* p. 66.

ONLINE

Rita Bergstein Home Page, http://www.ritabergstein.com (January 6, 2010).*

BLAKE, Quentin 1932-

Personal

Born December 16, 1932, in Sidcup, Kent, England; son of William (a civil servant) and Evelyn Blake. *Education:* Downing College, Cambridge, England, M.A., 1956; University of London Institute of Education, P.G. C.E., 1956-57; attended Chelsea School of Art, 1958-59.

Addresses

Home—London, England. *Agent*—A.P. Watt Ltd., 20 John St., London WCIN 2DR, England.

Career

Author, artist, editor, and educator. Illustrator for *Punch,* beginning 1948, and other British magazines, including *Spectator;* freelance illustrator, 1957—; Royal College of Art, London, England, tutor in School of Graphic Design, 1965-78, head of Illustration Department, 1978-86, visiting tutor, 1986-89,, senior fellow, 1988, visiting professor, beginning 1989. Has also worked as an English teacher at French Lycee in London, 1962-65. *Exhibitions:* Work has been exhibited at Workshop Gallery, London, England; 1972, 1973, 1974, 1976; National Theatre, London, 1984; Royal Academy, London, 1984, 1986, 1987; Bologna International Children's Book Fair, 1985; National Gallery, London, 2001; Dulwich Picture Gallery, London, 2004; Somerset House, London, 2004; Petit Palais, Paris, France, 2005; and in Genoa, Italy, 2009. *Military service:* Served in British Army Education Corps, 1951-53.

Awards, Honors

Several of Blake's books were named to Child Study Association of America's Children's Books of the Year list, including *Put on Your Thinking Cap,* 1969, *Arabel's Raven,* 1974, *Custard and Company,* 1985, and *The Giraffe and the Pelly and Me,* 1986; London *Guardian* Award, second prize, 1969, for *Patrick; New York Times* Best Illustrated Books of the Year designation, 1976, for *A Near Thing for Captain Najork,* and 1997, for *Clown;* Kate Greenaway Medal high commendation, British Library Association (BLA), 1980, for *The Wild Washerwomen;* Kate Greenaway Medal, and Children's Book Award, Federation of Children's Book Groups, both 1981, both for *Mister Magnolia;* named Royal Designer for Industry, 1981; Children's Book Award, Federation of Children's Book Groups, 1982, for *The BFG;* Kurt Maschler Award runner-up, National Book League (London, England), 1982, for *Rumbelow's Dance,* 1984, for *The Story of the Dancing Frog,* 1985, for *The Giraffe and the Pelly and Me,* and 1986, for *The Rain Door;* Silver Pencil award (Holland), 1985; named officer, Order of the British Empire, 1988; Reading Magic Award, 1989, for *Quentin Blake's ABC;* Kurt Maschler Award, 1990, for *All Join In;* Smarties Prize (ages six to eight), 1990, for *Esio Trot;* British Book Award (illustrated runner-up), 1990, for *Alpha-*

Quentin Blake (Reproduced by permission.)

beasts; University of Southern Mississippi medallion, 1993, for body of work; Ragazzi Award, Bologna Children's Book Fair, and Blue Ribbon citation, *Bulletin of the Center for Children's Books,* both 1996, both for *Clown; How Tom Beat Captain Najork and His Hired Sportsmen* and *The Witches* named Notable Books, American Library Association; *How Tom Beat Captain Najork and His Hired Sportsmen* and *The Wild Washerwomen* named to *Boston Globe/Horn Book* Award honor list; named inaugural Children's Laureate of the United Kingdom, 1999-2001; Hans Christian Andersen Award for illustration, International Board on Books for Young People, 2002; *Boston Globe/Horn Book* Award nomination, and Kate Greenaway Medal nomination, both 2005, both for *Michael Rosen's Sad Book;* decorated commander, Order of the British Empire, 2005; named chevalier, Ordre des Arts et des Lettres (France) 2007; J.M. Barrie Award, Action for Children's Arts, 2008; recipient of honorary degrees from London Institute, 2000, Royal College of Art, 2001, University of Northumbria, 2001, University of Cambridge, 2004, Institute of Education, University of Loughborough, Open University, and Anglia Ruskin University. Quentin Blake Award, funded by the Roald Dahl Foundation, was named for the illustrator.

Writings

SELF-ILLUSTRATED; FOR CHILDREN

Patrick, Jonathan Cape (London, England), 1968, Walck (New York, NY), 1969.

Jack and Nancy, Jonathan Cape (London, England), 1969.

Angelo, Jonathan Cape (London, England), 1970.

Snuff, Lippincott (Philadelphia, PA), 1973.

Lester at the Seaside, Collins Picture Lions (London, England), 1975.

(Compiler, with John Yeoman) *The Puffin Book of Improbable Records,* Puffin (London, England), 1975, published as *The Improbable Book of Records,* Atheneum (New York, NY), 1976.

The Adventures of Lester, British Broadcasting Corporation (London, England), 1978.

(Compiler) *Custard and Company: Poems by Ogden Nash,* Kestrel (London, England), 1979, Little, Brown (Boston, MA), 1980.

Mister Magnolia, Merrimack, 1980, Random Century (London, England), 1991.

Quentin Blake's Nursery Rhyme Book, Jonathan Cape (London, England), 1983, Harper (New York, NY), 1984.

The Story of the Dancing Frog, Jonathan Cape (London, England), 1984, Knopf (New York, NY), 1985.

Mrs. Armitage on Wheels, Jonathan Cape (London, England), 1987, Knopf (New York, NY), 1988.

Quentin Blake's ABC, Knopf (New York, NY), 1989.

All Join In, Jonathan Cape (London, England), 1990, Little, Brown (Boston, MA), 1991.

Quentin Blake's Nursery Collection, Jonathan Cape (London, England), 1991.

Cockatoos, Little, Brown (Boston, MA), 1992.

Simpkin, Jonathan Cape (London, England), 1993, Viking (New York, NY), 1994.

(Compiler) *The Quentin Blake Book of Nonsense Verse,* Viking (New York, NY), 1994.

(Compiler) *The Penguin Book of Nonsense Verse,* Penguin (New York, NY), 1995.

Clown, Jonathan Cape (London, England), 1995, Holt, 1996.

The Quentin Blake Book of Nonsense Stories, Viking (New York, NY), 1996.

Mrs. Armitage and the Big Wave, Harcourt (San Diego, CA), 1997.

Ten Frogs, Pavilion (London, England), 1997, Michael di Capua Books/HarperCollins (New York, NY), 2000.

The Green Ship, Jonathan Cape (London, England), 1998.

Zagazoo, Orchard Books (New York, NY), 1998.

(With John Cassidy) *Drawing for the Artistically Undiscovered,* Klutz Press, 1998.

Fantastic Daisy Artichoke, Rand, 2001.

Loveykins, Peachtree Press (Atlanta, GA), 2003.

Tell Me a Picture, Millbrook Press (Brookfield, CT), 2003.

Mrs. Armitage: Queen of the Road, Peachtree Press (Atlanta, GA), 2003.

ILLUSTRATOR

Patrick Campbell, *Come Here till I Tell You,* Hutchinson (London, England), 1960.

John Yeoman, *A Drink of Water and Other Stories,* Faber (London, England), 1960.

Evan Hunter, *The Wonderful Button,* Abelard (New York, NY), 1961.

Frances Gray Patton, *Good Morning, Miss Dove,* Penguin (London, England), 1961.

John Moore, editor, *The Boys' Country Book,* Collins (London, England), 1961.

Rosemary Weir, *Albert the Dragon,* Abelard (New York, NY), 1961.

John Yeoman, *The Boy Who Sprouted Antlers,* Faber (London, England), 1961, revised edition, Collins (London, England), 1977.

Edward Korel, *Listen and I'll Tell You,* Blackie (London, England), 1962, Lippincott (Philadelphia, PA), 1964.

John Moreton, *Punky: Mouse for a Day,* Faber (London, England), 1962.

Ezo, *My Son-in-Law the Hippopotamus,* Abelard (New York, NY), 1962.

Patrick Campbell, *Constantly in Pursuit,* Hutchinson (London, England), 1962.

Patrick Campbell, *Brewing Up in the Basement,* Hutchinson (London, England), 1963.

Patrick Campbell, *How to Become a Scratch Golfer,* Blond (London, England), 1963.

Rupert Croft-Cooke, *Tales of a Wicked Uncle,* Jonathan Cape (London, England), 1963.

Richard Schickel, *The Gentle Knight,* Abelard (New York, NY), 1964.

Joan Tate, *The Next-Doors,* Heinemann (London, England), 1964.

Rosemary Weir, *Albert the Dragon and the Centaur,* Abelard (New York, NY), 1964.

Rosemary Weir, *The Further Adventures of Albert the Dragon,* Abelard (New York, NY), 1964.

Ennis Rees, *Riddles, Riddles Everywhere,* Abelard (New York, NY), 1964.

Fred Loads, Alan Gemmell, and Bill Sowerbutts, *Gardeners' Question Time,* British Broadcasting Corporation (London, England), 1964, second series, 1966.

J.P. Martin, *Uncle,* Jonathan Cape (London, England), 1964, Coward (New York, NY), 1966, reprinte, New York Review of Books (New York, NY), 2007.

James Britton, editor, *The Oxford Books of Stories for Juniors,* three volumes, Oxford University Press (Oxford, England), 1964–1966.

Nils-Olof Franzen, *Agaton Sax and the Diamond Thieves,* Deutsch (London, England), 1965, translated by Evelyn Ramsden, Delacorte (New York, NY), 1967.

Ennis Rees, *Pun Fun,* Abelard (New York, NY), 1965.

Bill Hartley, *Motoring and the Motorist,* BBC (London, England), 1965.

Charles Connell, *Aphrodisiacs in Your Garden,* Mayflower, 1965.

Patrick Campbell, *The P-P-Penguin Patrick Campbell,* Penguin (London, England), 1965.

Patrick Campbell, *Rough Husbandry,* Hutchinson (London, England), 1965.

J.P. Martin, *Uncle Cleans Up,* Jonathan Cape (London, England), 1965, Coward (New York, NY), 1967, reprinted, New York Review of Books (New York, NY), 2008.

Barry Ruth, *Home Economics,* Heinemann (London, England), 1966.

Jules Verne, *Around the World in Eighty Days,* Chatto & Windus (London, England), 1966.

Thomas L. Hirsch, *Puzzles for Pleasure and Leisure,* Abelard (New York, NY), 1966.

J.P. Martin, *Uncle and His Detective,* Jonathan Cape (London, England), 1966.

Robert Tibber, *Aristide,* Hutchinson (London, England), 1966, Dial (New York, NY), 1967.

J.P. Martin, *Uncle and the Treacle Trouble,* Jonathan Cape (London, England), 1967.

Marjorie Bilbow and Antony Bilbow, *Give a Dog a Good Name,* Hutchinson (London, England), 1967.

Joan Tate, *Bits and Pieces,* Heinemann (London, England), 1967.

Ennis Rees, *Tiny Tall Tales,* Abelard (New York, NY), 1967.

Joan Tate, *Luke's Garden,* Heinemann (London, England), 1967.

Helen J. Fletcher, *Put on Your Thinking Cap,* Abelard (New York, NY), 1968.

G. Broughton, *Listen and Read with Peter and Molly,* British Broadcasting Corporation (London, England), 1968.

John Yeoman, *The Bear's Winter House,* World Publishing Company (New York, NY), 1969.

Gordon Fraser, editor, *Your Animal Book,* Gordon Fraser, 1969.

H.P. Rickman, *Living with Technology,* Zenith Books (London, England), 1969.

G. Broughton, *Success with English: The Penguin Course,* Penguin (London, England), 1969.

Nathan Zimelman, *The First Elephant Comes to Ireland,* Follett (Chicago, IL), 1969.

James Reeves, *Mr. Horrox and the Gratch,* Abelard (New York, NY), 1969.

Ennis Rees, *Gillygaloos and the Gollywhoppers: Tall Tales about Mythical Monsters,* Abelard (New York, NY), 1969.

J.P. Martin, *Uncle and Claudius the Camel,* Jonathan Cape (London, England), 1969.

Nils-Olof Franzen, *Agaton Sax and the Scotland Yard Mystery,* Delacorte (New York, NY), 1969.

John Yeoman, *Alphabet Soup* (poem), Faber (London, England), 1969, Follett (Chicago, IL), 1970.

Nils-Olof Franzen, *Agaton Sax and the Incredible Max Brothers,* Delacorte (New York, NY), 1970.

Gillian Edwards, *Hogmanay and Tiffany: The Names of Feasts and Fasts,* Geoffrey Bles, 1970.

D. Mackay, B. Thompson, and P. Schaub, *The Birthday Party,* Longman (London, England), 1970.

Elizabeth Bowen, *The Good Tiger,* Jonathan Cape (London, England), 1970.

Helen J. Fletcher, *Puzzles and Quizzles,* Platt, 1970.

Thomas Corddry, *Kibby's Big Feat,* Follett (Chicago, IL), 1970.

John Yeoman, *The Bear's Water Picnic,* Blackie (London, England), 1970, Macmillan (New York, NY), 1971.

H. Thomson, *The Witch's Cat,* Addison-Wesley, 1971.

J.B.S. Haldane, *My Friend Mr. Leakey,* Puffin (London, England), 1971.

Ruth Craft, *Play School Play Ideas,* Penguin, 1971.

Aristophanes, *The Birds,* translated by Dudley Fitts, Royal College of Art, 1971.

Marcus Cunliffe, *The Ages of Man: From Sav-age to Sew-age,* American Heritage, 1971.

Nils-Olof Franzen, *Agaton Sax and the Criminal Doubles,* Deutsch (London, England), 1971.

John Yeoman, *Sixes and Sevens,* (London, England), 1971, Macmillan (New York, NY), 1972.

Nils-Olof Franzen, *Agaton Sax and the Colossus of Rhodes,* Deutsch (London, England), 1972.

G. Broughton, *Peter and Molly,* British Broadcasting Corporation (London, England), 1972.

John Yeoman, *Mouse Trouble,* Hamish Hamilton (London, England), 1972, Macmillan (New York, NY), 1973.

Natalie Savage Carlson, *Pigeon of Paris,* Blackie (London, England), 1972, Scholastic, Inc. (New York, NY), 1975.

Sid Fleischman, *McBroom's Wonderful One-Acre Farm,* Chatto & Windus (London, England), 1972, Greenwillow (New York, NY), 1992.

Norman Hunter, *Wizards Are a Nuisance,* British Broadcasting Corporation (London, England), 1973.

Julia Watson, editor, *The Armada Lion Book of Young Verse,* Collins (London, England), 1973.

R.C. Scriven, *The Thingummy-jig,* British Broadcasting Corporation (London, England), 1973.

F. Knowles and B. Thompson, *Eating,* Longman (London, England), 1973.

Nils-Olof Franzen, *Agaton Sax and the London Computer Plot,* Deutsch (London, England), 1973.

J.P. Martin, *Uncle and the Battle for Badgertown,* Jonathan Cape (London, England), 1973.

Joan Aiken, *Arabel and the Escaped Black Mamba,* British Broadcasting Corporation (London, England), 1973, published as *Arabel, Mortimer, and the Escaped Black Mamba,* Barn Owl Books (London, England), 2001.

Michael Rosen, *Mind Your Own Business,* Deutsch (London, England), 1974.

Nils-Olof Franzen, *Agaton Sax and the League of Silent Exploders,* Deutsch (London, England), 1974.

Clement Freud, *Grimble,* Penguin (London, England), 1974, published as *Grimble at Christmas,* Jonathan Cape (London, England), 2008.

Dr. Seuss, *Great Day for Up!,* Random House (New York, NY), 1974.

Bronnie Cunningham, editor, *The Puffin Joke Book,* Penguin (London, England), 1974.

Joan Aiken, *The Bread Bin,* British Broadcasting Corporation (London, England), 1974.

John Yeoman, *Beatrice and Vanessa,* Hamish Hamilton (London, England), 1974, Macmillan (New York, NY), 1975.

Russell Hoban, *How Tom Beat Captain Najork and His Hired Sportsmen,* Atheneum (New York, NY), 1974, reprinted, David R. Godine (Boston, MA), 2006.

Joan Aiken, *Tales of Arabel's Raven,* Jonathan Cape (London, England), 1974, published as *Arabel's Raven,* Doubleday (New York, NY), 1974, reprinted, Harcourt (Orlando, FL), 2007.

Willis Hall, *The Incredible Kidnapping,* Heinemann (London, England), 1975.

Willis Hall, *Kidnapped at Christmas,* Heinemann (London, England), 1975.

G. Broughton, *Peter and Molly's Revision Book,* British Broadcasting Corporation (London, England), 1975.

Nils-Olof Franzen, *Agaton Sax and the Haunted House,* Deutsch (London, England), 1975.

Russell Hoban, *A Near Thing for Captain Najork,* Jonathan Cape (London, England), 1975, Atheneum (New York, NY), 1976, reprinted, David R. Godine (Boston, MA), 2006.

Roald Dahl, *Danny: The Champion of the World,* Jonathan Cape (London, England), 1975, Knopf (New York, NY), 2002.

Nils-Olof Franzen, *Agaton Sax and the Big Rig,* Deutsch (London, England), 1976.

Lewis Carroll, *The Hunting of the Snark,* Folio Society (London, England), 1976.

Sylvia Plath, *The Bed Book,* Faber (London, England), 1976.

Adele De Leeuw, *Horseshoe Harry and the Whale,* Parents Magazine Press, 1976.

Joan Aiken, *Mortimer's Tie* (also see below), British Broadcasting Corporation (London, England), 1976.

Ellen Blance and Ann Cook, *Monster Books,* twenty-four volumes, Longman (London, England),1976–1978.

Sid Fleischman, *Here Comes McBroom!,* Chatto & Windus (London, England), 1976, Greenwillow (New York, NY), 1992.

John Yeoman, *The Young Performing Horse,* Hamish Hamilton (London, England), 1977, Parents Magazine Press (New York, NY), 1978.

Margaret Mahy, *The Nonstop Nonsense Book,* Dent (London, England), 1977, Margaret K. McElderry Books (New York, NY), 1989.

Sara Brewton, John E. Brewton, and John B. Blackburn, editors, *Of Quarks, Quasars, and Other Quirks: Quizzical Poems for the Supersonic Age,* Harper (New York, NY), 1977.

Michael Rosen, *Wouldn't You Like to Know?,* Deutsch (London, England), 1977.

Carole Ward, *Play School Ideas 2,* British Broadcasting Corporation (London, England), 1977.

Stella Gibbons, *Cold Comfort Farm,* Folio Society (London, England), 1977.

Ted Allan, *Willie the Squowse,* McClelland & Stewart (Toronto, Ontario, Canada), 1977, Hastings House, 1978.

Roald Dahl, *The Enormous Crocodile,* Knopf (New York, NY), 1978.

Nils-Olof Franzen, *Agaton Sax and Lispington's Grandfather Clock,* Deutsch (London, England), 1978.

Bronnie Cunningham, editor, *Funny Business,* Penguin (London, England), 1978.

Patrick Campbell, *A Feast of True Fandangles,* W.H. Allen (London, England), 1979.

Michael Rosen, *The Bakerloo Flea,* Longman (London, England), 1979.

Joan Aiken, *Mortimer and the Sword Excalibur* (also see below), British Broadcasting Corporation (London, England), 1979.

Joan Aiken, *The Spiral Stair* (also see below), British Broadcasting Corporation (London, England), 1979.

Joan Aiken, *Arabel and Mortimer* (includes *Mortimer's Tie, The Spiral Stair,* and *Mortimer and the Sword Excalibur*), British Broadcasting Corporation (London, England), 1979, Doubleday (New York, NY), 1981, reprinted, Harcourt (Orlando, FL), 2007.

John Yeoman, *The Wild Washerwomen: A New Folktale,* Greenwillow (New York, NY), 1979, reprinted, Andersen Press (Minneapolis, MN), 2009.

Joan Aiken, *Mortimer's Portrait on Glass,* British Broadcasting Corporation (London, England), 1980.

Joan Aiken, *The Mystery of Mr. Jones's Disappearing Taxi,* British Broadcasting Corporation (London, England), 1980.

Helen Young, *What Difference Does It Make, Danny?,* Deutsch (London, England), 1980.

Russell Hoban, *The Twenty Elephant Restaurant,* Jonathan Cape (London, England), 1980.

Russell Hoban, *Ace Dragon Ltd.,* Jonathan Cape (London, England), 1980, Merrimack Book Service (Salem, NH), 1981.

Roald Dahl, *The Twits,* Knopf (New York, NY), 1980, reprinted, 2002.

Michael Rosen, *You Can't Catch Me!,* Deutsch (London, England), 1981.

Evelyn Waugh, *Black Mischief,* Folio Society (London, England), 1981.

Jonathan Gathorne-Hardy, *Cyril Bonhamy v. Madam Big,* Jonathan Cape (London, England), 1981.

Tony Lacey, editor, *Up with Skool!,* Kestrel (London, England), 1981.

Sid Fleischman, *McBroom and the Great Race,* Chatto & Windus (London, England), 1981.

Roald Dahl, *George's Marvellous Medicine,* Jonathan Cape (London, England), 1981, published as *George's Marvelous Medicine,* Knopf (New York, NY), 1982, reprinted, 2002.

Roald Dahl, *The BFG,* Farrar, Straus (New York, NY), 1982.

John Yeoman, *Rumbelow's Dance,* Hamish Hamilton (London, England), 1982.

Tim Rice and Andrew Lloyd Webber, *Joseph and the Amazing Technicolor Dreamcoat,* Holt (New York, NY), 1982.

Roald Dahl, *Roald Dahl's Revolting Rhymes,* Jonathan Cape (London, England), 1982, Knopf (New York, NY), 1983, reprinted, 2002.

Jonathan Gathorne-Hardy, *Cyril Bonhamy and the Great Drain Robbery,* Jonathan Cape (London, England), 1983.

Evelyn Waugh, *Scoop,* Folio Society (London, England), 1983.

Joan Aiken, *Mortimer's Cross,* Jonathan Cape (London, England), 1983, Harper (New York, NY), 1984.

Roald Dahl, *Roald Dahl's Dirty Beasts,* Jonathan Cape (London, England), 1983, Penguin (New York, NY), 1986, published as *Dirty Beasts,* Puffin (New York, NY), 2002.

Roald Dahl, *The Witches,* Farrar, Straus (New York, NY), 1983, Random House (London, England), 1995.

John Yeoman, *The Hermit and the Bear,* Deutsch (London, England), 1984.

George Orwell, *Animal Farm,* Folio Society (London, England), 1984.

Rudyard Kipling, *How the Camel Got His Hump,* Macmillan (London, England), 1984, P. Bedrick Books, 1985.

Jonathan Gathorne-Hardy, *Cyril Bonhamy and Operation Ping,* Jonathan Cape (London, England), 1984.

Michael Rosen, *Quick, Let's Get out of Here,* Deutsch (London, England), 1984.

Jeff Brown, *A Lamp for the Lambchops,* Methuen (London, England), 1985.

Roald Dahl, *The Giraffe and the Pelly and Me,* Farrar, Straus (New York, NY), 1985.

Margaret Mahy, *The Great Piratical Rumbustification and the Librarian and the Robbers,* David Godine (London, England), 1986, Morrow (New York, NY), 1993.

Jan Mark, *Frankie's Hat,* Kestrel (London, England), 1986.

Dr. Pete Rowan, *Can You Get Warts from Touching Toads?: Ask Dr. Pete,* Messner, 1986.

Russell Hoban, *The Marzipan Pig,* Farrar, Straus (New York, NY), 1986.

Michael Rosen, *Don't Put Mustard in the Custard,* Deutsch (London, England), 1986.

Michael Rosen, *Under the Bed,* Prentice-Hall (New York, NY), 1986.

Michael Rosen, *Smelly Jelly Smelly Fish,* Prentice-Hall (New York, NY), 1986.

Russell Hoban, *The Rain Door,* Gollancz (London, England), 1986, Crowell (New York, NY), 1987.

Michael Rosen, *Hard-Boiled Legs: The Breakfast Book,* Prentice-Hall (New York, NY), 1987.

Michael Rosen, *Spollyollydiddlytiddlyitis: The Doctor Book,* Walker Books (London, England), 1987.

Joan Aiken, *Mortimer Says Nothing,* Harper (New York, NY), 1987.

Michael Rosen, *Down at the Doctor's: The Sick Book,* Simon & Schuster (New York, NY), 1988.

John Yeoman, *Our Village* (poems), Atheneum (New York, NY), 1988.

Roald Dahl, *Matilda,* Jonathan Cape (London, England), 1988, Random House (New York, NY), 1994.

John Yeoman, *Old Mother Hubbard's Dog Dresses Up,* Walker Books (London, England), 1989, Houghton Mifflin (Boston, MA), 1990.

John Yeoman, *Old Mother Hubbard's Dog Learns to Play,* Walker Books (London, England), 1989, Houghton Mifflin (Boston, MA), 1990.

John Yeoman, *Old Mother Hubbard's Dog Needs a Doctor,* Walker Books (London, England), 1989, Houghton Mifflin (Boston, MA), 1990.

John Yeoman, *Old Mother Hubbard's Dog Takes up Sport,* Walker Books (London, England), 1989, Houghton Mifflin (Boston, MA), 1990.

Roald Dahl, *Rhyme Stew,* Jonathan Cape (London, England), 1989, Viking (New York, NY), 1990.

Roald Dahl, *Esio Trot,* Viking (New York, NY), 1990.

Joan Aiken, *Arabel and the Escaped Black Mamba,* British Broadcasting Corporation (London, England), 1990.

Jeff Brown, *Stanley and the Magic Lamp,* Methuen (London, England), 1990.

Russell Hoban, *Monsters,* Scholastic, Inc. (New York, NY), 1990.

Dick King-Smith, *Alphabeasts,* Gollancz (London, England), 1990, Simon & Schuster (New York, NY), 1992.

John Yeoman, *The World's Laziest Duck and Other Amazing Records,* Macmillan (London, England), 1991.

John Masefield, *The Midnight Folk,* Heinemann (London, England), 1991.

Hilaire Belloc, *Algernon and Other Cautionary Tales,* Jonathan Cape (London, England), 1991.

Roald Dahl, *The Dahl Diary,* Puffin (London, England), 1991.

Roald Dahl, *Roald Dahl's Guide to Railway Safety,* British Railways Board, 1991.

Roald Dahl, *The Vicar of Nibbleswicke,* Random Century (London, England), 1991, Viking (New York, NY), 1992.

John Masefield, *The Box of Delights,* Heinemann (London, England), 1992.

Joan Aiken and Lizza Aiken, *Mortimer and Arabel,* British Broadcasting Corporation (London, England), 1992.

Bianca Pitzorno, *Tornatrás,* Mondadori (Milan, Italy), 1993.

John Yeoman, *The Family Album,* Hamish Hamilton (London, England), 1993.

John Yeoman, *Featherbrains,* Hamish Hamilton (London, England), 1993.

John Yeoman, *The Singing Tortoise and Other Animal Folktales,* Gollancz (London, England), 1993, Morrow (New York, NY), 1994.

Roald Dahl, *My Year,* Viking (New York, NY), 1994.

Roald Dahl, *Roald Dahl's Revolting Recipes,* compiled by Josie Fison and Felicity Dahl, photographs by Jan Baldwin, Viking (New York, NY), 1994.

Hilaire Belloc, *The Winter Sleepwalker,* Jonathan Cape (London, England), 1994.

John Yeoman, *Mr. Nodd's Ark,* Hamish Hamilton (London, England), 1995.

John Yeoman, *The Do-It-Yourself House That Jack Built,* Atheneum (New York, NY), 1995.

Michael Rosen, *The Best of Michael Rosen,* Wetlands Press (Berkeley, CA), 1995.

Joan Aiken, *A Handful of Gold,* Jonathan Cape (London, England), 1995.

Hilaire Belloc, *Cautionary Verses,* Red Fox (London, England), 1995.

Carol Ann Duffy, *Meeting Midnight,* Jonathan Cape (London, England), 1995.

Charles Dickens, *A Christmas Carol,* Simon & Schuster (New York, NY), 1995.

Sylvia Sherry, *Elephants Have Right of Way,* Jonathan Cape (London, England), 1995.

Roald Dahl, *The Magic Finger,* Viking (New York, NY), 1995.

Roald Dahl, *The Complete Adventures of Charlie and Mr. Willy Wonka* (includes *Charlie and the Chocolate Factory* and *Charlie and the Great Glass Elevator*), Viking (New York, NY), 1995.

Roald Dahl, *Charlie and the Chocolate Factory,* Puffin (London, England), 1995, Puffin (New York, NY), 1998, 40th anniversary edition, Knopf (New York, NY), 2004.

Roald Dahl, *James and the Giant Peach,* Viking (New York, NY), 1995.

Roald Dahl, *The Roald Dahl Quiz Book 2,* compiled by Sylvia Bond and Richard Maher, Puffin (London, England), 1996.

John Yeoman, reteller, *Sinbad the Sailor,* Pavilion (London, England), 1996.

Catherine Anholt and Emma Quentin, editors, *The Candlewick Book of First Rhymes,* Candlewick Press (Cambridge, MA), 1996.

Roald Dahl, *Fantastic Mr. Fox,* Viking (London, England), 1996, Puffin (New York, NY), 1998.

John Hedgecoe, *Breakfast with Dolly,* Collins (London, England), 1997.

John Julius Norwich, *The Twelve Days of Christmas,* St. Martin's Press (New York, NY), 1998.

Roald Dahl, *Charlie and the Great Glass Elevator,* Puffin (London, England), 1998, Knopf (New York, NY), 2001.

John Yeoman, reteller, *The Princes' Gifts: Magic Folktales from around the World,* Pavilion (London, England), 1999.

J.P. Martin, *Uncle Stories,* Red Fox (London, England), 2000.

William Steig, *Wizzil,* Farrar, Straus (New York, NY), 2000.

Bianca Pitzorno, *Polissena del Porcello,* Mondadori (Milan, Italy), 2000.

Russell Hoban, *Trouble on Thunder Mountain,* Orchard Books (New York, NY), 2000.

Roald Dahl, *The Wonderful Story of Henry Sugar and Six More,* Puffin (London, England), 2000, Knopf (New York, NY), 2001.

Roald Dahl, *Even More Revolting Recipes,* compiled by Felicity Dahl, Viking (New York, NY), 2001.

Marie-Aude Murail and Elvire Murail, *Santa's Last Present,* Peachtree Press (Atlanta, GA), 2003.

Wendy Cooling, compiler, *D Is for Dahl: A Gloriumptious A-Z Guide to the World of Roald Dahl,* Penguin (London, England), 2004, Viking (Atlanta, GA), 2005.

(With others) Roald Dahl, *Vile Verses,* Viking (New York, NY), 2005.

Michael Rosen, *Michael Rosen's Sad Book,* Candlewick Press (Cambridge, MA), 2005.

Michael Morpurgo, *On Angel Wings,* Candlewick Press (Cambridge, MA), 2007.

(And author of introduction) Daniel Pennac, *The Rights of the Reader,* translated by Sarah Adams, Candlewick Press (Cambridge, MA), 2008.

(With others; and coeditor with Michael Morpurgo) *The Birthday Book,* Jonathan Cape (London, England), 2008.

David Walliams, *The Boy in the Dress,* HarperCollins (London, England), 2008.

David Walliams, *Mr. Stink,* HarperCollins (London, England), 2009.

OTHER

(And illustrator) *A Band of Angels* (for adults), Gordon Fraser (London, England), 1969.

(Author of introduction, and contributor) *Magic Pencil: Children's Book Illustration Today,* British Library (London, England), 2002.

Illustrator for "Jackanory," BBC-TV. Contributor of illustrations to periodicals, including *Punch* and *Spectator.*

Adaptations

Several of Blake's works have been adapted as filmstrips and as audio books; *Clown* was adapted for the stage and toured the United Kingdom, 2005-07.

Sidelights

Named the inaugural children's laureate of the United Kingdom in 1999, British author and illustrator Quentin Blake is regarded by many critics as a master artist whose line drawings and watercolors are touched with genius. Dubbed a "wizard with a scribbly line and a color wash," by *Booklist* critic Michael Cart, Blake has written and illustrated numerous well-received books for children and has provided the pictures for over two hundred titles by other authors for children and adults. "Blake is beyond brilliant," asserted London *Daily Telegraph* contributor Melanie McDonagh. "He's anarchic, moral, infinitely subversive, sometimes vicious, socially acute, sparse when he has to be, exuberantly lavish in the detail when he feels like it."

Considered an especially inventive and adaptable illustrator, Blake has created a highly recognizable style—called "calligraphic" by Brian Alderson in *Horn Book*—that ranges from the childlike to the highly sophisticated. Blake generally uses squiggly black lines heightened with color to express a variety of characteristics and expressions with a minimum of strokes. Full of life and fluid movement, the humor, drama, and spirit of his illustrations are thought to make them appealing to viewers, especially children. According to Lindsay Duguid in the *Times Educational Supplement,* "Blake's work is unmistakable: gob-struck youths and formless maidens, wicked small boys and batty old ladies, desperate desperadoes, parrots, monkeys, cats, mice and frogs, all rendered in a characteristically insouciant squiggly line, heightened with colour." Although these pictures may appear casual, they are acknowledged for their artistry and technical skill; in addition, Blake is praised for his keen observation of human nature as well as for the depth and pathos with which he underscores many of his works.

Lauded as a gifted humorist and storyteller, Blake invests his works with a strong theatricality and includes elements of fantasy in many of his books, which he writes in both prose and verse. Blake uses familiar motifs—the folktale, the cumulative tale, the alphabet book, the counting book, and the nursery rhyme—to provide his young audience with works that are considered both original and delightful. He often uses historical settings such as the Middle Ages and the eighteenth and nineteenth centuries to introduce elements of social history along with his broadly comic yet incisive characterizations. Writing in the London *Times,* Kate Quill

***Blake's collaborations with noted author Roald Dahl include the popular story* Matilda.**

remarked that the illustrator's "love of the ridiculous and depictions of wide-eyed, inquisitive children and eccentric animals have formed part of the landscape of childhood, his books popular with successive generations of children and the parents who read to them." Quill went on to praise "Blake's gently anarchic world," adding, "His style—scratchy, freewheeling linework fizzing with energy holds fast to memory, as recognisable as E.H. Shepard, Edward Ardizzone or John Tenniel."

Blake has been celebrated by critics as both creator and collaborator. *Signal* critic Elaine Moss called him "the genius who turns a difficult manuscript into a thoroughly acceptable and beckoning book," while *Times Educational Supplement* reviewer Naomi Lewis asserted that "any book which has Quentin Blake as an illustrator is in luck, for who can match his zany wit and euphoria, his engaging charm, his wild assurance of line?" In *Horn Book* Alderson named him "the laureate of happiness," and added that "thought and graphic wizardry . . . underline almost the whole of Quentin Blake's oeuvre."

The son of a civil servant and a homemaker, Blake grew up in Sidcup, Kent, a suburb of London, England. He once told *SATA,* "I can remember drawing on the back of my exercise books as far back as primary

school. I wasn't especially encouraged by anyone. Aside from children's comics, there wasn't a great deal of illustrated material available when I was a young boy. If you were growing up in a wealthy family, you would perhaps be conscious of Arthur Rackham. But in general, children had no notion of 'an illustrator.' Once I got past children's books, I became an omnivorous reader. I read anything and everything."

Blake began submitting prose and pictures to the *Chronicle,* the school magazine of Chiselhurst Grammar School. "My most significant experience at Chiselhurst was meeting Alfred Jackson, a cartoonist for *Punch* and other magazines," he recalled. "His wife, my Latin teacher, took an interest in my drawings, and arranged a meeting between us. I was fifteen at the time, and had no idea how one went about submitting drawings to magazines. After my informative meeting with Jackson, however, I began to send my work to *Punch.* . . . [Eventually,] they accepted a few small drawings. I was drawn to the work of Ronald Searle and André François. I was influenced by them, not in terms of style, but because each in his own way seemed to be absolutely unrestricted by the conventions of illustration." When asked by Moss in *Signal* if his early success helped his parents to support Blake's leanings toward a career in humorous art, he responded that they wanted security for him, "something like banking or teaching."

After graduating from Chiselhurst, Blake served in the Army Education Corps for two years, teaching English at Aldershot and illustrating a reader for illiterate soldiers. After completing his national service, he went to Downing College Cambridge to study English. "I had decided against art school," he recalled, "because I wanted an education in literature. Had I enrolled in art school I knew that I would lose the opportunity to study literature. I could still continue to draw." Blake studied for three years at Cambridge, where he drew for their undergraduate magazines as well as for *Punch.* In 1956, he went to the University of London for a year of teacher's training. "On the verge of becoming a teacher," Blake noted, "I completed the training program and took the qualifications, but took no full-time job and went back to what I had always intended for myself: art and illustration."

Becoming a freelance artist, Blake was hired to do a drawing a week for *Punch* and also began working for the literary magazine *Spectator.* In addition, he became a part-time student at Chelsea College of Art, "because," he said, "I wanted to learn more about life drawing and painting." Blake enrolled at Chelsea in order to study with Brian Robb, a noted painter, illustrator, and cartoonist who taught at the school. His early cartoons, he recalled, "were funny, which was their main objective. I was not at all interested in political satire, which is probably why my career developed more in the direction of book illustration than cartooning. I was drawn to the drama of illustration and the theatricality of it. Books offered a continuity of narrative, which was very important to me. I was interested in storytelling and in showing how people react, how they move, and how they're placed in a scene. I was fascinated with the way

Blake teams up with beloved children's book author William Steig on the picture book **Wizzil.** (Illustration copyright © 2000 by Quentin Blake. All rights reserved. Used by permission of Farrar, Straus & Giroux, LLC.)

one could tell a story by visually portraying the action of the characters. Of course, I didn't identify this as a motive at the time, but it certainly had a lot to do with my development in the direction of book illustration."

At the age of thirty-six, Blake created his first children's book, *Patrick,* a picture-book fantasy about a young man who fiddles his way through Ireland on a magical violin. Years earlier, he had begun illustrating books for other authors. Throughout his career, Blake has provided the pictures for writers such as Lewis Carroll, Sylvia Plath, Rudyard Kipling, Dr. Seuss, Jules Verne, Margaret Mahy, George Orwell, John Masefield, Joan Tate, Evelyn Waugh, and Aristophanes. He is especially well known for his illustrations for the children's books of Joan Aiken, Michael Rosen, Sid Fleischman, J.P. Martin, and Nils-Olof Franzen. However, some of Blake's greatest artistic successes have been his illustrations for the works of Roald Dahl, Russell Hoban, and John Yeoman, the last a friend with whom Blake attended Cambridge and with whom he has co-written some texts. "I like working with other people's words—I think of it as a kind of theatre on the page," he remarked in a *Time Out London* online interview. "When you've got someone else's manuscript, . . . it's a bit like being the director of a play. You decide what it's going to look like, and you're guided by the text but you have to bring it forward from the text, so that you actually see the surroundings and you decide what those characters are wearing and the way they move and behave."

Reviewing Blake's illustrations for Hoban's *How Tom Beat Captain Najork and His Hired Sportsmen,* Moss declared that the artist is "perhaps the only illustrator who could have given visual form to [Hoban's] text without underplaying or overplaying the absurdity." Mary Nickerson, reviewing the same title in *School Library Journal,* called attention to Blake's "loony, pop-eyed characters" who "enliven some of the best current English books." Writing of his illustrations for Yeoman's *The Wild Washerwoman, Horn Book* reviewer Paul Heins noted that "the preposterous, joyful narrative and the expressive caricaturing of the slapdash line drawings washed with color are perfectly balanced." "The team of John Yeoman and Quentin Blake is way out on its own, far ahead of the field," declared Marcus Crouch in a *Junior Bookshelf* review of *The Wild Washerwoman.* "This is genuine, all-pervading humor, untouched with satire but firmly based in real values."

Some of Blake's most endearing and signature work can be found in his classic illustrations for Dahl's sardonic tales, such as *The Enormous Crocodile, The Twits, George's Marvelous Medicine, Matilda,* and *Charlie and the Chocolate Factory.* "What was so wonderful to me was that so many of Roald's stories were fantastical, unrealistic, so I was free to do what I wanted. I could let my style develop," Blake told Stuart Jeffries in the London *Guardian.* "Think of *The Twits* or *The*

BFG—they don't really take place in a realistic world. They come from my head." According to McDonagh, "The diabolic ingenuity of Dahl came into its own only when he wrote for children. In conjunction with Blake, there was a kind of alchemy. It is a world where the good are rewarded in the story, and championed in the pictures, and where the creeps and bullies are punished in the plot and damned by the way they were drawn."

Beginning in the late 1960s, Blake began to alternate his work on original picture books, comic fantasies, concept books, and compilations with illustration projects for books by others. One of his most acclaimed original works is *Mister Magnolia,* the story of how the cheerful, dashing title character searches for and is presented with a boot to match the one he is wearing. Called a "masterpiece" by Alderson, *Mister Magnolia* is also one of the author's favorites among his books; he told *SATA,* "It's not autobiographical, but reflects the things I like in *pictures.*" Blake tells a rhyming nonsense tale in which flute, newt, hoot, rooty-toot and other words guide the story. *Growing Point* reviewer Margery Fisher cited his use of "typically active line and emphatic colour and his comic detail," and in *Book Window,* Margaret Walker claimed that Blake "has excelled himself" with *Mister Magnolia.*

One book that demonstrates Blake's sensitivity and understanding of the human condition particularly well is *The Story of the Dancing Frog.* Recounted as family history by a mother to her small daughter, the tale describes how Great Aunt Gertrude, who has recently been widowed, is prevented from drowning herself by the sight of a frog dancing on a lily pad. Gertrude and the frog, which she names George, become increasingly successful on the strength of George's talent; they tour the world before retiring to the south of France. In his book *The Telling Line: Essays on Fifteen Contemporary Book Illustrators,* Douglas Martin called *The Story of the Dancing Frog* "storytelling and illustrative book designing at its most accomplished."

Blake's *Simpkin* is a picture book with a rhyming text that is noted for expressing the duality of a small boy's nature while explaining the concept of opposites. In his review in *Junior Bookshelf,* Crouch asserted: "This artist grows more assured with every book." *The Singing Tortoise and Other Animal Folktales* contains international cautionary tales from the nineteenth and early twentieth centuries collected by John Yeoman. Blake decorates the work with what a *Publishers Weekly* reviewer described as "[his] inimitably puckish art."

With *Clown,* Blake creates a wordless story about how a discarded toy clown searches for a home for himself and his stuffed animal friends, all of whom have been tossed into a trash can in a tough urban neighborhood. Thrown through the window of a run-down apartment where a crying baby is being cared for by her older sister, the clown cheers up the girl and the infant with jug-

gling tricks, helps with the dishes, sweeps, and even changes the baby's diapers. After rescuing the other toys, he goes back to the apartment, where the children's tired mother returns to find a clean house and smiling offspring. As *Horn Book* reviewer Flowers maintained, "Only Quentin Blake's remarkable skill as an artist could produce such a touching, endearing story." Writing in *School Library Journal*, Carol Ann Wilson commented that "Blake succeeds admirably in presenting a multilayered and thought-provoking tale that will capture readers' imaginations." Jim Gladstone, writing in the *New York Times Book Review*, noted the "pitch-perfect details and often unsettling undertones" of the story, and concluded that Blake "delivers a Dickensian happy ending that can easily be read as very unhappy, uniting the city's underclass: the children, the poor, and the wide-eyed toys." In fact, Blake has also illustrated a new edition of Charles Dickens' *A Christmas Carol* that was, like *Clown*, published in 1995. *Horn Book* reviewer Flowers wrote that "everything is handsome about this edition. . . . It would be hard to think of a more quintessentially Dickensian illustrator."

Blake has also written a number of comic adventures about the unflappable Mrs. Armitage. In *Mrs. Armitage and the Big Wave*, the gray-haired heroine is off to catch a big wave with her surfboard, accompanied by her faithful dog, Breakspear. However, on the way out from shore she always thinks of some absurd thing she most desperately needs and then paddles back to the beach. "Awash with droll particulars, Blake's winsome cartoon art ensures that this tale will have even young landlubbers dipping eagerly," wrote a contributor for *Publishers Weekly*. In *Mrs. Armitage: Queen of the Road*, the eccentric title character hits the streets after inheriting a dilapidated, old jalopy. "Blake's lively, scribbled, color-washed sketches find the humor in the chaotic action," *Booklist* contributor Gillian Engberg noted of the book.

In another original title, *Zagazoo*, the postman brings George and Bella a delightful pink creature that suddenly and quite frighteningly morphs into a variety of repellent creatures: a warthog, a dragon, a hairy monster. "Blake's devotees . . . will most appreciate this quirky tale," noted a writer for *Publishers Weekly*. Abbott Combes, writing in the *New York Times Book Review*, praised Blake's "dead-on illustrations and 574 well-suited words [that] capture perfectly the joy of bringing someone new into the world." In *The Green Ship*, two youngsters come upon a topiary ship and explore its leafy treetop only to lose their perch over the years as nature returns the carefully pruned domain to a tree. "An aura of melancholy pervades this imaginative tale," commented a reviewer for *Publishers Weekly*. A self-illustrated tale, *Loveykins* centers on the relationship between Angela Bowling, a caring but eccentric woman, and Augustus, the young bird she rescues and nurtures. "Blake's images of Angela fretting and fawning over her beloved bird are hilarious," a *Publishers Weekly* critic noted.

In *Wizzil*, Blake's collaboration with William Steig, a bored witch causes trouble when she decides to take revenge on an old man. Her actions ultimately backfire, though, providing a happy ending. "*Wizzil* is literary ambrosia," declared a contributor to *Horn Book*. "Blake's pen-and-ink and watercolor illustrations, full of energy and humor and movement . . . are sublime." A reviewer for *Publishers Weekly* concluded, "Steig and Blake start with unrefined nastiness, then blindside their characters (and readers) with a comical but sincere look at love." "Blake's lively watercolor cartoons, filled with humorous detail, are a delightful companion to this ultimately good-natured tale of transformation and rebirth," observed Rosalyn Pierini in a *School Library Journal* review.

Collaborating with Hoban again on *Trouble on Thunder Mountain*, Blake serves up illustrations in the service of environmentalism. The O'Saurus family, threatened by the transformation of their mountain into a hi-tech theme park, resorts to faith and glue to rectify matters. In *School Library Journal*, Lauralyn Persson called *Trouble on Thunder Mountain* a "quirky story full of humor and drama," and praised Blake's "effortless" watercolors, which manage to capture "so much emotion with just a few sketchy lines."

Blake has also contributed the artwork to *Michael Rosen's Sad Book*, in which the author recounts the depression he experienced following the death of his eighteen-year-old son. "When the book is at its darkest—and Blake's black-and-gray line work wrests every bit of the agony from the understated words—there is despair," Ilene Cooper stated in *Booklist*. As time passes and Rosen learns to cope with his grief, Blake's illustrations reflect his changing mood; in the book's final spread, Joanna Rudge Long noted in *Horn Book*, "a glowing last candle casts its hopeful light on the bereaved father, pen in hand in the retreating gloom." Blake has also teamed with British comedian David Walliams on *Mr. Stink*, a chapter book for young readers about the unlikely friendship between a lonely little girl and a smelly tramp. According to Alison Roberts, writing in the London *Evening Standard*, "Blake's pictures—particularly his illustration of Mr Stink's smell, a sort of mucky cloud that makes people faint and gag—draw you into the book. There is something very comforting and familiar about a Blake illustration, yet the pictures always hit you with their complete freshness of vision and perfectly judged wit."

"Blake is a remarkable and true artist," remarked *Financial Times* contributor William Packer, "for all that he has made his career in the critically under-acknowledged field of illustration, and children's illustration at that." Writing in *Horn Book*, Blake commented, "I embrace the simplicity of both the story and the pictures, in which there may not seem to be, for the grownup, much to talk about." He concluded, "I don't have children, but am still in touch with the child in

me, and this has been immensely important to me as an artist. Part of keeping one's child-self alive is not being embarrassed to admit it exists."

Biographical and Critical Sources

BOOKS

Children's Literature Review, Volume 31, Gale (Detroit, MI), 1994.

Kingman, Lee, and others, compilers, *Illustrators of Children's Books: 1967-1976,* Horn Book (Boston, MA), 1968.

Martin, Douglas, *The Telling Line: Essays on Fifteen Contemporary Book Illustrators,* Julia MacRae Books, 1989.

Peppin, Brigid, and Lucy Micklethwait, *Book Illustrators of the Twentieth Century,* Arco, 1984.

Silvey, Anita, editor, *The Essential Guide to Children's Books and Their Creators,* Houghton Mifflin (Boston, MA), 2002.

PERIODICALS

Booklist, January 15, 1995, Ilene Cooper, review of *Roald Dahl's Revolting Recipes,* p. 916; October 15, 1995, Sally Estes, review of *A Christmas Carol,* p. 401; April 15, 1996, Carolyn Phelan, review of *Clown,* p. 1445; January 1, 1998, Carolyn Phelan, review of *The Seven Voyages of Sinbad the Sailor,* pp. 808-809; October 1, 2000, Michael Cart, review of *Wizzil,* p. 337; February 1, 2002, Carolyn Phelan, review of *Roald Dahl's Even More Revolting Recipes,* p. 935; November 15, 2003, Gillian Engberg, review of *Mrs. Armitage: Queen of the Road,* p. 598; May 15, 2005, Ilene Cooper, "Being Sad," review of *Michael Rosen's Sad Book,* p. 1658; November 1, 2005, GraceAnne A. DeCandido, review of *Vile Verses,* p. 45.

Book Window, spring, 1980, Margaret Walker, review of *Mister Magnolia,* p. 12.

Christian Science Monitor, March 4, 2005, Christopher Andreae, "Blake's Ecstasy of Being," p. 18.

Daily Telegraph (London, England), April 13, 2002, Melanie McDonagh, "Once upon a Time, Children's Books Were Looked Down On."

Financial Times (London, England), February 20, 2001, William Packer, "When Every Picture Tells a Story," p. 16.

Growing Point, May, 1980, Margery Fisher, review of *Mister Magnolia,* p. 3708.

Guardian (London, England), April 19, 2003, Joanna Carey, "Dances with Frogs"; September 28, 2007, Stuart Jeffries, "A Free Hand: After Almost 60 Years in the Business, Quentin Blake Is One of Britain's—Perhaps the World's—Best-loved Illustrators."

Horn Book, January-February, 1980, Paul Heins, review of *The Wild Washerwoman,* pp. 50-51; September-October, 1981, Quentin Blake, "Wild Washerwomen, Hired Sportsmen, and Enormous Crocodiles," pp. 505-513; January-February, 1986, Ann A. Flowers, review of *The Giraffe and the Pelly and Me,* pp. 46-47; September-October, 1995, Brian Alderson, "All Join In: The Generous Art of Quentin Blake," pp. 562-571; January-February, 1996, Ann A. Flowers, review of *A Christmas Carol,* p. 73; July-August, 1996, Ann A. Flowers, review of *Clown,* p. 444; March-April, 1998, Ann A. Flowers, review of *The Seven Voyages of Sinbad the Sailor,* p. 228; May-June, 2000, review of *Wizzil,* p. 466; May-June, 2002, Brian Alderson, "Back to the Laurel Grove," p. 283; May-June, 2005, Joanna Rudge Long, review of *Michael Rosen's Sad Book,* p. 313.

Junior Bookshelf, February, 1980, Marcus Crouch, review of *The Wild Washerwoman,* p. 19; February, 1994, Marcus Crouch, review of *Simpkin,* pp. 12-13.

Kirkus Reviews, February 15, 2003, review of *Loveykins,* p. 299; August 15, 2003, review of *Mrs. Armitage,* p. 1069.

New Statesman, October 31, 1969, review of *Jack and Nancy,* p. 628; November 9, 1973, review of *Snuff,* p. 705; November 21, 1980, review of *Mister Magnolia,* p. 19.

New York Times Book Review, January 15, 1989, Vicki Weissman, review of *Mathilda,* p. 31; September 22, 1996, Jim Gladstone, review of *Clown,* p. 28; November 16, 1997, Ruth Reichl, review of *Roald Dahl's Revolting Recipes,* p. 38; September 20, 1998, Lisa Shea, review of *Mrs. Armitage and the Big Wave,* p. 33; December 5, 1999, Abbott Combes, review of *Zagazoo,* p. 95.

Publishers Weekly, May 16, 1994, review of *The Singing Tortoise and Other Animal Folktales,* p. 64; December 18, 1995, review of *The Best of Michael Rosen,* pp. 54-55; March 25, 1996, review of *Clown,* p. 83; March 16, 1998, review of *Mrs. Armitage and the Big Wave,* pp. 62-63; July 26, 1999, review of *Zagazoo,* p. 89; July 3, 2000, review of *Wizzil,* p. 70; November 27, 2000, review of *The Green Ship,* p. 76; February 10, 2003, review of *Loveykins,* p. 185; April 4, 2005, review of *Michael Rosen's Sad Book,* p. 58; October 22, 2007, review of *On Angel Wings,* p. 53.

School Library Journal, October, 1980, Mary Nickerson, review of *How Tom Beat Captain Najork and His Hired Sportsmen,* p. 119; May, 1996, Carol Ann Wilson, review of *Clown,* p. 84; December, 1997, John Sigwald, review of *The Seven Voyages of Sinbad,* p. 150; May, 1998, Anne Connor, review of *Mrs. Armitage and the Big Wave,* p. 106; July, 2000, Lauralyn Persson, review of *Trouble on Thunder Mountain,* p. 80; August, 2000, Rosalyn Pierini, review of *Wizzil,* p. 165; November, 2001, Carolyn Jenks, review of *Roald Dahl's Even More Revolting Recipes,* p. 144; October, 2003, Shelley B. Sutherland, review of *Mrs. Armitage,* p. 114; November, 2005, Kirsten Cutler, review of *Vile Verses,* p. 155; October, 2007, Anne Connor, review of *On Angel Wings,* p. 102.

Sewanee Review, winter, 1998, Michael L. Hall, review of *The Penguin Book of Nonsense Verse,* pp. 112-117.

Signal, January, 1975, Elaine Moss, "Quentin Blake," pp. 33-39.

Spectator, December 5, 1970, review of *Angelo,* p. R14; April 16, 1977, review of *Snuff,* p. 27; January 17, 2004, Andrew Lambirth, "Hogarth's Heirs," p. 41.

Times (London, England), February 10, 2001, Emma Pomfret, "Every Picture Tells a Story," p. 18; December 11, 2004, Kate Quill, "Anarchy for Children—and Adults," p. 88; December 14, 2005, Valerie Grove, "Blake's Cherubs Tickle a French Institution," p. 22; November 15, 2008, Amanda Craig, "A Tale Drawn to Perfection," review of *The Birthday Book,* p. 15.

Times Educational Supplement, March 28, 1980, review of *Mister Magnolia,* p. 28; October 31, 1980, review of *Angelo,* p. 24; November 19, 1982, Naomi Lewis, "Once upon a Line," p. 32; June 9, 1989, Lindsay Duguid, "Artist Enchanter," p. B9.

Times Literary Supplement, November 9, 1984, John Mole, "Space to Dance," p. 1294; May 6, 1988, Linda Taylor, review of *Mathilda,* p. 513; July 7, 1989, review of *Quentin Blake's ABC,* p. 757.

Wilson Library Bulletin, June, 1995, Cathi Dunn MacRae, review of *Roald Dahl's Revolting Recipes,* p. 125.

ONLINE

Contemporary Writers Web site, http://www.contemporarywriters.com/ (January 1, 2010), "Quentin Blake."

Quentin Blake Home Page, http://www.quentinblake.com (January 1, 2010).

Time Out London Online, http://www.timeout.com/london/ (December 18, 2006), interview with Blake.*

*   *   *

BOORAEM, Ellen

Personal

Born in MA; partner of Robert Shillady (a painter). *Education:* Wheaton College, degree.

Addresses

Home—Brooklin, ME. *Agent*—Kate Schafer Testerman, KT Literary, Highlands Ranch, CO 80129. *E-mail*—evb9@myfairpoint.net.

Career

Author. Journalist and editor for New England newspapers for thirty years, including as managing editor and writer at *Weekly Packet,* Blue Hill, ME, and arts and special sections editor at *Ellsworth American,* Ellsworth, ME.

Writings

The Unnameables, Harcourt (Orlando, FL), 2008.
Small Persons with Wings, Dial (New York, NY), 2011.

Ellen Booraem (Photograph by Sherry Streeter. Reproduced by permission.)

Contributor of articles and reviews to *Ellsworth American.*

Sidelights

After spending much of her working career as a journalist and editor of weekly newspapers in New England, Ellen Booraem turned her hand to children's literature in 2008, publishing her first work, *The Unnameables.* Set on a present-day island simply called Island, *The Unnameables* traces the story of Medford Runyuin, a teenaged boy growing up in a society that has remained unchanged since the late 1600s. Medford is the son of parents native to the mainland who drowned at sea. Rescued and raised by the Carver family, he struggles to fit in with the island society's single-minded focus on creating only functional objects and living according to a set of rules recorded in a 300-year-old book. Upon reaching age fourteen, Island children receive their work assignments from the elders and assume a new surname based on that skill, such as Baker, Carpenter, or Potter. For Medford, however, the elders instruct him to live in isolation and prove himself worthy of a trade. Living apart from the others suits the boy well, allowing him secretly to make the decorative wood carvings that are considered "unnameable" by the Islanders as they serve no utilitarian function. When a half-man, half-goat creature arrives, a traveler whose efforts to perfect his control of the wind have brought him to Island, Medford gains a new understanding of his talent and its potential to transform Island life.

In a review of *The Unnameables,* a *Kirkus Reviews* critic called Booraem's novel "an ever-surprising, genre-defying page-turner," and *School Library Journal* contributor Sharon Rawlins wrote that the story "has a style and charm of its own." *Kliatt* contributor Donna Scanlon also found *The Unnameables* to be an inventive work for children, describing it as "fresh, original, and appealing." In her review, Scanlon cited in particular the author's "rich, intricate narrative," which is

Cover of Booraem's evocative young-adult novel The Unnameables, *which finds a boy trapped in a culture cut off from modern society.* (Jacket photographs © Cary Wolinsky/Aurora/Getty Images (goat), David McLain/Aurora/Getty Images (cane), DEX Images/Getty Images (wood shavings). Reproduced by permission.)

"laced with enough humor to leaven the story," and added that *The Unnameables* invites repeated readings "just to spend more time with the characters." Writing in *Booklist*, Ian Chipman concluded his review if *The Unnameables* by predicting that "patient readers who like a little quirk in their fantasy will enjoy this stick-it-to-the-status-quo romp."

Biographical and Critical Sources

PERIODICALS

Booklist, November 15, 2008, Ian Chipman, review of *The Unnameables,* p. 58.

Horn Book, January-February, 2009, Deirdre F. Baker, review of *The Unnameables,* p. 89.

Kirkus Reviews, September 1, 2008, review of *The Unnameables.*

Kliatt, November, 2008, Donna Scanlon, review of *The Unnameables,* p. 8.

School Library Journal, November, 2008, Sharon Rawlins, review of *The Unnameables,* p. 115.

ONLINE

Ellen Booraem Home Page, http://www.ellenbooraem.com (December 29, 2009).

Ellen Booraem Web Log, http://ellenbooraem.blogspot.com (December 29, 2009).

C

CALDER, Lyn
See CALMENSON, Stephanie

*   *   *

CALMENSON, Stephanie 1952-
(Lyn Calder)

Personal

Born November 28, 1952, in Brooklyn, NY; daughter of Kermit (a podiatrist and educator) and Edith (a medical secretary) Calmenson. *Education:* Brooklyn College of the City University of New York, B.A. (magna cum laude), 1973; New York University, M.A., 1976.

Addresses

Home—New York, NY. *E-mail*—stephanie@stephanie calmenson.com.

Career

Teacher of early childhood grades at public schools in Brooklyn, NY, 1974-75; Doubleday and Co., New York, NY, editor of children's books, 1976-80; Parents Magazine Press, New York, NY, editorial director of Read-Aloud Book Club, 1980-84; author of children's books, 1984—.

Member

Authors Guild, Authors League of America, PEN, Society of Children's Book Writers and Illustrators, National Arts Club.

Writings

FOR CHILDREN

(Editor) *Never Take a Pig to Lunch and Other Funny Poems about Animals,* illustrated by Hilary Knight, Doubleday (New York, NY), 1982.

My Book of the Seasons, illustrated by Eugenie Fernandes, Western Publishing (New York, NY), 1982.

One Little Monkey, illustrated by Ellen Appleby, Parents Magazine Press (New York, NY), 1982.

Barney's Sand Castle, illustrated by Sheila Becker, Western Publishing (New York, NY), 1983.

That's Not Fair!, Grosset & Dunlap (New York, NY), 1983.

The Kindergarten Book, illustrated by Beth L. Weiner, Grosset & Dunlap (New York, NY), 1983.

Where Will the Animals Stay?, Parents Magazine Press (New York, NY), 1983.

The Birthday Hat: A Grandma Potamus Story, illustrated by Susan Gantner, Grosset & Dunlap (New York, NY), 1983.

Where Is Grandma Potamus?, illustrated by Susan Gantner, Grosset & Dunlap (New York, NY), 1983.

The After School Book, illustrated by Beth L. Weiner, Grosset & Dunlap (New York, NY), 1984.

Ten Furry Monsters, illustrated by Maxie Chambliss, Parents Magazine Press (New York, NY), 1984.

All Aboard the Goodnight Train, illustrated by Normand Chartier, Grosset & Dunlap (New York, NY), 1984.

Waggleby of Fraggle Rock, illustrated by Barbara McClintock, Holt (New York, NY), 1985.

Ten Items or Less, Western Publishing (New York, NY), 1985.

Rainy Day Walk, Parachute Press (New York, NY), 1985.

(Compiler, with Joanna Cole) *The Laugh Book: A New Treasury of Humor for Children,* illustrated by Marylin Hafner, Doubleday (New York, NY), 1986.

The Toy Book, Western Publishing (New York, NY), 1986.

What Babies Do, Western Publishing (New York, NY), 1986.

The Little Bunny, the Shaggy Little Monster, the Little Chick, illustrated by Maxie Chambliss, Simon & Schuster (New York, NY), 1986.

Little Duck's Moving Day, illustrated by Cathy Cruikshank, Western Publishing (New York, NY), 1986.

(Compiler, with Joanna Cole) *The Read-Aloud Treasury for Young Children,* illustrated by Ann Schweninger, Doubleday (New York, NY), 1987.

Fido, illustrated by Maxie Chambliss, Scholastic, Inc. (New York, NY), 1987.

Tiger's Bedtime, Western Publishing (New York, NY), 1987.

The Bambi Book, Western Publishing (New York, NY), 1987.

The Giggle Book, illustrated by Maxie Chambliss, Parents Magazine Press (New York, NY), 1987.

Where's Rufus?, illustrated by Maxie Chambliss, Parents Magazine Press (New York, NY), 1987.

One Red Shoe (The Other One's Blue!), Western Publishing (New York, NY), 1987.

Spaghetti Manners, Western Publishing (New York, NY), 1987.

"The Busy Garage," "Who Said Moo?," "A Visit to the Firehouse," Parachute Press (New York, NY), 1987.

The Children's Aesop: Selected Fables, illustrated by Robert Byrd, Doubleday (New York, NY), 1988.

Little Duck and the New Baby, Western Publishing (New York, NY), 1988.

Ho! Ho! Ho! Christmas Jokes and Riddles, illustrated by Byron Smith, Weekly Reader Books (Middletown, CT), 1988.

No Stage Fright for Me!, illustrated by Rose Mary Berlin, Western Publishing (New York, NY), 1988.

The Little Witch Sisters, illustrated by R.W. Alley, Parents Magazine Press (New York, NY), 1989.

(With others) *All about Me: Featuring Jim Henson's Sesame Street Muppets,* illustrated by Richard Brown and others, in conjunction with Children's Television Workshop, Western Publishing (New York, NY), 1989.

What Am I? Very First Riddles, illustrated by Karen Gundersheimer, Harper & Row(New York, NY), 1989.

(With Joanna Cole) *Safe from the Start: Your Child's Safety from Birth to Age Five,* illustrated by Lauren Jarrett, Facts on File (New York, NY), 1989.

The Principal's New Clothes, illustrated by Denise Brunkus, Scholastic, Inc. (New York, NY), 1989.

101 Silly Summer Jokes, Scholastic, Inc. (New York, NY), 1989.

101 Funny Bunny Jokes, Scholastic, Inc. (New York, NY), 1989.

(Compiler, with Joanna Cole) *Miss Mary Mack and Other Children's Street Rhymes,* illustrated by Alan Tiegreen, Morrow Junior Books (New York, NY), 1990.

(Compiler, with Joanna Cole) *Ready, Set, Read! The Beginning Reader's Treasury,* illustrated by Anne Burgess and others, Doubleday (New York, NY), 1990.

Wanted: Warm, Furry Friend, illustrated by Amy Schwartz, Macmillan (New York, NY), 1990.

(Compiler, with Joanna Cole) *The Scary Book,* illustrated by Chris Demarest and others, Morrow Junior Books (New York, NY), 1991.

Zip, Whiz, Zoom, illustrated by Dorothy Stott, Little, Brown (Boston, MA), 1991.

The Addams Family (novelization), Scholastic, Inc. (New York, NY), 1991.

Hopscotch, the Tiny Bunny, illustrated by Barbara Lanza, Western Publishing (New York, NY), 1991.

Dinner at the Panda Palace, illustrated by Nadine Bernard Westcott, HarperCollins (New York, NY), 1991.

(Author of adaptation) *Walt Disney Presents: The Little Mermaid,* illustrated by Franc Mateu, Golden Books (New York, NY), 1991, published as *Disney's The Little Mermaid,* Random House (New York, NY), 2003.

(Compiler, with Joanna Cole) *The Eentsy, Weentsy Spider: Fingerplays and Action Rhymes,* illustrated by Alan Tiegreen, Morrow Junior Books (New York, NY), 1991.

Come to My Party, illustrated by Beth Weiner Lipson, Parents Magazine Press (New York, NY), 1991.

(Compiler, with Joanna Cole) *Pat-a-Cake and Other Play Rhymes,* illustrated by Alan Tiegreen, Morrow Junior Books (New York, NY), 1992.

Babies, illustrated by Kathy Wilburn, Western Publishing (New York, NY), 1992.

Roller Skates!, illustrated by True Kelley, Scholastic, Inc. (New York, NY), 1992.

It Begins with an A, illustrated by Marisabina Russo, Hyperion Books for Children (New York, NY), 1993.

(Compiler, with Joanna Cole) *Six Sick Sheep: 101 Tongue Twisters,* illustrated by Alan Tiegreen, Morrow (New York, NY), 1993.

Tom and Jerry: The Movie (novelization), Scholastic, Inc. (New York, NY), 1993.

The Little Witch Sisters, illustrated by R.W. Alley, Parents Magazine Press (New York, NY), 1993.

(Adaptator) *Race to Danger* (based on *Young Indiana Jones Chronicles*), Random House (New York, NY), 1993.

(Compiler, with Joanna Cole) *Pin the Tail on the Donkey and Other Party Games,* illustrated by Alan Tiegreen, Morrow (New York, NY), 1993.

Kinderkittens: Show-and-Tell, illustrated by Diane de Groat, Scholastic, Inc. (New York, NY), 1994.

Marigold and Grandma on the Town, illustrated by Mary Chalmers, Harper Collins (New York, NY), 1994.

Walt Disney's Winnie the Pooh and Tigger Too, illustrated by Vaccaro Associates, Inc., Disney Press (New York, NY), 1994.

Rosie: A Visiting Dog's Story, photographs by Justin Sutcliffe, Clarion (New York, NY), 1994.

(With Joanna Cole) *Crazy Eights and Other Card Games,* illustrated by Alan Tiegreen, Morrow (New York, NY), 1994.

Hotter than a Hot Dog!, illustrated by Elivia Savadier, Little, Brown (Boston, MA), 1994.

(Compiler, with Joanna Cole) *Why Did the Chicken Cross the Road?, and Other Riddles, Old and New,* illustrated by Alan Tiegreen, Morrow (New York, NY), 1994.

Where Is Eeyore's Tail?, Disney Press (New York, NY), 1994.

(Compiler, with Joanna Cole) *A Pocketful of Laughs: Stories, Poems, Jokes, and Riddles,* illustrated by Marylin Hafner, Doubleday (New York, NY), 1995.

Kinderkittens: Who Took the Cookie from the Cookie Jar?, illustrated by Diane de Groat, Scholastic, Inc. (New York, NY), 1995.

(Compiler, with Joanna Cole) *Ready, Set, Read—and Laugh! A Funny Treasury for Beginning Readers,* Doubleday (New York, NY), 1995.

(Compiler, with Joanna Cole) *Yours till Banana Splits: 201 Autograph Rhymes,* illustrated by Alan Tiegreen, Morrow (New York, NY), 1995.

(Compiler with Joanna Cole) *The Gator Girls,* illustrated by Lynn Munsinger, Morrow (New York, NY), 1995.

Engine, Engine, Number Nine, illustrated by Paul Meisel, Hyperion (New York, NY), 1996.

Who Am I?, Hyperion (New York, NY), 1996.

(With Joanna Cole) *Bug in a Rug: Reading Fun for Just-Beginners,* illustrated by Alan Tiegreen, Morrow (New York, NY), 1996.

(Compiler, with Joanna Cole) *Give a Dog a Bone: Stories, Poems, Jokes, and Riddles about Dogs,* illustrated by John Speirs, Scholastic, Inc. (New York, NY), 1996.

My Dog's the Best, illustrated by Marcy Dunn Ramsey, Scholastic, Inc. (New York, NY), 1997.

(With Joanna Cole) *The Rain or Shine Activity Book: Fun Things to Make and Do,* illustrated by Alan Tiegreen, Morrow (New York, NY), 1997.

(With Joanna Cole) *Rockin' Reptiles,* illustrated by Lynn Munsinger, Morrow (New York, NY), 1997.

First Steps, illustrated by Toni Delaney, Golden Books (New York, NY), 1998.

(With Joanna Cole) *Get Well, Gators!,* illustrated by Lynn Munsinger, Morrow (New York, NY), 1998.

Shaggy, Waggy Dogs (and Others), photographs by Justin Sutcliffe, Clarion (New York, NY), 1998.

The Teeny, Tiny Teacher, illustrated by Denis Roche, Scholastic, Inc. (New York, NY), 1998.

(With Joanna Cole and Michael Street) *Marbles: 101 Ways to Play,* illustrated by Alan Tiegreen, Morrow (New York, NY), 1998.

(With Joanna Cole) *Gator Halloween,* illustrated by Lynn Munsinger, Morrow (New York, NY), 1999.

(With Joanna Cole and Michael Street) *Fun on the Run: Travel Games and Songs,* illustrated by Alan Tiegreen, Morrow (New York, NY), 1999.

What's My Job?, illustrated by Alice and Paul Sharp, Scholastic, Inc. (New York, NY), 2000.

The Frog Principal, illustrated by Denise Brunkus, Scholastic, Inc. (New York, NY), 2001.

Good for You!: Toddler Rhymes for Toddler Times, illustrated by Melissa Sweet, HarperCollins (New York, NY), 2001.

Perfect Puppy, illustrated by Thomas F. Yezerski, Clarion, 2001.

Welcome Baby!: Baby Rhymes for Baby Times, illustrated by Melissa Sweet, HarperCollins (New York, NY), 2002.

Kindergarten Kids: Riddles, Rebuses, Wiggles, Giggles, and More!, illustrated by Melissa Sweet, HarperCollins (New York, NY), 2005.

Birthday at the Panda Palace, illustrated by Doug Cushman, HarperCollins (New York, NY), 2007.

May I Pet Your Dog?: The How-to Guide for Kids Meeting Dogs (and Dogs Meeting Kids), illustrated by Jan Ormerod, Clarion (New York, NY), 2007.

Jazzmatazz!, illustrated by Bruce Degen, HarperCollins (New York, NY), 2008.

Late for School!, illustrated by Sachiko Yoshikawa, Carolrhoda Books (Minneapolis, MN), 2008.

Contributor of educational stories and fiction to books and to magazines, including *Humpty Dumpty.*

UNDER PSEUDONYM LYN CALDER; FOR CHILDREN

Bambi and the Butterfly, Western Publishing (New York, NY), 1983.

The Three Bears, Western Publishing (New York, NY), 1983.

Happy Birthday, Buddy Blue, Western Publishing (New York, NY), 1984.

Blast Off, Barefoot Bear!, Cloverdale Press (New York, NY), 1985.

Gobo and the Prize from Outer Space, Holt (New York, NY), 1986.

The Gloworm Bedtime Book, Random House (New York, NY), 1986.

The Sesame Street ABC Book, Western Publishing (New York, NY), 1986.

The Sesame Street Book of First Times, Western Publishing (New York, NY), 1986.

The Little Red Hen, Western Publishing (New York, NY), 1987.

Little Red Riding Hood, Western Publishing (New York, NY), 1987.

If You Were a Cat, illustrated by Cornelius Van Wright, Prentice-Hall (Englewood Cliffs, NJ), 1989.

If You Were a Fish, Prentice-Hall (Englewood Cliffs, NJ), 1989.

If You Were a Bird, Prentice-Hall (Englewood Cliffs, NJ), 1989.

If You Were an Ant, Prentice-Hall (Englewood Cliffs, NJ), 1989.

Mickey Visits the Fair: A Book about Numbers, illustrated by Mones, Western Publishing (New York, NY), 1990.

Blue-Ribbon Friends, illustrated by Vaccaro Associates, Disney Press (New York, NY), 1991.

Gold-Star Homework, illustrated by Vaccaro Associates, Disney Press (New York, NY), 1991.

Good Night, Magellan, illustrated by Tom Brannon, Western Publishing (New York, NY), 1991.

The Perfect Bow, illustrated by Sue Shakespeare, Western Publishing (New York, NY), 1991.

Walt Disney Presents: The Little Mermaid, Ariel above the Sea, illustrated by Franc Mateu, Western Publishing (New York, NY), 1991.

What Will I Wear?, illustrated by Franc Mateu, Western Publishing (New York, NY), 1991.

Magellan's Hats, illustrated by Jim Mahon and David Prebenna, Western Publishing (New York, NY), 1991.

Walt Disney's Alice's Tea Party, illustrated by Jesse Clay, Disney Press (New York, NY), 1992.

That's What Friends Are For, illustrated by Vaccaro Associates, 1992.

Sebastian's Story, Western Publishing (New York, NY), 1992.

Lemonade for Sale, illustrated by Vaccaro Associates, Western Publishing (New York, NY), 1992.

Where's Fifi?, illustrated by Vaccaro Associates, Western Publishing (New York, NY), 1992.

Walt Disney's Minnie Mouse and the Friendship Lockets, illustrated by Russell Hicks, Michael Horowitz, and Eric Binder, Western Publishing (New York, NY), 1993.

Also author of *Minnie 'n' Me Stories.*

Sidelights

A former educator, Stephanie Calmenson is the author of more than one hundred children's books, some published under the pseudonym Lyn Calder. Calmenson deals with goofy principals, frisky alligators, and rhymes galore in her picture books and chapter books that tease and please young readers. She has written counting tales, alphabet rhymes, fractured fairy tales, chapter books, and concept books for young readers, and even rhymes for toddlers and babies, all with her signature sprightly tone. Among her popular titles are *Dinner at the Panda Palace, The Gator Girls,* written with Joanna Cole, and *Jazzmatazz!* "To have become a children's book writer is a happy surprise for me," Calmenson once told *SATA.* "I have always loved books, language, and working with children."

Despite her many literary successes, Calmenson had little confidence in her writing abilities as a child. There were clues, however, that an author lurked within. Her delight in reading was one, and her letter-writing habit was another. "I wrote to a pen pal on the other side of the world," Calmenson once commented. "I wrote to friends and family when I went away to summer camp; I wrote to companies and to magazines, letting them know what I thought of their product or point of view. I see now that this was a good way to begin writing because letters are not scrutinized the way school compositions are."

Calmenson's love of children led her into education. She taught for a few years in the Brooklyn public schools but lost her job due to budget cutbacks. She later worked as an editorial secretary and then editor of children's books at Doubleday. Meanwhile, she also attended graduate school in the evenings, hoping to strengthen her teaching credentials. "All that changed when I was studying for my master's degree in elementary education," she recalled. "Two courses were required: 'Introduction to Children's Literature' and 'Writing for Children.' In the first, I discovered how much I loved children's picture books; I devoured them. My enthusiasm spilled over to the second class, and when my very first story was published in a children's magazin I was off and running."

Calmenson once described her goals to *SATA:* "Before beginning a book, I always ask the same question: What will this book give to a child? Will it be a love of language? A feeling of being valued? An introduction to numbers or letters? A belly laugh to ease a difficult growing-up day? When I'm satisfied with the answer, I begin to write."

Calmenson often finds inspiration in everyday occurrences, and such was the case with *Dinner at the Panda Palace.* She once told *SATA,* "I remember exactly when I got the idea for that book. I overheard a young boy as he was walking into a restaurant say to his mother, 'Mommy, I am going to ask for a table for two.' Right then and there, I decided to write a counting book in which diners, from one to a group of ten, ask for tables at a restaurant. I love animals and know that most children do, too. So the diners became an assortment of animals: 'An elephant came first with a trunk that was gray. He'd been out on the road selling peanuts all day. I'm enormously hungry. My bag weighs a ton. I would like to sit down. Have you a table for one?' There are monkeys swinging across the chandeliers, peacocks showing off their plumage, and so on. Now I had a book that was a counting book and an animal identification book." Reviewing *Dinner at the Panda Palace,* a *Publishers Weekly* contributor praised Calmenson's "rhyming verse and innovative cast of characters" that provide the book with "zip."

A sequel to *Dinner at the Panda Palace, Birthday at the Panda Palace* features the same cast of characters. According to the author, "This continuation of the story contains the added fun of a rebus element. This time, it is Mouse's birthday and her friends come bearing gifts. The greatest gift of all turns out to be from Mr. Panda as he surprises Mouse with a visit from her country mice relations (including the three blind mice) who live far away, and mouse ends her birthday, as all children should, feeling like a star." According to a contributor in *Kirkus Reviews,* the "popular theme and winning ending" in *Birthday at the Panda Palace* ". . . will encourage repeated readings with gleeful shouts at the appropriate time."

Calmenson's other poetry books include the rhyme collections *Welcome, Baby!: Baby Rhymes for Baby Times, Good for You!: Toddler Rhymes for Toddler Times,* and *Kindergarten Kids: Riddles, Rebuses, Wiggles, Giggles and More! Welcome, Baby!* is a joyous celebration of a baby's first year of life. Everyday events, such as meal time and bath time; milestones, including baby's first steps, first words, and first birthday; and basic concepts such as ABC's, colors, and more are put into words that infants enjoy hearing, repeating, and acting out. As Lauren Peterson wrote in *Booklist,* Calmenson's "poems and pictures mirror the physical and emotional development of children from birth to about 18 months." The poems were described by Kristin de Lacoste in *School Library Journal* as "whimsical and lively and sure to grab the attention of even the littlest listeners."

Good for You! is a celebration of all the things a toddler can do and learn. There are poems about using the potty, getting dressed, and having lunch at a diner, as well as a funny lesson on good manners provided by a group of not-so-well behaved animals. Writing in *Publishers Weekly,* a critic remarked that Calmenson and illustrator Melissa Sweet "open the door to the world of poetry

and the playfulness of language, and usher toddlers through it." A critic for *Kirkus Reviews* also praised this gathering of two dozen rhymes as a "wonderfully affirming collection" that is both "perky and pertinent." Bina Williams, writing in *School Library Journal,* called *Good for You!* a "winning collection," and *Booklist* critic Annie Ayres called it an "an altogether buoyant book." Describing her inspiration for the work, Calmenson remarked in an interview on the *Cynthia Leitich Smith* Web site, "I love the company of toddlers. They're so busy! And they're learning so much so fast. I wanted to put their experience into words. I chose to write catchy-rhythm rhymes because they're most fun for toddlers (and for me) and because rhyming helps with language development."

Also featuring Sweet's illustrations, *Kindergarten Kids* celebrates and reassures youngest students, from their morning greetings to end-of-the-day good-byes, with lots of learning and action, including a pizza party, a Halloween parade, a chance to conquer a challenge in the poem "Puzzled," and an opportunity to see that no one is perfect in "Oops!" Mary Hazelton, writing in *School Library Journal,* called *Kindergarten Kids* an "appealing collection of original rhymes and riddles," and *Horn Book* reviewer Susan Dove Lempke observed that the collection gives young readers "a well-rounded peek into kindergarten life."

More rhyming fun for the very young is served up in *Engine, Engine, Number Nine,* Calmenson's adaptation of the traditional rhyme. In her take on the poem, Calmenson has the county fair as the ultimate destination. A reviewer for *Publishers Weekly* found this to be "a gently comic premise." In the course of the cumulative rhyme, Calmenson packs her engine with more and more human and animal passengers. The same reviewer called the book "a cheery, workmanlike effort." In *Jazzmatazz!,* a shivering mouse slips inside a warm house and begins to play the piano, prompting the homeowner's dog to begin drumming on his dish and the cat to fiddle around with a carpet beater and spoon. Soon, the entire neighborhood has joined in the fun, creating a whirlwind of sound. "The rhythmic text uses onomatopoeic words and a jazzy refrain," Krista Hutley remarked in *Booklist. Jazzmatazz!,* was described as "a bright, syncopated jam session sure to please storytime audiences" by a contributor in *Kirkus Reviews.*

Calmenson is often asked by young readers where she gets all the ideas for her books. As she explained to *SATA,* "An idea can emerge from an observation, a dream, a memory, a feeling, a wish. What are my subjects? As long as I am having fun with the language, I can write about anything. I have written books about numbers, letters, everyday objects. I have written about being brave enough to tell the truth; about not having to be perfect; about not judging others too quickly. I have written about friends, families, and . . . about my own dog, Rosie, who is a working dog."

In *Rosie: A Visiting Dog's Story,* Calmenson explains how she trained her Tibetan terrier, Rosie, to visit hospital rooms, nursing homes, and other such places to bring laughter and companionship into the lives of those who are sick or lonely. Calmenson describes how to choose a dog for this purpose and how to prepare for the visits. The text is simple in keeping with the author's audience. She concludes her book with the addresses of various associations that can supply readers with more information. Margaret A. Bush, in a *Horn Book* review, called *Rosie* an "appealing photo-documentary," and in a *Booklist* review Ellen Mandel deemed it "valuable and charming."

Another book about canines, *Perfect Puppy,* follows the fictional story of a puppy who tries his hardest to be perfect. After making a mistake and running away, the pup learns he need not be perfect to be loved. *School Library Journal* reviewer Rachel Fox described the book as "a heartwarming story told from the dog's perspective," while Mandel predicted that Calmenson's book will help youngsters "be understanding, patient trainers for their soon-to-be perfect puppies."

Dogs are once again at the center of things in *Shaggy, Waggy Dogs (and Others),* as a young girl seeks just the right pet. In the course of her search, introduces readers to thirty dog breeds, with accompanying color pictures. Each dog is also introduced with a rhyming text. *Booklist* contributor Ellen Mandel praised Calmenson's "carefully considered words" which "encourage responsible, committed dog ownership." In *May I Pet Your Dog?: The How-to Guide for Kids Meeting Dogs (and Dogs Meeting Kids)* an amiable dachshund named Harry patiently guides readers through the rules of human-canine interaction. As he accompanies a young boy who meets a variety of pooches, including a puppy and a guide dog, Harry explains how to approach dogs safely, how to recognize a dog's temperament, and how to pet a dog properly. "The already dog-savvy will appreciate the respect this book gives to their skill," Roger Sutton commented in *Horn Book,* and a critic in *Kirkus Reviews* stated that young readers "will find this volume useful and encouraging."

The versatile Calmenson has also retold many folktales and fables in various works. *The Children's Aesop: Selected Fables,* for instance, is a retelling of twenty-eight fables. She includes a large number of stories that contain human characters and also supplies her characters' motivations. For example, in the well-known fable about the tortoise and the hare, she gives both creatures' points of view. Aesop's morals are printed at the bottom of each page. Calmenson preserves the "informal, colloquial tone of the writing," Carolyn Phelan remarked in her *Booklist* review of *The Children's Aesop.*

The Principal's New Clothes is an adaptation of Hans Christian Andersen's story. The vain, clothes-conscious elementary school principal, Mr. Bundy, is the equivalent of the emperor, the two untrustworthy tailors work

on the outfit in the gymnasium, and the unveiling takes place at a school assembly. A kindergartner points out that the principal is only wearing underwear, and the children throw articles of clothing at him in an attempt to help. The principal reappears wearing the odd assortment and presents the child with a gold star for her honesty. "These modern-day trappings invite readers to set their favorite folktales in their own neighborhoods," concluded Susan Hepler in *School Library Journal.*

Calmenson reprises her vain principal in *The Frog Principal,* a parody of the Grimm Brothers' "The Frog Prince." In this tale, Mr. Bundy is searching for an educational show and brings in Marty Q. Marvel, who accidentally turns the principal into a frog. However, the indomitable Mr. Bundy does not let this little setback get him down; he still performs the tasks of a principal, and ultimately turns back into his old self. However, first he indulges in a little game of leapfrog with the students and even takes a dip in a classroom sink to the astonishment of the pupils. *Booklist* critic Lauren Peterson noted that the "silly plot" in *The Frog Principal* is very believably written," and Patti Gonzales, writing in *School Library Journal,* lauded Calmenson's version of the fairy tale for "adding quirky humor and delightful situations" to the original story.

Another adaptation of an older tale appears in *The Teeny Tiny Teacher,* and here Calmenson also features a school setting. As a contributor for *Publishers Weekly* noted, the story "combines school and ghost story in this knock-off of the classic folktale." In this story, a very small teacher and her even tinier pupils must deal with a wee bone which seems to be invested with a small, ghostly voice. This mysterious ghostly presence will not leave the teeny people alone until it gets its bone back. The teacher and pupils are so small that in Denis Roche's illustrations they use dice to sit on, and when they take a walk in the park, the flowers stand like trees overhead. *Horn Book* reviewer Joanna Rudge Long praised Calmenson's "reassuring, playful ending" in this adaptation of Joseph Jacobs' tale "Teeny Tiny." Janice M. Del Negro, writing in the *Bulletin of the Center for Children's Books,* noted that young listeners "will get a kick of this academic variant" of the traditional cumulative tale.

Calmenson's *Hotter than a Hot Dog!* is about the special relationship between a girl and her grandmother as they escape the city heat by spending the afternoon on the beach. "The delightful slice of city life is made real by the author's use of concrete details," according to Maeve Visser Knoth in *Horn Book.* Jan Shepherd Ross, in a *School Library Journal* review, described the text as "lyrical" and lauded the description of the beach through the girl's sense of sight, smell, touch, and taste. Writing in *Publishers Weekly,* a critic claimed that "Calmenson's bubbly narrative voice convincingly mimics a child's own storytelling." *Booklist* contributor Ilene Cooper also had praise for the title, noting that the "humor and natural tone of a text" are equaled "by the wit of the art."

Marigold and Grandma on the Town is very similar in theme to *Hotter than a Hot Dog!,* although the girl and her grandmother are now cast as bunnies. With thoughtful detail, Calmenson tells the story of little bunny Marigold feeding ducks in a park and acts up in a coffee shop. Marigold's temper tantrums and worries are realistically portrayed. Marigold's grandmother buys her a hat, and, on the way home, they get their picture taken in a photo booth. "Lively characters, childlike dilemmas, and cheerful artwork make this newest 'I Can Read' just right for the intended audience," declared Maeve Visser Knoth in *Horn Book,* and Deborah Stevenson wrote in the *Bulletin of the Center for Children's Books* that "events are individually mild but collectively important."

Wanted: Warm, Furry Friend is another story about bunnies. When gray rabbit Ralph first sets eyes on white rabbit Alice, he feels instant dislike, which she reciprocates. Ralph answers a personal ad and believes the writer is his soul mate, not realizing that it is Alice with whom he is corresponding. While sparks fly between the two whenever they meet, they are tender to one another in their letters. "The telling is delicious," remarked a critic in *Publishers Weekly.*

From bunnies, Calmenson turns her hand to alligators in a series of books about best friends Allie and Amy Gator, cowritten with Joanna Cole and illustrated by Lynn Munsinger. In *The Gator Girls,* the two friends are planning how they will spend summer vacation together. Disrupting the girl's plans, Allie's parents suddenly inform her that they have enrolled her at Camp Wogga-Bog for the summer. Allie and Amy now have to fly through their entire list of activities in the few days before Allie goes off to summer camp. They manage to do this, despite the interference of their pesky neighbor, Marvin. *Booklist* reviewer Mary Harris Veeder felt that "the joys of true blue friendship are humorously realized" in *The Gator Girls.*

Friends Allie and Amy are on hand for more action in *Rockin' Reptiles,* a "comic take on a recognizable childhood dilemma," according to Stephanie Zvirin in *Booklist.* The girls' friendship is put to the test with the arrival of Gracie, a new gator in the neighborhood. When the newcomer has an extra ticket to a rock concert, she must decide whether to give it to Amy or Allie. Again, the friends manage to solve their problem without losing their friendship, this time turning to a fortuneteller for help. Maggie McEwen, writing in *School Library Journal,* concluded that "Readers who are ready for a challenge will relish this spirited tale."

The gator girls' third outing comes in *Get Well, Gators!,* which relates the efforts of the duo to come up with a song for the town's street fair. When Allie comes down with swamp flu and is kept in bed, she grows fearful that no one will even notice that she is not present at the fair. Meanwhile, Amy feels insecure about performing alone. Finally the spirited duo comes up

with a creative solution to their predicament. *Booklist* contributor Kay Weisman found *Get Well, Gators!* "funny," recommending it to "first chapter-book readers."

Gator Halloween finds Amy and Allie each hoping to win the prize for best costume at the annual Halloween parade, and both gators put much time and effort into their costumes. However, when the day for the parade comes around, the two become involved in helping to search for a lost pet and arrive late for the parade. Rosie Peasley, reviewing the book in *School Library Journal,* predicted that readers will enjoy Calmenson and Cole's "warm and cheerful holiday selection," and Zvirin praised the book's "over-the-top comedy."

Calmenson has also created several other beginner books. *It Begins with an A* is an alphabet book with two-line, rhyming riddles on each page. Calmenson uses small words and short sentences, mindful of her young readers. The answers to the riddles and a review of the alphabet are on the last two pages of the book. This book is "full of things relevant to a child's life," noted Kathryn Broderick in *Booklist. What Am I? Very First Riddles* is another book of rhyming riddles aimed at young listeners. The answers are revealed in the text and in the pictures, making it easy for young children to answer them. The riddles are based on everyday objects and on items that are special to children, such as ice cream, a birthday cake, and a rainbow. The rhymes are kept brief, just four lines long, and there are fifteen riddles in all. Ellen Fader declared in *Horn Book* that "children will be reading this book to themselves in no time at all." With *Why Did the Chicken Cross the Road?, and Other Riddles Old and New,* Calmenson also serves up a "wide variety of clever riddles," according to Carolyn Phelan writing in *Booklist,* while *Give a Dog a Bone,* presents riddles, jokes, and stories about canine friends.

Calmenson once told *SATA:* "I have been an elementary school teacher, a children's book editor, and am now a full-time writer. While I am no longer in a classroom, I continue to think of myself as a teacher, speaking to children through my books. My primary goal when writing is to create books kids *want* to read. I go on from there. Through my words, I get to explore the world with children. And, for me, that is pure joy."

Biographical and Critical Sources

PERIODICALS

Booklist, April 1, 1992, Carolyn Phelan, review of *The Children's Aesop: Selected Fables,* pp. 1452-1453; June 1 and 15, 1993, Kathryn Broderick, review of *It Begins with an A,* p. 1842; April 1, 1994, Ilene Cooper, review of *Hotter than a Hot Dog!,* p. 1458; April 15, 1994, Ellen Mandel, review of *Rosie: A Visiting Dog's Story,* pp. 1536-1537; October 15, 1994, Carolyn Phelan, review of *Why Did the Chicken Cross the Road?, and Other Riddles Old and New,* p. 429; April 15, 1995, Mary Harris Veeder, review of *The Gator Girls,* p. 1497; September 1, 1996, p. 133; March 1, 1997, Stephanie Zvirin, review of *Rockin' Reptiles,* p. 1162; May 1, 1998, Ellen Mandel, review of *Shaggy, Waggy Dogs (and Others),* p. 1519; August, 1998, GraceAnne A. DeCandido, review of *The Teeny Tiny Teacher,* p. 2010; November 15, 1998, Kay Weisman, review of *Get Well, Gators!,* p. 590; September 1, 1999, Stephanie Zvirin, review of *Gator Halloween,* p. 145; September 15, 2001, Annie Ayres, review of *Good for You!,* p. 225; September 15, 2001, Lauren Peterson, review of *The Frog Principal,* p. 230; March 1, 2002, Ellen Mandel, review of *Perfect Puppy,* p. 1139; December 1, 2002, Lauren Peterson, review of *Welcome Baby!: Baby Rhymes for Baby Times,* p. 669; August, 2005, Ilene Cooper, review of *Kindergarten Kids: Riddles, Rebuses, Wiggles, Giggles, and More!,* p. 2038; January 1, 2008, Krista Hutley, review of *Jazzmatazz!,* p. 94.

Bulletin of the Center for Children's Books, March, 1994, Deborah Stevenson, review of *Marigold and Grandma on the Town,* p. 217; October, 1998, Janice M. Del Negro, review of *The Teeny Tiny Teacher,* p. 53.

Horn Book, May-June, 1989, Ellen Fader, review of *What Am I? Very First Riddles,* p. 353; March-April, 1994, Maeve Visser Knoth, review of *Marigold and Grandma on the Town,* p. 194; May-June, 1994, Maeve Visser Knoth, review of *Hotter than a Hot Dog!,* pp. 309-310; July-August, 1994, Margaret A. Bush, review of *Rosie,* pp. 470-471; September-October, 2005, Susan Dove Lempke, review of *Kindergarten Kids,* p. 595; July-August, 2007, Roger Sutton, review of *May I Pet Your Dog?: The How-to Guide for Kids Meeting Dogs (and Dogs Meeting Kids),* p. 410.

Kirkus Reviews, August 15, 2001, review of *Good for You!,* p. 1207; July 1, 2002, review of *Welcome, Baby!,* p. 950; June 15, 2005, review of *Kindergarten Kids,* p. 679; April 1, 2007, review of *May I Pet Your Dog?;* June 1, 2007, review of *Birthday at the Panda Palace;* December 1, 2007, review of *Jazzmatazz!*

Publishers Weekly, October 26, 1990, review of *Wanted: Warm, Furry Friend,* p. 68; March 8, 1991, review of *Dinner at the Panda Palace,* p. 73; April 26, 1993, review of *It Begins with an A,* p. 77; February 28, 1994, review of *Hotter than a Hot Dog!,* p. 87; February 24, 1997, review of *Engine, Engine, Number Nine,* p. 89; August 3, 1998, review of *The Teeny Tiny Teacher,* p. 85; June 28, 1999, review of *Games for Hitting the Road,* p. 81; August 23, 1999, review of *Give a Dog a Bone,* p. 61; August 20, 2001, review of *Good for You!,* p. 78; April 16, 2007, "Pets on Parade," review of *May I Pet Your Dog?,* p. 54.

School Library Journal, March, 1990, Susan Hepler, review of *The Principal's New Clothes,* p. 154; May, 1994, Jan Shepherd Ross, review of *Hotter than a Hot Dog!,* p. 89; April, 1997, Maggie McEwen, review of *Rockin' Reptiles,* p. 91; July, 1997, Karen James, review of *Engine, Engine, Number Nine,* p. 60; July,

1998, Carol Kolb Phillips, review of *Shaggy, Waggy Dogs (and Others),* p. 86; October, 1998, Dina Sherman, review of *Get Well, Gators!,* p. 87; September, 1999, Rosie Peasley, review of *Gator Halloween,* p. 176; October, 2001, Patti Gonzales, review of *The Frog Principal,* pp. 106-107; October, 2001, Bina Williams, review of *Good for You!,* p. 136; March, 2002, Rachel Fox, review of *Perfect Puppy,* p. 172; September, 2002, Kristin de Lacoste, review of *Welcome Baby!,* p. 210; August, 2005, Mary Hazelton, review of *Kindergarten Kids,* p. 112; April, 2007, Amanda Moss, review of *May I Pet Your Dog?,* p. 96; September, 2007, Marge Loch-Wouters, review of *Birthday at the Panda Palace,* p. 160.

ONLINE

Cynthia Leitich Smith Web site, http://www.cynthialeitich smith.com/ (April 1, 2008), "The Story behind the Story: Stephanie Calmenson on *Good for You!: Toddler Rhymes for Toddler Times.*"

Stephanie Calmenson Home Page, http://www.stephanie calmenson.com (April 1, 2008).*

*   *   *

CASILLA, Robert 1959-

Personal

Born April 16, 1959, in Jersey City, NJ; son of Miriam Casilla; married Carmen Torres (a real estate adjuster), May 1, 1982; children: Robert, Jr., Emily. *Ethnicity:* "Puerto Rican heritage." *Education:* School of Visual Arts, B.F.A., 1982. *Religion:* Christian. *Hobbies and other interests:* Family, museums, fine art, running, baseball, movies.

Addresses

Home—New Fairfield, CT. *Home and office*—5 Erin Dr., New Fairfield, CT 06812. *Agent*—Libby Ford Artist Representative, 320 E. 57th St., Ste. 10B, New York, NY 10022. *E-mail*—robert@robertcasilla.com.

Career

Freelance illustrator, 1983—. Designer of postage stamps for Sierra Leone, Federated States of Micronesia, and Marshall Islands. Teacher of middle-school through high school art at Dolan Art Academy/Children's Aid Society. Presenter at schools. *Exhibitions:* Work included in exhibitions of Society of Illustrators, New York, NY.

Member

Society of Illustrators, Society of Children's Book Writers and Illustrators, Connecticut Watercolor Society.

Awards, Honors

Washington Irving Children's Book Choice Award for Illustration, 1996, Notable Book selection, American Library Association, and Pick of the List selection,

Robert Casilla (Reproduced by permission.)

American Booksellers Association, both for *The Little Painter of Sabana Grande;* Children's Choice designation, 2000; *Smithsonian* magazine Notable Book designation, 2002; Cooperative Children's Book Center Choice designation, 2003; Pura Belpré Illustrator Award Honor Book designation, 2004.

Illustrator

David A. Adler, *Martin Luther King, Jr.: Free at Last,* Holiday House (New York, NY), 1986.

Elizabeth Howard, *The Train to Lulu's,* Bradbury Press (New York, NY), 1988.

Myra Cohn Livingston, *Poems for Fathers,* Holiday House (New York, NY), 1989.

David A. Adler, *Jackie Robinson: He Was the First,* Holiday House (New York, NY), 1989.

David A. Adler, *A Picture Book of Martin Luther King, Jr.,* Holiday House (New York, NY), 1989.

Eileen Roe, *Con mi hermano/With My Brother,* Bradbury Press (New York, NY), 1991.

David A. Adler, *A Picture Book of Eleanor Roosevelt,* Holiday House (New York, NY), 1991.

David A. Adler, *A Picture Book of John F. Kennedy,* Holiday House (New York, NY), 1991.

David A. Adler, *A Picture Book of Simón Bolívar,* Holiday House (New York, NY), 1992.

David A. Adler, *A Picture Book of Jesse Owens,* Holiday House (New York, NY), 1992.

Patricia Murkin, *The Little Painter of Sabana Grande,* Bradbury Press (New York, NY), 1993.

David A. Adler, *A Picture Book of Rosa Parks,* Holiday House (New York, NY), 1993.

Gary Soto, *The Pool Party,* Delacorte Press (New York, NY), 1993.

David A. Adler, *A Picture Book of Jackie Robinson,* Holiday House (New York, NY), 1994.

Jonelle Toriseva, *Rodeo Day,* Bradbury Press (New York, NY), 1994.

Gary Soto, *Boys at Work,* Delacorte Press (New York, NY), 1995.

Jane Q. Saxton, reteller, *The Good Samaritan,* Time-Life for Children (Alexandria, VA), 1996.

Natasha Wing, *Jalapeño Bagels,* Atheneum (New York, NY), 1996.

David A. Adler, *A Picture Book of Thurgood Marshall,* Holiday House (New York, NY), 1997.

Jo Harper, *The Legend of Mexicatl,* Turtle Books (New York, NY), 1998.

John Micklos, Jr., *Daddy Poems,* Boyds Mills Press (Honesdale, PA), 2000.

L. King Pérez, *First Day in Grapes,* Lee & Low (New York, NY), 2002.

Carolyn Marsden, *Mama Had to Work on Christmas,* Viking (New York, NY), 2003.

Jane Medina, *The Dream on Blanca's Wall/El sueño en la pared de Blanca: Poems in English and Spanish,* Wordsong (Honesdale, PA), 2004.

Gary Hines, *Midnight Forests: A Story of Gifford Pinchot and Our National Forests,* Boyds Mills Press (Honesdale, PA), 2005.

April Jones Prince, *Jackie Robinson: He Led the Way,* Grosset & Dunlap (New York, NY), 2008.

Anne C. Bromley, *The Lunch Thief,* Tilbury House Publishers (Gardiner, ME), 2009.

Francine Poppo Rich, *Larry Bird: The Boy from French Lick,* Blue Marlin Publications, 2009.

Contributor of illustrations to the *New York Times, Reader's Digest* and *Highlights for Children.*

Works illustrated by Casilla have been translated into Spanish.

Sidelights

Robert Casilla is an award-winning illustrator of children's books who is known for the warmth and detail he brings to his work. Using watercolors, line drawings, and pastels, Casilla creates realistic renderings that critics consider especially appropriate for the many picture-book biographies he has illustrated for author David A. Adler. Raised by parents born in Puerto Rico, the illustrator brings to his work a multicultural perspective that has enhanced books such as *The Pool Party* and *Boys at Work,* both by noted author Gary Soto, as well as Jo Harper's *The Legend of Mexicatl,* which tells the story of a boy chosen by the Great Spirit to lead his people out of the desert and into the region now known as Mexico. Using watercolors in earthy shades of gold, rust, and brown, Casilla's illustrations for *The Legend of Mexicatl* (published simultaneously in Spanish as *La*

leyenda de Mexicatl) "complement the text perfectly," according to *School Library Journal* reviewer Monica Scheliga Carnesi, "infusing the story with both realism and magic."

Casilla has collaborated with Adler on several illustrated biographies of a number of men and women who have excelled at their field and made important contributions to society as well. Athlete Jackie Robinson joins civil rights advocates Rosa Parks and Dr. Martin Luther King, Jr., as well as U.S. Supreme Court Justice Thurgood Marshall and first lady Eleanor Roosevelt, in a series of books that a *Publishers Weekly* contributor praised as "a highly effective . . . way to introduce the life and legacy of important Americans" to pre-readers. In each book, Casilla creates full-page watercolor paintings representing significant events from the subject's life, giving special attention to portraits and period details. Praising *A Picture Book of Thurgood Marshall* in *School Library Journal,* Margaret Bush noted that the author and illustrator work together to "offer a succinct, visually handsome presentation of the youth and the career highlights of the history-making Marshall." The

Casilla captures the charisma of a beloved sports hero in his work for April Jones Prince's picture book Jackie Robinson: He Led the Way.

life of the Alabama-born woman who sparked the civil-rights movement of the twentieth century is depicted in *A Picture Book of Rosa Parks.* Here Casilla uses "dramatic color" in illustrations that reveal the historic backdrop to Parks' life—from Ku Klux Klan rallies lit by flaming torches to inspiring speeches by Dr. King—and include intimate portraits of Parks that "capture the ordinary person who made a difference," in the words of *Booklist* contributor Hazel Rochman.

Poems reflecting the special relationship between children and their fathers are the center of *Daddy Poems,* edited by John Micklos, Jr. In creating the illustrations for this poetry collection, Casilla used his own two children as models. The illustrator depicts children as they "dance, snuggle, and rest across the warmly illustrated pages," remarked Jeanie Burnett in her *Childhood Education* review. Praising the collection of twenty poems as a wonderful way to reinforce the many different relationships children may have with a father, *School Library Journal* reviewer Nina Lindsay commended in particular Casilla's "realistic paintings of families of diverse backgrounds." Another verse collection, Jane Medina's bilingual *The Dream on Blanca's Wall/El sueño en la pared de Blanca: Poems in English and Spanish*, was dubbed "a winner" by a *Kirkus Reviews* writer on the strength of Casilla's "lifelike and inviting" drawings.

The life of a migrant farmworker family is the focus of L. King Pérez's picture book *First Day in Grapes,* another book featuring Casilla's art. The story follows Chico as he begins third grade in a new school where he knows no one and where he will only stay until the grape harvest is complete and his family moves on to the next job. Although an initially unhappy Chico prepares to be hounded by schoolyard bullies and given homework he is unable to complete, he discovers that he has a skill with math due to his work in the fields and returns home from his first day confident and excited about the school year to come. Casilla's colored pencil-and-watercolor illustrations "excel in conveying Chico's emotions through facial expressions," noted a *Kirkus Reviews* critic, while in *School Library Journal,* Rosalyn Pierini complimented the illustrator's work for adding "warmth and color to this portrait of life in rural California."

In his work for Carolyn Marsden's elementary-grade chapter book *Mama Had to Work on Christmas,* Casilla captures the warmth of a Mexican migrant farmworker family's holiday season in "moving, realistic" drawings that "bring home the painful truth about class differences," according to *Booklist* reviewer Hazel Rochman. *Midnight Forests: A Story of Gifford Pinchot and Our National Forests,* a picture-book biography about the nineteenth-century forester who helped President Theodore Roosevelt establish America's national forest system, pairs Casilla's earth-toned watercolor art with a text by Gary Hines. In *Booklist* Carolyn Phelan praised the artist's "dignified pencil-and-watercolor" illustra-

tions, and Julie Leibach wrote in her *Audubon* review that the artist's "nostalgic" images recall the turn of the twentieth century, a time in which "natural resources seemed limitless and conservation was a strange new idea."

In addition to illustrating children's books, Casilla also works with clients as a professional artist, and he has created art for magazines and even designed a postage stamp. He lives and works in Hastings-on-Hudson, New York, with his wife, Carmen, and his children Emily and Robert, Jr. When not working in his studio, Casilla enjoys spending time with young people and sharing what he does for a living; he visits schools and explains to students how the book illustration process works, from reading the manuscript and meeting with the author through "thumbnail" sketches, finished drawings, and final watercolor paintings.

Casilla once commented: "When I illustrate biographies, I try to learn as much as possible about the person I am illustrating so when I am working on the art, I feel I know the person very well. I find great rewards and satisfaction in illustrating for children. I hope to be able to help kids learn and grow and enjoy reading."

Biographical and Critical Sources

PERIODICALS

Audubon, March-April, 2007, Julie Leibach, review of review of *Midnight Forests: A Story of Gifford Pinchot and Our National Forests,* p. 133.

Booklist, March 1, 1993, Julie Corsaro, review of *The Little Painter of Sabana Grande,* p. 1237; October 15, 1993, Hazel Rochman, review of *A Picture Book of Rosa Parks,* p. 444; June 1, 1996, Stephanie Zvirin, review of *Jalapeño Bagels,* p. 1737; November 15, 1997, Carolyn Phelan, review of *A Picture Book of Thurgood Marshall,* p. 552; November 15, 1998, Isabel Schon, review of *La leyenda de Mexicatl,* p. 599; November 15, 2002, Linda Perkins, review of *First Day in Grapes,* p. 612; September 1, 2003, Hazel Rochman, review of *Mama Had to Work on Christmas,* p. 133; May 15, 2005, Carolyn Phelan, review of *Midnight Forests,* p. 1655.

Childhood Education, winter, 2000, Jeanie Burnett, review of *Daddy Poems,* p. 107.

Kirkus Reviews, October 1, 2002, review of *First Day in Grapes,* p. 1477; November 1, 2003, review of *Mama Had to Work on Christmas,* p. 1318; April 1, 2004, review of *The Dream on Blanca's Wall/El sueño en la pared de Blanca: Poems in English and Spanish,* p. 334.

Publishers Weekly, November 24, 1989, review of *A Picture Book of Martin Luther King, Jr.,* p. 71; February 15, 1993, review of *The Little Painter of Sabana Grande,* p. 237; September 22, 2003, review of *Mama Had to Work on Christmas,* p. 72.

School Library Journal, May, 1988, Jeanette Lambert, review of *The Train to Lulu's,* p. 84; November, 1994, Charlene Strickland, review of *Rodeo Day,* p. 92; December, 1994, Tom S. Hurburt, review of *A Picture Book of Jackie Robinson,* p. 94; July, 1996, Beth Tegart, review of *Jalapeño Bagels,* p. 75; January, 1998, Margaret Bush, review of *A Picture Book of Thurgood Marshall,* p. 96; May, 1998, Monica Scheliga Carnesi, review of *La leyenda de Mexicatl,* p. 161; October, 2002, Nina Lindsay, review of *Daddy Poems,* and Rosalyn Pierini, review of *First Day in Grapes,* p. 125; September 22, 2003, review of *Mama Had to Work on Christmas,* p. 72; April, 2005, Kathy Piehl, review of *Midnight Forests,* p. 123.

ONLINE

Author-Illustrator Source, http://author-illustr-source.com/ (June 11, 2003), "Robert Casilla, Illustrator."

Robert Casilla Home Page, http://robertcasilla.com (January 10, 2010).

Robert Casilla Fine Arts Web site, http://www.robcasilla fineart.com (December 29, 2009).

*   *   *

CHODOS-IRVINE, Margaret

Personal

Born in CA; married; has children. *Education:* University of Oregon, B.A. (anthropology), B.A. (art).

Addresses

Office—3018 45th Ave. S.W., Seattle, WA 98116. *Agent*—Linda Pratt, Sheldon Fogelman Agency, 10 E. 40th St., Ste. 3205, New York, NY 10016. *E-mail*—margaret@chodos-irvine.com.

Career

Artist, author, and children's book illustrator. Formerly worked as a commercial illustrator. Presenter at schools.

Awards, Honors

American Bookseller Association Pick of the Lists designation, Cooperative Center of Books for Children Choice designation, and Oppenheim Toy Portfolio Gold Award, all 2000, all for *Buzz* by Janet S. Wong; Caldecott Honor Book designation, and *Parents* magazine Best Book of the Year designation, both 2004, both for *Ella Sarah Gets Dressed;* Oppenheim Toy Portfolio Gold Award, 2000, for *Hello, Arctic!* by Theodore Taylor; International Reading Association Notable Books for a Global Society selection, 2000, for *Apple Pie 4th of July* by Wong; American Library Association Notable Book designation, 2007, for *Best Best Friends.*

Margaret Chodos-Irvine (Photograph by Gloria Da Pra. Reproduced by permission.)

Writings

SELF-ILLUSTRATED

Ella Sarah Gets Dressed, Harcourt (San Diego, CA), 2003.
Best Best Friends, Harcourt (Orlando, FL), 2006.

ILLUSTRATOR

Ursula Le Guin, *Always Coming Home,* Harper & Row (New York, NY), 1985, reprinted, University of California Press (Berkeley, CA), 2000.

Arthur Griffin, *Ah mo: Indian Legends from the Northwest,* Hancock House (Blain, WA), 1990.

Janet S. Wong, *Buzz,* Harcourt (San Diego, CA), 2000.

Theodore Taylor, *Hello, Arctic!,* Harcourt (San Diego, CA), 2000.

Janet S. Wong, *Apple Pie 4th of July,* Harcourt (San Diego, CA), 2000.

Betsy R. Rosenthal, *My House Is Singing,* Harcourt (Orlando, FL), 2004.

Janet S. Wong, *Hide and Seek,* Harcourt (Orlando, FL), 2005.

Robin Cruise, *Only You,* Harcourt (Orlando, FL), 2007.

Susan Marie Swanson, *To Be like the Sun,* Harcourt (Orlando, FL), 2008.

Sidelights

Printmaker Margaret Chodos-Irvine puts her imagination to the test as she adorns the pages of children's

books that include original tales as well as stories such as *Apple Pie 4th of July* and *Hide and Seek* by Janet S. Wong, *Hello, Arctic!* by Theodore Taylor, and *My House Is Singing* by Betsy R. Rosenthal. Chodos-Irvine's innovative, stylized patterns and her use of vivid color have been praised for adding dimension to her work, which spans techniques such as chine colle, monotyping, collography, and linocut. Asked about her approach to illustration, the Seattle-based artist commented on the Harcourt Web site: "I think of the manuscript as the recipe of a book; it includes the basic ingredients but you have to figure out the instructions. . . . I look at the manuscript as the basis of the book and I have to figure out exactly what the manuscript needs me to do."

Wong's *Apple Pie 4th of July* tells the story of a young Chinese-American girl whose parents own a Chinese food store. The girl becomes frustrated with her parents on the Fourth of July because she believes that Americans will not want their cultural food. Surprised when the orders for Chinese food arrive on the patriotic holiday, the girl also decides to savor the taste of another culture, and shares a homemade apple pie with her family and friends. *Hide and Seek,* a counting story by Wong in which a father and son join the family dog in an event-filled day, pairs a spare text with "bold, high-contrast" prints that mimic the "big, solid forms" of cut-paper collage, according to a *Publishers Weekly* critic. Alicia Eames, writing in *School Library Journal,* called *Apple Pie 4th of July* "cheerfully bright and crisp," and praised Chodos-Irvine for "capturing the spirit of the day as well as the changing emotions of the main character" in her woodcut illustrations. According to the *Publishers Weekly* critic, *Hide and Seek* "is really the illustrator's show"; as Jennifer M. Brabander wrote in *Horn Book,* the book's art is "clean, bold, [and] colorful," while *School Library Journal* contributor Angela J. Reynolds called Chodos-Irvine's brightly colored images "large and interesting enough to capture attention."

Chodos-Irvine creates an awe-inspiring landscape for kids to enjoy in *Hello, Arctic!* Never having been to the Arctic herself, she researched the area, studying the beauty that exists there. Depicting the subtlety of the changing Arctic seasons proved to be a challenge, and Chodos-Irvine carefully considered color choices, form, and texture in creating her artwork for Taylor's story. A reviewer for *Publishers Weekly* maintained that the artist's "otherworldly prints, rendered from a variety of techniques, provide a breathtaking accompaniment" to *Hello, Arctic!* and capture the visual essence of the frigid polar region. A more welcoming environment is the focus of *My House Is Singing,* and here the artist captures the warmth of Rosenthal's poems about a cozy home with "flat, patterned" images that provide young readers with "lots of space . . . to contemplate the music of their own dwellings," according to *Horn Book* contributor Kitty Flynn.

Only You, a picture book by Robin Cruise, combines Chodos-Irvine's rhyming text with pastel-toned illustrations that benefit from "pure, saturated colors" and

"shapes [that] are large, simple, and effective," according to *Booklist* critic Ilene Cooper. The artist's "now-trademark prints are the wholly perfect accompaniment" to Cruise's poetic text, wrote a *Kirkus Reviews* writer, the critic adding that the artist's ability to capture a toddler's *joie de vivre* "is unparalleled." In *Publishers Weekly* a critic cited the book's close-up images as "capturing the unalloyed affection . . . that defines" the love between toddler and parent, adding that its images of family scenes "seem fresh and unsentimental." Another family-centered tale, Susan Marie Swanson's *To Be like the Sun,* features linoleum block prints by Chodos-Irvine that "bring subtle layers of interpretation to" Swanson's text, according to *School Library Journal* reviewer Heidi Estrin.

In addition to illustrating the work of other authors, Chodos-Irvine has also created the original self-illustrated picture books *Ella Sarah Gets Dressed* and *Best Best Friends.* In *Ella Sarah Gets Dressed,* a simple story inspired by her oldest daughter, budding fashionista Ella Sarah demands to wear her most colorful, highly patterned clothing, despite all suggestions from more conservative family members. When her friends show up for a tea party, their garb is as flamboyant and colorful as Ella Sarah's, making everyone realize that the young girl's taste is perfectly appropriate for the occasion. Reviewing the Caldecott Honor-winning book for *School Library Journal,* Linda M. Kenton praised Chodos-Irvine's work as a surefire storytime hit, noting that her "exuberant illustrations . . . dance and tumble across the page." "By conveying her heroine's perspective so convincingly," added a *Publishers Weekly* critic, "Chodos-Irvine makes the book's ending a triumph—and one that should strike a chord with dress-up fans everywhere."

In *Best Best Friends* Chodos-Irvine combines what *Booklist* contributor Jennifer Mattson described as "spot-on words and crisp, gaily patterned" illustrations to capture the close friendship between Clare and Mary. Even the best of friends sometimes face challenges, and in Chodos-Irvine's story Mary's birthday earns the preschooler a level of attention that makes Clare feel left out. Although Clare's jealousy flares into an unkind statement, the two children find a way to set things right by the end of the school day. Noting the many ethnicities represented within the girls' preschool class, Maryann H. Owen added in her *School Library Journal* critic of *Best Best Friends* that the author/artist uses "a warm palette" to "give a retro feel to the story." Dubbing the picture book "a small, perfect tale of conflict and resolution," a *Kirkus Reviews* writer praised Chodos-Irvine's prints for *Best Best Friends* as "full of pattern, color, shape and form."

Biographical and Critical Sources

PERIODICALS

Booklist, July, 2000, Kathy Broderick, review of *Buzz,* p. 2044; October 1, 2002, GraceAnne A. DeCandido, re-

view of *Hello, Arctic!,* p. 339; January 1, 2003, review of *Apple Pie Fourth of July,* p. 799; June 1, 2003, Gillian Engberg, review of *Ella Sarah Gets Dressed,* p. 1768; April 1, 2004, Gillian Engberg, review of *My House Is Singing,* p. 1367; May 1, 2006, Jennifer Mattson, review of *Best Best Friends,* p. 84; February 15, 2007, Ilene Cooper, review of *Only You,* p. 83; April 15, 2008, Gillian Engberg, review of *To Be like the Sun,* p. 51.

Horn Book, March-April, 2004, Kitty Flynn, review of *My House Is Singing,* p. 195; May-June, 2005, Jennifer M. Brabander, review of *Hide and Seek,* p. 318.

Kirkus Reviews, April 15, 2002, review of *Apple Pie Fourth of July,* p. 582; May 1, 2003, review of *Ella Sarah Gets Dressed,* p. 675; April 1, 2006, review of *Best Best Friends,* p. 344; March 1, 2007, review of *Only You,* p. 220; March 15, 2008, review of *To Be like the Sun.*

Publishers Weekly, June 5, 2000, review of *Buzz,* p. 92; July 29, 2002, review of *Hello, Arctic!,* p. 70; April 28, 2003, review of *Ella Sarah Gets Dressed,* p. 68; March 28, 2005, review of *Hide and Seek,* p. 78; February 26, 2007, review of *Only You,* p. 88.

School Library Journal, December, 2000, Trev Jones, review of *Buzz,* p. 56; May, 2002, Alicia Eames, review of *Apple Pie Fourth of July,* p. 132; November, 2002, Sally R. Dow, review of *Hello, Arctic!,* p. 138; July, 2003, Linda M. Kenton, review of *Ella Sarah Gets Dressed,* p. 88; April, 2005, Angela J. Reynolds, review of *Hide and Seek,* p. 116; June, 2006, Maryann H. Owen, review of *Best Best Friends,* p. 108; April, 2008, Heidi Estrin, review of *To Be like the Sun,* p. 123.

ONLINE

Margaret Chodos-Irvine Home Page, http://www.chodos-irvine.com (January 10, 2010).

Harcourt Web site, http://www.harcourtbooks.com/ (February 5, 2004), interview with Chodos-Irvine.

D

DeLANGE, Alex Pardo
See PARDO DeLANGE, Alex

* * *

DILLON, Anna
See SCOTT, Michael

* * *

DOGAR, Sharon 1962-

Personal

Born 1962, in Liverpool, England; married; children: two sons, one daughter. *Education:* Attended college in London, England.

Addresses

Home—Oxford, England. *Agent*—Rosemary Canter, PFD, Drury House, 34-43 Russell St., London WC2B 5HA, England.

Career

Writer and social worker.

Writings

Waves, Chicken House/Scholastic (New York, NY), 2007.

Adaptations

Waves was adapted as an audiobook.

Sidelights

British social worker Sharon Dogar published her debut young-adult novel, *Waves,* in 2007. The work concerns the eerie, supernatural bond between Hal, a British teen-ager, and his comatose sister, Charley. "For me, a book usually starts with a picture," Dogar told an interviewer on the *Embracing the Child* Web site. "One day I saw Hal—he just leapt into my mind, just the way he is in the prologue. He had his back to me, and I knew there was something he both did and didn't want to look at (Charley's picture). The minute I had that vision, I knew I would write a book about him."

In *Waves,* Hal's family decides to take its annual vacation to Brackinton, a seaside haven where Charley nearly drowned just one year earlier. Angry at leaving his sister behind, Hal determines to learn the true cause of her accident. As he investigates the events of that fateful night, Hal's thoughts mingle with those of Charley, and he begins to resolve the mystery. "At the centre of this story is a brave evocation of closeness between a brother and sister that veers beyond the boundaries of what is comfortable," London *Guardian* critic Diane Samuels remarked, adding that the author "is not afraid to delve into murky emotional territory and hold together different levels of reality, conscious and unconscious, permitted and forbidden." Young adults "who don't balk at nonlinear narratives will sink into Dogar's lyrical, free-associative writing," observed *Booklist* reviewer Jennifer Mattson. *School Library Journal* critic Ginny Gustin wrote that, "both suspenseful and thoughtful, action packed and atmospheric," *Waves* "is compelling and memorable."

Biographical and Critical Sources

PERIODICALS

Booklist, December 1, 2006, Jennifer Mattson, review of *Waves,* p. 38.
Guardian (London, England), April 28, 2007, Diane Samuels, "Riding the Surf," review of *Waves,* p. 20.
Kirkus Reviews, March 15, 2007, review of *Waves,*
Kliatt, March, 2007, Claire Rosser, review of *Waves,* p. 10.

Publishers Weekly, February 19, 2007, review of *Waves,* p. 170.

School Library Journal, May, 2007, Ginny Gustin, review of *Waves,* p. 132.

ONLINE

Chicken House Web site, http://www.doublecluck.com/ (March 1, 2009), "Sharon Dogar."

Embracing the Child Web site, http://www.embracingthe child.org/ (March 1, 2007), interview with Dogar.

Scholastic Web site, www.scholastic.com/kids/ (March 1, 2009), "Sharon Dogar."*

*   *   *

DORAN, Colleen 1963-

Personal

Born July 24, 1963. *Education:* Attended college. *Hobbies and other interests:* Hiking, gardening, spending time with family.

Addresses

Office—Colleen Doran Studios, 435-2 Oriana Rd., PMB 610, Newport News, VA 23608. *Agent*—Artist's Choice, Spencer R. Beck, 102 East Ave., 2nd Fl. N., East Norwalk, CT 06851.

Career

Illustrator, conceptual artist, cartoonist, and writer. Colleen Doran Studios, Newport News, VA, owner. Former draughtsman, Yorktown Shipwreck Archeological Project. Creator of original art and images for license. Artist-in-residence at Smithsonian Institute, 2006. Presenter at seminars. *Exhibitions:* Art exhibited at Four Color Images Gallery, New York, NY; Kunstlerhaus, Stuttgart, Germany; Porto, Portugal; Milan, Italy; Secession Gallery, Vienna, Austria; Gijon Cultural Center, Gijon, Spain; San Francisco Cartoon Art Museum, San Francisco, CA; and Museum of Cartoon Art, Rye Brook, NY.

Member

American Society of Portrait Artists, Association of Science Fiction and Fantasy Artists, National Cartoonists Society.

Awards, Honors

Chesley Award, Spectrum Award, and Eisner Award nominations, all 2001, all for *A Distant Soil;* Delphi Institute grant; guest of honor, San Diego Comic Con.

Writings

SELF-ILLUSTRATED

A Distant Soil: Immigrant Song, Donning Company (Norfolk, VA), 1987, reprinted, Image Comics, 2001.

Colleen Doran (Reproduced by permission.)

A Distant Soil: Knights of the Angel, Donning Company (Norfolk, VA), 1989, published as *The Ascendant,* Image Comics, 2001.

A Distant Soil: The Aria, Image Comics, 2001.

A Distant Soil: Coda, Image Comics, 2006.

Girl to Grrrl Manga: How to Draw the Hottest Shoujo Manga, Impact Books (Cincinnati, OH), 2007.

Manga Pro Superstar Workshop: How to Create and Sell Comics and Graphic Novels, Impact Books (Cincinnati, OH), 2008.

ILLUSTRATOR

Warren Ellis, *Orbiter* (graphic novel), DC Comics/Vertigo (New York, NY), 2003.

The Complete J.R.R. Tolkien Sourcebook: An Enthusiast's Guide to Middle-Earth and Beyond, New Page Books, 2003.

J. Michael Straczynski, *The Book of Lost Souls: Introductions All Around,* Marvel/Icon (New York, NY), 2007.

Peter David, *Mascot to the Rescue!,* HarperCollins (New York, NY), 2008.

Contributor to books, including *The Forbidden Book* (graphic novel), *Manga Mania: How to Draw Japanese Comics,* Watson Guptill, *Anime Mania,* Watson Guptill,

and *The Nightmare Factory,* Atomic Comics, 2007. Author/illustrator of comic-book series, including *A Distant Soil,* Aria Press, 1991-95, Image Comics, 1995—; and (with Keith Giffen) *Reign of the Zodiac,* DC Comics/Vertigo, 2003—. Contributor to comic-book series, including *Sandman: Dream Country* by Neil Gaiman, DC Comics/Vertigo; *Wonder Woman: The Once and Future Story; Clive Barker's Hellraiser,* Marvel/Epic Comics; *Clive Barker's Nightbreed,* Marvel/Epic Comics; *Anne Rice's The Master of Rampling Gate,* Innovation Comics; *Tori Amos: Comic Book Tatoo,* Image Comics, and *Captain America, Star Trek, Silver Surfer, Amazing Spiderman, The Legion of Superheroes, Valor, Shade, The Death Gallery, Amethyst: Princess of Gemworld, Power Pack, Manga Mania, Anime Mania,* and *Lucifer.* Contributor to periodicals, including *Disney Adventures, Young Readers Digest, CPM Magazine,* and *Play Station* magazine.

Consultant editor to *Drawing Action Comics: Easel Does It,* by Lee Townsend, Harper Design (New York, NY), 2005.

Sidelights

Colleen Doran is a graphic novelist and comic book artist who is best known for "A Distant Soil," a comic-book series she first created at age twelve and which has gone on to sell over 500,000 copies. Her comic-book series "Reign of the Zodiac" tells of a war between the twelve royal families of the zodiac. In addition to her own work, Doran has also created artwork for projects by numerous other writers, such as Neil Gaiman, Tom Ligotti, and Warren Ellis. In more recent years, she has also worked as an illustrator in the children's-book field.

Doran always wanted to be an artist. At the age of five, she won an art contest sponsored by the Walt Disney Company. Seven years later, while recovering from a serious bout with pneumonia that left her bedridden for weeks, she spent a great deal of time drawing. A gift of a box of comic books inspired Doran to channel her art in a new direction, and it was then that she began writing and drawing "A Distant Soil." The comic series tells of a young brother and sister who are born into an alien religious dynasty. Jason and Liana have extraordinary psychic powers. Liana, in fact, is an Avatar, one of her people's most powerful religious leaders because of her ability to focus their life force to use as a weapon against their enemies. When another Avatar sees Liana as a rival, the siblings flee to Earth but are followed by an assassination team from their home planet. "A Distant Soil" has its origins in the myriad influences that inspired its then-preteen creator, from Arthurian legend to the "Superman" comics, and it also deals with contemporary issues such as gay rights.

Doran attended her first science-fiction convention at age fifteen, and when her work was displayed to the public it sold out. In addition, the owner of an advertising agency was so impressed with Doran's drawings that she hired the teen as an illustrator for commercial projects that included a S.W.A.T. team training manual and literature for Planned Parenthood. Although Doran attempted to combine her work as a professional artist with college, she ultimately opted for her job.

Doran's artwork soon attracted attention in science-fiction circles, and WaRP Graphics began publishing "A Distant Soil." However, the publisher rewrote her stories and changed her art, and nine issues later Doran broke her contract and regained full ownership of the comic. A new contract with the Donning Company resulted in the series' release in the trade paperbacks *A Distant Soil: Immigrant Song* and *A Distant Soil: Knights of the Angel.*

Although Donning went out of business soon after, Doran found work with comic-book publishers to work on such popular characters as Spiderman, Wonder Woman, Sandman, and the Legion of Super Heroes. Now, as she explained at the A Distant Soil Web site, "I was getting a chance to have some fun, work with real profession-

Doran's illustration projects include creating detailed illustrations for Warren Ellis's picture book **Orbiter.** (Illustration © Warren Ellis and Colleen Doran. All rights reserved. Used with permission of DC Comics.)

als, and I decided to get my life back to normal after WaRP and Donning. I bought a home, got a cat and went to work."

In 1991 Doran formed Aria Press to republish "A Distant Soil," and after the twelfth issue she started producing new material. In 1995, after Marvel Comics took control of their own distribution, the independent distribution network for smaller publishers fell apart. Although Aria Press experienced financial problems, a call from Erik Larsen of Image Comics saved the day when he offered to take over publication of Doran's popular series. In addition to its release in comic-book format by Image Comics, "A Distant Soil" has also been collected in several book-length anthologies.

In her other work in comics, Doran has collaborated with writer Warren Ellis on the graphic novel *Orbiter,* a hard science-fiction saga about the Venture, a space shuttle that returns to Earth after an unexplained absence of ten years. The shuttle is covered with a strange organic material, and the machinery has been revised with an alien technology. Only one crew member is found on board and he is in a catatonic state and unable to speak. The government brings in a crack scientific team to explain what has happened. According to Steve Raiteri, reviewing *Orbiter* for *Library Journal,* "fans of Doran . . . will see a different side of her . . . in the realistic work here." A critic for *Publishers Weekly* concluded that Doran "handles cataclysmic disaster scenes, detailed technical exposition and tender human moments with equal deftness."

A collaboration with writer Keith Giffen resulted in *Reign of the Zodiac,* which describes a world where the twelve houses of the zodiac are embodied in twelve royal families that vie for power. The characteristics of each family are based on the traditional virtues attributed to each zodiacal house. The clothing and architecture of the members of the house of Pisces, for example, are drawn from the fishing communities of Northern Europe, while those of the house of Leo are simple and unadorned.

Working with J. Michael Straczynski, Doran has also contributed to Marvel's *The Book of Lost Souls: Introductions All Around.* Praising this work, which finds a man living in the nineteenth century deterred from committing suicide with an offer of rescuing five troubled individuals living in the twenty-first century, *Library Journal* reviewer Steve Raiteri described the comic as "an interesting take on the Garden of Eden story." Calling Straczynski's text "portentous and intriguing," the critic also cited Doran's "excellent artwork," which juxtaposes "gorgeous Art Nouveu-esque" images with "a grittier style."

Doran joins writer Peter David in turning to younger readers in *Mascot to the Rescue!,* a middle-grade novel that mixed a chapter book with graphic-novel elements. In the story, twelve-year-old Josh Miller is a fan of a superhero sidekick named Mascot, and he finds it uncanny that the fictional Mascot's life seems to mirror his own. When he learns that Mascot will be killed off in the "Captain Major" comic-book series, Josh determines to prevent the sidekick's death, embarking on a humorous quest that intrigues his friends, frustrates his teachers, and worries his parents. Calling *Mascot to the Rescue!* a "breathless, funny novel," a *Kirkus Reviews* contributor added that "David and Doran know their comic-book stuff." In *School Library Journal,* Laura Lutz also enjoyed the novel but bemoaned the fact that Doran's "action-packed and dynamic" illustrations are "too few" in number.

A prolific artist and writer, Doran continues to contribute to a wide variety of illustrated works, and is an active voice for professionalism in her field. "I try very hard to give my readers the best art and story I can . . . ," she noted on the A Distant Soil Web site. "I hope I can be an inspiration to other young artists out there who experience doubt and setbacks. Don't give up your dream!"

Biographical and Critical Sources

PERIODICALS

Bulletin of the Center for Children's Books, October, 2008, April Spisak, review of *Mascot to the Rescue!,* p. 68.
Comics Buyer's Guide, March 3, 1995, Jeff Mason, interview with Doran.
Kirkus Reviews, October 1, 2008, review of *Mascot to the Rescue!*
Library Journal, September 1, 2003, Steve Raiteri, review of *Orbiter,* p. 140; January 1, 2007, Steve Raiteri, review of *The Book of Lost Souls: Introductions All Around,* p. 79.
Magazine of Fantasy and Science Fiction, October-November, 2003, Charles de Lint, review of *Orbiter,* p. 49.
Publishers Weekly, September 15, 2003, review of *Orbiter,* p. 46.
School Library Journal, November, 2008, Laura Lutz, review of *Mascot to the Rescue!,* p. 118.

ONLINE

A Distant Soil Web site, http://www.adistantsoil.com/ (January 10, 2010).
Colleen Doran Web site, http://www.colleendoran.com (January 10, 2010).
Westfield Comics Web site, http://westfieldcomics.com/ (February, 1998), interview with Doran.

OTHER

Scenes from the Small Press: Colleen Doran (film).*

DRAKE, Salamanda
See BARLOW, Steve

*   *   *

DUNBAR, Polly 1980-

Personal

Born 1980, in the Cotswalds, England; daughter of Joyce Dunbar (a writer). *Education:* Attended Norwich Art School; Brighton University, degree (illustration), 1999.

Addresses

Home—London, England. *Agent*—Celia Catchpole, 56 Gilpin Ave., London SW14 8QY, England. *E-mail*—polly@pollydunbar.com.

Career

Writer and illustrator. Puppeteer.

Awards, Honors

Cuffie Award for Most Promising New Illustrator, *Publishers Weekly,* for *Flyaway Katie* and *Dog Blue;* NASEN/*Times Educational Supplement* Special Education Needs Children's Book Award, 2006, for *Looking after Louis* by Lesley Ely; Best Children's Show honor, Brighton Festival, 2006, for puppet-theater adaptation of *Shoe Baby* by Joyce Dunbar; Nestlé Children's Book Prize Silver Award for Children under Five, and Booktrust Early Years Award in preschool category, both 2007, both for *Penguin;* International Board on Books for Young People Honor Book designation, 2008, for *Here's a Little Poem* edited by Jane Yolen and Andrew Fusek Peters.

Writings

SELF-ILLUSTRATED

Help! I'm out with the In-Crowd, and Other Saturday Nightmares, Kingfisher (London, England), 1996.
Help! I've Forgotten My Brain, and Other Exam Nightmares, Kingfisher (London, England), 1996.
Scrooge: Hole Story, Scholastic (London, England), 2002.
Henry VIII: Hole Story, Scholastic (London, England), 2002.
Cleopatra: Hole Story, Scholastic (London, England), 2002.
Flyaway Katie, Candlewick (Cambridge, MA), 2004.
Dog Blue, Candlewick (Cambridge, MA), 2004.
Penguin, Candlewick (Cambridge, MA), 2007.

SELF-ILLUSTRATED; "TILLY AND FRIENDS" SERIES

Happy Hector, Candlewick Press (Cambridge, MA), 2008.
Hello, Tilly, Candlewick Press (Cambridge, MA), 2008.
Doodle Bites, Candlewick Press (Somerville, MA), 2009.

Polly Dunbar (Photograph courtesy of Polly Dunbar. Reproduced by permission.)

Good Night, Tiptoe, Candlewick Press (Somerville, MA), 2009.
Where's Tumpty?, Candlewick Press (Somerville, MA), 2009.
Pretty Prue, Candlewick Press (Somerville, MA), 2009.

ILLUSTRATOR

Sherry Ashworth, *Fat,* Scholastic (London, England), 1997.
Elizabeth Laird, editor, *Me and My Electric,* Mammoth (London, England), 1998.
Jeanette Baker, *A Survivor's Guide to School,* Wayland (Hove, England), 1999.
Jeanette Baker, *A Survivor's Guide to Love, Etc.,* Wayland (Hove, England), 1999.
Jeanette Baker, *A Survivor's Guide to Friends,* Wayland (Hove, England), 1999.
Jeanette Baker, *A Survivor's Guide to Families,* Wayland (Hove, England), 1999.
Myra Barrs and Sue Ellis, editors, *A Saucepan on His Head, and Other Nonsense Poems,* Walker (London, England), 2001.
Sandra Cain and Michelle Maxwell, *The Total Volunteering Book,* A & C Black (London, England), 2001.
Sherry Ashworth, *English Literature: Exam Success without the Stress,* Scholastic (London, England), 2001.
June Crebbin, *The Dragon Test,* Walker (London, England), 2003.

June Crebbin, *Hal the Highwayman,* Walker (London, England), 2003.

Pippa Goodhart, *Ratboy,* Barrington Stoke (Edinburgh, Scotland), 2004.

Lesley Ely, *Looking after Louis,* Albert Whitman (Morton Grove, IL), 2004.

June Crebbin, *Lucy and the Firestone,* Walker (London, England), 2004.

June Crebbin, *Hal the Pirate,* Walker (London, England), 2004.

Joyce Dunbar, *Shoe Baby* (also see below), Candlewick (Cambridge, MA), 2005.

Margaret Mahy, *Down the Back of the Chair,* Clarion (New York, NY), 2006.

Pippa Goodhart, *The Runaway Chair,* Barrington Stoke (Edinburgh, Scotland), 2006.

Jane Yolen and Andrew Fusek Peters, editors, *Here's a Little Poem: A Very First Book of Poetry,* Candlewick (Cambridge, MA), 2007.

David Almond, *My Dad's a Bird Man,* Candlewick (Cambridge, MA), 2007.

Lesley Ely, *Measuring Angels,* Frances Lincoln (London, England), 2008.

Margaret Mahy, *Bubble Trouble,* Clarion Books (New York, NY), 2009.

The Boy Who Climbed into the Moon, Candlewick Press (Somerville, MA), 2010.

OTHER

(Adaptor, with Katherine Morton) *Shoe Baby* (puppet play based on the picture book by Joyce Dunbar), produced at Brighton Festival, 2006.

Sidelights

Award-winning artist Polly Dunbar has been writing and illustrating books professionally since she was sixteen years old. Her first two books, *Help! I'm out with the In-Crowd, and Other Saturday Nightmares* and *Help! I've Forgotten My Brain, and Other Exam Nightmares,* are "cartoon books inspired by teenage antics," as Dunbar wrote on her home page. Since those debut titles, Dunbar has written and illustrated several books of her own, as well as providing illustrations for other writers, including her mother, prolific children's writer Joyce Dunbar.

Collaborating with author Lesley Ely, Dunbar produced *Looking after Louis,* a story about accepting differences. The story is told from the point of view of a young girl who sits next to Louis, an autistic boy, in her class. "Dunbar's childlike paintings cleverly show how Louis is essentially the same as the other kids," wrote Kathleen Kelly MacMillan in *School Library Journal.* A *Kirkus Reviews* contributor noted the illustrator's use of "sketchy scenes rendered in a childlike, cartoon style."

A joint project of Dunbar and mom Joyce Dunbar, *Shoe Baby* finds a young baby traveling to fantastic locations in a shoe. "The mixed-media artwork is particularly en-

ticing," wrote Ilene Cooper in *Booklist,* and a *Kirkus Reviews* contributor noted that Polly Dunbar's "delightful mixed-media collage illustrations of eccentric creatures great and small burst forth with . . . glee."

Dunbar's work with well-known poet Margaret Mahy includes *Down the Back of the Chair* and *Bubble Trouble.* In *Down the Back of the Chair* Dunbar's "cacophonous, sunny, paint-and-paper collages" pair with Mahy's text, according to *Booklist* critic Gillian Engberg. A *Kirkus Reviews* contributor noted that the "whimsical creatures, juicy colors and . . . motion" in Dunbar's art "match the kinetic energy of the text." In the "mountains of mayhem" that readers encounter in *Bubble Trouble,* Dunbar's "energetic watercolor and cut-paper" illustrations contribute to the "over-the-top silliness" of Mahy's tale, according to *School Library Journal* contributor Marianne Saccardi. According to *Horn Book* contributor Robin L. Smith, "every little detail" in Mahy's "raucous story is depicted in the [illustrator's] dramatic spreads" for the large-format picture book.

In addition to illustration, Dunbar has also created several self-illustrated books. In *Flyaway Katie* she tells a story about the power of imagination to drive away the doldrums. Katie wakes up feeling gray, quite literally: her world is colorful, but Katie is depicted in gray tones. Trying to make herself feel more cheerful, she dons a bright green hat and yellow tights. As she adds more and more color to her ensemble, the colors begin to whirl and Katie is transformed into a colorful bird. Spending the afternoon flying about, Katie arrives home—happily pink—just in time for her bath. "The magical makeover, a literal flight of fancy, will make

Dunbar's endearing illustrations are beloved by children due to her depiction of strong family bonds. (Courtesy of Polly Dunbar.)

readers' spirits soar, too," wrote a *Publishers Weekly* critic, and Cooper predicted that young readers will enjoy the "neatly framed pictures that eventually burst into a mixed-media multihued whirl." Asserting that the picture book is "told at just the right pace," Wanda Meyers-Hines wrote in *School Library Journal* that Dunbar's "whimsical story presents a gentle reminder of the power of a child's imagination," and a *Kirkus Reviews* contributor deemed *Flyaway Katie* "a joyous cure for a case of the doldrums."

Another self-illustrated picture book by Dunbar, *Dog Blue* also focuses on the power of imagination. Here Bertie wants a dog in his favorite color, blue. Because he does not have a real-life pup, Bertie creates one in his mind, playing with his imaginary dog and fetching his own sticks. When a spotted dog arrives in Bertie's life, the boy is disappointed that it is not blue, but instead of turning away, he names the dog Blue and now has a friend to play with. "Young Bertie's joy comes through loud and clear" in both the story and the artwork, according to a *Kirkus Reviews* contributor. Although she found the story's resolution gratifying, Jennifer Mattson wrote in *Booklist* that "it's Bertie's ingenious self-sufficiency that truly resonates." A *Publishers Weekly* contributor also praised the picture book, writing that *Dog Blue* features "polished artwork and skilled pacing."

In *Penguin,* another of Dunbar's award-winning original picture books, she focuses on a boy named Ben, who is dismayed to learn that his new pet penguin is unable to talk. When Ben employs drastic measures in an effort to elicit a comment from Penguin—even blasting the bird into outer space—his efforts backfire and the pet ultimately reveals his visual method of communication. Calling *Penguin* a "brief, brisk" tale, Randall Enos predicted in *Booklist* that "its message" about the importance of "communication and mutual respect bears repeated reading." The author/illustrator's "winsome mixed media illustrations carry the day" in *Penguin* noted a *Publishers Weekly* contributor, the critic calling the book's art "child-centered, deceptively simple, and satisfying."

Dunbar's self-illustrated "Tilly and Friends" series focuses on a little girl who lives with an unusual group of housemates: Tiptoe the rabbit, Hector the pig, Doodle the alligator, Pru the chicken, and Tumpty the elephant. Geared for toddlers, the simple stories in *Hello Tilly, Happy Hector, Doodle Bites,* and *Goodnight Tiptoe,* capture a child's attention through their humor and use of onomatopoeia. Dunbar matches her text for *Happy Hector* with "lovely, soothing drawings in gentle pastel colors," according to *School Library Journal* contributor Madigan McGillicuddy. In *Pretty Pru,* in which the chicken discovers that her housemates have made use of all the cosmetics in her handbag, the author/illustrator pairs her "gentle" story of forgiveness with "colorful and expressive mixed-media" images, according to Anne Beier in another *School Library Journal* review. Calling *Where's Tumpty?* a "delightful" installment in the "Tilly and Friends" series, Cooper praised it as an effective read-aloud choice that features a "diverse group of friends with personality."

Along with writing and illustrating, Dunbar is also a member of the Long Nose Puppets Theater Company, a collection of friends from her university days that stages puppet-show versions of her picture books. Based in Brighton, England, the Long Nose Puppets Theatre Company has produced award-winning adaptations of *Shoe Baby, Flyaway Katie,* and *Penguin* at theatres, schools, and festivals throughout the United Kingdom.

Biographical and Critical Sources

PERIODICALS

Booklist, April 15, 2004, Connie Fletcher, review of *Looking after Louis,* p. 1445; June 1, 2004, Ilene Cooper, review of *Flyaway Katie,* p. 1740; July, 2004, Jennifer Mattson, review of *Dog Blue,* p. 1846; June 1, 2005, Ilene Cooper, review of *Shoe Baby,* p. 1821; May 1, 2006, Gillian Engberg, review of *Down the Back of the Chair,* p. 92; June 1, 2007, Randall Enos, review of *Penguin,* p. 84; March 1, 2009, Ilene Cooper, review of *Where's Tumpty?,* p. 53.
Horn Book, September-October, 2004, Joanna Rudge Long, review of *Dog Blue,* p. 566; May-June, 2009, Robin L. Smith, review of *Bubble Trouble,* p. 284.

Dunbar creates humorous artwork for Here's a Little Poem, *an anthology compiled by Jane Yolen and Andrew Fusek Peters.* (Illustration copyright © 2007 by Polly Dunbar. Reproduced by permission of Candlewick Press, Inc., on behalf of Walker Books, London.)

Margaret Mahy's lighthearted story in **Bubble Trouble** *is enhanced by Dunbar's colorful collage and watercolor art.* (Illustration copyright © 2008 by Polly Dunbar. All rights reserved. Reprinted by permission of Clarion Books, an imprint of Houghton Mifflin Harcourt Publishing Company.)

Kirkus Reviews, March 15, 2004, review of *Looking after Louis,* p. 268; June 15, 2004, review of *Flyaway Katie,* p. 576; July 1, 2004, review of *Dog Blue,* p. 627; July 1, 2005, review of *Shoe Baby,* p. 733; May 15, 2006, review of *Down the Back of the Chair,* p. 520.

New York Times Book Review, May 13, 2007, Joanna Rudge Long, review of *Here's a Little Poem: A Very First Book of Poetry,* p. 16.

Publishers Weekly, July 5, 2004, review of *Flyaway Katie,* p. 54; August 30, 2004, review of *Dog Blue,* p. 53; September 5, 2005, review of *Shoe Baby,* p. 60; April 10, 2006, review of *Down the Back of the Chair,* p. 70; July 23, 2007, review of *Penguin,* p. 66.

School Library Journal, April, 2004, Kathleen Kelly MacMillan, review of *Looking after Louis,* p. 109; September, 2004, Janet M. Bair, review of *Dog Blue,* and Wanda Meyers-Hines, review of *Flyaway Katie,* p. 158; August, 2005, Marianne Saccardi, review of *Shoe Baby,* p. 93; June, 2006, Carol L. MacKay, review of *Down the Back of the Chair,* p. 122; May, 2008, Margaret A. Chang, review of *My Dad's a Birdman,* p. 92; May, 2009, Anne Beier, review of *Pretty Prue,* p. 74; March, 2009, review of *Measuring Angels,* p. 112; May, 2009, Marianne Saccardi, review of *Bubble Trouble,* p. 83; June, 2009, Madigan McGillicuddy, reviews of *Happy Hector* and *Hello Tilly,* p. 84.

Sunday Times (London, England), October 21, 2007, Nicolette Jones, review of *My Dad's a Birdman,* p. 49.

Times Educational Supplement, October 27, 2006, Karen Gold, "All Together Now," p. 30, Jane Doonan, "Art World Is Their Oyster," p. 34.

Tribune Books (Chicago, IL), July 2, 2006, Mary Harris Russell, review of *Down the Back of the Chair,* p. 7.

ONLINE

Houghton Mifflin Web site, http://www.houghtonmifflin books.com/ (January 10, 2010), "Polly Dunbar."

Images of Delight Web site, http://www.imagesofdelight. com/ (January 10, 2010), "Polly Dunbar."

Long Nose Puppets Web log, http://www.longnosepuppets. com/ (January 10, 2010), "Polly Dunbar."

Meet the Author Web site, http://www.meettheauthor.co.uk/ (July 3, 2007), video interview with Dunbar.

Polly Dunbar Home Page, http://www.pollydunbar.com (January 10, 2010).

E-F

EDGSON, Alison

Personal

Born in County Down, Northern Ireland; married; husband's name Jeff. *Education:* University of Ulster, degree. *Hobbies and other interests:* Running, cycling.

Addresses

Home—Usk Valley, Wales.

Career

Illustrator of children's books. Worked previously in computer department of a bank.

Illustrator

Three Billy Goats Gruff, Child's Play (Auburn, ME), 2005.

Andrew Peters, *Bear and Turtle and the Great Lake Race,* Child's Play (Auburn, ME), 2006.

Alison Ritchie, *Me and My Dad!,* Good Books (Intercourse, PA), 2007.

Claire Freedman, *Follow That Bear If You Dare!,* Good Books (Intercourse, PA), 2008.

Linda Jennings, *Little Puppy Lost,* Good Books (Intercourse, PA), 2008.

Marni McGee, *Silly Goose,* Good Books (Intercourse, PA), 2008.

Alison Ritchie, *Me and My Mom!,* Good Books (Intercourse, PA), 2009.

Catherine Walters, *The Magical Snowman,* Good Books (Intercourse, PA), 2009.

Sidelights

After studying visual communication at the University of Ulster in Belfast, Northern Ireland, Alison Edgson began turning her talents to children's illustration, providing the artwork for texts by Alison Ritchie, Claire Freedman, and Linda Jennings, among others. Bear characters feature prominently in works by the first two writers, as Ritchie depicts the special relationship fathers and sons share through a pair of loving bears in *Me and My Dad!* while Freedman offers young readers a story about a young rabbit that loves bears and hopes to track one down in *Follow That Bear If You Dare!* According to a *Publishers Weekly* reviewer, Edgson's illustrations elevate *Me and My Dad!* "above the ordinary with her impressionistic settings and backgrounds." In her *School Library Journal* review, G. Alyssa Parkinson described the pictures in the same book as "bright, with soft, rounded edges," allowing the fearsome creatures to be "depicted realistically" but not in a way "frightening" to young children. Also writing in *School Library Journal,* Ieva Bates found Edgson's figures in *Follow That Bear If You Dare!* "soft and cuddly," further highlighting them as "endearing."

A different animal appears in Jennings' *Little Puppy Lost,* as a young canine becomes separated from its siblings while playing in the park on a snowy winter day. Scared by a large barking dog, the little puppy runs away quickly, only to find itself in unfamiliar surroundings. Asking other animals in the park for help, the pup receives advice both useful and discouraging. The tension in *Little Puppy Lost* quickly becomes resolved, however, as the youngster's concerned mother locates her missing pup. "Soft-focus illustrations lend a quiet, dreamy, wintry quality to the attractive spreads," observed Linda Staskus in a *School Library Journal* review, while *Booklist* critic Ilene Cooper wrote that Edgson's artwork provides a main character "with real expression on his face." Cooper went on to recommend *Little Puppy Lost* as a good selection for reading aloud to larger groups, calling the illustrations "appealing even from afar."

Biographical and Critical Sources

PERIODICALS

Booklist, May 1, 2007, Ilene Cooper, review of *Me and My Dad!,* p. 84; June 1, 2008, Connie Fletcher, re-

view of *Follow That Bear If You Dare!,* p. 87; December 1, 2008, Ilene Cooper, review of *Little Puppy Lost,* p. 58.

Kirkus Reviews, May 1, 2007, review of *Me and My Dad!;* September 15, 2008, review of *Little Puppy Lost.*

Publishers Weekly, March 12, 2007, review of *Me and My Dad!,* p. 56.

School Library Journal, August, 2007, G. Alyssa Parkinson, review of *Me and My Dad!,* p. 90; August, 2008, Ieva Bates, review of *Follow That Bear If You Dare!,* p. 89; June, 2008, Catherine Callegari, review of *Silly Goose,* p. 110; December, 2008, Linda Staskus, review of *Little Puppy Lost,* p. 92; May, 2009, Rebecca Dash, review of *Me and My Mom!,* p. 87.*

*   *   *

EVANS, Freddi Williams 1957-

Personal

Born February 13, 1957, in Jackson, MS; daughter of R.L. (a minister) and Carrie (a teacher) Williams; married (divorced); children: Akita, Melvin. *Education:* Tougaloo College, B.A. (music) and B.A. (psychology; magna cum laude), 1977; Hahnemann University, M.C.A.T., 1979; attended University of New Orleans, 1990-92. *Politics:* Democrat. *Religion:* Baptist. *Hobbies and other interests:* Traveling, reading, conducting research.

Addresses

Home—New Orleans, LA.

Career

Author, artist, therapist, educator, and administrator. Southern Home for Children, Philadelphia, PA, music therapist, 1978-80; worked as creative arts specialist, 1981-82; Jefferson Parish Public Schools, Harvey, LA, artist and teacher, 1985-94, artist and administrator, 1994—. Artist-in-residence, Louisiana Division of the Arts, 1995-2001, and New Orleans Arts Council, 1995, 1997-2001. Consultant to Amistad Research Center, 2001 and 2004, New Orleans Public Schools, 2001-05, Mississippi Whole Schools Institute, 2004, VSA Arts of Louisiana, 1999-2004, and Jackson State University, 2007-08. Private practice of music therapy, 1986-94; Jefferson Parish Juvenile Court Services, creative arts therapist. Delgado Community College, part-time instructor, 1981-82. Congo Square Research Initiative, participant, 1999; also affiliated with Highlands for Children Foundation, Chautauqua Institute, National Faculty Teacher Institute at Dillard University, Start with the Arts Consultant Institute, and Louisiana Department of Education.

Member

Society of Children's Book Writers and Illustrators, Louisiana Reading Association, NOMMO Literary Society, Phi Delta Kappa, Alpha Kappa Alpha.

Freddi Williams Evans (Reproduced by permission.)

Awards, Honors

Regional Artists Project grant, 1995; Fulbright scholar in Zimbabwe, 1995, and South Africa, 2000; Council for Basic Education grant, 1997; Maizie Malveaux Very Special Arts Award, 1998, for outstanding service to Louisiana students with disabilities; New Orleans Jazz and Heritage Foundation grant, 1999; Louisiana State Department of Education grants, 1999, 2000; Louisiana Endowment for the Humanities grant, 2001; special congressional recognition for outstanding contribution to the arts, 2002; Outstanding Achievement Award (literature), The Links, Inc. (New Orleans chapter), 2002; Notable Social Studies Trade Book for Young People designation, National Council for the Social Studies/Children's Book Council, Platinum Book Award, Oppenheim Toy Portfolio, 2002, and Mississippi Authors' Award, Mississippi Library Association, 2004, all for *A Bus of Our Own.*

Writings

A Bus of Our Own, illustrated by Shawn Costello, Albert Whitman (Morton Grove, IL), 2001.

The Battle of New Orleans: The Drummer's Story, illustrated by Emile Henriquez, Pelican Publishing (Gretna, LA), 2005.

Hush Harbor: Praying in Secret, illustrated by Erin Bennet Banks, Carolrhoda Books (Minneapolis, MN), 2008.

Also author of picture book, *Ngoma in Congo Square.* Creator of multidisciplinary performance piece, "I Hear the Drums," performed in Jackson, MS, and New Orleans, LA. Work represented in anthologies, including *Educators as Authors,* Louisiana Reading Association, 1992; *Kente Cloth,* University of Texas Press (Austin, TX), 1997; and *From a Bend in the River: 100 New Orleans Poets,* Runagate Press, 1998. Contributor to periodicals, including *Louisiana Weekly, Preservation in Print, Fertile Ground Literary Journal, African American,* and *New Orleans Tribune.*

Sidelights

In her historical fiction *A Bus of Our Own* and *Hush Harbor: Praying in Secret,* Freddi Williams Evans explores little-known episodes from U.S. history that are based on the slave narratives collected throughout the American South by the government-sponsored Works Progress Administration during the 1930s. An arts educator and administrator, Evans once told *SATA,* "I grew up among extended family members in my hometown of Madison, Mississippi. I lived with my parents and two brothers and frequently visited old relatives who told me stories about how their lives used to be. My writings grew out of a desire to share those family stories as well as the untold and 'under-told' stories of other African Americans."

A Bus of Our Own is based on actual events from the late 1940s and early 1950s. As Evans recalled, her debut title "is about my family and hometown. I first heard about the bus at my uncle's funeral and began to inquire about it on the way to the graveyard. Based on real events, *A Bus of Our Own* celebrates the bonding together of the community in the 1940s and 1950s to make life better for the children." The work concerns a

Evans' civil-war-themed story in **The Battle of New Orleans** *is paired with Emile Henriquez' pen-and-watercolor illustrations.* (Pelican Publishing Company, 2005. Illustration copyright © 2005 by Emile Henriquez. All rights reserved. Reproduced by permission.)

Mississippi youngster who, tiring of the daily five-mile walk to school during which she endures the jeers of her white classmates, inspires members of her community to purchase a school bus for black children. According to *Booklist* contributor Hazel Rochman, "the drama is in the facts about what ordinary people did together."

In *The Battle of New Orleans,* a work told in verse, Evans looks at the final conflict of the War of 1812 though the eyes of Jordan B. Noble, an African-American teenager who served as the drummer for General Andrew Jackson. Evans turns her attention to the ways enslaved Africans in the American South managed to preserve their traditions and practice their religious beliefs in *Hush Harbor.* This work centers on Simmy, a young boy who acts as a lookout while other slaves hold clandestine nighttime prayer meetings in remote locations. "Evans captures the drama and tension" of the often dangerous situations, commented *School Library Journal* critic Grace Oliff in her review of *Hush Harbor,* and Ilene Cooper, writing in *Booklist,* similarly noted that the work "captures some of the fear and horror associated with slavery."

Biographical and Critical Sources

PERIODICALS

Black Issues Book Review, January-February, 2002, Lydia Omolola Okutoro, review of *A Bus of Our Own,* p. 79.
Booklist, August, 2001, Hazel Rochman, review of *A Bus of Our Own,* p. 2128; October 1, 2008, Ilene Cooper, review of *Hush Harbor: Praying in Secret,* p. 51.
Kirkus Reviews, October 1, 2008, review of *Hush Harbor.*
School Library Journal, September, 2001, Thomas Pitchford, review of *A Bus of Our Own,* p. 188; November, 2005, Judith Constantinides, review of *The Battle of New Orleans: The Drummer's Story,* p. 90; November, 2008, Grace Oliff, review of *Hush Harbor,* p. 88.

ONLINE

Pelican Publishing Company Web site, http://pelicanpub. com/ (January 1, 2010), "Freddi Williams Evans."

*   *   *

FOX, Mem 1946-
(Merrion Frances Fox)

Personal

Born March 5, 1946, in Melbourne, Victoria, Australia; daughter of Wilfrid Gordon McDonald (a missionary) and Nancy Walkden (a writer) Partridge; married Mal-

Mem Fox (Photograph by Donica Bettanin. Reproduced by permission.)

colm Fox (a teacher), January 2, 1969; children: Chloë Catienne. *Education:* Attended Rose Bruford Drama School, London, 1968; Finders University, South Australia, B.A., 1978; South Australian College of Advanced Education, B.Ed., 1979, graduate diploma, 1981. *Politics:* Labour. *Religion:* Christian.

Addresses

Home—Adelaide, South Australia, Australia. *Agent*—Jenny Darling, P.O. Box 413, Toorak, Victoria 3142, Australia.

Career

Writer, educator, and television host. Cabra Dominican School, Adelaide, South Australia, drama teacher, 1970-72; South Australian College of Advanced Education-Sturt (now Flinders University), Adelaide, South Australia, lecturer, 1973-86, senior lecturer, beginning 1987, associate professor of literacy studies until 1996. Speaker and lecturer at literary conferences and other events; educational consultant.

Member

South Australian Story Telling Guild (founder, 1978; president, 1981), Actors Equity, Australian Society of

Authors, National Council for Teachers of English, Primary English Teachers Association (Australia), Children's Book Council (Australia), Association for Study of Australian Literature.

Awards, Honors

Australian Children's Book Council Picture Book of the Year high commendation, and New South Wales Premier's Literary Award for Best Children's Book, both 1984, both for *Possum Magic;* Australian Picture Book of the Year shortlist, and Child Study Association of America's Children's Books of the Year designation, both 1985, and *New York Times* Notable Books designation, 1986, all for *Wilfrid Gordon McDonald Partridge;* Dromkeen Medal for distinguished services to children's literature, 1990; Advance Australia Award, 1991, for outstanding contribution to Australian literature; medal from Australia Day Honors awards, 1993; honorary doctorate of Letters, University of Wollongong, Australia, 1996; South Australia Great Award for literature, 2001; Woman of Achievement Award, Zonta International, 2002; Prime Minister's Centenary Medal, 2003; Australian of the Year for South Australia, 2003; named Australian of the Year finalist, 2004; honorary D.Let., University of Flinders, 2004; appointed Hans Christian Andersen Australian ambassador by Crown Prince Frederik of Denmark, 2005; Children's Language and Literature Achievement Award, Speech Pathology Association of Australia, 2007.

Writings

FOR CHILDREN

Possum Magic, illustrated by Julie Vivas, Omnibus (Norwood, South Australia, Australia), 1983, Harcourt (New York, NY), 1990, tenth-anniversary commemorative edition, Omnibus, 1993, adapted as *The Little Book of Possum Magic,* Omnibus (Malvern, South Australia, Australia), 2006.

Wilfrid Gordon McDonald Partridge, illustrated by Julie Vivas, Omnibus (Norwood, South Australia, Australia), 1984, Kane Miller (New York, NY), 1985.

A Cat Called Kite, illustrated by Kevin Hawley, Ashton Scholastic (Auckland, New Zealand), 1985.

Hattie and the Fox, illustrated by Patricia Mullins, Ashton Scholastic (Sydney, New South Wales, Australia), 1986, Bradbury (New York, NY), 1987, reprinted, Ashton Scholastic, 2006.

Sail Away: The Ballad of Skip and Nell, illustrated by Pamela Lofts, Ashton Scholastic (Sydney, New South Wales, Australia), 1986, reprinted, 2006.

Arabella, the Smallest Girl in the World, illustrated by Vicky Kitanov, Ashton Scholastic (Sydney, New South Wales, Australia), 1986.

Just like That, illustrated by Kilmeny Niland, Hodder & Stoughton (Sydney, New South Wales, Australia), 1986.

Zoo-Looking, illustrated by Rodney McCrae, Martin Educational (Cammeray, New South Wales, Australia), 1986, illustrated by Candace Whitman, Mondo (Greenvale, NY), 1996.

Koala Lou, illustrated by Pamela Lofts, J. Dent (London, England), 1986, Harcourt Brace Jovanovich (San Diego, CA), 1988, reprinted, Puffin (Camberwell, Victoria, Australia), 2005.

A Bedtime Story, illustrated by Elivia Savadier, Martin Educational (Cammeray, New South Wales, Australia), 1987, Mondo (Greenvale, NY), 1996.

The Straight Line Wonder, illustrated by Mark Rosenthal, Martin Educational (Cammeray, New South Wales, Australia), 1987, Mondo (Greenvale, NY), 1996.

Goodnight Sleep Tight, illustrated by Helen Semmler, Century Hutchinson (Melbourne, Victoria, Australia), 1988.

Shoes from Grandpa, illustrated by Patricia Mullins, Ashton Scholastic (Sydney, New South Wales, Australia), 1988, Orchard Books (New York, NY), 1990.

Night Noises, illustrated by Terry Denton, Omnibus (Norwood, South Australia, Australia), 1988, Harcourt Brace Jovanovich (San Diego, CA), 1989, reprinted, Penguin (Camberwell, Victoria, Australia), 2005.

Guess What?, illustrated by Vivienne Goodman, Omnibus (Norwood, South Australia, Australia), 1988, Harcourt Brace Jovanovich (San Diego, CA), 1990, reprinted, Omnibus, 2007.

Sophie, illustrated by Craig Smith, Drakeford Watts (Melbourne, Victoria, Australia), 1989, illustrated by Aminah Brenda Lynn Robinson, Harcourt Brace Jovanovich (San Diego, CA), 1994.

Feathers and Fools, illustrated by Lorraine Ellis, Ashwood House (Melbourne, Victoria, Australia), 1989, illustrated by Nicholas Wilton, Harcourt Brace Jovanovich (San Diego, CA), 1996.

Hattie and the Fox in: Goodness, Gracious Me!, Macmillan (New York, NY), 1992.

With Love at Christmas, illustrated by Fay Palmka, Lutheran Press (Adelaide, New South Wales, Australia), 1992.

Time for Bed, illustrated by Jane Dyer, Harcourt Brace Jovanovich (San Diego, CA), 1993.

Tough Boris, illustrated by Kathryn Brown, Harcourt Brace Jovanovich (San Diego, CA), 1994, reprinted, Puffin (Camberwell, Victoria, Australia), 2005.

Wombat Divine, illustrated by Kerry Argent, Harcourt Brace Jovanovich (San Diego, CA), 1996.

Boo to a Goose, illustrated by David Miller, Hodder Children's Books (Rydalmere, New South Wales, Australia), 1996, Dial Books (New York, NY), 1999.

Whoever You Are, illustrated by Leslie Staub, Harcourt Brace Jovanovich (San Diego, CA), 1997.

Because of the Bloomers, illustrated by Terry Denton, Harcourt Brace Jovanovich (San Diego, CA), 1998.

Sleepy Bears, illustrated by Kerry Argent, Harcourt Brace Jovanovich (San Diego, CA), 1999.

Harriet, You'll Drive Me Wild!, illustrated by Marla Frazee, Harcourt Brace Jovanovich (San Diego, CA), 2000.

The Magic Hat, illustrated by Tricia Tusa, Harcourt (San Diego, CA), 2002.

Where Is the Green Sheep?, illustrated by Judy Horacek, Harcourt (Orlando, FL), 2004.

Hunwick's Egg, illustrated by Pamela Lofts, Harcourt (Orlando, FL), 2004.

Fairy, Fairy Quite Contrary, illustrated by Greg Swearingen, Harcourt (Orlando, FL), 2005.

A Particular Cow, illustrated by Terry Denton, Harcourt (Orlando, FL), 2006.

Where the Giant Sleeps, illustrated by Vladimir Radunsky, Harcourt (Orlando, FL), 2007.

Ten Little Fingers and Ten Little Toes, illustrated by Helen Oxenbury, Harcourt (Orlando, FL), 2008.

Dragon Fire, illustrated by Roland Harvey, Penguin (Camberwell, Victoria, Australia), 2009.

Hello, Baby!, illustrated by Steve Jenkins, Beach Lane Books (New York, NY), 2009.

The Goblin and the Empty Chair, illustrated by Leo and Diane Dillon, Beach Lane Books (New York, NY), 2009.

Two Little Monkeys, illustrated by Jill Barton, Beach Lane Books (New York, NY), 2010.

(With Olivia Rawson) *What Makes You Laugh?,* illustrated by Kerry Argent, Penguin (Camberwell, Victoria, Australia), 2010.

OTHER

How to Teach Drama to Infants without Really Crying, Ashton Scholastic (Sydney, New South Wales, Australia), 1984, published as *Teaching Drama to Young Children,* Heinemann (London, England), 1986.

Mem's the Word, Penguin (Ringwood, Victoria, Australia), 1990, published as *Dear Mem Fox, I Have Read All Your Books Even the Pathetic Ones, and Other Incidents in the Life of a Children's Book Author,* Harcourt Brace Jovanovich (San Diego, CA), 1992.

Memories: An Autobiography, McDougal, Littell (Evanston, IL), 1992.

Radical Reflections: Passionate Opinions on Teaching, Learning, and Living, Harcourt Brace Jovanovich (San Diego, CA), 1993.

Reading Magic: How Your Child Can Learn to Read before School, and Other Read-Aloud Miracles, illustrated by Judy Horacek, Pan Macmillan (Sydney, New South Wales, Australia), 2001, published as *Reading Magic: Why Reading Aloud to Our Children Will Change Their Lives Forever,* Harcourt (New York, NY), 2001, revised edition, 2008.

Contributor to periodicals and education textbooks and teacher references.

Fox's books have been translated into other languages, including Hebrew, Portuguese, Swedish, Danish, and German.

Adaptations

Possum Magic was adapted as an animated short film, with teacher's guide, by Weston Woods/Scholastic, 2001. *Where Is the Green Sheep?* was adapted as the stage play *The Green Sheep,* produced by the Windmill Performing Arts, c. 2007.

Sidelights

Beloved as a writer in her native Australia, author and educator Mem Fox is the author of *Possum Magic,* one of the best-known children's books ever published by a native Australian. The story of a grandmother possum whose magic accidentally turns her grandchild invisible, *Possum Magic* has been followed by numerous other picture books—among them *Wombat Divine, Where Is the Green Sheep?, Koala Lou,* and *Time for Bed*—that reveal Fox's sly humor and enthusiasm for Aussie culture and history. Featuring a "beguiling bunch" of Australian animals, *Wombat Divine* has also found fans in the United States; its holiday theme—the book focuses on a young wombat who wants desperately to be cast in his school's nativity play—and its "playful approach to Christmas" make it unique, according to a *Publishers Weekly* reviewer.

Like *Wombat Divine,* many of Fox's other books have also found a large following with U.S. readers; *Time for Bed* spent twelve months on best-seller lists and has been ranked by some critics as a modern picture-book classic. Fox also writes for adults, although these writings take the form of nonfiction rather than fiction. Her book *Reading Magic: Why Reading Aloud to Our Children Will Change Their Lives Forever* is designed to help parents of very young children inspire an interest in reading, while *Radical Reflections: Passionate Opinions on Teaching, Learning, and Living* addresses the concerns of older parents and teachers.

Fox was born in Australia in 1946, but was living with her missionary parents in Rhodesia (now Zimbabwe) at age six months. As she once recalled to *SATA:* "I grew up among black people, and until I was five or so, I believed I was black. I was the only white child at the mission school, blind to my own whiteness and absolutely astonished when the local authorities told my parents I would be required to attend a school for white children." Although she was a bit of a tomboy, Fox also loved to read, particularly nineteenth-century novels. "My parents had many, many books, mostly classics. I tore through them all. But the world of books—*those* books at any rate—was a fantasy world completely removed from my way of life."

After completing her education in an all-white school, Fox moved to England to attend drama school and become an actress. "I arrived in London in the heyday of Carnaby Street, the Beatles, miniskirts, pantyhose, and works like psychedelic," she once recalled. "Never exposed to television, I had no clue about what to expect on a daily basis on the street." In London, Fox's acting skills allowed her to be a bit of a reactionary with regard to the entrenched class prejudices she discovered within British society. "The whole [class] system, and the attitudes that went with it, disgusted me," Fox recalled. "I played with it as though it were a diabolical toy. Because I can do accents well, I experimented: I'd go into a posh store and talk posh or Cockney depending on what reaction I was trying to elicit—dark fun that."

While studying acting in London, Fox met Malcolm Fox, the man she would later marry, and they traveled to Australia as an adventure but have continued to make that continent their home. Fox eventually became a teacher, and introduced her students to books written by Australians as well as to classics of English literature by Jane Austen and Thomas Hardy. She also started to write for children. *Possum Magic* was published in 1983 after being rewritten twenty-three times, and then rejected by nine publishers who dubbed it "too Australian." "The irony," Fox maintained, ". . . is that *Possum Magic* is the best-selling children's book in the history of Australia, has won a number of awards, and been published internationally."

"I write 'up' to children, never 'down,'" explained Fox. "I write to move children. All of my ideas for books come from my life. I frequently tell my students, 'I've no imagination at all.' *Possum Magic* came about because I was enraged that my daughter had no books to help her identify herself as an Australian, to help her feel proud of her country and heritage. *Wilfrid Gordon McDonald Partridge* came out of my very close relationship with my grandfather who, like Miss Nancy in the book, lived to be ninety-six." *Wilfrid Gordon McDonald Partridge,* the first book by Fox to be published in the United States, focuses on a small boy with a very long name (the name is that of Fox's own father). Helping an elderly friend named Miss Nancy cope with her failing memory, the boy listens to her stories and the stories of her friends in a local nursing home.

Sophie recalls Fox's early childhood and her African friends as it tells the story of an African-American girl who has a special bond with her grandfather. When the elderly man finally passes away, Sophie keeps him alive in her heart by sharing his stories with her own children, in a story that *Booklist* contributor Henrietta M. Smith described as "quietly moving." In contrast, *Harriet, You'll Drive Me Wild!* introduces a mother and daughter who, although often at odds, ultimately have a loving relationship. Harriet always seems to be making a mess by spilling her food, accidentally breaking things, and generally causing her mother grief. Sometimes her mother's frustration reaches the boiling point, and yelling follows, but like Harriet and her accidents, she did not intend to make her daughter feel bad. While some critics found *Harriet, You'll Drive Me Wild!* to be less-than-reassuring to young children who want to believe their parents are always in control, *Booklist* reviewer Hazel Rochman noted that Fox relates "a scenario that nearly every young preschooler . . . will recognize" and that the outbursts of pent-up anger result in an affectionate reconciliation and a situation in which both parent and child "can be open about their feelings." *Harriet, You'll Drive Me Wild!* was welcomed by a *Horn Book* reviewer who praised "its acceptance of both a child's penchant for trouble and a parent's occasional outburst—both happen, 'just like that,' and both will be forgiven."

Fox creates a book that *Horn Book* contributor Betty Carter praised as "perfectly attuned to a toddler's sense of playful discovery" in *Where Is the Green Sheep?* In an easy-to-read text, she introduces youngsters to a flock of rambunctious sheep pre-dyed-in-the-wool: red, blue, and yellow sheep flying kites, skateboarding, partying, jumping from diving boards, and even snorkeling. The elusive green sheep is nowhere to be found, however, until readers reach the final page and find it fast asleep. Noting the book's value in teaching basic vocabulary through rhythmic "repetitive phrases," Blair Christolon commented in a review for *School Library Journal* that *Where Is the Green Sheep?* is "a welcome addition to the year's flock of easy-readers," while a *Kirkus Reviews* critic described the book as "a perfectly simple text with a patterned language and rhythm just right for toddlers." In *Booklist* Ilene Cooper dubbed *Where Is the Green Sheep?* a "neat and satisfying wedding of text and art," noting that Judy Horacek's humorous line-and-watercolor artwork adds to the book's humor.

Fox deals with a more villainous subject in *Tough Boris,* as hideous pirate Boris von der Borch snatches center stage. Narrated by the pirate's cabin boy, the book extols Boris's piratical virtues: he is "tough," "scruffy," "greedy," and the like, but this grim exterior hides a soft spot that appears when his beloved parrot dies and Tough Boris sheds a tear. Praising the book as a "celebration of a glorious villain," *Booklist* contributor Rochman also noted that *Tough Boris* "is full of surprises, both in the simple text and in the dramatic underlying story" told in the illustrations by Kathryn Brown.

Children in a local park are given a show in *The Magic Hat,* as a magical chapeau blows through the area, landing momentarily on the head of all the adults and transforming them into the animal each most represents. A woman with a young child becomes a kangaroo carrying the child in its pouch, while a grouchy old man is transformed into a frog. Finally a wizard appears to set things right. The energetic artwork by Tricia Tusa enhances what Cooper described as Fox's "bouncy rhyme" to create a book perfect for story hour. The "unbridled enjoyment" of the children in *The Magic Hat* "will almost certainly evoke the same response from readers," added an enthusiastic *Publishers Weekly* contributor.

In *A Particular Cow* Fox treats readers to what a *Publishers Weekly* critic characterized as a "read-aloud gem" that "contains an absurdly appropriate plot." In Fox's story, readers meet a cow that lives a very regimented life. Every Saturday, the cow goes on the same walk with the same result: nothing out of the ordinary ever happens. One day, however, the bovine gets tangled in a clothesline where a pair of underwear is hanging in her path. From there everything falls into disarray, as the cow's fall into a mail cart sets the cart into motion. Fortunately, a strange sequence of events ultimately finds the cow safely back at home. Brought to life in

Terry Denton's cartoon art, Fox's story features the "slapstick humor and verbal dexterity" that is known to "delight youngsters," according to the *Publishers Weekly* critic, while in *School Library Journal* Marge Loch Wouters quipped that "udders and undies combine to make [*A Particular Cow*] . . . a sure hit."

Fox pairs her sing-song rhyming text for *Ten Little Fingers and Ten Little Toes* with Helen Oxenbury's engaging art. With every turn of the page, readers greet a new pair of babies, each infant possessing the requisite number of fingers and toes, although they represent a variety of ethnicities and cultures. As each new infant duo appears, the pages become increasingly crowded, until eight infants are collected. Finally one more infant is introduced to the group: it is the narrator's baby and in addition to fingers and toes it also has a kiss from Mommy that sets it apart from the playschool pack. In *Horn Book* Kitty Flynn described *Ten Little Fingers and Ten Little Toes* as a "love song to one very special baby" that combines Oxenbury's "irresistible round-headed tots" and "Fox's lilting verse." In *Booklist* Gillian Engberg dubbed the picture book "a standout for its beautiful simplicity," and Jessica Bruder wrote in the *New York Times Book Review* that the book's "words roll out easy and familiar, as if they'd been handed down to children for decades." Also praising Fox's "bouncing and well-constructed rhyme," London *Sunday Times* contributor Nicolette Jones added that *Ten Little Fingers and Ten Little Toes* "celebrates the diversity of babies from around the world."

"A novel is like an oak tree with all its branches," Fox once explained in discussing her long career as a writer. "A picture book, however, is more like a polished plank of wood. With it, you cannot exceed the bare minimum. Because you haven't many words to play with, rhythm is extremely important. In fact, I believe that rhythm is the most important element in the text of a picture book. There must be no evidence of strain; the story must fall into place apparently effortlessly." Her advice to aspiring writers: "Don't be easily discouraged. To write well is very difficult. Draft and redraft. And if publishers knock you back, just remember, it's all part of it."

Biographical and Critical Sources

PERIODICALS

Booklist, March 1, 1994, Hazel Rochman, review of *Tough Boris,* p. 1269; October 1, 1994, Janice Del Negro, review of *Sophie,* p. 332; June 1, 1996, Susan Dove Lempke, review of *Zoo-Looking,* p. 1731; October 15, 1996, Ilene Cooper, review of *Wombat Divine,* p. 434; October 1, 1997, Linda Perkins, review of *Whoever You Are,* p. 334; October 15, 1997, Susan Dove Lempke, review of *Straight Line Wonder,* p. 414; February 1, 1998, Hazel Rochman, review of *Boo to a Goose,* p. 922; October 1, 1998, Sue-Ellen Beauregard, review of *Wilfrid Gordon McDonald Partridge,* p. 349; November 15, 1999, Susan Dove Lempke, review of *Sleepy Bears,* p. 634; March 1, 2000, Hazel Rochman, review of *Harriet, You'll Drive Me Wild!,* p. 1250; February 15, 2001, Henrietta M. Smith, review of *Sophie,* p. 1160; August, 2001, Hazel Rochman, review of *Reading Magic: Why Reading Aloud to Our Children Will Change Their Lives Forever,* p. 2067; April 15, 2002, Ilene Cooper, review of *The Magic Hat,* p. 1408; March 1, 2004, Ilene Cooper, review of *Where Is the Green Sheep?,* p. 1193; November 15, 2008, Gillian Engberg, review of *Ten Little Fingers and Ten Little Toes,* p. 45; May 15, 2009, Gillian Engberg, review of *Hello Baby!,* p. 46.

Horn Book, May-June, 1994, Elizabeth S. Watson, review of *Tough Boris,* p. 313; March, 2000, review of *Harriet, You'll Drive Me Wild!,* p. 184; May-June, 2004, Betty Carter, review of *Where Is the Green Sheep?,* p. 312; January-February, 2009, Kitty Flynn, review of *Ten Little Fingers and Ten Little Toes,* p. 78.

Kirkus Reviews, March 1, 2002, review of *The Magic Hat,* p. 334; March 15, 2004, review of *Where Is the Green Sheep?,* p. 269; April 1, 2009, review of *Hello Baby!*

Library Journal, August 2001, Margaret Cardwell, review of *Reading Magic,* p. 148.

New York Times Book Review, November 9, 2009, Jessica Bruder, review of *Ten Little Fingers and Ten Little Toes,* p. 39.

Publishers Weekly, August 9, 1993, review of *Time for Bed,* p. 475; October 10, 1994, review of *Sophie,* p. 70; June 17, 1996, review of *Zoo-Looking,* p. 64; August 19, 1996, review of *A Bedtime Story,* p. 67; September 30, 1996, review of *Wombat Divine,* p. 90; August 18, 1997, review of *The Straight Line Wonder,* p. 93; November 3, 1997, review of *Whoever You Are,* p. 84; March 2, 1998, review of *Boo to a Goose,* p. 67; July 19, 1999, review of *Sleepy Bears,* p. 193; September 27, 1999, review of *Wombat Divine,* p. 64; March 20, 2000, review of *Harriet, You'll Drive Me Wild!,* p. 91; May 29, 2000, review of *Feathers and Fools,* p. 84; February 11, 2002, review of *The Magic Hat,* p. 184; June 9, 2003, review of *Harriet, You'll Drive Me Wild!,* p. 54; March 8, 2004, review of *Where Is the Green Sheep?,* p. 72; January 24, 2005, review of *Hunwick's Egg,* p. 242; July 17, 2006, review of *A Particular Cow,* p. 155; October 29, 2007, review of *Where the Giant Sleeps,* p. 54.

School Library Journal, April, 2000, Kate McClelland, review of *Harriet, You'll Drive Me Wild!,* p. 104; September, 2001, Shauna Yusko, review of *Reading Magic,* p. 262; December, 2001, Erin Caskey, review of *Possum Magic,* p. 67; April, 2002, Wendy Lukehart, review of *The Magic Hat,* p. 110; February, 2003, Lee Bock, review of *Wilfrid Gordon McDonald Partridge,* p. 96; February, 2003, Lee Bock, review of *Whoever You Are,* p. 96; March, 2004, Andrew Medlar, review of *Koala Lou,* p. 67; April, 2004, Blair

Christolon, review of *Where Is the Green Sheep?,* p. 110; March, 2005, Linda L. Walkins, review of *Huwick's Egg,* p. 171; September, 2006, Marge Loch-Wouters, review of *A Particular Cow,* p. 171; November, 2007, Kathy Krasniewicz, review of *Where the Giant Sleeps,* p. 90; December, 2008, Amy Lilien-Harper, review of *Ten Little Fingers and Ten Little Toes,* p. 90.
Sunday Times (London, England), October 18, 2008, Nicolette Jones, review of *Ten Little Fingers and Ten Little Toes,* p. 49.
Teacher Librarian, June, 2000, Shirley Lewis, review of *Harriet, You'll Drive Me Wild!,* p. 49.

ONLINE

Mem Fox Web site, http://www.memfox.net (January 10, 2010).
Pan Macmillan Australia Web site, http://www.panmac millan.com.au/ (October 21, 2004), "Mem Fox."*

* * *

FOX, Merrion Frances
See FOX, Mem

G

GIBSON, Sarah P. 1962-

Personal

Born 1962, in ME; married; children: Seth, Irene. *Education:* Syracuse University, degree (journalism); Louisiana State University, M.A. (library and information science). *Hobbies and other interests:* Travel.

Addresses

Home—ME. *E-mail*—info@sarahpgibson.com.

Career

Librarian and author of books for children. Worked as a librarian in an international school in Brazil; worked throughout the Middle East. Presenter at schools.

Writings

Lisa's Snow Day, illustrated by Gretchen Duane, Gannett Books (Portland, ME), 1988.
The Truth about Horses, Friends, and My Life as a Coward, illustrated by Glin Dibley, Marshall Cavendish Children (Tarrytown, NY), 2008.

Contributor to periodicals, including *Cricket.*

Biographical and Critical Sources

PERIODICALS

Kirkus Reviews, September 15, 2008, review of *The Truth about Horses, Friends, and My Life as a Coward.*
School Library Journal, November, 2008, Jane Cronkhite, review of *The Truth about Horses, Friends, and My Life as a Coward,* p. 120.

ONLINE

Sarah P. Gibson Home Page, http://www.sarahpgibson. com (January 10, 2010).

* * *

GOODMAN KOZ, Paula
(Paula G. Koz)

Personal

Born in Perú; married; husband's name Gabe; children: Nadia, Daniel. *Education:* Bryn Mawr, B.A.; attended National Academy of Design and New School of Social Research (now New School University).

Addresses

Home—Williamsburg, VA. *E-mail*—vitabreve@cox.net.

Career

Illustrator. Worked as a copywriter at a medical advertising agency for five years; freelance illustrator, beginning c. 2004.

Awards, Honors

Sydney Taylor Honor Book designation, Association of Jewish Libraries, 2006, for *Shlemiel Crooks.*

Illustrator

Anna Olswanger, *Shlemiel Crooks,* Junebug Books (Montgomery, AL), 2005.
(As Paula G. Koz) Peter Huggins, *In the Company of Owls,* Junebug Books (Montgomery, AL), 2008.

Contributor of illustrations to periodicals, including the *New York Times.*

Sidelights

After a five-year stint in the advertising industry, Paula Goodman Koz refocused her career goals and became a freelance illustrator. Beginning by creating artwork for

periodicals, including the *New York Times,* she took a time-out to raise her young children. When she reentered the art world in the mid-2000s, Goodman Koz added children's illustration to her list of accomplishments.

In her debut work, Goodman Koz provided the pictures for Anna Olswanger's *Shlemiel Crooks,* a story about two bumbling thieves intent on swiping kosher wine meant for the Jewish Passover holiday. Set in St. Louis, Missouri, during the spring of 1919, *Shlemiel Crooks* features Reb Elias Olschwanger, a purveyor of wines, who becomes involved in a heated discussion at the synagogue about the first Passover. In Reb Elias's retelling, the Israelites fled Egypt with riches taken from Pharaoh's treasure and then witnessed the parted Red Sea engulf the pursuing Egyptian leader and his men. As Reb Elias is debating his ideas in the synagogue, the two dimwitted crooks are attempting to steal wine from his shop, influenced by the ghost of the biblican pharaoh himself. However, the would-be robbers make too much noise, alerting neighbors to the scene and thwarting the efforts of the criminals.

Critics responded positively to the artwork of Goodman Koz that is featured in the pages of *Shlemiel Crooks.* Writing in *School Library Journal,* Teri Markson noted that "the boldly colored, expressive illustrations enhance the humor" of the story, while in *Booklist* Hazel Rochman suggested that the artist's "woodcuts give life to the city neighborhood, the foolish villains, and the lively arguments." A *Publishers Weekly* critic gave special attention to Goodman Koz's efforts as well, claiming that "her attention to old-world detail and a few funny scenes of the crooks . . . give [*Shlemiel Crooks*] . . . plenty of visual charm."

Biographical and Critical Sources

PERIODICALS

Booklist, May 15, 2005, Hazel Rochman, review of *Shlemiel Crooks,* p. 1660.
New York Times Book Review, April 10, 2005, review of *Shlemiel Crooks,* p. 21.
Publishers Weekly, March 28, 2005, review of *Shlemiel Crooks,* p. 82.
School Library Journal, June, 2005, Teri Markson, review of *Shlemiel Crooks,* p. 123.

ONLINE

Paula Goodman Koz Home Page, http://paulagoodman koz.com (December 30, 2009).

* * *

GRANT, Judyann Ackerman

Personal

Married; has children.

Addresses

Home—Mannsfield, NY.

Career

Author. Raises chickens.

Writings

Chicken Said, "Cluck!", illustrated by Sue Truesdell, HarperCollins (New York, NY), 2008.

Biographical and Critical Sources

PERIODICALS

Horn Book, November, 2008, Martha V. Parravano, review of *Chicken Said, "Cluck!",* p. 92.
School Library Journal, November, 2008, Teresa Pfeifer, review of *Chicken Said, "Cluck!",* p. 88.

ONLINE

HarperCollins Web site, http://www.harpercollins.com/ (January 10, 2010), "Judith Ackerman Grant."*

* * *

GREEN, Jessica

Personal

Born in Australia; married; children: three.

Addresses

Home—Newcastle, New South Wales, Australia.

Career

Author and educator. Has taught primary school in Australia for over thirty years.

Writings

NOVELS

Diary of a Would-Be Princess: The Journal of Jillian James, 5B, Scholastic Australia (Gosford, New South Wales, Australia), 2005, Charlesbridge (Watertown, MA), 2007.
A Tyranny of Toads (sequel to *Diary of a Would-Be Princess*), Scholastic Australia (Gosford, New South Wales, Australia), 2006.

PICTURE BOOKS

Scratch Kitten and the Battle for the Pirate's Shoulder, illustrated by Mitch Vane, Little Hare Books (Surry Hill, New South Wales, Australia), 2008.

Scratch Kitten in the Quest for the Top Spot, illustrated by Mitch Vane, Little Hare Books (Surry Hill, New South Wales, Australia), 2008.

Sidelights

Australian writer and educator Jessica Green is the author of the middle-grade novel *Diary of a Would-Be Princess: The Journal of Jillian James, 5B* and its sequel, *A Tyranny of Toads.* In *Diary of a Would-Be Princess,* Green introduces readers to fifth-grader Jillian James, who attends Flora Heights Primary School in rural Australia. A social outcast, Jillian longs to be part of the popular girls' "princess" clique. Her only real connection, however, is with Nigel, a nerdy classmate who helps Jillian with her math homework. During the school year, Jillian grows closer to Nigel and his group of misfit friends, and she records her thoughts in a daily journal. "Green injects plenty of humor and turns Jillian's diary into a meaningful creative training ground for winning a prestigious speaking competition," noted a *Kirkus Reviews* contributor. "Although Jillian is a character who takes getting used to, she's definitely worth knowing," remarked Tina Zubak in *School Library Journal,* and *Booklist* critic Kay Weisman stated that Green's "delightful look at universal middle-grade concerns will work equally well for reading aloud or reading alone."

Jillian begins her final year of primary school in horrible fashion *A Tyranny of Toads.* Not only is she forced to sit next to her worst enemy, but her new teacher has taken an instant dislike to her. Sally Murphy, writing in *Aussiereviews.com,* called *A Tyranny of Toads* "an enjoyable read for upper primary aged readers."

Biographical and Critical Sources

PERIODICALS

Booklist, March 1, 2007, Kay Weisman, review of *Diary of a Would-Be Princess: The Journal of Jillian James, 5B,* p. 83.

Kirkus Reviews, January 15, 2007, review of *Diary of a Would-Be Princess,* p. 73.

School Library Journal, March, 2007, Tina Zubak, review of *Diary of a Would-Be Princess,* p. 209.

ONLINE

Aussiereviews.com, http://www.aussiereviews.com/ (March 1, 2008), Sally Murphy, reviews of *Diary of a Would-Be Princess* and *A Tyranny of Toads.*

Scholastic Australia Web site, http://www.scholastic.com.au/ (March 16, 2009), "Jessica Green."*

*   *   *

GREENBERG, Jan 1942-

Personal

Born December 29, 1942, in St. Louis, MO; daughter of Alexander (a manufacturer) and Lilian (an advertising executive) Schonwald; married Ronald Greenberg (an art dealer), August 31, 1963; children: Lynne, Jeanne, Jacqueline. *Education:* Washington University, B.A. (English), 1964; Webster University, M.A.T. (communications), 1971. *Hobbies and other interests:* Hiking, traveling, reading, playing bridge.

Addresses

Home and office—3 Brentmoor Park, St. Louis, MO 63105. *E-mail*—jngreenb@aol.com.

Career

Teacher and author. St. Louis Public Schools, St. Louis, MO, teacher, 1969-72; Forest Park Community College, St. Louis, instructor in English composition, 1973-75; Webster University, St. Louis, director and instructor in aesthetic education, 1974-79; *St. Louis Post-Dispatch,* St. Louis, book reviewer, 1975-80; CEMREL (National Education Laboratory), St. Louis, researcher, 1976-78; freelance writer, beginning 1978. Presenter of workshops and lectures on aesthetic education, writing, biography, nonfiction, and fiction for young readers, 1979—. Member of council, Aspen Music Festival and Aspen Art Museum.

Member

PEN, Society of Children's Book Writers and Illustrators.

Awards, Honors

American Library Association (ALA) Best Books for Young Adults citation, 1984, for *No Dragons to Slay,* 2001, for *Vincent Van Gogh;* Webster University Distinguished Alumni Award, 1986; *Boston Globe/Horn Book* Award, 1998, and Norman Sugarman Award, both for *Chuck Close, up Close;* Michael J. Printz Honor Book designation, 2001, for *Heart to Heart;* Robert J. Sibert Award Honor Book designation, 2001, for *Vincent van Gogh,* 2002, for *Action Jackson;* ALA Notable Book designation, 2008, for *Christo and Jeanne-Claude;* International Reading Association Notable Book for a Global Society designation, and National Council of Teachers of English Notable Children's Book in Language Arts, both 2008, and CCBC Choice designation, 2009, all for *Side by Side.*

Writings

A Season in-Between, Farrar, Straus (New York, NY), 1979.

Jan Greenberg (Reproduced by permission.)

The Iceberg and Its Shadow, Farrar, Straus (New York, NY), 1980.

The Pig-out Blues, Farrar, Straus (New York, NY), 1982.

No Dragons to Slay, Farrar, Straus (New York, NY), 1983.

Bye, Bye, Miss American Pie, Farrar, Straus (New York, NY), 1985.

Exercises of the Heart, Farrar, Straus (New York, NY), 1986.

Just the Two of Us, Farrar, Straus (New York, NY), 1988.

(With Sandra Jordan) *The Painter's Eye: Learning to Look at Contemporary American Art,* Delacorte (New York, NY), 1991.

(With Sandra Jordan) *The Sculptor's Eye: Looking at Contemporary American Art,* DK Ink (New York, NY), 1993.

(With Sandra Jordan) *The American Eye: Eleven Artists of the Twentieth Century,* Delacorte (New York, NY), 1995.

(With Sandra Jordan) *Chuck Close up Close* (biography), DK Ink (New York, NY), 1998.

(With Sandra Jordan) *Frank O. Gehry: Outside In,* DK Ink (New York, NY), 2000.

(With Sandra Jordan) *Vincent Van Gogh: Portrait of an Artist,* Delacorte (New York, NY), 2001.

(Editor) *Heart to Heart: New Poems Inspired by Twentieth-Century American Art,* Harry N. Abrams (New York, NY), 2001.

(With Sandra Jordan) *Action Jackson,* illustrated by Robert Andrew Parker, Roaring Brook Press (Brookfield, CT), 2002.

Romare Bearden: Collage of Memories, Harry N. Abrams (New York, NY), 2003.

(With Sandra Jordan) *Runaway Girl: The Artist Louise Bourgeois,* Harry N. Abrams (New York, NY), 2003.

(With Sandra Jordan) *Andy Warhol: Prince of Pop,* Delacorte Press (New York, NY), 2004.

(Editor) *Side by Side: New Poems Inspired by Art from around the World,* Abrams Books for Young Readers (New York, NY), 2008.

(With Sandra Jordan) *Christo and Jeanne-Claude: Through the Gates and Beyond,* Roaring Book Press (New York, NY), 2008.

(With Sandra Jordan) *Ballet for Martha: Making Appalachian Spring,* Roaring Book Press (New York, NY), 2010.

Sidelights

Jan Greenberg is the author of teen fiction that focuses on young people who experience the ordinary, day-to-day problems of growing up in a complex society. In recent years she has expanded her writing for young people to reflect her passion for contemporary American art, as in the picture book *Action Jackson,* about the author Jackson Pollock, and *Romare Bearden: Collage of Memories,* about the African-American collage artist. Greenberg has also paired up with coauthor Sandra Jordan to create well-received overviews of modern art as well as biographies of individual artists. As an editor, she has also produced the award-winning verse anthologies *Heart to Heart: New Poems Inspired by Twentieth-Century American Art* and *Side by Side: New Poems Inspired by Art from around the World.*

Born in St. Louis, Missouri, in 1942, Greenberg quickly developed a love of books and reading. "My parents' library was filled with an assortment of books ranging from Plato's *Dialogues* to *Gone with the Wind,*" she once recalled to *SATA.* "It was there in that cozy room with a fireplace that I developed my eclectic tastes in literature." When Greenberg was ten years old, she began keeping a journal, a practice she has continued to maintain throughout her adult life.

Graduating with a degree in English in 1964, Greenberg worked for several years as a teacher, and went on to receive a master's degree in 1971. In the 1970s, she and her husband, Ronald Greenberg, began collecting contemporary American art, and soon their house was filled to overflowing, the walls covered "with bright canvases, the yard with large steel sculpture." The couple eventually opened an art gallery in their Midwest community that quickly became a center for young artists and musicians. "The energy and excitement engendered by my contact with other artists inspired me to write and develop my own creative skills," explained Greenberg.

As the author of teen fiction and nonfiction, Greenberg finds writing to be a process of discovery, as her young protagonists develop life skills by facing life's prob-

lems. "My books deal with domestic issues: illness or death in a family, sibling rivalry, or problems with friends or parents," Greenberg noted of such books as *The Pig-out Blues* and *Just the Two of Us.* Her first novel, *A Season in-Between,* is the story of a thirteen-year-old girl who must face the illness and death of her father while engaged in a host of adolescent worries, fears, and concerns. Published in 1979, it was followed a year later by *An Iceberg and Its Shadow.* In 1982 she released one of her most popular novels, *The Pig-out Blues,* in which Jodie struggles with weight fluctuations as well as a tense relationship with her ultra-thin mother. As a coveted part to play Juliet opposite a dishy Romeo in her school's annual play becomes available to Jodie, a crash diet is the order of the day, resulting in unforeseen consequences.

Just the Two of Us also finds a young teen coping none too well with the minefield of everyday life. It is not bad enough that Holly Hornby must struggle to finish the seventh grade; now her mother has totally disrupted her future by deciding to leave Manhattan and move to a small town in Iowa. Holly convinces her mom to let her remain in the city for the summer, and takes up residence at the Applebaum house, home to her best buddy, Max. By summer's end, Holly learns that life with the Applebaums is not as wonderful as she expected and she looks forward to joining her mother in Iowa. Reviewing *Just the Two of Us* for *Booklist,* Bar-

bara Elleman praised Greenberg for her "firm but easy touch with characters," adding that the book's "lively plot is believable and well paced."

When writing fiction, Greenberg thinks of herself as "a storyteller. I write books with a beginning, a middle, and an end. Most of my stories take place in the Midwest. But . . . my books could take place in suburbia almost anywhere in America." According to Greenberg, when she meets with groups of young people, they often asked her "what kind of a miserable childhood did I have to invent such weird and cranky characters. The truth is that my childhood wasn't unusually miserable at all. Yes, I had eye allergies and boy troubles. I was too tall, I thought my parents too strict, my teachers unfair. But then," she added, "these complaints and a host of new ones cropped up in regular cycles with my own daughters as well." In fact, Greenberg credits her experiences parenting teens through a series of adolescent traumas as the impetus for her fiction-writing career. "The fact is," she once explained to *SATA,* "that trauma is the business of adolescence, and along with these traumas, large or small, come negative feelings. . . . After my first novel, some people told me how courageous I was to admit weakness and negative feelings in print. But writing is an act of sharing. A book is never a total figment of the imagination. It begins as a stomach ache, a slight quiver of discomfort. It's like falling in or out of love. If the feeling is strong enough, a book may evolve. Or maybe not. But when something happens and a year later I'm holding a new novel in my hand, I

Greenberg and Sandra Jordan bring to life the story of controversial artist Jackson Pollack in **Action Jackson,** *featuring artwork by Robert Andrew Parker.* (Illustration copyright © 2002 by Robert Andrew Parker. All rights reserved. Reprinted by arrangement with of Henry Holt & Company, LLC.)

want to jump up and down, throw confetti, and stop everyone on the street and say, 'Look what I've done.'"

Beginning in the 1990s Greenberg paired up with Jordan to publish books focusing on the field of art. The first, *The Painter's Eye: Learning to Look at Contemporary American Art*, describes basic elements of artistic composition amid a wealth of visual examples and interviews with artists, resulting in a work that a *Publishers Weekly* contributor dubbed "an ingeniously choreographed duet of text and image" that aids young people in understanding the role of contemporary art and the significance of their response to it. A companion volume, *The Sculptor's Eye*, was released two years later, its wealth of material "woven together with a clear and perceptive text," according to *Horn Book* contributor Lolly Robinson. In *American Eye: Eleven Artists of the Twentieth Century*, Greenberg and Jordan present biographies of such major artists as Thomas Hart Benton, Stuart Davis, Jackson Pollock, and Georgia O'Keeffe and explain the significance of several modern masterworks. Calling their examination one of "clarity and insight," *Horn Book* reviewer Lolly Robinson added that the focus of *American Eye* "is placed on understanding the artist as a person in order to begin to understand each artist's frame of reference for his or her work."

Individual artists Vincent Van Gogh, Chuck Close, Christo, Louise Bourgeois, and Frank O. Gehry also benefit as the subject of highly praised biographies by Greenberg and Jordan. In *Chuck Close up Close*, the life and work of the artist known in the 1960s for his oversized, highly detailed, and often outrageous neck-up portraits is examined. Published to coincide with a retrospective of Close's work in New York City, *Chuck Close up Close* "is a simply written yet fascinating account of how nearly insurmountable obstacles can often spur artistic growth," according to *New York Times Book Review* contributor Elizabeth Spires, the critic also noting the disabilities endured by the artist throughout his life. A contributor to *Publishers Weekly* deemed the book equally praiseworthy, calling it "an ideal example of an artist biography." Noting that van Gogh stands among the world's "most enigmatic" painters, Lolly Robinson added in her *Horn Book* review of Greenberg and Jordan's *Vincent van Gogh: Portrait of an Artist* that the book chronicles "a fascinating" life story that may also resonate with teens "struggling to figure out who they are, who they will become, and why they are (secretly) so weird."

Frank O. Gehry: Outside In drew the same positive response from critics, as Greenberg and Jordan explain Gehry's approach to space and materials as it developed against the backdrop of his life and culminated in such whimsical, original works as the Guggenheim Museum in Bilbao, Spain. "This book is a journey through the creative process," noted Paul Goldberger in a laudatory appraisal for the *New York Times Book Review*. While noting that *Frank O. Gehry* would not be suitable for readers under age ten, Goldberger went on to comment

that the Goldberg-Jordan collaboration "may be one of the few books for young readers to address honestly not just the payoffs of artistic success but also the risks."

Greenberg and Jordan focus on other pivotal artists of the twentieth century in *Andy Warhol: Prince of Pop* and the picture book *Action Jackson*, the latter illustrated by Robert Andrew Parker. Jackson, a highly influential artist known for for creating dripped paintings of massive scale, suffered from depression while also becoming one of the most widely known artists of his generation. In *Action Jackson* the coauthors "have again pushed the nonfiction envelope with [their] . . . astonishing biography" of the "action painter and abstract expressionist," according to a *Kirkus Reviews* contributor, while a *Publishers Weekly* critic dubbed the work "outstanding." Reviewing *Andy Warhol*, *School Library Journal* contributor Daryl Grabarek described the work as a "competent, well-documented biography" that features "a good balance of personal and art history," while in *Kirkus Reviews* a reviewer noted the coauthors' success at accomplishing "a difficult task."

Warhol, the artist known for his acrylic paintings of the Campbell soup can and celebrities such as Marilyn Monroe, inspired the 1960s Pop-art focus on consumer culture through his paintings, films, and lifestyle. *Andy Warhol* stands as "riveting biography," the critic added, citing Greenberg and Jordan for producing "an almost awed (and frequently very funny)" profile of Warhol's eccentric life.

The first female sculptor to be the focus of a major exhibition at New York City's Museum of Modern Art is the focus of *Runaway Girl: The Artist Louise Bourgeois*. In their profile, Greenberg and Jordan follow Bourgeois's life from her troubled childhood through her development as an abstract artist and her impact upon others that culminated in her 1982 museum retrospective. Noting that the book includes interviews with the artist herself, Delia Fritz called *Runaway Girl* a "superb" study and predicted in her *School Library Journal* review that the book will serve readers as a "perfect starting point for research on . . . 20th century sculpture." In *Booklist* Gillian Engberg asserted that in "clear, elegant prose," the coauthors "make challenging art accessible and exciting to teen readers," and Lolly Robinson wrote in her *Horn Book* that in *Runaway Girl* "Bourgeois's emotional honesty and the authors' infectious admiration for their subject create an uplifting book."

Described by *Booklist* contributor Ilene Cooper as a "thoughtful, eye-opening, and meticulous" profile of two artists known for their ephemeral outdoor textile sculptures, *Christo and Jeanne-Claude: Through the Gates and Beyond* focuses on Christo and his partner. In the book, Greenberg and Jordan follow the careers of these flamboyant artists, who are known for their work wrapping buildings, trees, islands, and other outdoor structures in public spaces with textiles to transform

landscapes. The Gates in Central Park, which used twenty-three miles of vivid orange fabric, drew over a million visitors to the park. These impermanent works have been experienced by most people through photographs because the opportunity to witness them first hand lasts only days. A *Kirkus Reviews* writer praised *Christo and Jeanne-Claude* as "an immoderately engaging profile" of two of the "most visible and widely known public artists" of our day, citing the book's compelling mix of artist interviews and large-scale color photographs. Greenberg and Jordan present readers with a crucial challenge, the critic added: to "think long thoughts about the nature of art and their . . . response to it."

Reviewing Greenberg's poetry collection *Heart to Heart,* Kathleen Whalin noted in *School Library Journal* that, "if a picture book is defined as a marriage of word and art, then *Heart to Heart* [ranks as] . . . a picture book of the highest quality." Gillian Engberg, writing in *Booklist,* predicted of the companion verse anthology, *Side by Side,* that young readers should identify "with the poems' universal themes, including identity, childhood memories, nature's mysterious power, and the powerful emotions and experiences that link us all."

Commenting on the Greenberg-Jordan contributions to children's literature and art, *Bulletin of the Center for Children's Books* contributor Deborah Stevenson claimed that "no literary gallery can be complete without titles" from the pair. "The provocation of thought,

encouragement of curiosity, and exploration of what all kinds of art can mean and do are the real contributions of this team's *oeuvre.* These books are truly state of the art."

Biographical and Critical Sources

PERIODICALS

Booklist, January 15, 1989, Barbara Elleman, review of *Just the Two of Us,* pp. 870-871; March 15, 1994, Stephanie Zvirin, review of *The Sculptor's Eye: Looking at Contemporary American Art,* p. 1377; March 15, 1996, review of *The American Eye: Eleven Artists of the Twentieth Century,* p. 1274; April 1, 1999, Stephanie Zvirin, review of *Chuck Close up Close,* p. 1382; December 15, 2000, Gillian Engberg, review of *Frank O. Gehry: Outside In,* p. 810; March 15, 2001, Gillian Engberg, review of *Heart to Heart: New Poems Inspired by Twentieth-Century American Art,* p. 1394, and interview with Greenberg, p. 1395; August, 2001, Gilian Engberg, review of *Vincent Van Gogh: Portrait of an Artist,* p. 2117; April 15, 2003, Gillian Engberg, review of *Runaway Girl: The Artist Louise Bourgeois,* p. 1469; September 15, 2003, Hazel Rochman, review of *Romare Bearden: Collage of Memories,* p. 238; June 1, 2004, Gillian Engberg, review of *Andy Warhol: Prince of Pop,* p. 1753; May 1, 2008, Gillian Engberg, review of *Side by Side: New Poems Inspired by Art from Around the World,* p. 89; November 1, 2008, Ilene Cooper, review of *Christo and Jeanne-Claude: Through the Gates and Beyond,* p. 52.

Horn Book, March, 1994, Lolly Robinson, review of *The Sculptor's Eye,* p. 223; January-February, 1996, Lolly Robinson, review of *The American Eye,* p. 91; September, 2000, Lolly Robinson, review of *Frank O. Gehry,* p. 594; November-December, 2001, Lolly Robinson, review of *Vincent Van Gogh,* p. 770; November-December, 2002, Lolly Robinson, review of *Action Jackson,* p. 775; July-August, 2003, Lolly Robinson, review of *Runaway Girl,* p. 478; November-December, 2003, Barbara Bader, review of *Romare Bearden,* p. 764.

Kirkus Reviews, August 15, 2002, review of *Action Jackson,* p. 1223; August 15, 2003, review of *Romare Bearden,* p. 1073; October 1, 2004, review of *Andy Warhol,* p. 960; October 1, 2008, review of *Christo and Jean-Claude.*

Kliatt, July, 2003, Jennifer Banas, review of *Vincent Van Gogh,* p. 51.

New York Times Book Review, May 17, 1998, Elizabeth Spires, review of *Chuck Close up Close,* p. 32; November 19, 2000, Paul Goldberger, "The Master Builder," p. 30; November 17, 2002, Peter Plagens, review of *Action Jackson,* p. 44; June 1, 2003, review of *Runaway Girl,* p. 24.

Publishers Weekly, April 25, 1994, review of *The Painter's Eye,* p. 81; July 3, 2000, review of *Chuck Close up Close,* p. 73; March 12, 2001, review of *Heart to Heart,* p. 87; July 22, 2002, review of *Action Jackson,* p. 178.

Cover of Greenberg's edited poetry collection **Heart to Heart,** *featuring a painting by Stuart Davis.* (Harry Abrams, Inc, 2001. Reproduced by permission of VAGA, New York.)

School Library Journal, April, 2001, Kathleen Whalin, review of *Heart to Heart,* p. 160; May, 2003, Delia Fritz, review of *Runaway Girl,* p. 169; August 25, 2003, review of *Romare Bearden,* p. 64; September, 2003, Heather E. Miller, review of *Romare Bearden,* p. 232; April, 2004, Wendy Lukehart, review of *Action Jackson,* p. 62; November, 2004, Daryl Grabarek, review of *Andy Warhol,* p. 164; July, 2008, Shawn Brommer, review of *Side by Side,* p. 112.

Voice of Youth Advocates, February, 1989, Beth E. Andersen, review of *Just the Two of Us,* p. 284; October, 1990, Susan Levine, review of *The Pig-out Blues,* p. 257.

Women's Review of Books, November, 2003, Patricia G. Berman, review of *Runaway Girl,* p. 1.

ONLINE

Bulletin of the Center for Children's Books Web site, http:// alexia.lis.uiui.edu/puboff/bccb/ (September 1, 2000), Deborah Stevenson, "True Blue: Jan Greenberg and Sandra Jordan."

Missouri Writes for Kids Web site, http://mowrites4kids. drury.edu/ (January 10, 2010), "Jan Greenberg."

*　　*　　*

GUIBERSON, Brenda Z. 1946-

Personal

Surname is pronounced "*guy*-berson"; born December 10, 1946, in Denver, CO; daughter of Carl Nicholas (a civil engineer) and Ruth Ellen (a homemaker) Zangar; married William R. Guiberson (a business agent), August, 1973; children: Jason. *Education:* University of Washington, B.A. (art and English). *Hobbies and other interests:* Hiking, kayaking, bird watching, spending time with friends and family.

Addresses

Home—Seattle, WA. *E-mail*—brenda@brendazguiber son.com.

Career

Writer. Worked as a copywriter, letter carrier, stained-glass worker and woodworker, manager, and counselor. Teacher at University of Washington.

Awards, Honors

Parent's Choice Picture Book Award, Teacher's Choice designation, International Reading Association/Children's Book Council (IRA/CBC), Notable Trade Book in Language Arts designation, National Council of Teachers of English, and El Paso Prickly Pear Award, all for *Cactus Hotel;* Best Book of the Year citation, *School Library Journal,* Pick of the List selection, American Booksellers Association (ABA), California Children's Media Award, and Outstanding Science

Brenda Z. Guiberson (Photograph by Mary W. Gallagher. Reproduced by permission.)

Trade Book designation, National Science Teachers Association (NSTA)/CBC, all for *Spoonbill Swamp;* Outstanding Science Trade Book designation, NSTA/CBC, for *Lobster Boat;* Outstanding Science Trade Book designation, NSTA/CBC, and Orbis Pictus nomination, both for *Spotted Owl;* Rhode Island Children's Book Award nomination, for *Lighthouses;* Best Book of the Year citation, *School Library Journal,* Pick of the List, ABA, Society of School Librarians International Science Honor for K-6, and Chicago Public Library Best of the Best selection, all for *Into the Sea;* Best Book designation, Bank Street College, and Capitol Choice selection, Cooperative Children's Book Center, both 2002, both for *The Emperor Lays an Egg;* Orbis Pictus Recommended designation, Kansas State Reading Circle award, and John Burroughs Medal for Outstanding Natural History Writing, all for *Ice Bears;* NSTA/CBC Recommended designation, *Booklist* Top-Ten Sci Tech designation, and American Booksellers Association Book Sense nomination, all 2004, and Outstanding Children's Book Award finalist, Animal Behavior Society, 2005, all for *Rain, Rain, Rainforest;* Oppenheim Platinum Award, Outstanding Science Trade Book designation, NSTA/CBC, and *Booklist* Top-Ten Sci Tech designation, all 2009, all for *Life in the Boreal Forest.*

Writings

Turtle People, Atheneum (New York, NY), 1990.

Cactus Hotel, illustrated by Megan Lloyd, Henry Holt (New York, NY), 1991.

Instant Soup, Atheneum (New York, NY), 1991.

Spoonbill Swamp, illustrated by Megan Lloyd, Henry Holt (New York, NY), 1992.

Lobster Boat, illustrated by Megan Lloyd, Henry Holt (New York, NY), 1993.

(Self-illustrated) *Salmon Story,* Henry Holt (New York, NY), 1993.

(Self-illustrated) *Spotted Owl: Bird of the Ancient Forest,* Henry Holt (New York, NY), 1994.

Winter Wheat, illustrated by Megan Lloyd, Henry Holt (New York, NY), 1995.

(Self-illustrated) *Lighthouses: Watchers at Sea,* Henry Holt (New York, NY), 1995.

Into the Sea, illustrated by Alix Berenzy, Henry Holt (New York, NY), 1996.

Teddy Roosevelt's Elk, illustrated by Patrick O'Brien, Henry Holt (New York, NY), 1997.

(Self-illustrated) *Mummy Mysteries: Tales from North America,* Henry Holt (New York, NY), 1998.

Exotic Species: Invaders in Paradise, Twenty-first Century Books (Brookfield, CT), 1999.

(Self-illustrated) *Tales of the Haunted Deep,* Henry Holt (New York, NY), 2000.

The Emperor Lays an Egg, illustrated by Joan Paley, Henry Holt (New York, NY), 2001.

Ocean Life, Scholastic, Inc. (New York, NY), 2001.

Sharks, Scholastic Reference (New York, NY), 2002.

Rain, Rain, Rain Forest, illustrated by Steve Jenkins, Henry Holt (New York, NY), 2004.

(Self-illustrated) *Mud City: A Flamingo Story,* Henry Holt (New York, NY), 2005.

Ice Bears, illustrated by Ilya Spirin, Henry Holt (New York, NY), 2008.

Life in the Boreal Forest, illustrated by Gennady Spirin, Henry Holt (New York, NY), 2009.

(Self-illustrated) *Disasters: Natural and Man-made Catastrophes through the Centuries,* Henry Holt (New York, NY), 2010.

Earth: Feeling the Heat, illustrated by Chad Wallace, Henry Holt (New York, NY), 2010.

Moon Bear, illustrated by Ed Young, Henry Holt (New York, NY), 2010.

Sidelights

Brenda Z. Guiberson writes informative picture books for young readers that are inspired by her interest in science and nature. Many of her books, such as *Salmon Story* and *Teddy Roosevelt's Elk,* are set in the Pacific Northwest, where the author lives, while others, such as *Mud City: A Flamingo Story,* have their origins in family travels. Still others, such as *Earth: Feeling the Heat, Life in the Boreal Forest, Rain, Rain, Rain Forest, Moon Bear,* and *Disasters: Natural and Man-made Catastrophes through the Centuries,* introduce readers to environmental issues of importance in their own lives.

"Becoming a writer was not on my mind as a child," Guiberson once told *SATA.* "I had five sisters and two brothers and, for a while, three foster children in the family. We never sat around much and were usually out along the Columbia River, which ran past our backyard in Richland, Washington.

"In high school and college I took many science classes and was a little surprised to finally end up with degrees in fine art and English. Along the way, I tried out several things: copywriter, letter carrier, stained-glass worker and woodworker, manager, and counselor.

"The idea of creating children's books started with my son, Jason. He used to bring home dozens of books from the library and ask to hear them over and over again. We were having a good time and it sank in. After years in this training ground, I finally got up the courage to write. Now I don't want to stop."

In Guiberson's first book, *Turtle People,* a Washington state sixth grader named Richie finds an ancient stone bowl while playing on an island near his home. He used to hunt for Native American artifacts with his father, but his father has moved away. Richie is fascinated by the idea of the Turtle People, and wonders why they became so enamored of the slow-moving creature. On his own, he thinks about what lessons he might learn from the turtle. Eventually Richie and his pal track down an expert to answer their questions. *Horn Book* reviewer Carolyn K. Jenks called Richie "a likable, sensitive boy . . . enough in touch with reality to describe his world with liveliness and humor."

Guiberson returns to the turtle once again with *Into the Sea,* a picture book illustrated by Alix Berenzy. Words and images tell the story of the massive female sea turtle who takes twenty years to mature. It must make an arduous journey in order to lay its eggs on land, and, when the new turtles hatch themselves, they must hurry to the sea on new legs before land predators find them. "Well-chosen details convey the vulnerability of the young animal," remarked *Horn Book* reviewer Margaret A. Bush, while *Booklist* critic Kay Weisman commended the "vivid prose" in *Into the Sea* that recounts "ample real-life drama."

Guiberson has worked with several illustrators in her career as a writer, and her collaborations with artist Megan Lloyd have resulted in several books. Inspired by a trip to Arizona's Sonora Desert, *Cactus Hotel* recounts the life story of a legendary saguaro cactus, a species that can live for 200 years. Some reach fifty feet in height and might weigh eight tons, but they also provide an important link in the desert ecosystem, as a home for birds, insects and various small creatures of the region. "Guiberson's simple, understandable text gives an enjoyable lesson in desert ecology," remarked Leone McDermott in a *Booklist* review of *Cactus Hotel.*

Another work by Guiberson and Lloyd, *Spoonbill Swamp* describes life in a swamp that is home to a spoonbill crane and its new offspring. The swamp also shelters another new mother, an alligator, which preys

Guiberson tells a story of the southwest in* Cactus Hotel, *a picture book brought to life in Megan Lloyd's art. (Illustration © 1991 by Megan Lloyd. Reprinted by arrangement with Henry Holt & Company, LLC.)

on the spoonbill. As Guiberson told *SATA,* the book "began after trips out into the waterways of Louisiana and Florida. I thought about those places quite a bit and wanted to know about the action and drama that went on in all those moments that I could not be there. I wanted to know why cacti have holes and what happens when all the sleeping creatures wake up hungry." *Spoonbill Swamp* recounts the activities of both families over the course of one day as they search for food and protect their young. "Readers will feel an uncommon pull between the innocence of both mothers," noted a *Publishers Weekly* reviewer.

Teaming up with painter Gennady Spirin, Guiberson presents the ecosystem that covers much of the planet's northern hemisphere in *Life in the Boreal Forest.* More than just describing the many animals that make this region their home, Guiberson also discusses the ecology of the area and explains the complex ecosystem's fragile balance and how it may be threatened. Praising Spirin's "gorgeously intricate" paintings for the book, *Booklist* critic Debra Foote recommended the author's "effective" technique of "showing, rather than telling, how an ecosystem works." Another effective collaboration, this time with collage artist Steve Jenkins, resulted

in *Rain, Rain, Rainforest,* which brings to life another intricate ecosystem. Monkeys, sloths, colorful birds, and a myriad insects make their way through Guiberson's story, which follows a scientist as he gathers samples of unusual plants. Dubbing Guiberson "one of the best science writers around for younger readers," a *Kirkus Reviews* writer praised *Rain, Rain, Rainforest* as a "vivid, engrossing" nature title, while in *Booklist* Gillian Engberg noted that the author "doesn't shy away from the realities of predators and death" in her informative study.

In Guiberson's self-illustrated *Salmon Story* she concentrates on the Pacific salmon species, chronicling the amazing life cycle of this fish, which can travel thousands of miles to the ocean, then return to the stream in which it was born. Once plentiful in the inland and coastal waters of the Northwest, the salmon was revered by the Native American population of the area, whose sustenance depended on it. The species is now in a precarious state due to generations of human interference. Overfishing, the construction of hydroelectric power dams, and the polluting effects of industrialization in the region have decimated its numbers over the years. She also writes of the salmon's exceptionally determined nature: it can perform great leaps to get somewhere, and salmon are known to never turn back along their spawning journey—if they encounter the wall of a dam, for instance, they will try to get through it until they die. Later chapters discuss how environmental activists and scientists are working to help restore the natural habitat of the fish. "This makes ecology urgent and compelling," noted Hazel Rochman in *Booklist,* while Susan Oliver, writing for *School Library Journal,* maintained that Guiberson provides "a lucid explanation of how environmental abuses affect the balance of nature."

Focusing on a Pacific Northwest ecosystem, *Spotted Owl: Bird of the Ancient Forest* mixes Guiberson's text and illustrations to describe the old-growth forests of the region that was once the quiet home to the majestic spotted owl. That environment was impacted by logging, and Guiberson also discusses the timber industry in the region and the economic hardship caused when the industry fell into decline. A bird of a different sort altogether is her focus in *Mud City,* a self-illustrated picture book that finds a flamingo family raising their young chick in a mangrove swamp. Praising *Mud City,* Carolyn Phelan noted in *Booklist* that Guiberson's "watercolor illustrations are well observed" and mesh well with her "informative" text. A *Kirkus Reviews* writer also cited the book, maintaining that the author "has done her usual efficient job" of providing "an insiders' view of a very alien way of life."

Another self-illustrated work, *Lighthouses: Watchers at Sea,* reveals the history of such structures dating back to ancient times. As Guiberson notes, lighthouses were built to withstand the fiercest of elements, and she provided her own technical illustrations to show how light-

houses were constructed and the means by which their vital lights were kept burning for years. She also discusses the special breed of people who once chose lighthouse-keeping a livelihood until the task became an automated one. Lastly, the book touches upon some of the ghost stories associated with various lighthouses. Deborah Stevenson, writing for *Bulletin of the Center for Children's Books,* claimed that *Lighthouses* provides "a neat, understandable, and sometimes haunting treatment" of its subject.

In *Teddy Roosevelt's Elk* Guiberson explains how a species of North American elk received its unusual name. As a young man, Theodore Roosevelt traveled through the Dakota Territory twice and was devastated on his second visit when he witnessed the destruction wrought by humans because of mining and logging. When he became a U.S. president, Roosevelt created the legislation that survives as America's national parks. Guiberson's text then heads west to Washington state, where a species of elk named in the president's honor reside in the Olympic National Park. The book provides interesting facts about these magnificent creatures, chronicling a year in the life of a young elk calf. Guiberson makes it plain that, although they live in a protected environment, the elks' survival is not an assured one. *Bulletin of the Center for Children's Books* critic Elizabeth Bush praised the "intimate yet unsentimentalized narrative that acknowledges that challenges for supremacy . . . or even death by starvation" lie ahead for the young elk.

Guiberson takes readers to chilly climes in *An Emperor Lays an Egg* and *Ice Bears,* the latter featuring artwork by Ilya Spirin. In *An Emperor Lays an Egg* she follows a family of penguins from egg laying and hatching to the growth of their young family, treating readers to many facts about these interesting birds in the process. Described by *Horn Book* contributor Danielle J. Ford as a "story of growth and survival," *Ice Bears* takes a similar path in its focus on a polar bear family and the efforts of the two cubs to learn to hunt for food in their harsh Arctic environment. In *An Emperor Lays an Egg* Guiberson's "vivid prose" and "memorable images" mesh with artist Joan Paley's "exceptionally beautiful" cut-paper-and-painted collage art, concluded Phelan, while in *School Library Journal* Cathie E. Bashaw predicted that the large-format picture book "is sure to delight readers" while also introducing "the wonderful diversity of the Earth's habitats." Praising Spirin's "expressive illustrations" for capturing the nature of the polar bear, Ford added that *Ice Bears* "effectively emphasizes" the seasonal changes that affect the bears' activity. "Guiberson uses precise verbs and onomatopoeia" in creating the text for her nonfiction picture book, noted *School Library Journal* critic Ellen Heath, and in *Booklist* Randall Enos cited *Ice Bears* for both its "lush, realistic watercolor illustrations" and the author's ability to mesh both "variety and drama" within in her short text.

The collected photographs and images in *Mummy Mysteries: Tales from North America* reveal that many different kinds of preserved remains have been found throughout the continent. Unlike their ancient Egyptian counterparts, these mummies were not always intentionally preserved. Guiberson notes that modern scientists have learned much from them nevertheless. A blue bison carcass found in Alaska, dating back some 36,000 years, bore wound marks from a lion, for example. Scientists can only speculate about why the lions that once roamed this region disappeared. The remains of nineteenth-century explorers, icebound in the Hudson Bay area, reveal that lead poisoning may have spelled their doom. "For readers who like mysteries that unravel slowly, this book will be a joy," remarked Cathryn A. Camper in a *School Library Journal* review of *Mummy Mysteries.*

In *Exotic Species: Invaders in Paradise* Guiberson presents another unusual look at nature and its continual surprises. Here, the topic is disruptions in nature when foreign species arrive: the introduction of zebra mussels into the Great Lakes, for instance, or what happened as starlings, a European import, disrupted the ornithological hierarchy in the New World. The stories recount how such alien invaders affect the food chain and general ecosystem, and discuss measures that are sometimes taken to combat them. Guiberson also shows how nature can do the work of keeping an ecosystem in balance if not overwhelmed. John Peters, writing for *Booklist,* found that Guiberson's book "examines a controversial subject from several angles and presents convincing arguments for its importance." *School Library Journal* reviewer Arwen Marshall found *Exotic Species* to be "well balanced," and singled out the author for being "careful to look at both the positive and negative aspects of these invasions."

I like to write both fiction and nonfiction," Guiberson once told *SATA*. "I like to write about subjects that are interesting and exciting to me. Writers can make anything happen and write about places that they would like to go.

"It takes a lot of research to write about what might happen at some random moment in time. A writer can't say that a kangaroo rat stops for a drink of water when research reveals that this creature never drinks. And if an alligator is cold-blooded, then how does it behave? It takes a lot of observation and digging into books, field reports, and museums to find out. This is something I really enjoy. In writing *Turtle People,* I ended up reading the entire journals of Lewis and Clark. For *Cactus Hotel,* I gleaned information from the desert, museums, and scientists. For *Mummy Mysteries,* I visited ancient ruins and searched university archives and special collections. For other books, I have swam near dolphins and sea turtles, climbed lighthouses, hiked through forests, and have met so many wonderful people willing to help me with the research process.

"For someone who has always been interested in science and the visual arts, writing or illustrating a book combines many things that I like to do. Opportunities to investigate connections between people, creatures, and environments around the world are fun, surprising, and full of meaning."

Cover of Guiberson's nonfiction picture book Exotic Species, *which describes the threat to small ecosystems.* (Twenty-first Century Books, 1999. Photograph courtesy of Animals, Animals, © Stephen Dalton. Reproduced by permission.)

Biographical and Critical Sources

PERIODICALS

Booklist, June 15, 1991, Leone McDermott, review of *Cactus Hotel,* p. 1969; April 15, 1993, Emily Melton, review of *Lobster Boat,* p. 1511; January 1, 1994, Hazel Rochman, review of *Salmon Story,* p. 819; January 1, 1995, Carolyn Phelan, review of *Spotted Owl: Bird of the Ancient Forest,* pp. 817-818; November 1, 1995, Hazel Rochman, review of *Lighthouses: Watchers at Sea,* p. 466; November 15, 1995, Julie Corsaro, review of *Winter Wheat,* p. 562; September 15, 1996, Kay Weisman, review of *Into the Sea,* p. 243; September 15, 1997, John Peters, review of *Teddy Roosevelt's Elk,* p. 237; July, 1999, John Peters, review of *Exotic Species: Invaders in Paradise,* p. 1940; December 1, 2001, Carolyn Phelan, review of *The Emperor Lays an Egg,* p. 658; May 1, 2004, Gillian Engberg, review of *Rain, Rain, Rain Forest,* p. 1557;

May 15, 2005, Carolyn Phelan, review of *Mud City: A Flamingo Story,* p. 1662; October 15, 2008, Randall Enos, review of *Ice Bears,* p. 43; July 1, 2009, Diane Foote, review of *Life in the Boreal Forest;* November 1, 2009, Hazel Rochman, review of *Earth: Feeling the Heat.*

Bulletin of the Center for Children's Books, January, 1994, Carol Fox, review of *Salmon Story,* p. 155; December, 1995, Deborah Stevenson, review of *Lighthouses,* pp. 127-128; October, 1997, Elizabeth Bush, review of *Teddy Roosevelt's Elk,* p. 52; February, 1999, Elizabeth Bush, review of *Mummy Mysteries: Tales from North America,* pp. 203-204.

Horn Book, January, 1991, Carolyn K. Jenks, review of *Turtle People,* p. 67; November, 1996, Margaret A. Bush, review of *Into the Sea,* p. 759; January-February, 2002, Danielle J. Ford, review of *The Emperor Lays an Egg,* p. 97; July-August, 2004, Danielle J. Ford, review of *Rain, Rain, Rain Forest,* p. 467; January-February, 2009, Danielle J. Ford, review of *Ice Bears,* p. 115.

Kirkus Reviews, August 15, 1991, review of *Instant Soup,* p. 1089; February 15, 1992, review of *Spoonbill Swamp,* p. 254; April 1, 1993, review of *Lobster Boat,* p. 455; April 1, 2004, review of *Rain, Rain, Rainforest;* June 1, 2005, review of *Mud City,* p. 636.

New York Times Book Review, November 9, 2008, Ann Hodgman, review of *Ice Bears,* p. 36.

Publishers Weekly, January 13, 1992, review of *Spoonbill Swamp,* p. 56.

School Library Journal, July, 1991, Diane Nunn, review of *Cactus Hotel,* p. 68; July, 1993, Carolyn Jenks, review of *Lobster Boat,* p. 60; April, 1994, Susan Oliver, review of *Salmon Story,* pp. 119-120; January, 1995, Kathy Piehl, review of *Spotted Owl,* p. 118; May, 1997, review of *Into the Sea* and *Spoonbill Swamp,* p. 57; December, 1998, Cathryn H. Camper, review of *Mummy Mysteries,* p. 136; September, 1999, Arwen Marshall, review of *Exotic Species,* p. 234; November, 2000, Elaine Baran Black, review of *Tales of the Haunted Deep,* p. 142; December, 2001, Cathie E. Bashaw, review of *The Emperor Lays an Egg,* p. 121; October, 2008, Ellen Heath, review of *Ice Bears,* p. 131.

ONLINE

Brenda Z. Guiberson Home Page, http://www.brendazguiberson.com (January 10, 2010).

H

HERLONG, Madaline
See HERLONG, M.H.

* * *

HERLONG, M.H.
(Madaline Herlong)

Personal
Married; children: four sons. *Education:* College of William and Mary, degree 1976; earned J.D.

Addresses
Home—New Orleans, LA. *E-mail*—mhherlong@ thegreatwidesea.com.

Career
Author, educator, and attorney. Has worked as a high-school English teacher and law-school instructor.

Writings

The Great Wide Sea, Viking (New York, NY), 2008.

Sidelights
Author M.H. Herlong experienced a varied career prior to penning literature for young-adult readers, working as a high-school English teacher and also practicing law. Enjoying sailing with her husband as a favored pastime, Herlong gave her first novel, *The Great Wide Sea,* a nautical theme, focusing on a family of three boys who take a year-long voyage with their father after the death of their mother. While the oldest son, fifteen-year-old Ben Byron, finds his father's decision to sell everything thing they own to buy a sailboat a bit rash, he nonetheless goes along with the plan, still

shocked at the sudden loss of his mother in a fiery car crash two months earlier. The boys must mature quickly as they discover life at sea more challenging than anticipated. Their situation turns from challenging to threatening when their father becomes lost at sea and

Cover of M.H. Herlong's young-adult novel The Great Wide Sea, *featuring artwork by Robert Hunt.* (Jacket art copyright © Robert Hunt, 2008. Reproduced by permission of Viking, a division of Penguin Putnam Books for Young Readers.)

the brothers end up on a deserted island after a powerful storm. Parentless, Ben must take charge of his two younger siblings, all the while wondering if his father's disappearance was an accident or as an intentional attempt at suicide.

Herlong received several positive reviews for her efforts in *The Great Wide Sea,* with *Horn Book* contributor Christine M. Heppermann calling out the author's "precise, adrenaline-raising descriptive prose" for special attention. Other critics offered positive comments about the story's main character, with *Booklist* reviewer Carolyn Phelan describing Ben as "a sympathetic protagonist" and *School Library Journal* contributor Melyssa Malinowski writing that "the protagonist's emotions ring true." Herlong also earned notice for her ability to develop an "adventure tale full of peril," in the words of Aimee Cole in *Kliatt,* and Phelan concluded her review by calling *The Great Wide Sea* a "page-turner of an adventure story" as well as "a convincing, compelling, and ultimately moving novel."

Biographical and Critical Sources

PERIODICALS

Booklist, November 15, 2008, Carolyn Phelan, review of *The Great Wide Sea,* p. 58.

Horn Book, January-February, 2009, Christine M. Heppermann, review of *The Great Wide Sea,* p. 93.

Kirkus Reviews, September 15, 2008, review of *The Great Wide Sea.*

Kliatt, September, 2008, Aimee Cole, review of *The Great Wide Sea,* p. 12.

School Library Journal, March, 2009, Melyssa Malinowski, review of *The Great Wide Sea,* p. 145.

ONLINE

Great Wide Sea Home Page, http://www.thegreatwidesea. com (December 31, 2009).*

* * *

HOFFMAN, Mary 1945-
(Mary Margaret Hoffman, Mary Lassiter)

Personal

Born April 20, 1945, in Eastleigh, Hampshire, England; daughter of Origen Herman (a railway telecommunications inspector) and Ivegh (a homemaker) Hoffman; married Stephen James Barber (a social worker), December 22, 1972; children: Sarah Rhiannon, Rebecca Imogen, Jessica Rowena. *Ethnicity:* "White." *Education:* Newham College, Cambridge University, B.A., 1967; University College London, postgraduate diploma

Mary Hoffman (Reproduced by permission.)

(linguistics), 1970. *Politics:* "Disillusioned Labour voter/pro animal rights." *Religion:* Anglo-Catholic. *Hobbies and other interests:* Swimming, cooking, cats, doing the *Times* crossword, old roses.

Addresses

Home—Carterton, Oxfordshire, England. *Agent*—Pat White, Rogers, Coleridge & White, 20 Powis Mews, London W11 1JN, England. *E-mail*—maryhoffman@ stravaganza.co.uk.

Career

Journalist and author. Open University, Milton Keynes, England, lecturer in continuing education, 1975-80; reading consultant for British Broadcasting Corporation school television series *Look and Read,* 1977-95; Campaigner for libraries. Founder and editor of *Armadillo* (review publication for children's literature), 1999—.

Member

Society of Authors (chairperson, 2005), National Union of Journalists, International Board on Books for Young People (Hans Christian Andersen Medal panelist, 1981, 1987; member of Children's Writers and Illustrators Committee), Library Association (honorary fellow), Scattered Authors Society, Oxfordshire Children's Book Group.

Awards, Honors

NestléeSmarties Book Prize shortlist, British Book Trust, 1987, for *Nancy No-Size,* and 1993, for *Henry's Baby;* Kurt Maschler Award shortlist, British Book Trust, 1995, for *Song of the Earth;* Books for the Teen Age selection, New York Public Library, 2003, for *Stravaganza: City of Masks;* W.H. Smith "People's Choice" Book Awards shortlist, 2004, for *Stravaganza: City of Stars;* London *Guardian* Children's Fiction Prize shortlist, Agatha Award nominee, and Outstanding International Books selection, U.S. Board on Books for Young People, all 2008, all for *The Falconer's Knot.*

Writings

FICTION

White Magic (novel), Rex Collings (London, England), 1975.

(With Chris Callery) *Buttercup Buskers' Rainy Day,* illustrated by Margaret Chamberlain, Heinemann (London, England), 1982.

The Return of the Antelope (based on the television series by Willis Hall), illustrated by Faith Jacques, Heinemann (London, England), 1985.

Beware, Princess!, illustrated by Chris Riddell, Heinemann (London, England), 1986.

The Second-Hand Ghost, illustrated by Eileen Browne, MMB/Deutsch (London, England), 1986.

King of the Castle, illustrated by Alan Marks, Hamish Hamilton (London, England), 1986.

A Fine Picnic, illustrated by Leon Baxter, Silver Burdett (Chicago, IL), 1986.

Animal Hide and Seek, illustrated by Leon Baxter, Macdonald (London, England), 1986, Silver Burdett (Chicago, IL), 1987.

The Perfect Pet, illustrated by Leon Baxter, Silver Burdett (Chicago, IL), 1986.

Clothes for Sale, illustrated by Leon Baxter, Silver Burdett (Chicago, IL), 1986.

Nancy No-Size, illustrated by Jennifer Northway, Methuen (Oxford, England), 1987.

Specially Sarah, illustrated by Joanna Carey, Methuen (London, England), 1987.

Dracula's Daughter, illustrated by Chris Riddell, Barron's (Hauppauge, NY), 1988, reprinted, Crabtree Publishing (New York, NY), 2006.

My Grandma Has Black Hair, illustrated by Joanna Burroughes, Dial (New York, NY), 1988.

Catwalk, illustrated by Joanna Burroughes, Methuen (London, England), 1989.

All about Lucy, illustrated by Joanna Carey, Methuen (London, England), 1989.

Min's First Jump, illustrated by John Rogan, Hamish Hamilton (London, England), 1989.

Mermaid and Chips, illustrated by Bernice McMullen, Heinemann (London, England), 1989.

Dog Powder, illustrated by Paul Warren, Heinemann (London, England), 1989.

Just Jack, illustrated by Joanna Carey, Methuen (London, England), 1990.

(Editor) *Ip, Dip, Sky Blue,* Collins (London, England), 1990.

Leon's Lucky Lunchbreak, illustrated by Polly Noakes, Dent (London, England), 1991.

The Babies' Hotel, Dent (London, England), 1991.

Max in the Jungle, illustrated by John Rogan, Hamish Hamilton (London, England), 1991.

The Ghost Menagerie, illustrated by Laura L. Seeley, Orchard Books (London, England), 1992, published as *The Four-egged Ghosts,* Dial (New York, NY), 1994.

Henry's Baby, illustrated by Susan Winter, Dorling Kindersley (New York, NY), 1993.

Cyril MC, Viking (New York, NY), 1993.

Bump in the Night, Collins (London, England), 1993.

Song of the Earth, illustrated by Jane Ray, Orion (London, England), 1995, published as *Earth, Fire, Water, Air,* Dutton (New York, NY), 1995.

Trace in Space, Hodder & Stoughton (London, England), 1995.

A Vanishing Tail, Orchard Books (London, England), 1996.

Quantum Squeak, Orchard Books (London, England), 1996.

Special Powers, Hodder & Stoughton (London, England), 1997.

A First Bible Story Book, illustrated by Julie Downing, Dorling Kindersley (New York, NY), 1997.

An Angel Just like Me, illustrated by Cornelius Van Wright and Ying-Hwa Hu, Dial (New York, NY), 1997.

(Editor) *Stacks of Stories,* Hodder (London, England), 1997.

Comet, Orchard Books (London, England), 1997.

A Twist in the Tail: Animal Stories from around the World, illustrated by Jan Ormerod, Holt (New York, NY), 1998.

Clever Katya: A Fairy Tale from Old Russia, illustrated by Marie Cameron, Barefoot Books (Brooklyn, NY), 1998.

Virtual Friend, illustrated by Shaun McLaren, Barrington Stoke (Edinburgh, Scotland), 1998.

Sun, Moon and Stars, illustrated by Jane Ray, Dutton (New York, NY), 1998.

Three Wise Women, illustrated by Lynne Russell, Phyllis Fogelman Books (New York, NY), 1999.

(Reteller) *A First Myths Storybook: Myths and Legends for the Very Young from around the World,* illustrated by Roger Langton and Kevin Kimber, DK Publishing (London, England), 1999, published as *A First Book of Myths: Myths and Legends for the Very Young from around the World,* DK Publishing (New York, NY), 1999.

Parables: Stories Jesus Told, illustrated by Jackie Morris, Phyllis Fogelman Books (New York, NY), 2000.

The Barefoot Book of Brother and Sister Tales, illustrated by Emma Shaw-Smith, Barefoot Books (New York, NY), 2000.

Women of Camelot: Queens and Enchantresses at the Court of King Arthur, illustrated by Christian Balit, Abbeville Press (New York, NY), 2000.

The Macmillan Treasury of Nursery Stories, illustrated by Anna Currey, Macmillan (London, England), 2000,

published as *Puss in Boots and Other Stories,* Macmillan (London, England), 2001.

Virtual Friend Again, illustrated by Shaun McLaren, Barrington Stoke (Edinburgh, Scotland), 2001.

Miracles: Wonders Jesus Worked, illustrated by Jackie Morris, Phyllis Fogelman Books (New York, NY), 2001.

A First Book of Fairy Tales, illustrated by Julie Downing, DK Publishing (New York, NY), 2001.

The Gingerbread Man and Other Stories, illustrated by Anna Currey, Macmillan (London, England), 2001.

How to Be a Cat, illustrated by Pam Martins, Frances Lincoln (London, England), 2001.

The Colour of Home, illustrated by Karin Littlewood, Frances Lincoln (London, England), 2002, published as *The Color of Home,* Phyllis Fogelman Books (New York, NY), 2002.

A First Book of Jewish Bible Stories, illustrated by Julie Downing, DK Publishing (New York, NY), 2002.

Hansel and Gretel and other stories, illustrated by Anna Currey, Macmillan (London, England), 2002.

Sleeping Beauty and Other Stories, illustrated by Anna Currey, Macmillan (London, England), 2002.

Animals of the Bible, illustrated by Jackie Morris, Frances Lincoln (London, England), 2002, Phyllis Fogelman Books (New York, NY), 2003.

Seven Wonders of the Ancient World, illustrated by M.P. Robertson, Frances Lincoln (London, England), 2003.

(Editor, with daughter Rhiannon Lassiter) *Lines in the Sand: New Writing on War and Peace,* Disinformation Company (New York, NY), 2003.

The Falconer's Knot: A Story of Friars, Flirtation and Foul Play, Bloomsbury (New York, NY), 2007.

Kings and Queens of the Bible, illustrated by Christina Balit, Holt (New York, NY), 2007.

Several of Hoffman's books have been translated into Spanish.

"GRACE" SERIES

Amazing Grace, illustrated by Caroline Binch, Dial (New York, NY), 1991.

Grace and Family, illustrated by Caroline Binch, Frances Lincoln (London, England), 1995, published as *Boundless Grace,* Dial (New York, NY), 1995.

Starring Grace, illustrated by Caroline Binch, Phyllis Fogelman Books (New York, NY), 2000.

Encore, Grace!, illustrated by June Allen, Phyllis Fogelman Books (New York, NY), 2003.

Bravo, Grace!, illustrated by June Allen, Phyllis Fogelman Books (New York, NY), 2005.

Princess Grace, illustrated by Cornelius Van Wright and Ying-Hwa Hu, Dial Books (New York, NY), 2008.

"STRAVAGANZA" SERIES

Stravaganza: City of Masks, Bloomsbury (New York, NY), 2002.

Stravaganza: City of Stars, Bloomsbury (New York, NY), 2003.

Stravaganza: City of Flowers, Bloomsbury (New York, NY), 2005.

Stravaganza: City of Secrets, Bloomsbury (New York, NY), 2008.

NONFICTION

Whales and Sharks, Brimax (London, England), 1986.

(With Trevor Weston) *Dangerous Animals,* Brimax (London, England), 1986.

Amazing Mammals Kit, Dorling Kindersley (London, England), 1993.

"ANIMALS IN THE WILD" SERIES

Tiger, Belitha/Windward (London, England), 1983, Raintree (New York, NY), 1984, revised edition, Belitha/Windward, 1988.

Monkey, Belitha/Windward (London, England), 1983, Raintree (New York, NY), 1985, revised edition, Belitha/Windward, 1988.

Elephant, Belitha/Windward (London, England), 1983, Raintree (New York, NY), 1985, revised edition, Belitha/Windward, 1988.

Panda, Belitha/Windward (London, England), 1983, Raintree (New York, NY), 1985, revised edition, Belitha/Windward (London, England), 1988.

Lion, Raintree (New York, NY), 1985.

Zebra, Raintree (New York, NY), 1985.

Hippopotamus, Raintree (New York, NY), 1985.

Gorilla, Raintree (New York, NY), 1985.

Wild Cat, Raintree (New York, NY), 1986.

Giraffe, Raintree (New York, NY), 1986.

Snake, Raintree (New York, NY), 1986.

Bear, Raintree (New York, NY), 1986.

Wild Dog, Raintree (New York, NY), 1987.

Seal, Raintree (New York, NY), 1987.

Antelope, Raintree (New York, NY), 1987.

Bird of Prey, Raintree (New York, NY), 1987.

FOR ADULTS

Reading, Writing, and Relevance, Hodder & Stoughton (London, England), 1976.

(Under name Mary Lassiter) *Our Names, Our Selves,* Heinemann (London, England), 1983.

Contributor to *Times Educational Supplement.* Reviewer for *School Librarian, Guardian, Telegraph,* and other periodicals. Author of monthly column in *Mother* (magazine), 1984-87.

Adaptations

Amazing Grace and *Boundless Grace* were both adapted for the theater, performed by the Minneapolis Theatre Company, in 1995 and 1998 respectively; several of Hoffman's titles have been adapted as audiobooks.

Sidelights

A British author of more than ninety books for young readers, Mary Hoffman produces works for elementary-grade and older readers that take a new slant on inter-

personal relationships. Confronting such issues as sexism, racism, and discrimination against the elderly by portraying non-traditional characters leading fulfilling lives and coping with prejudice and discrimination in a positive manner, Hoffman is credited with adding a level of sophistication to books for preschool children and beginning readers alike. The bubbly and enthusiastic protagonist of her best-selling *Amazing Grace* provides an example that encourages young children to think beyond stereotypical roles and boundaries. Discussing the highly regarded work with Nikki Gamble of *Write Away* online Hoffman stated: "I wrote, 'Once upon a time there was a little girl called Grace who loved stories.' I've often said since that it's not quite as momentous as, 'In a hole in the ground there lived a Hobbit,' but it was almost like that for me because it really did change the nature of my career."

Other popular works from Hoffman include chapter books such as *Beware, Princess!* and picture books such as *Sun, Moon, and Stars.* Hoffman's works about the Bible and mythology have also attracted young readers. With her juvenile novel *Stravaganza: City of Masks,* the first title of a critically acclaimed series, the prolific author charted a new course for her writing.

Raised in London during the 1950s, Hoffman has vivid memories of her own childhood, during which she claims she did not give much thought to "all those serious grown-up things" that would later appear in her work. In an essay for *Something about the Author Autobiography Series* (*SAAS*), she characterized her youth as

Hoffman presents the highlights of the life of Jesus in her picture book Miracles, *featuring stylized art by Jackie Morris.* (Illustration © 2001 by Jackie Morris. Reproduced in the European Union and the British Commonwealth by permission of Frances Lincoln, Ltd., in the rest of the world by permission of Phyllis Fogelman Books, a division of Penguin Young Readers Group, a member of Penguin Group (USA) Inc., 345 Hudson St., New York, NY 10014. All rights reserved.)

"the years which made me the person I am now. Whenever I write, I am in touch with the five year old or seven year old or nine year old who is still inside me." With her aptitude for writing and languages and a love of English literature gained during her school years, Hoffman further found herself unsure of her future occupation after graduating from Cambridge University. Working as a tutor and teacher of English, Latin, and Anglo-Saxon, she soon settled in to write a full-length novel about a young boy and girl living in Italy who discover a unicorn and thereafter have to take care of it. After a year and a half of hard work, during which time Hoffman also accepted work as a book reviewer for the *Times Literary Supplement,* this first novel, *White Magic,* was completed; it was published in 1975.

With one published novel under her belt, Hoffman was determined to pursue a career as a writer. In 1980, after working for five years as a lecturer at the Open University, she left her job to become a freelance author of children's literature. As Hoffman characterized that time in her life in *SAAS,* "the books and articles came thick and fast"—over thirty-five works of fiction or nonfiction bearing her name were published during the 1980s. Among them was the sixteen-volume "Animals in the Wild" series. Each book in the series discusses a particular kind of animal, ranging from antelopes to zebras, and provides an introduction to the animal's habitat, behavior, and the effects of man's interference on the species. "These are sharply conservationist," their author once admitted of the series to *SATA,* "and I do care very much about the way humans treat animals. (This is not the same as *not* caring about the way humans treat humans, by the way.) I am a vegetarian myself and have been for [several decades] and I regard fur coats as an ultimate obscenity."

In the mid-1970s, during the height of the feminist movement, Hoffman joined a women's group that examined children's books for racism, sexism, ageism, and socioeconomic prejudice. As a result, she became very conscious of creating balanced stories yet realized the importance of remaining "funny, lively, and linguistically inventive." As the author herself once noted in *SATA,* "propaganda is boring." "In my own books, I try for strong and memorable heroines," Hoffman explained, citing her 1986 books *Beware, Princess!* and *Dracula's Daughter* as examples. This trend continues in the 1988 picture book *My Grandma Has Black Hair,* wherein the author creates a whimsical character that is unlike any grandmother known to most of the story-hour crowd in their books, but very recognizable in real life. The young narrator admits that her independent, free-spirited grandma is "a little nutty," but prefers her to the stereotypical white-haired, apron-and slipper-clad, cookie-baking little old lady of most fiction. The granddaughter ultimately recognizes that adoring her family and telling wonderful stories is all that is really important in order to be a wonderful granny. "Children who have nonstereotypical grandmothers should especially relate to this story," predicted *Booklist* reviewer Ilene Cooper.

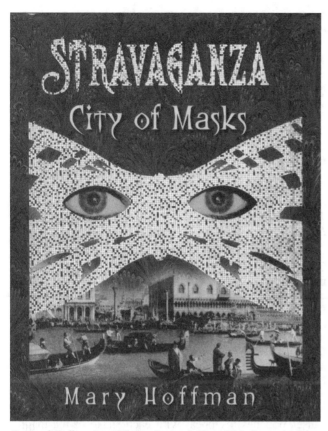

Cover of Hoffman's middle-grade novel City of Masks, *part of her "Stravaganza" series set in a parallel universe.* (Bloomsbury USA Children's Books, 2002. Reprinted by permission of St. Martin's Press, LLC.)

Many of Hoffman's books for young people are geared toward the preschool crowd, while others provide a fun challenge for beginning readers. A nontraditional approach to family relationships is contained within the illustrated pages of *Henry's Baby*. At first worried that having a baby brother will make him uncool with the group of boys that he wants to join, young Henry Moon finds out that his diaper-clad sibling is actually a novelty. "This picture book demonstrates that having a gentle, nurturing side can be masculine," noted *Five Owls* contributor Stephen Fraser, praising the volume for addressing the problems of young boys. In the picture book *Nancy No-Size*, the problems of being the middle child are addressed, in this case within a biracial family where siblings' differences extend beyond personalities to skin color as well.

Among Hoffman's books for slightly older readers, perhaps her most popular story is *Amazing Grace*. Called a "superb picture book to challenge stereotypes" by *School Librarian* contributor Chris Stephenson, *Amazing Grace* features a feisty young black protagonist with a love of acting and stories. Grace is determined to land the title role in her elementary school's production of *Peter Pan*, even though Peter was a boy—and white at that—as Grace's classmates remind her. Betsy Hearne lauded the picture book in the *Bulletin of the Center for Children's Books*, describing Hoffman's main character as "a girl whose love of stories empowers her to over-

come race and gender prejudice to do what she dreams." Hearne also noted that Hoffman's *Amazing Grace* "demonstrates the potency of imagination by being potently imaginative." Writing in *Horn Book,* Mary M. Burns called the story "a dynamic introduction to one of the most engaging protagonists in contemporary picture books." *Booklist* contributor Hazel Rochman was also favorably impressed by the book, calling it a "wonderful upbeat story . . . grounded in reality."

Producing *Amazing Grace* was a turning point for Hoffman, who based the book's main character in *Amazing Grace* on her own childhood. "I had already written about forty books by the time *Amazing Grace* was published in 1991," Hoffman noted on her home page. "But it is fair to say that it was Grace who changed my life." The book proved especially popular in the United States, where it was adapted for a theater production in Minneapolis, Minnesota, in 1995. Spin-off products also include a doll based on Grace.

Hoffman and illustrator Caroline Binch journeyed to Gambia in West Africa to produce a sequel to the story, *Grace and Family,* published in the United States as *Boundless Grace*. The work depicts Grace at eight and having to deal with the divorce of her parents and an absent father, back in Africa with a new family. Grace decides that she would like to visit him there. In the company of her grandmother, and filled with anxiety about the visit, she flies to Gambia to see him, his new wife, and her two step-siblings. Expecting an evil stepmother, she is happily surprised by the warmth this second family feels for her, and she is also pleasantly surprised to find that her father—now quite successful—has missed her all along. She learns the lesson that "families are what you make them," as a reviewer for *Publishers Weekly* quoted from the story. The same contributor also noted that Hoffman "has once again imbued her story with an abundance of familial understanding." Although Rochman maintained that the plot of *Boundless Grace* "doesn't ring true," for Burns, writing in *Horn Book,* the sequel "like Grace, transcends social, cultural, and geographic boundaries." The critic for *Publishers Weekly* also wrote that, in spite of the "more predictable plot line, this [sequel] is as assured and as uplifting as its predecessor."

Grace takes center stage again in *Starring Grace,* a chapter book in which the young charmer is on summer vacation and leads a group of friends in various amateur theatrics that somehow manage to lead to real situations. Playing circus, the group later visits a real circus, a mysterious neighbor is discovered when they are playing ghostbusters, and a bit of playing doctor allows them to deal with a real emergency when it arises. In the final chapter, they eventually land parts in an actual theater production. A contributor for *Horn Book* maintained that Grace is "as appealingly irrepressible as ever" in *Starring Grace,* but that "the book as a whole lacks urgency and individuality." Nancy Menaldi-Scanlan, writing in *School Library Journal,* noted that

Caroline Binch creates the detailed pencil art in Hoffman's middle-grade novel Encore, Grace! (Illustration copyright © 2000 by Caroline Binch. All rights reserved. Reproduced by permission of Dial Books for Young Readers, a division of Penguin Putnam Books for Young Readers Group, a member of Penguin Group (USA) Inc., 345 Hudson Street, New York, NY 10014.)

the "text reads easily and is filled with humor," going on to recommend the book as a "fast-paced choice for reluctant readers."

In *Encore, Grace!* the youngster deals with an assortment of challenges, including the death of a beloved neighbor and the impending move of a close friend. Grace also experiences jealousy when a bright new student takes command of the class play. Hoffman's protagonist "provides a wonderful role model for today's multicultural school community," noted a *Kirkus Reviews* critic. Grace faces a number of changes in her life, including her mother's second marriage, a move to a new home, and a friend's struggle with anorexia, in *Bravo, Grace!* According to *School Library Journal* contributor Amanda Rose Conover, "Hoffman does a fine job with this story about life, love, friendships, and real problems that many children face." In *Princess Grace,* the title character decides to shun convention and dress in Kente cloth for the school parade. In the words of London *Times* critic Amanda Craig, "feminism is all about making more choices available to women, and that includes those of traditional femininity." A contributor in *Kirkus Reviews* observed that Grace "is able to rethink traditional limits and provoke change."

Reviewers have compared Hoffman's picture book *The Color of Home* to the stories about Grace. In this case, the protagonist is a young immigrant Somali boy, Hassan, who is attending his first day of school in America and feeling homesick. Everything about his new life, including learning about culture and language, is a struggle. Yet when art supplies are handed out to the class, Hassan finally finds a way to communicate his feelings, painting two pictures of his life in Somalia and his hopes for a happy future. In a review of *The Color of Home,* Rochman noted that Hoffman "tells another moving story." Similarly, a critic for *Kirkus Reviews* compared Hassan to "another victorious child in *Amazing Grace.*" Reviewing the title in *School Library Journal,* Ajoke' T.I. Kokodoko called *The Color of Home* a "sensitively told story [that] also demonstrates the value of art therapy."

Other books by Hoffman that are designed for beginning readers include several stories involving the otherworldly. *The Second-Hand Ghost* introduces readers to Lisa, a girl who suddenly finds herself the owner of a small, troubled ghost that has been stitched up inside the pocket of an old jacket. The miniature spirit's search for a way to end its supernatural state and find eternal rest becomes the focus of this humorous tale. In the offbeat *Dog Powder,* a boy named Colin is unable to have a dog of his own due to his landlord's restrictions. Then he is sold a bottle of Dawn-to-Dusk Dog Powder, which causes pooches to appear with each shake of the magical dust. Problems arise when too many ephemeral hounds start causing chaos for Colin in this story that a *Junior Bookshelf* reviewer characterized as "charming, skillfully crafted," and "heart-warming." Sprites, spirits, and pets are all combined in Hoffman's *The Four-legged Ghosts,* in which young Alex Brodie receives a white mouse for his birthday and discovers that the small rodent has the ability to summon forth ghostly pets from years past. "Likable characters, lively action, and a fresh take" on traditional themes characterize the easy-reader, according to a *Kirkus Reviews* contributor. A contributor for *Publishers Weekly* also commended the book, calling it a "rollicking fantasy about furry phantoms," and a "spirited supernatural tale." Sequels to *The Four-legged Ghosts* include *A Vanishing Tail* and *Quantum Squeak.*

Hoffman takes a look at Christmas traditions in two titles, *An Angel Just like Me* and *The Three Wise Women.* In *An Angel Just like Me* Tyler, a young black boy, tries to find a black angel for the family Christmas tree. However, he soon discovers how impossible such a mission is, until his friend Carl finally carves him one. Janice M. DelNegro, writing in the *Bulletin of the Center for Children's Books,* found this to be "a palatable message story with a strong emotional core." DelNegro also thought that young Tyler "is appealingly tenacious" in his quest. Hoffman's *Three Wise Women* is a retelling of the Yuletide tale of the three wise men who follow the star of Bethlehem to find the newly born Jesus. In Hoffman's rendition, the three women carry gifts of freshly baked bread, a kiss, and a story. A contributor for *Publishers Weekly* noted that "a touch of girl power imbues . . . [this] magical tale."

Hoffman also retells folktales, legends, fairy tales, myths, fables, and stories from the Bible. In *Clever Katya: A Fairy Tale from Old Russia,* she retells a Russian folktale about a wise little girl who solves the Czar's riddles. Denise Anton Wright, reviewing the book in *School Library Journal,* thought it was "a satisfying and accessible retelling." *Booklist*'s Susan Dove Lempke praised the character of Katya as a "refreshing contrast to the helpless woman in *Rumpelstiltskin.*" More folktales are gathered in *A Twist in the Tail: Animal Stories from around the World,* "an attractive, if not unique, collection of ten folktales starring tricksters of land, sea, and sky," according to a reviewer for *Publishers Weekly.* The tales, taken from Asia, Africa, Australia and the Americas, are "pure pleasure and much needed," according to *Horn Book*'s Burns. *Booklist*'s Stephanie Zvirin also found the title to be a "spirited collection of animal tales."

Fourteen myths and legends from a variety of sources are retold in *A First Myths Storybook: Myths and Legends for the Very Young from around the World,* a book published in the United States as *A First Book of Myths.* Liz Dubber, writing in *School Librarian,* likewise called *A First Myths Storybook* "a very welcome addition." A more eclectic approach is taken in *The Barefoot Book of Brother and Sister Tales,* a compilation of stories from around the world celebrating the sibling bond. From the German story of "Hansel and Gretel" to the Armenian tale "The Red Cow," these stories deal with cruel stepmothers, witches, and queens in "clear, captivating language, each the perfect length for a bedtime read," according to Gillian Engberg in a *Booklist* review. The Arthurian legend gets a different spin in Hoffman's *Women of Camelot: Queens and Enchantresses at the Court of King Arthur,* a collection of nine tales dealing with various females from the land of the Round Table, including Guinevere and Morgan le Fay.

The Bible provides more inspiration for retellings from Hoffman. Among these collections are *A First Bible Story Book, Miracles: Wonders Jesus Worked, Parables: Stories Jesus Told,* and *Animals of the Bible.* The last three of these were done in collaboration with illustrator Jackie Morris and earned critical acclaim. In a review of *Parables,* a *Publishers Weekly* reviewer noted that Hoffman "steps beyond mere retellings" and described *Parables* as an "intimate, thought-provoking picture book." Patricia Pearl Dole, writing in *School Library Journal,* found the same book to be "excellent, accurate, [and] thoughtful." Another contributor for *Publishers Weekly,* in a review of *Miracles,* called this companion volume "a thoughtful, accessible overview" and "a book sure to be welcomed by children and those helping them to interpret scripture." Stories from the serpent in the Garden of Eden to Noah and his ark are gathered in *Animals of the Bible,* "an ideal introduction to the Bible for the very young," according to Susan Oliver in *School Library Journal.*

Hoffman returns to the longer novel form in *Stravaganza: City of Masks,* a story of "political intrigue . . . against the glittering backdrop of an alternate Venice,"

according to a critic for *Kirkus Reviews.* A time-slip novel, the tale involves fifteen-year-old Lucien, who is undergoing chemotherapy in present-day London. Falling asleep with a strange book in hand, the boy wakes up in an enchanted sixteenth-century city, Bellezza, a Venice-like place in the land of Talia where he meets Arianna, a beautiful young girl who is dressed as a boy. Lucien can only return to London by finding that book again. Caught up in the political intrigues of the time and now known as Luciano, he becomes an adept of "stravagation," or traveling between worlds. The first book of a fantasy series, *City of Masks* "will likely intrigue more sophisticated readers," noted a reviewer for *Publishers Weekly,* the critic also praising the "Renaissance backdrop [that] sets an elegant mood for the [story's] time-travel toggling." Karin Snelson, reviewing the novel in *Booklist,* lauded Hoffman for creating an "utterly fascinating, . . . rich, rip-roaring adventure" and predicted that the novel "will no doubt whet readers' appetites for Italian history and culture."

In *Stravaganza: City of Stars,* a sequel, London teenager Georgia finds herself transported to Talia, where she meets Lucien, her former classmate, and learns of the miraculous birth of a winged horse. Georgia also forms a strong bond with Falco, a crippled prince from the powerful de Chimici family, and helps Falco stravagate to England so he can seek the benefits of modern medicine. A contributor in *Kirkus Reviews* described *Stravaganza: City of Stars* as "a fine read on its own, and a compelling entry in an addictive series." *Stravaganza: City of Flowers* centers on Sky Meadows, a London teenager who finds himself enmeshed in a political feud between the rival Giglia and di Chimici clans after he also magically travels to Talia. In the words of *School Library Journal* reviewer Eva Mitnick, "the world of Talia is presented in vivid sensory detail that immediately sweeps readers into the story."

Hoffman produces another highly regarded work of historical fiction with *The Falconer's Knot: A Story of Friars, Flirtation, and Foul Play.* Set in fourteenth-century Umbria, the novel concerns sixteen-year-old Silvano, a wealthy nobleman who seeks refuge in a Franciscan friary after he is suspected of murder. Silvano finds himself attracted to Chiara, a novice at a nearby abbey, and when two of the monks are killed, they join forces to investigate the crimes. *The Falconer's Knot* "is a spirited thriller that prances off the page with its author's lively enjoyment of her subject," remarked London *Times* reviewer Amanda Craig. "Beautifully produced, it is a pleasure to handle as well as to read." According to Diane Samuels, writing in the London *Guardian,* "Hoffman's medieval murder mystery has all the elements needed to weave a satisfying web of intrigue, tinged with religion and high art. This is a pacy and highly enjoyable read."

On Hoffman's frequent visits to classrooms around her native England to talk to her young fans, children are always curious about her life as a writer. "Why I am a

writer is because it's the only thing I am good enough at to do professionally," Hoffman once explained to *SATA*. "I am very lucky to do for a job the thing that I enjoy most. I love everything to do with writing—from buying the paper to proofreading. . . . You know the way that some people are stage-struck? So much so that they'll even make tea or find props? Well, I'm the same about books—page-struck, perhaps? I can never quite believe that this is what I am, this is really what I do and I am not making it up. It still surprises me every time I look at my bookcases that house my titles."

Biographical and Critical Sources

BOOKS

Hoffman, Mary, essay in *Something about the Author Autobiography Series,* Volume 24, Gale (Detroit, MI), 1997.

St. James Guide to Children's Writers, 5th edition, St. James Press (Detroit, MI), 2000.

PERIODICALS

Booklist, June 1, 1988, Ilene Cooper, review of *My Grandma Has Black Hair,* p. 1676; April 15, 1995, Hazel Rochman, review of *Boundless Grace,* p. 1506; January 1-15, 1996, Susan Dove Lempke, review of *Earth, Fire, Water, Air,* p. 829; October 1, 1998, Susan Dove Lempke, review of *Clever Katya: A Fairy Tale from Old Russia,* p. 332; November 1, 1998, Ilene Cooper, review of *Sun, Moon, and Stars,* p. 486; November 15, 1998, Stephanie Zvirin, review of *A Twist in the Tail: Animal Stories from around the World,* p. 583; February 15, 2000, Hazel Rochman, review of *Starring Grace,* p. 1112; October 1, 2000, Shelley Townsend-Hudson, review of *Parables: Stories Jesus Told,* p. 356; November 15, 2000, Gillian Engberg, review of *The Barefoot Book of Brother and Sister Tales,* p. 641; October 1, 2001, Ilene Cooper, review of *Parables,* p. 333, and *Miracles: Wonders Jesus Worked,* p. 337; October 15, 2002, Karin Snelson, review of *Stravaganza: City of Masks,* p. 407, and Hazel Rochman, review of *The Color of Home,* p. 410; January 1, 2003, Ilene Cooper, review of *Animals of the Bible,* pp. 897-898; September 15, 2003, Carolyn Phelan, review of *Stravaganza: City of Stars,* p. 238; December 1, 2003, Hazel Rochman, review of *Encore, Grace!,* p. 666; February 1, 2004, Hazel Rochman, review of *Lines in the Sand: New Writing on War and Peace,* p. 968; March 1, 2005, Carolyn Phelan, review of *Stravaganza: City of Flowers,* p. 1181; April 15, 2005, Hazel Rochman, review of *Bravo, Grace!,* p. 1456; March 15, 2007, Gillian Engberg, review of *The Falconer's Knot: A Story of Friars, Flirtation, and Foul Play,* p. 48.

Bulletin of the Center for Children's Books, September, 1992, Betsy Hearne, review of *Amazing Grace,* pp. 3-4; March, 1998, Janice M. Del Negro, review of *An Angel Just like Me,* pp. 245-246.

Children's Digest, March, 2000, review of *A First Book of Myths: Myths and Legends for the Very Young from around the World,* p. 22.

Five Owls, May-June, 1994, Stephen Fraser, review of *Henry's Baby,* p. 106.

Guardian (London, England), July 14, 2007, Diane Samuels, "High Art, Low Deeds," review of *the Falconer's Knot,* p. 20.

Horn Book, July-August, 1995, Mary M. Burns, review of *Boundless Grace,* p. 450; November-December, 1998, Mary M. Burns, review of *A Twist in the Tail,* p. 746; March-April, 2000, review of *Starring Grace,* p. 196.

Journal of Adolescent & Adult Literacy, October, 2003, Jean Boreen, review of *Stravaganza: City of Masks,* p. 189; May, 2004, Jean Boreen, review of *Stravaganza: City of Stars,* p. 709.

Junior Bookshelf, December, 1989, review of *Dog Powder,* p. 278; October, 1991, p. 204; April, 1996, review of *Song of the Earth,* pp. 73-74.

Kirkus Reviews, August 1, 1993, review of *The Four-legged Ghost,* p. 1002; October 15, 1999, review of *Three Wise Women,* p. 1654; August 15, 2002, review of *The Color of Home,* pp. 1225-1226; September 15, 2002, review of *Stravaganza: City of Masks,* p. 1392; February 15, 2003, review of *Animals of the Bible,* p. 307; September 15, 2003, review of *Stravaganza: City of Stars,* p. 1175; November 15, 2003, review of *Encore, Grace!,* p. 1360; April 1, 2005, review of *Bravo, Grace!,* p. 418; May 15, 2005, review of *Stravaganza: City of Flowers,* p. 591; March 15, 2007, review of *The Falconer's Knot;* December 15, 2007, review of *Princess Grace.*

Kliatt, January, 2005, Joni Spurrier, review of *Stravaganza: City of Masks,* p. 20.

Publishers Weekly, July 12, 1993, review of *The Four-legged Ghosts,* p. 80; May 8, 1995, review of *Boundless Grace,* p. 294; September 14, 1998, review of *A Twist in the Tail,* p. 67; November 16, 1998, review of *Sun, Moon, and Stars,* p. 73; September 27, 1999, review of *Three Wise Women,* p. 61; May 15, 2000, "A Grace Note," p. 119; July 24, 2000, review of *Parables,* p. 91; October 9, 2000, review of *The Barefoot Book of Brother and Sister Tales,* p. 90; July 30, 2001, review of *Miracles,* p. 82; December 10, 2001, review of *Starring Grace,* p. 73; September 30, 2002, review of *Stravaganza: City of Masks,* p. 72; March 31, 2003, review of *Animals of the Bible,* p. 63; February 26, 2007, review of *The Falconer's Knot,* p. 90.

School Librarian, November, 1991, Chris Stephenson, review of *Amazing Grace,* p. 140; autumn, 1999, Liz Dubber, review of *A First Myths Storybook: Myths and Legends for the Very Young from around the World,* p. 136.

School Library Journal, October, 1998, Denise Anton Wright, review of *Clever Katya,* pp. 124-125; February, 1999, Patricia Pearl Dole, review of *A First Bible Story Book,* p. 97; September, 1999, Gunny Gustin, review of *A First Book of Myths,* p. 213; October, 1999, Tracy Taylor, review of *Three Wise Women,* p. 68; July, 2000, Nancy Menaldi-Scanlan, review of *Starring Grace,* p. 80; November, 2000, Patricia Pearl Dole, review of *Parables,* p. 142; January, 2001, Grace

Oliff, review of *The Barefoot Book of Brother and Sister Tales,* p. 118; October, 2001, Patricia Pearl Dole, review of *Miracles,* p. 142; September, 2002, Ajoke' T.I. Kokodoko, review of *The Color of Home,* p. 194; November, 2002, Patricia A. Dollisch, review of *Stravaganza: City of Masks,* p. 168; April, 2003, Susan Oliver, review of *Animals of the Bible,* p. 150; December, 2003, Tina Zubak, review of *Encore, Grace!,* p. 114; January, 2004, Jane G. Connor, review of *Stravaganza: City of Stars,* p. 130; August, 2004, Harriett Fargnoli, review of *Seven Wonders of the Ancient World,* p. 110; May, 2005, Eva Mitnick, review of *Stravaganza: City of Flowers,* p. 128; August, 2005, Amanda Rose Conover, review of *Bravo, Grace!,* p. 97; April, 2007, Quinby Frank, review of *The Falconer's Knot,* p. 138.

Teacher Librarian, June, 2000, Jessica Higgs, review of *A First Book of Myths,* p. 54.

Times (London, England), April 14, 2007, Amanda Craig, "There's a Conspiracy Here," review of *The Falconer's Knot,* p. 15; October 13, 2007, Amanda Craig, "Pretty, but Not in Pink," review of *Princess Grace,* p. 15.

ONLINE

Mary Hoffman Home Page, http://www.maryhoffman.co.uk (March 1, 2008).

Stravaganza Web site, http://www.stravaganza.co.uk/ (March 1, 2008).

Write Away Web site, http://www.writeaway.org.uk/ (March 1, 2008), Nikki Gamble, interview with Hoffman.*

*   *   *

HOFFMAN, Mary Margaret
See HOFFMAN, Mary

*   *   *

HORACEK, Judy 1961-

Personal

Born November 12, 1961, in Australia. *Education:* University of Melbourne, B.A. (fine art and English), 1991; diploma (museum studies).

Addresses

Home—Canberra, Australian Capital Territory, Australia. *Agent*—Jenny Darling and Associates, P.O. Box 413, Toorak, Victoria 3142, Australia.

Career

Cartoonist and author of books for children. Presenter at schools; speaker. *Exhibitions:* Work included in exhibitions at galleries in Australia, including Helen Maxwell Gallery, Canberra, Australia.

Awards, Honors

Honorable mention, Centre for Australian Cultural Studies National Awards, 1999, for *If the Fruit Fits . . . ;* Children's Book Council of Australia (CBCA) Book of the Year Award in Early Childhood category, 2005, for *Where Is the Green Sheep?;* Australian Capital Territory Creative Arts fellowship, 2007; Notable Book designation, CBCA, 2008, for *The Story of Growl.*

Writings

CARTOON COLLECTIONS

Life on the Edge, introduction by Dale Spender, Spinifex (North Melbourne, Victoria, Australia), 1992, second edition, 2003.

Unrequited Love, Numbers 1-100, McPhee Gribble (Melbourne, Victoria, Australia), 1994.

Woman with Altitude, Hodder (Rydalmere, New South Wales, Australia), 1998.

Lost in Space, Allen & Unwin (St. Leonards, New South Wales, Australia), 1998.

If the Fruit Fits . . . , introduction by Peter Nicholson, Hodder (Sydney, New South Wales, Australia), 1999.

I Am Woman, Hear Me Draw, National Museum of Australia (Canberra, Australian Capital Territory, Australia), 2003.

Make Cakes Not War, Scribe (Carlton North, Victoria, Australia), 2006, Andrews McMeel (Kansas City, MO), 2007.

FOR CHILDREN

(Illustrator) Mem Fox, *Where Is the Green Sheep?,* Harcourt (Orlando, FL), 2004.

(And illustrator) *The Story of Growl,* Penguin (Camberwell, Victoria, Australia), 2006, Kane/Miller (La Jolla, CA), 2008.

(And illustrator) *These Are My Feet,* Penguin (Camberwell, Victoria, Australia), 2008.

(And illustrator) *These Are My Hands,* Penguin (Camberwell, Victoria, Australia), 2009.

OTHER

(Illustrator) Sancia Robinson and Foong Ling Kong, *Mary Jane: Living through Anorexia and Bulimia Nervosa,* Random House Australia (Milson's Point, New South Wales, Australia), 1996.

Joan Kirner and Moira Rayner, *The Women's Power Pocket Book,* Penguin (Ringwood, Victoria, Australia), 2000.

Mem Fox, *Reading Magic: How Your Child Can Learn to Read before School, and Other Read-Aloud Miracles,* Pan Macmillan (Sydney, New South Wales, Australia), 2001, published as *Reading Magic: Why Reading Aloud to Our Children Will Change Their Lives Forever,* Harcourt (New York, NY), 2001, revised edition, 2008.

Contributor of cartoons to periodicals, including the *Age, Australian Book Review, Canberra Times,* and *Weekend Australian Magazine.*

Adaptations

Horacek's cartoon images have been adapted as designs for housewares and other consumer products.

Sidelights

Judy Horacek is an Australian cartoonist and humorist whose wry images capture the whimsies of life from a women's viewpoint. Horacek also uses her talent to comment on the timely political and social issues that surface in Australian discourse, and her cartoons have been collected in a series of anthologies that include *Life on the Edge, If the Fruit Fits . . . ,* and *I Am Woman, Hear Me Draw.* Her most popular cartoon art has been adapted as graphic designs that can be found emblazoned on everything from tea towels and coffee mugs to refrigerator magnets, and she also produces greeting cards and a line of limited-edition prints. Discussing her decision to become a cartoonist, Horacek noted on her home page: "Dad got *Pick of Punch* (the annual collection produced from the English humour magazine *Punch*) for Christmas every year, and I read the cartoons from when I was old enough to read). I wasn't influenced by specific artists as much as I was influenced by the idea of cartoons: that there were people in the world drawing pictures to make other people laugh or exclaim or think."

Horacek was inspired to focus on a younger audience by an e-mail from well-known Australia children's writer Mem Fox, who saw in one of Horacek's cartoons the spark of an entertaining children's story. Joining together, the two women produced *Where Is the Green Sheep?,* a concept book for toddlers that pairs Fox's "perfectly simple" text with Horacek's "clear . . . cartoon-style drawings," according to a *Kirkus Reviews* writer. Also praising the book's "amusing" illustrations, which features the artist's characteristic use of heavy lines and flat gouache tints, *Booklist* contributor Ilene Cooper added that *Where Is the Green Sheep?* will inspire "laughs and interactive play . . . among readers and listeners."

Horacek's work with Fox on *Where Is the Green Sheep?* convinced her to explore other avenues in children's literature, and she combines her cartoon art with an original story in *The Story of Growl.* The simple text introduces readers to a long-toothed purple monster who enjoys making a growling sound while walking along the street near her castle home. When her growling frightens a family taking tea, Growl is admonished to stay silent. Unable to make noise, the monster grows sad, but when her growling saves her neighborhood from a robber, her neighbors realize that the monster's noisiness may not be so bad after all. In *Kirkus Reviews* a reviewer wrote that "Horacek gets all the details just right" in *The Story of Growl,* a picture book "to read over and over," according to the critic. In *Publishers Weekly* a reviewer described the book's illustrations as "goofy cartoons" that feature "a genial, contemporary look" as well as a purple heroine with "Pokemonesque charm."

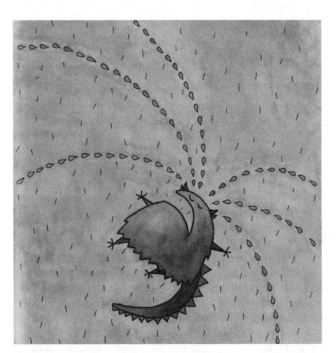

Cartoonist Judy Horacek treats picture-book fans to a quirky tale in **The Story of Growl.** (Kane/Miller Book Publishers, 2008. Copyright © Judy Horacek, 2007. All rights reserved. Reproduced by permission.)

Biographical and Critical Sources

PERIODICALS

Booklist, March 1, 2004, Ilene Cooper, review of *Where Is the Green Sheep?,* p. 1193.

Horn Book, May-June, 2004, Betty Carter, review of *Where Is the Green Sheep?,* p. 312.

Kirkus Reviews, March 15, 2004, review of *Where Is the Green Sheep?,* p. 269: September 15, 2008, review of *The Story of Growl.*

Publishers Weekly, March 8, 2004, review of *Where Is the Green Sheep?,* p. 72; September 1, 2008, review of *The Story of Growl,* p. 53.

School Library Journal, April, 2004, Blair Christolon, review of *Where Is the Green Sheep?,* p. 110; October, 2008, Ieva Bates, review of *The Story of Growl,* p. 112.

ONLINE

Judy Horacek Home Page, http://horack.com.au (January 10, 2010).*

J

JENNINGS, Linda 1937-
(Linda M. Jennings)

Personal
Born 1937, in England.

Addresses
Home—London, England.

Career
Author of books for children.

Writings

(Reteller, as Linda M. Jennings) *A First Jack and the Beanstalk,* illustrated by John Patience, Hodder & Stoughton (London, England), 1979.

(Reteller, as Linda M. Jennings) *A First Red Riding Hood,* illustrated by Glenys Amrus, Hodder & Stoughton (London, England), 1979.

(Reteller, as Linda M. Jennings) Ulf Löfgren, *Hans Andersen's The Tinder Box,* illustrated by Löfgren, Hodder & Stoughton (London, England), 1980.

(Reteller, as Linda M. Jennings) Ulf Löfgren, *Hans Andersen's The Emperor's New Clothes,* illustrated by Löfgren, Hodder & Stoughton (London, England), 1980.

(Reteller, as Linda M. Jennings) Ulf Löfgren, *Hans Andersen's Tomfool,* illustrated by Löfgren, Hodder & Stoughton (London, England), 1981.

(Reteller, as Linda M. Jennings) Ulf Löfgren, *Hans Andersen's The Swineherd,* illustrated by Löfgren, Hodder & Stoughton (London, England), 1981.

(Reteller, as Linda M. Jennings) Ulf Löfgren, *The Thief,* illustrated by Löfgren, Hodder & Stoughton (London, England), 1982.

(Reteller, as Linda M. Jennings) *The Prince and the Firebird,* illustrated by Krystyna Turska, Hodder & Stoughton (London, England), 1982.

(Reteller, as Linda M. Jennings) The Brothers Grimm, *The Musicians of Bremen,* illustrated by Martin Ursell, 1984, Silver Burdett (Morristown, NJ), 1985.

(Compiler, as Linda M. Jennings) *Poems, Prayers, and Graces,* illustrated by Sally Gregory, Hodder & Stoughton (London, England), 1984.

The Sleeping Beauty: The Story of the Ballet, illustrated by Francesca Crespi, Hodder & Stoughton (London, England), 1984.

(Adaptor, as Linda M. Jennings) *Coppelia,* illustrated by Krystyna Turska, Silver Burdett (Morristown, NJ), 1985.

(Compiler, as Linda M. Jennings) *Sing a Song of Seasons,* illustrated by Sally Gregory, Hodder & Stoughton (London, England), 1985.

(Reteller, as Linda M. Jennings) The Brothers Grimm, *The Golden Goose,* illustrated by Martin Ursell, Silver Burdett (Morristown, NJ), 1985.

(As Linda M. Jennings) *Crispin and the Dancing Piglet,* illustrated by Krystyna Turska, Hodder & Stoughton (London, England), 1986, Silver Burdett (Morristown, NJ), 1987.

Merrydale Treasure Hunt, illustrated by Laini, Crown (New York, NY), 1986.

(Reteller) The Brothers Grimm, *The Wolf and the Seven Little Kids,* illustrated by Martin Ursell, Silver Burdett (Morristown, NJ), 1986.

(As Linda M. Jennings) *Fred's Garden,* illustrated by Martin Ursell, Hodder & Stoughton (London, England), 1987.

(Compiler, as Linda M. Jennings) *Fairies and Phantoms,* illustrated by Sally Gregory, Hodder & Stoughton (London, England), 1987.

(Compiler, as Linda M. Jennings) *The Hippopotamus's Birthday, and Other Poems about Animals and Birds,* illustrated by Roger Hughes, Hodder & Stoughton (London, England), 1987.

(Adaptor, as Linda M. Jennings) *The Mule's Tale,* based on a story by Alphonse Daudet, Hodder & Stoughton (London, England), 1988.

(As Linda M. Jennings) *Benny's Visit,* illustrated by Krystyna Turska, Hodder & Stoughton (London, England), 1988.

(Adaptor) *The Peter Pan Picture Book,* based on the play by J.M. Barrie, Hodder & Stoughton (London, England), 1991.

Batman and Other Animals, illustrated by Jacqui Thomas, Blackie (London, England), 1992.

Animal Stories, illustrated by Val Biro, Award Publications (London, England), 1992.

(Adaptor) *Jack and the Beanstalk* (play; includes audio-cassette), illustrated by David Mostyn, HarperCollins (London, England), 1992.

(Reteller) Carlo Collodi, *Pinocchio,* Ladybird, 1993.

Five-Minute Tales for Bedtime, illustrated by Hilda Offen, Dean, 1993.

Luke's Dog, illustrated by Jacqui Thomas, Blackie (London, England), 1993.

Buster, illustrated by Catherine Walters, Magi Publications (London, England), 1993.

Scramcat, illustrated by Rhian Nest James, Crocodile Books (New York, NY), 1993.

The Dog Who Found Christmas, illustrated by Catherine Walters, Dutton Children's Books (New York, NY), 1993.

(Selector) *A Treasury of Stories from around the World,* illustrated by Victor Ambrus, Kingfisher (London, England), 1993, published as *The Kingfisher Treasury of Stories from around the World,* Kingfisher (Boston, MA), 2004.

Luke's Holiday, illustrated by Jacqui Thomas, Blackie (London, England), 1994.

Witches Galore, and Other Magical Stories, illustrated by Val Biro, Award Publications (London, England), 1994.

(Reteller) *A Treasury of Bedtime Stories,* illustrated by Leo Hartas and others, Award Publications (London, England), 1995.

(Reteller) *The Story of Baby Jesus,* illustrated by Gwen and Pat Tourret, Ladybird (Loughborough, England), 1995.

The Toad Prince, illustrated by Georgien Overwater, Macdonald Young (Hemel Hempstead, England), 1995.

Batty Beasts (pop-up book), illustrated by Louise Gardner, Levinson (London, England), 1995.

Fred, illustrated by Basia Bogdanowicz, Magi (London, England), 1995.

Creepy Crawlies (pop-up book), illustrated by Louise Gardner, Levinson (London, England), 1995.

Ghosts (pop-up book), illustrated by Louise Gardner, Levinson (London, England), 1995.

Millie, illustrated by Catherine Walters, Magi (London, England), 1995.

Jellybaby and Other Problem Pets, illustrated by Jacqui Thomas, Puffin (London, England), 1995.

Monsters, illustrated by Louise Gardner, Levinson (London, England), 1995.

The Brave Little Bunny, illustrated by Catherine Walters, Dutton Children's Books (New York, NY), 1995.

Tom's Tail, illustrated by Tim Warnes, Little, Brown (Boston, MA), 1995.

(Abridger) Charles Dickens, *A Tale of Two Cities,* introduced by Roddy Doyle, Puffin (London, England), 1995, reprinted, 2009.

(Abridger) Charles Dickens, *Great Expectations,* Puffin (London, England), 1995.

(Abridger) Jane Austen, *Pride and Prejudice,* Puffin (London, England), 1995.

Come Back, Buster, illustrated by Catherine Walters, Magi (London, England), 1996.

(Reteller) *Fairy Tales,* illustrated by Gavin Rowe, Brimax (Newmarket, England), 1996.

(Abridger) Jane Austen, *Sense and Sensibility,* Puffin (London, England), 1996.

The Best Christmas Present of All, illustrated by Catherine Walters, Dutton Children's Books (New York, NY), 1996.

(Compiler) *A Treasury of Pony Stories,* illustrated by Anthony Lewis, Kingfisher (London, England), 1996, published as *The Kingfisher Treasury of Pony Stories,* Kingfisher (New York, NY), 2003.

Easy Peasy!, illustrated by Tanya Linch, Farrar, Straus & Giroux (New York, NY), 1997.

Lonely Misty, illustrated by Julia Malim, Little Tiger Press (Waukesha, WI), 1997.

Penny and Pup, illustrated by Jane Chapman, Little Tiger Press (Wauwatosa, WI), 1997.

This Little Piggy, illustrated by Valeria Petrone, Levinson Books (London, England), 1997.

Kitty's Fish Dinner, illustrated by Tanya Linch, Magi (London, England), 1997.

Where Can Horace Hide!, illustrated by Elizabeth Bell, Magi (London, England), 1997.

Steady Eddie and His Brilliant Idea, Little Rocket (London, England), 1998.

Mary Had a Little Lamb, illustrated by Tania Hurt-Newton, Levinson Children's Books (London, England), 1998.

(Reteller) *Sleeping Beauty,* illustrated by Claire Pound, Ladybird (London, England), 1999.

Nine Naughty Kittens, illustrated by Caroline Jayne Church, Little Tiger (London, England), 1999.

(Reteller) *Cinderella,* illustrated by Claire Pound, Ladybird (London, England), 1999.

My First Picture Book of Farm Animals, illustrated by Lesley Smith, Award (London, England), 1999.

My First Picture Book of Baby Animals, illustrated by Lesley Smith, Award (London, England), 1999.

My First Picture Book of Wild Animals, illustrated by Lesley Smith, Award (London, England), 1999.

(Reteller) *Beauty and the Beast,* illustrated by Claire Pound, Ladybird (London, England), 1999.

(Reteller) *The Princess and the Pea,* illustrated by Kay Widdowson, Ladybird (London, England), 1999.

Titus's Troublesome Tooth, illustrated by Gwyneth Williamson, Little Tiger (London, England), 2000.

A Tale of Two Pandas, illustrated by Adrienne Kennaway, Happy Cat (Manningtree, England), 2000.

What Do I Do with My Tail?, illustrated by Alan Fredman, Award (London, England), 2000.

Whose Ears Are Those?, illustrated by Alan Fredman, Award (London, England), 2000.

Hide and Seek Birthday Treat, illustrated by Joanna Partis, Barron's (Hauppauge, NY), 2001.

(With Kes Gray) *Toffee and Marmalade: Two Pet Stories,* Oxford University Press (Oxford, England), 2002.

(As Linda M. Jennings) *Dudley and the Lost Mouse,* illustrated by Maggie Downer, Award (London, England), 2003.

Dudley's Cat Flap, illustrated by Maggie Downer, Award (London, England), 2003.

Dudley's Box, illustrated by Maggie Downer, Award (London, England), 2003.

My Christmas Book of Stories and Carols, illustrated by Anne Grahame Johnstone, Award (London, England), 2004.

Little Puppy Lost, illustrated by Alison Edgson, Good Books (Intercourse, PA), 2008.

Author's books have been translated into several languages, including Bengali, Chinese, Punjabi, Somali, Spanish, Urdu, Vietnamese, and Welsh.

Biographical and Critical Sources

PERIODICALS

Booklist, February 15, 1995, Ellen Mandel, review of *The Brave Little Bunny,* p. 1092; March 15, 1995, Mary Harris Veeder, review of *Tom's Tail,* p. 1334; September 1, 1996, Kathy Broderick, review of *The Best Christmas Present of All,* p. 136; April 1, 1997, Julie Corsaro, review of *Easy Peasy!,* p. 1338; December 1, 2008, Ilene Cooper, review of *Little Puppy Lost,* p. 58.

Kirkus Reviews, September 15, 2008, review of *Little Puppy Lost.*

Publishers Weekly, May 1, 1995, review of *Tom's Tail,* p. 58; March 3, 1997, review of *Easy Peasy!,* p. 74.

School Library Journal, December, 2008, Linda Staskus, review of *Little Puppy Lost,* p. 92.*

*   *   *

JENNINGS, Linda M.
See JENNINGS, Linda

K

KELLEY, Marty 1971-

Personal

Born March 5, 1971, in Manchester, NH; married; wife's name Kerri; children: Alex, Victoria. *Education:* Earned teaching degree; attended School of the Museum of Fine Arts (Boston, MA).

Addresses

Home—NH. *Office*—7 East Lull Pl., New Boston, NH 03070. *E-mail*—martykelley@hotmail.com.

Career

Author, painter, illustrator, and sculptor. Has worked as an elementary school teacher, newspaper art director, and cartoonist. Musical performer with Steve Blunt on CD *Fun with Steve and Marty: Let's Have a Reading Party.*

Writings

SELF-ILLUSTRATED

Fall Is Not Easy, Zino Press Children's Books (Madison, WI),1998.
The Rules, Zino Press Children's Books (Madison, WI), 2000.
Summer Stinks, Zino Press Children's Books (Madison, WI), 2001.
Winter Woes, Zino Press Children's Books (Madison, WI), 2003.
Spring Goes Squish: A Vibrant Volume of Vociferous Vernal Verse, Zino Press Children's Books (Madison, WI), 2008.
Twelve Terrible Things, Tricycle Press (Berkeley, CA), 2008.
The Messiest Desk, Zino Press Children's Books (Madison, WI), 2009.

Marty Kelley (Reproduced by permission.)

Sidelights

Author-illustrator Marty Kelley is known for combining the gloomy and scary with the hysterically funny in his picture books. In *Fall Is Not Easy* a tree mourns the fact that it is unable to change to traditional fall colors of orange and red. Instead, the tree produces rainbow-colored leaves embellished with polka dots, stripes, and other patterns that resemble everything from a smiley face to a hamburger. Kelley's "clear and unassuming" paintings "reflect a good understanding of a young child's sense of humor," Carolyn Phelan commented in her *Booklist* review of the picture book.

In *The Rules* Kelley's rhyming text lists many of the rules that adults give children, while his illustrations show kids breaking each one. In *School Library Journal* Gay Lynn Van Vleck cited the book's "wry humor" and "irreverent" artwork and concluded that, for parents hoping to talk about safety with their kids, Kelley's "bouncy, quick read will be a great icebreaker."

Kelley continues exploring the gloomy side of the seasons in *Summer Stinks, Winter Woes,* and *Spring Goes Squish: A Vibrant Volume of Vociferous Vernal Verse.* The problems with summer—from ants to bug zappers—are detailed in a rhymed alphabetical list in the first, while readers of the next two books learn that Winter's challenges include slipping on ice and frozen boogers and spring is rife with loud thunderstorms, bumpy potholes, allergies, and errant baseballs. The winter fears outlined in *Winter Woes* involve "various gut-wrenching and hilarious difficulties," as Rebecca Sheridan remarked in *School Library Journal,* adding that Kelley's "watercolor illustrations extend the text." "The cheery color illustrations add the perfect touch to this delightful story," a *Children's Bookwatch* critic similarly noted about *Spring Goes Squish.* Even if children harbor worries about spring, predicted Van Vleck, "they won't be able to resist a grin thanks to Kelley's watercolors."

Kelley deals with scarier subjects in *Twelve Terrible Things.* With just a few words and paintings from a you-are-there perspective, the artist depicts childhood tragedies ranging from a dropped ice cream cone to a dead pet goldfish. A *Kirkus Reviews* critic maintained that the book's realistic illustrations make these everyday problems "delightfully exaggerated" and concluded that *Twelve Terrible Things* "turns the terrible into the terrific." As Madeline Walton-Hadlock concluded in a *School Library Journal* review of the picture book, Kelley's "minimal text and detailed artwork combine to convey a macabre humor that is bound to ensnare even the most hesitant of readers."

The Messiest Desk was inspired by Kelley's experiences as a second-grade teacher and shows what happens when a boy's school desk becomes so messy that it swallows him whole and a classmate has to go in with a plunger to rescue the boy from the mountainous mess. Praising the book, a *Children's Bookwatch* reviewer wrote that Kelley "hides humor in every sly detail" of his "zany, fun-filled story."

Kelley plans to continue writing about things that make kids laugh, including boogers and messes and other terrible things that come out of his imagination. "I have to hold back, if anything," Kelley told Sarah M. Earle in New Hampshire's *Concord Monitor.* "If I were totally cut free, I don't know what would happen." Writing for kids and speaking in classrooms can be a tiring job, he added, but "I really, really genuinely enjoy what I'm doing."

Biographical and Critical Sources

PERIODICALS

Booklist, January 1, 1999, Carolyn Phelan, review of *Fall Is Not Easy,* p. 888.
Children's Bookwatch, April, 2009, review of *Spring Goes Squish!;* October, 2009, review of *The Messiest Desk.*
Kirkus Reviews, September 15, 2008, review of *Twelve Terrible Things.*

Kelley captures the hijinks of an energetic childhood in his self-illustrated picture book **Twelve Terrible Things.** (Illustration copyright © 2008 by Marty Kelley. All rights reserved. Used by permission of Tricycle Press, an imprint of Crown Publishing Group, a division of Random House, Inc.)

New York Times Book Review, November 9, 2008, Daniel Handler, "Fright Club," p. L19.
School Library Journal, December, 2000, Gay Lynn Van Vleck, review of *The Rules,* p. 112; October, 2001, DeAnn Tabuchi, review of *Summer Stinks,* p. 122; April, 2005, Rebecca Sheridan, review of *Winter Woes,* p. 105; October, 2008, Madeline Walton-Hadlock, review of *Twelve Terrible Things,* p. 114; May, 2009, Gay Lynn Van Vleck, review of *Spring Goes Squish!,* p. 82.

ONLINE

Concord Monitor Online (Concord, NH), http://www.concordmonitor.com/ (October 4, 2009), Sarah M. Earle, "There's No Hiding the Kid Inside."
Marty Kelley Home Page, http://www.martykelley.com (January 6, 2010).

* * *

KIMMELMAN, Leslie 1958-

Personal

Born April 19, 1958, in Philadelphia, PA; married Ray Kimmelman, 1984; children: Natalie, Gregory. *Education:* Middlebury College, B.A. (magna cum laude), 1980. *Religion:* Jewish.

Addresses

Home—Ardsley, NY.

Career

William Morrow Publishers, New York, NY, editorial assistant for children's books, 1980-82; Taft Corp., Washington, DC, marketing associate, 1982-83; Harper & Row Publishers, New York, NY, children's book editor, 1983-89; writer and freelance editor, beginning 1989; Sesame Street Books, part-time editor, and former senior editor of *Sesame Street Magazine.*

Awards, Honors

Pick of the List citation, American Booksellers Association, and Notable Book in the Field of Social Studies designation, American Library Association, both 1989, both for *Frannie's Fruits;* Sydney Taylor Book Award Notable Book designation, 2000, for *Dance, Sing, Remember.*

Writings

PICTURE BOOKS

Frannie's Fruits, illustrated by Petra Mathers, Harper (New York, NY), 1989.

Me and Nana, illustrated by Marilee Robin Burton, Harper (New York, NY), 1990.

Hanukkah Lights, Hanukkah Nights, illustrated by John Himmelman, HarperCollins (New York, NY), 1992.

Hooray! It's Passover!, illustrated by John Himmelman, HarperCollins (New York, NY), 1996.

Sound the Shofar! A Story of Rosh Hashanah and Yom Kippur, illustrated by John Himmelman, HarperCollins (New York, NY), 1998.

Dance, Sing, Remember: A Celebration of Jewish Holidays, illustrated by Ora Eitan, HarperCollins (New York, NY), 2000.

The Runaway Latkes, illustrated by Paul Yalowitz, Albert Whitman (Morton Grove, IL), 2000.

Round the Turkey: A Grateful Thanksgiving, illustrated by Nancy Cote, Albert Whitman (Morton Grove, IL), 2002.

Happy Fourth of July, Jenny Sweeney!, illustrated by Nancy Cote, Albert Whitman (Morton Grove, IL), 2003.

Emily and Bo, Best Friends, illustrated by True Kelley, Holiday House (New York, NY), 2005.

How Do I Love You?, illustrated by Lisa McCue, HarperCollins (New York, NY), 2005.

In the Doghouse: An Emma and Bo Story, illustrated by True Kelley, Holiday House (New York, NY), 2006.

Everybody Bonjours!, illustrated by Sarah McMenemy, Alfred A. Knopf (New York, NY), 2008.

Mind Your Manners, Alice Roosevelt!, illustrated by Adam Gustavson, Peachtree Publishers (Atlanta, GA), 2009.

The Little Red Hen and the Passover Matzah, illustrated by Paul Meisel, Holiday House (New York, NY), 2010.

Sidelights

In her children's books author Leslie Kimmelman focuses on strong family relationships. Whether working together, enjoying special outings, or sharing the special joy of a holiday season, Kimmelman's books portray loving families wherein young children are nurtured and allowed to participate. Praised for her simple, clearly written texts, Kimmelman entertains the picture-book set with *Frannie's Fruits, Hanukkah Lights, Hanukkah Nights,* and *Everybody, Bonjours!,* while older children gain confidence in their growing mastery of an important skill in her "Emma and Bo" beginning readers. Her picture-book biography of the high-spirited daughter of U.S. president Theodore Roosevelt, *Mind Your Manners, Alice Roosevelt!,* was praised by a *Publishers Weekly* contributor for its "lively" description "of a very independent girl."

In *Frannie's Fruits,* Kimmelman's first picture book, parents and children work side by side at the bustling, seasonal fruit-and-vegetable stand named for the family dog. There is much to be done, as the fresh produce must be washed, polished, and piled high, the flowers trimmed and freshened, and merchandise shelved and priced. Told through the eyes of the family's youngest daughter, the book chronicles the day's events and each customer's purchases and eccentricities, including, as Hanna B. Zeiger noted in *Horn Book,* everyone from

Leslie Kimmelman's imaginative story **The Runaway Latkes** *features colorful artwork by Paul Yalowitz.* (Albert Whitman & Company 2000. Illustration copyright © 2000 by Paul Yalowitz. All rights reserved. Reproduced by permission.)

"the sour woman who wants a dozen lemons to the romantic couple buying the biggest bouquet of flowers." The critic praised *Frannie's Fruits* as "a welcome addition to stories about people working and enjoying their work."

Me and Nana captures the special bond that exists between young Natalie and her sprightly, slightly unusual grandmother, a woman with whom the girl enjoys spending time. Writing in *Booklist*, Ellen Mandel remarked that Kimmelman and illustrator Marilee Robin Burton "invite readers to be part of the warm and loving twosome's perfect relationship."

In *Emily and Bo, Best Friends* and *In the Doghouse: An Emma and Bo Story* Kimmelman collaborates with artist True Kelley to create entertaining stories for beginning readers. Readers first meet Emma, her family, and her dog Bo in the four chapters of *Emily and Bo, Best Friends,* while *In the Doghouse,* finds them on a trip to the lake and witnessing Bo's successful attempt to nab Emma's ice-cream treat. "Kimmelman writes with simplicity and wit" in capturing the ups and downs of her young heroine's day, concluded Carolyn Phelan in her *Booklist* review of *In the Doghouse*, while *School Library Journal* critic Bobbee Pennington recommended the book as "a solid choice" for young readers on the strength of its "simple and natural" text.

In *Everybody Bonjours!*, a story illustrated by Sarah McMenemy, Kimmelman treats readers to what a *Publishers Weekly* contributor described as a "light-as-souffle salute" to Paris, France, while in *How Do I Love You?* she teams with artist Lisa McCue to present a counting story that enumerates the many manifestations of love between a mother alligator and her young. "Kimmelman's versifying is economic, energetic and admirably varies," wrote a *Publishers Weekly* reviewer in appraising *How Do I Love You?*, while in *School Library Journal* Julie R. Ranelli described *Everybody Bonjours!* as "a clever introduction to a foreign culture as seen through a child's eyes."

Happy Fourth of July, Jenny Sweeney! finds a young girl caught up in the excitement of her town's Independence Day celebration. Jenny decides to take part in the bustle by washing her family dog, and the book recounts the preparations of the girl's family and neighbors in getting ready for the parade. Kimmelman describes the festivities in rhyming couplets enhanced by illustrations that *School Library Journal* reviewer Linda M. Kenton noted "honor America's melting pot" through the inclusion of an ethnically diverse neighborhood. Reflecting pride in the heritage the holiday represents, Kimmelman closes her book with a page detailing information regarding the flag, the Liberty Bell, and the signers of the Declaration of Independence.

Many of Kimmelman's books focus on the traditions of the Jewish faith. In *Hanukkah Lights, Hanukkah Nights* the "warmth of family love and joy of holiday celebra-

Kimmelman tells the story of a group of enthusiastic travelers in her picture book Everybody, Bonjours, *featuring artwork by Sarah McMenemy.* (Illustration copyright © 2008 by Sarah McMenemy. All rights reserved. Used by permission of Alfred A. Knopf, an imprint of Random House Children's Books, a division of Random House, Inc.)

tion light up" what a *School Library Journal* reviewer called a "simple narrative." Each of the eight nights of Hanukkah is described by Kimmelman in two sentences on a double-page spread. The rituals and activities associated with the holiday are illustrated by various family members as they engage in lighting candles, flipping latkes, and giving holiday blessings. Jewish traditions are blended with a well-known story in *The Little Red Hen and the Passover Matzah,* illustrated by Paul Meisel.

Eleven Jewish holidays are given broader coverage in Kimmelman's *Dance, Sing, Remember: A Celebration of Jewish Holidays,* which describes not only the well-known Rosh Hashanah and Hannukkah but also Shavot, Shabbat, and Yom Hashoah. In *School Library Journal,* Teri Markson noted that Kimmelman's text is "wonderfully written, simple yet informative," while Stephanie Zvirin added in *Booklist* that the author introduces the holidays "in a lively, dramatic way, limiting details so as not to overwhelm [the] very young." Praising the book as "valuable for its inclusion of several holidays rarely (if ever) mentioned in secular children's literature," *Horn Book* reviewer Lauren Adams added that *Dance, Sing, Remember,* with its illustrations by Ora Eitan, "is truly an invitation to celebrate."

Biographical and Critical Sources

PERIODICALS

Booklist, October 15, 1990, Ellen Mandel, review of *Me and Nana,* p. 447; March 15, 1996, Ellen Mandel, review of *Hooray! It's Passover,* p. 1266; October 1, 2000, Stephanie Zvirin, review of *Dance, Sing, Remember: A Celebration of Jewish Holidays,* p. 356; May 15, 2003, Karen Hutt, review of *Happy Fourth of July, Jenny Sweeney!,* p. 1672; April 15, 2006, Carolyn Phelan, review of *In the Doghouse: An Emma and Bo Story,* p. 52.

Horn Book, May-June, 1989, Hanna B. Zeiger, review of *Frannie's Fruits,* pp. 359-360; November, 2000, Lauren Adams, review of *Dance, Sing, Remember,* p. 769.

Kirkus Reviews, March 15, 2003, review of *Happy Fourth of July, Jenny Sweeney!,* p. 470; November 15, 2005, review of *How Do I Love You?,* p. 1234; March 15, 2006, review of *In the Doghouse,* p. 294; March 15, 2008, review of *Everybody Bonjours!;* August 15, 2009, review of *Mind Your Manners, Alice Roosevelt!*

Publishers Weekly, September 7, 1992, review of *Hanukkah Lights, Hanukkah Nights,* p. 62; February 12, 1996, review of *Hooray! It's Passover,* p. 72; July 27, 1998, review of *Sound the Shofar,* p. 70; September 15, 2000, review of *The Runaway Latkes,* p. 66; December 5, 2005, review of *How Do I Love You?,* p. 54; March 24, 2008, review of *Everybody Bonjours!,* p. 70; September 7, 2009, review of *Mind Your Manners, Alice Roosevelt!,* p. 43.

School Library Journal, October, 1992, review of *Hanukkah Lights, Hanukkah Nights,* p. 42; October, 2000, review of *The Runaway Latkes,* p. 65, and Teri Markson, review of *Dance, Sing, Remember,* p. 148; September, 2002, Genevieve Gallagher, review of *Round the Turkey: A Grateful Thanksgiving,* p. 195; July, 2003, Linda M. Kenton, review of *Happy Fourth of July, Jenny Sweeney!,* p. 100; February, 2006, Kathy Piehl, review of *How Do I Love You?,* p. 104; May, 2006, Bobbee Pennington, review of *In the Doghouse,* p. 91; April, 2008, Julie R. Ranelli, review of *Everybody Bonjours!,* p. 114; September, 2009, Lisa Egly Lehmuller, review of *Mind Your Manners, Alice Roosevelt!,* p. 127.

ONLINE

Leslie Kimmelman Home Page, http://lesliekimmelman.net (January 10, 2010).*

*   *   *

KIRSCH, Vincent X.

Personal

Born in Massena, NY. *Education:* Syracuse University, B.A. (advertising design). *Hobbies and other interests:* Puppetry, animation, theatre, travel.

Addresses

Home—Brooklyn Heights, NY. *E-mail*—studio@vincent xkirsch.com.

Career

Author and illustrator. Scenic and poster designer in theatres and on Broadway; former art director for television networks; visual merchandiser in luxury retail; freelance designer and illustrator. Presenter at schools, bookstores, and hospitals.

Writings

SELF-ILLUSTRATED

Natalie and Naughtily, Bloomsbury Children's Books (New York, NY), 2008.

Two Little Boys from Toolittle Toys, Bloomsbury Children's Books (New York, NY), 2010.

Forsythia and Me, Farrar, Straus & Giroux (New York, NY), 2010.

Sidelights

Vincent X. Kirsch told *SATA:* "After pursuing work in children's books for over twenty years, my big break came in 2006 when an editor at BloomsburyUSA noticed an illustration of mine in the *New York Times Book Review.* After looking at my sketchbook full of characters, she noticed two little sketches and wanted me to work on a book for these two characters: a neat and prim little girl named Natalie and a zany wild child named Naughtily.

"I used a spectacular department store as the setting for their story. The store is based on Bergdorf Goodman in New York City, where I worked for three years designing the window displays.

"Over the years, waiting for my first opportunity in children's books, I worked in the evenings and on weekends, creating new characters, writing stories, building puppets and toy theaters, and creating sample dummy books for many book ideas.

"I never really gave up on my aspiration to create books for children of all ages, though it looked as though I might not ever have the chance. The delay has made me appreciate the work even more than it ordinarily would."

Biographical and Critical Sources

PERIODICALS

Children's Bookwatch, September, 2008, review of *Natalie and Naughtily.*

Kirkus Reviews, October 1, 2008, review of *Natalie and Naughtily.*

School Library Journal, November, 2008, Lisa Glasscock, review of *Natalie and Naughtily,* p. 92.

ONLINE

Vincent X. Kirsch Home Page, http://www.vincentxkirsch. com (January 10, 2009).

Vincent X. Kirsch Web log, http://vincentxkirsch.blogspot. com (December 25, 2009).*

*   *   *

KLEIN, Lisa 1958-
(Lisa M. Klein)

Personal

Born 1958, in Peoria, IL; daughter of Gerald and Mary Klein; married Robert Reed (a financial planner); children: two sons. *Education:* Marquette University, B.A.; Indiana University, Ph.D. (literature).

Addresses

Home and office—Columbus, OH. *E-mail*—lisamklein@ columbus.rr.com.

Career

Writer and educator. Ohio State University, Columbus, assistant professor of English literature, 1989-98. Director of writing for children conference, 1998-2000.

Awards, Honors

National Endowment for the Humanities research grant; Books for the Teen Age selection, New York Public Library, for *Ophelia.*

Writings

NOVELS

Ophelia, Bloomsbury (New York, NY), 2006.
Two Girls of Gettysburg, Bloomsbury (New York, NY), 2008.
Lady MacBeth's Daughter, Bloomsbury (New York, NY), 2009.

NONFICTION

(As Lisa M. Klein) *The Exemplary Sidney and the Elizabethan Sonneteer* (dissertation), University of Delaware Press (Newark, DE), 1998.
(As Lisa M. Klein) *Be It Remembered: The Story of Trinity Episcopal Church on Capitol Square,* Orange Frazer Press (Wilmington, OH), 2003.

Lisa Klein (Photograph by Gretchen Garner. Reproduced by permission.)

Sidelights

A former professor of English, Lisa Klein is the author of *Ophelia* and *Lady MacBeth's Daughter,* two books inspired by her love of William Shakespeare's dramas. "I've long had this kind of 'hero worship' of Shakespeare," Klein remarked in a *Compulsive Reader* online interview. "He is one person I'd like to meet in the afterlife. Or I'd like to time travel to Elizabethan London and follow him around, go to all his plays. My own rewriting of Shakespeare's stories is an effort to understand and participate in his creativity."

Klein's young-adult novel *Ophelia* resulted from a series of surprising events. Denied tenure, after teaching at Ohio State University for eight years, Klein was then extended the opportunity to write a history of the Trinity Episcopal Church in Columbus. While completing this volume, she developed an interest in the stories of history. At the same time, her experience organizing and directing a conference for children's authors inspired her to "try my own hand at writing," as she stated on her home page. "I think that all English professors secretly long to write books that will be read by regular people (not just other English professors). So when I left teaching, I had the time and the freedom to write a novel."

In *Ophelia,* a reimagining of Shakespeare's *Hamlet,* Klein's title character survives the chaotic and tragic events at Elsinore Castle, escaping with a dangerous secret. First introduced as a ten-year-old tomboy, Ophelia develops into a strong-willed member of Queen Ger-

trude's court and later secretly marries Hamlet. "Klein stays close to the original plot, but adds new layers of meaning by filling in Ophelia's experiences," noted Gillian Engberg in *Booklist.* According to a critic in *Publishers Weekly,* the author "smoothly weaves in lines from the play and keeps her characterizations true to the playwright's, even as she rounds out the back story." Writing in *School Library Journal,* Nancy Menaldi-Scanlan praised Klein's decision to set *Ophelia* in the late-sixteenth century, commenting that "her detail-rich text conveys considerable information about courtly life, intrigue, and the societal mores of the times."

Two Girls of Gettysburg, Klein's second novel, concerns two cousins who find themselves on opposite sides of the battle line during the U.S. Civil War. After her father and brother enlist in the Union Army, fifteen-year-old Lizzie Allbauer must take charge of the family's butcher shop in Gettysburg, Pennsylvania. Her cousin, Rosanna, however, returns to her hometown of Richmond, Virginia, and begins working as an army nurse for the Confederacy. Lizzie and Rosanna meet again when war comes to Gettysburg in July of 1863. "Terrific action and lively characterizations move the story along well," Anne O'Malley commented in her *Booklist* review of *Two Girls of Gettysburg,* and in *School Library Journal* Kim Dare wrote that "Klein's weaving of the young women's stories to a shared conclusion gives a fresh perspective on the complexities of the Civil War."

Lady MacBeth's Daughter, another work based on a Shakespearean tragedy, centers on Albia, the banished child of Macbeth and Grelach. Raised in secret by a trio of soothsayers, Albia develops the gift of second sight, forseeing the bloody events that will lead to her father's takeover of the crown. "As in *Ophelia,* Klein nimbly inserts feminist themes and vivid detail into the story," Engberg stated of *Lady MacBeth's Daughter,* while in *School Library Journal* Kathleen E. Graver described Albia as "a compelling character who fights for the good of her country and refuses to allow anyone to use her as a political pawn."

Biographical and Critical Sources

PERIODICALS

Booklist, November 1, 2006, Gillian Engberg, review of *Ophelia,* p. 66; September 1, 2008, Anne O'Malley, review of *Two Girls of Gettysburg,* p. 92; August 1, 2009, Gillian Engberg, review of *Lady Macbeth's Daughter,* p. 56.

Kirkus Reviews, September 15, 2008, review of *Two Girls of Gettysburg;* October 1, 2009, review of *Lady Macbeth's Daughter.*

Publishers Weekly, December 4, 2006, review of *Ophelia,* p. 59.

School Library Journal, February, 1, 2007, Nancy Menaldi-Scanlan, review of *Ophelia,* p. 122; Kim Dare, review of *Two Girls of Gettysburg,* p. 126; December, 2009, Kathleen E. Gruver, review of *Lady Macbeth's Daughter,* p. 124.

ONLINE

Compulsive Reader Web log, http://www.thecompulsive reader.com/ (October 31, 2009), interview with Klein.

Lisa Klein Home Page, http://authorlisaklein.com (January 1, 2010).

*   *   *

KLEIN, Lisa M.
    See KLEIN, Lisa

*   *   *

KOZ, Paula G.
    See GOODMAN KOZ, Paula

L

LANDOWNE, Youme 1970-
(Youme)

Personal

Born 1970, in Woods Hole, MA. *Education:* Attended Friends World College (now Global College), Machakos, Kenya, and Kyoto, Japan, 1990; New School for Social Research (now New School University), B.A., 1992.

Addresses

Home—Brooklyn, NY.

Career

Author and illustrator of children's books. Muralist and artist for community organizations, including Groundswell, New York, NY, 2000-08, InterNos, Santiago de Cuba, 2001-02, Unified for Global Healing, Atlantic Yards Footprint, Brooklyn, NY, 2006-08, and Precita Eyes Mural Art Center, San Francisco, CA. New School University, New York, NY, teacher, 2007-08.

Awards, Honors

Jane Addams Book Award for Younger Children, Jane Addams Peace Association, 2005, for *Sélavi, That Is Life: A Haitian Story of Hope;* Top Ten Great Graphic Novels for Teens selection, American Library Association, 2009, for *Pitch Black: Don't Be Skerd.*

Writings

SELF-ILLUSTRATED

(As Youme) *Sélavi, That Is Life: A Haitian Story of Hope,* Cinco Puntos Press (El Paso, TX), 2004.
(With Anthony Horton) *Pitch Black: Don't Be Skerd,* Cinco Puntos Press (El Paso, TX), 2008.

Mali under the Night Sky: A Lao Story of Home, Cinco Puntos Press (El Paso, TX), 2010.

Contributor to Kenya's *Rainbow* magazine.

Sidelights

In addition to creating murals for community art organizations, artist Youme Landowne has also illustrated a self-authored book for children and collaborated with Anthony Horton on the graphic novel *Pitch Black: Don't Be Skerd.* Her original self-illustrated picture book, *Sélavi, That Is Life: A Haitian Story of Hope,* takes place among a group of orphans living on the street in Port-au-Prince, Haiti, and focuses in particular on a boy named Sélavi. Displaced from their families through violence, illness, or poverty, the group of street children works to create a safe haven, only to witness their home's eventual destruction at the hands of arsonists. Rebuilding their orphanage, the children also create a radio station to broadcast their stories, sharing their hopes, experiences, and accomplishments with a wider audience.

Winner of the 2005 Jane Addams Book Award for Younger Children, *Sélavi, That Is Life* also earned positive comments from reviewers, both for the quality of the narrative as well as its colorful artwork. "Beautiful illustrations using watercolor, photographs, collage, and techniques like batik make vivid Selavi's life," wrote a *Kirkus Reviews* critic, while *School Library Journal* Barbara S. Wysocki noted that Landowne provides "a realistic view of children whose lives are sometimes disconcerting and sometimes hopeful."

Described as a "beautiful, gritty biography" by *School Library Journal* contributor Lauren Anduri, *Pitch Black* tells the story of a African American named Anthony Horton who resides in the deep, dark tunnels of New York City's labyrinthine subway system. Abandoned not only by his birth parents but also by his adopted family, Horton found himself living on the streets before social-service workers learned of his situation and

Youme Landowne collaborates with artist Anthony Horton to produce the graphic novel Pitch Black. (Cinco Puntos Press, 2008. Illustration copyright © 2008 by Youme Landowne and Anthony Horton. All rights reserved. Reproduced by permission.)

assigned him to a homeless youth shelter. Conditions there, however, proved worse than being homeless for Horton, so the young man began to searching for alternative living arrangements. Hiding from police in the subway system one day introduced Horton to a new option deep under the city. Making his home in the darkness, the homeless man joined a small group of individuals living in the secluded parts of the transit system where later he began expressing himself through artwork he created on the walls of his subterranean home. On a chance encounter on the subway, Landowne met the now-adult Horton, striking up the relationship that resulted in the joint effort *Pitch Black.*

Many reviewers described *Pitch Black* as an unflinching look at life on the margins of society, captured through black-and-white illustrations in a graphic-novel format. "The horrors attendant on homelessness are not sugarcoated," observed a *Kirkus Reviews* contributor, who described the collaboration as "powerful." In her *School Library Journal* review, Anduri predicted that young-adult readers will be attracted to the "unflinching look at homelessness" as to well as the creators' skill at identifying "hope and inspiration in the dark."

Biographical and Critical Sources

PERIODICALS

Kirkus Reviews, April 15, 2004, review of *Sélavi, That Is Life: A Haitian Story of Hope,* p. 396; September 15, 2008, review of *Pitch Black: Don't Be Skerd.*

School Library Journal, July, 2004, Barbara S. Wysocki, review of *Sélavi, That Is Life,* p. 80; March, 2005, Kathleen T. Isaacs, review of review of *Sélavi, That Is Life,* p. 67; March, 2009, Lauren Anduri, review of *Pitch Black,* p. 173.

ONLINE

New York Times City Room Web Log, http://cityroom.blogs.nytimes.com/ (October 7, 2008), Sewell Chan, "Graphic Tale of Life in Subway Tunnels."
Youme Landowne Home Page, http://youme.landowne.org (December 31, 2009).*

*   *   *

LASSITER, Mary
See HOFFMAN, Mary

*   *   *

LAYSON, Annelex Hofstra 1938(?)-

Personal

Born c. 1938, in Java, Dutch East Indies (now Indonesia); immigrated to Holland, c. 1949; immigrated to United States; daughter of a Dutch naval pilot; married Bill Layson; children: Ingrid, Neil. *Education:* Degree (nursing).

Addresses

Home—Northern VA.

Career

Writer. Worked as a nurse; retired.

Writings

(With Herman J. Viola) *Lost Childhood: My Life in a Japanese Prison Camp during World War II* (memoir), National Geographic (Washington, DC), 2008.

Biographical and Critical Sources

BOOKS

Layson, Annelex Hofstra, with Herman J. Viola, *Lost Childhood: My Life in a Japanese Prison Camp during World War II*, National Geographic (Washington, DC), 2008.

PERIODICALS

Horn Book, January-February, 2009, Joanna Rudge Long, review of *Lost Childhood,* p. 118.
Kirkus Reviews, September 15, 2008, review of *Lost Childhood.*

ONLINE

Annelex Hofstra Layson Home Page, http://lostchildhood. net (January 10, 2010).*

*   *   *

LESZCZYNSKI, Diana

Personal

Born in England; married.

Addresses

Home—CA. *Agent*—Ellen Levine, Trident Media Group, 44 Madison Ave., 36th Fl., New York, NY 10010. *E-mail*—diana@dianaleszczynski.com.

Career

Writer. Has been a reporter, researcher, yoga instructor, and film developer.

Awards, Honors

Smithsonian magazine Notable Children's Books designation, 2008, and Green Earth Book Awards Honour Book, both for *Fern Verdant and the Silver Rose.*

Writings

Fern Verdant and the Silver Rose, Alfred A. Knopf (New York, NY), 2008.

Sidelights

Writer Diana Leszczynski was born in England and immigrated to Canada with her parents as a child. After moving several times, her family settled in a new subdivision, and because they were one of the first families to live there it created a lonely situation for Leszczynski. With no other children nearby to play with, the girl started reading anything she could find. Leszczynski's desire to write stretches back to that summer, when she discovered the books of Lewis Carroll and the mysteries of Nancy Drew and others. However, on the way to writing her first book for children, Leszczynski had a varied career as a reporter, film developer, and yoga instructor.

In Leszczynski's first book for children, *Fern Verdant and the Silver Rose,* Fern is the daughter of two botanists who love plants. Although Fern dislikes plants, after her mother disappears, the girl discovers that she has a kinship with them. This skill allows Fern to find her kidnapped mother and stop the anti-environment villain Henry Saagwalla. Beth L. Meister, reviewing *Fern Verdant and the Silver Rose* for *School Library Journal,* stated that while Leszczynski's descriptions of "the adults are a bit exaggerated, Fern's search for her mother and the decisions she is forced to make add depth to her character." A critic for *Kirkus Reviews* commented that, although the villain's motives lack cohesion, *Fern Verdant and the Silver Rose* is enriched by the author's "clever, witty narration, . . . likable and earnest main character and . . . plant community filled with unique personalities."

Biographical and Critical Sources

PERIODICALS

Kirkus Reviews, October 1, 2008, review of *Fern Verdant and the Silver Rose.*
School Library Journal, February, 2009, Beth L. Meister, review of *Fern Verdant and the Silver Rose,* p. 102.

ONLINE

Books 4 Your Kids Web site, http://www.books4yourkids. com/ (January 3, 2010), interview with Leszczynski.
Diana Leszczynski Home Page, http://www.dianaleszczyn ski.com (January 3, 2010).*

*   *   *

LEVERT, Mireille 1956-

Personal

Born December 20, 1956, in St.-Jean-sur-Richelieu, Québec, Canada. *Education:* University of Québec,

Montréal, B.A. (art); earned teaching credentials. *Hobbies and other interests:* Music, dance, films, theatre, sculpture, bicycling, cooking for friends.

Addresses

Home—Montréal, Québec, Canada.

Career

Author and illustrator. Worked variously as a window dresser, bookseller, art teacher, and muralist; freelance illustrator beginning 1975. *Exhibitions:* Work has been exhibited in Canada, France, Italy, Japan, and the United States.

Awards, Honors

Diploma of Honor, Premio Internacional Catalonia d'Illustración (Barcelona, Spain), *Studio* magazine merit award, Mr. Christie Book Award finalist, and Governor General's Award finalist, all 1990, all for *Jeremiah and Mrs. Ming* by Sharon Jennings; Mr. Christie Book Award finalist, and Governor General's Award finalist, both 1992, both for *When Jeremiah Found Mrs. Ming* by Jennings; Governor-General's Award for Illustration, 1993, for *Sleep Tight, Mrs. Ming* by Jennings; Canada Council for the Arts Award for Children's Literature (Illustration), 2001, for *An Island in the Soup;* Canadian Children's Book Centre Our Choice designation, and National Association for Humane and Environmental Education Recommended Book designation, both 2003, both for *Tina and the Penguin* by Heather Dyer; numerous other awards for art.

Writings

SELF-ILLUSTRATED

Le train, Ovále (Sillery, Québec, Canada), 1984, translated as *The Train,* Lorimer (Toronto, Ontario, Canada), 1984.

Jeux d'hiver, Éditions Chouette (Montréal, Québec, Canada), 1988, translated as *Winter Games,* 1988.

(Reteller) *Little Red Riding Hood,* Douglas & McIntyre (Toronto, Ontario, Canada), 1995.

Charlotte s'habille, Annick Press (Toronto, Ontario, Canada), 1997, translated as *Molly's Clothes,* 1997.

Charlotte se lave, Annick Press (Toronto, Ontario, Canada), 1997, translated as *Molly's Bath,* 1997.

Charlotte déjeune, Annick Press (Toronto, Ontario, Canada), 1997, translated as *Molly's Breakfast,* 1997.

Charlotte joue, Annick Press (Toronto, Ontario, Canada), 1997, translated as *Molly's Toys,* 1997.

Charlotte dessine, Annick Press (Toronto, Ontario, Canada), 1997, translated as *Molly Draws,* 1998.

Charlotte compte, Annick Press (Toronto, Ontario, Canada), 1997, translated as *Molly's Counts,* 1998.

Les nuits de Rose, Dominique et compagnie (Saint-Lambert, Québec, Canada), 1998, translated as *Rose by Night,* Douglas & McIntyre (Toronto, Ontario, Canada), 1998.

(Reteller) *Goldilocks and the Three Bears,* Golden Book (New York, NY), 2000.

An Island in the Soup, Douglas & McIntyre (Toronto, Ontario, Canada), 2001.

Le secret de Luciole, Dominique et compagnie (Lambert, Québec, Canada), 2004, translated as *Lucy's Secret,* Groundwood Books (Toronto, Ontario, Canada), 2004.

Tommy dans la galaxie, Dominique et compagnie (Saint-Lambert, Québec, Canada), 2004.

Émile Pantalon, Dominique et compagnie (Saint-Lambert, Québec, Canada), 2005, translated by Sarah Quinn as *Eddie Longpants,* Groundwood Books (Berkeley, CA), 2005.

Contes de la forêt, Dominique et compagnie (Saint-Lambert, Québec, Canada), 2006.

La princesse qui avait presque tout, illustrated by Josée Masse, Dominique et compagnie (Saint-Lambert, Québec, Canada), 2006, translated as *The Princess Who Had almost Everything,* Tundra Books (Toronto, Ontario, Canada), 2008.

Le sorcier amoureux, illustrated by Marie Lafrance, Dominique et compagnie (Saint-Lambert, Québec, Canada), 2007, translated as *A Wizard in Love,* Tundra Books (Toronto, Ontario, Canada), 2009.

Capucine et Lupin: pour toujours, Dominique et compagnie (Saint-Lambert, Québec, Canada), 2008, translated by Elisa Amado as *Tulip and Lupin Forever,* Tundra Books (Toronto, Ontario, Canada), 2009.

(Reteller) *Le petit chaperon rouge, d'après les frères Grimm,* Éditions Imagine (Montréal, Québec, Canada), 2009.

ILLUSTRATOR

Jean-Marie Poupart, *Une journée dans la vie de Craquelin 1er, roi de Soupe-au-Lait,* Leméac (Montréal, Québec, Canada), 1981.

Jean-Marie Poupart, *Drôle de pique-nique pour le roi Craquelin,* Leméac (Montréal, Québec, Canada), 1982.

Cécile Cloutier, *La girafe,* Pierre Tisseyre (Montréal, Québec, Canada), 1984.

Barbara Smucker, *Un monde hors du temps,* Pierre Tisseyre (Montréal, Québec, Canada), 1985.

Christine L'Heureux, *Les déguisements d'Amélie,* Éditions La Courte Échelle (Montréal, Québec, Canada), 1986.

Sharon Jennings, *Jeremiah and Mrs. Ming,* Annick Press (Toronto, Ontario, Canada), 1992.

Sharon Jennings, *When Jeremiah Found Mrs. Ming,* Annick Press (Toronto, Ontario, Canada), 1992.

Sharon Jennings, *Sleep Tight, Mrs. Ming,* Annick Press (Toronto, Ontario, Canada), 1993.

Donna Jakob, *Tiny Toes,* Hyperion Books for Children (New York, NY), 1995.

Marthe Faribault, *Le petit chaperon rouge,* Héritage (Lambert, Québec, Canada), 1995.

Karen Hoenecke, *The Pea or the Flea?,* School Zone Publishing (Grand Haven, WI), 2000.

Heather Dyer, *Tina and the Penguin,* Kids Can Press (Toronto, Ontario, Canada), 2002.

Gilles Tibo, *Parfois, j'exagère!,* Éditions du Renouveau Pédagogique (Saint-Lambert, Québec, Canada), 2004.

Greg Brown, *Down at the Sea Hotel: A Greg Brown Song* (with sound recording), Secret Mountain (Montréal, Québec, Canada), 2007.

Carl Norac, *Ne dites pas à maman que je suis dans les nuages,* Éditions Imagine (Montréal, Québec, Canada), 2007.

Sidelights

Mireille Levert is an award-winning artist and author whose work is well known to young children in her home province of Quebec, Canada, as well as to those throughout the country's English-speaking provinces in translation. Her illustrations for Sharon Jennings "Jeremiah and Mrs. Ming" stories earned Levert much acclaim and several major awards, and her original self-illustrated picture book *An Island in the Soup* was honored with the Canada Council for the Arts Award for Illustrated Children's Literature in 2001. Other books by Levert include her "Charlotte"/"Molly" board-book series and the imaginative stories *Eddie Longpants, The Princess Who Had Almost Everything,* and *Tulip and Lupin Forever.*

Born in 1956, in St-Jean-sur-Richelieu, Québec, Levert knew she wanted to be an artist by the time she was in middle school. After taking several classes at a nearby community college, she transferred to the University of Québec in Montréal to earn her bachelor's degree. Intending at first to be an art teacher, Levert instead gravitated toward book illustration, and her work has been published in both French-and English-language books

Mireille Levert's self-illustrated picture book Tulip and Lupin Forever *depicts the close friendship of two engaging characters.* (Groundwood Books, 2008. Illustration copyright © 2009 by Mireille Levert. Reproduced by permission.)

and magazines since 1975. Levert works primarily in water color, gouache, and acrylic paint on textured paper.

In *An Island in the Soup* Levert captures the thoughts of an imaginative toddler named Victor as he revisions his dinnertime bowl of soup as a treacherous swamp filled with strange creatures. Other foodstuffs are also transformed, as Victor fights his way out of the swamp, and soon celery trees, a hail of peas, and a fire-breathing dragon shaped like a roasted red pepper appear. Praising Levert's colorful, energetic art, Hazel Rochman predicted in *Booklist* that young readers "will enjoy the playful combination of the wild and the mundane" in *An Island in the Soup,* while *School Library Journal* contributor Maryanne H. Owen maintained that Levert's "boldly tinted watercolor illustrations are the [book's] highlight." Calling the book a "delectable concoction," *Quill & Quire* reviewer Sherie Posesorski concluded that the author/illustrator successfully captures a young child's "comic, scarily fanciful vision of the word" in watercolor paintings that "energetically swirl with movement in mischievous invention."

Levert focuses on bullying in her picture book *Eddie Longpants,* which is opened top to bottom rather than side to side. In the story, a very tall Eddie is teased by his classmates, and Pete the bully is relentless in his taunting. When Eddie's even-taller mom comes to school, Pete turns his teasing her way with unfortunate results. Showing himself to be the bigger person, Eddie ultimately rescues the bully from an unfortunate predicament, resolving what a *Publishers Weekly* contributor described as "a sweetly humorous portrayal of loving kindness." Reviewing *Eddie Longpants* in *Resource Links,* Anna S. Rinaldi also praised Levert's picture book, recommending it for use in classrooms as "a forum for children to share their feelings, experiences and positive solutions to bullying and celebrating diversity."

A bored and bratty girl takes on the title role in Levert's *The Princess Who Had Almost Everything,* and nothing that anyone does seems to satisfy her or capture her interest. Finally, a gift of colorful paper and a lesson in origami taps the girl's natural creativity. In true fairytale fashion, she eventually marries the gift giver, who is, after all, a handsome and clever prince. In *School Library Journal* Linda M. Kenton praised Levert's "rich palette" of colors, which include "bold reds" and "landscape greens," and dubbed *The Princess Who Had Almost Everything* "enjoyable." In addition to praising the book's illustrations, a *Kirkus Reviews* writer described Levert's story as "an enchanting lesson in the importance of simple gifts and self-entertainment."

Another self-illustrated book by Levert, *Lucy's Secret,* recounts "a sunny story of discovery," according to *Booklist* reviewer Gillian Engberg. In the story, Lucy and her aunt Zinnia plant flower seeds, but then Lucy must patiently wait for beautiful flowers to appear while nature takes its course. In the story, Levert introduces

readers to the germination process and the role of water, sunshine, and rich soil, and her brightly colored artwork pairs well with her "lyrical phrases" according to *School Library Journal* contributor Rachel G. Payne. In *Lucy's Secret* Levert shares with readers "a magical world filled with flowers and new life," maintained *Resource Links* contributor Denise Parrott, the critic also praising the author/illustrator's successful mix of a "poetic, lulling text and clear, bold art."

In addition to creating original picture books, Levert continues to contribute to both English-and-French-language texts by other authors, including Jean-Marie Poupart, Carl Norac, Giles Tibo, and Heather Dyer. In her work for Dyer's *Tina and the Penguin,* a story about a girl who helps a penguin to escape from the local zoo, the artist "extends the silly scenarios in bright, gouache-and-watercolor illustrations," according to *Booklist* contributor Helen Rosenberg.

Biographical and Critical Sources

PERIODICALS

Booklist, April 1, 1995, Ilene Cooper, review of *Tiny Toes,* p. 1427; June 1, 2000, Ilene Cooper, review of *Goldilocks and the Three Bears,* p. 1901; July, 2001, Hazel Rochman, review of *An Island in the Soup,* p. 2019; January 1, 2003, Helen Rosenberg, review of *Tina and the Penguin,* p. 905; March 15, 2003, Gillian Engberg, review of *Lucy's Secret,* p. 1308; October 15, 2008, Patricia Austin, review of *The Princess Who Had Almost Everything,* p. 48.

Canadian Review of Materials, June 13, 2008, Gregory Bryan, review of *The Princess Who Had Almost Everything;* December 5, 2008, Gregory Bryan, review of *A Wizard in Love.*

Globe and Mail (Toronto, Ontario, Canada), November 9, 2002, Susan Perren, review of *Tina and the Penguin;* May 8, 2004, Susan Perren, review of *Lucy's Secret,* p. D19; October 22, 2005, Susan Perren, review of *Eddie Longpants,* p. D22; November 22, 2008, Susan Perren, review of *The Princess Who Had Almost Everything,* p. D14; June 6, 2009, Susan Perren, review of *A Wizard in Love,* p. F11.

Kirkus Reviews, August 15, 2002, review of *Tina and the Penguin,* p. 1222; August 15, 2005, review of *Eddie Longpants,* p. 918; September 15, 2008, review of *The Princess Who Had Almost Everything;* February 1, 2009, review of *Tulip and Lupin Forever.*

Publishers Weekly, April 17, 1995, review of *Tiny Toes,* p. 56; August 26, 2002, review of *Tina and the Penguin,* p. 67; December 12, 2005, review of *Eddie Longpants,* p. 65; February 9, 2009, review of *Tulip and Lupin Forever,* p. 48; February 23, 2009, review of *A Wizard in Love,* p. 49.

Quill & Quire, April, 1997, Fred Boer, review of "Molly Bear" series; April, 2001, Sherie Posesorski, review of *An Island in the Soup;* March, 2004, Bridget Donald, review of *Lucy's Secret;* December, 2007, Greg Brown, review of *Down at the Sea Hotel: a Greg Brown Song;* May, 2009, Chelsea Donaldson, review of *Tulip and Lupin Forever.*

Resource Links, December, 1998, Susan Leppington, review of *Rose by Night,* p. 4; February, 1999, Lisa Curnoe, reviews of *Molly Draws* and *Molly Counts,* pp. 3-4; October, 2004, Denise Parrott, review of *Lucy's Secret,* p. 6; February, 2006, Anna S. Rinaldis, review of *Eddie Longpants,* p. 6.

School Library Journal, June, 2001, Maryann H. Owen, review of *An Island in the Soup,* p. 122; April, 2004, Rachel G. Payne, review of *Lucy's Secret,* p. 118; January, 2009, Linda M. Kenton, review of *The Princess Who Had Almost Everything,* p. 78.

ONLINE

Annick Press Web site, http://www.annickpress.com/ (January 10, 2009), "Mireille Levert."

Kids Can Press Web site, http://www.kidscanpress.com/ (January 10, 2010), "Mireille Levert."*

* * *

LEVINSON, Nancy Smiler 1938-

Personal

Born November 5, 1938, in Minneapolis, MN; daughter of Paul (an attorney) and Minnie Smiler; married Irwin Levinson (a cardiologist), June 1, 1966; children: Matthew, Danny. *Education:* University of Minnesota, B.A., 1960. *Politics:* Democrat. *Religion:* Jewish. *Hobbies and other interests:* Reading, attending theater and symphonies.

Addresses

Home—Beverly Hills, CA. *E-mail*—nancy@nancysmilerlevinson.com; bookwag@aol.com.

Career

Author and editor. *Port Chester Daily Item,* Westchester, NY, reporter, 1960-61; Columbia University Language Laboratory, New York, NY, office worker, 1961-62; *Time* magazine, New York, NY, researcher, 1962-63; Bantam Books, Inc., New York, NY, associate editor, 1963-66; Head Start Program, Los Angeles, CA, teacher, 1967-68; freelance writer and editor, 1974—. Tutor of disabled children.

Member

Society of Children's Book Writers and Illustrators, Southern California Council on Literature for Children and Young People, Friends of Children and Literature.

Awards, Honors

Best Books for the Teen Age selection, New York Public Library, 1987, for *Getting High in Natural Ways,* and 2001, for *Magellan and the First Voyage around*

Nancy Smiler Levinson (Reproduced by permission.)

the World; Susan B. Anthony Community Award for Cultural Achievement, 1987; Distinguished Work of Nonfiction citations, Southern California Council on Literature for Children and Young People, 1987, for *I Lift My Lamp,* 1991, for *Christopher Columbus,* and 1993, for *Snowshoe Thompson.*

Writings

JUVENILE FICTION

World of Her Own, illustrated by Gene Feller, Harvey House (New York, NY), 1981, published as *Annie's World,* Gallaudet University Press (Washington, DC), 1990.

Silent Fear, illustrated by Paul Furan, Crestwood (Mankato, MN), 1981.

Make a Wish, Scholastic, Inc. (New York, NY), 1983.

The Ruthie Greene Show, Lodestar Books (New York, NY), 1985.

Second Chances (part of "Sweet Dreams" series), Bantam (New York, NY), 1985.

Clara and the Bookwagon, illustrations by Carolyn Croll, Harper (New York, NY), 1988.

Your Friend, Natalie Popper, Lodestar (New York, NY), 1991.

Snowshoe Thompson, illustrated by Joan Sandin, Harper-Collins (New York, NY), 1992.

Sweet Notes, Sour Notes, illustrated by Beth Peck, Lodestar Books (New York, NY), 1993.

Say Cheese!, illustrated by Valeria Petrone, Golden Books (New York, NY), 2000.

Prairie Friends, illustrated by Stacey Schuett, HarperCollins (New York, NY), 2003.

JUVENILE NONFICTION

Contributions of Women: Business (biography), Dillon (New York, NY), 1981.

The First Women Who Spoke Out (biography), Dillon (New York, NY), 1983.

(With Joanne Rocklin) *Getting High in Natural Ways: An Infobook for Young People of All Ages,* Hunter House (Claremont, CA), 1986, revised edition published as *Feeling Great: Reaching out to Life, Reaching in to Yourself—Without Drugs,* 1992.

I Lift My Lamp: Emma Lazarus and the Statue of Liberty, Lodestar Books (New York, NY), 1986.

Chuck Yeager: The Man Who Broke the Sound Barrier, Walker (New York, NY), 1988.

Christopher Columbus: Voyager to the Unknown, Lodestar Books (New York, NY), 1990.

Turn of the Century: Our Nation One Hundred Years Ago, Lodestar Books (New York, NY), 1994.

Thomas Alva Edison, Great Inventor, Scholastic, Inc. (New York, NY), 1996.

She's Been Working on the Railroad, Lodestar Books (New York, NY), 1997.

Death Valley: A Day in the Desert, illustrated by Diane Dawson Hearn, Holiday House (New York, NY), 2001.

Magellan and the First Voyage around the World, Clarion Books (New York, NY), 2001.

North Pole, South Pole, illustrated by Diane Dawson Hearn, Holiday House (New York, NY), 2002.

Cars, illustrated by Jacqueline Rogers, Holiday House (New York, NY), 2004.

Rain Forests, illustrated by Diane Dawson Hearn, Holiday House (New York, NY), 2008.

OTHER

Contributor of articles and stories to adult and children's magazines and newspapers, including *Seventeen, American Girl, Highlights for Children, Writer's Digest, Confrontation, Teen, Newsday, Library Journal, Los Angeles Times* "Reading Room" page, and *Los Angeles Herald Examiner.*

Sidelights

Nancy Smiler Levinson has been praised by critics for her finely crafted works of nonfiction, including *Death Valley: A Day in the Desert* and *Rainforests.* Levinson has earned special recognition for her biographies of

explorers and record breakers, including Christopher Columbus, Ferdinand Magellan, and Chuck Yeager, as well as the precursors of the feminist movement. Her well-received fictional works, such as *Clara and the Bookwagon* and *Prairie Friends,* have also garnered praise for their thoroughly researched historical contexts. "Writing for young readers is the most joyful and challenging work I have ever done," the author noted on her home page.

In *World of Her Own,* which a *Booklist* reviewer called "involving," sixteen-year-old Annie Meredith struggles to get along in public high school after attending private school for many years. Like most new students, Annie feels alienated. However, she must also deal with the school's lack of teachers willing to assist her as a partially deaf person. Some students also tease her, while others befriend her, and things eventually improve to the point that Annie even find romance. Reviewing the book's 1991 version, titled *Annie's World,* Roger Sutton wrote in *Bulletin of the Center for Children's Books* that the girl's experiences are "satisfyingly played out" in the novel while Sharron Freeman described Levinson's story as "simplistic" yet "interesting" in her *Voice of Youth Advocates* review. As Levinson once told *SATA* regarding *World of Her Own,* "It is my hope that the book's readers will become sensitive to the pain and problems of the lone young person across the classroom—and reach out."

First published as *Getting High in Natural Ways: An Infobook for Young People of All Ages,* the nonfiction title *Feeling Great: Reaching out to Life, Reaching in to Yourself—Without Drugs* allows Levinson and coauthor Joanne Rocklin to share with young people a variety of drug-free ways to feel good. According to a *Kliatt* contributor, the coauthors provide "clear but not patronizing" explanations about the benefits of various activities. Exercising, meditating, competing, writing in a journal, laughing, listening to music, and even walking on the beach are the alternatives included in what *Booklist* critic Stephanie Zvirin called a "low-key but sensible" work.

Levinson turns to history in some of her more recent novels. In what *School Library Journal* contributor Susan Pine called a "very sweet and sentimental story of a Jewish family in the 1920s," *Sweet Notes, Sour Notes* is enhanced by the author's attention to historical detail. Here, fourth-grader David pursues his latest ambition—to make the violin "sing" like the concert violinist he watched with his grandfather. David finally begins to play well enough to entertain his grandfather when the elderly man becomes bedridden. Along with learning to play the violin, as Emily Melton remarked in *Booklist,* David learns "important" lessons "about persistence, talent, hard work, and love." Writing in *Publishers Weekly,* a critic praised *Sweet Notes, Sour Notes* as "believable and genuinely beguiling."

In *Your Friend, Natalie Popper* Natalie confronts issues such as the aftermath of World War II, a polio outbreak,

and anti-Semitism while attending summer camp in 1946. In the opinion of *School Library Journal* contributor Joyce Adams Burner, while some details are "heavyhanded" and some characters "stereotypes," Levinson's novel "moves along quickly, and . . . [the author] shows insight and compassion" in her description of young friendships. Several other commentators praised *Your Friend, Natalie Popper* as well, *Five Owls* critic Norine Odland citing Levinson's "uncomplicated" and easy-to-read prose and *Bulletin of the Center for Children's Books* reviewer Zena Sutherland noting how the use of historical details "add[s] substance to the smoothly written story." In *Voice of Youth Advocates,* Rachel Gonsenhauser described *Your Friend, Natalie Popper* as a "very readable" coming-of-age story and recommended the book "highly."

Levinson's stories for younger readers include *Snowshoe Thompson,* which Roger Sutton described in *Bulletin of the Center for Children's Books* as "a satisfying blend of heartache . . . and action" and a *Kirkus Reviews* critic dubbed "an interesting vignette from the past." Through the voice of its young narrator, *Snowshoe Thompson* tells the story of one of the Scandinavian immigrants who brought skiing to Northern California. When Danny has trouble getting a letter to his father because of the deep snow, John "Snowshoe" Thompson saves the day by crafting a pair of skis, getting Danny's letter to his father, and even bringing back a note in return. "Don't miss this warm bit of historical fiction set in a cold, forbidding climate," advised Gale W. Sherman in a *School Library Journal* review of Levinson's book.

In *Clara and the Bookwagon* a farmer tells his young daughter, Clara, that she cannot stop at the local book station because books are only for the rich. When Clara befriends a woman with a wagonload of books, her father relents and is soon persuaded to let her borrow books and read them. Although Clara and her father are fictional, the character of the wagon woman is based on Mary Lemist Titcomb, the early twentieth-century librarian who drove the first bookmobile in the United States. In *Booklist* Ilene Cooper praised Levinson's ability to explain complex concepts to younger readers, while *School Library Journal* contributor Hayden E. Atwood called the "well-written" story is "a good example of historical fiction for the very young." In her *Bulletin of the Center for Children's Books* review, Betsy Hearne likewise recommended the book, calling *Clara and the Bookwagon* "one of those books you want to put in every six-year-old's hands."

In *Prairie Friends,* another work of historical fiction, Levinson offers a tale of friendship. Set on the Nebraska prairie in the mid-1800s, the work concerns young Betsy, a lonely pioneer girl who longs for a friend. When the Fitzroys move to the area from the city, Betsy learns that they have a daughter her age, and she excitedly prepares a cornhusk doll for her new neighbor. After she presents her gift to Emmeline, how-

ever, the newcomer accepts it without much enthusiasm. Although she is disappointed, Betsy vows to help the obviously homesick Emmeline learn to appreciate rural life. "Levinson evokes prairie life with a few well-chosen details," Marilyn Taniguchi commented in *School Library Journal.*

Levinson ventures into biography with *The First Women Who Spoke Out,* a profile of women considered to be precursors of the modern women's movement, such as Sarah and Angelina Grimke, Lucretia Mott, Sojourner Truth, Elizabeth Cady Stanton, and Lucy Stone. Writing in *Voice of Youth Advocates,* Kay Ann Cassell concluded that "Levinson's lively style makes this a very interesting and appealing book." In *Booklist* Ilene Cooper applauded Levinson's "enlightening first look" at feminist leaders, adding that each life story is told "concisely" and "clearly."

Another work about a well-known early twentieth-century American, *I Lift My Lamp: Emma Lazarus and the Statue of Liberty,* recalls the life of the woman who wrote the lines inscribed at the base of the Statue of Liberty: "Give me your tired, your poor, /Your huddled masses yearning to breathe free." Part of the "Jewish Biography" series, Levinson's biography/history includes information on Jewish immigration and the building of the statue as well as details of Lazarus's life. Lazarus was born to a prominent Jewish family, and that her poetry did not gain its passionate quality until she understood the suffering of Jewish immigrants. Among the many books published to honor the statue's centennial, *I Lift My Lamp* was singled out for praise. In *Kirkus Reviews,* a contributor called Leinson's book "well-written" and "fact-filled," while in *Horn Book,* Elizabeth S. Watson described the book as an "interesting" combination of history and biography. "Like the statue," concluded a *Publishers Weekly* reviewer, Levinson's "book is stirring."

Levinson's interest in social history comes through in such titles as *Turn of the Century: Our Nation One Hundred Years Ago* and *She's Been Working on the Railroad.* In the former, the author describes the later decades of the 1800s and the early 1900s, focusing on societal changes and life among the ordinary people, a treatment that Elizabeth Bush termed "refreshing" in her *Bulletin of the Center for Children's Literature* review. In this "fascinating look back," wrote Elizabeth S. Watson in *Horn Book,* Levinson discusses such aspects as communication and transportation, changes from agrarian to urban lifestyles, and the conditions among industrialists, immigrants, Native Americans, and African Americans. In the same vein, *She's Been Working on the Railroad* portrays the varied jobs that women held and the prejudice they suffered while working for the railroads in the mid-1800s. Levinson's book "makes interesting reading," wrote Carolyn Phelan in a *Booklist* review of *She's Been Working on the Railroad.*

Several of Levinson's books focus on explorers and pioneers in their fields. For instance, in *Chuck Yeager:*

The Man Who Broke the Sound Barrier, she draws readers into Yeager's life as a child, teen, World War II and Vietnam fighter pilot, and test pilot. *School Library Journal* contributor Eldon Younce praised *Chuck Yeager* for its "fresh, crisp, and fast-moving" prose, while a *Kirkus Reviews* critic noted that Levinson "does a good job of explaining why Yeager is famous." Marc K. Torrey commented in *Voice of Youth Advocates* that in *Chuck Yeager* Levinson "captures the excitement of Yeager's most spectacular adventures."

In reviewing *Christopher Columbus: Voyager to the Unknown* Jean H. Zimmerman wrote in *School Library Journal* that Levinson "incorporates recent scholarship and presents Columbus' character in an objective way," producing an "eminently readable" work. In a review of *Magellan and the First Voyage around the World, Horn Book* critic Mary M. Burns found the "clarity" of Levinson's text to be a strength of this "businesslike biography," and in *Booklist* Phelan termed it a "well-designed," "useful," and "interesting" biography of the Portuguese navigator. Writing in *School Library Journal,* Kim Donius appreciated the work as well, describing *Magellan and the First Voyage around the World* as an "unbiased and insightful biography," while a *Kirkus Reviews* critic concluded that Levinson's "thoughful study" clearly explains Magellan's historical importance.

Levinson has written several nonfiction titles for younger children, among them *Death Valley,* which looks at the flora and fauna of the national park in California. Writing in *Booklist,* Cooper described *Death Valley* as a "very nice presentation." Levinson explores the geography, climate, and wildlife of the northernmost and southernmost points on the globe in *North Pole, South Pole.* Using simple vocabulary and short sentences, she explains concepts such as the Earth's axis of rotation and the northern lights. Levinson's narrative "works well to distinguish the two areas as very different, while still sharing some common features," noted a critic in *Kirkus Reviews.* In *Rain Forests* readers are introduced to another type of ecosystem, and here Levinson's text "will serve equally well to inform and to entertain," as a contributor in *Kirkus Reviews* remarked. Levinson surveys both tropical rainforests, as found in the Congo Basin, Tasmania, and Costa Rica, for example, and temperate rainforests, and she introduces the plants and animals that live in each region. According to Phelan, *Rain Forests* "provides a good, basic introduction to the subject for young readers."

Levinson focuses on the development of the automobile industry in *Cars,* a work "full of fascinating details," according to a *Kirkus Reviews* contributor. After presenting an overview of the first "horseless carriages," including models by Karl Benz, Gottlieb Daimler, and Charles and Frank Duryea, Levinson discusses the concept of the assembly line that was made famous by Henry Ford, as well as the experiences of early drivers. The author also explores the many ways cars have af-

Levinson teams up with artist Diane Dawson Hearn to treat readers to a day in the desert in **Death Valley.**

fected modern society and the environment, for good or ill. *Cars* "presents a good introduction to the subject in a short text," according to Phelan.

Discussing her literary career in a *California Readers* interview with Ann Stalcup, Levinson remarked: "Since I write both fiction and nonfiction, I am asked which I like best, and my answer is always 'Both.' In fiction, it is rewarding to find that I can draw readers into caring about my characters and connecting with what they are experiencing and feeling. I enjoy researching and writing nonfiction because when something particularly interests me, such as an historical event or a person's biography, I have a strong urge to share the story."

Biographical and Critical Sources

PERIODICALS

Booklist, January 15, 1982, review of *World of Her Own,* p. 644; April 1, 1983, review of *Silent Fear,* p. 1022; June 1, 1983, Ilene Cooper, review of *The First*

Women Who Spoke Out, p. 1277; October 1, 1986, Stephanie Zvirin, review of *Getting High in Natural Ways: An Infobook for Young People of All Ages,* p. 214; April 1, 1988, Ilene Cooper, review of *Clara and the Bookwagon,* p. 1355; March 15, 1991, review of *Christopher Columbus: Voyager to the Unknown,* p. 1488; April 15, 1993, Emily Melton, review of *Sweet Notes, Sour Notes,* p. 1515; September 15, 1997, Carolyn Phelan, review of *She's Been Working on the Railroad,* pp. 228-229; April 15, 2001, Ilene Cooper, review of *Death Valley: A Day in the Desert,* p. 1568; February 1, 2002, Carolyn Phelan, review of *Magellan and the First Voyage around the World,* p. 935; January 1, 2003, Lauren Peterson, review of *Prairie Friends,* p. 891; November 15, 2004, Carolyn Phelan, review of *Cars,* p. 588; May 1, 2008, Carolyn Phelan, review of *Rain Forests,* p. 92.

Book Report, March-April, 1995, Marjorie Stumpf, review of *Turn of the Century: Our Nation One Hundred Years Ago,* p. 50.

Bulletin of the Center for Children's Books, January, 1986, review of *The Ruthie Greene Show,* p. 90; February, 1988, Betsy Hearne, review of *Clara and the Bookwagon,* p. 120; July, 1990, Roger Sutton, review of

Annie's World, p. 271; February, 1991, Zena Sutherland, review of *Your Friend, Natalie Popper,* p. 146; February, 1992, Roger Sutton, review of *Snowshoe Thompson,* pp. 160-161; January, 1995, Elizabeth Bush, review of *Turn of the Century,* p. 171; January, 1998, Elizabeth Bush, review of *She's Been Working on the Railroad,* pp. 163-164.

Children's Book Review Service, winter, 1982, review of *World of Her Own,* p. 58; May, 1983, review of *The First Women Who Spoke Out,* p. 103; January, 1986, review of *The Ruthie Greene Show,* p. 56; July, 1988, review of *Chuck Yeager: The Man Who Broke the Sound Barrier,* p. 147.

Five Owls, March, 1991, Norine Odland, review of *Your Friend, Natalie Popper,* p. 77.

Horn Book, May, 1986, Elizabeth S. Watson, review of *I Lift My Lamp: Emma Lazarus and the Statue of Liberty,* pp. 339-340; March, 1992, Michael O. Tunnell, "Books in the Classroom: Columbus and Historical Perspective," pp. 244-247; March, 1995, Elizabeth S. Watson, review of *Turn of the Century,* pp. 215-216; January-February, 2002, Mary M. Burns, review of *Magellan and the First Voyage around the World,* p. 102.

Kirkus Reviews, June 1, 1986, review of *I Lift My Lamp,* pp. 873-874; March 15, 1988, review of *Chuck Yeager,* p. 457; April 1, 1988, review of *Clara and the Bookwagon,* p. 541; December 15, 1991, review of *Snowshoe Thompson,* p. 1594; March 15, 2001, review of *Death Valley,* pp. 413-414; October 15, 2001, review of *Magellan and the First Voyage around the World,* p. 1487; November 15, 2002, review of *North Pole, South Pole,* p. 1696; February 1, 2003, review of *Prairie Friends,* p. 235; September 1, 2004, review of *Cars,* p. 870; March 1, 2008, review of *Rain Forests.*

Kliatt, fall, 1986, review of *Getting High in Natural Ways,* p. 47.

Language Arts, September, 1993, Miriam Martinez and Marcia F. Nash, review of *Snowshoe Thompson,* p. 420.

Publishers Weekly, March 21, 1986, review of *I Lift My Lamp,* p. 92; November 28, 1986, review of *Getting High in Natural Ways,* p. 80; June 14, 1993, review of *Sweet Notes, Sour Notes,* p. 71; November 19, 2001, review of *Magellan and the First Voyage around the World,* p. 69.

School Library Journal, August, 1981, Blair Christolon, review of *Business,* p. 76; March, 1982, review of *Silent Fear,* pp. 158-159; January, 1986, Virginia Opocensky, review of *The Ruthie Greene Show,* p. 74; January, 1986, review of *Second Chances,* p. 81; May, 1986, Ruth Shire, review of *I Lift My Lamp,* p. 94; May, 1988, Eldon Younce, review of *Chuck Yeager,* pp. 102-103; June, 1988, Hayden E. Atwood, review of *Clara and the Bookwagon,* p. 92; June, 1990, Jean H. Zimmerman, review of *Christopher Columbus,* p. 132; March, 1991, Joyce Adams Burner, review of *Your Friend, Natalie Popper,* p. 193; January, 1992, Gale W. Sherman, review of *Snowshoe Thompson,* p. 104; August, 1993, Susan Pine, review of *Sweet Notes, Sour Notes,* p. 164; December, 1994, Kellie Flynn, review of *Turn of the Century,* p. 136; December, 1997, Rebecca O'Connell, review of *She's Been Working on the Railroad,* p. 140; April, 2001, John Sigwald, review of *Death Valley,* p. 132; January, 2002, Kim Dorius, review of *Magellan and the First Voyage around the World,* p. 161; December, 2002, Blair Christolon, review of *North Pole, South Pole,* p. 126; March, 2003, Marilyn Taniguchi, review of *Prairie Friends,* p. 198; December, 2004, Tana Elias, review of *Cars,* p. 134; May, 2008, Kathy Piehl, review of *Rain Forests,* p. 116.

Stone Soup, January, 1999, Miranda Miller, review of *She's Been Working on the Railroad,* p. 14.

Voice of Youth Advocates, February, 1982, Sharron Freeman, review of *A World of Her Own,* p. 35; August, 1983, Kay Ann Cassell, review of *The First Women Who Spoke Out,* p. 154; August, 1988, Marc K. Torrey, review of *Chuck Yeager,* pp. 147-148; April, 1991, Rachel Gonsenhauser, review of *Your Friend, Natalie Popper,* p. 32.

ONLINE

California Readers Web site, http://www.californiareaders. org/ (January 1, 2010), Ann Stalcup, "Meet Nancy Smiler Levinson.

Nancy Smiler Levinson Home Page, http://www.nancysmilerlevinson.com (January 1, 2010).

*   *   *

LEWIS, Earl Bradley
See LEWIS, E.B.

*   *   *

LEWIS, E.B. 1956-
(Earl Bradley Lewis)

Personal

Born December 16, 1956, in Philadelphia, PA. *Education:* Attended Tyler School of Art, Temple University.

Addresses

Home—Hammonton, NJ. *Agent*—Dwyer & O'Grady Inc., P.O. Box 239, E. Lempster, NH 03605. *E-mail*—eblewis@eticomm.net.

Career

Artist and illustrator. Teacher in public schools for twelve years; University of the Arts, Philadelphia, PA, currently instructor in illustration. *Exhibitions:* Work included in permanent collection of Pew Charitable Trust.

Member

Society of Illustrators, Philadelphia Water Club Society.

Awards, Honors

Notable Book selection, American Library Association, 1996, for *Down the Road* by Alice Schertle; Notable Books for the Language Arts citation, 2002, for *The Other Side;* Coretta Scott King Award, 2003, for *Talkin' about Bessie,* by Nikki Grimes; Caldecott Honor Book, 2005, for *Coming on Home Soon* by Jacqueline Woodson.

Illustrator

Jane Kurtz, *Fire on the Mountain,* Simon & Schuster (New York, NY), 1993.

Doreen Rappaport, *The New King,* Dial (New York, NY), 1994.

Tololwa M. Mollel, *Big Boy,* Clarion Books (New York, NY), 1994.

Alice Schertle, *Down the Road,* Harcourt (San Diego, CA), 1994.

Dakari Hru, *The Magic Moonberry Jump Ropes,* Dial (New York, NY), 1995.

Mary Matthews, *Magid Fasts for Ramadan,* Clarion (New York, NY), 1995.

Jane Kurtz and Christopher Kurtz, *Only a Pigeon,* Simon & Schuster (New York, NY), 1995.

Nancy Antle, *Champions,* Dial (New York, NY), 1997.

Nancy Antle, *Staying Cool,* Dial (New York, NY), 1997.

Natasha Anastasia Tarpley, *I Love My Hair!,* Little, Brown (Boston, MA), 1997.

John Steptoe, *Creativity,* Clarion (New York, NY), 1997.

Gavin Curtis, *The Bat Boy and His Violin,* Simon & Schuster (New York, NY), 1998.

Fatima Shaik, *The Jazz of Our Street,* Dial (New York, NY), 1998.

Clifton L. Taulbert, *Little Cliff and the Porch People,* Dial (New York, NY), 1999.

T. Obinkaram Echewa, *The Magic Tree: A Folktale from Nigeria,* Morrow Junior Books (New York, NY), 1999.

Elizabeth Fitzgerald Howard, *Virgie Goes to School with Us Boys,* Simon & Schuster (New York, NY), 1999.

Tololwa M. Mollel, *My Rows and Piles of Coins,* Clarion (New York, NY), 1999.

Lucille Clifton, *The Times They Used to Be,* Doubleday (New York, NY), 2000.

Jane Kurtz, *Faraway Home,* Harcourt (San Diego, CA), 2000.

Doreen Rappaport and Lyndall Callan, *Dirt on Their Skirts: The Story of the Young Women Who Won the World Championship,* Dial (New York, NY), 2000.

Clifton L. Taulbert, *Little Cliff's First Day of School,* Dial (New York, NY), 2001.

Jacqueline Woodson, *The Other Side,* Putnam (New York, NY), 2001.

Natasha Anastasia Tarpley, *Bippity Bop Barbershop,* Little, Brown (Boston, MA), 2002.

Clifton L. Taulbert, *Little Cliff and the Cold Place,* Dial (New York, NY), 2002.

Nikki Grimes, *Talkin' about Bessie: The Story of Aviator Elizabeth Coleman,* Orchard (New York, NY), 2002.

Bebe Moore Campbell, *Sometimes My Mommy Gets Angry,* Putnam (New York, NY), 2003.

Natasha Anastasia Tarpley, *Joe-Joe's First Flight,* Knopf (New York, NY), 2003.

Dianna Hutts Aston, *When You Were Born,* Candlewick (Cambridge, MA), 2004.

Jacqueline Woodson, *Coming on Home Soon,* Putnam (New York, NY), 2004.

Margot Theis Raven, *Circle Unbroken: The Story of a Basket and Its People,* Farrar, Straus (New York, NY), 2004.

Mary Ann Rodman, *My Best Friend,* Viking (New York, NY), 2005.

Nikki Grimes, *Danitra Brown, Class Clown,* HarperCollins (New York, NY), 2005.

This Little Light of Mine, Simon & Schuster (New York, NY), 2005.

Richard Michelson, *Happy Feet: The Savoy Ballroom Lindy Hoppers and Me,* Gulliver (Orlando, FL), 2005.

Margot Theis Raven, *Christmas John and the Night Boat,* Farrar Straus (New York, NY), 2006.

Angela Johnson, *Lily Brown's Paintings,* Orchard (New York, NY), 2006.

Elisa Lynn Carbone, *Night Running: How James Escaped with the Help of His Faithful Dog,* Knopf (New York, NY), 2007.

Nancy I. Sanders, *D Is for Drinking Gourd: An African American Alphabet,* Sleeping Bear Press (Chelsea, MI), 2007.

Jerdine Nolen, *Pitching in for Eubie,* Amistad (New York, NY), 2007.

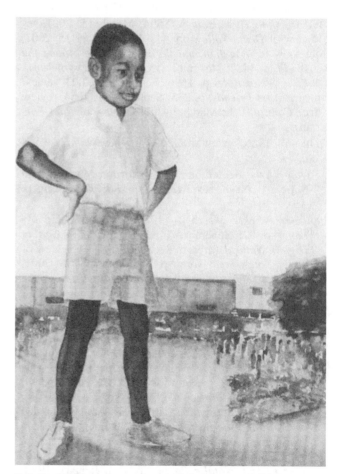

E.B. Lewis's illustration projects include his artwork for Tololwa M. Mollel's African-themed picture book **Big Boy.** (Illustration copyright © 1995 by E.B. Lewis. All rights reserved. Reprinted by permission of Clarion Books, an imprint of Houghton Mifflin Publishing Company.)

Trinka Hakes Noble, *The Legend of the Cape May Diamond,* Sleeping Bear Press (Chelsea, MI), 2007.

Hope Anita Smith, *Keeping the Night Watch,* Henry Holt (New York, NY), 2008.

Janet S. Wong, *Homegrown House,* Margaret K. McElderry Books (New York, NY), 2009.

Joseph Slate, *I Want to Be Free,* G.P. Putnam's Sons (New York, NY), 2009.

Geoffrey Norman, *Stars on the Ceiling,* G.P. Putnam's Sons (New York, NY), 2009.

Hester Bass, *The Secret World of Walter Anderson,* Candlewick Press (Cambridge, MA), 2009.

Robert D. San Souci, *Robin Hood and the Golden Arrow,* Orchard Books (New York, NY), 2010.

Sidelights

The work of award-winning illustrator E.B. Lewis has been praised for its depiction of light, as well as its color and detail. A popular illustrator whose awards include both a Caldecott Honor and the Coretta Scott King award, Lewis creates paintings that have enriched such picture books as Nikki Grimes' *Talkin' about Bessie: The Story of Aviator Elizabeth Coleman,* Jacqueline Woodson's *Coming on Home Soon* Joseph Slate's *I Want to Be Free,* and Janet S. Wong's *Homegrown House.* For Lewis, his achievement is as much a product of his strong work ethic as it is an outgrowth of his natural talent. It is also a love of the planning and the actual painting. "I have a love of the process, the doing," Lewis once noted. "For me, that's all there is."

For Lewis, a strong work ethic was something that took time to develop. A self-confessed class clown who flunked out of third grade, he began to reassess his strategy for success during sixth grade, at an assembly at his Philadelphia public school. At the close of his talk, a lecturer asked students in the auditorium what they planned to be when they grew up. When Lewis stood up and proclaimed that he intended to be a lawyer, his friends and teachers started laughing.

Determined to make something of his life, Lewis enrolled in Temple University's Tyler School of Art, majoring in graphic design and illustration while also studying art education. After graduation, he taught art in public schools while also developing a design practice and working at his true calling: fine-art painting. By the mid-1980s Lewis's watercolor paintings could be found in galleries as well as in private and corporate collections.

Although Lewis was not originally enthusiastic about book illustration, the prodding of an editor convinced him to take on his first assignment: creating art for Jane Kurtz's picture book *Fire on the Mountain.* Published in 1993, the book was praised by *School Library Journal* contributor Jos N. Holman, who wrote that Lewis's watercolors "captur[e] . . . the warmth and simplicity of the tale" and "bring the story to life, complementing the emotion, expression, and character of the printed words."

Lewis's skill in capturing strong African-American characters adds to Joseph Slate's story in **I Want to Be Free.** (Illustration copyright © 2009 by E.B. Lewis. Reproduced by permission of G.P. Putnam's Sons, a division of Penguin Putnam Books for Young Readers.)

Finding a sense of accomplishment in the book illustration process, which involves working with editors and authors as well as planning, Lewis has devoted much of his time since to creating illustrations for a range of children's books, including texts by such noted authors as Tololwa M. Mollel, Alice Schertle, Trinka Hakes Noble, and Lucille Clifton. His artwork for Mollel's *Big Boy* was received with typical enthusiasm by reviewers, among whom a *Publishers Weekly* commentator asserted: "Mollel's story is an engaging fantasy for little ones with big aspirations, but it is Lewis's crisp, understated watercolors that steal the show."

Talkin' about Bessie won Lewis the 2003 Coretta Scott King award for illustration. Relating the story of the African-American aviator who is noted for being the first woman of color to become a licensed pilot, Grimes's text is accompanied by "painterly illustrations" that "deepen" the story, according to Ellen Feldman in her *New York Times* review. "Lewis' paintings, subdued in tone and color, reflect the spirit of the verse through telling details and sensitive, impressionistic portrayals," wrote Carolyn Phelan in *Booklist,* while Harriett Fargnoli noted in *School Library Journal* that the work is "well conceived, well-executed, [and] handsomely illustrated."

Many of Lewis's works, particularly his illustrations depicting earlier periods in history, have won him praise from critics. Of the illustrations he created for Natasha Anastasia Tarpley's *Joe-Joe's First Flight,* which is set in 1922, *New York Times* contributor Daniel B. Schneider wrote that, "rich in period detail, yet slightly blurred and indistinct, as though traced from weathered old photographs," the artwork is "exquisitely well suited to the story." Marianne Saccardi, reviewing the same title for *School Library Journal,* noted that "Lewis's large watercolor paintings capture the flavor of this period."

Michael Cart, writing in *Booklist,* noted that Lewis's "warm watercolors . . . catch the affectionate spirit" of Clifton L. Taulbert's *Little Cliff and the Cold Place,* a picture book set in the 1950s. Lewis moves a decade ahead in illustrating *My Rows and Piles of Coins,* Mollel's picture book set in Tanzania during the 1960s. Grace Oliff, writing in *School Library Journal,* wrote that Lewis's "watercolor paintings authentically depict Tanzanian village life" during that period. In 2005 Lewis was awarded a Caldecott Honor Medal for his work on *Coming on Home Soon,* a story by Woodson that is set during World War II.

For Elisa Carbone's *Night Running: How James Escaped with the Help of His Faithful Dog,* Lewis's art transports readers to 1838 as a young slave named

James and his dog Zeus run away from a farm in West Virginia and head north to freedom. The book's illustrations "beautifully evoke" the rural setting of Carbone's tale, and also "bring James to life and convey Zeus's devotion to his owner," asserted *School Library Journal* contributor Carolyn Janssen. According to *Horn Book* writer Susan Dove Lempke, the artwork for *Night Running* is characteristic Lewis. "As always," the artist's "watercolors tenderly depict the people with the same beauty and verisimilitude as the nature surrounding them," Lempke wrote, while a *Publishers Weekly* critic praised Lewis's "dramatically illuminated" paintings for effectively "highlight[ing] the characters' peril." Describing another illustration project, Joseph Slate's *I Want to Be Free,* Hazel Rochman noted in *Booklist* that Slate's "powerful" story about a runaway slave's lust for freedom features "unforgettable" images by Lewis, and a *Publishers Weekly* contributor cited the book's "extraordinarily accomplished watercolors."

In addition to bringing to life the past, Lewis illustrates many books with contemporary settings. *When You Were Born* shows a family and neighbors welcoming a new baby, and in reviewing this work Sally R. Dow commented in *School Library Journal* that Lewis's "eye-catching images" for the book "are sophisticated yet childlike." Lewis used the text for the African-American spiritual "This Little Light of Mine" for his book of the same title. Focusing on one young boy's cheerful disposition as the light in the song, the book's art serves as an "evocative interpretation," according to a *Kirkus Reviews* contributor. Lewis has collaborated on several fictional stories with Grimes, including their *Danitra Brown, Class Clown,* which is set in a present-day classroom, while *My Best Friend,* written by Mary Ann Rodman, is a another modern story of friendship. He continues to illustrate titles, both modern and period, for such authors as Margo Theis Raven, Angela Johnson, and Jerdine Nolan.

When Lewis began his career as an artist, he did not expect to illustrate children's books; in fact, he turned down an illustration contract before rethinking his career path. "Some of the best artwork in the country is being done in children's books," the artist asserted to Kevin Riordan for the South Jersey *Courier-Post.* On his home page, Lewis described the types of books he chooses to illustrate: "I like the strong human interest stories," he wrote, "the kind that evoke emotion . . . stories that touch the heart."

Lewis teams up with author Doreen Rappaport to present a chapter from the history of women's sports in **Dirt on Their Skirts.** (Illustration copyright © 2000 by E.B. Lewis. Used by permission of Dial Books for Young Readers, a division of Penguin Young Readers Group, a member of Penguin Group (USA) Inc., 345 Hudson St., New York, NY 10014. All rights reserved.)

Biographical and Critical Sources

PERIODICALS

Booklist, October 15, 1994, Janice Del Negro, review of *Fire on the Mountain,* p. 432; November 1, 2002, Michael Cart, review of *Little Cliff and the Cold Place,* p. 509; November 15, 2002, Carolyn Phelan, review

Lewis captures the up-and-down energy between growing girls in his luminous illustrations for Mary Ann Rodman's **My Best Friend.** (Illustration copyright © 2005 by E.B. Lewis. Reproduced by permission of Viking, a division of Penguin Putnam Books for Young Readers.)

of *Talkin' about Bessie: The Story of Aviator Elizabeth Coleman,* p. 602; January 1, 2003, review of *Bippity Bop Barbershop,* p. 799; December 1, 2004, Hazel Rochman, review of *When You Were Born,* p. 658; October 15, 2006, Hazel Rochman, review of *Night Boat to Freedom,* p. 47; February 1, 2007, Gillian Engberg, review of *Lily Brown's Paintings,* p. 60; March 15, 2008, Hazel Rochman, review of *Keeping the Night Watch,* p. 53; December 1, 2008, Hazel Rochman, review of *I Want to Be Free,* p. 50.

Courier-Post (South Jersey, NJ), February 5, 2004, Kevin Riordan, "E.B. Lewis' Illustrations Help Bring Life to Books."

Horn Book, July-August, 2005, Michelle Martin, review of *My Best Friend,* p. 456; March-April, 2008, Susan Dove Lempke, review of *Night Running,* p. 201; July-August, 2008, Robin L. Smith, review of *Keeping the Night Watch,* p. 459.

Kirkus Reviews, October 15, 2002, review of *Talkin' about Bessie,* p. 1530; December 15, 2004, review of *This Little Light of Mine,* p. 1204; May 1, 2005, review of *My Best Friend,* p. 545; October 15, 2007, review of *Pitching in for Eubie;* March 15, 2008, review of *Keeping the Night Watch.*

Newton's Book Notes, May 19, 2005, Holly Newton, review of *This Little Light of Mine.*

New York Times, February 9, 2003, Ellen Feldman, review of *Talkin' about Bessie;* October 9, 2003, Daniel B. Schneider, review of *Joe-Joe's First Flight.*

Publishers Weekly, September, 1994, review of *Fire on the Mountain,* p. 69; January 23, 1995, review of *Big Boy,* p. 70; January 1, 2007, review of *Lily Brown's Paintings,* p. 49; November 26, 2007, review of *Pitching in for Eubie,* p. 52; December 24, 2007, review of *Night Running,* p. 55; January 19, 2009, review of *I Want to Be Free,* p. 59.

School Library Journal, December, 1994, Jos N. Holman, review of *Fire on the Mountain,* p. 99; April, 1996, p. 117; June, 2001, Marianne Saccardi, review of *Little Cliff's First Day of School,* p. 131; October, 2002, Harriett Fargnoli, review of *Talkin' about Bessie,* p. 183; July, 2003, Marianne Saccardi, review of *Joe-Joe's First Flight,* p. 108; September, 2003, Grace Oliff, review of *My Rows and Piles of Coins,* p. 85; December, 2004, Sally R. Dow, review of *When You Were Born,* p. 96; May, 2005, Catherine Threadgill, review of *My Best Friend,* p. 95; September, 2005, Mary Elam, review of *Danitra Brown, Class Clown,* p. 171; November, 2005, Nina Lindsay, review of *Happy Feet: The Savoy Ballroom Lindy Hoppers and Me,* p. 100; November, 2006, Nina Lindsay, review of *Night Boat to Freedom,* p. 109; January, 2008, Carolyn Janssen, review of *Night Running,* p. 83; January, 2009, Joan Kindig, review of *I Want to Be Free,* p. 86.

ONLINE

E.B. Lewis Home Page, http://www.eblewis.com (January 10, 2010).*

*   *   *

LITTLEWOOD, Karin

Personal

Born in Yorkshire, England. *Education:* Attended Botley Art College; earned degree from University of Northumbria; Manchester University, M.A. *Hobbies and other interests:* Canoeing, walking, cycling, gardening, travel, film.

Addresses

Home—London, England. *Office*—Courtyard Studio, Panther House, 38 Mount Pleasant, London WC1X 0AP, England. *Agent*—Eunice McMullen Children's Literary Agent Ltd., Low Ibbotsholme Cottage, Off Bridge Lane, Troutbeck Bridge, Windermere, Cumbria LA23 1HU, England. *E-mail*—karinl@btopenworld.com.

Career

Illustrator.

Awards, Honors

Children's Book Award shortlist, 2001, for *Ellie and the Butterfly Kitten;* Kate Greenaway Medal nomination, 2001, for *Swallow Journey.*

Illustrator

Ann Jungman, *Lucy and the Big Bad Wolf,* Dragon (London, England), 1986.

Ann Jungman, *Lucy and the Wolf in Sheep's Clothing,* Dragon (London, England), 1987.

How Does It Feel to Be a . . .?, illustrated by Karin Littlewood, ABC (London, England), 1993, published as *How Does It Feel?,* Thomasson-Grant (Charlottesville, VA), 1993.

Antonia Barber, *Gemma and the Baby Chick,* Scholastic, Inc. (New York, NY), 1993.

Elizabeth Morgan, *Can We Afford the Bidet?: A Guide to Setting up House in France,* Lennard (Harpenden, England), 1993.

Edward Blishen, editor, *Science Fiction Stories,* Kingfisher (New York, NY), 1993.

Althea, *Gita Gets Lost,* A. & C. Black (London, England), 1996.

Althea, *The Bullies,* A. & C. Black (London, England), 1996.

Althea, *The Birthday Party,* A. & C. Black (London, England), 1996.

Althea, *Alone at Home,* A. & C. Black (London, England), 1996.

Nicola Moon, *Billy's Sunflower,* Little Hippo (London, England), 1997.

Adèle Geras, *Sun Slices, Moon Slices,* Little Hippo (London, England), 1998.

Gillian Lobel, *Ellie and the Butterfly Kitten,* Orchard Books (London, England), 2000.

Mike Jubb, *Splosh!,* Scholastic, Inc. (London, England), 2000.

Vivian French, *Swallow Journey,* Zero to Ten (Slough, England), 2000.

Margaret Bateson Hill, *Chanda and the Mirror of Moonlight,* Zero to Ten (Slough, England), 2001.

Caroline Pitcher, *Ghost in the Glass,* Mammoth (London, England), 2001.

Kate Banks, *Mama's Little Baby,* Dorling Kindersley (New York, NY), 2001.

Mary Hoffman, *The Colour of Home,* Frances Lincoln (London, England), 2002, published as *The Color of Home,* Phyllis Fogelman Books (New York, NY), 2002.

Burt Bacharach and Hal David, *I Say a Little Prayer for You,* Chicken House (New York, NY), 2002.

Beverley Naidoo and Maya Naidoo, *Baba's Gift,* Puffin (London, England), 2004.

Sally Grindley, *Home for Christmas,* Frances Lincoln (London, England), 2004.

Helen Dunmore, *Tara's Tree House,* Egmont (London, England), 2004, Crabtree Publishing (New York, NY), 2006.

David Conway, *The Most Important Gift of All,* Gingham Dog Press (Cleveland, OH), 2006.

Kenneth Steven, *The Dragon Kite,* Tamarind Books (London, England), 2007.

Lesley Beake, *Home Now,* Charlesbridge (Watertown, MA), 2007.

Nicki Cornwell, *Christophe's Story,* Frances Lincoln (London, England), 2007.

Sidelights

British designer and illustrator Karin Littlewood has provided the artwork for more than twenty-five children's books, including *Swallow Journey,* which earned her a Kate Greenaway Medal nomination. *Swallow Journey,* written by Vivian French, follows a flock of birds as they migrate 6,000 miles from their birthplace in England to their winter home in southern Africa. "The drama is in Littlewood's double-page watercolor paintings from the swallows' viewpoint," noted *Booklist* contributor Hazel Rochman of the work.

Margaret Bateson Hill's *Chanda and the Mirror of Moonlight,* an adaptation of a Cinderella story from India, is told in both Hindi and English. The work concerns a young woman who receives a special mirror from her dying mother. When a handsome prince asks the woman to marry him, her evil stepmother tries to prevent the ceremony from happening, until the mirror reveals an important truth. Littlewood's "lavish illustrations are vivid and romantically realistic," Carol Johnson Shedd remarked in *School Library Journal.* In another multicultural work, *The Color of Home* by Mary Hoffman, a young immigrant boy who has fled his war-torn nation of Somalia faces a difficult adjustment on his first day of school in the United States. Through a painting he makes in art class, Hassan reveals the depths of his emotions, prompting his teacher to seek out a Somali interpreter. According to Rochman, "Littlewood's

Karen Littlewood's illustration projects include Lesley Beake's family-centered picture book Home Now. *(Charlesbridge, 2007. Illustration copyright © 2006 by Karin Littlewood. Reproduced by permission.)*

beautiful impressionistic watercolor paintings reveal the child's memories of his African village: the warmth and light and then the terror." Ajoke' T.I. Kokodoko, writing in *School Library Journal,* similarly noted that Littlewood's pictures "beautifully convey Hassan's sadness, fear, and ultimate happiness."

Littlewood has also served as the illustrator for *I Say a Little Prayer for You,* a version of the 1967 hit song written by Burt Bacharach and Hal David. The work focuses on an African-American girl and her mother as they make preparations for the youngster's birthday. "Sweeping, swirling, softly realistic watercolors in glowing shades are effectively arranged" throughout the work, commented Patricia Pearl Dole in *School Library Journal* review of the book. In *I Say a Little Prayer for You,* Littlewood's "vividly colored artwork sings its own bright song," concluded *Booklist* contributor Ilene Cooper. *Baba's Gift,* a story by South African-born writer Beverley Naidoo and her daughter, Maya, concerns the friendship between two black children and an East Indian youth. The tale, which reflects the authors' strong political convictions, "has been vividly illustrated by Karin Littlewood—the spare text set against rich watercolour hues," Dina Rabinovitch and Blake Morrison stated in their review of the book for the London *Guardian.*

Set on the African plains, David Conway's *The Most Important Gift of All* concerns young Ama, who wants to find the perfect present for her newborn brother. When Grandma Sis suggests that Ama give him love, the girl seeks help from a weaverbird, a giraffe, and a lion inorder to make sense of the woman's suggestion. "Littlewood's exquisite illustrations evoke the vast beauty and simmering daytime heat of Kenya," noted Mary Hazelon in *School Library Journal,* and Rochman observed that the "blend of the traditional storytelling pattern and contemporary realism is expressed in Littlewood's double-page spreads." A reviewer in *Publishers Weekly* also praised the illustrator's work, stating that "Littlewood's pictures soar. She covers the pages with exuberant brushstrokes and patches of sheer, radiant hues."

Another work set in Africa, Lesley Beake's *Home Now,* focuses on Sieta, a girl who moves to a new village after the death of her parents. During a class trip to the park, Sieta forms a strong connection with an orphaned elephant. "The book is tenderly and skillfully illustrated in vibrant watercolours," commented Nicolette Jones in the London *Sunday Times* and Heide Piehler, writing in *School Library Journal,* stated that Littlewood's "evocative watercolors" in *Home Now* "effectively convey the child's loneliness, isolation, and, finally, emotional rejuvenation."

Biographical and Critical Sources

PERIODICALS

Booklist, January 1, 2002, Hazel Rochman, review of *Swallow Journey,* p. 861; April 15, 2002, Ilene Cooper, review of *I Say a Little Prayer for You,* p. 1402; October 15, 2002, Hazel Rochman, review of *The Color of Home,* p. 410; April 1, 2006, Hazel Rochman, review of *The Most Important Gift of All,* p. 47; February 1, 2007, Julie Cummins, review of *Home Now,* p. 60; December 15, 2007, Suzanne Harold, review of *Christophe's Story,* p. 45.

Guardian (London, England), June 18, 2002, Lindsey Fraser, review of *The Colour of Home,* p. 61; February 25, 2004, Dina Rabinovitch and Blake Morrison, review of *Baba's Gift;* January 9, 2007, Kate Agnew, review of *Home Now,* p. 7.

Kirkus Reviews, August 15, 2002, review of *The Color of Home,* p. 1225; December 15, 2006, review of *Home Now,* p. 1264; June 1, 2007, review of *Christophe's Story.*

Publishers Weekly, January 18, 1993, review of *Gemma and the Baby Chick,* p. 468; March 4, 2002, review of *I Say a Little Prayer for You,* p. 78; April 3, 2006, review of *The Most Important Gift of All,* p. 71.

School Library Journal, May, 2002, Carol Johnson Shedd, review of *Chanda and the Mirror of Moonlight,* p. 132; July, 2002, Patricia Pearl Dole, review of *I Say a Little Prayer for You,* p. 102; September, 2002, Ajoke' T.I. Kokodoko, review of *The Color of Home,* p. 194; May, 2006, Mary Hazelon, review of *The Most Important Gift of All,* p. 85; March, 2007, Heide Piehler, review of *Home Now,* p. 151.

Sunday Times (London, England), November 19, 2006, Nicolette Jones, review of *Home Now,* p. 56.

Tribune Books (Chicago, IL), September 1, 2002, review of *The Color of Home,* p. 5.

ONLINE

Childrensillustrators.com, http://www2.childrensillustrators.com/ (April 1, 2008), "Karin Littlewood."

Eunice McMullen Web site, http://www.eunicemcmullen.co.uk/ (April 1, 2008), "Karin Littlewood."

Walker Books Web site, http://www.walkerbooks.com.au/ (April 1, 2008), "Karin Littlewood."*

*   *   *

LOWE, Steve
See BARLOW, Steve

M

MacLEAN, Jill 1941-

Personal

Born 1941, in England; immigrated to Canada in 1950; married; children: one son, one daughter. *Education:* Dalhousie University, B.S.; Atlantic School of Theology, M.A. *Hobbies and other interests:* Chamber and choral music; outdoors pursuits including canoeing, kayaking, snowmobiling, and boating.

Addresses

Home and office—New Bedford, Nova Scotia, Canada. *Agent*—c/o Writer's Federation of Nova Scotia, 1113 Marginal Rd., Halifax, Nova Scotia B3H 4P7, Canada.

Career

Author. Previously worked at Dalhousie University, Fisheries Research Board, Mount Allison University, and Sydney City Hospital; worked as a researcher on Prince Edward Island.

Awards, Honors

Ann Connor Brimer Award for Children's Literature; Book of the Year for Children finalist, Canadian Library Association, 2009; Hackmatack Children's Choice Book Award shortlist, 2010; KIND Children's Book Award honorable mention, Humane Society of the United States, 2009.

Writings

Jean Pierre Roma of the Company of the East of Isle St. Jean, Prince Edward Island Heritage Foundation (Charlottetown, Prince Edward Island, Canada), 1977, reprinted, Acorn Press (Charlottetown, Prince Edward Island, Canada), 2005.

The Brevity of Red (poetry), Signature Editions (Winnipeg, Manitoba, Canada), 2003.

The Nine Lives of Travis Keating, Fitzhenry & Whiteside (Markham, Ontario, Canada), 2008.

The Present Tense of Prinny Murphy, Fitzhenry & Whiteside (Markham, Ontario, Canada), 2010.

Sidelights

Jill MacLean emigrated from England to make her new home in Canada in 1950, and she has lived in the Maritime provinces for most of her life. An avid naturalist and writer, MacLean has visited the Northwest Territories, the Yukon, the coast of Labrador, and the high Arctic, as well as canoeing, kayaking, snowmobiling, walking, and boating around the Maritimes. As she noted on her Web log, her fictional characters take form in her head, and she starts writing notes on available scraps of paper as the conversation between author and character develops. MacLean's first book, the biography *Jean Pierre Roma of the Company of the East of Isle St. Jean,* was followed by *The Brevity of Red,* a compilation of poetry dealing with the author's grief over losing her mother, sister, and daughter before she turned forty.

MacLean's first children's book, *The Nine Lives of Travis Keating,* was written at the request of the author's grandson. The book tells the story of Travis Keating after the boy moves with his family to a small town in Newfoundland. Like many children who must adapt to a new location, Travis has difficulty finding new friends, and also finds himself confronting the school bully. Kara Schaff Dean, writing for *School Library Journal,* called *The Nine Lives of Travis Keating* as "a solid piece of contemporary fiction with an interesting story," while a critic for *Kirkus Reviews* called characterized the story as "not a complicated tale, but not heavy-handed either." MacLean's novel *The Present Tense of Prinny Murphy,* a sequel to *The Nine Lives of Travis Keating,* follows one of Travis's new friends, a girl named Prinny.

Cover of Jill MacLean's elementary-grade novel The Nine Lives of Travis Keating, *featuring artwork by Tara Anderson.* (Fitzhenry & Whiteside, 2008. Cover image courtesy of Tara Anderson. Reproduced by permission.)

Biographical and Critical Sources

PERIODICALS

Kirkus Reviews, October 1, 2008, review of *The Nine Lives of Travis Keating.*
School Library Journal, March, 2009, Kara Schaff Dean, review of *The Nine Lives of Travis Keating,* p. 148.

ONLINE

Jill MacLean Web log, http://jillmaclean.wordpress.com (January 3, 2010).
PEIbooks Web site, http://www.peibooks.ca/ (January 3, 2010), "Jill MacLean."
Writer's Federation of Nova Scotia Web site, http://www.writers.ns.ca/ (January 3, 2010), "Jill MacLean."*

*   *   *

MANNING, Maurie
See MANNING, Maurie J.

MANNING, Maurie J.
(Maurie Manning, Maurie Jo Manning)

Personal

Born July 22; children: one daughter.

Addresses

Home—CA. *E-mail*—maurie@mauriejmanning.com.

Career

Author and illustrator. Former illustrator and art director at educational software companies, including Jostens Learning.

Writings

SELF-ILLUSTRATED

The Aunts Go Marching, Boyds Mills Press (Honesdale, PA), 2003.
Kitchen Dance, Clarion Books (New York, NY), 2008.

ILLUSTRATOR

(As Maurie Manning; with others) Chris Engholm, *The Armenian Earthquake,* Lucent (San Diego, CA), 1989.
(As Maurie Manning; with others) Ronald Migneco, *The Crash of 1929,* Lucent (San Diego, CA), 1989.
(As Maurie Manning; with others) James House and Bradley Steffens, *The San Francisco Earthquake,* Lucent (San Diego, CA), 1989.
(As Maurie Manning; with Michael Spackman) Timothy Levi Biel, *Black Death,* Lucent (San Diego, CA), 1989.
(As Maurie Manning; with others) John Farris, *The Dust Bowl,* Lucent (San Diego, CA), 1989.
(As Maurie Manning; with Michael Spackman) Tom Stacey, *The Titanic,* Lucent (San Diego, CA), 1989.
(As Maurie Jo Manning) Clement Clarke Moore, *The Night before Christmas,* Bell Books (Honesdale, PA), 1992.
Jan M. Czech, *The Coffee Can Kid,* Child and Family Press (Washington, DC), 2002.
Sharon Hambrick, *Tommy's Clubhouse,* JourneyForth (Greenville, SC), 2003.
Kathleen T. Pelley, *The Giant King,* Child and Family Press (Washington, DC), 2003.
Christine Taylor-Butler, *Water Everywhere!,* Children's Press (New York, NY), 2004.
Sharon Hambrick, *Tommy's Rocket,* JourneyForth (Greenville, SC), 2004.
Sharon Hambrick, *Tommy's Race,* JourneyForth (Greenville, SC), 2004.
Marcie Aboff, *The Hot Shots,* Celebration Press (Parsippany, NJ), 2004.
Roz Rosenbluth, *Getting to Know Ruben Plotnick,* Flashlight Press (Brooklyn, NY), 2005.

Trudy Ludwig, *Sorry!,* Tricycle Press (Berkeley, CA), 2006.

John Farrell, *Dear Child,* Boyds Mills Press (Honesdale, PA), 2008.

Also illustrator (as Maurie Manning) of Olga Romero's *Big Max y yo* and Yanitzia Canetti's *Qué familión!,* both published by Hampton-Brown (Carmel, CA). Contributor to periodicals, including *Highlights for Children.*

Sidelights

In her career in children's literature, Maurie J. Manning has illustrated the works of other authors as well as published her own self-illustrated stories. In one of her early collaborations, Manning teamed up with author Jan M. Czech to produce *The Coffee Can Kid,* a story about a young adopted girl named Annie who wishes to hear the story of her birth after spotting the coffee-can container in which her new parents keep both her baby photo and a special letter from her biological mother. Listening to her father recount the story, the six year old learns that her young Korean birth mother recognized her own inability to provide for her daughter and loved the infant so much that she made arrangements for the girl to be cared for in America, where she would have plenty of food and opportunities for a better life. In *School Library Journal,* Judith Constantinides wrote that Manning's pictures "portray this early history with grace," while in *Booklist* Linda Perkins observed that

Maurie J. Manning captures the upbeat energy of a rambunctious, close-knit family in her self-illustrated picture book Kitchen Dance.

the artist's choice of "sunny yellows dominate the watercolor art, reflecting the tender, cheerful narrative."

Manning's *The Aunts Go Marching,* her self-illustrated and humorous adaptation of the traditional children's song, takes advantage of the homophone pair "aunt" and "ant" to write a story about a young girl who leads a parade of aunts through her neighborhood during a downpour. One by one, the ladies step out of their homes and follow the young girl's drumbeats to the town center until a final clap of thunder drives them all inside and out of the growing storm. "Manning's clever, full-color spreads are sure to provoke giggles among young listeners," remarked Nancy Menaldi-Scanlan in her *School Library Journal* review, while in *Horn Book* Joanna Rudge Long wrote that there is "enough vigor in these sturdy marching figures to energize the grayest day." *Booklist* contributor Ilene Cooper focused on "the unique perspectives used in the art" and predicted that children will enjoy repeated readings of *The Aunts Go Marching.*

Manning highlights other family members in her self-illustrated *Kitchen Dance.* While trying to fall asleep one evening, a young sister and brother hear strange noises coming from the downstairs kitchen, leading the pair to investigate the mysterious sounds. Much to their delight, the children discover their father serenading their mother in Spanish as the couple washes the dinner dishes together. Noticing an appreciative audience, the father includes his son and daughter in the song and dance, expressing his love for his family in boisterous verse. The books pages "radiate happiness in every line," wrote a *Kirkus Reviews* critic, the reviewer also expressing appreciation for Marklew's depiction of "a set of parents loving each other with such abandon and enthusiasm." In *School Library Journal* Mary N. Oluonye also found *Kitchen Dance* "full of vitality, simple, and touching," concluding her review by proclaiming the picture book to be "wonderful."

Biographical and Critical Sources

PERIODICALS

Booklist, July, 2002, Linda Perkins, review of *The Coffee Can Kid,* p. 1855; February 1, 2003, Ilene Cooper, review of *The Aunts Go Marching,* p. 81.
Horn Book, May-June, 2003, Joanna Rudge Long, review of *The Aunts Go Marching,* p. 330.
Kirkus Reviews, October 1, 2008, review of *Kitchen Dance.*
Publishers Weekly, October 13, 2008, review of *Kitchen Dance,* p. 53.
School Library Journal, July, 2002, Judith Constantinides, review of *The Coffee Can Kid,* p. 87; April, 2003, Nancy Menaldi-Scanlan, review of *The Aunts Go Marching,* p. 133; February, 2004, Kathleen Simonetta, review of *The Giant King,* p. 121; December, 2006, Catherine Callegari, review of *Sorry!,* p. 107; January, 2009, Mary N. Oluonye, review of *Kitchen Dance,* p. 81.

ONLINE

Maurie J. Manning Home Page, http://www.mauriejmanning.com (January 8, 2010).
Maurie J. Manning Web Log, http://www.thedigitalpencil.blogspot.com (January 7, 2010).*

*   *   *

MANNING, Maurie Jo
See MANNING, Maurie J.

*   *   *

MARKLEW, Gilly

Personal
Born in England.

Addresses
Home—England. *E-mail*—gill@gilly-marklew.co.uk.

Career
Artist and art instructor for adult education in England.

Illustrator
Patricia Cleveland-Peck, *City Cat, Country Cat,* Morrow (New York, NY), 1992, published as *Freckle and Clyde,* Collins (London, England), 1992.
Christine Pullein-Thompson, *I Want That Pony!,* Simon & Schuster (Hemel Hempstead, England), 1993.
Caroline Walsh, compiler, *The Little Book of Poems,* Kingfisher (New York, NY), 1993.
Joyce Faraday, reteller, *The Secret Garden* (adapted from Frances Hodgson Burnett's novel), Ladybird (Loughborough, England), 1994.
Richard Brown, *A Shoot of Corn,* Cambridge University Press (Cambridge, England), 1996.
Shelia Lane, *The Riddle Girl: An Anglo-Saxon Story,* Anglia Young Books (Saffron Walden, England), 1996.
Christine Pullein-Thompson, *The Pony Test,* Macdonald Young (Hove, England), 1997.
Antonia Barber, reteller, *Snow-White and Rose-Red,* Macdonald Young (Hove, England), 1997.
(And adaptor) *The Ugly Duckling,* Ladybird (London, England), 1998.
Christine Pullein-Thompson, *The Pony Picnic,* Macdonald Young (Hove, England), 1998.
Laurie Sheehan, *Chimney Child: A Victorian Story,* Anglia Young Books (Saffron Walden, England), 1998.
Diana Birkbeck, reteller, *The Watercress Girl* (adapted from Henry Mayhew's story "London Labour and the London Poor"), Heinemann (Oxford, England), 1999.
Fiona Waters, *Great Irish Heroes,* Gill & Macmillan (Dublin, Ireland), 2004.
Salamanda Drake (joint pseudonym of Steve Barlow and Steve Skidmore), *Dragonsdale,* Chicken House/Scholastic, Inc. (New York, NY), 2007.

Salamanda Drake, *Dragonsdale: Riding the Storm,* Chicken House/Scholastic, Inc. (New York, NY), 2008.

Sidelights

In addition to providing the artwork for a variety of works by British authors, illustrator Gilly Marklew has also teamed with Steve Barlow and Steve Skidmore, writers under the joint pen name Salamanda Drake, to create a fanciful series about a young girl and her fascination with dragons. *Dragonsdale,* the first book in the series, features sixteen-year-old Cara, who is charged with taking care of the dragons at the training center operated by her father. As much as she loves the creatures and wishes she could fly one on her own, Cara's father has forbidden her to ever ride on a dragon after a flying accident killed Cara's mother years earlier. Instead, the teen must be content to look after the mythical animals, developing a special relationship with a dragon named Skydancer. When Hortense, the indulged daughter of a local nobleman, selects Skydancer as her personal dragon to spite Cara after a quarrel, the youngster must decide if she can rise above her petty griev-

Gilly Marklew's illustration projects include the illustrations for Salamanda Drake's fantasy novel **Dragonsdale: Riding the Storm.** (Chicken House, 2008. Illustration copyright © 2008 by Gilly Marklew. Reproduced by permission of Scholastic, Inc.)

ances and come to Skydancer's rescue after a rocky flight with Hortense. For her efforts illustrating *Dragonsdale,* Marklew earned positive comments from reviewers, including *Booklist* contributor Jennifer Mattson, who called the pencil artwork "appealing," and a *Publishers Weekly* critic, who deemed the same pictures "exuberant."

In 2008, a second installment, *Dragonsdale: Riding the Storm,* appeared. In this episode, Cara's relationship with her best friend Breena becomes threatened by the manipulative Hortense. Wishing to become a member of the flight guard, Breena feels that her dragon riding skills are becoming overshadowed by Cara's superior ability. Yet when Breena fails to return to the stables after a solo ride in the country, Cara realizes that she alone can solve the mystery of the girl's disappearance and must set off on an adventure to save her friend. Once again, critics found Marklew's illustrations to be an attractive aspect of the middle-grade series. Reviewing the book in *Kirkus Reviews,* a contributor suggested that the "plentiful black-and-white illustrations" contribute to "the charm" of *Riding the Storm,* while *School Library Journal* contributor Tasha Saecker noted that Marklew's "black-and-white drawings add to the action" of Drake's novel.

Biographical and Critical Sources

PERIODICALS

Booklist, June 1, 2007, Jennifer Mattson, review of *Dragonsdale,* p. 70.
Kirkus Reviews, May 15, 2008, review of *Riding the Storm.*
Publishers Weekly, May 21, 2007, review of *Dragonsdale,* p. 55.
School Library Journal, June, 2007, Tasha Saecker, review of *Dragonsdale,* p. 96; October, 2008, Tasha Saecker, review of *Riding the Storm,* p. 106.*

*　　*　　*

MAXWELL, B.E. 1957-
(Bruce E. Maxwell)

Personal

Born 1957; married; wife's name Heather; children: two daughters.

Addresses

Home—CT.

Career

Author.

Writings

The Faerie Door, Harcourt (Orlando, FL), 2008.

Sidelights

Bruce Maxwell's eighth-grade English teacher introduced him to the works of J.R.R. Tolkien, inspiring the future author with a life-long fascination with fantasy fiction. Many years later, as a grown adult with children and grandchildren, Maxwell added to his favorite fictional genre by writing his own middle-grade novel. *The Faerie Door.*

The Faerie Door is based on a story that Maxwell told to his daughter and his niece. Inspired by the girls' love of the story, Maxwell decided to write it down, and ultimately dedicated the completed novel to them. The story follows Victoria Deveny, a girl living in 1890s Great Britain, and Elliot Good, a boy from the mid-sixties U.S.A., as they step through portals in their respective worlds and meet each other, as well as the Faerie Queen. The Faerie Queen sends the two children off through other portals, their task to defeat the Shadow Knight and defend her world. A contributor to *Kirkus Reviews* recommended *The Faerie Door* for sophisticated readers, noting that the novel's "plot and quest narrative are complex and intricate; the characters in

their quests are not always heroic or admirable." While *Booklist* reviewer Krista Hutley wrote that "the story feels . . . cobbled together from fantasy conventions," Christi Esterle remarked in *School Library Journal* that Maxwell employs traditional fantasy conventions, such as "evil sorceresses, . . . flying pirate ships, dragons, and ballet" in his time-travel story.

Biographical and Critical Sources

PERIODICALS

Booklist, November 15, 2008, Krista Hutley, review of *The Faerie Door,* p. 60.
Kirkus Reviews, September 15, 2008, review of *The Faerie Door.*
School Library Journal, February, 2009, Christi Esterle, review of *The Faerie Door,* p. 104.

ONLINE

Bruce Maxwell Home Page, http://www.bemaxwell.com (January 4, 2010).*

*   *   *

MAXWELL, Bruce E.
See MAXWELL, B.E.

*   *   *

McNAUGHTON, Colin 1951-

Personal

Born May 18, 1951, in Wallsend-upon-Tyne, England; son of Thomas (a pattern maker) and May McNaughton; married Françoise Julie, June 27, 1970; children: Ben, Timothy. *Education:* Central School of Art and Design, B.A., 1973; Royal College of Art, M.A., 1976.

Addresses

Home—London, England.

Career

Author and illustrator. Cambridge School of Art, Cambridge, England, art instructor; freelance author and illustrator, beginning 1976. *Exhibitions:* Work exhibited in galleries and museums, including at Discovery Museum, Newcastle upon Tyne, England, 1998.

Member

British Society of Authors.

Awards, Honors

First Prize for Didactic Literature, Cultural Activities Board of City of Trento/Children's Literature Department of University of Padua, Italy, 1978, for *C'era una*

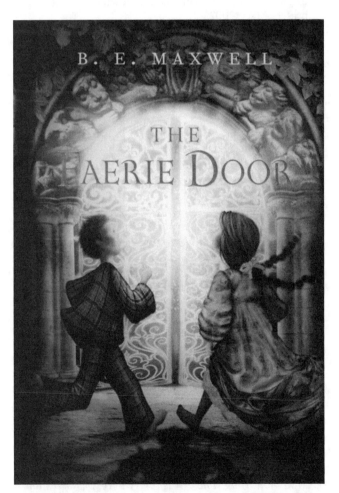

Cover of B.E. Maxwell's elementary-grade fantasy novel, **The Fairie Door,** *featuring artwork by Mehrdokht Amini.* (Jacket illustration © 2008 by Mehrdokht Amini. Reproduced by permission of Houghton Mifflin Harcourt Company. This material may not be reproduced in any form or by any means without prior written permission of the publisher.)

Colin McNaughton (Photograph by Michael Ann Mullen. Reproduced by permission.)

volta (Italian edition of combined volumes *Colin McNaughton ABC and Things* and *Colin McNaughton's 1, 2, 3 and Things*); Kurt Maschler Award shortlist, 1988, for *Jolly Roger and the Pirates of Abdul the Skinhead,* and award, 1991, for *Have You Seen Who's Just Moved Next Door to Us?;* Smarties Prize shortlist, 1988, for *Jolly Roger and the Pirates of Abdul the Skinhead,* and 1994, for *Suddenly!,* and award, 1996, for *Oops!;* British Book Design and Production Award, 1989, for *Jolly Roger and the Pirates of Abdul the Skinhead,* 1993, for *Who's That Banging on the Ceiling?,* and 1994, for *Making Friends with Frankenstein;* United Kingdom Reading Association Book Award, and Nottinghamshire Children's Acorn Award, both 1995, both for *Suddenly!;* Kate Greenaway Medal shortlist, 1995, for *Here Come the Aliens!;* Smarties' Gold Prize, 1996; Nottinghamshire Children's Book Award shortlist, 1997; Blue Peter Book Award shortlist, and Sheffield Children's Book Award Highly Commended designation, both 2001; Big 3 Children's Book Prize, Nottingham Libraries, 2002, 2003; Outstanding International Book designation, U.S. Board on Books for Young People/Children's Book Council, and Bank Street College Best Children's Book designation, both 2005, both for *Once upon an Ordinary School Day.*

Writings

SELF-ILLUSTRATED

Colin McNaughton's ABC and 1, 2, 3: A Book for All Ages for Reading Alone or Together, Doubleday (New York, NY), 1976, published seperately as *Colin McNaughton's ABC and Things* and *Colin McNaughton's 1, 2, 3 and Things,* Benn (London, England), 1976, published as *ABC and Things* and *1, 2, 3 and Things,* Macmillan (London, England), 1989.

(With Elizabeth Attenborough) *Walk, Rabbit, Walk,* Viking (New York, NY), 1977.

The Great Zoo Escape, Heinemann (London, England), 1978, Viking (New York, NY), 1979.

The Rat Race: The Amazing Adventures of Anton B. Stanton, Doubleday (New York, NY), 1978.

Anton B. Stanton and the Pirats, Doubleday (New York, NY), 1979, published as *The Pirats: The Amazing Adventures of Anton B. Stanton,* Benn (London, England), 1979.

Football Crazy, Heinemann (London, England), 1980, published as *Soccer Crazy,* Atheneum (New York, NY), 1981, reprinted, Mathew Price (Denton, TX), 2008.

King Nonn the Wiser, Heinemann (London, England), 1981.

If Dinosaurs Were Cats and Dogs, verses adapted by Alice Low, Four Winds Press (New York, NY), 1981, revised edition with verses by McNaughton, 1991.

Fat Pig, Benn (London, England), 1981, Puffin (New York, NY), 1987.

Crazy Bear, Holt (New York, NY), 1983.

"There's an Awful Lot of Weirdos in Our Neighborhood," and Other Wickedly Funny Verse, Simon & Schuster (New York, NY), 1987, published as *There's an Awful Lot of Weirdos in Our Neighbourhood: A Book of Rather Silly Verse and Pictures,* Walker (London, England), 1987, reprinted, Candlewick Press (Cambridge, MA), 2002.

Santa Clause Is Superman, Walker (London, England), 1988.

Jolly Roger and the Pirates of Abdul the Skinhead, Simon & Schuster (New York, NY), 1988, reprinted, Candlewick Press (Cambridge, MA), 2004.

Who's Been Sleeping in My Porridge? A Book of Silly Poems and Pictures, Ideals Children's Books, 1990, second edition published as *Who's Been Sleeping in My Porridge?: A Book of Wacky Poems and Pictures,* Candlewick Press (Cambridge, MA), 1998.

Watch out for the Giant-Killers!, Walker (London, England), 1991.

Guess Who's Just Moved in Next Door?, Random House (New York, NY), 1991, published as *Have You Seen Who's Just Moved in Next Door to Us?,* Walker (London, England), 1991.

Who's That Banging on the Ceiling?: A Multistory Story, Walker (London, England), 1992, Candlewick Press (Cambridge, MA), 1994.

Making Friends with Frankenstein: A Book of Monstrous Poems and Pictures, Walker (London, England), 1993, Candlewick Press (Cambridge, MA), 1994.

Captain Abdul's Pirate School, Candlewick Press (Cambridge, MA), 1994.

Merry Christmas, Sainsbury/Walker (London, England), 1994.

Here Come the Aliens!, Candlewick Press (Cambridge, MA), 1995.

Dracula's Tomb (pop-up book), Candlewick Press (Cambridge, MA), 1998.

Wish You Were Here (and I Wasn't): A Book of Poems and Pictures for Globe-Trotters, Candlewick Press (Cambridge, MA), 2000.

Don't Step on the Crack!, Dial (New York, NY), 2001.

Lemmy Was a Diver, Andersen (London, England), 2003.

Cushie Butterfield (She's a Little Cow), Collins (London, England), 2004.

Potty Poo-poo Wee-wee!, Candlewick Press (Cambridge, MA), 2005.

When I Grow Up, Candlewick Press (Cambridge, MA), 2005.

What Now, Cushie Butterfield?, HarperCollins (London, England), 2005.

Captain Abdul's Little Treasure, Candlewick Press (Cambridge, MA), 2006.

Nighty Night!, Walker Books (London, England), 2007.

We're off to Look for Aliens, Walker Books (London, England), 2007, Candlewick Press (Cambridge, MA), 2008.

Author's books have been translated into Welsh and Italian.

"PRESTON PIG" SERIES; SELF-ILLUSTRATED

Suddenly!, Andersen Press (London, England), 1994, Harcourt (New York, NY), 1995.

Boo!, Andersen Press (London, England), 1995, Harcourt (New York, NY), 1996.

Oops!, Andersen Press (London, England), 1996.

Preston's Goal!, Harcourt (San Diego, CA), 1998, published as *Goal!,* Anderson Press (London, England), 1998.

Yum!, Harcourt (New York, NY), 1999.

Shh! (Don't Tell Mr. Wolf!) (lift-the-flap book), Harcourt (San Diego, CA), 1999.

Little Suddenly! (board book), Harcourt (San Diego, CA), 2000.

Little Boo! (board book), Harcourt (San Diego, CA), 2000.

Little Goal! (board book), Collins (London, England), 2000, Harcourt (San Diego, CA), 2001.

Little Oops! (board book), Harcourt (San Diego, CA), 2001.

Oomph!, Harcourt (San Diego, CA), 2001.

S.W.A.L.K., Andersen (London, England), 2002.

"BOOKS OF OPPOSITES" SERIES; SELF-ILLUSTRATED

At Home, Philomel (New York, NY), 1982, published as *Long-Short: At Home,* Walker (London, England), 1982.

At Playschool, Philomel (New York, NY), 1982, published as *Over-Under: At Playschool,* Walker (London, England), 1982.

At the Party, Philomel (New York, NY), 1982, published as *Hide-Seek: At the Party,* Walker (London, England), 1982.

At the Park, Philomel (New York, NY), 1982, published as *In-Out: At the Park,* Walker (London, England), 1982.

At the Stores, Philomel (New York, NY) 1982, published as *Fat-Thin: At the Shops,* Walker (London, England), 1982.

"VERY FIRST BOOKS" SERIES; SELF-ILLUSTRATED

Spring, Walker (London, England), 1983, Dial (New York, NY), 1984.

Summer, Walker (London, England), 1983, Dial (New York, NY), 1984.

Autumn, Walker (London, England), 1983, Dial (New York, NY), 1984.

Winter, Walker (London, England), 1983, Dial (New York, NY), 1984.

FOR CHILDREN

Once upon an Ordinary School Day, illustrated by Satoshi Kitamura, Farrar, Straus & Giroux (New York, NY), 2004.

Not Last Night but the Night Before, illustrated by Emma Chichester Clark, Candlewick Press (Somerville, MA), 2009.

ILLUSTRATOR

James Reeves, compiler, *The Springtime Book: A Collection of Prose and Poetry,* Heinemann (London, England), 1976.

James Reeves, compiler, *The Autumn Book: A Collection of Prose and Poetry,* Heinemann (London, England), 1977.

Hester Burton, *A Grenville Goes to Sea,* Heinemann (London, England), 1977.

James Reeves, *Eggtime Stories,* Blackie & Son (London, England), 1978.

Mary McCaffrey, *The Mighty Muddle,* Eel Pie Publishing, 1979.

Jenny Hawkesworth, *A Handbook of Family Monsters,* Dent (London, England), 1980.

Wendy Wood, *The Silver Chanter: Traditional Scottish Tales and Legends,* Chatto & Windus (London, England), 1980.

Emil Pacholek, *A Ship to Sail the Seven Seas,* Kestrel (London England), 1980.

Allan Ahlberg, *Miss Brick the Builder's Baby,* Kestrel (London, England), 1981, Golden Press (New York, NY), 1982.

Allan Ahlberg, *Mr. and Mrs. Hay the Horse,* Kestrel (London, England), 1981.

Russell Hoban, *The Great Fruit Gum Robbery,* Walker (London, England), 1981, published as *The Great Gum Drop Robbery,* Philomel (New York, NY), 1982.

Russell Hoban, *They Came from Aargh,* Philomel (New York, NY), 1981.

Russell Hoban, *The Flight of Bembel Rudzuk,* Philomel (New York, NY), 1982.

Russell Hoban, *The Battle of Zormla,* Philomel (New York, NY), 1982.

Andrew Lang, compiler, *The Pink Fairy Book* (fairy tales), revised and edited by Brian Alderson, Viking (New York, NY), 1982.

Allan Ahlberg, *Mrs. Jolly's Joke Shop,* Kestrel (London, England), 1988.

Robert Louis Stevenson, *Treasure Island,* Holt (New York, NY), 1993.

Adrian Henry and others, *One of Your Legs Is Both the Same,* Macmillan (New York, NY), 1994.

Roger McGough and others, *Another Day on Your Foot and I Would Have Died,* Macmillan (New York, NY), 1996.

James Berry and others, *We Couldn't Provide Fish Thumbs,* Macmillan (New York, NY), 1997.

ILLUSTRATOR; "RED NOSE READERS" SERIES BY ALLAN AHLBERG

Help!, Random House (New York, NY), 1985.
Jumping, Random House (New York, NY), 1985.
Make a Face, Random House (New York, NY), 1985.
Big Bad Pig, Random House (New York, NY), 1985.
Fee Fi Fo Fum, Random House (New York, NY), 1985.
Happy Worm, Random House (New York, NY), 1985.
Bear's Birthday, Random House (New York, NY), 1985.
So Can I, Random House (New York, NY), 1985.
Shirley's Shops, Random House (New York, NY), 1986.
Push the Dog, Random House (New York, NY), 1986.
Crash, Bang, Wallop!, Random House (New York, NY), 1986.
Me and My Friend, Random House (New York, NY), 1986.
Blow Me Down, Random House (New York, NY), 1986.
Look Out for the Seals, Random House (New York, NY), 1986.
One Two Flea, Random House (New York, NY), 1986.
Tell Us a Story, Random House (New York, NY), 1986.
Put on a Show, Walker (London, England), 1995.
Who Stole the Pie, Walker (London, England), 1995.

ILLUSTRATOR; "FOLDAWAY" SERIES BY ALLAN AHLBERG

Circus, Granada/Collins (London, England), 1984.
Zoo, Granada/Collins (London, England), 1984.
Families, Granada/Collins (London, England), 1984.
Monsters, Granada/Collins (London, England), 1984.

Adaptations

Fat Pig was adapted as a rock musical in 1983 and produced in France, Germany, Austria, Great Britain, the United States, Finland, and Norway.

Sidelights

Award-winning British children's author and illustrator Colin McNaughton has delighted countless young readers on both sides of the Atlantic with his lighthearted stories and cartoon-like drawings. From humorous illustrated verse collections such as *Who's Been Sleeping in My Porridge? A Book of Silly Poems and Pictures* to the popular "Preston the Pig" stories for younger children, McNaughton continues to capture the fancy—and tickle the funny bones—of readers and critics alike.

Reflecting on his artistic style, McNaughton once told *SATA:* "The only picture books I knew as a child were the comic annuals I was given at Christmas: *Beano, Dandy, Topper, Eagle,* and *Lion.* Looking back it is not difficult to say that these comics were the main influ-

ence on my work. These and the films I saw every Saturday morning . . . pirate films, knights in shining armour, cowboys and Indians." This childhood love of comedy, excitement, and make believe continues to provide McNaughton with a unique ability to make children laugh. The author noted that, "although I am married, with two sons and a lovely French wife, I still like the same things—the escapism of the adventure film and the crazy madness of the comic. I guess I never grew up."

Born in Wallsend-upon-Tyne, England, in 1951, McNaughton attended the Central School of Art and Design. Graduating in 1973, he went on to take classes at the Royal College of Art, earning a master's degree in 1976. He began his professional career by illustrating the works of other authors, such as Hester Burton, Russell Hoban, and James Reeves, and quickly began to also write his own stories. One of McNaughton's first writing efforts, a 1977 collaboration with Elizabeth Attenborough titled *Walk, Rabbit, Walk,* received much praise from critics. In this easy-to-read book, a young rabbit on his way to a friend's house turns down modern methods of transport, including sports cars, helicopters, and even a hot air balloon ride, in favor of a pleasant walk on his own two feet. A *Junior Bookshelf* critic noted that McNaughton's illustrations "compliment the

Colin McNaughton's humorous self-illustrated books include **Don't Step on the Crack!** (Dial Books for Young Readers, 2000. Reproduced by permission of Dial Books for Young Readers, a division of Penguin Putnam Books for Young Readers.)

story perfectly," while Merrie Lou Cohen, writing in *School Library Journal,* praised the "refreshing text and nice homey illustrations" in *Walk, Rabbit, Walk,* going on to call the story "funny, imaginative, and full of rollicking action."

Another of McNaughton's successful partnerships has been with children's author Allan Ahlberg, with whom he has created the popular "Red Nose Reader" series. "Red Nose" books help readers understand concepts; for example, in *Big Bad Pig* McNaughton and Ahlberg explain the difference between big and little, while *Help!* tries to teach children to overcome their fears. In *Help!,* a small boy is frightened by the monsters, burglars, and other hideous creatures that invade his bedroom. Gathering his courage, the lad devises a clever plan to scare away all these uninvited guests. In a *School Library Journal* review of several of the duo's books, Louise L. Sherman applauded the "Red Nose" series for its "simple use of words and the clear comic illustrations," exclaiming that they "will tickle the funny bones of children." Reviewing *Help!* for *Publishers Weekly,* a critic deemed the collaborative early readers "absurd and amusing."

McNaughton's offbeat sense of humor also surfaces in his self-illustrated and award-winning *Guess Who's Just Moved in Next Door?* News of a new family joining the neighborhood spreads quickly from house to house. As readers follow the message being passed through the street, they cannot help but notice the odd characters that fill the town, including an apartment full of pirates, a clan of space creatures, and a group of pigs shopping for wigs. When the mystery neighbors finally arrive, the entire neighborhood of strange inhabitants appears horrified by the family's ordinariness. Describing the humor in the book—published in England as *Have You Seen Who's Just Moved in Next Door to Us?*—as "both cheeky and camp," a *Publishers Weekly* critic maintained that McNaughton's "rollicking verse will make reading aloud a zany treat." A reviewer in *Junior Bookshelf* also praised the book's creative verse, citing its author's "repetitions, detail, and . . . sure feel of what children enjoy."

Featuring a title that will captivate young children from the get go, *Potty Poo-Poo Wee-Wee!* focuses on a young dinosaur who avoids using the potty until his father, Daddysaurus, declares that he will no longer worry about his son's bathroom mishaps. In a perversity that is characteristic of many children, the young dino decides that it is now safe to adopt grown-up bathroom habits. Noting that McNaughton's brightly colored "polka-dot dinosaurs are from the goofy genus," Ilene Cooper added in *Booklist* that *Potty Poo-Poo Wee-Wee!* will serve parents as a segue into a "talk about potty training."

Also featuring what *School Library Journal* reviewer Piper Nyman described as "the trademark goofy humor and kid-friendly illustrations" that have won McNaugh-

Monsters big and small are the stock characters in McNaughton's verse collection **Making Friends with Frankenstein.** (Copyright © 1999 by Colin McNaughton. Reproduced by permission of Candlewick Press, Somerville, MA, on behalf of Walker Books, Ltd., London.)

ton so many fans, *We're off to Look for Aliens* features a book-within-a-book format. The story follows a dad who leaves his family to walk the dog while they read his newly published book. As readers learn, by reading the mini-book included in *We're off to Look for Aliens,* Dad's story finds a man and his dog encountering space aliens while walking through the neighborhood. Featuring a humorous twist, McNaughton's story was praised as "imaginative" by Nyman, while a *Kirkus Reviews* writer dubbed *We're off to Look for Aliens* "inspired metafictive read-aloud fun."

In addition to space aliens, pirates make an appearance in several books by McNaughton. In *Captain Abdul's Pirate School,* for example, the salty pirate crew decides to start a school to give young whippersnappers more backbone, while *Captain Abdul's Little Treasure* finds the pirate band helpless when ordered to babysit the captain's young infant. Written in the form of a diary purportedly penned by a student named Pickles, *Captain Abdul's Pirate School* reveals the pirates' educational philosophy to be one promoting sloth, cheating, sloppiness, and other tempting traits. Describing McNaughton's "scruffy pop-eyed pirates" as "an engaging lot," *Booklist* contributor Stephanie Zvirin called *Captain Abdul's Pirate School* "a sort of dream come true for young pirate fanciers." Reviewing *Captain Abdul's Little Treasure* in the same periodical, GraceAnne

A. DeCandido noted that the author/illustrator's use of "word balloons . . . and parodies of sea shanties and nursery rhymes add to the gleeful chaos."

A story about neighbors spying on their neighbors is recounted in humorous fashion in *Who's That Banging on the Ceiling?: A Multistory Story* Sharing space in a twelve-story apartment building, each resident takes ridiculous guesses about what the neighbors above them are doing to make such a racket. As readers turn the page, McNaughton reveals how the crazy apartment dwellers create so much noise: children bounce on the bed, young men gorge themselves at the table, and even King Kong tap-dances on the roof. Describing *Who's That Banging on the Ceiling?* as a "clever novelty book," *School Library Journal* contributor Kathy Piehl predicted that the tale will "amuse young audiences." *Booklist* reviewer Emily Melton suggested that, while the page design may challenge some readers, "the silly humor, the repetitive text, and giant fold-out will probably appeal to children."

Among McNaughton's self-illustrated books of witty verse is *Making Friends with Frankenstein: A Book of Monstrous Poems and Pictures*. In this volume a mad scientist actually "makes a friend" in his laboratory, ghosts act out a "phantomime," and witches who play in the sand become "sandwitches." Describing the poems as "deliciously outrageous," a *Publishers Weekly* reviewer commended McNaughton's "wacky cartoon characters, nimble puns, and clever spoofs." While noting that the book is filled with "disgusting bodily functions that children will find hilarious," Marjorie Lewis wrote in *School Library Journal* that the poems are well suited to reading aloud. Calling *Making Friends with Frankenstein* "a must for Halloween," *Booklist* contributor Hazel Rochman asserted that McNaughton's "nonsense verse and comic illustrations" will entertain children throughout the entire year.

Another rollicking poetry fest featuring McNaughton's illustrations, *Who's Been Sleeping in My Porridge?: A Book of Wacky Poems and Pictures* features everything from aliens, gorillas, and walking fish in the author/illustrator's irreverent verse. *Wish You Were Here (and I Wasn't): A Book of Poems and Pictures for Globe-Trotters* marks another poetry collection by "the sublimely silly McNaughton," in the opinion of a *Publishers Weekly* contributor. It includes boring poems to murmur on long car rides—"Are We Nearly There Yet?" and "I Feel Sick"—to verses about space aliens opting to leave their Earth vacation with a collection of souvenirs that includes the actual Eiffel Tower, Golden Gate Bridge, and Mount Everest instead of simple postcards. Describing the text as "redolent with puns, nonsense words, wisecracks and child-pleasing ickyness," the reviewer added that McNaughton himself appears in a number of the book's "goofy" illustrations.

Adding to his works featuring horrible monsters, creepy characters, and juicy illustrations, McNaughton has also published a number of stories about softer, more lovable creatures, illustrated in pencil and bright watercolor. In *Suddenly!* the artist presents an update on the "Three Little Pigs" story by introducing amiable soccer-playing Preston the pig. Completely unaware that a ferocious wolf is stalking him, young Preston goes about his daily business without a care. On his way home from school, the young piglet stops at the store to do an errand for his mother. Leaving for home, he succumbs to the lure of the playground. Upon each change of direction, Preston narrowly misses the sharp teeth of the increasingly frustrated Mr. Wolf, and the end of the story finds Preston safe at home and Mr. Wolf at the hospital. Writing in *Booklist,* Annie Ayres predicted that children will be entertained by this "deftly executed and designed" picture book. In a *School Library Journal* review, Lisa S. Murphy applauded *Suddenly!* for providing "zany fun that's perfect for young audiences," while a critic in *Junior Bookshelf* declared that the book "will be a big hit with small children."

Preston returns in several other books by McNaughton, including *Boo!, Preston's Goal!,* and *Oomph!* In *Preston's Goal!*—published in England as *Goal!* and called a "picture book of rare comic zest" by a *Books for Keeps* contributor—the young porker pays more attention to his soccer ball than he does to hungry Mr. Wolf lurking nearby, with chaotic results that feature "enough slapstick fun for every young soccer fan," in the opinion of *Booklist* contributor Shelley Townsend-Hudson. Praising the book's humor, *School Library Journal* reviewer Barbara Elleman noted that the author-illustrator employs a "light palette and easy lines" to create a tale

A team of intrepid young hunters takes the reins of McNaughton's self-illustrated We're Off to Look for Aliens.

evocative of "the shenanigans and fast pace of Saturday morning cartoons." Teresa Scragg enthused about *Goal!* in *School Librarian,* commenting that "very rarely do we see such fun in a picture book for young children."

The fairy tale "Little Red Riding Hood" joins "The Three Little Pigs" in McNaughton's *Oops!,* as Mr. Wolf tries to remember what he is supposed to do when Preston appears at Granny Pig's house with a basket of food. While noting that older readers will enjoy the author's "smart-aleck humor," a *Publishers Weekly* reviewer added that preschoolers will get a giggle from cartoons featuring "Mr. Wolf's snarly snout [and] buggy eyes." *Horn Book* review Cathryn M. Mercier praised McNaughton's "energetic yet clear" layout, which should appeal to children "old enough to get the jokes and young enough to delight in them again and again."

In *Yum!* Preston the pig decides that Mr. Wolf should find a more constructive—and less threatening—way of dealing with his hunger: get a job and earn money for groceries! But while the young pig earnestly searches for a proper career for the wily wolf—everything from astronaut to pilot to sailor—the cagey Mr. Wolf transforms every suggested vocation into a chance "for piggie pie and piggie stew—even if only in his dreams," noted *Booklist* reviewer Zvirin. Fortunately, a tangle with Preston's father armed with a heavy iron cooking pot puts an end to the wolf's carnivorous fantasies. *Oomph!* continues the saga of pig and pursuer as Preston goes on a trip to the beach and meets a new friend named Maxine. As young love blooms, Mr. Wolf is there to watch—sickened by all the sweetness—from his hiding place within McNaughton's "sunny" illustrations that feature "plenty of ocean greens and skies of blues," according to Ilene Cooper in *Booklist.* In each of the "Preston the Pig" stories, youngsters will enjoy the fresh take on the "Three Little Pigs" fable, "and the lazy wolf's far-from-subtle interest" in McNaughton's chubby young hero, according to *School Library Journal* reviewer Adele Greenlee.

One of several moveable books by McNaughton, *Shh! (Don't Tell Mr. Wolf)* is a lift-the-flap book for toddlers that finds Mr. Wolf increasingly injured after accidentally chancing upon friends of Preston while searching for the tricky pig. Noting that youngsters "will enjoy being Preston's accomplice in outfoxing the villain," *School Library Journal* reviewer Marilyn Ackerman also praised the book's large type and brightly colored illustrations. Other moveable books by McNaughton include *Little Oops!* and *Little Goal!,* both of which feature characters from the author/illustrator's popular "Preston the Pig" series. McNaughton's scary pop-up, *Dracula's Tomb,* serves up a characteristic dose of giggles and gore before closing "with a superbly engineered pop-up of Dracula, complete with sound effects," according to *School Librarian* contributor Mary Crawford.

Biographical and Critical Sources

BOOKS

McNaughton, Colin, *Making Friends with Frankenstein: A Book of Monstrous Poems and Pictures,* Walker (London, England), 1993, Candlewick Press (Cambridge, MA), 1994.

McNaughton, Colin, *Wish You Were Here (and I Wasn't): A Book of Poems and Pictures for Globe-Trotters,* Candlewick Press (Cambridge, MA), 2000.

PERIODICALS

Booklist, January 15, 1993, Emily Melton, review of *Who's That Banging on the Ceiling?: A Multistory Story,* p. 922; May 15, 1994, Hazel Rochman, review of *Making Friends with Frankenstein: A Book of Monstrous Poems and Pictures,* p. 1678; October 15, 1994, Stephanie Zvirin, review of *Captain Abdul's Pirate School,* p. 438; May 5, 1995, Annie Ayres, review of *Suddenly!,* p. 1652; October 1, 1997, Stephanie Zvirin, review of *Oops!,* p. 337; August, 1998, Shelley Townsend-Hudson, review of *Preston's Goal!,* p. 2015; September 1, 1999, Stephanie Zvirin, review of *Yum!,* p. 141; March 15, 2001, Ilene Cooper, review of *Oomph!,* p. 1405; August, 2005, Ilene Cooper, review of *Potty Poo-Poo Wee-Wee!,* p. 2035; May 1, 2006, GraceAnne A. DeCandido, review of *Captain Abdul's Little Treasure,* p. 93.

Books for Keeps, January, 1998, review of *Goal!,* p. 15.

Horn Book, January-February, 1998, Cathryn M. Mercier, review of *Oops!,* p. 66; July, 2001, review of *Don't Step on the Crack,* p. 441; March-April, 2005, Joanna Rudge Long, review of *Once upon an Ordinary School Day,* p. 192; July-August, 2006, Christine M. Heppermann, review of *Captain Abdul's Little Treasure,* p. 427.

Junior Bookshelf, December, 1977, review of *Walk, Rabbit, Walk,* p. 329; April, 1992, review of *Have You Seen Who's Just Moved in Next Door to Us?,* p. 56; December, 1994, review of *Suddenly!,* p. 204.

Kirkus Reviews, August 1, 1998, review of *Who's Been Sleeping in My Porridge?,* p. 1122; August 1, 1999, review of *Yum!,* p. 1229; April 15, 2001, review of *Don't Step on the Crack!,* p. 590; February 1, 2005, review of *Once upon an Ordinary School Day,* p. 178; May 1, 2005, review of *When I Grow Up,* p. 543; May 15, 2008, review of *We're off to Look for Aliens.*

Publishers Weekly, December 20, 1985, review of *Help!,* p. 66; August 9, 1991, review of *Guess Who's Just Moved in Next Door?,* p. 56; May 9, 1994, review of *Making Friends with Frankenstein,* p. 73; June 23, 1997, review of *Oops!,* p. 91; January 31, 2000, review of *Wish You Were Here (and I Wasn't): A Book of Poems and Pictures for Globe Trotter,* p. 106; March 14, 2005, review of *Once upon an Ordinary School Day,* p. 66; June 9, 2008, review of *We're off to Look for Aliens,* p. 49.

School Librarian, summer, 1998, Teresa Scragg, review of *Goal!,* p. 74; spring, 1999, Mary Crawford, review of *Dracula's Tomb,* p. 33.

School Library Journal, April, 1978, Merrie Lou Cohen, review of *Walk, Rabbit, Walk,* p. 73; April, 1986, Louise L. Sherman, reviews of *Big Bad Pig, Fee Fi Fo Fum, Happy Worm,* and *Help!,* all p. 67; February, 1991, Ann Stell, review of *Who's Been Sleeping in My Porridge?,* p. 73; October, 1991, Nancy Menaldi-Scanlan, review of *Guess Who's Just Moved in Next Door?,* p. 101; January, 1992, Christine A. Moesch, review of *If Dinosaurs Were Cats and Dogs,* p. 93; March, 1993, Kathy Piehl, review of *Who's That Banging on the Ceiling?,* p. 182; May, 1994, Marjorie Lewis, review of *Making Friends with Frankenstein,* p. 125; January, 1995, Kate McClelland, review of *Captain Abdul's Pirate School,* p. 90; June, 1995, Lisa S. Murphy, review of *Suddenly!,* p. 92; November, 1995, John Peters, review of *Here Come the Aliens!,* p. 79; September, 1996, Elisabeth Palmer Abarbanel, review of *Boo!,* p. 184; September, 1997, Lisa Marie Gangemi, review of *Oops!,* p. 186; October, 1998, Jane Marino, review of *Who's Been Sleeping in My Porridge?,* p. 126; November, 1998, Barbara Elleman, review of *Preston's Goal!,* p. 90; October, 1999, Adele Greenlee, review of *Yum!,* p. 120; May, 2000, Marilyn Ackerman, review of *Shh! (Don't Tell Mr. Wolf!),* p. 149; June, 2000, Anne Parker, review of *Wish You Were Here (and I Wasn't),* p. 134; June, 2001, Sally R. Dow, review of *Don't Step on the Crack!,* p. 126; July, 2001, DeAnn Tabuchi, review of *Oomph!,* p. 85; July, 2001, Olga R. Juharets, review of *Little Goal!* and *Little Oops!,* p. 85; July, 2001, DeAnn Tabuchi, review of *Oomph!,* p. 85; July, 2005, Marge Loch-Wouters, review of *When I Grow Up,* p. 78; August, 2005, Elaine Lesh Morgan, review of *Potty Poo-Poo Wee-Wee!,* p. 102; September, 2008, Piper Nyman, review of *We're off to Look for Aliens,* p. 154.

Times Educational Supplement, October 9, 1998, Elaine Williams, interview with McNaughton.

Times Literary Supplement, November 22, 1991, Tim Hilton, review of *Have You Seen Who's Just Moved in Next Door to Us?,* p. 23.

ONLINE

Images of Delight Web site, http://www.imagesofdelight.com/ (February 1, 2010), "Colin McNaughton."*

*   *   *

MESERVE, Jessica

Personal

Partner's name Dave; children: Elodie (daughter). *Education:* Edinburgh College of Art, B.A., M.A. (illustration).

Addresses

Home and office—Edmonton, Alberta, Canada.

Career

Writer and illustrator. Previously worked as a children's book designer.

Writings

SELF-ILLUSTRATED

Small, Andersen (London, England), 2006, published as *Small Sister,* Clarion (New York, NY), 2007.

Can Anybody Hear Me?, Clarion (New York, NY), 2008.

Bedtime without Arthur, Andersen (Minneapolis, MN), 2010.

ILLUSTRATOR

Mimi Thebo, *Drawing Together,* Walker (London, England), 2005.

Jeanne Willis, *Grandad and John,* Walker (London, England), 2007.

India Knight, *The Baby (But I'd Have Liked a Hamster),* Penguin (New York, NY), 2007.

Steve Voake, *Daisy Dawson Is on Her Way!,* Candlewick (Cambridge, MA), 2008.

Steve Voake, *Daisy Dawson and the Secret Pool,* Walker (London, England) 2008, published as *Daisy Dawson and the Secret Pond,* Candlewick (Cambridge, MA), 2009.

Steve Voake, *Daisy Dawson and the Big Freeze,* Candlewick (Cambridge, MA), 2010.

Sidelights

Jessica Meserve was born in the United States, grew up partially in the United Kingdom, and now lives in Canada. After completing her education in illustration at the Edinburgh College of Art, Meserve worked for four years as a children's book designer. In 2001 she decided to quit her job and start freelancing, and her work now appears in books written by authors such as Steve Voake, India Knight, Mimi Thebo, and Jeanne Willis, as well as in her original picture books *Small Sister, Can Anybody Hear Me?,* and *Bedtime without Arthur.*

Meserve's illustrations are featured in three of the titles in Voake's "Daisy Dawson" series. Suzanne Harold, writing in *Booklist,* described the artwork in *Daisy Dawson Is on Her Way!* as "well-placed black-and-white illustrations that grace almost every page." Andrea Tarr, a reviewer for *School Library Journal,* also cited the book's art, describing it as "sprightly illustrations in a variety of shapes." A critic for *Kirkus Reviews* commented that "Meserve's abundant comical sketches add bounce to this already-sweet wisp of a tale that gladdens the heart."

Meserve's first self-illustrated book, *Small,* was published in the United States as *Small Sister.* The story of a younger sister living in her older sibling's shadow,

Jessica Meserve creates expressive drawings in her work as illustrator of Steve Voake's Daisy Dawson Is on Her Way! *(Illustration copyright © 2007 by Jessica Meserve. Reproduced by permission of Candlewick Press, on behalf of Walker Books, London.)*

Small is illustrated with digital media. A *Kirkus Reviews* critic wrote that the illustrations "create the child-like vibrancy and immediacy necessary to bring to life this poignant tale of finding one's strengths," and *School Library Journal* critic Ieva Bates noted that "the details in the backdrops . . . are vividly depicted, and the outdoor scenes are colorful and soft." Ken Kilback, a reviewer for *Resource Links,* called *Small* "a lovely, touching, and reassuring story."

In Meserve's *Can Anybody Hear Me?* Quiet Jack has a very noisy family and must develop a louder voice. He does so after a series of adventures that gives Jack the power to make his family hear him. Catherine Callegari wrote in *School Library Journal* that, "despite the happy ending, some children may find Jack's invisibility a bit unnerving." However, a critic for *Kirkus Reviews* noted of *Can Anybody Hear Me?* that Meserve's use of "varied colors enliven the tale, conveying the shifts in mood" throughout her original story.

Biographical and Critical Sources

PERIODICALS

Booklist, May 1, 2008, Suzanne Harold, review of *Daisy Dawson Is on Her Way!,* p. 86.

Kirkus Reviews, May 1, 2007, review of *Small Sister;* May 15, 2008, review of *Daisy Dawson Is on Her Way!;* August 1, 2008, review of *Can Anybody Hear Me?*

Resource Links, April, 2007, Ken Kilback, review of *Small,* p. 8.

School Library Journal, June, 2007, Ieva Bates, review of *Small Sister,* p. 116; April, 2008, Andrea Tarr, review

of *Daisy Dawson Is on Her Way!,* p. 124; November, 2008, Catherine Callegari, review of *Can Anybody Hear Me?,* p. 96.

ONLINE

Jessica Meserve Home Page, http://jessicameserve.com (January 7, 2010).*

*　　　*　　　*

METAXAS, Eric 1963-

Personal

Born 1963, in New York, NY; married; children: one daughter. *Education:* Yale University, degree. *Religion:* Christian.

Addresses

Home—New York, NY.

Career

Author and storyteller. Rabbit Ears Productions, head writer and editorial director, 1988-92; *Breakpoint* (syndicated radio program), head writer for two years; Socrates in the City (lecture program), New York, NY, founder and host; commentator on radio and television; moderator of debates; featured speaker.

Awards, Honors

Yaddo fellowship; MacDowell Colony fellowship; three Grammy nominations for best children's recording; named honorary fellow, British-American Project, 2007.

Writings

FOR CHILDREN

The Fisherman and His Wife, illustrated by Diana Bryan, Rabbit Ears Books (Westport, CT), 1990.

The Story of Brer Rabbit and the Wonderful Tar Baby, illustrated by Henrik Drescher, Rabbit Ears Books (Saxonville, MA), 1990.

Jack and the Beanstalk, illustrated by Edward Sorel, Rabbit Ears Books (Westport, CT), 1991.

The Emperor's New Clothes, illustrated by Robert Van Nutt, Rabbit Ears Books (Westport, CT), 1991.

Puss in Boots, illustrated by Pierre Le-Tan, Rabbit Ears Books (Saxonville, MA), 1992.

The Fool and the Flying Ship, illustrated by Henrik Drescher, Rabbit Ears Books (Rowayton, CT), 1992.

The Boy and the Whale: A Christmas Fairy Tale, illustrated by Paul Lopez, Andrews McMeel (Kansas City, MO), 1994.

Peachboy, illustrated by Jeffrey Smith, Rabbit Ears Books (New York, NY), 1995.

Stormalong, illustrated by Don Vanderbeek, Rabbit Ears Books (New York, NY), 1995.

The Birthday ABC, Simon & Schuster Books for Young Readers (New York, NY), 1995.

The Monkey People, illustrated by Diana Bryan, Rabbit Ears Books (New York, NY), 1995.

Uncle Mugsy and the Terrible Twins of Christmas, Madison Square Press (New York, NY), 1995.

David and Goliath, illustrated by Douglas Fraser, Simon & Schuster (New York, NY), 1996.

Mose the Fireman, illustrated by Everett Peck, Rabbit Ears Books (New York, NY), 1996.

Pinocchio, illustrated by Brian Ajhar, Rabbit Ears Books (New York, NY), 1996.

Princess Scargo and the Birthday Pumpkin, illustrated by Karen Barbour, Rabbit Ears Books (New York, NY), 1996.

Squanto and the First Thanksgiving, illustrated by Michael Donato, Rabbit Ears Books (New York, NY), 1996.

The Wild Ride of Miss Impala George, Orchard (New York, NY), 1996.

A to Z, Tommy Nelson (Nashville, TN), 1998.

Bible ABC, illustrated by Jim Harris, Tommy Nelson (Nashville, TN), 1998.

The Gardener's Apprentice: A Folktale and Flower Journal, Creative Editions (Mankato, MN), 1998.

Squanto and the Miracle of Thanksgiving, illustrated by Shannon Stirnweis, Tommy Nelson (Nashville, TN), 1999.

Even Fish Slappers Need a Second Chance, illustrated by Greg Hardin and Robert Vann, ZonderKidz (Grand Rapids, MI), 2002.

God Made You Special, ZonderKidz (Grand Rapids, MI), 2002.

The Pirates Who Usually Don't Do Anything, illustrated by Ron Eddy and Robert Vann, ZonderKidz (Grand Rapids, MI), 2002.

King Midas and the Golden Touch, illustrated by Rodica Prato, Abdo Pub. (Edina, MN), 2006.

It's Time to Sleep, My Love (a Lullabye), illustrated by Nancy Tillman, Feiwel & Friends (New York, NY), 2008.

Author of other books, including *Prince of Egypt A to Z* (film tie-in).

SOUND RECORDINGS

The Fisherman and His Wife, Windham Hill Records (Stanford, CA), 1989.

Brer Rabbit and the Wonderful Tar Baby, Windham Hill Records (Stanford, CA), 1990.

The Emperor's New Clothes, Windham Hill Records (Stanford, CA), 1990.

Jack and the Beanstalk, Kid Rhino (Santa Monica, CA), 1991.

King Midas and the Golden Touch, Kid Rhino (Santa Monica, CA), 1991.

Peachboy, Kid Rhino (Santa Monica, CA), 1991.

Puss in Boots, Kid Rhino (Santa Monica, CA), 1991.

The Fool and the Flying Ship, Kid Rhino (Santa Monica, CA), 1991.

The Monkey People, Kid Rhino (Rowayton, CT), 1991.

David and Goliath, BMG Music (Rowayton, CT), 1992.

Princess Scargo and the Birthday Pumpkin, Rabbit Ears (Rowayton, CT), 1993.

The White Cat, Rabbit Ears (New York, NY), 2000.

OTHER

Don't You Believe It!, illustrated by Marc Dennis, St. Martin's Griffin (New York, NY), 1996.

Everything You Always Wanted to Know about God (but Were Afraid to Ask), WaterBrook Press (Colorado Springs, CO), 2005.

Amazing Grace: William Wilberforce and the Heroic Campaign to End Slavery, HarperSanFrancisco (New York, NY), 2007.

Everything ELSE You Always Wanted to Know about God (but Were Afraid to Ask), WaterBrook Press (Colorado Springs, CO), 2007.

Bonhoeffer: A Biography, HarperOne (New York, NY), 2009.

Everything You Always Wanted to Know about God (the Jesus Edition), WaterBrook Press (Colorado Springs, CO), 2010.

Author of scripts for videos, including for *Veggie Tales,* and *3-2-1-Penguins!.* Contributor to periodicals, including *New York Times, New York Times Book Review, Atlantic Monthly, Washington Post, Regeneration Quarterly, Books & Culture, Christianity Today, Mars Hill Review,* and *First Things.*

Sidelights

A humorist and commentator based in New York City, Eric Metaxas has also enjoyed a long career in children's publishing. After serving as head writer and editorial director for Rabbit Ears Productions, an award-winning animation and recording studio, he went on to write scripts for the "Veggie Tales" series of computer-animated Christian-themed videos. In addition, Metaxas has also written dozens of children's books that have been praised for their energetic and lighthearted texts. In reviewing *The Birthday ABC, Booklist* critic Julie Corsaro cited the story's "giddy verse," calling the volume "a clever concept executed in a striking theatrical design." Metaxas's retelling of a Colombian folk tale in *The Monkey People* was also praised by Susan Dove Lempke, a *Booklist* reviewer who made special note of the author's "easy storytelling style."

With its unique take on the Thanksgiving holiday celebrated by most Americans, Metaxas's *Squanto and the Miracle of Thanksgiving* follows the young Patuxet boy as he is kidnaped by Spaniards, taken by ship to Spain, and then taken in and educated by a group of monks before returning to his home village a decade later. Finding his tribe decimated by disease, Squanto decides to help William Bradford and the group of English Puritans attempting to establish a colony at Plymouth.

Squanto and the Miracle of Thanksgiving "approaches the holiday from an evangelical point of view," observed a *Publishers Weekly,* and it also accurately depicts "the holiday's religious roots and historical beginnings."

In the picture book *It's Time to Sleep, My Love* a bedtime story by Metaxas is brought to life in detailed photo-collage illustrations by artist Nancy Tillman. In *Booklist* Gillian Engberg wrote that the author's "lilting, picture-book lullaby" sustains its calming mood through a mix of "lulling sounds, repetition, and . . . short lines." Praising Tillman's "dramatic, digitally created" art, a *Kirkus Reviews* writer deemed *It's Time to Sleep, My Love* "a luxuriant bedtime retreat for children and parents alike."

In addition to his work for children, Metaxas is the author of *Everything Else You Always Wanted to Know*

about God (but Were Afraid to Ask), a work described by a *Publishers Weekly* contributor as a "cheeky question-and-answer book" addressing commonly asked questions about a higher power. In *Amazing Grace: William Wilberforce and the Heroic Campaign to End Slavery* he chronicles the life of Wilberforce, the English politician and orator who dedicated much of his life to outlawing slavery in Great Britain and its colonies. A popular commentator, Metaxas also contributes opinion pieces to publications that include the *Atlantic Monthly, Christianity Today,* and the *New York Times.*

Biographical and Critical Sources

PERIODICALS

Booklist, August, 1995, Julie Corsaro, review of *The Birthday ABC,* p. 1953; February 1, 1996, Susan Dove

Eric Metaxas's gentle bedtime story in **It's Time to Sleep, My Love** *is captured in detailed paintings by Nancy Tillman.* (Feiwel & Friends, 2008. Illustration

Lempke, review of *The Monkey People,* p. 935; October 15, 2008, Gillian Engberg, review of *It's Time to Sleep, My Love,* p. 47.

Christian Century, November 13, 2007, Jonathan R. Baer, review of *Amazing Grace: William Wilberforce and the Heroic Campaign to End Slavery,* p. 39.

First Things, February, 208, Anna Deborah Bingham, review of *Amazing Grace,* p. 49.

Kirkus Reviews, September 15, 2008, review of *It's Time to Sleep, My Love.*

Kliatt, January, 2008, Pat Dole, review of *Amazing Grace,* p. 48.

National Review, December 5, 2005, S.T. Karnick, review of *Everything You Always Wanted to Know about God (but Were Afraid to Ask),* p. 49.

Publishers Weekly, April 19, 1993, review of *Princess Scargo and the Birthday Pumpkin* (sound recording), p. 29; March 21, 1994, review of *Mose the Fireman* (sound recording), p. 29; September 27, 1999, review of *Squanto and the Miracle of Thanksgiving,* p. 50; August 29, 2005, review of *Everything You Always Wanted to Know about God (but Were Afraid to Ask),* p. 53.

School Library Journal, December, 2008, Bethany Isaacson, review of *It's Time to Sleep, My Love,* p. 96.

ONLINE

Eric Metaxas Home Page, http://www.ericmetaxas.com (January 10, 2010).*

*   *   *

MORDEN, Simon 1966(?)-

Personal

Born c. 1966, in England. *Education:* University of Sheffield, B.Sc. (geology; with honors); University of Newcastle, Ph.D. (planetary geophysics).

Addresses

Home—Gateshead, England. *Agent*—Antony Harwood Literary Agency, 103 Walton St., Oxford OX2 6EB, England. *E-mail*—bookofmorden@blueyonder.co.uk.

Career

Author and editor. Formerly worked as a school caretaker, administrative assistant, and assistant to a financial advisor. Part-time teaching assistant in primary school, Gateshead, England. *Focus* (magazine of British Science Fiction Association), editor beginning c. 2004. Judge for Arthur C. Clarke Awards, 2006.

Member

British Fantasy Society.

Awards, Honors

Bram Stoker Award for Best Short Story nomination, 2002, for "Hollow"; World Fantasy Award for Best Novella shortlist, 2005, for *Another War.*

Writings

Thy Kingdom Come (short stories), Lone Wolf Publications, 2002.

Heart, Razorblade Press, 2002.

Brilliant Things (short stories), Subway (Bristol, England), 2004.

Another War (novella), Telos, 2005.

The Lost Art, David Fickling Books (Oxford, England), 2007, David Fickling Books (New York, NY), 2008.

Contributor of short stories to periodicals, including *Noesis, Terror Tales,* and *This Way Up.* Work represented in anthologies, including *Hideous Progeny,* edited by Brian Willis, Razorblade Press, 2000; *Extremes: Fantasy and Horror from the Ends of the Earth,* edited by Brian Hopkins, Lone Wolf Publications, 2000; and *Extremes 2,* 2001.

Sidelights

Simon Morden has a background that makes him unusual among his fellow writers: he has degrees in geology and planetary geophysics. Interestingly, Morden decided to opt for writing about science rather than working as a scientist, and he worked as a teacher and

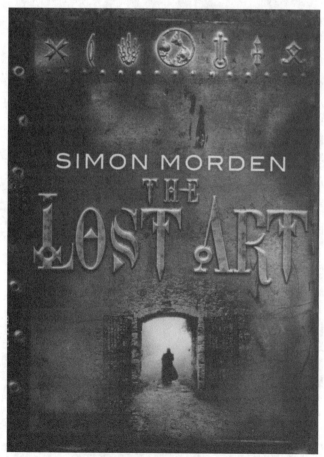

Cover of Simon Morden's fantasy novel The Lost Art, *featuring artwork by Henry Steadman.* (David Fickling Books, 2008. Photo of archway & figure: © Photolibrary.com. Reproduced by permission of Photolibrary.com.)

administrative assistant while developing his fiction-writing skills. Since the early 2000s, Morden has published acclaimed short stories that blend science fiction with elements of horror and fantasy, some of which have been anthologized in the books *Thy Kingdom Come* and *Brilliant Things.* In addition to his novella *Another War,* which he published in 2005, Morden has attracted teen readers with his book *The Lost Art.*

In *The Lost Art* Morden takes readers into an agrarian world where technological advances have culminated in catastrophe. Humans now live in a pre-industrial dark age known as the Reversal, and the knowledge of the past has been collected in books which are hidden in Siberia and guarded by a group of monks. When the book is stolen and most of its guardians murdered, Va survives and goes in search of the thieves. A warrior monk, Va gains companions as he travels, and he is eventually joined by Benzamir Michael Mahmood. Mahmood, a descendent of a group of humans who escaped prior to Earth's catastrophe, has been sent to protect the planet from those who are determined to destroy it. Calling *The Lost Art* "philosophically challenging," a *Kirkus Reviews* writer ranked the work as "action-packed science-fiction," and Lynn Rutan concluded in *Booklist* that Morden's "secret-laden plot" resolves in "a satisfying conclusion." *The Lost Art* "poses . . . questions about faith, purpose, and means to noble ends," observed Lesley Farmer in a *Kliatt* review, the critic adding that Morden's "satisfying read" will appeal to a range of readers, from middle school through adult.

Biographical and Critical Sources

PERIODICALS

Booklist, May 15, 2008, Lynn Rutan, review of *The Lost Art,* p. 56.
Kirkus Reviews, May 15, 2008, review of *The Lost Art.*
Kliatt, May, 2008, Lesley Farmer, review of *The Lost Art,* p. 14.
School Library Journal, November, 2008, Jennifer D. Montgomery, review of *The Lost Art,* p. 131.

ONLINE

Simon Morden Home Page, http://www.bookofmorden.com (January 1, 2010).*

* * *

MORTON, Christine
See MORTON-SHAW, Christine

MORTON-SHAW, Christine 1957-
(Christine Morton)

Personal

Born 1957, in England; married Greg Shaw (a writer); children. *Education:* Sheffield Hallam University, M.A. (creative writing).

Addresses

Home—Sheffield, England.

Career

Author of books for children and young adults.

Awards, Honors

Silver Award, Parents' Choice Foundation, for *Picnic Farm;* Best Children's Illustrated Book designation, English Association, 2001.

Writings

(As Christine Morton) *The Pig That Barked,* illustrated by Angie Sage, Hodder & Stoughton (London, England), 1992.
(As Christine Morton) *Don't Worry William,* illustrated by Nigel McMullen, Ladybird Books (Loughborough, England), 1995.
(As Christine Morton) *Picnic Farm,* illustrated by Sarah Barringer, Holiday House (New York, NY), 1998.
(As Christine Morton) *Run, Rabbit, Run,* illustrated by Eleanor Taylor, Bloomsbury Children's (London, England), 2001.
Magoozy, illustrated by Thomas Müller, Macmillan Children's (London, England), 2002.
Itzy Bitzy House, illustrated by Arthur Robins, Barron's Educational Series (Hauppauge, NY), 2004.
The Riddles of Epsilon, Katherine Tegen Books (New York, NY), 2005.
Mr Jack, illustrated by Thomas Müller, Macmillan Children's (London, England), 2005.
(With husband Greg Shaw) *Wake up, Sleepy Bear!,* illustrated by John Butler, Puffin (New York, NY), 2006.
The Hunt for the Seventh, Katherine Tegen Books (New York, NY), 2008.

Also author, under name Christine Morton, of "Stringalongs" and "Little Stringalongs" educational series, 1995-97. Contributor to anthologies, including *Bears for Bedtime! Storybook Collection,* Ladybird (London, England), 1999.

Author's work has been translated into German.

Sidelights

A British author who specializes in creating stories to entertain children and young adults, Christine Morton-Shaw began her writing career in the early 1990s, creating original picture-book stories such as *Wake up, Sleepy Bear!,* a rhyming tale about springtime that *School Library Journal* critic DeAnn Okamura recommended as "perfect for . . . one-on-one sharing." In addition to producing educational books in the "String-alongs" series, Morton-Shaw is known for her young-adult fantasy novels *The Riddles of Epsilon* and *The Hunt for the Seventh,* both of which have earned her fans in both her native United Kingdom and the United States.

In *The Riddles of Epsilon* readers meet fourteen-year-old Jessica White as she moves with her parents to an ancient house on an island off the coast of Scotland. Jess soon becomes aware that the house—and her family—is becoming overwhelmed by a ghostly presence that does not bode good. At night her dreams are haunted by the spirit of Sebastian Wren, who lived in the house a century before, while another spirit named Epsilon speaks to her during the daytime, sending riddles and poems during her Internet chats. Now, it is up to Jess to discover which spirit to trust and how to fight the darkness that threatens her family in a novel that *Kliatt* contributor Donna Scanlon described as "engrossing, cleverly constructed, and original." Noting Morton-Shaw's use of ciphers, clues, and the like, a *Kirkus Reviews* critic predicted that readers "looking for Christian symbolism will be rewarded" by the novel and dubbed *The Riddles of Epsilon* "a clever conundrum."

Another family move propels the supernatural action in *The Hunt for the Seventh.* Here Jim and Sal move to Minerva Hall with their father, who works for Lord Minerva as head gardener. Soon Jim meets up with a strange boy named Einstein, who hints at a dark secret within the history of the Minerva family. As Jim explores, he realizes that this secret has to do with the death of several children, the spirits of whom still reside at Minerva Hall. Praising the "fine plotting" in *The Hunt for the Seventh,* Jennifer D. Montgomery added in her *School Library Journal* review that "Morton-Shaw skillfully weaves ancient lore into a gripping mystery." A *Kirkus Reviews* writer recommended the middle-grade novel as "a fairly age-appropriate scary read," and in *Booklist* Todd Morning described *The Hunt for the Seventh* as "a classic ghost story with a modern twist."

Biographical and Critical Sources

PERIODICALS

Booklist, January 1, 2009, Todd Morning, review of *The Hunt for the Seventh,* p. 82.

Kirkus Reviews, April 15, 2005, review of *The Riddles of Epsilon,* p. 478; September 15, 2008, review of *The Hunt for the Seventh.*

Kliatt, March, 2007, Donna Scanlon, review of *The Riddles of Epsilon,* p. 26.

School Library Journal, August, 2005, Melissa Moore, review of *The Riddles of Epsilon,* p. 132; November, 2006, DeAnn Okamura, review of *Wake up, Sleepy Bear!,* p. 107; May, 2009, Jennifer D. Montgomery, review of *The Hunt for the Seventh,* p. 116.

Voice of Youth Advocates, June, 2005, Arlene Garcia and Sara Garcia, review of *The Riddles of Epsilon,* p. 150; December, 2008, Rayna Patton, review of *The Hunt for the Seventh,* p. 456.*

O-P

OFFILL, Jenny 1968-

Personal

Born 1968, in MA. *Education:* Attended Stanford Creative Writing Program, 1991-93.

Addresses

Home—Brooklyn, NY. *Office*—Brooklyn College, English Department, 2308 Boylan Hall, Brooklyn, NY 11210.

Career

Author and editor. Brooklyn College, Brookly, NY, instructor in writing; has also taught at Yale University and State University of New York at Purchase.

Awards, Honors

Stegner fellow, 1991-93; *Los Angeles Times* First Book Award finalist, for *Last Things.*

Writings

FOR CHILDREN

Seventeen Things I'm Not Allowed to Do Anymore, illustrated by Nancy Carpenter, Schwartz & Wade Books (New York, NY), 2007.

FOR ADULTS

Last Things, Farrar, Straus & Giroux (New York, NY), 1999.

(Editor, with Elissa Schappell) *The Friend Who Got Away: Twenty Women's True-life Tales of Friendships That Blew Up, Burned Out, or Faded Away,* Doubleday (New York, NY), 2005.

(Editor, with Elissa Schappell) *Money Changes Everything: Twenty-two Writers Tackle the Last Taboo with Tales of Sudden Windfalls, Staggering Debts, and Other Surprising Turns of Fortune,* Doubleday (New York, NY), 2007.

Contributor to periodicals, including *Story, Gettysburg Review, Black Warrior Review,* and *Boulevard.*

Sidelights

Jenny Offill is an author, editor, and educator who produced the highly regarded picture book *Seventeen Things I'm Not Allowed to Do Anymore* in 2007. Offill, who teaches at Brooklyn College, has also written *Last Things,* a critically acclaimed work for adults, and has served as coeditor, with Elissa Schappell, of a pair of well-received anthologies. Her shorter fiction has appeared in *Gettysburg Review* and *Boulevard,* among other publications.

Last Things, Offill's debut novel, concerns Grace Davitt, a young girl growing up in a small Vermont town with her stubborn, rationalist father and her mesmerizing but disturbed mother Anna. When Grace runs into trouble at school, Anna, an ornithologist, decides to educate her daughter at home using an irrational "cosmic calendar" that condenses the history of the universe into a single year. The youngster also receives informal instruction from her father, Jonathan, a chemistry teacher; her babysitter, Edgar, a teenage genius; and her Uncle Pete, who plays "Mr. Science" on television. According to *Ploughshares* contributor Fred Leebron, "when Grace begins to understand that she must choose between her father and her mother, her despair escalates to danger and—as in all the bits of stories that her

Jenny Offill's story of a girl in distress is captured in Nancy Carpenter's illustrations for **Seventeen Things I'm Not Allowed to Do Anymore.** (Illustration copyright © 2006 by Nancy Carpenter. All rights reserved. Used by permission of Schwartz & Wade Books, an imprint of Random House Children's Books, a division of Random House, Inc.)

mother has told her in these years—to the crucial sensation that she has learned many things but does not know which are true."

Last Things garnered strong reviews. "The novel is crisply written, economically constructed and so inventive that you read without a clue as to what anyone will say or do next," remarked *New York Times Book Review* critic Nancy Willard, the reviewer adding that "Offill's fresh voice, endearing and quirky, makes you willingly suspend disbelief." In *Booklist* Donna Seaman commented that the author "gives human form to the conflict between art and science, the cosmic and the prosaic," and a reviewer for *Publishers Weekly* described the novel as "a rare feat of remarkable constraint and nearly miraculous construction of a most unique family."

In *Seventeen Things I'm Not Allowed to Do Anymore* Offill introduces an imaginative young rule-breaker who has seemingly changed her ways. "I wanted to write a book that captured the mischievous side of childhood," the author stated in an online interview for Powells. com. "So many seem to be about teaching kids lessons, eat your spinach, don't talk back to your mother, go to bed, and they feel like rulebooks to me. I wanted a book that reflected kids as they really are, not as parents might wish them to be." In the work, the unnamed narrator lists a number of her now-forbidden behaviors, including stapling her brother's hair to his pillow and adding dead flies to the ice cube tray. "Kids will be intrigued by the pictures' playful sense of composition as well as the heroine's brazenness," remarked a critic in *Publishers Weekly,* and *Austin American-Statesman* reviewer Julia Null Smith noted that the "simple call and response" in Offill's narrative gives readers "a window

into this energetic, imaginative little girl and her wild, sometimes dangerous, and downright silly plans."

Biographical and Critical Sources

PERIODICALS

Austin American-Statesman, April 1, 2007, Julia Null Smith, "Seventeen Things Kids Will Want to Read Again," p. J5.

Booklist, April 1, 1999, Donna Seaman, review of *Last Things,* p. 1386; April 15, 2005, Whitney Scott, review of *The Friend Who Got Away: Twenty Women's Life Tales of Friendships That Blew Up, Burned Out, or Faded Away,* p. 1415; November 1, 2006, Hazel Rochman, review of *Seventeen Things I'm Not Allowed to Do Anymore,* p. 58.

International Herald Tribune, March 3, 2007, Alina Tugend, "Penny for Your Thoughts?," review of *Money Changes Everything: Twenty-two Writers Tackle the Last Taboo with Tales of Sudden Windfalls, Staggering Debts, and Other Surprising Turns of Fortune,* p. 19.

Kirkus Reviews, February 1, 2005, review of *The Friend Who Got Away,* p. 168; December 1, 2006, review of *Seventeen Things I'm Not Allowed to Do Anymore,* p. 1224.

Library Journal, May 15, 2005, Kay Brodie, review of *The Friend Who Got Away,* p. 129.

Newsweek, May 30, 2005, Kay Brodie, review of *The Friend Who Got Away,* p. 129.

New Yorker, June 21, 1999, review of *Last Things,* p. 216.

New York Times Book Review, June 13, 1999, Nancy Willard, "Oh Mom, Poor Mom," review of *Last Things.*

Ploughshares, fall, 1999, Fred Leebron, review of *Last Things,* p. 218.

Publishers Weekly, February 1, 1999, review of *Last Things,* p. 73; February 7, 2005, review of *The Friend Who Got Away,* p. 49; December 4, 2006, review of *Money Changes Everything,* p. 49; October 30, 2006, review of *Seventeen Things I'm Not Allowed to Do Anymore,* p. 60.

Review of Contemporary Fiction, fall, 1999, Evelin Sullivan, review of *Last Things,* p. 169.

School Library Journal, November, 2006, Catherine Threadgill, review of *Seventeen Things I'm Not Allowed to Do Anymore,* p. 107.

Times (London, England), August 14, 1999, Tim Teeman, "Women's World," review of *Last Things,* p. 22.

ONLINE

Powell's Web site, http://www.powells.com/ (March 10, 2008), "Kids' Q&A: Jenny Offill and Nancy Carpenter."

Friend Who Got Away Web site, http://www.thefriendwho gotaway.com/ (March 10, 2008).*

PARDO DeLANGE, Alex

Personal

Born in Caracas, Venezuela; married; children: three. *Education:* University of Miami, B.F.A.

Addresses

Home and office—Gainesville, FL.

Career

Illustrator.

Illustrator

Mary Dixon Lake, *My Circus Family,* Mondo (Greenvale, NY), 1995.

Ofelia Dumas Lachtman, *Pepita Talks Twice/Pepita habla dos veces,* Piñata Books (Houston, TX), 1995.

Diane Gonzales Bertrand, *Sip, Slurp, Soup, Soup/Caldo, caldo, caldo,* Piñata Books (Houston, TX), 1996.

Ofelia Dumas Lachtman, *Pepita Thinks Pink/Pepita y el color rosado,* Piñata Books (Houston, TX), 1998.

Ofelia Dumas Lachtman, *Pepita Takes Time/Pepita, siempre tarde,* Piñata Books (Houston, TX), 2001.

Ofelia Dumas Lachtman, *Pepita Finds Out/Lo que Pepita descubre,* Piñata Books (Houston, TX), 2002.

Alex Pardo DeLange's picture-book projects include creating the engaging artwork in Ofelia Dumas Lachtman's Pepita Packs Up. *(Illustration copyright © 2005 by Alex Pardo DeLange. Arte Público Press—University of Houston. Reproduced by permission.)*

Ofelia Dumas Lachtman, *Tina and the Scarecrow Skins/Tina y las pieles de espantapajaros,* Piñata Books (Houston, TX), 2002.

Diane Gonzales Bertrand, *The Empanadas That Abuela Made/Las empanadas que hacia la abuela,* Piñata Books (Houston, TX), 2003.

Ofelia Dumas Lachtman, *Pepita Packs Up/Pepita empaca,* Piñata Books (Houston, TX), 2005.

Ofelia Dumas Lachtman, *Pepita on Pepper Street/Pepita en la calle Pepper,* Piñata Books (Houston, TX), 2008.

Sidelights

Like the character Pepita, which she brings to life as illustrator of a series of books by Ofelia Dumas Lachtman, Alex Pardo DeLange is a child of two cultures. Born in Caracas, Venezuela, Pardo DeLange spent her teen years in Buenos Aires, Argentina, before moving to the United States. She attended the University of Miami to study fine arts and worked as a freelance designer for various design and advertising agencies before becoming an illustrator of children's books. On the Children's Literature Web site, Pardo DeLange noted: "I love illustrating children's books. It gives me the freedom to create fun and interesting characters, and to bring them to life." Pardo DeLange works in both digital art and water color combined with pen and ink to create her characters.

Pepita, the star of Lachtman's bi-lingual series, is an energetic young girl who struggles with issues familiar to many young people, such as being tardy, having to move, and making new friends. In *Pepita Talks Twice/Pepita habla dos veces,* the girl becomes frustrated with having to translate for others and decides to give up speaking Spanish altogether. Soon, however, Pepita realizes that speaking two languages is not just about language, but about being part of her family's culture. The other books in Lachtman's "Pepita" series continue that same multicultural theme.

As Ann Welton wrote in *School Library Journal,* Pardo DeLange's "full-page, pen-and-ink and watercolor cartoon illustrations extend the text" in *Pepita Finds Out/Lo que Pepita descubre,* while in *Pepita Takes Time/Pepita, siempre tarde* the "cartoon illustrations are clean and have considerable child appeal." Pardo DeLange uses a digital approach in her artwork for *Pepita Packs Up/Pepita empaca,* and Maria Otero-Boisvert wrote in *School Library Journal* that the illustrator's "simple computer-generated art depicts Hispanic characters in a pleasant setting." A *Kirkus Reviews* contributor described the same illustrations as "vivid," noting that the images "combine black outlines with pastel sweeps of color." Another *Kirkus Reviews* critic had praise for Pardo DeLange's work in *Pepita on Pepper Street/Pepita en la calle Pepper,* citing her contribution of "detailed, cartoon-style paintings."

Along with the "Pepita" books, Pardo DeLange has illustrated several stand-alone picture books by other writers. Her illustrations "cheerfully burst out of

crowded patterned borders" of the pages in *Sip, Slurp, Soup, Soup/Caldo, caldo, caldo,* a story by Diane Gonzales Bertrand, according to a *Publishers Weekly* contributor. In *The Empanadas That Abuela Made/Las empanadas que hacia la abuela,* another Bertrand tale, Pardo DeLange's images "have just the right verve and humor" to compliment the story, according to Welton.

Biographical and Critical Sources

PERIODICALS

Booklist, February 15, 2003, John Peters, review of *Tina and the Scarecrow Skins/Tina y las pieles de espantapajaros,* p. 1069.

Kirkus Reviews, November 15, 2005, review of *Pepita Packs Up/Pepita empaca,* p. 1234; September 15, 2008, review of *Pepita on Pepper Street/Pepita en la calle Pepper.*

Publishers Weekly, May 12, 1997, review of *Sip, Slurp Soup, Soup/Caldo, caldo, caldo,* p. 75.

School Library Journal, January, 2001, Ann Welton, review of *Pepita Takes Time/Pepita, siempre tarde,* p. 102; March, 2003, Ann Welton, reviews of *Tina and*

Pardo DeLange's collaboration with Lachtman continues, as their young heroine stars in **Pepita on Pepper Street.** *(Piñata Books, 2008. Illustration copyright © 2008 by Arte Público Press—University of Houston. Reprinted with permission of the publisher.)*

the Scarecrow Skins/*Tina y las pieles de espantapa-jaros* and *Pepita Finds Out/Lo que Pepita descubre,* both p. 227; December, 2003, Ann Welton, review of *The Empanadas That Abuela Made/Las empanadas que hacía la abuela,* p. 142; February, 2006, Maria Otero-Boisvert, review of *Pepita Packs Up/Pepita empaca,* p. 126.

ONLINE

Children's Literature Web site, http://www.childrenslit. com/ (January 6, 2010), "Alex Pardo DeLange."
LatinoTeca Web site, http://www.latinoteca.com/ (January 6, 2010), "Alex Pardo DeLange."*

*   *   *

PEARSON, Mary E. 1955-

Personal
Born August, 1955, in Lakewood, CA; daughter of Silas Odell (a fisherman) and Helen Frances (a postal clerk) Stark; married Dennis Pearson (a certified public accountant), 1974; children: Karen, Jessica. *Education:* California State University—Long Beach, B.F.A., 1978; San Diego State University, teaching credential, 1990. *Religion:* Christian. *Hobbies and other interests:* Reading, gardening, snow skiing, cooking, traveling, spending time with family.

Addresses
Home—P.O. Box 130997, Carlsbad, CA 92013-0997. *E-mail*—mary@marypearson.com.

Career
Author and educator. Teacher in San Marcos, CA, beginning 1990; freelance writer, beginning 1996.

Member
Society of Children's Book Writers and Illustrators, Assembly on Literature for Adolescents.

Awards, Honors
Year's Best Books for Older Children designation, *St. Louis Post Dispatch,* and Best Book Award Honor Book designation, Society of School Librarians International, both 2000, and Children's Choice Award, International Reading Association, Best Pick selection, *Jewish Family Times,* and Best Books for the Teen Age listee, New York Public Library, all 2001, all for *David v. God;* Best Book designation, Society of School Librarians International, 2001, and South Carolina Young-Adult Book Award, 2004, both for *Scribbler of Dreams;* Golden Kite Award, Society of Children's Book Writers and Illustrators, 2005, for *A Room on Lorelei Street;* Golden Kite Award Honor Book designation, 2008, and

Mary E. Pearson (Reproduced by permission.)

Andre Norton Award finalist, American Library Association Best Books for Young Adults designation, and Capitol Choices designation, both 2009, all for *The Adoration of Jenna Fox;* numerous state award honors.

Writings

BEGINNING READERS

Pickles in My Soup (easy reader), illustrated by Tom Payne, Children's Press (New York, NY), 1999.
Where Is Max?, illustrated by Samanatha L. Walker, Children's Press (New York, NY), 2000.
I Can Do It All, illustrated by Jeff Shelly, Children's Press (New York, NY), 2002.
Generous Me, illustrated by Gary Krejca, Children's Press (New York, NY), 2002.
Fast Dan, illustrated by Eldon C. Doty, Children's Press (New York, NY), 2002.

YOUNG-ADULT NOVELS

David v. God, Harcourt (San Diego, CA), 2000.
Scribbler of Dreams, Harcourt (San Diego, CA), 2001.
A Room on Lorelei Street, Henry Holt (New York, NY), 2005.

The Adoration of Jenna Fox, Henry Holt (New York, NY), 2008.

The Miles Between, Henry Holt (New York, NY), 2009.

Author's work has been translated into numerous languages, including Chinese, Dutch, Finnish, French, German, Japanese, Korean, Polish, and Spanish.

Adaptations

The Adoration of Jenna Fox was adapted for audiobook by Macmillan Audiobook (New York, NY), 2008, and adapted for a film by Twentieth Century-Fox. *The Miles Between, A Room on Lorelei Street,* and *Scribbler of Dreams* were adapted as audiobooks by Brilliance Audio.

Sidelights

Mary E. Pearson began her writing career creating entertaining stories for beginning readers and has gone on to find success in writing for young adults. In her award-winning novels such as *David v. God, Scribbler of Dreams, A Room on Lorelei Street,* and *The Miles Between,* Pearson focuses on teen characters who, when faced with choices and challenges, have a willingness to accept change and embrace the responsibilities that come with maturity. In reviewing *The Miles Between,* a novel about a teenaged loner who is given a rare glimpse of a different life, *Booklist* contributor Kara Dean wrote that "Pearson skillfully separates truth from illusion" in an "uplifting" novel that deals with sophisticated themes and thoughtful, compelling characters.

Pearson grew up in Southern California where, as a child, she used her imagination so well that each morning when she got up she pretended to be someone else and would not respond to her mother unless called by her "name of the day." While in school, perceptive teachers recognized and encouraged Pearson's talent. After earning a college degree and teaching certificate, she taught many different grades and, writing with her students rekindled her own interest in writing. "During Writing Workshop, I would sit with them and write, loving the process, loving the stories, and lo and behold deciding I would love to return to my first love," Pearson recalled on her home page.

In her first young-adult novel, *David v. God,* Pearson portrays the near-death experience of David, the class clown who demands an audience with God and challenges Him to a debate. At stake is life or death, and David must team up with Marie, the president of the high school Speech and Debate Club, to have a chance. "No leap of faith is required to enjoy this easy-to-read, fast-paced contemporary parable," Joel Shoemaker remarked in his *School Library Journal* review of the work.

Scribbler of Dreams is a romance between members of longtime feuding families. Pearson once told *SATA* about the novel's genesis: "I think our actions do have

consequences and sometimes they ripple much farther than we know. I wanted to explore that idea in *Scribbler of Dreams.* 'What if' someone did something and it rippled past even their own lifetime. 'What if' it kept rippling past generation and generation? Could that happen? And if that rippling effect became a 'tradition,' could one young person have the power to end it?" In her story, Pearson explores one girl's attempt to end a cycle of hate that has become a tradition in her family.

Scribbler of Dreams garnered mixed reviews. While a *Publishers Weekly* contributor moted the familiarity of the theme, the repetition in the plot, and the "highly unlikely denouement," other critics were more appreciative. In her review for *School Library Journal,* Rebecca Hogue Wojahn mentioned the "believable characters and a fast-moving, if somewhat transparent, plot" in *Scribbler of Dreams.* "*Romeo and Juliet* this isn't," wrote a *Kirkus Reviews* critic, "but fans of teen angst and undying-love stories will probably appreciate the effort." *Booklist* reviewer John Peters predicted that "fans of angst-laden teen romance will be glued" to *Scribbler of Dreams.*

Cover of Mary E. Pearson's young-adult novel The Adoration of Jenna Fox, *about a teenager's efforts to rebuild her life after a long illness.* (Henry Holt & Company, LLC, 2008. Jacket art ©: Gary Powell/Getty Images (background); Roy McMahon/Corbis (foreground). Reprinted by permission.)

Winner of the Golden Kite Award, Pearson's novel *A Room on Lorelei Street* takes place in Texas and focuses on seventeen-year-old Zoe. The teen is overwhelmed with responsibility, not only for her own survival but also for the care of her alcoholic mother and her little brother. With her brother now living with caring relatives, Zoe decides that it is time for her to also leave home. She works to support herself while finishing high school, and also deals with the grown-up worries of independent living, all the while wrestling with the emotional consequences of her choice. Is she being selfish, as her grandmother asserts, or has Zoe's choice been a healthy one? In *Kliatt* Claire Rosser described *A Room on Lorelei Street* as "a raw story" in which Pearson illustrates "how crippling it is to be the child of an alcoholic." In the novel the author combines what Sharon Morrison described in her *School Library Journal* assessment as an "at times lyrical" narrative containing a "powerful" message about self-actualization. In *A Room on Lorelei Street* Pearson "sophisticately crafts" a tense work of teen literature that is enriched by her depiction of what a *Kirkus Reviews* writer described as "a quietly cramped, small-town . . . community."

Unlike Zoe in *A Room on Lorelei Street*, the seventeen-year-old narrator of *The Adoration of Jenna Fox* is not motivated by her past experiences within a troubled family. Jenna Fox has no past: she has just come out of a long coma and she has no memories of her former life or the accident that caused her injury. The people who now claim her as their daughter and granddaughter seem strange to the teen, and when she returns to the place they assure her is "home," she feels displaced. With the help of friends at her new school, Jenna works to reconcile the person she learns she once was with the person she now knows herself to be. As time passes, and she learns about the family's abrupt cross-country relocation, Jenna senses that her questions spark tension and attempts at evasion among family members. Set in the near future, *The Adoration of Jenna Fox* allows Pearson "to generate suspense" and also encourages readers to consider the "ethical implications" of "advanced biomedical technology," according to *Horn Book* contributor Jonathan Hunt. Describing the novel as "part mystery and part science fiction," *Kliatt* contributor Janis Flint-Ferguson dubbed *The Adoration of Jenna Fox* both "fascinating and thought provoking," while in *School Library Journal* Meredith Robbins praised Pearson for "construct[ing] . . . a gripping, believable vision of a future dystopia."

"I think the vast amounts of poetry I read in high school and college had a tremendous influence on me," Pearson noted in a discussion with *Teacher Librarian* interviewer David Gill. She credits her interest in poetry with "contributing to my interest in young adult literature where every word must count. Even though my books are by no means slim, I do consider every word, and I'm always trying to trim them down. I always joke that one day I will truly get my stories down to their purest essence, and a whole novel will be read in one paragraph."

Biographical and Critical Sources

PERIODICALS

Booklist, April 15, 2001, John Peters, review of *Scribbler of Dreams*; July 1, 2009, Kara Dean, review of *The Miles Between*, p. 55.
Horn Book, May-June, 2008, Jonathan Hunt, review of *The Adoration of Jenna Fox*, p. 325.
Journal of Adolescent and Adult Literacy, November, 2003, review of *Scribbler of Dreams*, p. 215.
Kirkus Reviews, March 15, 2001, review of *Scribbler of Dreams*; May 15, 2005, review of *A Room on Lorelei Street*, p. 594.
Kliatt, July, 2005, Claire Rosser, review of *A Room on Lorelei Street*, p. 15; March, 2008, Janis Flint-Ferguson, review of *The Adoration of Jenna Fox*, p. 18.
Publishers Weekly, March 11, 2001, review of *Where Is Max?*; April 9, 2001, review of *Scribbler of Dreams*, p. 25; March 3, 2008, review of *The Adoration of Jenna Fox*, p. 49.
School Library Journal, April, 2000, Joel Shoemaker, review of *David v. God*; May 1, 2001, Rebecca Hogue Wojahn, review of *Scribbler of Dreams*, p. 158; August, 2005, Sharon Morrison, review of *A Room on Lorelei Street*, p. 132; May, 2008, Meredith Robbins, review of *The Adoration of Jenna Fox*, p. 136.
Teacher Librarian, December, 2007, David Gill, interview with Pearson, p. 60.

ONLINE

Mary E. Pearson Home Page, http://www.marypearson. com (December 24, 2009).
Mary E. Pearson Web log, http://marypearson.livejournal. com (December 24, 2009).*

*   *   *

POLCOVAR, Jane 1948-

Personal
Born September 23, 1948.

Addresses
Home—Saugerties, NY.

Career
Writer.

Writings

The Charming (young-adult novel), Bantam (New York, NY), 1984.
Hey, Good Looking! (young-adult novel; "Sweet Dreams" series), Bantam (New York, NY), 1985.
Harriet Tubman ("What Was It Like?" series), Children's Press (New York, NY), 1988.
Helen Keller ("What Was It Like?" series), Children's Press (New York, NY), 1988.

Rosalind Franklin and the Structure of Life, Morgan Reynolds (Greensboro, CA), 2006.

Biographical and Critical Sources

PERIODICALS

Booklist, December 1, 2006, Carolyn Phelan, review of *Rosalind Franklin and the Structure of Life,* p. 56.

Bulletin of the Center for Children's Books, January, 2007, Deborah Stevenson, review of *Rosalind Franklin and the Structure of Life,* p. 226.

School Library Journal, May, 1985, review of *The Charming,* p. 111; September, 1985, Kathy Fritts, review of *Hey, Good Looking!,* p. 152; March, 2007, Delia Carruthers, review of *Rosalind Franklin and the Structure of Life,* p. 234.

Voice of Youth Advocates, April, 1985, review of *The Charming,* p. 46.*

R

RAPPAPORT, Doreen 1939-

Personal
Born 1939, in New York, NY; married; husband a painter and sculptor. *Education:* Brandeis University, B.A. (music).

Addresses
Home—New York, NY; and Copake Falls, NY. *E-mail*—rapabook@aol.com.

Career
Teacher of music and reading in schools in New York and New Rochelle, NY, 1961-68; teacher at a freedom school, McComb, MS, 1965; writer.

Awards, Honors
Gradiva Award Honor designation, National Association for the Advancement of Psychoanalysis/World Association of Psychoanalysis, Best Book on Africa for Young Readers citation, African Studies Association, 100 Titles for Reading and Sharing selection, New York Public Library, and Notable Trade Book in the Field of Social Studies citation, National Council on the Social Studies (NCSS), all for *The New King;* Carter G. Woodson Honor Book designation, and Notable Trade Book in the Field of Social Studies selection, NCSS, both for *The Flight of Red Bird;* Coretta Scott King Honor Book designation, American Library Association (ALA), and Notable Book selection, ALA, both for *Freedom River;* Jane Addams Children's Book Award in picture-book category, 2002, Children's Choice selection, International Reading Association (IRA), Orbis Pictus Honor Book designation, National Council of Teachers of English, Caldecott Honor Book designation and Notable Book selection, both ALA, and Coretta Scott King Honor Book designation, all for *Martin's Big Words* illustrated by Bryan Collier; Flora Stieglitz Straus Award, Bank Street College of Education, Notable Trade Book

Doreen Rappaport (Reproduced by permission.)

in the Field of Social Studies citation, NCSS, 100 Titles for Reading and Sharing selection, New York Public Library, Fanfare citation, *Horn Book,* Gold Award, *Parents* magazine, and Best Book of the Year citation, *Child* magazine, all 2002, all for *No More!;* Notable Trade Book in the Field of Social Studies citations, NCSS, 1998, for *Escape from Slavery,* and 2002, for *We Are the Many;* IRA Notable Book for a Global Society designation, Best Children's Book of the Year designation,

Bank Street College of Education, and Image Award finalist, National Association for the Advancement of Colored People (NAACP), all 2005, all for *The School Is Not White!*; NAACP Image Award finalist, and *Parents' Choice* Silver Honor award, both 2005, both for *Nobody Gonna Turn Me 'Round;* Best Children's Book of the Year designation, Bank Street College of Education, and CCBC Choices Book of the Year selection, both 2005, both for *Freedom Ship;* CCBC Choices designation, 2008, for *Lady Liberty;* CCBC Choices Book of the Year selection, 100 Titles for Reading and Sharing selection, and IRA Teachers' Choice selection, all 2008, all for *Abe's Honest Words.*

Writings

NONFICTION

(With Susan Kempler and Michele Spirn) *A Man Can Be . . . ,* photographs by Russell Dian, Human Sciences Press (New York, NY), 1981.

(Editor) *American Women: Their Lives in Their Words,* Harper & Row (New York, NY), 1990.

Escape from Slavery: Five Journeys to Freedom, illustrated by Charles Lilly, Harper & Row (New York, NY), 1991.

Living Dangerously: American Women Who Risked Their Lives for Adventure, Harper & Row (New York, NY), 1991.

The Flight of Red Bird: The Life of Zitkala-Sa, Dial Books for Young Readers (New York, NY), 1997.

Freedom River, illustrated by Bryan Collier, Jump at the Sun (New York, NY), 2000.

Martin's Big Words: The Life of Dr. Martin Luther King, Jr., illustrated by Bryan Collier, Jump at the Sun (New York, NY), 2001.

We Are the Many: A Picture Book of American Indians, illustrated by Cornelius Van Wright and Ying-Hwa Hu, HarperCollins (New York, NY), 2002.

No More! Stories and Songs of Slave Resistance, illustrated by Shane W. Evans, Candlewick Press (Cambridge, MA), 2002.

(With Joan Verniero) *Victory or Death! Stories of the American Revolution,* illustrated by Greg Call, HarperCollins (New York, NY), 2003.

Free at Last! Stories and Songs of Emancipation, illustrated by Shane W. Evans, Candlewick Press (Cambridge, MA), 2004.

John's Secret Dreams: The Life of John Lennon, illustrated by Bryan Collier, Hyperion (New York, NY), 2004.

The School Is Not White! A True Story of the Civil Rights Movement, illustrated by Curtis James, Jump at the Sun (New York, NY), 2005.

In the Promised Land: Lives of Jewish Americans, illustrated by Cornelius Van Wright and Ying-Hwa Hu, HarperCollins (New York, NY), 2005.

Freedom Ship, illustrated by Curtis James, Hyperion Books for Children (New York, NY)2006.

Nobody Gonna Turn Me 'Round: Stories and Songs of the Civil Rights Movement, illustrated by Shane W. Evans, Candlewick Press (Cambridge, MA), 2006.

(With Joan Verniero) *United No More!: Stories of the Civil War,* illustrated by Rick Reeves, HarperCollins (New York, NY), 2006.

Abe's Honest Words: The Life of Abraham Lincoln, illustrated by Kadir Nelson, Hyperion Books for Children (New York, NY), 2008.

Lady Liberty: A Biography, illustrated by Matt Tavares, Candlewick Press (Cambridge, MA), 2008.

Eleanor, Quiet No More: The Life of Eleanor Roosevelt, illustrated by Gary Kelley, Disney/Hyperion Books (New York, NY), 2009.

Also creator of *Freedom River,* an animated video about the Underground Railroad, from Disney Educational Productions.

"BE THE JUDGE/BE THE JURY" SERIES; NONFICTION

The Lizzie Borden Trial, HarperCollins (New York, NY), 1992.

The Sacco-Vanzetti Trial, HarperCollins (New York, NY), 1992.

The Alger Hiss Trial, HarperCollins (New York, NY), 1993.

Tinker vs. Des Moines: Student Rights on Trial, HarperCollins (New York, NY), 1993.

FICTION

"But She's Still My Grandma!," illustrated by Bernadette Simmons, Human Sciences Press (New York, NY), 1982.

Trouble at the Mines, illustrated by Joan Sandin, Crowell (New York, NY), 1987.

The Boston Coffee Party, Harper & Row (New York, NY), 1988.

(Reteller) *The Journey of Meng: A Chinese Legend,* illustrated by Yang Ming-Yi, Dial Books for Young Readers (New York, NY), 1991.

(Reteller) *The Long-haired Girl: A Chinese Legend,* illustrated by Yang Ming-Yi, Dial Books for Young Readers (New York, NY), 1995.

The New King, illustrated by E.B. Lewis, Dial Books for Young Readers (New York, NY), 1995.

(With Lyndall Callan) *Dirt on Their Skirts: The Story of the Young Women Who Won the World Championship,* illustrated by E.B. Lewis, Dial Books for Young Readers (New York, NY), 2000.

The Secret Seder, illustrated by Emily Arnold McCully, Hyperion (New York, NY), 2005.

Sidelights

Doreen Rappaport is the author of numerous nonfiction and historical fiction books that attempt to convey U.S. and world history to children aged four to seventeen. Many of Rappaport's books draw heavily on primary sources and integrate the words of historical figures into the text. In addition to writing picture books that focus on the efforts of African Americans and their long jour-

ney toward racial equality, she has also produced fictional stories as well as the "Be the Judge/Be the Jury" series, which focuses on famous trials.

As a young woman Rappaport was a music and reading teacher, first in the ethnically diverse New York City and New Rochelle public schools, and later in a Southern "freedom school" for African-American students. Teaching in the Freedom School in McComb, Mississippi, was what first inspired her to write about history. The African Americans she met in Mississippi "were heroic" in their struggle to secure their rights, Rappaport recalled on her home page. "I knew there had to be many more 'unknown heroes,' people who helped change history. I set out to recover and write about this 'lost' history."

Rappaport worked with illustrator Shane W. Evans on a trilogy that chronicles the black experience in America from the slave trade in Africa to the civil-rights movement of the mid-twentieth century. In *No More! Stories and Songs of Slave Resistance*, Rappaport tells the stories of Underground Railroad conductor Harriet Tubman, slave rebellion leader Nat Turner, and other African Americans, creating composite characters and fictionalized accounts. The author's "research is documented," Hazel Rochman noted in *Booklist*, explaining that students requiring factual information can draw on Rappaport's bibliography. In addition to narratives, Rappaport also integrates folk tales and songs that were told and sung by African Americans. The collection of actual and fictional narratives, stories, and songs forms "an excellent account of the many ways in which slaves participated in bringing down the greatest evil in our nation's history," wrote a *Kirkus Reviews* contributor.

In *Free at Last! Stories and Songs of Emancipation* and *Nobody Gonna Turn Me 'Round: Stories and Songs of the Civil Rights Movement* Rappaport and Evans "reprise the passion and power that informed" *No More!*, according to a *Kirkus Reviews* contributor. Here readers are introduced to African-American culture from 1863 to 1954. Again, Rappaport tells the stories of famous blacks, such as intellectual Booker T. Washington and baseball player Jackie Robinson, as well as several less-famous people, interspersing her narratives with writings that include gospel songs and Langston Hughes's famous poem "I, Too, Sing America." *Nobody Gonna Turn Me 'Round* follows the latter years of the struggle for civil rights, ranging in its focus from the Montgomery bus boycott of 1955 to 1965 and the passage of the U.S. Voting Rights Act. As with *No More!*, the last two books include extensive bibliographies and reading lists. Calling the concluding volume "a moving portrayal" of the civil-rights era, *School Library Journal* Mary N. Oluonye added that Rappaport's series serves as "a wonderful resource to enhance curriculum units on African-American history."

Other books focusing on the civil-rights era include *The School Is Not White!: A True Story of the Civil Rights Movement*, in which Rappaport recounts the efforts of the eight African-American children who in 1965 formed the first wave of school desegregation in Drew, Mississippi. Setting her story against the backdrop of the historic *Brown vs. Board of Education* ruling, she follows the Carters, sharecroppers who were determined to provide their eight children with the education they had been denied. Although the family endured hardships, the author ends her story on a positive note, including an epilogue that lists the adult accomplishments of the eight Carter children. "Rappaport writes with an eloquent simplicity [that is] echoed in [illustrator Curtis] James' monumental figures," observed *Horn Book* contributor Joanna Rudge Long, the critic adding that the "fortitude, idealism, and hope" exhibited by the Carter family "make [*The School Is Not White!*] an inspiring story."

Martin's Big Words: The Life of Dr. Martin Luther King, Jr. is an atypical biography right from the start. Instead of title and author information, the cover features nothing but a close-up portrait of civil rights leader Dr. Martin Luther King, Jr. As in her other books, "the text is a mix of Rappaport's finely honed biographical narrative and appropriate quotes from King himself," explained *Horn Book* contributor Mary M. Burns. Although the text is designed for early readers, with short, simple sentences, it still covers all of the major events in King's life, from his childhood as the son of a

Doreen Rappaport presents the story of a noted civil-rights leader in **Martin's Big Words,** *featuring artwork by Bryan Collier.* (Illustration © 2001 by Bryan Collier. All rights reserved. Both reprinted by permission of Disney Hyperion, an imprint of Disney Book Group LLC.)

Rappaport tells a story of racial integration in **The School Is Not White!,** *a picture book illustrated by Curtis James.* (Illustration copyright © 2005 by Curtis James. All rights reserved. Reprinted by permission of Disney Hyperion, an imprint of Disney Book Group LLC.)

preacher in segregated Atlanta to his assassination in April of 1968. The title refers to the young King's determination to speak with big words just like his father did, but could also refer to the large-type font in which King's quotations are printed, noted reviewers. *Martin's Big Words* is "a stunning, reverent tribute" to Dr. King, concluded *School Library Journal* contributor Catherine Threadgill.

Other biographies by Rappaport include *John's Secret Smile: The Life of John Lennon* and *Eleanor, Quiet No More: The Life of Eleanor Roosevelt,* the latter a biography of the first lady whose work on the public stage earned her respect as First Lady of the World. Featuring illustrations by Gary Kelley, *Eleanor, Quiet No More* introduces young readers to a woman who "may not be immediately familiar," observed *Horn Book* contributor Betty Carter, the critic also noting Rappaport's inclusion of a timeline and detailed list of sources. *Abe's Honest Words: The Life of Abraham Lincoln,* illustrated by Kadir Nelson, sets the story of the life of the sixteenth U.S. president against a framework of his own words. "With language as lean as [Lincoln himself] . . . , Rappaport brings to light the major influences" that shaped the man's pivotal presidency, wrote Carter, the reviewer also citing Nelson's "handsome portraits," which "glow with background light."

Moving to an earlier period of U.S. history, in *Victory or Death! Stories of the American Revolution* Rappaport and coauthor Joan Verniero tell the stories of eight

famous and not-yet celebrated participants in the Revolutionary War. Although they cover such well-known figures as General George Washington and future first lady Abigail Adams, Rappaport and Verniero also write about multicultural figures on both sides, including Francis Salvador, a Jew from South Carolina who risked his life to rally his neighbors to the Patriot cause, and Grace Growden Galloway, a Philadelphia loyalist who attempted to defend her family's property from the rebellious Colonists. "Each chapter is very short and relies on vivid characterization," noted *Booklist* critic GraceAnne A. DeCandido, making it a good introduction to Revolutionary history for younger children. The narratives are arranged chronologically and "each story is set in its historical context," a critic commented in *Kirkus Reviews,* so "readers will learn a good deal of history and gain a sense of the ebb and flow of the war."

Coauthored with Verniero and illustrated by Rick Reeves, *United No More!: Stories of the Civil War* recounts in seven stories the pivotal events of the War between the States. In addition to the heroic charge on Fort Wagner by an African-American regiment and the surrender by General Robert E. Lee at Appomattox Court House, the book also reveals some lesser-known but equally human dramas that took place during wartime. Another compelling story is recounted in *Freedom Ship,* a picture book illustrated by James that recounts

the efforts, in May of 1862, of wheelman Robert Smalls. It was Small's leadership of a nine-member black crew in hijacking a Confederate steamer containing much-needed weapons that resulted in the delivery of the ship to Union forces and the freeing of all civilians on board. Narrated by a young boy, who heard the story from his father, *Freedom Ship* features "realistic chalk-pastel drawings" that bring the nighttime drama to life. Noting Rappaport's "lengthy note" about the life of Smalls, who eventually became the first black captain in the U.S. Navy, Hazel Rochman wrote in *Booklist* that the "personal narrative gives [*Freedom Ship*] . . . immediacy."

Based on a historical event but told through a fictional story, *Dirt on Their Skirts: The Story of the Young Women Who Won the World Championship* offers readers an account of the 1946 championship game of the All-American Girls Professional Baseball League. Formed in 1942, the league provided much-needed entertainment on the home front during and after World War II. In *Dirt on Their Skirts,* coauthored with Lyndall Callan, a young girl named Margaret watches the game from the stands with her mother, her brother, and her father, who has recently returned from the war. Concidering Racine Belles second basewoman Sophie Kurys a favorite, Margaret is thrilled when Kurys steals second base and eventually slides into home to win the game, a tough play, as Margaret's mother comments, if you are wearing a skirt. "With its economy of language and telling period details, this book provides an exciting slice of sports history and an appealing bit of Americana," Luann Toth wrote in *School Library Journal*. A *Publishers Weekly* critic commended Rappaport for "judiciously using end matter to relate a historical overview of the league," information which is useful for children to understand the importance of the story. By relegating the historical facts to the afterword, the *Publishers Weekly* reviewer continued, Rappaport and Callan can "serve up a fan's view of the game."

Biographical and Critical Sources

PERIODICALS

Black Issues Book Review, January-February, 2002, Clarence V. Reynolds, review of *Martin's Big Words: The Life of Dr. Martin Luther King, Jr.,* p. 80.

Booklist, September 1, 1992, Hazel Rochman, review of *The Lizzie Borden Trial,* pp. 45-46; August, 1993, Janice Del Negro, review of *Tinker vs. Des Moines: Student Rights on Trial,* p. 2048; January 1, 1994, Hazel Rochman, review of *The Alger Hiss Trial,* p. 815; January 15, 1995, Hazel Rochman, review of *The Long-haired Girl: A Chinese Legend,* p. 933; May 1, 1995, Hazel Rochman, review of *The New King,* pp. 1577-1578; July, 1997, Karen Hutt, review of *The Flight of Red Bird: The Life of Zitkala-Sa,* p. 1810; January 1, 2000, Todd Morning, review of *Dirt on Their Skirts: The Story of the Young Women Who Won the World Championship,* p. 936; October 1, 2000, Hazel Rochman, review of *Freedom River,* p. 341; October 1, 2001, Hazel Rochman, review of *Martin's Big Words,* p. 338; February 15, 2002, Hazel Rochman, review of *No More! Stories and Songs of Slave Resistance,* p. 1033; October 15, 2002, Hazel Rochman, review of *We Are the Many: A Picture Book of American Indians,* pp. 408-409; June 1, 2003, GraceAnne A. DeCandido, review of *Victory or Death! Stories of the American Revolution,* p. 1770; February 14, 2004, Hazel Rochman, review of *Free at Last! Stories and Songs of Emancipation,* p. 1076; October 1, 2006, Hazel Rochman, review of *Freedom Ship,* p. 60.

Book Report, January-February, 1994, Edna Boardman, review of *Tinker vs. Des Moines,* pp. 61-62.

Childhood Education, fall, 2002, Nancy S. Maldonado, review of *Freedom River,* pp. 63-64.

Horn Book, March-April, 1987, Hanna B. Zeiger, review of *Trouble at the Mines,* p. 212; September-October, 1988, Mary M. Burns, review of *The Boston Coffee Party,* pp. 623-624; March-April, 1991, Ellen Fader, review of *American Women: Their Lives in Their Words,* p. 219; November-December, 1991, Margaret A. Bush, review of *The Journey of Meng: A Chinese Legend,* pp. 748-749; January-February, 2002, Mary M. Burns, review of *Martin's Big Words,* pp. 105-106; March-April, 2002, Joanna Rudge Long, review of *No More!,* pp. 231-232; July-August, 2005, Joanna Rudge Long, review of *The School Is Not White!: A True Story of the Civil Rights Movement,* p. 489; March-April, 2006, Betty Carter, review of *United No More,* p. 208; November-December, 2008, Betty Carter, review of *Abe's Honest Words: The Life of Abraham Lincoln,* p. 724; March-April, 2009, Betty Carter, review of *Eleanor, Quiet No More,* p. 213.

Instructor, March, 1994, Judy Freeman, review of *Living Dangerously: American Women Who Risked Their Lives for Adventure,* p. 79.

Kirkus Reviews, August 15, 2001, review of *Martin's Big Words,* p. 1120; January 1, 2002, review of *No More!,* p. 49; August 15, 2002, review of *We Are the Many,* p. 1233; April 1, 2003, review of *Victory or Death!,* p. 539; December 15, 2003, review of *Free at Last!,* p. 1454; January 1, 2009, review of *Eleanor, Quiet No More.*

Language Arts, May, 2002, Mingshui Cai and Junko Yokata, review of *No More!,* p. 433; September, 2002, review of *Martin's Big Words,* p. 72.

New Yorker, November 26, 1990, Faith McNulty, review of *American Women,* p. 144.

New York Times Book Review, May 17, 1987, Lee Smith, review of *Trouble at the Mines,* p. 33; April 10, 1988, Elisabeth Griffith, review of *The Boston Coffee Party,* p. 39; January 13, 1991, Elizabeth Gleick, review of *American Women,* p. 21; November 18, 2001, James McMullan, review of *Martin's Big Words,* p. 47.

Publishers Weekly, April 10, 1987, review of *Trouble at the Mines,* p. 96; March 22, 1991, review of *Escape from Slavery: Five Journeys to Freedom,* p. 81; August 30, 1991, review of *The Journey of Meng,* pp.

82-83; October 11, 1991, review of *Living Danger-ously,* p. 64; February 27, 1995, review of *The Long-haired Girl,* p. 103; June 12, 1995, review of *The New King,* pp. 60-61; March 27, 2000, review of *Dirt on Their Skirts,* p. 79; October 8, 2001, review of *Martin's Big Words,* p. 64; December 17, 2001, review of *No More!,* p. 91; February 16, 2009, review of *Eleanor, Quiet No More,* p. 127.

Reading Teacher, November, 2002, review of *Martin's Big Words,* p. 259.

Reading Today, February-March, 2002, Lynne T. Burke, review of *Martin's Big Words,* p. 32.

School Library Journal, April, 1987, Mary Beth Burgoyne, review of *Trouble at the Mines,* p. 102; May, 1988, Sylvia S. Marantz, review of *The Boston Coffee Party,* p. 87; February, 1991, Ruth K. MacDonald, review of *American Women,* p. 100; May, 1991, Elizabeth M. Reardon, review of *Escape from Slavery,* pp. 105-106; December, 1991, April L. Judge, review of *Living Dangerously,* p. 127, and John Philbrook, review of *The Journey of Meng,* pp. 126-127; January, 1993, Sylvia V. Meisner, review of *The Lizzie Borden Trial,* p. 120; March, 1993, Beth Tegart, review of *The Sacco-Vanzetti Trial,* p. 216; January, 1994, Doris A. Fong, review of *Tinker vs. Des Moines,* p. 128; February, 1994, Todd Morning, review of *The Alger Hiss Trial,* p. 128; March, 1995, Margaret A. Chang, review of *The Long-haired Girl,* pp. 199-200; July, 1995, Donna L. Scanlon, review of *The New King,* p. 74; July, 1997, Lisa Mitten, review of *The Flight of the Red Bird,* p. 111; March, 2000, Luann Toth, review of *Dirt on Their Skirts,* p. 212; October, 2000, Cynde Marcengill, review of *Freedom River,* p. 152; October, 2001, Catherine Threadgill, review of *Martin's Big Words,* p. 146; February, 2002, Ginny Gustin, review of *No More!,* p. 150; September, 2002, Anne Chapman Callaghan, review of *We Are the Many,* p. 217; June, 2003, Jean Gaffney, review of *Victory or Death!,* p. 168; February, 2004, Tracy Bell, review of *Free at Last!,* p. 168; September, 2005, Holly T. Sneeringer, review of *The School Is Not White!,* p. 195; February, 2006, Mary Mueller, review of *United No More!,* p. 152; October, 2006, Mary N. Oluonye, review of *Nobody Gonna Turn Me 'Round: Stories and Songs of the Civil Rights Movement,* p. 182; November, 2006, Julie R. Ranelli, review of *Freedom Ship,* p. 108; October, 2008, Barbara Auerbach, review of *Abe's Honest Words,* p. 135.

ONLINE

BookPage, http://www.bookpage.com/ (February, 2004), Heidi Henneman, interview with Rappaport.

Doreen Rappaport Web Site, http://www.doreenrappaport. com/ (January 14, 2002).*

* * *

REED, Mike 1951-

Personal

Born 1951, in GA; married; children: two. *Education:* University of Michigan, B.F.A. *Hobbies and other interests:* Writing, tournament pocket billiards, books.

Addresses

Office—1314 Summit Ave., Minneapolis, MN 55403. *Agent*—MB Artists, 10 E. 29th St., Ste. 40G, New York, NY 10016; melambartists.com. *E-mail*—mike@mike reedart.com.

Career

Illustrator, animator, and educator. Worked as a background painter, character designer, and character animator for an animation studio; Reelworks (animation studio), cofounder; Minneapolis *Star Tribune,* Minneapolis, MN, columnist, beginning 1986, and features illustrator, for ten years; freelance commercial and editorial illustrator. College of Visual Arts, St. Paul, MN, adjunct professor of visual communications; has also taught at Minneapolis College of Art and Design and Rhode Island School of Design.

Awards, Honors

Texas Bluebonnet Award, 2008, for *On the Road;* awards from American Institute of Arts, Los Angeles Society of Illustrators, New York Society of Illustrators, and *Communication Arts.*

Writings

ILLUSTRATOR

Lauren L. Wohl, *Christopher Davis's Best Year Yet,* Hyperion Books for Children (New York, NY), 1995.

W. Nikola-Lisa, *Shake Dem Halloween Bones,* Houghton Mifflin (Boston, MA), 1997.

Margie Palatini, *Elf Help,* Hyperion Books for Children (New York, NY), 1998.

John K. Bollard, *Scholastic Children's Thesaurus,* Scholastic Reference (New York, NY), 1998, revised edition, 2006.

Joan Holub, *Space Dogs on Planet K-9,* Troll (Mahwah, NJ), 1998.

Kalli Dakos, *The Bug in Teacher's Coffee and Other School Poems,* HarperCollins (New York, NY), 1999.

Rita Williams-Garcia, *Catching the Wild Waiyuuzee,* Simon & Schuster Books for Young Readers (New York, NY), 2000.

Shana Corey, *Boats!,* Random House (New York, NY), 2001.

Christine Kole MacLean, *Even Firefighters Hug Their Moms,* Dutton Children's Books (New York, NY), 2002.

Stuart J. Murphy, *Racing Around,* HarperCollins (New York, NY), 2002.

Johanna Hurwitz, *Oh No, Noah!,* SeaStar Books (New York, NY), 2002.

John Frank, *A Chill in the Air: Nature Poems for Fall and Winter,* Simon & Schuster Books for Young Readers (New York, NY), 2003.

J.C. Greenburg, *Under Water,* Random House (New York, NY), 2003.

Heidi Kilgras, *Peanut,* Random House (New York, NY), 2003.

J.C. Greenburg, *In the Whale,* Random House (New York, NY), 2003.

Steven Kroll, *A Tale of Two Dogs,* Marshall Cavendish (New York, NY), 2004.

Lucy Nolan, *Smarter than Squirrels* ("Down Girl and Sit" series), Marshall Cavendish (New York, NY), 2004.

Coleen Paratore, *Twenty-six Big Things Small Hands Do,* Free Spirit Publishing (Minneapollis, MN), 2004.

Lucy Nolan, *On the Road* ("Down Girl and Sit" series), Marshall Cavendish (New York, NY), 2005.

Linda Hoffman Kimball, *Come with Me on Halloween,* Albert Whitman (Morton Grove, IL), 2005.

Tammi Sauer, *Cowboy Camp,* Sterling Publishing (New York, NY), 2005.

Andrew Clements, *A Million Dots,* Simon & Schuster Books for Young Readers (New York, NY), 2006.

Mitch Chivus, *Fartsy Claus,* HarperCollins (New York, NY), 2007.

Lucy Nolan, *Bad to the Bone* ("Down Girl and Sit" series), Marshall Cavendish (New York, NY), 2008.

Jamie Adoff, *Small Fry,* Dutton Children's Books (New York, NY), 2008.

Tim Myers, *Looking for Luna,* Marshall Cavendish (New York, NY), 2009.

Lucy Nolan, *Home on the Range* ("Down Girl and Sit" series), Marshall Cavendish (New York, NY), 2010.

Contributor of illustrations to periodicals, including *Business Week, Time, New York Times, USA Today, Los Angeles Times, Chicago Tribune,* and *PC World.*

OTHER

Author and illustrator of *The Netizens Guide to Flame Warriors,* http://www.flamewarriors.com. Author of digital imaging tutorials for Peach Pit Press, *How* magazine, and *Step-by-Step* magazine. Contributor to periodicals, including *Architecture Minnesota, Step-by-Step,* and Minneapolis *Star Tribune.*

Sidelights

Award-winning illustrator Mike Reed has provided the artwork for numerous children's books, including titles by such acclaimed authors as Steven Kroll, Rita Williams-Garcia, and Andrew Clements. A former animator who has created films for *Sesame Street* and *Nova,* Reed is the creator of *The Netizens Guide to Flame Warriors,* a rogue's gallery of characters found in cyberspace that became an internet sensation. In addition, Reed spent ten years as an illustrator for the Minneapolis *Star Tribune* and now performs work for advertising agencies, public relations firms, and editorial clients. "I am attracted to illustration because it is an accessible form of visual communication," Reed stated on his home page, adding that "drawing isn't just making marks on paper, it's a way of thinking."

Reed made his literary debut in 1995 by contributing the pictures to *Christopher Davis's Best Year Yet,* a work by Lauren L. Wohl. He followed that effort with *Shake Dem Halloween Bones,* a rhyming tale by W. Nikola-Lisa that features a host of fairytale characters, including Goldilocks, Rapunzel, and Tom Thumb. According to a *Publishers Weekly* critic, the "rubber-limbed dancers jitterbug with abandon through Reed's oddball oil paintings." Another holiday-themed story, Linda Hoffman Kimball's *Come with Me on Halloween,* centers on a young boy who helps his easily frightened father navigate an evening of trick-or-treating. Reed "creates well-lit scenes of spookery in glowing sunset hues," noted a reviewer in *Publishers Weekly.*

A young African-American girl playfully evades her mother's attempts to braid her hair in Rita Williams-Garcia's *Catching the Wild Waiyuuzee.* Reed's "dynamic illustrations" for this book drew praise from *School Library Journal* contributor Kathleen Kelly MacMillan. In another story of parental love, Christine Kole MacLean's *Even Firefighters Hug Their Moms,* a single-minded youngster will not interrupt his pretend games to give his mother a much-needed squeeze. In the words of *Booklist* reviewer Ilene Cooper, Reed's "dappled artwork" for MacLean's story "has a sturdy feeling that adds a realistic look to the world of imagination."

Reed has also illustrated a number of poetry books, including Jamie Adoff's *Small Fry,* which explores the advantages and disadvantages of being short in stature. "Colorful and textured illustrations add to the peppy text," Julie Roach noted in *School Library Journal.* A

Mike Reed's use of imaginative perspectives enhances his artwork for Jaime Adoff's story in **Small Fry.** (Illustration copyright © 2008 by Mike Reed. All rights reserved. Reproduced by permission of Dutton Children's Books, a division of Penguin Putnam Books for Young Readers.)

Chill in the Air: Nature Poems for Fall and Winter, a verse collection by John Frank, celebrates the outdoors. Here "Reed's amazing, windswept paintings capture the exhilaration and challenge of the two seasons," wrote Lee Bock in a review of the book for *School Library Journal.*

In Kroll's *A Tale of Two Dogs,* a mischievous puppy proves so exasperating to its new owners that they return the pup to the pound although they soon discover that they miss its rambunctiousness. "Reed's expressive, lively, almost three-dimensional paintings infuse plenty of humor into this tail-wagging, happy-ending picture book," Karin Snelson remarked in *Booklist.* In *A Million Dots,* Clements presents a variety of interesting facts to help young readers understand the concept of one million. Complimenting the "entertaining" narrative in *School Library Journal,* Grace Oliff noted that "Reed's humorous and eye-catching digital artwork adds to the appeal."

Reed has enjoyed a successful collaboration with Lucy Nolan on Nolan's chapter-book series about a pair of humorous canines named Down Girl and Sit. In *Smarter than Squirrels,* the well-meaning dogs create havoc for their owners while guarding the yard against intruders. "Lively, expressive black-and-white illustrations shot from a canine point-of-view animate Down Girl's hilarious first-person narrative," stated a contributor in *Kirkus Reviews. Booklist* critic Shelle Rosenfeld praised Reed's "witty, black-and-white art" in *On the Road,* which describes an adventure-filled camping trip, and in the same periodical Gillian Engberg cited the "action-filled drawings" as a highlight of *Bad to the Bone,* which finds the frisky canines headed to obedience school.

Biographical and Critical Sources

PERIODICALS

Booklist, October 1, 1997, Hazel Rochman, review of *Shake Dem Halloween Bones,* p. 338; November 15, 2000, Connie Fletcher, review of *Catching the Wild Waiyuuzee,* p. 651; November 15, 2002, Ilene Cooper, review of *Even Firefighters Hug Their Moms,* p. 611; April 15, 2004, Karin Snelson, review of *A Tale of Two Dogs,* p. 1446; November 15, 2005, Shelle Rosenfeld, review of *On the Road,* p. 52; November 15, 2008, Gillian Engberg, review of *Bad to the Bone,* p. 40.

Horn Book, November-December, 2005, Betty Carter, review of *On the Road,* p. 723.

Kirkus Reviews, May 1, 2002, review of *Oh No, Noah!,* p. 657; August 1, 2004, review of *Smarter Than Squirrels,* p. 747; October 1, 2008, review of *Small Fry.*

Los Angeles Times, December 12, 2003, Bob Baker, "A Flaming Desire."

Publishers Weekly, October 6, 1997, review of *Shake Dem Halloween Bones,* p. 49; April 22, 2002, review of *Oh No, Noah!,* p. 70; October 27, 2003, review of *A Chill in the Air: Nature Poems for Fall and Winter,* p. 68; August 1, 2005, review of *Come with Me on Halloween,* p. 64; June 12, 2006, review of *A Million Dots,* p. 51.

School Library Journal, November, 2000, Kathleen Kelly MacMillan, review of *Catching the Wild Waiyuuzee,* p. 137; October, 2002, Joy Fleishhacker, review of *Even Firefighters Hug Their Moms,* p. 120; September, 2003, Lee Bock, review of *A Chill in the Air,* p. 197; July, 2004, Teri Markson, review of *A Tale of Two Dogs,* p. 80; November, 2004, Debbie Whitbeck, review of *Smarter Than Squirrels,* p. 113; October, 2005, Julie Roach, review of *Come with Me on Halloween,* p. 116; July, 2006, Grace Oliff, review of *A Million Dots,* p. 70; October, 2007, Linda Israelson, review of *Fartsy Claus,* p. 96; November, 2008, Julie Roach, review of *Small Fry,* p. 104; January, 2009, Carrie Rogers-Whitehead, review of *Bad to the Bone,* p. 82.

ONLINE

Mike Reed Home Page, http://www.mikereedart.com (January 1, 2010).

Painter Studio Web site, http://apps.corel.com/painterx/us/ (January 1, 2010), interview with Reed.*

* * *

REIBSTEIN, Mark

Personal

Male. *Education:* Attended college.

Addresses

Home and office—Menlo Park, CA. *E-mail*—mreibstein @sbcglobal.net.

Career

Writer and educator.

Writings

Wabi Sabi, illustrated by Ed Young, Little, Brown (New York, NY), 2008.

Sidelights

Because Mark Reibstein grew up with children's book writer Roni Schotter as a family friend and role model, he knew early on that being a children's book writer was a career option. Before writing his own children's

Mark Reibstein (Reproduced by permission.)

book, however, Reibstein became a teacher. He has also traveled to many places, including Japan, where he was introduced to the concept of *wabi sabi.* The words, which come into Japanese tradition from China, are difficult to explain, and Reibstein talked to many people in trying to discover the meaning of the phrase. A loose translation of wabi sabi is the sense of the beauty in things that are not perfect, or that are simple and humble. After Reibstein translated this meaning into a story for children, he sought out Schotter, who became his advocate. Schotter introduced Reibstein to Caldecott winning artist Ed Young, setting the whole project on the path to publication.

In *Wabi Sabi,* a cat who shares her name with the title asks people to explain the meaning behind her name. Each animal she asks tells her that it is difficult to describe, and offers her an example of what the name means in a haiku. "It is a complex idea, and the cat's journey is an effective way of presenting it," wrote Kara Schaff Dean in *School Library Journal,* the critic adding that *Wabi Sabi* is "a book to be savored and contemplated." A *Kirkus Reviews* contributor wrote that "Reibstein's plain yet poetic text . . . deftly incorporates original and traditional Japanese haiku," while in *Booklist* Ilene Cooper wrote that "some of the allusions are beautiful" in the explanations Wabi Sabi receives. "Reibstein and Young have created a magnificent offering that is the embodiment of Wabi Sabi," Cooper concluded, and Joanna Rudge Long wrote her review of *Wabi Sabi* for the *New York Times Book Review* that author and illustrator "capture the essence of all of this with clarity, elegance and a kind of indirection that seems intrinsic to the subject."

Biographical and Critical Sources

PERIODICALS

Booklist, September 1, 2008, Ilene Cooper, review of *Wabi Sabi,* p. 98.
Horn Book, January-February, 2009, Lolly Robinson, review of *Wabi Sabi,* p. 83.
Kirkus Reviews, September 15, 2008, review of *Wabi Sabi.*
New York Times Book Review, November 9, 2008, Joanna Rudge Long, "Haiku for Cats," p. 35.
School Library Journal, September, 2008, Kara Schaff Dean, review of *Wabi Sabi,* p. 157.

ONLINE

Little Brown Web site, http://www.littlebrown.co.uk/ (January 8, 2010), "Mark Reibstein."

*   *   *

RENAUD, Anne 1957-

Personal

Born 1957, in Valleyfield, Québec, Canada. *Education:* Concordia University, B.A. (translation).

Addresses

Home—Westmount, Quebec, Canada. *Office*—4656 Sherbrooke St. W., Apt. 2, Westmount, Quebec H3Z 1G3, Canada. *E-mail*—earenaud@yahoo.com.

Career

Writer and translator.

Member

Canadian Society of Children's Author's Illustrators, and Performers, Writers' Union of Canada, Society of Children's Book Writers and Illustrators, Quebec Writer's Federation.

Awards, Honors

Hackmatack Children's Choice Book Award shortlist, and Silver Birch Award nomination, Ontario Library Association, both 2006, and Red Cedar Book Award shortlist, 2006-07, all for *A Bloom of Friendship;* Quebec Writers Federation Prize for Children and Young-Adult Literature nomination, 2008, and Hackmatack Children's Choice Book Award shortlist, 2009, both for *Pier Twenty-one;* Red Maple Award nomination, Ontario Library Association, 2009, for *Island of Hope and Sorrow.*

Writings

A Bloom of Friendship: The Story of the Canadian Tulip Festival ("My Canada" series), illustrated by Ashley Spires, Lobster Press (Montreal, Quebec, Canada), 2004.

Anne Renaud (Reproduced by permission.)

How the Sea Came to Marissa, illustrated by Maud Durland, Beyond Words Publishing (Hillsboro, OR), 2006.

Island of Hope and Sorrow: The Story of Grosse Île ("Canadian Immigration" series), illustrated by Aries Cheung, Lobster Press (Montreal, Quebec, Canada), 2007.

Pier 21: Stories from Near and Far ("Canadian Immigration" series), illustrated by Aries Cheung, Lobster Press (Montreal, Quebec, Canada), 2008.

Missuk's Snow Geese, illustrated by Geneviève Côté, Simply Read Books (Vancouver, British Columbia, Canada), 2008, translated by the author as *Missuk et les oies des neiges,* Dominique et Cie. (Montreal, Quebec, Canada), 2009.

Contributor of nonfiction and craft articles to periodicals, including *YESMag, Cricket, CHIRP, Helix, Highlights for Children, Faces, Odyssey,* and *Read.*

TRANSLATOR

Margaret Merrifield, *Viens t'asseoir avec moi,* illustrated by Heather Collins, Éditions Héritage (Saint-Lambert, Quebec, Canada), 1991.

Margaret Merrifield, *La lueur du matin,* illustrated by Heather Collins, Éditions Héritage (Saint-Lambert, Quebec, Canada), 1991.

Sidelights

Author and translator Anne Renaud has written a number of nonfiction works that explore Canada's history, particularly the story of that nation's immigration policies. Renaud, a frequent contributor to publications such as *Cricket, Highlights for Children,* and *Odyssey,* is also the author of picture books for young readers, including *Missuk's Snow Geese.* "I hope my books educate, entertain and inspire children," Renaud commented on her home page.

Renaud dedicated her first book, *A Bloom of Friendship: The Story of the Canadian Tulip Festival,* to her uncle, Thomas Delaney, who fought in World War II. The book examines a decades-old tradition held annu-

ally in Ottawa, Ontario, Canada. The festival celebrates Canada's commitment to providing a safe haven for members of the Dutch royal family during World War II as well as honoring Canadian troops involved in the liberation of Holland. To demonstrate her appreciation, Princess Juliana of the Netherlands presented 100,000 tulip bulbs to Canada in 1945, following her return to Holland; each fall since, 20,000 tulip bulbs have arrived in Ottawa. The first official Canadian Tulip Festival took place in 1953, spearheaded by renowned photographer Malak Karsh, and each year more than 600,000 visitors from North America, Europe, and Asia enjoy the festivities. Critics praised Renaud's work, which includes newspaper clippings and archival photographs. In the *Canadian Review of Materials,* Grace Sheppard observed that in *A Bloom of Friendship,* the author "has summed up many years of complicated events in a few pages and an easy-to-read timeline."

In *Island of Hope and Sorrow: The Story of Grosse Île,* Renaud traces the history of the island of Grosse Île. From 1832 to 1937, more than four million people sailed from Europe across the Atlantic to Canada with the dream of creating better lives for themselves in a new land. During this period, the tiny island of Grosse Île, located thirty miles downstream from the port of Quebec City, served as a quarantine station. Its mission was to prevent ship passengers from spreading diseases to the mainland. After its closure in 1937, Grosse Île served a research center for Canadian scientists during World War II; it is now designated as an historic site. *Island of Hope and Sorrow* also garnered solid reviews. As Laurie McNeill stated in *Quill & Quire,* Renaud "packs a great deal of knowledge into an accessible history" for young readers.

Renaud looks at another historically significant Canadian locale in *Pier 21: Stories from Near and Far.* Located in Halifax, Nova Scotia, Pier 21 welcomed more than one million newcomers to Canada from 1928 to 1971; it also served as a point of departure for hundreds of thousands of Canadian servicemen during World War II. Now a museum and a national historic site, Pier 21 is considered one of the "Seven Wonders of Canada." In her account, wrote *Canadian Review of Materials* critic Marilynne V. Black, "Renaud captures the human side of immigration. . . . She has the gift of succinctly capturing events with poignant and evocative language."

Based on Renaud's experiences in Northern Quebec, *Missuk's Snow Geese* introduces a young girl who dreams of becoming a skilled soapstone carver like her father. Leaving her igloo, Missuk finds inspiration in the snow geese that fly overhead, but she grows concerned when a huge storm blows in, threatening her father's hunt. When Missuk's father appears the next day, he offers a surprising anecdote about his safe return. "Families will relish this simple telling's child-empowering ending," observed a contributor in *Kirkus Reviews.*

Biographical and Critical Sources

PERIODICALS

Booklist, April 15, 2008, Carolyn Phelan, review of *Pier 21: Stories from Near and Far,* p. 44.

Canadian Review of Materials, January 20, 2006, Grace Sheppard, review of *A Bloom of Friendship: The Story of the Canadian Tulip Festival;* May 16, 2008, Marilynne V. Black, review of *Pier 21.*

Kirkus Reviews, September 15, 2008, review of *Missuk's Snow Geese.*

Quill & Quire, May, 2007, Laurie McNeill, review of *Island of Hope and Sorrow: The Story of Grosse Île.*

Resource Links, February, 2005, Victoria Pennell, review of *A Bloom of Friendship,* p. 27; April, 2007, Victoria Pennell, review of *Island of Hope and Sorrow,* p. 36; June, 2008, Victoria Pennell, review of *Pier 21,* p. 13.

ONLINE

Anne Renaud Home Page, http://annerenaud.net (January 1, 2010).

Canadian Society of Children's Author's Illustrators, and Performers Web site, http://www.canscaip.org/ (January 1, 2010), "Anne Renaud."

Renaud's story in **Missuk's Snow Geese** *is brought to life in Geneviève Côté's evocative paintings.* (Simply Read Books, 2008. Illustration © 2008 by Geneviève Côté. All rights reserved. Reproduced by permission.)

Writers' Union of Canada Web site, http://www.writers union.ca/ (January 1, 2010), "Anne Renaud."

*   *   *

ROGERS, Gregory 1957-

Personal

Born 1957, in Brisbane, Queensland, Australia. *Education:* Attended Queensland College of Art. *Hobbies and other interests:* Playing the cornetto, recorder, and baroque guitar; collecting antiques and books.

Addresses

Home—Brisbane, Queensland, Australia. *Agent*—Margaret Connolly & Associates, P.O. Box 945, Wahroonga, New South Wales 2076, Australia.

Career

Freelance illustrator and graphic designer, 1987—. Queensland Conservatorium of Music, South Bank, Queensland, Australia, former senior research assistant; Australian Commonwealth Government, former graphic designer; Queensland College of Art, Griffith University, lecturer in illustration; Illustration House, art teacher.

Awards, Honors

SGIO Art Award for photography, 1983; Children's Book Council Awards shortlist, 1993, for *Lucy's Bay;* Kate Greenaway Medal for illustration, Parent's Choice Award, and highly commended citation, Australian Book Publishers Association Awards, all 1995, all for *Way Home;* Wilderness Society Environment Award for Children's Literature, and Whitley Award for best children's book, Royal Zoological Society of New South Wales, both 2001, both for *The Platypus;* Australian Family Therapist's Award for Children's Literature, 2002, for *Princess Max;* Notable Children's Book selection, American Library Association, Aurealis Awards shortlist, Illustrators Australia Illustration Awards selection, and *New York Times* Best Illustrated Books selection, all 2004, all for *The Boy, the Bear, the Baron, the Bard;* Notable Book selection, Children's Book Council, 2007, for *Midsummer Knight.*

Writings

SELF-ILLUSTRATED

The Boy, the Bear, the Baron, the Bard, Roaring Brook Press (Brookfield, CT), 2004.

Midsummer Knight (sequel to *The Boy, the Bear, the Baron, the Bard*), Allen & Unwin (Crows Nest, New South Wales, Australia), 2006, Roaring Brook Press (Brookfield, CT), 2007.

ILLUSTRATOR

Kay Arthur, *Enter Bob Dickinson,* Rigby Education (Melbourne, Victoria, Australia), 1988.

Virginia King, *Grandma's Memories,* Mimosa Publications (Hawthorn, Victoria, Australia), 1989.

The Ball Game, Mimosa Publications (Hawthorn, Victoria, Australia), 1989.

Margaret Card, *Auntie Mary's Dead Goat,* Hill of Content (Melbourne, Victoria, Australia), 1990.

Susan Reid, *Zoe at the Fancy Dress Ball,* Mimosa Publications (Hawthorn, Victoria, Australia), 1990.

Susan Reid, *Lucy Meets a Dragon,* Mimosa Publications (Hawthorn, Victoria, Australia), 1990.

Ian Trevaskis, *The Postman's Race,* Random House Australia (Milsons Point, New South Wales, Australia), 1991.

Margaret Wild, *Space Travellers,* Scholastic, Inc. (New York, NY), 1992.

Gary Crew, *Lucy's Bay,* Jamroll Press (Nundah, Queensland, Australia), 1992.

Gary Crew, *Tracks,* Lothian (Port Melbourne, Victoria, Australia), 1992, Gareth Stevens (Milwaukee, WI), 1996.

Libby Hathorn, *Way Home,* Crown (New York, NY), 1994.

Susan McQuade, *Great-grandpa,* SRA School Group (Santa Rosa, CA), 1994.

Gary Crew, *The Bent-back Bridge,* Lothian (Port Melbourne, Victoria, Australia), 1995.

Nigel Gray, *Running away from Home,* Crown (New York, NY), 1996.

Robert Cormier, *The Moustache,* Angus & Robertson (Pymble, New South Wales, Australia), 1996.

Jeri Kroll, *What Goes with Toes?,* Houghton Mifflin (Boston, MA), 1996.

Jenny Pausacker, *The Rings,* Lothian (Port Melbourne, Victoria, Australia), 1997.

Peter Carey, *American Dreams,* HarperCollins (Pymble, New South Wales, Australia), 1997.

Gary Crew, *The Fort,* Lothian (Port Melbourne, Victoria, Australia), 1997.

Penny Hall, *Fraidy Cats,* Koala Books (Mascot, New South Wales, Australia), 1998.

Gary Crew, *The Bread of Heaven,* Lothian (Port Melbourne, Victoria, Australia), 1999.

Victor Kelleher, *Beyond the Dusk,* Random House Australia (Milsons Point, New South Wales, Australia), 2000.

Libby Hathorn, *The Gift,* Random House Australia (Milsons Point, New South Wales, Australia), 2000.

Jo Brice, *The Platypus: What Is It?,* Penguin (Ringwood, Victoria, Australia), 2000.

Laurie Stiller, *Princess Max,* Random House Australia (Milsons Point, New South Wales, Australia), 2001.

Gary Crew, *The Rainbow,* Lothian (Port Melbourne, Victoria, Australia), 2001.

Clare Scott-Mitchell and Kathlyn Griffith, editors, *One Hundred Australian Poems for Children,* Random House Australia (Milsons Point, New South Wales, Australia), 2002.

Janeen Brian, *Theseus and the Minotaur,* Pearson Education Australia (Frenchs Forest, New South Wales, Australia), 2002.

Sally Odgers, *Knightfall,* Koala Books (Mascot, New South Wales, Australia), 2002.

Jill Lewis, *Hans Christian Andersen,* Pearson Education Australia (Frenchs Forest, New South Wales, Australia), 2003.

Archimede Fusillo, *Game or Not?,* Puffin (Camberwell, Victoria, Australia), 2003.

Linsay Knight, *Thirty Australian Stories for Children,* Random House Australia (Milsons Point, New South Wales, Australia), 2003.

Helen Bethune, *Oliver the Acrobat,* Pearson Education Australia (Frenchs Forest, New South Wales, Australia), 2003.

Mark Carthew, *Tiddalick the Thirsty Frog,* Pearson Education Australia (Frenchs Forest, New South Wales, Australia), 2003.

Janeen Brian, *The Brothers Grimm,* Pearson Education Australia (Frenchs Forest, New South Wales, Australia), 2004.

Colin McNaughton, *King Nonn the Wiser,* Pearson Education Australia (Frenchs Forest, New South Wales, Australia), 2004.

Linsay Knight, *Thirty Australian Ghost Stories,* Random House Australia (Milsons Point, New South Wales, Australia), 2004.

Susan Green, *It's True!: Fashion Can Be Fatal,* Allen & Unwin (Crows Nest, New South Wales, Australia), 2004.

Pat Flynn, *Alex Jackson: Dropping In,* University of Queensland Press (St. Lucia, Queensland, Australia), 2004.

Jenny Wagner, *High Hopes on Sea,* University of Queensland Press (St. Lucia, Queensland, Australia), 2005.

Carol Faulkner, *Dads Have No Shame,* Puffin (Camberwell, Queensland, Australia), 2005.

Anne Ingram and Peggy O'Donnell, *Thirty Australian Legends and Icons,* Random House Australia (Milsons Point, New South Wales, Australia), 2006.

Christopher Cheng, *Thirty Amazing Australian Animals,* Random House Australia (North Sydney, New South Wales, Australia), 2007.

Tony Davis, *Roland Wright, Future Knight,* Random House Australia (North Sydney, New South Wales, Australia), 2007.

Tony Davis, *Roland Wright, Brand New Page,* Random House Australia (North Sydney, New South Wales, Australia), 2008.

Loretta Barnard, *Thirty Australian Sports Stories,* Random House Australia (North Sydney, New South Wales, Australia), 2008.

Sidelights

Gregory Rogers is an award-winning Australian author and illustrator. Born in Brisbane, Queensland, Australia, in 1957, Rogers studied at the Queensland College of Art and worked as a graphic designer for the Australian Commonwealth Government before taking up a career as a freelance illustrator in 1987. He has illustrated numerous books covers for Australian publishers, and his artwork has appeared in titles by such celebrated authors as Gary Crew, Robert Cormier, and Victor Kelle-

her. In 1995 Rogers became the first Australian to be awarded the prestigious Kate Greenaway Medal, garnering the honor for his illustrations in Libby Hathorn's *Way Home*. Rogers also teaches illustration classes and workshops, and he is a gifted musician who plays the cornetto, recorder, and baroque guitar.

Rogers made his literary debut in 1988, providing the artwork for *Enter Bob Dickinson*, an educational work by Kay Arthur. His art also appeared in *Space Travellers* by Margaret Wild, in which a homeless mother and son spend their nights in a city park, huddled inside a rocket-shaped sculpture. When Mandy and Zac are fortunate enough to share a room in a friend's house, they "donate" their shelter to another homeless person. "In Rogers's warm, grainy illustrations the characters are affectionately portrayed as more eccentric than poor," observed a *Publishers Weekly* contributor in a review of *Space Travellers*.

Another book, Hathorn's novel *Way Home*, focuses on Shane, a boy who also lives in dire circumstances. When Shane finds a stray kitten one evening, he bundles the creature inside his jacket and carries it to his home: a corner of a dark alley. "Hathorn's gritty evocation of life on the streets is matched by Rogers's darkly realistic visuals," a *Publishers Weekly* reviewer stated. In a lighter work, Nigel Gray's *Running away from Home*, six-year-old Sam is determined to live apart from his bossy father . . . , until the youngster realizes that he left his toothbrush back at the house. According to Susan Dove Lempke, writing in *Booklist*, Rogers' "subdued hues capture Sam's widely ranging moods very well."

Rogers' first self-illustrated title, *The Boy, the Bear, the Baron, the Bard*, was described as "one-of-a-kind fun" by a critic in *Kirkus Reviews*. In the wordless picture book, a little boy chasing his wayward soccer ball into an empty theater finds himself magically transported onto the stage of the Globe Theatre in Elizabethan London. Upon learning that a performance of his play has been interrupted, an enraged William Shakespeare begins chasing the youngster through town. During his flight, the child rescues and befriends a caged bear, frees an imprisoned baron from the Tower of London, and floats down the River Thames on a royal barge belonging to Queen Elizabeth I. "With its harried pace and sportive sight gags—not to mention its undignified rendering of Shakespeare—this chase comedy proves to be a bravura performance," observed a *Publishers Weekly* reviewer. *Booklist* contributor Joanna Rudge Long stated of *The Boy, the Bear, the Baron, the Bard* that "the characters are drawn with humor, affection, and style." Rogers' "sophisticated romp will attract the eyes of intermediate audiences," noted Nancy Menaldi-Scanlan in *School Library Journal*, "and could serve as a good prelude to the study of Shakespeare and his times."

In *Midsummer Knight*, a sequel to *The Boy, the Bear, the Baron, the Bard*, Bear discovers an enchanted forest that resembles the world of Shakespeare's *A Midsum-*

mer Night's Dream. Tossed into a palace dungeon with a kindhearted fairy boy, the king and queen of Fairyland, and their servants, Bear leads a revolt against a villainous fairy (who resembles the famous playwright). *Horn Book* critic Vicki Smith called *Midsummer Knight* "another grand, wordless romp through tunnels and palace," and *School Library Journal* reviewer Suzanne Myers Harold stated that "pen and watercolor illustrations add to the lighthearted tone and provide ample detail of the setting and the characters' emotions." According to a reviewer in *Publishers Weekly*, "Rogers expertly composes the fast-paced comic panels, specializing in towering bird's-eye views of the fairy forest and in crowded rooms busy with over-the-top silly action."

Biographical and Critical Sources

BOOKS

Collins, Paul, *Meet Australia's Children's Authors and Illustrators*, Macmillan Education Australia (South Yarra, Victoria, Australia), 2002.
Dromkeen Book of Australian Children's Illustrators, Scholastic Australia (Sydney, New South Wales, Australia), 1997.

PERIODICALS

Booklist, August, 1996, Susan Dove Lempke, review of *Running away from Home*, p. 1907; October 1, 2004, Francisca Goldsmith, review of *The Boy, the Bear, the Baron, the Bard*, p. 336; April 1, 2007, Kat Kan, review of *Midsummer Knight*, p. 61.
Horn Book, November-December, 2004, Joanna Rudge Long, review of *The Boy, the Bear, the Baron, the Bard*, p. 701; July-August, 2007, Vicky Smith, review of *Midsummer Knight*, p. 384.
Kirkus Reviews, September 15, 2004, review of *The Boy, the Bear, the Baron, the Bard*, p. 919; April 15, 2007, review of *Midsummer Knight*.
Publishers Weekly, April 12, 1993, review of *Space Travellers*, p. 63; August 1, 1994, review of *Way Home*, p. 79; September 20, 2004, review of *The Boy, the Bear, the Baron, the Bard*, p. 62; May 28, 2007, review of *Midsummer Knight*, p. 62.
School Library Journal, December, 2004, Nancy Menaldi-Scanlan, review of *The Boy, the Bear, the Baron, the Bard*, p. 118; June, 2007, Suzanne Myers Harold, review of *Midsummer Knight*, p. 122.

ONLINE

Allen & Unwin Web site, http://www.allenandunwin.com/ (March 10, 2008), "Gregory Rogers."
Margaret Connolly & Associates Web site, http://margaret connolly.com/ (December 21, 2007), "Writers' Rooms: Gregory Rogers."

*   *   *

ROUSS, Sylvia

Personal

Born in CA; married 1983; children: three. *Education:* California State University, Fresno, B.A.

Addresses

Home—CA. *E-mail*—info@sylviarouss.com.

Career

Author and educator. Teaches preschool in Los Angeles, CA. Presenter at book fairs in the United States and Israel.

Awards, Honors

Samuel Glasner Creative Teaching Award, Baltimore Board of Jewish Education, 1989; National Jewish Book Award; Sydney Taylor Honor Award for Younger Readers, Association of Jewish Libraries; *Storytelling World* Award.

Writings

Fun with Jewish Holiday Rhymes, illustrated by Lisa Steinberg, UAHC (New York, NY), 1992.

Sammy Spider's First Hanukkah, illustrated by Katherine Janus Kahn, Kar Ben (Rockville, MD), 1993.

Sammy Spider's First Passover, illustrated by Katherine Janus Kahn, Kar Ben (Rockville, MD), 1995.

Sammy Spider's First Rosh Hashana, illustrated by Katherine Janus Kahn, Kar Ben (Rockville, MD), 1996.

Sammy Spider's First Shabbat, illustrated by Katherine Janus Kahn, Kar Ben (Rockville, MD), 1997.

Sammy Spider's First Purim, illustrated by Katherine Janus Kahn, Kar Ben (Rockville, MD), 2000.

Sammy Spider's First Tu B'Shevat, illustrated by Katherine Janus Kahn, Kar Ben (Rockville, MD), 2000.

Sammy Spider's Hanukkah Fun Book, illustrated by Katherine Janus Kahn, Kar Ben (Minneapolis, MN), 2001.

Sammy Spider's Passover Fun Book, illustrated by Katherine Janus Kahn, Kar Ben (Minneapolis, MN), 2001.

Sammy Spider's Israel Fun Book, illustrated by Katherine Janus Kahn, Kar Ben (Minneapolis, MN), 2001.

The Littlest Pair, illustrated by Holly Hannon, Pitspopany Press (New York, NY), 2001.

The Littlest Frog, illustrated by Holly Hannon, Pitspopany Press (New York, NY), 2001.

Sammy Spider's First Trip to Israel: A Book about the Five Senses, illustrated by Katherine Janus Kahn, Kar Ben (Minneapolis, MN), 2002.

The Littlest Candlesticks, illustrated by Holly Hannon, Pitspopany Press (New York, NY), 2002.

My Baby Brother: What a Miracle!, illustrated by Liz Goulet Dubois, J. David (Middle Village, NY), 2002.

Aaron's Bar Mitzvah, illustrated by Liz Goulet Dubois, J. David (Middle Village, NY), 2003.

Tali's Jerusalem Scrapbook, illustrated by Nancy Oppenheimer, Pitspopany Press (New York, NY), 2003.

(With Joachim H. Joseph) *Reach for the Stars: A Little Torah's Journey,* Devorah (New York, NY), 2004.

Sammy Spider's First Sukkot, illustrated by Katherine Janus Kahn, Kar Ben (Minneapolis, MN), 2004.

No Rules for Michael, illustrated by Susan Simon, Kar Ben (Minneapolis, MN), 2004.

God's World, illustrated by Janet Zwebner, Simcha Media Group (NJ), 2005.

The Littlest Tree, illustrated by Ari Binus, Simcha Media Group (NJ), 2005.

The Littlest Maccabee, illustrated by Greg A. Cohen, Simcha Media Group (NJ), 2006.

Sammy Spider's Shabbat Fun Book, illustrated by Katherine Janus Kahn, Kar Ben (Minneapolis, MN), 2006.

Sammy Spider's First Haggadah, illustrated by Katherine Janus Kahn, Kar Ben (Minneapolis, MN), 2007.

Sammy Spider's First Shavuot, illustrated by Katherine Janus Kahn, Kar Ben (Minneapolis, MN), 2008.

The Littlest Fish, illustrated by Carlos Avalone, Pitspopany Press (New York, NY), 2008.

Sammy Spider's First Day of School, illustrated by Katherine Janus Kahn, Kar Ben (Minneapolis, MN), 2009.

Sammy Spider's First Simchat Torah, illustrated by Katherine Janus Kahn, Kar Ben (Minneapolis, MN), 2010.

Sidelights

Author and educator Sylvia Rouss has a passion for conveying concepts to young children. In addition to teaching preschool at Jewish community centers in both Baltimore and Los Angeles for more than twenty-five years, Rouss has created numerous concept books that combine basic themes such as counting or shapes with Jewish traditions. Her first book, *Fun with Jewish Holiday Rhymes,* was published in 1992, and shortly thereafter Rouss launched her long-running "Sammy Spider" series, which is illustrated by Katherine Janus Kahn. Rouss has also penned standalone titles as well as retellings of Bible stories in her "Littlest" series.

The first "Sammy Spider" book, *Sammy Spider's First Hanukkah,* sets the tone for much of the rest of the series. Sammy watches the Shapiro family as its members prepare for Hanukkah and he decides that he would rather spin dreidels than spider webs. Along with introducing Hanukkah concepts, Rouss incorporates learning numbers and colors in *Sammy Spider's First Hanukkah,* and a *Publishers Weekly* reviewer maintained that her

"spider story has charm." The author combines another Jewish holiday with a lesson on shapes in *Sammy Spider's First Passover,* about which a *Publishers Weekly* contributor wrote that "Rouss's text is lively and informative" despite its ambitious intent.

Sammy Spider's First Haggadah introduces young readers to the Passover Seder, as Sammy and the Shapiros remember the exodus from Egypt, and the lyrics of several traditional songs are included. Lisa Silverman, reviewing the book for *School Library Journal,* praised it as a "highly successful collaboration" between author and series artist Katherine Janus Kahn and ranked it as "perfect for the targeted age group." *Sammy Spider's First Day of School,* the first of the series in which young Josh Shapiro actually notices Sammy's presence, features Sammy's first visit to Josh's Jewish school. When Sammy is discovered by the students, Josh reminds them all of one of their lessons: to be kind to creatures, large or small. Rachel Kamin considered *Sammy Spider's First Day of School* to be "a welcome addition" to the series.

One of Rouss's stand-alone titles, *Tali's Jerusalem Scrapbook,* introduces readers to nine-year-old Tali, who is upset that her American family members are not going to visit Israel to celebrate her birthday because they worry that the middle eastern country is too dangerous. Tali and a friend discuss how things could be better if there were only Jews living in Jerusalem, and sage Mr. Feldman reminds them of the importance of diversity, without which things would be boring. Although Tali arrives at to no conclusions, she does hold out hope that her American relatives will join her for her birthday celebration next year. Sandra Kitain, writing in *School Library Journal,* called *Tali's Jerusalem Scrapbook* a "clearly written story" and recommended it for group discussions.

Rouss has also penned a number of Bible story retellings in her "Littlest" series. In *The Littlest Fish* she takes the perspective of a small fish that encounters the big whale that swallowed Jonah after the prophet said "No" to God. *The Littlest Maccabee* offers the story of the first Hanukkah from the perspective of a mouse, and *The Littlest Pair* offers the tale of Noah's Ark from the perspective of two termites. A frog's perspective on the plague of frogs that tormented Egypt is offered in *The Littlest Frog,* another book in the series. A *Kirkus Reviews* contributor noted of the "Littlest" library that Rouss effectively showcases "her creativity in interpreting Judaic principles for a child's perspective."

Biographical and Critical Sources

PERIODICALS

Kirkus Reviews, September 15, 2008, review of *The Littlest Fish.*
Los Angeles Times, March 26, 2002, Patricia Ward Biederman, "Los Angeles; A Writer Comforts Jewish Children Touched by Tragedy," p. B4.
Publishers Weekly, September 20, 1993, review of *Sammy Spider's First Hanukkah,* p. 32; March 20, 1995, review of *Sammy Spider's First Passover,* p. 59; February 23, 1998, review of *Sammy Spider's First Shabbat,* p. 66.
School Library Journal, August, 2001, Martha Link, review of *Sammy Spider's First Tu B'Shevat,* p. 160; December, 2002, Amy Kellman, review of *Sammy Spider's First Trip to Israel: A Book about the Five Senses,* p. 107; February, 2004, Sandra Kitain, review of *Tali's Jerusalem Scrapbook,* p. 122; June, 2004, Sandra Kitain, review of *No Rules for Michael,* p. 118; March, 2007, Lisa Silverman, review of *Sammy Spider's First Haggadah,* p. 200; July, 2008, Lisa Silverman, review of *Sammy Spider's First Shavuot,* p. 80; March, 2009, Rachel Kamin, review of *Sammy Spider's First Day of School,* p. 127.

ONLINE

Pitspopany Press Web site, http://www.pitspopany.com/ (January 6, 2010), "Sylvia Rouss."
Sylvia Rouss Home Page, http://www.sylviarouss.com (January 6, 2010).*

Sylvia A. Rouss's picture book Sammy Spider's First Hanukkah *features artwork by Katherine Janus Kahn.* (Kar-Ben Copies, Inc., 1993. Illustration copyright © 1993 by Katherine Janus Kahn. Reproduced by permission of The Lerner Publishing Group.)

S

SANDEMOSE, Iben 1950-

Personal

Born July 13, 1950, in Oslo, Norway; daughter of Jørgen Sandermose. *Education:* Statens Læerskole, degree, 1978.

Addresses

Home—Norway.

Career

Illustrator and author of books for children.

Awards, Honors

Oslo bys kunstnerpris, 2004; Bokkunstprisen, 2008.

Writings

SELF-ILLUSTRATED

Kort katt og genever, Cappelen (Oslo, Norway), 1984.

Det vokser Ikke Hvitløk På Skillebekk, Cappelen (Oslo, Norway), 1986.

Vingemus og kattejammer, Cappelen (Oslo, Norway), 1987.

Selv Løvene Gråt den natten, Aschehoug (Oslo, Norway), 1989.

Vil du være kæresten min?, Cappelen (Oslo, Norway), 1990.

Mellom sol og måne, Cappelen (Oslo, Norway), 1992.

Englepels, Cappelen (Oslo, Norway), 1995.

Et glass plumbo og en dusj?, Cappelen (Oslo, Norway), 2001.

To ganger i uken er lite. For lite, Cappelen (Oslo, Norway), 2001.

Fiat og Farmor, Cappelen (Oslo, Norway), 2002, translated as *Gracie and Grandma,* Mackenzie Smiles, (San Francisco, CA), 2007.

Fiat og Farmor undervann, Cappelen (Oslo, Norway), 2003, translated by Tonje Vetleseter as *Gracie and Grandma: Underwater,* Mackenzie Smiles (San Francisco, CA), 2008.

Fiat og Farmor, hemmeligheten, Cappelen (Oslo, Norway), 2003, translated by Tonje Verleseter as *Gracie and Grandma and the Itsy, Bitsy Seed,* Mackenzie Smiles (San Francisco, CA), 2009.

Lykkens frakk, Cappelen (Oslo, Norway), 2006.

Sov godt, pus, Cappelen (Oslo, Norway), 2006.

Fiat og Farmor og en til, Cappelen (Oslo, Norway), 2007.

Fiat og Farmor på Honolulu, Cappelen (Oslo, Norway), 2009.

OTHER

(With Bjarne Sandemose) *Ugler i Sandermosen* (biography), Cappelen (Oslo, Norway), 1999.

Biographical and Critical Sources

PERIODICALS

Kirkus Reviews, September 15, 2008, review of *Gracie and Grandma: Underwater.*

School Library Journal, July, 2009, Rachel Kamin, review *Gracie and Grandma and the Itsy, Bitsy Seed,* p. 68.

ONLINE

Cappelen Web site, http://www.cappelendamm.no/ (January 10, 2010), "Iben Sandemose."*

* * *

SAND-EVELAND, Cyndi

Personal

Born in Canada; married. *Hobbies and other interests:* Gardening.

Addresses

Home—British Columbia, Canada.

Career

Educator and writer. Teacher assistant for English-as-a-second-language students and students with learning disabilities; storyteller; interpreter.

Writings

(Self-illustrated) *Dear Toni,* Tundra Books (Plattsburgh, NY), 2008.

Biographical and Critical Sources

PERIODICALS

Kirkus Reviews, September 15, 2008, review of *Dear Toni.*
School Library Journal, February, 2009, Donna Atmur, review of *Dear Toni,* p. 110.

ONLINE

Cyndi Sand-Eveland Home Page, http://www.sand-eveland.ca (January 10, 2010).*

*   *   *

SCOTT, Michael 1959-
(Anna Dillon, Mike Scott)

Personal

Born September 28, 1959, in Dublin, Ireland.

Addresses

Home—Dublin, Ireland. *Agent*—Barry Krost, Barry Krost Management, 9229 Sunset Blvd., Ste. 215, Los Angeles, CA 90069. *E-mail*—michaeldillonscott@gmail.com; annadillonscott@gmail.com.

Career

Writer, beginning 1982. Also worked as a dealer in rare and antique books and as a television producer. Writer-in-residence in Dublin, Ireland, 1991.

Awards, Honors

Irish Book of the Year nomination, Kentucky Bluegrass Book Award nomination, and Rhode Island Book Award, all 2008, all for *The Alchemist;* Cybils Award nomination, 2009, for *The Sorceress;* Irish Book of the Year Award, and Dublin Airport Authority Irish Children's Book of the Year in Senior Category, both 2009, both for *The Magician.*

Writings

Irish Folk and Fairy Tales, Sphere (London, England), three volumes, 1983–84, published in one volume as *Irish Folk and Fairy Tales Omnibus,* Penguin Books (New York, NY), 1989.
The Song of the Children of Lir, De Vogel (Dublin, Ireland), 1983, published as *The Children of Lir,* Methuen (London, England), 1986.
A Celtic Odyssey: The Voyage of Maildun, Sphere (London, England), 1985.
The Last of the Fianna, illustrated by Gary Ward, Methuen (London, England), 1987.
Navigator: The Voyage of Saint Brendan, Methuen (London, England), 1988.
The Quest of the Sons, Methuen (London, England), 1988.
Green and Golden Tales: Irish Fairytales, illustrated by Joseph Gervin, Mercier Press (Cork, Ireland), 1988.
Irish Hero Tales, illustrated by Joseph Gervin, Mercier Press (Cork, Ireland), 1989.
Banshee, Mandarin (London, England), 1990.
The Story of Ireland, Dent (London, England), 1990.
Saint Patrick, translated by Brôd Nô Chuilinn and illustrated by Peter Haigh, Anna Livia Press (Dulbin, Ireland), 1990.
The River Gods, illustrated by Alan Nugent, Real Ireland Design (Bray, Ireland), 1991.
Image, Sphere (London, England), 1991.
The Seven Treasures: The Quest of the Sons of Tuireann, illustrated by Gary Ward, O'Brien Press (Dublin, Ireland), 1992.
Irish Myths and Legends, Warner (London, England), 1992.
The Piper's Ring, Dent (London, England), 1992.
Reflection, Warner (London, England), 1992.
Lottery, O'Brien Press (Dublin, Ireland), 1993.
Gemini Game, O'Brien Press (Dublin, Ireland), 1993.
Imp, Warner (London, England), 1993.
Irish Ghosts and Hauntings, Warner Books (London, England), 1994.
Fungie and the Magical Kingdom, Sonas (Dublin, Ireland), 1994.
Magical Irish Folk Tales, Mercier Press (Dublin, Ireland), 1995.
(With Morgan Llywelyn) *Ireland: A Graphic History,* illustrated by Eoin Coveney, Gill & Macmillan (Dublin, Ireland), 1995.
The Hallows, Signet (London, England), 1995.
Vampyre, Poolbeg Press (Dublin, Ireland), 1995.
Wolf Moon, O'Brien Press (Dublin, Ireland), 1995.
Nineteen Railway Street, Poolbeg Press (Dublin, Ireland), 1996.
(With Morgan Llywelyn) *Etruscans: Beloved of the Gods* ("Beloved of the Gods" series), Tor (New York, NY), 2000.

(With Armin Shimerman) *The Merchant Prince,* Pocket Books (New York, NY), 2000.

The Quiz Master, New Island (Dublin, Ireland), 2004.

(With Adrienne Barbeau) *Vampyres of Hollywood,* Thomas Dunne Books/St. Martin's Press (New York, NY), 2008.

Also author of scripts for movies and television. Contributor to anthologies, including *A Treasury of Irish Stories, The Irish Leprechaun Book, Shiver, Nightmares,* and *Big Pictures.*

Author's works have been translated into twenty languages.

"TALES FROM THE LAND OF ERIN" SERIES

A Bright Enchantment, Sphere (London, England), 1985.
A Golden Dream, Sphere (London, England), 1985.
A Silver Wish, Sphere (London, England), 1985.
Tales from the Land of Erin, Sphere (London, England), 1985.

"TALES OF THE BARD" SERIES

Magician's Law, Sphere (London, England), 1987.
Demon's Law, Sphere (London, England), 1988.
Death's Law, Sphere (London, England), 1989.
The Culai Heritage, Meisha Merlin Publishing (Atlanta, GA), 2001.

"DE DANNAN TALES" SERIES

Windlord, Wolfhound Press (Dublin, Ireland), 1991.
Earthlord, Wolfhound Press (Dublin, Ireland), 1992.
Firelord, Wolfhound Press (Dublin, Ireland), 1994.

"OTHER WORLD" SERIES

October Moon, O'Brien Press (Dublin, Ireland), 1992, Holiday House (New York, NY), 1994.
House of the Dead, O'Brien Press (Dublin, Ireland), 1993.

"ARCANA" SERIES

(With Morgan Llywelyn) *Silverhand,* Baen Books (Riverdale, NY), 1995.
(With Morgan Llywelyn) *Silverlight,* Baen Books (Riverdale, NY), 1996.

"SECRETS OF THE IMMORTAL NICHOLAS FLAMEL" SERIES

The Alchemyst, Delacorte (New York, NY), 2007.
The Magician, Delacorte (New York, NY), 2008.
The Sorceress, Delacorte (New York, NY), 2009.
The Necromancer, Delacorte (New York, NY), 2010.

NONFICTION

(Editor) *Hall's Ireland: Mr. and Mrs. Hall's Tour of 1840,* Sphere (London, England), 1984.

(Editor) John K'Eogh, *An Irish Herbal: The Botanalogia Universalis Hibernica,* Aquarian Press (New York, NY), 1986.

Celtic Wisdom for Business, Newleaf (Dublin, Ireland), 2001.

The Book of Celtic Wisdom: Poems, Proverbs, and Blessings, Warner Books (New York, NY), 2002.

Contributor to books, including *Irish Pubs, Irish Castles,* and *Irish Cottages.*

UNDER PSEUDONYM ANNA DILLON

Seasons, St. Martin's Press (New York, NY), 1988.
Another Time, Another Season, Sphere (London, England), 1989, published as *Another Season,* Poolbeg Press (Dublin, Ireland), 2003.
Season's End, Sphere (London, England), 1990.
Lies, Brookside (Dublin, Ireland), 1998.
The Affair, Poolbeg Press (Dublin, Ireland), 2004.
Consequences, Poolbeg Press (Dublin, Ireland), 2005.

UNDER NAME MIKE SCOTT

Judith and the Traveller, Wolfhound Press (Dublin, Ireland), 1991.
Judith and Spider, Wolfhound Press (Dublin, Ireland), 1992.
Good Enough for Judith, Wolfhound Press (Dublin, Ireland), 1994.

Adaptations

Film rights to "Secrets of the Immortal Nicholas Flamel" series were optioned to New Line Productions, 2007, and to Lorenzo diBonaventura Pictures, 2009. The online games "The Codex Master" and "The Challenges of the Elder" are based on "Secrets of the Immortal Nicholas Flamel."

Sidelights

Michael Scott, an Irish folklorist and mythologist, is the author of more than one hundred books for readers of all ages, including works of fantasy, science fiction, and horror. Considered an expert on Celtic lore, Scott published his first collection, *Irish Folk and Fairy Tales,* in 1983, and the well-respected work has remained in print ever since. In addition, Scott has written such acclaimed novels as *The Hallows, Silverhand,* and *The Alchemyst,* while also joining actress and writer Adrienne Barbeau to create the novel *Vampyres of Hollywood.* Writing in the *Magazine of Fantasy and Science Fiction,* Orson Scott Card described the author as "a man of musical speech, unflappable charm, and incisive wit."

Scott often uses his knowledge of Irish folklore in his novels. *Windlord, Earthlord,* and *Firelord,* which comprise Scott's "De Dannan Tales" series, are based on Celtic legend and concern a brother and sister who are transported back in time where they encounter shapeshifters, flying serpents, and sorcerers. The "Tales of

the Bard" series, which includes *Magician's Law, Demon's Law,* and *Death's Law,* chronicles the adventures of the bard Paedur, who travels through supernatural realms at the command of Mannam, the Lord of the Dead.

The Hallows, a work of horror, concerns a set of thirteen ancient artifacts that seal the gateway to the demon world. Known as the Hallows, the magical relics have been entrusted to the Guardians for more than half a century. Shadowy figures hoping to unleash the demons begin slaughtering the Guardians and activate the Hallows through a gory ritual. According to a contributor in the *St. James Guide to Horror, Ghost & Gothic Writers,* the author "uses techniques of dreams and historical flashback, and gives a mythological bias to the supernatural elements."

In *October Moon,* Rachel Stone, an American teen, moves to historic Seasonstown House in Ireland with her family. The Stones are tormented by a series of mysterious fires, however, and the police believe Rachel

Cover of Michael Scott's fantasy novel The Magician, *part of his "Secrets of the Immortal Nicholas Flamel" series featuring artwork by Michael Wagner.* (Cover art © 2008 by Michael Wagner. Used by permission of Delacorte Press, an imprint of Random House Children's Books, a division of Random House, Inc.)

may be the culprit. In truth, however, the fires are tied to a clan that is under an ancient spell. "Scott is a master of the naturally unfolding mystery," Card stated, "and the tension never lets up as he takes Rachel—and us—deeper into the darkness."

In *The Alchemyst,* the first book in Scott's "Secrets of the Immortal Nicholas Flamel" series, the author takes readers to San Francisco, as fifteen-year-old twins Sophie and Josh discover that bookstore owner Nick Fleming is really Nicholas Flamel. A fourteenth-century alchemist, Flamel guards the Book of Abraham the Mage, an ancient text of powerful spells. When golems serving the villainous Dr. John Dee steal the magical book, the twins, who possess magical powers, manage to escape with its two most important pages, placing their lives in danger. "After the requisite scene-setting and character introductions, the story takes off like a turbocharged magic carpet," noted Seattle *Post-Intelligencer* critic Cecelia Goodnow, and Sue Giffard, writing in *School Library Journal,* observed that "Scott keeps his sights on the small details of character and dialogue and provides evocative descriptions of people, mythical beings, and places." The "Secrets of the Immortal Nicholas Flamel" series plays out in the novels *The Magician, The Sorceress,* and *The Necromancer,* as Flamel and the twins seek to evade Dr. Dee and the evil Dark Elders.

In addition to his own fiction, Scott sometimes works in collaboration with other writers. Together with Morgan Llywelyn, an award-winning author of historical fiction and nonfiction, he has produced his two-volume "Arcana" series. Comprising the novels *Silverhand* and *Silverlight,* the series centers on young Caeled, a prophesied hero who can restore order to his world using the Arcana, the treasures of the Gods. "This rich tale shows how good fantasy can be," noted a *Publishers Weekly* contributor in a review of *Silverhand.* Other works co-authored with Llywelyn include *Ireland: A Graphic History* and *Etruscans: Beloved of the Gods,* the latter which recounts the exploits of Horatius, a supernatural being who must travel to the underworld to confront his demon father. In *Etruscans* the authors "evoke a vivid sense of time and place," observed *Library Journal* critic Jackie Cassada.

Scott's collaboration with Barbeau on *Vampyres of Hollywood* resulted in a novel that *Booklist* reviewer Diana Tixier Herald dubbed a "tongue-in-cheek romp" that finds B-movie star Osvanna Moore at the center of a strange sequence of grisly murders when she attempts to expand her Anticipation Studios. After several actors who have starred in her horror films are found dead, Osvanna finds herself at the top of the "prime suspect" list and attracting the attention of handsome police detective Peter King. As the murders continue, Peter and Osvanna join forces, and through their alternating narratives the tension—and their romantic entanglement—builds as they try to stop the "Cinema Slayer" from killing his or her next victim. While Patricia Altner

wrote in *School Library Journal* that the novel's "silly plot sometimes overwhelms," she nonetheless praised Scott's "witty" text, "insider knowledge," and an ability to create "interesting" characters. According to a *Publishers Weekly* critic, in *Vampyres of Hollywood* Scott and Barbeau treat readers to a "compulsively readable dark fantasy" that is "briskly paced" and full of "narrative tension."

Biographical and Critical Sources

BOOKS

St. James Guide to Horror, Ghost, and Gothic Writers, St. James Press (Detroit, MI), 1998.

PERIODICALS

Booklist, March 15, 1995, Sally Estes, review of *Silverhand*, p. 1313; May 1, 2007, Frances Bradburn, review of *The Alchemyst*, p. 86; August 1, 2008, Diana Tixier Herald, review of *Vampyres of Hollywood*, p. 53.

Kirkus Reviews, May 1, 2007, review of *The Alchemyst*.

Kliatt, May, 2007, Lesley Farmer, review of *The Alchemyst*, p. 19.

Library Journal, April 15, 2000, Jackie Cassada, review of *Etruscans: Beloved of the Gods*, p. 126; May 15, 2008, Patricia Altner, review of *Vampyres of Hollywood*, p. 87.

Magazine of Fantasy and Science Fiction, May, 1993, Orson Scott Card, review of *October Moon*, p. 36.

Publishers Weekly, November 15, 1994, review of *Gemini Game*, p. 70; March 13, 1995, review of *Silverhand*, p. 64; April 24, 2000, review of *Etruscans*, p. 66; January 21, 2002, Jackie Cassada, review of *The Book of Celtic Wisdom: Poems, Proverbs, and Blessings*, p. 74; March 5, 2007, review of *The Alchemyst*, p. 61; June 2, 2008, review of *Vampyres of Hollywood*, p. 29.

School Library Journal, May, 2007, Sue Giffard, review of *The Alchemyst*, p. 142; July, 2009, Tim Wadham, review of *The Sorceress*, p. 92.

Seattle Post-Intelligencer, June 10, 2007, Cecelia Goodnow, "The Alchemyst Could Be the Start of Something Harry Big in Young-Adult Fantasy."

ONLINE

Michael Scott Home Page, http://www.dillonscott.com (January 10, 2010).*

*   *   *

SCOTT, Mike
See SCOTT, Michael

SEDERMAN, Marty

Personal

Born in MA; daughter of Seymour Epstein (a psychologist); married; children: Casey, Derek. *Education:* Williams College, B.A. (economics); Harvard University, M.B.A.; Pennsylvania State University, M.S. (psychology). *Hobbies and other interests:* Watching and playing hockey, skiing.

Addresses

Home and office—NJ. *E-mail*—sederman@comcast.net.

Career

Market research consultant and author.

Writings

(With Seymour Epstein) *The Magic Box: When Parents Can't Be There to Tuck You In*, illustrated by Karen Stormer Brooks, Magination (Washington, DC), 2002.
Casey and Derek on the Ice, illustrated by Zachary Pullen, Chronicle (San Francisco, CA), 2008.

Sidelights

Marty Sederman, who holds a master's degree in psychology, began writing when her two boys were very young. Because Sederman's husband was often away from home on business trips, Sederman decided to develop a way to help her children cope with their father's absence. Mr. Sederman left behind a special box as a gift whenever he would go away, so the children would know he was thinking of them. The idea worked so well for her family that Sederman decided to share the technique with other parent. The result was *The Magic Box: When Parents Can't Be There to Tuck You In*, which Sederman co-wrote with her father, Dr. Seymour Epstein.

Like *The Magic Box*, Sederman's book *Casey and Derek on the Ice* was inspired by real life. Her children—who share the names of the book's main characters—were avid hockey players, as is Sederman. Using the classic poem "Casey at the Bat" as the basis for her tale, Sederman creates a tense hockey game, where a penalty shot made by Casey has the chance to tie the big game. "Hockey fans will relish the jargon," noted a critic for *Publishers Weekly*. Calling the tale "a contemporary nail-biter," a *Kirkus Reviews* contributor added that Sederman's "tight rhythms keep the story buoyant." Blair Christolon asserted in *School Library Journal* that "any sports enthusiast can enjoy this simple tale with basic brotherly concern."

Biographical and Critical Sources

PERIODICALS

Kirkus Reviews, September 15, 2008, review of *Casey and Derek on the Ice*.

Marty Sederman's sports-themed story in **Casey and Derek on the Ice** *features colorful acrylic paintings by Zachary Pullen.* (Illustration © 2008 by Zachary Pullen. All rights reserved. Used with permission of Chronicle Books, LLC, San Francisco. Visit ChronicleBooks.com.)

Publishers Weekly, October 20, 2008, review of *Casey and Derek on the Ice,* p. 50.
School Library Journal, January, 2009, Blair Christolon, review of *Casey and Derek on the Ice,* p. 84.

ONLINE

American Psychological Association Web site, http://www. apa.org/ (January 6, 2010), "Marty Sederman."
Marty Sederman Home Page, http://martysedermanbooks. com (January 6, 2010).*

* * *

SESKIN, Steve 1953-

Personal

Born 1953.

Addresses

E-mail—steve@steveseskin.com.

Career

Songwriter.

Awards, Honors

Video of the Year designation, Academy of Country Music, 1997, and award from Tennessee Task Force against Domestic Violence, both for "I Think about You" performed by Colin Raye; NSAI Song of the Year designation, and *Music Row* magazine Song of the Year citation, both 1999, both (with Chuck Jones) for "Don't Laugh at Me"; Song of the Year designation, Just Plain Folks Music Awards, 2004, for "Pictures"; Grammy Award nominations, for "Grown Men Don't Cry" and "Don't Laugh at Me."

Writings

SOUND RECORDINGS

Steve Seskin, RSM Records (San Francisco, CA), 1984.
Life's a Dance, Seskin Records (Richmond, CA), 1991.
Cactus in a Coffee Can, Sony/ATV Music (Santa Monica, CA), 1998.
(With Allen Shamblin) *Don't Laugh at Me* (also see below), Sony/ATV Music (Santa Monica, CA), 1998.
(With Tom Douglas) *Grown Men Don't Cry,* Sony/ATV Music (Milwaukee, WI), 2000.
(With others) *Steve Seskin Live,* 2005.

Author of numerous other song lyrics.

FOR CHILDREN

(With Allen Shamblin) *Don't Laugh at Me* (based on the music recording of the same title), illustrated by Glin Dibley, Tricycle Press (Berkeley, CA), 2002.

(With Allen Shamblin) *A Chance to Shine* (based on the song of the same title), illustrated by R. Gregory Christie, Tricycle Press (Berkeley, CA), 2005.
Sing My Song: A Kid's Guide to Songwriting, illustrated by Eve Aldridge, Tricycle Press (Berkeley, CA), 2008.

Author's work has been translated into Spanish.

Sidelights

Based in Nashville, Steve Seskin has had a long, successful career writing hit songs for musicians that include Tim McGraw, Kenny Chesney, Colin Raye, and even Peter, Paul, and Mary. Seskin also has a successful career as a performer, having recorded seventeen albums in which he performs his own music. A regular guest at school assemblies and workshops, he treats listeners to a range of songs geared toward young audiences.

Recorded by Peter, Paul, and Mary, Seskin's "Don't Laugh at Me" became the anthem for a project called

Glin Dibley creates the unique art that brings to life Steve Seskin and Allen Shamblin's story in **Don't Laugh at Me.** (Illustration copyright © 2002 by Glin Dibley. All rights reserved. Used by permission of Ten Speed Press, an imprint of Random House Children's Books, a division of Random House, Inc.)

Operation Respect, founded by group member Peter Yarrow. The goal of the program is to create an environment for school children that incorporates mutual respect, rejects bullying, and helps children to cope with differences. Seskin has also performed at Operation Respect assemblies, and the lyrics to "Don't Laugh at Me," which he cowrote with Allen Shamblin, has been adapted as a children's book.

In *Don't Laugh at Me* a boy with glasses, a girl with braces, and a child who has to use a wheel chair each speak to the audience, imploring them not to laugh or call names, since everyone is equal. The lyrics "laudably sound a call for tolerance," wrote a *Publishers Weekly* contributor. The picture book, which features a message from Peter Yarrow, also includes a CD recording featuring Seskin and Shamblin performing the song, as well as an instrumental version designed to encourage children to sing the song on their own.

Another song adaptation by Seskin and Shamblin resulted in *A Chance to Shine*, which also focuses on people who are different. Told from the perspective of an African-American child, the book shows how the child's father gives a homeless white man an opportunity to make his life better. The child notices how, once the homeless man has a job, he begins to succeed in his life and become a different person. Calling *A Chance to Shine* "thought provoking," Lynn K. Vanca wrote in *School Library Journal* that the "powerful book would be a good choice to stimulate classroom discussions." Although *Booklist* reviewer Hazel Rochman found the homeless man's transformation somewhat simplistic, she predicted that "what will draw children is the bond between the father and son."

Along with songwriting, Seskin also teaches others to write music. As he explained to Whittington in the *San Jose Mercury News:* "I can't really teach somebody to have an imagination. I can give them pointers on form, how to develop story, the very unique art of telling a large story in three to five minutes." Seskin transfers his enthusiasm for teaching to print in *Sing My Song: A Kid's Guide to Songwriting*. The how-to guide offers twelve examples for children to follow, explaining musical terms and showing different forms and patterns that songwriters use. A CD of the twelve songs accompanies the book. "Seskin has tapped a mother lode of musical enthusiasm in this book," wrote Mary Elam in her *School Library Journal* review of *Sing My Song* and a *Kirkus Reviews* writer recommended the book as an "inspired" choice for educators.

Biographical and Critical Sources

PERIODICALS

Booklist, April 15, 2006, Hazel Rochman, review of *A Chance to Shine*, p. 55.

Kirkus Reviews, September 15, 2002, review of *Don't Laugh at Me*, p. 1400; September 15, 2008, review of *Sing My Song: A Kid's Guide to Songwriting.*
Publishers Weekly, October 21, 2002, review of *Don't Laugh at Me*, p. 74.
San Jose Mercury News, March 22, 2006, Mark Whittington, "Songwriter's Advice: 'Get Your Soul onto Paper.'"
School Library Journal, September, 2006, Lynn K. Vanca, review of *A Chance to Shine*, p. 184; October, 2008, Mary Elam, review of *Sing My Song*, p. 136.
Sing Out!, spring, 2005, Rich Warren, review of *Steve Seskin: Live*, p. 134.

ONLINE

Steve Seskin Home Page, http://www.steveseskin.com (January 6, 2010).*

*　　　*　　　*

SHEINMEL, Courtney 1977-

Personal

Born June 21, 1977, in CA. *Education:* Barnard College, Columbia University, B.A. (English), 1999; Fordham University School of Law, J.D., 2002

Addresses

Home—New York, NY. *E-mail*—courtney@courtney sheinmel.com.

Career

Author. Formerly worked as an attorney. Teacher of fiction writing at Writopia Lab.

Awards, Honors

Cybils Award for Middle-grade Fiction nomination, 2008, for *My So-Called Family*, 2009, for *Positively.*

Writings

My So-Called Family, Simon & Schuster Books for Young Readers (New York, NY), 2008.
Positively, Simon & Schuster Books for Young Readers (New York, NY), 2009.
Sincerely Sophie/Sincerely Katie, Simon & Schuster Books for Young Readers (New York, NY), 2010.

Contributor to periodicals, including *Publishers Weekly.*

Sidelights

Although Courtney Sheinmel grew up with a love of writing and majored in English as a college undergraduate, she went on to earn her law degree. However, des-

tiny won out. "For a few years I had two jobs—on weekdays, I was working as a litigation associate at a law firm in Manhattan, and on weekends, I was writing," she explained on her home page. "When I finished my first book, I called a law school professor of mine who was also a novelist. He gave me an incredible gift—the name of his agent. I ended up signing with someone else in the same agency, and the book was sold . . . a month after that. I remember sitting in my office at the law firm, getting the call from my agent that the offer from Simon & Schuster had officially come in. It was one of the best moments of my life."

In her first novel, *My So-Called Family*, Sheinmel introduces a thirteen year old named Leah Hoffman-Ross. Like other girls her age, Leah wants to appear normal, especially now that she has to deal with being the new girl in her New York City school. Leah has a secret, however: even though she has an average-looking family with a mom, dad, and pesky brother, she was actually fathered by a test-tube donation at a reproduction clinic. When her online search for other children that were fathered by the same donor yields a half sister her age, Leah is determined to meet the girl. Although

Cover of Courtney Sheinmel's middle-grade novel My So-Called Family, *which finds a young teen dealing with a surprising revelation.* (Simon & Schuster Books for Young Readers, 2008. Jacket photography copyright © 2008 by Michael Frost Studio. Reproduced by permission of Michael Frost Inc.)

Booklist contributor Michael Cart acknowledged that *My So-Called Family* exhibits several pitfalls of many first novels, he lauded Sheinmel's story as "original" and "involving," adding that it will prompt young teens to "consider . . . the ever-changing meanings of that word family." In *School Library Journal* Natasha Forrester praised the novel's central teen character and maintained that the "solid story" presents "a fresh take on an issue that's rarely addressed." "Leah's [narrative] voice is right on key," observed a *Publishers Weekly* reviewer in an appraisal of *My So-Called Life,* the critic going on to dub Sheinmel's story "smart, original and full of vitality."

Positively was inspired by Sheinmel's volunteer experiences with the Elizabeth Glaser Pediatric AIDS Foundation, the leading national organization identifying and funding pediatric AIDS research. Diagnosed as HIV-positive at age four, Sheinmel's protagonist Emmy Price lives a relatively normal life, even experiencing the ubiquitous family breakup at age eight when her parents divorce. However, after her mother's death from AIDS, thirteen-year-old Emmy must move in with her dad and his pregnant second wife. Worried about her own health, missing her mom, and unsure where she belongs, Emmy knows she does not need a trip to summer camp. However, when the camp turns out to be for HIV-positive girls, the teen learns that others share her worries in a novel that a *Publishers Weekly* contributor cited for its "wrenchingly authentic and quietly powerful" narrative. In *Booklist,* Hazel Rochman echoed that assessment, concluding of *Positively* that the novel's "lively . . . narrative tells a gripping story . . . that will prompt group discussions."

Biographical and Critical Sources

PERIODICALS

Booklist, November 15, 2008, Michael Cart, review of *My So-Called Family,* p. 60; July 1, 2009, Hazel Rochman, review of *Positively,* p. 56.

Kirkus Reviews, September 15, 2008, review of *My So-Called Family;* August 1, 2009, review of *Positively.*

Publishers Weekly, October 20, 2008, review of *My So-Called Family,* p. 50; September 7, 2009, review of *Positively,* p. 47.

School Library Journal, December, 2008, Natasha Forrester, review of *My So-Called Family,* p. 137.

Voice of Youth Advocates, August, 2009, Ava Ehde, review of *Positively,* p. 232.

ONLINE

Courtney Sheinmel Home Page, http://www.courtneysheinmel.com (January 10, 2010).

Courtney Sheinmel Web log, http://courtneywrites.livejournal.com (January 10, 2010).

SIGSAWA, Keiichi 1972-

Personal

Born 1972, in Kanagawa, Japan. *Hobbies and other interests:* Traveling, riding motorcycles.

Addresses

Home—Japan.

Career

Author.

Awards, Honors

Dengeki Novel Awards finalist, for *Kino No Tabi.*

Writings

"BEAUTIFUL WORLD" NOVEL SERIES

Kino No Tabi: Book One of the Beautiful World (title means "Kino's Journey"; originally serialized in a Japanese magazine), illustrated by Kouhaku Kuroboshi, Tokyopop (Tokyo, Japan), 2006.
Kino No Tabi: Book Two: Where Nothing Is Written, illustrated by Kouhaku Kuroboshi, Tokyopop (Tokyo, Japan), 2008.

Also author of novels, including *Alison* and *Lillia and Treize.*

Adaptations

Kino No Tabi was adapted for television, 2003, for film, 2005, and as a video game.

Sidelights

Keiichi Sigsawa is the creator of the "Beautiful World" illustrated novel series featuring Kino, a young world traveler, and her companion, a talking motorcycle named Hermes. In *Kino No Tabi: Book One of the Beautiful World,* Sigsawa introduces his eleven-year-old narrator, a young girl who lives in the Land of Grownups. When they reach the age of twelve, members of her community undergo surgery that transforms them into adults who blindly follow orders. Days before her operation, the narrator meets an enigmatic stranger named Kino who miraculously brings a ruined motorcycle to life and ultimately inspires the girl to question the necessity of her society's rituals. After Kino is killed by the girl's father, she adopts his name and flees her village on Hermes. The pair travels through a dystopian landscape, encountering a village of telepaths and a town that settles disputes through violent contests.

Kino No Tabi received generally positive reviews. "The stories read, in turn, like sci-fi cautionary tales of progress-gone-wrong or classical philosophy lessons,"

Katie Haegele remarked in the *Philadelphia Inquirer.* While Haegele deemed *Kino No Tabi* "a quick and pleasurable read," the critic added that the first volume in Sigsawa's series "is shot through with a feeling of melancholy, even desolation, and the ideas behind the stories are sophisticated and spiritual." "Teens with an interest in politics and philosophy will probably enjoy this story," noted *School Library Journal* contributor Miranda Doyle, and a *Publishers Weekly* critic stated that "manga fans seeking more substance in their reading will likely embrace this series."

Biographical and Critical Sources

PERIODICALS

Philadelphia Inquirer, November 1, 2006, Katie Haegele, "An Androgynous Adventurer Unearths Human Nature's Perils in *Kino No Tabi: Book One of the Beautiful World.*"
Publishers Weekly, November 13, 2006, review of *Kino No Tabi,* p. 58.
School Library Journal, December, 2006, Miranda Doyle, review of *Kino No Tabi,* p. 154.

ONLINE

Anime News Network Web site, http://www.animenews network.com/ (September 1, 2005), Chih-Chieh Chang, "Interview: *Kino's Journey* Creator Keiichi Sigsawa."*

*   *   *

SOBOL, Richard

Personal

Children: Jonah.

Addresses

Home and office—Lexington, MA. *E-mail*—info@wild-foto.com.

Career

Photojournalist.

Writings

SELF-ILLUSTRATED

(With son, Jonah Sobol) *Seal Journey,* Cobblehill (New York, NY), 1993.

Governor: In the Company of Ann W. Richards, Governor of Texas, foreword by Richards, Cobblehill (New York, NY), 1994.

Senator: In the Company of Connie Mack, U.S. Senator from Florida, foreword by Mack, Cobblehill (New York, NY), 1995.

One More Elephant: The Fight to Save Wildlife in Uganda, Cobblehill (New York, NY), 1995.

Mayor: In the Company of Norman Rice, Mayor of Seattle, foreword by Rice, Cobblehill (New York, NY), 1996.

Abayudaya: The Jews of Uganda, music by Jeffrey A. Summit, Abbeville (New York, NY), 2002.

Adelina's Whales, Dutton (New York, NY), 2003.

An Elephant in the Backyard, Dutton (New York, NY), 2004.

Breakfast in the Rainforest: A Visit with Mountain Gorillas, afterword by Leonardo DiCaprio, Candlewick (Cambridge, MA), 2008.

This Life of Rice: From Seed to Supper, Candlewick (Somerville, MA), 2010.

PHOTOGRAPHER

Nancy Joyce, *Building Stata: The Design and Construction of Frank O. Gehry's Stata Center at MIT,* MIT Press (Cambridge, MA), 2004.

Cheryl Willis Hudson, *Construction Zone,* Candlewick (Cambridge, MA), 2006.

Contributor of photographs to periodicals, including *National Geographic, Time, Newsweek, People, Life, Fortune, Audubon, Wildlife Conservation,* and *Outside.*

Sidelights

Richard Sobol has worked for more than twenty-five years as a photojournalist. Along with contributing wildlife and political photographs to periodicals for adults, he is the author and photographer of several books for young readers. Sobol has also created photographs for several books by other writers, and his work has appeared in numerous high-profile periodicals.

Beginning with *Seal Journey,* most of Sobol's picture books feature wildlife photography and themes of conservation and wildlife protection. *Seal Journey,* which Sobol created with his son, Jonah Sobol, gives readers a peek into the world of baby harp seals. While "close-up views of the animals are the heart of the matter," according to Margaret A. Bush in *Horn Book,* the reviewer also complimented the Sobols' "informative, readable essay text."

Elephants star in both *One More Elephant: The Fight to Save Wildlife in Uganda* and *An Elephant in the Backyard,* the latter which is set in Thailand. The first tells of the restoration of the Queen Elizabeth National Park, a preserve for Uganda's dwindling elephant population. *Booklist* contributor Ellen Mandel commented on the "accessible text and crisply focused photographs" in

One More Elephant. The situation for elephants in the small village of Tha Klang is quite different: though also endangered, these Asian elephants are trained by humans from a young age and, in many ways, are treated as part of Thai families. "The text is packed with interesting tidbits about these large mammals . . . and day-to-day life in Tha Klang," wrote Blair Christolon in *School Library Journal,* while Gillian Engberg commented in a *Booklist* review of *An Elephant in the Backyard* on Sobol's "stunning color photographs" and "accessible, casual language."

Adelina's Whales takes readers to a small village in Baja California, where Adelina Mayoral lives with her family and where gray whales winter. "This documentary account is well constructed and beautifully assembled on the pages," wrote Margaret Bush in her *School Library Journal* review of the book. "Most of the story lies in the clear, candid photographs," Linda Perkins noted in *Booklist,* while a *Kirkus Reviews* contributor concluded that, "accessible on many levels," *Adelina's Whales* "gives a personal face to conservation."

Sobol moves from whales to gorillas in *Breakfast in the Rainforest: A Visit with Mountain Gorillas.* This book marked a return to Uganda for Sobol, this time describing his own journey through Uganda's mountainous rain forest. "Remarkable and well-captioned full-color photographs abound," according to *Booklist* critic Shauna Yusko, *Breakfast in the Rainforest* will "make readers feel a part of the trip." Kathy Piehl concluded in her review of the book for *School Library Journal* that Sobol's "admiration for the animals and the people working to protect them provides a personal perspective."

Along with his titles about wildlife conservation, Sobol follows his interest in the world of politics in photo essays that explain the role of different government representatives. In *Governor: In the Company of Ann W. Richards, Governor of Texas* Sobol introduced young readers to a governor who was, at the time, one of the few women in the United States in a major executive political position. The book's text "broadens the Texas perspective by look at the role of the governor of any state," according to Frances Bradburn in *Booklist.* In *Senator: In the Company of Connie Mack, U.S. Senator from Florida* Sobol introduced young readers to the legislative branch and several of the issues on which Mack was working at the time of the book. While giving readers "a feel for the frenetic, diverse pace of a U.S. senator," the scope of information included in the book felt somewhat overwhelming to Bradburn. *Mayor: In the Company of Norman Rice, Mayor of Seattle* is another installment in Sobol's series.

Sobol's work for other authors includes his collaboration with Cheryl Willis Hudson on *Construction Zone,* a picture book that follows the construction of the Massachusetts Institute of Technology's Strata Center from

Richard Sobol pairs detailed photographs with his informative study of mountain gorillas in **Breakfast in the Rainforest.** (Copyright © 2008 by Richard Sobol. Reproduced by permission ofCandlewick Press, Inc., Somerville, MA.)

its original architectural drawings to its completion. "Photos range from small close-ups to awesome two-page spreads picturing the city," Shelle Rosenfeld noted in *Booklist.* As a *Kirkus Reviews* contributor observed, Sobol's "color images are varied in perspective, but each captures the action." Sobol also provided the photographs for a more-in-depth profile of the Strata Center: *Building Stata: The Design and Construction of Frank O. Gehry's Stata Center at MIT.*

Biographical and Critical Sources

PERIODICALS

Booklist, October 15, 1994, Frances Bradburn, review of *Governor: In the Company of Ann W. Richards, Governor of Texas,* p. 423; January 15, 1995, Ellen Mandel, review of *One More Elephant: The Fight to Save Wildlife in Uganda,* p. 922; January 1, 1996, Frances Bradburn, review of *Senator: In the Company of Connie Mack, U.S. Senator from Florida,* p. 830; July, 2003, Linda Perkins, review of *Adelina's Whales,* p. 1883; June 1, 2004, Gillian Engberg, review of *An El-* *ephant in the Backyard,* p. 1736; September 1, 2006, Shelle Rosenfeld, review of *Construction Zone,* p. 131; October 15, 2008, Shauna Yusko, review of *Breakfast in the Rainforest: A Visit with Mountain Gorillas,* p. 38.

Horn Book, September-October, 1993, Margaret A. Bush, review of *Seal Journey,* p. 627.

Kirkus Reviews, June 1, 2003, review of *Adelina's Whales,* p. 811; May 15, 2004, review of *An Elephant in the Backyard,* p. 497; May 1, 2006, review of *Construction Zone,* p. 461; September 15, 2008, review of *Breakfast in the Rainforest.*

School Library Journal, September, 2003, Margaret Bush, review of *Adelina's Whales,* p. 206; July, 2004, Blair Christolon, review of *An Elephant in the Backyard,* p. 96; June, 2006, Carolyn Janssen, review of *Construction Zone,* p. 136; November, 2008, Kathy Piehl, review of *Breakfast in the Rainforest,* p. 148.

ONLINE

Random House Web site, http://www.randomhouse.com/ (January 6, 2010), "Richard Sobol."

Richard Sobol Home Page, http://www.wildfoto.com/ (January 6, 2010).

ZReportage Web site, http://www.zreportage.com/ (January 6, 2010), "Richard Sobol."*

* * *

STEIN, David Ezra

Personal

Born in Brooklyn, NY; married; wife's name Miriam. *Education:* Attended Parsons School of Design. *Hobbies and other interests:* Playing the cello, rock climbing, walking in the woods.

Addresses

Home—Queens, NY. *Agent*—Rebecca Sherman, Writers House, 21 W. 26th St., New York, NY 10010. *E-mail*—david@davidezra.com.

Career

Author and illustrator.

Awards, Honors

New York Public Library Best Books designation, 2007, and Ezra Jack Keats New Author Award, 2008, both for *Leaves.*

Writings

SELF-ILLUSTRATED PICTURE BOOKS

Cowboy Ned and Andy, Simon & Schuster Books for Young Readers (New York, NY), 2006.
Ned's New Friend, Simon & Schuster Books for Young Readers (New York, NY), 2007.
Leaves, Putnam (New York, NY), 2007.
Monster Hug!, Putnam (New York, NY), 2007.
The Nice Book, G.P. Putnam's Sons (New York, NY), 2008.
Pouch!, G.P. Putnam's Sons (New York, NY), 2009.
Interrupting Chicken, Candlewick Press (Somerville, MA), 2010.

Sidelights

David Ezra Stein began a successful career as a children's book author and illustrator almost immediately after graduating from New York's Parsons School of Design. In addition to winning the Ezra Jack Keats New Author award for his picture book *Leaves,* Stein has created a number of other books designed to engage young children, among them *Monster Hug!, The Nice Book,* and *Pouch!* "I have ideas every day," the author/illustrator explained to an interview for the *HipWriter Mama* Web log. "I believe everyone can. The 'trick' is to listen to and honor those ideas. Write them down. Draw them. Edison said something like, 'The best way to have a great idea is to have a lot of ideas.'"

Stein's first published picture books, *Cowboy Ned and Andy* and its companion *Ned's New Friend,* describe the friendship between a cowboy and his trusty horse as they travel the dusty desert ranges of the Old West with their herd of cattle. Comparing Stein's "realistic, simplistic" text in *Cowboy Ned and Andy* to the work of American novelist Ernest Hemingway, a *Publishers Weekly* contributor also praised the book's "spare" watercolor and ink art, which captures Andy the horse's efforts to find a way to celebrate his friend's birthday. The story of man and horse continues in *Ned's New Friend,* although here Andy is worried about his rider's interest in the pretty Miss Clementine. In Stein's engaging cartoon art, readers are ultimately reassured, explained *Booklist* contributor Gillian Engberg, and all ends well in a tale that focuses on "the gentle ups and downs that come with best friendship."

In *School Library Journal* Joy Fleishhacker had special praise for Stein's art, noting of *Cowboy Ned and Andy* that Andy the horse "is the star . . . , and his equine features comically convey concern, dejection, and ultimately, happiness" in Stein's "satisfying tale of friendship." Reviewing *Ned's New Friend* in the same periodical, Maura Bresnahan cited the book's art for its "scratchy charm," but added that the author/illustrator's "text is peppered with expressions and circumstances sure to bring a smile" to storyhour audiences.

In *Leaves* Stein introduces young children to a brown bear cub that lives on a small island. When autumn comes, the leaves that fall from the trees amaze the young bear, and as he attempts to reattach all the fallen leaves, without success, he grows tired. Ultimately, the bear uses the fallen leaves to make a soft bed in a comfy cave, where he sleeps away the winter and awakes to

David Ezra Stein pairs amusing cartoon illustrations with a simple, lighthearted text in his appropriately titled The Nice Book. *(Copyright © 2008 by David Ezra Stein. All rights reserved. Reproduced by permission of G.P. Putnam's Sons, a division of Penguin Putnam Books for Young Readers.)*

watch tiny new leaves spring to life along the branches of his beloved trees. Reviewing *Leaves* in *Booklist*, Carolyn Phelan commented on Stein's "precise text" and added that his "narrative works seamlessly" alongside the book's "freewheeling, expressive" tinted ink drawings. The author/illustrator's "illustrations conjure a place readers will wish they could visit," predicted a *Publishers Weekly* reviewer, and *School Library Journal* critic Kirsten Cutler praised *Leaves* as an "introspective little gem" of a picture book in which a "simple" text "and expressive small-scale pictures blend beautifully."

Other books by Stein include *Monster Hug!* and *The Nice Book,* both of which combine an entertaining story with the author's energetic art. In *Monster Hug!* two rotund monsters spend the day engaged in a range of childlike games that are supersized to accommodate the monsters' giant size. "Children will be delighted by the kinetic, slapstick scenes and the surprise ending" in *Monster Hug!,* predicted Engberg, while in *School Library Journal* Jayne Damron wrote that "Stein's rambunctious watercolors are as joyously messy" as the story's monstrous cast. In contrast, *The Nice Book* focuses on the simple gestures that distinguish nice from naughty, each act of niceness captured in ink and acrylic images featuring engaging animal characters. Praising *The Nice Book* as "charming," Linda Staskus recommended it in her *School Library Journal* as an aid to toddlers trying to understand "what adults mean when they say 'Be nice.'" A *Kirkus Reviews* writer dubbed the work "emotional literacy at its most basic," and in *Booklist* Randall Enos praised Stein's "alliterative" text in *The Nice Book* as a highlight of a picture book that is "enjoyable, informative, and just plain nice."

Biographical and Critical Sources

PERIODICALS

Booklist, June 1, 2007, Gillian Engberg, review of *Ned's New Friend,* p. 83; September 1, 2007, Carolyn Phelan, review of *Leaves,* p. 116; October 15, 2007, Gillian Engberg, review of *Monster Hug!,* p. 52; November 1, 2008, Randall Enos, review of *The Nice Book,* p. 48.

Kirkus Reviews, June 15, 2006, review of *Cowboy Ned and Andy,* p. 638; July 15, 2007, review of *Leaves;* August 1, 2007, review of *Monster Hug!;* October 1, 2008, review of *The Nice Book.*

Publishers Weekly, July 31, 2006, review of *Cowboy Ned and Andy,* p. 74; August 13, 2007, review of *Leaves,* p. 66.

School Library Journal, July, 2006, Joy Fleishhacker, review of *Cowboy Ned and Andy,* p. 87; August, 2007, Kirsten Cutler, review of *Leaves,* p. 94; September, 2007, Jayne Damron, review of *Monster Hug!,* p. 176; November, 2007, Maura Bresnahan, review of *Ned's New Friend,* p. 100; October, 2008, Linda Staskus, review of *The Nice Book,* p. 125.

ONLINE

David Ezra Stein Home Page, http://www.davidezra.com (January 10, 2010).

David Ezra Stein Web log, http://davidezrastein.blogspot.com (January 10, 2010).

Hip Writer Mama Web log, http://hipwritermama.blogspot.com/ (October 26, 2007), interview with Stein.*

*   *   *

STEWART, Joel

Personal

Born in England; son of Pete Stewart. *Education:* Falmouth College of Art, BTEC Foundation, 1997, B.A. (first class), 2000. *Hobbies and other interests:* Playing the chromatic button accordion and the five-string banjo.

Addresses

Home—England. *E-mail*—jstewart@joelstewart.co.uk.

Career

Illustrator. Moonsheep Studio, cofounder with Viviane Schwartz. *Exhibitions:* Work exhibited at Edinburgh Festival, 1999; Royal Institute of Painters in Watercolours, 2001; Original Art Show of Society of Illustrators, New York, NY, 2002, 2003; and Falmouth Art Gallery, 2003.

Awards, Honors

Hodder Book Jacket Award, 2000; Stoke-Roberts bursary, Worshipful Company of Painter-Stainers, 2001; Parents' Choice Silver Medal, 2002, for *The Adventures of a Nose.*

Writings

SELF-ILLUSTRATED

Me and My Mammoth, Macmillan (London, England), 2005.

The Trouble with Wenlocks, Doubleday (London, England), 2007.

Dexter Bexley and the Big Blue Beastie, Holiday House (New York, NY), 2007.

Addis Berner Bear Forgets, Farrar, Straus & Giroux (New York, NY), 2008.

Tree Soup, Doubleday (London, England), 2008.

ILLUSTRATOR

Carol Ann Duffy, *Underwater Farmyard,* Macmillan (London, England), 2002.

Viviane Schwarz, _The Adventures of a Nose,_ Candlewick Press (Cambridge, MA), 2002.

Nikki Siegen-Smith, compiler, _Sea Dream: Poems from under the Waves,_ Barefoot Books (New York, NY), 2002.

Julia Donaldson, _The Magic Paintbrush,_ Macmillan (London, England), 2003.

Lewis Carroll, _Jabberwocky,_ Candlewick Press (Cambridge, MA), 2003.

Carol Ann Duffy, _Moon Zoo,_ Macmillan (London, England), 2004.

Hans Christian Andersen, _Tales of Hans Christian Andersen,_ translated by Naomi Lewis, Candlewick Press (Cambridge, MA), 2004.

Malachy Doyle, _When a Zeeder Met a Xyder,_ Doubleday (London, England), 2006.

(Co-illustrator) Viviane Schwarz, _Shark and Lobster's Amazing Undersea Adventure,_ Candlewick Press (Cambridge, MA), 2006.

Tasha Pym, _Have You Ever Seen a Sneep?,_ Farrar, Straus & Giroux (New York, NY), 2009.

Michael Rosen, _Red Ted and the Lost Things,_ Candlewick Press (Somerville, MA), 2010.

Sidelights

The mixed-media illustrations of British artist Joel Stewart have appeared in original, self-illustrated picture books such as _Dexter Bexley and the Big Blue Beastie, Tree Soup,_ and _Addos Berner Bear Forgets._ In

Joel Stewart teams up with writer Viviane Schwartz to create the quirky picture book **The Adventures of a Nose.** (Illustration copyright © 2002 by Joel Stewart. Reproduced by permission of Candlewick Press, Inc. on behalf of Walker Books, London.)

addition, Stewart's artwork brings to life children's stories by contemporary writers such as Malachy Doyle, Carol Ann Duffy, and Michael Rosen as well as the childhood classics of Lewis Carroll and Hans Christian Andersen. Appraising his work in _Tales of Hans Christian Andersen,_ Margaret Chang noted in _School Library Journal_ that Stewart's "digitally created drawings shed fresh light on the stories," while in _Kirkus Reviews_ a writer made particular note of the "winsome, quirky illustrations" that embellish the "elegant" volume.

Stewart's illustrations for a new edition of the classic poem _Jabberwocky_ by _Alice in Wonderland_ author Charles Dodgson (under the Carroll pseudonym) were also highly praised by many critics, a _Kirkus Reviews_ contributor calling them "brilliantly original" and commenting that they "suit the wry humor of this nonsense poem . . . perfectly." Similarly, Nancy Palmer wrote in _School Library Journal_ that Stewart's "almost cartoonish" illustrations "nicely convey the lighthearted mysteriousness of the poem."

Working with author/artist Viviane Schwarz, Stewart created whimsical illustrations for _The Adventures of a Nose,_ an amusing story about a gigantic, anthropomorphized nose that wanders about on gray-flannel-clad legs (which grow out of its nostrils) in search of a place to call home. A _Publishers Weekly_ contributor called Stewart's illustrations for the story "ingenious," while London _Sunday Times_ reviewer Nicolette Jones predicted that the team of Stewart and Schwarz "clearly has a promising future." The "hand-inked" images Stewart contributes to a more-recent collaboration with Schwarz, _Shark and Lobster's Amazing Undersea Adventure,_ "spin out the story at just the right pace," according to _Booklist_ contributor Jennifer Mattson. Describing the book as "an intriguing stylistic cross between picture book and graphic novel," a _Kirkus Reviews_ writer added that in _Shark and Lobster's Amazing Undersea Adventure_ Schwarz's story gains a "visual zing" from Stewart's hand-lettered text and "ink-lined and digitally colored zany characters."

In his original self-illustrated picture book _Dexter Bexley and the Big Blue Beastie_ Stewart tells the story of a blue monster that decides that snacking on a young boy might be just the thing to raise his spirits. Unfortunately for Dexter Bexley, he is the first young boy that catches the beastie's eye. Fortunately, Dexter manages to distract the hungry monster with enough fun activities that the Big Blue Beastie forgets his tummy and makes a new friend. Noting Stewart's use of comic-book elements in _Dexter Bexley and the Big Blue Beastie,_ a _Publishers Weekly_ contributor praised the tale's "urbane, economical narrative," as well as the "mock-Victorian drawings" that recall the work of the late Edward Gorey. Randall Enos predicted in _Booklist_ that Stewart's story treats children to a "delightful romp from beginning to end," and _School Library Journal_ contributor Barbara Katz proclaimed the picture book to be "original, funny, and endearing."

Stewart brings to life a talented but absentminded ursine character in his self-illustrated picture book **Addis Berner Bear Forgets.** (Illustration copyright © 2008 by Joel Stewart. All rights reserved. Used by permission of Farrar, Straus & Giroux, LLC.)

Biographical and Critical Sources

PERIODICALS

Booklist, October 15, 2002, Gillian Engberg, review of *Sea Dream: Poems from under the Waves,* p. 402; January 1, 2005, Jennifer Mattson, review of *Tales of Hans Christian Andersen,* p. 848; July 1, 2006, Jennifer Mattson, review of *Shark and Lobster's Amazing Undersea Adventure,* p. 68; April 1, 2007, Randall Enos, review of *Dexter Bexley and the Big Blue Beastie,* p. 61; November 15, 2008, Ilene Cooper, review of *Addis Berner Bear Forgets,* p. 49.

Daily Telegraph (London, England), May 24, 2003, Toby Clements, review of *The Magic Paintbrush.*

Evening Standard (London, England), April 10, 2003, Damian Kelleher, review of *Underwater Farmyard,* p. 46.

Guardian (London, England), July 16, 2003, review of *The Adventures of a Nose,* p. 17; May 2, 2009, Julia Eccleshare, review of *Have You Ever Seen a Sneep?,* p. 14.

Horn Book, January-February, 2005, Joanna Rudge Long, review of *Tales of Hans Christian Andersen,* p. 88.

Kirkus Reviews, February 1, 2003, review of *Jabberwocky,* pp. 226-227; October 1, 2004, review of *Tales of Hans Christian Andersen,* p. 956; June 1, 2006, review of *Shark and Lobster's Amazing Undersea Adventure,* p. 580; September 15, 2008, review of *Addis Berner Bear Forgets;* April 1, 2007, review of *Dexter Bexley and the Big Blue Beastie.*

Publishers Weekly, February 25, 2002, review of *The Adventures of a Nose,* pp. 66-67; June 19, 2006, review of *Shark and Lobster's Amazing Undersea Adventure,* p. 61; February 26, 2007, review of *Dexter Bexley and the Big Blue Beastie,* p. 89.

School Library Journal, May, 2002, Sally R. Dow, review of *The Adventures of a Nose,* p. 126; December, 2002, Margaret Bush, review of *Sea Dream,* p. 170; July, 2003, Nancy Palmer, review of *Jabberwocky,* pp. 111-112; December, 2004, Margaret A. Chang, review of *Tales of Hans Christian Andersen,* p. 96; April, 2007, Barbara Katz, review of *Dexter Bexley and the Big Blue Beastie,* p. 116.

Sunday Times (London, England), March 24, 2002, review of *The Adventures of a Nose*, p. 46; March 6, 2005, Nicolette Jones, review of *Me and My Mammoth*, p. 54; January 8, 2006, Nicolette Jones, review of *When a Zeeder Met a Xyder*, p. 54; January 20, 2008, review of *Addis Berner Bear Forgets*, p. 48.

ONLINE

Joel Stewart Home Page, http://www.joelstewart.co.uk (January 10, 2010).*

* * *

SWEET, Melissa 1956-

Personal

Born 1956, in Wyckoff, NJ; married; children: one stepdaughter. *Education:* Endicott College, associate's degree; attended Kansas City Art Institute.

Addresses

Home—68 Main St., Rockport, ME 04856. *E-mail*—melissa@melissasweet.net.

Career

Illustrator, 1986—.

Awards, Honors

Pick of the Lists designation, American Booksellers Association, for *The Talking Pot* by Virginia Haviland; Parents' Choice Award, Parents' Choice Foundation, for *Llama in Pajamas* by Gisela Vos; Gold Award, Oppenheim Toy Portfolio, for *Bouncing Time;* Notable Social Studies Trade Book designation, National Council for the Social Studies (NCSS), 2000, for *Leaving Vietnam* by Sarah S. Kilburn;Outstanding Science Trade Books designation, National Science Teachers Association (NSTA), 2001, for *Girls Think of Everything,* by Catharine Thinmesh, and 2003, for *5,000-Year-Old Puzzle* by Claudia Logan; Minnesota Book Award, Minnesota Humanities Commission, NCSS Notable Social Studies Trade Book designation, and NSTA Outstanding Science Trade Book designation, all 2003, all for *The Sky's the Limit* by Thinmesh; Children's Book of Distinction honor, *Riverbank Review,* 2003, and Texas Bluebonnet Award, 2004, both for *Dirty Laundry Pile* by Paul B. Janeczko; New York Public Library Best Books designation, 2004, for *The Boy Who Drew Birds* by Jacqueline Davies; Lupine Award Honor designation, Maine Library Association, and named among *New York Times Book Review* Ten Best Illustrated Books, both 2005, both for *Carmine;* Golden Kite Award, Society of Children's Book Writers and Illustrators, 2005, for *Baby Bear's Chairs* by Jane Yolen; Caldecott Honor Book designation, 2009, for *A River of Words* by Jen Bryant.

Writings

SELF-ILLUSTRATED

(Adaptor) *Fiddle-i-Fee: A Farmyard Song for the Very Young,* Little Brown (Boston, MA), 1992.
Jingle Bells, HarperFestival (New York, NY), 2002.
Carmine: A Little More Red, Houghton Mifflin (New York, NY), 2005.
Tupelo Rides the Rails, Houghton Mifflin Company (Boston, MA), 2008.

ILLUSTRATOR

Virginia Haviland, reteller, *The Talking Pot: A Danish Folktale,* Joy Street Books (Boston, MA), 1990.
Deborah Heiligman, *Into the Night,* Harper & Row (New York, NY), 1990.
James Howe, *Pinky and Rex,* Atheneum (New York, NY), 1990.
James Howe, *Pinky and Rex Get Married,* Atheneum (New York, NY), 1990.
Maryann MacDonald, *Rosie Runs Away,* Atheneum (New York, NY), 1990.
James Howe, *Pinky and Rex and the Mean Old Witch,* Atheneum (New York, NY), 1991.
James Howe, *Pinky and Rex and the Spelling Bee,* Atheneum (New York, NY), 1991.
Maryann MacDonald, *Rosie's Baby Tooth,* Atheneum (New York, NY), 1991.
James Howe, *Pinky and Rex Go to Camp,* Atheneum (New York, NY), 1992.
C.B. Christiansen, *Sycamore Street,* Atheneum (New York, NY), 1993.
James Howe, *Pinky and Rex and the New Baby,* Atheneum (New York, NY), 1993.
Elizabeth O'Donnell, *Sing Me a Window,* Morrow Junior Books (New York, NY), 1993.
Charlotte Zolotow, *Snippets: A Gathering of Poems, Pictures, and Possibilities,* HarperCollins (New York, NY), 1993.
Maryann MacDonald, *Rosie and the Poor Rabbits,* Atheneum (New York, NY), 1994.
Bonnie Pryor, *Marvelous Marvin and the Wolfman Mystery,* Morrow Junior Books (New York, NY), 1994.
Joanne Ryder, *A House by the Sea,* Morrow Junior Books (New York, NY), 1994.
Gisela Voss, *Llama in Pajamas,* Museum of Fine Arts (Boston, MA), 1994.
Lee Bennett, selector, *Blast Off! Poems about Space,* HarperCollins (New York, NY), 1995.
James Howe, *Pinky and Rex and the Double-Dad Weekend,* Atheneum (New York, NY), 1995.
Bonnie Pryor, *Marvelous Martin and the Pioneer Ghost,* Morrow Junior Books (New York, NY), 1995.
Eileen Spinelli, *Naptime, Laptime,* Cartwheel Books (New York, NY), 1995.
Kathi Appelt, *The Bat Jamboree,* Morrow Junior Books (New York, NY), 1996.
C.B. Christiansen, *A Snowman on Sycamore Street,* Atheneum (New York, NY), 1996.

James Howe, *Pinky and Rex and the Bully,* Atheneum (New York, NY), 1996.

James Howe, *Pinky Rex and the New Neighbors,* Atheneum (New York, NY), 1997.

Dian Curtis Regan, *Monsters in Cyberspace,* Henry Holt (New York, NY), 1997.

Margaret Park Bridges, *Will You Take Care of Me?,* Morrow Junior Books (New York, NY), 1998.

James Howe, *Pinky and Rex and the Perfect Pumpkin,* Atheneum (New York, NY), 1998.

James Howe, *Pinky and Rex and the School Play,* Atheneum (New York, NY), 1998.

Dian Curtis Regan, *Monsters and My One True Love,* Henry Holt (New York, NY), 1998.

On Christmas Day in the Morning: A Traditional Carol, foreword by John Langstaff, Candlewick Press (Cambridge, MA), 1999.

Kathi Appelt, *Bats on Parade,* Morrow Junior Books (New York, NY), 1999.

Sarah S. Kilborne, *Leaving Vietnam: The Journey of Tuan Ngo, a Boat Boy,* Simon & Schuster (New York, NY), 1999.

Sarah Wilson, *Love and Kisses,* Candlewick Press (Cambridge, MA), 1999.

Kathi Appelt, *Bats around the Clock,* HarperCollins (New York, NY), 2000.

Samantha Berger, *It's Spring,* Scholastic, Inc. (New York, NY), 2000.

Maria Fleming, *Autumn Leaves Are Falling,* Scholastic, Inc. (New York, NY), 2000.

Patricia Hubbell, *Bouncing Time,* HarperCollins (New York, NY), 2000.

Joan MacPhail Knight, *Charlotte in Giverny,* Chronicle Books (San Francisco, CA), 2000.

Catherine Thimmesh, *Girls Think of Everything: Stories of Ingenious Inventions by Women,* Houghton Mifflin (Boston, MA), 2000.

Paul B. Janeczko, selector, *Dirty Laundry Pile,* HarperCollins (New York, NY), 2001.

Margaret Park Bridges, *Now What Can I Do?,* Seastar Books (New York, NY), 2001.

Stephanie Calmenson, *Good for You: Toddler Rhymes for Toddler Times,* HarperCollins (New York, NY), 2001.

James Howe, *Pinky and Rex and the Just-Right Pet,* Atheneum (New York, NY), 2001.

Cobi Ladner, editor, *Notes from Home: Twenty Canadian Writers Share Their Thoughts of Home,* McArthur (Toronto, Ontario, Canada), 2002.

Stephanie Calmenson, *Welcome, Baby!: Baby Rhymes for Baby Times,* HarperCollins (New York, NY), 2002.

Claudia Logan, *The 5,000-Year-Old Puzzle: Solving a Mystery of Ancient Egypt,* Farrar, Straus & Giroux (New York, NY), 2002.

Alice B. McGinty, *Ten Little Lambs,* Dial Books for Young Readers (New York, NY), 2002.

Catherine Thimmesh, *The Sky's the Limit: Stories of Discovery by Women and Girls,* Houghton Mifflin (New York, NY), 2002.

Nancy Carolstrom White, *Giggle-Wiggle Wake Up!,* Knopf (New York, NY), 2003.

Anna Grossnickle Hines, *My Grandma Is Coming to Town,* Candlewick Press (Cambridge, MA), 2003.

Joan Knight, *Charlotte in Paris,* Chronicle Books (San Francisco, CA), 2003.

Cynthia Rylant, *Moonlight, the Halloween Cat,* HarperCollins (New York, NY), 2003.

Lee Wardlaw, *Peek-a-Book: A Lift-the-Flap Bedtime Rhyme,* Dial Books for Young Readers (New York, NY), 2003.

Eve Bunting, *I Love You Too!,* Scholastic, Inc. (New York, NY), 2004.

Jacqueline Davies, *The Boy Who Drew Birds: A Story of John James Audubon,* Houghton Mifflin (Boston, MA), 2004.

Pamela Jane, *Spring Is Here! A Barnyard Counting Book,* Little Simon (New York, NY), 2004.

Joanne Ryder, *Won't You Be My Kissaroo?,* Harcourt (Orlando, FL), 2004.

Stephanie Calmenson, *Kindergarten Kids: Riddles, Rebuses, Wiggles, Giggles, and More!,* HarperCollins (New York, NY), 2005.

Judy Sierra, *Schoolyard Rhymes: Kids' Own Rhymes for Rope Skipping, Hand Clapping, Ball Bouncing, and Just Plain Fun,* Knopf (New York, NY), 2005.

Jane Yolen, *Baby Bear's Chairs,* Gulliver Books (Orlando, FL), 2005.

Joan Knight, *Charlotte in New York,* Chronicle Books (San Francisco, CA), 2006.

Joanne Ryder, *Won't You Be My Hugaroo?,* Harcourt (New York, NY), 2006.

Jane Yolen, *Baby Bear's Books,* Harcourt (Orlando, FL), 2006.

Jane Yolen, *Baby Bear's Big Dreams,* Harcourt (Orlando, FL), 2007.

Jacqueline Briggs Martin, *Chicken Joy on Redbean Road: A Bayou Country Romp,* Houghton Mifflin (Boston, MA), 2007.

Tony Johnston, *Off to Kindergarten,* Cartwheel Books (New York, NY), 2007.

Jen Bryant, *A River of Words: The Story of William Carlos Williams,* Eerdmans Books for Young Readers (Grand Rapids, MI), 2008.

Joan McPhail Knight, *Charlotte in London,* Chronicle Books (San Francisco, CA), 2008.

Judy Sierra, *Sleepy Little Alphabet: A Bedtime Story from Alphabet Town,* Alfred A. Knopf (New York, NY), 2009.

Cari Best, *Easy as Pie,* Farrar, Straus & Giroux (New York, NY), 2010.

Sidelights

Award-winning artist Melissa Sweet has illustrated dozens of children's books, including James Howe's "Pinky and Rex" picture-book series, Joan Knight's "Charlotte" series of travel journals written by Claude Monet's fictional daughter, and the award-winning *The Sky's the Limit: Stories of Discovery by Women and Girls,* written by Catherine Thimmesh. Awarded a Caldecott Honor Book citation for her illustrations for Jen Bryant's picture-book biography *A River of Words: The Story of William Carlos Williams,* Sweet has also created artwork for several original stories, among them *Carmine: A Little More Red, Tupelo Rides the Rails,* and *Fiddle-i-Fee: A Farmyard Song for the Very Young.*

Sweet grew up in northern New Jersey with her two brothers, and enjoyed living in a suburban neighborhood with lots of kids. She was not an avid reader, but was always making art. She later went to art school, thinking she would become a potter, but fell in love with drawing and painting. During her first year in art school, Sweet was re-introduced to Else Holmelund Minarik's children's book *Little Bear,* which features Maurice Sendak's art work. Sweet was inspired by Sendak's work, and decided to pursue a career in children's illustration.

For Sweet, the most intriguing aspect in creating art is the actual process: learning about the many materials and tools of art and keeping sketch books. Each work is unique and requires its own distinctive technique. In creating the artwork that brings to life Cynthia Rylant's *Moonlight, the Midnight Cat,* for instance, Sweet paints using acrylics in order to capture the rich colors of the night. Nancy White Carlson's *Giggle-Wiggle Wake-Up!,*

a children's book about a preschooler preparing for school, finds her replicating the pages of a school exercise book in order to reflect the mood of a classroom. Sweet often travels in order to do research for her work, especially for her nonfiction titles, and she finds inspiration for her artwork in the details of daily life during walks, gardening, and even while watching the antics of her pet dog Rufus.

Featuring Sweet's illustrations, Howe's "Pinky and Rex" series focuses on the adventures of a little girl named Rex and her best friend Pinky, a little boy. In *Pinky and Rex and the Bully* Pinky is teased by a classroom bully because the boy likes the color pink and enjoys playing with girls. The taunting Pinky endures from the bully causes the boy to question his identity until he is reassured by caring neighbor Mrs. Morgan, who tells him that it is okay to be different. In illustrating *Pinky and Rex and the Bully,* Sweet uses ink and watercolor to depict the children's experiences, "giving

Sweet captures the whimsical humor in Jacqueline Briggs Martin's farmyard story **Chicken Joy on Redbean Road.** (Illustration copyright © 2007 by Melissa Sweet. All rights reserved. Reprinted by permission of Houghton Mifflin Harcourt Publishing Company.)

the book a most appealing look," in the opinion of *Booklist* reviewer Carolyn Phelan. With her ink-and-watercolor technique, Sweet adds a personal touch to *Pinky and Rex and the New Neighbors,* which revolves around favorite neighbor Mrs. Morgan. Pinky and Rex are distraught when they find out that Mrs. Morgan will be moving away, and are tentative about befriending the new neighbors who replace the woman. In a review for *Booklist,* Phelan noted that in *Pinky and Rex and the New Neighbors,* "Sweet's ink-and-watercolor illustrations work their quiet charm again, depicting the characters and settings with clarity and warmth."

Other books featuring Sweet's illustrations include Judy Sierra's *Sleepy Little Alphabet: A Bedtime Story from Alphabet Town,* Bryant's *A River of Words,* and Joanne Ryder's *Won't You Be My Hugaroo?,* the last a rhyming story about an affectionate zebra and its loving caretaker that serves as a sequel to *Won't You Be My Kissaroo?* Praising *A River of Words* as a "fresh, accessible" introduction to the work of noted twentieth-century U.S. poet William Carlos Williams, a *Kirkus Reviews* writer added that Sweet's "artistically compelling" watercolor and collage illustrations for the book have a nostalgic quality that is both "vividly childlike, and highly sophisticated." Sweet's art also captures the personality of the "endearing animal characters" in *Won't You Be My Huggaroo?,* according to *Booklist* contributor Shelle Rosenfeld, the critic citing the "whimsical" mixed-media illustrations for making Ryder's story "a joy to read and view." In *Kirkus Reviews* a contributor also praised the collaboration between Ryder and Sweet, noting that the artist's "vivid" images "capture the vibrancy of a summer's outing on a glorious day."

In *Carmine,* Sweet employs her characteristic mixed-media technique in illustrating her own adaptation of the traditional story of Little Red Riding Hood. The book, which also serves as an alphabet book, introduces Carmine, a young artist who is infatuated with the color red. Caroline Ward, writing in *School Library Journal,* noted that the author/illustrator's use of mixed-media art "imitates the sketchbook of a child artist," and her "inventive layout employs a variety of techniques to engage viewers and move the story forward." *Carmine* begins when the girl's grandmother invites Carmine to her house to enjoy some of her homemade alphabet soup. The child is warned by the older woman not to dilly-dally on her way over because of the wolf that resides in the woods. As Carmine walks through the woods with her dog Rufus, she forgets her grandmother's advice and stops to paint a picture of some red poppies she sees on her way. Ultimately, her lingering results in some eventful surprises. Joanna Rudge Long, writing in *Horn Book,* concluded that Sweet's illustrations, "sparked with reds in all their bright variety— tells the story beautifully," while a *Publishers Weekly* contributor dubbed *Carmine* an "overall entertaining package."

Another self-illustrated picture book that features an original story, *Tupelo Rides the Rails* finds a dog and its beloved toy Mr. Bones looking for a loving home. When

Melissa Sweet tells the story of a traveling pup in her self-illustrated picture book **Tupelo Rides the Rails.**

Tupelo happens on a gang of dogs that is cared for by a kindly boxcar hobo, the pup joins the travelers on their next train ride and hears wonderful stories about brave dogs from Lassie to Toto. In *School Library Journal* Teresa Pfeifer described *Tupelo Rides the Rails* as "a richly rewarding book about the power of wishful thinking and kindness," while a *Publishers Weekly* contributor wrote that the story's "unusually expressive canine cast" is brought to life in "cheery watercolors and mixed media." Hazel Rochman had special praise for *Tupelo Rides the Rails,* writing in *Booklist* that Sweet's "tender" story of a dog's search for home "is packed with feeling and story."

Biographical and Critical Sources

PERIODICALS

Booklist, April 1, 1996, Carolyn Phelan, review of *Pinky and Rex and the Bully,* p. 1364; May 1, 1997, Carolyn Phelan, review of *Pinky and Rex and the New Neighbors,* p. 1503; August, 2005, Kay Weisman, review of *Schoolyard Rhymes: Kids' Own Rhymes for Rope Skipping, Hand Clapping, Ball Bouncing, and Just Plain Fun,* p. 242; March 1, 2006, Shelle Rosenfeld, review of *Won't You Be My Hugaroo?,* p. 101; February 15, 2007, Janice Del Negro, review of *Chicken Joy on Redbean Road: A Bayou Country Romp,* p. 84; August, 2007, Carolyn Phelan, review of *Baby Bear's Big Dreams,* p. 81, and Hazel Rochman, review of *Off to Kindergarten,* p. 83; January 1, 2008, Hazel Rochman, review of *Tupelo Rides the Rails,* p. 79; August 1, 2008, Gillian Engberg, review of *A River of Words:*

The Story of William Carlos Williams, p. 66; March 15, 2009, Ilene Cooper, review of *Charlotte in London,* p. 55; June, 2009, Bethany Isaacson, review of *The Sleepy Little Alphabet: A Bedtime Story from Alphabet Town,* p. 100.

Horn Book, July-August, 2005, Joanna Rudge Long, review of *Carmine: A Little More Red,* p. 460.

Kirkus Reviews, June 15, 2005, review of *Kindergarten Kids: Riddles, Rebuses, Wiggles, Giggles, and More!,* p. 679, and review of *Schoolyard Rhymes,* p. 690; February 15, 2006, review of *Won't You Be My Hugaroo?,* p. 190; July 15, 2007, review of *Baby Bear's Big Dreams.*

Publishers Weekly, May 16, 2005, review of *Carmine,* p. 62; April 21, 2008, review of *Tupelo Rides the Rails,* p. 57; May 1, 2009, review of *The Sleepy Little Alphabet,* p. 50.

School Library Journal, August, 2005, Caroline Ward, review of *Carmine,* p. 107; August, 2005, Mary Hazelton, review of *Kindergarten Kids,* p. 112; March, 2007, Marge Loch-Wouters, review of *Chicken Joy on Redbean Road,* p. 180; July, 2007, Rachel G. Payne, review of *Off to Kindergarten,* p. 78; March, 2008, Teresa Pfeifer, review of *Tupelo Rides the Rails,* p. 176; March, 2009, Meg Smith, review of *Charlotte in London,* p. 119.

ONLINE

Melissa Sweet Home Page, http://www.melissasweet.net (January 20, 2010).

T-U

TILLMAN, Nancy

Personal
Born in AL. *Education:* Rollins College, B.A., 1976.

Addresses
Home—Tualatin, OR. *E-mail*—nancy@nancytillman.com.

Career
Author and illustrator. Formerly worked in advertising; former greeting-card designer.

Writings

SELF-ILLUSTRATED

On the Night You Were Born, Feiwel & Friends (New York, NY), 2006.
The Spirit of Christmas, Feiwel & Friends (New York, NY), 2009.
Wherever You Are, Feiwel & Friends (New York, NY), 2010.

ILLUSTRATOR

Eric Metaxas, *It's Time to Sleep, My Love,* Feiwel & Friends (New York, NY), 2008.

Sidelights
Oregon-based painter and author Nancy Tillman left a career in advertising and greeting-card design to create warmhearted self-illustrated picture-book stories that include *Wherever You Are* and *The Spirit of Christmas,* as well as the reassuring read aloud *On the Night You Were Born.* In addition, her glowing, detailed images bring to life Eric Metaxas's bed-time picture book *It's Time to Sleep, My Love.*

Nancy Tillman (Reproduced by permission.)

Described by a *Kirkus Reviews* contributor as "a beautiful tribute to the uniqueness of every child," *On the Night You Were Born* recreates a magical night that finds animals engaging in joyous celebration throughout the world. From dancing polar bears to cheerful lady-bugs to a flock of geese winging their way homeward to a family reunion, the story is designed to inspire young children with the knowledge that every life is a miracle. In her review of *On the Night You Were Born, New York Times Book Review* contributor Julie Just cited Tillman's "riveting" mixed-media art, and a *Publishers Weekly* reviewer wrote that her "quietly celebratory" text avoids sentimentality and "has the authenticity of whispered conversation." Remarking on the book's value to loving parents, *Booklist* critic Gillian Engberg wrote that the "rhyming, rhythmic text" in *On the Night You Were Born* "includes lines that beg for

Nancy Tillman's inspiring ethereal art matches Eric Metaxas' soothing story in **It's Time to Sleep, My Love.** (Feiwel & Friends, 2008. Illustration copyright © 2008 by Nancy Tillman. All rights reserved. Reproduced by permission.)

participation," while in *School Library Journal* Carolyn Janssen praised the volume's combination of "painterly art and poetic . . . text."

Biographical and Critical Sources

PERIODICALS

Booklist, December 1, 2006, Gillian Engberg, review of *On the Night You Were Born,* p. 55; October 15, 2008, Gillian Engberg, review of *It's Time to Sleep, My Love,* p. 47.

Kirkus Reviews, October 1, 2005, review of *On the Night You Were Born,* p. 1091; September 15, 2008, review of *It's Time to Sleep, My Love.*

New York Times Book Review, February 11, 2007, Julie Just, review of *On the Night You Were Born,* p. 17.

Publishers Weekly, November 20, 2006, review of *On the Night You Were Born,* p. 57.

School Library Journal, March, 2007, Carolyn Janssen, review of *On the Night You Were Born,* p. 186; December, 2008, Bethany Isaaacson, review of *It's Time to Sleep, My Love,* p. 96.

ONLINE

Nancy Tillman Home Page, http://www.nancytillman.com (January 10, 2010).*

* * *

TURNER, Pamela S. 1957-

Personal

Born 1957, in CA; married Rob Turner; children: Connor, Travis, Kelsey. *Education:* University of California, Irvine, B.A. (social science); University of California, Berkeley, M.A. (public heath). *Hobbies and other interests:* SCUBA diving, snow-skiing, reading, kendo, travel.

Addresses

Home—Oakland, CA. *E-mail*—pstrst@pacbell.net.

Career

Writer. Worked as a legislative assistant for foreign affairs for a California congressman; former international heath consultant. Volunteer wildlife rehabilitator for Lindsay Wildlife Hospital.

Member

Authors League, Society of Children's Book Writers and Illustrators.

Awards, Honors

Golden Kite Honor designation, Society of Children's Book Writers and Illustrators, and Pennsylvania Young Reader's Choice Award, both 2004, both for *Hachiko;* Notable Book designation, American Library Association, Flora Stieglitz Straus Award, and Henry Bergh Award, American Society for the Protection of Animals, all 2006, all for *Gorilla Doctors;* Golden Kite Award, and Notable Book designation, National Science Teachers Association, both 2008, and Northern California Book Award for Children's Literature, all for *A Life in the Wild;* American Association for the Advancement of Science (AAAS)/Subaru SB&F Award finalist, 2008, and Best Children's Book designation, Bank Street College of Education, both for *Life on Earth . . . and Beyond;* Cybils Award nomination, for *A Life in the Wild* and *The Frog Scientist; Booklist* Top-Ten Sci-Tech Book for Youth selection and Editor's Choice selection, both 2009, and American Association for the Advancement of Science/Subaru SB&F Award, and Best Children's Book designation, Bank Street College of Education, both 2010, all for *The Frog Scientist.*

Writings

Hachiko: The True Story of a Loyal Dog, illustrated by Yan Nascimbene, Houghton Mifflin (Boston, MA), 2004.

Gorilla Doctors: Saving Endangered Great Apes, Houghton Mifflin (Boston, MA), 2005.

A Life in the Wild: George Schaller's Struggle to Save the Last Great Beasts, Farrar, Straus & Giroux (New York, NY), 2008.

Life on Earth—and Beyond: An Astrobiologist's Quest, Charlesbridge (Watertown, MA), 2008.

The Frog Scientist, Houghton Mifflin Books for Children (Boston, MA), 2009.

Prowling the Deep: Exploring the Hidden World of Ocean Predators, Walker & Co. (New York, NY), 2009.

Contributor to periodicals, including *Christian Science Monitor, Cobblestone, Cricket, Highlights for Children, National Geographic Kids, National Wildlife, Odyssey, Scientific American Explorations, Spider,* and *Writer.*

Sidelights

Inspired by her life-long love of animals and her interest in nature, Pamela S. Turner writes award-winning nonfiction books for young readers that focus on animal conservation and the men and women who dedicate their lives to that cause. *Gorilla Doctors: Saving Endangered Great Apes, A Life in the Wild: George Schaller's Struggle to Save the Last Great Beasts,* and *The Frog Scientist* include interviews with experts in their respective fields, and contain numerous photographs and maps that let readers visually explore the relevant region and its wildlife. In *Life on Earth—and*

Pamela S. Turner (Photograph by Jamie Westdahl. Reproduced by permission.)

Beyond: An Astrobiologist's Quest Turner provides a closer view of nature, profiling a scientist whose studies are on the microscopic level.

Turner's books have been inspired and enriched by her many travels; at various times she and her husband, Rob Turner, have made their home in Kenya, the Marshall Islands, South Africa, the Philippines, and Japan. All three of the couple's children were born overseas, each in a different country. Turner's first published book, *Hachiko: The True Story of a Loyal Dog,* was inspired by a story she learned while living in Tokyo, Japan, and is brought to life in dramatic stylized art by Yan Nascimbene. Commemorated by a prominent statue in Tokyo, Hachiko was a dog who lived with Dr. Ueno, and the pup became well know throughout the city as he patiently awaited his master's daily return from work at the train station. This went on for many years and, after the doctor's death, Hachiko continued to return to the train station each day, loyally waiting for the human companion who would never return until his own death a decade later. Nascimbene's watercolor illustrations, with their "austere elegance," effectively reflect the "suitably distant and subdued tone" of Turner's text, according to *Horn Book* contributor Jennifer M. Brabander. In *Booklist* Jennifer Mattson praised the "poignant true story" recounted in *Hachiko,* and predicted that Turner's story "will resonate with any child who has loved a dog."

Part of the "Scientists in the Field" series, Turner's *Gorilla Doctors* shares the series' focus on conservation in its story profiling the work of the Mountain Gorilla Vet-

Pamela S. Turner shares her passion for science in picture books such as **Life on Earth—and Beyond,** *which focuses on the work of a noted astrobiologist.* (Charlesbridge, 2008. Photo courtesy of NASA/JPL/Caltech.)

erinary Project. Based in Rwanda and Uganda, these veterinarians and epidemiologists track and protect the gorilla population in these east-central African nations from both biological and animal threats. Turner's "dramatic, present-tense" accounts of the project's expeditions to study or rescue gorillas depict "an unusually diverse group" of scientists, noted Jennifer Mattson in her *Booklist* review of *Gorilla Doctors*. In *School Library Journal* Patricia Manning praised the author's "readable text" as well as the book's "striking, full-color photographs," while a *Kirkus Reviews* writer dubbed Turner's work "outstanding."

Described by *Booklist* contributor Gillian Engberg as an "excellent introduction to animal conservation," *A Life in the Wild* focuses on naturalist George Schaller, who fled to the United States from Nazi Germany as a child and eventually became noted for his studies of lions, ti-

gers, and other wild animals. His methods were revolutionary for their time: rather than killing the animal and then extrapolating its habits from its corpse, Schaller observed wild creatures with his camera during field studies. "Turner's vivid, moment-by-moment descriptions of animal encounters will captivate readers," predicted Engberg, while in *School Library Journal* Ellen Heath dubbed *A Life in the Wild* as an "inspiring biography" that features "writing [that] is both clear and lively."

NASA astrobiologist Chris McKay and his exploration of extreme environments that share characteristics of remote planets is the focus of *Life on Earth—and Beyond*. Here Turner shadows the scientist's travels to such remote regions as Antarctica, Siberia, and Chile's sterile Atacama Desert. The "absorbing account" of McKay's adventures in gathering and studying micro-

bial life forms incorporates "enough detail to create vivid impressions" in readers' minds, according to Brabander, In addition to describing the physical challenges the scientist encounters, *Life on Earth—and Beyond* provides "an in-depth look at the richly rewarding career of a field scientist," according to *Horn Book* contributor Danielle J. Ford. In the opinion of a *Kirkus Reviews* writer, Turner's comprehensive work relays "a perspective on space exploration that is both down to earth and out of this world."

In an article for *Writer* magazine, Turner described her career as a writer. "I object to that old adage 'write what you know,'" she noted. "I write what I want to know. I look for topics that fascinate me, research them, and try to inject my own passion into my text." After finding a topic, the next challenge is presenting it in an interesting and readable way. "Take the books or articles you admire most—the ones you wish you'd written—and dissect them," Turner advised. "Try to figure out why you like the writing, and identify the techniques the writer used. Adapt those lessons to your own work."

Biographical and Critical Sources

PERIODICALS

Booklist, April 15, 2004, Jennifer Mattson, review of *Hachiko: The True Story of a Loyal Dog,* p. 1441; June 1, 2005, Jennifer Mattson, review of *Gorilla Doctors: Saving Endangered Great Apes,* p. 1804; February 1, 2008, Carolyn Phelan, review of *Life on Earth—and Beyond: An Astrobiologist's Quest,* p. 44; December 1, 2008, Gillian Engberg, review of *A Life in the Wild: George Schaller's Struggle to Save the Last Great Beasts,* p. 61.

Horn Book, July-August, 2004, Jennifer M. Brabander, review of *Hachiko,* p. 471; July-August, 2005, Danielle J. Ford, review of *Gorilla Doctors,* p. 484; September-October, 2008, Danielle J. Ford, review of *Life on Earth—and Beyond,* p. 615.

Kirkus Reviews, May 1, 2005, review of *Gorilla Doctors,* p. 547; October 1, 2008, review of *A Life in the Wild;* May 15, 2008, review of *Life on Earth—and Beyond.*

Publishers Weekly, May 17, 2004, review of *Hachiko,* p. 50.

School Library Journal, May, 2004, Carol Schene, review of *Hachiko,* p. 138; July, 2005, Patricia Manning, review of *Gorilla Doctors,* p. 123; March, 2008, John Peters, review of *Life on Earth—and Beyond,* p. 224; November, 2008, Ellen Heath, review of *A Life in the Wild,* p. 148.

ONLINE

Pamela S. Turner Home Page, http://www.pamelasturner. com (January 10, 2010).

UEGAKI, Chieri 1969-

Personal

Born February 21, 1969, in Quesnel, British Columbia, Canada; daughter of Takuo (a landscape architect) and Motoko (a homemaker) Uegaki; married Paul Douglas Mears (a builder), 1994. *Education:* University of British Columbia, B.F.A., 1990; attended Simon Fraser University.

Addresses

Home—Sechelt, British Columbia, Canada.

Career

Author of books for children.

Awards, Honors

Writers' Union of Canada "Writing for Children" competition finalist, 2000.

Writings

PICTURE BOOKS

Suki's Kimono, illustrated by Stéphane Jorisch, Kids Can Press (Toronto, Ontario, Canada), 2003.
Rosie and Buttercup, illustrated by Stéphane Jorisch, Kids Can Press (Toronto, Ontario, Canada), 2008.

Author's books have been translated into French.

Adaptations

Suki's Kimono was adapted as a Braille text.

Sidelights

Born in British Columbia, Canada, of Japanese parents, Chieri Uegaki creates stories for young children that reflect her cultural heritage. Uegaki's picture books, which include *Suki's Kimono* and *Rosie and Buttercup,* introduce engaging young characters that, whether human or animal, deal with everyday challenges with kindness and good humor.

Featuring artwork by Stéphane Jorisch, *Suki's Kimono* celebrates a nonconformist attitude and gives spunky young girls of any ethnicity a heroine to emulate. On the first day of school, Suki insists on wearing her beautiful blue kimono to school, because her grandmother gave it to her on a happy day they spent together. Despite the dire warnings of her older sisters—who strive to be cool in the latest fashions—Suki skips to school in her kimono and wooden clogs. At first the sisters' predictions seem to ring true. Other children snicker and tease, and Suki gets plenty of stares. However, the

teasing turns to admiration when Suki tells her new class about dancing with her grandmother at a festival. At the end of the day Suki's colorful costume attracts more notice than her sisters' high fashion. Uegaki's "charming book highlights the importance of being ourselves, reflecting what makes us distinctive," Kathryn McNaughton noted in *Resource Links*. "It also gives children the message that being true to what we value is worthwhile."

Reviewing Uegaki's picture-book debut, a *Kirkus Reviews* critic called *Suki's Kimono* "a wonderful story about being yourself, with the added bonus of teaching readers a little about Japanese culture." In *School Library Journal* Sue Morgan deemed the work "an appealing story of courage and independence," and a *Publishers Weekly* reviewer deemed the tale "appealing" due to its "true-to-life" young character. In her *Booklist* review of *Suki's Kimono* Linda Perkins called Uegaki's heroine "a lively, irrepressible girl, who gives new charm to a familiar story line."

In *Rosie and Buttercup* Uegaki again teams with Jorisch to "bring poise and polish to a well-worn subject," according to a *Publishers Weekly* contributor. In her story, she focuses on a young mouse named Rosie, who loves ballet and singing and enjoys her single-sister status in her loving family. When new baby sister Buttercup arrives, Rosie loves playing games with her, but as the years pass, the older sister becomes frustrated by little Buttercup's tendency to invade her time, attention, and toybox. In *School Library Journal* Erlene Bishop Killeen praised Jorisch's "pretty watercolors" with their detailed "touches of ribbons and flowers," and a *Kirkus Reviews* contributor wrote that the artwork in *Rosie and*

Buttercup "suits the easygoing tenor of [Uegaki's] . . . tale." In *Canadian Review of Materials*, Gregory Bryan wrote from a parent's perspective, concluding that the book "is a simple, yet entirely effective portrayal of sibling relationships" that is presented in "a realistic, engaging manner" by both author and illustrator.

Biographical and Critical Sources

PERIODICALS

Booklist, November 15, 2003, Linda Perkins, review of *Suki's Kimono,* p. 604.
Canadian Review of Materials, June 13, 2008, Gregory Bryan, review of *Rosie and Buttercup.*
Kirkus Reviews, October 1, 2003, review of *Suki's Kimono;* March 15, 2008, review of *Rosie and Buttercup.*
Quill & Quire, October, 2003, Jessica Kelley, review of *Suki's Kimono;* January, 2008, Carlyn Zwarenstein, review of *Rosie and Buttercup.*
New York Times Book Review, November 16, 2003, Marigny Dupuy, review of *Suki's Kimono,* p. 46.
Publishers Weekly, November 24, 2003, review of *Suki's Kimono,* p. 64; March 17, 2008, review of *Rosie and Buttercup,* p. 68.
Resource Links, October 1, 2003, Kathryn McNaughton, review of *Suki's Kimono.*
School Library Journal, December, 2003, Sue Morgan, review of *Suki's Kimono,* p. 129; May, 2008, Erlene Bishop Killeen, review of *Rosie and Buttercup,* p. 111.

ONLINE

Vancouver International Writers and Readers Festival, http://www.writersfest.bc.ca/ (June 4, 2004), "Chieri Uegaki."*

*   *   *

URBAIN, Cat 1956-
(Catherine Urbain)

Personal

Born 1956. *Education:* Wesleyan University, M.A. (art education).

Addresses

Home—Milford, CT. *E-mail*—urbaina@sbcglobal.net.

Career

Writer and educator. Grant writer for nonprofit organizations. Former teacher at private schools, Children's Museum of Manhattan, and at international film school;

Chieri Uegaki tells a story about a girl's desire to fit in with the crowd in Suki's Kimono, *featuring artwork by Stéphane Jorisch.* (Illustration © 2003 by Stéphane Jorisch. All rights reserved. Used by permission of Kids Can Press Ltd., Toronto.)

researcher for WNET; director of Connecticut Storytelling Center; Weston Woods Studio, member of staff; teacher of creative writing to middle-school students. Producer of video *The Children Want Peace.*

Member
Society of Children's Book Writers and Illustrators.

Awards, Honors
Tassy Walden Award finalist, 2008, for *Manuel and the Lobsterman.*

Writings

Manuel and the Lobsterman, Front Street (Asheville, NC), 2008.

Contributor to periodicals, including *Milford Living Magazine.*

Biographical and Critical Sources

PERIODICALS

Kirkus Reviews, October 1, 2008, review of *Manuel and the Lobsterman.*

ONLINE

Cat Urbain Home Page, http://www.booksbycat.com (January 10, 2010).

Chester Rotary Web site, http://www.chesterrotary.org/ (January 10, 2010).*

*   *   *

URBAIN, Catherine
See URBAIN, Cat

V

VANDE VELDE, Vivian 1951-

Personal
Born June 18, 1951, in New York, NY; daughter of Pasquale (a linotype operator) and Marcelle Brucato; married Jim Vande Velde (a computer analyst), April 20, 1974; children: Elizabeth. *Education:* Attended State University of New York at Brockport, 1969-70, and Rochester Business Institute, 1970-71. *Religion:* Roman Catholic. *Hobbies and other interests:* Reading, needlecrafts, "quiet family things."

Addresses
Home—Rochester, NY.

Career
Writer.

Member
Society of Children's Book Writers and Illustrators, Rochester Area Children's Writers and Illustrators.

Awards, Honors
Child Study Association Book of the Year designation, 1986, Bro-Dart Foundation Elementary School Library Collection inclusion, Notable Trade Books in the Language Arts designation, National Council of Teachers of English, Pick of the Lists citation, American Booksellers Association (ABA), and 100 Titles for Reading and Sharing inclusion, New York Public Library, all for *A Hidden Magic;* Author of the Month designation, *Highlights for Children,* 1988; Best Books for Young Adults citation, Quick Picks for Reluctant Young-Adult Readers citation, and Popular Paperbacks for Young Adults citation, all American Library Association (ALA), Pick of the Lists citation, ABA, Books for the Teen Age selection, New York Public Library, and Nevada Young Readers award, 1998, all for *Companions of the Night;*

Vivian Vande Velde (Reproduced by permission.)

Quick Picks for Reluctant Young-Adult Readers and Recommended Books for Reluctant Young-Adult Readers citations, ALA, and Books for the Teen Age selection, New York Public Library, all 1992, all for *Dragon's Bait;* Best Books for Young Adults and Quick Picks for Reluctant Young-Adult Readers citations, ALA, and Young Adult's Choice citation, International Reading Association (IRA), all 1995, all for *Tales from the Brothers Grimm and the Sisters Weird;* Books for the Teen Age selection, New York Public Library, IRA Young Adults Choice selection, and Quick Picks for Reluctant Young-Adult Readers citation, ALA, all 1997, all for *Curses, Inc., and Other Stories;* Quick Picks for Reluctant Young-Adult Readers citation, ALA, 1999, for *Ghost of a Hanged Man;* Best Books for Young Adults selection, and Quick Pick for Reluctant Young-Adult Readers citations, ALA, and Edgar Allan Poe Award for Best Young-Adult Mystery, Mystery Writers of America, all 2000, all for *Never Trust a Dead Man;* Society of School Librarians International Honor Book designation, and Children's Choice selection, IRA/Children's Book Council (CBC), both 2000, both for *Magic Can Be Murder;* Popular Paperbacks for Young

Adults citation, ALA, 2000, for *The Rumpelstiltskin Problem;* IRA Young Adults Choice selection, Books for the Teen Age selection, New York Public Library, and Best Books for Young Adults and Popular Paperbacks for Young Adults citations, ALA, all 2001, all for *Being Dead;* Black-eyed Susan Award, 100 Titles for Reading and Sharing selection, New York Public Library, ALA Best Books for Young Adults citation, Anne Spencer Lindbergh Prize in Children's Literature, 2002, Books for the Teen Age selection, New York Public Library, 2003, and Sunshine State Young Reader's Award, 2005-06, all for *Heir Apparent;* IRA Young Adults Choice selection, and Black-eyed Susan Award, both 2002, both for *There's a Dead Person Following My Sister Around;* Volunteer State Book Award, 2002, for *Smart Dog;* Paterson Prize for Books for Young People, 2004, for *Witch's Wishes;* Books for the Teen Age selection, New York Public Library, and Popular Paperbacks for Young Adults citation, ALA, both 2005, both for *Now You See It . . .* ; Quick Picks for Reluctant Young-Adult Readers citation, ALA, for *Remembering Raquel.*

Writings

Once upon a Test: Three Light Tales of Love, illustrated by Diane Dawson Hearn, Albert Whitman (Morton Grove, IL), 1984.

A Hidden Magic, illustrated by Trina Schart Hyman, Crown (New York, NY), 1985.

A Well-timed Enchantment, Crown (New York, NY), 1990, Magic Carpet Books (Orlando, FL), 2006.

User Unfriendly, Harcourt (San Diego, CA), 1991.

Dragon's Bait, Harcourt (San Diego, CA), 1992.

Tales from the Brothers Grimm and the Sisters Weird, Harcourt (San Diego, CA), 1995.

Companions of the Night, Harcourt (San Diego, CA), 1995.

Curses, Inc., and Other Stories, Harcourt (San Diego, CA), 1997.

The Conjurer Princess, HarperPrism (New York, NY), 1997.

The Changeling Prince, HarperPrism (New York, NY), 1998.

Ghost of a Hanged Man, Marshall Cavendish (Tarrytown, NY), 1998.

A Coming Evil, Houghton Mifflin (Boston, MA), 1998.

Smart Dog, Harcourt (San Diego, CA), 1998.

Spellbound, Science Fiction Book Club (New York, NY), 1998.

Never Trust a Dead Man, Harcourt (San Diego, CA), 1999.

There's a Dead Person Following My Sister Around, Harcourt (San Diego, CA), 1999.

Magic Can Be Murder, Harcourt (San Diego, CA), 2000.

Troll Teacher, illustrated by Mary Jane Auch, Holiday House (New York, NY), 2000.

The Rumpelstiltskin Problem, Houghton Mifflin (Boston, MA), 2000.

Alison, Who Went Away, Houghton Mifflin (Boston, MA), 2001.

Being Dead (stories), Harcourt (San Diego, CA), 2001.

Heir Apparent, Harcourt (San Diego, CA), 2002.

Wizard at Work, Harcourt (San Diego, CA), 2003.

Witch's Wishes, Holiday House (New York, NY), 2003.

Witch Dreams, Marshall Cavendish (Tarrytown, NY), 2005.

Now You See It . . ., Harcourt (Orlando, FL), 2005.

The Book of Mordred, Houghton Mifflin (Boston, MA), 2005.

Three Good Deeds, Harcourt (Orlando, FL), 2005.

All Hallows' Eve: Thirteen Stories, Harcourt (Orlando, FL), 2006.

Remembering Raquel, Harcourt (Orlando, FL), 2007.

Stolen, Marshall Cavendish (Tarrytown, NY), 2008.

Contributor to anthologies, including *A Wizard's Dozen: Stories of the Fantastic,* edited by Michael Stearns, Harcourt (Orlando, FL), 1993, *A Nightmare's Dozen: Stories from the Dark,* edited by Stearns, Harcourt, 1996, *The Best of Girls to the Rescue:,* edited by Bruce Lansky, Meadowbrook Press (Minnetonka, MN), 2002, *Gothic!: Ten Original Dark Tales,* edited by Deborah Noyes, Candlewick Press (New York, NY), 2004, and several volumes edited by Bruce Coville. Contributor of short stories to *Cricket, Disney Adventures, Electric Company, Highlights for Children, Kid City, School, Storyworks,* and *Young American.*

Sidelights

Vivian Vande Velde is the author of dozens of books for young readers that blend fantasy with mystery elements, or that turn fairy tales on their heads with fresh new perspectives and humorous touches. Offbeat, fantastic, and even sarcastic, Vande Velde's books contain intriguing, suspenseful situations and provocative messages that eschew traditional themes and genres. She has demonstrated versatility in her canon, writing works of both realism and science fiction, but she is best known for her mystery and fantasy novels. Vande Velde has written about vampires in *Companions of the Night,* played with the conventions of the Western genre in *The Ghost of the a Hanged Man,* and created a magical world in *Now You See It . . . .* As Vande Velde told Lori Atkins Goodson in the *ALAN Review,* "I write the kinds of stories I like to read. I enjoy fantasy and science fiction because I find those stories can deal with universal questions, and yet—because the specifics of the stories are fantastical—the stories are nonjudgmental and non-confrontational and might open a reader up to new ways of looking at things."

Born in New York City in 1951, Vande Velde developed an early love of reading and storytelling. "I can't remember a time when I wasn't making up stories," she once told *SATA.* "As a child, I would invent an adven-

ture for my stuffed animals and act it out—not a play, not for the rest of the family—but just for my own pleasure." Though Vande Velde admits she was just an average student (in fact, her writing efforts gained little notice from her teachers), she never wavered from her choice of careers. "I always knew I wanted to be an author," she remarked to Goodson, "but it was when I was in 8th grade and read T.H. White's *The Once and Future King* that I absolutely knew what kind of story I wanted to write."

After graduating from high school, Vande Velde moved on to college for a year but quit when she had exhausted all the literature course offerings she was interested in. Thereafter she attended a business school and trained as a secretary. Married in 1974, Vande Velde opted for life as a stay-at-home mom with a daughter, and she eventually enrolled in a writing course. Completing her first book, *A Hidden Magic,* proved more challenging than expected and, as Vande Velde recalled on her home page, "once I finished writing the book, getting it published was even harder. I sent it out to 32 different publishers over a two-year period, before number 33 said yes."

A Hidden Magic exemplifies the author's talent for transforming old tales into new ones. According to Karen P. Smith in *School Library Journal,* the work is a "delightful parody of the classic fairy tale genre." Vande Velde's princess, instead of being beautiful, is plain. Her handsome prince is far from noble—he's spoiled and vain. Moreover, the princess in the story does not have to be saved by a prince—she saves him. At the close of the story, the princess refuses to marry the prince, and readers may be surprised by the man she prefers. "[Vande] Velde's approach remains fresh and definitely amusing," remarked Smith.

It was another five years before Vande Velde published her next book, *A Well-timed Enchantment,* about a teenage girl who is sent back in time by T-shirt-wearing elves after she accidentally messes up history by dropping her digital watch into a wishing well. A subsequent novel, *User Unfriendly,* contains what Diane G. Yates described in *Voice of Youth Advocates* as an "interesting premise" that is "nicely developed with some lively fights and mildly scary situations." The story takes place in cyberspace and a teenager's basement. After Arvin's friend pirates an interactive computer game, he assures Arvin and five other high-school pals that it is okay to play. However, Arvin, his friends, and even his mother have no idea that playing the game without anyone monitoring their progress can be truly dangerous. As the friends begin to play the game, they discover that there are glitches and holes in the program. Soon they find themselves playing the roles of medieval characters and fighting for survival, with no hope of quitting the game before they finish their quest. To make matters worse, Arvin's mother begins to display terrifying symptoms of an unknown illness. To

help her, Arvin has to win the game by facing orcs and wolves and rescuing a princess who has been kidnapped. According to a *Kirkus Reviews* critic, the "adventures" in *User Unfriendly* "are vivid and diverting," and a *Publishers Weekly* critic predicted that some readers "will not be able to put this swashbuckler down."

Alys, the protagonist in *Dragon's Bait,* feels ready to die after she has been accused and condemned for witchcraft. Her punishment is to be devoured by a dragon, and she is tied up and left on a hilltop to await her fate. There is no one who can save Alys (her father died when he heard the sentence placed upon her), and she thinks her life is over. Instead of eating her, however, the dragon decides to help her. The dragon, Selendrile, is only a part-time dragon. He can assume human form, and by doing so, he helps Alys get back at those who falsely accused her. As a *Publishers Weekly* reviewer asserted, Vande Velde's "gently feminist slant" features in the book's "gripping adventure," which "probes the issues associated with revenge."

Cover of Vande Velde's middle-grade novel **Dragon's Bait,** *featuring artwork by Cliff Nielsen.* (Laurel-Leaf Books, 1997. Used by permission of Laurel-Leaf, an imprint of Random House Children's Books, a division of Random House, Inc.)

Companions of the Night garnered praise for its "brisk prose, engaging characters and a plot that keeps you quickly turning the pages," according to Charles de Lint in the *Magazine of Fantasy and Science Fiction*. Kerry Nowicki, just sixteen years old, drives out alone late at night to the Laundromat to recover her little brother's toy bear. Kerry finds something else, however: Ethan, a young man thought to be a vampire and about to be killed by a mob. When Kerry saves Ethan, she is accused of being a vampire herself, and when she returns home she finds that her father and brother have been kidnaped by the vampire hunters. Eventually, Kerry learns that Ethan really is a vampire, but she asks him to help her locate her family anyway. Despite the fact that she does not quite know whether to fear him or trust him, Kerry finds herself attracted to Ethan. As Deborah Stevenson wrote in the *Bulletin of the Center for Children's Books, Companions of the Night* is "an intellectual adventure more than a sensual one, its challenges more cerebral than hormonal. . . . It's a freshly written thriller, an offbeat love story, an engaging twist on the vampire novel, and an exciting tale of moral complexity." "*Companions of the Night* should attract a loyal following of its own," concluded Marilyn Makowski in her review of Vande Velde's novel for *School Library Journal*.

Tales from the Brothers Grimm and the Sisters Weird consists of thirteen familiar folktales that are revised in "both amusing and touching versions" as Ann A. Flowers explained in *Horn Book*. In one story, Rumpelstiltskin is a young, handsome elf. In another, Hansel and Gretel are murderers. The wolf in the story of Little Red Riding Hood is Granny's friend, the princess in the story of the Princess and the Pea requests more mattresses on her own, and the beauty in the Beauty and the Beast story is not pleased with the Beast's human appearance. "[Vande] Velde challenges readers' notions of good, bad, and ugly," observed Luann Toth in *School Library Journal,* while a *Kirkus Reviews* critic dubbed the work "terrific fun." Vande Velde returns to fairy tales with *The Rumpelstiltskin Problem,* a book that presents six variations on that tale. Susan L. Rogers, writing in *School Library Journal,* found this offering to be an "interesting experiment." A reviewer for *Publishers Weekly* had stronger praise for *The Rumpelstiltskin Problem,* writing that "Vande Velde's takes on this fairy tale are always humorous and often heartwarming."

In other fantasy novels, Vande Velde takes her penchant for unusual situations and combines it with in-depth examinations of moral issues. *The Conjurer Princess,* for instance, begins as a standard adventure when sixteen-year-old Lylene determines to rescue her older sister from the man who kidnapped her and murdered her fiancé on their wedding day. Lylene first turns to magic to aid her on her quest, promising to work for a wizard as payment for magical training. When magic proves less helpful than she had hoped, Lylene enlists the aid

Cover of Vande Velde's young-adult fantasy novel **The Conjure Princess,** *featuring artwork by David Loew.* (HarperPrism, 1997. Copyright © 1997 by Vivian Vande Velde. Used by permission of the illustrator, David Loew.)

of two soldiers who turn out to be violent mercenaries. Many people have been hurt by the time Lylene finds her sister, but now she realizes that perhaps her rescue attempt was ill-advised in the first place. As Diane G. Yates remarked in *Voice of Youth Advocates,* "Vande Velde packs a lot into an enjoyable, short, quickly read narrative," including a portrayal of Lylene's growing maturity.

The Changeling Prince likewise illuminates issues of fate and responsibility. Weiland has lived an uneasy existence since the sinister sorceress Daria transformed him from a wolf cub into a human child. He is only one of a group of similarly changed people who live their lives in fear of when Daria might suddenly become angry and return them to their animal forms. When Daria decides to leave her fortress and move into a town, Weiland has a new adjustment to make. He learns to live among the townspeople and eventually finds a friend in the thief Shile. As Daria's power becomes more malevolent, Weiland finally must make a stand.

Voice of Youth Advocates contributor Nancy Eaton found the protagonist in *The Changeling Prince* compelling, writing that "Weiland's detailed agonies of indecision evoke compassion in the reader: everything could go either way; there are no right choices." The result, the critic concluded, is a work that "raises thoughtful questions about individual responsibility."

In *Ghost of a Hanged Man* Vande Velde combines an element of the supernatural with yet another genre, the Western. The infamous criminal Jake Barnette is sentenced to hang in the summer of 1877, and no one really takes it seriously when he swears in court that he will take revenge against those responsible for his punishment. The next spring, however, floods spill through the town, forcing several coffins—including Barnette's—to emerge from the inundated cemetery. When the foreman of Barnette's jury and the judge who presided at the trial suddenly die, the young son of the town sheriff knows he must take action before his family is destroyed. "This unsettling novel has many appealing elements," Carrie Schadle noted in *School Library Journal,* the critic citing a sinister ghost, the Old West setting, and the scared yet brave protagonists. Janice M. Del Negro likewise found the "colorful characters" and "easy immediacy" of the dialogue appealing, and concluded in a review of *Ghost of a Hanged Man* for the *Bulletin of the Center for Children's Books* that "Vande Velde has a knack for creepy understatement that effectively delivers unexpected chills, and the climax . . . brings the book to its shuddery, satisfying conclusion."

A murder mystery also figures in *Never Trust a Dead Man,* albeit one with a more lighthearted approach. Seventeen-year-old Selwyn has been wrongly convicted of murder by those in his medieval village, and he has been sentenced to be entombed alive in the burial cave of his supposed victim, Farold. Selwyn has almost resigned himself to his fate when the imperious witch Elswyth enters the cave while looking for spell components. She offers to make a bargain with Selwyn: she will release him from the cave and give him one week to find the real killers in exchange for years of his service. Elswyth complicates the deal by resurrecting the spirit of the annoying Farold as a bat and disguising Selwyn as a beautiful girl. As this unlikely duo of sleuths searches for the answer, many mishaps and humorous truths follow in their wake. "Favoring the comic over the macabre," as Kitty Flynn wrote in *Horn Book,* "Vande Velde offers a funny and imaginative murder mystery that intrigues as much as it entertains." A *Kirkus Reviews* critic similarly hailed *Never Trust a Dead Man,* writing that "the sympathetic hero, original humor, sharp dialogue, and surprising plot twists make this read universally appealing and difficult to put down."

With *Magic Can Be Murder* Vande Velde "throws murder, witchcraft, and romance into the brew," according to Laura Glaser in *School Library Journal.* Nola and her witch mother live in something of a medieval netherworld, traveling from town to town to work. Despite all, Nola manages to use her powers to good effect, solving a murder, saving herself and her mother, and even finding true love in a book that is, according to Glaser, "most likely to cast a spell on Vande Velde's fans." In *Booklist* Helen Rosenberg praised *Magic Can Be Murder* as a "lighthearted mystery," concluding that kids "who like mystery and fantasy fans . . . will like this."

Being Dead is a collection of seven "deliciously creepy tales," according to Miranda Doyle in *School Library Journal.* In such stories as "Drop by Drop" and "Dancing with Marjorie's Ghost," the author chillingly examines the possibilities of an afterlife. A critic for *Kirkus Reviews* concluded that Vande Velde "again chills, charms, moves and startles with her customary effectiveness." Similarly, GraceAnne A. DeCandido, writing in *Booklist,* praised the author's "sure hand" and went on to predict that "these spirits are destined to find their

Cover of Vande Velde's novel A Hidden Magic, *featuring artwork by Trina Schart Hyman.* (Illustration copyright © 1985, 1997, by Trina Schart Hyman. Reproduced by permission of Houghton Mifflin Publishing Company. This material should not be reproduced in any form or by any means without the prior written permission of the publisher.)

Cover of Vande Velde's elementary-grade chapter book Smart Dog, *featuring cover art by David Sheldon.* (Illustration © 2007 by David Sheldon. Reproduced by permission of Houghton Mifflin Harcourt Publishing Company. This material may not be reproduced in any form or by any means without the prior written permission of the publisher.)

audience." According to *Horn Book* critic Anita L. Burkam, in *Being Dead* Vande Velde offers "a set of ghost stories for readers who enjoy being really scared."

According to a contributor for *Kirkus Reviews,* in *Heir Apparent* Vande Velde tells a "plausible, suspenseful" story of a girl in the near future who becomes trapped in a total-immersion virtual-reality game. Giannine becomes stranded in a game of kings and intrigue called "Heir Apparent" after some anti-fantasy protestors purposely damaged the programming equipment; if she does not become successor to the medieval throne within three days, her brain could suffer permanent damage. The critic for *Kirkus Reviews* added that the book is "riveting reading for experienced gamers and tyros alike." A reviewer for *Publishers Weekly* also had praise for the title, noting that "hilarious characters . . . plus fantastical elements . . . will spur readers on toward the satisfying conclusion." Similarly, Linda Miles, writing in *School Library Journal,* commented that "all of the elements of a good fantasy are present in this adventure." Miles further lauded the book as a "unique combination of futuristic and medieval themes."

Set in a medieval village, Vande Velde's suspenseful novel *Witch Dreams* concerns a teenager who uses her unusual ability to visualize other people's dreams to solve the murder of her own parents. "Vande Velde's spare prose style reflects the simple and harsh existence of Nyssa's village," a *Publishers Weekly* reviewer commented, and Donna Marie Wagner, writing in *School Library Journal,* asserted that the "surprising plot twists in *Witch Dreams* should please mystery fans." Vande Velde presents her take on a traitorous character from Arthurian legend in *The Book of Mordred,* "a richly imagined retelling of traditional lore," wrote Carolyn Phelan in *Booklist.* Told through the eyes of three women, Vande Velde's portrayal of the title character "flesh[es] out a portrait of the knight who betrayed Arthur and caused the breakup of the Round Table," *School Library Journal* critic June H. Keuhn observed. A twelve-year-old girl is at the heart of a bizarre mystery in *Stolen.* Found running through the woods at the edge of a village, Isabelle has no memory of her past, although the locals believe she may have been abducted years earlier by the same conjurer who has eluded capture after kidnaping a baby. *Stolen* "is a solid fantasy and mystery that builds in intrigue and suspense as more layers are added to the story," Amanda Raklovits wrote in *School Library Journal.*

Vande Velde offers lighter fare in a number of highly regarded novel for young readers. A young spellcaster's peaceful summer is interrupted by a series of humorous dilemmas in *Wizard at Work.* After bidding farewell to the students at his school for sorcerers, a wizard hoping to spend time tending to his garden instead finds himself rescuing princesses, dealing with rowdy unicorns, and finding a new home for a ghost. Vande Velde "hilarious twists on familiar folktales and deft, clever solutions to a succession of domestic crises," a *Kirkus Reviews* contributor noted. *Witch's Wishes,* another work for elementary-grade readers, centers on a helpful young trick-or-treater. When six-year-old Sarah offers comfort to a baffled witch, the conjurer repays the girl by giving her magical powers for the evening, resulting in one disaster after another. Although the work is intended for a younger audience than most of Vande Velde's titles, *School Library Journal* critic Heather Dieffenbach remarked that in *Witch's Wishes* "the author maintains the wry wit and entertaining fantasy for which she is known."

In *Now You See It . . .* fifteen-year-old Wendy discovers a pair of mysterious sunglasses that allows her to see a parallel world inhabited by a variety of strange creatures. After learning that one of her classmates is actually an embattled elf prince, Wendy enters Kazaran Dahaani to save his life. "Vande Velde's sly humor and snappy dialogue make this story a joy to read," remarked Saleena L. Davidson in *School Library Journal.* A mischievous boy learns a valuable lesson in *Three Good Deeds,* a "funny and thought-provoking tale in folkloric dress," according to a *Kirkus Reviews* critic. When young Howard is caught stealing from the neigh-

borhood witch, he is transformed into a goose and must complete a trio of tasks before he can return to human form. Writing in *Horn Book,* Robin Smith called *Three Good Deeds* "a lightweight, enjoyable transformation tale just right for fans of such farmyard tales as Dick King-Smith's *Babe.*"

Though Vande Velde is best known for creating stories that delve into the fantastic and supernatural, she has also explored more contemporaneous settings. In *Alison, Who Went Away,* fourteen-year-old Sibyl has not heard from her older sister, Alison, for three years. While Sibyl believes that her rebellious sister has merely run away, the truth may be far more ominous: Alison may have been the victim of a serial killer. Vande Velde's first venture into realistic fiction, *Alison, Who Went Away* is a "high-school story laced with a dose of sadness and mystery," according to *Booklist* critic Frances Bradburn. A teenager's untimely passing is the focus of *Remembering Raquel,* "a poignant novel about life and loss," observed Janis Flint-Ferguson in *Kliatt.* Told from the viewpoints of Raquel's classmates, on-line friends, and family members, as well as through the sensitive teen's own blog entries, *Remembering Raquel* "will make students think about the coincidental possibilities that propel their lives forward—and have the potential to bring them to an end," stated Nora G. Murphy in *School Library Journal.*

Vande Velde takes her role as an author of books for children and young adults quite seriously. "Writing for young people is the most important writing there is," she remarked to Goodson, adding "that there are only a relatively small number of books a child can read, and that is limited further by reading ability and interest in subject matter. So, it is a very short window of opportunity. And yet that is precisely the time of life when tastes and opinions are being formed—including, even, whether reading is worthwhile and if that child is going to grow up to be one of those adults who reads."

Biographical and Critical Sources

BOOKS

Children's Literature Review, Volume 145, Gale (Detroit, MI), 2009.

Moonshower, Candie, *Vivian Vande Velde: Author of Fantasy Fiction,* Enslow Publishers (Berkeley Heights, NJ), 2009.

Oxford Companion to Fairy Tales, edited by Jack Zipes, Oxford University Press (New York, NY), 2000, p. 534.

Reginald, Robert, *Science Fiction and Fantasy Literature, 1975-1991,* Gale (Detroit, MI), 1992.

PERIODICALS

ALAN Review, fall, 2004, Lori Atkins Goodson, interview with Vande Velde, pp. 21-24.

Booklist, April 1, 1995, Sally Estes, review of *Companions of the Night,* p. 1389; September 1, 1998, John Peters, review of *Smart Dog,* p. 121; November 15, 1998, Chris Sherman, review of *Ghost of a Hanged Man,* p. 591; April 1, 1999, Holly Koelling, review of *Never Trust a Dead Man,* p. 1402; September 1, 1999, Candace Smith, review of *There's a Dead Person Following My Sister Around,* p. 124; November 15, 2000, Marta Segal, review of *Troll Teacher,* p. 650; December 15, 2000, Helen Rosenberg, review of *Magic Can Be Murder,* p. 809; April 1, 2001, Frances Bradburn, review of *Alison, Who Went Away,* p. 1459; September 1, 2001, GraceAnne A. DeCandido, review of *Being Dead,* p. 97; February 1, 2003, Gillian Engberg, review of *Heir Apparent,* p. 982; April 15, 2003, GraceAnne A. DeCandido, review of *Wizard at Work,* p. 1466; December 1, 2003, Kay Weisman, review of *Witch's Wishes,* p. 669; September 15, 2005, Carolyn Phelan, review of *The Book of Mordred,* p. 60; October 1, 2006, Hazel Rochman, review of *All Hallows' Eve: Thirteen Stories,* p. 49.

Bulletin of the Center for Children's Books, July-August, 1995, Deborah Stevenson, review of *Companions of the Night,* pp. 373-374; October, 1998, Deborah Stevenson, review of *Ghost of a Hanged Man,* p. 75; October, 1999, Janice M. DelNegro, review of *There's a Dead Person Following My Sister Around,* p. 72; February, 2001, Janice M. DelNegro, review of *The Rumpelstiltskin Problem,* p. 239; September, 2001, Janice M. DelNegro, review of *Being Dead,* p. 29.

Horn Book, March-April, 1996, Ann A. Flowers, review of *Tales from the Brothers Grimm and the Sisters Weird,* pp. 201-202; May-June, 1998, Kitty Flynn, review of *Never Trust a Dead Man,* pp. 339-340; November-December, 1998, Kitty Flynn, review of *Ghost of a Hanged Man,* p. 742; November-December, 2001, Anita L. Burkam, review of *Being Dead,* p. 758; September-October, 2005, Robin Smith, review of *Three Good Deeds,* p. 589; September-October, 2006, Kitty Flynn, review of *All Hallows' Eve,* p. 598; November-December, 2008, Christine M. Heppermann, review of *Stolen,* p. 717.

Kirkus Reviews, August 1, 1991, review of *User Unfriendly,* p. 1017; August 1, 1992, review of *Dragon's Bait,* p. 994; August 1, 1995, review of *Tales from the Brothers Grimm and the Sisters Weird,* p. 1118; October 15, 1998, review of *A Coming Evil,* p. 1539; March 15, 1999, review of *Never Trust a Dead Man;* August 1, 2001, review of *Being Dead,* p. 1133; March 1, 2003, review of *Wizard at Work,* p. 401; September 15, 2005, review of *Three Good Deeds,* p. 1036.

Kliatt, January, 2004, Bethan Steward, review of *Being Dead,* p. 25; January, 2005, Janis Flint-Ferguson, review of *Now You See It . . .,* p. 11; November, 2007, Janis Flint-Ferguson, review of *Remembering Raquel,* p. 14.

Magazine of Fantasy and Science Fiction, October-November, 1995, Charles de Lint, review of *Companions of the Night,* pp. 57-58; June, 1996, Charles de Lint, review of *Tales from the Brothers Grim and the Sisters Weird,* p. 27; August, 1999, Michelle West, review of *Never Trust a Dead Man,* p. 45; March, 2002,

Michelle West, review of *Being Dead,* pp. 34-39; March, 2004, Charles de Lint, review of *Being Dead,* p. 30.

New York Times Book Review, March 9, 2003, review of *Heir Apparent,* p. 24.

Publishers Weekly, August 23, 1991, review of *User Unfriendly,* pp. 63-64; July 27, 1992, review of *Dragon's Bait,* p. 63; August 10, 1998, review of *Smart Dog,* p. 389; November 9, 1998, review of *Ghost of a Hanged Man,* p. 77; August 30, 1999, review of *Thre's a Dead Person Following My Sister Around,* p. 85; October 2, 2000, review of *Magic Can Be Murder,* p. 82, review of *The Rumpelstiltskin Problem,* p. 82; February 5, 2001, review of *Alison, Who Went Away,* p. 89; September 16, 2002, review of *Heir Apparent,* p. 69; January 17, 2005, review of *Now You See It . . .,* p. 56; October 31, 2005, review of *Witch Dreams,* p. 58; November 12, 2007, review of *Remembering Raquel,* p. 56.

School Library Journal, December, 1985, Karen P. Smith, review of *A Hidden Magic,* pp. 95-96; September, 1992, Margaret A. Chang, review of *Dragon's Bait,* p. 261; May, 1995, Marilyn Makowski, review of *Companions of the Night,* pp. 123-124; January, 1996, Luann Toth, review of *Tales from the Brothers Grimm and the Sisters Weird,* p. 126; October, 1998, Carrie Schadle, review of *Ghost of a Hanged Man,* p. 147; November, 1998, Cyrisse Jaffee, review of *A Coming Evil,* p. 131; May, 1999, Laura Glaser, review of *Never Trust a Dead Man,* p. 131; September, 1999, Timothy Capehart, review of *There's a Dead Person Following My Sister Around,* pp. 229-230; October, 2000, Gay Lynn Van Vleck, review of *Troll Teacher,* p. 140; November, 2000, Laura Glaser, review of *Magic Can Be Murder,* p. 164, Susan L. Rogers, review of *The Rumpelstiltskin Problem,* p. 177; April, 2001, Betty S. Evans, review of *Alison, Who Went Away,* p. 151; September, 2001, Miranda Doyle, review of *Being Dead,* p. 234; October, 2002, Lana Miles, review of *Heir Apparent,* p. 174; November, 2003, Heather Dieffenbach, review of *Witch's Wishes,* p. 116; January, 2005, Saleena L. Davidson, review of *Now You See It . . .,* p. 138; October, 2005, June H. Keuhn, review of *The Book of Mordred,* p. 176; November, 2005, Donna Marie Wagner, review of *Witch Dreams,* p. 150; December, 2007, Nora G. Murphy, review of *Remembering Raquel,* p. 146; November, 2008, Amanda Raklovits, review of *Stolen,* p. 138.

Voice of Youth Advocates, December, 1991, Diane G. Yates, review of *User Unfriendly,* p. 327; April, 1993, Kim Carter, review of *Dragon's Bait,* p. 48; October, 1995, Christy Tyson, review of *Companions of the Night,* pp. 238-239; February, 1998, Diane G. Yates, review of *The Conjurer Princess,* pp. 396-397; June, 1998, Nancy Eaton, review of *The Changeling Prince,* pp. 134, 136.

ONLINE

Debbi Michiko Florence Web site, http://www.debbi michikoflorence.com/ (January 1, 2010), interview with Vande Velde.

Houghton Mifflin Harcourt Web site, http://www.harcourt books.com/ (January 1, 2010), interview with Vande Velde.

Vivian Vande Velde Home Page, http://www.vivianvande velde.com (January 1, 2010).*

*   *   *

VAN LEEUWEN, Jean 1937-

Personal

Surname pronounced "Van *Loo*-en"; born December 26, 1937, in Glen Ridge, NJ; daughter of Cornelius (a clergyman) and Dorothy (a teacher) Van Leeuwen; married Bruce David Gavril (a digital computer-systems designer), July 7, 1968; children: David Andrew, Elizabeth Eva. *Education:* Syracuse University, B.A., 1959. *Hobbies and other interests:* Gardening, reading, antiques, music, tennis.

Addresses

Home—Chappaqua, NY. *E-mail*—jvl@jeanvanleeuwen. com.

Career

Author. Began career working for *TV Guide;* Random House, Inc., New York, NY, began as assistant editor, became associate editor of juvenile books, 1963-68; Viking Press, Inc., New York, NY, associate editor of juvenile books, 1968-70; Dial Press, New York, NY, senior editor of juvenile books, 1971-73. Also teaches at writing workshops.

Awards, Honors

New Jersey Institute of Technology award, 1972, for *I Was a 98-Pound Duckling,* and 1975 and 1976, for *Too Hot for Ice Cream;* Art Books for Children award, 1974, for adaptation of Hans Christian Andersen's *The Emperor's New Clothes;* Ethical Culture School award, 1975, William Allen White Award, 1978, and South Carolina Children's Book Award, 1979, all for *The Great Christmas Kidnapping Caper;* Best Books designation, 1979, American Library Association (ALA) Young-Adult Services Division (YALSA), for *Seems like This Road Goes on Forever*; Massachusetts Honor Book Award, 1981, for *The Great Cheese Conspiracy;* Pick of the Lists selection, American Booksellers Association (ABA), and Parents' Choice Remarkable Books for Literature selection, both for *The Great Rescue Operation;* International Reading Association Teachers' Choice selection, Pick of the Lists selection, ABA, and Best in Kids' Entertainment selection, *Parents'* magazine, all for *Going West; Booklist* Children's Editors' Choice designations, for *More Tales of Oliver Pig, Amanda Pig and Her Big Brother Oliver, Tales of Amanda Pig,* and *More Tales of Amanda Pig;* Pick of the Lists selections, ABA, for *More Tales of Oliver Pig,*

Amanda Pig and Her Big Brother Oliver, and *More Tales of Amanda Pig;* Child Study Association Children's Books of the Year designations, for *Amanda Pig and Her Big Brother Oliver, Benjy and the Power of Zingies,* and *Benjy in Business;* New York Public Library 100 Titles for Reading and Sharing selections, for *Oliver, Amanda, and Grandmother Pig* and *Going West;* Library of Congress Books of the Year awards, for *Oliver, Amanda, and Grandmother Pig, Tales of Amanda Pig, More Tales of Oliver Pig,* and *Amanda Pig and Her Big Brother Oliver;* ALA Notable Book designations, for *Tales of Amanda Pig* and *Amanda Pig and the Really Hot Day;* Theodor Seuss Geisel Award Honor Book designation, 2006, for *Amanda Pig and the Really Hot Day.*

Writings

(Editor) *A Time of Growing,* Random House (New York, NY), 1967.

Timothy's Flower, illustrated by Moneta Barnett, Random House (New York, NY), 1967.

One Day in Summer, illustrated by Richard Fish, Random House (New York, NY), 1969.

The Great Cheese Conspiracy, Random House (New York, NY), 1969.

(Adaptor) Hans Christian Andersen, *The Emperor's New Clothes,* illustrated by Jack Delano and Irene Delano, Random House (New York, NY), 1971.

I Was a 98-Pound Duckling, Dial (New York, NY), 1972.

Too Hot for Ice Cream, illustrated by Martha Alexander, Dial (New York, NY), 1974.

The Great Christmas Kidnapping Caper, illustrated by Steven Kellogg, Dial (New York, NY), 1975.

Seems like This Road Goes on Forever, Dial (New York, NY), 1979.

The Great Rescue Operation, illustrated by Margot Apple, Dial (New York, NY), 1982.

Benjy and the Power of Zingies, illustrated by Margot Apple, Dial (New York, NY), 1982.

Benjy in Business, illustrated by Margot Apple, Dial (New York, NY), 1983.

Benjy the Football Hero, illustrated by Gail Owens, Dial (New York, NY), 1985.

Dear Mom, You're Ruining My Life, Dial (New York, NY), 1989.

Going West, illustrated by Thomas B. Allen, Dial (New York, NY), 1991.

The Great Summer Camp Catastrophe, illustrated by Diane deGroat, Dial (New York, NY), 1992.

Emma Bean, illustrated by Juan Wijngaard, Dial (New York, NY), 1993.

Two Girls in Sister Dresses, illustrated by Linda Benson, Dial (New York, NY), 1994.

Bound for Oregon, Dial (New York, NY), 1994.

Across the Wide Dark Sea, illustrated by Thomas B. Allen, Dial (New York, NY), 1995.

Blue Sky, Butterfly, Dial (New York, NY), 1996.

A Fourth of July on the Plains, illustrated by Henri Sorensen, Dial (New York, NY), 1997.

Touch the Sky Summer, illustrated by Dan Andreasen, Dial (New York, NY), 1997.

Nothing Here but Trees, illustrated by Phil Boatwright, Dial (New York, NY), 1998.

Growing Ideas (biography), photographs by David Gavril, Richard C. Owen (Katonah, NY), 1998.

The Tickle Stories, illustrated by Mary Whyte, Dial (New York, NY), 1998.

The Strange Adventures of Blue Dog, illustrated by Marco Ventura, Dial (New York, NY), 1999.

Sorry, illustrated by Brad Sneed, Phyllis Fogelman Books (New York, NY), 2001.

"Wait for Me!" Said Maggie McGee, illustrated by Jacqueline Rogers, Phyllis Fogelman Books (New York, NY), 2001.

Lucy Was There . . ., Phyllis Fogelman Books (New York, NY), 2002.

The Amazing Air Balloon, illustrated by Marco Ventura, Phyllis Fogelman Books (New York, NY), 2003.

The Great Googlestein Museum Mystery, illustrated by R.W. Alley, Phyllis Fogelman Books (New York, NY), 2003.

When the White Man Came to Our Shores, illustrated by James Bernardin, Phyllis Fogelman Books (New York, NY), 2004.

Cabin on Trouble Creek, Dial (New York, NY), 2004.

Benny and Beautiful Baby Delilah, illustrated by LeUyen Pham, Dial (New York, NY), 2006.

Papa and the Pioneer Quilt, illustrated by Rebecca Bond, Dial (New York, NY), 2007.

"OLIVER AND AMANDA PIG" SERIES

Tales of Oliver Pig, illustrated by Arnold Lobel, Dial (New York, NY), 1979.

More Tales of Oliver Pig, illustrated by Arnold Lobel, Dial (New York, NY), 1981.

Amanda Pig and Her Big Brother Oliver, illustrated by Ann Schweninger, Dial (New York, NY), 1982.

Tales of Amanda Pig, illustrated by Ann Schweninger, Dial (New York, NY), 1983.

More Tales of Amanda Pig, illustrated by Ann Schweninger, Dial (New York, NY), 1985.

Oliver, Amanda, and Grandmother Pig, illustrated by Ann Schweninger, Dial (New York, NY), 1987.

Oliver and Amanda's Christmas, illustrated by Ann Schweninger, Dial (New York, NY), 1989.

Oliver Pig at School, illustrated by Ann Schweninger, Dial (New York, NY), 1990.

Amanda Pig on Her Own, illustrated by Ann Schweninger, Dial (New York, NY), 1991.

Oliver and Amanda's Halloween, illustrated by Ann Schweninger, Dial (New York, NY), 1992.

Oliver and Amanda and the Big Snow, illustrated by Ann Schweninger, Dial (New York, NY), 1995.

Amanda Pig, School Girl, Dial (New York, NY), 1997.

Amanda Pig and Her Best Friend Lollipop, illustrated by Ann Schweninger, Penguin Putnam (New York, NY), 1998.

Oliver and Albert, Friends Forever, illustrated by Ann Schweninger, Phyllis Fogelman Books (New York, NY), 2000.

Amanda Pig and the Awful, Scary Monster, illustrated by Ann Schweninger, Phyllis Fogelman Books (New York, NY), 2003.

Oliver the Mighty Pig, illustrated by Ann Schweninger, Dial (New York, NY), 2004.

Amanda Pig and the Really Hot Day, illustrated by Ann Schweninger, Dial (New York, NY), 2005.

Oliver Pig and the Best Fort Ever, illustrated by Ann Schweninger, Dial (New York, NY), 2006.

Amanda Pig and the Wiggly Tooth, illustrated by Ann Schweninger, Dial (New York, NY), 2007.

Amanda Pig, First Grader, illustrated by Ann Schweninger, Dial (New York, NY), 2007.

"HANNAH" TRIOLOGY

Hannah of Fairfield, illustrated by Donna Diamond, Dial (New York, NY), 1999.

Hannah's Helping Hands, illustrated by Donna Diamond, Phyllis Fogelman Books (New York, NY), 1999.

Hannah's Winter of Hope, illustrated by Donna Diamond, Phyllis Fogelman Books (New York, NY), 2000.

Adaptations

Some of Van Leeuwen's works have been adapted as audiobooks.

Sidelights

Jean Van Leeuwen is the award-winning author of dozens of books for young readers. Equally adept at entertaining readers in picture books as she is in chapter books and novels for middle graders and young adults, Van Leeuwen has charmed her audiences for more than four decades. "I like writing different kinds of stories: funny ones and serious ones, fantasy and real-life, stories about animals and people, children today and children who lived a long time ago," the author remarked on her home page. "I enjoy writing for different age groups, from preschool to middle school."

Van Leeuwen's stories about the jovial pig siblings Oliver and Amanda number in the double digits and have drawn praise from fans and critics alike. Other books that have remained popular over time include *The Great Cheese Conspiracy,* featuring a trio of meddlesome mice, and its several sequels. Van Leeuwen does not entertain only with animal protagonists, however. Characters in the "Benjy" stories, and in novels such as *Dear Mom, You're Ruining My Life,* deal with contemporary issues in both humorous and heart-wrenching ways. A prolific and versatile writer, Van Leeuwen also mines an historical vein in books such as *Going West* and *Cabin on Trouble Creek,* both of which are set during pioneering days in America.

Van Leeuwen had a long and close relationship with the printed word before she became a writer, and she loved to read as a child. She was working as a children's

Jean Van Leeuwen teams up with artist Ann Schweninger on the warm-hearted picture book **Amanda Pig, Schoolgirl.** (Illustration copyright © 1997 by Ann Schweninger. All rights reserved. Reproduced by permission of Dial Books for Young Readers, a division of Penguin Books USA, Inc.)

book editor when she rediscovered her childhood ambition to write and in 1967 joyfully saw the publication of her first book, *Timothy's Flower.* A reviewer for the *Bulletin of the Center for Children's Books* credited the "simple, unpretentious style" in this story of how a flower improves the life of a poor boy. Van Leeuwen's early works also include *A Time of Growing,* an edited anthology of fictional reminiscences of adolescence by established authors, and the picture book *One Day in Summer,* which was described by a *Bulletin of the Center for Children's Books* critic as a "quiet" story with possibly limited appeal due to the "static quality" of the plot.

During this time Van Leeuwen married Bruce Gavril, a computer-systems designer who became her technical consultant. Her husband was also the inspiration for the character of Raymond, star of *The Great Cheese Conspiracy* and its sequels. Van Leeuwen describes Raymond as the one "with brains": "a thinker, problem solver, and saver of seemingly useless objects—just like Bruce." *The Great Cheese Conspiracy* features three mice—Raymond; Marvin, the brave but foolhardy leader of the gang; and Fats, whose laziness and passion for food often land him and his friends in trouble—in a story about the trio's effort to rob a cheese store. Van Leeuwen's mouse books have typically received praise from critics. For example, one *Bulletin of the Center for Children's Books* reviewer, writing about *The Great Rescue Operation,* noted that Marvin, Raymond, and Fats "are distinct—if exaggerated—personalities, the style is colorful and breezy, [and] the plot—deliberately unrestrained—is nicely structured and paced."

In the first sequel to *The Great Cheese Conspiracy, The Great Christmas Kidnapping Caper,* the three mice move into a dollhouse in Macy's department store, where they are befriended by Mr. Dunderhoff, who annually plays Santa Claus. When Mr. Dunderhoff is abducted by the store's greedy competitor, the mice use all their ingenuity to rescue him. A *Bulletin of the Center for Children's Books* reviewer commented that the "story has a happy blend of humor in dialogue, Christmas setting, local color, and silly situations." The trio is put to the test again in *The Great Rescue Operation,* in which Marvin and Raymond wake up one day to find that Fats has disappeared along with the doll carriage in which he likes to nap. The friends' attempts to rescue Fats from what they fear is a horrible fate at the hands of a scientist lead to "slapstick humor and nonstop action," according to Caroline S. Parr in the *School Library Journal.* The three mice again leave Macy's in *The Great Summer Camp Catastrophe,* in which they are inadvertently packed off with a box of cookies to summer camp in Vermont. "What will grab readers," observed Jacqueline Rose in the *School Library Journal,* "is the action-packed plot, with its series of near disasters." In *The Great Googlestein Museum Mystery,* the trio of mice once again departs its snug home at Macy's department store and spends a fine time at the Guggenheim Museum. "As always, Van Leeuwen's characters are appealing, both for their mouselike behaviors and their childlike personalities," wrote *Booklist* critic Kay Weisman.

In the early years of her marriage to Gavril, Van Leeuwen published her first young-adult novel, *I Was a 98-Pound Duckling,* a comical account of Kathy's thirteenth summer, when she and her best friend are consumed with thoughts of boys and dates and attempt to follow the beauty regimen outlined in a teen magazine. Although several reviewers noted the lack of originality in the story's plot, a *Bulletin of the Center for Children's Books* contributor remarked that "Kathy tells her story . . . with such wry humor and candor that it gives a fresh vitality to a familiar pattern." In a *Publishers Weekly* review, a contributor declared that *I Was a 98-Pound Duckling* "is a witty and charming book."

In the early 1970s Van Leeuwen left publishing to care for her two small children, but she was also determined to continue to write. The result of her decision to stay home to raise her children is the series of first-reader books filled with stories about Oliver and Amanda Pig. Based on her experiences with her own children, *Tales of Oliver Pig* and the subsequent books in this series have been warmly received for their gentle humor and loving portrayal of the everyday trials and joys of living with small children. Mary Gordon, writing in the *New York Times Book Review,* stated that "one of the great values of these books is their ability to dramatize the ridiculous and trivial and sickeningly frequent fights that siblings engage in every day of their lives, and yet suggest the siblings' essential fondness for each other, their dependency, their mutual good will."

More Tales of Oliver Pig, the first sequel to Van Leeuwen's successful *Tales of Oliver Pig,* follows Oliver's first efforts at gardening, how he adjusts to being cared for by his grandmother, and his attempts to stall at bedtime. A *Bulletin of the Center for Children's Books* critic singled out the "gentle humor in the simple, fluent writing style" for praise in reviewing this work. In response to her daughter's request, Van Leeuwen's next work in the series shifts the focus away from Oliver and toward his younger sister, Amanda. The stories in *Amanda Pig and Her Big Brother Oliver*—Van Leeuwen's first collaboration with series illustrator Ann Schweninger—highlight Amanda's frustrations at being unable to do some of the things her big brother can do and her parents' sympathetic responses. "Never cloying, the humor is genuine, the incidents right on the younger-sibling mark," remarked a *School Library Journal* reviewer of the book.

Critics noted that Amanda is more than an envious younger sister in *Tales of Amanda Pig,* the next work in this series. The stories in this volume find her refusing to eat a fried egg, scaring the clock-monster in the front hall with the help of her father, and switching roles with her sleepy mother at bed-time. Although a reviewer in *School Library Journal* found "the domestic drama . . . a bit dull this time out," a contributor to *Kirkus Reviews* praised "the same irreproachable, unforced child psychology, and . . . sly by-play" in this installment. Amanda "maintains her pluck, imagination and vulnerability," in *More Tales of Amanda Pig,* according to a *School Library Journal* critic, as she plays house

Brad Sneed creates the paintings for Van Leeuwen's picture book Sorry, *which tells the story of two feuding brothers.* (Illustration copyright © 2001 by Bradley D. Sneed. Reproduced by permission of Phyllis Fogelman Books, a division of Penguin Putnam Books for Young Readers.)

Van Leeuwen follows the story of a prairie family in her picture book **Nothing Here but Trees,** *featuring paintings by Phil Boatwright.* (Illustration copyright © 1998 by Phil Boatwright. Reproduced by permission of Dial Books for Young Readers, a division of Penguin Putnam Books for Young Readers.)

with her brother, becomes jealous of visiting cousins, and gives her father her favorite toy for his birthday. *Horn Book* reviewer Karen Jameyson found Van Leeuwen's story her to be as "comfortable as an easy chair, as warm and filling as a cup of cocoa."

In *Oliver, Amanda, and Grandmother Pig* the Pig family enjoys a week-long visit by Grandmother Pig, who cannot do everything younger adults can do but can tell stories and give good hugs. This was followed by *Oliver and Amanda's Christmas,* in which the two young pigs learn to keep Christmas secrets, bake cookies, and select the perfect Christmas tree. Reviewers compared this work favorably with earlier books in the series, Betsy Hearne, writing in *Bulletin of the Center for Children's Books,* describing *Oliver and Amanda's Christmas* to be "as comfortable as tradition."

Oliver and Amanda are starting to grow up in *Oliver Pig at School,* as Oliver experiences his first day of kindergarten, befriends a scary classmate, and makes and eats a necklace in art class. Martha V. Parravano praised "the author's understanding of childhood experiences" in her review for *Horn Book.* In *Amanda Pig on Her Own* Amanda learns to enjoy the adventures she can have when her big brother is away at school. Reviewing the work in *Bulletin of the Center for Children's Books,* Ruth Ann Smith particularly enjoyed Van Leeuwen's ability to "combine gentle humor with ingenuous dialogue."

Van Leeuwen has continued her easy-reader series with seasonal tales such as *Oliver and Amanda's Halloween* and *Oliver and Amanda and the Big Snow.* In the former title, the little pigs make a jack-o'-lantern and help prepare doughnuts as they get ready for Halloween. Brother and sister have to learn to compromise over carving the pumpkin in "this warmhearted installment," as a critic described the book in *Publishers Weekly.* In *Oliver and Amanda and the Big Snow* the porcine siblings go out to play after a snow storm and Amanda proves herself adept at snow games. "The warm interactions among family members continue to make these gentle stories a delight for early readers," wrote Hanna B. Zeiger in a *Horn Book* review. In *Booklist* Carolyn Phelan also noted the "gentle humor" in Van Leeuwen's tale.

In *Amanda Pig, Schoolgirl* the young piglet meets a new friend whom she dubs Lollipop. Parravano praised this title for its "thorough understanding of the emotions and situations of childhood." Friendship is celebrated in two further titles in the series, *Amanda Pig and Her Best Friend Lollipop* and *Oliver and Albert, Friends Forever.* In the former title, Amanda continues extending into a wider world than family. She and her new friend have good times together at each other's houses and also have their first sleepover. "Amanda is as engaging a character as ever," concluded Parravano, and *Booklist* contributor Carolyn Phelan noted that this "pleasant entry" in the series is written with "simplicity and affection." Oliver makes friends with the new boy in school in *Oliver and Albert, Friends Forever,* which finds the two playing kickball and collecting bugs. Albert is not an easy friend at first, because he is bookish and ignorant of the rules of the easiest games, but Oliver finds Albert willing to learn and takes the classmate under his wing. Leslie S. Hilverding, reviewing the title in *School Library Journal,* felt that *Oliver and Albert, Friends Forever* provides a "sweet and simple beginning chapter book about friendship." Shelle Rosenfeld, writing in *Booklist,* also noted the theme of friendship, writing that Van Leeuwen "illustrates the importance of appreciating and respecting differences" in an "entertaining story."

In *Oliver the Mighty Pig* young Oliver receives a special cape for his birthday and imagines himself to be a superhero. When his cape becomes stained with juice and is thrown in the wash, however, Oliver feels drained and incomplete. In the opinion of *Booklist* critic Gillian Engberg, "many children will recognize the empowerment Oliver finds in his special object." In *Oliver Pig and the Best Fort Ever,* the little pig and his two friends enjoy a busy day and an adventurous night in their homemade structure. "Simple dialogue, short sentences, and repeated words make this a great selection for beginning readers," observed Mary Hazelton in *School Library Journal.*

Oliver's sister returns in *Amanda Pig and the Awful, Scary Monster,* in which the young pig learns to overcome her fear of the dark. According to Parravano, the

Van Leeuwen's story about a time-honored cure pairs with David Gavril's cartoon art in the picture book **Chicken Soup.** (Illustration copyright © 2009 by David Gavril. Reproduced by permission of Harry N. Abrams, Inc.)

team of Van Leeuwen and Schweninger "demonstrates a solid understanding of childhood feelings and family dynamics." Amanda reaches a major childhood milestone in *Amanda Pig and the Wiggly Tooth.* When she cannot locate the first tooth that she has lost, however, Amanda worries that the Tooth Fairy will not arrive. Amanda takes a further step toward maturity in *Amanda Pig, First Grader,* "another solid entry in a winning series," remarked Engberg. Frustrated with her inability to instantly learn to read, Amanda devotes her recess time to developing her vocabulary. In the words of *School Library Journal* contributor Mary Elam, Van Leeuwen's "message of perseverance in the face of new experiences is one that may . . . be shared aloud."

Van Leeuwen has also written several chapter books for slightly older readers featuring Benjy, a third-grade boy critics have described as a lovable academic and athletic underachiever. As a reviewer commented in *Horn Book,* "Like Henry Huggins, Ellen Tebbits, and Ramona, Benjy is an engaging personality—one not quickly forgotten." In *Benjy and the Power of Zingies* Benjy decides that his only chance against the school bully who picks on him is to build up his body by eating Zingies breakfast cereal. A *Bulletin of the Center for Children's Books* critic praised the book's "lighthearted" and "often funny" treatment of life in the third grade. In *Benjy in Business* Benjy attempts to earn enough money to buy a special baseball mitt he hopes will improve his game. "Benjy displays a sturdy tenac-

ity that makes his extended effort credible and enjoyable," commented Carolyn Noah in her *School Library Journal* of this installment. Ilene Cooper remarked in *Booklist* that some of the action in the third work in the series, *Benjy the Football Hero,* may be lost on readers not familiar with the rules of the game at the book's center, but the critic added that "this has the same good humor and engaging characters of the other Benjy books." About the series as a whole, Robert E. Unsworth remarked in *School Library Journal* that "Van Leeuwen has a fine ability to see the humor in the tribulations of nine year olds and she writes about them with understanding."

In her other picture books, Van Leeuwen often deals with family relations and friendship, among other themes. *Touch the Sky Summer* is narrated by Luke and tells of a special family vacation by the lake. "Children who have visited lakeside cabins will enjoy the vicarious experience, related in a natural-sounding text," wrote Phelan in a *Booklist* review. Opocensky also praised this story of a "happy family and an idyllic setting," calling *Touch the Sky Summer* a "warm, wonderful read." In *Sorry,* two brothers who have a disagreement over a bowl of oatmeal manage to turn the incident into a feud that lasts generations. "Familiar themes of feuding families and the power of a simple apology dominate this story," wrote Susan L. Rogers in a *School Library Journal* review of *Sorry.* Rogers went on to

note that Van Leeuwen's "folkloric comic satire with overtones of universal truths should appeal to a wide range of readers and listeners."

Family dynamics of a less-serious sort are at the center of *"Wait for Me!" Said Maggie McGee,* in which the youngest of eight children is left out of the games of her older siblings. Too young to ride a tricycle or reach the cookie jar, Maggie longs for the day when she can go to school. Once she does, she manages to help her older brother remember his lines in the school play and as a result becomes "one of the gang." "Maggie McGee is a spunky, appealing role model for the youngest among us," remarked Rosalyn Pierini in a *School Library Journal* review. Engberg had more laudatory words for the book, noting that, with "gentle, poignant humor, Van Leeuwen tells a charming, straightforward story most younger siblings can relate to."

Although she remains best known for her picture books and simple stories for first readers, Van Leeuwen has said that she has always enjoyed writing for older children and adolescents. *Dear Mom, You're Ruining My Life,* her novel for upper-elementary-school grades, was inspired by Van Leeuwen's daughter, Elizabeth. A critic in *Kirkus Reviews* called the resulting portrait of life in the sixth grade "a genuinely funny look at a roller-coaster year." Writing for middle graders, Van Leeuwen tells the story of an eleven year old trying to cope with her parents' separation in her novel *Blue Sky, Butterfly.* Young Twig feels isolated from both her mom and her older brother after her father leaves, and they all try and cope with the changed circumstances in their lives. Finally, through the intervention of a grandmother and the healing influences of a garden, Twig is able to deal with her life. Reviewing the novel in *Booklist,* Susan Dove Lempke noted that in *Blue Sky, Butterfly* Van Leeuwen "evokes the desolate period immediately following parental breakup" with "aching sharpness."

Van Leeuwen examines how a family copes with tragedy in *Lucy Was There . . .,* a novel described as "a tender and honest portrait of grief" by a contributor in *Publishers Weekly.* Twelve-year-old Morgan blames herself for the disappearance of her mother and younger brother, who never returned after a fateful plane flight. The preteen ultimately comes to accept her loss with the help of Lucy, a special dog that visits the girl in her dreams. "The story's a sad but life-affirming one," remarked a critic in *Kirkus Reviews,* "and Morgan's a realistically drawn preteen with whom readers will identify."

Van Leeuwen has also produced historical books for young readers, including *Going West,* which chronicles the fictional journey of seven-year-old Hannah as she and her family travel west by wagon train in the days of the pioneers. Another journal-style novel, *Bound for Oregon,* is based on the real-life journey of Mary Ellen Todd and her family on the Oregon trail in the 1850s. Although more serious than many of the works for which Van Leeuwen is best known, these books have been praised for the author's signature emphasis on a warm and supportive family atmosphere. A *Publishers Weekly* critic called *Going West* a "haunting evocation of times past," and further remarked: "Into a gentle text brimming with family warmth and love, Van Leeuwen . . . packs a wealth of emotional moments." Reviewing *Bound for Oregon,* a *Publishers Weekly* critic wrote that the "contrast between the tenderness of Mary Ellen's perceptions and the hardships of the frontier is deeply moving," while in *Horn Book* Ellen Fader praised the "especially vivid and well-rounded" characters and dubbed the book "inspiring reading."

In another historical novel, *Cabin on Trouble Creek,* Van Leeuwen provides a fictional account of an actual incident from 1803. Twelve-year-old Daniel and younger brother Will stay in Ohio when their father returns to Pennsylvania to gather the rest of their family. As winter arrives, the boys find themselves alone and starving, until a Native-American trapper teaches them some essential survival skills. According to a *Kirkus Reviews* critic, *Cabin on Trouble Creek* "works as both a solid historical novel and as an exciting survival tale."

Van Leeuwen looks at the first manned hot-air balloon flight in America in *The Amazing Air Balloon.* The work centers on thirteen-year-old Edward Warren, a blacksmith's apprentice who joins the crew of balloon owner Peter Carnes in 1784. "Van Leeuwen, of course, takes creative liberty," remarked a *Kirkus Reviews* contributor, "but her account is solidly based on fact and embellished with details that reflect 18th-century reality."

History for a younger audience also finds its way into several of Van Leeuwen's picture books. *Across the Wide Dark Sea* tells of life on the *Mayflower* as the ship makes its way across the Atlantic Ocean to the New World. Storms and suffering make the nine-week trip harrowing, and upon arrival there is a harsh winter and unfamiliar Indians to contend with. Reviewing *Across the Wide Dark Sea*, Phelan praised Van Leeuwen for "telling a particular story that reflects the broader immigrant experience."

Reviewers have consistently praised the warm yet realistic celebrations of family life found in Van Leeuwen's books, also emphasizing her gentle humor and insightful portrayal of common childhood experiences. "Writing is hard work . . . ," the author stated on the Penguin Group Web site. "But I can't imagine any other work that I could enjoy more. There is excitement in creating something that didn't exist before. And a writer is always learning something new, about herself or the world. But perhaps the most satisfying moment comes after a book is published and a letter arrives in the mail from a child telling me, 'I read your book. And I understand what you're saying.' That, for me, is the biggest reward of writing."

Biographical and Critical Sources

BOOKS

Something about the Author Autobiography Series, Volume 8, Gale (Detroit, MI), 1989.

PERIODICALS

Booklist, September 1, 1985, Ilene Cooper, review of *Benjy the Football Hero,* p. 72; July, 1993, Annie Ayres, review of *Emma Bean,* p. 1977; May 1, 1992, Stephanie Zvirin, review of *The Great Summer Camp Catastrophe,* p. 1603; April 1, 1994, Carolyn Phelan, review of *Two Girls in Sister Dresses,* p. 1453; October 1, 1994, Carolyn Phelan, review of *Bound for Oregon,* p. 329; September 15, 1995, Carolyn Phelan, review of *Across the Wide Sea,* p. 161; January 1, 1996, Carolyn Phelan, review of *Oliver and Amanda and the Big Snow,* p. 850; June 1, 1996, Susan Dove Lempke, review of *Blue Sky, Butterfly,* p. 1724; May 15, 1997, Hazel Rochman, review of *A Fourth of July on the Plains,* p. 1582; June 1, 1997, Carolyn Phelan, review of *Touch the Sky Summer,* p. 1723; May 1, 1998, Linda Perkins, review of *The Tickle Stories,* p. 1524; July, 1998, Carolyn Phelan, review of *Amanda Pig and Her Best Friend Lollipop,* p. 1892; September 1, 1998, Hazel Rochman, review of *Nothing Here but Trees,* p. 129; March 1, 1999, Hazel Rochman, review of *Hannah of Fairfield,* p. 1215; August, 2000, Connie Fletcher, review of *Hannah's Winter of Hope,* p. 2142; December 1, 2000, Shelle Rosenfeld, review of *Oliver and Albert, Friends Forever,* p. 727; May 15, 2001, Gillian Engberg, review of *"Wait for Me!" Said Maggie McGee,* p. 1761; June 1, 2001, Shelle Rosenfeld, review of *Sorry,* p. 1896; September 1, 2002, Chris Sherman, review of *Lucy Was There . . .,* 126; February 1, 2003, Kay Weisman, review of *The Great Googlestein Museum Mystery,* p. 996; March 1, 2004, Gillian Engberg, review of *Oliver the Mighty Pig,* p. 1199; June 1, 2004, Sally Estes, review of *Cabin on Trouble Creek,* p. 1734; June 1, 2005, Carolyn Phelan, review of *Amanda Pig and the Really Hot Day,* p. 1826; April 15, 2006, Carolyn Phelan, review of *Oliver Pig and the Best Fort Ever,* p. 55; August, 2007, Gillian Engberg, review of *Amanda Pig, First Grader,* p. 82.

Bulletin of the Center for Children's Books, June, 1968, review of *Timothy's Flower,* p. 166; July, 1969, review of *One Day in Summer,* p. 184; September, 1973, review of *I Was a 98-Pound Duckling,* p. 19; February, 1975, review of *Too Hot for Ice Cream,* p. 100; November, 1975, review of *The Great Christmas Kidnapping Caper;* October, 1979, review of *Seems like This Road Goes on Forever;* July, 1981, review of *More Tales of Oliver Pig,* p. 221; July-August, 1982, review of *The Great Rescue Operation,* p. 217; March, 1983, review of *Benjy and the Power of Zingies;* January, 1986, leeuwen of *More Tales of Amanda Pig,* p. 98; May, 1989, review of *Dear Mom, You're Ruining My Life,* pp. 238-239; October, 1989, Betsy Hearne,

review of *Oliver and Amanda's Christmas,* p. 47; March, 1991, Ruth Ann Smith, review of *Amanda Pig on Her Own,* pp. 180-181; December, 1995, Susan Dove Lempke, review of *Oliver and Amanda and the Big Snow,* p. 143.

Horn Book, April, 1983, review of *Benjy and the Power of Zingies,* pp. 168-169; March-April, 1986, Karen Jameyson, review of *More Tales of Amanda Pig,* pp. 199-200; September, 1987, Karen Jameyson, review of *Oliver, Amanda, and Grandmother Pig,* pp. 606-607; September-October, 1990, Martha V. Parravano, review of *Oliver Pig at School,* p. 599; March-April, 1995, Ellen Fader, review of *Bound for Oregon,* p. 197; September-October, 1995, Hanna B. Zeiger, review of *Oliver and Amanda and the Big Snow,* p. 628; May-June, 1997, Martha V. Parravano, review of *Amanda Pig, Schoolgirl,* p. 329; July-August, 1998, Martha V. Parravano, review of *Amanda Pig and Her Best Friend Lollipop,* pp. 499-500; July-August, 2003, Martha V. Parravano, review of *Amanda Pig and the Awful, Scary Monster,* p. 468.

Kirkus Reviews, September 1, 1983, review of *Tales of Amanda Pig;* May 15, 1989, review of *Dear Mom, You're Ruining My Life,* p. 772; September 1, 1998, review of *Nothing Here but Trees,* p. 1294; January 1, 1999, review of *Hannah of Fairfield,* p. 73; May 15, 2002, review of *Lucy Was There . . .,* p. 742; March 1, 2003, review of *The Amazing Air Balloon,* p. 400; March 15, 2003, review of *The Great Googlestein Museum Mystery,* p. 480; May 15, 2004, review of *Trouble on Trouble Creek,* p. 499; March 15, 2006, review of *Benny and Beautiful Baby Delilah,* p. 302.

New York Times Book Review, November 11, 1979, review of *Seems like This Road Goes on Forever;* April 25, 1982, Doris Orgel, "Mice in Macy's"; November 10, 1985, Mary Gordon, "Pig Tales"; January 10, 1988, review of *Oliver, Amanda, and Grandmother Pig,* p. 36.

Publishers Weekly, September 25, 1972, review of *I Was a 98-Pound Duckling;* October 7, 1974, review of *Too Hot for Ice Cream,* p. 63; September 8, 1975, review of *The Great Christmas Kidnapping Caper;* December 13, 1991, review of *Going West,* p. 55; September 2, 1992, review of *Oliver and Amanda's Halloween,* p. 59; August 2, 1993, p. 79; September 5, 1994, review of *Bound for Oregon,* p. 112; May 19, 1997, review of *A Fourth of July on the Plains,* pp. 75-76; May 21, 2001, review of *Sorry,* p. 107; May 27, 2002, review of *Lucy Was There . . .,* p. 60; December 9, 2002, review of *The Amazing Air Balloon,* p. 84; October 11, 2004, review of *The Great Cheese Conspiracy,* p. 27; May 14, 2007, review of *Papa and the Pioneer Quilt,* p. 53.

School Library Journal, August, 1982, Caroline S. Parr, review of *The Great Rescue Operation,* p. 123; December, 1982, review of *Amanda Pig and Her Big Brother Oliver,* p. 75; December, 1983, Carolyn Noah, review of *Benjy in Business,* p. 70; December, 1983, review of *Tales of Amanda Pig,* p. 80; May, 1985, Robert E. Unsworth, review of *Benjy the Football Hero,* p. 111; December, 1985, review of *More Tales of Amanda Pig,* p. 110; April, 1992, Jacqueline Rose,

review of *The Great Summer Camp Catastrophe,* p. 126; December, 1995, Gale W. Sherman, review of *Oliver and Amanda and the Big Snow,* p. 92; July, 1997, Virginia Opocensky, review of *Touch the Sky Summer* and *Amanda Pig, School Girl,* p. 77; November, 1999, Cheryl Cufari, review of *Hannah's Helping Hands,* pp. 131-132; November, 2000, Leslie S. Hilverding, review of *Oliver and Albert, Friends Forever,* p. 136; May, 2001, Susan L. Rogers, review of *Sorry,* p. 138; July, 2001, Rosalyn Pierini, review of *"Wait for Me!" Said Maggie McGee,* p. 90; May, 2003, Shara Alpern, review of *The Great Googlestein Museum Mystery,* p. 131; July, 2003, Anne Knickerbocker, review of *Amanda Pig and the Awful, Scary Monster,* p. 108; March, 2004, Nancy A. Gifford, review of *Oliver the Mighty Pig,* p. 186; July, 2004, Kristen Oravec, review of *Cabin on Trouble Creek,* p.

113; March, 2006, Martha Topol, review of *Benny and Beautiful Baby Delilah,* p. 204; July, 2006, Mary Hazelton, review of review of *Oliver Pig and the Best Fort Ever,* 88; March, 2007, Lee Bock, review of *Papa and the Pioneer Quilt,* p. 188; July, 2007, Mary Elam, review of *Amanda Pig, First Grader,* p. 86.

ONLINE

Houghton Mifflin Education Place Web site, http://www.eduplace.com/ (March 10, 2008), "Meet Jean Van Leeuwen."

Jean Van Leeuwen Home Page, http://www.jeanvanleeuwen.com (December 10, 2010).

Penguin Group Web site, http://us.penguingroup.com/ (March 1, 2008), "Jean Van Leeuwen."*

WATSON, Richard Jesse 1951-

Personal

Born January 15, 1951, in Ridgecrest, CA; son of Jesse Robert (a physicist) and Elsie M. (an artist and homemaker) Watson; married Rebecca Sue Davis (an artist, writer, and homemaker), December 27, 1970; children: Jesse Joshua, Faith Christina, Benjamin James. *Education:* Attended Pasadena City College and Art Center College of Design (Pasadena, CA). *Politics:* Democrat. *Religion:* Christian. *Hobbies and other interests:* Reading, international folk dancing, hiking, sculpting.

Addresses

Home—Port Townsend, WA. *Agent*—Rubin Pfeffer, East/West Literary Agency, Boston, MA; rpfeffer@eastwestliteraryagency.com. *E-mail*—rjw@olympus.net.

Career

Graphic designer and illustrator. U.S. Post Office, Pasadena, CA, letter carrier, 1971-75; World Vision International, Monrovia, CA, assistant art director, 1975-79; Hallmark Cards, Inc., Kansas City, MO, artist, 1979-82; freelance graphic designer and illustrator, beginning 1982. Presenter at schools, libraries, and museums; keynote speaker. *Exhibitions:* Work exhibited at Society of Illustrators Western Exhibition, Los Angeles, CA, 1985, 1990; American Institute of Graphic Arts, New York, NY, 1987; Master Eagle Gallery, New York, NY, 1987; Society of Illustrators, New York, NY, 1987, 1989, 2003; Springfield Art Association, Springfield, IL, 1989; Every Picture Tells a Story Gallery of Fine Art, Los Angeles, 1989, 2000; American Booksellers Convention Exhibit, New York, NY, 1989; Green Valley Public Library Gallery, Las Vegas, NV, 1990; Repartee Gallery, Salt Lake City, UT, 1995; Whatcom Museum of History and Art, Bellingham, WA, 1995-96; Belleview Art Museum, Belleview, WA, 1996; Mazza Centennial Collection, University of Findlay, Findlay, OH, 1996-2010; Pak Place Science and Arts Center, Asheville, NC, 1998;

Richard Jesse Watson (Photograph by Susi Watson. Reproduced by permission.)

Hamilton Gallery, Montreat Anderson College, Montreat, NC, 1998, 2000; Lookout Gallery, Regent College, Vancouver, British Columbia, Canada, 2000; Grove Park Inn, Asheville, 2000; Art of Illustration Gallery, Seattle, WA, 2001-02; Whidbey Island Center for the Arts, Langely, WA, 2001; Books of Wonder Gallery, New York, NY, 2005; Rancho Mirage Library Grand Opening Exhibit, Rancho Mirage, CA, 2006; and Golden Kite Award Exhibit, National Center for Children's Illustrated Literature, Abilene, TX, 2010.

Awards, Honors

Best Book Design designation, American Institute of Graphic Arts, 1986, and Parent's Choice Award for Illustration, Parent's Choice Foundation, 1987, both for *Bronwen, the Traw, and the Shape-Shifter* by James Dickie; Ezra Jack Keats fellow, University of Minnesota Kerlan Collection, 1987; Graphic Arts Award for Best Printed Children's Book, Printing Industries of America, and *Booklist* Editor's Choice selection, both 1989, and Golden Kite Award, Society of Children's Book Writers, 1990, all for *Tom Thumb;* Best Picture Book of the Year designation, *People* magazine, and Children's Choice designation, International Reading Association (IRA), both 1990, both for *The High Rise*

Glorious Skittle Skat Roarious Sky Pie Angel Food Cake by Nancy Willard; C.S. Lewis Gold Medal for Children's Picture Books, 1995, for *One Wintry Night* by Ruth Bell Graham; Teachers' Choice Award, IRA, 2002, for *The Waterfall's Gift* by Joanne Ryder; *New York Times* Top Ten Children's Books listee, 2006, for *The Night before Christmas.*

Writings

SELF-ILLUSTRATED

(Reteller) *Tom Thumb,* Harcourt (New York, NY), 1989.
The Magic Rabbit, Blue Sky Press (New York, NY), 2005.

ILLUSTRATOR

James Dickey, *Bronwen, the Traw, and the Shape-Shifter: A Poem in Four Parts,* Harcourt (New York, NY), 1986.

Betsy James, *The Dream Stair,* Harper (New York, NY), 1989.

Nancy Willard, *The High Rise Glorious Skittle Skat Roarious Sky Pie Angel Food Cake,* Harcourt (New York, NY), 1990.

Ruth Bell Graham, *One Wintry Night,* Baker Books (Grand Rapids, MI), 1994.

Joanne Ryder, *The Waterfall's Gift,* Sierra Club Books for Children (San Francisco, CA), 2001.

Margaret Hodges, adaptor, *The Legend of Saint Christopher: From the Golden Legend Englished by William Caxton, 1483,* Eerdmans Books for Young Readers (Grand Rapids, MI), 2002.

Clement C. Moore, *The Night before Christmas,* new edition, HarperCollins (New York, NY), 2006.

Benjamin James Watson, *The Boy Who Went Ape,* Blue Sky Press (New York, NY), 2008.

Contributor to *Speak! Children's Book Illustrators Brag about Their Dogs,* edited by Michael J. Rosen, Harcourt (New York, NY), 1993; *Writers in the Kitchen,* compiled by Trisha Gardella, Boyds Mills Press (Honesdale, PA), 1998; and *Oz: The Hundredth Anniversary Celebrarion,* edited by Peter Glassman, HarperCollins (New York, NY), 2000.

Sidelights

Richard Jesse Watson is an artist and author whose original stories are featured in his picture books *Tom Thumb* and *The Magic Rabbit.* Watson's work for other authors includes contributions to Nancy Willard's picture book *The High Rise Glorious Skittle Skat Roarious Sky Pie Angel Food Cake* and poet James Dickey's *Bronwen, the Traw, and the Shapeshifter: A Poem in Four Parts.* A creative collaborating with his son, Benjamin James Watson, resulted in *The Boy Who Went Ape,* a story about a boy's fun-filled trip to the zoo that

Booklist contributor John Peters praised as full of "enough silly details . . . to reward repeat" readings. Also writing in praise of the father-son picture book, Mary Hazelton noted in her *School Library Journal* review of *The Boy Who Went Ape* that Watson's "terrific illustrations" are energized by "irregular lines and blasts of color" and contribute to a picture book that is "lively and full of humor."

"I can't remember a time when I wasn't doing art of one kind or another," Watson once told *SATA.* "My mother, an artist as well, encouraged my efforts and provided me with all sorts of supplies. My father was a scientist, hung upon realism. 'That doesn't quite look right,' he used to say. So I was always trying to get the drawings to 'look right.' My mom, on the other hand, was very free, liked abstract work, and argued endlessly with my dad about modern art. I was fascinated by their conversations and continually weighed the merits of their respective viewpoints.

"I doodled my way through school and was privileged to study the paintings at the Los Angeles County Museum and to take art classes at the Pasadena Art Museum. My talents were encouraged, nurtured, and inspired. From the beginning, there was a narrative bent to my art work. I would create a story in my mind and make images to bring the story to conclusion. During high school and college my art became socially oriented."

Watson collaborates with his son, Benjamin James Watson, on creating the picture book **The Boy Who Went Ape.** (Blue Sky Press, 2008. Illustration copyright © 2008 by Richard Jesse Watson. Reproduced by permission of Scholastic, Inc.)

After touring Europe and then getting married, Watson worked on a Quaker dairy farm in Ohio, then returned to Pasadena with his growing family, supporting it by working jobs such as a welder and letter carrier. A job as a graphic designer with the Christian humanitarian organization World Vision allowed him to attend the Pasadena Art Center. Four years on staff at Hallmark Cards proved to be "somewhat like graduate school," as Watson later explained. "I learned a great deal about color and techniques, and got some wonderful training painting flowers. It became oppressive, however. I like to experiment, but Hallmark was uncomfortable with that. Their highly skilled artists were hired to replicate colors, styles, forms of whatever was deemed 'hot' in fashion shows and art galleries in Paris and New York." In 1983 Watson returned to California and began his career in children's books.

Watson's original self-illustrated picture book *The Magic Rabbit* exhibits his talent for creating detailed paintings that are characterized by vivid colors and a nostalgic storybook feel. In the story, Rabbit lives in a black top hat and is able to perform a number of magic tricks. Although Rabbit is lonely, he eventually finds the perfect companion in another magic hat that he finds hidden inside his own. Although Ilene Cooper noted in *Booklist* that *The Magic Rabbit* features a "slight" story, she maintained that young readers will be captivated by the book's "spectacular art, which fuses realism with fantasy." Cooper hailed Watson as "an excellent colorist," while in *School Library Journal* Maryann H. Owen noted that the "richly hued oil paintings" that bring to life *The Magic Rabbit* are commendable for their "varying perspectives and textures." In the opinion of a *Kirkus Reviews* writer, the artist's original picture book serves as "a strong showcase for Watson's technical versatility."

In his work for an early picture-book project, Willard's *The High Rise Glorious Skittle Skat Roarious Sky Pie Angel Food Cake,* Watson's "captivating images . . . add an extra touch of magic and mystery to this already magical, mysterious fairy tale," according to a *Publishers Weekly* writer. Margaret Hodges' retelling *The Legend of Saint Christopher: From the Golden Legend Englished by William Caxton, 1483* also benefits from Watson's detailed representational painting, which a *Publishers Weekly* contributor described as "a startling blend of the ancient and the timeless." Reviewing Watson's strikingly realistic paintings for Ruth Bell Graham's *One Wintry Night, Booklist* critic Shelley Townsend-Hudson called the work "unusually arresting, [and] offering plenty of visual subtext to support the ambitious undertaking," while a *Publishers Weekly* critic praised it as "richly detailed and, at times, vividly realistic." *The Waterfall's Gift,* a picture book with a text by Joanne Ryder, benefits from "Watson's detailed egg tempera illustrations," which "add the final layer to this beautifully crafted book," according to *School Library Journal* contributor Holly T. Sneeringer.

"My basic process doesn't change that much from book to book," Watson once explained of his illustration work. "I tend to begin every project with physical ac-

tivity: hiking, splitting wood, burning brush, Gradually I focus on the story and gear up for research. Invariably I over-research, but that, too, seems to be part of my process. I'm extremely interested in the effects of light and often make approximate models of characters or scenes. For *Tom Thumb* my wife sewed costumes from which I worked—a real luxury. Usually, I'll make do with physical 'improvisations,' say a sweatshirt turned inside out. The end of a book is always very hard. I work constantly, become quite unsocial (I have to admit), and feel at once exhausted and exhilarated.

"I paint for the child inside me: that true, unpretentious person who meets the world with wonder and awe and acceptance. Some people think that drawings for children should be very simple. Some should. Some shouldn't. As a child I loved highly detailed art. I want to create pictures in which I can get lost and in which a child can wander and be transported to someplace new."

"When I take the dive into making a book," Watson more-recently added, "I am aware that the book is already underway. It is like the mushroom. We see the fruiting body when the mushroom finally pops up after a johnny-come-lately rain. But underground the mycelium (a network of fine, almost microscopic filaments) have been at work for quite a while. So, too, the creative person has been subconsciously working out an idea, a concept, trying to get at an inner itch. Many of my best ideas begin in my journals. I jot a thought. I scribble a sighting (whether an 'inny' or an 'outy'). These ideas continue to grow in the dark.

"Each book I have made is inevitably wrapped up in many layers of life. While trying to write or illustrate a book, there is the narrative arc of bills which beckon like banshees, and kids with their soccer games. Babies are born, forest fires engulf the neighborhood, cars crash, elderly parents unwittingly set fire to their microwaves, and the power of love prevails.

"But back in the refuge of my studio I find the privilege of working with various authors, editors, and art directors to be one of my greatest joys. Each collaboration has a different and amazing narrative.

"My family is a great joy to me. My wife, Susi, and I made it a priority to read and draw with our children before bedtime each night. Now that our children are grown with families of their own, they continue that tradition with their own children. The love of books must have rubbed off, because each of our children has pursued getting published: Jesse Joshua Watson, Benjamin James Watson, and Faith Christina (Watson) Pray. They are all artists, musicians, writers, and now published authors or illustrators. (At this writing, our daughter, Faith, has her first novel that is being submitted by her agent to publishers.)

"I am a blessed man."

Biographical and Critical Sources

PERIODICALS

Booklist, September 1, 1995, Shelley Townsend-Hudson, review of *One Wintry Night,* p. 56; October 1, 2002, Ilene Cooper, review of *The Legend of Saint Christopher: From the Golden Legend Englished by William Caxton, 1483,* p. 342; January 1, 2005, Ilene Cooper, review of *The Magic Rabbit,* p. 876; November 1, 2008, John Peters, review of *The Boy Who Went Ape,* p. 45.

Kirkus Reviews, December 15, 2004, review of *The Magic Rabbit,* p. 1210; October 1, 2008, review of *The Boy Who Went Ape.*

New York Times Book Review, January 28, 1990, review of *Tom Thumb;* May 12, 1991, review of *The High Rise Glorious Skittle Skat Roarious Sky Pie Angel Food Cake.*

Publishers Weekly, April 13, 1990, review of *The Dream Stair,* p. 63; August 31, 1990, review of *The High Rise Glorious Skittle Skat Roarious Sky Pie Angel Food Cake,* p. 67; September 18, 1995, review of *One Wintry Night,* p. 96; September 30, 2002, review of *The Legend of Saint Christopher,* p. 69.

School Library Journal, August, 2001, Holly T. Sneeringer, review of *The Waterfall's Gift,* p. 160; November, 2002, Jane G. Connor, review of *The Legend of Saint Christopher,* p. 144; April, 2005, Maryann H. Owen, review of *The Magic Rabbit,* p. 114; December, 2008, Mary Hazelton, review of *The Boy Who Went Ape,* p. 106.

ONLINE

Richard Jesse Watson Home Page, http://www.richard jessewatson.com (January 10, 2010).

Richard Jesse Watson Web log, http://www.richardjesse watson.blogspot.com (January 10, 2010).

*   *   *

WATSON, Sasha

Personal

Born July 23, in Boston, MA. *Education:* Barnard College, B.A. (French literature and translation), 1997; New York University, M.A. (French literature), 2003.

Addresses

Home—Boston, MA. *Agent*—Rosemary Stimola, Stimola Literary Studio, 306 Chase Ct., Edgewater, NJ 07020. *E-mail*—sasha_watson@yahoo.com.

Career

Writer, poet, and translator. Has also taught French literature at Barnard College and New York University.

Writings

Vidalia in Paris (young-adult novel), Viking (New York, NY), 2008.

Contributor to periodicals, including *Los Angeles Times, Publishers Weekly,* and *ARTnews,* and to Web magazines, including *Double X* and *Arthur.* Contributor of poetry to periodicals, including *Tarpaulin Sky* and *Bird Song.*

TRANSLATOR

Louis Zukofsky, *The Writing of Guillaume Apollinaire: Le Style Apollinaire,* edited and with introduction by Serge Gavronsky, Wesleyan University Press (Middletown, CT), 2004.

Yves Chaland, *Freddy Lombard: Chaland Anthology, Volume One,* Humanoids/DC Comics (New York, NY), 2004.

Yves Chaland and Yann Lepennetier, *Freddy Lombard: Chaland Anthology, Volume Two,* Humanoids/DC Comics (New York, NY), 2005.

(With Justin Kelly) Alexandro Jodorowsky, *The Epic Conspiracy* ("Incal" series), illustrated by Moebius, Humanoids/DC Comics (New York, NY), 2005.

Emmanuel Guibert, *Sardine in Outer Space,* illustrated by Joann Sfar, First Second (New York, NY), 2006.

Emmanuel Guibert, *Sardine in Outer Space Two,* illustrated by Joann Sfar, First Second (New York, NY), 2006.

Emmanuel Guibert, *Space Pirate: Sardine in Outer Space,* illustrated by Joann Sfar, First Second (New York, NY), 2008.

Emmanuel Guibert, *Space Pirate: Sardine vs. the Brainwashing Machine,* illustrated by Joann Sfar, First Second (New York, NY), 2008.

Contributor of poetry translations to periodicals, including *TriQuarterly.*

Sidelights

Dedicated Francophile Sasha Watson is the author of *Vidalia in Paris,* a highly regarded novel that centers on a high-school student who earns a scholarship to study art in the "City of Light." Watson, who has also translated works by such authors as Guillaume Apollinaire, Joyce Mansour, Charles Albert Cingria, Yves Chaland, and Emmanuel Guibert, noted in a *Story Sirens* interview that she enjoys the rewards of writing for a young adult audience. "Adolescence is when people define themselves and start making choices about the kind of person they want to be," Watson commented. "I find that process fascinating. It's also a time of life that's filled with hope and potential, and I love writing with that anything-is-possible sense of a character's life."

Watson's interest in Paris began at a young age, during her initial visit to the French capital. "I first went there with my mother, who was studying French, when I was

four years old," the author recalled in an interview on the *Penguin Books* Web site. "I was lucky to learn to speak French at that age, and that's something I've used ever since. I also studied in Paris in both college and graduate school, and I've spent a lot of time there outside of school as well." Because of Watson's frequent visits to the city, it has earned a special place in her heart. "I really love Paris, not only because it's so beautiful but because I have a history there. It feels like another home to me."

The idea for *Vidalia in Paris,* Watson's debut novel, stemmed from an article she came across about a most unusual art lover. "When I was starting to write *Vidalia,*" she remarked in her Penguin Books interview, "I read a story about an art thief who had spent years stealing small works of art from museums and churches in Europe, only to keep them in his small apartment in Switzerland. What interested me was that he was stealing these things, not to make money, but because he loved them. So I thought, what if a young girl who loved art fell in love with someone who stole art? And a part of Vidalia was born."

Cover of Sasha Watson's entertaining young-adult novel Vidalia in Paris, *featuring cover art by Tim Ashton.* (Jacket illustration copyright © 2008, by Tim Ashton. Reproduced by permission of Viking, a division of Penguin Putnam Books for Young Readers.)

In the work, Watson introduces Vidalia Sloane, a budding artist entering her senior year of high school who leaps at the chance to study abroad one summer. Once in Paris, Vidalia immerses herself in the experience, taking classes at the Beaux-Arts under the tutelage of the harsh Monsieur Benoît, enjoying the many spectacular sights of the city, and entering a relationship with Marco, a mysterious young art dealer. Although Marco's charm and sophistication prove irresistible to Vidalia, his involvement with an art theft ring forces the teen to examine what is truly important to her. "For me, the true story here is about an artist finding out that she is an artist," Watson stated in her *Penguin Books* interview. "At the end of her adventures, it's Vidalia's art that sustains and nourishes her, not romance and not the excitement of a glamorous life. Vidalia's story ends with a scene of her drawing, because that's really where her heart is."

Vidalia in Paris garnered solid reviews. A *Publishers Weekly* contributor remarked that the crime element "energetically drives the plot," and Ilene Cooper, writing in *Booklist,* similarly noted that "the main push and pull of the narrative—Vidalia's relationship with the scheming Marco—fascinates throughout." Other critics cited the Parisian setting as a strength of the work, According to a contributor in *Kirkus Reviews,* "Watson portrays Paris with a doting accuracy and delineates all the torments of first love," and Cynthia Winfield described the work in *Voice of Youth Advocates* as an "artfully constructed Parisian adventure, which is ultimately a compelling mystery with no hint of formulaic structure."

"One of the great joys of publishing *Vidalia in Paris* has been meeting readers, many of whom love art, Paris, or writing," Watson commented to *SATA.* "I'm always happy to enter into conversation about these (and other!) subjects with readers. I've taken special pleasure in offering writing workshops as well. Being in a position to encourage young writers and artists to find their voices and the courage to put their work out into the world, adds an incredible layer of richness to my writing life."

Biographical and Critical Sources

PERIODICALS

Booklist, November 15, 2008, Ilene Cooper, review of *Vidalia in Paris,* p. 58.

Kirkus Reviews, September 15, 2008, review of *Vidalia in Paris.*

Publishers Weekly, September 1, 2008, review of *Vidalia in Paris,* p. 54.

School Library Journal, April, 2009, Melyssa Malinowski, review of *Vidalia in Paris,* p. 144.

Voice of Youth Advocates, December, 2008, Cynthia Winfield, review of *Vidalia in Paris,* p. 442.

ONLINE

Compulsive Reader Web log, http://www.thecompulsive
reader.com/ (November 13, 2008), "Insight from Sasha
Watson, Author of *Vidalia in Paris.*"
Penguin Books Web site, http://us.penguingroup.com/
(January 10, 2010), interview with Watson.
Sasha Watson Home Page, http://sashawatson.com (Janu-
ary 10, 2010).
Story Siren Web log, http://www.thestorysiren.com/ (De-
cember 18, 2008), "Author Tales: Sasha Watson."

*   *   *

WINGET, Susan

Personal

Born in Charlotte, NC; married Al Winget; children:
Mac, Erin, Sam. *Education:* University of North Carolina, Chapel Hill, B.A. (art), 1975.

Addresses

Home—Charlotte, NC. *Office*—Winget Art, 13735 Steele
Creek Rd., Charlotte, NC 28273. *Agent*—Courtney
Davis, Inc., 340 Main St., Franklin, TN 37064. *E-mail*—
wingetart@aol.com.

Career

Illustrator, designer, and author. Water colorist, beginning 1982; founder, Winget Art Studio; creator of housewares design lines for Lang Graphics, beginning 1987,
and Burnes of Boston, among others. *Exhibitions:* Work
exhibited in galleries and included in private and corporate collections around the world.

Writings

SELF-ILLUSTRATED

Susan Winget's The Changing Seasons, Meredith Press
(New York, NY), 1992.
Tucker's Four-Carrot School Day, HarperCollins (New
York, NY), 2005.
Tucker's Apple-Dandy Day, HarperCollins (New York,
NY), 2006.
Friends Forever!, Harvest House (Eugene, OR), 2006.
My Friend You've Been an Angel, Harvest House (Eugene,
OR), 2006.
Sam the Snowman, HarperCollins (New York, NY), 2008.

ILLUSTRATOR

Rhonda S. Hogan, compiler, *Happiness Is Homemade,*
Brownlow (Fort Worth, TX), 1999.

Hearts at Home: Celebrating Where Love Lives, Brown-
low Pub. (Fort Worth, TX), 1999.
Alice Gray, compiler, *Stories for the Teacher's Heart,*
Multnomah Publishers (Sisters, OR), 2002.
Mark Kimball Moulton, *The Visit,* Ideals Children's Books
(Nashville, TN), 2003.
Mark Kimball Moulton, *Everyday Angels,* Ideals Chil-
dren's Books (Nashville, TN), 2004.

Sidelights

Working from a studio on her 80-acre family farm near
Charlotte, North Carolina, Susan Winget has become
nationally known for her folk-art paintings and her
country-themed designs. In addition to creating artwork
for use on a range of home decor items, Winget has
also produced several books that feature the nostalgic
images of country life that have gained her fans
throughout the United States.

Born in Charlotte, Winget began marketing her watercolor paintings after graduating from the University of
North Carolina and marrying her husband, Al Winget.
While raising their three children, she successfully grew
her business to the point that her studio building was
expanded to house a full-time staff that now includes
several other artists. Farm animals such as cows, sheep,
and roosters, as well as fruits, vegetables, and flowers,
often appear in Winget's detailed, country-themed paintings.

Winget's original self-illustrated picture books include
*Tucker's Four-Carrot School Day, Tucker's Apple-
Dandy Day,* and *Sam the Snowman.* In *Tucker's Four-
Carrot School Day* she introduces a class of young farm
animals that includes Tucker the rabbit. In the story,
Tucker copes with first-day jitters and ultimately makes
new friends with the help of his kindly teacher, Miss
Blossom. In *Publishers Weekly* a critic described
Winget's picture-book debut as full of "homey touches"
that exude "comfort and tranquility."

When readers rejoin Tucker in *Tucker's Apple-Candy
Day,* the rabbit has joined his class on a trip to a local
fruit orchard. Although he has promised to bring home
some apples for a pie, the young rabbit becomes dis-
tracted by the many activities available. Fortunately,
Tucker's parents are sympathetic, creating what *Booklist*
contributor Connie Fletcher called a "sweet resolution"
to Winget's colorfully illustrated story. The author/illus-
trator's ink and watercolor artwork brings to life "the
comfort and security of family life," concluded Carolyn
Janssen in her *School Library Journal* review of *Tucker's Apple-Dandy Day,* and *Booklist* critic Kay Weisman
dubbed *Tucker's Four-Carrot School Day* as "a good
choice for opening-day story hours."

In *Sam the Snowman* a snowchild desires to learn the
art of making snow, but he is unable to do so until he
meets Sarah and Tommy in a nearby forest. Hoping to
treat the siblings to a glistening, shimmering, wintry-

looking day, Sam again fails in his snow-making attempt. However, when the children give Sam a striped scarf to make him feel better, the snowchild so happily spins his broom that he transforms the forest into a wintry wonderland. Describing the illustrations in *School Library Journal,* reviewer Susan Weitz noted that the animal characters in Winget's "reassuring" picture book "resemble stuffed animals while . . . children are as round and rosy as dolls." While calling the setting of *Sam the Snowman* "over-the-top idyllic," *Booklist* contributor Abby Nolan concluded that it is "not a bad world for readers . . . to visit every now and again."

Biographical and Critical Sources

PERIODICALS

Booklist, August, 2005, Kay Weisman, review of *Tucker's Four-Carrot School Day,* p. 2042; September 1, 2006, Connie Fletcher, review of *Tucker's Apple-Dandy Day,* p. 142; October 15, 2008, Abby Nolan, review of *Sam the Snowman,* p. 48.
Kirkus Reviews, September 15, 2008, review of *Sam the Snowman.*
Publishers Weekly, July 11, 2005, review of *Tucker's Four-Carrot School,* p. 91.
School Library Journal, September, 2005, Marge Loch-Wouters, review of *Tucker's Four-Carrot School Day,* p. 188; September, 2006, Carolyn Janssen, review of *Tucker's Apple-Dandy Day,* p. 188; December, 2008, Susan Weitz, review of *Sam the Snowman,* p. 107.

ONLINE

Susan Winget Home Page, http://www.wingetart.com (January 10, 2010).*

*　　*　　*

WINNICK, Karen B. 1946-

Personal

Born June 28, 1946, in NY; daughter of Sanford (a certified public accountant) and Miriam Binkoff; married Gary Winnick (a bond broker), December 24, 1972; children: Adam Scott, Alex, Matt. *Education:* Syracuse University, B.F.A., 1968; graduate study at New York University and School of Visual Arts. *Religion:* Jewish.

Addresses

Home—New York, NY. *E-mail*—karen@karenbwinnick. com.

Career

Artist and writer. Grey Advertising, New York, NY, art director, 1970; Lois Holland Calloway, New York, NY, graphics designer, 1972-75; freelance artist and writer, beginning 1975.

Member

Art Directors Club.

Awards, Honors

Pennsylvania Children's Book Award nomination, 1996, for *Mr. Lincoln's Whiskers;* Best Books designation, Bank Street College of Education, 2000, for *Sybil's Night Ride,* 2006, for *Cassie's Sweet Berry Pie,* 2008, for *Lucy's Cave;* Georgia Children's Book Award nomination, 2010, for *The Night of the Fireflies.*

Writings

SELF-ILLUSTRATED

Patch and the Strings, Lippincott (Philadelphia, PA), 1977.
Sandro's Dolphin, Lothrop, Lee & Shepard Books (New York), 1980.
Mr. Lincoln's Whiskers, Boyds Mills Press (Honesdale, PA), 1996.
Sybil's Night Ride, Boyds Mill Press (Honesdale, PA), 2000.
A Year Goes Round: Poems for the Months, Boyds Mills Press (Honesdale, PA), 2001.
Barn Sneeze, Boyds Mills Press (Honesdale, PA), 2002.
The Night of the Fireflies, illustrated by Yoriko Ito, Boyds Mills Press (Honesdale, PA), 2004.
Cassie's Sweet Berry Pie: A Civil War Story, Boyds Mills Press (Honesdale, PA), 2005.
Lucy's Cave: A Story of Vicksburg, 1863, Boyds Mills Press (Honesdale, PA), 2008.

Sidelights

In books that include *Mr. Lincoln's Whiskers, Cassie's Sweet Berry Pie: A Civil War Story,* and *Lucy's Cave: A Story of Vicksburg,* author and artist Karen B. Winnick creates picture-book stories that mix her interest in history with her desire to focus on strong-willed young girls. "I like to show strong girls in my stories because I want my readers to believe in their own abilities," Winnick noted on her home page. "Hopefully they will be inspired to trust their instincts, follow their beliefs, and rely on their own resourcefulness."

A letter sent from eleven-year-old Grace Bedell to the tall, lanky lawyer running for election as the sixteenth president of the United States is the focus of *Mr. Lincoln's Whiskers.* Although several other books are based on Grace's letter encouraging Lincoln to grow whiskers to make him look more presidential, Winnick enriches her tale with research that included reading original correspondence, tracking Grace to her home in upstate New York, and studying the history of Lincoln's presidential campaign. Based on the real-life story of an eleven-year-old girl living in Vicksburg, Mississippi in 1863, *Lucy's Cave* depicts the plight of the Confederate families forced to flee in the face of General Grant's in-

Karen B. Winnick tells the story of a resourceful young southerner in her civil-war story **Cassie's Sweet Berry Pie.** (Boyds Mills Press, 2005. Illustration copyright © 2005 by Karen Winnick. All rights reserved. Reproduced by permission.)

vading Union forces and hide in the caves near Vicksburg, Lucy McRae and her family join many others, surviving for over six weeks on meager rations. Winnick's picture-book text is based on McRae's actual narrative, and she pairs it with original oil paintings rendered in a primitive style that reflects her story's cultural setting.

Also set in the Confederate south, *Cassie's Sweet Berry Pie* finds older sister Cassie entrusted with the safety of her younger siblings when word comes that Union soldiers are raiding farms nearby. To demonstrate Cassie's quick thinking and resourcefulness, the author/illustrator creates "homespun" oil paintings that depict the "plucky heroine," according to *Booklist* critic Julie Cummins. Also reviewing *Cassie's Sweet Berry Pie*, Catherine Threadgill wrote in *School Library Journal* that "Winnick's engaging story is straightforward and easy to follow."

While most of Winnick's picture books take place during the U.S. Civil War, *Sybil's Night Ride* returns young readers to the first months of the American Revolution, as British troops attempted to route patriots from the farms of central Connecticut. When she learns that a nearby town has been set afire, sixteen-year-old Sybil Ludington jumps on her horse Star and rides to warn her father's colonial regiment so that they can save both property and lives on the night of April 26, 1777. In her *Booklist* review of *Sybil's Night Ride,* Ellen Mandel had special praise for Winnick's earth-toned illustrations, writing that her textured gouache paintings "evoke . . . the feelings of . . . flashing white raindrops cutting through the black night."

Biographical and Critical Sources

PERIODICALS

Booklist, December 15, 1996, Ilene Cooper, review of *Mr. Lincoln's Whiskers,* p. 734; March 1, 2000, Ellen Mandel, review of *Sybil's Night Ride,* p. 1253; May 15, 2002, Helen Rosenberg, review of *Barn Sneeze,* p. 1603; October 1, 2004, Karen Hutt, review of *The Night of the Fireflies,* p. 399; February 15, 2005, Julie Cummins, review of *Cassie's Sweet Berry Pie: A Civil War Story,* p. 1085.
Kirkus Reviews, October 1, 2008, review of *Lucy's Cave: A Civil War Story.*
School Library Journal, November, 2001, Sally R. Dow, review of *A Year Goes Round: Poems for the Months,* p. 2001; June, 2002, Melinda Piehler, review of *Barn Sneeze,* p. 116; October, 2004, Catherine Threadgill, review of *The Night of the Fireflies,* p. 136; March, 2005, Catherine Threadgill, review of *Cassie's Sweet Berry Pie,* p. 190; December, 2008, Kim T. Ha, review of *Lucy's Cave,* p. 107.

ONLINE

Karen B. Winnick Home Page, http://www.karenbwinnick.com (January 10, 2010).

*   *   *

WOOD, Jacqueline
See WOOD, Jakki

*   *   *

WOOD, Jakki 1957-
(Jacqueline Wood)

Personal

Born 1957, in England.

Addresses

Home—West Malvern, England.

Career

Author and illustrator of books for children.

Writings

SELF-ILLUSTRATED, UNLESS OTHERWISE NOTED

A Cat's Tail, Dinosaur (London, England), 1987.

In the Park, Hodder & Stoughton (London, England), 1989.

In the Canal, Hodder & Stoughton (London, England), 1989.

In the Countryside, Hodder & Stoughton (London, England), 1989.

Who's in My Garden?, Collins (London, England), 1989.

Happy Christmas, Ginger!, Collins (London, England), 1989.

One Bear with Bees in His Hair, ABC (London, England), 1990, Dutton Children's Books (New York, NY), 1991.

Dads Are Great Fun, ABC (London, England), 1991, published as *Dads Are Such Fun,* Simon & Schuster Books for Young Readers (New York, NY), 1992.

Moo Moo, Brown Cow, Have You Any . . . , illustrated by Rog Bonner, ABC Books (London, England), 1991, Harcourt Brace Jovanovich (San Diego, CA), 1992.

Animal Parade: A Wildlife Alphabet, Maxwell Macmillan International (New York, NY), 1993.

Fiddle-i-fee: A Noisy Nursery Rhyme, Bradbury Press (New York, NY), 1994.

Number Parade: A Wildlife Counting Book, Frances Lincoln (London, England), 1994.

One Tortoise, Ten Wallabies: A Wildlife Counting Book, Bradbury Press (New York, NY), 1994.

Jakki Wood's Animal Hullabaloo: A Wildlife Noisy Book, Macmillan Books for Young Readers (New York, NY), 1995, published as *Noisy Parade: A Hullabaloo Safari,* Francis Lincoln (London, England), 2002.

Bumper to Bumper: A Traffic Jam, Simon & Schuster Books for Young Readers (New York, NY), 1996.

The Deep Blue Sea: An Ocean Wildlife Book, Frances Lincoln (London, England), 1998, published as *Across the Big Blue Sea: An Ocean Wildlife Book,* National Geographic Society (Washington, DC), 1998.

March of the Dinosaurs: A Prehistoric Counting Book, Frances Lincoln (London, England), 1999.

Never Say Boo to a Goose!, illustrated by Clare Beaton, Barefoot Books (Cambridge, MA), 2002.

Baby Parade, Frances Lincoln (London, England), 2003.

A Hole in the Road, Frances Lincoln (London, England), 2008.

"IF YOU CHOOSE ME" BEGINNING READERS

Puppy, Franklin Watts (New York, NY), 1998.

Guinea Pig, Franklin Watts (New York, NY), 1998.

Kitten, Franklin Watts (New York, NY), 1998.

Rabbit, Franklin Watts (New York, NY), 1998.

"ROUNDABOUTS" SERIES

Anita Ganeri, *Into Space,* Barron's (New York, NY), 1993.

Kate Petty, *Maps and Journeys,* Barron's (Hauppauge, NY), 1993.

Anita Ganeri, *Deserts,* Barron's (New York, NY), 1993.

Anita Ganeri, *Rain Forests,* Barron's (Hauppauge, NY), 1993.

Kate Petty, *Our Globe, Our World,* Barron's (Hauppauge, NY), 1993.

Kate Petty, *The Ground below Us,* Barron's (Hauppauge, NY), 1993.

Kate Petty, *The Sky above Us,* Barron's Educational Series (Hauppauge, NY), 1993.

Anita Ganeri, *Under the Sea,* Barron's (New York, NY), 1993.

ILLUSTRATOR

Ann Morris, *The Bread Book,* Dinosaur (London, England), 1987.

Kate Petty, *A Stormy Day,* Hodder & Stoughton (London, England), 1988.

Kate Petty, *A Sunny Day,* Hodder & Stoughton (London, England), 1988.

Kate Petty, *A Windy Day,* Hodder & Stoughton (London, England), 1988.

Ann Turnbull, *There's a Monster under My Bed,* Aurum, 1990.

Donna Bryant, *My Dog Jessie,* Frances Lincoln (London, England), 1991.

Donna Bryant, *My Rabbit Bobbie,* Frances Lincoln (London, England), 1991.

Donna Bryant, *My Cat Buster,* Frances Lincoln (London, England), 1991.

Donna Bryant, *My Guinea Pigs Pip and Gus,* Frances Lincoln (London, England), 1991.

Joyce Dunbar, *Four Fierce Kittens,* Orchard Books (London, England), 1991

Lone Morton, *Goodnight Everyone: Buenas noches a todos,* B. Small Publishing, 1995.

Geraldine Taylor and Jill Harker, *Joe and the Farm Goose,* Picture Ladybird (Loughborough, England), 1995.

Sidelights

Jakki Wood is a prolific British writer and artist whose self-illustrated picture books and chapter books have entertained young children since the late 1980s. In addition to her own stories, which include *Fiddle-i-fee: A Noisy Nursery Rhyme, Bumper to Bumper: A Traffic Jam,* and *A Hole in the Road,* as well as the "If You Choose Me" series of pet-centered beginning readers, Wood has also contributed artwork to texts by authors that include Kate Petty, Donna Bryant, and Joyce Dunbar.

An early self-illustrated work by Wood, *One Bear with Bees in His Hair* is a counting tale that follows an ever-increasing number of honey bears as they enjoy a succession of lighthearted activities. Reviewing the book for *Publishers Weekly,* a critic praised Wood's "simple yet sprightly" text and "whimsical artwork." In *One Tortoise, Ten Wallabies: A Wildlife Counting Book,* an-

Jakki Wood's child-friendly illustrations and her simple text combine in popular board-book stories such as **Bumper to Bumper.** (Frances Lincoln Children's Books, 1996. Illustration copyright © 1996 by Jakki Wood. All rights reserved. Reproduced by permission.)

other concept book for the very young, she takes the action to the ocean in a story awash with "sheer exuberance," according to *Booklist* contributor Ilene Cooper.

In *Bumper to Bumper* Wood uses a busy city rush-hour to treat young children to an introduction to common cars, trucks, and other motorized vehicles and their uses. Her ink-and-watercolor images combine with her simple text to "provide elements of comic action," observed Carolyn Phelan in her *Booklist* review, while in *Publishers Weekly* a reviewer noted that "no two vehicles are alike, and each is clearly labeled." Construction equipment and its uses are profiled in a similar fashion in *A Hole in the Road,* another book that combines a brief text and engaging watercolor illustrations. "Wood incorporates great details into the art" in *A Hole in the Road,* asserted *School Library Journal* reviewer Lynn K. Vanca, and the human characters in her images reflect a "multicultural" work force.

In *Across the Big Blue Sea: An Ocean Wildlife Book* and *Animal Hullabaloo: A Wildlife Noisy Book* Wood draws from her engaging anima menagerie in introducing young children to the many creatures that share Planet Earth. In *Across the Big Blue Sea* a toy boat drifts from the coast of California across the seas to Australia, then to Africa, and ultimately to the coast of Great Britain where it is discovered by a young boy. On its voyage, the small craft encounters myriad fish and dolphins, as well as penguins and other water birds, resulting in what *Booklist* contributor Ellen Mandel described as a "sometimes lighthearted, occasionally dramatic, and always inviting" travelogue. Wood's "cheerful" watercolor paintings also enliven *Animal Hullabaloo,* according to a *Publishers Weekly* reviewer, the critic describing a picture book in which noisy animals from farm and field, suburban back yards, and the grasslands of Africa gather on the book's pages.

Biographical and Critical Sources

PERIODICALS

Booklist, June 1, 1994, Ilene Cooper, review of *Fiddle-i-fee: A Noisy Nursery Rhyme,* p. 1846; November 1, 1994, Ilene Cooper, review of *One Tortoise, Ten Wallabies: A Wildlife Counting Book,* p. 511; June 1, 1996, Carolyn Phelan, review of *Bumper to Bumper: A Traffic Jam,* p. 1737; May 1, 1998, Ellen Mandel, review of *Across the Big Blue Sea: An Ocean Wildlife Book,* p. 1524; December 1, 2002, Kathy Broderick, review of *Never Say Boo to a Goose!,* p. 680.

Kirkus Reviews, September 1, 2002, review of *Never Say Boo to a Goose!,* p. 1324; September 15, 2008, review of *A Hole in the Road.*

Publishers Weekly, December 14, 1990, review of *One Bear with Bees in His Hair,* p. 65; January 25, 1993, review of *Animal Parade,* p. 85; October 2, 1995, review of *Animal Hullabaloo: A Wildlife Noisy Book,* p. 72; June 10, 1996, review of *Bumper to Bumper,* p. 98; April 13, 1998, review of *Across the Big Blue Sea,* p. 74.

School Library Journal, November, 2002, Susan Pine, review of *Never Say Boo to a Goose!,* p. 140; December, 2008, Lynn K. Vanca, review of *A Hole in the Road,* p. 108.*

*   *   *

WOODRUFF, Elvira 1951-

Personal

Born June 19, 1951, in Somerville, NJ; daughter of John (a truck driver) and Francis G. (a nurse) Pirozzi; married David Woodruff (divorced); children: Noah, Jess. *Education:* Attended Adelphi University, 1970-71, and Boston University, 1971-72.

Addresses

Home—Martins Creek, PA.

Career

Writer. Worked variously as a janitor, gardener, baker, window decorator, ice-cream truck driver, storyteller, and library aide; owner of toy, clothing, and miscellany store in Clinton, NJ.

Awards, Honors

Numerous child-voted state awards, including Missouri Mark Twain Book Award, Oklahoma Sequoyah Children's Book Award, and West Virginia Children's Book Award, all for *Dear Napoleon, I Know You're Dead, But—*.

Writings

Awfully Short for the Fourth Grade, illustrated by Will Hillenbrand, Holiday House (New York, NY), 1989.

Tubtime, illustrated by Suçie Stevenson, Holiday House (New York, NY), 1990.

The Summer I Shrank My Grandmother, illustrated by Katherine Coville, Holiday House (New York, NY), 1990.

The Wing Shop, illustrated by Stephen Gammell, Holiday House (New York, NY), 1991.

Show and Tell, illustrated by Denise Brunkus, Holiday House (New York, NY), 1991.

Back in Action, illustrated by Will Hillenbrand, Holiday House (New York, NY), 1991.

Mrs. McClosky's Monkeys, illustrated by Jill Kastner, Scholastic, Inc. (New York, NY), 1991.

George Washington's Socks, Scholastic, Inc. (New York, NY), 1991.

The Disappearing Bike Shop, Holiday House (New York, NY), 1992.

Dear Napoleon, I Know You're Dead, But—, illustrated by Noah and Jess Woodruff, Holiday House (New York, NY), 1992.

The Secret Funeral of Slim Jim the Snake, Holiday House (New York, NY), 1993.

Ghosts Don't Get Goose Bumps, illustrated by Joel Iskowitz, Holiday House (New York, NY), 1993.

The Magnificent Mummy Maker, Scholastic, Inc. (New York, NY), 1994.

Dear Levi: Letters from the Overland Trail, illustrated by Ruth Peck, Knopf (New York, NY), 1994.

A Dragon in My Backpack, illustrated by Denise Brunkus, Troll Associates (Metuchen, NJ), 1996.

The Orphan of Ellis Island: A Time Travel Adventure, Scholastic, Inc. (New York, NY), 1997.

Dear Austin: Letters from the Underground Railroad, illustrated by Nancy Carpenter, Knopf (New York, NY), 1998.

The Christmas Doll, Scholastic, Inc. (New York, NY), 1998.

The Memory Coat, illustrated by Michael Dooling, Scholastic, Inc. (New York, NY), 1998.

Can You Guess Where We're Going?, illustrated by Cynthia Fisher, Holiday House (New York, NY), 1998.

The Ghost of Lizard Light, Knopf (New York, NY), 1999.

The Ravenmaster's Secret: Escape from the Tower of London, Scholastic, Inc. (New York, NY), 2003.

Small Beauties: The Journey of Darcy Heart O'Hara, illustrated by Adam Rex, Alfred A. Knopf (New York, NY), 2006.

Fearless, Scholastic, Inc. (New York, NY), 2007.

Adaptations

The Christmas Doll was adapted for the stage by Joan Cushing and produced in Charlotte, NC, 2007.

Sidelights

Elvira Woodruff combines history and magic in equal measure in her novels and picture books for young readers. With stories such as *Awfully Short for the Fourth Grade* and *The Disappearing Bike Shop,* the time-travel fantasy *Dear Napoleon, I Know You're Dead, But—,* and the historical novels *The Ravenmaster's Secret: Escape from the Tower of London* and *Fearless,* she spans a broad readership, from the read-aloud set to middle graders. Reviewing *The Summer I Shrank My Grandmother,* a *Publishers Weekly* contributor commented

Elvra Woodruff's imaginative story in **The Wing Shop** *is brought to life in Stephen Gammell's detailed illustrations.* (Illustration copyright © 1991 by Stephen Gammell. Reproduced by permission of Holiday House, Inc.)

that "Woodruff seems to know all the tricks for holding a middle grade audience: blending elements of magic, fast-paced action and a dab of levity, she produces an irresistible tale."

"Becoming a writer has been one of the most pleasant surprises I've had in my life," Woodruff once told *SATA*. Born in New Jersey, she wrote her first poem at age nine. "I can remember sitting at the dining room table with my pencil and paper and feeling as if I had just discovered something really wonderful," she recalled. "I had. It was the joy of creating. It was the same feeling I had when I completed my first piece of embroidery, planted my first garden, painted my first picture."

Despite this discovery, it would be several decades before Woodruff embraced her calling as a writer. After attending college as an English literature major for two years, she left for the world of work, and for the next fifteen years held a series of jobs that included receptionist, window-dresser, and library aide. She also married and raised two sons, which provided her a second exposure to children's books. "It was like coming back to an old love," she once recalled to *SATA*. Taking up writing in her thirties, Woodruff was fortunate to have the aid of her cousin, author and illustrator Frank Asch, who provided advice with both manuscript preparation and the steps to selecting a publisher. "He looked over my work, offered suggestions, and basically held my hand through the births of those first efforts." Woodruff's first manuscript, the picture-book text *Mrs. Mc-Closky's Monkeys,* was eventually published, but only after several other Woodruff titles had arrived on bookstore shelves.

After a divorce required her to earn a more stable income, and the sale of her second manuscript, *Tubtime,* suggested that there was a living to be made in children's books, Woodruff converted her sewing table to a desk and exchanged her sewing machine for a computer. Her instincts proved correct: during her first years she published three or more books a year, moving from picture books such as *The Wing Shop* and *Show and Tell* to historical novels for older readers. In the early 1990s she added speaker to her profession, and began to talk to young people about what it is like to be an author.

In *Tubtime,* which Ilene Cooper praised in *Booklist* for showing that "bath time has never been more fun," three little sisters take a bath together after a mud fight. While talking on the telephone downstairs, their mother keeps yelling up to the children to see if they are doing all right. Meanwhile, the girls have begun blowing soap bubbles, and each becomes magically stuffed with an animal: a chicken, a frog, even an alligator. "The fantastic happenings in the bathroom . . . escalate with impunity," Cooper added, concluding that *Tubtime* "bubbl[es] . . . over with good cheer." Praised as "lighthearted" by *School Library Journal* reviewer Liza Bliss, *Tubtime* contains the fantasy elements that have been featured in many of Woodruff's more recent works.

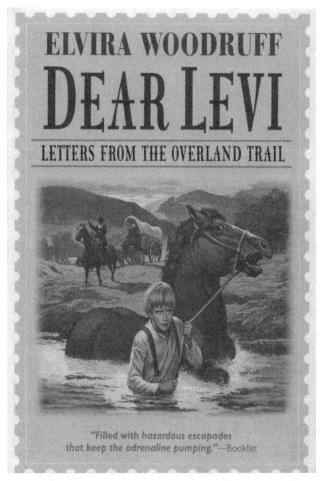

Cover of Woodruff's historical epistolary novel Dear Levi, *featuring artwork by Bill Maughan.* (Cover art copyright © 1998 by Bill Maughan. Used by permission of Alfred A. Knopf, an imprint of Random House Children's Books, a division of Random House, Inc.)

More fantasy is served up in *The Wing Shop,* which tells the story of a boy who is disappointed by his family's move to a new neighborhood until he views it from up on high via a pair of special wings purchased at Featherman's Wing Shop. In another picture book, *Show and Tell,* a boy searching for the perfect object for a class presentation finds a bottle of bubbles in the grass; when the bubbles land on his teacher and fellow students, they cause these people to shrink down to the size of a spec and float about the room and then out the window on an airborne adventure. Once safely enlarged and back in class, all agree that Andy's was the best show and tell ever. *Horn Book* contributor Nancy Vasilakis commented of *The Wing Shop* that Woodruff's "simple story, with its reassuring theme of change and acceptance, is filled out and given added meaning by Stephen Gammell's exuberant and wildly improbable illustrations." *Show and Tell* also received praise; "Any kid who has ever brought a dopey item for show-and-tell . . . will relish Andy's success," concluded Cooper in a review of the story for *Booklist.*

Illustrated by Adam Rex, Woodruff's picture book *Small Beauties: The Journey of Darcy Heart O'Hara* draws on the author's love of history in its story about an Irish

Cover of Woodruff's middle-grade novel **The Ravenmaster's Secret,** *featuring cover art by Dan Craig.* (Jacket illustration copyright © 2003 by Dan Craig. Reproduced by permission of Scholastic, Inc.)

girl who, in 1835, learns that she and her family must leave their home for America due to the potato famine that has destroyed the region's main source of food. Noting the deep emotions in Woodruff's story, Hazel Rochman added praise *Booklist* for the book's pairing of "simple, poetic storytelling" and Rex's dramatic graphite-and-oil artwork. In her "smooth and descriptive prose," the author "subtly captures the lilt of the Irish dialect," wrote Lee Bock in his *School Library Journal* review of *Small Beauties,* and a contributor to *Kirkus Reviews* praised the book for setting "a little history in a lovely story."

In the first of Woodruff's popular middle-grade novels, *Awfully Short for the Fourth Grade,* young Noah finds a packet of magic dust in the gumball machine. Surprisingly, the dust actually works, making the boy shrink to the size of his plastic toy action figures. Now Lilliputian in size, he joins his toys in an adventure, proving how treacherous the school yard can be for a little guy. Noah and his new companions have several close shaves with the school bully and a rapacious hamster before he returns to normal size. A critic for *Kirkus Reviews* noted that "Woodruff wins some chuckles with her humorous depiction of grade-school subcultures . . . and her topic will be dear to the heart of any child who collects little

plastic creatures." Elaine Fort Weischedel concluded in *School Library Journal* that *Awfully Short for the Fourth Grade* "is pleasant fare and a promising debut for Woodruff," while *Booklist* reviewer Denise Wilms dubbed the book a "breezy adventure, with particular appeal for boys."

Noah returns in *Back in Action,* in which the nine year old is still a fan of plastic action figures. This time, he brings friend Nate along on his small-scale adventures, but when the shrinking powder brings Nate's toy monster to life, the boy's adventures become a battle for survival; Noah must learn some fast leadership skills in order to deploy his action figures and battle the hungry monster. Elaine E. Knight, writing in *School Library Journal,* noted that Woodruff affirms "the value of individual initiative and cooperative effort" in her "light-fantasy adventure," while in *Booklist* contributor Linda Callaghan deemed the book's mix of action tale and fantasy "ripe with clever plot action, excitement, and humor." Kathryn Pierson Jennings commented in a review of *Back in Action* for the *Bulletin of the Center for Children's Books* that the novelist "knows boys' fantasies—endless candy, a working space station and plane to fly in, and a real army."

George Washington's Socks takes the reader back to the American Revolution as Matthew, his sister Kate, and three friends board an old rowboat and are transported back in time. Poorly dressed for the weather, Kate receives the gift of a pair of warm socks from the chivalrous Washington himself. Renaissance artist Leonardo da Vinci plays a supporting role in *The Disappearing Bike Shop,* in which Tyler and best friend Freckle grow suspicious over a bike shop that seems to disappear and reappear on a vacant lot. Finally building up their courage, they enter the shop and encounter the strange owner, Quigley, who has a secret room full of inventions and amazing drawings. Later, working on a school report on Leonardo da Vinci, Tyler becomes convinced that Quigley is the reincarnation of the Italian inventor/ artist. *School Library Journal* contributor Jana R. Fine noted that "Woodruff's story combines mystery, suspense, and an element of danger into a rollicking good adventure," and added that "readers will be drawn into the smoothly building plot and find that the past can be truly exciting."

Napoleon Bonaparte plays a walk-on role in *Dear Napoleon, I Know You're Dead, But—,* a story centering on another school assignment. Writing letters to historical figures can be boring . . . that is, until the intended recipient actually begins to write back. When Marty's letter to the long-dead French emperor is relayed via the boy's crusty but lovable grandfather, Marty receives a surprise: a response, postmarked from Paris, from Emperor Napoleon Bonaparte himself! Marty thinks it is one of Grandfather's tricks, until the elderly man dies, and after the funeral a grieving Marty receives a letter from artist Vincent Van Gogh. Todd Morning, reviewing *Dear Napoleon, I Know You're Dead, But—* in

School Library Journal, wrote that Woodruff's book maintains "a nice balance . . . between the story's serious elements and the humorous, fantastic parts," and added that the "affectionate relationship between Marty and his grandfather is particularly well rendered."

History takes on another time-travel aspect in *The Orphan of Ellis Island.* In this novel Dominic has no heritage to share in his fifth-grade discussion on family backgrounds because he has spent much of his life in foster care. A visit to New York's Ellis Island with his class as well as his effort to escape an uncomfortable moment result in a trip back in time. Finding himself in Italy in 1908, Dominic is befriended by orphaned brothers en route for America, and he shares their immigrant adventures in this "enjoyable and informative tale," according to Susan L. Rogers in *School Library Journal.*

A more-conventional sort of history is served up in the companion books *Dear Levi: Letters from the Overland Trail* and *Dear Austin: Letters from the Underground Railway.* In both titles Woodruff employs the epistolary format to tell her historical tales. *Dear Levi* follows Austin Ives, a twelve-year-old orphan, as he sets out in 1851 for the Oregon Territory and writes to his brother, Levi, in Pennsylvania about the adventures he experiences on his pioneering trip. *Booklist* reviewer Deborah Abbott concluded that *Dear Levi* makes for "solid reading," while Elizabeth Bush noted in the *Bulletin of the Center for Children's Books* that "Woodruff presents a bounty of information in a format that will be especially valued as a classroom readaloud." Discussing the sequel in *School Library Journal,* Janet Gillen noted that Levi's letters back to his brother in *Dear Austin* telling of his adventures aiding escaping slaves on the Underground Railroad serve as an "emotional and gripping tale of one boy's confrontations with the issue of slavery and its significance in American history."

In *The Ravenmaster's Secret* Woodruff takes her interest in history farther afield, setting the middle-grade novel in England. The year is 1735, a brutal time that is overshadowed by Scotland's efforts to gain independence from English rule. Eleven-year-old Forrest lives at the Tower of London, a prison where some of the inmates are condemned to face death at a public hanging. Forrest's father, a ravenmaster, cares for the birds living in the tower and also brings food to the prisoners held there. When one of the prisoners condemned to death turns out to be a young Scottish rebel named Maddy, Forrest sees a new side of the Scottish cause. Together with his pet raven Tuck, Forrest helps Maddy plot her path to freedom in a novel that *School Library Journal* reviewer Bruce Ann Shook praised for containing "suspense, excitement, and interesting characters." In *Booklist* Carolyn Phelan cited *The Ravenmaster's Secret* as "an absorbing historical adventure with a unique and colorful setting," adding that Woodruff's inclusion of a glossary of period terms and a background essay on the Tower of London is an "unusual but welcome" aid for young history buffs. A *Publishers Weekly* reviewer

added that Woodruff "has much to say about the nature of war, judgment and prejudice" in her thoughtful text, while a *Childhood Education* reviewer dubbed *The Ravenmaster's Secret* "a real page turner."

Another work of historical fiction, *Fearless* is set in the early 1700s, and follows eleven-year-old Digory Beale and younger brother Cubby as they travel from their home in Cornwall to Plymouth, England, in search of their father, a sailor who has been missing since a harsh storm. Alone and vulnerable to scaliwags, the boys are jailed as thieves and sentenced to death until a quirky inventor named Henry Winstanley rescues them and makes Digory his apprentice. In bringing to life the difficulties of life in eighteenth-century England, Woodruff captures the realities of people living along the Cornish coast, "adding authenticity with many colorful local expressions," according to *Booklist* critic Todd Morning. In *School Library Journal* Nancy P. Reeder praised *Fearless* as "fascinating" and "well-written," noting that Woodruff bases her novel on the life of the actual Winstanley, "one of the leading inventors of the day," and his efforts to perfect the lighthouse technology that would save the loss of life caused by ships run ground on England's treacherous rocky coastline

Cover of Woodruff's young-adult mystery Fearless, *featuring artwork by Bagram Ibatoulline.* (Jacket art copyright © 2008 by Bagram Ibatoulline. Reproduced by permission of Scholastic, Inc.)

Whether writing lighthearted fare about the shrinking adventures of a fourth-grader, or more hard-hitting stories of young people caught in the maw of history, Woodruff employs a keen observer's eye and a wry sense of humor. "I've found that writing is an organic process, unfolding from one's life," she once told *SATA*. "What you have to do as a writer is feel, look, and listen. Your stories then become a celebration of these observations."

Biographical and Critical Sources

PERIODICALS

Booklist, January 1, 1990, Denise Wilms, review of *Awfully Short for the Fourth Grade,* p. 922; April 1, 1990, Ilene Cooper, review of *Tubtime,* p. 1561 September 15, 1991, Ilene Cooper, review of *Show and Tell,* pp. 167-168; January 15, 1992, Linda Callaghan, review of *Back in Action,* p. 941 July, 1994, Deborah Abbott, review of *Dear Levi: Letters from the Overland Trail,* p. 1949; January 1, 2004, Carolyn Phelan, review of *The Ravenmaster's Secret: Escape from the Tower of London,* p. 864; August 1, 2006, Hazel Rochman, review of *Small Beauties: The Journey of Darcy Heart O'Hara,* p. 94; May 1, 2008, Todd Morning, review of *Fearless,* p. 86.

Bulletin of the Center for Children's Books, January, 1992, Kathryn Pierson Jennings, review of *Back in Action,* p. 142; September, 1994, Elizabeth Bush, review of *Dear Levi,* pp. 28-29.

Childhood Education, summer, 2004, review of *The Ravenmaster's Secret,* p. 215.

Horn Book, May-June, 1991, Nancy Vasilakis, review of *The Wing Shop,* p. 327.

Kirkus Reviews, September 1, 1989, review of *Awfully Short for the Fourth Grade,* p. 1335; October 15, 2003, review of *The Ravenmaster's Secret,* p. 1277; August 15, 2006, review of *Small Beauties,* p. 854; March 15, 2008, review of *Fearless.*

New York Times Book Review, June 16, 1991, review of *The Wing Shop,* p. 25.

Publishers Weekly, November 2, 1990, review of *The Summer I Shrank My Grandmother,* p. 74; September 25, 2000, review of *The Christmas Doll,* p. 74; January 5, 2004, review of *The Ravenmaster's Secret,* p. 62.

School Library Journal, November, 1989, Elaine Fort Weischedel, review of *Awfully Short for the Fourth Grade,* p. 116; July, 1990, Liza Bliss, review of *Tubtime,* p. 66; June, 1991, Ruth Semrau, review of *Mrs. McClosky's Monkeys,* p. 93; November, 1991, Eve Larkin, review of *The Wing Shop,* p. 109, and Bruce Anne Shook, review of *George Washington's Socks,* p. 125; December, 1991, Elaine E. Knight, review of *Back in Action,* pp. 119-120; May, 1992, Jana R. Fine, review of *The Disappearing Bike Shop,* p. 117; October, 1992, Todd Morning, review of *Dear Napoleon, I Know You're Dead, But—,* pp. 123-124; May, 1997, Susan L. Rogers, review of *The Orphan of Ellis Island,* p. 140; October, 1998, Janet Gillen, review of *Dear Austin: Letters from the Underground Railway,* p. 148; October, 2000, review of *The Christmas Doll,* p. 64; January, 2004, Bruce Anne Shook, review of *The Ravenmaster's Secret,* p. 138; September, 2006, Lee Bock, review of *Small Beauties,* p. 188; April, 2008, Nancy P. Reeder, review of *Fearless,* p. 154.

ONLINE

Elvira Woodruff Home Page, http://www.ewoodruff.com (January 10, 2010).*

Y-Z

YEE, Paul 1956-

Personal

Born October 1, 1956, in Spalding, Saskatchewan, Canada; son of Gordon and Gim May Yee. *Education:* University of British Columbia, B.A., 1978, M.A. (Canadian history), 1983. *Hobbies and other interests:* Cycling, swimming.

Addresses

Home—Toronto, Ontario, Canada. *E-mail*—paulyee@sympatico.ca.

Career

Writer. City of Vancouver Archives, Vancouver, British Columbia, Canada, assistant city archivist, 1980-88; Archives of Ontario, Toronto, Ontario, Canada, portfolio manager, 1988-91; Ontario Ministry of Citizenship, policy analyst, 1991-97.

Member

Writers Union of Canada, Canadian Society of Children's Authors, Illustrators, and Performers.

Awards, Honors

Honourable Mention, Canada Council Prizes for Children's Literature, 1986, for *The Curses of Third Uncle;* Vancouver Book Prize, 1989, for *Saltwater City;* British Columbia Book Prize for Children's Literature, I.O.D.E. Violet Downey Book Award, Sheila A. Egoff Children's Book Prize, and Parents' Choice Honor Book designation, all 1990, all for *Tales from Gold Mountain;* Ruth Schwartz Award, Canadian Booksellers Association, 1992, for *Roses Sing on New Snow,* and 1997, for *Ghost Train;* Governor General's Award, Canada Council, 1996, and Prix Enfantasie (Switzerland), 1998, both for *Ghost Train;* YALSA Best Books for Young Adults listee, 1998, for *Breakaway;* Kiryama Pacific Rim Prize Notable Book designation, 2002, and Sunburst Award

Paul Yee (Reproduced by permission.)

nomination, and Books for the Teen Age listee, New York Public Library, both 2003, all for *Dead Man's Gold;* Vancouver Book Award finalist, 2004, and Rocky Mountain Book Award shortlist, 2006, both for *The Bone Collector's Son;* Christie Harris Illustrated Children's Literature Prize nomination, 2006, for *Bamboo* illustrated by Shaoli Wang.

Writings

FICTION FOR CHILDREN AND YOUNG ADULTS

Teach Me to Fly, Skyfighter!, and Other Stories, illustrated by Sky Lee, Lorimer (Toronto, Ontario, Canada), 1983.

The Curses of Third Uncle (novel), Lorimer (Toronto, Ontario, Canada), 1986.

Tales from Gold Mountain: Stories of the Chinese in the New World, illustrated by Simon Ng, Groundwood Books (Toronto, Ontario, Canada), 1989, Macmillan (New York, NY), 1990.

Roses Sing on New Snow: A Delicious Tale, illustrated by Harvey Chan, Macmillan (New York, NY), 1991.

Breakaway (novel), Groundwood Books (Toronto, Ontario, Canada), 1994.

Moonlight's Luck, illustrated by Terry Yee, Macmillan (New York, NY), 1995.

Ghost Train, illustrated by Harvey Chan, Groundwood Books (New York, NY), 1996.

The Boy in the Attic, illustrated by Gu Xiong, Groundwood Books (Toronto, Ontario, Canada), 1998.

Dead Man's Gold, and Other Stories, illustrated by Harvey Chan, Douglas & McIntyre (Berkley, CA), 2002.

The Jade Necklace, illustrated by Grace Lin, Interlink, 2002.

The Bone Collector's Son, Tradewind Books (Vancouver, British Columbia, Canada), 2003, Marshall Cavendish (New York, NY), 2004.

A Song for Ba, illustrated by Jan Peng Wang, Douglas & McIntyre (Berkeley, CA), 2004.

Bamboo, illustrated by Shaoli Wang, Tradewind Books (Vancouver, British Columbia, Canada), 2005.

What Happened This Summer (stories), Tradewind Books (Vancouver, British Columbia, Canada), 2006.

Shu-Li and Tamara, illustrated by Shaoli Wang, Tradewind Books (Vancouver, British Columbia, Canada), 2007.

Learning to Fly, Orca Book Publishers (Victoria, British Columbia, Canada), 2008.

Shu-Li and Diego, illustrated by Shaoli Wang, Tradewind Books (Vancouver, British Columbia, Canada), 2009.

NONFICTION

Saltwater City: An Illustrated History of the Chinese in Vancouver, Douglas & McIntyre (Vancouver, British Columbia, Canada), 1988, University of Washington (Seattle, WA), 1989, reprinted, Douglas & McIntyre (Berkeley, CA), 2006.

Struggle and Hope: The Story of Chinese Canadians, Umbrella Press (Toronto, Ontario, Canada), 1996.

Chinatown: An Illustrated History of the Chinese Communities of Victoria, Vancouver, Calgary, Winnipeg, Toronto, Ottawa, Montréal, and Halifax, James Lorimer (Toronto, Ontario, Canada), 2005.

Yee's work has been translated into several languages, including French.

Adaptations

Roses Sing on New Snow was adapted as a videocassette produced by the National Film Board of Canada, 2002. "The Friends of Kwan Ming," from *Tales from Gold Mountain,* was adapted as an animated film by the National Film Board of Canada, 2002. *Ghost Train* was adapted for the stage by Lorraine Kimsa for Young People's Theatre of Toronto, 2001.

Sidelights

Paul Yee is an award-winning Canadian writer whose Chinese heritage and experiences growing up in the Chinatown region of Vancouver, British Columbia, have inspired many of his highly acclaimed books for younger readers. While writing primarily for Canadian children of Chinese ancestry who desire to learn about themselves and their heritage, Yee's books have also found audiences among children of many backgrounds living in both Canada and the United States. Among Yee's books are the short-story collections *Tales from Gold Mountain: Stories of the Chinese in the New World, Dead Man's Gold, and Other Stories,* and *What Happened This Summer,* as well as picture books and novels that include *Breakaway, The Curses of Third Uncle,* and *Learning to Fly.* Despite his relatively small output, "by fusing the unique details of ethnic experience with the universal concerns for identity and love," a *Canadian Children's Books* essayist maintained, Yee has "made a notable contribution to Canadian children's literature."

Born in Spalding, Saskatchewan, in 1956, Yee had what he once termed a "typical Chinese-Canadian childhood, caught between two worlds, and yearning to move away from the neighborhood." While he wrote short stories

Cover of Yee's novel **Learning to Fly,** *which focuses on a Chinese immigrant trying to find his place within his new Canadian culture.* (Orca Book Publishers, 2008. Cover photography © by Getty Images. Reproduced by permission.)

as a hobby, he never considered making writing his profession. Instead, after graduating from high school Yee attended the University of British Columbia and ultimately earned his M.A. in history in 1983. Although Yee has taught informally at several institutions in British Columbia, the focus of his career has been on his work as an archivist and policy analyst, organizing and analyzing information for government agencies in Canada.

Although it seems a far cry from archivist/analyst to children's book author, Yee found the step to be a natural one, given his circumstances and interests. "Back in 1983, I was involved in doing work for Chinatown, such as organizing festivals, exhibits, and educational programs," he explained. "Even though I had written some short stories, I had not done anything in children's literature. A Canadian publishing company, Lorimer, knowing about my work in the Chinese community, asked me to write a children's book that would employ my knowledge of Chinese-Canadian life as a background." The result of this request was *Teach Me to Fly, Skyfighter!, and Other Stories,* Yee's first book for children.

Yee's second short-story collection, *Tales from Gold Mountain,* was published in 1989 to high praise from critics. Lee Galda and Susan Cox, writing in *Reading Teacher,* observed that the eight stories included in the book "give . . . voice to the previously unheard generations of Chinese immigrants whose labor supported the settlement of the west coast of Canada and the United States." Yee includes stories about the conflict between the manager of a fish cannery and his greedy boss; a young man who arranges the burial of Chinese railroad workers after he meets his father's ghost; a young woman's gift of ginger root to save her fiancée's life; a wealthy merchant who exchanges his twin daughters for sons; and clashes between old traditions and new influences. Betsy Hearne noted in the *Bulletin of the Center for Children's Books* that "Yee never indulges in stylistic pretensions" in blending realism and legend, and praised the stories for containing "mythical overtones that lend the characters unforgettable dimension—humans achieving supernatural power in defying their fate of physical and cultural oppression." *School Library Journal* contributor Margaret A. Chang praised Yee for "further expand[ing] and enhanc[ing] understanding of the Chinese immigrant experience," while a *Horn Book* reviewer praised *Tales from Gold Mountain* for interweaving "the hardships and dangers of frontier life in a new country with the ancient attitudes and traditions brought over from China" and predicted that the images created "will stay with the reader for a long time."

Dead Man's Gold and Other Stories contains ten tales that combine real life and the supernatural, while the nine tales in *What Happened This Summer* focus on the experiences of Chinese immigrants spending their teen years in Canada. Against the backdrop of a harsh exist-

ence comprised of hard labor in gold mines, on railroads, and in family-run businesses, the protagonists in *Dead Man's Gold, and Other Stories* long for home and family as they face prejudices while trying to build a better life. In these stories, each accompanied by an appropriately haunting illustration by Harvey Chan, Yee's characters are also tested by unearthly horrors of one sort or another. Calling *Dead Man's Gold, and Other Stories* "a remarkable piece of literature," Laura Reilly added in *Resource Links* that Yee's tales "have surprising twists that compel the reader to read on," and *Booklist* critic Jennifer Mattson dubbed *What Happened This Summer* "a thoughtful examination of a little-known cultural clash."

Yee's first novel, *The Curses of Third Uncle,* is a work of historical fiction that deals with the period of the early twentieth century in which Sun Yat-Sen's revolutionary movement fought against the Chinese Empire. Dr. Sun Yat-Sen, called the "Father of Modern China," had led nine uprisings against the empire by the time he visited Vancouver in 1910 and 1911. Yee's protagonist, fourteen-year-old Lillian, lives in Vancouver's Chinatown and misses her father, who often travels back to China and throughout the British Columbian frontier, presumably to take care of his clothing business. He is actually a secret agent for Dr. Sun's revolutionary movement. At one point in his travels, Lillian's father fails to return. His absence is economically hard on the family, but Lillian will not believe her father has deserted them. Her third uncle, however, threatens to send Lillian's family back to China. In her attempts to locate her father by traveling through British Columbia, Lillian discovers that he has been betrayed by his brother, who has been paid to turn him over to his enemies. Reviewing the novel in *Emergency Librarian,* Christine Dewar called *The Curses of Third Uncle* "a story that is exciting but contrived, with an attractive and reasonably motivated heroine." *Quill & Quire* writer Annette Goldsmith similarly commented that Yee's novel is "an exciting, fast-pace, well-written tale," and praised the author for his use of legendary Chinese female warriors to reinforce Lillian's story.

Set in Vancouver's Chinatown in 1932 during the Great Depression, *Breakaway* "explores questions of identity and belonging by detailing conflicts between generations and cultures," according to a *Canadian Children's Books* essayist. A senior in high school, Kwok-Ken Wong hopes a soccer scholarship will save him from an otherwise dismal future working on his father's farm. When his plans are dashed and racism prevents him from playing the sport he loves, Kwok-Ken grows disillusioned but ultimately grows in understanding as he begins to appreciate the strengths of his cultural heritage. Reviewing *Breakaway* in *Quill & Quire,* Patty Lawlor called the book "a well-written novel with staying power" that would be useful in discussions of racism. While noting that the novel's ending is "rather abrupt," *Canadian Review of Materials* contributor Mar-

Cover of Yee's middle-grade novel **Breakaway,** *featuring cover art by* **Laurie McGaw.** (Groundwood Books, 1997. Reproduced by permission of Groundwood Books.)

garet Mackey praised Yee's novel for painting "a valuable picture of a fascinating and complex time and world."

In *The Bone Collector's Son,* a novel that *Horn Book* contributor Vicky Smith described as "an unusual ghost story," Yee sets his story in 1907 Vancouver. Here fourteen-year-old Bing-wing Chan is forced to help his father dig up the bones of dead Chinese and return them to their homeland. Although the superstitious teen manages to avoid helping with the grisly task by finding another job, he worries for his father's health after a headless corpse is unearthed and the man now seems to be failing rapidly. For Jason Shen, the seventeen-year-old protagonist in *Learning to Fly,* present-day life is also troubled because of the boy's isolation. Recently arrived from China, Jason feels isolated in small-town Canada, but when he finds acceptance with a group of trouble makers the teen is ultimately forced to reassess his choices. Praising *The Bone Collector's Son* as "a gripping story of a boy caught between physical and

spiritual worlds," *Booklist* reviewer Gillian Engberg added that Yee "skillfully" weaves together themes of prejudice and the desire for cultural roots. In reviewing *Learning to Fly,* *Booklist* contributor Hazel Rochman described the novel as a "gripping friendship story" in which Yee's "clipped dialogue perfectly echoes" the teen's efforts to deal with adversity. In *Kliatt* Sharon Blumberg also recommended the novel as a "quick read for reluctant YA readers," and a *Kirkus Reviews* critic wrote that Yee's "spare writing style . . . is well suited" to the reluctant-reader genre.

In addition to novels and short fiction for older readers, Yee has also made the Chinese-Canadian heritage come vividly to life for younger readers. Maylin, the heroine of his picture book *Roses Sing on New Snow,* embodies the difference between the Old World and the New World when she explains to the governor of South China, who is visiting her father's Chinatown restaurant to learn the secrets of her delicious recipes, that "this is a dish of the New World. . . . You cannot re-create it in the Old." Although efforts are made to push Maylin aside and allow the men of the family to take credit for the restaurant's excellent fare, after her father and brothers cannot reproduce the meals served to the governor, Maylin is called forth and ultimately shown to be one of the most talented cooks in Chinatown. Hearne noted in the *Bulletin of the Center for Children's Books* that "vivid art and clean writing are graced by a neatly feminist ending."

Other picture books by Yee include *The Jade Necklace, The Boy in the Attic,* and the award-winning *Ghost Train. The Jade Necklace* focuses on Yenyee, a young girl whose fisherman father presents her with a necklace with a carved jade fish, then is lost at sea soon after. Giving the necklace to the sea in the hope that it will return her father to her, Yenyee goes on to immigrate to the New World as a nanny before the sea responds to her request in a surprising way. In *Quill & Quire* Sherie Posesorski praised *The Jade Necklace* as "a coming-of-age tale that's both contemporary and timeless, realistic and symbolic," and added that Yee's prose "seamlessly marries the formality of the storyteller's voice with the intimacy of a child's perspective."

An immigrant family's tradition of performing in traditional Chinese opera is threatened in *A Song for Ba,* a story brought to life in detailed paintings by illustrated by Jan Peng Wang. Wei Lim enjoys watching both his father and grandfather perform the traditional male and female roles in Chinese opera, but in their new home in Canada, Chinese residents prefer modern movies over traditional stage entertainments. While his father encourages Wei Lim to adopt the new ways, Grandfather teaches the boy several of the traditional opera roles before he returns to China. As the months go by and audiences continue to dwindle, the boy fears that he will never have the chance to take his turn on the family's stage. However, he finds a way to help his father rekindle interest in the art form when a new production is

staged in a picture book *Resource Links* contributor Laura Reilly described as a "powerful tale" that combines the real-life "hardships of Chinese immigrants" with a "touching story of the evolving relationship between father and son." Also reviewing *A Song for Ba*, a *Kirkus Reviews* writer recommended Yee's picture book as "an unusual immigrant story [that] offers a fascinating glimpse into an unfamiliar art form," while *Booklist* critic Linda Perkins cited it as "an excellent choice for music and cultural studies."

Winner of Canada's prestigious Governor General's award, *Ghost Train* focuses on a talented young artist named Choon-yi. The boy's father, a railway worker, is killed only days before Choon-yi arrives from China to join him, leaving the talented boy to find his own way in life. In *The Boy in the Attic* seven-year-old Chinese immigrant Kai-ming discovers the ghost of a boy who died in Kai-ming's new Canadian home eighty years before. Through the intervention of a magic butterfly, the two boys are able to break through their language barrier and converse, helping Kai-ming make the transition to his new country. Praising Yee's use of the ghost as a metaphor, *Quill & Quire* contributor Freida Ling described *The Boy in the Attic* as a tale of "human courage, resourcefulness, and the adaptability required to uproot yourself from your homeland and start over in a strange country."

Yee's award-winning picture book Ghost Train *is brought to life in Harvey Chan's evocative art.* (Illustration copyright © 1996 by Harvey Chan. All rights reserved. Reproduced by permission of Groundwood Books.)

A story for beginning readers that is illustrated by Shaoli Wang, *Shu-Li and Tamara* focuses on two fourth-grade girls who become good friends despite their differing backgrounds. Although a fellow classmate starts spreading a rumor suggesting that Tamara has stolen money from the school's bake-sale proceeds, Shu-Li stands by her new friend. Despite warnings from her parents, she continues to defend Tamara when more money goes missing, and ultimately her clear thinking helps point attention to the true thief. Noting the story's multicultural focus, *Booklist* critic Carolyn Phelan recommended *Shu-Li and Tamara* for its focus on "cultural differences" as well as "themes on friendship and loyalty," while in *Resource Links* Michelle Gowans described Yee's book as "a terrific little story that celebrates diversity."

Although Yee's primary career was as an historian, he has found no difficulty making the switch to fiction. Nevertheless, he once remarked that he finds fiction writing more "arduous because instead of merely reporting what has happened in nonfiction, fiction requires the creation of a story" that will be believable and enjoyable. "The difference between nonfiction and fiction is the difference between reliable reporting and imaginative creating," he concluded.

Biographical and Critical Sources

BOOKS

Canadian Children's Books: A Critical Guide to Authors and Illustrators, Oxford University Press (Toronto, Ontario, Canada), 2000, pp. 493-496.
Children's Literature Review, Volume 44, Gale (Detroit, MI), 1997, pp. 156-166.
Oxford Companion to Children's Literature, 2nd edition, Oxford University Press (New York, NY), 1997, pp. 1194-1195.
St. James Guide to Children's Writers, 5th edition, St. James Press (Detroit, MI), 1999, pp. 1148-1149.
Yee, Paul, *Saltwater City: An Illustrated History of the Chinese in Vancouver*, Douglas & McIntyre (Vancouver, British Columbia, Canada), 1988, University of Washington (Seattle, WA), 1989.
Yee, Paul, *Tales from Gold Mountain: Stories of the Chinese in the New World*, Groundwood Books (Toronto, Ontario, Canada), 1989, Macmillan (New York, NY), 1990.

PERIODICALS

Booklist, March 15, 1990, Denise Wilms, review of *Tales from Gold Mountain: Stories of the Chinese in the New World*, p. 1464; March 1, 1999, Sally Estes, review of *Tales from Gold Mountain*, p. 1212; November 1, 2002, Hazel Rochman, *Dead Man's Gold and Other Stories*, p. 494; April 1, 2004, Linda Perkins,

review of *A Song for Ba*, p. 1364; December 1, 2005, Gillian Engberg, review of *The Bone Collector's Son*, p. 38; June 1, 2006, Jennifer Mattson, review of *Bamboo*, p. 78; November 1, 2006, Jennifer Hubert, review of *What Happened This Summer*, p. 46; April 1, 2008, Carolyn Phelan, review of *Shu-Li and Tamara*, p. 57; October, 1, 2008, Hazel Rochman, review of *Learning to Fly*, p. 38.

Bulletin of the Center for Children's Books, January, 1990, Betsy Hearne, review of *Tales from the Gold Mountain*, p. 178; July, 1992, B. Hearne, review of *Roses Sing on New Snow: A Delicious Tale*, p. 307.

Canadian Children's Literature, autumn, 1996, Marie Davis, "A Backward Way of Thanking People," pp. 50-68; winter, 1996, James Greenlaw, "Chinese Canadian Fathers and Sons," pp. 106-108.

Canadian Literature, spring, 1988, "Different Dragons," p. 168; winter, 1999, review of *The Boy in the Attic*, p. 204.

Canadian Review of Materials, September, 1994, Margaret Mackey, review of *Breakaway*, p. 139.

Emergency Librarian, May-June, 1995, David Jenkinson, "Portraits: Paul Yee," pp. 61-64; May, 1987, Christine Dewar, review of *The Curses of Third Uncle*, p. 51.

Horn Book, July, 1990, review of *Tales from the Gold Mountain*, pp. 459-460; March-April, 1992, Elizabeth S. Watson, review of *Roses Sing on New Snow*, p. 196; November-December, 2005, Vicky Smith, review of *The Bone Collector's Son*, p. 730.

Kirkus Reviews, May 15, 2002, review of *The Jade Necklace*, p. 744; April 15, 2004, review of *A Song for Ba*, p. 403; October 1, 2005, review of *The Bone Collector's Son*, p. 1093; September 15, 2008, review of *Learning to Fly.*

Quill & Quire, October, 1983, Frieda Wishinsky, review of *Teach Me to Fly, Skyfighter!*, p. 16; December, 1986, Annette Goldsmith, "Illuminating Adventures with Young People from Long Ago," p. 14; April, 1994, Patty Lawlor, review of *Breakaway*, p. 39; October, 1998, Freida Ling, review of *The Boy in the Attic*, p. 42; May, 2002, Sherie Posesorski, review of *The Jade Necklace*, p. 32.

Reading Teacher, April, 1991, Lee Galda and Susan Cox, review of *Tales from Gold Mountain*, p. 585.

Resource Links, June, 2002, Rosemary Anderson, review of *The Jade Necklace*, p. 46; December, 2002, Laura Reilly, review of *Dead Man's Gold, and Other Stories*, p. 35; October, 2004, Laura Reilly, review of *A Song for Ba*, p. 11; February, 2006, Anne Burke, review of *Bamboo*, p. 14; December, 2007, Michelle Gowans, review of *Shu-Li and Tamara*, p. 36.

School Library Journal, May, 1990, Margaret A. Chang, review of *Tales from Gold Mountain*, p. 121; December, 1998, Diane S. Marton, review of *The Boy in the Attic*, p. 96; September, 2002, Margaret A. Chang, review of *The Jade Necklace*, p. 209; June, 2004, Margaret A. Chang, review of *A Song for Ba*, p. 122; February, 2007, Miranda Doyle, review of *What Happened This Summer*, p. 130; September, 2008, Teri Markson, review of *Shu-Li and Tamara*, p. 161; March, 2009, Joanna K. Fabicon, review of *Learning to Fly*, p. 159.

ONLINE

Canadian Children's Book Centre Web site, http://www.bookcentre.ca/ (March 11, 2003), "Paul Yee."
Paul Yee Home Page, http://www.paulyee.ca (January 10, 2010).
Ryerson University Asian Heritage in Canada Web site, http://www.ryerson.ca/ (January 10, 2010), "Paul Yee."

OTHER

Meet the Author: Paul Yee (video), School Services of Canada, 1991.

* * *

YOUME
See LANDOWNE, Youme

* * *

YOUNG, Ed 1931-
(Ed Tse-chun Young)

Personal

Born November 28, 1931, in Tianjin, China; immigrated to United States, 1951; naturalized U.S. citizen; son of Qua-Ling (an engineer) and Yuen Teng Young; married, 1962 (divorced, 1969); married Natasha Gorky, June 1, 1971; children: Antonia, one younger daughter. *Education:* Attended City College of San Francisco, 1952, and University of Illinois at Urbana-Champaign, 1952-54; Art Center College of Design (Pasadena, CA), B.F.A., 1957; graduate study at Pratt Institute, 1958-59.

Addresses

Home—Hastings-on-Hudson, NY. *Agent*—Edward Necarsulmer III, McIntosh & Otis, 353 Lexington Ave., New York, NY 10016.

Career

Children's book illustrator and author. Mel Richman Studio, New York, NY, illustrator and designer, 1957-62; Pratt Institute, Brooklyn, NY, instructor in visual communications, 1960-66; Shu Jung Tai Chi Chuan School, New York, NY, secretary and instructor, 1964-73, director, 1973; Sarah Lawrence College, Bronxville, NY, instructor, beginning 1975. Has also taught at Pratt Institute, Naropa Institute, Yale University, and University of California at Santa Cruz.

Awards, Honors

American Institute of Graphic Arts award, 1962, for *The Mean Mouse and Other Mean Stories* by Janice Urdry, Notable Book designation, American Library As-

sociation, 1967, for *The Emperor and the Kite* edited by Jane Yolen, 1981, for *High on a Hill,* 1982, for *Yeh Shen* by Ah-Ling Louie, 1988, for *Cats Are Cats* edited by Nancy Larrick, 1989, for *Lon Po Po,* for 1992, for *Seven Blind Mice,* 2001, for *The Hunter* by Mary Casanova, 2008, for *Wabi Sabi* by Mark Reibstein; Caldecott Medal Honor designation, 1968, for *The Emperor and the Kite; Horn Book* Honor List designation, and Child Study Association Book Award, both 1969, both for *Chinese Mother Goose Rhymes; The Girl Who Loved the Wind* was named a Children's Book Showcase Title, 1973; Anne Izard Storyteller's Choice designation, 1983, for *Up a Tree,* 1988, for *Cats Are Cats,* 2000, for *The Hunter;* Child Study Association Book of the Year designation, 1978, for *The Terrible Nung Gwama;* Trento Graphic Arts Award, 1980, for *The Lion and the Mouse; New York Times* Best Illustrated Children's Book Award, 1984, for *Up a Tree,* 1988, for *Cats Are Cats; Horn Book* Honor List designation, 1986, for *Foolish Rabbit's Big Mistake* by Rafe Martin; Caldecott Medal, and *Boston Globe/Horn Book* Award, both 1990, both for *Lon Po Po;* U.S. nominee for Hans Christian Andersen Award, 1992, 2002; *Boston Globe/Horn Book* Award, 1992, and Caldecott Honor listee, 1993, both for *Seven Blind Mice;* New York Public Library 100 Titles for Reading and Sharing, 1992, for *Seven Blind Mice,* 1997, for *Pinocchio,* 2000, for *The Hunter,* 2004, for both *I, Doko* and *The Sons of the Dragon King;* Aesop's Accolade Award, 1996, for *The Turkey Girl* by Penny Pollock; Mazza Medallion of Excellence for Artistic Diversity, 2002; Washington Irving Children's Choice Book Award, 1997, for *Pinocchio,* 2000, for *The Hunter;* Asian Pacific Award, and *New York Times* Best Illustrated Children's Book award, both 2008, both for *Wabi Sabi.*

Writings

SELF-ILLUSTRATED; FOR CHILDREN

(With Hilary Beckett) *The Rooster's Horns: A Chinese Puppet Play to Make and Perform,* Collins (New York, NY), 1978.

(Reteller) *The Terrible Nung Gwama: A Chinese Folktale,* Collins (New York, NY), 1978.

(Adaptor) *The Lion and the Mouse: An Aesop Fable,* Doubleday (New York, NY), 1979.

High on a Hill: A Book of Chinese Riddles, Collins (New York, NY), 1980.

Up a Tree, Harper (New York, NY), 1983.

The Other Bone, Harper (New York, NY), 1984.

(Translator) *Lon Po Po: A Red-Riding Hood Story from China,* Philomel (New York, NY), 1989.

(Reteller) *Seven Blind Mice,* Philomel (New York, NY), 1992.

(Reteller) *Moon Mother: A Native-American Creation Tale,* HarperCollins (New York, NY), 1993.

(Reteller) *Red Thread,* Philomel (New York, NY), 1993.

(Reteller) *Little Plum,* Philomel (New York, NY), 1994.

(Reteller) *Donkey Trouble,* Atheneum Books for Young Readers (New York, NY), 1995.

(Adaptor) *Pinocchio,* Philomel (New York, NY), 1995.

(Reteller) *Night Visitors,* Philomel (New York, NY), 1995.

Cat and Rat: The Legend of the Chinese Zodiac, Holt (New York, NY), 1995.

(Reteller) *Mouse Match: A Chinese Folktale,* Silver Whistle, 1997.

(Adaptor) *Genesis,* Laura Geringer Books (New York, NY), 1997.

Voices of the Heart, Scholastic, Inc. (New York, NY), 1997.

(Reteller) *The Lost Horse: A Chinese Folktale,* Silver Whistle, 1998.

Monkey King, HarperCollins (New York, NY), 2001.

The Boy Who Wanted Knowledge, Penguin Putnam (New York, NY), 2002.

What about Me?, Philomel (New York, NY), 2002.

(Adaptor) *The Sons of the Dragon King: A Chinese Legend,* Atheneum (New York, NY), 2004.

I, Doko: The Tale of a Basket, Philomel (New York, NY), 2004.

Nikki Grimes, *Tai Chi Morning: Snapshots of China,* Cricket Books (Chicago, IL), 2004.

Beyond the Great Mountains: A Visual Poem about China, Chronicle Books (San Francisco, CA), 2005.

My Mei Mei, Philomel (New York, NY), 2006.

Hook, Roaring Brook Press (New York, NY), 2009.

ILLUSTRATOR

Janice M. Udry, *The Mean Mouse and Other Mean Stories,* Harper (New York, NY), 1962.

Leland B. Jacobs and Sally Nohelty, editors, *Poetry for Young Scientists,* Holt (New York, NY), 1964.

Margaret Hillert, *The Yellow Boat,* Follett (Chicago, IL), 1966.

Jane Yolen, editor, *The Emperor and the Kite,* World Publishing (Chicago, IL), 1967, reprinted, Penguin Putnam (New York, NY), 1988.

Robert Wyndam, editor, *Chinese Mother Goose Rhymes,* World Publishing (Chicago, IL), 1968, reprinted, Penguin Putnam (New York, NY), 1998.

Kermit Krueger, *The Golden Swans: A Picture Story from Thailand,* World Publishing (Chicago, IL), 1969.

Mel Evans, *The Tiniest Sound,* Doubleday (New York, NY), 1969.

Jane Yolen, *The Seventh Mandarin,* Seabury (New York, NY), 1970.

Renee K. Weiss, *The Bird from the Sea,* Crowell (New York, NY), 1970.

Diane Wolkstein, *Eight Thousand Stones: A Chinese Folktale,* Doubleday (New York, NY), 1972.

Jane Yolen, *The Girl Who Loved the Wind,* Crowell (New York, NY), 1972.

L.C. Hunt, editor, *The Horse from Nowhere,* Holt (New York, NY), 1973.

Donnarae MacCann and Olga Richard, *The Child's First Books,* 1973.

Elizabeth F. Lewis, *Young Fu of the Upper Yangtze,* new edition, Holt (New York, NY), 1973.

Diane Wolkstein, *The Red Lion: A Tale of Ancient Persia,* Crowell (New York, NY), 1977.

Feenie Ziner, *Cricket Boy: A Chinese Tale,* Doubleday (New York, NY), 1977.

N.J. Dawood, *Tales from the Arabian Nights,* Doubleday (New York, NY), 1978.

Diane Wolkstein, *White Wave: A Chinese Tale,* Crowell (New York, NY), 1979.

Priscilla Jaquith, *Bo Rabbit Smart for True: Folktales from the Gullah,* Philomel (New York, NY), 1981.

Al-Ling Louie, *Yeh-Shen: A Cinderella Story from China,* Putnam (New York, NY), 1982.

Mary Scioscia, *Bicycle Rider,* Harper (New York, NY), 1983.

Rafe Martin, *Foolish Rabbit's Big Mistake,* Putnam (New York, NY), 1985.

Jean Fritz, *The Double Life of Pocahontas,* Putnam (New York, NY), 1985.

Margaret Leaf, *Eyes of the Dragon,* Lothrop (New York, NY), 1987.

James Howe, *I Wish I Were a Butterfly,* Harcourt (San Diego, CA), 1987.

Tony Johnston, *Whale Song,* Harcourt (San Diego, CA), 1987.

Richard Lewis, *In the Night, Still Dark,* Atheneum (New York, NY), 1988.

Nancy Larrick, editor, *Cats Are Cats,* Philomel (New York, NY), 1988.

Robert Frost, *Birches,* Holt (New York, NY), 1988.

Oscar Wilde, *The Happy Prince,* new edition, Simon & Schuster (New York, NY), 1989.

Lafcadio Hearn, *The Voice of the Great Bell,* retold by Margaret Hodges, Little, Brown (Boston, MA), 1989.

Ruth Y. Radin, *High in the Mountains,* Macmillan (New York, NY), 1989.

Nancy Larrick, editor, *Mice Are Nice,* Philomel (New York, NY), 1990.

Richard Lewis, *All of You Was Singing,* Atheneum (New York, NY), 1991.

Nancy White Carlstrom, *Goodbye, Geese,* Philomel (New York, NY), 1991.

Barabara Savage Horton, *What Comes in Spring?,* Knopf (New York, NY), 1992.

Mary Calhoun, *While I Sleep,* Morrow (New York, NY), 1992.

Audrey Osofsky, *Dreamcatcher,* Orchard Books (New York, NY), 1992.

Laura Krauss Melmed, *The First Song Ever Sung,* Lothrop (New York, NY), 1993.

Eleanor Coerr, *Sadako,* Putnam (New York, NY), 1993.

Isaac Olaleye, *Bitter Bananas,* Boyds Mills Press (Honesdale, PA), 1994.

Shulamith Levey Oppenheim, reteller, *Iblis,* Harcourt (San Diego, CA), 1994.

Penny Pollock, reteller, *The Turkey Girl: A Zuni Cinderella Story,* Little, Brown (Boston, MA), 1996.

Lisa Westberg Peters, *October Smiled Back,* Holt (New York, NY), 1996.

Jack London, *White Fang,* new edition, Viking (New York, NY), 1999.

Mary Casanova, *The Hunter: A Chinese Folktale,* Simon & Schuster (New York, NY), 2000.

Dorothea P. Seeber, *A Pup Just for Me—A Boy Just for Me,* Philomel (New York, NY), 2000.

Tony Johnston, *Desert Song,* Sierra Club Books for Children (San Francisco, CA), 2000.

Andrea Cheng, *Shanghai Messenger,* Lee & Low (New York, NY), 2005.

Robert Burleigh, *Tiger of the Snows: Tenzing Norgay: The Boy Whose Dream Was Everest,* Atheneum Books for Young Readers (New York, NY), 2006.

Dennis Haseley, *Twenty Heartbeats,* Roaring Brook Press (New York, NY), 2008.

Mark Reibstein, *Wabi Sabi,* Little, Brown (New York, NY), 2008.

Margaret Hillert, *The Yellow Boat,* Norwood House Press (Chicago, IL), 2009.

Kimiko Kajikawa, *Tsunami!,* Philomel Books (New York, NY), 2009.

Brenda Z. Guiberson, *Moon Bear,* Holt (New York, NY), 2010.

Also illustrator of film *Sadako and the Thousand Paper Cranes,* based on the story by Eleanor Coerr.

Sidelights

A critically acclaimed illustrator of children's books since he began his career in the early 1960s, Ed Young often draws on the folklore and folktales of his native China for inspiration. Creating artwork for the texts of others as well as illustrating original tales and adaptations, Young's visual images have helped young readers understand historical China from the days of the Han dynasty onward. His awards include Caldecott honors for illustrating Jane Yolen's *The Emperor and the Kite* and his own retelling of an Indian story in *Seven Blind Mice* as well as a Caldecott medal for his translation of *Lon Po Po: A Red Riding Hood Story from China.* Often working with charcoals and pastels on rice paper, Young captures the feel of Chinese art in his illustrations. Not surprisingly, he cites the philosophy of Chinese painters as his inspiration. "Young is one of those illustrators not to be missed," wrote M.P. Dunleavey in the *New York Times Book Review,* "especially if you share his fondness for legends from far-off lands, retold to appeal to young Americans." In addition to such exotic tales, Young has embraced the native heritage of his adopted home, retelling Native-American myths in books such as *Moon Mother: A Native-American Creation Tale.* He has also explored a variety of other cultures, adapting European fairy and folk tales, stories from the Old Testament, and a tale from Middle Eastern traditions in *What about Me?*

Born in a Chinese coal-mining town and raised in Shanghai and Hong Kong, Young exhibited a talent for drawing early in life. After he immigrated to the United States on a student visa at age nineteen, he first studied architecture but soon turned to art. Following graduation from the Los Angeles Art Center College of Design, Young moved to New York City, where he embarked on a career in advertising design. During his

PAPERSTAR

The Emperor and the Kite

by JANE YOLEN   illustrated by ED YOUNG

One of Ed Young's early illustration projects was creating artwork for Jane Yolen's **The Emperor and the Kite.** (Illustration copyright © 1967, 1988 by Ed Young. Reproduced by permission of Penguin Putnam Inc.)

lunch breaks, he sketched animals at the city zoo, and when the studio for which he worked went out of business, a friend suggested that Young try his hand at illustrating children's books. Although he was reluctant—he did not want to draw cartoons, as he mistakenly thought all children's books were—Young agreed to illustrate Janice M. Udry's *The Mean House, and Other Mean Stories* for Harper & Row.

When it was published in 1962, *The Mean House, and Other Mean Stories* won an award from the American Institute of Graphic Artists. Since then Young has written or retold—and illustrated—many stories for children, and has also contributed artwork to books by other authors, including the *Horn Book* honor listees *Chinese*

Mother Goose Rhymes and *Foolish Rabbit's Big Mistake* by Rafe Martin. Young's original work *Up a Tree* was included among the *New York Times'* list of best illustrated children's books in 1984.

The Caldecott Honor is one of the most prestigious awards available to book illustrators, and Young's name appears on the Caldecott honor role several times, in several different capacities. For his 1968 work for Yolen's *The Emperor and the Kite,* he received a Caldecott honor, and his self-illustrated retelling *Seven Blind Mice* earned another place on the award's honor list. The Caldecott Medal came to Young in 1990 in recognition of his self-illustrated *Lon Po Po.* The story of three sisters who outwit an evil wolf that sneaks into

their home, *Lon Po Po* was translated from the Chinese by Young. Reviewing the title in *School Library Journal,* John Philbrook commented that the author/illustrator's "gripping variation of Red Riding Hood . . . possesses that matter-of-fact veracity that characterizes the best fairy tales," and further noted that Young's "outstanding achievement . . . will be pored over again and again." Writing in the *Los Angeles Times Book Review,* George Shannon observed that, "rather than illustrating only the words of his tale . . . Young has given new life to its metaphoric essence and created a book to savor." A "must for folklore and storytelling collections" was Carolyn Phelan's assessment of *Lon Po Po* in a *Booklist* review.

As with *Lon Po Po,* Young shares Chinese myth and folklore with Western readers through his illustrated retellings. A *Kirkus Reviews* writer described Young's self-illustrated *Red Thread* as "another spellbinding Chinese tale" with "an imaginative, innovative use of traditional elements of Chinese art." In recounting this story of matchmaking and destiny, "Young dapples his pages with delectable clouds of pastels and watercolors," the same writer added, while Phelan remarked on the "ethereal" look of the book's artwork. *Little Plum,* another Chinese fable, has the tiny defeating the powerful when a boy the size of a plum seed outsmarts an evil lord and overcomes the lord's soldiers. "The narration moves as nimbly as Little Plum himself," commented Elizabeth Bush in a review of *Little Plum* for the *Bulletin of the Center for Children's Books.* Bush further noted that "Young has a field day playing with perspectives in his ruggedly textured pastels."

With *Monkey King* Young adapts Chinese myth for a "strikingly designed Buddhist tale," as *Booklist* critic Gillian Engberg described the picture book. With the explosion of a rock, a monkey suddenly emerges, setting off this trickster tale as the monkey outwits adversaries and also gets himself on the wrong side of others. "Young's dynamic artwork and his mercurial transitions between spreads mimic Monkey's own shape-shifting," noted a reviewer for *Publishers Weekly,* characterizing *Monkey King* as "deliciously unpredictable reading." Engberg further remarked in *Booklist* that Young's language is "lively and rich," and his cut-paper collages "beautifully illustrate the action-hero excitement."

In *Cat and Rat: The Legend of the Chinese Zodiac* Young explains how the enmity between the two animals began 5,000 years ago in a race in which the first dozen finishers would have a year named after them. In a *Booklist* review, Phelan observed that "Young captures the emotional content of the scenes with quick, sure strokes of charcoal and pastels on rice paper." Margaret A. Chang, writing in *School Library Journal,* praised the author/illustrator's ability to relate "his story in lively, spare prose."

In both *Voices of the Heart* and *Beyond the Great Mountains: A Visual Poem about China* Young shares his knowledge of Chinese calligraphy and also reveals the Chinese mind by exploring the meaning behind Chinese characters. In the first he examines twenty-six symbols that represent personal traits such as virtue, shame, and mercy, while in the second he focuses on pictographic seal-style characters representing aspects of the natural world. "I was interested in doing two things," Young explained to *Publishers Weekly* interviewer Valiska Gregory in discussing *Beyond the Great Mountains.* "I wanted to introduce the Chinese mind, how it interprets and emotion in a different way than the Western mind, and I wanted to figure out a way that Westerners could understand that difference. My mission was to create a bridge between the two cultures."

With *Voices of the Heart* "Young pushes the envelope of picture-book illustration once again," creating an "unusual combination of image and language," wrote Janice M. Del Negro in the *Bulletin of the Center for Children's Books,* the critic adding that the book serves as "a powerful combination of words and imagery." Philbrook, writing in *School Library Journal,* called *Voices of the Heart* "perhaps [Young's] most conceptually brilliant work to date," and concluded: "Though certainly an interesting introduction to Chinese characters, this highly original tour de force will awaken children to the relation between language and thought, providing many hours of fascination and discussion." Calling the illustrations for *Beyond the Mountains* "Matisse-inspired," a *Kirkus Reviews* writer found the book to be a "lovely tribute to 'the hidden wisdom of symbols.'"

Young returns to more traditional Chinese fare with *Night Visitors, Mouse Match: A Chinese Folktale, The Lost Horse,* and *The Sons of the Dragon King.* In *Night Visitors* a young man believes that, because all living things are equally worthy, when ants plague his father's storehouse, he must find a way to get rid of the insects without killing them. Julie Cummins, writing in *School Library Journal,* noted that the "deftly crafted story concludes with a message of respect for all forms of life," while Rochman called attention to "exquisite illustrations" that "express the changing point of view that is the heart of the story." In *Mouse Match* a father mouse travels to the four corners of the Earth in search of the perfect husband for his daughter. Rejected in turn by the Sun, the Moon, and others, the father finally discovers that the best choice is also the most obvious. A reviewer for *Booklist* noted that Young's folktale retelling "is inventively illustrated with collages and innovatively designed with pages that fold out to tell the story," while a contributor to *Kirkus Reviews* called the work a "polished, effective presentation that . . . redefines [Young's] role as a picture-book creator."

Chinese values are further revealed in *The Lost Horse,* in which a man who loves his fantastic horse comes to discover that things are not as good or bad as they appear on the surface. "This story is an excellent springboard for a discussion of the changing nature of life," noted Marianne Saccardi in a *School Library Journal*

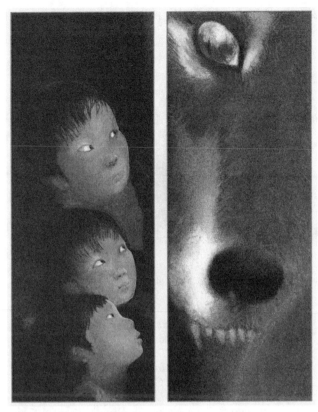

Young's award-winning picture book Lon Po Po *presents an Asian variant of the Red Riding Hood story.* (Paperstar, 1989. Copyright © 1989 by Ed Young. Reproduced by permission.)

review of the book. Commenting on Young's collage artwork, which features pastel and water color, a contributor for *Kirkus Reviews* commented that the book's "sensitive illustrations portray both the panoramic sweeps of life in ancient China, and the individual characters in the story." A writer for *Publishers Weekly* maintained that *The Lost Horse* "may be among the Caldecott Medalist's finest works."

Another story that couches an important lesson in its colorful story, *The Sons of the Dragon King* follows nine self-indulgent dragon princes as they are sent forth by their kingly father to seek the means by which their unique abilities can create goodness in the world. Although all are spoiled, one boy is also loud, one is a good swimmer, and one is strong. By story's end each son has used his unique talent for good. Along with cut-paper collage, Young "depicts each son in an expressive ink wash" that is full of "movement and humor," noted a *Kirkus Reviews* writer, while a *Publishers Weekly* writer noted that the book possesses "a design as elegant and lively as the prose is clear."

Mining other cultural traditions has also yielded a wealth of inspiration for Young. Praised as "a superb rendition of a tale with universal resonance," *I, Doko: The Tale of a Basket* is a Nepalese story about learning to value each of life's stages. A 1992 Caldecott honor book, *Seven Blind Mice,* is a retelling of the Indian story "The Blind Men and the Elephant." "The story

unfolds in a series of striking paper collages ingeniously arranged on a background of black bordered in white," according to Mandy Cheetham in a *Magpies* review. Cheetham thought that "the sheer artistry and delight of both text and illustrations will ensure that it becomes a classic for pre-school storytime programmes," and a *School Library Journal* critic deemed *I, Doko* a "perfect picture book" that is "brilliantly elegant in design and artwork."

A Native-American story that recalls the story of the Ugly Duckling, *Hook* finds a mother hen worried about the odd-looking "chick" that hatches from an abandoned egg, until the bird takes flight and proves to be an eagle. Modernized Sufi texts yield *What about Me?,* a story by Young that finds a young man's search for knowledge come full circle when, with the initial guidance of a Grand Master, he learns that in the act of giving one often receives. Praising *Hook* as an "inspirational story of perseverance and courage," Kristin McKulski added in *Booklist* that the author/illustrator's "graceful, sketchlike" illustrations bring to life the tale's "southwestern setting." "Young seems incapable of making anything less than a beautiful book," commented *School Library Journal* contributor Dona Ratterree in a review of *What about Me?,* the reviewer also praising the book's "elegant design and clever cut-paper and watercolor collages." Dubbing Young's illustrations "dazzling," Mary M. Burns wrote in *Horn Book* that the artwork in *What about Me?* features characters who are "agile, rhythmic, graceful, and emotionally charged."

Young has also borrowed from LaFontaine and Aesop, as in his retelling of *Donkey Trouble,* in which a simple man and his grandson go off to market to sell their donkey. On the way, however, they are mocked for the manner in which they are traveling and finally, after trying to please everyone, end up pleasing no one. Young transplants this tale to a Mid-Eastern desert, creating a "striking picture book" and "an elegant retelling," according to Judith Constantinides in *School Library Journal.* A writer for *Kirkus Reviews* called the same book a "timeless interpretation of an ancient fable." Additionally, Young has adapted more modern tales, such as Carlo Collodi's *Pinocchio,* as well as Oscar Wilde's fairy tale, *The Happy Prince.* In *Moon Mother,* he introduces a Native-American creation myth. "Images within images add visual layers of meaning to the complex creation myth, which Young tells with deceptive simplicity" noted Janice Del Negro in a *Booklist* review. "The landscapes are as large as the story," commented Ruth K. MacDonald in *School Library Journal,* "as timeless as history."

While most of Young's books present universal themes, one book focuses on the thing closest to the artist's heart: his family. Praised by *School Library Journal* contributor Kate McClelland as "a simple story of family bonds unerringly told," *My Mei-Mei* focuses on the growing relationship between the two daughters Young and his wife adopted from China. The story follows

older sister Antonia as she wishes for a "mei-mei" (little sister), then realizes that the new family member demands an unfair amount of attention. Ultimately, *My Mei-Mei* depicts what a *Kirkus Reviews* writer called a "tender celebration of love flowering between sisters" as the baby grows and Antonia realizes the important role she has in her mei mei's life. As Gillian Engberg noted in *Booklist,* Young's story depicts "the small moments that hold [the sisters] . . . fiercely together," while his "vibrant collage illustrations joyously extend the spare, direct words."

Young continues to find numerous opportunities to share the themes that underlay his personal philosophy in illustrating the stories of others. In Dennis Haseley's *Twenty Heartbeats* the artist's "arresting limited-color collage work" captures the nuanced story about the nature of true art, according to a *Kirkus Reviews* writer. Young "uses a panoply of papers to create collages that tell the story of a sacrifice that saved hundreds of lives" in his work for Kimiko Kajikawa's *Tsunami!* according to *School Library Journal* contributor Kathy Krasniewicz. His "hauntingly beautiful" pastel images for Robert Burleigh's *Tiger of the Snows: Tenzing Norgay, the Boy Whose Dream Was Everest* "capture the mystery and grandeur" of the mountainous setting, wrote *School Library Journal* contributor Be Astengo, and a *Kirkus Reviews* writer praised the book's "spectacular pastels."

Young's "beautiful collages have an almost 3-D effect and perfectly complement the spiritual, lyrical text" in Mark Reibstein's *Wabi Sabi,* according to *School Library Journal* writer Kara Schaff Dean. Named a *New York Times* best illustrated children's book, *Wabi Sabi* focuses on a cat's desire to discover the meaning of its name. With that simple promise, the story also deals with Chinese culture and its interest in origins. In his art for the book, which Joanna Rudge Long described in her *New York Times Book Review* appraisal of *Wabi Sabi* as "rich in leaf greens and glowing reds." Young captures "the textures of hair, straw, crazed paint or rough paper." He also "captures moments of transcendent beauty . . . and his art incorporates traditional haiku references," the critic added.

Despite his busy writing schedule, Young reserves time to work with children in schools around the country, reading stories and inspiring young artists to create illustrations. In a Scholastic Web site interview, he offered advice to young people considering a career in writing or book illustration. In addition to a desire to tell stories, and perhaps a desire to tell stories in pictures, future author/illustrators should have "an interest in everything—music, nature, art," recommended Young. "And [they should] be open to everything that comes their way." "Do not rely on training from school because training for an artist is a lifetime endeavor."

Biographical and Critical Sources

BOOKS

Children's Literature Review, Volume 27, Gale (Detroit, MI), 1992.
St. James Guide to Children's Writers, 5th edition, St. James Press (Detroit, MI), 1999.
Silvey, Anita, editor, *Children's Books and Their Creators,* Houghton Mifflin (Boston, MA), 1995.

PERIODICALS

Booklist, November 15, 1989, Carolyn Phelan, review of *Lon Po Po: A Red-Riding Hood Story from China,* p. 672; March 1, 1993, Carolyn Phelan, review of *Red Thread,* p. 1233; October 15, 1993, Janice Del Negro, review of *Moon Mother: A Native-American Creation Tale,* pp. 439-440; September 15, 1995, Hazel Rochman, review of *Night Visitor,* p. 174; November 1, 1995, Carolyn Phelan, review of *Cat and Rat: The Legend of the Chinese Zodiac,* p. 1995; January 1, 1998, review of *Mouse Match: A Chinese Folktale,* p. 736; February 1, 2001, Gillian Engberg, review of *Monkey King,* p. 1058; May 15, 2004, Jennifer Mattson, review of *The Sons of the Dragon King: A Chinese Legend,* p. 1617; December 1, 2004, Jennifer Mattson, review of *I, Doko: The Tale of a Basket,* p. 652; November 1, 2005, Carolyn Phelan, review of *Beyond the Great Mountains: A Visual Poem about China,* p. 48; January 1, 2006, Gillian Engberg, review of *My Mei Mei,* p. 104; May 1, 2008, Carolyn Phelan, review of *Twenty Heartbeats,* p. 94; September 1, 2008, Ilene Cooper, review of *Wabi Sabi,* p. 98; June 1, 2009, Kristen McKulski, review of *Hook,* p. 64.
Bulletin of the Center for Children's Books, October, 1994, Elizabeth Bush, review of *Little Plum,* p. 71; April, 1997, Janice M. Del Negro, review of *Voices of the Heart,* p. 301.
Five Owls, March-April, 2006, Jennifer M. Brabander, review of *My Mei Mei,* p. 178.
Horn Book, July-August, 2002, Mary M. Burns, review of *What about Me?,* p. 477; November-December, 2004, Joanna Rudge Long, review of *I, Doko,* p. 704; May-June, 2009, Joanna Rudge Long, review of *Hook,* p. 288.
Kirkus Reviews, January 1, 1993, review of *Red Thread,* p. 70; September 15, 1995, review of *Donkey Trouble,* p. 1360; October 1, 1997, review of *Mouse Match,* p. 1540; April 1, 1998, review of *The Lost Horse,* p. 504; April 15, 2004, review of *The Sons of the Dragon King,* p. 403; November 15, 2004, review of *I, Doko,* p. 1095; September 1, 2005, review of *Beyond the Great Mountains,* p. 985; February 1, 2006, review of *My Mei Mei,* p. 139; May 15, 2006, review of *Tiger of the Snows: Tenzing Norgay, the Boy Whose Dream Was Everest,* p. 514; March 15, 2008, review of *Twenty Heartbeats;* September 15, 2008, review of *Wabi Sabi;* December 1, 2008, review of *Tsunami!*

Los Angeles Times Book Review, December 10, 1989, George Shannon, "Of Metaphors and a Boy Flat as a Page," p. 9.

Magpies, November, 1994, Mandy Cheetham, review of *Seven Blind Mice,* p. 24.

New York Times Book Review, May 5, 1996, M.P. Dunleavey, review of *Cat and Rat* and *Night Visitors,* p. 27; November 13, 2005, Beth Gutcheon, review of *My Mei Mei,* p. 40; November 9, 2008, Joanna Rudge Long, review of *Wabi Sabi,* p. 35.

Publishers Weekly, April 27, 1998, review of *The Lost Horse,* p. 66; January 15, 2001, review of *Monkey King,* p. 74; May 24, 2004, review of *The Sons of the Dragon King,* p. 61; November 8, 2004, review of *I, Doko,* p. 54; September 19, 2005, Valiska Gregory, "East Meets West," p. 65, and review of *Beyond the Great Mountains,* p. 64; January 9, 2006, review of *My Mei Mei,* p. 52; June 5, 2006, review of *Tiger of the Snows,* p. 64.

School Library Journal, December, 1989, John Philbrook, review of *Lon Po Po,* p. 97; November, 1993, Ruth K. MacDonald, review of *Moon Mother,* p. 103; October, 1995, Julie Cummins, review of *Night Visitors,* p. 130; December, 1995, Margaret A. Chang, review of *Cat and Rat,* p. 101; December, 1995, Judith Constantinides, review of *Donkey Trouble,* p. 101; June, 1997, John Philbrook, review of *Voices of the Heart,* p. 150; April, 1998, Marianne Saccardi, review of *The Lost Horse,* p. 127; January, 2000, review of *Seven Blind Mice,* p. 58; December, 2000, Daryl Grabarek, review of *Desert Song,* p. 112; February 2001, Carol Ann Wilson, review of *Monkey King,* p. 108; June, 2002, Dona Ratterree, review of *What about Me?,* p. 127; June, 2004, Grace Oliff, review of *The Sons of the Dragon King,* p. 134; November, 2004, Lauralyn Persson, review of *I, Doko,* p. 120; October, 2005, Carol L. MacKay, review of *Beyond the Great Mountains,* p. 196; February, 2006, Kate McClelland, review of *My Mei Mei,* p. 112; June, 2006, Be Astengo, review of *Tiger of the Snows,* p. 134; April, 2008, Wendy Lukehart, review of *Twenty Heartbeats,* p. 110; September, 2008, Kara Schaff Dean, review of *Wabi Sabi,* p. 157; December 8, 2008, review of *Tsunami!,* p. 57; January, 2009, Kathy Krasniewicz, review of *Tsunami!,* p. 76; June, 2009, Margaret Bush, review of *Hook,* p. 102.

Washington Post Book World, July 4, 2004, Elizabeth Ward, review of *The Sons of the Dragon King,* p. 11.

ONLINE

Ed Young Home Page, http://edyoungart.com (January 10, 2010).

Scholastic Web site, http://www.books.scholastic.com/ (September 23, 2006), interview with Young.

National Center for Children's Illustrated Literature Web site, http://www.nccil.org/ (September 23, 2006), "Meet the Artist: Ed Young."*

*   *   *

YOUNG, Ed Tse-chun
See YOUNG, Ed

YUM, Hyewon

Personal

Born in Seoul, South Korea; married; children: two sons. *Education:* Seoul National University, degree; School of Visual Arts, M.F.A.

Addresses

Home—Brooklyn, NY. *E-mail*—me@hyewonyum.com.

Career

Artist and illustrator.

Member

Society of Children's Book Writers and Illustrators.

Awards, Honors

Golden Kite Award for Illustration, Society of Children's Book Writers and Illustrators, 2008, and Bologna Ragazzi award honorable mention, 2009, both for *Last Night.*

Writings

SELF-ILLUSTRATED

Last Night, Farrar, Straus & Giroux (New York, NY), 2008.

There Are No Scary Wolves, Farrar, Straus & Giroux (New York, NY), 2010.

Sidelights

In the award-winning *Last Night,* Hyewon Yum tells the story of a little girl who finds solace in pleasant dreams after being sent to be early by her mother. Created while

Hyewon Yum (Reproduced by permission.)

Yum tells a dreamlike story conjured by a young girl in her debut picture book, **Last Night.** (Illustration copyright © 2008 by Hyewon Yum. All rights reserved. Used by permission of Farrar, Straus & Giroux, LLC.)

Yum was an M.F.A. student at New York City's School of Visual Arts, the wordless picture book serves as a fitting stage for the artist's detailed linoleum block images. While also creating illustrations for a variety of commercial clients, Yum has continued her work in picture books with *There Are No Scary Wolves,*

In *Last Night* the little girl's dreams follow an act of mild defiance: she did not want to finish her dinner and has been consequently sent to bed early. Curling up with her stuffed bear, the girl drifts off to dreams where the bear is grown to life size and dances with her in a forest of other friendly animals. Noting that Yum's evocative carvings, featuring shades of pink and yellow, "are appropriate for the open-ended mystery" in her story, *Horn Book* critic Lolly Robinson added that the artist's gestured and highly textured technique "requires much planning and time-consuming execution." The story "will strike a chord with many children," predicted Ilene Cooper in a *Booklist* review of *Last Night,* while in *School Library Journal* Kirsten Cutler wrote that the "sweet poignancy" of Yum's quiet story "is palpable." Writing in *Publishers Weekly,* a reviewer concluded of *Last Night:* "Some picture books are written for children; this one gives a sense of what it's like to be one."

Biographical and Critical Sources

PERIODICALS

Booklist, November 15, 2008, Ilene Cooper, review of *Last Night,* p. 44.

Horn Book, January-February, 2009, Lolly Robinson, review of *Last Night,* p. 87.
Kirkus Reviews, September 15, 2008, review of *Last Night.*
Publishers Weekly, September 1, 2008, review of *Last Night,* p. 53.
School Library Journal, September, 2008, Kirsten Cutler, review of *Last Night,* p. 161.

ONLINE

Hyewon Yum Home Page, http://www.hyewonyum.com (January 10, 2010).
Macmillan Web site, http://us.macmillan.com/ (January 10, 2010), "Hyewon Yum."

*   *   *

ZIMMERMANN, Karl 1943-
(Karl R. Zimmermann)

Personal

Born 1943, in Chicago, IL; married Laurel Ann Chenet, 1966; children: Jennifer, Emily. *Education:* Princeton University, B.A.; New York University, M.A. (English), 1968.

Addresses

Home—Oradell, NJ. *E-mail*—karl@karlzimmermann. com.

Career

Educator and author. Englewood School for Boys (now Dwight-Englewood), teacher, beginning 1965; teacher

and administrator for private schools for twenty-five years; Browning Associates (consulting firm), worked with schools for twenty years. Freelance writer, beginning 1970. Lecturer and tour host.

Member

American Society of Journalists and Authors.

Writings

AND PHOTOGRAPHER

(As Karl R. Zimmermann) *CZ: The Story of the California Zephyr,* Starrucca Valley Publications (Starrucca, PA), 1972.

(As Karl R. Zimmermann) *Erie Lackawanna East,* Quadrant Press (New York, NY), 1975.

(As Karl R. Zimmermann) *The Remarkable GG1,* Quadrant Press (New York, NY), 1977.

(As Karl R. Zimmermann) *A Decade of D&H,* Delford Press (Oradell, NJ), 1978.

Amtrak at Milepost 10, PTJ Pub. (Park Forest, IL), 1981.

(Author of text) *Ed Nowak's New York Central,* PTJ Pub. (Homewood, IL), 1983.

Santa Fe Streamliners: The Chiefs and Their Tribesmen, Quadrant Press (New York, NY), 1987.

(With Roger Cook) *The Western Maryland Railway: Fireballs and Black Diamonds,* Garrigues House (Laurys Station, PA), 1992.

Michigan's Railroad Car Ferries, privately published, 1993.

Domeliners: Yesterday's Trains of Tomorrow, Kalmbach Books (Waukesha, WI), 1998.

(With Roger Cook) *Magnetic North: Canadian Steam in Twilight,* Boston Mills Press (Erin, Ontario, Canada), 1999.

Twentieth Century Limited, M.B.I. Publishing Co. (St. Paul, MN), 2002.

Burlington's Zephyrs, M.B.I. Publishing Co. (St. Paul, MN), 2004.

The GrandLuxe Express: Traveling in High Style, Indiana University Press (Bloomington, IN), 2007.

Contributor to numerous periodicals, including *Amtrak Express, Bon Appétit, Boston Globe, Chicago Tribune, Chronos, Classic Trains, Cruise Travel, Gourmet, Outdoor Life, Locomotive & Railway Preservation, Los Angeles Times, Miami Herald, New York Times, Railroad and Railfan, Railroad Model Craftsman, Trains, Travel & Leisure, Washington Post, Western Outdoors,* and *Writer.* Contributing editor to *Americana* and *International Railway Traveler;* contributing editor and North American Intercity Rail columnist to *Passenger Train Journal.*

FOR CHILDREN; AND PHOTOGRAPHER

Steam Locomotives: Whistling, Chugging, Smoking Iron Horses of the Past, Boyds Mills Press (Honesdale, PA), 2004.

All Aboard!: Passenger Trains around the World, Boyds Mills Press (Honesdale, PA), 2006.

Steamboats: The Story of Lakers, Ferries, and Majestic Paddle-wheelers, Boyds Mills Press (Honesdale, PA), 2007.

Ocean Liners: Crossing and Cruising the Seven Seas, Boyds Mills Press (Honesdale, PA), 2008.

Sidelights

Although he spent his career in education, Karl Zimmermann has also channeled his lifelong fascination with trains and train travel into a second career as an expert on the subject. A writer, photographer, and lecturer, has written or coauthored numerous books and hundreds of articles, introducing readers to the history and technology of trains as well as steamboats, ocean liners, baseball, and other icons of America's history and culture.

Zimmermann relives a journey he took with his then-teenaged coauthor Roger Cook in 1958 in *Magnetic North: Canadian Steam in Twilight.* The teens' trip—from New York City to Montréal, Québec, Canada—inspired several more journeys to see the then-vanishing steam trains, and cemented their shared passion for trains that has forged their writing collaboration. Describing rail journeys throughout eastern Canada, *Magnetic North* relates "a story that Cook and Zimmermann are well-suited to tell," asserted Carl A. Swanson in *Trains* magazine. Praising the book's detailed and now-historical photographs, Swanson added that *Magnetic North* serves as "a wonderful memoir of a fascinating era."

In addition to his books for the general reader, Zimmermann has also authored his multi-volume "Transportation" series for younger children. The series, which includes *All Aboard!: Passenger Trains around the World, Steamboats: The Story of Lakers, Ferries, and Majestic Paddle-Wheelers, Steam Locomotives: Whistling, Chugging, Smoking Iron Horses of the Past,* and *Ocean Liners: Crossing and Cruising the Seven Seas,* combines a discussion of the history of various modes of transportation with Zimmermann's colorful photographs.

Described by *Booklist* contributor Hazel Rochman as an "enthusiastic account" of modern train travel, *All Aboard!* covers passenger trains worldwide. In *Steam Locomotives* Zimmermann shares his passion for pre-diesel trains in a large-format photo-essay that mixes photographs and factual information about the role steam technology played in transportation history. Reviewing *Steam Locomotives* in *Kirkus Reviews,* a writer praised the "vivid appreciation" Zimmermann inspires through his "lively, opinionated history." Noting the nostalgic quality of the book, the reviewer remarked that the list of sites where steam trains still run is "poignantly short," and *Booklist* contributor Kay Weisman maintained that Zimmermann's "crisp, clear photographs" bring a freshness to the appealing topic.

Ocean Liners takes a similar approach in its focus on passenger liners and cruise ships, chronicling the advances in shipbuilding that led to the creation of the largest transportation vehicles on earth and encouraged a thriving cross-Atlantic tourism industry. In *Steamboats* attention turns to the boats that travel interior lakes and waterways, transfixing young readers with a "text [that] will captivate the mechanically curious," according to Engberg. Appraising *Ocean Liners* for *Kirkus Reviews,* a contributor noted that Zimmermann's inclusion of a "plethora of facts and details never detracts from [his] . . . obvious love of these stately ships." Also praising the book, John Peters noted in *Booklist* that *Ocean Liners* will inspire young readers with a respect for "the magnificence of these floating hotels."

Biographical and Critical Sources

PERIODICALS

Booklist, February 1, 2004, Kay Weisman, review of *Steam Locomotives: Whistling, Chugging, Smoking Iron Horses of the Past,* p. 973; February 15, 2006, Hazel Rochman, review of *All Aboard!: Passenger Trains around the World,* p. 96; January 1, 2007, Gillian Engberg, review of *Steamboats: The Story of Lakers, Ferries, and Majestic Paddle-Wheelers,* p. 96; December 1, 2008, John Peters, review of *Ocean Liners: Crossing and Cruising the Seven Seas,* p. 65.

Kirkus Reviews, January 15, 2004, review of *Steam Locomotives,* p. 91; December 15, 2006, review of *Steamboats,* p. 1275; September 15, 2008, review of *Ocean Liners.*

School Library Journal, April, 2007, Eldon Younce, review of *Steamboats,* p. 167.

Trains, February, 2000, Carl A. Swanson, review of *Magnetic North: Canadian Steam in Twilight,* p. 84.

ONLINE

Karl Zimmermann Home Page, http://www.karlzimmermann.com (January 10, 2010).

*   *   *

ZIMMERMANN, Karl R.
See ZIMMERMANN, Karl

Illustrations Index

(In the following index, the number of the *volume* in which an illustrator's work appears is given *before* the colon, and the *page number* on which it appears is given *after* the colon. For example, a drawing by Adams, Adrienne appears in Volume 2 on page 6, another drawing by her appears in Volume 3 on page 80, another drawing in Volume 8 on page 1, and so on and so on. . . .)

YABC

Index references to *YABC* refer to listings appearing in the two-volume *Yesterday's Authors of Books for Children,* also published by Gale, Cengage Learning. *YABC* covers prominent authors and illustrators who died prior to 1960.

A

Aas, Ulf *5:* 174
Abbe, S. van
 See van Abbe, S.
Abel, Raymond *6:* 122; *7:* 195; *12:* 3; *21:* 86; *25:* 119
Abelliera, Aldo *71:* 120
Abolafia, Yossi *60:* 2; *93:* 163; *152:* 202
Abrahams, Hilary *26:* 205; *29:* 24, 25; *53:* 61
Abrams, Kathie *36:* 170
Abrams, Lester *49:* 26
Abulafia, Yossi *154:* 67; *177:* 3
Accardo, Anthony *191:* 3, 8
Accornero, Franco *184:* 8
Accorsi, William *11:* 198
Acs, Laszlo *14:* 156; *42:* 22
Acuna, Ed *198:* 79
Adams, Adrienne *2:* 6; *3:* 80; *8:* 1; *15:* 107; *16:* 180; *20:* 65; *22:* 134, 135; *33:* 75; *36:* 103, 112; *39:* 74; *86:* 54; *90:* 2, 3
Adams, Connie J. *129:* 68
Adams, John Wolcott *17:* 162
Adams, Lynn *96:* 44
Adams, Norman *55:* 82
Adams, Pam *112:* 1, 2
Adams, Sarah *98:* 126; *164:* 180
Adams, Steve *209:* 64
Adamson, George *30:* 23, 24; *69:* 64
Addams, Charles *55:* 5
Addison, Kenneth *192:* 173
Addy, Sean *180:* 8
Ade, Rene *76:* 198; *195:* 162
Adinolfi, JoAnn *115:* 42; *176:* 2
Adkins, Alta *22:* 250
Adkins, Jan *8:* 3; *69:* 4; *144:* 2, 3, 4; *210:* 11, 17, 18, 19
Adler, Kelynn *195:* 47
Adler, Peggy *22:* 6; *29:* 31
Adler, Ruth *29:* 29
Adlerman, Daniel *163:* 2
Adragna, Robert *47:* 145
Agard, Nadema *18:* 1
Agee, Jon *116:* 8, 9, 10; *157:* 4; *196:* 3, 4, 5, 6, 7, 8
Agre, Patricia *47:* 195
Aguirre, Alfredo *152:* 218
Ahjar, Brian *207:* 126
Ahl, Anna Maria *32:* 24
Ahlberg, Allan *68:* 6, 7, 9; *165:* 5

Ahlberg, Janet *68:* 6, 7, 9
Aicher-Scholl, Inge *63:* 127
Aichinger, Helga *4:* 5, 45
Aitken, Amy *31:* 34
Akaba, Suekichi *46:* 23; *53:* 127
Akasaka, Miyoshi *YABC 2:* 261
Akib, Jamel *181:* 13; *182:* 99
Akino, Fuku *6:* 144
Alain *40:* 41
Alajalov *2:* 226
Albert, Chris *200:* 64
Alborough, Jez *86:* 1, 2, 3; *149:* 3
Albrecht, Jan *37:* 176
Albright, Donn *1:* 91
Alcala, Alfredo *91:* 128
Alcantará, Felipe Ugalde *171:* 186
Alcorn, John *3:* 159; *7:* 165; *31:* 22; *44:* 127; *46:* 23, 170
Alcorn, Stephen *110:* 4; *125:* 106; *128:* 172; *150:* 97; *160:* 188; *165:* 48; *201:* 113; *203:* 39; *207:* 3
Alcott, May *100:* 3
Alda, Arlene *44:* 24; *158:* 2
Alden, Albert *11:* 103
Aldridge, Andy *27:* 131
Aldridge, George *105:* 125
Aldridge, Sheila *192:* 4
Alejandro, Cliff *176:* 75
Alex, Ben *45:* 25, 26
Alexander, Ellen *91:* 3
Alexander, Lloyd *49:* 34
Alexander, Martha *3:* 206; *11:* 103; *13:* 109; *25:* 100; *36:* 131; *70:* 6, 7; *136:* 3, 4, 5; *169:* 120
Alexander, Paul *85:* 57; *90:* 9
Alexeieff, Alexander *14:* 6; *26:* 199
Alfano, Wayne *80:* 69
Aliki
 See Brandenberg, Aliki
Allamand, Pascale *12:* 9
Allan, Judith *38:* 166
Alland, Alexandra *16:* 255
Allen, Gertrude *9:* 6
Allen, Graham *31:* 145
Allen, Jonathan *131:* 3, 4; *177:* 8, 9, 10
Allen, Joy *168:* 185
Allen, Pamela *50:* 25, 26, 27, 28; *81:* 9, 10; *123:* 4, 5
Allen, Raul *207:* 94
Allen, Rowena *47:* 75

Allen, Thomas B. *81:* 101; *82:* 248; *89:* 37; *104:* 9
Allen, Tom *85:* 176
Allender, David *73:* 223
Alley, R.W. *80:* 183; *95:* 187; *156:* 100, 153; *169:* 4, 5; *179:* 17
Allison, Linda *43:* 27
Allon, Jeffrey *119:* 174
Allport, Mike *71:* 55
Almquist, Don *11:* 8; *12:* 128; *17:* 46; *22:* 110
Aloise, Frank *5:* 38; *10:* 133; *30:* 92
Alsenas, Linas *186:* 2
Alter, Ann *206:* 4, 5
Althea
 See Braithwaite, Althea
Altschuler, Franz *11:* 185; *23:* 141; *40:* 48; *45:* 29; *57:* 181
Alvin, John *117:* 5
Ambrus, Victor G. *1:* 6, 7, 194; *3:* 69; *5:* 15; *6:* 44; *7:* 36; *8:* 210; *12:* 227; *14:* 213; *15:* 213; *22:* 209; *24:* 36; *28:* 179; *30:* 178; *32:* 44, 46; *38:* 143; *41:* 25, 26, 27, 28, 29, 30, 31, 32; *42:* 87; *44:* 190; *55:* 172; *62:* 30, 144, 145, 148; *86:* 99, 100, 101; *87:* 66, 137; *89:* 162; *134:* 160
Ames, Lee J. *3:* 12; *9:* 130; *10:* 69; *17:* 214; *22:* 124; *151:* 13
Amini, Mehrdokht *211:* 119
Amon, Aline *9:* 9
Amoss, Berthe *5:* 5
Amstutz, Andre *152:* 102
Amundsen, Dick *7:* 77
Amundsen, Richard E. *5:* 10; *24:* 122
Ancona, George *12:* 11; *55:* 144; *145:* 7; *208:* 13
Anderson, Alasdair *18:* 122
Andersen, Bethanne *116:* 167; *162:* 189; *175:* 17; *191:* 4, 5
Anderson, Bob *139:* 16
Anderson, Brad *33:* 28
Anderson, Brian *211:* 8
Anderson, C.W. *11:* 10
Anderson, Carl *7:* 4
Anderson, Catherine Corley *72:* 2
Anderson, Cecil *127:* 152
Anderson, David Lee *118:* 176
Anderson, Derek *169:* 9; *174:* 180
Anderson, Doug *40:* 111
Anderson, Erica *23:* 65
Anderson, Laurie *12:* 153, 155
Anderson, Lena *99:* 26

Anderson, Peggy Perry *179:* 2
Anderson, Sara *173:* 3
Anderson, Scoular *138:* 13; *201:* 6
Anderson, Susan *90:* 12
Anderson, Tara *188:* 132; *211:* 115
Anderson, Wayne *23:* 119; *41:* 239; *56:* 7; *62:* 26; *147:* 6; *202:* 4, 5
Andreasen, Daniel *86:* 157; *87:* 104; *103:* 201, 202; *159:* 75; *167:* 106, 107; *168:* 184; *180:* 247; *186:* 9
Andrew, Ian *111:* 37; *116:* 12; *166:* 2
Andrew, John *22:* 4
Andrews, Benny *14:* 251; *31:* 24; *57:* 6, 7; *183:* 8
Andrews, Vaughn *166:* 28
Anelay, Henry *57:* 173
Angel, Marie *47:* 22
Angelo, Valenti *14:* 8; *18:* 100; *20:* 232; *32:* 70
Anglund, Joan Walsh *2:* 7, 250, 251; *37:* 198, 199, 200
Anholt, Catherine *74:* 8; *131:* 7; *141:* 5
Anholt, Laurence *141:* 4
Anno, Mitsumasa *5:* 7; *38:* 25, 26, 27, 28, 29, 30, 31, 32; *77:* 3, 4; *157:* 10, 11
Antal, Andrew *1:* 124; *30:* 145
Antram, David *152:* 133
Apostolou, Christy Hale
    See Hale, Christy
Apple, Margot *33:* 25; *35:* 206; *46:* 81; *53:* 8; *61:* 109; *64:* 21, 22, 24, 25, 27; *71:* 176; *77:* 53; *82:* 245; *92:* 39; *94:* 180; *96:* 107; *152:* 4, 5; *162:* 192, 194; *173:* 44
Appleyard, Dev *2:* 192
Aragones, Sergio *48:* 23, 24, 25, 26, 27
Araneus *40:* 29
Arbo, Cris *103:* 4
Archambault, Matt *85:* 173; *138:* 19, 20; *143:* 33; *145:* 144; *179:* 103; *187:* 7
Archer, Janet *16:* 69; *178:* 156
Ardizzone, Edward *1:* 11, 12; *2:* 105; *3:* 258; *4:* 78; *7:* 79; *10:* 100; *15:* 232; *20:* 69,178; *23:* 223; *24:* 125; *28:* 25, 26, 27, 28, 29, 30, 31,33, 34, 35, 36, 37; *31:* 192, 193; *34:* 215, 217; *60:* 173; *64:* 145; *87:* 176; *YABC 2:* 25
Arena, Jill *176:* 49
Arenella, Roy *14:* 9
Argemi, David *197:* 2
Argent, Kerry *103:* 56; *138:* 17; *158:* 134
Arihara, Shino *201:* 98
Arisman, Marshall *162:* 50
Armer, Austin *13:* 3
Armer, Laura Adams *13:* 3
Armer, Sidney *13:* 3
Armitage, David *47:* 23; *99:* 5; *155:* 4
Armitage, Eileen *4:* 16
Armstrong, George *10:* 6; *21:* 72
Armstrong, Shelagh *102:* 114
Armstrong-Ellis, Carey *185:* 196
Arno, Enrico *1:* 217; *2:* 22, 210; *4:* 9; *5:* 43; *6:* 52; *29:* 217, 219; *33:* 152; *35:* 99; *43:* 31, 32, 33; *45:* 212, 213, 214; *72:* 72; *74:* 166; *100:* 169
Arnold, Alli *187:* 40, 41
Arnold, Caroline *174:* 5
Arnold, Emily *76:* 7, 9, 10
Arnold, Katya *115:* 11; *168:* 2, 3
Arnold, Tedd *116:* 14; *133:* 152; *160:* 5; *208:* 24, 25, 26, 176
Arnosky, Jim *22:* 20; *70:* 9, 10, 11; *118:* 3, 5; *160:* 8, 10; *189:* 5, 7, 8, 9, 10
Arnsteen, Katy Keck *105:* 97; *116:* 145
Arsenault, Isabelle *207:* 7
Arrowood, Clinton *12:* 193; *19:* 11; *65:* 210
Artell, Mike *89:* 8
Arting, Fred J. *41:* 63
Artzybasheff, Boris *13:* 143; *14:* 15; *40:* 152, 155
Aruego, Ariane *6:* 4

Aruego, José *4:* 140; *6:* 4; *7:* 64; *33:* 195; *35:* 208; *68:* 16, 17; *75:* 46; *93:* 91, 92; *94:* 197; *109:* 65, 67; *125:* 2, 3, 4, 5; *127:* 188; *143:* 25; *178:* 17, 19, 74; *188:* 166; *202:* 164
Arzoumanian, Alik *177:* 12; *194:* 115
Asare, Meshack *86:* 9; *139:* 19
Ascensios, Natalie *105:* 139
Asch, Frank *5:* 9; *66:* 2, 4, 6, 7, 9, 10; *102:* 18, 19,21; *154:* 12
Ashby, Gail *11:* 135
Ashby, Gil *146:* 4
Ashby, Gwynneth *44:* 26
Ashley, C.W. *19:* 197
Ashmead, Hal *8:* 70
Ashton, Tim *211:* 204
Aska, Warabe *56:* 10
Assel, Steven *44:* 153; *77:* 22, 97
Astrop, John *32:* 56
Atene, Ann *12:* 18
Atherton, Lisa *38:* 198
Atkinson, Allen *60:* 5
Atkinson, J. Priestman *17:* 275
Atkinson, Janet *86:* 147; *103:* 138
Atkinson, Mike *127:* 74
Atkinson, Wayne *40:* 46
Attard, Karl *196:* 22, 23
Attebery, Charles *38:* 170
Atwell, Debby *150:* 6
Atwood, Ann *7:* 9
Aubrey, Meg Kelleher *77:* 159
Auch, Herm *173:* 7, 8
Auch, Mary Jane *173:* 7
Augarde, Steve *25:* 22; *159:* 7; *210:* 43, 44
Austerman, Miriam *23:* 107
Austin, Margot *11:* 16
Austin, Robert *3:* 44
Austin, Virginia *81:* 205; *127:* 221
Auth, Tony *51:* 5; *192:* 18
Avendano, Dolores *158:* 74
Avedon, Richard *57:* 140
Averill, Esther *1:* 17; *28:* 39, 40, 41
Axeman, Lois *2:* 32; *11:* 84; *13:* 165; *22:* 8; *23:* 49; *61:* 116; *101:* 124
Axtel, David *155:* 110
Ayer, Jacqueline *13:* 7
Ayer, Margaret *15:* 12; *50:* 120
Ayers, Alan *91:* 58; *107:* 169
Ayliffe, Alex *95:* 164
Ayto, Russell *111:* 5; *112:* 54; *206:* 7, 8
Azarian, Mary *112:* 9, 10; *114:* 129; *117:* 171; *137:* 163; *171:* 4, 5; *181:* 161; *188:* 128

B

B.T.B.
    See Blackwell, Basil T.
Babbitt, Bradford *33:* 158
Babbitt, Natalie *6:* 6; *8:* 220; *68:* 20; *70:* 242, 243; *194:* 8, 9
Baca, Maria *104:* 5
Bacchus, Andy *94:* 87
Bacha, Andy *109:* 169
Bachelet, Gilles *196:* 18
Bachem, Paul *48:* 180; *67:* 65; *144:* 206
Back, Adam *63:* 125
Back, George *31:* 161
Backes, Nick *190:* 72
Backhouse, Colin *78:* 142
Bacon, Bruce *4:* 74
Bacon, Paul *7:* 155; *8:* 121; *31:* 55; *50:* 42; *56:* 175; *62:* 82, 84
Bacon, Peggy *2:* 11, 228; *46:* 44
Baek, Matthew J. *169:* 95; *202:* 8
Baer, Julie *161:* 2
Baicker-McKee, Carol *177:* 15; *180:* 215
Bailey, Peter *58:* 174; *87:* 221; *194:* 12
Bailey, Sheila *155:* 11
Baker, Alan *22:* 22; *61:* 134; *93:* 11, 12; *146:* 6, 7, 10

Baker, Charlotte *2:* 12
Baker, Garin *89:* 65
Baker, Jeannie *23:* 4; *88:* 18, 19, 20
Baker, Jim *22:* 24
Baker, Joe *82:* 188; *111:* 55; *124:* 70; *197:* 73
Baker, Keith *179:* 6, 7
Baker, Leslie *112:* 214; *132:* 103, 246; *180:* 74, 246
Baldacci, Rudy *184:* 9
Baldridge, Cyrus LeRoy *19:* 69; *44:* 50
Baldus, Zachary *152:* 231; *187:* 60
Balet, Jan *11:* 22
Balian, Lorna *9:* 16; *91:* 16
Balit, Christina *102:* 24; *159:* 9; *162:* 118, 119
Ballantyne, R.M. *24:* 34
Ballis, George *14:* 199
Balouch, Kristen *176:* 11
Baltzer, Hans *40:* 30
Banbery, Fred *58:* 15
Banfill, A. Scott *98:* 7; *112:* 59
Bang, Molly Garrett *24:* 37, 38; *69:* 8, 9, 10; *111:* 7,9, 10, 11; *140:* 11; *158:* 37, 38, 39; *195:* 3
Banik, Yvette Santiago *21:* 136
Banks, Erin Bennett *211:* 12
Banner, Angela
    See Maddison, Angela Mary
Bannerman, Helen *19:* 13, 14
Banning, Greg *202:* 98
Bannon, Laura *6:* 10; *23:* 8
Bantock, Nick *74:* 229; *95:* 6
Banyai, Istvan *185:* 209; *193:* 14, 16; *209:* 155
Baptist, Michael *37:* 208
Baracca, Sal *135:* 206
Baranaski, Marcin *182:* 113
Barasch, Lynne *126:* 16; *186:* 15
Barbarin, Lucien C., Jr. *89:* 88
Barbour, Karen *96:* 5; *74:* 209; *170:* 16
Bare, Arnold Edwin *16:* 31
Bare, Colleen Stanley *32:* 33
Barger, Jan *147:* 11
Bargery, Geoffrey *14:* 258
Barkat, Jonathan *149:* 177; *164:* 254; *181:* 106; *184:* 186; *196:* 11; *198:* 148
Barker, Carol *31:* 27
Barker, Cicely Mary *49:* 50, 51
Barkley, James *4:* 13; *6:* 11; *13:* 112
Barks, Carl *37:* 27, 28, 29, 30, 31, 32, 33, 34
Barling, Joy *62:* 148
Barling, Tom *9:* 23
Barlow, Gillian *62:* 20
Barlow, Perry *35:* 28
Barlowe, Dot *30:* 223
Barlowe, Wayne *37:* 72; *84:* 43; *105:* 5
Barnard, Bryn *88:* 53; *13:* 55; *169:* 13; *193:* 194
Barneda, David *206:* 11
Barner, Bob *29:* 37; *128:* 33; *136:* 19, 20; *177:* 27
Barnes, Hiram P. *20:* 28
Barnes, Tim *137:* 28
Barnes-Murphy, Rowan *88:* 22
Barnett, Charles II *175:* 150
Barnett, Ivan *70:* 14
Barnett, Moneta *16:* 89; *19:* 142; *31:* 102; *33:* 30, 31, 32; *41:* 153; *61:* 94, 97
Barney, Maginel Wright *39:* 32, 33, 34; *YABC 2:* 306
Barnum, Jay Hyde *11:* 224; *20:* 5; *37:* 189, 190
Baron, Alan *80:* 3; *89:* 123
Barr, George *60:* 74; *69:* 64
Barragan, Paula S. *134:* 116; *186:* 158
Barrall, Tim *115:* 152
Barraud, Martin *189:* 38
Barrauds *33:* 114
Barrer-Russell, Gertrude *9:* 65; *27:* 31
Barret, Robert *85:* 134
Barrett, Angela *40:* 136, 137; *62:* 74; *75:* 10; *76:* 142; *144:* 137; *145:* 14
Barrett, Jennifer *58:* 149

Barrett, John E. *43:* 119
Barrett, Moneta *74:* 10
Barrett, Peter *55:* 169; *86:* 111
Barrett, Robert *62:* 145; *77:* 146; *82:* 35
Barrett, Ron *14:* 24; *26:* 35
Barron, John N. *3:* 261; *5:* 101; *14:* 220
Barrow, Ann *136:* 27
Barrows, Walter *14:* 268
Barry, Ethelred B. *37:* 79; *YABC 1:* 229
Barry, James *14:* 25
Barry, Katharina *2:* 159; *4:* 22
Barry, Robert E. *6:* 12
Barry, Scott *32:* 35
Barshaw, Ruth McNally *203:* 9
Bartenbach, Jean *40:* 31
Barth, Ernest Kurt *2:* 172; *3:* 160; *8:* 26; *10:* 31
Bartholomew, Caty *208:* 153
Bartholomew, Marie *200:* 66
Bartlett, Alison *101:* 88; *165:* 93; *209:* 51
Barton, Byron *8:* 207; *9:* 18; *23:* 66; *80:* 181; *90:* 18, 19, 20, 21; *126:* 29, 30
Barton, Harriett *30:* 71
Barton, Jill *129:* 108; *135:* 120; *145:* 185, 189; *184:* 177
Bartram, Robert *10:* 42
Bartsch, Jochen *8:* 105; *39:* 38
Bascove, Barbara *45:* 73
Base, Graeme *101:* 15, 16, 17, 18; *162:* 8, 10, 12
Baseman, Gary *174:* 12
Bash, Barbara *132:* 9
Baskin, Leonard *30:* 42, 43, 46, 47; *49:* 125, 126, 128, 129,133; *173:* 120
Bass, Saul *49:* 192
Bassett, Jeni *40:* 99; *64:* 30
Basso, Bill *99:* 139; *189:* 134
Batchelor, Joy *29:* 41, 47, 48
Bate, Norman *5:* 16
Bates, Amy June *188:* 170; *189:* 27, 28
Bates, Leo *24:* 35
Batet, Carmen *39:* 134
Batherman, Muriel *31:* 79; *45:* 185
Battaglia, Aurelius *50:* 44
Batten, John D. *25:* 161, 162
Batten, Mary *162:* 14, 15
Battles, Asa *32:* 94, 95
Bauer, Carla *193:* 6
Bauer, Jutta *150:* 32
Bauernschmidt, Marjorie *15:* 15
Baum, Allyn *20:* 10
Baum, Willi *4:* 24, 25; *7:* 173
Bauman, Leslie *61:* 121
Baumann, Jill *34:* 170
Baumhauer, Hans *11:* 218; *15:* 163, 165, 167
Baxter, Glen *57:* 100
Baxter, Leon *59:* 102
Baxter, Robert *87:* 129
Bayer, Herbert *181:* 16
Bayley, Dorothy *37:* 195
Bayley, Nicola *40:* 104; *41:* 34, 35; *69:* 15; *129:* 33, 34, 35
Baylin, Mark *158:* 233
Baynes, Pauline *2:* 244; *3:* 149; *13:* 133, 135,137, 141; *19:* 18, 19, 20; *32:* 208, 213, 214; *36:* 105, 108; *59:* 12, 13, 14, 16, 17, 18, 20; *100:* 158, 159, 243; *133:* 3, 4
Beach, Lou *150:* 150; *207:* 117, 118
Beame, Rona *12:* 40
Bean, Jonathan *196:* 102
Bear's Heart *73:* 215
Beard, Dan *22:* 31, 32
Beard, J.H. *YABC 1:* 158
Bearden, Romare *9:* 7; *22:* 35
Beardshaw, Rosalind *169:* 22; *190:* 22
Beardsley, Aubrey *17:* 14; *23:* 181; *59:* 130, 131
Bearman, Jane *29:* 38
Beaton, Cecil *24:* 208
Beaton, Clare *125:* 28; *208:* 67
Beauce, J.A. *18:* 103

Beaujard, Sophie *81:* 54
Beccia, Carlyn *189:* 29
Bechtold, Lisze *208:* 29
Beck, Charles *11:* 169; *51:* 173
Beck, Ian *138:* 27; *182:* 150; *190:* 25
Beck, Melinda *203:* 112
Beck, Ruth *13:* 11
Becker, Harriet *12:* 211
Beckerman, Jonathan *208:* 194
Beckett, Sheilah *25:* 5; *33:* 37, 38
Beckhoff, Harry *1:* 78; *5:* 163
Beckhorn, Susan Williams *189:* 32
Beckman, Kaj *45:* 38, 39, 40, 41
Beckman, Per *45:* 42, 43
Beddows, Eric *72:* 70
Bedford, F.D. *20:* 118, 122; *33:* 170; *41:* 220, 221,230, 233
Bee, Joyce *19:* 62
Bee, William *188:* 6
Beeby, Betty *25:* 36
Beech, Carol *9:* 149
Beech, Mark *192:* 122
Beek *25:* 51, 55, 59
Beeke, Tiphanie *177:* 127; *204:* 140
Beekman, Doug *125:* 146, 148
Beerbohm, Max *24:* 208
Beeson, Bob *108:* 57
Begin, Mary Jane *82:* 13; *206:* 13
Beha, Philippe *172:* 85
Behr, Joyce *15:* 15; *21:* 132; *23:* 161
Behrens, Hans *5:* 97
Beier, Ellen *135:* 170; *139:* 47; *183:* 164
Beinicke, Steve *69:* 18
Beisner, Monika *46:* 128, 131; *112:* 127
Belden, Charles J. *12:* 182
Belina, Renate *39:* 132
Bell, Corydon *3:* 20
Bell, Graham *54:* 48
Bell, Julia *151:* 214
Bell, Julie *159:* 172; *165:* 18
Bell, Thomas P. *76:* 182
Bellamy, Glen *127:* 15
Beltran, Alberto *43:* 37
Bemelmans, Ludwig *15:* 19, 21; *100:* 27
Ben-Ami, Doron *75:* 96; *84:* 107; *108:* 132; *110:* 63; *159:* 157; *197:* 142
Bendall-Brunello, John *150:* 4; *157:* 163; *185:* 3, 4; *203:* 5
Benda, Wladyslaw T. *15:* 256; *30:* 76, 77; *44:* 182
Bender, Robert *77:* 162; *79:* 13; *160:* 23
Bendick, Jeanne *2:* 24; *68:* 27, 28
Benioff, Carol *121:* 42; *175:* 23
Benner, Cheryl *80:* 11
Bennett, Charles H. *64:* 6
Bennett, Erin Susanne *166:* 216
Bennett, F.I. *YABC 1:* 134
Bennett, James *146:* 240
Bennett, Jill *26:* 61; *41:* 38, 39; *45:* 54
Bennett, Rainey *15:* 26; *23:* 53
Bennett, Richard *15:* 45; *21:* 11, 12, 13; *25:* 175
Bennett, Susan *5:* 55
Benny, Mike *142:* 78; *203:* 13, 14; *207:* 85
Benoit, Elise *77:* 74
Benson, Linda *60:* 130; *62:* 91; *75:* 101; *79:* 156; *134:* 129
Benson, Patrick *68:* 162; *147:* 17, 18, 19, 20
Bentley, Carolyn *46:* 153
Bentley, James *149:* 30
Bentley, Roy *30:* 162
Benton, Jim *172:* 22
Benton, Thomas Hart *2:* 99
Berelson, Howard *5:* 20; *16:* 58; *31:* 50
Berenstain, Jan *12:* 47; *64:* 33, 34, 36, 37, 38, 40, 42, 44; *135:* 25, 28, 31, 35
Berenstain, Stan *12:* 47; *64:* 33, 34, 36, 37, 38, 40, 42, 44; *135:* 25, 28, 31, 35
Berenzy, Alix *65:* 13; *73:* 6; *78:* 115
Berg, Joan *1:* 115; *3:* 156; *6:* 26, 58
Berg, Ron *36:* 48, 49; *48:* 37, 38; *67:* 72

Bergen, David *115:* 44; *207:* 34
Berger, Barbara *77:* 14
Berger, Carin *185:* 6
Berger, William M. *14:* 143; *YABC 1:* 204
Bergherr, Mary *74:* 170; *151:* 123
Bergin, Mark *114:* 8, 9; *143:* 95; *160:* 26, 27
Bergstreser, Douglas *69:* 76
Bergum, Constance R. *121:* 14, 15; *208:* 31, 32, 33; *209:* 176
Bering, Claus *13:* 14
Berkeley, Jon *139:* 218
Berkowitz, Jeanette *3:* 249
Berman, Paul *66:* 14
Bernal, Richard *154:* 176
Bernadette
　See Watts, Bernadette
Bernardin, James *112:* 24; *167:* 94
Bernasconi, Pablo *183:* 10, 11
Bernath, Stefen *32:* 76
Bernhard, Durga *80:* 13
Bernstein, Michel J. *51:* 71
Bernstein, Ted *38:* 183; *50:* 131
Bernstein, Zena *23:* 46
Berridge, Celia *86:* 63
Berrill, Jacquelyn *12:* 50
Berry, Erick
　See Best, Allena
Berry, Holly *205:* 116; *210:* 49, 50
Berry, William D. *14:* 29; *19:* 48
Berry, William A. *6:* 219
Berson, Harold *2:* 17, 18; *4:* 28, 29, 220; *9:* 10; *12:* 19; *17:* 45; *18:* 193; *22:* 85; *34:* 172; *44:* 120; *46:* 42; *80:* 240
Bertholf, Bret *187:* 9; *189:* 32, 33
Berton, Patsy *99:* 16
Bertschmann, Harry *16:* 1
Besco, Don *70:* 99
Beskow, Elsa *20:* 13, 14, 15
Bess, Clayton *63:* 94
Best, Allena *2:* 26; *34:* 76
Betera, Carol *74:* 68
Bethell, Thomas N. *61:* 169
Bethers, Ray *6:* 22
Bettina
　See Ehrlich, Bettina
Betts, Ethel Franklin *17:* 161, 164, 165; *YABC 2:* 47
Betz, Rudolf *59:* 161
Bewick, Thomas *16:* 40, 41, 43, 44, 45, 47; *54:* 150; *YABC 1:* 107
Beyer, Paul J. III *74:* 24
Bezencon, Jacqueline *48:* 40
Biamonte, Daniel *40:* 90
Bianchi, John *91:* 19
Bianco, Pamela *15:* 31; *28:* 44, 45, 46
Bible, Charles *13:* 15
Bice, Clare *22:* 40
Biedrzycki, David *186:* 170
Bierman, Don *57:* 184
Biggers, John *2:* 123
Biggs, Brian *192:* 38; *196:* 15; *207:* 170
Bikadoroff, Roxanna *201:* 74
Bileck, Marvin *3:* 102; *40:* 36, 37
Bilibin, Ivan *61:* 8, 9, 12, 13, 14, 15, 151, 152, 154, 162
Billington, Patrick *98:* 71
Billout, Guy *144:* 38, 39
Bimen, Levent *5:* 179
Binch, Caroline *81:* 18; *140:* 15, 16; *144:* 115; *211:* 82
Binder, Hannes *169:* 163
Bing, Christopher *126:* 34
Binger, Bill *121:* 46
Binks, Robert *25:* 150
Binzen, Bill *24:* 47
Birch, Reginald *15:* 150; *19:* 33, 34, 35, 36; *37:* 196,197; *44:* 182; *46:* 176; *YABC 1:* 84; *2:* 34, 39
Birchall, Mark *123:* 188
Bird, Esther Brock *1:* 36; *25:* 66
Birdsong, Keith *167:* 85

Birkett, Georgie *204:* 121
Birkett, Rachel *78:* 206
Birling, Paul *109:* 30
Birmingham, Christian *132:* 243; *143:* 114; *209:* 58
Birmingham, Lloyd P. *12:* 51; *83:* 13
Biro, Val *1:* 26; *41:* 42; *60:* 178; *67:* 23, 24; *84:* 242, 243
Bischoff, Ilse *44:* 51
Bishop, Don *199:* 133
Bishop, Gavin *97:* 17, 18; *144:* 42, 44
Bishop, Kathleen Wong *115:* 67
Bishop, Rich *56:* 43
Bite, I. *60:* 14
Bittinger, Ned *93:* 117; *205:* 115
Bjorklund, Lorence *3:* 188, 252; *7:* 100; *9:* 113; *10:* 66; *19:* 178; *33:* 122, 123; *35:* 36, 37, 38, 39,41, 42, 43; *36:* 185; *38:* 93; *47:* 106; *66:* 194; *YABC 1:* 242
Bjorkman, Steve *91:* 199; *160:* 110; *198:* 18
Black Sheep *164:* 100
Blackburn, Loren H. *63:* 10
Blackall, Sophie *194:* 140; *209:* 157
Blackford, John *137:* 105; *180:* 36
Blackwell, Basil T. *YABC 1:* 68, 69
Blackwood, Freya *199:* 9
Blackwood, Gary L. *118:* 17
Blades, Ann *16:* 52; *37:* 213; *50:* 41; *69:* 21; *99:* 215
Blair, Jay *45:* 46; *46:* 155
Blaisdell, Elinore *1:* 121; *3:* 134; *35:* 63
Blake, Anne Catharine *189:* 71
Blake, Francis *198:* 4
Blake, Quentin *3:* 170; *10:* 48; *13:* 38; *21:* 180; *26:* 60; *28:* 228; *30:* 29, 31; *40:* 108; *45:* 219; *46:* 165, 168; *48:* 196; *52:* 10, 11, 12,13, 14, 15, 16, 17; *73:* 41, 43; *78:* 84, 86; *80:* 250, 251; *84:* 210, 211, 212; *87:* 177; *96:* 24, 26, 28; *124:* 79; *125:* 32, 34; *181:* 139; *211:* 26, 27
Blake, Robert J. *37:* 90; *53:* 67; *54:* 23; *160:* 28, 29
Blake, William *30:* 54, 56, 57, 58, 59, 60
Blanchard, N. Taylor *82:* 140
Blass, Jacqueline *8:* 215
Blazek, Scott R. *91:* 71
Bleck, Cathie *118:* 116
Bleck, Linda *204:* 124
Blegvad, Erik *2:* 59; *3:* 98; *5:* 117; *7:* 131; *11:* 149; *14:* 34, 35; *18:* 237; *32:* 219; *60:* 106; *66:* 16, 17, 18, 19; *70:* 233; *76:* 18; *82:* 106; *87:* 45; *100:* 188; *129:* 125; *132:* 17, 18, 19, 20; *176:* 14; *200:* 100; *YABC 1:* 201
Blessen, Karen *93:* 126
Bliss, Corinne Demas *37:* 38
Bliss, Harry *196:* 27, 28, 29
Blitt, Barry *179:* 199; *187:* 13
Bloch, Lucienne *10:* 12
Blondon, Herve *129:* 48; *183:* 22
Bloom, Lloyd *35:* 180; *36:* 149; *47:* 99; *62:* 117; *68:* 231; *72:* 136; *75:* 185; *83:* 99; *108:* 19
Bloom, Suzanne *172:* 23, 24
Blossom, Dave *34:* 29
Blumenschein, E.L. *YABC 1:* 113, 115
Blumer, Patt *29:* 214
Blundell, Kim *29:* 36
Bluthenthal, Diana Cain *93:* 32; *104:* 106; *177:* 26
Blythe, Benjamin *128:* 7
Blythe, Gary *112:* 52; *181:* 166; *182:* 64; *185:* 7; *186:* 116, 117
Boake, Kathy *176:* 185
Board, Perry *171:* 99
Boardman, Gwenn *12:* 60
Boatwright, Phil *211:* 195
Bober, Richard *125:* 145; *132:* 40
Bobri *30:* 138; *47:* 27
Bock, Vera *1:* 187; *21:* 41
Bock, William Sauts *8:* 7; *14:* 37; *16:* 120; *21:* 141; *36:* 177; *62:* 203

Bodecker, N(iels) M(ogens) *8:* 13; *14:* 2; *17:* 55, 56, 57; *73:* 22, 23, 24
Boehm, Linda *40:* 31
Bogacki, Tomek *138:* 31, 32; *144:* 123; *202:* 13
Bogan, Paulette *197:* 152; *201:* 17
Bogdan, Florentina *107:* 43
Bohdal, Susi *22:* 44; *101:* 20
Bohlen, Nina *58:* 13
Boies, Alex *96:* 53
Bok, Chip *205:* 16
Bolam, Emily *101:* 216; *159:* 12; *205:* 59
Bolian, Polly *3:* 270; *4:* 30; *13:* 77; *29:* 197
Bolle, Frank *87:* 100; *208:* 101
Bollen, Roger *79:* 186; *83:* 16
Bolling, Vickey *114:* 44
Bollinger, Peter *101:* 7; *128:* 198; *172:* 26
Bolognese, Don *2:* 147, 231; *4:* 176; *7:* 146; *17:* 43; *23:* 192; *24:* 50; *34:* 108; *36:* 133; *71:* 24, 25; *103:* 131; *129:* 39, 40
Bolster, Rob *186:* 169
Bolton, A.T. *57:* 158
Bond, Arnold *18:* 116
Bond, Barbara Higgins *21:* 102
Bond, Bruce *52:* 97
Bond, Felicia *38:* 197; *49:* 55, 56; *89:* 170; *90:* 171; *126:* 37
Bond, Higgins *177:* 22, 23; *209:* 175
Bonn, Pat *43:* 40
Bonner, Hannah *197:* 13, 14
Bonners, Susan *41:* 40; *85:* 36; *94:* 99, 100; *151:* 105, 106
Bono, Mary *184:* 73
Bonsall, Crosby *23:* 6
Boon, Debbie *103:* 6; *144:* 188
Boon, Emilie *86:* 23, 24
Boone, Debbie *165:* 77
Boore, Sara *60:* 73
Bootman, Colin *155:* 13; *159:* 35; *174:* 192
Booth, Franklin *YABC 2:* 76
Booth, George *191:* 13
Booth, Graham *32:* 193; *37:* 41, 42
Borda, Juliette *102:* 188
Bordier, Georgette *16:* 54
Boren, Tinka *27:* 128
Borges, Jose Francisco *119:* 62
Borja, Robert *22:* 48
Born, Adolf *49:* 63
Bornstein, Ruth *14:* 44; *88:* 45, 46; *107:* 30
Borten, Helen *3:* 54; *5:* 24
Bosin, Blackbear *69:* 104
Bossom, Naomi *35:* 48
Bostock, Mike *83:* 221; *114:* 14; *188:* 205
Boston, Peter *19:* 42
Bosustow, Stephen *34:* 202
Boszko, Ron *75:* 47
Bottner, Barbara *14:* 46
Boucher, Joelle *41:* 138
Boulat, Pierre *44:* 40
Boulet, Susan Seddon *50:* 47
Bouma, Paddy *118:* 25; *128:* 16
Bour, Daniele *66:* 145
Bourke-White, Margaret *15:* 286, 287; *57:* 102
Boutavant, Marc *200:* 136
Boutet de Monvel, M. *30:* 61, 62, 63, 65
Bowen, Betsy *105:* 222
Bowen, Richard *42:* 134
Bowen, Ruth *31:* 188
Bower, Ron *29:* 33
Bowers, David *95:* 38; *115:* 20; *127:* 169, 170; *165:* 57; *207:* 11
Bowers, Tim *185:* 35; *201:* 41
Bowman, Claire *174:* 177
Bowman, Eric *151:* 23
Bowman, Leslie *85:* 203; *105:* 108; *116:* 76; *128:* 234; *182:* 24, 25
Bowman, Peter *146:* 214, 215; *150:* 115
Bowser, Carolyn Ewing *22:* 253
Boxall, Ed *178:* 28
Boyd, Aaron *158:* 242
Boyd, Patti *45:* 31

Boyle, Eleanor Vere *28:* 50, 51
Boynton, Sandra *57:* 13, 14, 15; *107:* 36, 37; *152:* 12, 13, 14
Bozzo, Frank *4:* 154
Brabbs, Derry *55:* 170
Brace, Eric *132:* 193, 194; *152:* 71; *184:* 195; *197:* 6; *201:* 54
Brackers de Hugo, Pierre *115:* 21
Bradford, June *158:* 138
Bradford, Ron *7:* 157
Bradley, David P. *69:* 105
Bradley, Richard D. *26:* 182
Bradley, William *5:* 164
Brady, Irene *4:* 31; *42:* 37; *68:* 191
Bragg, Michael *32:* 78; *46:* 31
Bragg, Ruth Gembicki *77:* 18
Brainerd, John W. *65:* 19
Braithwaite, Althea *23:* 12, 13; *119:* 16
Brak, Syd *146:* 187
Bralds, Braldt *90:* 28; *91:* 151
Bram, Elizabeth *30:* 67
Bramley, Peter *4:* 3
Brandenberg, Aliki *2:* 36, 37; *24:* 222; *35:* 49, 50, 51,52, 53, 54, 56, 57; *75:* 15, 17; *92:* 205; *113:* 18, 19, 20; *157:* 28; *156:* 111
Brandenburg, Alexa *75:* 19
Brandenburg, Jim *47:* 58; *150:* 212
Brandi, Lillian *31:* 158
Brandon, Brumsic, Jr. *9:* 25
Brannen, Sarah S. *202:* 15
Bransom, Paul *17:* 121; *43:* 44
Braren, Loretta Trezzo *87:* 193
Brassard, France *186:* 22
Braun, Wendy *80:* 17, 18
Brautigam, Don *115:* 175, 176
Brazell, Derek *75:* 105; *79:* 9
Breathed, Berkeley *86:* 27, 28, 29; *161:* 13, 14
Breckenreid, Julia *192:* 209
Breen, Steve *186:* 23
Brennan, Steve *83:* 230; *101:* 184
Brenner, Fred *22:* 85; *36:* 34; *42:* 34
Brett, Bernard *22:* 54
Brett, Harold M. *26:* 98, 99, 100
Brett, Jan *30:* 135; *42:* 39; *71:* 31, 32; *130:* 23, 24, 25, 26, 27; *171:* 15, 16
Brewer, Paul *106:* 115; *145:* 202
Brewer, Sally King *33:* 44
Brewster, Patience *40:* 68; *45:* 22, 183; *51:* 20; *66:* 144; *89:* 4; *97:* 30, 31
Brick, John *10:* 15
Brickman, Robin D. *131:* 88; *142:* 150; *155:* 18; *178:* 109; *184:* 32
Bridge, David R. *45:* 28
Bridgman, L.J. *37:* 77
Bridwell, Norman *4:* 37; *138:* 36, 37, 40
Brierley, Louise *91:* 22; *96:* 165; *183:* 51
Briggs, Harry *172:* 187
Briggs, Raymond *10:* 168; *23:* 20, 21; *66:* 29, 31, 32; *131:* 28, 29; *184:* 15, 16
Brigham, Grace A. *37:* 148
Bright, Robert *24:* 55
Brighton, Catherine *107:* 39; *206:* 23
Brinckloe, Julie *13:* 18; *24:* 79, 115; *29:* 35; *63:* 140; *81:* 131
Brion *47:* 116
Brisley, Joyce L. *22:* 57
Brisson, James F. *110:* 60
Brittingham, Geoffrey *88:* 37
Brix-Henker, Silke *81:* 194
Broadway, Hannah *208:* 104
Brock, Charles E. *15:* 97; *19:* 247, 249; *23:* 224, 225; *36:* 88; *42:* 41, 42, 43, 44, 45; *100:* 189; *YABC 1:* 194, 196, 203
Brock, Emma *7:* 21
Brock, Henry Matthew *15:* 81; *16:* 141; *19:* 71; *34:* 115; *40:* 164; *42:* 47, 48, 49; *49:* 66
Brocksopp, Arthur *57:* 157
Broda, Ron *136:* 180; *174:* 123
Brodkin, Gwen *34:* 135
Brodovitch, Alexi *52:* 22
Bromhall, Winifred *5:* 11; *26:* 38

Bromley, Lizzy *159:* 179
Bronson, Linda *150:* 210; *174:* 133; *203:* 16, 17
Brooke, L. Leslie *16:* 181, 182, 183, 186; *17:* 15, 16, 17; *18:* 194
Brooker, Christopher *15:* 251
Brooker, Kyrsten *111:* 94; *140:* 28; *162:* 111; *175:* 108; *186:* 42, 225; *199:* 12; *201:* 30
Brooks, Erik *166:* 52; *182:* 30
Brooks, Karen Stormer *186:* 110
Brooks, Maya Itzna *92:* 153
Brooks, Ron *94:* 15; *197:* 188
Brooks, S.G. *178:* 127
Broomfield, Maurice *40:* 141
Brotman, Adolph E. *5:* 21
Brown, Buck *45:* 48
Brown, Calef *179:* 18; *210:* 206
Brown, Christopher *62:* 124, 125, 127, 128
Brown, Craig McFarland *73:* 28; *84:* 65
Brown, Dan *61:* 167; *115:* 183, 184; *116:* 28, 29; *193:* 190; *200:* 21, 23
Brown, David *7:* 47; *48:* 52
Brown, Denise *11:* 213
Brown, Don *172:* 29
Brown, Elbrite *195:* 39; *198:* 5
Brown, Ford Madox *48:* 74
Brown, Hunter *191:* 111, 112
Brown, Judith Gwyn *1:* 45; *7:* 5; *8:* 167; *9:* 182, 190; *20:* 16, 17, 18; *23:* 142; *29:* 117; *33:* 97; *36:* 23, 26; *43:* 184; *48:* 201, 223; *49:* 69; *86:* 227; *110:* 188; *153:* 7
Brown, Kathryn *98:* 26
Brown, Lisa *187:* 175
Brown, Laurie Krasny *99:* 30
Brown, Marc (Tolon) *10:* 17, 197; *14:* 263; *51:* 18; *53:* 11, 12, 13, 15, 16, 17; *75:* 58; *80:* 24, 25, 26; *82:* 261; *99:* 29; *145:* 22, 23, 25, 27; *162:* 198
Brown, Marcia *7:* 30; *25:* 203; *47:* 31, 32, 33, 34, 35,36, 37, 38, 39, 40, 42, 43, 44; *YABC 1:* 27
Brown, Margery W. *5:* 32, 33; *10:* 3
Brown, Martin *101:* 43
Brown, Mary Barrett *97:* 74
Brown, Palmer *36:* 40
Brown, Paul *25:* 26; *26:* 107
Brown, Richard *61:* 18; *67:* 30
Brown, Rick *78:* 71; *150:* 154
Brown, Robert S. *85:* 33
Brown, Rod *157:* 142
Brown, Ruth *55:* 165; *86:* 112, 113; *105:* 16, 17, 18; *171:* 178
Brown, Trevor *99:* 160; *139:* 247; *189:* 206
Browne, Anthony *45:* 50, 51, 52; *61:* 21, 22, 23, 24, 25; *105:* 21, 22, 23, 25
Browne, Dik *8:* 212; *67:* 32, 33, 35, 37, 39
Browne, Gordon *16:* 97; *64:* 114, 116, 117, 119, 121
Browne, Hablot K. *15:* 65, 80; *21:* 14, 15, 16, 17, 18, 19,20; *24:* 25
Browne, Jane *165:* 222
Browning, Coleen *4:* 132
Browning, Mary Eleanor *24:* 84
Bruce, Robert *23:* 23
Brude, Dick *48:* 215
Bruel, Nick *166:* 41; *205:* 17, 18
Brule, Al *3:* 135
Brumbeau, Jeff *157:* 29
Bruna, Dick *43:* 48, 49, 50; *76:* 27, 28
Brundage, Frances *19:* 244
Brunhoff, Jean de *24:* 57, 58
Brunhoff, Laurent de *24:* 60; *71:* 35, 36, 37
Brunkus, Denise *84:* 50; *123:* 117; *178:* 209; *193:* 99; *204:* 10, 11, 12; *209:* 202
Brunson, Bob *43:* 135
Bryan, Ashley *31:* 44; *72:* 27, 28, 29; *107:* 92; *116:* 192; *132:* 24; *178:* 33, 34, 35; *208:* 83
Bryant, Laura J. *176:* 36; *183:* 168
Bryant, Michael *93:* 74
Brychta, Alex *21:* 21
Bryer, Diana *107:* 121

Bryson, Bernarda *3:* 88, 146; *39:* 26; *44:* 185; *131:* 40
Buba, Joy *12:* 83; *30:* 226; *44:* 56
Buchanan, George *166:* 198
Buchanan, Lilian *13:* 16
Buchanan, Rachel *171:* 71
Bucholtz-Ross, Linda *44:* 137
Buchs, Thomas *40:* 38
Buck, Margaret Waring *3:* 30
Buckhardt, Marc *172:* 59
Buckley, Mike *166:* 180
Budwine, Greg *175:* 172
Buehner, Mark *104:* 12, 15; *105:* 160; *119:* 98; *157:* 188; *159:* 39, 40, 43; *192:* 111
Buehr, Walter *3:* 31
Buff, Conrad *19:* 52, 53, 54
Buff, Mary *19:* 52, 53
Bull, Charles Livingston *18:* 207; *88:* 175, 176
Bullen, Anne *3:* 166, 167
Buller, Jon *205:* 21
Bullock, Kathleen *77:* 24
Bumgarner-Kirby, Claudia *77:* 194
Burbank, Addison *37:* 43
Burchard, Peter Duncan *3:* 197; *5:* 35; *6:* 158, 218; *143:* 17
Burckhardt, Marc *94:* 48; *110:* 89; *196:* 41; *199:* 116
Burger, Carl *3:* 33; *45:* 160, 162
Burgeson, Marjorie *19:* 31
Burgess, Anne *76:* 252
Burgess, Gelett *32:* 39, 42
Burgess, Mark *157:* 31
Burke, Jim *179:* 19; *185:* 63
Burke, Phillip *95:* 117
Burkert, Nancy Ekholm *18:* 186; *22:* 140; *24:* 62, 63,64, 65; *26:* 53; *29:* 60, 61; *46:* 171; *YABC 1:* 46
Burkhardt, Bruce *142:* 86
Burkhardt, Melissa A. *142:* 86
Burleson, Joe *104:* 35; *172:* 139
Burn, Doris *6:* 172
Burn, Jeffrey *89:* 125; *152:* 132
Burn, Ted
    See Burn, Thomas E.
Burn, Thomas E. *151:* 41
Burnard, Damon *115:* 23
Burnett, Lindy *210:* 59
Burnett, Virgil *44:* 42
Burningham, John *9:* 68; *16:* 60, 61; *59:* 28, 29, 30,31, 32, 33, 35; *111:* 18, 19, 21; *160:* 37
Burns, Howard M. *12:* 173
Burns, Jim *47:* 70; *86:* 32; *91:* 197; *123:* 16
Burns, M.F. *26:* 69
Burns, Raymond *9:* 29
Burns, Robert *24:* 106
Burr, Dan *65:* 28; *108:* 134; *164:* 203; *182:* 68
Burr, Dane *12:* 2
Burra, Edward *YABC 2:* 68
Burrell, Galen *56:* 76
Burri, Rene *41:* 143; *54:* 166
Burridge, Marge Opitz *14:* 42
Burris, Burmah *4:* 81
Burroughs, John Coleman *41:* 64
Burroughs, Studley O. *41:* 65
Burton, Marilee Robin *46:* 33
Burton, Virginia Lee *2:* 43; *44:* 49, 51; *100:* 46, 47; *YABC 1:* 24; *147:* 56
Busoni, Rafaello *1:* 186; *3:* 224; *6:* 126; *14:* 5; *16:* 62, 63
Butchkes, Sidney *50:* 58
Butler, Geoff *94:* 20
Butler, Ralph *116:* 212
Butterfield, Ned *1:* 153; *27:* 128; *79:* 63
Butterworth, Ian *184:* 48, 49
Butterworth, Nick *106:* 43, 44; *149:* 34
Buxton, John *123:* 12
Buzelli, Christopher *105:* 149
Buzonas, Gail *29:* 88
Buzzell, Russ W. *12:* 177

Byard, Carole *39:* 44; *57:* 18, 19, 20; *60:* 60; *61:* 93, 96; *69:* 210; *78:* 246; *79:* 227
Byars, Betsy *46:* 35
Byfield, Barbara Ninde *8:* 18
Byfield, Graham *32:* 29
Bynum, Janie *176:* 50
Byrd, Robert *13:* 218; *33:* 46; *158:* 70
Byrd, Samuel *123:* 104

C

Cabat, Erni *74:* 38
Cabban, Vanessa *138:* 73; *176:* 39; *185:* 65
Cabrera, Jane *103:* 24; *152:* 27; *182:* 33, 34
Caceres, Ana Palmero *198:* 106
Caddy, Alice *6:* 41
Cady, Harrison *17:* 21, 23; *19:* 57, 58
Caffrey, Aileen *72:* 223; *141:* 154
Cairns, Julia *177:* 37
Caldecott, Randolph *16:* 98, 103; *17:* 32, 33, 36, 38, 39; *26:* 90; *100:* 49, 50; *YABC 2:* 172
Calder, Alexander *18:* 168
Calderón, Gloria *179:* 5
Calderon, W. Frank *25:* 160
Caldwell, Ben *105:* 75; *149:* 60; *195:* 61
Caldwell, Clyde *98:* 100; *116:* 39; *208:* 145
Caldwell, Doreen *23:* 77; *71:* 41
Caldwell, John *46:* 225
Call, Greg *126:* 135; *165:* 49; *182:* 105, 163; *197:* 18, 19; *200:* 159; *209:* 166
Callahan, Kevin *22:* 42
Callahan, Philip S. *25:* 77
Callan, Jamie *59:* 37
Calvin, James *61:* 92
Camburn-Bracalente, Carol A. *118:* 22
Cameron, Chad *190:* 144
Cameron, Julia Margaret *19:* 203
Cameron, Scott *99:* 18
Camm, Martin *140:* 208, 209, 210
Campbell, Ann *11:* 43; *123:* 182; *183:* 68
Campbell, Bill *89:* 39
Campbell, Ken *126:* 143; *205:* 162
Campbell, Robert *55:* 120
Campbell, Rod *51:* 27; *98:* 34
Campbell, Walter M. *YABC 2:* 158
Camps, Luis *28:* 120, 121; *66:* 35
Canga, C.B. *187:* 165
Caniglia, Jeremy *201:* 89
Cann, Helen *124:* 50; *141:* 78; *170:* 138; *179:* 22, 23
Cannell, Jon *196:* 43
Cannon, Janell *78:* 25; *128:* 40
Canright, David *36:* 162
Cantone, AnnaLaura *182:* 146; *196:* 80
Canty, Thomas *85:* 161; *92:* 47; *113:* 192; *134:* 60; *185:* 117
Canyon, Christopher *150:* 44; *151:* 112
Caparo, Antonio Javier *204:* 128
Caporale, Wende *70:* 42
Capp, Al *61:* 28, 30, 31, 40, 41, 43, 44
Cappon, Manuela *154:* 64
Caras, Peter *36:* 64
Caraway, Caren *57:* 22
Caraway, James *3:* 200, 201
Carbe, Nino *29:* 183
Cares, Linda *67:* 176
Carigiet, Alois *24:* 67
Carle, Eric *4:* 42; *11:* 121; *12:* 29; *65:* 32,33, 34, 36; *73:* 63, 65; *163:* 55, 56
Carling, Amelia Lau *164:* 46
Carlino, Angela *168:* 43; *188:* 20
Carlson, Nancy L. *41:* 116; *56:* 25; *90:* 45; *144:* 48, 50
Carlluccio, Maria *175:* 129
Carmi, Giora *79:* 35; *149:* 40; *208:* 126
Carpenter, Nancy *76:* 128; *86:* 173; *89:* 171; *131:* 186; *134:* 8; *138:* 215; *153:* 204; *159:* 93; *165:* 232; *211:* 134

Carr, Archie 37: 225
Carrick, Donald 5: 194; 39: 97; 49: 70; 53: 156; 63: 15, 16, 17, 18, 19, 21; 80: 131; 86: 151; 118: 24
Carrick, Malcolm 28: 59, 60
Carrick, Paul 118: 26; 194: 28
Carrick, Valery 21: 47
Carrier, Lark 71: 43
Carroll, Jim 88: 211; 140: 177; 153: 99; 195: 75
Carroll, Lewis
See Dodgson, Charles L.
Carroll, Michael 72: 5
Carroll, Pamela 84: 68; 128: 214; 199: 130
Carroll, Ruth 7: 41; 10: 68
Carter, Abby 81: 32; 97: 121; 102: 61; 163: 139; 164: 125; 184: 22, 23; 191: 85
Carter, Barbara 47: 167, 169
Carter, David A. 114: 24, 25; 170: 42, 43
Carter, Don 124: 54; 184: 100; 192: 43, 44, 45
Carter, Harry 22: 179
Carter, Helene 15: 38; 22: 202, 203; YABC 2: 220, 221
Carter, Penny 173: 91
Cartlidge, Michelle 49: 65; 96: 50, 51
Cartwright, Reg 63: 61, 62; 78: 26; 143: 4
Cartwright, Shannon 176: 81
Carty, Leo 4: 196; 7: 163; 58: 131
Cary 4: 133; 9: 32; 20: 2; 21: 143
Cary, Page 12: 41
Casale, Paul 71: 63; 109: 122; 136: 28
Case, Chris 209: 23
Case, Sandra E. 16: 2
Caseley, Judith 87: 36; 159: 47, 48, 49
Casilla, Robert 78: 7; 167: 124; 211: 41
Casino, Steve 85: 193
Cassel, Lili
See Wronker, Lili Cassel
Cassel-Wronker, Lili
See Wronker, Lili Cassel
Cassels, Jean 8: 50; 150: 119; 173: 37; 186: 182
Cassen, Melody 140: 51
Cassity, Don 104: 24
Cassler, Carl 75: 137, 138; 82: 162
Casson, Hugh 65: 38, 40, 42, 43
Castellon, Federico 48: 45, 46, 47, 48
Castle, Jane 4: 80
Castro, Antonio 84: 71
Casu, Danny "casroc" 201: 10
Catalano, Dominic 94: 79; 163: 60, 61; 162: 54
Catalanotto, Peter 63: 170; 70: 23; 71: 182; 72: 96; 74: 114; 76: 194, 195; 77: 7; 79: 157; 80: 28, 67; 83: 157; 85: 27; 108: 11; 113: 30, 31, 33, 34, 36; 114: 27, 28, 29; 117: 53; 124: 168; 159: 54, 55; 195: 19, 20, 21, 22, 24, 174; 200: 156; 207: 103; 209: 184
Catania, Tom 68: 82
Cather, Carolyn 3: 83; 15: 203; 34: 216
Catrow, David 117: 179; 152: 31, 33; 173: 24; 206: 29
Cauley, Lorinda Bryan 44: 135; 46: 49
Cayard, Bruce 38: 67
Cazet, Denys 52: 27; 99: 39, 40; 163: 65, 66; 191: 25, 27, 28
Ceccoli, Nicoletta 181: 39; 188: 99; 199: 118; 209: 6
Cecil, Randy 127: 132, 133; 187: 16, 17; 191: 168; 209: 5
Cellini, Joseph 2: 73; 3: 35; 16: 116; 47: 103
Cepeda, Joe 90: 62; 109: 91; 134: 172; 159: 57, 58, 164; 197: 157; 203: 69, 95
Chabrian, Debbi 45: 55
Chabrian, Deborah 51: 182; 53: 124; 63: 107; 75: 84; 79: 85; 82: 247; 89: 93; 101: 197
Chagnon, Mary 37: 158
Chalmers, Mary 3: 145; 13: 148; 33: 125; 66: 214
Chamberlain, Christopher 45: 57

Chamberlain, Margaret 46: 51; 106: 89; 188: 193
Chamberlain, Nigel 78: 140
Chambers, C.E. 17: 230
Chambers, Dave 12: 151
Chambers, Jill 134: 110
Chambers, Mary 4: 188
Chambliss, Maxie 42: 186; 56: 159; 93: 163, 164; 103: 178; 186: 33, 34; 196: 39
Champlin, Dale 136: 124
Chan, Harvey 96: 236; 99: 153; 143: 218; 179: 144; 211: 219
Chan, Peter 207: 21
Chandler, David P. 28: 62
Chaney, Howard 139: 27
Chang, Warren 101: 209
Chapel, Jody 68: 20
Chapman, C.H. 13: 83, 85, 87
Chapman, Frederick T. 6: 27; 44: 28
Chapman, Gaye 203: 133
Chapman, Gaynor 32: 52, 53
Chapman, Jane 145: 186; 150: 56; 166: 220; 174: 202; 176: 43, 44; 179: 131; 202: 189
Chapman, Lynne 175: 31; 197: 25; 208: 44
Chappell, Warren 3: 172; 21: 56; 27: 125
Charles, Donald 30: 154, 155
Charlip, Remy 4: 48; 34: 138; 68: 53, 54; 119: 29, 30; 210: 63, 64
Charlot, Jean 1: 137, 138; 8: 23; 14: 31; 48: 151; 56: 21
Charlot, Martin 64: 72
Charlton, Michael 34: 50; 37: 39
Charmatz, Bill 7: 45
Chartier, Normand 9: 36; 52: 49; 66: 40; 74: 220; 145: 169; 168: 91; 177: 108
Chase, Lynwood M. 14: 4
Chast, Roz 97: 39, 40
Chastain, Madye Lee 4: 50
Chateron, Ann 152: 19
Chatterton, Martin 68: 102; 152: 19
Chau, Tungwai 140: 35
Chauncy, Francis 24: 158
Chayka, Doug 145: 97; 177: 150; 196: 46
Chee, Cheng-Khee 79: 42; 81: 224; 180: 245
Chen, Chih-sien 90: 226
Chen, Tony 6: 45; 19: 131; 29: 126; 34: 160
Chen, Yong 183: 34
Cheney, T.A. 11: 47
Cheng, Andrea 205: 28
Cheng, Judith 36: 45; 51: 16
Chermayeff, Ivan 47: 53
Cherry, David 93: 40
Cherry, Lynne 34: 52; 65: 184; 87: 111; 99: 46, 47
Chesak, Lina 135: 118
Chess, Victoria 12: 6; 33: 42, 48, 49; 40: 194; 41: 145; 69: 80; 72: 100; 92: 33, 34; 104: 167
Chessare, Michele 41: 50; 56: 48; 69: 145
Chesterton, G.K. 27: 43, 44, 45, 47
Chestnutt, David 47: 217
Chesworth, Michael 75: 24, 152; 88: 136; 94: 25; 98: 155; 160: 42; 207: 23, 24, 25
Chetham, Celia 134: 34
Chetwin, Grace 86: 40
Cheung, Irving 158: 96
Chevalier, Christa 35: 66
Chew, Ruth 7: 46; 132: 147
Chewning, Randy 92: 206
Chichester Clark, Emma 72: 121; 77: 212; 78: 209; 87: 143; 117: 37, 39, 40; 144: 138; 156: 24, 25; 209: 26
Chifflart 47: 113, 127
Child, Lauren 119: 32; 183: 30, 31
Chin, Alex 28: 54
Chitwood, Susan Tanner 163: 16
Cho, Shinta 8: 126
Chodos-Irvine, Margaret 52: 102, 103, 107; 152: 44
Choi, Yangsook 171: 134; 173: 135; 178: 38, 39, 40

Chollat, Emilie 170: 203
Chollick, Jay 25: 175
Choma, Christina 99: 169
Chomey, Steve 188: 53
Chorao, Kay 7: 200, 201; 8: 25; 11: 234; 33: 187; 35: 239; 69: 35; 70: 235; 123: 174; 193: 179
Chow, Frances J. Soo Ping 206: 36
Chowdhury, Subrata 62: 130; 162: 22, 23
Christelow, Eileen 38: 44; 83: 198, 199; 90: 57, 58; 184: 26
Christensen, Bonnie 93: 100; 153: 67
Christensen, Gardell Dano 1: 57
Christensen, James C. 140: 226
Christiana, David 90: 64; 135: 13; 171: 7; 195: 26, 27
Christiansen, Per 40: 24
Christie, R. Gregory 116: 107; 127: 20, 21; 162: 179; 164: 114; 165: 137; 174: 157; 179: 172; 185: 17, 18, 19; 200: 2; 204: 85
Christy, Howard Chandler 17: 163, 164, 165, 168, 169; 19: 186, 187; 21: 22, 23, 24, 25
Christy, Jana 194: 21
Chronister, Robert 23: 138; 63: 27; 69: 167
Church, Caroline Jayne 179: 27
Church, Frederick YABC 1: 155
Chute, Marchette 1: 59
Chwast, Jacqueline 1: 63; 2: 275; 6: 46, 47; 11: 125; 12: 202; 14: 235
Chwast, Seymour 3: 128, 129; 18: 43; 27: 152; 92: 79; 96: 56, 57, 58; 146: 32, 33; 197: 99
Cieslawksi, Steve 101: 142; 127: 116; 158: 169, 171; 190: 174
Cinelli, Lisa 146: 253
Cirlin, Edgard 2: 168
Clairin, Georges 53: 109
Clapp, John 105: 66; 109: 58; 126: 7; 129: 148; 130: 165; 195: 48
Clark, Brenda 119: 85; 153: 55
Clark, David 77: 164; 134: 144, 145
Clark, Emma Chichester
See Chichester Clark, Emma
Clark, Victoria 35: 159
Clarke, Greg 169: 134
Clarke, Gus 72: 226; 134: 31
Clarke, Harry 23: 172, 173
Clarke, Peter 75: 102
Claverie, Jean 38: 46; 88: 29
Clavis, Philippe Goossens 182: 167
Clay, Wil 203: 29
Clayton, Elaine 159: 60; 209: 32
Clayton, Robert 9: 181
Cleary, Brian P. 186: 37
Cleaver, Elizabeth 8: 204; 23: 36
Cleland, T.M. 26: 92
Clemens, Peter 61: 125
Clement, Charles 20: 38
Clement, Gary 186: 79; 191: 32
Clement, Janet 182: 50
Clement, Nathan 200: 30
Clement, Rod 97: 42
Clement, Stephen 88: 3
Clementson, John 84: 213
Clemesha, David 192: 49, 50
Clevin, Jorgen 7: 50
Clifford, Judy 34: 163; 45: 198
Clokey, Art 59: 44
Clouse, Dennis 187: 158
Clouse, James 84: 15
Clouse, Nancy L. 78: 31; 114: 90
Clover, Peter 152: 45
Cneut, Carll 156: 166; 165: 67; 197: 26
Coalson, Glo 9: 72, 85; 25: 155; 26: 42; 35: 212; 53: 31; 56: 154; 94: 37, 38, 193
Cober, Alan E. 17: 158; 32: 77; 49: 127
Cober-Gentry, Leslie 92: 111
Cocca-Leffler, Maryann 80: 46; 136: 60; 139: 193; 194: 31, 33, 34
Cochran, Bobbye 11: 52
CoConis, Ted 4: 41; 46: 41; 51: 104

Cocozza, Chris 87: 18; 110: 173; 111: 149
Cockroft, Jason 152: 20
Coerr, Eleanor 1: 64; 67: 52
Coes, Peter 35: 172
Cogancherry, Helen 52: 143; 69: 131; 77: 93; 78: 220; 109: 204; 110: 129; 203: 92
Coggins, Jack 2: 69
Cohen, Alix 7: 53
Cohen, Miriam 155: 23, 24
Cohen, Nancy R. 165: 35
Cohen, Santiago 164: 26
Cohen, Sheldon 105: 33, 34; 166: 46, 47
Cohen, Vincent O. 19: 243
Cohen, Vivien 11: 112
Coker, Paul 51: 172
Colbert, Anthony 15: 41; 20: 193
Colby, C.B. 3: 47
Cole, Babette 58: 172; 96: 63, 64; 155: 29
Cole, Brock 68: 223; 72: 36, 37, 38, 192; 127: 23; 136: 64, 65; 197:
Cole, Gwen 87: 185
Cole, Henry 178: 120; 181: 42, 43; 189: 60
Cole, Herbert 28: 104
Cole, Michael 59: 46
Cole, Olivia H.H. 1: 134; 3: 223; 9: 111; 38: 104
Cole, Rachael 209: 39
Colin, Paul 102: 59; 123: 118; 126: 152; 192: 129
Colley, Jacqui 202: 20
Collicott, Sharleen 98: 39; 143: 29, 30
Collier, Bryan 126: 54; 151: 166; 174: 16, 17, 18; 204: 18, 19; 208: 84; 211: 143
Collier, David 13: 127
Collier, John 27: 179; 208: 154
Collier, Steven 50: 52
Collier-Morales, Roberta 168: 61
Collins, Heather 66: 84; 67: 68; 81: 40; 98: 192, 193; 129: 95, 96, 98
Collins, Matt 167: 90
Collins, Ross 140: 23, 24; 200: 36, 37; 209: 54
Colman, Audrey 146: 161
Colón, Raul 108: 112; 113: 5; 117: 167; 134: 112; 146: 23; 159: 92; 166: 73; 180: 107; 186: 156; 190: 6; 193: 24, 205; 202: 21, 22, 23
Colonna, Bernard 21: 50; 28: 103; 34: 140; 43: 180; 78: 150
Comport, Sally Wern 117: 169; 169: 104; 190: 42; 207: 50
Conde, J.M. 100: 120
Condon, Grattan 54: 85 Condon, Ken 161: 44; 195: 28, 29
Cone, Ferne Geller 39: 49
Cone, J. Morton 39: 49
Conklin, Paul 43: 62
Connelly, James 198: 12
Connolly, Howard 67: 88
Connolly, Jerome P. 4: 128; 28: 52
Connolly, Peter 47: 60
Conoly, Walle 110: 224
Conover, Chris 31: 52; 40: 184; 41: 51; 44: 79
Constantin, Pascale 207: 159
Contreras, Gerry 72: 9
Converse, James 38: 70
Conway 62: 62
Conway, Michael 69: 12; 81: 3; 92: 108
Cook, Ande 188: 135
Cook, G.R. 29: 165
Cook, Joel 108: 160
Cookburn, W.V. 29: 204
Cooke, Donald E. 2: 77
Cooke, Tom 52: 118
Coomaraswamy, A.K. 50: 100
Coombs, Charles 43: 65
Coombs, Deborah 139: 175
Coombs, Patricia 2: 82; 3: 52; 22: 119; 51: 32, 33, 34, 35, 36, 37, 38, 39, 40, 42, 43

Cooney, Barbara 6: 16, 17, 50; 12: 42; 13: 92; 15: 145; 16: 74, 111; 18: 189; 23: 38, 89, 93; 32: 138; 38: 105; 59: 48, 49, 51, 52, 53; 74: 222; 81: 100; 91: 25; 96: 71, 72, 74; 100: 149; YABC2: 10
Cooper, Elisha 157: 38, 39
Cooper, Floyd 79: 95; 81: 45; 84: 82; 85: 74; 91: 118; 96: 77, 78; 103: 149; 144: 54; 145: 151; 159: 198; 176: 133, 134; 187: 26, 27, 28, 29; 188: 22; 199: 175
Cooper, Heather 50: 39
Cooper, Helen 102: 42, 43, 44
Cooper, Mario 24: 107
Cooper, Marjorie 7: 112
Cope, Jane 61: 201; 108 52
Copeland, Mark 180: 12
Copelman, Evelyn 8: 61; 18: 25
Copley, Heather 30: 86; 45: 57
Corace, Jen 208: 48
Corbett, Grahame 30: 114; 43: 67
Corbino, John 19: 248
Corcos, Lucille 2: 223; 10: 27; 34: 66
Cordell, Matthew 197: 93; 199: 20, 21
Corey, Robert 9: 34
Corlass, Heather 10: 7
Cornell, James 27: 60
Cornell, Jeff 11: 58
Cornell, Laura 94: 179; 95: 25
Corr, Christopher 204: 98
Corrigan, Barbara 8: 37
Corrigan, Patrick 145: 149
Corwin, Judith Hoffman 10: 28
Corwin, Oliver 191: 119
Cory, Fanny Y. 20: 113; 48: 29
Cosentino, Ralph 169: 32
Cosgrove, Margaret 3: 100; 47: 63; 82: 133
Costabel, Eva Deutsch 45: 66, 67
Costanza, John 58: 7, 8, 9
Costello, Chris 86: 78
Costello, David F. 23: 55
Côté, Geneviéve 184: 37, 39; 210: 256; 211: 151
Cote, Nancy 126: 139; 156: 101; 174: 101; 182: 53, 54, 55
Cottenden, Jeff 190: 45
Couch, Greg 94: 124; 110: 13; 162: 31; 168: 149; 199: 22
Councell, Ruth Tietjen 79: 29
Courtney, Cathy 58: 69, 144; 59: 15; 61: 20, 87
Courtney, R. 35: 110
Counihan, Claire 133: 106
Cousineau, Normand 89: 180; 112: 76
Cousins, Lucy 172: 53, 54; 205: 34, 35
Couture, Christin 41: 209
Covarrubias, Miguel 35: 118, 119, 123, 124, 125
Coville, Katherine 32: 57; 36: 167; 92: 38
Covington, Neverne 113: 87
Cowdrey, Richard 169: 170; 178: 205; 204: 22, 23
Cowell, Cressida 140: 39
Cowell, Lucinda 77: 54
Cowles, Rose 203: 164, 167
Cox 43: 93
Cox, Charles 8: 20
Cox, David 56: 37; 90: 63; 119: 38
Cox, Palmer 24: 76, 77
Cox, Steve 140: 96
Coxe, Molly 69: 44
Coxon, Michele 158: 80
Crabb, Gordon 70: 39
Crabtree, Judith 98: 42
Craft, Kinuko 22: 182; 36: 220; 53: 122, 123, 148,149; 74: 12; 81: 129; 86: 31; 89: 139; 127: 27, 28, 29; 132: 142; 139: 38
Craig, Daniel 177: 67; 180: 11; 185: 203; 211: 212
Craig, David 136: 198; 205: 37
Craig, Helen 49: 76; 62: 70, 71, 72; 69: 141; 94: 42, 43, 44; 112: 53; 135: 101, 102

Crane, Alan H. 1: 217
Crane, H.M. 13: 111
Crane, Jack 43: 183
Crane, Jordan 174: 21
Crane, Walter 18: 46, 47, 48, 49, 53, 54, 56, 57, 59, 60, 61; 22: 128; 24: 210, 217; 100: 70, 71
Cravath, Lynne W. 98: 45; 182: 58, 59
Crawford, Denise 137: 213
Crawford, Will 43: 77
Credle, Ellis 1: 69
Czernecki, Stefan 154: 104; 178: 68, 69
Crespi, Francesca 87: 90
Cressy, Michael 124: 55; 203: 132
Crews, Donald 32: 59, 60; 76: 42, 43, 44
Crews, Nina 97: 49
Crichlow, Ernest 74: 88; 83: 203
Crilley, Mark 210: 71
Croft, James 150: 57
Crofut, Bob 80: 87; 81: 47
Crofut, Susan 23: 61
Croll, Carolyn 80: 137; 102: 52
Cross, Peter 56: 78; 63: 60, 65
Crowe, Elizabeth 88: 144
Crowell, Pers 3: 125
Cruikshank, George 15: 76, 83; 22: 74, 75, 76, 77, 78, 79,80, 81, 82, 84, 137; 24: 22, 23
Crump, Fred H. 11: 62
Cruz, Ray 6: 55; 70: 234; 123: 173; 172: 192
Csatari, Joe 44: 82; 55: 152; 63: 25, 28; 102: 58
Cuetara, Mittie 158: 85
Cuffari, Richard 4: 75; 5: 98; 6: 56; 7: 13,84, 153; 8: 148, 155; 9: 89; 11: 19; 12: 55, 96,114; 15: 51, 202; 18: 5; 20: 139; 21: 197; 22: 14, 192; 23: 15, 106; 25: 97; 27: 133; 28: 196; 29: 54; 30: 85; 31: 35; 36: 101; 38: 171; 42: 97; 44: 92, 192; 45: 212, 213; 46: 36, 198; 50: 164; 54: 80, 136, 137, 145; 56: 17; 60: 63; 66: 49, 50; 70: 41; 71: 132; 77: 157; 78: 58, 149; 79: 120; 85: 2, 152
Cugat, Xavier 19: 120
Cumings, Art 35: 160
Cummings, Chris 29: 167
Cummings, Michael 159: 142
Cummings, Pat 42: 61; 61: 99; 69: 205; 71: 57,58; 78: 24, 25; 93: 75; 107: 49, 50; 164: 259; 203: 45, 46
Cummings, Richard 24: 119
Cunette, Lou 20: 93; 22: 125
Cunningham, Aline 25: 180
Cunningham, David 11: 13
Cunningham, Imogene 16: 122, 127
Cunningham, Kelley 176: 159
Cupples, Pat 107: 12; 126: 109; 182: 13; 198: 68
Curlee, Lynn 98: 48; 141: 39; 190: 48
Currey, Anna 190: 145; 202: 130, 132
Curry, John Steuart 2: 5; 19: 84; 34: 36; 144: 126
Curry, Tom 127: 131; 185: 25, 26
Curtis, Bruce 23: 96; 30: 88; 36: 22
Curtis, Neil 167: 30
Curtis, Stacy 205: 38
Cusack, Margaret 58: 49, 50, 51
Cushman, Doug 65: 57; 101: 39, 40; 133: 179; 157: 45; 186: 157; 210: 76, 77
Cutting, Ann 196: 194
Cyrus, Kurt 132: 39; 179: 36, 37
Czechowski, Alicia 95: 21; 171: 37
Czernecki, Stefan 117: 173

D

Dabcovich, Lydia 25: 105; 40: 114; 99: 75, 76
Dacey, Bob 82: 175; 152: 65
d'Achille, Gino 127: 175, 176
Dailey, Don 78: 197
Dain, Martin J. 35: 75

Dale, Penny *127:* 224; *151:* 57; *160:* 89; *197:* 75

Dale, Rae *72:* 197

Daley, Joann *50:* 22

Dalton, Anne *40:* 62; *63:* 119

Daly, Deborah M. *74:* 213

Daly, Jim *103:* 60; *150:* 48

Daly, Jude *138:* 118, 119

Daly, Nicholas *37:* 53; *76:* 48, 49

Daly, Niki *107:* 15; *114:* 38, 39, 40; *164:* 86; *192:* 53; *198:* 26, 27

Daly, Paul *97:* 205

Dalziel, Brothers *33:* 113

D'Amato, Alex *9:* 48; *20:* 25

D'Amato, Janet *9:* 48; *20:* 25; *26:* 118

D'Amico, Steve *170:* 52

Danalis, Johnny *167:* 27

D'Andrea, Domenick *183:* 108

Daniel, Alan *23:* 59; *29:* 110; *76:* 50, 53, 55, 56; *153:* 76 *115:* 74; *134:* 70

Daniel, Lea *76:* 53, 55; *153:* 76

Daniel, Lewis C. *20:* 216

Daniels, Beau *73:* 4

Daniels, Steve *22:* 16

Daniels, Stewart *56:* 12

Dann, Bonnie *31:* 83

Dann, Penny *82:* 128

Danska, Herbert *24:* 219

Danyell, Alice *20:* 27

Dardik, Helen *208:* 200

Darley, F.O.C. *16:* 145; *19:* 79, 86, 88, 185; *21:* 28,36; *35:* 76, 77, 78, 79, 80, 81; *YABC 2:* 175

Darling, Lois *3:* 59; *23:* 30, 31

Darling, Louis *1:* 40, 41; *2:* 63; *3:* 59; *23:* 30,31; *43:* 54, 57, 59; *121:* 53

Darnell, K.L. *210:* 247

Darrow, David R. *84:* 101

Darrow, Whitney, Jr. *13:* 25; *38:* 220, 221

Darwin, Beatrice *43:* 54

Darwin, Len *24:* 82

Dastolfo, Frank *33:* 179

Dauber, Liz *1:* 22; *3:* 266; *30:* 49

Daugherty, James *3:* 66; *8:* 178; *13:* 27, 28, 161; *18:* 101; *19:* 72; *29:* 108; *32:* 156; *42:* 84; *YABC 1:* 256; *2:* 174

d'Aulaire, Edgar Parin *5:* 51; *66:* 53

d'Aulaire, Ingri Parin *5:* 51; *66:* 53

Davalos, Felipe *99:* 197; *159:* 66; *174:* 163

Davenier, Christine *125:* 88; *127:* 32; *128:* 152; *179:* 39, 40

Davick, Linda *151:* 124; *208:* 187

David, Jacques-Louis *193:* 22

David, Jonathan *19:* 37

Davidson, Kevin *28:* 154

Davidson, Raymond *32:* 61

Davie, Helen K. *77:* 48, 49

Davies, Andy Robert *205:* 169

Davis, Allen *20:* 11; *22:* 45; *27:* 222; *29:* 157; *41:* 99; *47:* 99; *50:* 84; *52:* 105

Davis, Bette J. *15:* 53; *23:* 95

Davis, Dimitris *45:* 95

Davis, Eleanor *209:* 33

Davis, Hendon *151:* 122

Davis, Jack E. *145:* 139; *175:* 84, 85; *208:* 102; *210:* 81, 82

Davis, Jim *32:* 63, 64

Davis, Katie *152:* 52, 53, 54; *208:* 52

Davis, Lambert *110:* 23, 24; *176:* 58

Davis, Marguerite *31:* 38; *34:* 69, 70; *100:* 34; *YABC 1:* 126, 230

Davis, Nelle *69:* 191

Davis, Paul *78:* 214

Davis, Rich *206:* 38

Davis, Stuart *211:* 69

Davis, Yvonne LeBrun *94:* 144

Davisson, Virginia H. *44:* 178

DaVolls, Andy *85:* 53

Dawson, Diane *24:* 127; *42:* 126; *52:* 130; *68:* 104

Dawson, Willow *208:* 54

Day, Alexandra *67:* 59; *97:* 54; *166:* 65; *169:* 40; *197:* 50, 51, 52, 54

Day, Larry *169:* 88; *185:* 59

Day, Rob *94:* 110; *127:* 24; *197:* 32

Dean, Bob *19:* 211

Dean, David *192:* 55

de Angeli, Marguerite *1:* 77; *27:* 62, 65, 66, 67, 69, 70, 72; *100:* 75, 76; *YABC 1:* 166

DeArmond, Dale *70:* 47

Deas, Michael *27:* 219, 221; *30:* 156; *67:* 134; *72:* 24; *75:* 155; *84:* 206; *88:* 124

Deas, Rich *191:* 87; *193:* 10

deBarros, Jim *196:* 60

Debon, Nicolas *151:* 60; *177:* 46

de Bosschere, Jean *19:* 252; *21:* 4; *186:* 44, 45

De Bruyn, M(onica) G. *13:* 30, 31

Decker, C.B. *172:* 120

De Cuir, John F. *1:* 28, 29

Deeter, Catherine *74:* 110; *103:* 150; *137:* 50

Degen, Bruce *40:* 227, 229; *57:* 28, 29; *56:* 156; *75:* 229; *76:* 19; *81:* 36, 37; *92:* 26; *93:* 199; *97:* 56, 58, 59; *124:* 40; *147:* 39, 40, 41; *168:* 23; *205:* 45, 46

De Grazia *14:* 59; *39:* 56, 57

DeGrazio, George *88:* 40

deGroat, Diane *9:* 39; *18:* 7; *23:* 123; *28:* 200, 201; *31:* 58, 59; *34:* 151; *41:* 152; *43:* 88; *46:* 40, 200; *49:* 163; *50:* 89; *52:* 30, 34; *54:* 43; *63:* 5; *70:* 136; *71:* 99; *73:* 117,156; *77:* 34; *85:* 48; *86:* 201; *87:* 142; *90:* 72, 73, 143; *95:* 182; *111:* 123; *118:* 160; *126:* 8; *130:* 130; *138:* 93, 94; *169:* 46, 47

de Groot, Lee *6:* 21

Deines, Brian *110:* 139

DeJohn, Marie *89:* 78

Dekhteryov, B. *61:* 158

de Kiefte, Kees *94:* 107

Delacre, Lulu *36:* 66; *156:* 35; *202:* 10, 53; *209:* 36

Delaney, A. *21:* 78

Delaney, Michael *180:* 16

Delaney, Molly *80:* 43

Delaney, Ned *28:* 68; *56:* 80; *102:* 11

DeLapine, Jim *79:* 21

De La Roche Saint Andre, Anne *75:* 37

de Larrea, Victoria *6:* 119, 204; *29:* 103; *72:* 203; *87:* 199

DeLeon, Melanie *210:* 43

Delessert, Étienne *7:* 140; *46:* 61, 62, 63, 65, 67, 68; *130:* 38, 39, 40, 41, 42; *179:* 46, 47, 48, 49; *YABC 2:* 209

Delezenne, Christine *186:* 126

Del Negro, Janice *196:* 161

DeLorenzo, Christopher *154:* 149

Delulio, John *15:* 54

DeLuna, Tony *88:* 95

Demarest, Chris L. *45:* 68, 69, 70; *73:* 172, 173, 176; *78:* 106; *82:* 48, 49; *89:* 212; *92:* 86; *128:* 57, 58; *175:* 46, 48

De Mejo, Oscar *40:* 67

De Muth, Roger *205:* 184

Demi *11:* 135; *15:* 245; *66:* 129, 130; *89:* 216; *102:* 66, 67, 68; *210:* 86, 87, 89

Denetsosie, Hoke *13:* 126; *82:* 34

Denise, Christopher *147:* 43, 44; *176:* 101; *193:* 35, 36, 37; *201:* 37

Dennis, Morgan *18:* 68, 69; *64:* 89

Dennis, Wesley *2:* 87; *3:* 111; *11:* 132; *18:* 71, 72, 73, 74; *22:* 9; *24:* 196, 200; *46:* 178; *69:* 94, 96; *129:* 62

Denos, Julia *202:* 26

Denslow, W.W. *16:* 84, 85, 86, 87; *18:* 19, 20, 24; *29:* 211; *100:* 21

Denton, Kady MacDonald *110:* 82; *130:* 70; *181:* 54, 55, 56; *192:* 75

Denton, Terry *72:* 163; *174:* 26; *186:* 52; *196:* 83, 84

DePalma, Mary Newell *132:* 114; *139:* 75; *185:* 30, 31; *186:* 121

dePaola, Tomie *8:* 95; *9:* 93; *11:* 69; 25; 103; *28:* 157; *29:* 80; *39:* 52, 53; *40:* 226; *46:* 187; *59:* 61, 62, 63, 64, 65, 66, 67, 68, 69, 71, 72, 74; *62:* 19; *108:* 63, 67, 68, 70; *155:* 62, 64, 66; *180:* 105; *200:* 47, 48, 49, 50

Deraney, Michael J. *77:* 35; *78:* 148

deRosa, Dee *70:* 48; *71:* 210; *91:* 78

Dervaux, Isabelle *111:* 117

DeSaix, Deborah Durland *180:* 15; *188:* 24

De Saulles, Tony *119:* 39

de Seve, Peter *146:* 261; *207:* 78

Deshaprabhu, Meera Dayal *86:* 192

Desimini, Lisa *86:* 68; *94:* 47; *96:* 7; *104:* 107; *125:* 194; *131:* 180; *172:* 56

de St. Menin, Charles *70:* 17

Detmold, Edward J. *22:* 104, 105, 106, 107; *35:* 120; *64:* 5; *YABC 2:* 203

Detrich, Susan *20:* 133

Deutermann, Diana *77:* 175

DeVelasco, Joseph E. *21:* 51

de Veyrac, Robert *YABC 2:* 19

DeVille, Edward A. *4:* 235

de Visser, John *55:* 119

Devito, Bert *12:* 164

Devlin, Harry *11:* 74; *74:* 63, 65; *136:* 77, 78

Dewan, Ted *108:* 73; *157:* 55; *165:* 129

Dewar, Nick *133:* 122

Dewdney, Anna *184:* 43, 44

Dewey, Ariane *7:* 64; *33:* 195; *35:* 208; *68:* 16,17; *75:* 46; *93:* 91; *94:* 197; *109:* 65, 66, 67; *125:* 2, 3, 4, 5; *127:* 188; *143:* 25; *178:* 17, 19, 74; *188:* 166; *202:* 164

Dewey, Jennifer (Owings) *58:* 54; *64:* 214; *65:* 207; *88:* 169; *103:* 45

Dewey, Kenneth *39:* 62; *51:* 23; *56:* 163

de Zanger, Arie *30:* 40

Diakité, Baba Wagué *174:* 28

Diamond, Donna *21:* 200; *23:* 63; *26:* 142; *35:* 83, 84, 85, 86, 87, 88, 89; *38:* 78; *40:* 147; *44:* 152; *50:* 144; *53:* 126; *69:* 46, 47, 48, 201; *71:* 133; *123:* 19

Dias, Ron *71:* 67

Diaz, David *80:* 213; *96:* 83, 84; *108:* 228; *110:* 29; *149:* 106; *150:* 63; *179:* 160; *184:* 95, 97; *189:* 51, 52, 53

Dibley, Glin *138:* 83; *141:* 128; *211:* 162

DiCesare, Joe *70:* 38; *71:* 63, 106; *79:* 214; *93:* 147; *116:* 217; *143:* 111; *166:* 57

Dick, John Henry *8:* 181

Dickens, Frank *34:* 131

Dickey, Robert L. *15:* 279

Dickson, Mora *84:* 21

Didier, Sam *166:* 114

Dietz, James *128:* 223; *193:* 136

di Fate, Vincent *37:* 70; *90:* 11; *93:* 60; *109:* 219, 220

Di Fiori, Lawrence *10:* 51; *12:* 190; *27:* 97; *40:* 219; *93:* 57; *130:* 45

Digby, Desmond *97:* 180

Dignan, James *196:* 143

Di Grazia, Thomas *32:* 66; *35:* 241

Dillard, Annie *10:* 32

Dillard, Sarah *136:* 186

Dillon, Corinne B. *1:* 139

Dillon, Diane *4:* 104, 167; *6:* 23; *13:* 29; *15:* 99; *26:* 148; *27:* 136, 201; *51:* 29, 48, 51, 52, 53, 54,55, 56, 57, 58, 59, 60, 61, 62; *54:* 155; *56:* 69; *58:* 127,128; *61:* 95; *62:* 27; *64:* 46; *68:* 3; *69:* 209; *74:* 89; *79:* 92; *86:* 89; *92:* 28, 177; *93:* 7, 210; *94:* 239, 240; *97:* 167; *106:* 58, 59,61, 64; *107:* 3; *139:* 246; *167:* 77; *189:* 202; *191:* 191; *194:* 45, 46, 48, 49

Dillon, Leo *4:* 104, 167; *6:* 23; *13:* 29; *15:* 99; *26:* 148; *27:* 136, 201; *51:* 29, 48, 51, 52, 53, 54,55, 56, 57, 58, 59, 60, 61, 62; *54:* 155; *56:* 69; *58:* 127,128; *61:* 95; *62:* 27; *64:* 46; *68:* 3; *69:* 209; *74:* 89; *79:* 92; *86:*

89; *92:* 28, 177; *93:* 7, 210; *94:* 239, 240; *97:* 167; *106:* 58, 59,61, 64; *107:* 3; *139:* 246; *167:* 77; *189:* 202; *191:* 191; *194:* 45, 46, 48, 49
Dillon, Sharon Saseen *59:* 179, 188
DiMaccio, Gerald *121:* 80
DiMaggio, Joe *36:* 22
DiMassi, Gina *169:* 17
Dinan, Carol *25:* 169; *59:* 75
Dines, Glen *7:* 66, 67
Dinesen, Thomas *44:* 37
Dinh, Pham Viet *167:* 184
Dinnerstein, Harvey *42:* 63, 64, 65, 66, 67, 68; *50:* 146
Dinsdale, Mary *10:* 65; *11:* 171
Dinyer, Eric *86:* 148; *109:* 163; *110:* 239; *124:* 11; *150:* 69; *170:* 4; *171:* 30
Dion, Nathalie *170:* 124
DiRocco, Carl *181:* 23
DiSalvo-Ryan, DyAnne *59:* 77; *62:* 185; *117:* 46; *144:* 64; *150:* 153; *186:* 162
Disney, Walt *28:* 71, 72, 73, 76, 77, 78, 79, 80, 81, 87, 88, 89,90, 91, 94
DiTerlizzi, Tony *105:* 7; *147:* 22; *154:* 31, 32, 33
Divito, Anna *83:* 159
Dixon, Don *74:* 17; *109:* 196
Dixon, Larry *127:* 125
Dixon, Maynard *20:* 165
Doares, Robert G. *20:* 39
Dob, Bob *205:* 14
Dobias, Frank *22:* 162
Dobrin, Arnold *4:* 68
Dobson, Steven Gaston *102:* 103
Dockray, Tracy *139:* 77
Docktor, Irv *43:* 70
Dodd, Ed *4:* 69
Dodd, Emma *203:* 57
Dodd, Julie *74:* 73
Dodd, Lynley *35:* 92; *86:* 71; *132:* 45, 46, 47
Dodge, Bill *96:* 36; *118:* 7, 8, 9; *133:* 135
Dodgson, Charles L. *20:* 148; *33:* 146; *YABC 2:* 98
Dodson, Bert *9:* 138; *14:* 195; *42:* 55; *54:* 8; *60:* 49; *101:* 125
Dodson, Liz Brenner *105:* 117; *111:* 15
Dohanos, Stevan *16:* 10
Dolce, J. Ellen *74:* 147; *75:* 41
Dolch, Marguerite P. *50:* 64
Dolesch, Susanne *34:* 49
Dollar, Diane *57:* 32
Dolobowsky, Mena *81:* 54
Dolson, Hildegarde *5:* 57
Domanska, Janina *6:* 66, 67; *YABC 1:* 166
Domi *134:* 113
Dominguez, El *53:* 94
Domjan, Joseph *25:* 93
Domm, Jeffrey C. *84:* 69; *135:* 70
Donahey, William *68:* 209
Donahue, Dorothy *76:* 170
Donahue, Vic *2:* 93; *3:* 190; *9:* 44
Donald, Elizabeth *4:* 18
Donalty, Alison *149:* 195, 196, 197
Donato *85:* 59; *149:* 204; *191:* 19
Donato, Michael A. *200:* 143
Doner, Kim *208:* 57
Doney, Todd L.W. *87:* 12; *93:* 112; *98:* 135; *101:* 57; *104:* 40; *118:* 163; *135:* 162, 163; *151:* 18
Donna, Natalie *9:* 52
Donohue, Dorothy *95:* 2; *132:* 30; *176:* 54, 55; *178:* 77, 78, 79
Dooling, Michael *82:* 19; *105:* 55; *106:* 224; *125:* 135; *171:* 46; *172:* 12; *176:* 120; *197:* 89
Doran, Ben-Ami *128:* 189
Doran, Colleen *211:* 48
Dore, Gustave *18:* 169, 172, 175; *19:* 93, 94, 95, 96, 97, 98,99, 100, 101, 102, 103, 104, 105; *23:* 188; *25:* 197, 199

Doremus, Robert *6:* 62; *13:* 90; *30:* 95, 96, 97; *38:* 97
Dorfman, Ronald *11:* 128
Doriau *86:* 59; *91:* 152
Dorman, Brandon *197:* 35; *204:* 6; *210:* 104
Dormer, Frank W. *200:* 55
Dorros, Arthur *78:* 42, 43; *91:* 28
Doruyter, Karel *165:* 105
dos Santos, Joyce Audy *57:* 187, 189
Doty, Roy *28:* 98; *31:* 32; *32:* 224; *46:* 157; *82:* 71; *142:* 7
Doucet, Bob *132:* 238; *169:* 159
Dougherty, Charles *16:* 204; *18:* 74
Doughty, Rebecca *177:* 174
Doughty, Thomas *118:* 31; *140:* 60
Douglas, Aaron *31:* 103
Douglas, Carole Nelson *73:* 48
Douglas, Goray *13:* 151
Dow, Brian *150:* 92
Dowd, Jason *132:* 51, 52; *164:* 244
Dowd, Vic *3:* 244; *10:* 97
Dowden, Anne Ophelia *7:* 70, 71; *13:* 120
Dowdy, Mrs. Regera *29:* 100
Downard, Barry *202:* 32
Downes, Belinda *180:* 29
Downing, Julie *60:* 140; *81:* 50; *86:* 200; *99:* 129
Doyle, Janet *56:* 31
Doyle, Richard *21:* 31, 32, 33; *23:* 231; *24:* 177; *31:* 87
Draper, Angie *43:* 84
Drath, Bill *26:* 34
Drawson, Blair *17:* 53; *126:* 65
Dray, Matt *177:* 47
Drescher, Henrik *105:* 60, 62, 63; *172:* 72
Drescher, Joan *30:* 100, 101; *35:* 245; *52:* 168; *137:* 52
Dressell, Peggy *186:* 41
Drew, Janet *201:* 177
Drew, Patricia *15:* 100
Dronzek, Laura *199:* 28, 29; *207:* 69
Drummond, Allan *209:* 41
Drummond, V.H. *6:* 70
Drury, Christian Potter *105:* 97; *186:* 224
Dubanevich, Arlene *56:* 44
Dubin, Jill *205:* 56
Dubois, Claude K. *196:* 2
Dubois, Gerard *182:* 9
DuBurke, Randy *187:* 89
Ducak, Danilo *99:* 130; *108:* 214
Duchesne, Janet *6:* 162; *79:* 8
Duda, Jana *102:* 155; *209:* 134
Dudash, Michael *32:* 122; *77:* 134; *82:* 149
Duer, Douglas *34:* 177
Duewell, Kristina *195:* 76
Duffy, Daniel Mark *76:* 37; *101:* 196; *108:* 147, 148
Duffy, Joseph *38:* 203
Duffy, Pat *28:* 153
Dugan, Karen *181:* 26; *202:* 35
Dugin, Andrej *77:* 60
Dugina, Olga *77:* 60
Duke, Chris *8:* 195; *139:* 164
Duke, Kate *87:* 186; *90:* 78, 79, 80, 81; *192:* 21, 59, 60, 61, 63
Duke, Marion *165:* 87
Dulac, Edmund *19:* 108, 109, 110, 111, 112, 113, 114, 115, 117; *23:* 187; *25:* 152; *YABC 1:* 37; *2:* 147
Dulac, Jean *13:* 64
Dumas, Philippe *52:* 36, 37, 38, 39, 40, 41, 42, 43, 45; *119:* 40, 41, 42
Dunaway, Nancy *108:* 161
Dunbar, James *76:* 63
Dunbar, Polly *181:* 60, 61; *211:* 51, 52, 53
Duncan, Beverly *72:* 92
Duncan, John *116:* 94
Dunn, H.T. *62:* 196
Dunn, Harvey *34:* 78, 79, 80, 81
Dunn, Iris *5:* 175
Dunn, Phoebe *5:* 175

Dunne, Jeanette *72:* 57, 173, 222
Dunnick, Regan *176:* 51; *178:* 83, 84
Dunnington, Tom *3:* 36; *18:* 281; *25:* 61; *31:* 159; *35:* 168; *48:* 195; *79:* 144; *82:* 230
Dunn-Ramsey, Marcy *117:* 131
Dunrea, Olivier *59:* 81; *118:* 53, 54; *124:* 43
Dupasquier, Philippe *86:* 75; *104:* 76; *151:* 63
duPont, Lindsay Harper *207:* 39
DuQuette, Keith *90:* 83; *155:* 73, 74
Durand, Delphine *200:* 56
Durham, Sarah *192:* 248
Durney, Ryan *208:* 122
Duroussy, Nathalie *146:* 150
Durrell, Julie *82:* 62; *94:* 62
Dutz *6:* 59
Duvoisin, Roger *2:* 95; *6:* 76, 77; *7:* 197; *28:* 125; *30:* 101, 102, 103, 104, 105, 107; *47:* 205; *84:* 254
Dyer, Dale *141:* 71
Dyer, Jane *75:* 219; *129:* 28; *147:* 49, 50, 51; *168:* 121; *190:* 4; *191:* 57, 59, 60; *203:* 4
Dypold, Pat *15:* 37

E

E.V.B.
    See Boyle, Eleanor Vere (Gordon)
Eachus, Jennifer *29:* 74; *82:* 201; *164:* 153
Eadie, Bob *63:* 36
Eagle, Bruce *95:* 119
Eagle, Ellen *82:* 121; *89:* 3
Eagle, Jeremy *141:* 71
Eagle, Michael *11:* 86; *20:* 9; *23:* 18; *27:* 122; *28:* 57; *34:* 201; *44:* 189; *73:* 9; *78:* 235; *85:* 43
Earl-Bridges, Michele *159:* 128
Earle, Edwin *56:* 27
Earle, Olive L. *7:* 75
Earle, Vana *27:* 99
Earley, Lori *132:* 2; *186:* 4; *195:* 8
Early, Margaret *72:* 59
East, Stella *131:* 223
Eastman, P.D. *33:* 57
Easton, Reginald *29:* 181
Eaton, Tom *4:* 62; *6:* 64; *22:* 99; *24:* 124
Ebbeler, Jeffrey *193:* 62; *206:* 45
Ebel, Alex *11:* 89
Eberbach, Andrea *192:* 115
Ebert, Len *9:* 191; *44:* 47
Echevarria, Abe *37:* 69
Echo Hawk, Bunky *187:* 192
Eckersley, Maureen *48:* 62
Eckert, Horst *72:* 62
Ede, Janina *33:* 59
Edens, Cooper *49:* 81, 82, 83, 84, 85; *112:* 58
Edens, John *109:* 115
Edgar, Sarah E. *41:* 97
Edgerton, Perky *195:* 144
Edliq, Emily S. *131:* 107
Edrien *11:* 53
Edwards, Freya *45:* 102
Edwards, George Wharton *31:* 155
Edwards, Gunvor *2:* 71; *25:* 47; *32:* 71; *54:* 106
Edwards, Jeanne *29:* 257
Edwards, Linda Strauss *21:* 134; *39:* 123; *49:* 88, 89
Edwards, Michelle *152:* 62, 63
Edwards, Wallace *170:* 55
Egan, Tim *155:* 76, 77, 78
Egge, David *102:* 71
Eggenhofer, Nicholas *2:* 81
Eggleton, Bob *74:* 40; *81:* 190, 191; *105:* 6; *121:* 183; *149:* 203; *166:* 215
Egielski, Richard *11:* 90; *16:* 208; *33:* 236; *38:* 35; *49:* 91, 92, 93, 95, 212, 213, 214, 216; *79:* 122; *106:* 67, 68, 69; *134:* 135; *144:* 244; *163:* 82, 84; *207:* 125

Ehlert, Lois *35:* 97; *69:* 51; *112:* 7; *113:* 208; *128:* 63, 64, 65; *172:* 77, 79, 80
Ehrlich, Bettina *1:* 83
Eitan, Ora *160:* 165
Eichenberg, Fritz *1:* 79; *9:* 54; *19:* 248; *23:* 170; *24:* 200; *26:* 208; *50:* 67, 68, 69, 70, 71, 72, 73,74, 75, 77, 79, 80, 81; *60:* 165; *100:* 137; *YABC 1:* 104, 105; *2:* 213
Einsel, Naiad *10:* 35; *29:* 136
Einsel, Walter *10:* 37
Einzig, Susan *3:* 77; *43:* 78; *67:* 155; *129:* 154
Eisner, Will *165:* 82, 83
Eitzen, Allan *9:* 56; *12:* 212; *14:* 226; *21:* 194; *38:* 162; *76:* 218
Eldridge, H. *54:* 109
Eldridge, Harold *43:* 83
Elgaard, Greta *19:* 241
Elgin, Kathleen *9:* 188; *39:* 69
Ellacott, S.E. *19:* 118
Elliot, David *192:* 26; *208:* 62, 63
Elliott, Mark *93:* 69; *105:* 108; *107:* 123; *140:* 53; *165:* 189; *173:* 67; *195:* 95; *203:* 67; *210:* 99
Elliott, Sarah M. *14:* 58
Ellis, Dianne *130:* 208
Ellis, Jan Davey *88:* 50; *115:* 80
Ellis, Richard *130:* 47, 48
Ellison, Chris *196:* 66; *199:* 131; *207:* 193
Ellison, Pauline *55:* 21
Elmer, Richard *78:* 5
Elmore, Larry *90:* 8
Elschner, Géraldine *183:* 38
Elwell, Peter *195:* 150
Elwell, Tristan *110:* 39; *121:* 182; *127:* 46; *137:* 144; *141:* 173; *151:* 236; *158:* 264; *167:* 119, 120, 121; *169:* 20; *190:* 12; *202:* 16
Elzbieta *88:* 80, 81
Emberley, Ed *8:* 53; *70:* 53, 54; *146:* 65, 69, 70
Emberley, Michael *34:* 83; *80:* 72; *119:* 47, 48; *147:* 100; *158:* 115; *189:* 62, 64; *203:* 87, 89
Emerling, Dorothy *104:* 27
Emery, Leslie *49:* 187
Emmett, Bruce *49:* 147; *80:* 175; *101:* 206
Emry-Perrott, Jennifer *61:* 57
Emshwiller, Ed *174:* 45
Endle, Kate *191:* 167; *207:* 41
Engel, Diana *70:* 57
Engle, Mort *38:* 64
Englebert, Victor *8:* 54
English, Mark *101:* 207
Enik, Ted *142:* 39
Enos, Randall *20:* 183
Enright, Maginel Wright *19:* 240, 243; *39:* 31, 35, 36
Enrique, Romeo *34:* 135
Ensor, Barbara *180:* 30
Epstein, Stephen *50:* 142, 148
Erdogan, Buket *174:* 179
Erdrich, Louise *141:* 62
Erhard, Walter *1:* 152
Erickson, Jim *196:* 190
Erickson, Phoebe *11:* 83; *59:* 85
Erikson, Mel *31:* 69
Eriksson, Eva *63:* 88, 90, 92, 93; *203:* 99; *207:* 44
Ering, Timothy Basil *131:* 100; *176:* 63, 64; *202:* 29; *204:* 8
Erlbruch, Wolf *181:* 66
Ernst, Lisa Campbell *47:* 147; *95:* 47; *154:* 46, 47, 48; *164:* 88
Esco, Jo *61:* 103
Escourido, Joseph *4:* 81
Escrivá, Viví *119:* 51; *181:* 36
Essakalli, Julie Klear *200:* 58
Este, Kirk *33:* 111
Estep, David *73:* 57
Estes, Eleanor *91:* 66
Estoril, Jean *32:* 27

Estrada, Pau *74:* 76
Estrada, Ric *5:* 52, 146; *13:* 174
Etchemendy, Teje *38:* 68
Etheredges, the *73:* 12
Etienne, Kirk-Albert *145:* 184
Ets, Marie Hall *2:* 102
Ettlinger, Doris *171:* 98; *186:* 106; *197:* 126
Eulalie *YABC 2:* 315
Evans, Greg *73:* 54, 55, 56; *143:* 40, 41
Evans, Katherine *5:* 64
Evans, Leslie *144:* 227; *207:* 57
Evans, Shane W. *159:* 142; *160:* 190; *168:* 39; *188:* 88; *196:* 66, 67, 68
Everitt, Betsy *151:* 110
Ewart, Claire *76:* 69; *145:* 59, 60
Ewing, Carolyn *66:* 143; *79:* 52
Ewing, Juliana Horatia *16:* 92
Eyolfson, Norman *98:* 154

F

Fabian, Limbert *136:* 114
Facklam, Paul *132:* 62
Falconer, Ian *125:* 66; *179:* 59
Falconer, Pearl *34:* 23
Falkenstern, Lisa *70:* 34; *76:* 133; *78:* 171; *127:* 16; *191:* 151
Falls, C.B. *1:* 19; *38:* 71, 72, 73, 74
Falter, John *40:* 169, 170
Falwell, Cathryn *118:* 77; *137:* 185; *196:* 71, 72
Fancher, Lou *138:* 219; *141:* 64; *144:* 199; *177:* 51
Fanelli, Sara *89:* 63; *126:* 69
Faria, Rosana *150:* 143
Faricy, Patrick *185:* 182
Farooqi, Musharraf Ali *207:* 46
Farmer, Andrew *49:* 102
Farmer, Peter *24:* 108; *38:* 75
Farnsworth, Bill *93:* 189; *116:* 147; *124:* 8; *135:* 52; *146:* 242, 243, 244; *182:* 176; *186:* 31, 83, 84, 85; *191:* 197
Farquharson, Alexander *46:* 75
Farrell, David *40:* 135
Farrell, Russell *196:* 38
Farris, David *74:* 42
Fasolino, Teresa *118:* 145
Fatigati, Evelyn *24:* 112
Fatus, Sophie *182:* 74; *190:* 218
Faul-Jansen, Regina *22:* 117
Faulkner, Jack *6:* 169
Faulkner, Matt *161:* 174; *167:* 75
Fava, Rita *2:* 29
Fax, Elton C. *1:* 101; *4:* 2; *12:* 77; *25:* 107
Fay *43:* 93
Fearnley, Jan *153:* 82, 83; *205:* 63, 64, 65
Fearrington, Ann *146:* 80
Federspiel, Marian *33:* 51
Fedorov, Nickolai Ivanovich *110:* 102
Feelings, Tom *5:* 22; *8:* 56; *12:* 153; *16:* 105; *30:* 196; *49:* 37; *61:* 101; *69:* 56, 57; *93:* 74; *105:* 88
Fehr, Terrence *21:* 87
Feiffer, Jules *3:* 91; *8:* 58; *61:* 66, 67, 70, 74, 76,77, 78; *111:* 47, 48, 49, 50; *132:* 122; *157:* 62; *201:* 48, 49, 50
Feigeles, Neil *41:* 242
Feldman, Elyse *86:* 7
Feller, Gene *33:* 130
Fellows, Muriel H. *10:* 42
Felstead, Cathie *116:* 85
Felts, Shirley *33:* 71; *48:* 59
Fennell, Tracy *171:* 69
Fennelli, Maureen *38:* 181
Fenton, Carroll Lane *5:* 66; *21:* 39
Fenton, Mildred Adams *5:* 66; *21:* 39
Ferguson, Peter *177:* 30, 31; *181:* 154; *197:* 4; *199:* 40
Ferguson, Walter W. *34:* 86

Fernandes, Eugenie *77:* 67; *205:* 68
Fernandes, Stanislaw *70:* 28
Fernandez, Fernando *77:* 57
Fernandez, Laura *77:* 153; *101:* 117; *131:* 222; *170:* 119; *175:* 182
Ferrari, Alex *188:* 121
Ferrington, Susan *172:* 22
Fetz, Ingrid *11:* 67; *12:* 52; *16:* 205; *17:* 59; *29:* 105; *30:* 108, 109; *32:* 149; *43:* 142; *56:* 29; *60:* 34; *85:* 48; *87:* 146
Fiammenghi, Gioia *9:* 66; *11:* 44; *12:* 206; *13:* 57, 59; *52:* 126, 129; *66:* 64; *85:* 83; *91:* 161; *166:* 169
Fiedler, Joseph Daniel *96:* 42; *113:* 173; *129:* 164; *146:* 17; *159:* 68; *162:* 104
Field, Rachel *15:* 113
Fielding, David *70:* 124
Fieser, Stephen *152:* 36
Fine, Howard *145:* 159; *159:* 64; *165:* 134; *174:* 129; *181:* 68
Fine, Peter K. *43:* 210
Finger, Helen *42:* 81
Fink, Sam *18:* 119
Finlay, Winifred *23:* 72
Finney, Pat *79:* 215
Fiore, Peter *99:* 196; *125:* 139; *144:* 225; *160:* 169; *180:* 72
Fiorentino, Al *3:* 240
Firehammer, Karla *174:* 202
Firmin, Charlotte *29:* 75; *48:* 70
Firmin, Peter *58:* 63, 64, 65, 67, 68, 70, 71
Firth, Barbara *81:* 208; *127:* 218; *179:* 62
Fischel, Lillian *40:* 204
Fischer, Hans *25:* 202
Fischer, Scott *207:* 37
Fischer-Nagel, Andreas *56:* 50
Fischer-Nagel, Heiderose *56:* 50
Fisher, Carolyn *154:* 50
Fisher, Chris *79:* 62; *158:* 248; *188:* 195
Fisher, Cynthia *117:* 45; *137:* 118; *195:* 40
Fisher, Jeffrey *142:* 80
Fisher, Leonard Everett *3:* 6; *4:* 72, 86; *6:* 197; *9:* 59; *16:* 151, 153; *23:* 44; *27:* 134; *29:* 26; *34:* 87, 89, 90, 91, 93, 94, 95, 96; *40:* 206; *50:* 150; *60:* 158; *73:* 68, 70, 71, 72, 73; *176:* 71, 72, 73; *208:* 131; *YABC 2:* 169
Fisher, Lois *20:* 62; *21:* 7
Fisher, Valorie *177:* 55
Fisk, Nicholas *25:* 112
Fitschen, Marilyn *2:* 20, 21; *20:* 48
Fitz-Maurice, Jeff *175:* 2
Fitzgerald, F.A. *15:* 116; *25:* 86, 87
Fitzgerald, Joanne *157:* 153, 154; *198:* 34, 35
Fitzgerald, Royce *205:* 5
Fitzhugh, Louise *1:* 94; *9:* 163; *45:* 75, 78
Fitzhugh, Susie *11:* 117
Fitzpatrick, Jim *109:* 130
Fitzpatrick, Marie-Louise *125:* 69, 70; *189:* 72, 73
Fitzsimmons, Arthur *14:* 128
Fix, Philippe *26:* 102
Flack, Marjorie *21:* 67; *100:* 93; *YABC 2:* 122
Flagg, James Montgomery *17:* 227
Flavin, Teresa *132:* 115; *186:* 119
Flax, Zeona *2:* 245
Fleetwood, Tony *171:* 51
Fleishman, Seymour *14:* 232; *24:* 87
Fleming, Denise *71:* 179; *81:* 58; *126:* 71, 72, 73; *173:* 52, 53
Fleming, Guy *18:* 41
Flesher, Vivienne *85:* 55
Fletcher, Claire *80:* 106; *157:* 159
Flint, Russ *74:* 80
Floate, Helen *111:* 163
Floca, Brian *155:* 88, 89; *190:* 10, 66, 67
Floethe, Richard *3:* 131; *4:* 90
Floherty, John J., Jr. *5:* 68
Flook, Helen *160:* 81
Flora, James *1:* 96; *30:* 111, 112
Florczak, Robert *166:* 51

Florian, Douglas *19:* 122; *83:* 64, 65; *125:* 71, 72, 74, 76; *128:* 130; *177:* 58, 60
Flory, Jane *22:* 111
Flower, Renee *125:* 109
Floyd, Gareth *1:* 74; *17:* 245; *48:* 63; *62:* 35,36, 37, 39, 40, 41; *74:* 245; *79:* 56
Fluchere, Henri A. *40:* 79
Flynn, Alice *183:* 2
Flynn, Barbara *7:* 31; *9:* 70
Fogarty, Thomas *15:* 89
Foley, Greg *190:* 69
Folger, Joseph *9:* 100
Folkard, Charles *22:* 132; *29:* 128, 257, 258
Foott, Jeff *42:* 202
Forberg, Ati *12:* 71, 205; *14:* 1; *22:* 113; *26:* 22; *48:* 64, 65
Ford, George *24:* 120; *31:* 70, 177; *58:* 126; *81:* 103; *107:* 91; *136:* 100; *194:* 47; *208:* 81
Ford, Gilbert *199:* 10
Ford, H.J. *16:* 185, 186
Ford, Jason *174:* 119
Ford, Pamela Baldwin *27:* 104
Fordham, John *168:* 160, 161
Foreman, Michael *2:* 110, 111; *67:* 99; *73:* 78, 79, 80,81, 82; *93:* 146; *135:* 55, 56, 57; *184:* 58, 59
Forrester, Victoria *40:* 83
Forsey, Chris *140:* 210
Fortnum, Peggy *6:* 29; *20:* 179; *24:* 211; *26:* 76, 77, 78; *39:* 78; *58:* 19, 21, 23, 27; *YABC 1:* 148
Fortune, Eric *191:* 52
Foster, Brad W. *34:* 99
Foster, Genevieve *2:* 112
Foster, Gerald L. *78:* 198; *198:* 40
Foster, Jon *146:* 18; *198:* 7
Foster, Laura Louise *6:* 79
Foster, Marian Curtis *23:* 74; *40:* 42
Foster, Sally *58:* 73, 74
Foucher, Adele *47:* 118
Foust, Mitch *168:* 50
Fowler, Jim *184:* 190
Fowler, Mel *36:* 127
Fowler, Richard *87:* 219
Fowles, Shelley *165:* 127; *205:* 72
Fox, Charles Phillip *12:* 84
Fox, Christyan *188:* 36
Fox, Jim *6:* 187
Fox, Nathan *208:* 64
Fox-Davies, Sarah *76:* 150; *182:* 63; *199:* 42, 43
Frace, Charles *15:* 118
Frailey, Joy *72:* 108
Frame, Paul *2:* 45, 145; *9:* 153; *10:* 124; *21:* 71; *23:* 62; *24:* 123; *27:* 106; *31:* 48; *32:* 159; *34:* 195; *38:* 136; *42:* 55; *44:* 139; *60:* 39, 40, 41, 42, 43, 44, 46; *73:* 183
Frampton, David *85:* 72; *102:* 33; *139:* 182; *152:* 37; *189:* 171
Francis, Guy *198:* 164
Francois, Andre *25:* 117
Francoise
　See Seignobosc, Francoise
Frank, Lola Edick *2:* 199
Frank, Mary *4:* 54; *34:* 100
Franke, Phil *45:* 91
Frankel, Alona *66:* 70
Frankel, Julie *40:* 84, 85, 202
Frankenberg, Robert *22:* 116; *30:* 50; *38:* 92, 94, 95; *68:* 111
Frankfeldt, Gwen *84:* 223; *110:* 92
Frankland, David *169:* 137; *182:* 164; *201:* 159
Franklin, Ashton *165:* 144
Franklin, John *24:* 22
Franson, Leanne R. *111:* 57, 58; *151:* 7
Frascino, Edward *9:* 133; *29:* 229; *33:* 190; *48:* 80, 81, 82, 83, 84, 85, 86
Frasconi, Antonio *6:* 80; *27:* 208; *53:* 41, 43, 45, 47,48; *68:* 145; *73:* 226; *131:* 68

Fraser, Betty *2:* 212; *6:* 185; *8:* 103; *31:* 72,73; *43:* 136; *111:* 76
Fraser, Eric *38:* 78; *41:* 149, 151
Fraser, F.A. *22:* 234
Fraser, James *171:* 68
Fraser, Mary Ann *137:* 63
Frasier, Debra *69:* 60; *112:* 67; *182:* 81, 82, 83
Fraustino, Lisa Rowe *146:* 87
Frazee, Marla *72:* 98; *105:* 79, 80; *151:* 67, 68; *164:* 165; *171:* 190, 191; *187:* 53, 54,55, 56, 143
Frazetta, Frank *41:* 72; *58:* 77, 78, 79, 80, 81, 82, 83
Frazier, Craig *177:* 63
Freas, John *25:* 207
Fredrickson, Mark *103:* 33
Freeland, Michael J. *118:* 115
Freeman, Don *2:* 15; *13:* 249; *17:* 62, 63, 65, 67, 68; *18:* 243; *20:* 195; *23:* 213, 217; *32:* 155; *55:* 129
Freeman, Irving *67:* 150
Freeman, Laura *144:* 111; *200:* 62, 63
Freeman, Pietri *140:* 223
Freeman, Tom *167:* 118
Freeman, Tor *164:* 93
Fregosi, Claudia *24:* 117
Fremaux, Charlotte Murray *138:* 29; *141:* 95
French, Fiona *6:* 82, 83; *75:* 61; *109:* 170; *132:* 79, 80, 81, 82
French, Martin *163:* 4
Frendak, Rodney *126:* 97, 98
Freschet, Gina *175:* 73
Freynet, Gilbert *72:* 221
Fried, Janice *202:* 121
Friedman, Judith *43:* 197; *131:* 221
Friedman, Marvin *19:* 59; *42:* 86
Frinta, Dagmar *36:* 42
Frith, Michael K. *15:* 138; *18:* 120
Fritz, Ronald *46:* 73; *82:* 124
Fromm, Lilo *29:* 85; *40:* 197
Frost, A.B. *17:* 6, 7; *19:* 123, 124, 125, 126, 127, 128, 129,130; *100:* 119; *YABC 1:* 156, 157, 160; *2:* 107
Frost, Helen *183:* 51
Frost, Kristi *118:* 113
Frost, Michael *209:* 209; *209:* 44
Froud, Brian *150:* 82, 83
Froud, Wendy *151:* 237
Fry, Guy *2:* 224
Fry, Rosalie *3:* 72; *YABC 2:* 180, 181
Fry, Rosalind *21:* 153, 168
Fryer, Elmer *34:* 115
Fuchs, Bernie *110:* 10; *162:* 46
Fuchs, Erich *6:* 84
Fuchshuber, Annegert *43:* 96
Fufuka, Mahiri *32:* 146
Fuge, Charles *144:* 91, 93
Fujikawa, Gyo *39:* 75, 76; *76:* 72, 73, 74
Fulford, Deborah *23:* 159
Fuller, Margaret *25:* 189
Fulweiler, John *93:* 99
Funai, Mamoru *38:* 105
Funfhausen, Christian *196:* 30
Funk, Tom *7:* 17, 99
Furchgott, Terry *29:* 86
Furness, William Henry, Jr. *94:* 18
Furukawa, Mel *25:* 42
Fusari, Erika *164:* 227

G

Gaadt, David *78:* 212; *121:* 166; *201:* 171
Gaadt, George *71:* 9
Gaber, Susan *99:* 33; *115:* 57, 58; *164:* 195; *169:* 61, 62, 63; *185:* 50, 51; *188:* 124
Gaberell, J. *19:* 236
Gable, Brian *195:* 68, 69
Gabler, Mirko *99:* 71; *195:* 32

Gackenbach, Dick *19:* 168; *41:* 81; *48:* 89, 90, 91, 92,93, 94; *54:* 105; *79:* 75, 76, 77
Gad, Victor *87:* 161
Gaetano, Nicholas *23:* 209
Gaffney-Kessell, Walter *94:* 219; *174:* 188
Gag, Flavia *17:* 49, 52
Gag, Wanda *100:* 101, 102; *YABC 1:* 135, 137, 138, 141, 143
Gagnon, Cecile *11:* 77; *58:* 87
Gaillard, Jason *200:* 69; *204:* 74
Gal, Laszlo *14:* 127; *52:* 54, 55, 56; *65:* 142; *68:* 150; *81:* 185; *96:* 104, 105
Galazinski, Tom *55:* 13
Galbraith, Ben *200:* 70
Galdone, Paul *1:* 156, 181, 206; *2:* 40, 241; *3:* 42,144; *4:* 141; *10:* 109, 158; *11:* 21; *12:* 118, 210; *14:* 12; *16:* 36, 37; *17:* 70, 71, 72, 73, 74; *18:* 111, 230; *19:* 183; *21:* 154; *22:* 150, 245; *33:* 126; *39:* 136, 137; *42:* 57; *51:* 169; *55:* 110; *66:* 80, 82, 139; *72:* 73; *100:* 84
Gale, Cathy *140:* 22; *143:* 52
Gall, Chris *176:* 79, 80
Gallagher, Jack *187:* 100
Gallagher, S. Saelig *105:* 154; *198:* 91
Gallagher, Sears *20:* 112Gallagher-Cole, Mernie *206:* 56
Galloway, Ewing *51:* 154
Galouchka, Annouchka Gravel *95:* 55; *182:* 40
Galster, Robert *1:* 66
Galsworthy, Gay John *35:* 232
Galvez, Daniel *125:* 182
Gamble, Kim *112:* 64, 65; *124:* 77; *183:* 40, 42, 43, 56, 57; *187:* 170
Gammell, Stephen *7:* 48; *13:* 149; *29:* 82; *33:* 209; *41:* 88; *50:* 185, 186, 187; *53:* 51, 52, 53, 54, 55, 56,57, 58; *54:* 24, 25; *56:* 147, 148, 150; *57:* 27, 66; *81:* 62, 63; *87:* 88; *89:* 10; *106:* 223; *126:* 2; *128:* 71, 73, 74, 77; *154:* 34; *211:* 210
Gamper, Ruth *84:* 198
Gampert, John *58:* 94
Ganly, Helen *56:* 56
Gannett, Ruth Chrisman *3:* 74; *18:* 254; *33:* 77, 78
Gannon, Ned *205:* 6
Gantschev, Ivan *45:* 32
Garafano, Marie *73:* 33
Garbot, Dave *131:* 106
Garbutt, Bernard *23:* 68
Garcia *37:* 71
Garcia, Manuel *74:* 145
Garcia-Franco, Rebecca *173:* 46
Gardiner, Lindsey *178:* 128; *186:* 137
Gardner, Earle *45:* 167
Gardner, Joan *40:* 87
Gardner, Joel *40:* 87, 92
Gardner, John *40:* 87
Gardner, Lucy *40:* 87
Gardner, Richard
　See Cummings, Richard
Gardner, Sally *171:* 177; *177:* 66, 68
Gargiulo, Frank *84:* 158
Garland, Michael *36:* 29; *38:* 83; *44:* 168; *48:* 78, 221, 222; *49:* 161; *60:* 139; *71:* 6, 11; *72:* 229; *74:* 142; *89:* 187; *93:* 183; *104:* 110; *131:* 55; *139:* 209; *168:* 56; *208:* 72, 73, 75
Garland, Peggy *60:* 139
Garland, Sarah *62:* 45; *135:* 67, 68; *171:* 118
Garn, Aimee *75:* 47
Garner, Joan *128:* 170
Garneray, Ambroise Louis *59:* 140
Garnett, Eve *3:* 75
Garnett, Gary *39:* 184
Garns, Allen *80:* 125; *84:* 39; *165:* 231; *209:* 44
Garófoli, Viviana *186:* 123
Garraty, Gail *4:* 142; *52:* 106
Garrett, Agnes *46:* 110; *47:* 157
Garrett, Edmund H. *20:* 29

Garrett, Tom *107:* 194
Garrick, Jacqueline *67:* 42, 43; *77:* 94
Garrison, Barbara *19:* 133; *104:* 146; *109:* 87
Garro, Mark *108:* 131; *128:* 210
Garvey, Robert *98:* 222
Garza, Carmen Lomas *80:* 211; *182:* 86
Garza, Xavier *184:* 64
Gates, Frieda *26:* 80
Gaughan, Jack *26:* 79; *43:* 185
Gaver, Becky *20:* 61
Gavril, David *211:* 196
Gawing, Toby *72:* 52
Gay, Marie-Louise *68:* 76, 77, 78; *102:* 136; *126:* 76, 78, 81, 83; *127:* 55, 56; *179:* 70, 72, 73, 74
Gay, Zhenya *19:* 135, 136
Gaydos, Tim *62:* 201
Gazsi, Ed *80:* 48
Gazso, Gabriel *73:* 85
Geary, Clifford N. *1:* 122; *9:* 104; *51:* 74
Geary, Rick *142:* 44, 46
Gee, Frank *33:* 26
Geehan, Wayne *157:* 181
Geer, Charles *1:* 91; *3:* 179; *4:* 201; *6:* 168; *7:* 96; *9:* 58; *10:* 72; *12:* 127; *39:* 156,157, 158, 159, 160; *42:* 88, 89, 90, 91; *55:* 111, 116
Geerinck, Manuel *173:* 128
Gehm, Charlie *36:* 65; *57:* 117; *62:* 60, 138
Geis, Alissa Imre *189:* 77
Geisel, Theodor Seuss *1:* 104, 105, 106; *28:* 108, 109, 110,111, 112, 113; *75:* 67, 68, 69, 70, 71; *89:* 127, 128; *100:* 106, 107, 108
Geisert, Arthur *92:* 67, 68; *133:* 72, 73, 74; *165:* 97, 98; *171:* 64, 65
Geldart, William *15:* 121; *21:* 202
Genia *4:* 84
Gentry, Cyrille R. *12:* 66
Genzo, John Paul *136:* 74
George, Jean *2:* 113
George, Lindsay Barrett *95:* 57; *155:* 97, 98
Geraghty, Paul *130:* 60, 61
Gerard, Jean Ignace *45:* 80
Gerard, Rolf *27:* 147, 150
Gerber, Mark *61:* 105
Gerber, Mary Jane *112:* 124; *171:* 56
Gerber, Stephanie *71:* 195
Gerdstein, Mordecai *169:* 105
Gergely, Tibor *54:* 15, 16
Geritz, Franz *17:* 135
Gerlach, Geff *42:* 58
Gerrard, Roy *78:* 78; *90:* 96, 97, 98, 99
Gerritsen, Paula *177:* 69
Gershinowitz, George *36:* 27
Gerstein, Mordicai *31:* 117; *47:* 80, 81, 82, 83, 84, 85, 86; *51:* 173; *69:* 134; *107:* 122; *142:* 49, 52; *165:* 209; *176:* 119; *178:* 95, 97, 99
Gervase *12:* 27
Geter, Tyrone *146:* 249; *150:* 86
Getz, Arthur *32:* 148
Gévry, Claudine *188:* 47
Gewirtz, Bina *61:* 81
Giancola, Donato *95:* 146; *164:* 226
Gibala-Broxholm, Scott *205:* 76
Gibbons, Gail *23:* 78; *72:* 77, 78, 79; *82:* 182; *104:* 65; *160:* 99, 100; *201:* 59, 60, 62
Gibbs, Tony *40:* 95
Gibran, Kahlil *32:* 116
Gibson, Barbara Leonard *205:* 77
Gider, Iskender *81:* 193
Giebfried, Rosemary *170:* 135
Giesen, Rosemary *34:* 192, 193
Giffard, Hannah *83:* 70
Giguere, George *20:* 111
Gilbert, John *19:* 184; *54:* 115; *YABC 2:* 287
Gilbert, W.S. *36:* 83, 85, 96
Gilbert, Yvonne *116:* 70; *128:* 84; *149:* 119; *185:* 69; *192:* 25; *195:* 81
Gilchrist, Jan Spivey *72:* 82, 83, 84, 85, 87; *77:* 90; *105:* 89, 91; *130:* 63, 64; *155:* 105, 107; *182:* 67
Giles, Will *41:* 218

Gili, Phillida *70:* 73
Gill, Margery *4:* 57; *7:* 7; *22:* 122; *25:* 166; *26:* 146, 147
Gillen, Denver *28:* 216
Gillette, Henry J. *23:* 237
Gilliam, Stan *39:* 64, 81
Gillies, Chuck *62:* 31
Gilliland, Jillian *87:* 58
Gillman, Alec *98:* 105
Gilman, Esther *15:* 124
Gilman, Phoebe *104:* 70, 71
Ginsberg, Sari *111:* 184
Ginsburg, Max *62:* 59; *68:* 194 *Girard, Roge 161:* 30
Girouard, Patrick *155:* 100
Giovanopoulos, Paul *7:* 104; *60:* 36
Giovine, Sergio *79:* 12; *93:* 118; *139:* 118; *205:* 114
Gist, E.M. *206:* 60
Githens, Elizabeth M. *5:* 47
Gladden, Scott *99:* 108; *103:* 160; *193:* 46, 47
Gladstone, Gary *12:* 89; *13:* 190
Gladstone, Lise *15:* 273
Glanzman, Louis S. *2:* 177; *3:* 182; *36:* 97, 98; *38:* 120, 122; *52:* 141, 144; *71:* 191; *91:* 54, 56
Glaser, Byron *154:* 59, 60
Glaser, Milton *3:* 5; *5:* 156; *11:* 107; *30:* 26; *36:* 112; *54:* 141; *151:* 70
Glass, Andrew *36:* 38; *44:* 133; *48:* 205; *65:* 3; *68:* 43, 45; *90:* 104, 105; *150:* 89
Glass, Marvin *9:* 174
Glasser, Judy *41:* 156; *56:* 140; *69:* 79; *72:* 101
Glattauer, Ned *5:* 84; *13:* 224; *14:* 26
Glauber, Uta *17:* 76
Gleeson, J.M. *YABC 2:* 207
Glegg, Creina *36:* 100
Glienke, Amelie *63:* 150
Gliewe, Unada *3:* 78, 79; *21:* 73; *30:* 220
Gliori, Debi *72:* 91; *138:* 82; *162:* 37; *189:* 79, 81, 82
Glovach, Linda *7:* 105
Gobbato, Imero *3:* 180, 181; *6:* 213; *7:* 58; *9:* 150; *18:* 39; *21:* 167; *39:* 82, 83; *41:* 137, 251; *59:* 177
Goble, Paul *25:* 121; *26:* 86; *33:* 65; *69:* 68, 69; *131:* 79, 80
Goble, Warwick *46:* 78, 79; *194:* 143
Godal, Eric *36:* 93
Godkin, Celia *145:* 84, 86
Godfrey, Michael *17:* 279
Godon, Ingrid *166:* 163; *186:* 99
Goede, Irene *208:* 87
Goembel, Ponder *42:* 124
Goffe, Toni *61:* 83, 84, 85; *89:* 11; *90:* 124; *178:* 118
Goffstein, M.B. *8:* 71; *70:* 75, 76, 77
Golbin, Andre *15:* 125
Gold, Robert *166:* 151, 152
Goldfeder, Cheryl *11:* 191
Goldfinger, Jennifer P. *185:* 71
Goldsborough, June *5:* 154, 155; *8:* 92; *14:* 226; *19:* 139; *54:* 165
Goldsmith, Robert *110:* 77
Goldstein, Barry *198:* 147
Goldstein, Leslie *5:* 8; *6:* 60; *10:* 106
Goldstein, Nathan *1:* 175; *2:* 79; *11:* 41, 232; *16:* 55
Goldstrom, Robert *98:* 36; *145:* 51, 52
Golembe, Carla *79:* 80, 81; *136:* 91; *144:* 113; *193:* 53
Golin, Carlo *74:* 112
Gomez, Elena *188:* 122; *191:* 72
Gomez, Elizabeth *127:* 70; *133:* 76
Gomi, Taro *64:* 102; *103:* 74, 76
Gon, Adriano *101:* 112
Gonsalve, Ron *178:* 213
Gonzalez, Maya Christina *104:* 3; *136:* 92
Goodall, John S. *4:* 92, 93; *10:* 132; *66:* 92, 93; *YABC 1:* 198

Goode, Diane *15:* 126; *50:* 183; *52:* 114, 115; *76:* 195; *84:* 94; *99:* 141; *114:* 76, 77, 78; *170:* 99, 101
Goodelman, Aaron *40:* 203
Goodenow, Earle *40:* 97
Goodfellow, Peter *62:* 95; *94:* 202
Goodman, Joan Elizabeth *50:* 86
Goodman, Vivienne *82:* 251; *146:* 181, 182
Goodnow, Patti *117:* 33
Goodwin, Harold *13:* 74
Goodwin, Philip R. *18:* 206
Goor, Nancy *39:* 85, 86
Goor, Ron *39:* 85, 86
Goossens, Philippe *195:* 71
Gorbachev, Valeri *89:* 96; *112:* 97; *143:* 63, 64; *184:* 66, 67, 68, 101
Gordon, Gwen *12:* 151
Gordon, Margaret *4:* 147; *5:* 48, 49; *9:* 79
Gordon, Mike *101:* 62, 63, 64
Gordon, Russell *136:* 204; *137:* 214
Gordon, Walter *138:* 9
Gore, Leonid *89:* 51; *94:* 74; *136:* 8; *158:* 117; *166:* 136; *168:* 36; *170:* 107; *181:* 94; *185:* 73
Gorecka-Egan, Erica *18:* 35
Gorey, Edward *1:* 60, 61; *13:* 169; *18:* 192; *20:* 201; *29:* 90, 91, 92, 93, 94, 95, 96, 97, 98, 99, 100; *30:* 129; *32:* 90; *34:* 200, 65: 48; *68:* 24, 25; *69:* 79; *70:* 80, 82, 83, 84; *85:* 136; *127:* 62
Gorsline, Douglas *1:* 98; *6:* 13; *11:* 113; *13:* 104; *15:* 14; *28:* 117, 118; *YABC 1:* 15
Gorton, Julia *108:* 94; *178:* 81, 82
Gosfield, Josh *118:* 165, 166; *149:* 67
Gosner, Kenneth *5:* 135
Gosney, Joy *167:* 142
Gotlieb, Jules *6:* 127
Goto, Scott *115:* 86; *136:* 69; *203:* 77, 78
Gott, Barry *197:* 95
Gottlieb, Dale *67:* 162; *107:* 16; *149:* 6
Goudey, Ray *97:* 86
Gough, Alan *91:* 57
Gough, Philip *23:* 47; *45:* 90
Gould, Chester *49:* 112, 113, 114, 116, 117, 118
Gould, Jason *151:* 232
Gourbault, Martine *177:* 159
Govern, Elaine R. *26:* 94
Gower, Teri *102:* 184
Gowing, Toby *60:* 25; *63:* 33; *78:* 70, 252; *83:* 228; *86:* 187; *93:* 145; *108:* 133; *110:* 217; *184:* 125
Grabianski *20:* 144
Grabianski, Janusz *39:* 92, 93, 94, 95
Graboff, Abner *35:* 103, 104
Graef, Renée *61:* 188; *72:* 207; *204:* 45; *210:* 249
Grafe, Max *156:* 173; *178:* 237; *192:* 240; *198:* 51
Graham, A.B. *11:* 61
Graham, Bob *101:* 66, 67, 68; *151:* 74, 75; *187:* 65, 67, 68, 70
Graham, Georgia *188:* 3; *190:* 75
Graham, L. *7:* 108
Graham, Margaret Bloy *11:* 120; *18:* 305, 307
Graham, Mark *88:* 208; *159:* 153; *182:* 3
Grahame-Johnstone, Janet *13:* 61
Grahame-Johnstone, Anne *13:* 61
Grainger, Sam *42:* 95
Gralley, Jean *166:* 86
Gramatky, Hardie *1:* 107; *30:* 116, 119, 120, 122, 123
Gran, Julie *168:* 118
Granahan, Julie *84:* 84
GrandPré, Mary *84:* 131; *109:* 199; *118:* 76; *180:* 65; *184:* 70, 71, 180; *192:* 87
Grandström, Brita *176:* 139
Grandville, J.J. *45:* 81, 82, 83, 84, 85, 86, 87, 88; *47:* 125; *64:* 10
Granger, Paul *39:* 153
Granström, Brita *162:* 35; *167:* 46

Grant, (Alice) Leigh *10:* 52; *15:* 131; *20:* 20; *26:* 119; *48:* 202
Grant, Gordon *17:* 230, 234; *25:* 123, 124, 125, 126; *52:* 69; *YABC 1:* 164
Grant, Melvyn *159:* 186, 187; *170:* 48, 49
Grant, Michelle *210:* 95
Grant, Renee *77:* 40
Grant, Shirley *109:* 45
Graves, Elizabeth *45:* 101
Graves, Keith *167:* 89; *191:* 74
Gray, Harold *33:* 87, 88
Gray, Les *82:* 76; *83:* 232
Gray, Reginald *6:* 69
Greco, Tony *184:* 6
Greder, Armin *76:* 235
Green, Ann Canevari *62:* 48
Green, Eileen *6:* 97
Green, Elizabeth Shippen *139:* 109
Green, Jonathan *86:* 135; *105:* 109
Green, Ken *111:* 68
Green, Michael *32:* 216
Green, Robina *87:* 138
Green, Jonathan *157:* 105
Greene, Jeffrey *117:* 93
Greenaway, Kate *17:* 275; *24:* 180; *26:* 107; *41:* 222, 232; *100:* 115, 116; *YABC 1:* 88, 89; *2:* 131, 133, 136,138, 139, 141
Greenberg, Melanie Hope *72:* 93; *80:* 125; *101:* 174; *133:* 180; *186:* 189
Greenseid, Diane *178:* 106, 107
Greenstein, Elaine *150:* 100
Greenwald, Sheila *1:* 34; *3:* 99; *8:* 72
Greger, Carol *76:* 86
Gregorian, Joyce Ballou *30:* 125
Gregory, Emilian *177:* 146; *187:* 10
Gregory, Fran *130:* 4; *140:* 93
Gregory, Frank M. *29:* 107
Greiffenhagen, Maurice *16:* 137; *27:* 57; *YABC 2:* 288
Greiner, Robert *6:* 86
Gretter, J. Clemens *31:* 134
Gretz, Susanna *7:* 114
Gretzer, John *1:* 54; *3:* 26; *4:* 162; *7:* 125; *16:* 247; *18:* 117; *28:* 66; *30:* 85, 211; *33:* 235; *56:* 16
Grey, Mini *166:* 90; *192:* 71
Grey Owl *24:* 41
Gri *25:* 90
Grieder, Walter *9:* 84
Griesbach/Martucci *59:* 3
Grifalconi, Ann *2:* 126; *3:* 248; *11:* 18; *13:* 182; *46:* 38; *50:* 145; *66:* 99, 100, 101, 104, 106; *69:* 38; *70:* 64; *87:* 128; *90:* 53; *93:* 49; *128:* 48; *133:* 79, 81; *210:* 111
Griffin, Gillett Good *26:* 96
Griffin, James *30:* 166
Griffin, John Howard *59:* 186
Griffin, Rachel *131:* 23
Griffith, Gershom *94:* 214
Griffiths, Dave *29:* 76
Griffiths, Dean *168:* 180; *169:* 182
Grimly, Gris *186:* 102; *192:* 112; *197:* 86
Grimsdell, Jeremy *83:* 75
Grimwood, Brian *82:* 89
Gringhuis, Dirk *6:* 98; *9:* 196
Gripe, Harald *2:* 127; *74:* 98
Grisha *3:* 71
Grobler, Piet *201:* 100
Grohmann, Susan *84:* 97
Gropper, William *27:* 93; *37:* 193
Gros *60:* 199
Grose, Helen Mason *YABC 1:* 260; *2:* 150
Grossman, Nancy *24:* 130; *29:* 101
Grossman, Robert *11:* 124; *46:* 39
Groth, John *15:* 79; *21:* 53, 54; *83:* 230
Grover, Lorie Ann *168:* 59
Grubb, Lisa *160:* 116
Grue, Lisa *187:* 193
Gruelle, Johnny *35:* 107
Gschwind, William *11:* 72
Guarnaccia, Steven *201:* 170, 173

Guay-Mitchell, Rebecca *110:* 95, 96; *135:* 240; *180:* 76; *181:* 71, 73
Guback, Georgia *88:* 102
Guerguerion, Claudine *105:* 73
Guevara, Susan *97:* 87; *167:* 49; *194:* 54
Guggenheim, Hans *2:* 10; *3:* 37; *8:* 136
Guhathaakurta, Ajanta *183:* 199
Guida, Lisa Chauncy *172:* 188
Guilbeau, Honore *22:* 69
Guillette, Joseph *137:* 37
Guisewite, Cathy *57:* 52, 53, 54, 56, 57
Gukova, Julia *95:* 104; *154:* 103; *168:* 195
Gundersheimer, Karen *35:* 240; *82:* 100
Gunderson, Nick *57:* 120
Gunnella *192:* 144
Gurney, James *76:* 97; *86:* 32
Gurney, John Steven *75:* 39, 82; *110:* 175; *143:* 67, 68; *169:* 172
Gusman, Annie *38:* 62
Gustafson, Scott *34:* 111; *43:* 40
Gustavson, Adam *104:* 10; *171:* 183; *176:* 87; *197:* 94; *204:* 35
Guthridge, Bettina *108:* 79; *186:* 92
Guthrie, R. Dale *64:* 143
Guthrie, Robin *20:* 122
Gutierrez, Akemi *172:* 87; *205:* 135
Gutierrez, Alan *136:* 31, 32
Gutierrez, Rudy *97:* 162; *203:* 79
Gutmann, Bessie Pease *73:* 93, 94
Gwynne, Fred *41:* 94, 95
Gyberg, Bo-Erik *38:* 131

H

Haas, Irene *17:* 77; *87:* 46; *96:* 117
Hack, Konrad *51:* 127
Hader, Berta H. *16:* 126
Hader, Elmer S. *16:* 126
Haeffele, Deborah *76:* 99
Haemer, Alan *62:* 109
Hafner, Marylin *22:* 196, 216; *24:* 44; *30:* 51; *35:* 95; *51:* 25, 160, 164; *86:* 16; *105:* 196; *121:* 93, 94; *149:* 208, 209; *179:* 82, 83, 84, 115; *190:* 200; *201:* 29
Hagerty, Sean *62:* 181
Hague, Michael *32:* 128; *48:* 98, 99, 100, 101, 103, 105,106, 107, 108, 109, 110; *49:* 121; *51:* 105; *64:* 14, 15; *79:* 134; *80:* 91, 92; *83:* 135; *100:* 241; *102:* 29; *129:* 101, 103, 104; *185:* 80, 81, 82
Hair, Jonathan *115:* 135
Halas, John *29:* 41, 47, 48
Haldane, Roger *13:* 76; *14:* 202
Hale, Bruce *203:* 83
Hale, Christy *79:* 124; *84:* 200; *114:* 201; *128:* 2, 3; *146:* 203; *158:* 243; *167:* 99; *179:* 87
Hale, Irina *26:* 97
Hale, James Graham *88:* 207
Hale, Kathleen *17:* 79; *66:* 114, 116, 118
Hale, Nathan *210:* 115, 116
Haley, Amanda *205:* 82, 83
Haley, Gail E. *43:* 102, 103, 104, 105; *78:* 65, 67; *136:* 106, 107
Hall, Amanda *96:* 110
Hall, Chuck *30:* 189
Hall, Douglas *15:* 184; *43:* 106, 107; *86:* 100; *87:* 82; *129:* 72
Hall, H. Tom *1:* 227; *30:* 210
Hall, Melanie *116:* 48, 49; *169:* 77, 78
Hall, Sydney P. *31:* 89
Hall, Tim *164:* 196; *202:* 41
Hall, Vicki *20:* 24
Hallinan, P.K. *39:* 98
Hallman, Tom *98:* 166
Hally, Greg *101:* 200; *151:* 224
Halperin, Wendy Anderson *96:* 151; *125:* 96, 97, 98, 99; *139:* 22; *140:* 84; *200:* 77, 78; *210:* 157
Halpern, Joan *10:* 25

Halpern, Shari *174:* 172
Halsey, Megan *96:* 172; *114:* 185; *180:* 8; *185:* 85
Halstead, Virginia *125:* 105
Halverson, Janet *49:* 38, 42, 44
Hallensleben, Georg *134:* 5, 6; *172:* 17
Hamanaka, Sheila *71:* 100
Hamann, Brad *78:* 151
Hamann, Sigune *104:* 115
Hamberger, John *6:* 8; *8:* 32; *14:* 79; *34:* 136; *88:* 78
Hamil, Tom *14:* 80; *43:* 163
Hamilton, Bill and Associates *26:* 215
Hamilton, Helen S. *2:* 238
Hamilton, J. *19:* 83, 85, 87
Hamilton, Laurie *116:* 210
Hamilton, Todd Cameron *84:* 15
Hamlin, Janet *97:* 136; *124:* 90; *137:* 157; *182:* 117
Hamlin, Louise *71:* 135
Hammill, Matt *206:* 65
Hammond, Chris *21:* 37
Hammond, Elizabeth *5:* 36, 203
Hampshire, Michael *5:* 187; *7:* 110, 111; *48:* 150; *51:* 129
Hampson, Denman *10:* 155; *15:* 130
Hampton, Blake *41:* 244
Handford, Martin *64:* 105, 106, 107, 109
Handforth, Thomas *42:* 100, 101, 102, 103, 104, 105, 107
Handville, Robert *1:* 89; *38:* 76; *45:* 108, 109
Hane, Roger *17:* 239; *44:* 54
Haney, Elizabeth Mathieu *34:* 84
Hanke, Ted *71:* 10
Hankinson, Phil *181:* 164
Hanley, Catherine *8:* 161
Hann, Jacquie *19:* 144
Hanna, Cheryl *91:* 133
Hanna, Wayne A. *67:* 145
Hannon, Mark *38:* 37
Hanrahan, Kelly-Anne *203:* 142
Hansen, Gaby *159:* 11; *186:* 25
Hansen, Mia *149:* 76
Hanson, Joan *8:* 76; *11:* 139
Hanson, Peter E. *52:* 47; *54:* 99, 100; *73:* 21; *84:* 79; *116:* 144
Hansson, Gunilla *64:* 111, 112
Hardcastle, Nick *121:* 82; *175:* 185
Hardy, David A. *9:* 96; *119:* 74
Hardy, Paul *YABC 2:* 245 Haring, Keith *145:* 65
Harlan, Jerry *3:* 96
Harlin, Greg *89:* 194; *103:* 82; *118:* 161; *121:* 167; *182:* 76; *201:* 172
Harman, Dominic *206:* 48
Harness, Cheryl *106:* 80; *131:* 87; *178:* 111; *200:* 39
Harnischfeger *18:* 121
Harper, Arthur *YABC 2:* 121
Harper, Betty *126:* 90
Harper, Jamie *174:* 71
Harper, Piers *79:* 27; *105:* 102; *161:* 67
Harrington, Glenn *82:* 18; *94:* 66, 68; *185:* 118
Harrington, Jack *83:* 162
Harrington, Richard *5:* 81
Harris, Andrew N. *191:* 78
Harris, Jim *127:* 130; *183:* 4
Harris, John *83:* 25
Harris, Nick *86:* 177
Harris, Susan Yard *42:* 121
Harrison, Florence *20:* 150, 152
Harrison, Harry *4:* 103
Harrison, Jack *28:* 149
Harrison, Mark *105:* 157; *165:* 190
Harrison, Ted *56:* 73
Harsh, Fred *72:* 107
Harston, Jerry *105:* 143
Hart, Lewis *98:* 115
Hart, Thomas *181:* 165
Hart, William *13:* 72

Hartland, Jessie *171:* 80, 81; *186:* 165
Hartung, Susan Kathleen *150:* 107, 108; *173:* 106; *175:* 106; *192:* 78; *211:* 19
Hartelius, Margaret *10:* 24
Hartshorn, Ruth *5:* 115; *11:* 129
Harvey, Amanda *145:* 44
Harvey, Bob *48:* 219
Harvey, Gerry *7:* 180
Harvey, Lisa *97:* 21
Harvey, Paul *88:* 74
Harvey, Roland *71:* 88; *123:* 63; *179:* 94
Haskamp, Steve *195:* 36
Hassall, Joan *43:* 108, 109
Hassell, Hilton *YABC 1:* 187
Hassett, John *162:* 59
Hasselriis, Else *18:* 87; *YABC 1:* 96
Hastings, Glenn *89:* 183
Hastings, Ian *62:* 67
Hauman, Doris *2:* 184; *29:* 58, 59; *32:* 85, 86, 87
Hauman, George *2:* 184; *29:* 58, 59; *32:* 85, 86, 87
Hausherr, Rosmarie *15:* 29
Hawkes, Kevin *78:* 72; *104:* 198; *105:* 197; *112:* 109; *126:* 87; *144:* 88; *149:* 210; *150:* 110, 135; *156:* 94; *164:* 35; *186:* 18; *190:* 197; *198:* 152; *201:* 70, 71, 72
Hawkins, Jacqui *112:* 86; *162:* 64
Hawkinson, John *4:* 109; *7:* 83; *21:* 64
Hawkinson, Lucy *21:* 64
Hawthorne, Mike *140:* 228
Haxton, Elaine *28:* 131
Haydock, Robert *4:* 95
Hayes, Geoffrey *26:* 111; *44:* 133; *91:* 85; *207:* 63
Hayes, Karel *207:* 65
Haynes, Max *72:* 107
Hays, Michael *73:* 207; *83:* 93; *139:* 197; *146:* 202, 250; *202:* 47
Haywood, Carolyn *1:* 112; *29:* 104
Heale, Jonathan *104:* 117
Healy, Daty *12:* 143
Healy, Deborah *58:* 181, 182; *101:* 111
Heap, Sue *102:* 207; *150:* 113, 114; *187:* 84, 85, 87
Hearn, Diane Dawson *79:* 99; *113:* 13; *209:* 71, 72; *211:* 106
Hearon, Dorothy *34:* 69
Heaslip, William *57:* 24, 25
Hechtkopf, H. *11:* 110
Heck, Ed *173:* 81
Hector, Julian *205:* 85
Hedderwick, Mairi *30:* 127; *32:* 47; *36:* 104; *77:* 86; *145:* 91, 93, 95
Heffernan, Phil *146:* 197; *195:* 172
Hefter, Richard *28:* 170; *31:* 81, 82; *33:* 183
Hehenberger, Shelly *126:* 91
Heigh, James *22:* 98
Heighway, Richard *25:* 160; *64:* 4
Heighway-Bury, Robin *159:* 89
Heine, Helme *67:* 86; *135:* 91, 92
Heinly, John *45:* 113
Hellard, Susan *81:* 21; *204:* 82; *209:* 92
Hellebrand, Nancy *26:* 57
Heller, Linda *46:* 86
Heller, Ruth M. *66:* 125; *77:* 30, 32
Hellmuth, Jim *38:* 164
Helms, Georgeann *33:* 62
Helquist, Brett *142:* 203; *146:* 133, 134; *156:* 10; *173:* 25; *180:* 106; *187:* 90, 91; *193:* 12
Helweg, Hans *41:* 118; *50:* 93; *58:* 22, 26
Hemphill, Helen *179:* 95
Henba, Bobbie *90:* 195
Henderson, Dave *73:* 76; *75:* 191, 192, 193, 194; *82:* 4
Henderson, Douglas *103:* 68
Henderson, Kathy *55:* 32; *155:* 118
Henderson, Keith *35:* 122
Henderson, Meryl *127:* 58, 60; *169:* 81
Hendrix, John *187:* 133; *208:* 106, 107, 108
Hendry, Linda *80:* 104; *83:* 83; *164:* 216

Hengeveld, Dennis *142:* 86
Henkes, Kevin *43:* 111; *108:* 106, 107, 108
Henneberger, Robert *1:* 42; *2:* 237; *25:* 83
Henriksen, Harold *35:* 26; *48:* 68
Henriquez, Celeste *103:* 137
Henriquez, Elsa *82:* 260
Henriquez, Emile F. *89:* 88; *211:* 56
Henry, Everett *29:* 191
Henry, Matthew *117:* 58
Henry, Paul *93:* 121; *194:* 125
Henry, Thomas *5:* 102
Hensel *27:* 119
Henshaw, Jacqui *141:* 127
Henstra, Friso *8:* 80; *36:* 70; *40:* 222; *41:* 250; *73:* 100, 101
Henterly, Jamichael *93:* 4
Heo, Yumi *89:* 85, 86; *94:* 89, 90; *146:* 40, 137, 138; *163:* 227; *201:* 192
Hepple, Norman *28:* 198
Herbert, Helen *57:* 70
Herbert, Jennifer *189:* 47
Herbert, Wally *23:* 101
Herbster, Mary Lee *9:* 33
Herder, Edwin *182:* 104
Herge
  See Remi, Georges
Hermansen, Pal *133:* 113
Hermanson, Dennis *10:* 55
Hermes, Gertrude *54:* 161
Herr, Margo *57:* 191
Herr, Susan *83:* 163
Herriman, George *140:* 74, 75, 76, 77, 78
Herriman, Lisa *87:* 190
Herring, Michael *121:* 76; *182:* 103
Herrington, Roger *3:* 161
Herscovici, C. *165:* 240
Hescox, Richard *85:* 86; *90:* 30; *139:* 35
Heslop, Mike *38:* 60; *40:* 130
Hess, Lydia J. *85:* 17
Hess, Mark *111:* 146; *113:* 207
Hess, Paul *134:* 47; *166:* 133; *193:* 13
Hess, Richard *42:* 31
Hester, Ronnie *37:* 85
Heuser, Olga J. *121:* 116
Heusser, Sibylle *168:* 195
Heustis, Louise L. *20:* 28
Hewgill, Jodi *201:* 90
Hewitson, Jennifer *74:* 119; *124:* 167
Hewitt, Kathryn *80:* 126; *149:* 105; *184:* 93; *196:* 36
Hewitt, Margaret *84:* 112
Heyduck-Huth, Hilde *8:* 82
Heyer, Carol *74:* 122; *130:* 72, 73; *192:* 35; *203:* 78
Heyer, Hermann *20:* 114, 115
Heyer, Marilee *102:* 108
Heyman, Ken *8:* 33; *34:* 113
Heyne, Ulrike *146:* 151
Heywood, Karen *48:* 114
Hickling, P.B. *40:* 165
Hickman, Stephen *85:* 58; *136:* 33; *171:* 128
Hierstein, Judy *56:* 40; *162:* 168
Higashi, Sandra *154:* 59, 60
Higginbottom, J. Winslow *8:* 170; *29:* 105, 106
Higgins, Chester *101:* 79
Higham, David *50:* 104
Hilb, Nora *176:* 8
Hildebrandt, Greg *8:* 191; *55:* 35, 36, 38, 39, 40, 42, 46; *172:* 110
Hildebrandt, Tim *8:* 191; *55:* 44, 45, 46
Hilder, Rowland *19:* 207
Hill, Eric *66:* 127, 128; *133:* 91
Hill, Gregory *35:* 190
Hill, Pat *49:* 120
Hillenbrand, Will *84:* 115; *92:* 76, 80; *93:* 131; *104:* 168; *128:* 137; *145:* 187; *146:* 184; *147:* 105, 106, 107; *152:* 59; *184:* 179; *195:* 34, 180; *196:* 125; *210:* 122, 123, 124
Hilliard, Richard *183:* 74
Hillier, Matthew *45:* 205

Hillman, Priscilla *48:* 115
Hills, Tad *113:* 4; *137:* 147; *173:* 83; *208:* 199
Himler, Ronald *6:* 114; *7:* 162; *8:* 17, 84, 125; *14:* 76; *19:* 145; *26:* 160; *31:* 43; *38:* 116; *41:* 44, 79; *43:* 52; *45:* 120; *46:* 43; *54:* 44, 83; *58:* 180; *59:* 38; *68:* 146; *69:* 231; *70:* 98; *71:* 177, 178; *77:* 219; *79:* 212; *83:* 62; *89:* 5; *91:* 160; *92:* 91, 92, 93; *94:* 93; *95:* 69, 174, 194; *99:* 99, 112; *113:* 92; *118:* 114; *137:* 73, 74, 77, 167; *163:* 99; *165:* 138; *178:* 9, 220; *183:* 77, 79, 80, 81; *184:* 80, 83
Himmelman, John *47:* 109; *65:* 87; *94:* 96, 97; *159:* 85
Hinds, Bill *37:* 127, 130
Hines, Anna Grossnickle *51:* 90; *74:* 124; *95:* 78, 79,80, 81
Hines, Bob *135:* 149, 150
Hirao, Amiko *203:* 98
Hiroko *99:* 61
Hiroshige *25:* 71
Hirsh, Marilyn *7:* 126
Hiscock, Bruce *137:* 80, 81; *204:* 51, 53
Hissey, Jane *103:* 90; *130:* 81
Hitch, Jeff *99:* 206; *128:* 86
Hitz, Demi *11:* 135; *15:* 245; *66:* 129, 130; *152:* 94, 95
Hnizdovsky, Jacques *32:* 96; *76:* 187
Ho, Kwoncjan *15:* 132
Hoban, Lillian *1:* 114; *22:* 157; *26:* 72; *29:* 53; *40:* 105, 107, 195; *41:* 80; *69:* 107, 108; *71:* 98; *77:* 168; *106:* 50; *113:* 86; *136:* 118
Hoban, Tana *22:* 159; *104:* 82, 83, 85
Hobbie, Jocelyn *190:* 78; *196:* 92
Hobbie, Nathaniel *196:* 92
Hobbs, Leigh *166:* 95
Hoberman, Norman *5:* 82
Hobson, Sally *77:* 185
Hockerman, Dennis *39:* 22; *56:* 23
Hodgell, P.C. *42:* 114
Hodges, C. Walter *2:* 139; *11:* 15; *12:* 25; *23:* 34; *25:* 96; *38:* 165; *44:* 197; *45:* 95; *100:* 57; *YABC 2:* 62, 63
Hodges, David *9:* 98
Hodgetts, Victoria *43:* 132
Hofbauer, Imre *2:* 162
Hoff, Syd *9:* 107; *10:* 128; *33:* 94; *72:* 115,116, 117, 118; *138:* 114, 115
Hoffman, Rosekrans *15:* 133; *50:* 219; *63:* 97
Hoffman, Sanford *38:* 208; *76:* 174; *88:* 160, 161; *151:* 156
Hoffmann, Felix *9:* 109
Hoffnung, Gerard *66:* 76, 77
Hofsinde, Robert *21:* 70
Hogan, Inez *2:* 141
Hogan, Jamie *192:* 94; *198:* 177
Hogarth, Burne *41:* 58; *63:* 46, 48, 49, 50, 52, 53, 54, 55,56
Hogarth, Paul *41:* 102, 103, 104; *YABC 1:* 16
Hogarth, William *42:* 33
Hogenbyl, Jan *1:* 35
Hogner, Nils *4:* 122; *25:* 144
Hogrogian, Nonny *3:* 221; *4:* 106, 107; *5:* 166; *7:* 129; *15:* 2; *16:* 176; *20:* 154; *22:* 146; *25:* 217; *27:* 206; *74:* 127, 128, 129, 149, 152; *127:* 99; *YABC 2:* 84, 94
Hokanson, Lars *93:* 111; *172:* 137
Hokusai *25:* 71
Hol, Colby *126:* 96
Holberg, Richard *2:* 51
Holbrook, Kathy *107:* 114
Holdcroft, Tina *38:* 109
Holden, Caroline *55:* 159
Holder, Heidi *36:* 99; *64:* 9
Holder, Jim *204:* 163
Holder, Jimmy *151:* 224
Hole, Stian *204:* 55
Holiday, Henry *YABC 2:* 107
Holl, F. *36:* 91
Holland, Brad *45:* 59, 159
Holland, Gay W. *128:* 105
Holland, Janice *18:* 118

Holland, Marion *6:* 116
Holldobler, Turid *26:* 120
Holliday, Keaf *144:* 236
Holling, Holling C. *15:* 136, 137
Hollinger, Deanne *12:* 116
Holm, Sharon Lane *114:* 84; *115:* 52
Holmes, B. *3:* 82
Holmes, Bea *7:* 74; *24:* 156; *31:* 93
Holmes, Dave *54:* 22
Holmes, Lesley *135:* 96
Holmgren, George Ellen *45:* 112
Holmlund, Heather D. *150:* 140
Holt, Norma *44:* 106
Holt, Pater *151:* 188
Holtan, Gene *32:* 192
Holub, Joan *149:* 72
Holyfield, John *149:* 231
Holz, Loretta *17:* 81
Hom, Nancy *79:* 195
Homar, Lorenzo *6:* 2
Homer, Winslow *128:* 8; *YABC 2:* 87
Honey, Elizabeth *112:* 95, 96; *137:* 93, 94
Honeywood, Varnette P. *110:* 68, 70
Hong, Lily Toy *76:* 104
Honigman, Marian *3:* 2
Honore, Paul *42:* 77, 79, 81, 82
Hood, Alun *69:* 145, 218; *72:* 41; *80:* 226; *87:* 4; *95:* 139
Hood, Susan *12:* 43
Hook, Christian *104:* 103
Hook, Frances *26:* 188; *27:* 127
Hook, Jeff *14:* 137; *103:* 105
Hook, Richard *26:* 188
Hooks *63:* 30
Hooper, Hadley *177:* 145
Hoover, Carol A. *21:* 77
Hoover, Russell *12:* 95; *17:* 2; *34:* 156
Hope, James *141:* 116
Hopkins, Chris *99:* 127
Hopkinson, Leigh *202:* 70
Hopman, Philip *178:* 184
Hoppe, Paul *209:* 85
Hoppin, Augustus *34:* 66
Horacek, Judy *211:* 86
Horacek, Petr *163:* 117
Horder, Margaret *2:* 108; *73:* 75
Horen, Michael *45:* 121
Horne, Daniel *73:* 106; *91:* 153; *109:* 127; *110:* 232; *164:* 176
Horne, Richard *111:* 80
Horowitz, Dave *204:* 58
Horse, Harry *128:* 195; *169:* 86
Horton, Anthony *211:* 98
Horvat, Laurel *12:* 201
Horvath, David *192:* 95
Horvath, Ferdinand Kusati *24:* 176
Horvath, Maria *57:* 171
Horwitz, Richard *57:* 174
Hotchkiss, De Wolfe *20:* 49
Hough, Charlotte *9:* 112; *13:* 98; *17:* 83; *24:* 195
Houlihan, Ray *11:* 214
House, Caroline *183:* 121
Housman, Laurence *25:* 146, 147
Houston, James *13:* 107; *74:* 132, 134, 135
Hovland, Gary *88:* 172; *171:* 148
Hoyt, Eleanor *158:* 231
How, W.E. *20:* 47
Howard, Alan *16:* 80; *34:* 58; *45:* 114
Howard, Arthur *165:* 111, 112; *190:* 5
Howard, J.N. *15:* 234
Howard, John *33:* 179
Howard, Kim *116:* 71
Howard, Paul *142:* 126, 129; *144:* 187
Howard, Rob *40:* 161
Howarth, Daniel *170:* 34
Howe, John *79:* 101; *80:* 150; *115:* 47; *176:* 106; *207:* 32, 35
Howe, Phillip *79:* 117; *175:* 115
Howe, Stephen *1:* 232
Howell, Karen *119:* 123

Howell, Pat *15:* 139
Howell, Troy *23:* 24; *31:* 61; *36:* 158; *37:* 184; *41:* 76, 235; *48:* 112; *56:* 13; *57:* 3; *59:* 174; *63:* 5; *74:* 46; *89:* 188; *90:* 231; *95:* 97; *98:* 130; *99:* 189; *153:* 156, 157, 158; *176:* 104; *199:* 96, 98
Howes, Charles *22:* 17
Hoyt, Ard *145:* 141; *190:* 82; *207:* 148
Hranilovich, Barbara *127:* 51
Hu, Ying-Hwa *116:* 107; *152:* 236; *173:* 171
Huang, Benrei *137:* 55
Huang, Zhong-Yang *117:* 30, 32
Hubbard, Woodleigh Marx *98:* 67; *115:* 79; *160:* 138
Hubley, Faith *48:* 120, 121, 125, 130, 131, 132, 134
Hubley, John *48:* 125, 130, 131, 132, 134
Hudak, Michal *143:* 74
Hudnut, Robin *14:* 62
Huerta, Catherine *76:* 178; *77:* 44, 45; *90:* 182; *210:* 202
Huffaker, Sandy *10:* 56
Huffman, Joan *13:* 33
Huffman, Tom *13:* 180; *17:* 212; *21:* 116; *24:* 132; *33:* 154; *38:* 59; *42:* 147
Hughes, Arthur *20:* 148, 149, 150; *33:* 114, 148, 149
Hughes, Darren *95:* 44
Hughes, David *36:* 197
Hughes, Shirley *1:* 20, 21; *7:* 3; *12:* 217; *16:* 163; *29:* 154; *63:* 118; *70:* 102, 103, 104; *73:* 169; *88:* 70; *110:* 118, 119; *159:* 103
Hugo, Victor *47:* 112
Huliska-Beith, Laura *204:* 108
Hull, Cathy *78:* 29
Hull, Richard *95:* 120; *123:* 175; *172:* 195
Hulsmann, Eva *16:* 166
Hume, Lachie *189:* 93
Hummel, Berta *43:* 137, 138, 139
Hummel, Lisl *29:* 109; *YABC 2:* 333, 334
Humphrey, Henry *16:* 167
Humphreys, Graham *25:* 168
Humphries, Tudor *76:* 66; *80:* 4; *124:* 4, 5
Huneck, Stephen *183:* 88, 89
Hunt, James *2:* 143
Hunt, Jonathan *84:* 120
Hunt, Paul *119:* 104; *129:* 135; *139:* 160; *173:* 112
Hunt, Robert *110:* 206, 235; *147:* 136, 137; *170:* 3; *211:* 76
Hunt, Scott *190:* 143
Hunter, Anne *133:* 190; *178:* 150
Huntington, Amy *180:* 99
Hurd, Clement *2:* 148, 149; *64:* 127, 128, 129, 131, 133, 134,135, 136; *100:* 37, 38
Hurd, Peter *24:* 30, 31,; *YABC 2:* 56
Hurd, Thacher *46:* 88, 89; *94:* 114, 115, 116; *123:* 81, 82, 84
Hurlimann, Ruth *32:* 99
Hurst, Carol Otis *185:* 92
Hurst, Philip *196:* 79
Hurst, Tracey *192:* 238
Hussar, Michael *114:* 113; *117:* 159
Hustler, Tom *6:* 105
Hutchins, Laurence *55:* 22
Hutchins, Pat *15:* 142; *70:* 106, 107, 108; *178:* 131, 132
Hutchinson, Sascha *95:* 211
Hutchinson, William M. *6:* 3, 138; *46:* 70
Hutchison, Paula *23:* 10
Hutton, Clarke *YABC 2:* 335
Hutton, Kathryn *35:* 155; *89:* 91
Hutton, Warwick *20:* 91
Huyette, Marcia *29:* 188
Hyatt, John *54:* 7
Hyatt, Mitch *178:* 162
Hyde, Maureen *82:* 17; *121:* 145, 146
Hyman, David *117:* 64
Hyman, Miles *210:* 132

Hyman, Trina Schart *1:* 204; *2:* 194; *5:* 153; *6:* 106; *7:* 138, 145; *8:* 22; *10:* 196; *13:* 96; *14:* 114; *15:* 204; *16:* 234; *20:* 82; *22:* 133; *24:* 151; *25:* 79, 82; *26:* 82; *29:* 83; *31:* 37, 39; *34:* 104; *38:* 84, 100, 128; *41:* 49; *43:* 146; *46:* 91, 92, 93, 95, 96, 97, 98, 99, 100, 101, 102, 103, 104, 105,108, 109, 111, 197; *48:* 60, 61; *52:* 32; *60:* 168; *66:* 38; *67:* 214; *72:* 74; *75:* 92; *79:* 57; *82:* 95, 238; *89:* 46; *95:* 91, 92, 93; *100:* 33, 199; *132:* 12; *147:* 33, 35, 36; *167:* 58, 60; *177:* 189, 190; *211:* 188

I

Ibarra, Rosa *147:* 91
Ibatoulline, Bagram *156:* 48; *174:* 33, 82; *202:* 30; *211:* 213
Ichikawa, Satomi *29:* 152; *41:* 52; *47:* 133, 134,135, 136; *78:* 93, 94; *80:* 81; *146:* 143, 145, 146; *208:* 117, 118, 119
Ide, Jacqueline *YABC 1:* 39
Ilsley, Velma *3:* 1; *7:* 55; *12:* 109; *37:* 62; *38:* 184
Imai, Ayano *190:* 85, 86
in den Bosch, Nicole *150:* 204
Inga *1:* 142
Ingman, Bruce *134:* 50; *182:* 91, 92
Ingpen, Robert *109:* 103, 104; *132:* 138; *137:* 177; *166:* 103; *181:* 140
Ingraham, Erick *21:* 177; *84:* 256; *103:* 66
Inkpen, Mick *99:* 104, 105; *106:* 44
Innerst, Stacy *149:* 104
Innocenti, Roberto *21:* 123; *96:* 122; *159:* 111, 197; *199:* 176
Inoue, Yosuke *24:* 118
Iofin, Michael *97:* 157
Iosa, Ann *63:* 189
Ipcar, Dahlov *1:* 124, 125; *49:* 137, 138, 139, 140, 141, 142,143, 144, 145; *147:* 122, 124, 126
Irvin, Fred *13:* 166; *15:* 143, 144; *27:* 175
Irving, Jay *45:* 72
Irving, Laurence *27:* 50
Isaac, Joanne *21:* 76
Isaacs, Gary *170:* 188
Isadora, Rachel *43:* 159, 160; *54:* 31; *79:* 106, 107,108; *121:* 100, 102; *165:* 116, 117; *204:* 61, 63, 64
Ishmael, Woodi *24:* 111; *31:* 99
Ives, Ruth *15:* 257
Iwai, Melissa *149:* 233; *183:* 92; *199:* 115

J

Jabar, Cynthia *101:* 201; *210:* 134, 135
Jackness, Andrew *94:* 237
Jackson, Julian *91:* 104, 106
Jackson, Michael *43:* 42
Jackson, Shelley *79:* 71; *99:* 109; *187:* 82
Jacob, Murv *89:* 30
Jacobi, Kathy *62:* 118
Jacobs, Barbara *9:* 136
Jacobs, Lou, Jr. *9:* 136; *15:* 128
Jacobsen, Laura *176:* 98; *177:* 85, 86
Jacobson, Rick *222:* 170; *119*
Jacobus, Tim *79:* 140; *109:* 126; *129:* 180
Jacques, Robin *1:* 70; *2:* 1; *8:* 46; *9:* 20; *15:* 187; *19:* 253; *32:* 102, 103, 104; *43:* 184; *73:* 135; *YABC 1:* 42
Jaeggi, Yoshiko *186:* 184
Jaffee, Al *66:* 131, 132
Jagr, Miloslav *13:* 197
Jahn-Clough, Lisa *88:* 114; *152:* 104; *193:* 70, 71
Jahnke, Robert *84:* 24

Jainschigg, Nicholas *80:* 64; *91:* 138; *95:* 63; *99:* 25; *108:* 50; *171:* 41
Jakesavic, Nenad *85:* 102
Jakobsen, Kathy *116:* 83
Jakubowski, Charles *14:* 192
Jambor, Louis *YABC 1:* 11
James, Ann *73:* 50; *82:* 113; *158:* 61; *183:* 44
James, Brian *140:* 91
James, Curtis E. *182:* 93
James, Derek *35:* 187; *44:* 91; *61:* 133; *74:* 2; *80:* 57; *86:* 88; *130:* 30; *179:* 29
James, Gilbert *YABC 1:* 43
James, Gordon C. *195:* 89
James, Harold *2:* 151; *3:* 62; *8:* 79; *29:* 113; *51:* 195; *74:* 90
James, Kennon *126:* 211
James, Robin *50:* 106; *53:* 32, 34, 35
James, Simon *202:* 73, 74
James, Will *19:* 150, 152, 153, 155, 163
Janosch
    See Eckert, Horst
Janovitch, Marilyn *68:* 168
Janovitz, Marilyn *87:* 187; *130:* 198; *194:* 91
Jansons, Inese *48:* 117
Jansson, Tove *3:* 90; *41:* 106, 108, 109, 110, 111, 113, 114
Jaques, Faith *7:* 11, 132, 133; *21:* 83, 84; *69:* 114,116; *73:* 170
Jaques, Frances Lee *29:* 224
Jarrett, Clare *201:* 77
Jauss, Anne Marie *1:* 139; *3:* 34; *10:* 57, 119; *11:* 205; *23:* 194
Jay, Alison *158:* 97, 98; *183:* 126, 127; *196:* 95, 96, 97, 98; *200:* 72, 73, 74
Jeffers, Oliver *175:* 111
Jeffers, Susan *17:* 86, 87; *25:* 164, 165; *26:* 112; *50:* 132, 134, 135; *70:* 111, 112, 113; *137:* 107, 108, 109, 110, 111; *202:* 77, 78
Jefferson, Louise E. *4:* 160
Jenkin-Pearce, Susie *78:* 16
Jenkins, Debra Reid *85:* 202; *114:* 89; *173:* 134
Jenkins, Jean *98:* 79, 102
Jenkins, Leonard *157:* 169; *167:* 128; *189:* 96, 97; *190:* 89
Jenkins, Patrick *72:* 126
Jenkins, Steve *124:* 177; *154:* 90, 91, 92, 93; *185:* 194; *188:* 81, 82, 83, 84, 85, 86
Jenks, Aleta *73:* 117; *124:* 225
Jenkyns, Chris *51:* 97
Jensen, Bruce *95:* 39
Jensinius, Kirsten *56:* 58
Jeram, Anita *89:* 135; *102:* 122, 123; *129:* 112; *154:* 96, 97, 98; *164:* 154; *203:* 123, 124
Jernigan, E. Wesley *85:* 92
Jerome, Karen A. *72:* 194
Jeruchim, Simon *6:* 173; *15:* 250
Jeschke, Susan *20:* 89; *39:* 161; *41:* 84; *42:* 120
Jessel, Camilla *29:* 115
Jessell, Tim *159:* 3; *177:* 87; *181:* 95; *205:* 4
Jeyaveeran, Ruth *182:* 100
Jiang, Cheng An *109:* 108
Jiang, Wei *109:* 108
Jimenez, Maria *77:* 158; *93:* 127
Jobling, Curtis *138:* 74
Jocelyn, Marthe *118:* 83; *137:* 219; *163:* 119, 120; *198:* 62
Joerns, Consuelo *38:* 36; *44:* 94
John, Diana *12:* 209
John, Helen *1:* 215; *28:* 204
Johns, Elizabeth *127:* 33
Johns, Jasper *61:* 172
Johns, Jeanne *24:* 114
Johnson, Adrian *143:* 50
Johnson, Bruce *9:* 47
Johnson, Cathy *92:* 136
Johnson, Crockett
    See Leisk, David
Johnson, D. William *23:* 104

Johnson, D.B. *183:* 98, 139
Johnson, David *175:* 18; *191:* 91
Johnson, Gillian *119:* 175; *164:* 217
Johnson, Harper *1:* 27; *2:* 33; *18:* 302; *19:* 61; *31:* 181; *44:* 46, 50, 95
Johnson, Ingrid *37:* 118
Johnson, James Ralph *1:* 23, 127
Johnson, James David *12:* 195
Johnson, Jane *48:* 136
Johnson, Joel Peter *98:* 18; *128:* 111; *201:* 13
Johnson, John E. *34:* 133
Johnson, Kevin *72:* 44
Johnson, Kevin Eugene *109:* 215
Johnson, Larry *47:* 56; *123:* 107; *159:* 203
Johnson, Layne *187:* 94; *209:* 63
Johnson, Margaret S. *35:* 131
Johnson, Meredith Merrell *71:* 181; *83:* 158; *89:* 103; *104:* 88
Johnson, Milton *1:* 67; *2:* 71; *26:* 45; *31:* 107; *60:* 112; *68:* 96
Johnson, Pamela *16:* 174; *52:* 145; *62:* 140; *73:* 116; *85:* 64
Johnson, Paul Brett *83:* 95; *132:* 119
Johnson, Stephen T. *80:* 15; *131:* 35; *141:* 96; *145:* 40; *164:* 187; *175:* 32; *189:* 99, 100; *208:* 43
Johnson, Steve *138:* 219; *141:* 64; *144:* 199; *177:* 51
Johnson, William R. *38:* 91
Johnson-Petrov, Arden *115:* 206
Johnston, David McCall *50:* 131, 133
Johnston, Lynne *118:* 85, 87, 89
Johnstone, Anne *8:* 120; *36:* 89
Johnstone, Janet Grahame *8:* 120; *36:* 89
Jonas, Ann *50:* 107, 108, 109; *135:* 113
Jones, Bob *71:* 5; *77:* 199
Jones, Carol *5:* 131; *72:* 185, 186; *153:* 111, 112
Jones, Chuck *53:* 70, 71
Jones, Curtis *211:* 144
Jones, Davy *89:* 176
Jones, Douglas B. *185:* 192; *202:* 82
Jones, Elizabeth Orton *18:* 124, 126, 128, 129
Jones, Harold *14:* 88; *52:* 50
Jones, Holly *127:* 3
Jones, Jeff *41:* 64
Jones, Laurian *25:* 24, 27
Jones, Margaret *74:* 57
Jones, Noah Z. *182:* 37; *203:* 159
Jones, Randy *131:* 104
Jones, Richard *127:* 222
Jones, Robert *25:* 67
Jones, Wilfred *35:* 115; *YABC 1:* 163
Jordan, Charles *89:* 58
Jordan, Jess *158:* 136; *203:* 111
Jordan, Martin George *84:* 127
Jordan, Richard *84:* 36
Jorgenson, Andrea *91:* 111
Jorisch, Stéphane *153:* 56, 193; *177:* 29; *178:* 138, 139; *187:* 23; *211:* 182
Joseph, James *53:* 88
Joudrey, Ken *64:* 145; *78:* 6
Joyce, William *72:* 131, 132, 133, 134; *73:* 227; *145:* 37
Joyner, Jerry *34:* 138
Joyner, Loraine M. *209:* 17
Joysmith, Brenda *210:* 237
Juan, Ana *175:* 38; *179:* 111, 112
Jucker, Sita *5:* 93
Judge, Lita *192:* 99
Judkis, Jim *37:* 38
Juhasz, Victor *31:* 67
Jullian, Philippe *24:* 206; *25:* 203
Jung, Tom *91:* 217
Junge, Alexandra *183:* 37
Junge, Walter *67:* 150
Jupo, Frank *7:* 148, 149
Jurisch, Stephane *154:* 105
Justice, Martin *34:* 72

K

Kabatova-Taborska, Zdenka *107:* 153
Kachik, John *165:* 230
Kaczman, James *156:* 98
Kadair, Deborah Ousley *184:* 45, 89
Kahl, David *74:* 95; *97:* 35; *109:* 174; *110:* 213; *198:* 15
Kahl, M.P. *37:* 83
Kahl, Virginia *48:* 138
Kahn, Katherine Janus *90:* 135; *211:* 155
Kakimoo, Kozo *11:* 148
Kalett, Jim *48:* 159, 160, 161
Kalin, Victor *39:* 186
Kalis, Jennifer *207:* 82
Kalman, Maira *96:* 131, 132; *137:* 115
Kalmenoff, Matthew *22:* 191
Kalow, Gisela *32:* 105
Kamen, Gloria *1:* 41; *9:* 119; *10:* 178; *35:* 157; *78:* 236; *98:* 82
Kaminsky, Jef *102:* 153
Kandell, Alice *35:* 133
Kane, Henry B. *14:* 90; *18:* 219, 220
Kane, Robert *18:* 131
Kanfer, Larry *66:* 141
Kangas, Juli *200:* 88
Kappes, Alfred *28:* 104
Karalus, Bob *41:* 157
Karas, G. Brian *80:* 60; *99:* 179; *115:* 41; *118:* 50; *136:* 168; *145:* 166; *149:* 245; *159:* 65; *171:* 192; *178:* 142, 143; *202:* 38; *209:* 142
Karasz, Ilonka *128:* 163
Karlin, Eugene *10:* 63; *20:* 131
Karlin, Nurit *63:* 78; *103:* 110
Karpinski, Tony *134:* 160
Kasamatsu, Shiro *139:* 155
Kasparavicius, Kestutis *139:* 210
Kassian, Olena *64:* 94
Kastner, Jill *79:* 135; *117:* 84, 85
Kasuya, Masahiro *41:* 206, 207; *51:* 100
Kasza, Keiko *191:* 99, 100, 101, 102, 103
Katona, Robert *21:* 85; *24:* 126
Katz, Avi *199:* 55
Katz, Karen *158:* 123
Kauffer, E. McKnight *33:* 103; *35:* 127; *63:* 67
Kaufman, Angelika *15:* 156
Kaufman, Joe *33:* 119
Kaufman, John *13:* 158
Kaufman, Stuart *62:* 64; *68:* 226; *137:* 44
Kaufmann, John *1:* 174; *4:* 159; *8:* 43, 1; *10:* 102; *18:* 133, 134; *22:* 251
Kaye, Graham *1:* 9; *67:* 7, 8
Kaye, M.M. *62:* 95
Kazalovski, Nata *40:* 205
Keane, Bil *4:* 135
Kearney, David *72:* 47; *121:* 83
Keating, Pamel T. *77:* 37
Keats, Ezra Jack *3:* 18, 105, 257; *14:* 101, 102; *33:* 129; *57:* 79, 80, 82, 83, 84, 87
Keegan, Charles *166:* 211
Keegan, Marcia *9:* 122; *32:* 93
Keeler, Patricia A. *81:* 56; *183:* 102, 103
Keely, Jack *119:* 95
Keely, John *26:* 104; *48:* 214
Keen, Eliot *25:* 213
Keep, Richard C. *170:* 122
Keeping, Charles *9:* 124, 185; *15:* 28, 134; *18:* 115; *44:* 194, 196; *47:* 25; *52:* 3; *54:* 156; *69:* 123, 124; *74:* 56; *155:* 9
Keeter, Susan *168:* 46; *183:* 192
Keith, Eros *4:* 98; *5:* 138; *31:* 29; *43:* 220; *52:* 91, 92, 93, 94; *56:* 64, 66; *60:* 37; *79:* 93
Keleinikov, Andrei *65:* 101, 102
Kelen, Emery *13:* 115
Keller, A.J. *62:* 198
Keller, Arthur I. *26:* 106
Keller, Dick *36:* 123, 125
Keller, Holly *45:* 79; *76:* 118, 119, 120, 121; *108:* 137, 138, 140; *157:* 117, 118, 119
Keller, Katie *79:* 222; *93:* 108

Keller, Laurie *196:* 105, 106
Keller, Ronald *45:* 208
Kelley, Gary *183:* 105
Kelley, Marty *211:* 91
Kelley, True *41:* 114, 115; *42:* 137; *75:* 35; *92:* 104, 105; *124:* 62; *130:* 100, 101; *179:* 120, 121, 122; *192:* 251
Kellogg, Steven *8:* 96; *11:* 207; *14:* 130; *20:* ; *201:* 38 58; *29:* 140, 141; *30:* 35; *41:* 141; *57:* 89, 90, 92,93, 94, 96; *59:* 182; *73:* 141; *77:* 129; *130:* 105, 106; *177:* 94, 95, 96, 97; *199:* 57; *YABC 1:* 65, 73
Kelly, Billy *158:* 143
Kelly, Geoff *97:* 196; *112:* 25
Kelly, Irene *147:* 134; *210:* 144, 145
Kelly, John *194:* 186
Kelly, Joseph *174:* 94
Kelly, Kathleen M. *71:* 109
Kelly, Laura *89:* 217
Kelly, True *163:* 87
Kelly, Walt *18:* 136, 137, 138, 139, 140, 141, 144, 145, 146, 148, 149
Kemble, E.W. *34:* 75; *44:* 178; *YABC 2:* 54, 59
Kemly, Kathleen *209:* 165
Kemp-Welsh, Lucy *24:* 197; *100:* 214
Kendall, Jane *150:* 105; *186:* 109
Kendall, Peter *152:* 85
Kendrick, Dennis *79:* 213
Kennaway, Adrienne *60:* 55, 56; *171:* 88, 89
Kennedy, Doug *189:* 104
Kennedy, Paul Edward *6:* 190; *8:* 132; *33:* 120
Kennedy, Richard *3:* 93; *12:* 179; *44:* 193; *100:* 15; *YABC 1:* 57
Kent, Jack *24:* 136; *37:* 37; *40:* 81; *84:* 89; *86:* 150; *88:* 77
Kent, Rockwell *5:* 166; *6:* 129; *20:* 225, 226, 227,229; *59:* 144
Kenyon, Tony *81:* 201; *127:* 74
Kepes, Juliet *13:* 119
Kerins, Anthony *76:* 84
Kerr, Judity *24:* 137
Kerr, Phyllis Forbes *72:* 141
Kessler, Leonard *1:* 108; *7:* 139; *14:* 107, 227; *22:* 101; *44:* 96; *67:* 79; *82:* 123
Kest, Kristin *168:* 99; *173:* 23
Kesteven, Peter *35:* 189
Ketcham, Hank *28:* 140, 141, 142
Kettelkamp, Larry *2:* 164
Key, Alexander *8:* 99
Khalsa, Dayal Kaur *62:* 99
Kiakshuk *8:* 59
Kid, Tom *207:* 54
Kidd, Chip *94:* 23
Kidd, Richard *152:* 110
Kidd, Tom *64:* 199; *81:* 189; *185:* 173
Kiddell-Monroe, Joan *19:* 201; *55:* 59, 60; *87:* 174; *121:* 112
Kidder, Harvey *9:* 105; *80:* 41
Kidwell, Carl *43:* 145
Kieffer, Christa *41:* 89
Kiesler, Kate *110:* 105; *136:* 142
Kiff, Ken *40:* 45
Kilbride, Robert *37:* 100
Kilby, Don *141:* 144
Kim, David *201:* 79; *202:* 97
Kim, Glenn *99:* 82
Kimball, Anton *78:* 114; *119:* 105
Kimball, Yeffe *23:* 116; *37:* 88
Kimber, Murray *171:* 91
Kimmel, Warren *176:* 112
Kincade, Orin *34:* 116
Kindersley, Barnabas *96:* 110
Kindred, Wendy *7:* 151
King, Colin *53:* 3
King, Robin *10:* 164, 165
King, Stephen Michael *141:* 31; *197:* 191
King, Tara Calahan *139:* 172
King, Tony *39:* 121
Kingman, Dong *16:* 287; *44:* 100, 102, 104
Kingsley, Charles *YABC 2:* 182

Kingston, Julie *147:* 14
Kingston, Maxine Hong *53:* 92
Kinney, Jeff *187:* 97
Kipling, John Lockwood *YABC 2:* 198
Kipling, Rudyard *YABC 2:* 196
Kipniss, Robert *29:* 59
Kirchherr, Astrid *55:* 23
Kirchhoff, Art *28:* 136
Kirk, Daniel *153:* 115, 116, 117; *173:* 101; *196:* 113, 114, 115, 116
Kirk, David *117:* 88, 89; *161:* 97, 98
Kirk, Ruth *5:* 96
Kirk, Steve *170:* 37
Kirk, Tim *32:* 209, 211; *72:* 89; *83:* 49
Kirmse, Marguerite *15:* 283; *18:* 153
Kirsch, Vincent X. *124:* 207
Kirschner, Ruth *22:* 154
Kirwan, Wednesday *198:* 73
Kish, Ely *73:* 119; *79:* 2
Kitamura, Satoshi *62:* 102; *98:* 91; *101:* 147; *138:* 2; *143:* 83, 85, 86; *201:* 83
Kiss, Andrew *168:* 115
Kitchel, JoAnn E. *133:* 32
Kitchen, Bert *70:* 126; *193:* 49
Kittelsen, Theodor *62:* 14
Kiuchi, Tatsuro *114:* 71
Kiwak, Barbara *172:* 135
Klahr, Susan *176:* 196
Klapholz, Mel *13:* 35
Klee, Jutte *209:* 136
Klein, Bill *89:* 105
Klein, Robert *55:* 77
Klein, Suzanna *63:* 104
Kleinman, Zalman *28:* 143
Kleven, Elisa *173:* 96, 97
Kliban, B. *35:* 137, 138
Kline, Michael *127:* 66
Klise, M. Sarah *180:* 117, 118; *181:* 97
Knabel, Lonnie *73:* 103; *75:* 187, 228; *194:* 216
Kneen, Maggie *140:* 139
Knight, Ann *34:* 143
Knight, Christopher *13:* 125
Knight, Hilary *1:* 233; *3:* 21; *15:* 92, 158, 159; *16:* 258, 259, 260; *18:* 235; *19:* 169; *35:* 242; *46:* 167; *52:* 116; *69:* 126, 127; *132:* 129; *YABC 1:* 168, 169, 172
Knorr, Laura *200:* 91
Knorr, Peter *126:* 92, 93
Knotts, Howard *20:* 4; *25:* 170; *36:* 163
Knutson, Barbara *112:* 134; *202:* 108
Knutson, Kimberley *115:* 90
Kobayashi, Ann *39:* 58
Kochalka, James *196:* 120, 121, 122
Kocsis, J.C.
　　See Paul, James
Kodman, Stanislawa *201:* 85
Koehler, Hanne Lore *176:* 203
Koehn, Ilse *34:* 198; *79:* 123
Koelsch, Michael *99:* 182; *107:* 164; *109:* 239; *138:* 142; *150:* 94; *176:* 105; *187:* 63; *198:* 63
Koering, Ursula *3:* 28; *4:* 14; *44:* 5; *64:* 140,141; *85:* 46
Koerner, Henry
　　See Koerner, W.H.D.
Koerner, W.H.D. *14:* 216; *21:* 88, 89, 90, 91; *23:* 211
Koetsch, Mike *166:* 68
Koffler, Camilla *36:* 113
Kogan, Deborah Ray *161:* 101, 102
Koide, Yasuko *50:* 114
Kolado, Karen *102:* 228
Komoda, Kiyo *9:* 128; *13:* 214
Kompaneyets, Marc *169:* 92
Konashevich, Vladimir *61:* 160
Konashevicha, V. *YABC 1:* 26
Konigsburg, E.L. *4:* 138; *48:* 141, 142, 144, 145; *94:* 129, 130; *126:* 129, 130, 131; *194:* 95, 98
Kono, Erin Eitter *177:* 99

Kooiker, Leonie *48:* 148
Koonook, Simon *65:* 157
Koontz, Robin Michal *136:* 155
Koopmans, Loek *101:* 121
Kopelke, Lisa *154:* 107
Kopper, Lisa *72:* 152, 153; *105:* 135, 136
Korach, Mimi *1:* 128, 129; *2:* 52; *4:* 39; *5:* 159; *9:* 129; *10:* 21; *24:* 69
Koren, Edward *5:* 100; *65:* 65, 67
Kosaka, Fumi *164:* 130
Koscielniak, Bruce *99:* 122; *153:* 120, 121, 122
Koshkin, Alexander *92:* 180
Kossin, Sandy *10:* 71; *23:* 105
Kostin, Andrej *26:* 204
Kosturko, Bob *164:* 56
Kotzky, Brian *68:* 184
Kovacevic, Zivojin *13:* 247
Kovalski, Maryann *58:* 120; *84:* 88; *97:* 124, 125, 126; *158:* 3; *186:* 80
Kozjan, Drazen *209:* 99
Krahn, Fernando *2:* 257; *34:* 206; *49:* 152
Kramer, Anthony *33:* 81
Kramer, David *96:* 162; *109:* 132; *150:* 220
Kramer, Frank *6:* 121
Krantz, Kathy *35:* 83
Kratter, Paul *139:* 65
Kraus, Robert *13:* 217; *65:* 113; *93:* 93, 94
Krause, Jon *176:* 62
Krauss, Trisha *174:* 10
Kredel, Fritz *6:* 35; *17:* 93, 94, 95, 96; *22:* 147; *24:* 175; *29:* 130; *35:* 77; *YABC 2:* 166, 300
Kreloff, Eliot *189:* 107, 108; *205:* 182
Krementz, Jill *17:* 98; *49:* 41
Krenina, Katya *117:* 106; *125:* 133; *176:* 117
Kresin, Robert *23:* 19
Krieger, Salem *54:* 164
Kriegler, Lyn *73:* 29
Krinitz, Esther Nisenthal *193:* 196
Krommes, Beth *128:* 141; *149:* 136; *181:* 100, 101; *184:* 105; *188:* 125; *208:* 135; *209:* 185
Krone, Mike *101:* 71
Kronheimer, Ann *135:* 119
Krosoczka, Jarrett J. *155:* 142; *200:* 93, 94
Kruck, Gerald *88:* 181
Krudop, Walter Lyon *199:* 19
Krupinski, Loretta *67:* 104; *102:* 131; *161:* 105, 106
Krupp, Robin Rector *53:* 96, 98
Krush, Beth *1:* 51, 85; *2:* 233; *4:* 115; *9:* 61; *10:* 191; *11:* 196; *18:* 164, 165; *32:* 72; *37:* 203; *43:* 57; *60:* 102, 103, 107, 108, 109
Krush, Joe *2:* 233; *4:* 115; *9:* 61; *10:* 191; *11:* 196; *18:* 164, 165; *32:* 72, 91; *37:* 203; *43:* 57; *60:* 102, 103, 107, 108, 109
Krych, Duane *91:* 43
Krykorka, Vladyana *96:* 147; *143:* 90, 91; *168:* 14
Kubick, Dana *165:* 91
Kubinyi, Laszlo *4:* 116; *6:* 113; *16:* 118; *17:* 100; *28:* 227; *30:* 172; *49:* 24, 28; *54:* 23; *167:* 149
Kubricht, Mary *73:* 118
Kucharik, Elena *139:* 31
Kuchera, Kathleen *84:* 5
Kuhn, Bob *17:* 91; *35:* 235
Kulikov, Boris *163:* 185; *185:* 23; *205:* 99, 100
Kulka, Joe *188:* 110
Kukalis, Romas *90:* 27; *139:* 37
Kuklin, Susan *63:* 82, 83, 84
Kunhardt, Dorothy *53:* 101
Kunhardt, Edith *67:* 105, 106
Kunstler, Mort *10:* 73; *32:* 143
Kurchevsky, V. *34:* 61
Kurczok, Belinda *121:* 118
Kurelek, William *8:* 107
Kuriloff, Ron *13:* 19
Kurisu, Jane *160:* 120
Kuskin, Karla *2:* 170; *68:* 115, 116; *111:* 116

Kutzer, Ernst *19:* 249
Kuzma, Steve *57:* 8; *62:* 93
Kuznetsova, Berta *74:* 45
Kvasnosky, Laura McGee *93:* 103; *142:* 83; *182:* 108
Kwas, Susan Estelle *179:* 116
Kyong, Yunmee *165:* 139

L

LaBlanc, Andre *24:* 146
Laboccetta, Mario *27:* 120
LaBrose, Darcie *157:* 134
Labrosse, Darcia *58:* 88; *108:* 77; *178:* 89
LaCava, Vince *95:* 118
Laceky, Adam *32:* 121
Lacis, Astra *85:* 117
Lacome, Julie *174:* 96, 97
La Croix *YABC 2:* 4
Ladd, London *206:* 50
Ladwig, Tim *98:* 212; *117:* 76
La Farge, Margaret *47:* 141
LaFave, Kim *64:* 177; *72:* 39; *97:* 146; *99:* 172; *106:* 123; *149:* 126; *196:* 128, 129
Lafontaine, Roger *167:* 158
Lafrance, Marie *197:* 109
Lagarrigue, Jerome *136:* 102; *187:* 81
Laimgruber, Monika *11:* 153
Laite, Gordon *1:* 130, 131; *8:* 209; *31:* 113; *40:* 63; *46:* 117
Laliberté, Louise-Andrée *169:* 98
LaMarche, Jim *46:* 204; *61:* 56; *94:* 69; *114:* 22; *129:* 163; *162:* 78, 80
Lamb, Jim *10:* 117
Lambase, Barbara *101:* 185; *150:* 221; *166:* 234
Lambert, J.K. *38:* 129; *39:* 24
Lambert, Sally Anne *133:* 191
Lambert, Saul *23:* 112; *33:* 107; *54:* 136
Lambert, Stephen *109:* 33; *174:* 99
Lambo, Don *6:* 156; *35:* 115; *36:* 146
Lamontagne, Jacques *166:* 227
Lamut, Sonja *57:* 193
Lamut, Sonya *85:* 102
Landa, Peter *11:* 95; *13:* 177; *53:* 119
Landau, Jacob *38:* 111
Landis, Joan *104:* 23; *203:* 32
Landon, Lucinda *79:* 31
Landshoff, Ursula *13:* 124
Landström, Lena *146:* 165, 166
Landström, Olof *146:* 166, 168; *170:* 22
Lane, Daniel *112:* 60
Lane, John R. *8:* 145
Lane, John *15:* 176, 177; *30:* 146
Lane, Nancy *166:* 74
Lang, G.D. *48:* 56
Lang, Gary *73:* 75
Lang, Jerry *18:* 295
Langdo, Bryan *186:* 187; *191:* 113, 114, 115
Lange, Dorothea *50:* 141
Langley, Jonathan *162:* 128
Langner, Nola *8:* 110; *42:* 36
Lanino, Deborah *105:* 148
Lantz, Paul *1:* 82, 102; *27:* 88; *34:* 102; *45:* 123
Larkin, Bob *84:* 225
Laroche, Giles *126:* 140; *146:* 81
LaRochelle, David *171:* 97
Larrecq, John *44:* 108; *68:* 56
Larsen, Suzanne *1:* 13
Larson, Gary *57:* 121, 122, 123, 124, 125, 126, 127
Larsson, Carl *35:* 144, 145, 146, 147, 148, 149, 150, 152, 153, 154
Larsson, Karl *19:* 177
Lartitegui, Ana G. *105:* 167
LaRue, Jenna *167:* 20
La Rue, Michael D. *13:* 215

Lasker, Joe *7:* 186, 187; *14:* 55; *38:* 115; *39:* 47; *83:* 113, 114, 115
Latham, Barbara *16:* 188, 189; *43:* 71
Lathrop, Dorothy *14:* 117, 118, 119; *15:* 109; *16:* 78, 79, 81; *32:* 201, 203; *33:* 112; *YABC 2:* 301
Lattimore, Eleanor Frances *7:* 156
Lauden, Claire *16:* 173
Lauden, George, Jr. *16:* 173
Laune, Paul *2:* 235; *34:* 31
Laure, Jason *49:* 53; *50:* 122
Lauter, Richard *63:* 29; *67:* 111; *77:* 198
Lavallee, Barbara *74:* 157; *92:* 154; *96:* 126; *145:* 193; *166:* 125, 126; *186:* 155; *192:* 172
Lave, Fitz Hugh *59:* 139
Lavis, Stephen *43:* 143; *87:* 137, 164, 165
Layton, Neal *152:* 120, 121; *182:* 65; *187:* 103, 105, 106
Law, Jenny *201:* 31
Lawrason, June *168:* 30
Lawrence, John *25:* 131; *30:* 141; *44:* 198, 200
Lawrence, Stephen *20:* 195
Lawson, Carol *6:* 38; *42:* 93, 131; *174:* 56; *189:* 89; *209:* 59
Lawson, George *17:* 280
Lawson, Robert *5:* 26; *6:* 94; *13:* 39; *16:* 11; *20:* 100, 102, 103; *54:* 3; *66:* 12; *100:* 144, 145; *YABC 2:* 222, 224, 225, 227, 228, 229, 230, 231, 232, 233, 234, 235, 237, 238, 239, 240, 241
Layfield, Kathie *60:* 194
Lazare, Jerry *44:* 109; *74:* 28
Lazarevich, Mila *17:* 118
Lazarus, Claire *103:* 30
Lazarus, Keo Felker *21:* 94
Lazzaro, Victor *11:* 126
Lea, Bob *166:* 208; *203:* 108
Lea, Tom *43:* 72, 74
Leacroft, Richard *6:* 140
Leaf, Munro *20:* 99
Leake, Donald *70:* 41
Leander, Patricia *23:* 27
Lear, Edward *18:* 183, 184, 185
Lear, Rebecca *149:* 46
Lebenson, Richard *6:* 209; *7:* 76; *23:* 145; *44:* 191; *87:* 153
Le Cain, Errol *6:* 141; *9:* 3; *22:* 142; *25:* 198; *28:* 173; *68:* 128, 129; *86:* 49
Lechon, Daniel *113:* 211
Leder, Dora *129:* 172
Ledger, Bill *181:* 58
Leduc, Bernard *102:* 36
Lee, Alan *62:* 25, 28
Lee, Bryce *99:* 60; *101:* 195; *196:* 53
Lee, Chinlun *181:* 138; *182:* 112
Lee, Declan *191:* 20
Lee, Dom *83:* 118, 120; *93:* 123; *121:* 121, 126; *146:* 174, 175, 206, 207; *174:* 204
Lee, Doris *13:* 246; *32:* 183; *44:* 111
Lee, Hector Viveros *115:* 96
Lee, Ho Baek *200:* 160
Lee, Jeanne M. *158:* 56
Lee, Jared *93:* 200; *157:* 229
Lee, Jody *81:* 121; *82:* 225; *91:* 155; *100:* 182
Lee, Jody A. *127:* 124, 126, 127
  See also Lee, Jody
Lee, Manning de V. *2:* 200; *17:* 12; *27:* 87; *37:* 102, 103, 104; *YABC 2:* 304
Lee, Marie G. *138:* 157
Lee, Paul *97:* 100; *105:* 72, 209; *109:* 177; *128:* 113; *202:* 45
Lee, Robert J. *3:* 97; *67:* 124
Lee, Victor *96:* 228; *105:* 182; *140:* 196; *208:* 191
Lee, Virginia *208:* 139, 140
Leech, Dorothy *98:* 76
Leech, John *15:* 59
Leedy, Loreen *84:* 142; *128:* 144, 145, 146; *175:* 125, 126, 127
Leeman, Michael *44:* 157

Leeming, Catherine *87:* 39
Lees, Harry *6:* 112
LeFever, Bill *88:* 220, 221
Legenisel *47:* 111
Legrand, Edy *18:* 89, 93
Lehman, Barbara *73:* 123; *170:* 130
Lehrman, Rosalie *2:* 180
Leichman, Seymour *5:* 107
Leick, Bonnie *205:* 104
Leighton, Clare *25:* 130; *33:* 168; *37:* 105, 106, 108,109
Leisk, David *1:* 140, 141; *11:* 54; *30:* 137, 142, 143,144
Leister, Brian *89:* 45; *106:* 37; *114:* 67; *149:* 236
Leloir, Maurice *18:* 77, 80, 83, 99
Lemaître, Pascal *144:* 175; *176:* 130; *189:* 135
Lemieux, Michele *100:* 148; *139:* 153
Lemke, Horst *14:* 98; *38:* 117, 118, 119
Lemke, R.W. *42:* 162
Lemon, David Gwynne *9:* 1
LeMoult, Adolph *82:* 116
Lenn, Michael *136:* 89
Lennon, John *114:* 100
Lennox, Elsie *95:* 163; *143:* 160
Lenski, Lois *1:* 144; *26:* 135, 137, 139, 141; *100:* 153, 154
Lent, Blair *1:* 116, 117; *2:* 174; *3:* 206, 207; *7:* 168, 169; *34:* 62; *68:* 217; *133:* 101; *183:* 60
Leonard, Richard *91:* 128
Leonard, Tom *207:* 95
Leone, Leonard *49:* 190
Lerner, Carol *86:* 140, 141, 142
Lerner, Judith *116:* 138
Lerner, Sharon *11:* 157; *22:* 56
Leroux-Hugon, Helene *132:* 139
Leslie, Cecil *19:* 244
Lessac, Frané *80:* 182, 207; *96:* 182; *202:* 58; *209:* 104
Lessing, Erich *167:* 52; *173:* 60
Lester, Alison *50:* 124; *90:* 147, 148; *129:* 130
Lester, Mike *208:* 50
Lethcoe, Jason *191:* 116, 117
Le Tord, Bijou *49:* 156; *95:* 112
Leutz, Emanuel *165:* 27
Levai, Blaise *39:* 130
Levert, Mireille *211:* 101
Levin, Ted *12:* 148
Levine, David *43:* 147, 149, 150, 151, 152; *64:* 11
Levine, Joe *71:* 88
Levine, Marge *81:* 127
Levinson, David *178:* 232
Levit, Herschel *24:* 223
Levstek, Ljuba *131:* 192; *134:* 216; *149:* 65; *168:* 180
Levy, Jessica Ann *19:* 225; *39:* 191
Levy, Lina *117:* 126
Lewin, Betsy *32:* 114; *48:* 177; *90:* 151; *91:* 125; *92:* 85; *115:* 105; *169:* 110, 111; *178:* 47; *186:* 188; *194:* 201
Lewin, Ted *4:* 77; *8:* 168; *20:* 110; *21:* 99,100; *27:* 110; *28:* 96, 97; *31:* 49; *45:* 55; *48:* 223; *60:* 20, 119, 120; *62:* 139; *66:* 108; *71:* 12; *72:* 21; *74:* 226; *76:* 139, 140; *77:* 82; *79:* 87; *85:* 49, 177; *86:* 55; *88:* 182; *93:* 28, 29; *94:* 34, 182, 194; *99:* 156; *104:* 8; *115:* 123; *118:* 74; *119:* 114, 116; *131:* 54; *145:* 99; *165:* 151; *177:* 75; *178:* 42; *190:* 30; *192:* 86; *195:* 101, 102; *203:* 52
Lewis, Allen *15:* 112
Lewis, E.B. *88:* 143; *93:* 109; *119:* 79; *124:* 113; *128:* 49; *151:* 167; *168:* 110; *173:* 121; *174:* 66; *176:* 7; *184:* 150; *185:* 191; *211:* 108, 109, 110, 111
Lewis, H.B. *170:* 124
Lewis, J. Patrick *162:* 83
Lewis, Jan *81:* 22
Lewis, Kim *136:* 165
Lewis, Richard W. *52:* 25

Lewis, Robin Baird *98:* 193
Leydon, Rita Floden *21:* 101
Li, Xiojun *187:* 172
Liao, Jimmy *202:* 100
Lichtenheld, Tom *152:* 125, 126
Lieblich, Irene *22:* 173; *27:* 209, 214
Lieder, Rick *108:* 197; *199:* 58, 59, 60
Lies, Brian *92:* 40; *141:* 101; *150:* 138; *190:* 97, 98, 99,
Liese, Charles *4:* 222
Life, Kay *79:* 49
Lifton, Robert Jay *66:* 154
Lightburn, Ron *86:* 153; *91:* 122
Lightfoot, Norman R. *45:* 47
Lignell, Lois *37:* 114
Lill, Debra *121:* 70
Lilly, Charles *8:* 73; *20:* 127; *48:* 53; *72:* 9,16; *77:* 98; *102:* 94
Lilly, Ken *37:* 224
Lim, John *43:* 153
Limona, Mercedes *51:* 183
Lin, Grace *143:* 217; *162:* 86, 87; *174:* 185
Lincoln, Patricia Henderson *27:* 27; *78:* 127
Lindahn, Ron *84:* 17
Lindahn, Val *84:* 17
Lindberg, Howard *10:* 123; *16:* 190
Lindberg, Jeffrey *64:* 77; *77:* 71; *79:* 54; *80:* 149; *174:* 109; *179:* 52
Linden, Seymour *18:* 200, 201; *43:* 140
Lindenbaum, Pija *144:* 143; *183:* 113
Linder, Richard *27:* 119
Lindman, Maj *43:* 154
Lindsay, Norman *67:* 114
Lindsay, Vachel *40:* 118
Lindstrom, Jack *145:* 118
Line, Les *27:* 143
Linell
　See Smith, Linell
Lionni, Leo *8:* 115; *72:* 159, 160, 161
Lipinsky, Lino *2:* 156; *22:* 175
Lippincott, Gary A. *70:* 35; *119:* 118
Lippman, Peter *8:* 31; *31:* 119, 120, 160
Lisi, Victoria *89:* 145
Lisker, Emily *169:* 114
Lisker, Sonia O. *16:* 274; *31:* 31; *44:* 113, 114
Lisowski, Gabriel *47:* 144; *49:* 157
Lissim, Simon *17:* 138
Little, Ed *89:* 145; *151:* 53
Little, Harold *16:* 72
Little, Mary E. *28:* 146
Littlewood, Karen *165:* 126; *211:* 112
Litty, Julie *111:* 63
Litzinger, Rosanne *151:* 101; *176:* 118; *196:* 133, 134, 135; *208:* 129; *209:* 147
Liu, Lesley *143:* 72
Lively, Lorna *19:* 216
Livingston, Susan *95:* 22
Liwska, Renata *164:* 113; *199:* 25, 69
Ljungkvist, Laura *180:* 120
Llerena, Carlos Antonio *19:* 181
Lloyd, Errol *11:* 39; *22:* 178
Lloyd, Megan *77:* 118; *80:* 113; *97:* 75; *117:* 94, 95; *189:* 121, 122; *208:* 128; *211:* 72
Lloyd, Sam *183:* 116, 117
Lo, Beth *165:* 154
Lo, Koon-chiu *7:* 134
Loates, Glen *63:* 76
Lobel, Anita *6:* 87; *9:* 141; *18:* 248; *55:* 85,86, 87, 88, 93, 104; *60:* 67; *78:* 263; *82:* 110; *96:* 157, 159; *101:* 84; *132:* 35; *162:* 93, 94
Lobel, Arnold *1:* 188, 189; *5:* 12; *6:* 147; *7:* 167, 209; *18:* 190, 191; *25:* 39, 43; *27:* 40; *29:* 174; *52:* 127; *55:* 89, 91, 94, 95, 97, 98, 99, 100, 101, 102,103, 105, 106; *60:* 18, 31; *66:* 181, 183; *75:* 57; *82:* 246; *136:* 146
Lobel, Gillian *190:* 21
Locker, Thomas *109:* 134
Lodge, Bernard *107:* 125, 126; *153:* 93
Loeb, Jeph *153:* 177
Lodge, Jo *112:* 119
Loefgren, Ulf *3:* 108

Loescher, Ann *20:* 108
Loescher, Gil *20:* 108
Loew, David *93:* 184; *171:* 120; *211:* 187
Lofting, Hugh *15:* 182, 183; *100:* 161, 162
Lofts, Pamela *60:* 188
Loh, George *38:* 88
Lomberg, Jon *58:* 160
Lonette, Reisie *11:* 211; *12:* 168; *13:* 56; *36:* 122; *43:* 155
Long, Ethan *168:* 146; *178:* 12; *182:* 120, 121; *196:* 124
Long, Laurel *162:* 135; *190:* 11; *203:* 113, 114
Long, Loren *99:* 176; *172:* 65; *182:* 78; *188:* 114, 115
Long, Melinda *152:* 128
Long, Miles *115:* 174
Long, Sally *42:* 184
Long, Sylvia *74:* 168; *132:* 63; *179:* 134
Longoni, Eduardo *73:* 85
Longtemps, Ken *17:* 123; *29:* 221; *69:* 82
Looser, Heinz *YABC 2:* 208
Lopez, Loretta *190:* 100
López, Rafael *197:* 160; *198:* 85
Lopshire, Robert *6:* 149; *21:* 117; *34:* 166; *73:* 13
Lord, John Vernon *21:* 104; *23:* 25; *51:* 22
Lorenz, Albert *40:* 146; *115:* 127
Loretta, Sister Mary *33:* 73
Lorraine, Walter H. *3:* 110; *4:* 123; *16:* 192; *103:* 119
Los, Marek *146:* 22; *193:* 23
Loss, Joan *11:* 163
Louderback, Walt *YABC 1:* 164
Lousada, Sandra *40:* 138
Louth, Jack *149:* 252; *151:* 191, 192
Love, Judy *173:* 43; *196:* 40
Low, Joseph *14:* 124, 125; *18:* 68; *19:* 194; *31:* 166; *80:* 239
Low, William *62:* 175; *80:* 147; *112:* 194; *150:* 202; *169:* 175; *177:* 110; *192:* 27
Lowe, Vicky *177:* 130
Lowenheim, Alfred *13:* 65, 66
Lowenstein, Sallie *116:* 90, 91
Lowitz, Anson *17:* 124; *18:* 215
Lowrey, Jo *8:* 133
Lubach, Vanessa *142:* 152
Lubell, Winifred *1:* 207; *3:* 15; *6:* 151
Lubin, Leonard B. *19:* 224; *36:* 79, 80; *45:* 128, 129,131, 132, 133, 134, 135, 136, 137, 139, 140, 141; *70:* 95; *YABC2:* 96
Lucas, David *208:* 148
Lucht, Irmgard *82:* 145
Ludwig, Helen *33:* 144, 145
Lufkin, Raymond *38:* 138; *44:* 48
Luhrs, Henry *7:* 123; *11:* 120
Lujan, Tonita *82:* 33
Lupo, Dom *4:* 204
Lustig, Loretta *30:* 186; *46:* 134, 135, 136, 137
Lutes, Jason *210:* 163
Luthardt, Kevin *172:* 125, 126
Luxbacher, Irene *153:* 145
Luzak, Dennis *52:* 121; *99:* 142
Lydbury, Jane *82:* 98
Lydecker, Laura *21:* 113; *42:* 53
Lynch, Charles *16:* 33
Lynch, Marietta *29:* 137; *30:* 171
Lynch, P.J. *126:* 228; *129:* 110; *132:* 247; *183:* 64; *207:* 184
Lyne, Alison Davis *188:* 118, 198
Lyon, Carol *102:* 26
Lyon, Elinor *6:* 154
Lyon, Fred *14:* 16
Lyon, Tammie *175:* 170
Lyons, Oren *8:* 193
Lyster, Michael *26:* 41

M

Maas, Dorothy *6:* 175
Maas, Julie *47:* 61
Macaulay, David *46:* 139, 140, 141, 142, 143, 144, 145, 147, 149, 150; *72:* 167, 168, 169; *137:* 129, 130, 131, 132
MacCarthy, Patricia *69:* 141
Macdonald, Alister *21:* 55
Macdonald, Roberta *19:* 237; *52:* 164
MacDonald, Norman *13:* 99
MacDonald, Ross *201:* 103
MacDonald, Suse *54:* 41; *109* 138; *130:* 156; *193:* 106, 107, 109, 110
Mace, Varian *49:* 159
MacEachern, Stephen *206:* 2
Macguire, Robert Reid *18:* 67
Machetanz, Fredrick *34:* 147, 148
MacInnes, Ian *35:* 59
MacIntyre, Elisabeth *17:* 127, 128
Mack, Jeff *161:* 128; *194:* 119, 120
Mack, Stan *17:* 129; *96:* 33
Mackay, Donald *17:* 60
MacKaye, Arvia *32:* 119
Mackenzie, Robert *204:* 78
Mackenzie, Stuart *73:* 213
MacKenzie, Garry *33:* 159
Mackie, Clare *87:* 134
Mackinlay, Miguel *27:* 22
MacKinstry, Elizabeth *15:* 110; *42:* 139, 140, 141, 142, 143,144, 145
MacLeod, Lee *91:* 167
Maclise, Daniel *YABC 2:* 257
Macnaughton, Tina *182:* 145
MacRae, Tom *181:* 112
Madden, Don *3:* 112, 113; *4:* 33, 108, 155; *7:* 193; *78:* 12; *YABC 2:* 211
Maddison, Angela Mary *10:* 83
Madsen, Jim *146:* 259; *152:* 237; *184:* 106; *197:* 21; *202:* 103, 104
Maestro, Giulio *8:* 124; *12:* 17; *13:* 108; *25:* 182; *54:* 147; *59:* 114, 115, 116, 117, 118, 121, 123, 124, 125,126, 127; *68:* 37, 38; *106:* 129, 130, 131, 136, 137, 138
Maffia, Daniel *60:* 200
Maggio, Viqui *58:* 136, 181; *74:* 150; *75:* 90; *85:* 159; *90:* 158; *109:* 184; *193:* 113
Magnus, Erica *77:* 123
Magnuson, Diana *28:* 102; *34:* 190; *41:* 175
Magoon, Scott *181:* 104
Magovern, Peg *103:* 123
Maguire, Sheila *41:* 100
Magurn, Susan *91:* 30
Mahony, Will *37:* 120
Mahony, Will *85:* 116
Mahood, Kenneth *24:* 141
Mahurin, Matt *164:* 225; *175:* 95; *189:* 37; *196:* 14; *209:* 163
Maik, Henri *9:* 102
Maione, Heather *106:* 5; *178:* 8; *189:* 126, 127; *193:* 58
Maisto, Carol *29:* 87
Maitland, Antony *1:* 100, 176; *8:* 41; *17:* 246; *24:* 46; *25:* 177, 178; *32:* 74; *60:* 65, 195; *67:* 156; *87:* 131; *101:* 110
Majewski, Dawn W. *169:* 92
Mak, Kam *72:* 25; *75:* 43; *87:* 186; *97:* 24; *102:* 154; *149:* 195; *186:* 28; *209:* 132
Makie, Pam *37:* 117
Maktima, Joe *116:* 191
Maland, Nick *99:* 77
Male, Alan *132:* 64
Malone, James Hiram *84:* 161
Malone, Nola Langner *82:* 239
Malone, Peter *191:* 121, 122, 123
Malsberg, Edward *51:* 175
Malvern, Corinne *2:* 13; *34:* 148, 149
Manchess, Gregory *165:* 241; *203:* 119
Mancusi, Stephen *63:* 198, 199
Mandelbaum, Ira *31:* 115

Manders, John *138:* 152, 155; *188:* 171; *190:* 92; *199:* 5
Manet, Edouard *23:* 170
Mangiat, Jeff *173:* 127
Mangurian, David *14:* 133
Manham, Allan *42:* 109; *77:* 180; *80:* 227
Manley, Matt *103:* 167; *117:* 98; *172:* 49
Manna, Giovanni *178:* 44
Manniche, Lise *31:* 121
Manning, Jane *96:* 203
Manning, Jo *63:* 154
Manning, Lawrence *191:* 153
Manning, Maurie J. *211:* 116
Manning, Mick *176:* 139
Manning, Samuel F. *5:* 75
Mantel, Richard *57:* 73; *63:* 106; *82:* 255
Mantha, John *205:* 164
Maraja *15:* 86; *YABC 1:* 28; *2:* 115
Marcellino, Fred *20:* 125; *34:* 222; *53:* 125; *58:* 205; *61:* 64, 121, 122; *68:* 154, 156, 157, 158, 159; *72:* 25; *86:* 184; *98:* 181; *118:* 129, 130, 131; *149:* 218; *194:* 7
Marchesi, Stephen *34:* 140; *46:* 72; *50:* 147; *66:* 239; *70:* 33; *73:* 18, 114, 163; *77:* 47, 76,147; *78:* 79; *80:* 30; *81:* 6; *89:* 66; *93:* 21,130; *94:* 94; *97:* 66; *98:* 96; *114:* 115, 116
Marchiori, Carlos *14:* 60
Marciano, John Bemelmans *118:* 133; *167:* 110, 111, 112
Marcus, Barry David *139:* 248; *145:* 18
Maren, Julie *199:* 73
Margules, Gabriele *21:* 120
Mariana
  See Foster, Marian Curtis
Mariano, Michael *52:* 108
Marino, Dorothy *6:* 37; *14:* 135
Mario, Heide Stetson *101:* 202
Maris, Ron *71:* 123
Maritz, Nicolaas *85:* 123
Mark, Mona *65:* 105; *68:* 205; *116:* 213
Markham, R.L. *17:* 240
Marklew, Gilly *211:* 118
Marks, Alan *104:* 104; *109:* 182; *164:* 92; *185:* 134; *187:* 120, 121, 122
Marks, Cara *54:* 9
Marks, Colin *203:* 129
Marokvia, Artur *31:* 122
Marquez, Susan *108:* 121
Marrella, Maria Pia *62:* 116
Marriott, Pat *30:* 30; *34:* 39; *35:* 164, 165, 166; *44:* 170; *48:* 186, 187, 188, 189, 191, 192, 193; *91:* 92
Mars, W.T. *1:* 161; *3:* 115; *4:* 208, 225; *5:* 92, 105, 186; *8:* 214; *9:* 12; *13:* 121; *27:* 151; *31:* 180; *38:* 102; *48:* 66; *62:* 164, 165; *64:* 62; *68:* 229; *79:* 55
Marschall, Ken *85:* 29
Marsh, Christine *3:* 164
Marsh, James *73:* 137
Marsh, Reginald *17:* 5; *19:* 89; *22:* 90, 96
Marshall, Anthony D. *18:* 216
Marshall, Felicia *170:* 190
Marshall, James *6:* 160; *40:* 221; *42:* 24, 25, 29; *51:* 111, 112, 113, 114, 115, 116, 117, 118, 119, 120, 121; *64:* 13; *75:* 126, 127, 128, 129; *102:* 10, 12
Marshall, Janet *97:* 154
Marstall, Bob *55:* 145; *84:* 153, 170; *104:* 145; *154:* 166, 167, 168
Martchenko, Michael *50:* 129, 153, 155, 156, 157; *83:* 144,145; *154:* 137, 138, 139
Marten, Ruth *129:* 52
Martin, Brad *199:* 186
Martin, Charles E. *70:* 144
Martin, David Stone *24:* 232; *62:* 4
Martin, Fletcher *18:* 213; *23:* 151
Martin, Rene *7:* 144; *42:* 148, 149, 150
Martin, Richard E. *51:* 157; *131:* 203
Martin, Ron *32:* 81
Martin, Stefan *8:* 68; *32:* 124, 126; *56:* 33

Martin, Whitney *166:* 137
Martinez, Ed *58:* 192; *72:* 231; *77:* 33; *80:* 214; *167:* 123
Martinez, John *6:* 113; *118:* 13; *139:* 143
Martinez, Sergio *158:* 190
Martini, Angela *183:* 161
Martiniere, Stephan *171:* 130
Marton, Jirina *95:* 127, 128; *144:* 145
Martorell, Antonio *84:* 6; *97:* 161
Martucci, Griesbach *52:* 106
Marvin, Frederic *83:* 86
Marx, Robert F. *24:* 143
Marzollo, Jean *190:* 127
Masefield, Judith *19:* 208, 209
Masheris, Robert *78:* 51
Masiello, Ralph *186:* 171
Mason, George F. *14:* 139
Mason, Robert *84:* 96
Masse, Josée *208:* 45
Massey, Barbara *68:* 142
Massie, Diane Redfield *16:* 194
Massie, Kim *31:* 43
Mataya, David *121:* 66
Mathers, Petra *119:* 135; *163:* 104; *176:* 143, 144; *187:* 142; *196:* 101
Mathewuse, James *51:* 143
Mathieu, Joseph *14:* 33; *39:* 206; *43:* 167; *56:* 180; *79:* 126; *94:* 147; *185:* 140
Matje, Martin *169:* 177, 178; *172:* 180
Matsubara, Naoko *12:* 121
Matsuda, Shizu *13:* 167
Matsuoka, Mei *192:* 135
Matte, L'Enc *22:* 183
Mattelson, Marvin *36:* 50, 51
Mattheson, Jenny *180:* 132
Matthews, Elizabeth *194:* 128
Matthews, F. Leslie *4:* 216
Matthews, Tina *190:* 130
Mattingly, David *71:* 76, 77; *82:* 64; *91:* 216, 217; *109:* 25
Matulay, Laszlo *5:* 18; *43:* 168
Matus, Greta *12:* 142
Maughan, Bill *181:* 31; *211:* 211
Mauldin, Bill *27:* 23
Mauterer, Erin Marie *119:* 5
Mawicke, Tran *9:* 137; *15:* 191; *47:* 100
Mawson, Matt *74:* 115
Max, Peter *45:* 146, 147, 148, 149, 150
Maxie, Betty *40:* 135
Maxwell, John Alan *1:* 148
May, Steve *204:* 30
Mayan, Earl *7:* 193
Mayer, Bill *200:* 138
Mayer, Danuta *117:* 103
Mayer, Marianna *32:* 132
Mayer, Mercer *11:* 192; *16:* 195, 196; *20:* 55, 57; *32:* 129, 130, 132, 133, 134; *41:* 144, 248, 252; *58:* 186; *73:* 140, 142, 143; *137:* 137, 138
Mayforth, Hal *166:* 77
Mayhew, James *85:* 121; *138:* 187; *149:* 140; *204:* 81
Mayhew, Richard *3:* 106
Mayo, Gretchen Will *38:* 81; *84:* 166
Mays, Victor *5:* 127; *8:* 45, 153; *14:* 245; *23:* 50; *34:* 155; *40:* 79; *45:* 158; *54:* 91; *66:* 240
Mazal, Chanan *49:* 104
Maze, Deborah *71:* 83
Mazellan, Ron *75:* 97, 98; *210:* 169
Mazetti, Alan *112:* 72
Mazille, Capucine *96:* 168
Mazza, Adriana Saviozzi *19:* 215
Mazzella, Mary Jo *82:* 165
Mazzetti, Alan *45:* 210
McAfee, Steve *135:* 146; *167:* 176; *191:* 84; *210:* 117
McAlinden, Paul *112:* 128
McBride, Angus *28:* 49; *103:* 40
McBride, Will *30:* 110
McCaffery, Janet *38:* 145

McCall, Bruce *209:* 119
McCallum, Graham *78:* 78
McCallum, Stephen *141:* 143; *156:* 5; *166:* 228
McCann, Gerald *3:* 50; *4:* 94; *7:* 54; *41:* 121
McCarthy, Dan *174:* 74
McCarthy, Linda *177:* 128
McCarthy, Meghan *168:* 134; *199:* 74
McCauley, Adam *157:* 36; *184:* 199; *193:* 100; *209:* 122
McCay, Winsor *41:* 124, 126, 128, 129, 130, 131; *134:* 77, 79
McClary, Nelson *1:* 111
McClements, George *196:* 146
McClennan, Connie *210:* 181
McClintock, Barbara *57:* 135; *95:* 130; *146:* 190
McClintock, Theodore *14:* 141
McCloskey, Robert *1:* 184, 185; *2:* 186, 187; *17:* 209; *39:* 139, 140, 141, 142, 143, 146, 147, 148; *85:* 150, 151; *100:* 172, 173, 174
McClung, Robert *2:* 189; *68:* 166, 167
McClure, Gillian *31:* 132; *150:* 53
McConnel, Jerry *31:* 75, 187
McConnell, Mary *102:* 49
McCord, Kathleen Garry *78:* 236
McCormack, John *66:* 193
McCormick, A.D. *35:* 119
McCormick, Dell J. *19:* 216
McCrady, Lady *16:* 198; *39:* 127
McCrea, James *3:* 122; *33:* 216
McCrea, Ruth *3:* 122; *27:* 102; *33:* 216
McCue, Lisa *65:* 148, 149; *77:* 54; *80:* 132; *175:* 33; *177:* 133, 135
McCully, Emily Arnold *2:* 89; *4:* 120, 121, 146, 197; *5:* 2, 129; *7:* 191; *11:* 122; *15:* 210; *33:* 23; *35:* 244; *37:* 122; *39:* 88; *40:* 103; *50:* 30,31, 32, 33, 34, 35, 36, 37; *52:* 89, 90; *57:* 6; *62:* 3; *70:* 195; *86:* 82; *96:* 192; *97:* 93; *110:* 143,144; *117:* 47; *167:* 96; *210:* 175, 176
McCurdy, Michael *13:* 153; *24:* 85; *81:* 160; *82:* 157, 158; *86:* 125; *97:* 92; *117:* 178; *132:* 6; *147:* 159, 160
McCusker, Paul *99:* 19
McDaniel, Jerry *132:* 135
McDaniel, Preston *160:* 206; *170:* 139
McDermott, Beverly Brodsky *11:* 180
McDermott, Gerald *16:* 201; *74:* 174, 175; *163:* 150, 151
McDermott, Mike *96:* 187
McDonald, Jill *13:* 155; *26:* 128
McDonald, Mercedes *169:* 118
McDonald, Ralph J. *5:* 123, 195
McDonnell, Flora *146:* 199, 200
McDonnell, Patrick *179:* 153, 154
McDonough, Don *10:* 163
McElligott, Matt *196:* 147
McElmurry, Jill *137:* 148; *163:* 141; *202:* 186
McElrath-Eslick, Lori *129:* 145; *142:* 21; *173:* 123; *202:* 194; *204:* 88, 89
McEntee, Dorothy *37:* 124
McEwan, Keith *88:* 116; *165:* 122, 123
McEwen, Katharine *169:* 34
McFall, Christie *12:* 144
McFeely, Daniel *160:* 213
McGaw, Laurie *109:* 243; *143:* 216; *211:* 218
McGee, Barbara *6:* 165
McGee, Marni *163:* 153
McGillvray, Kim *158:* 171; *165:* 213; *186:* 183; *190:* 175
McGinley-Nally, Sharon *131:* 19
McGinnis, Robert *110:* 113; *177:* 80
McGovern, Tara *98:* 171
McGraw, Sheila *83:* 146
McGregor, Barbara *200:* 155
McGregor, Malcolm *23:* 27
McGrory, Anik *193:* 120
McGuire, Robert *204:* 57; *209:* 86
McGuirk, Leslie *152:* 159
McHale, John *138:* 190

McHenry, E.B. *193:* 122
McHugh, Tom *23:* 64
McIntosh, Jon *42:* 56
McKay, Donald *2:* 118; *32:* 157; *45:* 151, 152
McKean, Dave *150:* 71; *174:* 156; *197:* 83, 118
McKeating, Eileen *44:* 58
McKee, David *10:* 48; *21:* 9; *70:* 154, 155; *107:* 139, 140, 141; *134:* 218; *158:* 148, 149, 150, 151
McKee, Diana *109:* 185
McKelvey, Patrick *164:* 141
McKendry, Joe *170:* 136
McKeveny, Tom *164:* 60; *173:* 79
McKie, Roy *7:* 44
McKie, Todd *205:* 181
McKillip, Kathy *30:* 153
McKinney, Ena *26:* 39
McKinnon, James *136:* 75
McKowen, Scott *172:* 63; *202:* 49
McLachlan, Edward *5:* 89
McLaren, Chesley *133:* 53
McLaren, Kirsty *123:* 99; *124:* 226
Mclean, Andrew *113:* 117, 118, 120, 121; *172:* 130, 131
Mclean, Janet *172:* 130
McLean, Meg *94:* 196
McLean, Sammis *32:* 197
McLean, Wilson *90:* 29; *113:* 195
McLoughlin, John C. *47:* 149
McLoughlin, Wayne *102:* 230; *134:* 178
McMahon, Robert *36:* 155; *69:* 169
McManus, Shawn *85:* 71
McMenemy, Sarah *156:* 139 ; *211:* 93
McMillan, Bruce *22:* 184
McMullan, James *40:* 33; *67:* 172; *87:* 142; *99:* 63, 64; *189:* 133; *196:* 51
McMullen, Nigel *146:* 177
McNeely, Tom *162:* 55
McNaught, Harry *12:* 80; *32:* 136
McNaughton, Colin *39:* 149; *40:* 108; *92:* 144, 145, 146; *134:* 104, 106; *211:* 122, 123, 124
McNicholas, Maureen *38:* 148
McNicholas, Shelagh *173:* 61; *191:* 125, 126
McPhail, David *14:* 105; *23:* 135; *37:* 217, 218, 220,221; *47:* 151, 152, 153, 154, 155, 156, 158, 159, 160, 162, 163, 164; *71:* 211; *81:* 139, 140, 142; *86:* 123; *132:* 150; *140:* 129, 131, 132; *183:* 134, 135, 137; *189:* 132
McPhee, Richard B. *41:* 133
McPheeters, Neal *78:* 132; *86:* 90; *99:* 162; *111:* 141; *142:* 162
McQuade, Jacqueline *124:* 223
McQueen, Lucinda *28:* 149; *41:* 249; *46:* 206; *53:* 103
McQuillan, Mary *153:* 97; *200:* 140
McVay, Tracy *11:* 68
McVicker, Charles *39:* 150
Mead, Ben Carlton *43:* 75
Meade, Holly *90:* 102; *94:* 101; *149:* 8; *151:* 107
Mecray, John *33:* 62
Meddaugh, Susan *20:* 42; *29:* 143; *41:* 241; *77:* 50; *84:* 173, 174, 175, 176, 177, 178; *125:* 160, 161, 162; *176:* 148, 149, 150, 151
Meehan, Dennis B. *56:* 144
Meents, Len W. *73:* 147, 150
Meers, Tony *99:* 113
Meisel, Paul *98:* 137; *124:* 18; *162:* 180; *179:* 16; *181:* 62; *194:* 154
Melanson, Luc *149:* 229; *198:* 97, 98
Melendez, Francisco *72:* 180
Melling, David *202:* 199
Melnychuk, Monika *153:* 65
Melo, Esperança *196:* 90
Melo, John *16:* 285; *58:* 203
Meloni, Maria Teresa *98:* 62
Meltzer, Ericka
　　See O'Rourke, Ericka
Menasco, Milton *43:* 85
Menchin, Scott *188:* 129

Mendelson, Steven T. *86:* 154
Mendelssohn, Felix *19:* 170
Mendola, Christopher *88:* 223
Meng, Heinz *13:* 158
Merian, Maria Sibylla *140:* 88
Mero, Lee *34:* 68
Merrell, David *205:* 3
Merrill, Frank T. *16:* 147; *19:* 71; *YABC 1:* 226, 229,273
Merriman, Rachel *98:* 108; *114:* 122; *149:* 142
Merveille, David *200:* 142
Meryman, Hope *27:* 41
Meryweather, Jack *10:* 179
Meseldzija, Petar *168:* 97
Meserve, Jessica *184:* 137; *211:* 127
Messick, Dale *64:* 150, 151, 152
Meth, Harold *24:* 203
Meyer, Herbert *19:* 189
Meyer, Renate *6:* 170
Meyers, Bob *11:* 136
Meyers, Nancy *172:* 124
Meynell, Louis *37:* 76
Micale, Albert *2:* 65; *22:* 185
Miccuci, Charles *82:* 163; *144:* 150
Micich, Paul *164:* 163
Middleton, Jeffrey *177:* 173
Middleton, Joshua *208:* 146
Middleton-Sandford, Betty *2:* 125
Mieke, Anne *45:* 74
Mighell, Patricia *43:* 134
Miglio, Paige *101:* 203; *151:* 223; *201:* 118, 119; *204:* 162
Mikec, Larry *204:* 125
Mikolaycak, Charles *9:* 144; *12:* 101; *13:* 212; *21:* 121; *22:* 168; *30:* 187; *34:* 103, 150; *37:* 183; *43:* 179; *44:* 90; *46:* 115, 118, 119; *49:* 25; *78:* 121, 122, 205, 207; *81:* 4
Milelli, Pascal *129:* 66; *135:* 153; *187:* 45
Miles, Elizabeth *117:* 77
Miles, Jennifer *17:* 278
Milgrim, David *158:* 157; *187:* 125, 126, 128
Milhous, Katherine *15:* 193; *17:* 51
Millais, John E. *22:* 230, 231
Millar, H.R. *YABC 1:* 194, 195, 203
Millard, C.E. *28:* 186
Millard, Kerry *105:* 124; *204:* 93, 94
Miller, Don *15:* 195; *16:* 71; *20:* 106; *31:* 178
Miller, Edna *29:* 148
Miller, Edward *115:* 64; *183:* 140, 141
Miller, Frank J. *25:* 94
Miller, Grambs *18:* 38; *23:* 16
Miller, Ian *99:* 128
Miller, Jane *15:* 196
Miller, Marcia *13:* 233
Miller, Marilyn *1:* 87; *31:* 69; *33:* 157
Miller, Mitchell *28:* 183; *34:* 207
Miller, Phil *175:* 150
Miller, Shane *5:* 140
Miller, Virginia *81:* 206
Millman, Isaac *172:* 18
Mills, Elaine *72:* 181
Mills, Judith Christine *130:* 168, 169
Mills, Lauren *92:* 170
Mills, Yaroslava Surmach *35:* 169, 170; *46:* 114
Millsap, Darrel *51:* 102
Milone, Karen *89:* 169
Milord, Susan *147:* 163, 164; *200:* 144
Milton, Debbie *162:* 161
Mims, Ashley *170:* 51
Miner, Julia *98:* 69
Minor, Wendell *39:* 188; *52:* 87; *56:* 171; *58:* 116; *62:* 56; *66:* 109; *74:* 93; *78:* 129; *94:* 67; *117:* 12, 13; *124:* 84, 86; *136:* 121; *164:* 168, 169; *170:* 71; *199:* 79, 80, 81, 82
Minter, Daniel *176:* 154; *179:* 177
Mirocha, Paul *81:* 133; *192:* 148; *194:* 36
Misako Rocks! *192:* 149, 150
Mitchell, Judith *109:* 117
Mitchell, Mark *91:* 208
Mitchell, Tracy *190:* 15

Mitgutsch, Ali *76:* 161
Mitsuhashi, Yoko *45:* 153
Miyake, Yoshi *38:* 141
Mizumura, Kazue *10:* 143; *18:* 223; *36:* 159
Mochi, Ugo *8:* 122; *38:* 150
Mock, Paul *55:* 83; *123:* 32
Modarressi, Mitra *90:* 236; *126:* 168; *173:* 165, 166; *200:* 147, 148
Modell, Frank *39:* 152
Mogenson, Jan *74:* 183
Mohn, Susan *89:* 224
Mohr, Mark *133:* 201
Mohr, Nicholasa *8:* 139; *113:* 127
Molan, Christine *60:* 177; *84:* 183
Moldon, Peter L. *49:* 168
Molk, Laurel *92:* 150
Mollica, Gene *197:* 11
Momaday, N. Scott *48:* 159
Mombourquette, Paul *112:* 91; *126:* 142
Monk, Julie *165:* 231; *191:* 96
Monks, Lydia *189:* 136, 137
Monroy, Manuel *199:* 192
Montgomery, Lucy *150:* 126
Montgomery, Michael G. *208:* 159
Montgomery-Higham, Amanda *169:* 131
Monteiel, David *201:* 95
Montiel, David *69:* 106; *84:* 145
Montijo, Rhode *193:* 164
Montresor, Beni *2:* 91; *3:* 138; *38:* 152, 153, 154,155, 156, 157, 158, 159, 160; *68:* 63
Montserrat, Pep *128:* 135; *181:* 119; *184:* 53
Moon, Carl *25:* 183, 184, 185
Moon, Eliza *14:* 40
Moon, Ivan *22:* 39; *38:* 140
Moore, Adrienne *67:* 147
Moore, Agnes Kay Randall *43:* 187
Moore, Cyd *117:* 107, 108; *159:* 137, 138; *186:* 148, 149, 151; *203:* 15
Moore, Gustav *127:* 181, 182; *170:* 162, 163
Moore, Jackie *128:* 79
Moore, Janet *63:* 153
Moore, Margie *176:* 156
Moore, Mary *29:* 160
Moore, Patrick *184:* 121
Moore, Yvette *101:* 11, 12; *154:* 141
Mora, Giovanni *179:* 127; *184:* 11
Mora, Raul Mina *20:* 41
Moraes, Odilon *102:* 144
Morales, Yuyi *154:* 144
Moran, Rosslyn *111:* 26
Moran, Tom *60:* 100
Mordan, C.B. *193:* 115
Mordvinoff, Nicolas *15:* 179
Moreno, René King *169:* 59; *190:* 133, 209
Morgan, Barbara *169:* 116
Morgan, Jacqui *58:* 57
Morgan, Mary *114:* 133, 134, 135; *123:* 11
Morgan, Tom *42:* 157
Morgan, Pierr *173:* 148
Morgenstern, Michael *158:* 7, 57; *171:* 103; *174:* 60
Morice, Dave *93:* 142
Morin, Paul *73:* 132; *79:* 130; *88:* 140; *137:* 143
Moriuchi, Mique *177:* 203
Morning, Tuesday *205:* 25
Morozumi, Atsuko *110:* 155
Morrill, Leslie *18:* 218; *29:* 177; *33:* 84; *38:* 147; *42:* 127; *44:* 93; *48:* 164, 165, 167, 168, 169, 170,171; *49:* 162; *63:* 136, 180; *70:* 72; *71:* 70, 91,92; *72:* 228; *80:* 163, 164, 165; *90:* 121; *121:* 88; *178:* 117
Morrill, Rowena A. *84:* 16; *98:* 163
Morris *47:* 91
Morris, Frank *55:* 133; *60:* 28; *76:* 2
Morris, Harry O. *119:* 138
Morris, Jackie *128:* 194; *144:* 119; *151:* 146; *202:* 126, 127; *204:* 83; *211:* 80
Morris, Jennifer E. *179:* 157
Morris, Oradel Nolen *128:* 180
Morris, Tony *62:* 146; *70:* 97

Morrison, Bill *42:* 116; *66:* 170; *69:* 40
Morrison, Gordon *87:* 150; *113:* 93; *128:* 181, 182; *183:* 144, 145, 146
Morrison, Frank *169:* 162; *205:* 156
Morrison, Taylor *159:* 144, 145; *187:* 131
Morrow, Gray *2:* 64; *5:* 200; *10:* 103, 114; *14:* 175
Morse, Scott *200:* 149, 150
Morton, Lee Jack *32:* 140
Morton, Marian *3:* 185
Mosberg, Hilary *117:* 195; *118:* 164; *149:* 55
Moser, Barry *56:* 68, 117, 118, 119, 120, 121, 122, 123, 124; *59:* 141; *60:* 160; *79:* 91, 147, 149, 151, 152; *82:* 81; *90:* 118; *91:* 35; *95:* 210; *97:* 91, 93; *102:* 152; *126:* 4; *128:* 175; *133:* 141; *138:* 167, 171, 174; *153:* 205; *174:* 130; *185:* 152, 154; *195:* 163; *204:* 115; *209:* 201
Moser, Cara *90:* 118; *138:* 167
Moses, Grandma *18:* 228
Moses, Will *178:* 170, 171
Moskof, Martin Stephen *27:* 152
Mosley, Francis *57:* 144
Moss, Donald *11:* 184
Moss, Geoffrey *32:* 198
Moss, Marissa *71:* 130; *104:* 127; *163:* 156
Most, Bernard *48:* 173; *91:* 142, 143; *134:* 120
Mowll, Joshua *188:* 133
Mowry, Carmen *50:* 62
Moxley, Sheila *96:* 174; *169:* 26; *206:* 16
Moyers, William *21:* 65
Moyler, Alan *36:* 142
Mozley, Charles *9:* 87; *20:* 176, 192, 193; *22:* 228; *25:* 205; *33:* 150; *43:* 170, 171, 172, 173, 174; *YABC2:* 89
Mueller, Hans Alexander *26:* 64; *27:* 52, 53
Mugnaini, Joseph *11:* 35; *27:* 52, 53; *35:* 62
Mujica, Rick *72:* 67; *88:* 95; *111:* 53; *180:* 185; *197:* 70
Mullen, Douglas *180:* 178
Muller, Robin *86:* 161
Muller, Steven *32:* 167
Muller, Jorg *35:* 215; *67:* 138, 139
Mulock, Julie *163:* 112
Mullins, Edward S. *10:* 101
Mullins, Patricia *51:* 68
Multer, Scott *80:* 108
Munari, Bruno *15:* 200
Munch, Edvard *140:* 143
Munowitz, Ken *14:* 148; *72:* 178, 179
Muñoz, Claudio *208:* 161
Munoz, William *42:* 160
Munro, Roxie *58:* 134; *136:* 177; *137:* 218; *184:* 133, 134
Munsinger, Lynn *33:* 161; *46:* 126; *71:* 92; *82:* 80; *89:* 218; *92:* 125; *94:* 157, 158, 159, 160; *98:* 196; *103:* 198; *142:* 143; *145:* 133, 134, 136; *153:* 203; *176:* 162; *177:* 140, 141, 142; *189:* 113, 114, 116, 117; *201:* 42
Munson, Russell *13:* 9
Munster, Sebastian *166:* 107
Munzar, Barbara *149:* 75
Murdocca, Salvatore *73:* 212; *98:* 132; *111:* 168; *157:* 228; *164:* 257
Murphy, Bill *5:* 138; *130:* 170
Murphy, Jill *37:* 142; *70:* 166; *142:* 132, 134
Murphy, Kelly *130:* 212; *143:* 119; *176:* 158; *190:* 135
Murphy, Liz *210:* 183
Murphy, Mary *196:* 158
Murphy, Tom *192:* 40
Murr, Karl *20:* 62
Murray, Joe *175:* 37
Murray, Ossie *43:* 176
Mussino, Attilio *29:* 131; *100:* 164
Mutchler, Dwight *1:* 25
Myers, Bernice *9:* 147; *36:* 75; *81:* 146, 147, 148
Muth, Jon J. *165:* 169; *167:* 109; *190:* 227; *193:* 59
Myers, Christopher *183:* 150; *193:* 139

Myers, Duane O. *99:* 145
Myers, Tim *147:* 168
Myers, V.G. *142:* 41
Myers, Lou *11:* 2

N

Nachreiner, Tom *29:* 182
Nacht, Merle *65:* 49
Nadler, Ellis *88:* 91
Nagle, Shane *180:* 223
Nagy, Ian *195:* 64
Najaka, Marlies *62:* 101
Nakai, Michael *30:* 217; *54:* 29
Nakata, Hiroe *157:* 156; *162:* 30; *205:* 124, 125
Nakatani, Chiyoko *12:* 124
Narahashi, Keiko *77:* 188; *82:* 213; *115:* 142, 143, 144
Nascimbene, Yan *133:* 128; *173:* 132, 133
Nash, Lesa *87:* 135
Nash, Linell *46:* 175
Nash, Scott *130:* 36; *188:* 196
Naso, John *33:* 183
Nason, Thomas W. *14:* 68
Nasser, Muriel *48:* 74
Nast, Thomas *21:* 29; *28:* 23; *51:* 132, 133, 134, 135,136, 137, 138, 139, 141
Nasta, Vincent *78:* 185
Natale, Vincent *76:* 3; *78:* 125; *112:* 47; *166:* 81; *174:* 189; *185:* 212; *197:* 59
Natchev, Alexi *96:* 177
Nathan, Charlott *125:* 151
Nathan, Cheryl *150:* 104; *186:* 112
Natti, Susanna *20:* 146; *32:* 141, 142; *35:* 178; *37:* 143; *71:* 49; *93:* 98; *125:* 166, 168; *126:* 228; *151:* 6; *178:* 8; *188:* 106
Navarra, Celeste Scala *8:* 142
Naylor, Penelope *10:* 104
Nazz, James *72:* 8
Nebel, M. *45:* 154
Neebe, William *7:* 93
Needham, Dave *196:* 85
Needler, Jerry *12:* 93
Neel, Alice *31:* 23
Neely, Beth *119:* 184
Neely, Keith R. *46:* 124
Neff, Leland *78:* 74
Negri, Rocco *3:* 213; *5:* 67; *6:* 91, 108; *12:* 159
Negrin, Fabian *174:* 125; *175:* 15
Neidigh, Sherry *128:* 53; *204:* 101, 102, 103
Neilan, Eujin Kim *180:* 241; *200:* 151, 152
Neill, John R. *18:* 8, 10, 11, 21, 30; *100:* 22
Neilsen, Cliff *158:* 131; *177:* 112, 121; *209:* 8
Neilsen, Terese *116:* 74
Nelson, Craig *62:* 151; 153; *183:* 86
Nelson, Gail White *68:* 140
Nelson, Jennifer *129:* 152; *199:* 132
Nelson, Kadir *151:* 185; *154:* 146, 147; *157:* 189, 222; *181:* 122, 124; *197:* 155
Nelson, S.D. *131:* 34; *181:* 126, 127
Ness, Evaline *1:* 164, 165; *2:* 39; *3:* 8; *10:* 147; *12:* 53; *26:* 150, 151, 152, 153; *49:* 30, 31, 32; *56:* 30; *60:* 113
Neubecker, Robert *170:* 143
Neville, Vera *2:* 182
Nevins, Daniel *191:* 173
Nevwirth, Allan *79:* 168
Newberry, Clare Turlay *1:* 170
Newbold, Greg *108:* 125; *145:* 199; *151:* 23; *193:* 178; *197:* 10; *199:* 92, 93
Newfeld, Frank *14:* 121; *26:* 154
Newman, Andy *149:* 61; *195:* 63
Newman, Ann *43:* 90
Newman, Barbara Johansen *191:* 137, 138
Newsham, Ian *143:* 162

Newsom, Carol *40:* 159; *44:* 60; *47:* 189; *65:* 29; *70:* 192; *80:* 36; *85:* 137, 138; *92:* 167; *191:* 82
Newsom, Tom *49:* 149; *71:* 13, 62; *75:* 156; *91:* 113
Newton, Jill *83:* 105; *200:* 154
Ng, Michael *29:* 171
Ng, Simon *167:* 7
Nguyen, Vincent *189:* 49
Nicholson, William *15:* 33, 34; *16:* 48
Nickens, Bessie *104:* 153
Nicklaus, Carol *45:* 194; *62:* 132, 133
Nickle, John *181:* 128
Nickless, Will *16:* 139
Nicholas, Corasue *154:* 20
Nicolas *17:* 130, 132, 133; *YABC 2:* 215
Niebrugge, Jane *6:* 118
Nielsen, Cliff *95:* 207, 208; *105:* 58; *114:* 112; *124:* 12; *125:* 91, 92; *132:* 224; *135:* 187; *136:* 40; *137:* 168; *145:* 54; *149:* 28; *158:* 129; *165:* 64, 158; *168:* 169; *170:* 6; *175:* 114, 116; *187:* 75, 76; *194:* 107; *197:* 172; *201:* 14; *208:* 192; *211:* 186
Nielsen, Jon *6:* 100; *24:* 202
Nielsen, Kay *15:* 7; *16:* 211, 212, 213, 215, 217; *22:* 143; *YABC 1:* 32, 33
Niemann, Christoph *191:* 141
Nikola-Lisa, W. *180:* 180
Niland, Deborah *25:* 191; *27:* 156; *135:* 50; *172:* 143
Niland, Kilmeny *25:* 191; *75:* 143
Nino, Alex *59:* 145
Ninon *1:* 5; *38:* 101, 103, 108
Nissen, Rie *44:* 35
Nithael, Mark *158:* 237
Nivola, Claire A. *78:* 126; *140:* 147; *208:* 164
Nixon, K. *14:* 152
Nobati, Eugenia *194:* 118
Noble, Louise *61:* 170
Noble, Marty *97:* 168; *125:* 171
Noble, Trinka Hakes *39:* 162; *84:* 157
Noda, Takayo *168:* 143
Noguchi, Yoshie *30:* 99
Nolan, Dennis *42:* 163; *67:* 163; *78:* 189; *82:* 225; *83:* 26; *92:* 169, 170; *103:* 166; *111:* 35; *112:* 213; *127:* 171; *166:* 161; *194:* 218
Noll, Sally *82:* 171
Nolte, Larry *121:* 63, 65
Nones, Eric Jon *61:* 111; *76:* 38; *77:* 177
Noonan, Daniel *100:* 224
Noonan, Julia *4:* 163; *7:* 207; *25:* 151; *91:* 29; *95:* 149
Norcia, Ernie *108:* 155; *140:* 47
Nordenskjold, Birgitta *2:* 208
Noreika, Robert *173:* 20
Norling, Beth *149:* 153, 154; *209:* 77
Norman, Elaine *77:* 72, 176; *94:* 35; *136:* 63; *178:* 42
Norman, Mary *36:* 138, 147
Norman, Michael *12:* 117; *27:* 168
Northway, Jennifer *85:* 96
Nostlinger, Christiana *162:* 131
Novak, Linda *166:* 205
Novak, Matt *104:* 132, 133; *165:* 173, 174; *204:* 104, 106
Novelli, Luca *61:* 137
Nugent, Cynthia *106:* 189; *205:* 126, 127; *209:* 180
Numeroff, Laura Joffe *28:* 161; *30:* 177
Nurse, Chris *164:* 91
Nussbaumer, Paul *16:* 219; *39:* 117
Nutt, Ken *72:* 69; *97:* 170
Nyce, Helene *19:* 219
Nygren, Tord *30:* 148; *127:* 164

O

Oakley, Graham *8:* 112; *30:* 164, 165; *84:* 188,189, 190, 191, 192
Oakley, Thornton *YABC 2:* 189

Oberheide, Heide *118:* 37
Obligado, Lilian *2:* 28, 66, 67; *6:* 30; *14:* 179; *15:* 103; *25:* 84; *61:* 138, 139, 140, 141, 143
Oblinski, Rafael *190:* 139
Obrant, Susan *11:* 186
O'Brien, Anne Sibley *53:* 116, 117; *155:* 115
O'Brien, John *41:* 253; *72:* 12; *89:* 59, 60; *98:* 16; *161:* 185; *169:* 16; *180:* 196
O'Brien, Patrick *193:* 142, 143, 144
O'Brien, Teresa *87:* 89
O'Brien, Tim *93:* 25; *136:* 94; *164:* 57; *169:* 57; *173:* 55; *175:* 86; *184:* 192; *191:* 134; *193:* 137; *210:* 159
O'Clair, Dennis *127:* 25
O'Connor, George *183:* 153
Odell, Carole *35:* 47
Odem, Mel *99:* 164; *167:* 84, 87
O'Donohue, Thomas *40:* 89
Oechsli, Kelly *5:* 144, 145; *7:* 115; *8:* 83, 183; *13:* 117; *20:* 94; *81:* 199
Ofer, Avi *208:* 143
Offen, Hilda *42:* 207
Ogden, Bill *42:* 59; *47:* 55
Ogg, Oscar *33:* 34
Ogle, Nancy Gray *163:* 144
Ohi, Ruth *90:* 175, 177; *131:* 63; *135:* 106; *175:* 107; *179:* 55
Ohlsson, Ib *4:* 152; *7:* 57; *10:* 20; *11:* 90; *19:* 217; *41:* 246; *82:* 106; *92:* 213
Ohtomo, Yasuo *37:* 146; *39:* 212, 213
O'Keefe, Jennifer *136:* 184
O'Kelley, Mattie Lou *36:* 150
Olbinski, Rafal *149:* 27; *158:* 77; *203:* 36
O'Leary, Chris *208:* 166
Oleynikov, Igor *202:* 134
Oliver, Isaac *171:* 182
Oliver, Jenni *23:* 121; *35:* 112
Oliver, Narelle *152:* 192; *197:* 129, 130
Oller, Erika *128:* 186; *134:* 126
Olschewski, Alfred *7:* 172
Olsen, Ib Spang *6:* 178, 179; *81:* 164
Olson, Alan *77:* 229
Olson-Brown, Ellen *183:* 154
Olugebefola, Ademola *15:* 205
O'Malley, Kevin *94:* 180; *106:* 8; *113:* 108; *136:* 70; *157:* 193; *191:* 146; *203:* 78
O'Neil, Dan IV *7:* 176
O'Neill, Catharine *72:* 113; *84:* 78; *134:* 153
O'Neill, Jean *22:* 146
O'Neill, Martin *187:* 39; *203:* 118
O'Neill, Michael J. *54:* 172
O'Neill, Rose *48:* 30, 31
O'Neill, Steve *21:* 118
Ono, Chiyo *7:* 97
Orbaan, Albert *2:* 31; *5:* 65, 171; *9:* 8; *14:* 241; *20:* 109
Orbach, Ruth *21:* 112
Orback, Craig *197:* 132
Orfe, Joan *20:* 81
Org, Ed *119:* 93
Ormai, Stella *72:* 129
Ormerod, Jan *55:* 124; *70:* 170, 171; *90:* 39; *132:* 172, 173, 174; *147:* 98
Ormsby, Virginia H. *11:* 187
O'Rourke, Ericka *108:* 216; *117:* 194; *111:* 142; *119:* 194; *137:* 152; *150:* 134; *167:* 64; *172:* 164; *188:* 163; *191:* 172; *201:* 15; *203:* 75; *209:* 130
O'Rourke, Ericka Meltzer
    See O'Rourke, Ericka
Orozco, Jose Clemente *9:* 177
Orr, Forrest W. *23:* 9
Orr, N. *19:* 70
Ortiz, Vilma *88:* 158
Osborn, Kathy *152:* 232; *199:* 101, 102; *206:* 67
Osborn, Robert *65:* 49
Osborne, Billie Jean *35:* 209
Osmond, Edward *10:* 111
O'Sullivan, Tom *3:* 176; *4:* 55; *78:* 195
Otani, June *124:* 42; *156:* 53

Otis, Rebecca *185:* 92
Ottley, Matt *147:* 221; *171:* 133
Otto, Svend *22:* 130, 141; *67:* 188, 189
Oudry, J.B. *18:* 167
Oughton, Taylor *5:* 23; *104:* 136
Overeng, Johannes *44:* 36
Overlie, George *11:* 156
Owens, Carl *2:* 35; *23:* 521
Owens, Gail *10:* 170; *12:* 157; *19:* 16; *22:* 70; *25:* 81; *28:* 203, 205; *32:* 221, 222; *36:* 132; *46:* 40; *47:* 57; *54:* 66, 67, 68, 69, 70, 71, 72, 73; *71:* 100; *73:* 64; *77:* 157; *80:* 32; *82:* 3; *99:* 226
Owens, Mary Beth *113:* 202, 203; *191:* 148, 149
Owens, Nubia *84:* 74
Oxenbury, Helen *3:* 150, 151; *24:* 81; *68:* 174, 175,176; *81:* 209; *84:* 213, 245; *129:* 56; *149:* 159; *184:* 181
Oz, Robin *88:* 167; *185:* 181

P

Padgett, Jim *12:* 165
Page, Gail *205:* 128
Page, Homer *14:* 145
Page, Mark *162:* 70
Paget, Sidney *24:* 90, 91, 93, 95, 97
Paget, Walter *64:* 122
Paillot, Jim *173:* 89
Pajouhesh, Noushin *160:* 121
Pak *12:* 76
Pak, Yu Cha *86:* 174
Paladino, Lance *134:* 30
Palazzo, Tony *3:* 152, 153
Palecek, Josef *56:* 136; *89:* 158
Palen, Debbie *135:* 88; *195:* 148, 149
Palencar, John Jude *84:* 12, 45; *85:* 87; *92:* 187; *99:* 128; *110:* 204; *150:* 122; *171:* 86; *207:* 36
Palin, Nicki *81:* 201; *89:* 161
Palladini, David *4:* 113; *40:* 176, 177, 178, 179, 181,224, 225; *50:* 138; *78:* 186
Pallarito, Don *43:* 36
Palmer, Carol *158:* 230; *195:* 187
Palmer, Heidi *15:* 207; *29:* 102
Palmer, Jan *42:* 153; *82:* 161
Palmer, Judd *153:* 160, 161
Palmer, Juliette *6:* 89; *15:* 208
Palmer, Kate Salley *104:* 143; *154:* 169
Palmer, Lemuel *17:* 25, 29
Palmisciano, Diane *110:* 62; *162:* 26; *202:* 138, 139
Palmquist, Eric *38:* 133
Panesis, Nicholas *3:* 127
Panter, Gary *182:* 191
Panton, Doug *52:* 99
Paparone, Pamela *129:* 174
Papas, William *11:* 223; *50:* 160
Papin, Joseph *26:* 113
Papish, Robin Lloyd *10:* 80
Papp, Robert *198:* 41; *205:* 130
Paradis, Susan *40:* 216
Paraquin, Charles H. *18:* 166
Pardo DeLange, Alex *179:* 128; *211:* 135, 136
Paris, Peter *31:* 127
Parisi, Elizabeth B. *141:* 82; *164:* 57
Park, Nick *113:* 143
Park, Seho *39:* 110
Park, W.B. *22:* 189
Parker, Ant *82:* 87, 88; *104:* 121
Parker, Lewis *2:* 179
Parker, Nancy Winslow *10:* 113; *22:* 164; *28:* 47, 144; *52:* 7; *69:* 153; *91:* 171, 174; *132:* 175
Parker, Robert *4:* 161; *5:* 74; *9:* 136; *29:* 39

Parker, Robert Andrew *11:* 81; *29:* 186; *39:* 165; *40:* 25; *41:* 78; *42:* 123; *43:* 144; *48:* 182; *54:* 140; *74:* 141; *91:* 24; *111:* 115; *151:* 201; *154:* 156; *200:* 163, 164; *211:* 67
Parker-Rees, Guy *149:* 145; *193:* 149, 150
Parkin, Trevor *140:* 151
Parkins, David *114:* 123; *146:* 176; *176:* 168; *192:* 107
Parkinson, Kathy *71:* 143; *144:* 234
Parkinson, Keith *70:* 66
Parks, Gordon, Jr. *33:* 228
Parnall, Peter *5:* 137; *16:* 221; *24:* 70; *40:* 78; *51:* 130; *69:* 17, 155; *136:* 22, 23, 24
Parnall, Virginia *40:* 78
Paros, Jennifer *210:* 197
Parow, Lorraine *158:* 127
Parr, Todd *134:* 139, 140; *179:* 163, 164, 165
Parrish, Anne *27:* 159, 160
Parrish, Dillwyn *27:* 159
Parrish, Maxfield *14:* 160, 161, 164, 165; *16:* 109; *18:* 12, 13; *YABC 1:* 149, 152, 267; *2:* 146, 149
Parry, David *26:* 156
Parry, Marian *13:* 176; *19:* 179
Parsons, Garry *197:* 135
Partch, Virgil *45:* 163, 165
Pascal, David *14:* 174
Paschkis, Julie *177:* 153, 154
Pasquier, J.A. *16:* 91
Pastel, Elyse *201:* 123
Pasternak, Robert *119:* 53
Paterson, Diane *13:* 116; *39:* 163; *59:* 164, 165, 166,167; *72:* 51, 53; *129:* 175; *177:* 156, 157
Paterson, Helen *16:* 93
Patkau, Karen *112:* 123
Paton, Jane *15:* 271; *35:* 176
Patricelli, Leslie *207:* 129
Patrick, John *139:* 190
Patrick, Pamela *90:* 160; *93:* 211; *105:* 12
Patrick, Tom *190:* 103
Patterson, Geoffrey *54:* 75
Patterson, Robert *25:* 118
Patti, Joyce *187:* 145, 146
Patz, Nancy *111:* 40; *154:* 161
Paul, James *4:* 130; *23:* 161
Paul, Korky *102:* 85
Paull, Grace *24:* 157; *87:* 127
Paulsen, Ruth Wright *79:* 160, 164; *189:* 146
Pavlov, Elena *80:* 49
Payne, Adam S. *135:* 166
Payne, C.F. *145:* 138, 140; *179:* 168
Payne, Joan Balfour *1:* 118
Payne, Tom *170:* 27
Payson, Dale *7:* 34; *9:* 151; *20:* 140; *37:* 22
Payzant, Charles *21:* 147
Peacock, Ralph *64:* 118
Peake, Mervyn *22:* 136, 149; *23:* 162, 163, 164; *YABC2:* 307
Pearson, Larry *38:* 225
Pearson, Tracey Campbell *64:* 163, 164, 167, 168, 169; *118:* 51; *156:* 169, 171, 172; *163:* 140
Peat, Fern B. *16:* 115
Peck, Anne Merriman *18:* 241; *24:* 155
Peck, Beth *66:* 242; *79:* 166; *80:* 136; *91:* 34; *95:* 9; *101:* 77; *164:* 197; *190:* 170
Peddicord, Jane Ann *199:* 106
Pedersen, Janet *193:* 152
Pedersen, Judy *66:* 217; *121:* 36; *172:* 67
Pedersen, Vilhelm *YABC 1:* 40
Pederson, Sharleen *12:* 92
Pedlar, Elaine *161:* 45
Peek, Merle *39:* 168
Peet, Bill *2:* 203; *41:* 159, 160, 161, 162, 163; *78:* 158, 159, 160, 161
Peguero, Adrian *116:* 133
Peguero, Gerard *116:* 133
Pels, Winslow Pinney *55:* 126
Peltier, Leslie C. *13:* 178
Peltzer, Marc *202:* 92

Penberthy, Mark *171:* 78
Pendle, Alexy *7:* 159; *13:* 34; *29:* 161; *33:* 215; *86:* 62
Pendola, Joanne *76:* 203; *81:* 125; *105:* 181; *178:* 152, 153
Pene du Bois, William *4:* 70; *10:* 122; *26:* 61; *27:* 145, 211; *35:* 243; *41:* 216; *68:* 180, 181; *73:* 45
Penfound, David *102:* 185
Pennington, Eunice *27:* 162
Peppe, Mark *28:* 142
Peppe, Rodney *4:* 164, 165; *74:* 187, 188, 189
Pepper, Hubert *64:* 143
Percy, Graham *63:* 2
Pericoli, Matteo *178:* 177
Perini, Ben *173:* 77
Perkins, David *60:* 68
Perkins, Lucy Fitch *72:* 199
Perkins, Lynne Rae *172:* 146
Perl, Susan *2:* 98; *4:* 231; *5:* 44, 45, 118; *6:* 199; *8:* 137; *12:* 88; *22:* 193; *34:* 54, 55; *52:* 128; *YABC 1:* 176
Perrone, Donna *78:* 166
Perry, Marie Fritz *165:* 180
Perry, Patricia *29:* 137; *30:* 171
Perry, Roger *27:* 163
Perske, Martha *46:* 83; *51:* 108, 147
Persson, Stina *175:* 166
Pesek, Ludek *15:* 237
Petach, Heidi *149:* 166; *200:* 207
Peters, David *72:* 205; *182:* 116
Petersen, Jeff *181:* 95
Petersham, Maud *17:* 108, 147, 148, 149, 150, 151, 152, 153
Petersham, Miska *17:* 108, 147, 148, 149, 150, 151, 152, 153
Peterson, Eric *109:* 125
Peterson, Nisse *99:* 27
Peterson, R.F. *7:* 101
Peterson, Russell *7:* 130
Petie, Haris *2:* 3; *10:* 41, 118; *11:* 227; *12:* 70
Petricic, Dusan *153:* 75, 76, 77; *170:* 12; *172:* 13; *176:* 170; *179:* 56
Petrides, Heidrun *19:* 223
Petrone, Valeria *159:* 160; *171:* 92; *186:* 173; *204:* 49
Petrosino, Tamara *177:* 40; *193:* 154, 155
Petruccio, Steven James *67:* 159; *127:* 5
Pettingill, Ondre *64:* 181; *70:* 64
Peyo *40:* 56, 57
Peyton, K.M. *15:* 212
Pfeifer, Herman *15:* 262
Pfister, Marcus *83:* 165, 166, 167; *146:* 152; *150:* 160; *207:* 132, 134, 135, 136
Pfloog, Jan *124:* 60
Pham, LeUyen *160:* 48; *175:* 154, 156; *179:* 149; *201:* 124, 125, 126, 127; *204:* 28; *208:* 206
Phelan, Matt *182:* 160; *184:* 222
Phillips, Craig *70:* 151; *207:* 74
Phillips, Douglas *1:* 19
Phillips, F.D. *6:* 202
Phillips, Louise *133:* 67
Phillips, Matt *184:* 173
Phillips, Thomas *30:* 55
Philpot, Glyn *54:* 46
Phiz
  See Browne, Hablot K.
Piatti, Celestino *16:* 223
Pica, Steve *115:* 181
Picarella, Joseph *13:* 147
Picart, Gabriel *121:* 165; *201:* 169
Pichon, Liz *174:* 139
Pickard, Charles *12:* 38; *18:* 203; *36:* 152
Picken, George A. *23:* 150
Pickens, David *22:* 156
Pickering, Jimmy *195:* 152; *197:* 163
Pienkowski, Jan *6:* 183; *30:* 32; *58:* 140, 141, 142,143, 146, 147; *73:* 3; *87:* 156, 157; *131:* 189
Pieper, Christiane *200:* 168

Pignataro, Anna *163:* 220 *Pileggi, Steve 145:* 122
Pilkey, Dav *68:* 186; *115:* 164, 166; *166:* 173, 174, 175
Pimlott, John *10:* 205
Pincus, Harriet *4:* 186; *8:* 179; *22:* 148; *27:* 164, 165; *66:* 202
Pini, Wendy *89:* 166
Pinkett, Neil *60:* 8
Pinkney, Brian *81:* 184, 185; *94:* 107; *113:* 146, 147; *117:* 121, 166; *132:* 145; *158:* 108, 191; *160:* 189; *200:* 8
Pinkney, Jerry *8:* 218; *10:* 40; *15:* 276; *20:* 66; *24:* 121; *33:* 109; *36:* 222; *38:* 200; *41:* 165, 166, 167, 168, 169, 170, 171, 173, 174; *44:* 198; *48:* 51; *53:* 20; *56:* 61, 68; *58:* 184; *60:* 59; *61:* 91; *71:* 146, 148, 149; *72:* 17; *73:* 149; *74:* 159,192; *75:* 45; *80:* 206; *81:* 44; *85:* 144; *95:* 50; *107:* 158, 159, 160; *108:* 164; *112:* 114, 115; *133:* 58; *195:* 140
Pinkwater, Daniel Manus *8:* 156; *46:* 180, 181, 182, 185, 188, 189, 190; *151:* 161 *76:* 178, 179, 180; *210:* 203
Pinkwater, Manus
  See Pinkwater, Daniel Manus
Pinkwater, Jill *114:* 160, 161; *158:* 179; *188:* 143, 145, 146
Pinto, Ralph *10:* 131; *45:* 93
Pinto, Sara *200:* 165
Pinon, Mark *74:* 22
Piven, Hanoch *173:* 142
Pistolesi *73:* 211
Pitcairn, Ansel *188:* 10
Pittman, Helena Clare *71:* 151
Pitz, Henry C. *4:* 168; *19:* 165; *35:* 128; *42:* 80; *YABC 2:* 95, 176
Pitzenberger, Lawrence J. *26:* 94
Pitzer, Susanna *181:* 131
Player, Stephen *82:* 190
Plecas, Jennifer *84:* 201; *106:* 124; *149:* 168; *205:* 180
Ploog, Mike *180:* 19
Plowden, David *52:* 135, 136
Plume, Ilse *170:* 149
Plummer, William *32:* 31
Podevin, Jean François *184:* 185
Podwal, Mark *56:* 170, 173; *101:* 154, 155, 157; *149:* 176; *160:* 194
Pogany, Willy *15:* 46, 49; *19:* 222, 256; *25:* 214; *44:* 142, 143, 144, 145, 146, 147, 148
Pohrt, Tom *67:* 116; *104:* 80; *152:* 199; *195:* 154; *199:* 85
Poirson, V.A. *26:* 89
Polacco, Patricia *74:* 195, 196, 197, 198; *123:* 121, 122; *180:* 189, 190, 191, 193, 194
Polgreen, John *21:* 44
Polhemus, Coleman *210:* 209
Politi, Leo *1:* 178; *4:* 53; *21:* 48; *47:* 173,174, 176, 178, 179, 180, 181
Pollema-Cahill, Phyllis *123:* 126
Pollen, Samson *64:* 80
Polonsky, Arthur *34:* 168
Polseno, Jo *1:* 53; *3:* 117; *5:* 114; *17:* 154; *20:* 87; *32:* 49; *41:* 245
Pomaska, Anna *117:* 148
Pons, Bernadette *184:* 100
Ponter, James *5:* 204
Poole, Colin *111:* 27
Poortvliet, Rien *6:* 212; *65:* 165, 166, 167
Pope, Kevin *183:* 158
Popp, Wendy *72:* 122; *158:* 68
Poppel, Hans *71:* 154, 155
Porfirio, Guy *76:* 134
Portal, Colette *6:* 186; *11:* 203
Porter, George *7:* 181
Porter, Janice Lee *175:* 37; *164:* 37
Porter, John *113:* 47
Porter, Pat Grant *84:* 112; *125:* 101
Porter, Sue *146:* 246, 247
Porter, Walter *124:* 175
Posada, Mia *187:* 151

Posen, Michael *175:* 82
Posthuma, Sieb *150:* 163
Postier, Jim *202:* 140; *204:* 25
Postma, Lidia *79:* 17
Potter, Beatrix *100:* 194, 195; *132:* 179, 180, 181, 182; *YABC 1:* 208, 209, 210, 212, 213
Potter, Giselle *117:* 123; *143:* 44; *144:* 170, 197; *149:* 7; *150:* 165; *187:* 152, 153; *190:* 198; *196:* 152; *200:* 12
Potter, Katherine *104:* 147; *171:* 135; *173:* 136
Potter, Miriam Clark *3:* 162
Poulin, Stephane *98:* 140, 141
Poullis, Nick *146:* 210
Powell, Constance Buffington *174:* 141
Powell, Gary *151:* 208
Powell, Ivan *67:* 219
Power, Margaret *105:* 122
Powers, Daniel *161:* 173
Powers, Richard M. *1:* 230; *3:* 218; *7:* 194; *26:* 186
Powledge, Fred *37:* 154
Powzyk, Joyce *74:* 214
Poydar, Nancy *96:* 149; *190:* 180, 181, 182
Pracher, Richard *91:* 166
Prachaticka, Marketa *126:* 126
Prange, Beckie *181:* 169
Prap, Lila *177:* 165
Prater, John *103:* 142, 143, 144; *149:* 172
Pratt, Charles *23:* 29
Pratt, George *116:* 208
Pratt, Pierre *150:* 73; *166:* 183; *168:* 172; *201:* 27; *208:* 171, 172, 173
Prebenna, David *73:* 174
Preiss-Glasser, Robin *123:* 176; *152* 40; *172:* 194
Press, Jenny *116:* 95
Preston, Mark *152:* 162
Pretro, Korinna *91:* 126
Prevost, Mikela *209:* 111
Price, Christine *2:* 247; *3:* 163, 253; *8:* 166
Price, Cynthia *118:* 156
Price, Edward *33:* 34
Price, Garrett *1:* 76; *2:* 42
Price, Hattie Longstreet *17:* 13
Price, Norman *YABC 1:* 129
Price, Willard *48:* 184
Priceman, Marjorie *81:* 171; *136:* 169; *156:* 200; *168:* 153, 154; *188:* 45
Priestley, Alice *168:* 33
Priestley, Chris *198:* 144
Primavera, Elise *26:* 95; *58:* 151; *73:* 37; *80:* 79; *86:* 156; *105:* 161
Primrose, Jean *36:* 109
Prince, Alison *86:* 188, 189
Prince, Leonora E. *7:* 170
Pritchett, Shelley *116:* 148
Prittie, Edwin J. *YABC 1:* 120
Proimos, James *176:* 4
Proimos, John *173:* 144
Prosmitsky, Jenya *132:* 33
Provensen, Alice *37:* 204, 215, 222; *70:* 176, 177, 178, 180, 71: 213; *147:* 184; *191:* 190
Provensen, Martin *37:* 204, 215, 222; *70:* 176, 177, 178, 180; *71:* 213; *191:* 190
Pucci, Albert John *44:* 154
Pudlo *8:* 59
Puggaard, Ulla *196:* 25
Pullen, Zachary *211:* 161
Pulver, Harry, Jr. *129:* 159
Pulver, Robin *160:* 4
Punchatz, Don *99:* 57
Purdy, Susan *8:* 162
Pursell, Weimer *55:* 18
Purtscher, Alfons *97:* 6
Puskas, James *5:* 141
Pyk, Jan *7:* 26; *38:* 123
Pyle, Chuck *99:* 149; *191:* 83
Pyle, Howard *16:* 225, 226, 227, 228, 230, 231, 232, 235; *24:* 27; *34:* 124, 125, 127, 128; *59:* 132; *100:* 198

Q

Quackenbush, Robert *4:* 190; *6:* 166; *7:* 175, 178; *9:* 86; *11:* 65, 221; *41:* 154; *43:* 157; *70:* 185, 186; *71:* 137; *85:* 47; *92:* 148; *133:* 154, 164, 169
Qualls, Sean *177:* 167, 168; *193:* 43
Quennell, Marjorie (Courtney) *29:* 163, 164
Quidor, John *19:* 82
Quirk, John *62:* 170
Quirk, Thomas *12:* 81

R

Rackham, Arthur *15:* 32, 78, 214-227; *17:* 105, 115; *18:* 233; *19:* 254; *20:* 151; *22:* 129, 131, 132, 133; *23:* 175; *24:* 161, 181; *26:* 91; *32:* 118; *64:* 18; *100:* 9, 16, 203, 204; *YABC 1:* 25, 45, 55, 147; *2:* 103, 142, 173, 210
Racz, Michael *56:* 134
Raczka, Bob *191:* 155, 156
Radcliffe, Andrew *82:* 215
Rader, Laura *101:* 219; *197:* 147; *203:* 53
Radunsky, Vladimir *177:* 170; *192:* 30
Rafilson, Sidney *11:* 172
Raglin, Tim *125:* 24
Raible, Alton *1:* 202, 203; *28:* 193; *35:* 181; *110:* 207
Raine, Patricia *82:* 74; *88:* 154
Ramá, Sue *173:* 45; *185:* 186; *190:* 184
Ramhorst, John *117:* 11
Ramirez, Gladys *177:* 19
Ramirez, Jose *207:* 27
Ramsey, James *16:* 41
Ramsey, Marcy Dunn *82:* 11; *180:* 186
Ramus, Michael *51:* 171
Rand, Paul *6:* 188
Rand, Ted *67:* 9, 10, 121, 123; *74:* 190; *84:* 170; *103:* 170; *112:* 6; *114:* 73; *139:* 168; *143:* 194; *156:* 154; *161:* 9, 10; *200:* 38; *204:* 7
Randazzo, Tony *81:* 98
Randell, William *55:* 54
Rane, Walter *93:* 144; *143:* 109; *184:* 126
Rankin, Joan *163:* 40
Rankin, Laura *176:* 173, 174; *179:* 150
Ransome, Arthur *22:* 201
Ransome, James E. *74:* 137; *75:* 80; *84:* 181; *94:* 108; *117:* 115; *123:* 128, 129, 130; *158:* 101, 102; *159:* 205; *178:* 188, 189, 190
Rantz, Don *119:* 184
Rao, Anthony *28:* 126
Raphael, Elaine *23:* 192; *71:* 24, 25
Rappaport, Eva *6:* 190
Raschka, Chris *80:* 187, 189, 190; *97:* 211; *115:* 210; *117:* 151, 152, 153, 154; *143:* 195; *145:* 153; *166:* 190, 191; *170:* 114; *207:* 140, 143, 144, 145; *208:* 82
Rash, Andy *158:* 178; *162:* 172; *210:* 204
Raskin, Ellen *2:* 208, 209; *4:* 142; *13:* 183; *22:* 68; *29:* 139; *36:* 134; *38:* 173, 174, 175, 176, 177, 178,179, 180, 181; *60:* 163; *86:* 81
Rathmann, Peggy *93:* 32; *94:* 168; *157:* 212, 214
Ratkus, Tony *77:* 133
Ratzkin, Lawrence *40:* 143
Rau, Margaret *9:* 157
Raverat, Gwen *YABC 1:* 152
Ravid, Joyce *61:* 73
Ravielli, Anthony *1:* 198; *3:* 168; *11:* 143
Ravilious, Robin *77:* 169
Rawlins, Donna *72:* 198; *73:* 15, 129
Rawlins, Janet *76:* 79
Rawlings, Steve *143:* 139; *151:* 54; *208:* 150
Rawlinson, Debbie *75:* 132

Ray, Deborah Kogan *8:* 164; *29:* 238; *50:* 112, 113; *62:* 119; *78:* 191; *203:* 149, 150, 151
Ray, Jane *96:* 166; *97:* 104; *152:* 208; *190:* 221; *196:* 165
Ray, Ralph *2:* 239; *5:* 73
Rayann, Omar *162:* 205; *186:* 29, 30
Rayevsky, Robert *64:* 17; *70:* 173; *80:* 204; *117:* 79; *190:* 187, 188
Raymond, Larry *31:* 108; *97:* 109
Rayner, Hugh *151:* 170
Rayner, Mary *22:* 207; *47:* 140; *72:* 191; *87:* 171, 172; *192:* 104
Rayner, Shoo
  See Rayner, Hugh
Raynes, John *71:* 19
Raynor, Dorka *28:* 168
Raynor, Paul *24:* 73
Rayyan, Omar *110:* 222; *112:* 17; *125:* 131
Razzi, James *10:* 127
Read, Alexander D. *20:* 45
Reader, Dennis *71:* 157
Reasoner, Charles *53:* 33, 36, 37
Rebenschied, Shane *203:* 76
Reczuch, Karen *115:* 132; *145:* 131
Redlich, Ben *163:* 221; *198:* 193
Reddy, Mike *203:* 67
Reed, Joseph *116:* 139
Reed, Lynn Rowe *115:* 173; *171:* 146; *208:* 177
Reed, Mike *211:* 147
Reed, Tom *34:* 171
Reeder, Colin *74:* 202; *77:* 113
Rees, Mary *134:* 219
Reese, Bob *60:* 135
Reeve, Philip *171:* 50
Reeves, Eira B. *130:* 173, 174; *141:* 151
Reeves, Rick *181:* 179
Reeves, Rosie *202:* 200
Regan, Dana *117:* 116
Regan, Laura *103:* 198; *153:* 206
Reichert, Renée *169:* 127
Reid, Barbara *82:* 178; *92:* 17; *93:* 169, 170
Reid, Stephen *19:* 213; *22:* 89
Reim, Melanie *104:* 151; *150:* 98
Reinert, Kirk *89:* 138; *195:* 129
Reinertson, Barbara *44:* 150; *62:* 103
Reiniger, Lotte *40:* 185
Reisberg, Mira *119:* 2
Reisch, Jesse *158:* 130
Reiser, Lynn *81:* 175; *138:* 184; *180:* 200
Reiss, John J. *23:* 193
Relf, Douglas *3:* 63
Relyea, C.M. *16:* 29; *31:* 153
Remi, Georges *13:* 184
Remington, Frederic *19:* 188; *41:* 178, 179, 180, 181, 183,184, 185, 186, 187, 188; *62:* 197
Remkiewicz, Frank *67:* 102; *77:* 171; *80:* 130; *113:* 107; *152:* 116; *152:* 211, 212; *157:* 148
Rendon, Maria *116:* 141; *192:* 134; *134:* 152
Renfro, Ed *79:* 176
Renier, Aaron *202:* 141; *207:* 119
Renlie, Frank *11:* 200
Reschofsky, Jean *7:* 118
Rethi *60:* 181
Rethi, Lili *2:* 153; *36:* 156
Reusswig, William *3:* 267
Revell, Cindy *195:* 93
Rex, Adam *156:* 172; *169:* 91; *186:* 178, 179
Rex, Michael *157:* 147; *191:* 159, 160
Rey, H.A. *1:* 182; *26:* 163, 164, 166, 167, 169; *69:* 172, 173, 174, 175; *86:* 195, 196, 197; *100:* 211; *YABC 2:* 17
Rey, Luis V. *201:* 162
Reynolds, Adrian *192:* 159, 160
Reynolds, Doris *5:* 71; *31:* 77
Reynolds, Peter H. *142:* 12; *179:* 175, 176; *202:* 113, 114
Rhead, Louis *31:* 91; *100:* 228
Rhodes, Andrew *38:* 204; *50:* 163; *54:* 76; *61:* 123, 124; *87:* 200

Ribbons, Ian *3:* 10; *37:* 161; *40:* 76
Ricci, Regolo *93:* 22; *164:* 148
Rice, Elizabeth *2:* 53, 214
Rice, Eve *34:* 174, 175; *91:* 172
Rice, James *22:* 210; *93:* 173
Rich, Martha *195:* 16
Richards, Chuck *170:* 154
Richards, George *40:* 116, 119, 121; *44:* 179
Richards, Henry *YABC 1:* 228, 231
Richardson, Ernest *2:* 144
Richardson, Frederick *18:* 27, 31
Richardson, John *110:* 88
Richman, Hilda *26:* 132
Richmond, George *24:* 179
Riddell, Chris *114:* 170, 195; *166:* 179; *199:* 164, 166, 167
Riddle, Tohby *74:* 204; *151:* 179
Riding, Peter *63:* 195
Rieniets, Judy King *14:* 28
Riger, Bob *2:* 166
Riggio, Anita *73:* 191; *85:* 63; *137:* 184; *172:* 165
Riley, Jon *74:* 70
Riley, Kenneth *22:* 230
Riley, Terry *203:* 100
Riley-Webb, Charlotte *153:* 143
Rinaldi, Angelo *165:* 60, 69
Ringgold, Faith *71:* 162; *114:* 173, 174, 176; *187:* 160, 161, 163
Ringi, Kjell *12:* 171
Rios, Tere
  See Versace, Marie
Ripper, Charles L. *3:* 175
Ripplinger, Henry *117:* 31
Ritchie, William *74:* 183
Ritter, John *175:* 14
Ritz, Karen *41:* 117; *72:* 239; *87:* 125; *102:* 7; *106:* 6
Rivas, Victor *209:* 193
Rivers, Ruth *178:* 193
Rivkin, Jay *15:* 230
Rivoche, Paul *45:* 125
Roach, Marilynne *9:* 158
Robbin, Jodi *44:* 156, 159
Robbins, Frank *42:* 167
Robbins, Ken *147:* 191, 192
Robbins, Ruth *52:* 102
Roberts, Cliff *4:* 126
Roberts, David *154:* 4, 6; *191:* 162; *196:* 184; *197:* 105; *210:* 257
Roberts, Doreen *4:* 230; *28:* 105
Roberts, Jim *22:* 166; *23:* 69; *31:* 110
Roberts, Tony *109:* 195, 214
Roberts, W. *22:* 2, 3
Robertson, M.P. *197:* 153
Robins, Arthur *137:* 172; *151:* 225; *204:* 161
Robinson, Aminah Brenda Lynn *86:* 205; *103:* 55; *159:* 175
Robinson, Charles [1870-1937] *17:* 157, 171, 172, 173, 175, 176; *24:* 207; *25:* 204; *YABC 2:* 308, 309, 310, 331
Robinson, Charles *3:* 53; *5:* 14; *6:* 193; *7:* 150; *7:* 183; *8:* 38; *9:* 81; *13:* 188; *14:* 248, 249; *23:* 149; *26:* 115; *27:* 48; *28:* 191; *32:* 28; *35:* 210; *36:* 37; *48:* 96; *52:* 33; *53:* 157; *56:* 15; *62:* 142; *77:* 41; *111:* 148
Robinson, Jerry *3:* 262
Robinson, Joan G. *7:* 184
Robinson, Lolly *90:* 227
Robinson, T.H. *17:* 179, 181, 182, 183; *29:* 254
Robinson, W. Heath *17:* 185, 187, 189, 191, 193, 195, 197, 199, 202; *23:* 167; *25:* 194; *29:* 150; *YABC 1:* 44; *2:* 183
Rocco, John *187:* 4; *188:* 151; *208:* 180, 181, 182
Roche, Christine *41:* 98
Roche, Denis *99:* 184; *180:* 32; *196:* 168
Roche, P.K. *57:* 151, 152
Rocker, Fermin *7:* 34; *13:* 21; *31:* 40; *40:* 190,191

Rocklen, Margot *101:* 181
Rockwell, Anne *5:* 147; *33:* 171, 173; *71:* 166, 167,168; *114:* 183, 184; *194:* 152, 155
Rockwell, Gail *7:* 186
Rockwell, Harlow *33:* 171, 173, 175
Rockwell, Lizzy *114:* 182; *162:* 182; *185:* 189
Rockwell, Norman *23:* 39, 196, 197, 199, 200, 203, 204, 207; *41:* 140, 143; *123:* 47; *YABC 2:* 60
Rockwood, Richard *119:* 75
Rodanas, Kristina *156:* 183, 184
Rodegast, Roland *43:* 100
Rodgers, Frank *69:* 177
Rodriguez, Albert G. *182:* 50
Rodriguez, Christina *184:* 12
Rodriguez, Edel *204:* 86
Rodriguez, Joel *16:* 65
Rodriguez, Robert *145:* 145
Rodriguez-Howard, Pauline *177:* 18
Roe, Monika *210:* 94
Roeckelein, Katrina *134:* 223
Roennfeldt, Robert *66:* 243
Roever, J.M. *4:* 119; *26:* 170
Roffey, Maureen *33:* 142, 176, 177
Rogasky, Barbara *46:* 90
Rogé *173:* 160
Rogers, Carol *2:* 262; *6:* 164; *26:* 129
Rogers, Chris M. *150:* 59; *196:* 61
Rogers, Forest *87:* 160; *101:* 76
Rogers, Frances *10:* 130
Rogers, Gregory *104:* 76; *126:* 57; *171:* 26
Rogers, Jacqueline *78:* 249; *80:* 34; *86:* 54
103: 70; *115:* 72; *129:* 173; *131:* 57, 225; *143:* 211; *153:* 100; *193:* 186; *203:* 51
Rogers, Sherry *191:* 66
Rogers, Walter S. *31:* 135, 138; *67:* 65, 168; *100:* 81
Rogers, William A. *15:* 151, 153, 154; *33:* 35
Rogoff, Barbara *95:* 20
Rohmann, Eric *103:* 152; *198:* 151
Rojankovsky, Feodor *6:* 134, 136; *10:* 183; *21:* 128,129, 130; *25:* 110; *28:* 42; *68:* 120
Rolfsen, Alf *62:* 15
Rolston, Steve *209:* 154
Romain, Trevor *134:* 157
Roman, Barbara J. *103:* 171
Romas *114:* 111; *165:* 63
Romano, Robert *64:* 68
Romero, Alejandro *187:* 185
Roos, Maryn *168:* 198
Root, Barry *80:* 212; *90:* 196; *146:* 78; *156:* 165; *159:* 161; *182:* 18, 172
Root, Kimberly Bulcken *86:* 72; *98:* 21; *108:* 111; *127:* 114; *159:* 162; *176:* 134; *192:* 163
Roper, Bob *65:* 153
Roraback, Robin *111:* 156
Rorer, Abigail *43:* 222; *85:* 155
Rosales, Melodye *80:* 35
Rosamilia, Patricia *36:* 120
Rose, Carl *5:* 62
Rose, David S. *29:* 109; *70:* 120
Rose, Gerald *68:* 200, 201; *86:* 48
Rose, Ted *93:* 178
Rosen, Elizabeth *205:* 137
Rosenbaum, Jonathan *50:* 46
Rosenberg, Amye *74:* 207, 208
Rosenberry, Vera *87:* 22, 26; *144:* 212, 213; *158:* 120
Rosenblum, Richard *11:* 202; *18:* 18
Rosenstiehl, Agnès *203:* 153
Rosier, Lydia *16:* 236; *20:* 104; *21:* 109; *22:* 125; *30:* 151, 158; *42:* 128; *45:* 214; *77:* 227, 228
Rosing, Jens *85:* 142
Ross
See Thomson, Ross
Ross, Christine *83:* 172, 173
Ross, Clare Romano *3:* 123; *21:* 45; *48:* 199
Ross, Dave *32:* 152; *57:* 108
Ross, Graham *199:* 4
Ross, Herbert *37:* 78

Ross, John *3:* 123; *21:* 45
Ross, Johnny *32:* 190
Ross, Larry *47:* 168; *60:* 62
Ross, Ruth *109:* 233
Ross, Tony *17:* 204; *56:* 132; *65:* 176, 177, 179; *90:* 123; *123:* 186, 187, 190; *130:* 188, 190, 191, 192; *132:* 242; *174:* 159; *176:* 181, 182, 183; *202:* 198
Rossetti, Dante Gabriel *20:* 151, 153
Rostant, Larry *180:* 221; *194:* 108; *195:* 96; *197:* 12; *207:* 53; *210:* 189
Roth, Arnold *4:* 238; *21:* 133
Roth, Julie Jersild *180:* 206
Roth, Marci *135:* 223
Roth, R.G. *184:* 50
Roth, Rob *105:* 98; *146:* 41
Roth, Robert *176:* 159
Roth, Roger *61:* 128; *190:* 192
Roth, Stephanie *136:* 171, 172
Roth, Susan L. *80:* 38; *93:* 78; *134:* 165, 166; *181:* 145, 146
Rothenberg, Joani Keller *162:* 190, 191
Rothman, Michael *139:* 62; *184:* 34 Rotman, Jeffrey L. *145:* 30
Rotondo, Pat *32:* 158
Roughsey, Dick *35:* 186
Rouille, M. *11:* 96
Rounds, Glen *8:* 173; *9:* 171; *12:* 56; *32:* 194; *40:* 230; *51:* 161, 162, 166; *56:* 149; *70:* 198, 199; *YABC 1:* 1, 2, 3; *112:* 163
Roundtree, Katherine *114:* 88; *168:* 102
Rovetch, Lissa *201:* 164
Rowan, Evadne *52:* 51
Rowe, Eric *111:* 161
Rowe, Gavin *27:* 144; *72:* 47; *88:* 201
Rowe, John *132:* 70, 71; *180:* 126
Rowell, Kenneth *40:* 72
Rowen, Amy *52:* 143
Rowena *116:* 101
Rowland, Andrew *164:* 136
Rowland, Jada *83:* 73
Rowles, Daphne *58:* 24
Roy, Jeroo *27:* 229; *36:* 110
Royo *118:* 32; *144:* 105, 106, 108; *165:* 19; *166:* 166
Rubel, Nicole *18:* 255; *20:* 59; *81:* 66, 67; *95:* 169, 170; *119:* 60; *135:* 177, 179, 180; *169:* 68; *181:* 150
Rubel, Reina *33:* 217
Rud, Borghild *6:* 15
Ruddell, Gary *110:* 238; *116:* 207
Rudolph, Norman Guthrie *17:* 13
Rue, Leonard Lee III *37:* 164
Rueda, Claudia *183:* 170, 171
Ruelle, Karen Gray *126:* 193
Ruff, Donna *50:* 173; *72:* 203; *78:* 49; *80:* 120,121; *93:* 162; *164:* 121
Ruffins, Reynold *10:* 134, 135; *41:* 191, 192, 193, 194, 195, 196; *125:* 187, 188, 189; *162:* 197
Ruhlin, Roger *34:* 44
Ruiz, Art *95:* 154; *110:* 91
Rumford, James *193:* 167
Runnerstroem, Bengt Arne *75:* 161
Ruse, Margaret *24:* 155
Rush, Ken *98:* 74
Rush, Peter *42:* 75
Russell, Charles M. *167:* 171
Russell, E.B. *18:* 177, 182
Russell, Jim *53:* 134
Russell, P. Craig *80:* 196; *146:* 102; *162:* 186
Russo, Marisabina *84:* 51; *106:* 164; *151:* 183; *188:* 153, 154, 155, 156
Russo, Susan *30:* 182; *36:* 144
Russon, Mary *87:* 145
Ruth, Greg *183:* 125
Ruth, Rod *9:* 161
Rutherford, Alexa *110:* 108
Rutherford, Jenny *78:* 5
Rutherford, Meg *25:* 174; *34:* 178, 179; *69:* 73; *72:* 31

Rutland, Jonathan *31:* 126
Ruurs, Margriet *147:* 195
Ruzzier, Sergio *159:* 176, 177; *163:* 184; *210:* 214, 216
Ryan, Amy *188:* 50
Ryan, Will *86:* 134
Ryden, Hope *8:* 176
Rylant, Cynthia *112:* 170, 172
Rymer, Alta M. *34:* 181
Ryniak, Christopher *178:* 11
Rystedt, Rex *49:* 80

S

Saaf, Chuck *49:* 179
Saaf, Donald *101:* 220; *124:* 180
Sabaka, Donna R. *21:* 172
Sabin, Robert *45:* 35; *60:* 30; *99:* 161
Sabuda, Robert *170:* 166, 167, 168
Sacker, Amy *16:* 100
Saelig, S.M. *129:* 73; *173:* 59
Saffioti, Lino *36:* 176; *48:* 60
Saflund, Birgitta *94:* 2
Sagsoorian, Paul *12:* 183; *22:* 154; *33:* 106; *87:* 152
Sahara, Tony *168:* 106; *177:* 181; *178:* 228; *186:* 132; *207:* 89
Sahlberg, Myron *57:* 165
Saidens, Amy *145:* 162; *191:* 131; *210:* 129
Saint Exupery, Antoine de *20:* 157
Saint James, Synthia *152:* 220; *188:* 90; *200:* 7
Saldutti, Denise *39:* 186; *57:* 178
Sale, Morton *YABC 2:* 31
Sale, Tim *153:* 177
Salerno, Steven *150:* 79; *176:* 188; *202:* 39
Salter, George *72:* 128, 130
Saltzberg, Barney *135:* 184, 185; *194:* 160
Saltzman, David *86:* 209
Salwowski, Mark *71:* 54
Salzman, Yuri *86:* 12
Sambourne, Linley *YABC 2:* 181
Sampson, Katherine *9:* 197
Samson, Anne S. *2:* 216
San Souci, Daniel *40:* 200; *96:* 199, 200; *113:* 171; *157:* 149; *170:* 69; *192:* 167, 168
Sancha, Sheila *38:* 185
Sanchez, Enrique O. *155:* 84
Sand, George X. *45:* 182
Sandberg, Lasse *15:* 239, 241
Sanders, Beryl *39:* 173
Sanderson, Ruth *21:* 126; *24:* 53; *28:* 63; *33:* 67; *41:* 48, 198, 199, 200, 201, 202, 203; *43:* 79; *46:* 36,44; *47:* 102; *49:* 58; *62:* 121, 122; *85:* 3; *109:* 207, 208, 209, 210; *172:* 157, 158
Sandia *119:* 74
Sandin, Joan *4:* 36; *6:* 194; *7:* 177; *12:* 145,185; *20:* 43; *21:* 74; *26:* 144; *27:* 142; *28:* 224, 225; *38:* 86; *41:* 46; *42:* 35; *59:* 6; *80:* 136; *94:* 188; *140:* 116; *153:* 179, 180; *197:* 168
Sandland, Reg *39:* 215
Sandoz, Edouard *26:* 45, 47
Sanford, John *66:* 96, 97
Sanger, Amy Wilson *205:* 140
Sankey, Tom *72:* 103
Sano, Kazuhiko *153:* 208; *195:* 171; *203:* 21
Santat, Dan *188:* 160
Santiago, Wilfred *210:* 48
Santore, Charles *54:* 139; *200:* 171, 172
Santoro, Christopher *74:* 215
Santos, Jesse J. *99:* 24
Sapieha, Christine *1:* 180
Saport, Linda *123:* 137, 138
Sara
See De La Roche Saint Andre, Anne
Sardinha, Rick *175:* 151
Sarg, Tony *YABC 2:* 236

Sargent, Claudia *64:* 181
Sargent, Robert *2:* 217
Saris *1:* 33
Sarony *YABC 2:* 170
Saroff, Phyllis V. *202:* 160
Sasaki, Goro *170:* 46
Sasek, Miroslav *16:* 239, 240, 241, 242
Sassman, David *9:* 79
Satty *29:* 203, 205
Sauber, Robert *40:* 183; *76:* 256; *78:* 154; *87:* 92
Saunders, Dave *85:* 163, 164, 165
Savadier, Elivia *84:* 50; *145:* 45; *164:* 206
Savage, Naomi *56:* 172
Savage, Steele *10:* 203; *20:* 77; *35:* 28
Savage, Stephen *174:* 182
Savio *76:* 4
Savitt, Sam *8:* 66, 182; *15:* 278; *20:* 96; *24:* 192; *28:* 98
Sawyer, Kem Knapp *84:* 228, 229
Say, Allen *28:* 178; *69:* 182, 183, 232; *110:* 194, 195,196; *161:* 154, 155
Sayles, Elizabeth *82:* 93; *105:* 155; *109:* 116; *180:* 64
Scabrini, Janet *13:* 191; *44:* 128
Scanlan, Peter *83:* 27; *153:* 165; *187:* 149
Scanlon, Paul *83:* 87
Scannell, Reece *105:* 105
Scarry, Huck *35:* 204, 205
Scarry, Richard *2:* 220, 221; *18:* 20; *35:* 193, 194, 195,196, 197, 198, 199, 200, 201, 202; *75:* 165, 167, 168
Schachner, Judith Byron *88:* 180; *92:* 163; *93:* 102; *142:* 82; *178:* 199, 200; *190:* 140
Schade, Susan *205:* 21
Schaeffer, Mead *18:* 81, 94; *21:* 137, 138, 139; *47:* 128
Schaffer, Amanda *90:* 206
Schanzer, Rosalyn *138:* 192, 193
Scharl, Josef *20:* 132; *22:* 128
Scheel, Lita *11:* 230
Scheffler, Axel *180:* 23, 24
Scheib, Ida *29:* 28
Schermer, Judith *30:* 184
Schick, Eleanor *82:* 210, 211; *144:* 222
Schick, Joel *16:* 160; *17:* 167; *22:* 12; *27:* 176; *31:* 147, 148; *36:* 23; *38:* 64; *45:* 116, 117; *52:* 5, 85; *104:* 159
Schields, Gretchen *75:* 171, 203
Schindelman, Joseph *1:* 74; *4:* 101; *12:* 49; *26:* 51; *40:* 146; *56:* 158; *73:* 40
Schindler, Edith *7:* 22
Schindler, S.D. *38:* 107; *46:* 196; *74:* 162; *75:* 172, 173; *99:* 133; *112:* 177; *118:* 185, 186; *121:* 71; *136:* 159; *143:* 45; *149:* 120; *156:* 30; *169:* 135; *171:* 161, 162, 163; *172:* 9; *186:* 163; *194:* 109; *195:* 35; *198:* 170, 171, 172
Schlesinger, Bret *7:* 77
Schmid, Eleanore *12:* 188; *126:* 196, 197
Schmiderer, Dorothy *19:* 224
Schmidt, Bill *73:* 34; *76:* 220, 222, 224
Schmidt, Elizabeth *15:* 242
Schmidt, George Paul *132:* 122
Schmidt, Karen Lee *54:* 12; *71:* 174; *92:* 56; *94:* 190, 191; *127:* 103
Schmidt, Lynette *76:* 205
Schmitz, Tamara *207:* 147
Schneider, Christine M. *171:* 165
Schneider, Howie *181:* 159
Schneider, Rex *29:* 64; *44:* 171
Schnurr, Edward *170:* 62
Schoberle, Cecile *80:* 200; *92:* 134
Schoenherr, Ian *32:* 83; *173:* 41
Schoenherr, John *1:* 146, 147, 173; *3:* 39, 139; *17:* 75; *29:* 72; *32:* 83; *37:* 168, 169, 170; *43:* 164, 165; *45:* 160, 162; *51:* 127; *66:* 196, 197, 198; *68:* 83; *72:* 240; *75:* 225; *88:* 176
Scholder, Fritz *69:* 103
Schomburg, Alex *13:* 23

Schongut, Emanuel *4:* 102; *15:* 186; *47:* 218, 219; *52:* 147, 148, 149, 150; *185:* 27
Schoonover, Frank *17:* 107; *19:* 81, 190, 233; *22:* 88,129; *24:* 189; *31:* 88; *41:* 69; *YABC 2:* 282, 316
Schories, Pat *164:* 210
Schottland, Miriam *22:* 172
Schramm, Ulrik *2:* 16; *14:* 112
Schreiber, Elizabeth Anne *13:* 193
Schreiber, Ralph W. *13:* 193
Schreiter, Rick *14:* 97; *23:* 171; *41:* 247; *49:* 131
Schroeder, Binette *56:* 128, 129
Schroeder, E. Peter *12:* 112
Schroeder, Ted *11:* 160; *15:* 189; *30:* 91; *34:* 43
Schrotter, Gustav *22:* 212; *30:* 225
Schubert, Dieter *101:* 167, 168
Schubert-Gabrys, Ingrid *101:* 167, 168
Schucker, James *31:* 163
Schuett, Stacey *72:* 137; *208:* 204
Schulder, Lili *146:* 29
Schulke, Debra *57:* 167
Schulke, Flip *57:* 167
Schulz, Barbara *167:* 24
Schulz, Charles M. *10:* 137, 138, 139, 140, 141, 142; *118:* 192, 193, 194, 196, 199
Schutzer, Dena *109:* 32
Schwark, Mary Beth *51:* 155; *72:* 175
Schwartz, Amy *47:* 191; *82:* 100; *83:* 178, 179, 180,181; *129:* 107; *131:* 197, 198; *189:* 166, 168
Schwartz, Carol *124:* 41; *130:* 199
Schwartz, Charles *8:* 184
Schwartz, Daniel *46:* 37
Schwartz, Joanie *124:* 170
Schwartzberg, Joan *3:* 208
Schwarz, Viviane *204:* 132
Schweitzer, Iris *2:* 137; *6:* 207
Schweninger, Ann *29:* 172; *82:* 246; *159:* 202; *168:* 166; *211:* 193
Schwinger, Laurence *84:* 44; *91:* 61
Scofield, Penrod *61:* 107; *62:* 160
Scott, Anita Walker *7:* 38
Scott, Art *39:* 41
Scott, Frances Gruse *38:* 43
Scott, Julian *34:* 126
Scott, Roszel *33:* 238
Scott, Sally *87:* 27
Scott, Steve *166:* 230, 231; *171:* 93
Scott, Trudy *27:* 172
Scrace, Carolyn *143:* 95, 96
Scrambly, Crab *198:* 196
Scribner, Joanne *14:* 236; *29:* 78; *33:* 185; *34:* 208; *78:* 75; *164:* 237; *203:* 73
Scrofani, Joseph *31:* 163; *74:* 225
Scroggs, Kirk *187:* 169
Seaman, Mary Lott *34:* 64
Searle, Ronald *24:* 98; *42:* 172, 173, 174, 176, 177, 179; *66:* 73, 74; *70:* 205, 206, 207
Searle, Townley *36:* 85
Sebree, Charles *18:* 65
Sedacca, Joseph M. *11:* 25; *22:* 36
Seder, Jason *108:* 102
Seeger, Laura Vaccaro *172:* 162
Seegmiller, Don *174:* 57
Seely, David *164:* 173
Seeley, Laura L. *97:* 105
Segal, John *178:* 202
Segar, E.C. *61:* 179, 181
Segur, Adrienne *27:* 121
Seibold, J. Otto *83:* 188, 190, 191; *149:* 212, 214, 215, 216; *196:* 177, 179
Seignobosc, Francoise *21:* 145, 146
Sejima, Yoshimasa *8:* 187
Selig, Sylvie *13:* 199
Seltzer, Isadore *6:* 18; *133:* 59
Seltzer, Meyer *17:* 214
Selven, Maniam *144:* 133
Selway, Martina *169:* 157

Selznick, Brian *79:* 192; *104:* 25; *117:* 175; *126:* 156; *134:* 171; *158:* 76, 78; *169:* 70; *171:* 172, 173; *191:* 106; *192:* 130; *197:* 158; *203:* 35; *205:* 92; *210:* 219, 220, 221, 222
Sempe, Jean-Jacques *47:* 92; *YABC 2:* 109
Sendak, Maurice *1:* 135, 190; *3:* 204; *7:* 142; *15:* 199; *17:* 210; *27:* 181, 182, 183, 185, 186, 187, 189,190, 191, 192, 193, 194, 195, 197, 198, 199, 203; *28:* 181, 182; *32:* 108; *33:* 148, 149; *35:* 238; *44:* 180, 181; *45:* 97, 99; *46:* 174; *73:* 225; *91:* 10, 11 *YABC1:* 167; *113:* 163, 165, 167, 168; *118:* 153; *127:* 161
Senders, Marci *180:* 79
Sengler, Johanna *18:* 256
Senn, Steve *60:* 145
Seredy, Kate *1:* 192; *14:* 20, 21; *17:* 210
Sergeant, John *6:* 74
Servello, Joe *10:* 144; *24:* 139; *40:* 91; *70:* 130, 131; *146:* 159
Seton, Ernest Thompson *18:* 260-269, 271
Seuss, Dr.
  See Geisel, Theodor
Severin, John Powers *7:* 62
Sewall, Marcia *15:* 8; *22:* 170; *37:* 171, 172, 173; *39:* 73; *45:* 209; *62:* 117; *69:* 185, 186; *71:* 212; *90:* 232; *96:* 127; *102:* 101; *107:* 129; *119:* 176, 177, 178, 180
Seward, James *70:* 35
Seward, Prudence *16:* 243
Sewell, Helen *3:* 186; *15:* 308; *33:* 102; *38:* 189, 190, 191, 192
Seymour, Stephen *54:* 21
Sfar, Joann *182:* 183
Shachat, Andrew *82:* 179
Shadbolt, Robert *203:* 68
Shahn, Ben *39:* 178; *46:* 193
Shalansky, Len *38:* 167
Shanks, Anne Zane *10:* 149
Shannon, David *57:* 137; *107:* 184; *112:* 216; *135:* 12; *152:* 223, 224, 225; *158:* 192
Sharp, Paul *52:* 60
Sharp, William *6:* 131; *19:* 241; *20:* 112; *25:* 141
Sharratt, Nick *102:* 207, 208; *104:* 163; *153:* 198; *175:* 176; *192:* 208; *199:* 141, 142, 143, 184, 187, 188
Shaw, Barclay *74:* 14, 16; *118:* 138
Shaw, Charles *21:* 135; *38:* 187; *47:* 124; *126:* 219
Shaw, Charles G. *13:* 200
Shaw-Smith, Emma *144:* 117
Shea, Edmund *56:* 19
Shearer, Ted *43:* 193, 194, 195, 196
Sheban, Chris *182:* 185; *190:* 102, 104; *202:* 28; *204:* 112, 114; *209:* 150; *210:* 107
Shecter, Ben *16:* 244; *25:* 109; *33:* 188, 191; *41:* 77
Shed, Greg *74:* 94; *84:* 204; *129:* 149, 167: 91; *179:* 192
Sheeban, Chris *144:* 190; *158:* 163
Shefcik, James *48:* 221, 222; *60:* 141
Shefelman, Karl *58:* 168
Shefelman, Tom *204:* 137
Shefts, Joelle *48:* 210
Shein, Bob *139:* 189
Sheinkin, Stephen *204:* 139
Shekerjian, Haig *16:* 245
Shekerjian, Regina *16:* 245; *25:* 73
Sheldon, David *184:* 174; *185:* 204; *211:* 189
Shelley, John *186:* 223
Shemie, Bonnie *96:* 207
Shenton, Edward *45:* 187, 188, 189; *YABC 1:* 218, 219, 221
Shepard, Ernest H. *3:* 193; *4:* 74; *16:* 101; *17:* 109; *25:* 148; *33:* 152, 199, 200, 201, 202, 203, 204, 205, 206,207; *46:* 194; *98:* 114; *100:* 111, 178, 179, 217, 219, 220,221; *YABC 1:* 148, 153, 174, 176, 180, 181

Shepard, Mary *4:* 210; *22:* 205; *30:* 132, 133; *54:* 150, 152, 153, 157, 158; *59:* 108, 109, 111; *100:* 246
Shepherd, Amanda *198:* 14
Shepherd, Irana *171:* 112
Sheppard, Kate *195:* 176
Shepperson, Rob *96:* 153; *177:* 163; *178:* 204; *197:* 34; *205:* 108
Sheridan, Brian *196:* 193
Sherman, Theresa *27:* 167
Sherwan, Earl *3:* 196
Shields, Charles *10:* 150; *36:* 63
Shields, Leonard *13:* 83, 85, 87
Shiffman, Lena *139:* 167; *168:* 136
Shigley, Neil K. *66:* 219
Shillabeer, Mary *35:* 74
Shilston, Arthur *49:* 61; *62:* 58
Shimin, Symeon *1:* 93; *2:* 128, 129; *3:* 202; *7:* 85; *11:* 177; *12:* 139; *13:* 202, 203; *27:* 138; *28:* 65; *35:* 129; *36:* 130; *48:* 151; *49:* 59; *56:* 63, 65, 153
Shine, Andrea *104:* 165; *128:* 34
Shinn, Everett *16:* 148; *18:* 229; *21:* 149, 150, 151; *24:* 218
Shinn, Florence Scovel *63:* 133, 135
Shore, Robert *27:* 54; *39:* 192, 193; *YABC 2:* 200
Shortall, Leonard *4:* 144; *8:* 196; *10:* 166; *19:* 227, 228, 229, 230; *25:* 78; *28:* 66, 167; *33:* 127; *52:* 125; *73:* 12, 212
Shortt, T.M. *27:* 36
Shpitalnik, Vladimir *83:* 194
Shropshire, Sandy *170:* 191
Shtainments, Leon *32:* 161
Shulevitz, Uri *3:* 198, 199; *17:* 85; *22:* 204; *27:* 212; *28:* 184; *50:* 190, 191, 192, 193, 194, 195, 196,197, 198, 199, 201; *106:* 181, 182, 183; *165:* 203, 205; *166:* 138
Shulman, Dee *180:* 140
Shupe, Bobbi *139:* 80, 81
Shute, A.B. *67:* 196
Shute, Linda *46:* 59; *74:* 118
Siberell, Anne *29:* 193
Sibley, Don *1:* 39; *12:* 196; *31:* 47
Sibthorp, Fletcher *94:* 111, 112
Sidjakov, Nicolas *18:* 274
Siebel, Fritz *3:* 120; *17:* 145
Siebold, J. Otto *158:* 227
Siegel, Hal *74:* 246
Sieger, Ted *189:* 172
Siegl, Helen *12:* 166; *23:* 216; *34:* 185, 186
Silin-Palmer, Pamela *184:* 102
Sill, John *140:* 194; *141:* 157
Sills, Joyce *5:* 199
Silva, Simon *108:* 122
Silver, Maggie *85:* 210
Silveria, Gordon *96:* 44
Silverstein, Alvin *8:* 189
Silverstein, Shel *33:* 211; *92:* 209, 210
Silverstein, Virginia *8:* 189
Silvey, Joe *135:* 203
Simard, Remy *95:* 156
Simmons, Elly *110:* 2; *127:* 69; *134:* 181
Simon, Eric M. *7:* 82
Simon, Hilda *28:* 189
Simon, Howard *2:* 175; *5:* 132; *19:* 199; *32:* 163, 164, 165
Simont, Marc *2:* 119; *4:* 213; *9:* 168; *13:* 238,240; *14:* 262; *16:* 179; *18:* 221; *26:* 210; *33:* 189, 194; *44:* 132; *58:* 122; *68:* 117; *73:* 204, 205, 206; *74:* 221; *126:* 199, 200; *133:* 195; *164:* 128
Sims, Agnes *54:* 152
Sims, Blanche *44:* 116; *57:* 129; *75:* 179, 180; *77:* 92; *104:* 192; *152:* 117; *156:* 160; *160:* 70; *168:* 174, 175; *198:* 17
Singer, Edith G. *2:* 30
Singer, Gloria *34:* 56; *36:* 43
Singer, Julia *28:* 190
Singh, Jen *178:* 146
Siomades, Lorianne *134:* 45; *204:* 48

Simont, Marc *163:* 40
Siracusa, Catherine *68:* 135; *82:* 218
Sís, Peter *67:* 179, 181, 183, 184, 185; *96:* 96, 98; *106:* 193, 194, 195; *149:* 224, 226; *180:* 177; *192:* 180, 182
Sivard, Robert *26:* 124
Sivertson, Liz *116:* 84
Skardinski, Stanley *23:* 144; *32:* 84; *66:* 122; *84:* 108
Slack, Michael *185:* 108; *189:* 173, 174
Slackman, Charles B. *12:* 201
Slade, Christian *193:* 187; *204:* 134
Slade, Paul *61:* 170
Slark, Albert *99:* 212; *205:* 161
Slater, Rod *25:* 167
Slavin, Bill *182:* 14, 15; *196:* 90; *199:* 148, 149, 150
Sloan, Joseph *16:* 68
Sloane, Eric *21:* 3; *52:* 153, 154, 155, 156, 157, 158, 160
Sloat, Teri *164:* 231
Slobodkin, Louis *1:* 200; *3:* 232; *5:* 168; *13:* 251; *15:* 13, 88; *26:* 173, 174, 175, 176, 178, 179; *60:* 180
Slobodkina, Esphyr *1:* 201
Slonim, David *166:* 167, 168
Slonim, David *166:* 167, 168
Small, David *50:* 204, 205; *79:* 44; *95:* 189, 190, 191; *126:* 203, 204; *136:* 119; *143:* 201, 202, 203; *144:* 246; *150:* 5; *161:* 176; *183:* 181, 182, 183, 184; *200:* 211
Small, W. *33:* 113
Smalley, Janet *1:* 154
Smath, Jerry *198:* 179, 180
Smedley, William T. *34:* 129
Smee, David *14:* 78; *62:* 30
Smee, Nicola *167:* 156
Smith, A.G., Jr. *35:* 182
Smith, Ali *204:* 68
Smith, Alvin *1:* 31, 229; *13:* 187; *27:* 216; *28:* 226; *48:* 149; *49:* 60
Smith, Andy *188:* 20; *207:* 151
Smith, Anne *194:* 147
Smith, Anne Warren *41:* 212
Smith, Barry *75:* 183
Smith, Brian *200:* 183
Smith, Carl *36:* 41
Smith, Cat Bowman *146:* 39; *164:* 219; *201:* 55, 184
Smith, Craig *97:* 197; *172:* 175; *206:* 40
Smith, Donald A. *178:* 7
Smith, Doris Susan *41:* 139
Smith, Douglas *189:* 159
Smith, Duane *171:* 152; *208:* 97
Smith, E. Boyd *19:* 70; *22:* 89; *26:* 63; *YABC 1:* 4, 5, 240, 248, 249
Smith, Edward J. *4:* 224
Smith, Elwood H. *157:* 231; *181:* 79; *203:* 160, 161, 162
Smith, Eunice Young *5:* 170
Smith, Gary *113:* 216
Smith, George *102:* 169
Smith, Howard *19:* 196
Smith, J. Gerard *95:* 42
Smith, Jacqueline Bardner *27:* 108; *39:* 197
Smith, Jay J. *61:* 119
Smith, Jeff *93:* 191
Smith, Jessie Willcox *15:* 91; *16:* 95; *18:* 231; *19:* 57, 242; *21:* 29, 156, 157, 158, 159, 160, 161; *34:* 65; *100:* 223; *YABC 1:* 6; *2:* 180, 185, 191, 311, 325
Smith, Jos. A. *52:* 131; *72:* 120; *74:* 151; *84:* 147, 148; *85:* 146; *87:* 96; *94:* 219; *96:* 97; *104:* 33; *108:* 126, 127, 128; *111:* 140; *136:* 145; *181:* 173; *200:* 213; *201:* 94
Smith, Kenneth R. *47:* 182
Smith, Kevin Warren *89:* 112
Smith, Kristin *209:* 197
Smith, L.H. *35:* 174
Smith, Lane *76:* 211, 213; *88:* 115; *105:* 202, 203,204, 205; *131:* 207; *160:* 217, 221; *179:* 183, 184, 185, 186; *199:* 122, 123, 124, 126

Smith, Lee *29:* 32
Smith, Linell Nash *2:* 195
Smith, Maggie Kaufman *13:* 205; *35:* 191; *110:* 158; *178:* 226; *190:* 204; *209:* 145
Smith, Mavis *101:* 219
Smith, Moishe *33:* 155
Smith, Philip *44:* 134; *46:* 203
Smith, Ralph Crosby *2:* 267; *49:* 203
Smith, Robert D. *5:* 63
Smith, Sally J. *84:* 55
Smith, Susan Carlton *12:* 208
Smith, Terry *12:* 106; *33:* 158
Smith, Virginia *3:* 157; *33:* 72
Smith, William A. *1:* 36; *10:* 154; *25:* 65
Smith-Moore, J.J. *98:* 147
Smolinski, Dick *84:* 217
Smoljan, Joe *112:* 201
Smollin, Mike *39:* 203
Smyth, Iain *105:* 207
Smyth, M. Jane *12:* 15
Smythe, Fiona *151:* 213
Smythe, Theresa *141:* 37
Snair, Andy *176:* 4
Sneed, Brad *125:* 25; *191:* 175, 176; *211:* 194
Snyder, Andrew A. *30:* 212
Snyder, Jerome *13:* 207; *30:* 173
Snyder, Joel *28:* 163
So, Meilo *162:* 201; *208:* 188
Soentpiet, Chris K. *97:* 208; *110:* 33; *159:* 184; *161:* 10; *163:* 130
Sofia *1:* 62; *5:* 90; *32:* 166; *86:* 43
Sofilas, Mark *93:* 157
Sogabe, Aki *207:* 153
Sohn, Jiho *182:* 78
Sokol, Bill *37:* 178; *49:* 23
Sokolov, Kirill *34:* 188
Solbert, Ronni *1:* 159; *2:* 232; *5:* 121; *6:* 34; *17:* 249
Solomon, Michael *174:* 115
Solonevich, George *15:* 246; *17:* 47
Soma, Liana *81:* 118
Soman, David *90:* 122; *102:* 126; *140:* 120; *93:* 188; *43, 89; *200:* 180, 181
Sommer, Robert *12:* 211
Song, Jae *203:* 27
Soo, Kean *201:* 185
Sorel, Edward *4:* 61; *36:* 82; *65:* 191, 193; *126:* 214
Sorensen, Henri *196:* 58
Sorensen, Henrik *62:* 16
Sorensen, Svend Otto *22:* 130, 141; *67:* 188, 189
Sorra, Kristin *155:* 80
Sosa, Hernan *198:* 66
Sostre, Maria *187:* 36
Sotomayor, Antonio *11:* 215
Souhami, Jessica *112:* 128; *176:* 193
Sousa, Natalie C. *209:* 89
Souza, Diana *71:* 139
Sovak, Jan *115:* 190
Soyer, Moses *20:* 177
Spaenkuch, August *16:* 28
Spafford, Suzy *160:* 228
Spain, Valerie *105:* 76
Spain, Sunday Sahara *133:* 204
Spalenka, Greg *149:* 69; *151:* 228; *184:* 195; *191:* 21; *196:* 12; *198:* 181, 182, 201; *208:* 92
Spanfeller, James *1:* 72, 149; *2:* 183; *19:* 230, 231,232; *22:* 66; *36:* 160, 161; *40:* 75; *52:* 166; *76:* 37
Sparks, Mary Walker *15:* 247
Spears, Rick *182:* 187
Speidel, Sandra *78:* 233; *94:* 178; *134:* 180; *210:* 67
Speirs, John *67:* 178
Spence, Geraldine *21:* 163; *47:* 196
Spence, Jim *38:* 89; *50:* 102
Spencer, Laurie *113:* 12
Spencer, Mark *57:* 170
Spengler, Kenneth J. *146:* 256

Sperling, Andrea *133:* 182
Spiegel, Beth *184:* 203
Spiegel, Doris *29:* 111
Spiegelman, Art *109:* 227
Spier, Jo *10:* 30
Spier, Peter *3:* 155; *4:* 200; *7:* 61; *11:* 78; *38:* 106; *54:* 120, 121, 122, 123, 124, 125, 126, 127, 128, 129, 130,131, 132, 133, 134
Spilka, Arnold *5:* 120; *6:* 204; *8:* 131
Spirin, Gennady *95:* 196, 197; *113:* 172; *128:* 9; *129:* 49; *134:* 210; *153:* 9; *204:* 143, 144, 145
Spiro, Ruth *208:* 197
Spivak, I. Howard *8:* 10; *13:* 172
Spohn, David *72:* 233
Spohn, Kate *87:* 195; *147:* 201, 202
Spollen, Christopher J. *12:* 214
Spooner, Malcolm *40:* 142
Spowart, Robin *82:* 228; *92:* 149; *133:* 131; *176:* 163; *177:* 183, 184
Sprague, Kevin *150:* 60; *196:* 62
Spranger, Nina *201:* 199
Sprattler, Rob *12:* 176
Spring, Bob *5:* 60
Spring, Ira *5:* 60
Springer, Harriet *31:* 92
Spudvilas, Anne *110:* 74; *197:* 192; *199:* 154
Spurll, Barbara *78:* 199; *88:* 141, 142; *99:* 215
Spurrier, Steven *28:* 198
Spuvilas, Anne *85:* 114
Spy
    See Ward, Leslie
Squires, Stuart *127:* 74
St. Aubin, Bruno *179:* 54
St. John, J. Allen *41:* 62
Staake, Bob *209:* 168, 169
Stabin, Victor *101:* 131; *164:* 158
Stadler, John *62:* 33; *204:* 149
Staffan, Alvin E. *11:* 56; *12:* 187
Stahl, Ben *5:* 181; *12:* 91; *49:* 122; *71:* 128; *87:* 206; *112:* 107
Stair, Gobin *35:* 214
Stallwood, Karen *73:* 126
Stamaty, Mark Alan *12:* 215
Stammen, JoEllen McAllister *113:* 14
Stampnick, Ken *51:* 142
Stanbridge, Joanne *150:* 91
Stanley, Diane *3:* 45; *37:* 180; *80:* 217, 219
Stanley, Sanna *145:* 228
Starcke, Helmut *86:* 217
Stark, Ken *197:* 102
Starr, Branka *73:* 25
Stasiak, Krystyna *49:* 181; *64:* 194
Staub, Leslie *103:* 54
Staunton, Ted *112:* 192
Stawicki, Matt *164:* 250
Stead, L. *55:* 51, 56
Steadman, Broeck *97:* 185, 186; *99:* 56; *121:* 48; *208:* 190
Steadman, Henry *211:* 130
Steadman, Ralph *32:* 180; *123:* 143, 145
Stearn, Nick *183:* 26
Steckler, June *90:* 178
Steele, Robert Gantt *169:* 174
Steichen, Edward *30:* 79
Steig, William *18:* 275, 276; *70:* 215, 216, 217, 218; *111:* 173, 174, 175, 176, 177
Stein, David Ezra *211:* 168
Stein, Harve *1:* 109
Steinberg, Saul *47:* 193
Steinel, William *23:* 146
Steiner, Charlotte *45:* 196
Steiner, Joan *110:* 219; *199:* 160, 161
Steirnagel, Michael *80:* 56
Stemp, Eric *60:* 184
Stephens, Alice Barber *66:* 208, 209
Stephens, Charles H. *YABC 2:* 279
Stephens, Pam *198:* 69
Stephens, Pat *126:* 110; *128:* 101
Stephens, William M. *21:* 165
Steptoe, Javaka *151:* 203, 204; *190:* 169

Steptoe, John *8:* 197; *57:* 9; *63:* 158, 159, 160, 161,163, 164, 165, 166, 167; *96:* 4; *105:* 87
Stern, Simon *15:* 249, 250; *17:* 58; *34:* 192, 193
Sterret, Jane *53:* 27
Stetsios, Debbie *165:* 108, 109
Steven, Kat *158:* 237
Stevens, David *62:* 44
Stevens, Helen *189:* 31; *207:* 83
Stevens, Janet *40:* 126; *57:* 10, 11; *80:* 112; *90:* 221, 222; *109:* 156; *130:* 34; *166:* 202; *176:* 53, 116; *193:* 199, 200, 202; *208:* 127
Stevens, Mary *11:* 193; *13:* 129; *43:* 95
Stevenson, Harvey *66:* 143; *80:* 201, 221; *153:* 60; *191:* 166
Stevenson, James *42:* 182, 183; *51:* 163; *66:* 184; *71:* 185, 187, 188; *78:* 262; *87:* 97; *113:* 182, 183,184, 185; *161:* 182, 183
Stevenson, Sucie *92:* 27; *104:* 194, 195; *112:* 168; *160:* 202; *194:* 172, 173; *195:* 166
Stewart, April Blair *75:* 210
Stewart, Arvis *33:* 98; *36:* 69; *60:* 118; *75:* 91; *127:* 4
Stewart, Charles *2:* 205
Stewart, Joel *151:* 205; *211:* 170, 171
Stieg, William *172:* 58
Stiles, Fran *26:* 85; *78:* 56; *82:* 150
Stillman, Susan *44:* 130; *76:* 83
Stimpson, Tom *49:* 171
Stimson, James *208:* 46
Stinemetz, Morgan *40:* 151
Stinson, Paul *110:* 86
Stirnweis, Shannon *10:* 164
Stites, Joe *86:* 96
Stobbs, William *1:* 48, 49; *3:* 68; *6:* 20; *17:* 117, 217; *24:* 150; *29:* 250; *60:* 179; *87:* 204, 205,206
Stock, Catherine *37:* 55; *65:* 198; *72:* 7; *99:* 225; *114:* 197, 198, 199; *126:* 3; *145:* 161; *161:* 82; *173:* 149; *208:* 210
Stockman, Jack *113:* 24
Stoeke, Janet Morgan *90:* 225; *136:* 196; *202:* 182, 183
Stoerrle, Tom *55:* 147
Stolp, Jaap *49:* 98
Stolp, Todd *89:* 195
Stone, David L. *87:* 154
Stone, David *9:* 173
Stone, David K. *4:* 38; *6:* 124; *9:* 180; *43:* 182; *60:* 70
Stone, Helen V. *6:* 209
Stone, Helen *44:* 121, 122, 126
Stone, Kazuko G. *134:* 43
Stone, Kyle M. *202:* 185
Stone, Phoebe *86:* 212; *134:* 213; *162:* 188; *205:* 145
Stone, Steve *166:* 213; *208:* 185
Stone, Tony *150:* 34, 35
Storrings, Michael *191:* 108
Stoud, Virginia A. *89:* 31
Stover, Jill *82:* 234
Strachan, Bruce *205:* 146
Stratton, Helen *33:* 151
Stratton-Porter, Gene *15:* 254, 259, 263, 264, 268, 269
Straub, Matt *192:* 176
Straub, Phillip *197:* 22
Streano, Vince *20:* 173
Street, Janet Travell *84:* 235
Streeter, Clive *121:* 2
Strickland, Shadra *209:* 179
Stringer, Lauren *129:* 187; *154:* 172, 173; *161:* 127; *183:* 187, 188
Strodl, Daniel *47:* 95
Strogart, Alexander *63:* 139
Stromoski, Rick *111:* 179; *124:* 161, 190
Strong, Joseph D., Jr. *YABC 2:* 330
Stroyer, Poul *13:* 221
Strugnell, Ann *27:* 38
Struzan, Drew *117:* 6
Stubbs, William *73:* 196

Stubis, Talivaldis *5:* 182, 183; *10:* 45; *11:* 9; *18:* 304; *20:* 127
Stubley, Trevor *14:* 43; *22:* 219; *23:* 37; *28:* 61; *87:* 26
Stuck, Marion *104:* 44
Stuecklen, Karl W. *8:* 34, 65; *23:* 103
Stull, Betty *11:* 46
Stutzman, Mark *119:* 99
Stutzmann, Laura *73:* 185
Suarez, Maribel *162:* 208; *200:* 202
Suave, Gordon *209:* 66
Suba, Susanne *4:* 202, 203; *14:* 261; *23:* 134; *29:* 222; *32:* 30
Sue, Majella Lue *209:* 182
Sueling, Barbara *98:* 185
Sueling, Gwenn *98:* 186
Sugarman, Tracy *3:* 76; *8:* 199; *37:* 181, 182
Sugimoto, Yugo *170:* 144
Sugita, Yutaka *36:* 180, 181
Suh, John *80:* 157
Sullivan, Dorothy *89:* 113
Sullivan, Edmund J. *31:* 86
Sullivan, James F. *19:* 280; *20:* 192
Sully, Tom *104:* 199, 200; *182:* 77
Sumichrast, Jozef *14:* 253; *29:* 168, 213
Sumiko *46:* 57
Summers, Leo *1:* 177; *2:* 273; *13:* 22
Summers, Mark *118:* 144
Summers, Mike *190:* 176
Sutton, Judith *94:* 164
Svarez, Juan *56:* 113
Svendsen, Mark *181:* 176
Svolinsky, Karel *17:* 104
Swain, Carol *172:* 182
Swain, Su Zan Noguchi *21:* 170
Swan, Susan *22:* 220, 221; *37:* 66; *60:* 146; *145:* 205; *181:* 168
Swann, Susan *86:* 55
Swanson, Karl *79:* 65; *89:* 186
Swarner, Kristina *203:* 62
Swayne, Sam *53:* 143, 145
Swayne, Zoa *53:* 143, 145
Swearingen, Greg *152:* 56; *165:* 135; *173:* 2
Sweat, Lynn *25:* 206; *57:* 176; *73:* 184; *168:* 178
Sweet, Darrell K. *60:* 9; *69:* 86; *74:* 15; *75:* 215; *76:* 130, 131; *81:* 96, 122; *82:* 253; *83:* 11; *84:* 14; *85:* 37; *89:* 140; *90:* 6; *91:* 137,139; *95:* 160, 161; *126:* 25; *185:* 175; *195:* 132
Sweet, Darrell K. *1:* 163; *4:* 136; *164:* 175
Sweet, Melissa *71:* 94; *72:* 172; *111:* 82; *139:* 53, 58; *141:* 88; *142:* 231; *155:* 121; *159:* 121, 122; *172:* 185; *188:* 127; *209:* 81; *211:* 174, 175
Sweet, Ozzie *31:* 149, 151, 152
Sweetland, Robert *12:* 194
Swiatkowska, Gabi *132:* 43; *175:* 139; *180:* 218; *183:* 176
Swope, Martha *43:* 160; *56:* 86, 87, 89
Sylvada, Peter *154:* 174
Sylvester, Natalie G. *22:* 222
Szafran, Gene *24:* 144
Szasz, Susanne *13:* 55, 226; *14:* 48
Szekeres, Cyndy *2:* 218; *5:* 185; *8:* 85; *11:* 166; *14:* 19; *16:* 57, 159; *26:* 49, 214; *34:* 205; *60:* 150, 151, 152, 153, 154; *73:* 224; *74:* 218; *131:* 213, 215
Szpura, Beata *81:* 68; *119:* 65; *168:* 201

T

Taback, Simms *40:* 207; *52:* 120; *57:* 34; *80:* 241; *104:* 202, 203; *170:* 176, 177; *205:* 183
Taber, Patricia *75:* 124
Tabor, Nancy Maria Grande *89:* 210; *161:* 188
Taddei, Richard *112:* 13, 14
Tadgell, Nicole *150:* 77; *161:* 20; *177:* 186; *209:* 16

Tadiello, Ed *133:* 200
Tafuri, Nancy *39:* 210; *75:* 199, 200; *92:* 75; *130:* 215, 216, 217
Tailfeathers, Gerald *86:* 85
Tait, Douglas *12:* 220; *74:* 105, 106
Takabayashi, Mari *113:* 112; *130:* 22; *156:* 169
Takahashi, Hideko *136:* 160; *187:* 6; *209:* 152, 187
Takakjian, Portia *15:* 274
Takashima, Shizuye *13:* 228
Talarczyk, June *4:* 173
Talbott, Hudson *84:* 240; *163:* 100
Tallarico, Tony *116:* 197
Tallon, Robert *2:* 228; *43:* 200, 201, 202, 203, 204, 205,206, 207, 209
Tamaki, Jillian *201:* 188
Tamas, Szecsko *29:* 135
Tamburine, Jean *12:* 222
Tandy, H.R. *13:* 69
Tandy, Russell H. *65:* 9; *100:* 30, 131
Tang, Charles *81:* 202; *90:* 192
Tang, Susan *80:* 174; *108:* 158
Tang, You-shan *63:* 100
Tankersley, Paul *69:* 206; *133:* 219
Tannenbaum, Robert *48:* 181
Tanner, Jane *87:* 13; *97:* 37
Tanner, Tim *72:* 192; *84:* 35
Tanobe, Miyuki *23:* 221
Tarabay, Sharif *110:* 149; *113:* 123; *169:* 83
Tarkington, Booth *17:* 224, 225
Tarlow, Phyllis *61:* 198
Tate, Don *159:* 141, 191; *183:* 69; *186:* 120
Tauss, Herbert *95:* 179
Tauss, Marc *117:* 160; *126:* 155; *178:* 221; *197:* 7
Tavares, Matt *159:* 192, 193; *198:* 188, 189, 190; *199:* 86
Taylor, Ann *41:* 226
Taylor, Dahl *129:* 157
Taylor, Geoff *93:* 156; *197:* 173, 175; *204:* 151, 152
Taylor, Isaac *41:* 228
Taylor, Mike *143:* 99, 100
Teague, Mark *83:* 6; *139:* 241; *170:* 180, 181; *205:* 150, 151
Teale, Edwin Way *7:* 196
Teason, James *1:* 14
Teckentrup, Britta *200:* 191, 192
Teeple, Lyn *33:* 147
Tee-Van, Helen Damrosch *10:* 176; *11:* 182
Teicher, Dick *50:* 211
Teichman, Mary *77:* 220; *124:* 208; *127:* 22; *197:* 33
Temertey, Ludmilla *96:* 232; *104:* 43, 45; *109:* 244
Tempest, Margaret *3:* 237, 238; *88:* 200
Temple, Frances *85:* 185, 186, 187
Temple, Herbert *45:* 201
Templeton, Owen *11:* 77
ten Cate, Marijke *183:* 193
Tenggren, Gustaf *18:* 277, 278, 279; *19:* 15; *28:* 86; *YABC2:* 145
Tennent, Julie *81:* 105
Tenneson, Joyce *153:* 166
Tenney, Gordon *24:* 204
Tenniel, John *74:* 234, 235; *100:* 89; *YABC 2:* 99; *153:* 63
Tepper, Matt *116:* 80
Terkel, Ari *103:* 162
Terry, Michael *180:* 209
Terry, Will *131:* 73; *205:* 155
Teskey, Donald *71:* 51
Tessler, Manya *200:* 193
Thacher, Mary M. *30:* 72
Thackeray, William Makepeace *23:* 224, 228
Thamer, Katie *42:* 187
Tharlet, Eve *146:* 149
Thelwell, Norman *14:* 201
Theobalds, Prue *40:* 23
Theurer, Marilyn Churchill *39:* 195

Thiesing, Lisa *89:* 134; *95:* 202; *156:* 190; *159:* 195
Thiewes, Sam *133:* 114
Thistlethwaite, Miles *12:* 224
Thollander, Earl *11:* 47; *18:* 112; *22:* 224
Thomas, Allan *22:* 13
Thomas, Art *48:* 217
Thomas, Eric *28:* 49
Thomas, Harold *20:* 98
Thomas, Jacqui *125:* 95
Thomas, Jan *197:* 180
Thomas, Mark *42:* 136
Thomas, Martin *14:* 255
Thomas, Middy *177:* 114
Thompson, Arthur *34:* 107
Thompson, Carol *85:* 189; *95:* 75; *102:* 86; *147:* 166; *189:* 179, 180, 181; *190:* 84; *207:* 18
Thompson, Colin *95:* 204
Thompson, Ellen *51:* 88, 151; *60:* 33; *67:* 42; *77:* 148; *78:* 75, 219; *79:* 122, 170; *84:* 219; *85:* 97; *87:* 37; *88:* 192, 194; *89:* 80; *93:* 37; *98:* 59; *132:* 14
Thompson, George W. *22:* 18; *28:* 150; *33:* 135
Thompson, John *58:* 201; *102:* 226; *124:* 154; *128:* 228; *129:* 157; *150:* 49; *185:* 160; *191:* 192
Thompson, Julie *44:* 158
Thompson, Katherine *132:* 146
Thompson, K. Dyble *84:* 6
Thompson, Miles *152:* 77
Thompson, Sharon *74:* 113; *158:* 60; *165:* 87
Thomson, Arline K. *3:* 264
Thomson, Bill *186:* 160
Thomson, Hugh *26:* 88
Thomson, Ross *36:* 179
Thorkelson, Gregg *95:* 183, 184; *98:* 58; *165:* 30, 31
Thorn, Lori *189:* 119
Thornberg, Dan *104:* 125
Thornburgh, Rebecca McKillip *143:* 37
Thorne, Diana *25:* 212
Thornhill, Jan *77:* 213
Thorpe, Peter *58:* 109
Thorvall, Kerstin *13:* 235
Threadgall, Colin *77:* 215
Thurber, James *13:* 239, 242, 243, 245, 248, 249
Thurman, Mark *63:* 173; *168:* 116
Tibbles, Jean-Paul *115:* 200
Tibbles, Paul *45:* 23
Tibo, Gilles *67:* 207; *107:* 199, 201
Tichenor, Tom *14:* 207
Tichnor, Richard *90:* 218
Tiegreen, Alan *36:* 143; *43:* 55, 56, 58; *77:* 200; *94:* 216, 217; *121:* 54, 59
Tierney, Tom *113:* 198, 200, 201
Tildes, Phyllis Limbacher *210:* 240
Tilley, Debbie *102:* 134; *133:* 226; *137:* 101; *159:* 96; *190:* 211, 212
Tillman, Nancy *211:* 129, 178
Tilney, F.C. *22:* 231
Timbs, Gloria *36:* 90
Timmins, Harry *2:* 171
Timmons, Bonnie *194:* 189
Tinkelman, Murray *12:* 225; *35:* 44
Titherington, Jeanne *39:* 90; *58:* 138; *75:* 79; *135:* 161
Tjader, Ella *209:* 14
Tobin, Nancy *145:* 197
Toddy, Irving *172:* 144
Tokunbo, Dimitrea *181:* 183; *187:* 182, 183
Tolbert, Jeff *128:* 69
Toledo, Francisco *197:* 182; *198:* 199
Toledo, Natalia *197:* 182
Tolford, Joshua *1:* 221
Tolkien, J.R.R. *2:* 243; *32:* 215
Tolman, Marije *195:* 43
Tolmie, Ken *15:* 292
Tomei, Lorna *47:* 168, 171

Tomes, Jacqueline *2:* 117; *12:* 139
Tomes, Margot *1:* 224; *2:* 120, 121; *16:* 207; *18:* 250; *20:* 7; *25:* 62; *27:* 78, 79; *29:* 81, 199; *33:* 82; *36:* 186, 187, 188, 189, 190; *46:* 129; *56:* 71; *58:* 183; *70:* 228; *75:* 73, 75; *80:* 80; *83:* 97; *90:* 205
Tommaso, Rich *200:* 198
Toner, Raymond John *10:* 179
Tong, Gary *66:* 215
Tongier, Stephen *82:* 32
Tooke, Susan *173:* 162
Toothill, Harry *6:* 54; *7:* 49; *25:* 219; *42:* 192
Toothill, Ilse *6:* 54
Topolski, Feliks *44:* 48
Torbert, Floyd James *22:* 226
Torgersen, Don *55:* 157
Torline, Kevin *169:* 171
Tormey, Bertram M. *75:* 3, 4
Torrecilla, Pablo *176:* 207
Torres, Leyla *156:* 199, 201
Torrey, Helen *87:* 41
Torrey, Marjorie *34:* 105
Torrey, Richard *189:* 182; *205:* 24
Toschik, Larry *6:* 102
Totten, Bob *13:* 93
Toy, Julie *128:* 112
Trachok, Cathy *131:* 16
Tracy, Libba *82:* 24
Trago, Keith *158:* 253
Trail, Lee *55:* 157
Trang, To Ngoc *167:* 180
Trang, Winson *89:* 151
Trapani, Iza *116:* 202
Travers, Bob *49:* 100; *63:* 145
Treatner, Meryl *95:* 180
Tremain, Ruthven *17:* 238
Tresilian, Stuart *25:* 53; *40:* 212
Trez, Alain *17:* 236
Trezzo, Loretta *86:* 45
Trier, Walter *14:* 96
Trimby, Elisa *47:* 199
Trinkle, Sally *53:* 27
Triplett, Gina *182:* 193; *188:* 100; *198:* 38
Tripp, F.J. *24:* 167
Tripp, Wallace *2:* 48; *7:* 28; *8:* 94; *10:* 54,76; *11:* 92; *31:* 170, 171; *34:* 203; *42:* 57; *60:* 157; *73:* 182
Trivas, Irene *53:* 4; *54:* 168; *82:* 46, 101
Trnka, Jiri *22:* 151; *43:* 212, 213, 214, 215; *YABC 1:* 30, 31
Trondheim, Lewis *182:* 183
Troughton, Joanna *37:* 186; *48:* 72
Troyer, Johannes *3:* 16; *7:* 18
Trudeau, G.B. *35:* 220, 221, 222; *48:* 119, 123, 126, 127,128, 129, 133; *168:* 189
Trueman, Matthew *165:* 208; *183:* 191
Truesdell, Sue *55:* 142; *108:* 219, 220
Tryon, Leslie *84:* 7; *139:* 214; *143:* 10; *181:* 10
Tseng, Jean *72:* 195; *94:* 102; *119:* 126; *151:* 106; *173:* 138, 139; *200:* 158
Tseng, Mou-sien *72:* 195; *94:* 102; *119:* 126; *151:* 106; *173:* 138, 139; *200:* 158
Tsinajinie, Andy *2:* 62
Tsinganos, Jim *180:* 142
Tsugami, Kyuzo *18:* 198, 199
Tucker, Ezra *156:* 31
Tuckwell, Jennifer *17:* 205
Tudor, Bethany *7:* 103
Tudor, Tasha *18:* 227; *20:* 185, 186, 187; *36:* 111; *69:* 196, 198; *100:* 44; *YABC 2:* 46, 314; *160:* 234
Tuerk, Hanne *71:* 201
Tugeau, Jeremy *199:* 170; *203:* 96
Tulloch, Maurice *24:* 79
Tunis, Edwin *1:* 218, 219; *28:* 209, 210, 211, 212
Tunnicliffe, C.F. *62:* 176; 177; 178, 179; 181
Turkle, Brinton *1:* 211, 213; *2:* 249; *3:* 226; *11:* 3; *16:* 209; *20:* 22; *50:* 23; *67:* 50; *68:* 65; *79:* 205, 206, 207; *128:* 47; *YABC 1:* 79

Turnbull, Christopher J. *143:* 99, 100
Turner, Gwenda *59:* 195
Turner, Helen *203:* 154
Turska, Krystyna *12.* 103; *31:* 173, 174, 175; *56:* 32,34; *100:* 66
Tusa, Tricia *72:* 242; *111:* 180, 181; *157:* 165; *164:* 186; *189:* 40; *201:* 9; *207:* 163, 164
Tusan, Stan *6:* 58; *22:* 236, 237
Tworkov, Jack *47:* 207
Tyers, Jenny *89:* 220
Tylden-Wright, Jenny *114:* 119
Tyrol, Adelaide Murphy *103:* 27
Tyrrell, Frances *107:* 204
Tzimoulis, Paul *12:* 104

U

Uchida, Yoshiko *1:* 220
Uderzo *47:* 88
Udovic, David *189:* 185; *195:* 201
Ueno, Noriko *59:* 155
Ugliano, Natascia *196:* 186
Ulm, Robert *17:* 238
Ulrich, George *73:* 15; *75:* 136, 139; *99:* 150
Ulriksen, Mark *101:* 58; *182:* 43; *210:* 243
Unada *84:* 67
See Gliewe, Unada
Underhill, Liz *53:* 159
Underwood, Beck *192:* 36
Underwood, Clarence *40:* 166
Unger, Jim *67:* 208
Ungerer, Tomi *5:* 188; *9:* 40; *18:* 188; *29:* 175; *33:* 221, 222, 223, 225; *71:* 48; *106:* 209, 210, 211, 212
Unwin, Nora S. *3:* 65, 234, 235; *4:* 237; *44:* 173, 174; *YABC 1:* 59; *2:* 301
Upitis, Alvis *145:* 179
Urban, Helle *149:* 243
Urbanovic, Jackie *86:* 86; *189:* 186, 187
Uris, Jill *49:* 188, 197
Ursell, Martin *50:* 51
Utpatel, Frank *18:* 114
Utz, Lois *5:* 190

V

Vagin, Vladimir *66:* 10; *142:* 215
Vaillancourt, Francois *107:* 199
Vainio, Pirkko *123:* 157, 158
Valério, Geraldo *180:* 225; *194:* 116
Vallejo, Boris *62:* 130; *72:* 212; *91:* 38; *93:* 61
Van Abbe, S. *16:* 142; *18:* 282; *31:* 90; *YABC 2:* 157, 161
Van Allsburg, Chris *37:* 205, 206; *53:* 161, 162, 163, 165,166, 167, 168, 169, 170, 171; *105:* 215, 216, 217, 218; *156:* 176, 177, 178
Vance, James *65:* 28
Van Der Linde, Henry *99:* 17
van der Meer, Ron *98:* 204, 205
van der Meer, Atie *98:* 204, 205
Vandivert, William *21:* 175
Van Dongen, H.R. *81:* 97
Van Dusen, Chris W. *173:* 169
Vane, Mitch *210:* 160
Van Everen, Jay *13:* 160; *YABC 1:* 121
Van Fleet, John *165:* 12, 13
Van Frankenhuyzen, Gijsbert *145:* 230; *149:* 164; *184:* 151; *210:* 248
van Genechten, Guido *165:* 226
van Haeringen, Annemarie *193:* 206
Van Horn, William *43:* 218
van Hout, Mies *195:* 191; *207:* 58
van Kampen, Vlasta *194:* 217
van Lawick, Hugo *62:* 76, 79
Van Lieshout, Maria *201:* 196
Van Loon, Hendrik Willem *18:* 285, 289, 291

Van Munching, Paul *83:* 85
van Ommen, Sylvia *186:* 192
Van Patter, Bruce *183:* 195
Van Rynbach, Iris *102:* 192
Van Sciver, Ruth *37:* 162
VanSeveren, Joe *63:* 182
Van Stockum, Hilda *5:* 193
Van Wassenhove, Sue *202:* 193
Van Wely, Babs *16:* 50; *79:* 16
Van Wright, Cornelius *72:* 18; *102:* 208; *116:* 107; *152:* 236; *173:* 170, 171; *199:* 185
Van Zyle, Jon *103:* 125; *160:* 181, 182; *176:* 199, 200
Vardzigulyants, Ruben *90:* 54
Varga, Judy *29:* 196
Vargo, Kurt *79:* 224
Varley, Susan *61:* 199; *63:* 176, 177; *101:* 148; *134:* 220
Varon, Sara *195:* 208
Vasconcellos, Daniel *80:* 42
Vasiliu, Mircea *2:* 166, 253; *9:* 166; *13:* 58; *68:* 42
Vaughn, Frank *34:* 157
Vavra, Robert *8:* 206
Vawter, Will *17:* 163
Vayas, Diana *71:* 61
Vazquez, Carlos *125:* 184
Veeder, Larry *18:* 4
Velasquez, Eric *45:* 217; *61:* 45; *63:* 110, 111; *88:* 162; *90:* 34, 144; *94:* 213; *107:* 147; *132:* 192; *138:* 213; *159:* 126; *181:* 184; *184:* 96; *191:* 16; *192:* 234; *208:* 37
Velasquez, Jose A. *63:* 73
Velez, Walter *71:* 75; *91:* 154; *121:* 181; *168:* 49; *207:* 52
Velthuijs, Max *110:* 228, 229
Vendrell, Carme Sole *42:* 205
Venezia, Mike *54:* 17
Venti, Anthony Bacon *124:* 103; *126:* 26
Venturo, Piero *61:* 194, 195
Ver Beck, Frank *18:* 16, 17
Verkaaik, Ben *110:* 209
Verling, John *71:* 27
Verney, John *14:* 225; *75:* 8
Vernon, Ursula *204:* 157
Verrier, Suzanne *5:* 20; *23:* 212
Versace, Marie *2:* 255
Verstraete, Randy *108:* 193
Vestal, H.B. *9:* 134; *11:* 101; *27:* 25; *34:* 158
Vestergaard, Hope *190:* 203
Vicatan *59:* 146
Vickrey, Robert *45:* 59, 64
Victor, Joan Berg *30:* 193
Vieceli, Emma *210:* 245
Viereck, Ellen *3:* 242; *14:* 229
Vigna, Judith *15:* 293; *102:* 194, 195, 196, 197
Vila, Laura *207:* 172
Vilato, Gaspar E. *5:* 41
Villiard, Paul *51:* 178
Vimnera, A. *23:* 154
Vincent, Eric *34:* 98
Vincent, Felix *41:* 237
Vincent, Gabrielle *121:* 175
Vip *45:* 164
Viskupic, Gary *83:* 48
Vitale, Stefano *109:* 71, 107; *114:* 219, 220; *123:* 106; *138:* 232; *180:* 228, 229
Vivas, Julie *51:* 67, 69; *96:* 225; *197:* 190; *199:* 71
Voake, Charlotte *114:* 221, 222; *180:* 232
Vo-Dinh, Mai *16:* 272; *60:* 191
Vogel, Ilse-Margret *14:* 230
Voigt, Erna *35:* 228
Vojnar, Kamil *95:* 31; *114:* 4; *115:* 62; *121:* 90; *124:* 72; *130:* 31; *141:* 81; *146:* 196; *150:* 123; *158:* 5, 6; *158:* 154; *171:* 119, 188; *179:* 15; *180:* 112; *203:* 74
Vojtech, Anna *42:* 190; *108:* 222, 223; *150:* 203; *174:* 173
von Buhler, Cynthia *149:* 237; *162:* 177; *177:* 205; *180:* 77; *185:* 214, 215, 216

von Roehl, Angela *126:* 191
von Schmidt, Eric *8:* 62; *50:* 209, 210
von Schmidt, Harold *30:* 80
Vosburgh, Leonard *1:* 161; *7:* 32; *15:* 295, 296; *23:* 110; *30:* 214; *43:* 181
Voss, Tom *127:* 104
Voter, Thomas W. *19:* 3, 9
Vroman, Tom *10:* 29
Vulliamy, Clara *72:* 65

W

Waber, Bernard *47:* 209, 210, 211, 212, 213, 214; *95:* 215, 216, 217; *156:* 203, 205, 206, 207
Wachenje, Benjamin *194:* 170
Wack, Jeff *95:* 140; *110:* 90
Wagner, John *8:* 200; *52:* 104
Wagner, Ken *2:* 59
Wagner, Michael *211:* 159
Waide, Jan *29:* 225; *36:* 139
Wainwright, Jerry *14:* 85
Waites, Joan C. *171:* 2
Wakeen, Sandra *47:* 97
Wakiyama, Hanako *171:* 96; *192:* 236; *200:* 16
Waldherr, Kris *81:* 186
Waldman, Bruce *15:* 297; *43:* 178
Waldman, Neil *35:* 141; *50:* 163; *51:* 180; *54:* 78; *77:* 112; *79:* 162; *82:* 174; *84:* 5, 56, 106; *94:* 232, 233, 234; *96:* 41; *111:* 139; *113:* 9; *118:* 30; *142:* 220, 223; *203:* 173, 174
Waldrep, Richard *111:* 147; *198:* 202
Walker, Brian *144:* 128
Walker, Charles *1:* 46; *4:* 59; *5:* 177; *11:* 115; *19:* 45; *34:* 74; *62:* 168; *72:* 218
Walker, Dugald Stewart *15:* 47; *32:* 202; *33:* 112
Walker, Gil *8:* 49; *23:* 132; *34:* 42
Walker, Jeff *55:* 154; *123:* 116
Walker, Jim *10:* 94
Walker, Mort *8:* 213
Walker, Norman *41:* 37; *45:* 58
Walker, Stephen *12:* 229; *21:* 174
Wallace, Beverly Dobrin *19:* 259
Wallace, Cly *87:* 93
Wallace, Ian *53:* 176, 177; *56:* 165, 166; *58:* 4; *98:* 4; *101:* 191; *112:* 124; *141:* 197, 198, 199, 200; *151:* 212
Wallace, John *105:* 228
Wallace, Nancy Elizabeth *141:* 204; *186:* 195, 197, 199
Wallenta, Adam *123:* 180
Waller, S.E. *24:* 36
Wallner, Alexandra *15:* 120; *156:* 183
Wallner, John C. *9:* 77; *10:* 188; *11:* 28; *14:* 209; *31:* 56, 118; *37:* 64; *51:* 186, 187, 188, 189, 190, 191,192, 193, 194, 195; *52:* 96; *53:* 23, 26; *71:* 99; *73:* 158; *89:* 215; *141:* 9
Wallner, John *162:* 17
Wallower, Lucille *11:* 226
Walotsky, Ron *93:* 87
Walsh, Ellen Stoll *99:* 209; *147:* 219; *194:* 194, 195, 196
Walsh, Rebecca *158:* 193
Walsh, Vivian *149:* 215; *158:* 227
Walters, Anita *205:* 163
Walters, Audrey *18:* 294
Walther, Tom *31:* 179
Walton, Garry *69:* 149
Walton, Tony *11:* 164; *24:* 209; *153:* 8; *177:* 73
Waltrip, Lela *9:* 195
Waltrip, Mildred *3:* 209; *37:* 211
Waltrip, Rufus *9:* 195
Wan *12:* 76
Wang, Suling *191:* 183
Warburton, Sarah *154:* 187
Wappers, G. *121:* 40

Ward, Fred 52: 19
Ward, Helen 72: 244; 144: 240, 242
Ward, John 42: 191; 96: 54; 97: 110; 123: 105; 124: 71; 173: 66
Ward, Keith 2: 107; 132: 69
Ward, Leslie 34: 126; 36: 87
Ward, Lynd 1: 99, 132, 133, 150; 2: 108, 158, 196, 259; 18: 86; 27: 56; 29: 79, 187, 253, 255; 36: 199,200, 201, 202, 203, 204, 205, 206, 207, 209; 43: 34; 56: 28; 60: 116; 100: 65
Ward, Peter 37: 116
Waring, Geoff 172: 84
Warhola, James 92: 5; 115: 85, 87; 118: 174, 175, 177; 176: 84; 187: 189, 190
Warner, Ben 159: 171
Warner, Peter 14: 87
Warnes, Tim 175: 159; 202: 188
Warnick, Elsa 113: 223
Warren, Betsy 2: 101
Warren, Jim 85: 81
Warren, Marion Cray 14: 215
Warshaw, Jerry 30: 197, 198; 42: 165
Wasden, Kevin 102: 162
Washington, Nevin 20: 123
Washington, Phyllis 20: 123
Wasserman, Amy L. 92: 110; 209: 95
Waterman, Stan 11: 76
Watkins-Pitchford, D.J. 6: 215, 217
Watling, James 67: 210; 78: 112; 101: 81; 117: 189, 190; 127: 119, 120
Watson, Aldren A. 2: 267; 5: 94; 13: 71; 19: 253; 32: 220; 42: 193, 194, 195, 196, 197, 198, 199, 200, 201; YABC 2: 202
Watson, G. 83: 162
Watson, Gary 19: 147; 36: 68; 41: 122; 47: 139
Watson, J.D. 22: 86
Watson, Jesse Joshua 197: 124; 199: 181; 202: 136
Watson, Karen 11: 26
Watson, Mary 117: 193
Watson, Richard Jesse 62: 188, 189; 211: 201
Watson, Wendy 5: 197; 13: 101; 33: 116; 46: 163; 64: 12; 74: 242, 243; 91: 21; 142: 228
Watt, Mélanie 136: 206; 193: 211
Wattenberg, Jane 174: 200; 185: 46; 187: 108
Watterson, Bill 66: 223, 225, 226
Watts, Bernadette 4: 227; 103: 182, 183
Watts, James 59: 197; 74: 145; 86: 124
Watts, John 37: 149
Watts, Leslie Elizabeth 150: 207; 165: 106; 209: 67
Watts, Stan 116: 205
Weatherby, Mark Alan 77: 141
Webb, Jennifer 110: 79
Webb, Lanny 142: 175
Webb, Sophie 135: 214
Webber, Helen 3: 141
Webber, Irma E. 14: 238
Weber, Erik 56: 19, 20
Weber, Florence 40: 153
Weber, Jill 127: 227, 228; 189: 163; 208: 157; 209: 190, 191
Weber, Roland 61: 204
Weber, Sam 190: 227
Weber, William J. 14: 239
Webster, Jean 17: 241
Weeks, Sarah 162: 39
Wegman, William 78: 243
Wegner, Fritz 14: 250; 20: 189; 44: 165; 86: 62
Weidenear, Reynold H. 21: 122
Weigel, Jeff 170: 193
Weihs, Erika 4: 21; 15: 299; 72: 201; 107: 207, 208
Weil, Lisl 7: 203; 10: 58; 21: 95; 22: 188,217; 33: 193
Weiman, Jon 50: 162, 165; 52: 103; 54: 78, 79, 81; 78: 80; 82: 107; 93: 82; 97: 69; 105: 179; 193: 65

Weiner, Sandra 14: 240
Weiner, Scott 55: 27
Weinhaus, Karen Ann 53: 90; 71: 50; 86: 124
Weinman, Brad 197: 20
Weinstock, Robert 204: 165, 166
Weisgard, Leonard 1: 65; 2: 191, 197, 204, 264, 265; 5: 108; 21: 42; 30: 200, 201, 203, 204; 41: 47; 44: 125; 53: 25; 85: 196, 198, 200, 201; 100: 139,207; YABC 2: 13
Weisman, David 173: 47
Weiss, Ellen 44: 202
Weiss, Emil 1: 168; 7: 60
Weiss, Harvey 1: 145, 223; 27: 224, 227; 68: 214; 76: 245, 246, 247
Weiss, Nicki 33: 229
Weissman, Bari 49: 72; 90: 125; 139: 142
Weitzman, David L. 172: 199
Welch, Sheila Kelly 130: 221
Welkes, Allen 68: 218
Wellington, Monica 99: 223; 157: 259, 260, 261
Welliver, Norma 76: 94
Wellner, Fred 127: 53
Wells, Frances 1: 183
Wells, H.G. 20: 194, 200
Wells, Haru 53: 120, 121
Wells, Robert E. 184: 208
Wells, Rosemary 6: 49; 18: 297; 60: 32; 66: 203; 69: 215, 216; 114: 227; 118: 149, 150; 156: 188, 189, 190, 191; 207: 180, 181, 182, 183
Wells, Rufus III 56: 111, 113
Wells, Susan 22: 43
Wendelin, Rudolph 23: 234
Wengenroth, Stow 37: 47
Weninger, Brigitte 189: 192, 194
Werenskiold, Erik 15: 6; 62: 17
Werner, Honi 24: 110; 33: 41; 88: 122
Werth, Kurt 7: 122; 14: 157; 20: 214; 39: 128
Wesson,
West, Harry A. 124: 38
Westcott, Nadine Bernard 68: 46; 84: 49; 86: 133; 106: 199; 111: 78; 113: 111; 130: 224; 139: 54; 158: 256; 194: 199
Westerberg, Christine 29: 226
Westerduin, Anne 105: 229
Westerman, Johanna 162: 206
Weston, Martha 29: 116; 30: 213; 33: 85, 100; 53: 181, 182, 183, 184; 77: 95; 80: 152; 119: 196,197, 198, 199; 127: 189; 133: 196; 209: 199
Wetherbee, Margaret 5: 3
Wexler, Jerome 49: 73; 150: 129
Whalley, Peter 50: 49
Whatley, Bruce 186: 93, 95; 207: 127
Wheatley, Arabelle 11: 231; 16: 276
Wheeler, Cindy 49: 205
Wheeler, Dora 44: 179
Wheelright, Rowland 15: 81; YABC 2: 286
Whelan, Michael 56: 108; 70: 27, 29, 67, 68, 148; 74: 18; 84: 14; 91: 195, 196; 95: 147; 98: 150, 151; 106: 157; 113: 218, 220; 116: 99, 100
Whelan, Patrick 135: 145
Whistler, Rex 16: 75; 30: 207, 208
White, Craig 110: 130; 119: 193; 130: 33; 179: 31
White, David Omar 5: 56; 18: 6
White, Joan 83: 225
White, Martin 51: 197; 85: 127
Whitear 32: 26
Whitehead, Beck 86: 171
Whitehead, S.B. 154: 132
Whithorne, H.S. 7: 49
Whitman, Candace 208: 208
Whitney, George Gillett 3: 24
Whitney, Jean 99: 53
Whitson, Paul 102: 161
Whittam, Geoffrey 30: 191
Whyte, Mary 96: 127
Wiberg, Harald 38: 127; 93: 215

Wick, Walter 77: 128
Wickstrom, Sylvie 106: 87; 169: 180
Wickstrom, Thor 200: 205
Widener, Terry 105: 230; 106: 7; 163: 23; 200: 17; 209: 195
Wiese, Kurt 3: 255; 4: 206; 14: 17; 17: 18, 19; 19: 47; 24: 152; 25: 212; 32: 184; 36: 211,213, 214, 215, 216, 217, 218; 45: 161; 100: 92
Wiesner, David 33: 47; 51: 106; 57: 67; 58: 55; 64: 78, 79, 81; 69: 233; 72: 247, 248, 249, 251,252, 253, 254; 83: 134; 104: 31; 117: 197, 199, 200, 202; 139: 223, 224; 151: 51; 181: 189, 190
Wiesner, William 4: 100; 5: 200, 201; 14: 262
Wiggins, George 6: 133
Wijngaard, Juan 111: 36; 114: 124
Wikkelsoe, Otto 45: 25, 26
Wikland, Ilon 5: 113; 8: 150; 38: 124, 125, 130; 127: 162
Wikler, Madeline 114: 233
Wilbur, C. Keith, M.D. 27: 228
Wilburn, Kathy 53: 102; 68: 234
Wilcox, Cathy 105: 123
Wilcox, J.A.J. 34: 122
Wilcox, Lydia 207: 187
Wilcox, R. Turner 36: 219
Wild, Jocelyn 46: 220, 221, 222; 80: 117
Wilde, George 7: 139
Wildsmith, Brian 16: 281, 282; 18: 170, 171; 66: 25; 69: 224, 225, 227; 77: 103; 83: 218; 124: 214,217, 219
Wildsmith, Mike 140: 229
Wilhelm, Hans 58: 189, 191; 73: 157; 77: 127; 135: 229, 230, 233, 234; 196: 209
Wilkin, Eloise 36: 173; 49: 208, 209, 210
Wilkinson, Barry 50: 213
Wilkinson, Gerald 3: 40
Wilkon, Jozef 31: 183, 184; 71: 206, 207, 209; 133: 222
Wilks, Mike 34: 24; 44: 203
Willems, Mo 154: 245, 246, 247; 180: 236, 237, 239
Willey, Bee 103: 129; 139: 159; 173: 115
Willhoite, Michael A. 71: 214
William, Maria 168: 51
Williams, Berkeley, Jr. 64: 75
Williams, Ferelith Eccles 22: 238
Williams, Garth 1: 197; 2: 49, 270; 4: 205; 15: 198, 302, 304, 307; 16: 34; 18: 283, 298, 299, 300, 301; 29: 177, 178, 179, 232, 233, 241, 242, 243, 244, 245, 248; 40: 106; 66: 229, 230, 231, 233, 234; 71: 192; 73: 218, 219, 220; 78: 261; 100: 251, 252, 255; 136: 117; YABC 2: 15, 16, 19
Williams, J. Scott 48: 28
Williams, Jennifer 102: 201
Williams, Jenny 60: 202; 81: 21; 88: 71
Williams, Kent 180: 18
Williams, Kit 44: 206, 207, 208, 209, 211, 212
Williams, Marcia 97: 214; 159: 208, 209
Williams, Maureen 12: 238
Williams, Patrick 14: 218
Williams, Richard 44: 93; 72: 229; 74: 133; 78: 155, 237; 91: 178; 110: 212; 136: 201, 202, 203; 152: 115
Williams, Sam 124: 222; 153: 11; 177: 201, 202; 180: 34
Williams, Sophy 135: 236
Williams, Vera B. 53: 186, 187, 188, 189; 102: 201, 202, 203; 210: 65
Williamson, Alex 177: 180; 205: 50
Williamson, Mel 60: 9
Willingham, Fred 104: 206; 154: 157
Willis, Adam 181: 75; 209: 11
Willmore, J.T. 54: 113, 114
Wilsdorf, Anne 180: 122; 189: 124; 191: 195
Wilson, Anne 160: 114
Wilson, Charles Banks 17: 92; 43: 73
Wilson, Connie 113: 179
Wilson, Dagmar 10: 47

Wilson, Dawn *67:* 161; *81:* 120; *113:* 158
Wilson, Edward A. *6:* 24; *16:* 149; *20:* 220, 221; *22:* 87; *26:* 67; *38:* 212, 214, 215, 216, 217
Wilson, Forrest *27:* 231
Wilson, Gahan *35:* 234; *41:* 136
Wilson, George *76:* 87
Wilson, Helen Miranda *140:* 61
Wilson, Jack *17:* 139
Wilson, Janet *77:* 154; *96:* 114; *99:* 219, 220; *153:* 64 *106:* 122; *130:* 210; *145:* 178; *173:* 64
Wilson, John *22:* 240
Wilson, Maurice *46:* 224
Wilson, Patten *35:* 61
Wilson, Peggy *15:* 4; *84:* 20
Wilson, Phil *181:* 29
Wilson, Rowland B. *30:* 170
Wilson, Sarah *50:* 215
Wilson, Tom *33:* 232
Wilson, W.N. *22:* 26
Wilson-Max, Ken *170:* 196; *180:* 181
Wilton, Nicholas *103:* 52; *183:* 111
Wilwerding, Walter J. *9:* 202
Wimmer, Mike *63:* 6; *70:* 121; *75:* 186; *76:* 21,22, 23; *91:* 114; *97:* 45, 68; *98:* 28; *107:* 130; *146:* 21; *149:* 47; *173:* 126; *193:* 21, 25; *194:* 204, 205
Winborn, Marsha *78:* 34; *99:* 70; *192:* 20
Winch, John *165:* 233
Winchester, Linda *13:* 231
Wind, Betty *28:* 158
Windham, Kathryn Tucker *14:* 260
Windham, Sophie *184:* 212
Winfield, Alison *115:* 78
Winfield, Wayne *72:* 23
Wing, Gary *64:* 147
Wing, Ron *50:* 85
Wingerter, Linda S. *132:* 199; *174:* 181; *200:* 196
Winick, Judd *124:* 227, 228, 229
Winn-Lederer, Ilene *202:* 91
Winnick, Karen B. *211:* 207
Winslow, Will *21:* 124
Winstead, Rosie *180:* 243
Winsten, Melanie Willa *41:* 41
Winter, Jeanette *151:* 240, 241, 242; *184:* 215, 217, 218, 219
Winter, Milo *15:* 97; *19:* 221; *21:* 181, 203, 204, 205; *64:* 19; *YABC 2:* 144
Winter, Paula *48:* 227
Winter, Susan *163:* 177; *182:* 201
Winters, Greg *70:* 117
Winters, Nina *62:* 194
Wise, Louis *13:* 68
Wiseman, Ann *31:* 187
Wiseman, B. *4:* 233
Wishnefsky, Phillip *3:* 14
Wiskur, Darrell *5:* 72; *10:* 50; *18:* 246
Wisniewski, David *95:* 220, 221
Wisniewski, Robert *95:* 10; *119:* 192
Witschonke, Alan *153:* 149, 150
Witt, Dick *80:* 244
Wittmann, Patrick *162:* 204
Wittman, Sally *30:* 219
Wittner, Dale *99:* 43
Wittwer, Hala *158:* 267; *195:* 80
Woehr, Lois *12:* 5
Wohlberg, Meg *12:* 100; *14:* 197; *41:* 255
Wohnoutka, Mike *137:* 68; *190:* 199; *195:* 218; *205:* 132
Wojtowycz, David *167:* 168
Woldin, Beth Weiner *34:* 211
Wolf, Elizabeth *133:* 151; *208:* 175
Wolf, J. *16:* 91
Wolf, Janet *78:* 254
Wolf, Linda *33:* 163
Wolfe, Corey *72:* 213
Wolfe, Gillian *199:* 193

Wolff, Ashley *50:* 217; *81:* 216; *156:* 216, 217; *170:* 57; *174:* 174; *184:* 72; *203:* 181, 182, 183, 184
Wolff, Glenn *178:* 230
Wolfsgruber, Linda *166:* 61
Wondriska, William *6:* 220
Wong, Janet S. *98:* 225; *152:* 43
Wong, Nicole *174:* 13
Wonsetler, John C. *5:* 168
Wood, Audrey *50:* 221, 222, 223; *81:* 219, 221; *198:* 206
Wood, Don *50:* 220, 225, 226, 228, 229; *81:* 218, 220; *139:* 239, 240
Wood, Grant *19:* 198
Wood, Heather *133:* 108
Wood, Ivor *58:* 17
Wood, Jakki *211:* 209
Wood, Muriel *36:* 119; *77:* 167; *171:* 55; *187:* 46
Wood, Myron *6:* 220
Wood, Owen *18:* 187; *64:* 202, 204, 205, 206, 208, 210
Wood, Rob *193:* 48
Wood, Ruth *8:* 11
Woodbridge, Curtis *133:* 138; *204:* 113
Wooding, Sharon L. *66:* 237
Woodruff, Liza *132:* 239; *182:* 46, 204
Woodruff, Thomas *171:* 73
Woods, John, Jr. *109:* 142
Woodson, Jack *10:* 201
Woodson, Jacqueline *94:* 242
Woodward, Alice *26:* 89; *36:* 81
Wool, David *26:* 27
Woolley, Janet *112:* 75
Woolman, Steven *106:* 47; *163:* 73
Wooten, Vernon *23:* 70; *51:* 170
Worboys, Evelyn *1:* 166, 167
Word, Reagan *103:* 204
Wormell, Christopher *154:* 251; *202:* 206
Worth, Jo *34:* 143
Worth, Wendy *4:* 133
Wosmek, Frances *29:* 251
Wrenn, Charles L. *38:* 96; *YABC 1:* 20, 21
Wright, Barbara Mullarney *98:* 161
Wright, Cliff *168:* 203
Wright, Dare *21:* 206
Wright-Frierson, Virginia *58:* 194; *110:* 246
Wright, George *YABC 1:* 268
Wright, Joseph *30:* 160
Wronker, Lili Cassel *3:* 247; *10:* 204; *21:* 10
Wu, Donald *200:* 18
Wummer, Amy *154:* 181; *168:* 150; *176:* 85; *201:* 202, 203
Wyant, Alexander Helwig *110:* 19
Wyatt, David *97:* 9; *101:* 44; *114:* 194; *140:* 20; *167:* 13; *188:* 48
Wyatt, Stanley *46:* 210
Wyeth, Andrew *13:* 40; *YABC 1:* 133, 134
Wyeth, Jamie *41:* 257
Wyeth, N.C. *13:* 41; *17:* 252, 253, 254, 255, 256, 257, 258, 259, 264, 265, 266, 267, 268; *18:* 181; *19:* 80, 191, 200; *21:* 57, 183; *22:* 91; *23:* 152; *24:* 28, 99; *35:* 61; *41:* 65; *100:* 206; *YABC1:* 133, 223; *2:* 53, 75, 171, 187, 317
Wyman, Cherie R. *91:* 42
Wynne, Patricia J. *210:* 260

X

Xuan, YongSheng *119:* 202, 207, 208; *140:* 36; *187:* 21

Y

Yaccarino, Dan *141:* 208, 209; *147:* 171; *192:* 244, 245; *207:* 168
Yakovetic, Joe *59:* 202; *75:* 85

Yalowitz, Paul *93:* 33; *211:* 92
Yamaguchi, Marianne *85:* 118
Yamasaki, James *167:* 93
Yang, Belle *170:* 198
Yang, Jay *1:* 8; *12:* 239
Yap, Weda *6:* 176
Yaroslava
    See Mills, Yaroslava Surmach
Yashima, Taro *14:* 84
Yates, John *74:* 249, 250
Yates, Kelly *208:* 214
Yayo *178:* 88
Yee, Cora *166:* 233
Yee, Wong Herbert *115:* 216, 217; *172:* 204, 205; *194:* 59
Yelchin, Eugene *204:* 4
Yeo, Brad *135:* 121; *192:* 106
Yerxa, Leo *181:* 195
Yezerski, Thomas F. *162:* 29
Ylla
    See Koffler, Camilla
Yohn, F.C. *23:* 128; *YABC 1:* 269
Yoo, Taeeun *191:* 198
Yorinks, Adrienne *144:* 248; *200:* 214
Yorke, David *80:* 178
Yoshida, Toshi *77:* 231
Yoshikawa, Sachiko *168:* 104; *177:* 28; *181:* 196, 197
Youll, Paul *91:* 218
Youll, Stephen *92:* 227; *118:* 136, 137; *164:* 248; *202:* 92
Young, Amy L. *185:* 218; *190:* 46
Young, Cybéle *167:* 9
Young, Ed *7:* 205; *10:* 206; *40:* 124; *63:* 142; *74:* 250, 251, 252, 253; *75:* 227; *81:* 159; *83:* 98; *94:* 154; *115:* 160; *137:* 162; *YABC 2:* 242; *173:* 174, 175, 176; *205:* 29
Young, Mary O'Keefe *77:* 95; *80:* 247; *134:* 214; *140:* 213; *211:* 223, 225
Young, Noela *8:* 221; *89:* 231; *97:* 195
Young, Paul *190:* 222
Young, Selina *153:* 12; *201:* 204, 205
Yum, Hyewon *211:* 228
Yun, Cheng Mung *60:* 143

Z

Zacharow, Christopher *88:* 98
Zacks, Lewis *10:* 161
Zadig *50:* 58
Zaffo, George *42:* 208
Zagwyn, Deborah Turney *138:* 227
Zahares, Wade *193:* 219
Zaid, Barry *50:* 127; *51:* 201
Zaidenberg, Arthur *34:* 218, 219, 220
Zalben, Jane Breskin *7:* 211; *79:* 230, 231, 233; *170:* 202
Zallinger, Jean *4:* 192; *8:* 8, 129; *14:* 273; *68:* 36; *80:* 254; *115:* 219, 220, 222
Zallinger, Rudolph F. *3:* 245
Zakrajsek, Molly *177:* 146
Zappa, Ahmet *180:* 250
Zebot, George *83:* 214
Zecca, Katherine *207:* 195
Zeck, Gerry *40:* 232
Zeff, Joe *181:* 98
Zeifert, Harriet *154:* 265, 267
Zeiring, Bob *42:* 130
Zeldich, Arieh *49:* 124; *62:* 120
Zeldis, Malcah *86:* 239; *94:* 198; *146:* 265, 266
Zelinsky, Paul O. *14:* 269; *43:* 56; *49:* 218-223; *53:* 111; *68:* 195; *102:* 219, 222, 221, 222; *154:* 255, 256, 257; *171:* 141; *185:* 96
Zelvin, Diana *72:* 190; *76:* 101; *93:* 207
Zemach, Kaethe *149:* 250

Zemach, Margot *3:* 270; *8:* 201; *21:* 210, 211; *27:* 204, 205, 210; *28:* 185; *49:* 22, 183, 224; *53:* 151; *56:* 146; *70:* 245, 246; *92:* 74
Zeman, Ludmila *153* 212
Zemsky, Jessica *10:* 62
Zepelinsky, Paul *35:* 93
Zerbetz, Evon *127:* 34; *158:* 109
Zezejl, Daniel *197:* 74
Zhang, Ange *101:* 190; *172:* 41
Zhang, Son Nang *163:* 113; *170:* 206
Ziegler, Jack *84:* 134
Zimdars, Berta *129:* 155
Zimet, Jay *147:* 94; *152:* 74; *196:* 75

Zimic, Tricia *72:* 95
Zimmer, Dirk *38:* 195; *49:* 71; *56:* 151; *65:* 214; *84:* 159; *89:* 26; *147:* 224
Zimmer, Tracie Vaughn *169:* 183
Zimmerman, Andrea *192:* 49, 50
Zimmermann, H. Werner *101:* 223; *112:* 197
Zimnik, Reiner *36:* 224
Zingone, Robin *180:* 134
Zinkeisen, Anna *13:* 106
Zinn, David *97:* 97
Zoellick, Scott *33:* 231
Zollars, Jaime *190:* 190
Zonia, Dhimitri *20:* 234, 235

Zorn, Peter A., Jr. *142:* 157
Zudeck, Darryl *58:* 129; *63:* 98; *80:* 52
Zug, Mark *88:* 131; *204:* 169
Zulewski, Tim *164:* 95
Zuma *99:* 36
Zvorykin, Boris *61:* 155
Zweifel, Francis *14:* 274; *28:* 187
Zwerger, Lisbeth *54:* 176, 178; *66:* 246, 247, 248; *130:* 230, 231, 232, 233; *181:* 92; *194:* 224, 225, 226
Zwinger, Herman H. *46:* 227
Zwolak, Paul *67:* 69, 71, 73, 74

Author Index

The following index gives the number of the volume in which an author's biographical sketch, Autobiography Feature, Brief Entry, or Obituary appears.

This index includes references to all entries in the following series, which are also published by The Gale Group.

YABC—*Yesterday's Authors of Books for Children: Facts and Pictures about Authors and Illustrators of Books for Young People from Early Times to 1960*

CLR—*Children's Literature Review: Excerpts from Reviews, Criticism, and Commentary on Books for Children*

SAAS—*Something about the Author Autobiography Series*

A

Aardema, Verna 1911-2000 .... *107*
  Obituary *119*
  Earlier sketches in SATA *:4, 68*
  See also CLR *17*
  See also SAAS *8*
Aaron, Chester 1923- *74*
  Earlier sketch in SATA *9*
  See also SAAS *12*
Aaseng, Nate
  See Aaseng, Nathan
Aaseng, Nathan 1953- *172*
  Brief entry *38*
  Earlier sketches in SATA *51, 88*
  See also CLR *54*
  See also SAAS *12*
Abadzis, Nick 1965- *193*
Abalos, Rafael 1956- *197*
Abalos, Rafael 1956-
  See Abalos, Rafael
Abbas, Jailan 1952- *91*
Abbey, Lynn
  See Abbey, Marilyn Lorraine
Abbey, Marilyn Lorraine 1948- *156*
Abbott, Alice
  See Borland, Kathryn Kilby
  and Speicher, Helen Ross S(mith)
Abbott, Jacob 1803-1879 .... *22*
Abbott, Manager Henry
  See Stratemeyer, Edward L.
Abbott, R(obert) Tucker 1919-1995 .... *61*
  Obituary *87*
Abbott, Sarah
  See Zolotow, Charlotte
Abbott, Tony 1952- *205*
  Earlier sketch in SATA *159*
Abdelsayed, Cindy 1962- *123*
Abdul, Raoul 1929- *12*
Abeele, Veronique van den *196*
Abel, Raymond 1911- *12*
Abell, Kathleen 1938- *9*
Abelove, Joan *110*
Abels, Harriette S(heffer) 1926- *50*
Abercrombie, Barbara 1939- *182*
  Earlier sketch in SATA *16*
Abercrombie, Barbara Mattes
  See Abercrombie, Barbara

Abercrombie, Lynn
  See Sorrells, Walter
Abernethy, Robert G(ordon) 1927- *5*
Abisch, Roslyn Kroop 1927- *9*
Abisch, Roz
  See Abisch, Roslyn Kroop
Ablow, Gail 1962- *198*
Abodaher, David J. (Naiph) 1919- *17*
Abolafia, Yossi 1944-
  See Abulafia, Yossi
Abouzeid, Chris *175*
Abrahall, Clare Hoskyns
  See Hoskyns-Abrahall, Clare (Constance Drury)
Abrahams, Hilary (Ruth) 1938- *29*
Abrahams, Peter 1947- *194*
Abrahams, Robert David 1905-1998 .... *4*
Abramovitz, Anita (Zeltner Brooks) 1914- ... *5*
Abrams, Joy 1941- *16*
Abrams, Lawrence F. *58*
  Brief entry *47*
Abrashkin, Raymond 1911-1960 .... *50*
Abulafia, Yossi 1944- *177*
  Brief entry *46*
  Earlier sketch in SATA *60*
Acampora, Paul *175*
Accardo, Anthony *191*
Acer, David *206*
Achebe, Albert Chinualumogu
  See Achebe, Chinua
Achebe, Chinua 1930- *40*
  Brief entry *38*
  Earlier sketch in SATA *38*
  See also CLR *20*
Ackerman, Diane 1948- *102*
Ackerman, Eugene (Francis) 1888-1974 ..... *10*
Ackerman, Karen 1951- *126*
Ackerman, Susan Yoder 1945- *92*
Ackison, Wendy Wassink 1956- *103*
Ackley, Peggy Jo 1955- *58*
Ackroyd, Peter 1949- *153*
Acorn, John (Harrison) 1958- *79*
Acredolo, Linda (Potter) 1947- *159*
Acs, Laszlo (Bela) 1931- *42*
  Brief entry *32*
Acuff, Selma Boyd 1924- *45*
Ada, Alma Flor 1938- *181*
  Earlier sketches in SATA *43, 84, 143*
  See also CLR *62*

Adair, Gilbert 1944- *98*
Adair, Ian 1942- *53*
Adair, Margaret Weeks (?)-1971 .... *10*
Adam, Cornel
  See Lengyel, Cornel Adam
Adam, Mark
  See Alexander, Marc
Adam, Robert 1948- *93*
Adams, Adrienne 1906- *90*
  Earlier sketch in SATA *8*
  See also CLR *73*
Adams, Andy 1859-1935
  See YABC *1*
Adams, Barbara Johnston 1943- *60*
Adams, Bruin
  See Ellis, Edward S.
Adams, Captain Bruin
  See Ellis, Edward S.
Adams, Captain J. F. C.
  See Ellis, Edward S.
Adams, Dale
  See Quinn, Elisabeth
Adams, Daniel
  See Nicole, Christopher (Robin)
Adams, Debra
  See Speregen, Devra Newberger
Adams, Douglas 1952-2001 .... *116*
  Obituary *128*
Adams, Douglas Noel
  See Adams, Douglas
Adams, Edith
  See Shine, Deborah
Adams, Florence 1932- *61*
Adams, Harriet S(tratemeyer) 1892(?)-1982 . *1*
  Obituary *29*
Adams, Harrison
  See Rathborne, St. George (Henry)
  and Stratemeyer, Edward L.
Adams, Hazard 1926- *6*
Adams, Hazard Simeon
  See Adams, Hazard
Adams, John Anthony 1944- *67*
Adams, Laurie 1941- *33*
Adams, Lowell
  See Joseph, James (Herz)
Adams, Nicholas
  See Pine, Nicholas
Adams, Nicholas
  See Smith, Sherwood

Adams, Nicholas
 See Doyle, Debra
 and Macdonald, James D.
Adams, Pam 1919- *112*
Adams, Pamela
 See Adams, Pam
Adams, Richard 1920- *69*
 Earlier sketch in SATA 7
 See also CLR *121*
Adams, Richard George
 See Adams, Richard
Adams, Ruth Joyce *14*
Adams, Tricia
 See Kite, Pat
Adams, William Taylor 1822-1897 .... *28*
Adam Smith, Janet (Buchanan)
 1905-1999 .... *63*
Adamson, Gareth 1925-1982(?) *46*
 Obituary *30*
Adamson, George 1906-1989
 Obituary *63*
Adamson, George (Worsley) 1913-2005 ..... *30*
Adamson, Graham
 See Groom, Arthur William
Adamson, Joy(-Friederike Victoria)
 1910-1980 .... *11*
 Obituary *22*
Adamson, Wendy Writson 1942- *22*
Addasi, Maha 1968- *205*
Addison, Kenneth 1949(?)-2005 .... *187*
Addison, Kenneth L.
 See Addison, Kenneth
Addona, Angelo F. 1925- *14*
Addy, Sharon Hart 1943- *192*
 Earlier sketch in SATA *108*
Addy, Ted
 See Winterbotham, R(ussell) R(obert)
Adelberg, Doris
 See Orgel, Doris
Adelson, Leone 1908- *11*
Adinolfi, JoAnn *176*
Adkins, Jan 1944- *210*
 Autobiography Feature *210*
 Earlier sketches in SATA 8, 69, 144
 See also CLR 77
 See also SAAS 19
Adler, C(arole) S(chwerdtfeger) 1932- *126*
 Earlier sketches in SATA 26, 63, 102
 See also CLR 78
 See also SAAS 15
Adler, David A. 1947- *178*
 Earlier sketches in SATA 14, 70, 106, 151
 See also CLR 108
Adler, Irene
 See Penzler, Otto
 and Storr, Catherine (Cole)
Adler, Irving 1913- *29*
 Autobiography Feature *164*
 Earlier sketch in SATA 1
 See also CLR 27
 See also SAAS 15
Adler, Larry 1939- *36*
Adler, Peggy *22*
Adler, Ruth 1915-1968 .... *1*
Adlerman, Daniel (Ezra) 1963- *163*
 Earlier sketch in SATA 96
Adlerman, Kim
 See Adlerman, Kimberly M(arie)
Adlerman, Kimberly M(arie) 1964- *163*
 Earlier sketch in SATA 96
Adoff, Arnold 1935- *96*
 Earlier sketches in SATA 5, 57
 See also CLR 7
 See also SAAS 15
Adoff, Jaime *163*
Adoff, Jaime Levi
 See Adoff, Jaime
Adorjan, Carol (Madden) 1934- *71*
 Earlier sketch in SATA 10
Adrian, Frances
 See Polland, Madeleine A(ngela Cahill)

Adrian, Mary
 See Jorgensen, Mary Venn
Adshead, Gladys L(ucy) 1896-1985 .... *3*
Aesop 620(?)B.C.-560(?)B.C. *64*
 See also CLR 14
Aesop, Abraham
 See Newbery, John
Affabee, Eric
 See Stine, R.L.
Agapida, Fray Antonio
 See Irving, Washington
Agard, John 1949- *138*
Agard, Nadema 1948- *18*
Agarwal, Deepa 1947- *141*
Agee, Jon 1960- *196*
 Earlier sketches in SATA *116, 157*
Agell, Charlotte 1959- *150*
 Earlier sketch in SATA 99
Agent Orange
 See Moseley, James W(illett)
Aghill, Gordon
 See Garrett, Randall
 and Silverberg, Robert
Agle, Nan Hayden 1905- *3*
 See also SAAS 10
Agnew, Edith J(osephine) 1897-1988 .... *11*
Agonito, Joseph *177*
Agonito, Rosemary 1937- *177*
Ahern, Margaret McCrohan 1921- *10*
Ahl, Anna Maria 1926- *32*
Ahlberg, Allan 1938- *165*
 Brief entry *35*
 Earlier sketches in SATA 68, 120
 See also CLR 18
Ahlberg, Janet 1944-1994 .... *120*
 Brief entry *32*
 Obituary *83*
 Earlier sketch in SATA 68
 See also CLR 18
Aho, Julia Kay
 See Kay, Julia
Aichinger, Helga 1937- *4*
Aiken, Clarissa (M.) Lorenz 1899-1992 ..... *12*
 Obituary *109*
Aiken, Conrad 1889-1973 .... *30*
 Earlier sketch in SATA 3
Aiken, Conrad Potter
 See Aiken, Conrad
Aiken, Joan (Delano) 1924-2004 .... *73*
 Autobiography Feature *109*
 Obituary *152*
 Earlier sketches in SATA 2, 30
 See also CLR 90
 See also SAAS 1
Aillaud, Cindy Lou 1955- *184*
Ainsley, Alix
 See Steiner, Barbara A(nnette)
Ainsworth, Catherine Harris 1910- *56*
Ainsworth, Norma 1911-1987 .... *9*
Ainsworth, Ruth (Gallard) 1908- *73*
 Earlier sketch in SATA 7
Ainsworth, William Harrison 1805-1882 .... *24*
Aistrop, Jack 1916- *14*
Aitken, Amy 1952- *54*
 Brief entry *40*
Aitken, Dorothy 1916- *10*
Aitmatov, Chingiz 1928-2008 .... *56*
Aitmatov, Chingiz Torekulovich
 See Aitmatov, Chingiz
Akaba, Suekichi 1910- *46*
Akers, Floyd
 See Baum, L. Frank
Akib, Jamel *181*
Aks, Patricia 1926-1994 .... *68*
Alagoa, Ebiegberi Joe 1933- *108*
Alain
 See Brustlein, Daniel
Alajalov, Constantin 1900-1987
 Obituary *53*
Alalou, Ali *203*
Alalou, Elizabeth *203*

Alan, David
 See Horsfield, Alan
Alan, Robert
 See Silverstein, Robert Alan
Alarcon, Francisco X. 1954- *104*
Alarcon, Francisco Xavier
 See Alarcon, Francisco X.
Alarcon, Karen Beaumont
 See Beaumont, Karen
Albert, Burton 1936- *22*
Albert, Louise 1928- *157*
Albert, Michael 1966- *202*
Albert, Richard E. 1909-1999 .... *82*
Albert, Susan Wittig 1940- *107*
Alberts, Frances Jacobs 1907-1989 .... *14*
Albertson, Susan
 See Wojciechowski, Susan
Albion, Lee Smith *29*
Alborough, Jez 1959- *149*
 Earlier sketch in SATA 86
Albrecht, Lillie (Vanderveer H.)
 1894-1985 .... *12*
Albyn, Carole Lisa 1955- *83*
Alchemy, Jack
 See Gershator, David
Alcock, Gudrun 1908- *56*
 Brief entry *33*
Alcock, Vivien (Dolores) 1924-2003 .... *76*
 Brief entry *38*
 Obituary *148*
 Earlier sketch in SATA 45
 See also CLR 26
Alcorn, John 1935- *31*
 Brief entry *30*
Alcorn, Stephen 1958- *207*
 Earlier sketch in SATA 110
Alcott, Louisa May 1832-1888 .... *100*
 See also YABC 1
 See also CLR 109
Alda, Arlene 1933- *205*
 Brief entry *36*
 Earlier sketches in SATA 44, 106, 158
 See also CLR 93
Alden, Isabella (Macdonald) 1841-1930 ... *115*
 See also YABC 2
Alden, Sue
 See Francis, Dorothy
Alderman, Clifford Lindsey 1902-1988 .... *3*
Alderson, Sue Ann 1940- *59*
 Brief entry *48*
Alding, Peter
 See Jeffries, Roderic
Aldis, Dorothy (Keeley) 1896-1966 .... *2*
Aldiss, Brian W. 1925- *34*
Aldiss, Brian Wilson
 See Aldiss, Brian W.
Aldon, Adair
 See Meigs, Cornelia Lynde
Aldous, Allan (Charles) 1911- *27*
Aldrich, Ann
 See Meaker, Marijane
Aldrich, Bess Streeter 1881-1954
 See CLR 70
Aldrich, Thomas (Bailey) 1836-1907 .... *114*
 Earlier sketch in SATA 17
Aldridge, (Harold Edward) James 1918- *87*
Aldridge, Josephine Haskell *14*
Aldridge, Sheila 1974- *192*
Aleas, Richard
 See Appelt, Kathi
Alegria, Malin 1974(?)- *190*
Alegria, Ricardo E(nrique) 1921- *6*
Aleksin, Anatolii Georgievich 1924- *36*
Alenov, Lydia 1948- *61*
Alex, Ben (a pseudonym) 1946- *45*
Alex, Marlee (a pseudonym) 1948- *45*
Alexander, Anna B(arbara Cooke) 1913- *1*
Alexander, Anne
 See Alexander, Anna B(arbara Cooke)
Alexander, Ellen 1938- *91*
Alexander, Frances (Laura) 1888-1979 .... *4*

Alexander, Janet 1907-1994 97
  Earlier sketch in SATA *1*
Alexander, Jocelyn Anne Arundel 1930- 22
Alexander, Linda 1935- 2
Alexander, Lloyd 1924-2007 135
  Obituary 182
  Earlier sketches in SATA *3, 49, 81, 129*
  See also CLR *48*
  See also SAAS *19*
Alexander, Lloyd Chudley
  See Alexander, Lloyd
Alexander, Marc 1929- 117
Alexander, Martha 1920- 136
  Earlier sketches in SATA *11, 70*
Alexander, Rae Pace
  See Alexander, Raymond Pace
Alexander, Raymond Pace 1898-1974 22
Alexander, Robert 200
Alexander, Rod
  See Pellowski, Michael (Joseph)
Alexander, Sally Hobart 1943- 84
Alexander, Sue 1933-2008 136
  Obituary 195
  Earlier sketches in SATA *12, 89*
  See also SAAS *15*
Alexander, Vincent Arthur 1925-1980
  Obituary 23
Alexeieff, Alexandre A. 1901-1979 14
Alger, Horatio, Jr.
  See Stratemeyer, Edward L.
Alger, Horatio, Jr. 1832-1899 16
  See also CLR *87*
Alger, Leclaire (Gowans) 1898-1969 15
Aliki
  See Brandenberg, Aliki
Alkema, Chester Jay 1932- 12
Al-Khalili, Jim 1962- 124
Alkiviades, Alkis 1953- 105
Alkouatli, Claire 186
Allaby, John Michael
  See Allaby, Michael
Allaby, Michael 1933- 167
Allamand, Pascale 1942- 12
Allan, Mabel Esther 1915-1998 75
  Earlier sketches in SATA *5, 32*
  See also CLR *43*
  See also SAAS *11*
Allan, Nicholas 1956- 123
  Earlier sketch in SATA *79*
Allan-Meyer, Kathleen 1918- 51
  Brief entry 46
Allard, Harry
  See Allard, Harry G(rover), Jr.
Allard, Harry G(rover), Jr. 1928- 102
  Earlier sketch in SATA *42*
  See also CLR *85*
Allee, Marjorie Hill 1890-1945 17
Allen, Adam
  See Epstein, Beryl
  and Epstein, Samuel
Allen, Alex B.
  See Heide, Florence Parry
Allen, Allyn
  See Eberle, Irmengarde
Allen, Betsy
  See Harrison, Elizabeth (Allen) Cavanna
Allen, Bob 1961- 76
Allen, Gertrude E(lizabeth) 1888-1984 9
Allen, Grace
  See Hogarth, Grace (Weston Allen)
Allen, Jeffrey (Yale) 1948- 42
Allen, John
  See Perry, Ritchie (John Allen)
Allen, Jonathan 1957- 177
  Earlier sketch in SATA *131*
Allen, Jonathan Dean
  See Allen, Jonathan
Allen, Judy (Christina) 1941- 124
  Earlier sketch in SATA *80*
Allen, Kenneth S. 1913-1981 56
Allen, Leroy 1912- 11

Allen, Linda 1925- 33
Allen, Marjorie 1931- 22
Allen, Maury 1932- 26
Allen, Merritt Parmelee 1892-1954 22
Allen, Nancy Kelly 1949- 171
  Earlier sketch in SATA *127*
Allen, Nina (Stroemgren) 1935- 22
Allen, Pamela (Kay) 1934- 123
  Earlier sketches in SATA *50, 81*
  See also CLR *44*
Allen, Raul 205
Allen, Rodney F. 1938-1999 27
Allen, Roger MacBride 1957- 105
Allen, Ruth
  See Peterson, Esther (Allen)
Allen, Samuel W(ashington) 1917- 9
Allen, T. D.
  See Allen, Terril Diener
Allen, Terril Diener 1908- 35
Allen, Terry D.
  See Allen, Terril Diener
Allen, Thomas B. 1929- 193
  Earlier sketches in SATA *45, 140*
Allen, Thomas Benton
  See Allen, Thomas B.
Allen, Tom
  See Allen, Thomas B.
Allende, Isabel 1942- 163
  See also CLR *99*
Allerton, Mary
  See Govan, (Mary) Christine Noble
Alley, Robert W.
  See Alley, R.W.
Alley, R.W. 211
  Earlier sketch in SATA *169*
Alleyn, Ellen
  See Rossetti, Christina
Allington, Richard L(loyd) 1947- 39
  Brief entry 35
Allison, Amy 1956- 138
Allison, Bob 14
Allison, Diane Worfolk 78
Allison, Jennifer 173
Allison, Linda 1948- 43
Allison, Margaret
  See Klam, Cheryl
Allman, Barbara 1950- 137
Allmendinger, David F(rederick), Jr.
  1938- 35
Allred, Alexandra Powe 1965- 144
Allred, Gordon T(hatcher) 1930- 10
Allsop, Kenneth 1920-1973 17
Allsopp, Sophie 188
Alma, Ann 1946- 201
Almedingen, E. M.
  See Almedingen, Martha Edith von
Almedingen, Martha Edith von 1898-1971 ... 3
Almon, Russell
  See Clevenger, William R.
  and Downing, David A(lmon)
Almond, David 1951- 158
  Earlier sketch in SATA *114*
  See also CLR *85*
Almond, Linda Stevens 1881(?)-1987
  Obituary 50
Almquist, Don 1929- 11
Alonzo, Sandra 199
Alphin, Elaine Marie 1955- 139
  Autobiography Feature 139
  Earlier sketches in SATA *80, 130*
Alsenas, Linas 1979- 186
Alsop, Mary O'Hara 1885-1980 34
  Obituary 24
  Earlier sketch in SATA *2*
Alter, Anna 1974- 206
  Earlier sketch in SATA *135*
Alter, Judith (MacBain) 1938- 101
  Earlier sketch in SATA *52*
Alter, Judy
  See Alter, Judith (MacBain)
Alter, Robert Edmond 1925-1965 9

Alter, Stephen 1956- 187
Althea
  See Braithwaite, Althea
Altman, Linda Jacobs 1943- 21
Altman, Suzanne
  See Orgel, Doris
  and Schecter, Ellen
Alton, Steve 169
Altschuler, Franz 1923- 45
Altsheler, Joseph A(lexander) 1862-1919
  See YABC *1*
Alvarez, John
  See del Rey, Lester
Alvarez, Joseph A. 1930- 18
Alvarez, Julia 1950- 129
al-Windawi, Thura
  See Windawi, Thura al-
Alyer, Philip A.
  See Stratemeyer, Edward L.
Amado, Elisa 193
Amann, Janet 1951- 79
Amato, Carol A. 1942- 92
Amato, Mary 1961- 178
  Earlier sketch in SATA *140*
Ambrose, Stephen E. 1936-2002 138
  Earlier sketch in SATA *40*
Ambrose, Stephen Edward
  See Ambrose, Stephen E.
Ambrus, Gyozo Laszlo 1935- 1
  See also SAAS *4*
Ambrus, Victor G.
  See Ambrus, Gyozo Laszlo
Amend, Bill 1962- 147
Amerman, Lockhart 1911-1969 3
Ames, Evelyn 1908-1990 13
  Obituary 64
Ames, Gerald 1906-1993 11
  Obituary 74
Ames, Lee J(udah) 1921- 151
  Earlier sketch in SATA *3*
Ames, Mildred 1919-1994 85
  Earlier sketches in SATA *22, 81*
Amico, Tom 1960(?)- 176
Amit, Ofra 1966- 205
Ammon, Richard 1942- 124
Amon, Aline 1928- 9
Amoss, Berthe 1925- 112
  Earlier sketch in SATA *5*
Anastasio, Dina 1941- 94
  Brief entry 30
  Earlier sketch in SATA *37*
Anaya, Rudolfo 1937-
  See CLR *129*
Anaya, Rudolfo A.
  See Anaya, Rudolfo
Anaya, Rudolpho Alfonso
  See Anaya, Rudolfo
Anckarsvard, Karin Inez Maria 1915-1969 ... 6
Ancona, George 1929- 208
  Autobiography Feature 208
  Earlier sketches in SATA *12, 85, 145, 192*
  See also SAAS *18*
Anders, C. J.
  See Bennett, Cherie
Anders, Isabel 1946- 101
Anders, Lou 176
Andersdatter, Karla M(argaret) 1938- 34
Andersen, Bethanne 1954- 191
Andersen, Hans Christian 1805-1875 100
  See also YABC *1*
  See also CLR *113*
Andersen, Ted
  See Boyd, Waldo T.
Andersen, Yvonne 1932- 27
Anderson, Bernice G(oudy) 1894-1997 33
Anderson, Bob 1944- 139
  Earlier sketch in SATA *136*
Anderson, Brad(ley Jay) 1924- 33
  Brief entry 31
Anderson, Brian 1974- 211

Anderson, C. C.
See Anderson, Catherine Corley
Anderson, C(larence) W(illiam)
1891-1971 .... *11*
Anderson, Carolyn Dunn
See Dunn, Carolyn
Anderson, Catherine C.
See Anderson, Catherine Corley
Anderson, Catherine Corley 1909-2001 ...... *72*
Anderson, Clifford
See Gardner, Richard (M.)
Anderson, Daryl Shon 1963- *93*
Anderson, Dave
See Anderson, David
Anderson, David 1929- *60*
Anderson, Derek 1969- *169*
Anderson, Eloise Adell 1927- *9*
Anderson, George
See Groom, Arthur William
Anderson, Grace Fox 1932- *43*
Anderson, J(ohn) R(ichard) L(ane)
1911-1981 .... *15*
Obituary *27*
Anderson, Jodi Lynn *182*
Anderson, John David 1975- *197*
Anderson, John L. 1905- *2*
Anderson, Joy 1928- *1*
Anderson, Kevin J. 1962- *117*
Earlier sketch in SATA *74*
Anderson, Kevin James
See Anderson, Kevin J.
Anderson, Kirsty 1978- *108*
Anderson, K.J.
See Moesta, Rebecca
Anderson, Laurie Halse 1961- *186*
Earlier sketches in SATA *95, 132*
See also CLR *138*
Anderson, LaVere Francis Shoenfelt
1907-1998 .... *27*
Anderson, Leone Castell 1923- *53*
Brief entry *49*
Anderson, Lisa G. 1963- *108*
Anderson, Lonzo
See Anderson, John L.
Anderson, Lucia (Lewis) 1922- *10*
Anderson, Madelyn Klein 1926-2005 .... *28*
Anderson, Margaret J(ean) 1931- *27*
See also SAAS *8*
Anderson, Marilyn D. 1943- *144*
Anderson, Mary 1939- *82*
Earlier sketch in SATA *7*
See also SAAS *23*
Anderson, Matthew Tobin
See Anderson, M.T.
Anderson, Mona 1910-2004 .... *40*
Anderson, Mrs. Melvin
See Anderson, Catherine Corley
Anderson, M.T. 1968- *182*
Earlier sketches in SATA *97, 146*
Anderson, Norman Dean 1928- *22*
Anderson, Peggy Perry 1953- *179*
Earlier sketch in SATA *84*
Anderson, Poul 1926-2001 .... *90*
Autobiography Feature *106*
Brief entry *39*
See also CLR *58*
Anderson, Poul William
See Anderson, Poul
Anderson, Rachel 1943- *86*
Earlier sketch in SATA *34*
See also SAAS *18*
Anderson, Rebecca M.
See Moesta, Rebecca
Anderson, Rebecca Moesta
See Moesta, Rebecca
Anderson, Richard
See Anderson, J(ohn) R(ichard) L(ane)
Anderson, Sara *173*
Anderson, Scoular *201*
Anderson, (Tom) Scoular *138*
Anderson, Susan 1952- *90*

Anderson, Thomas Scoular
See Anderson, Scoular
Anderson, W. B.
See Schultz, James Willard
Anderson, Wayne 1946- *202*
Earlier sketches in SATA *56, 147*
Andersson, Kenneth 1970- *200*
Andre, Evelyn M(arie) 1924- *27*
Andreasen, Dan *186*
Andreassen, Karl
See Boyd, Waldo T.
Andreassi, K. Robert
See DeCandido, Keith R.A.
Andree, Louise
See Coury, Louise Andree
Andrew, Ian 1962- *166*
Earlier sketch in SATA *116*
Andrew, Ian Peter
See Andrew, Ian
Andrew, Prudence (Hastings) 1924- *87*
Andrews, Benny 1930-2006 .... *31*
Obituary *178*
Andrews, Eleanor Lattimore
See Lattimore, Eleanor Frances
Andrews, Elton V.
See Pohl, Frederik
Andrews, F(rank) Emerson 1902-1978 .... *22*
Andrews, J(ames) S(ydney) 1934- *4*
Andrews, Jan 1942- *167*
Brief entry *49*
Earlier sketches in SATA *58, 98*
Andrews, Julie 1935- *153*
Earlier sketch in SATA *7*
See also CLR *85*
Andrews, Laura
See Coury, Louise Andree
Andrews, Roy Chapman 1884-1960 .... *19*
Andrews, Tamra 1959- *129*
Andrews, V(irginia) C(leo) 1924(?)-1986
Obituary *50*
Andrews, Wendy
See Sharmat, Marjorie Weinman
Andrews, William G(eorge) 1930- *74*
Andrezel, Pierre
See Blixen, Karen
Andriani, Renee
See Williams-Andriani, Renee
Andriola, Alfred J. 1912-1983
Obituary *34*
Andrist, Ralph K. 1914-2004 .... *45*
Andronik, Catherine M. *189*
Andryszewski, Tricia 1956- *148*
Earlier sketch in SATA *88*
Angel, Ann 1952- *192*
Angel, Carl *178*
Angel, Marie 1923- *47*
Angeles, Peter A. 1931- *40*
Angeletti, Roberta 1964- *124*
Angeli, Marguerite (Lofft) de
See de Angeli, Marguerite (Lofft)
Angell, Judie 1937- *78*
Earlier sketch in SATA *22*
See also CLR *33*
Angell, Madeline 1919- *18*
Angelo, Valenti 1897- *14*
Angelou, Maya 1928- *136*
Earlier sketch in SATA *49*
See also CLR *53*
Angier, Bradford -1997 .... *12*
Angle, Kimberly Greene *203*
Angle, Paul M(cClelland) 1900-1975
Obituary *20*
Anglund, Joan Walsh 1926- *2*
See also CLR *94*
Ango, Fan D.
See Longyear, Barry B(rookes)
Angrist, Stanley W(olff) 1933- *4*
Anholt, Catherine 1958- *131*
Earlier sketch in SATA *74*
Anholt, Laurence 1959- *141*
Earlier sketch in SATA *74*

Anita
See Daniel, Anita
Anmar, Frank
See Nolan, William F.
Annett, Cora
See Scott, Cora Annett (Pipitone)
Annie-Jo
See Blanchard, Patricia
and Suhr, Joanne
Annixter, Jane
See Sturtzel, Jane Levington
Annixter, Paul
See Sturtzel, Howard A(llison)
Anno, Mitsumasa 1926- *157*
Earlier sketches in SATA *5, 38, 77*
See also CLR *122*
Anrooy, Francine Van
See Van Anrooy, Francine
Ansary, Mir Tamim 1948- *140*
Anstey, Caroline 1958- *81*
Antell, Will D. 1935- *31*
Anthony, Barbara
See Barber, Antonia
Anthony, C. L.
See Smith, Dorothy Gladys
Anthony, Edward 1895-1971 .... *21*
Anthony, John
See Beckett, Ronald Brymer
and Ciardi, John (Anthony)
and Sabini, John Anthony
Anthony, Joseph Patrick 1964- *103*
Anthony, Patricia 1947- *109*
Anthony, Piers 1934- *129*
Autobiography Feature *129*
Earlier sketch in SATA *84*
See also CLR *118*
See also SAAS *22*
Anthony, Susan C(arol) 1953- *87*
Anticaglia, Elizabeth 1939- *12*
Antilles, Kem
See Moesta, Rebecca
Antle, Nancy 1955- *102*
Antolini, Margaret Fishback 1904-1985
Obituary *45*
Anton, Michael J(ames) 1940- *12*
Antonacci, Robert J(oseph) 1916- *45*
Brief entry *37*
Anvil, Christopher 1925-2009 .... *102*
Anzaldua, Gloria (Evanjelina) 1942-2004
Obituary *154*
Aoki, Hisako 1942- *45*
Apfel, Necia H(alpern) 1930- *51*
Brief entry *41*
Aphrodite, J.
See Livingston, Carole
Apikuni
See Schultz, James Willard
Apostolina, M. *184*
Apostolina, Michael
See Apostolina, M.
Apostolou, Christine Hale 1955- *179*
Earlier sketches in SATA *82, 128*
Appel, Allen (R.) 1945- *115*
Appel, Benjamin 1907-1977 .... *39*
Obituary *21*
Appel, Martin 1948- *45*
Appel, Martin Eliot
See Appel, Martin
Appel, Marty
See Appel, Martin
Appelbaum, Diana Muir Karter 1953- *132*
Appelt, Kathi 1954- *190*
Earlier sketches in SATA *83, 129*
Apperley, Dawn 1969- *135*
Appiah, Peggy 1921-2006 .... *84*
Earlier sketch in SATA *15*
See also SAAS *19*
Apple, Margot *152*
Brief entry *42*
Earlier sketch in SATA *64*
Applebaum, Stan 1922- *45*

Applegate, K.A.
　See Applegate, Katherine
Applegate, Katherine 1956- 196
　Earlier sketches in SATA 109, 162
　See also CLR 90
Applegate, Katherine Alice
　See Applegate, Katherine
Appleton, Victor
　See Barrett, Neal, Jr.
　and Doyle, Debra
　and Macdonald, James D.
　and Stratemeyer, Edward L.
　and Vardeman, Robert E(dward)
Appleton, Victor II
　See Goulart, Ron
Apsler, Alfred 1907-1982 10
Aragones, Sergio 1937- 48
　Brief entry 39
Araujo, Frank P. 1937- 86
Arbo, Cris 1950- 103
Arbuckle, Dorothy Fry 1910-1982
　Obituary 33
Arbuthnot, May Hill 1884-1969 2
Archambault, John 163
　Earlier sketches in SATA 67, 112
Archbold, Rick 1950- 97
Archer, Colleen Rutherford 1949- 164
Archer, Frank
　See O'Connor, Richard
Archer, Jules 1915- 85
　Earlier sketch in SATA 4
　See also SAAS 5
Archer, Lily 1981- 193
Archer, Marion Fuller 1917- 11
Archer, Nathan
　See Watt-Evans, Lawrence
Archer, Peggy 1947- 199
Archibald, Joe
　See Archibald, Joseph S(topford)
Archibald, Joseph S(topford) 1898-1986 3
　Obituary 47
Ard, William
　See Jakes, John
Ardagh, Philip 1961- 154
Ardai, Charles 1969- 85
Arden, Barbi
　See Stoutenburg, Adrien (Pearl)
Arden, William
　See Lynds, Dennis
Ardizzone, Edward (Jeffrey Irving)
　1900-1979 28
　Obituary 21
　Earlier sketch in SATA 1
　See also CLR 3
Ardley, Neil (Richard) 1937- 121
　Earlier sketch in SATA 43
Arehart-Treichel, Joan 1942- 22
Arena, Felice 1968- 151
Arenella, Roy 1939- 14
Argent, Kerry 1960- 138
Arguelles, Francisco Xavier
　See Stork, Francisco X.
Argueta, Jorge 179
Arihara, Shino 1973- 201
Arkin, Alan 1934- 59
　Brief entry 32
Arkin, Alan Wolf
　See Arkin, Alan
Arksey, Neil 158
Arlen, Leslie
　See Nicole, Christopher (Robin)
Arley, Robert
　See Jackson, Mike
Armer, Alberta (Roller) 1904-1986 9
Armer, Laura Adams 1874-1963 13
Armistead, John 1941- 130
Armitage, David 1943- 155
　Brief entry 38
　Earlier sketch in SATA 99
Armitage, Frank
　See Carpenter, John

Armitage, Ronda (Jacqueline) 1943- 155
　Brief entry 38
　Earlier sketches in SATA 47, 99
Armour, Richard (Willard) 1906-1989 14
　Obituary 61
Armstrong, Alan 1939- 172
Armstrong, Alan W.
　See Armstrong, Alan
Armstrong, George D. 1927- 10
Armstrong, Gerry (Breen) 1929- 10
Armstrong, Jeannette (C.) 1948- 102
Armstrong, Jennifer 1961- 165
　Autobiography Feature 120
　Earlier sketches in SATA 77, 111
　See also CLR 66
　See also SAAS 24
Armstrong, Louise 43
　Brief entry 33
Armstrong, Martin Donisthorpe
　1882-1974 115
Armstrong, Matthew 1975- 188
Armstrong, Matthew S.
　See Armstrong, Matthew
Armstrong, Ralph Richard
　See Armstrong, Richard
Armstrong, Richard 1903-1986 11
Armstrong, William H(oward) 1914-1999 4
　Obituary 111
　See also CLR 117
　See also SAAS 7
Armstrong-Ellis, Carey (Fraser) 1956- 145
Arndt, Ursula (Martha H.) 56
　Brief entry 39
Arneson, D(on) J(on) 1935- 37
Arnett, Caroline
　See Cole, Lois Dwight
Arnett, Jack
　See Goulart, Ron
Arnette, Robert
　See Silverberg, Robert
Arno, Enrico 1913-1981 43
　Obituary 28
Arnold, Ann 1953(?)- 207
Arnold, Caroline 1944- 174
　Brief entry 34
　Earlier sketches in SATA 36, 85, 131
　See also CLR 61
　See also SAAS 23
Arnold, Elizabeth 1944- 164
Arnold, Elliott 1912-1980 5
　Obituary 22
Arnold, Emily 1939- 134
　Autobiography Feature 134
　Earlier sketches in SATA 5, 50, 76, 110
　See also CLR 46
　See also SAAS 7
　See McCully, Emily Arnold
Arnold, Gillian Clare
　See Cross, Gillian
Arnold, Katya 1947- 168
　Earlier sketches in SATA 82, 115
Arnold, Louise 175
Arnold, Marsha Diane 1948- 147
　Earlier sketch in SATA 93
Arnold, Nick 1961- 113
Arnold, Oren 1900-1980 4
Arnold, Susan (Riser) 1951- 58
Arnold, Tedd 1949- 208
　Earlier sketches in SATA 69, 116, 160
Arnoldy, Julie
　See Bischoff, Julia Bristol
Arnosky, James Edward 1946- 189
　Earlier sketches in SATA 70, 118
　See also CLR 93
Arnosky, Jim
　See Arnosky, James Edward
Arnott, Kathleen 1914- 20
Arnov, Boris, Jr. 1926- 12
Arnow, Harriette (Louisa) Simpson
　1908-1986 42
　Obituary 47

Arnsteen, Katy Keck 1934- 68
Arnstein, Helene S(olomon) 1915- 12
Arntson, Herbert E(dward) 1911-1982 12
Aroner, Miriam 82
Aronin, Ben 1904-1980
　Obituary 25
Aronson, Marc 1950- 189
　Autobiography Feature 189
　Earlier sketches in SATA 126, 175
Aronson, Marc Henry
　See Aronson, Marc
Aronson, Sarah 196
Aronson, Virginia 1954- 122
Arora, Shirley (Lease) 1930- 2
Arrasmith, Patrick 176
Arrick, Fran
　See Angell, Judie
Arrigan, Mary 1943- 142
Arrington, Aileen 183
Arrington, Stephen L. 1948- 97
Arrington, Stephen Lee
　See Arrington, Stephen L.
Arrley, Richmond
　See Delany, Samuel R., Jr.
Arrowood, (McKendrick Lee)
　Clinton 1939- 19
Arrowsmith, Pat 1930- 59
Arsenault, Isabelle 1978- 207
Artell, Mike 1948- 183
　Earlier sketches in SATA 89, 134
Arthur, Robert (Andrew) 1909-1969
　See Arthur, Robert, (Jr.)
Arthur, Robert, (Jr.) 1909-1969 118
Arthur, Ruth M(abel) 1905-1979 26
　Earlier sketch in SATA 7
Artis, Vicki Kimmel 1945- 12
Artzybasheff, Boris (Miklailovich)
　1899-1965 14
Aruego, Ariane
　See Dewey, Ariane
Aruego, Jose 1932- 178
　Earlier sketches in SATA 6, 68, 125
　See also CLR 5
Aruego, Jose Espiritu
　See Aruego, Jose
Arundel, Honor (Morfydd) 1919-1973 4
　Obituary 24
　See also CLR 35
Arundel, Jocelyn
　See Alexander, Jocelyn Anne Arundel
Arvey, Michael 1948- 79
Arzoumanian, Alik 177
Asare, Meshack (Yaw) 1945- 139
　Earlier sketch in SATA 86
Asaro, Catherine 1955- 165
　Earlier sketch in SATA 101
Asaro, Catherine Ann 1955-
　See Asaro, Catherine
Asay, Donna Day 1945- 127
Asbjornsen, Peter Christen 1812-1885 15
　See also CLR 104
Asch, Frank 1946- 154
　Earlier sketches in SATA 5, 66, 102
Ash, Jutta 1942- 38
Ashabranner, Brent 1921- 166
　Earlier sketches in SATA 1, 67, 130
　See also CLR 28
　See also SAAS 14
Ashabranner, Brent Kenneth
　See Ashabranner, Brent
Ashbless, William
　See Blaylock, James P.
　and Powers, Tim
Ashby, Gil 1958- 146
Ashby, Gwynneth 1922- 44
Ashby, Ruth 170
Ashby, Yvonne 1955- 121
Ashe, Arthur (Robert, Jr.) 1943-1993 65
　Obituary 87
Ashe, Geoffrey (Thomas) 1923- 17
　Autobiography Feature 125

Ashe, Mary Ann
 See Lewis, Mary
Asher, Bridget
 See Baggott, Julianna
Asher, Sandra Fenichel
 See Asher, Sandy
Asher, Sandy 1942- 71
 Autobiography Feature 158
 Brief entry 34
 Earlier sketch in SATA *36*
 See also SAAS *13*
Asheron, Sara
 See Moore, Lilian
Ashey, Bella
 See Breinburg, Petronella
Ashford, Daisy
 See Ashford, Margaret Mary
Ashford, Jeffrey
 See Jeffries, Roderic
Ashford, Margaret Mary 1881-1972 10
Ashland, Monk 1972- 207
Ashley, Bernard (John) 1935- 155
 Brief entry 39
 Earlier sketches in SATA *47, 79*
 See also CLR *4*
Ashley, Elizabeth
 See Salmon, Annie Elizabeth
Ashley, Ray
 See Abrashkin, Raymond
Ashman, Linda 1960- 203
 Earlier sketch in SATA *150*
Ashton, Lorayne
 See Gottfried, Theodore Mark
Ashton, Warren T.
 See Adams, William Taylor
Asimov, Isaac 1920-1992 74
 Earlier sketches in SATA *1, 26*
 See also CLR *79*
Asinof, Eliot 1919-2008 6
Asinof, Eliot Tager
 See Asinof, Eliot
Aska, Warabe
 See Masuda, Takeshi
Asprin, Robert 1946-2008 92
Asprin, Robert L.
 See Asprin, Robert
Asprin, Robert Lynn
 See Asprin, Robert
Asquith, Cynthia Mary Evelyn (Charteris)
 1887-1960 107
Asquith, Ros 153
Astley, Juliet
 See Lofts, Norah (Robinson)
Aston, Dianna Hutts 1964- 176
Aston, James
 See White, T(erence) H(anbury)
Ata, Te 1895-1995 119
Atene, Ann
 See Atene, (Rita) Anna
Atene, (Rita) Anna 1922- 12
Atheling, William, Jr.
 See Blish, James
Atkins, Catherine 160
Atkins, Jeannine 1953- 172
 Earlier sketch in SATA *113*
Atkinson, Allen G. 1953(?)-1987 60
 Brief entry 46
 Obituary 55
Atkinson, M. E.
 See Frankau, Mary Evelyn Atkinson
Atkinson, Margaret Fleming 14
Atteberry, Kevan J. 186
Attema, Martha 1949- 156
 Earlier sketch in SATA *94*
Atticus
 See Davies, Hunter
 and Fleming, Ian
 and Pawle, Gerald Strachan
 and Wilson, (Thomas) Woodrow

Atwater, Florence (Hasseltine Carroll)
 1896-1979 66
 Earlier sketch in SATA *16*
 See also CLR *19*
Atwater, Montgomery Meigs 1904-1976 15
Atwater, Richard (Tupper) 1892-1948 66
 Brief entry 27
 Earlier sketch in SATA *54*
 See also CLR *19*
Atwater-Rhodes, Amelia 1984- 170
 Earlier sketch in SATA *124*
Atwell, Debby 1953- 150
 Earlier sketch in SATA *87*
Atwood, Ann (Margaret) 1913-1992 7
Atwood, Margaret 1939- 170
 Earlier sketch in SATA *50*
Atwood, Margaret Eleanor
 See Atwood, Margaret
Aubrey, Meg Kelleher 1963- 83
Aubry, Claude B. 1914-1984 29
 Obituary 40
Auch, Herm 173
Auch, Mary Jane 173
 Earlier sketch in SATA *138*
Auch, M.J.
 See Auch, Mary Jane
Auclair, Joan 1960- 68
Auel, Jean 1936- 91
Auel, Jean M.
 See Auel, Jean
Auel, Jean Marie
 See Auel, Jean
Auer, Martin 1951- 77
Augarde, Steve 1950- 210
 Earlier sketches in SATA *25, 159*
Augelli, John P(at) 1921- 46
Augustine, Mildred
 See Benson, Mildred
Ault, Phil
 See Ault, Phillip H(alliday)
Ault, Phillip H(alliday) 1914- 23
Ault, Rosalie Sain 1942- 38
Ault, Roz
 See Ault, Rosalie Sain
Aung, (Maung) Htin 1909- 21
Auntie Deb
 See Coury, Louise Andree
Auntie Louise
 See Coury, Louise Andree
Aunt Weedy
 See Alcott, Louisa May
Auseon, Andrew 1976- 166
Austen, Carrie
 See Bennett, Cherie
Austin, Carrie
 See Seuling, Barbara
Austin, Elizabeth S. 1907-1977 5
Austin, Harry
 See McInerny, Ralph
Austin, Margot 1909(?)-1990 11
 Obituary 66
Austin, Michael 178
Austin, Oliver L(uther), Jr. 1903-1988 7
 Obituary 59
Austin, Patricia 1950- 137
Austin, R. G.
 See Gelman, Rita Golden
 and Lamb, Nancy
Austin, Virginia 1951- 152
 Earlier sketch in SATA *80*
Auteur, Hillary
 See Gottfried, Theodore Mark
Auth, Tony
 See Auth, William Anthony, Jr.
Auth, William Anthony, Jr. 1942- 192
Autry, Gloria Diener
 See Allen, Terril Diener
Auvil, Peggy A 1954- 122
Auvil, Peggy Appleby
 See Auvil, Peggy A
Aveni, Anthony F. 1938- 181

Aveni, Anthony Francis
 See Aveni, Anthony F.
Averbeck, Jim 1963- 201
Averill, Esther (Holden) 1902-1992 28
 Obituary 72
 Earlier sketch in SATA *1*
Avery, A. A.
 See Montgomery, Rutherford George
Avery, Al
 See Montgomery, Rutherford George
Avery, Gillian (Elise) 1926- 137
 Autobiography Feature 137
 Earlier sketches in SATA *7, 75*
 See also SAAS *6*
Avery, Kay 1908- 5
Avery, Lorraine
 See Older, Effin
 and Older, Jules
Avery, Lynn
 See Cole, Lois Dwight
Avi 1937- 190
 Earlier sketches in SATA *14, 71, 108, 156*
 See also CLR *68*
Avishai, Susan 1949- 82
Avril, Francois 1961- 191
Avril, Lynne
 See Cravath, Lynne W.
Awdry, Christopher Vere 1940- 67
Awdry, Wilbert Vere 1911-1997 94
 See also CLR *23*
Axelrod, Amy 131
Axelsen, Stephen 1953- 165
Axton, David
 See Koontz, Dean
Ayars, James S(terling) 1898-1986 4
Aye, A. K.
 See Edwards, Hazel (Eileen)
Ayer, Eleanor H. 1947-1998 121
 Earlier sketch in SATA *78*
Ayer, Jacqueline 1930- 13
Ayer, Margaret (?)-1981 15
Aylesworth, Jim 1943- 139
 Earlier sketches in SATA *38, 89*
 See also CLR *89*
Aylesworth, Thomas G(ibbons) 1927-1995 . 88
 Earlier sketch in SATA *4*
 See also CLR *6*
 See also SAAS *17*
Ayliffe, Alex 190
Aylward, Marcus
 See Alexander, Marc
Aymar, Brandt 1911- 22
Ayme, Marcel (Andre) 1902-1967 91
 See also CLR *25*
Ayres, Becky
 See Hickox, Rebecca (Ayres)
Ayres, Katherine 1947- 187
Ayres, Pam 1947- 90
Ayres, Patricia Miller 1923-1985
 Obituary 46
Aytmatov, Chingiz
 See Aitmatov, Chingiz
Ayto, Russell 1960- 206
 Earlier sketches in SATA *111, 166*
Azaid
 See Zaidenberg, Arthur
Azar, Penny 1952- 121
Azarian, Mary 1940- 171
 Earlier sketch in SATA *112*
Azore, Barbara 1934- 188

B

Baastad, Babbis Friis
 See Friis-Baastad, Babbis Ellinor
Bab
 See Gilbert, W(illiam) S(chwenck)
Babbis, Eleanor
 See Friis-Baastad, Babbis Ellinor

Babbitt, Lucy Cullyford 1960- 85
Babbitt, Natalie 1932- 194
   Earlier sketches in SATA 6, 68, 106
   See also CLR 141
   See also SAAS 5
Babbitt, Natalie Zane Moore
   See Babbitt, Natalie
Babcock, Chris 1963- 83
Babcock, Dennis 1948- 22
Babcock, Dennis Arthur
   See Babcock, Dennis
Baber, Carolyn Stonnell 1936- 96
Baboni, Elena 198
Baca, Ana 1967- 191
Baca, Maria 1951- 104
Bach, Alice (Hendricks) 1942- 93
   Brief entry 27
   Earlier sketch in SATA 30
Bach, Bellamy
   See Windling, Terri
Bach, Mary 1960- 125
Bach, Richard 1936- 13
Bach, Richard David
   See Bach, Richard
Bache, Ellyn 1942- 124
Bachel, Beverly K. 1957- 142
Bachelet, Gilles 1952- 196
Bachman, Fred 1949- 12
Bachman, Richard
   See King, Stephen
Bachrach, Deborah 80
Backus, James Gilmore 1913-1989
   Obituary 63
Backus, Jim
   See Backus, James Gilmore
Bacmeister, Rhoda W(arner) 1893-1991 11
Bacon, Betty
   See Bacon, Elizabeth
Bacon, Elizabeth 1914-2001 3
   Obituary 131
Bacon, Joan Chase
   See Bowden, Joan Chase
Bacon, Josephine Dodge (Daskam)
   1876-1961 48
Bacon, Margaret Frances
   See Bacon, Peggy
Bacon, Margaret Hope 1921- 6
Bacon, Martha Sherman 1917-1981 18
   Obituary 27
   See also CLR 3
Bacon, Melvin 1950- 93
Bacon, Melvin L.
   See Bacon, Melvin
Bacon, Peggy 1895-1987 50
Bacon, R(onald) L(eonard) 1924- 84
   Earlier sketch in SATA 26
Baddiel, Ivor 1963- 210
Baden, Robert 1936- 70
Baden-Powell, Robert (Stephenson Smyth)
   1857-1941 16
Badt, Karin L(uisa) 1963- 91
Bae, Hyun-Joo 186
Baehr, Kingsley M. 1937- 89
Baehr, Patricia 1952- 65
Baehr, Patricia Goehner
   See Baehr, Patricia
Baek, Matthew J. 1971- 202
Baer, Jill
   See Gilbert, (Agnes) Joan (Sewell)
Baer, Judy 1951- 71
Baer, Julie 1960- 161
Baer-Block, Roxanna 172
Baerg, Harry J(ohn) 1909-1996 12
Baeten, Lieve 1954- 83
Bagert, Brod 1947- 191
   Earlier sketch in SATA 80
Baggette, Susan K. 1942- 126
Baggott, Julianna 1969- 197
Bagnold, Enid 1889-1981 25
   Earlier sketch in SATA 1
Baguley, Elizabeth 1959- 199

Bahlke, Valerie Worth -1994
   See Worth, Valerie
Bahous, Sally 1939- 86
Bahr, Mary (Madelyn) 1946- 95
Bahr, Robert 1940- 38
Bahti, Tom 1926-1972 57
   Brief entry 31
Bai, Durga 211
Baicker-McKee, Carol 1958- 177
Bailey, Alice Cooper 1890-1978 12
Bailey, Anne 1958- 71
Bailey, Bernadine (Freeman) 1901-1995 14
Bailey, Carolyn Sherwin 1875-1961 14
Bailey, Debbie 1954- 123
Bailey, Donna (Veronica Anne) 1938- 68
Bailey, Jane H(orton) 1916- 12
Bailey, John (Robert) 1940- 52
Bailey, Len 193
Bailey, Linda 1948- 182
   Earlier sketch in SATA 107
Bailey, Maralyn Collins (Harrison) 1941- ... 12
Bailey, Matilda
   See Radford, Ruby L(orraine)
Bailey, Maurice Charles 1932- 12
Bailey, Pearl (Mae) 1918-1990 81
Bailey, Peter 1946- 194
Bailey, Ralph Edgar 1893-1982 11
Bailey, Sheila (Lucas) 1960- 155
Baillie, Allan 1943- 151
   Earlier sketch in SATA 87
   See also CLR 49
   See also SAAS 21
Baillie, Allan Stuart
   See Baillie, Allan
Baines, John (David) 1943- 71
Bains, Larry
   See Sabin, Louis
Baird, Alison 1963- 138
Baird, Bil 1904-1987 30
   Obituary 52
Baird, Thomas (P.) 1923-1990 45
   Brief entry 39
   Obituary 64
Baird, William Britton
   See Baird, Bil
Baity, Elizabeth Chesley 1907-1989 1
Baiul, Oksana 1977- 108
Bajoria, Paul 1964- 187
Bakeless, John (Edwin) 1894-1978 9
Bakeless, Katherine Little 1895-1992 9
Baker, Alan 1951- 146
   Earlier sketches in SATA 22, 93
Baker, Augusta 1911-1998 3
Baker, Barbara 1947- 192
Baker, Betty Lou 1928-1987 73
   Obituary 54
   Earlier sketch in SATA 5
Baker, Carin Greenberg 1959- 79
Baker, Charlotte 1910- 2
Baker, Christina
   See Kline, Christina Baker
Baker, Christopher W. 1952- 144
Baker, Deirdre 1955- 195
Baker, E.D. 190
Baker, (Mary) Elizabeth (Gillette) 1923- 7
Baker, Gayle Cunningham 1950- 39
Baker, James W. 1924- 65
   Earlier sketch in SATA 22
Baker, James W. 1926- 122
Baker, Janice E(dla) 1941- 22
Baker, Jeanette 178
Baker, Jeannie 1950- 156
   Earlier sketches in SATA 23, 88
   See also CLR 28
Baker, Jeffrey J(ohn) W(heeler) 1931- 5
Baker, Jim
   See Baker, James W.
Baker, Keith 1953- 179
Baker, Ken 1962- 133
Baker, Laura Nelson 1911- 3
Baker, Margaret 1890-1965 4

Baker, Margaret J(oyce) 1918- 12
   See also SAAS 8
Baker, Mary Gladys Steel 1892-1974 12
Baker, (Robert) Michael (Graham) 1938- 4
Baker, Nina (Brown) 1888-1957 15
Baker, Pamela J. 1947- 66
Baker, Rachel 1904-1978 2
   Obituary 26
Baker, Roberta 206
Baker, Rosalie F. 1945- 166
Baker, Samm Sinclair 1909-1997 12
   Obituary 96
Baker, Sharon Reiss 1962- 207
Baker, Susan (Catherine) 1942-1991 29
Balaam
   See Lamb, G(eoffrey) F(rederick)
Balan, Bruce 1959- 113
Balcavage, Dynise 1965- 137
Balch, Glenn 1902-1989 3
   Obituary 83
   See also SAAS 11
Baldacci, David 1960- 184
Baldacci, David G.
   See Baldacci, David
   and Baldacci, David
Balderose, Nancy Ward 1952- 93
Balderson, Margaret 1935- 151
Baldini, Michelle 205
Baldry, Cherith 1947- 167
   Earlier sketch in SATA 72
Balducci, Carolyn 1946- 5
Balducci, Carolyn Feleppa
   See Balducci, Carolyn
Baldwin, Alex
   See Griffin, W.E.B.
Baldwin, Anne Norris 1938- 5
Baldwin, Clara 11
Baldwin, Gordo
   See Baldwin, Gordon C(ortis)
Baldwin, Gordon C(ortis) 1908-1983 12
Baldwin, James 1841-1925 24
Baldwin, James 1924-1987 9
   Obituary 54
Baldwin, Louis 1919- 110
Baldwin, Margaret
   See Weis, Margaret
Baldwin, Stan(ley C.) 1929- 62
   Brief entry 28
Bales, Carol Ann 1940- 57
   Brief entry 29
Balet, Jan (Bernard) 1913- 11
Balgassi, Haemi 1971- 131
Balian, Lorna 1929- 91
   Earlier sketch in SATA 9
Balit, Christina 1961- 159
   Earlier sketch in SATA 102
Ball, Duncan 1941- 73
Ball, Zachary
   See Janas, Frankie-Lee
   and Masters, Kelly R(ay)
Ballantine, Lesley Frost
   See Frost, Lesley
Ballantyne, R(obert) M(ichael) 1825-1894 . 24
   See also CLR 137
Ballard, James G.
   See Ballard, J.G.
Ballard, James Graham
   See Ballard, J.G.
Ballard, Jane
   See Gorman, Carol
Ballard, J.G. 1930-2009 93
   Obituary 203
Ballard, Jim G.
   See Ballard, J.G.
Ballard, John 1945- 110
Ballard, Lowell C(lyne) 1904-1986 12
   Obituary 49
Ballard, (Charles) Martin 1929- 1
Ballard, Mignon F. 1934- 64
   Brief entry 49

Ballard, Mignon Franklin
See Ballard, Mignon F.
Ballard, Robert D(uane) 1942- 85
See also CLR 60
Ballard, Robin 1965- 126
Balliett, Blue 1955- 156
Ballinger, Bryan 1968- 161
Ballouhey, Pierre 1944- 90
Balogh, Penelope 1916-1975 1
Obituary 34
Balouch, Kristen 176
Balow, Tom 1931- 12
Baltazzi, Evan S(erge) 1921- 90
Balterman, Marcia Ridlon 1942- 22
Baltimore, J.
See Catherall, Arthur
Baltzer, Hans (Adolf) 1900- 40
Balzano, Jeanne (Koppel) 1912- 7
Bambara, Toni Cade 1939-1995 112
Bamfylde, Walter
See Bevan, Tom
Bamman, Henry A. 1918- 12
Banat, D. R.
See Bradbury, Ray
Bancroft, Griffing 1907-1999 6
Bancroft, Laura
See Baum, L. Frank
Bandel, Betty 1912- 47
Baner, Skulda Vanadis 1897-1964 10
Banerjee, Anjali 174
Banfill, A. Scott 1956- 98
Bang, Betsy 1912- 48
Brief entry 37
Bang, Garrett
See Bang, Molly
Bang, Molly 1943- 158
Earlier sketches in SATA 24, 69, 111
See also CLR 8
Bang, Molly Garrett
See Bang, Molly
Bang-Campbell, Monika 1975(?)- 195
Earlier sketch in SATA 140
Banjo, The
See Paterson, A(ndrew) B(arton)
Banke, Cecile de
See de Banke, Cecile
Banks, Erin Bennett 1978- 211
Banks, Kate 1960- 200
Earlier sketches in SATA 134, 172
Banks, Laura Stockton Voorhees 1908(?)-1980
Obituary 23
Banks, Lynne Reid
See Reid Banks, Lynne
Banks, Merry 197
Banks, Michael A. 1951- 101
Banks, Paul 1952- 174
Banks, Sara (Jeanne Gordon Harrell) 26
See Harrell, Sara (Jeanne) Gordon
Bannatyne-Cugnet, Elizabeth Jo-Anne
See Bannatyne-Cugnet, Jo
Bannatyne-Cugnet, Jo 1951- 101
Banner, Angela
See Maddison, Angela Mary
Bannerman, Helen (Brodie Cowan Watson)
1862(?)-1946 19
See also CLR 144
Banning, Evelyn I. 1903-1993 36
Bannon, Laura (?)-1963 6
Bannor, Brett 1959- 143
Banta, Susan 181
Bantock, Nick 1950(?)- 95
Banyai, Istvan 193
Barakat, Ibtisam 1963- 186
Barasch, Lynne 1939- 186
Earlier sketches in SATA 74, 126
Barbalet, Margaret 1949- 77
Barbary, James
See Baumann, Amy Beeching
and Beeching, Jack
Barbash, Shepard 1957- 84
Barbe, Walter Burke 1926- 45

Barber, Antonia 1932- 163
Earlier sketch in SATA 29
Barber, Atiim Kiambu
See Barber, Tiki
Barber, Lynda
See Graham-Barber, Lynda
Barber, Lynda Graham
See Graham-Barber, Lynda
Barber, Richard (William) 1941- 35
Barber, Ronde 1975- 182
Barber, Tiki 1975- 182
Barbera, Joe 1911-2006 51
Obituary 179
Barbera, Joseph
See Barbera, Joe
Barbera, Joseph Roland
See Barbera, Joe
Barberis, Juan C(arlos) 1920- 61
Barbour, Karen 1956- 170
Earlier sketches in SATA 63, 121
Barbour, Ralph Henry 1870-1944 16
Barclay, Bill
See Moorcock, Michael
Barclay, Isabel
See Dobell, I(sabel) M(arian) B(arclay)
Barclay, William Ewert
See Moorcock, Michael
Barclay, William Ewert
See Moorcock, Michael
Bardhan-Quallen, Sudipta 168
Bardoe, Cheryl 181
Bare, Arnold Edwin 1920- 16
Bare, Colleen Stanley 32
Bar-el, Dan 199
Barenholtz, Bernard 1914-1989
Obituary 64
Bargar, Gary W. 1947-1985 63
Barger, Jan 1948- 147
Barish, Matthew 1907-2000 12
Barkan, Joanne 127
Earlier sketch in SATA 77
Barker, Albert W. 1900- 8
Barker, Carol (Minturn) 1938- 31
Barker, Cicely Mary 1895-1973 49
Brief entry 39
See also CLR 88
Barker, Melvern 1907-1989 11
Barker, S. Omar 1894-1985 10
Barker, Squire Omar
See Barker, S. Omar
Barker, Will 1913-1983 8
Barkin, Carol 1944- 52
Earlier sketch in SATA 42
Barklem, Jill 1951- 96
See also CLR 31
Barkley, Brad 178
Barkley, James Edward 1941- 6
Barks, Carl 1901-2000 37
Barley, Janet Crane 1934- 95
Barlow, Steve 1952- 211
Barnaby, Ralph S(tanton) 1893-1986 9
Barnard, A. M.
See Alcott, Louisa May
Barnard, Bryn 1956- 169
Earlier sketch in SATA 115
Barne, Kitty
See Barne, Marion Catherine
Barne, Marion Catherine 1883-1957 97
Barneda, David 206
Barner, Bob 1947- 136
Earlier sketch in SATA 29
Barnes, Dawn 1957- 175
Barnes, Derrick 191
Barnes, Derrick D.
See Barnes, Derrick
Barnes, (Frank) Eric Wollencott
1907-1962 22
Barnes, Joyce Annette 1958- 85
Barnes, Laura T. 1958- 119
Barnes, Loutricia
See Barnes-Svarney, Patricia L(ou)

Barnes, Malcolm 1909(?)-1984
Obituary 41
Barnes, Michael 1934- 55
Barnes-Murphy, Frances 1951- 88
Barnes-Murphy, Rowan 1952- 88
Barnes-Svarney, Patricia L(ou) 1953- 67
Barnet, Nancy 1954- 84
Barnett, Ivan 1947- 70
Barnett, Lincoln (Kinnear) 1909-1979 36
Barnett, Moneta 1922-1976 33
Barnett, Naomi 1927- 40
Barney, Maginel Wright 1881(?)-1966 39
Brief entry 32
Barnhart, Clarence L(ewis) 1900-1993 48
Obituary 78
Barnouw, Adriaan Jacob 1877-1968
Obituary 27
Barnouw, Victor 1915-1989 43
Brief entry 28
Barnstone, Willis 1927- 20
Barnum, Jay Hyde 1888(?)-1962 20
Barnum, P. T., Jr.
See Stratemeyer, Edward L.
Barnum, Richard 67
Earlier sketch in SATA 1
Barnum, Theodore
See Stratemeyer, Edward L.
Barnwell, Ysaye M. 1946- 200
Baron, Kathy 1954- 90
Baron, Virginia Olsen 1931- 46
Brief entry 28
Barr, Donald 1921-2004 20
Obituary 152
Barr, George 1907-1992 2
Barr, Jene 1922-1985 16
Obituary 42
Barr, Nevada 1952- 126
Earlier sketch in SATA 115
Barrer, Gertrude
See Barrer-Russell, Gertrude
Barrer-Russell, Gertrude 1921- 27
Barrett, Angela (Jane) 1955- 145
Earlier sketch in SATA 75
Barrett, Ethel 87
Brief entry 44
Barrett, Joyce Durham 1943- 138
Barrett, Judi
See Barrett, Judith
Barrett, Judith 1941- 26
See also CLR 98
See Barrett, Judi
Barrett, Robert T(heodore) 1949- 92
Barrett, Ron 1937- 14
Barrett, Susan (Mary) 1938- 113
Barrett, Tracy 1955- 207
Earlier sketches in SATA 84, 115, 156
Barrett, William E(dmund) 1900-1986
Obituary 49
Barretta, Gene 176
Barretton, Grandall
See Garrett, Randall
Barrie, Baronet
See Barrie, J. M.
Barrie, J. M. 1860-1937 100
See also YABC 1
See also CLR 124
Barrie, James Matthew
See Barrie, J. M.
Barringer, William 1940-1996 153
Barrington, Michael
See Moorcock, Michael
Barris, George 1925- 47
Barrol, Grady
See Bograd, Larry
Barron, Rex 1951- 84
Barron, T.A. 1952- 192
Earlier sketches in SATA 83, 126
See also CLR 86
Barron, Thomas Archibald
See Barron, T.A.

Barron, Tom
   See Barron, T.A.
Barrow, Lloyd H. 1942- 73
Barrows, Annie 1962- 180
Barry, Dan 1958- 177
Barry, Dana (Marie Malloy) 1949- 139
Barry, James P(otvin) 1918- 14
Barry, Katharina Watjen 1936- 4
Barry, Robert (Everett) 1931- 6
Barry, Scott 1952- 32
Barry, Sheila Anne -2003 91
Barshaw, Ruth McNally 203
Bartell, Susan S. 175
Bartenbach, Jean 1918- 40
Barth, Edna 1914-1980 7
   Obituary 24
Barth, Kelly L. 1964- 152
Barthelme, Donald 1931-1989 7
   Obituary 62
Barth-Grozinger, Inge 1950- 185
Bartholomew, Barbara 1941- 86
   Brief entry 42
Bartholomew, Jean
   See Beatty, Patricia (Robbins)
Bartlett, Alison 153
Bartlett, Philip A. 1
Bartlett, Robert Merrill 1899-1995 12
Bartoletti, Susan Campbell 1958- 173
   Earlier sketches in SATA 88, 129, 135
Barton, Byron 1930- 126
   Earlier sketches in SATA 9, 90
Barton, Jill(ian) 1940- 75
Barton, May Hollis 67
   Earlier sketch in SATA 1
Barton, Pat
   See Arrowsmith, Pat
Bartos-Hoeppner, Barbara 1923- 5
Bartram, Simon 156
Bartsch, Jochen 1906- 39
Baruch, Dorothy W(alter) 1899-1962 21
Barunga, Albert 1912(?)-1977 120
Baryshnikov, Mikhail 1948- 192
Bas, Rutger
   See Rutgers van der Loeff-Basenau, An(na)
   Maria Margaretha
Base, Graeme 1958- 162
   Earlier sketches in SATA 67, 101
   See also CLR 22
Base, Graeme Rowland
   See Base, Graeme
Baseman, Gary 1960- 174
Bash, Barbara 1948- 132
Bashevis, Isaac
   See Singer, Isaac Bashevis
Bashevis, Yitskhok
   See Singer, Isaac Bashevis
Bashista, Adrienne Ehlert 203
Basile, Gloria Vitanza 1929- 180
Baskin, Leonard 1922-2000 120
   Brief entry 27
   Earlier sketch in SATA 30
Baskin, Nora Raleigh 1961- 189
   Earlier sketch in SATA 129
Bason, Lillian 1913- 20
Bass, L. G.
   See Geringer, Laura
Bassett, Jeni 1959- 64
   Brief entry 43
Bassett, John Keith
   See Keating, Lawrence A.
Bassett, Lisa 1958- 61
Bassil, Andrea
   See Nilsen, Anna
Bastyra, Judy 108
Basye, Dale E. 205
Bataille, Marion 1963- 209
Bat-Ami, Miriam 1950- 150
   Autobiography Feature 150
   Earlier sketches in SATA 82, 122
Bate, Lucy 1939-1993 18
Bate, Norman (Arthur) 1916- 5

Bateman, Colin 1962- 172
Bateman, Donna M. 190
Bateman, Teresa 1957- 168
   Earlier sketch in SATA 112
Bates, Amy June 189
Bates, Barbara S(nedeker) 1919- 12
Bates, Betty
   See Bates, Elizabeth
Bates, Dianne 1948- 147
Bates, Elizabeth 1921- 19
Bates, Ivan 175
Bates, Katharine Lee 1859-1929 113
Bates, Martine
   See Leavitt, Martine
Bateson, Catherine 1960- 197
   Earlier sketch in SATA 157
Batey, Tom 1946- 52
   Brief entry 41
Bath, Kevin P.
   See Bath, K.P.
Bath, K.P. 1959- 171
Batherman, Muriel
   See Sheldon, Muriel
Batson, Larry 1930- 35
Batt, Tanya Robyn 1970- 131
Battaglia, Aurelius 1910- 50
   Brief entry 33
Batten, H(arry) Mortimer 1888-1958 25
Batten, Mary 1937- 162
   Earlier sketches in SATA 5, 102
Batterberry, Ariane Ruskin 1935- 13
Batterberry, Michael Carver 1932- 32
Battle-Lavert, Gwendolyn 1951- 155
   Earlier sketches in SATA 85, 131
Battles, (Roxy) Edith 1921- 7
Baudouy, Michel-Aime 1909- 7
Bauer, A.C.E. 201
Bauer, Caroline Feller 1935- 98
   Brief entry 46
   Earlier sketch in SATA 52
   See also SAAS 24
Bauer, Fred 1934- 36
Bauer, Helen 1900-1988 2
Bauer, Joan 1951- 160
   Earlier sketch in SATA 117
Bauer, Jutta 1955- 150
Bauer, Marion Dane 1938- 192
   Autobiography Feature 144
   Earlier sketches in SATA 20, 69, 113, 144
   See also SAAS 9
Bauer, Michael Gerard 1955(?)- 167
Bauer, Steven 1948- 125
Bauerschmidt, Marjorie 1926- 15
Baughman, Dorothy 1940- 61
Baum, Allyn Z(elton) 1924-1997 98
   Earlier sketch in SATA 20
Baum, L. Frank
   See Thompson, Ruth Plumly
Baum, L. Frank 1856-1919 100
   Earlier sketch in SATA 18
   See also CLR 107
Baum, Louis 1948- 182
   Brief entry 52
   Earlier sketch in SATA 64
Baum, Louis F.
   See Baum, L. Frank
Baum, Lyman Frank
   See Baum, L. Frank
Baum, Maxie 188
Baum, Willi 1931- 4
Baumann, Amy Beeching 1922- 10
Baumann, Amy Brown Beeching
   See Baumann, Amy Beeching
Baumann, Hans 1914- 2
   See also CLR 35
Baumann, Kurt 1935- 21
Baumgartner, Barbara 1939- 86
Baurys, Flo(rence) 1938- 122
Bausum, Ann 173

Bawden, Nina 1925- 132
   Earlier sketches in SATA 4, 72
   See also CLR 51
   See also SAAS 16
Bawden, Nina Mary Mabey
   See Bawden, Nina
Baxter, Valerie
   See Meynell, Laurence Walter
Bay, Jeanette Graham 1928- 88
Bayer, Harold
   See Gregg, Andrew K.
Bayer, Jane E. (?)-1985
   Obituary 44
Bayley, Nicola 1949- 129
   Earlier sketches in SATA 41, 69
Baylor, Byrd 1924- 136
   Earlier sketches in SATA 16, 69
   See also CLR 3
Baynes, Pauline 1922-2008 133
   Obituary 196
   Earlier sketches in SATA 19, 59
Baynes, Pauline Diana
   See Baynes, Pauline
Bayoc, Cbabi 186
BB
   See Watkins-Pitchford, Denys James
Beach, Charles
   See Reid, (Thomas) Mayne
Beach, Charles Amory 1
Beach, Edward L. 1918-2002 12
   Obituary 140
Beach, Edward Latimer
   See Beach, Edward L.
Beach, Lisa 1957- 111
Beach, Lynn
   See Lance, Kathryn
Beach, Stewart T(aft) 1899-1979 23
Beachcroft, Nina 1931- 18
Beagle, Peter S. 1939- 130
   Earlier sketch in SATA 60
Beagle, Peter Soyer
   See Beagle, Peter S.
Beaglehole, Helen 1946- 117
Beake, Lesley 1949- 209
Beale, Fleur 107
Beale, Alex W(inkler III) 1921-1980 8
   Obituary 22
Beales, Valerie 1915- 74
Beals, Carleton 1893-1979 12
Beals, Frank Lee 1881-1972
   Obituary 26
Beam, Matt 1970- 187
Beame, Rona 1934- 12
Beamer, (George) Charles (Jr.) 1942- 43
Bean, Jonathan 1979- 194
Bean, Normal
   See Burroughs, Edgar Rice
Beaney, Jan
   See Udall, Jan Beaney
Beaney, Jane
   See Udall, Jan Beaney
Bear, Carolyn
   See Rayban, Chloe
Bear, Greg 1951- 105
   Earlier sketch in SATA 65
Bear, Gregory Dale
   See Bear, Greg
Bearanger, Marie
   See Messier, Claire
Beard, Charles A(ustin) 1874-1948 18
Beard, Dan(iel Carter) 1850-1941 22
Beard, Darleen Bailey 1961- 96
Bearden, Romare (Howard) 1914(?)-1988 22
   Obituary 56
Beardmore, Cedric
   See Beardmore, George
Beardmore, George 1908-1979 20
Beardshaw, Rosalind 1969- 190
Beardsley, Martyn R. 1957- 150
Bearman, Jane (Ruth) 1917- 29
Beaton, Clare 1947- 125

Beatty, Elizabeth
  See Holloway, Teresa (Bragunier)
Beatty, Hetty Burlingame 1907-1971 5
Beatty, Jerome, Jr. 1918- 5
Beatty, John (Louis) 1922-1975 6
  Obituary 25
Beatty, Patricia (Robbins) 1922-1991 73
  Obituary 68
  Earlier sketches in SATA *1, 30*
  See also SAAS *4*
Beaty, Andrea 186
Beaty, Mary (T.) 1947- 146
Beaudoin, Sean 210
Beaumont, Karen 1954- 204
Beccia, Carlyn 189
Bechard, Margaret 1953- 164
  Earlier sketch in SATA *85*
Bechtel, Louise Seaman 1894-1985 4
  Obituary 43
Bechtold, Lisze 208
Beck, Barbara L. 1927- 12
Beck, Ian 1947- 190
  Earlier sketch in SATA *138*
  See Beck, Ian Archibald
Beck, Peggy 1949- 171
Beck, Scott 197
Becker, Beril 1901-1999 11
Becker, Bonny 184
Becker, Deborah Zimmett 1955- 138
Becker, Helaine 1961- 142
Becker, John (Leonard) 1901- 12
Becker, John E(mil) 1942- 148
Becker, Joyce 1936- 39
Becker, May Lamberton 1873-1958 33
Becker, Neesa 1951- 123
Becker, Shari 174
Beckerman, Chad W. 198
Beckett, Sheilah 1913- 33
Beckhorn, Susan Williams 1953- 189
Beckles Willson, Robina 1930- 27
Beckman, Delores 1914-1994 51
Beckman, Gunnel 1910- 6
  See also CLR *25*
  See also SAAS *9*
Beckman, Kaj
  See Beckman, Karin
Beckman, Karin 1913- 45
Beckman, Per (Frithiof) 1913- 45
Bedard, Michael 1949- 154
  Earlier sketch in SATA *93*
  See also CLR *35*
Beddor, Frank 194
Beddows, Eric
  See Nutt, Ken
Bedford, A. N.
  See Watson, Jane Werner
Bedford, Annie North
  See Watson, Jane Werner
Bedford, David 159
Bedoukian, Kerop 1907-1981 53
Bee, Jay
  See Brainerd, John W(hiting)
Bee, William 188
Beebe, B. F.
  See Johnson, B. F.
Beebe, (Charles) William 1877-1962 19
Beeby, Betty 1923- 25
Beech, Mark 1971- 191
Beech, Webb
  See Griffin, W.E.B.
Beecham, Jahnna 161
Beechcroft, William
  See Hallstead, William F(inn III)
Beeching, Jack 1922- 14
Beeke, Tiphanie 163
Beeler, Janet
  See Shaw, Janet
Beeler, Nelson F(rederick) 1910-1978 13
Beere, Peter 1951- 97
Beers, Dorothy Sands 1917- 9
Beers, Lorna 1897-1989 14

Beers, V(ictor) Gilbert 1928- 130
  Earlier sketch in SATA *9*
Beeton, Max
  See Redding, Robert Hull
Begay, Shonto 1954- 137
Begaye, Lisa Shook
  See Beach, Lisa
Begin, Mary Jane 1963- 82
Begin-Callanan, Mary Jane
  See Begin, Mary Jane
Begley, Kathleen A. 1948- 21
Begley, Kathleen Anne
  See Begley, Kathleen A.
Beha, Philippe 211
Behan, Leslie
  See Gottfried, Theodore Mark
Behler, Deborah A. 1947- 145
Behler, John L. 1943-2006 145
  Obituary 173
Behler, John Luther
  See Behler, John L.
Behn, Harry 1898-1973 2
  Obituary 34
Behnke, Frances L. 8
Behr, Joyce 1929- 15
Behrens, June York 1925- 19
Behrman, Carol H(elen) 1925- 144
  Earlier sketch in SATA *14*
Beifuss, John, (Jr.) 1959- 92
Beil, Karen Magnuson 1950- 124
Beiler, Edna 1923- 61
Beinicke, Steve 1956- 69
Beirne, Barbara 1933- 71
Beiser, Arthur 1931- 22
Beiser, Germaine 1931- 11
Belair, Richard L. 1934- 45
Belaney, Archibald Stansfeld 1888-1938 24
  See also CLR *32*
Belbin, David 1958- 164
  Earlier sketch in SATA *106*
Belden, Wilanne Schneider 1925- 56
Belfrage, Sally 1936-1994 65
  Obituary 79
Belknap, B. H.
  See Ellis, Edward S.
Belknap, Boynton
  See Ellis, Edward S.
Belknap, Boynton M.D.
  See Ellis, Edward S.
Bell, Anthea 1936- 148
  Earlier sketch in SATA *88*
Bell, Cathleen Davitt 1971- 203
Bell, Cece 202
Bell, Clare (Louise) 1952- 99
Bell, Corydon Whitten 1894-1980 3
Bell, David Owen 1949- 99
Bell, Emerson
  See Stratemeyer, Edward L.
Bell, Emily Mary
  See Cason, Mabel Earp
Bell, Frank
  See Benson, Mildred
Bell, Gertrude (Wood) 1911-1987 12
Bell, Gina
  See Balzano, Jeanne (Koppel)
Bell, Hilari 1958- 197
  Earlier sketch in SATA *151*
Bell, Jadrien
  See Golden, Christie
Bell, Janet
  See Clymer, Eleanor
Bell, Janet Cheatham 1937- 127
Bell, Krista 1950- 126
Bell, Krista Anne Blakeney
  See Bell, Krista
Bell, Margaret E(lizabeth) 1898-1990 2
Bell, Mary Reeves 1946- 88
Bell, Norman (Edward) 1899- 11
Bell, Raymond Martin 1907-1999 13
Bell, Siobhan 177
Bell, Thelma Harrington 1896-1985 3

Bell, William 1945- 90
  See also CLR *91*
Bellairs, John (Anthony) 1938-1991 160
  Obituary 66
  Earlier sketches in SATA *2, 68*
  See also CLR *37*
Beller, Susan Provost 1949- 128
  Earlier sketch in SATA *84*
  See also CLR *106*
Bellingham, Brenda 1931- 99
  Brief entry 51
Bello, Rosario de
  See De Bello, Rosario
Belloc, Hilaire 1870-1953 112
  See also YABC *1*
  See also CLR *102*
Belloc, Joseph Hilaire Pierre Sebastien Rene
  Swanton
  See Belloc, Hilaire
Belloc, Joseph Peter Rene Hilaire
  See Belloc, Hilaire
Belloc, Joseph Pierre Hilaire
  See Belloc, Hilaire
Belloli, Andrea P. A. 1947- 86
Bell-Rehwoldt, Sheri 1962- 199
Bellville, Cheryl Walsh 1944- 54
  Brief entry 49
Bell-Zano, Gina
  See Balzano, Jeanne (Koppel)
Belpre, Pura 1899-1982 16
  Obituary 30
Belting, Natalia Maree 1915-1997 6
Belton, John Raynor 1931- 22
Belton, Sandra 1939- 186
  Earlier sketches in SATA *85, 134*
Belton, Sandra Yvonne
  See Belton, Sandra
Beltran, Alberto 1923- 43
Beltran-Hernandez, Irene 1945- 74
Belvedere, Lee
  See Grayland, Valerie (Merle Spanner)
Bemelmans, Ludwig 1898-1962 100
  Earlier sketch in SATA *15*
  See also CLR *93*
Benander, Carl D. 1941- 74
Benary, Margot
  See Benary-Isbert, Margot
Benary-Isbert, Margot 1889-1979 2
  Obituary 21
  See also CLR *12*
Benasutti, Marion 1908-1992 6
Benatar, Raquel 1955- 167
Benchley, Nathaniel (Goddard) 1915-1981 . 25
  Obituary 28
  Earlier sketch in SATA *3*
Benchley, Peter 1940-2006 164
  Earlier sketches in SATA *3, 89*
Benchley, Peter Bradford
  See Benchley, Peter
Bendall-Brunello, John 185
Bender, Edna 1941- 92
Bender, Esther 1942- 88
Bender, Lucy Ellen 1942- 22
Bender, Robert 1962- 160
  Earlier sketch in SATA *79*
Bendick, Jeanne 1919- 135
  Earlier sketches in SATA *2, 68*
  See also CLR *5*
  See also SAAS *4*
Bendick, Robert L(ouis) 1917- 11
Benedetto, William R. 1928- 180
Benedetto, William Ralph
  See Benedetto, William R.
Benedict, Andrew
  See Arthur, Robert, (Jr.)
Benedict, Dorothy Potter 1889-1979 11
  Obituary 23
Benedict, Lois Trimble 1902-1967 12
Benedict, Rex 1920-1995 8
Benedict, Stewart H(urd) 1924- 26
Beneduce, Ann Keay 128

Benet, Laura 1884-1979 3
  Obituary 23
Benet, Stephen Vincent 1898-1943
  See YABC 1
Benet, Sula 1906-1982 21
  Obituary 33
Ben-Ezer, Ehud 1936- 122
Benezra, Barbara (Beardsley) 1921- 10
Benham, Leslie 1922- 48
Benham, Lois (Dakin) 1924- 48
Benham, Mary Lile 1914-1991 55
Benjamin, E. M. J.
  See Bache, Ellyn
Benjamin, Floella 1949- 206
Benjamin, Nora
  See Kubie, Nora Gottheil Benjamin
Benjamin, Saragail Katzman 1953- 86
Benner, Cheryl 1962- 80
Benner, Judith Ann 1942- 94
Bennett, Alice
  See Ziner, Florence
Bennett, Cherie 1960- 158
  Earlier sketch in SATA *97*
Bennett, Dorothea
  See Young, Dorothea Bennett
Bennett, Erin Susanne
  See Banks, Erin Bennett
Bennett, Holly 1957- 181
Bennett, James (W.) 1942- 153
  Autobiography Feature 153
  Earlier sketches in SATA *93, 148*
Bennett, Jay 1912- 87
  Brief entry 27
  Earlier sketch in SATA *41*
  See also SAAS 4
Bennett, Jill (Crawford) 1934- 41
Bennett, John 1865-1956
  See YABC 1
Bennett, Penelope (Agnes) 1938- 94
Bennett, Rachel
  See Hill, Margaret (Ohler)
Bennett, Rainey 1907-1998 15
  Obituary 111
Bennett, Richard 1899- 21
Bennett, Russell H(oradley) 1896- 25
Bennett, Veronica 1953- 178
Bennett, William (John) 1943- 102
Benning, Elizabeth
  See Rice, Bebe Faas
Benny, Mike 1964- 203
Benson, Elizabeth P(olk) 1924- 65
Benson, Kathleen 1947- 183
  Earlier sketches in SATA *62, 111*
Benson, Linda M(aria) 1959- 84
Benson, Mildred 1905-2002 100
  Obituary 135
  Earlier sketches in SATA *1, 65, 67*
Benson, Mildred Augustine Wirt
  See Benson, Mildred
Benson, Mildred Wirt
  See Benson, Mildred
Benson, Millie
  See Benson, Mildred
Benson, Patrick 1956- 147
Benson, Sally 1900-1972 35
  Obituary 27
  Earlier sketch in SATA *1*
Bentley, Judith (McBride) 1945- 89
  Earlier sketch in SATA *40*
Bentley, Karen
  See Taschek, Karen
Bentley, Nancy (L.) 1946- 78
Bentley, Nicolas Clerihew 1907-1978
  Obituary 24
Bentley, Phyllis Eleanor 1894-1977 6
  Obituary 25
Bentley, Roy 1947- 46
Bentley, William (George) 1916- 84
Benton, Jim 1963- 172
ben Uzair, Salem
  See Horne, Richard Henry Hengist

Bercaw, Edna Coe 1961- 124
Berck, Judith 1960- 75
Berelson, Howard 1940- 5
Berends, Polly Berrien 1939- 50
  Brief entry 38
Berenstain, Jan 1923- 135
  Earlier sketches in SATA *12, 64, 129*
  See also CLR 150
  See also SAAS 20
Berenstain, Janice
  See Berenstain, Jan
Berenstain, Michael 1951- 45
Berenstain, Mike
  See Berenstain, Michael
Berenstain, Stan 1923-2005 135
  Obituary 169
  Earlier sketches in SATA *12, 64, 129*
  See also CLR 150
  See also SAAS 20
Berenstain, Stanley
  See Berenstain, Stan
Berenzy, Alix 1957- 168
  Earlier sketch in SATA *65*
Beresford, Elisabeth 1928- 141
  Earlier sketches in SATA *25, 86*
  See also SAAS 20
Berg, Adriane G(ilda) 1948- 152
Berg, Dave
  See Berg, David
Berg, David 1920-2002 27
  Obituary 137
Berg, Elizabeth 1948- 104
Berg, Jean Horton 1913-1995 6
Berg, Joan
  See Victor, Joan Berg
Berg, Ron 1952- 48
Bergaust, Erik 1925-1978 20
Bergel, Colin J. 1963- 137
Bergen, Joyce 1949- 95
Berger, Barbara (Helen) 1945- 77
Berger, Carin 185
Berger, Gilda 1935- 88
  Brief entry 42
Berger, Josef 1903-1971 36
Berger, Melvin H. 1927- 158
  Autobiography Feature 124
  Earlier sketches in SATA *5, 88*
  See also CLR 32
  See also SAAS 2
Berger, Phil 1942-2001 62
Berger, Samantha (Allison) 1969- 140
Berger, Terry 1933- 8
Bergey, Alyce (Mae) 1934- 45
Bergin, Mark 1961- 160
  Earlier sketch in SATA *114*
Berglin, Ruth Marie 1970- 181
Bergman, Donna 1934- 73
Bergman, Mara 1956- 196
Bergman, Tamar 1939- 95
Bergren, Lisa T.
  See Bergren, Lisa Tawn
Bergren, Lisa Tawn 200
Bergsma, Jody Lynn 163
Bergstein, Rita M. 211
Bergum, Constance R. 1952- 208
  Earlier sketch in SATA *121*
Berk, Ari 208
Berkebile, Fred D(onovan) 1900-1978
  Obituary 26
Berkeley, Jon 1962- 204
Berkes, Marianne 173
Berkey, Barry Robert 1935- 24
Berkowitz, Freda Pastor 1908-1994 12
Berkus, Clara Widess 1909- 78
Berlan, Kathryn Hook 1946- 78
Berlfein, Judy Reiss 1958- 79
Berlin, Eric 1968- 195
Berliner, Don 1930- 33
Berliner, Franz 1930- 13
Berlitz, Charles (L. Frambach) 1914-2003 . 32
  Obituary 151

Berman, Linda 1948- 38
Berman, Paul (Lawrence) 1949- 66
Berna, Paul 1910-1994 15
  Obituary 78
  See also CLR 19
Bernadette
  See Watts, (Anna) Bernadette
Bernard, Bruce 1928-2000 78
  Obituary 124
Bernard, George I. 1949- 39
Bernard, Jacqueline (de Sieyes) 1921-1983 .. 8
  Obituary 45
Bernard, Patricia 1942- 181
  Earlier sketch in SATA *106*
Bernard, Trish
  See Bernard, Patricia
Bernardin, James (B.) 1966- 112
Bernardo, Anilu 184
Bernards, Neal 1963- 71
Bernasconi, Pablo 1973- 183
Bernays, Anne 1930- 32
Bernhard, Durga T. 1961- 80
Bernhard, Emery 1950- 80
Bernheimer, Kate 201
Bernier-Grand, Carmen T. 1947- 202
Bernstein, Daryl (Evan) 1976- 81
Bernstein, Joanne E(ckstein) 1943- 15
Bernstein, Margery 1933- 114
Bernstein, Nina 1949- 180
Bernstein, Theodore M(enline) 1904-1979 . 12
  Obituary 27
Berrien, Edith Heal
  See Heal, Edith
Berrill, Jacquelyn (Batsel) 1905- 12
Berrington, John
  See Brownjohn, Alan
Berry, B. J.
  See Berry, Barbara J.
Berry, Barbara J. 1937- 7
Berry, Erick
  See Best, (Evangel) Allena Champlin
Berry, Holly 1957- 210
Berry, James 1924- 110
  Earlier sketch in SATA *67*
  See also CLR 143
Berry, Jane Cobb 1915(?)-1979
  Obituary 22
Berry, Joy
  See Berry, Joy Wilt
Berry, Joy Wilt 1944- 58
  Brief entry 46
Berry, Lynne 190
Berry, William D(avid) 1926- 14
Bersani, Shennen 1961- 164
Berson, Harold 1926- 4
Bertagna, Julie 1962- 151
Bertholf, Bret 189
Bertin, Charles-Francois
  See Berlitz, Charles (L. Frambach)
Bertolet, Paul
  See McLaughlin, Frank
Berton, Pierre (Francis de Marigny) 1920-2004
  99
  Obituary 158
Bertrand, Cecile 1953- 76
Bertrand, Diane Gonzales 1956- 177
  Earlier sketch in SATA *106*
Bertrand, Lynne 1963- 164
  Earlier sketch in SATA *81*
Beskow, Elsa (Maartman) 1874-1953 20
  See also CLR 17
Bess, Clayton
  See Locke, Robert
Besson, Luc 1959- 199
Best, (Evangel) Allena Champlin 1892-1974
  2
  Obituary 25
Best, Cari 1951- 200
  Earlier sketches in SATA *107, 149*
Best, (Oswald) Herbert 1894-1980 2

Bestall, A(lfred) E(dmeades) 1892-1986 97
  Obituary 48
Betancourt, Jeanne 1941- 148
  Brief entry 43
  Earlier sketches in SATA 55, 96
Beth, Mary
  See Miller, Mary Beth
Bethancourt, T. Ernesto
  See Paisley, Tom
Bethel, Dell 1929- 52
Bethell, Jean (Frankenberry) 1922- 8
Bethers, Ray 1902-1973 6
Bethke, Bruce Raymond 1955- 114
Bethlen, T.D.
  See Silverberg, Robert
Bethune, J. G.
  See Ellis, Edward S.
Bethune, J. H.
  See Ellis, Edward S.
Betteridge, Anne
  See Potter, Margaret
Bettina
  See Ehrlich, Bettina Bauer
Bettmann, Otto Ludwig 1903-1998 46
Bettoli, Delana 187
Betts, James
  See Haynes, Betsy
Betz, Eva Kelly 1897-1968 10
Bevan, Tom 1868-1930(?)
  See YABC 2
Bevis, Mary 1939- 202
Bewick, Thomas 1753-1828 16
Beyer, Audrey White 1916- 9
Beyer, Paul J. III 1950- 74
Beynon, John
  See Harris, John (Wyndham Parkes Lucas)
    Beynon
Bezencon, Jacqueline (Buxcel) 1924- 48
Bhatia, Jamunadevi 1919- 48
Bhatia, June
  See Bhatia, Jamunadevi
Bial, Morrison David 1917- 62
Bial, Raymond 1948- 165
  Earlier sketches in SATA 76, 116
Biala
  See Brustlein, Janice Tworkov
Biale, Rachel 1952- 99
Bialk, Elisa
  See Krautter, Elisa (Bialk)
Bianchi, John 1947- 91
Bianchi, Robert S(teven) 1943- 92
Bianco, Margery
  See Bianco, Margery Williams
Bianco, Margery Williams 1881-1944 15
  See also CLR 146
Bianco, Pamela 1906- 28
Bibby, Violet 1908-1996 24
Bible, Charles 1937- 13
Bibo, Bobette
  See Gugliotta, Bobette
Bice, Clare 1909-1976 22
Bickerstaff, Isaac
  See Swift, Jonathan
Bidner, Jenni 1963- 193
Biegel, Paul 1925- 79
  Earlier sketch in SATA 16
  See also CLR 27
  See also SAAS 18
Biemiller, Carl L(udwig), Jr.) 1912-1979 40
  Obituary 21
Bienenfeld, Florence L(ucille) 1929- 39
Bierhorst, John (William) 1936- 149
  Autobiography Feature 149
  Earlier sketches in SATA 6, 91
  See also SAAS 10
Biggar, Joan R(awlins) 1936- 120
Biggle, Lloyd, Jr. 1923-2002 65
Biggs, Brian 1968- 192
Bilal, Abdel W(ahab) 1970- 92
Bilbrough, Norman 1941- 111
Bildner, Phil 173

Bileck, Marvin 1920- 40
Bilibin, Ivan (Iakolevich) 1876-1942 61
Bill, Alfred Hoyt 1879-1964 44
Billam, Rosemary 1952- 61
Billings, Charlene W(interer) 1941- 41
Billingsley, Franny 1954- 132
Billington, Elizabeth T(hain) 50
  Brief entry 43
Billout, Guy (Rene) 1941- 144
  Earlier sketch in SATA 10
  See also CLR 33
Bilson, Geoffrey 1938-1987 99
Binch, Caroline (Lesley) 1947- 140
  Earlier sketch in SATA 81
Bing, Christopher (H.) 126
Bingham, Caroline 1962- 158
Bingham, Jane M. 1941- 163
Bingham, Jane Marie
  See Bingham, Jane M.
Bingham, Janet 1959- 200
Bingham, Kelly 1967- 207
Bingham, Sam(uel A.) 1944- 96
Bingley, Margaret (Jane Kirby) 1947- 72
Binkley, Anne
  See Rand, Ann (Binkley)
Binzen, Bill
  See Binzen, William
Binzen, William 24
Birch, David (W.) 1913-1996 89
Birch, Reginald B(athurst) 1856-1943 19
Birchman, David 1949- 72
Birchmore, Daniel A. 1951- 92
Bird, Carmel 1940- 124
Bird, E(lzy) J(ay) 1911- 58
Birdsall, Jeanne 1952(?)- 170
Birdseye, Tom 1951- 148
  Earlier sketches in SATA 66, 98
Birenbaum, Barbara 1941- 65
Birmingham, Lloyd P(aul) 1924- 83
  Earlier sketch in SATA 12
Birmingham, Ruth
  See Sorrells, Walter
Birney, Betty G. 1947- 169
  Earlier sketch in SATA 98
Biro, B.
  See Biro, B. S.
Biro, B. S. 1921- 1
  See also CLR 28
  See also SAAS 13
Biro, Val
  See Biro, B. S.
Bischoff, Julia Bristol 1899-1970 12
Bishop, Bonnie 1943- 37
Bishop, Claire Huchet 1899(?)-1993 14
  Obituary 74
  See also CLR 80
Bishop, Courtney
  See Ruemmler, John D(avid)
Bishop, Curtis (Kent) 1912-1967 6
Bishop, Elizabeth 1911-1979
  Obituary 24
Bishop, Gavin 1946- 144
  Earlier sketch in SATA 97
Bishop, Kathleen Wong 1954- 120
Bishop, Kathy
  See Bishop, Kathleen Wong
Bishop, Nic 1955- 161
  Earlier sketch in SATA 107
Bisset, Donald 1910-1995 86
  Earlier sketch in SATA 7
Bisson, Terry 1942- 99
Bisson, Terry Ballantine
  See Bisson, Terry
Bitter, Gary G(len) 1940- 22
Bixby, William (Courtney) 1920-1986 6
  Obituary 47
Bjoerk, Christina 1938- 99
  Earlier sketch in SATA 67
  See also CLR 22
Bjork, Christina
  See Bjoerk, Christina

Bjorklund, Lorence F. 1913-1978 35
  Brief entry 32
Bjorkman, Steve 163
Black, Algernon David 1900-1993 12
  Obituary 76
Black, Holly 1971- 210
  Earlier sketch in SATA 147
Black, Irma Simonton 1906-1972 2
  Obituary 25
Black, Mansell
  See Trevor, Elleston
Black, MaryAnn
  See Easley, MaryAnn
Black, Susan Adams 1953- 40
Blackall, Bernie 1956- 126
Blackall, Sophie 182
Blackburn, Claire
  See Altman, Linda Jacobs
Blackburn, John(ny) Brewton 1952- 15
Blackburn, Joyce Knight 1920- 29
Blacker, Terence 1948- 194
Blacker, Tina
  See Louise, Tina
Blackett, Veronica Heath 1927- 12
Blackie, Jean Cutler 1943- 79
Blacklin, Malcolm
  See Chambers, Aidan
Blacklock, Dyan 1951- 112
Blackman, Malorie 1962- 196
  Earlier sketches in SATA 83, 128
Blackton, Peter
  See Wilson, Lionel
Blackwood, Alan 1932- 70
Blackwood, Freya 199
Blackwood, Gary
  See Blackwood, Gary L.
Blackwood, Gary L. 1945- 169
  Earlier sketches in SATA 72, 118
Blade, Alexander
  See Garrett, Randall
    and Hamilton, Edmond
    and Silverberg, Robert
Blades, Ann (Sager) 1947- 69
  Earlier sketch in SATA 16
  See also CLR 15
Bladow, Suzanne Wilson 1937- 14
Blaine, Chris
  See Gardner, Craig Shaw
Blaine, John
  See Goodwin, Harold L(eland)
Blaine, Marge
  See Blaine, Margery Kay
Blaine, Margery Kay 1937- 11
Blair, Alison
  See Lerangis, Peter
Blair, Anne Denton 1914-1993 46
Blair, David Nelson 1954- 80
Blair, Eric
  See Orwell, George
Blair, Jay 1953- 45
Blair, Lucile
  See Yeakley, Marjory Hall
Blair, Margaret Whitman 1951- 124
Blair, Mary 1911-1978 195
Blair, Pauline Hunter
  See Clarke, Pauline
Blair, Ruth Van Ness 1912-1999 12
Blair, Shannon
  See Kaye, Marilyn
Blair, Walter 1900-1992 12
  Obituary 72
Blaisdell, Bob
  See Blaisdell, Robert
Blaisdell, Robert 1959- 105
Blake, Bronwyn 1940- 149
Blake, Francis 198
Blake, Jon 1954- 171
  Earlier sketch in SATA 78
Blake, Olive
  See Supraner, Robyn

Author Index

Blake, Quentin 1932- *211*
  Earlier sketches in SATA *9, 52, 96, 125*
  See also CLR *31*
Blake, Robert 1949- *42*
Blake, Robert J. *160*
Blake, Walker E.
  See Griffin, W.E.B.
Blake, William 1757-1827 .... *30*
  See also CLR *52*
Blakely, Gloria 1950- *139*
Blakely, Roger K. 1922- *82*
Blakeney, Jay D.
  See Chester, Deborah
Blakey, Nancy 1955- *94*
Blanc, Esther S. 1913-1997 .... *66*
Blanc, Mel 1908-1989
  Obituary *64*
Blanchard, Patricia *125*
Blanchet, M(uriel) Wylie 1891-1961 .... *106*
Blanco, Richard L(idio) 1926- *63*
Bland, E.
  See Nesbit, E.
Bland, Edith Nesbit
  See Nesbit, E.
Bland, Fabian
  See Nesbit, E.
Blane, Gertrude
  See Blumenthal, Gertrude
Blank, Clarissa Mabel 1915-1965 .... *62*
Blankenship, LeeAnn 1944- *181*
Blassingame, Wyatt Rainey 1909-1985 ...... *34*
  Obituary *41*
  Earlier sketch in SATA *1*
Blatchford, Claire H. 1944- *94*
Blauer, Ettagale 1940- *49*
Bleck, Linda *207*
Bledsoe, Glen L. 1951- *108*
Bledsoe, Glen Leonard
  See Bledsoe, Glen L.
Bledsoe, Karen E. 1962- *167*
  Earlier sketch in SATA *108*
Bledsoe, Karen Elizabeth
  See Bledsoe, Karen E.
Bledsoe, Lucy Jane 1957- *162*
  Earlier sketch in SATA *97*
Bleeker, Sonia
  See Zim, Sonia Bleeker
Blegen, Daniel M. 1950- *92*
Blegvad, Erik 1923- *132*
  Earlier sketches in SATA *14, 66*
Blegvad, Lenore 1926- *176*
  Earlier sketches in SATA *14, 66*
Bley, Anette 1967- *188*
Blish, James 1921-1975 .... *66*
Blish, James Benjamin
  See Blish, James
Blishen, Edward (William) 1920-1996 .... *66*
  Obituary *93*
  Earlier sketch in SATA *8*
Bliss, Corinne Demas 1947- *131*
  Earlier sketch in SATA *37*
  See Demas, Corinne
Bliss, Frederick
  See Card, Orson Scott
Bliss, Gillian
  See Paton Walsh, Jill
Bliss, Harry 1964- *196*
  Earlier sketch in SATA *156*
Bliss, Reginald
  See Wells, H. G.
Bliss, Ronald G(ene) 1942- *12*
Blitt, Barry *187*
Bliven, Bruce, Jr. 1916-2002 .... *2*
Blixen, Karen 1885-1962 .... *44*
Blizzard, Gladys S. (?)-1992 .... *79*
Blobaum, Cindy 1966- *123*
Bloch, Lucienne 1909-1999 .... *10*
Bloch, Marie Halun 1910-1998 .... *6*
  See also SAAS *9*
Bloch, Robert (Albert) 1917-1994 .... *12*
  Obituary *82*

Blochman, Lawrence G(oldtree)
  1900-1975 .... *22*
Block, Francesca Lia 1962- *158*
  Earlier sketches in SATA *80, 116*
  See also CLR *116*
  See also SAAS *21*
Block, Irvin 1917- *12*
Blomgren, Jennifer (Alice) 1954- *136*
Blood, Charles Lewis 1929- *28*
Bloom, Barbara Lee 1943- *146*
Bloom, Freddy 1914-2000 .... *37*
  Obituary *121*
Bloom, Lloyd 1947- *108*
  Brief entry *43*
Bloom, Suzanne 1950- *172*
Bloomfield, Michaela 1966- *70*
Bloor, Edward 1950- *201*
  Earlier sketches in SATA *98, 155*
Bloor, Edward William
  See Bloor, Edward
Blos, Joan W. 1928- *153*
  Autobiography Feature *153*
  Brief entry *27*
  Earlier sketches in SATA *33, 69, 109*
  See also CLR *18*
  See also SAAS *11*
Blos, Joan Winsor
  See Blos, Joan W.
Blough, Glenn O(rlando) 1907-1995 .... *1*
Blue, Rose 1931- *166*
  Autobiography Feature *117*
  Earlier sketches in SATA *5, 91, 93*
  See also SAAS *24*
Blue, Zachary
  See Stine, R.L.
Bluemle, Elizabeth *209*
Bluggage, Oranthy
  See Alcott, Louisa May
Blumberg, Leda 1956- *59*
Blumberg, Rhoda 1917- *123*
  Earlier sketches in SATA *35, 70*
  See also CLR *21*
Blume, Judy 1938- *195*
  Earlier sketches in SATA *2, 31, 79, 142*
  See also CLR *69*
Blume, Judy Sussman
  See Blume, Judy
Blume, Lesley M.M. 1975- *180*
Blumenthal, Deborah *204*
  Earlier sketch in SATA *161*
Blumenthal, Gertrude 1907-1971
  Obituary *27*
Blumenthal, Shirley 1943- *46*
Blutig, Eduard
  See Gorey, Edward (St. John)
Bly, Janet (Chester) 1945- *43*
Bly, Stephen A(rthur) 1944- *116*
  Earlier sketch in SATA *43*
Blyler, Allison Lee 1966- *74*
Blythe, Gary 1959- *185*
Blyton, Carey 1932-2002 .... *9*
  Obituary *138*
Blyton, Enid 1897-1968 .... *25*
  See also CLR *31*
Blyton, Enid Mary
  See Blyton, Enid
Bo, Ben
  See Richardson, V.A.
Boardman, Fon Wyman, Jr. 1911-2000 ...... *6*
Boardman, Gwenn R.
  See Petersen, Gwenn Boardman
Boase, Wendy 1944-1999 .... *28*
  Obituary *110*
Boatner, Mark Mayo III 1921- *29*
Bobbe, Dorothie de Bear 1905-1975 .... *1*
  Obituary *25*
Bober, Natalie S. 1930- *134*
  Earlier sketch in SATA *87*
  See also SAAS *23*
Bobette, Bibo
  See Gugliotta, Bobette

Bobri, Vladimir V. 1898-1986 .... *47*
  Brief entry *32*
Bobritsky, Vladimir
  See Bobri, Vladimir V.
Bochak, Grayce 1956- *76*
Bock, Hal
  See Bock, Harold I.
Bock, Harold I. 1939- *10*
Bock, William Sauts Netamux'we 1939- *14*
Bodanis, David *179*
Bode, Janet 1943-1999 .... *96*
  Obituary *118*
  Earlier sketch in SATA *60*
Bode, N.E.
  See Baggott, Julianna
Bodecker, N(iels) M(ogens) 1922-1988 ...... *73*
  Obituary *54*
  Earlier sketch in SATA *8*
Bodeen, S. A. 1965- *158*
  Earlier sketch in SATA *114*
Boden, Hilda
  See Bodenham, Hilda Morris
Bodenham, Hilda Morris 1901- *13*
Bodett, Thomas Edward 1955- *70*
Bodett, Tom
  See Bodett, Thomas Edward
Bodie, Idella F(allaw) 1925- *89*
  Earlier sketch in SATA *12*
Bodker, Cecil
  See Bodker, Cecil
Bodker, Cecil 1927- *133*
  Earlier sketch in SATA *14*
  See also CLR *23*
Bodsworth, (Charles) Fred(erick) 1918- *27*
Boeckman, Charles 1920- *12*
Boegehold, Betty (Doyle) 1913-1985
  Obituary *42*
Boelts, Maribeth 1964- *200*
  Earlier sketches in SATA *78, 163*
Boerst, William J. 1939- *170*
  Earlier sketch in SATA *121*
Boesch, Mark J(oseph) 1917- *12*
Boesen, Victor 1908- *16*
Bogacki, Tomek 1950- *138*
Bogaerts, Gert 1965- *80*
Bogan, Paulette 1960- *201*
  Earlier sketch in SATA *129*
Bogart, Jo Ellen 1945- *92*
  See also CLR *59*
Boggs, Ralph Steele 1901-1994 .... *7*
Bograd, Larry 1953- *89*
  Earlier sketch in SATA *33*
  See also SAAS *21*
Bogue, Gary 1938- *195*
Bogue, Gary L.
  See Bogue, Gary
Bohdal, Susi 1951- *101*
  Earlier sketch in SATA *22*
Bohlen, Nina 1931- *58*
Bohlmeijer, Arno 1956- *94*
Bohner, Charles (Henry) 1927- *62*
Bohnhoff, Maya Kaathryn 1954- *88*
Boiger, Alexandra *178*
Boissard, Janine 1932- *59*
Bojunga, Lygia
  See Nunes, Lygia Bojunga
Bojunga-Nunes, Lygia
  See Nunes, Lygia Bojunga
Bok, Arthur
  See Bok, Chip
Bok, Chip 1952- *205*
Bolam, Emily 1969- *206*
Boland, Janice *98*
Bolden, Tonya 1959- *188*
  Earlier sketches in SATA *79, 138*
Bolden, Tonya Wilyce
  See Bolden, Tonya
Boles, Paul Darcy 1916-1984 .... *9*
  Obituary *38*
Bolian, Polly 1925- *4*

Bollen, Roger 1941(?)- *83*
   Brief entry *29*
Bolliger, Max 1929- *7*
Bollinger, Max 1929- *167*
Bollinger, Peter *172*
Bolognese, Don(ald Alan) 1934- *129*
   Earlier sketches in SATA *24, 71*
Bolognese, Elaine 1933- *23*
Bolotin, Norman (Phillip) 1951- *93*
Bolton, Carole 1926- *6*
Bolton, Elizabeth
   See St. John, Nicole
Bolton, Evelyn
   See Bunting, Eve
Bonar, Veronica
   See Bailey, Donna (Veronica Anne)
Bond, B. J.
   See Heneghan, James
Bond, Bruce 1939- *61*
Bond, Felicia 1954- *126*
   Earlier sketch in SATA *49*
Bond, Gladys Baker 1912- *14*
Bond, Higgins 1951- *177*
   Earlier sketch in SATA *83*
Bond, J. Harvey
   See Winterbotham, R(ussell) R(obert)
Bond, (Thomas) Michael 1926- *157*
   Earlier sketches in SATA *6, 58*
   See also CLR *95*
   See also SAAS *3*
Bond, Nancy 1945- *159*
   Autobiography Feature *159*
   Earlier sketches in SATA *22, 82*
   See also CLR *11*
   See also SAAS *13*
Bond, Nancy Barbara
   See Bond, Nancy
Bond, Rebecca 1972- *130*
Bond, Ruskin 1934- *87*
   Earlier sketch in SATA *14*
Bondie, J. D.
   See Cunningham, Chet
Bondoux, Anne-Laure 1971- *175*
Bone, Ian 1956- *158*
   Earlier sketch in SATA *117*
Bonehill, Captain Ralph
   See Stratemeyer, Edward L.
Bonestell, Chesley 1888-1986
   Obituary *48*
Bonham, Barbara Thomas 1926- *7*
Bonham, Frank 1914-1989 .... *49*
   Obituary *62*
   Earlier sketch in SATA *1*
   See also SAAS *3*
Boniface, William 1963- *182*
   Earlier sketch in SATA *102*
Bonino, Louise
   See Williams, Louise Bonino
Bonk, John J. *189*
Bonn, Pat
   See Bonn, Patricia Carolyn
Bonn, Patricia Carolyn 1948- *43*
Bonner, Hannah *197*
Bonner, Mary Graham 1890-1974 .... *19*
Bonner, Mike 1951- *121*
Bonners, Susan 1947- *85*
   Brief entry *48*
Bonnett-Rampersaud, Louise *173*
Bonning, Tony 1948- *169*
Bonsall, Crosby Barbara (Newell)
   1921-1995 .... *23*
   Obituary *84*
Bonsall, Joseph S. 1948- *119*
Bonsignore, Joan 1959- *140*
Bontemps, Arna 1902-1973 .... *44*
   Obituary *24*
   Earlier sketch in SATA *2*
   See also CLR *6*
Bontemps, Arnaud Wendell
   See Bontemps, Arna
Bonzon, Paul-Jacques 1908-1978 .... *22*

Boock, Paula 1964- *134*
Booher, Dianna Daniels 1948- *33*
Book, Rick 1949- *119*
Book, Rita
   See Holub, Joan
Bookman, Charlotte
   See Zolotow, Charlotte
Boon, Debbie 1960- *103*
Boon, Emilie (Laetitia) 1958- *86*
Boone, Charles Eugene
   See Boone, Pat
Boone, Pat 1934- *7*
Booraem, Ellen *211*
Boorman, Linda (Kay) 1940- *46*
Boorstin, Daniel J(oseph) 1914-2004 .... *52*
Boos, Ben 1971- *206*
Booth, Coe *187*
Booth, Ernest Sheldon 1915-1984 .... *43*
Booth, George 1926- *191*
Booth, Graham (Charles) 1935- *37*
Bootman, Colin *159*
Borden, Louise 1949- *190*
   Autobiography Feature *141*
   Earlier sketches in SATA *68, 104, 141*
Bordier, Georgette 1924- *16*
Borgman, James
   See Borgman, Jim
Borgman, James Mark
   See Borgman, Jim
Borgman, Jim 1954- *122*
Borgo, Lacy Finn 1972- *194*
Boring, Mel 1939- *168*
   Earlier sketch in SATA *35*
Borja, Corinne 1929- *22*
Borja, Robert 1923- *22*
Borland, Hal
   See Borland, Harold Glen
Borland, Harold Glen 1900-1978 .... *5*
   Obituary *24*
Borland, Kathryn Kilby 1916- *16*
Borlenghi, Patricia 1951- *79*
Born, Adolf 1930- *49*
Bornstein, Ruth Lercher
   See Bornstein-Lercher, Ruth
Bornstein-Lercher, Ruth 1927- *88*
   Autobiography Feature *107*
   Earlier sketch in SATA *14*
Borski, Lucia Merecka *18*
Borten, Helen Jacobson 1930- *5*
Bortolotti, Dan 1969- *157*
Borton, Elizabeth
   See Trevino, Elizabeth B(orton) de
Borton, Lady 1942- *98*
Borton de Trevino, Elizabeth
   See Trevino, Elizabeth B(orton) de
Bortstein, Larry 1942-2010 .... *16*
Bortz, Alfred B(enjamin) 1944- *139*
   Earlier sketch in SATA *74*
Bortz, Fred
   See Bortz, Alfred B(enjamin)
Bosch, Pseudonymous *199*
Bosco, Jack
   See Holliday, Joseph
Boshell, Gordon 1908-1991 .... *15*
Boshinski, Blanche 1922- *10*
Bosman, Paul 1929- *107*
Bosse, Malcolm (Joseph, Jr.) 1926-2002 .. *136*
   Earlier sketch in SATA *35*
Bosserman, (Charles) Phillip 1931- *84*
Bossom, Naomi 1933- *35*
Bostock, Mike 1962- *114*
Boston, L(ucy) M(aria Wood) 1892-1990 ... *19*
   Obituary *64*
   See also CLR *3*
Bostrom, Kathleen (Susan) Long 1954- *139*
Bostrom, Kathy
   See Bostrom, Kathleen (Susan) Long
Boswell, Addie *208*
Boswell, Addie Kay
   See Boswell, Addie
Bosworth, J. Allan 1925- *19*

Bothwell, Jean (?)-1977 .... *2*
Botkin, B(enjamin) A(lbert) 1901-1975 ...... *40*
Botsford, Ward 1927-2004 .... *66*
Botting, Douglas (Scott) 1934- *43*
Bottner, Barbara 1943- *170*
   Autobiography Feature *121*
   Earlier sketches in SATA *14, 93*
   See also SAAS *26*
Bottone, Frank G., Jr. 1969- *141*
Bouchard, David 1952- *117*
Boucher, (Clarence) Carter 1954- *129*
Boudelang, Bob
   See Pell, Ed(ward)
Boughton, Richard 1954- *75*
Boulet, Susan Seddon 1941- *50*
Boulle, Pierre (Francois Marie-Louis)
   1912-1994 .... *22*
   Obituary *78*
Boulton, Jane 1921- *91*
Bouma, Paddy 1947- *128*
Bour, Daniele 1939- *62*
Bourbonniere, Sylvie 1966- *182*
Bourdon, David 1934-1998 .... *46*
Bourgeois, Paulette 1951- *153*
Bourne, Lesley
   See Marshall, Evelyn
Bourne, Miriam Anne 1931-1989 .... *16*
   Obituary *63*
Boutavant, Marc 1970- *200*
Boutet de Monvel, (Louis) M(aurice)
   1850(?)-1913 .... *30*
   See also CLR *32*
Bouwman, H.M. *209*
Bova, Ben 1932- *133*
   Earlier sketches in SATA *6, 68*
   See also CLR *96*
Bova, Benjamin William
   See Bova, Ben
Bovaird, Anne E(lizabeth) 1960- *90*
Bow, Patricia 1946- *168*
Bowden, Joan Chase 1925- *51*
   Brief entry *38*
Bowe, Julie 1962- *194*
Bowen, Alexandria Russell *97*
Bowen, Andy Russell
   See Bowen, Alexandria Russell
Bowen, Anne 1952- *202*
   Earlier sketch in SATA *170*
Bowen, Betty Morgan
   See West, Betty
Bowen, Catherine (Shober) Drinker
   1897-1973 .... *7*
Bowen, David
   See Bowen, Joshua David
Bowen, Fred 1953- *136*
Bowen, Joshua David 1930- *22*
Bowen, Rhys
   See Quin-Harkin, Janet
Bowen, Robert Sydney 1900-1977 .... *52*
   Obituary *21*
Bowermaster, Jon 1954- *135*
   Earlier sketch in SATA *77*
Bowers, Terrell L. 1945- *101*
Bowers, Terry
   See Bowers, Terrell L.
Bowers, Tim *185*
Bowie, C. W.
   See Old, Wendie C(orbin)
   and Wirths, Claudine (Turner) G(ibson)
Bowie, Jim
   See Norwood, Victor G(eorge) C(harles)
   and Stratemeyer, Edward L.
Bowkett, Stephen 1953- *67*
Bowler, Jan Brett
   See Brett, Jan
Bowler, Tim 1953- *209*
   Earlier sketch in SATA *149*
Bowman, Catherine
   See Smith, Cat Bowman
Bowman, Crystal 1951- *105*
Bowman, James Cloud 1880-1961 .... *23*

Bowman, John S(tewart) 1931- *16*
Bowman, Kathleen (Gill) 1942- *52*
  Brief entry *40*
Bowman, Leslie
  See Bowman, Leslie W.
Bowman, Leslie W. *182*
Bowsher, Melodie *195*
Boxall, Ed *178*
Boyce, Frank Cottrell *182*
Boyce, George A(rthur) 1898- *19*
Boyd, Candy Dawson 1946- *72*
  See also CLR 50
Boyd, Pauline
  See Schock, Pauline
Boyd, Selma
  See Acuff, Selma Boyd
Boyd, Waldo T. 1918- *18*
Boyden, Linda 1948- *143*
Boyer, Allen B. 1963- *153*
Boyer, Robert E(rnst) 1929- *22*
Boyes, Vivien 1952- *106*
Boyes, Vivien Elizabeth
  See Boyes, Vivien
Boyle, Ann (Peters) 1916- *10*
Boyle, Eleanor Vere (Gordon) 1825-1916 .. *28*
Boyle, Robert H. 1928- *65*
Boylston, Helen Dore 1895-1984 .... *23*
  Obituary *39*
Boyne, John 1971- *181*
Boynton, Sandra (Keith) 1953- *152*
  Brief entry *38*
  Earlier sketches in SATA *57, 107*
  See also CLR 105
Boz
  See Dickens, Charles
Braasch, Gary *201*
Bracken, Charles
  See Pellowski, Michael (Joseph)
Brackers de Hugo, Pierre 1960- *115*
Brackett, Dolli Tingle 1911-1993 .... *137*
Brackett, Virginia 1950- *166*
  Earlier sketch in SATA *121*
Brackett, Virginia Roberts Meredith
  See Brackett, Virginia
Bradbury, Bianca (Ryley) 1908-1982 .... *56*
  Earlier sketch in SATA *3*
Bradbury, Edward P.
  See Moorcock, Michael
Bradbury, Ray 1920- *123*
  Earlier sketches in SATA *11, 64*
Bradbury, Ray Douglas
  See Bradbury, Ray
Bradby, Marie *161*
Bradfield, Carl 1942- *91*
Bradford, Ann (Liddell) 1917- *56*
  Brief entry *38*
Bradford, Barbara Taylor 1933- *66*
Bradford, Karleen 1936- *96*
  Earlier sketch in SATA *48*
Bradford, Lois J(ean) 1936- *36*
Bradford, Richard (Roark) 1932-2002 .... *59*
  Obituary *135*
Bradley, Duane
  See Sanborn, Duane
Bradley, Kimberly Brubaker 1967- *179*
Bradley, Marion Zimmer 1930-1999 .... *139*
  Obituary *116*
  Earlier sketch in SATA *90*
Bradley, Timothy J. *193*
Bradley, Virginia 1912- *23*
Bradley, Will
  See Strickland, Brad
Bradman, Tony 1954- *152*
  Earlier sketch in SATA *81*
Bradshaw, Gillian (Joan) 1949- *118*
Bradshaw, Gillian 1956- *127*
Bradshaw, Gillian Marucha
  See Bradshaw, Gillian
Bradstreet, T. J.
  See Thesman, Jean

Brady, Esther Wood 1905-1987 .... *31*
  Obituary *53*
Brady, Irene 1943- *4*
Brady, Kimberley S. 1953- *101*
Brady, Kimberley Smith
  See Brady, Kimberley S.
Brady, Lillian 1902- *28*
Bragdon, Elspeth MacDuffie 1897-1980 ...... *6*
Bragdon, Lillian Jacot *24*
Brager, Bruce L. 1949- *146*
Bragg, Mabel Caroline 1870-1945 .... *24*
Bragg, Michael 1948- *46*
Bragg, Ruth Gembicki 1943- *77*
Brahm, Sumishta 1954- *58*
Brailsford, Frances
  See Wosmek, Frances
Brainerd, John W(hiting) 1918- *65*
Braithwaite, Althea 1940- *23*
  Autobiography Feature *119*
  See also SAAS 24
Bram, Elizabeth 1948- *30*
Brancato, Robin F(idler) 1936- *97*
  See also CLR 32
  See also SAAS 9
Branch, Muriel Miller 1943- *152*
  Earlier sketch in SATA *94*
Brand, Christianna
  See Lewis, Mary
Brand, Rebecca
  See Charnas, Suzy McKee
Brande, Robin *194*
Brandel, Marc 1919- *71*
Brandenberg, Alexa (Demetria) 1966- *97*
Brandenberg, Aliki 1929- *157*
  Earlier sketches in SATA *2, 35, 75, 113*
  See also CLR 71
Brandenberg, Franz 1932- *75*
  Earlier sketches in SATA *8, 35*
Brandenburg, Jim 1945- *87*
Brandhorst, Carl T(heodore) 1898-1988 ..... *23*
Brandis, Marianne 1938- *149*
  Earlier sketches in SATA *59, 96*
Brandon, Brumsic, Jr. 1927- *9*
Brandon, Curt
  See Bishop, Curtis (Kent)
Brandreth, Gyles 1948- *28*
Brandreth, Gyles Daubeney
  See Brandreth, Gyles
Brandt, Catharine 1905-1997 .... *40*
Brandt, Keith
  See Sabin, Louis
Brandt, Sue R(eading) 1916- *59*
Branfield, John (Charles) 1931- *11*
Branford, Henrietta 1946-1999 .... *106*
Branley, Franklyn M(ansfield)
  1915-2002 .... *136*
  Earlier sketches in SATA *4, 68*
  See also CLR 13
  See also SAAS 16
Brannen, Sarah S. *202*
Branscum, Robbie (Tilley) 1937-1997 .... *72*
  Obituary *96*
  Earlier sketch in SATA *23*
  See also SAAS 17
Bransom, (John) Paul 1885-1979 .... *43*
Brashares, Ann 1967- *188*
  Earlier sketch in SATA *145*
  See also CLR 113
Brassard, France 1963- *186*
Braswell, E.J.
  See Lynn, Tracy
Braswell, Elizabeth J.
  See Lynn, Tracy
Braswell, Liz
  See Lynn, Tracy
Bratton, Helen 1899-1986 .... *4*
Bratun, Katy 1950- *160*
  Earlier sketch in SATA *83*
Braude, Michael 1936- *23*
Braun, Lilian Jackson 1916(?)- *109*
Brautigan, Richard 1935-1984 .... *56*

Brautigan, Richard Gary
  See Brautigan, Richard
Bray, Libba *203*
  Earlier sketch in SATA *159*
Bray, Martha E.
  See Bray, Libba
Braymer, Marjorie Elizabeth 1911-1988 .... *6*
Breathed, Berke 1957- *161*
  Earlier sketch in SATA *86*
Breathed, Guy Berkeley
  See Breathed, Berke
Brecht, Edith 1895-1975 .... *6*
  Obituary *25*
Breck, Vivian
  See Breckenfeld, Vivian Gurney
Breckenfeld, Vivian Gurney 1895-1992 .... *1*
Breda, Tjalmar
  See DeJong, David C(ornel)
Bredeson, Carmen 1944- *163*
  Earlier sketch in SATA *98*
Breen, Steve 1970- *186*
Breinburg, Petronella 1927- *11*
  See also CLR 31
Breisky, William J(ohn) 1928- *22*
Brenaman, Miriam *172*
Brennan, Caitlin
  See Tarr, Judith
Brennan, Gale (Patrick) 1927- *64*
  Brief entry *53*
Brennan, Herbie 1940- *183*
  Earlier sketch in SATA *140*
Brennan, James Herbert
  See Brennan, Herbie
Brennan, Jan
  See Brennan, Herbie
Brennan, J.H.
  See Brennan, Herbie
Brennan, Joseph Lomas 1903-2000 .... *6*
Brennan, Linda Crotta 1952- *130*
Brennan, Tim
  See Conroy, John Wesley
Brennan-Nelson, Denise *203*
Brenner, Anita 1905-1974 .... *56*
Brenner, Barbara (Johnes) 1925- *124*
  Earlier sketches in SATA *4, 42, 76*
  See also SAAS 14
Brenner, Fred 1920- *36*
  Brief entry *34*
Brent, Hope 1935(?)-1984
  Obituary *39*
Brent, Stuart *14*
Breskin, Jane
  See Zalben, Jane Breskin
Breslin, Theresa *128*
  Autobiography Feature *128*
  Earlier sketch in SATA *70*
Breslow, Maurice 1935- *72*
Breslow, Maurice A
  See Breslow, Maurice
Breslow, Susan 1951- *69*
Brett, Bernard 1925- *22*
Brett, Grace N(eff) 1900-1975 .... *23*
Brett, Jan 1949- *171*
  Earlier sketches in SATA *42, 71, 130*
  See also CLR 27
Brett, Jan Churchill
  See Brett, Jan
Brett Bowler, Jan
  See Brett, Jan
Brewer, Heather 1973- *196*
Brewer, James D. 1951- *108*
Brewer, Sally King 1947- *33*
Brewster, Benjamin
  See Folsom, Franklin (Brewster)
Brewster, Hugh 1950- *191*
  Earlier sketch in SATA *95*
Brewster, Patience 1952- *97*
Brewton, John E(dmund) 1898-1982 .... *5*
Brian, Janeen (Paulette) 1948- *141*
Briant, Ed *180*
Brick, John 1922-1973 .... *10*

Brickman, Robin D. 1954- *155*
Bride, Nadja
    See Nobisso, Josephine
Bridgers, Sue Ellen 1942- *90*
    Autobiography Feature *109*
    Earlier sketch in SATA *22*
    See also CLR *18*
    See also SAAS *1*
Bridges, Laurie
    See Bruck, Lorraine
Bridges, Ruby (Nell) 1954- *131*
Bridges, William (Andrew) 1901-1984 .... *5*
Bridwell, Norman (Ray) 1928- *138*
    Earlier sketches in SATA *4, 68*
    See also CLR *96*
Brier, Howard M(axwell) 1903-1969 .... *8*
Brierley, (Louise) 1958- *59*
Briggs, Katharine Mary 1898-1980 .... *101*
    Obituary *25*
Briggs, Peter 1921-1975 .... *39*
    Obituary *31*
Briggs, Raymond 1934- *184*
    Earlier sketches in SATA *23, 66, 131*
    See also CLR *10*
Briggs, Raymond Redvers
    See Briggs, Raymond
Bright, Paul 1949- *182*
Bright, Robert Sr.) 1902-1988 .... *63*
    Obituary *60*
    Earlier sketch in SATA *24*
Bright, Robert Douglas
    See Bright, Robert Sr.)
Bright, Sarah
    See Shine, Deborah
Brightfield, Richard 1927- *65*
    Brief entry *53*
Brightfield, Rick
    See Brightfield, Richard
Brighton, Catherine 1943- *206*
    Earlier sketches in SATA *65, 107*
Brill, Marlene Targ 1945- *124*
    Earlier sketch in SATA *77*
Brimberg, Stanlee 1947- *9*
Brimner, Larry Dane 1949- *170*
    Autobiography Feature *112*
    Earlier sketch in SATA *79*
Brin, David 1950- *65*
Brin, Ruth Firestone 1921- *22*
Brinckloe, Julie 1950- *13*
Brinckloe, Julie Lorraine
    See Brinckloe, Julie
Brindel, June (Rachuy) 1919- *7*
Brindle, Max
    See Fleischman, Sid
Brindze, Ruth 1903-1984 .... *23*
Brink, Carol Ryrie 1895-1981 .... *100*
    Obituary *27*
    Earlier sketches in SATA *1, 31*
    See also CLR *149*
Brinsmead, H. F(ay)
    See Brinsmead, H(esba) F(ay)
Brinsmead, H. F.
    See Brinsmead, H(esba) F(ay)
Brinsmead, H(esba) F(ay) 1922- *78*
    Earlier sketch in SATA *18*
    See also CLR *47*
    See also SAAS *5*
Briquebec, John
    See Rowland-Entwistle, (Arthur) Theodore
    (Henry)
Brisbane, Henry R.
    See Ellis, Edward S.
Brisco, P. A.
    See Matthews, Patricia
Brisco, Patty
    See Matthews, Patricia
    and Matthews, Clayton (Hartley)
Briscoe, Jill (Pauline) 1935- *56*
    Brief entry *47*
Brisley, Joyce Lankester 1896-1978 .... *22*
    Obituary *84*

Brissenden, Connie
    See Brissenden, Constance
Brissenden, Constance 1947- *150*
Brisson, Pat 1951- *177*
    Autobiography Feature *133*
    Earlier sketches in SATA *67, 128, 133*
Britt, Albert 1874-1969
    Obituary *28*
Britt, Dell 1934- *1*
Brittain, Bill
    See Brittain, William
Brittain, C. Dale 1948- *82*
Brittain, William 1930- *76*
    Earlier sketch in SATA *36*
    See also SAAS *7*
Brittingham, Geoffrey (Hugh) 1959- *76*
Brittney, L. *209*
Britton, Kate
    See Stegeman, Janet Allais
Britton, Louisa
    See McGuire, Leslie (Sarah)
Britton, Rick 1952- *82*
Bro, Margueritte (Harmon) 1894-1977 .... *19*
    Obituary *27*
Broach, Elise 1963- *173*
Broadhead, Helen Cross 1913- *25*
Broadway, Hannah *208*
Brochmann, Elizabeth 1938- *41*
Brock, Betty (Carter) 1923-2003 .... *4*
    Obituary *150*
Brock, C(harles) E(dmund) 1870-1938 .... *42*
    Brief entry *32*
Brock, Delia
    See Ephron, Delia
Brock, Emma L(illian) 1886-1974 .... *8*
Brock, H(enry) M(atthew) 1875-1960 .... *42*
Brockett, Eleanor Hall 1913-1967 .... *10*
Brockman, C(hristian) Frank 1902-1985 ..... *26*
Brockmeier, Kevin 1972- *176*
Broda, Ron 1954- *209*
Broderick, Dorothy M. 1929- *5*
Brodeur, Ruth Wallace
    See Wallace-Brodeur, Ruth
Brodie, Sally
    See Cavin, Ruth (Brodie)
Brodsky, Beverly
    See McDermott, Beverly Brodsky
Brody, Wendy
    See Staub, Wendy Corsi
Broeger, Achim 1944- *31*
Broekel, Rainer Lothar 1923- *38*
Broekel, Ray
    See Broekel, Rainer Lothar
Broekstra, Lorette 1964- *189*
    Earlier sketch in SATA *124*
Brogden, Sherryl
    See Jordan, Sherryl
Broger, Achim
    See Broeger, Achim
Broida, Marian *154*
Brokamp, Marilyn 1920- *10*
Broman, Fred
    See Moseley, James W(illett)
Bromhall, Winifred *26*
Brommer, Gerald F(rederick) 1927- *28*
Brondfield, Jerome 1913-1998 .... *22*
Brondfield, Jerry
    See Brondfield, Jerome
Bronner, Stephen Eric 1949- *101*
Bronowski, Jacob 1908-1974 .... *55*
Bronson, Alice
    See Watkins, Dawn L.
Bronson, Linda *203*
Bronson, Lynn
    See Lampman, Evelyn Sibley
Bronson, Wilfrid Swancourt 1894-1985
    Obituary *43*
Brook, Judith (Penelope) 1926- *59*
    Brief entry *51*
Brook, Judy
    See Brook, Judith (Penelope)

Brooke, L(eonard) Leslie 1862-1940 .... *17*
    See also CLR *20*
Brooke, William J. 1946- *139*
Brooke-Haven, P.
    See Wodehouse, P. G.
Brooker, Kyrsten *199*
Brookins, Dana 1931- *28*
Brooks, Anita
    See Abramovitz, Anita (Zeltner Brooks)
Brooks, Bill 1939- *59*
Brooks, Bruce 1950- *112*
    Brief entry *53*
    Earlier sketch in SATA *72*
    See also CLR *25*
Brooks, Caryl 1924- *84*
Brooks, Charlotte K(endrick) 1918-1998 .... *24*
    Obituary *112*
Brooks, Erik 1972- *182*
    Earlier sketch in SATA *152*
Brooks, George
    See Baum, L. Frank
Brooks, Gwendolyn 1917-2000 .... *6*
    Obituary *123*
    See also CLR *27*
Brooks, Gwendolyn Elizabeth
    See Brooks, Gwendolyn
Brooks, Jerome 1931- *23*
Brooks, Kevin 1959- *197*
    Earlier sketch in SATA *150*
Brooks, Kevin M.
    See Brooks, Kevin
Brooks, Laurie *209*
Brooks, Lester 1924- *7*
Brooks, Martha 1944- *134*
    Autobiography Feature *134*
    Earlier sketches in SATA *68, 121*
Brooks, Maurice (Graham) 1900- *45*
Brooks, Polly Schoyer 1912- *12*
Brooks, Ron 1948- *94*
    Brief entry *33*
Brooks, Ronald George
    See Brooks, Ron
Brooks, Terry 1944- *60*
Brooks, Walter R(ollin) 1886-1958 .... *17*
Brooks-Hill, Helen (Mason) 1908-1994 ...... *59*
Broome, Errol 1937- *158*
    Earlier sketch in SATA *105*
Brophy, Nannette 1963- *73*
Brosnan, James Patrick 1929- *14*
Brosnan, Jim
    See Brosnan, James Patrick
Brostoff, Anita 1931- *132*
Brothers Grimm
    See Grimm, Jacob Ludwig Karl
    and Grimm, Wilhelm Karl
Brothers Hildebrandt, The
    See Hildebrandt, Greg
    and Hildebrandt, Tim
Broun, Emily
    See Sterne, Emma Gelders
Brouwer, S. W.
    See Brouwer, Sigmund (W.)
Brouwer, Sigmund (W.) 1959- *109*
Brow, Thea 1934- *60*
Brower, Millicent *8*
Brower, Pauline 1929- *22*
Browin, Frances Williams 1898-1986 .... *5*
Brown, Alexis
    See Baumann, Amy Beeching
Brown, Anne Ensign 1937- *61*
Brown, Beverly Swerdlow *97*
Brown, Bill
    See Brown, William L(ouis)
Brown, Billye Walker
    See Cutchen, Billye Walker
Brown, Bob
    See Brown, Robert Joseph
Brown, Buck 1936- *45*
Brown, Calef *179*
Brown, Cassie 1919-1986 .... *55*
Brown, Charlotte Lewis *181*

Brown, Conrad 1922- *31*
Brown, Craig McFarland 1947- *73*
Brown, David
 See Brown, David A(lan)
 and Myller, Rolf
Brown, Dee 1908-2002 .... *110*
 Obituary *141*
 Earlier sketch in SATA *5*
Brown, Dee Alexander
 See Brown, Dee
Brown, Don 1949- *200*
 Earlier sketch in SATA *172*
Brown, Drew T. III 1955- *83*
Brown, Drollene P. 1939- *53*
Brown, Elbrite *198*
Brown, Eleanor Frances 1908-1987 .... *3*
Brown, Elizabeth Ferguson 1937- *153*
Brown, Elizabeth M(yers) 1915- *43*
Brown, Fern G. 1918- *34*
Brown, (Robert) Fletch 1923- *42*
Brown, Fornan 1901-1996 .... *71*
 Obituary *88*
Brown, George Earl 1883-1964 .... *11*
Brown, George Mackay 1921-1996 .... *35*
Brown, Irene Bennett 1932- *3*
Brown, Irving
 See Adams, William Taylor
Brown, Ivor (John Carnegie) 1891-1974 ...... *5*
 Obituary *26*
Brown, Jane Clark 1930- *81*
Brown, Janet Mitsui *87*
Brown, Jo 1964- *170*
Brown, Joanne 1933- *147*
Brown, Joe David 1915-1976 .... *44*
Brown, Joseph E(dward) 1929- *59*
 Brief entry *51*
Brown, Judith Gwyn 1933- *20*
Brown, Kathryn 1955- *168*
 Earlier sketch in SATA *98*
Brown, Kathy
 See Brown, Kathryn
Brown, Ken (James) *129*
Brown, Kevin 1960- *101*
Brown, Laurene Krasny 1945- *99*
 Earlier sketch in SATA *54*
Brown, Laurie Krasny
 See Brown, Laurene Krasny
Brown, Lloyd Arnold 1907-1966 .... *36*
Brown, Mahlon A.
 See Ellis, Edward S.
Brown, Marc (Tolon) 1946- *145*
 Earlier sketches in SATA *10, 53, 80*
 See also CLR *29*
Brown, Marcia (Joan) 1918- *47*
 Earlier sketch in SATA *7*
 See also CLR *12*
Brown, Margaret Wise 1910-1952 .... *100*
 See also YABC *2*
 See also CLR *107*
Brown, Margery (Wheeler) *78*
 Earlier sketch in SATA *5*
Brown, Marion Marsh 1908-2001 .... *6*
Brown, Myra Berry 1918- *6*
Brown, Palmer 1919- *36*
Brown, Pamela (Beatrice) 1924-1989 .... *5*
 Obituary *61*
Brown, Peter 1979- *178*
Brown, Rachel W.N. 1947- *203*
Brown, Reeve Lindbergh
 See Lindbergh, Reeve
Brown, Richard E. 1946- *61*
Brown, Robert Joseph 1907-1989 .... *14*
Brown, Roderick (Langmere) Haig-
 See Haig-Brown, Roderick (Langmere)
Brown, Rosalie
 See Moore, Rosalie (Gertrude)
Brown, Roswell
 See Webb, Jean Francis (III)
Brown, Roy (Frederick) 1921-1982 .... *51*
 Obituary *39*

Brown, Ruth 1941- *170*
 Earlier sketch in SATA *105*
Brown, Scott 1971- *134*
Brown, Sue Ellen 1954- *81*
Brown, Tricia 1954- *114*
Brown, Vinson 1912-1991 .... *19*
Brown, Walter R(eed) 1929- *19*
Brown, Will
 See Ainsworth, William Harrison
Brown, William L(ouis) 1910-1964 .... *5*
Browne, Anthony 1946- *163*
 Brief entry *44*
 Earlier sketches in SATA *45, 61, 105*
 See also CLR *19*
Browne, Anthony Edward Tudor
 See Browne, Anthony
Browne, Dik
 See Browne, Richard Arthur Allen
Browne, Hablot Knight 1815-1882 .... *21*
Browne, Matthew
 See Rands, William Brighty
Browne, Nicki M.
 See Browne, N.M.
Browne, Nicky Matthews
 See Browne, N.M.
Browne, N.M. 1960- *167*
Browne, Richard Arthur Allen 1917-1989 .. *67*
 Brief entry *38*
Browne, Vee F(rances) 1956- *90*
Browning, Robert 1812-1889
 See YABC *1*
 See also CLR *97*
Brownjohn, Alan 1931- *6*
Brownlee, Walter 1930- *62*
Brownlie, Betty 1946- *159*
Brownlow, Kevin 1938- *65*
Brownlow, Mike *183*
Brownridge, William R(oy) 1932- *94*
Broyles, Anne 1953- *201*
Bruce, Dorita Fairlie 1885-1970
 Obituary *27*
Bruce, (William) Harry 1934- *77*
Bruce, Mary 1927- *1*
Bruchac, Joseph III
 See Bruchac, Joseph
Bruchac, Joseph 1942- *176*
 Autobiography Feature *176*
 Earlier sketches in SATA *42, 89, 131*
 See also CLR *46*
Bruchac, Margaret M.
 See Bruchac, Marge
Bruchac, Marge *181*
Bruck, Lorraine 1921- *55*
 Brief entry *46*
Bruel, Nick *205*
 Earlier sketch in SATA *166*
Bruel, Robert O. 1929-2002 .... *189*
Bruemmer, Fred 1929- *47*
Brugman, Alyssa (F.) 1974- *152*
Brumbeau, Jeff 1955- *157*
Bruna, Dick 1927- *76*
 Brief entry *30*
 Earlier sketch in SATA *43*
 See also CLR *7*
Brunhoff, Jean de 1899-1937 .... *24*
 See also CLR *116*
Brunhoff, Laurent de 1925- *150*
 Earlier sketches in SATA *24, 71*
 See also CLR *116*
Brunkus, Denise *204*
Brunskill, Elizabeth Ann Flatt
 See Flatt, Lizann
Brush, Karen A(lexandra) 1960- *85*
Brussel-Smith, Bernard 1914- *58*
Brust, Steven 1955- *121*
 Earlier sketch in SATA *86*
Brust, Steven K. Zoltan
 See Brust, Steven
Brustlein, Daniel 1904- *40*
Brustlein, Janice Tworkov -2000 .... *40*
 Obituary *126*

Brutschy, Jennifer 1960- *84*
Bryan, Ashley 1923- *178*
 Earlier sketches in SATA *31, 72, 132*
 See also CLR *66*
Bryan, Ashley F.
 See Bryan, Ashley
Bryan, Dorothy M. 1896(?)-1984
 Obituary *39*
Bryan, Jennifer *190*
Bryan, Sean *192*
Bryant, Bernice (Morgan) 1908-1976 .... *11*
Bryant, Jen 1960- *175*
 Earlier sketch in SATA *94*
Bryant, Jennifer
 See Bryant, Jen
Bryant, Jennifer Fisher
 See Bryant, Jen
Bryant, Laura J. *176*
Brychta, Alex 1956- *21*
Brynie, Faith H. 1946- *113*
Brynie, Faith Hickman
 See Brynie, Faith H.
Bryson, Bernarda 1903-2004 .... *9*
Buba, Joy Flinsch 1904- *44*
Buchan, Bryan 1945- *36*
Buchan, John 1875-1940
 See YABC *2*
Buchan, Stuart 1942-1987
 Obituary *54*
Buchanan, Debby 1952- *82*
Buchanan, Deborah Leevonne
 See Buchanan, Debby
Buchanan, Jane 1956- *160*
Buchanan, Paul 1959- *116*
Buchanan, Sue 1939- *139*
Buchheimer, Naomi Barnett
 See Barnett, Naomi
Buchignani, Walter 1965- *84*
Buchmann, Stephen L. *194*
Buchwald, Art 1925-2007 .... *10*
Buchwald, Arthur
 See Buchwald, Art
Buchwald, Emilie 1935- *7*
Buck, Gisela 1941- *101*
Buck, Lewis 1925- *18*
Buck, Margaret Waring 1905-1997 .... *3*
Buck, Nola
 See Godwin, Laura
Buck, Pearl S. 1892-1973 .... *25*
 Earlier sketch in SATA *1*
Buck, Pearl Sydenstricker
 See Buck, Pearl S.
Buck, Siegfried 1941- *101*
Buckalew, Clare B.
 See Dunkle, Clare B.
Buckeridge, Anthony (Malcolm)
 1912-2004 .... *85*
 Earlier sketch in SATA *6*
Buckholtz, Eileen (Garber) 1949- *54*
 Brief entry *47*
Buckingham, Royce 1966- *210*
Buckingham, Royce Scott
 See Buckingham, Royce
Buckler, Ernest 1908-1984 .... *47*
Buckless, Andrea K. 1968- *117*
Buckley, Helen E(lizabeth) 1918- *90*
 Earlier sketch in SATA *2*
Buckley, James, Jr. 1963- *166*
 Earlier sketch in SATA *114*
Buckley, Michael *177*
Buckley, Susan *184*
Buckley, Susan Washburn
 See Buckley, Susan
Buckley-Archer, Linda *185*
Buckmaster, Henrietta
 See Stephens, Henrietta Henkle
Bucks, Brad
 See Holub, Joan
Budd, E. S.
 See Sirimarco, Elizabeth
Budd, Lillian (Peterson) 1897-1989 .... *7*

Budhos, Marina *173*
Buehler, Stephanie Jona 1956- *83*
Buehner, Caralyn (M.) 1963- *159*
  Earlier sketch in SATA *104*
Buehner, Mark 1959- *159*
  Earlier sketch in SATA *104*
Buehr, Walter Franklin 1897-1971 .... *3*
Buell, Ellen Lewis
  See Cash, Ellen Lewis Buell
Buell, Janet 1952- *185*
  Earlier sketch in SATA *106*
Buergel, Paul-Hermann H. 1949- *83*
Buettner, Dan 1960- *95*
Buff, Conrad 1886-1975 .... *19*
Buff, Mary (E. Marsh) 1890-1970 .... *19*
Buffett, Jimmy 1946- *110*
  Earlier sketch in SATA *76*
Buffie, Margaret 1945- *161*
  Earlier sketches in SATA *71, 107*
  See also CLR *39*
Bugbee, Emma 1888(?)-1981
  Obituary *29*
Bugni, Alice 1951- *122*
Buhhos, Marina Tamar
  See Budhos, Marina
Bujold, Lois McMaster 1949- *136*
Bulfinch, Thomas 1796-1867 .... *35*
Bulion, Leslie 1958- *209*
  Earlier sketch in SATA *161*
Bull, Angela (Mary) 1936- *45*
Bull, Emma 1954- *190*
  Autobiography Feature *103*
  Earlier sketch in SATA *99*
Bull, Norman John 1916- *41*
Bull, Peter (Cecil) 1912-1984
  Obituary *39*
Bull, Schuyler M. 1974- *138*
Bulla, Clyde R. 1914-2007 .... *139*
  Obituary *182*
  Earlier sketches in SATA *2, 41, 91*
  See also SAAS *6*
Bullard, Lisa 1961- *142*
Buller, Jon *205*
Bullock, Kathleen (Mary) 1946- *77*
Bullock, Robert (D.) 1947- *92*
Bulpin, (Barbara) Vicki *92*
Bulwer-Lytton, Edward 1803-1873 .... *23*
Bulwer-Lytton, Edward George Earle Lytton
  See Bulwer-Lytton, Edward
Bumstead, Kathleen Mary 1918-1987 .... *53*
Bundles, A'Lelia Perry 1952- *76*
Bunge, Daniela 1973- *207*
Bunin, Catherine 1967- *30*
Bunin, Sherry 1925- *30*
Bunkers, Suzanne L. 1950- *136*
Bunting, A.E.
  See Bunting, Eve
Bunting, Anne Evelyn
  See Bunting, Eve
Bunting, Eve 1928- *196*
  Earlier sketches in SATA *18, 64, 110, 158*
  See also CLR *82*
Bunting, Glenn (Davison) 1957- *22*
Bunyan, John 1628-1688
  See CLR *124*
Bupp, Walter
  See Garrett, Randall
Burack, Sylvia K. 1916-2003 .... *35*
  Obituary *143*
Burbank, Addison (Buswell) 1895-1961 ..... *37*
Burch, Joann J(ohansen) *75*
Burch, Robert J(oseph) 1925- *74*
  Earlier sketch in SATA *1*
  See also CLR *63*
Burchard, Peter Duncan 1921- *143*
  Earlier sketches in SATA *5, 74*
  See also SAAS *13*
Burchard, S. H.
  See Burchard, Sue
Burchard, Sue 1937- *22*
Burchardt, Nellie 1921- *7*

Burckhardt, Marc 1962- *196*
Burdett, Lois *117*
Burdick, Eugene (Leonard) 1918-1965 .... *22*
Burford, Eleanor
  See Hibbert, Eleanor Alice Burford
Burg, Shana 1968- *204*
Burgan, Michael 1960- *167*
  Earlier sketch in SATA *118*
Burger, Carl 1888-1967 .... *9*
Burgess, Ann Marie
  See Gerson, Noel Bertram
Burgess, Barbara Hood 1926- *69*
Burgess, Em
  See Burgess, Mary Wyche
Burgess, (Frank) Gelett 1866-1951 .... *32*
  Brief entry *30*
Burgess, Mark *157*
Burgess, Mary Wyche 1916- *18*
Burgess, Melvin 1954- *198*
  Earlier sketches in SATA *96, 146*
Burgess, Michael
  See Gerson, Noel Bertram
Burgess, Robert F(orrest) 1927- *4*
Burgess, Starling
  See Tudor, Tasha
Burgess, Thornton Waldo 1874-1965 .... *17*
Burgess, Trevor
  See Trevor, Elleston
Burgwyn, Mebane Holoman 1914-1992 .... *7*
Burke, David 1927- *46*
Burke, Diana G.
  See Gallagher, Diana G.
Burke, Diana Gallagher
  See Gallagher, Diana G.
Burke, Dianne O'Quinn 1940- *89*
Burke, Janine 1952- *139*
Burke, Jim 1973- *179*
Burke, John
  See O'Connor, Richard
Burke, Katie 1953- *168*
Burke, Patrick 1958- *114*
Burke, Ralph
  See Garrett, Randall
  and Silverberg, Robert
Burkert, Nancy Ekholm 1933- *24*
  See also SAAS *14*
Burkett, D. Brent *194*
Burke-Weiner, Kimberly 1962- *95*
Burks, Brian 1955- *95*
Burland, Brian (Berkeley) 1931- *34*
Burland, C. A.
  See Burland, Cottie (Arthur)
Burland, Cottie (Arthur) 1905-1983 .... *5*
Burleigh, Robert 1936- *193*
  Earlier sketches in SATA *55, 98, 146*
Burlingame, (William) Roger 1889-1967 ...... *2*
Burman, Alice Caddy 1896(?)-1977
  Obituary *24*
Burman, Ben Lucien 1896-1984 .... *6*
  Obituary *40*
Burn, Doris 1923- *1*
Burn, Ted
  See Burn, Thomas E.
Burn, Thomas E. 1940- *150*
Burnard, Damon 1963- *115*
Burnett, Constance Buel 1893-1975 .... *36*
Burnett, Frances Eliza Hodgson
  See Burnett, Frances Hodgson
Burnett, Frances Hodgson 1849-1924 .... *100*
  See also YABC *2*
  See also CLR *122*
Burnett, Lindy *210*
Burnett Bossi, Lisa *193*
Burney, Anton
  See Hopkins, (Hector) Kenneth
Burnford, Sheila (Philip Cochrane Every)
  1918-1984 .... *3*
  Obituary *38*
  See also CLR *2*
Burnham, Gretchen
  See Sprague, Gretchen

Burnham, Nicole 1970- *161*
Burnham, Niki
  See Burnham, Nicole
Burnham, Sophy 1936- *65*
Burningham, John 1936- *160*
  Earlier sketches in SATA *16, 59, 111*
  See also CLR *9*
Burningham, Robin Yoko
  See Racoma, Robin Yoko
Burns, Diane L. 1950- *81*
  See also SAAS *24*
Burns, Eloise Wilkin
  See Wilkin, Eloise
Burns, Florence M. 1905-1988 .... *61*
Burns, Khephra 1950- *92*
Burns, Loree Griffin *193*
Burns, Marilyn 1941- *96*
  Brief entry *33*
Burns, Olive Ann 1924-1990 .... *65*
Burns, Paul C. *5*
Burns, Ray
  See Burns, Raymond (Howard)
Burns, Raymond (Howard) 1924- *9*
Burns, Theresa 1961- *84*
Burns, William A. 1909-1999 .... *5*
Burr, Dan 1951- *65*
Burr, Lonnie 1943- *47*
Burrell, Roy E(ric) C(harles) 1923- *72*
Burroughs, Edgar Rice 1875-1950 .... *41*
Burroughs, Jean Mitchell 1908- *28*
Burroughs, Polly 1925- *2*
Burroway, Janet (Gay) 1936- *23*
Burstein, Chaya M(alamud) 1923- *64*
Burstein, Fred 1950- *83*
Burstein, John 1949- *54*
  Brief entry *40*
Burstein, Stanley M.
  See Burstein, Stanley Mayer
Burstein, Stanley Mayer 1941- *175*
Bursztynski, Sue 1953- *114*
Burt, Jesse Clifton 1921-1976 .... *46*
  Obituary *20*
Burt, Olive Woolley 1894-1981 .... *4*
Burtinshaw, Julie *185*
Burton, Gennett 1945- *95*
Burton, Hester (Wood-Hill) 1913-2000 .... *74*
  Earlier sketch in SATA *7*
  See also CLR *1*
  See also SAAS *8*
Burton, Leslie
  See McGuire, Leslie (Sarah)
Burton, Marilee Robin 1950- *82*
  Earlier sketch in SATA *46*
Burton, Maurice 1898-1992 .... *23*
Burton, Rebecca 1970- *183*
Burton, Robert (Wellesley) 1941- *22*
Burton, Virginia Lee 1909-1968 .... *100*
  Earlier sketch in SATA *2*
  See also CLR *11*
Burton, William H(enry) 1890-1964 .... *11*
Busby, Ailie *192*
Busby, Cylin 1970- *118*
Busby, Edith (A. Lake) (?)-1964
  Obituary *29*
Busby, John 1942- *209*
Buscaglia, (Felice) Leo(nardo) 1924-1998 .. *65*
Buscaglia, Leo F.
  See Buscaglia, (Felice) Leo(nardo)
Busch, Phyllis S. 1909- *30*
Bush, Anne Kelleher
  See Kelleher, Anne
Bush, Catherine 1961- *128*
Bush, Jenna 1981- *208*
Bush, Laura 1946- *208*
Bushmiller, Ernest Paul 1905-1982 .... *31*
Bushmiller, Ernie
  See Bushmiller, Ernest Paul
Bushnell, Jack 1952- *86*
Busoni, Rafaello 1900-1962 .... *16*
Buss, Helen M.
  See Clarke, Margaret

Busse, Sarah Martin *194*
Busselle, Rebecca 1941- *80*
Bustard, Anne 1951- *173*
Butcher, Kristin 1951- *140*
Butenko, Bohdan 1931- *90*
Butler, Beverly Kathleen 1932- *7*
Butler, Bill
    See Butler, William Vivian
    and Butler, Ernest Alton
    and Butler, William Huxford
Butler, Charles 1963- *175*
    Earlier sketch in SATA *121*
Butler, Charles Cadman
    See Butler, Charles
Butler, Dori Hillestad 1965- *207*
    Earlier sketch in SATA *164*
Butler, Dorothy 1925- *73*
Butler, Geoff 1945- *94*
Butler, M. Christina 1934- *170*
    Earlier sketch in SATA *72*
Butler, Octavia 1947-2006 .... *84*
    See also CLR *65*
Butler, Octavia E.
    See Butler, Octavia
Butler, Octavia Estelle
    See Butler, Octavia
Butler, Vivian
    See Butler, William Vivian
Butler, William
    See Butler, William Vivian
Butler, William Vivian 1927-1987 .... *79*
Butters, Dorothy Gilman
    See Gilman, Dorothy
Butterworth, Emma Macalik 1928- *43*
Butterworth, Nick 1946- *149*
    Earlier sketch in SATA *106*
Butterworth, Oliver 1915-1990 .... *1*
    Obituary *66*
Butterworth, W.E.
    See Griffin, W.E.B.
Butterworth, William E.
    See Griffin, W.E.B.
Butterworth, William Edmund III
    See Griffin, W.E.B.
Butts, Ed 1951- *177*
Butts, Edward P.
    See Butts, Ed
Butts, Ellen R(ubinstein) 1942- *93*
Buxton, Ralph
    See Silverstein, Alvin
    and Silverstein, Virginia B.
Buzzeo, Toni 1951- *135*
Byalick, Marcia 1947- *141*
    Earlier sketch in SATA *97*
Byard, Carole (Marie) 1941- *57*
Byars, Betsy 1928- *163*
    Autobiography Feature *108*
    Earlier sketches in SATA *4, 46, 80*
    See also CLR *72*
    See also SAAS *1*
Byars, Betsy Cromer
    See Byars, Betsy
Byfield, Barbara Ninde 1930- *8*
Byman, Jeremy 1944- *129*
Bynum, Janie *133*
Byrd, Elizabeth 1912-1989 .... *34*
Byrd, Nicole
    See Zach, Cheryl (Byrd)
Byrd, Robert (John) 1942- *158*
    Earlier sketches in SATA *33, 112*
Byrne, Mary Gregg 1951- *162*

C

C. 3. 3.
    See Wilde, Oscar
C. E. M.
    See Mastrangelo, Charles E(lmer)
Cabaniss, J(ames) Allen 1911-1997 .... *5*

Cabat, Erni 1914- *74*
Cabban, Vanessa 1971- *176*
Cable, Mary 1920- *9*
Cabot, Meg 1967- *175*
    Earlier sketch in SATA *127*
    See also CLR *85*
Cabot, Meggin
    See Cabot, Meg
Cabot, Meggin Patricia
    See Cabot, Meg
Cabot, Patricia
    See Cabot, Meg
Cabral, O. M.
    See Cabral, Olga
Cabral, Olga 1909- *46*
Cabrera, Cozbi A. 1963- *177*
Cabrera, Jane 1968- *182*
    Earlier sketches in SATA *103, 152*
Cabrera, Marcela 1966- *90*
Caddy, Alice
    See Burman, Alice Caddy
Cade, Toni
    See Bambara, Toni Cade
Cadmus and Harmonia
    See Buchan, John
Cadnum, Michael 1949- *165*
    Earlier sketches in SATA *87, 121*
    See also CLR *78*
Caduto, Michael J. 1955- *103*
Cadwallader, Sharon 1936- *7*
Cady, (Walter) Harrison 1877(?)-1970 .... *19*
Caffey, Donna (J.) 1954- *110*
Cagle, Malcolm W(infield) 1918- *32*
Cahn, Rhoda 1922- *37*
Cahn, William 1912-1976 .... *37*
Cain, Arthur H(omer) 1913-1981 .... *3*
Cain, Christopher
    See Fleming, Thomas
Cain, Sheridan 1952- *186*
Caine, Geoffrey
    See Walker, Robert W.
Caines, Jeannette (Franklin) 1938- *78*
    Brief entry *43*
    See also CLR *24*
Cairns, Trevor 1922- *14*
Calabro, Marian 1954- *79*
Caldecott, Moyra 1927- *22*
Caldecott, Randolph (J.) 1846-1886 .... *100*
    Earlier sketch in SATA *17*
    See also CLR *110*
Calder, Charlotte 1952- *125*
Calder, David 1932-1997 .... *105*
Calder, Lyn
    See Calmenson, Stephanie
Calder, Marie D(onais) 1948- *96*
Calderone-Stewart, Lisa
    See Calderone-Stewart, Lisa-Marie
Calderone-Stewart, Lisa-Marie 1958- *123*
Caldwell, Doreen (Mary) 1942- *71*
Caldwell, John C(ope) 1913-1984 .... *7*
Caletti, Deb 1963- *171*
Calhoun, B. B. 1961- *98*
Calhoun, Chad
    See Barrett, Neal, Jr.
    and Cunningham, Chet
    and Goulart, Ron
Calhoun, Dia 1959- *183*
    Earlier sketch in SATA *129*
Calhoun, Mary
    See Wilkins, Mary Huiskamp
Calhoun, T.B.
    See Bisson, Terry
Cali, Davide 1972- *190*
Calif, Ruth 1922- *67*
Calkins, Franklin
    See Stratemeyer, Edward L.
Call, Greg *197*
Call, Hughie Florence 1890-1969 .... *1*
Callahan, Dorothy M(onahan) 1934- *39*
    Brief entry *35*
Callahan, Philip Serna 1923- *25*

Callan, Jamie 1954- *59*
Callan, Jim 1951- *181*
Callaway, Bernice (Anne) 1923- *48*
Callaway, Kathy 1943- *36*
Callen, Larry
    See Callen, Lawrence Willard, Jr.
Callen, Lawrence Willard, Jr. 1927- *19*
Calley, Karin 1965- *92*
Calmenson, Stephanie 1952- *211*
    Brief entry *37*
    Earlier sketches in SATA *51, 84, 139*
Calvert, Elinor H.
    See Lasell, Elinor H.
Calvert, John
    See Leaf, (Wilbur) Munro
Calvert, Pam 1966- *205*
Calvert, Patricia 1931- *132*
    Earlier sketches in SATA *45, 69*
    See also SAAS *17*
Camburn, Carol A.
    See Camburn-Bracalente, Carol A.
Camburn-Bracalente, Carol A. 1962- *118*
Cameron, Ann 1943- *129*
    Earlier sketches in SATA *27, 89*
    See also SAAS *20*
Cameron, Edna M. 1905-1999 .... *3*
Cameron, Eleanor (Frances) 1912-1996 ...... *25*
    Obituary *93*
    Earlier sketch in SATA *1*
    See also CLR *72*
    See also SAAS *10*
Cameron, Elizabeth
    See Nowell, Elizabeth Cameron
Cameron, Elizabeth Jane 1910-1976 .... *32*
    Obituary *30*
Cameron, Ian
    See Payne, Donald Gordon
Cameron, M(alcolm) G(ordon) Graham
    See Graham-Cameron, M(alcolm) G(ordon)
Cameron, M. Graham
    See Graham-Cameron, M(alcolm) G(ordon)
Cameron, Mike Graham
    See Graham-Cameron, M(alcolm) G(ordon)
Cameron, Polly 1928- *2*
Cameron, Scott 1962- *84*
Camp, Charles L. 1893-1975
    Obituary *31*
Camp, Lindsay 1957- *133*
Camp, Madeleine L'Engle
    See L'Engle, Madeleine
Camp, Walter (Chauncey) 1859-1925
    See YABC *1*
Campbell, (Elizabeth) Andrea 1963- *50*
Campbell, Ann R. 1925- *11*
Campbell, Bill 1960- *89*
Campbell, Bruce
    See Epstein, Samuel
Campbell, Camilla 1905-1992 .... *26*
Campbell, Carole R. 1939- *125*
Campbell, Hope 1925- *20*
Campbell, Hugh 1930- *90*
Campbell, Jane
    See Edwards, Jane Campbell
Campbell, Julie
    See Tatham, Julie Campbell
Campbell, Patricia J(ean) 1930- *45*
Campbell, Patty
    See Campbell, Patricia J(ean)
Campbell, Peter A. 1948- *99*
Campbell, R. W.
    See Campbell, Rosemae Wells
Campbell, Robin
    See Strachan, Ian
Campbell, Rod 1945- *98*
    Brief entry *44*
    Earlier sketch in SATA *51*
Campbell, Rosemae Wells 1909- *1*
Campbell, Sarah C. 1966- *207*
Camper, Cathy 1956- *170*
Campion, Nardi Reeder 1917-2007 .... *22*
Campling, Elizabeth 1948- *53*

Campoy, F. Isabel 1946- *181*
    Earlier sketch in SATA *143*
Camps, Luis 1928- *66*
Canales, Viola 1957- *141*
Candell, Victor 1903-1977
    Obituary *24*
Canfield, Dorothea F.
    See Fisher, Dorothy (Frances) Canfield
Canfield, Dorothea Frances
    See Fisher, Dorothy (Frances) Canfield
Canfield, Dorothy
    See Fisher, Dorothy (Frances) Canfield
Canfield, Jack 1944- *164*
Canfield, Jane White 1897-1984 .... *32*
    Obituary *38*
Canfield, Muriel 1935- *94*
Caniff, Milton 1907-1988
    Obituary *58*
Caniff, Milton Arthur Paul
    See Caniff, Milton
Cann, Helen 1969- *179*
    Earlier sketch in SATA *124*
Cann, Kate 1954- *152*
    Earlier sketch in SATA *103*
Cannan, Joanna
    See Pullein-Thompson, Joanna Maxwell
Cannell, Jon *196*
Cannell, Jonathan C.
    See Cannell, Jon
Cannon, A.E. *202*
    Earlier sketches in SATA *93, 163*
Cannon, Ann Edwards
    See Cannon, A.E.
Cannon, Bettie (Waddell) 1922- *59*
Cannon, Curt
    See Hunter, Evan
Cannon, Eileen E(mily) 1948- *119*
Cannon, Frank
    See Mayhar, Ardath
Cannon, Janell 1957- *128*
    Earlier sketch in SATA *78*
    See also CLR *120*
Cannon, Marian G. 1923- *85*
Cannon, Taffy
    See Cannon, Eileen E(mily)
Cantone, AnnaLaura *182*
Canusi, Jose
    See Barker, S. Omar
Canyon, Christopher 1966- *150*
    Earlier sketch in SATA *104*
Caparo, Antonio
    See Caparo, Antonio Javier
Caparo, Antonio Javier *205*
Capek, Michael 1947- *142*
    Earlier sketch in SATA *96*
Capes, Bernard (Edward Joseph)
    1854-1918 .... *116*
Caple, Kathy *193*
Caple, Laurie 1958- *201*
Caplin, Alfred Gerald 1909-1979 .... *61*
    Obituary *21*
Caponigro, John Paul 1965- *84*
Capote, Truman 1924-1984 .... *91*
Capp, Al
    See Caplin, Alfred Gerald
Cappel, Constance 1936- *22*
Cappetta, Cynthia 1949- *125*
Cappo, Nan Willard 1955- *143*
Capps, Benjamin (Franklin) 1922- *9*
Cappy Dick
    See Cleveland, George
Captain Kangaroo
    See Keeshan, Robert J.
Captain Wheeler
    See Ellis, Edward S.
Captain Young of Yale
    See Stratemeyer, Edward L.
Capucilli, Alyssa Satin 1957- *203*
    Earlier sketches in SATA *115, 163*
Capucine
    See Mazille, Capucine

Caraher, Kim(berley Elizabeth) 1961- *105*
Caraker, Mary 1929- *74*
Caras, Roger A(ndrew) 1928-2001 .... *12*
    Obituary *127*
Caravantes, Peggy 1935- *140*
Caraway, Caren 1939- *57*
Carbone, Elisa 1954- *173*
    Earlier sketches in SATA *81, 137*
Carbone, Elisa Lynn
    See Carbone, Elisa
Carbonnier, Jeanne 1894-1974 .... *3*
    Obituary *34*
Card, Orson Scott 1951- *127*
    Earlier sketch in SATA *83*
    See also CLR *116*
Care, Felicity
    See Coury, Louise Andree
Carew, Jan 1925- *51*
    Brief entry *40*
Carew, Jan Rynveld
    See Carew, Jan
Carey, Bonnie
    See Marshall, Bonnie C.
Carey, Charles W., Jr. 1951- *170*
Carey, Ernestine Gilbreth 1908-2006 .... *2*
    Obituary *177*
Carey, Janet Lee 1954(?)- *185*
Carey, Lisa *110*
Carey, M. V.
    See Carey, Mary V(irginia)
Carey, Mary V(irginia) 1925-1994 .... *44*
    Brief entry *39*
Carey, Peter 1943- *94*
Carey, Peter Philip
    See Carey, Peter
Carey, Valerie Scho 1949- *60*
Carheden, Goorel Kristina
    See Naaslund, Goorel Kristina
Carigiet, Alois 1902-1985 .... *24*
    Obituary *47*
    See also CLR *38*
Carini, Edward 1923- *9*
Carkeet, David 1946- *75*
Carle, Eric 1929- *163*
    Earlier sketches in SATA *4, 65, 120*
    See also CLR *72*
    See also SAAS *6*
Carleton, Captain L. C.
    See Ellis, Edward S.
Carleton, Captain Latham C.
    See Ellis, Edward S.
Carleton, Latham C.
    See Ellis, Edward S.
Carley, V(an Ness) Royal 1906-1976
    Obituary *20*
Carling, Amelia Lau 1949- *164*
    Earlier sketch in SATA *119*
Carlisle, Carolyn
    See Hawes, Louise
Carlisle, Clark
    See Holding, James (Clark Carlisle, Jr.)
Carlisle, Olga Andreyev 1930- *35*
Carlock, Miriam
    See Eyerly, Jeannette
Carls, Claudia 1978- *198*
Carlsen, G(eorge) Robert 1917- *30*
Carlsen, Ruth C(hristoffer) 1918- *2*
Carlson, Bernice Wells 1910- *8*
Carlson, Christopher C. *202*
Carlson, Dale (Bick) 1935- *1*
Carlson, Daniel (Bick) 1960- *27*
Carlson, Kirsten 1968- *192*
Carlson, Kirsten M.
    See Carlson, Kirsten
Carlson, Laurie 1952- *173*
    Earlier sketch in SATA *101*
Carlson, Laurie Winn
    See Carlson, Laurie
Carlson, Melody 1956- *171*
    Earlier sketch in SATA *113*

Carlson, Nancy L.
    See Carlson, Nancy L(ee)
Carlson, Nancy L(ee) 1953- *144*
    Brief entry *45*
    Earlier sketches in SATA *56, 90*
Carlson, Natalie Savage 1906-1997 .... *68*
    Earlier sketch in SATA *2*
    See also SAAS *4*
Carlson, Susan Johnston 1953- *88*
Carlson, Vada F. 1897- *16*
Carlstrom, Nancy White 1948- *156*
    Brief entry *48*
    Earlier sketches in SATA *53, 92*
Carlton, Keith
    See Robertson, Keith (Carlton)
Carlton, Susan 1960- *195*
Carlyon, Richard *55*
Carman, Patrick 1966- *197*
    Earlier sketch in SATA *161*
Carmer, Carl (Lamson) 1893-1976 .... *37*
    Obituary *30*
Carmer, Elizabeth Black 1904- *24*
Carmi, Giora 1944- *149*
    Earlier sketch in SATA *79*
Carmichael, Carrie
    See Carmichael, Harriet
Carmichael, Harriet *40*
Carmody, Isobelle 1958- *191*
    Earlier sketch in SATA *161*
Carmody, Isobelle Jane
    See Carmody, Isobelle
Carney, Elizabeth 1981- *199*
Carney, Jeff 1962- *196*
Carney, Mary Lou 1949- *170*
Carol, Bill J.
    See Knott, William C(ecil, Jr.)
Caron, Romi
    See Caron-Kyselkova', Romana
Caron-Kyselkova', Romana 1967- *94*
Caroselli, Remus F(rancis) 1916- *36*
Carpelan, Bo 1926- *8*
Carpelan, Bo Gustaf Bertelsson
    See Carpelan, Bo
Carpenter, (John) Allan 1917- *81*
    Earlier sketch in SATA *3*
Carpenter, Angelica Shirley 1945- *153*
    Earlier sketch in SATA *71*
Carpenter, Frances 1890-1972 .... *3*
    Obituary *27*
Carpenter, John 1948- *58*
Carpenter, John Howard
    See Carpenter, John
Carpenter, Johnny
    See Carpenter, John
Carpenter, Patricia (Healy Evans) 1920- *11*
Carr, Glyn
    See Styles, (Frank) Showell
Carr, Harriett H(elen) 1899-1977 .... *3*
Carr, Jan 1953- *132*
    Earlier sketch in SATA *89*
Carr, M. J.
    See Carr, Jan
Carr, Mary Jane 1899-1988 .... *2*
    Obituary *55*
Carr, Philippa
    See Hibbert, Eleanor Alice Burford
Carr, Roger Vaughan 1937- *95*
Carrel, Annette Felder 1929- *90*
Carrick, Carol (Hatfield) 1935- *118*
    Earlier sketches in SATA *7, 63*
    See also SAAS *18*
Carrick, Donald (F.) 1929-1989 .... *63*
    Earlier sketch in SATA *7*
Carrick, Malcolm 1945- *28*
Carrick, Paul 1972- *194*
Carrier, Lark 1947- *71*
    Brief entry *50*
Carrier, Roch 1937- *166*
    Earlier sketch in SATA *105*
Carrighar, Sally 1898-1985 .... *24*

Carrillo, Patricia S.
See Carrillo, P.S.
Carrillo, P.S. 209
Carrington, G. A.
See Cunningham, Chet
Carrington, Marsha Gray 1954- 168
Earlier sketch in SATA *111*
Carris, Joan 1938- 182
Brief entry 42
Earlier sketch in SATA *44*
Carris, Joan Davenport
See Carris, Joan
Carroll, Curt
See Bishop, Curtis (Kent)
Carroll, Elizabeth
See Barkin, Carol
and James, Elizabeth
Carroll, Jaye
See Carroll, Michael
Carroll, Jenny
See Cabot, Meg
Carroll, (Archer) Latrobe 1894-1996 7
Carroll, Laura
See Parr, Lucy
Carroll, Lewis 1832-1898 100
See also YABC *2*
See also CLR *108*
Carroll, Michael 1966- 203
Carroll, Raymond 1924- 86
Brief entry 47
Carruth, Hayden 1921-2008 47
Obituary 197
Carryl, Charles E. 1841-1920 114
Carryl, Charles Edward
See Carryl, Charles E.
Carse, Robert 1902-1971 5
Carson, J(ohn) Franklin 1920-1981 1
Obituary 107
Carson, Mary Kay 1964- 200
Earlier sketch in SATA *150*
Carson, Rachel 1907-1964 23
Carson, Rachel Louise
See Carson, Rachel
Carson, Rosalind
See Chittenden, Margaret
Carson, S. M.
See Gorsline, (Sally) Marie
Carson, William C. 1928- 154
Carter, Abby 184
Carter, Alden R 1947- 137
Earlier sketch in SATA *67*
See also CLR *22*
See also SAAS *18*
Carter, Alden Richardson
See Carter, Alden R
Carter, Andy 1948- 134
Carter, Angela 1940-1992 66
Obituary 70
Carter, Angela Olive
See Carter, Angela
Carter, Anne Laurel 1953- 209
Earlier sketch in SATA *135*
Carter, Asa Earl
See Carter, Forrest
Carter, Avis Murton
See Allen, Kenneth S.
Carter, Bruce
See Hough, Richard (Alexander)
Carter, Carol S(hadis) 1948- 124
Carter, David A. 1957- 170
Earlier sketch in SATA *114*
Carter, Don 1958- 192
Earlier sketch in SATA *124*
Carter, Dorothy Sharp 1921- 8
Carter, Forrest 1927(?)-1979 32
Carter, Helene 1887-1960 15
Carter, (William) Hodding, Jr. 1907-1972 2
Obituary 27
Carter, James Earl, Jr.
See Carter, Jimmy
Carter, Jimmy 1924- 79

Carter, Katharine J(ones) 1905-1984 2
Carter, Lin(wood Vrooman) 1930-1988 91
Carter, Mike 1936- 138
Carter, Nick
See Avallone, Michael (Angelo, Jr.)
and Ballard, (Willis) Todhunter
and Crider, Bill
and Cassiday, Bruce (Bingham)
and Chastain, Thomas
and Dey, Frederic (Merrill) Van Rensselaer
and Garside, Jack
and Hayes, Ralph E(ugene)
and Henderson, M(arilyn) R(uth)
and Lynds, Dennis
and Lynds, Gayle (Hallenbeck)
and Randisi, Robert J.
and Rasof, Henry
and Stratemeyer, Edward L.
and Smith, Martin Cruz
and Swain, Dwight V(reeland)
and Vardeman, Robert E(dward)
and Wallmann, Jeffrey M(iner)
and White, Lionel
Carter, Peter 1929- 57
Carter, Phyllis Ann
See Eberle, Irmengarde
Carter, Samuel (Thomson) III 1904-1988 ... 37
Obituary 60
Carter, William E. 1926-1983 1
Obituary 35
Cartlidge, Michelle 1950- 96
Brief entry 37
Earlier sketch in SATA *49*
Cartner, William Carruthers 1910- 11
Cartwright, Ann 1940- 78
Cartwright, Reg(inald Ainsley) 1938- 64
Cartwright, Sally 1923- 9
Carusone, Al 1949- 89
Carvell, Marlene 172
Carver, John
See Gardner, Richard (M.)
Carwell, L'Ann
See McKissack, Patricia C.
Cary
See Cary, Louis F(avreau)
Cary, Barbara Knapp 1912(?)-1975
Obituary 31
Cary, Kate 1967(?)- 174
Cary, Louis F(avreau) 1915- 9
Caryl, Jean
See Kaplan, Jean Caryl Korn
Casanova, Mary 1957- 186
Earlier sketches in SATA *94, 136*
Cascone, A.G.
See Cascone, Annette
and Cascone, Gina
Cascone, Annette 1960- 103
Cascone, Gina 1955- 103
Case, Chris 1976- 209
Case, Marshal T(aylor) 1941- 9
Case, Michael
See Howard, Robert West
Caseley, Judith 1951- 159
Brief entry 53
Earlier sketch in SATA *87*
Casewit, Curtis W(erner) 1922-2002 4
Casey, Barbara (Louise) 1944- 147
Earlier sketch in SATA *79*
Casey, Brigid 1950- 9
Casey, Tina 1959- 141
Cash, Ellen Lewis Buell 1905-1989
Obituary 64
Cash, Megan Montague 160
Cashore, Kristin 1976(?)- 206
Casilla, Robert 1959- 211
Earlier sketches in SATA *75, 146*
Cason, Mabel Earp 1892-1965 10
Cass, Joan E(velyn) 1
Cass-Beggs, Barbara 1904- 62
Cassedy, Patrice (Rinaldo) 1953- 149

Cassedy, Sylvia 1930-1989 77
Obituary 61
Earlier sketch in SATA *27*
See also CLR *26*
Cassel, Lili
See Wronker, Lili Cassel
Cassels, Jean 173
Cassidy, Anne 1952- 166
Cassidy, Cathy 1962- 183
Casson, Hugh Maxwell 1910-1999 65
Obituary 115
Cassutt, Michael 1954- 78
Cassutt, Michael Joseph
See Cassutt, Michael
Castaldi, Elicia 194
Castaldo, Nancy Fusco 1962- 151
Earlier sketch in SATA *93*
Castaneda, Omar S. 1954- 71
Castell, Megan
See Williams, Jeanne
Castellanos, Jane Mollie Robinson
  1913-2001 9
Castellon, Federico 1914-1971 48
Castellucci, Cecil 1969- 176
Castillo, Edmund L. 1924-2005 1
Obituary 167
Castillo, Lauren 195
Castle, Lee
See Ogan, George F.
and Ogan, Margaret E. (Nettles)
Castle, Paul
See Howard, Vernon (Linwood)
Castle, Robert
See Hamilton, Edmond
Castrovilla, Selene 1966- 186
Caswell, Brian 1954- 171
Earlier sketch in SATA *97*
Caswell, Helen (Rayburn) 1923- 12
Catalano, Dominic 1956- 163
Earlier sketch in SATA *76*
Catalano, Grace (A.) 1961- 99
Catalanotto, Peter 1959- 195
Autobiography Feature 113
Earlier sketches in SATA *70, 114, 159*
See also CLR *68*
See also SAAS *25*
Catanese, P.W. 1961- 179
Cate, Annette LeBlanc 196
Cate, Dick
See Cate, Richard Edward Nelson
Cate, Richard Edward Nelson 1932- 28
Cather, Willa 1873-1947 30
See also CLR *98*
Catherall, Arthur 1906-1980 74
Earlier sketches in SATA *3, 4*
Cathon, Laura E(lizabeth) 1908-1991 27
Catlett, Elizabeth 1919(?)- 82
Catlin, Wynelle 1930- 13
Catlow, Nikalas
See Catlow, Niki
Catlow, Niki 1975- 193
Cato, Heather 105
Cato, Sheila 114
Catran, Ken 1944- 190
Catrow, David 206
See Catrow, David J. III
Catrow, David J. III 152
See Catrow, David
Catt, Louis
See French, Vivian
Cattell, James 1954- 123
Catton, (Charles) Bruce 1899-1978 2
Obituary 24
Catz, Max
See Glaser, Milton
Caudell, Marian 1930- 52
Caudill, Rebecca 1899-1985 1
Obituary 44
Cauley, Lorinda Bryan 1951- 46
Brief entry 43

Caulfield, Peggy F. 1926-1987
  Obituary 53
Cauman, Samuel 1910-1971 48
Causley, Charles (Stanley) 1917-2003 66
  Obituary 149
  Earlier sketch in SATA 3
  See also CLR 30
Cavallaro, Ann (Abelson) 1918- 62
Cavallo, Diana 1931- 7
Cavanagh, Helen (Carol) 1939- 98
  Brief entry 37
  Earlier sketch in SATA 48
Cavanah, Frances 1899-1982 31
  Earlier sketch in SATA 1
Cavanna, Betty
  See Harrison, Elizabeth (Allen) Cavanna
Cavanna, Elizabeth
  See Harrison, Elizabeth (Allen) Cavanna
Cave, Kathryn 1948- 123
  Earlier sketch in SATA 76
Cavendish, Peter
  See Horler, Sydney
Cavin, Ruth (Brodie) 1918- 38
Cavoukian, Raffi 1948- 68
Cawley, Winifred 1915- 13
Cazeau, Charles J(ay) 1931- 65
Cazet, Denys 1938- 191
  Brief entry 41
  Earlier sketches in SATA 52, 99, 163
Cazzola, Gus 1934- 73
Cebulash, Mel 1937- 91
  Earlier sketch in SATA 10
Ceccoli, Nicoletta 181
Cecil, Randy 1968- 187
Cecka, Melanie 199
Ceder, Georgiana Dorcas -1985 10
Celenza, Anna Harwell 133
Celestino, Martha Laing
  See Laing, Martha
Cepeda, Joe 159
Cerf, Bennett (Alfred) 1898-1971 7
Cerf, Christopher (Bennett) 1941- 2
Cermak, Martin
  See Duchacek, Ivo D(uka)
Cerullo, Mary M. 1949- 145
  Earlier sketch in SATA 86
Cervon, Jacqueline
  See Moussard, Jacqueline
Cetin, Frank Stanley 1921- 2
Chabon, Michael 1963- 145
Chaconas, D.J.
  See Chaconas, Dori
Chaconas, Dori 1938- 208
  Earlier sketches in SATA 145, 175
Chaconas, Doris J.
  See Chaconas, Dori
Chadwick, Lester 67
  Earlier sketch in SATA 1
Chaffee, Allen 3
Chaffin, Lillie D(orton) 1925- 4
Chaikin, Miriam 1924- 152
  Earlier sketches in SATA 24, 102
Chall, Marsha Wilson 150
Challand, Helen J(ean) 1921- 64
Challans, Mary
  See Renault, Mary
Chalmers, Mary (Eileen) 1927- 6
  See also SAAS 14
Chamberlain, Barbara A.
  See Azore, Barbara
Chamberlain, Margaret 1954- 46
Chamberlin, Kate 1945- 105
Chamberlin, Mary 1960- 177
Chamberlin, Rich 177
Chamberlin, Richard
  See Chamberlin, Rich
Chambers, Aidan 1934- 171
  Earlier sketches in SATA 1, 69, 108
  See also CLR 151
  See also SAAS 12

Chambers, Bradford 1922-1984
  Obituary 39
Chambers, Catherine E.
  See St. John, Nicole
Chambers, John W. 1933- 57
  Brief entry 46
Chambers, Kate
  See St. John, Nicole
Chambers, Margaret Ada Eastwood 1911- 2
Chambers, Peggy
  See Chambers, Margaret Ada Eastwood
Chambers, Robert W(illiam) 1865-1933 ... 107
Chambliss, Maxie 186
Chan, Gillian 1954- 147
  Earlier sketch in SATA 102
Chan, Peter 1980(?)- 207
Chance, James T.
  See Carpenter, John
Chance, John T.
  See Carpenter, John
Chance, Stephen
  See Turner, Philip (William)
Chandler, Caroline A(ugusta) 1906-1979 22
  Obituary 24
Chandler, David P(orter) 1933- 28
Chandler, Edna Walker 1908-1982 11
  Obituary 31
Chandler, Jennifer
  See Westwood, Jennifer
Chandler, Karen 1959- 122
Chandler, Linda S(mith) 1929- 39
Chandler, Pauline 175
Chandler, Robert 1953- 40
Chandler, Ruth Forbes 1894-1978 2
  Obituary 26
Chandonnet, Ann F. 1943- 92
Chaney, Jill 1932- 87
Chang, Chih-Wei 1966- 111
Chang, Cindy 1968- 90
Chang, Margaret 1941- 71
Chang, Margaret Scrogin
  See Chang, Margaret
Chang, Raymond 1939- 142
  Earlier sketches in SATA 71, 142 PEN
Chanin, Michael 1952- 84
Channel, A. R.
  See Catherall, Arthur
Chapian, Marie 1938- 29
Chapin, Alene Olsen Dalton 1915(?)-1986
  Obituary 47
Chapin, Tom 1945- 83
Chapman, Allen 67
  Earlier sketch in SATA 1
Chapman, Cheryl O(rth) 1948- 80
Chapman, (Constance) Elizabeth (Mann)
  1919- 10
Chapman, Gaye 1970- 200
Chapman, Gaye Coralie
  See Chapman, Gaye
Chapman, Gaynor 1935- 32
Chapman, Gillian 1955- 120
Chapman, Jane 1970- 176
  Earlier sketch in SATA 122
Chapman, Jean 104
  Earlier sketch in SATA 34
  See also CLR 65
Chapman, John Stanton Higham 1891-1972
  Obituary 27
Chapman, Lee
  See Bradley, Marion Zimmer
Chapman, Lynne 1960- 197
Chapman, Lynne F(erguson) 1963- 150
  Earlier sketch in SATA 94
Chapman, Maristan
  See Chapman, John Stanton Higham
Chapman, Vera (Ivy May) 1898-1996 33
Chapman, Walker
  See Silverberg, Robert
Chappell, Audrey 1954- 72
Chappell, Crissa-Jean 198

Chappell, Warren 1904-1991 68
  Obituary 67
  Earlier sketch in SATA 6
  See also SAAS 10
Chapra, Mimi 182
Charbonneau, Eileen 1951- 118
  Earlier sketch in SATA 84
Charbonnet, Gabrielle 1961- 81
Chardiet, Bernice (Kroll) 1927(?)- 27
Charest, Emily MacLachlan 198
Charles, Donald
  See Meighan, Donald Charles
Charles, Louis
  See Stratemeyer, Edward L.
Charles, Nicholas
  See Kuskin, Karla
Charles, Nicholas J.
  See Kuskin, Karla
Charles, Norma 153
Charles, Veronika Martenova 182
Charlip, Remy 1929- 119
  Earlier sketches in SATA 4, 68
  See also CLR 8
Charlot, Jean 1898-1979 8
  Obituary 31
Charlot, Martin (Day) 1944- 64
Charlton, Michael (Alan) 1923- 34
Charlton-Trujillo, e.E. 189
Charmatz, Bill 1925-2005 7
Charnas, Suzy McKee 1939- 110
  Earlier sketch in SATA 61
Charosh, Mannis 1906- 5
Chartier, Normand L. 1945- 66
Chase, Alice
  See McHargue, Georgess
Chase, Alyssa 1965- 92
Chase, Andra 1942- 91
Chase, Emily
  See Aks, Patricia
  and Garwood, Julie
  and Sachs, Judith
  and White, Carol
Chase, Mary (Coyle) 1907-1981 17
  Obituary 29
Chase, Mary Ellen 1887-1973 10
Chase, Richard 1904-1988 64
  Obituary 56
Chase, Samantha
  See Glick, Ruth (Burtnick)
Chast, Roz 1954- 97
Chastain, Madye Lee 1908-1989 4
Chataway, Carol 1955- 140
Chatterjee, Debjani 1952- 83
Chauncy, Nan(cen Beryl Masterman)
  1900-1970 6
  See also CLR 6
Chaundler, Christine 1887-1972 1
  Obituary 25
Chayka, Doug 196
Chbosky, Stephen 1972- 164
Cheaney, Janie B.
  See Cheaney, J.B.
Cheaney, J.B. 1950- 188
Chee, Cheng-Khee 1934- 79
Cheese, Chloe 1952- 118
Chekhonte, Antosha
  See Chekhov, Anton
Chekhov, Anton 1860-1904 90
Chekhov, Anton Pavlovich
  See Chekhov, Anton
Chelushkin, Kirill 1968- 186
Chen, Anthony 1929- 6
Chen, Chih-Yuan 1975- 155
Chen, Ju-Hong 1941- 78
Chen, Pauline 1966- 202
Chen, Sara
  See Odgers, Sally Farrell
Chen, Tony
  See Chen, Anthony
Chen, Yong 1963- 183
Chen, Yuan-tsung 1932- 65

Chenault, Nell
    See Smith, Linell Nash
Chenery, Janet (Dai) 1923- 25
Cheney, Cora 1916-1999 3
    Obituary 110
Cheney, Glenn (Alan) 1951- 99
Cheney, Lynne V. 1941- 152
Cheney, Lynne Vincent
    See Cheney, Lynne V.
Cheney, Ted
    See Cheney, Theodore Albert
Cheney, Theodore A. Rees
    See Cheney, Theodore Albert
Cheney, Theodore Albert 1928- 11
Cheng, Andrea 1957- 205
    Earlier sketches in SATA *128, 172*
Cheng, Christopher 1959- 173
    Earlier sketch in SATA *106*
Cheng, Judith 1955- 36
Cheng, Shan
    See Jiang, Cheng An
Cheripko, Jan 1951- 155
    Earlier sketch in SATA *83*
Chermayeff, Ivan 1932- 47
Chernenko, Dan
    See Chernenko, Dan
Chernoff, Dorothy A.
    See Ernst, (Lyman) John
Chernoff, Goldie Taub 1909- 10
Cherry, Carolyn Janice
    See Cherryh, C.J.
Cherry, Lynne 1952- 99
    Earlier sketch in SATA *34*
Cherryh, C.J. 1942- 172
    Earlier sketch in SATA *93*
Cherryholmes, Anne
    See Price, Olive
Cheshire, Simon 172
Chesler, Bernice 1932-2002 59
Chess, Victoria (Dickerson) 1939- 92
    Earlier sketch in SATA *33*
Chessa, Francesca 191
Chester, Deborah 1957- 85
Chester, Kate
    See Guccione, Leslie Davis
Chesterton, G. K. 1874-1936 27
Chesterton, Gilbert Keith
    See Chesterton, G. K.
Chesworth, Michael 207
    Earlier sketch in SATA *160*
Chetin, Helen 1922- 6
Chetwin, Grace 86
    Brief entry 50
Chevalier, Christa 1937- 35
Chevalier, Tracy 1962- 128
Chew, Ruth 1920- 7
Chichester Clark, Emma 1955- 209
    Earlier sketches in SATA *117, 156, 69*
Chidsey, Donald Barr 1902-1981 3
    Obituary 27
Chiefari, Janet D. 1942- 58
Chien, Catia 193
Chien-min, Lin
    See Rumford, James
Child, L. Maria
    See Child, Lydia Maria
Child, Lauren 1965- 183
    Earlier sketches in SATA *119, 160*
Child, Lincoln 1957- 113
Child, Lincoln B.
    See Child, Lincoln
Child, Lydia Maria 1802-1880 67
Child, Mrs.
    See Child, Lydia Maria
Child, Philip 1898-1978 47
Children's Shepherd, The
    See Westphal, Arnold Carl
Childress, Alice 1920-1994 81
    Earlier sketches in SATA *7, 48*
    See also CLR *14*

Childs, H(alla) Fay (Cochrane) 1890-1971 ... *1*
    Obituary 25
Chilton, Charles (Frederick William)
    1917- 102
Chima, Cinda Williams 192
Chimaera
    See Farjeon, Eleanor
Chin, Richard (M.) 1946- 52
Chinery, Michael 1938- 26
Chin-Lee, Cynthia 1958- 102
Chin-Lee D., Cynthia
    See Chin-Lee, Cynthia
Chippendale, Lisa A. 158
Chipperfield, Joseph Eugene 1912-1980(?) . 87
    Earlier sketch in SATA *2*
Chisholm, P. F.
    See Finney, Patricia
Chislett, Gail (Elaine) 1948- 58
Chittenden, Elizabeth F. 1903-1999 9
Chittenden, Margaret 1935- 28
Chittum, Ida 1918- 7
Chitwood, Suzanne Tanner 1958- 160
Chmielarz, Sharon Lee 1940- 72
Choate, Judith (Newkirk) 1940- 30
Chocolate, Debbi 1954- 96
Chocolate, Deborah M. Newton
    See Chocolate, Debbi
Chodos-Irvine, Margaret 211
    Earlier sketch in SATA *152*
Choi, Sook Nyul 1937- 73
    Autobiography Feature 126
    See also CLR *53*
Choi, Yangsook 178
Choldenko, Gennifer 1957- 182
    Earlier sketch in SATA *135*
Chorao, (Ann Mc)Kay (Sproat) 1936- 162
    Earlier sketches in SATA *8, 69*
Choron, Sandra (Zena Samelson) 1950- ... 146
Choung, Eun-hee 199
Chown, Marcus 1959- 137
Choyce, Lesley 1951- 165
    Earlier sketch in SATA *94*
Choyce, Lesley Willis
    See Choyce, Lesley
Chrisman, Arthur Bowie 1889-1953 124
    See also YABC *1*
Christelow, Eileen 1943- 184
    Autobiography Feature 120
    Brief entry 35
    Earlier sketches in SATA *38, 90*
Christensen, Bonnie 1951- 157
    Earlier sketch in SATA *110*
Christensen, Gardell Dano 1907-1991 .... *1*
Christensen, Laurie
    See Steding, Laurie
Christensen, Barbara 1940- 40
Christgau, Alice Erickson 1902-1977 13
Christian, Mary Blount 1933- 9
Christiana, David 195
Christie, Agatha 1890-1976 36
Christie, Agatha Mary Clarissa
    See Christie, Agatha
Christie, Ann Philippa
    See Pearce, Philippa
Christie, Gregory
    See Christie, R. Gregory
Christie, Philippa
    See Pearce, Philippa
Christie, R. Gregory 1971- 185
    Earlier sketch in SATA *127*
Christopher, John
    See Youd, Samuel
Christopher, Louise
    See Hale, Arlene
Christopher, Matt(hew Frederick)
    1917-1997 80
    Obituary 99
    Earlier sketches in SATA *2, 47*
    See also CLR *119*
    See also SAAS *9*
Christopher, Milbourne 1914(?)-1984 46

Christy, Howard Chandler 1873-1952 21
Chrustowski, Rick 176
Chrystie, Frances N(icholson) 1904-1986 ... 60
Chu, Daniel 1933- 11
Chukovsky, Kornei (Ivanovich)
    1882-1969 34
    Earlier sketch in SATA *5*
Church, Caroline Jayne 179
Church, Richard 1893-1972 3
Churchill, E(lmer) Richard 1937- 11
Churchill, Elizabeth
    See Hough, Richard (Alexander)
Chute, B(eatrice) J(oy) 1913-1987 .... *2*
    Obituary 53
Chute, Marchette (Gaylord) 1909-1994 .... *1*
Chwast, Jacqueline 1932- *6*
Chwast, Seymour 1931- 146
    Earlier sketches in SATA *18, 96*
Ciardi, John (Anthony) 1916-1986 65
    Obituary 46
    Earlier sketch in SATA *1*
    See also CLR *19*
    See also SAAS *26*
Ciccone, Madonna Louise Veronica
    See Madonna
Ciment, James D. 1958- 140
Cirrone, Dorian 182
Cisneros, Sandra 1954-
    See CLR *123*
Citra, Becky 1954- 137
Citrin, Michael 1965(?)- 183
Claflin, Willy 1944- 208
Clair, Andree 19
Clampett, Bob 1914(?)-1985 44
    Obituary 38
Clampett, Robert
    See Clampett, Bob
Clapp, John 1968- 109
Clapp, Patricia 1912- 74
    Earlier sketch in SATA *4*
    See also SAAS *4*
Clare, Ellen
    See Sinclair, Olga
Clare, Helen
    See Clarke, Pauline
Claremont, Chris 1950- 87
Claremont, Christopher Simon
    See Claremont, Chris
Clark, Ann Nolan 1896-1995 82
    Obituary 87
    Earlier sketch in SATA *4*
    See also CLR *16*
    See also SAAS *16*
Clark, Champ 1923-2002 47
Clark, Christopher (Anthony) Stuart
    See Stuart-Clark, Christopher (Anthony)
Clark, Clara Gillow 1951- 154
    Earlier sketch in SATA *84*
Clark, David
    See Hardcastle, Michael
Clark, David Allen
    See Ernst, (Lyman) John
Clark, Emma Chichester
    See Chichester Clark, Emma
Clark, Frank J(ames) 1922- 18
Clark, Garel
    See Garelick, May
Clark, Halsey
    See Deming, Richard
Clark, Joan
    See Benson, Mildred
Clark, Joan 1934- 182
    Earlier sketches in SATA *59, 96*
Clark, Leonard 1905-1981 30
    Obituary 29
Clark, M. R.
    See Clark, Mavis Thorpe
Clark, Margaret (D.) 1943- 126
Clark, Margaret Goff 1913- 82
    Earlier sketch in SATA *8*
Clark, Mary Higgins 1929- 46

Clark, Mavis Thorpe 1909-1999 .... *74*
  Earlier sketch in SATA *8*
  See also CLR *30*
  See also SAAS *5*
Clark, Merle
  See Gessner, Lynne
Clark, Patricia Denise 1921- *117*
Clark, Patricia Finrow 1929- *11*
Clark, Ronald Harry 1904-1999 .... *193*
Clark, Ronald William 1916-1987 .... *2*
  Obituary *52*
Clark, Sherryl 1956- *149*
Clark, Van D(eusen) 1909-1974 .... *2*
Clark, Virginia
  See Gray, Patricia (Clark)
Clark, Walter Van Tilburg 1909-1971 .... *8*
Clarke, Arthur
  See Clarke, Arthur C.
Clarke, Arthur C. 1917-2008 .... *115*
  Obituary *191*
  Earlier sketches in SATA *13, 70*
  See also CLR *119*
Clarke, Arthur Charles
  See Clarke, Arthur C.
Clarke, Clorinda 1917- *7*
Clarke, Gus 1948- *134*
Clarke, J.
  See Clarke, Judith
Clarke, James Hall
  See Rowland-Entwistle, (Arthur) Theodore
  (Henry)
Clarke, Joan B. 1921- *42*
  Brief entry *27*
Clarke, John
  See Laklan, Carli
  and Sontup, Dan(iel)
Clarke, Judith 1943- *164*
  Earlier sketches in SATA *75, 110*
  See also CLR *61*
Clarke, Julia 1950- *138*
Clarke, Kenneth 1957- *107*
Clarke, Lea
  See Rowland-Entwistle, (Arthur) Theodore
  (Henry)
Clarke, Margaret 1941-
  See CLR *99*
Clarke, Mary Stetson 1911-1994 .... *5*
Clarke, Michael
  See Newlon, (Frank) Clarke
Clarke, Pauline 1921- *131*
  Earlier sketch in SATA *3*
  See also CLR *28*
Clarke-Rich, Elizabeth L. 1934- *103*
Clarkson, E(dith) Margaret 1915- *37*
Clarkson, Ewan 1929- *9*
Claudia, Susan
  See Goulart, Ron
  and Johnston, William
Claverie, Jean 1946- *38*
Clay, Patrice 1947- *47*
Clay, Wil *203*
Clayman, Deborah Paula
  See Da Costa, Deborah
Claypool, Jane
  See Miner, Jane Claypool
Clayton, Elaine 1961- *209*
  Earlier sketches in SATA *94, 159*
Clayton, Lawrence (Otto, Jr.) 1945- *75*
Clayton, Sandra 1951- *110*
Cle, Troy *202*
Clea, Super
  See Hantman, Clea
Cleary, Beverly 1916- *121*
  Earlier sketches in SATA *2, 43, 79*
  See also CLR *72*
  See also SAAS *20*
Cleary, Beverly Atlee Bunn
  See Cleary, Beverly
Cleary, Brian P. 1959- *186*
  Earlier sketches in SATA *93, 132*

Cleaver, Bill
  See Cleaver, William J.
Cleaver, Carole 1934- *6*
Cleaver, Elizabeth (Ann Mrazik)
  1939-1985 .... *23*
  Obituary *43*
  See also CLR *13*
Cleaver, Hylton Reginald 1891-1961 .... *49*
Cleaver, Vera 1919-1993 .... *76*
  Earlier sketch in SATA *22*
  See also CLR *6*
Cleaver, Vera Allen
  See Cleaver, Vera
Cleaver, William J. 1920-1981 .... *22*
  Obituary *27*
  See also CLR *6*
Cleishbotham, Jebediah
  See Scott, Sir Walter
Cleland, Mabel
  See Widdemer, Mabel Cleland
Clem, Margaret H(ollingsworth) 1923- *90*
Clemens, Samuel
  See Twain, Mark
Clemens, Samuel Langhorne
  See Twain, Mark
Clemens, Virginia Phelps 1941- *35*
Clement, Gary *191*
Clement, Janet *182*
Clement, Nathan 1966- *200*
Clement, Priscilla Ferguson 1942- *171*
Clement, Rod *97*
Clement-Moore, Rosemary *188*
Clements, Andrew 1949- *203*
  Earlier sketches in SATA *104, 158*
Clements, Bruce 1931- *178*
  Earlier sketches in SATA *27, 94*
Clemesha, David *192*
Clemons, Elizabeth
  See Nowell, Elizabeth Cameron
Clerk, N. W.
  See Lewis, C. S.
Cleveland, Bob
  See Cleveland, George
Cleveland, George 1903(?)-1985
  Obituary *43*
Cleveland-Peck, Patricia *80*
Cleven, Cathrine
  See Cleven, Kathryn Seward
Cleven, Kathryn Seward *2*
Clevenger, William R. 1954- *84*
Clevenger, William Russell
  See Clevenger, William R.
Clevin, Joergen 1920- *7*
Clevin, Jorgen
  See Clevin, Joergen
Clewes, Dorothy (Mary) 1907-2003 .... *86*
  Obituary *138*
  Earlier sketch in SATA *1*
Clifford, David
  See Rosenberg, Eth Clifford
Clifford, Eth
  See Rosenberg, Eth Clifford
Clifford, Harold B(urton) 1893-1988 .... *10*
Clifford, Margaret Cort 1929- *1*
Clifford, Martin
  See Hamilton, Charles (Harold St. John)
Clifford, Mary Louise Beneway 1926- *23*
Clifford, Peggy
  See Clifford, Margaret Cort
Clifford, Rachel Mark
  See Lewis, Brenda Ralph
Clifton, Lucille 1936-2010 .... *128*
  Earlier sketches in SATA *20, 69*
  See also CLR *5*
Clifton, Thelma Lucille
  See Clifton, Lucille
Climo, Shirley 1928- *166*
  Autobiography Feature *110*
  Brief entry *35*
  Earlier sketches in SATA *39, 77*
  See also CLR *69*

Cline-Ransome, Lesa *201*
Clinton, Catherine 1952- *203*
Clinton, Cathryn 1957- *136*
Clinton, Dirk
  See Silverberg, Robert
Clinton, Jon
  See Prince, J(ack) H(arvey)
Clippinger, Carol *193*
Clish, (Lee) Marian 1946- *43*
Clive, Clifford
  See Hamilton, Charles (Harold St. John)
Clokey, Art 1921- *59*
Cloudsley-Thompson, J(ohn) L(eonard)
  1921- *19*
Clouse, Nancy L. 1938- *78*
Clover, Peter 1952- *152*
Clutha, Janet Paterson Frame
  See Frame, Janet
Clymer, Eleanor 1906-2001 .... *85*
  Obituary *126*
  Earlier sketch in SATA *9*
  See also SAAS *17*
Clyne, Patricia (Edwards) *31*
Cneut, Carll 1969- *197*
Coalson, Glo 1946- *94*
  Earlier sketch in SATA *26*
Coates, Anna 1958- *73*
Coates, Belle 1896-1986 .... *2*
Coates, Ruth Allison 1915- *11*
Coats, Alice M(argaret) 1905-1976 .... *11*
Coatsworth, Elizabeth (Jane) 1893-1986 ... *100*
  Obituary *49*
  Earlier sketches in SATA *2, 56*
  See also CLR *2*
Cobalt, Martin
  See Mayne, William (James Carter)
Cobb, Jane
  See Berry, Jane Cobb
Cobb, Mary 1931- *88*
Cobb, Vicki 1938- *136*
  Autobiography Feature *136*
  Earlier sketches in SATA *8, 69, 131*
  See also CLR *2*
  See also SAAS *6*
Cobbett, Richard
  See Pluckrose, Henry (Arthur)
Cober, Alan E(dwin) 1935-1998 .... *7*
  Obituary *101*
Cobham, Sir Alan
  See Hamilton, Charles (Harold St. John)
Coburn, Jake 1978- *155*
Cocagnac, Augustin Maurice(-Jean) 1924- ... *7*
Cocca-Leffler, Maryann 1958- *194*
  Earlier sketches in SATA *80, 136*
Cochran, Bill *187*
Cochran, Bobbye A. 1949- *11*
Cochran, Thomas 1955- *198*
Cockett, Mary *3*
Cocks, Peter *204*
Cocovini, Abby *202*
Coddell, Esme Raji
  See Codell, Esme Raji
Codell, Esme Raji 1968- *160*
Cody, C. S.
  See Waller, Leslie
Cody, Jess
  See Cunningham, Chet
Coe, Anne (E.) 1949- *95*
Coe, Douglas
  See Epstein, Beryl
  and Epstein, Samuel
Coe, Lloyd 1899(?)-1976
  Obituary *30*
Coen, Rena Neumann 1925- *20*
Coerr, Eleanor (Beatrice) 1922- *67*
  Earlier sketch in SATA *1*
Cofer, Judith Ortiz 1952- *164*
  Earlier sketch in SATA *110*
Coffelt, Nancy 1961- *189*
Coffey, Brian
  See Koontz, Dean

Coffin, Geoffrey
  See Mason, F(rancis) van Wyck
Coffin, M. T.
  See Stanley, George Edward
Coffman, Ramon Peyton 1896-1989 4
Cogan, Karen 1954- 125
Coggins, Jack (Banham) 1911-2006 2
Cohen, Barbara 1932-1992 77
  Obituary 74
  Earlier sketch in SATA 10
  See also SAAS 7
Cohen, Daniel (E.) 1936- 70
  Earlier sketch in SATA 8
  See also CLR 43
  See also SAAS 4
Cohen, Deborah Bodin 1968- 180
Cohen, Jan Barger
  See Barger, Jan
Cohen, Jene Barr
  See Barr, Jene
Cohen, Joan Lebold 1932- 4
Cohen, Judith Love 1933- 78
Cohen, Miriam 1926-1955 155
  Earlier sketches in SATA 29, 106
  See also SAAS 11
Cohen, Nora 75
Cohen, Paul S. 1945- 58
Cohen, Peter Zachary 1931- 150
  Earlier sketch in SATA 4
Cohen, Robert Carl 1930- 8
Cohen, Sholom 1951- 94
Cohn, Angelo 1914-1997 19
Cohn, Diana 194
Cohn, Rachel 1968- 161
Coit, Margaret Louise 1922-2003 2
  Obituary 142
Colato Lainez, Rene 1970- 176
Colbert, Anthony 1934-2007 15
Colbert, Nancy A. 1936- 139
Colby, C(arroll) B(urleigh) 1904-1977 35
  Earlier sketch in SATA 3
Colby, Jean Poindexter 1909-1993 23
Cole, Annette
  See Steiner, Barbara A(nnette)
Cole, Babette 1949- 155
  Earlier sketches in SATA 61, 96
Cole, Betsy 1940- 83
Cole, Brock 1938- 200
  Earlier sketches in SATA 72, 136
  See also CLR 18
Cole, Davis
  See Elting, Mary
Cole, Hannah 1954- 74
Cole, Henry 1955- 181
Cole, Jack -1974
  See Stewart, John
Cole, Jackson
  See Curry, Thomas Albert
  and Germano, Peter B.
  and Heckelmann, Charles N(ewman)
  and Newton, D(wight) B(ennett)
  and Schisgall, Oscar
Cole, Jennifer
  See Zach, Cheryl (Byrd)
Cole, Joanna 1944- 168
  Brief entry 37
  Earlier sketches in SATA 49, 81, 120
  See also CLR 40
Cole, Lois Dwight 1903-1979 10
  Obituary 26
Cole, Michael 1947- 59
Cole, Samantha
  See Cole, Stephen
Cole, Sheila 1939- 171
  Earlier sketch in SATA 24, 95
Cole, Sheila R.
  See Cole, Sheila
Cole, Sheila Rotenberg
  See Cole, Sheila
Cole, Stephen 1971- 161

Cole, William (Rossa) 1919-2000 71
  Earlier sketch in SATA 9
  See also SAAS 9
Coleman, Andrew
  See Pine, Nicholas
Coleman, Clare
  See Bell, Clare (Louise)
  and Easton, M(alcolm) Coleman
Coleman, Janet Wyman 184
Coleman, Loren 1947- 164
Coleman, Loren Elwood, Jr.
  See Coleman, Loren
Coleman, Mary Ann 1928- 83
Coleman, Michael
  See Jones, Allan Frewin
Coleman, Michael 1946- 199
  Autobiography Feature 133
  Earlier sketches in SATA 108, 133
Coleman, Rowan 187
Coleman, William L(eRoy) 1938- 49
  Brief entry 34
Coles, Robert (Martin) 1929- 23
Colfer, Eoin 1965- 197
  Earlier sketch in SATA 148
  See also CLR 112
Colin, Ann
  See Ure, Jean
Collard, Sneed B. III 1959- 184
  Earlier sketches in SATA 84, 139
Colledge, Anne 1939- 142
Colley, Jacqui 1965- 202
Collicott, Sharleen 1937- 143
  Earlier sketch in SATA 98
Collier, Bryan 204
  Earlier sketches in SATA 126, 174
Collier, Christopher 1930- 70
  Earlier sketch in SATA 16
  See also CLR 126
Collier, Ethel 1903-1999 22
Collier, James Lincoln 1928- 166
  Earlier sketches in SATA 8, 70
  See also CLR 126
  See also SAAS 21
Collier, Jane
  See Collier, Zena
Collier, Kristi 182
Collier, Steven 1942- 61
Collier, Zena 1926- 23
Collings, Gillian 1939- 102
Collington, Peter 1948- 99
  Earlier sketch in SATA 59
Collins, Ace 1953- 82
Collins, Andrew J.
  See Collins, Ace
Collins, David R(aymond) 1940-2001 121
  Earlier sketch in SATA 7
Collins, Heather 1946- 81
Collins, Hunt
  See Hunter, Evan
Collins, Michael
  See Lynds, Dennis
Collins, Michael 1930- 58
Collins, Pat(ricia) Lowery 1932- 151
  Earlier sketch in SATA 31
Collins, Paul 1954- 126
Collins, Ross 1972- 200
Collins, Ruth Philpott 1890-1975
  Obituary 30
Collins, Suzanne 180
Collins, Yvonne 194
Collinson, A. S.
  See Collinson, Alan S.
Collinson, Alan S. 1934- 80
Collinson, Roger (Alfred) 1936- 133
Collison, Linda 1953- 185
Collodi, Carlo 1826-1890 100
  Earlier sketch in SATA 29
  See also CLR 120
Colloms, Brenda 1919- 40

Colman, Hila 53
  Earlier sketch in SATA 1
  See also SAAS 14
Colman, Morris 1899(?)-1981
  Obituary 25
Colman, Penny (Morgan) 1944- 160
  Autobiography Feature 160
  Earlier sketches in SATA 77, 114
Colman, Warren (David) 1944- 67
Colombo, John Robert 1936- 50
Colon, Raul 156
Colon, Raul 1952- 202
Colonius, Lillian 1911-1992 3
Colorado, Antonio J.
  See Colorado (Capella), Antonio J(ulio)
Colorado (Capella), Antonio J(ulio)
  1903-1994 23
  Obituary 79
Colquhoun, Glenn 1964- 165
Colston, Fifi E. 1960- 150
Colt, Martin
  See Epstein, Beryl
  and Epstein, Samuel
Colum, Padraic 1881-1972 15
  See also CLR 36
Columbus, Chris 1959- 97
Columbus, Christopher
  See Columbus, Chris
Columella
  See Moore, Clement Clarke
Colver, Anne 1908- 7
Colvin, James
  See Moorcock, Michael
Colwell, Eileen (Hilda) 1904-2002 2
Colwyn, Stewart
  See Pepper, Frank S.
Coman, Carolyn 1951- 197
  Earlier sketch in SATA 127
Combs, Lisa M.
  See McCourt, Lisa
Combs, Robert
  See Murray, John
Comfort, Jane Levington
  See Sturtzel, Jane Levington
Comfort, Mildred Houghton 1886-1976 3
Comins, Ethel M(ae) 11
Comins, Jeremy 1933- 28
Commager, Henry Steele 1902-1998 23
  Obituary 102
Comora, Madeleine 190
Compere, Mickie
  See Davidson, Margaret
Compestine, Ying Chang 1963- 187
  Earlier sketch in SATA 140
Comport, Sally Wern 190
Compton, Patricia A. 1936- 75
Comte, The Great
  See Hawkesworth, Eric
Comus
  See Ballantyne, R(obert) M(ichael)
Comyns, Nance
  See Comyns-Toohey, Nantz
Comyns-Toohey, Nantz 1956- 86
Conan Doyle, Arthur
  See Doyle, Sir Arthur Conan
Condie, Ally 204
Condie, Allyson B.
  See Condie, Ally
Condit, Martha Olson 1913- 28
Condon, Bill 1949- 142
Condon, Judith 83
Condon, Ken 195
Condy, Roy 1942- 96
Cone, Ferne Geller 1921- 39
Cone, Molly (Lamken) 1918- 151
  Autobiography Feature 151
  Earlier sketches in SATA 1, 28, 115
  See also SAAS 11
Cone, Patrick 1954- 89
Coney, Michael G. 1932-2005 61
  Obituary 170

Coney, Michael Greatrex
  See Coney, Michael G.
Coney, Mike
  See Coney, Michael G.
Conford, Ellen 1942- 162
  Earlier sketches in SATA 6, 68, 110
  See also CLR 71
Conger, Lesley
  See Suttles, Shirley (Smith)
Conklin, Gladys Plemon 1903- 2
Conklin, Paul S. 1929(?)-2003 43
  Brief entry 33
  Obituary 147
Conkling, Hilda 1910-1986 23
Conlan, Kathleen Elizabeth 1950- 145
Conlan, Kathy
  See Conlan, Kathleen Elizabeth
Conley, Robyn 1963- 125
Conley-Weaver, Robyn
  See Conley, Robyn
Conlon-McKenna, Marita 1956- 71
Conly, Jane Leslie 1948- 164
  Earlier sketches in SATA 80, 112
Conly, Robert Leslie 1918(?)-1973 23
  See also CLR 2
Connell, Kirk
  See Chapman, John Stanton Higham
Connell, Tom 206
Connelly, Marc(us Cook) 1890-1980
  Obituary 25
Connolly, Jerome P(atrick) 1931- 8
Connolly, Pat 1943- 74
Connolly, Peter 1935- 105
  Earlier sketch in SATA 47
Conover, Chris 1950- 31
Conquest, Owen
  See Hamilton, Charles (Harold St. John)
Conrad, Joseph 1857-1924 27
Conrad, Pam 1947-1996 133
  Brief entry 49
  Obituary 90
  Earlier sketches in SATA 52, 80
  See also CLR 18
  See also SAAS 19
Conroy, Jack
  See Conroy, John Wesley
Conroy, John Wesley 1899-1990 19
  Obituary 65
Conroy, Robert
  See Goldston, Robert (Conroy)
Constable, Kate 1966- 172
Constant, Alberta Wilson 1908-1981 22
  Obituary 28
Constantin, Pascale 185
Conway, Celeste 210
Conway, Diana C(ohen) 1943- 91
Conway, Gordon
  See Hamilton, Charles (Harold St. John)
Cook, Ande 192
Cook, Bernadine 1924- 11
Cook, Fred J(ames) 1911-2003 2
  Obituary 145
Cook, Glen 1944- 171
  Earlier sketch in SATA 108
Cook, Glen Charles
  See Cook, Glen
Cook, Hugh 1956- 85
Cook, Hugh, Walter Gilbert
  See Cook, Hugh
Cook, Jean Thor 1930- 94
Cook, Joel 1934- 79
Cook, Joseph Jay 1924- 8
Cook, Lisa Broadie 157
Cook, Lyn
  See Waddell, Evelyn Margaret
Cook, Roy
  See Silverberg, Robert
Cook, Sally 207
Cook, Trish 175
Cooke, Ann
  See Cole, Joanna

Cooke, Arthur
  See Lowndes, Robert A(ugustine) W(ard)
Cooke, Barbara
  See Alexander, Anna B(arbara Cooke)
Cooke, David Coxe 1917- 2
Cooke, Donald Ewin 1916-1985 2
  Obituary 45
Cooke, Frank E. 1920- 87
Cooke, Jean (Isobel Esther) 1929- 74
Cooke, John Estes
  See Baum, L. Frank
Cooke, Trish 1962- 129
Cookson, Catherine (McMullen) 1906-1998 . 9
  Obituary 116
Cooley, Beth 210
Cooley, Elizabeth
  See Cooley, Beth
Cooley, Regina Francoise 1940- 177
Coolidge, Olivia E(nsor) 1908- 26
  Earlier sketch in SATA 1
Cooling, Wendy 169
  Earlier sketch in SATA 111
Coombs, Charles I(ra) 1914-1994 43
  Earlier sketch in SATA 3
  See also SAAS 15
Coombs, Chick
  See Coombs, Charles I(ra)
Coombs, Jonathan 204
Coombs, Kate 190
Coombs, Patricia 1926- 51
  Earlier sketch in SATA 3
  See also SAAS 22
Cooney, Barbara 1917-2000 96
  Obituary 123
  Earlier sketches in SATA 6, 59
  See also CLR 23
Cooney, Caroline B. 1947- 179
  Brief entry 41
  Earlier sketches in SATA 48, 80, 113, 130
Cooney, Doug 181
Cooney, Nancy Evans 1932- 42
Coontz, Otto 1946- 33
Cooper, Ann (Catharine) 1939- 104
Cooper, Dutch
  See Kuyper, Sjoerd
Cooper, Elisha 1971- 157
  Earlier sketch in SATA 99
Cooper, Elizabeth Keyser -1992 47
Cooper, Floyd 187
  Earlier sketches in SATA 96, 144
  See also CLR 60
Cooper, Gordon 1932- 23
Cooper, Helen 1963- 169
  Earlier sketch in SATA 102
Cooper, Henry S(potswood) F(enimore), Jr.
  1933- 65
Cooper, Ilene 1948- 145
  Earlier sketches in SATA 66, 97
Cooper, James Fenimore 1789-1851 19
  See also CLR 105
Cooper, John R. 1
Cooper, Kay 1941- 11
Cooper, Lee Pelham 1926- 5
Cooper, Lester (Irving) 1919-1985 32
  Obituary 43
Cooper, Lettice (Ulpha) 1897-1994 35
  Obituary 82
Cooper, Louise 1952-2009 152
Cooper, M.E.
  See Lerangis, Peter
Cooper, M.E.
  See Davis, Maggie S.
Cooper, Melrose
  See Kroll, Virginia L.
Cooper, Michael L. 1950- 181
  Earlier sketches in SATA 79, 117
Cooper, Patrick 1949- 134
Cooper, Susan 1935- 151
  Earlier sketches in SATA 4, 64, 104
  See also CLR 67
  See also SAAS 6

Cooper, Susan Mary
  See Cooper, Susan
Cope, Jane U(rsula) 1949- 108
Copeland, Helen 1920- 4
Copeland, Mark 1956- 180
Copeland, Paul W. 23
Coplans, Peta 1951- 84
Copley (Diana) Heather Pickering 1918- 45
Coppard, A(lfred) E(dgar) 1878-1957
  See YABC 1
Copper, Melinda 1952- 172
Copper, Melinda McConnaughey
  See Copper, Melinda
Corace, Jen 208
Coralie
  See Anderson, Catherine Corley
Corbett, Grahame 43
  Brief entry 36
Corbett, Scott 1913- 42
  Earlier sketch in SATA 2
  See also CLR 1
  See also SAAS 2
Corbett, Sue 174
Corbett, W(illiam) J(esse) 1938- 102
  Brief entry 44
  Earlier sketch in SATA 50
  See also CLR 19
Corbin, Sabra Lee
  See Malvern, Gladys
Corbin, William
  See McGraw, William Corbin
Corbman, Marjorie 1987- 179
Corby, Dan
  See Catherall, Arthur
Corcoran, Barbara (Asenath) 1911-2003 77
  Autobiography Feature 125
  Earlier sketch in SATA 3
  See also CLR 50
  See also SAAS 20
Corcos, Lucille 1908-1973 10
Cordell, Alexander
  See Graber, Alexander
Cordell, Matthew 1975- 199
Corder, Zizou
  See Young, Louisa
Corella, Joseph
  See Odgers, Sally Farrell
Coren, Alan 1938-2007 32
  Obituary 187
Corey, Dorothy 23
Corey, Shana 1974- 133
Corfe, Thomas Howell 1928- 27
Corfe, Tom
  See Corfe, Thomas Howell
Corfield, Robin Bell 1952- 74
Corlett, William 1938-2005 46
  Brief entry 39
Cormack, M(argaret) Grant 1913- 11
Cormack, Maribelle B. 1902-1984 39
Cormier, Robert 1925-2000 83
  Obituary 122
  Earlier sketches in SATA 10, 45
  See also CLR 55
Cormier, Robert Edmund
  See Cormier, Robert
Cornelius, Carol 1942- 40
Cornelius, Kay 1933- 157
Cornell, J.
  See Cornell, Jeffrey
Cornell, James (Clayton, Jr.) 1938- 27
Cornell, Jean Gay 1920- 23
Cornell, Jeffrey 1945- 11
Cornell, Laura 189
Cornish, D.M. 1972- 185
Cornish, Sam(uel James) 1935- 23
Cornwall, Nellie
  See Sloggett, Nellie
Cornwell, Autumn 195
Corr, Christopher 1955- 189
Correy, Lee
  See Stine, G(eorge) Harry

Corrick, James A. 1945- 76
Corrigan, (Helen) Adeline 1909- 23
Corrigan, Barbara 1922- 8
Corrigan, Eireann 1977- 163
Corrin, Sara 1918- 86
Brief entry 48
Corrin, Stephen 86
Brief entry 48
Corsi, Wendy
See Staub, Wendy Corsi
Cort, M. C.
See Clifford, Margaret Cort
Cort, Margaret
See Clifford, Margaret Cort
Corwin, Judith H(offman) 1946- 10
Corwin, Oliver
See Corwin, Oliver J.
Corwin, Oliver J. 206
Cory, Rowena
See Lindquist, Rowena Cory
Cosby, Bill 1937- 110
Earlier sketch in SATA 66
Cosby, William Henry, Jr.
See Cosby, Bill
and Cosby, Bill
Cosentino, Ralph 169
Cosgrave, John O'Hara II 1908-1968
Obituary 21
Cosgrove, Margaret (Leota) 1926- 47
Cosgrove, Stephen E(dward) 1945- 53
Brief entry 40
Coskey, Evelyn 1932- 7
Cosner, Shaaron 1940- 43
Cossi, Olga 1921- 102
Earlier sketch in SATA 67
Costabel, Eva Deutsch 1924- 45
Costabel-Deutsch, Eva
See Costabel, Eva Deutsch
Coste, Marion 1938- 183
Costello, David 174
Costello, David F(rancis) 1904-1990 23
Cte, Genevieve 1964- 184
Cote, Nancy 1952- 182
Cott, Jonathan 1942- 23
Cottam, Clarence 1899-1974 25
Cotten, Cynthia 188
Cottle, Joan 1960- 135
Cottler, Joseph 1899-1996 22
Cottonwood, Joe 1947- 92
Cottrell, Leonard 1913-1974 24
Cottringer, Anne 1952- 150
Earlier sketch in SATA 97
Couch, Greg 199
Coulman, Valerie 1969- 161
Couloumbis, Audrey 173
Counsel, June 1926- 70
Countryman, The
See Whitlock, Ralph
Courlander, Harold 1908-1996 6
Obituary 88
Coursen, Valerie 1965(?)- 102
Courtis, Stuart Appleton 1874-1969
Obituary 29
Courtland, Tyler
See Stevens, Serita
Courtney, Dayle
See Goldsmith, Howard
Coury, Louise Andree 1895(?)-1983
Obituary 34
Cousins, Linda 1946- 90
Cousins, Lucy 1964- 205
Earlier sketch in SATA 172
Cousins, Margaret 1905-1996 2
Obituary 92
Cousteau, Jacques-Yves 1910-1997 98
Earlier sketch in SATA 38
Couture, Christin 1951- 73
Couvillon, Jacques 195
Covert, Ralph 1968- 197

Coville, Bruce 1950- 155
Autobiography Feature 155
Earlier sketches in SATA 32, 77, 118
Covington, Dennis 109
Covington, Linda
See Windsor, Linda
Cowan, Catherine 121
Cowan, Rebecca M.
See Moesta, Rebecca
Cowan, Rebecca Moesta
See Moesta, Rebecca
Coward, Fiona 1963- 178
Cowdrey, Richard 1959- 204
Cowell, Cressida 1966- 140
Cowen, Eve
See Werner, Herma
Cowen, Ida 1898-1993 64
Cowie, Leonard W(allace) 1919- 4
Cowles, Kathleen
See Krull, Kathleen
Cowley, Cassia Joy
See Cowley, Joy
Cowley, Joy 1936- 164
Autobiography Feature 118
Earlier sketches in SATA 4, 90
See also CLR 55
See also SAAS 26
Cowley, Marjorie 1925- 111
Cox, (Christopher) Barry 1931- 62
Cox, Clinton 1934- 108
Earlier sketch in SATA 74
Cox, David (Dundas) 1933- 56
Cox, Donald William 1921- 23
Cox, Jack
See Cox, John Roberts
Cox, John Roberts 1915-1981 9
Cox, Judy 1954- 198
Earlier sketches in SATA 117, 160
Cox, Marion Monroe 1898-1983
Obituary 34
Cox, Palmer 1840-1924 24
See also CLR 24
Cox, Vic 1942- 88
Cox, Vicki 1945- 158
Cox, Victoria
See Garretson, Victoria Diane
Cox, Wallace 1924-1973 25
Cox, Wally
See Cox, Wallace
Cox, William R(obert) 1901-1988 46
Brief entry 31
Obituary 57
Coxe, Molly 1959- 101
Earlier sketch in SATA 69
Coxon, Michele 1950- 158
Earlier sketch in SATA 76
Coy, Harold 1902-1986 3
Coy, John 1958- 171
Earlier sketch in SATA 120
Craats, Rennay 1973- 131
Crabtree, Judith 1928- 98
Earlier sketch in SATA 63
Cracker, Edward E.B.
See Odgers, Sally Farrell
Craft, Elizabeth 1971(?)- 204
Craft, K. Y.
See Craft, Kinuko Y(amabe)
Craft, Kinuko
See Craft, Kinuko Y(amabe)
Craft, Kinuko Y(amabe) 1940- 127
Earlier sketch in SATA 65
Craft, Ruth 1935- 87
Brief entry 31
Craig, A. A.
See Anderson, Poul
Craig, Alisa
See MacLeod, Charlotte (Matilda)
Craig, David 205
See James, Bill
Craig, Helen 1934- 94
Earlier sketches in SATA 46, 49

Craig, Joe 1979- 198
Craig, Joe Alexander
See Craig, Joe
Craig, John Eland
See Chipperfield, Joseph Eugene
Craig, John Ernest 1921- 23
Craig, Kit
See Reed, Kit
Craig, M. F.
See Craig, Mary (Francis) Shura
Craig, M. Jean 17
Craig, M. S.
See Craig, Mary (Francis) Shura
Craig, Margaret (Maze) 1911-1964 9
Craig, Mary
See Craig, Mary (Francis) Shura
Craig, Mary Shura
See Craig, Mary (Francis) Shura
Craig, Mary (Francis) Shura 1923-1991 86
Obituary 65
Earlier sketch in SATA 6
See also SAAS 7
Craig, Ruth 1922- 95
Craik, Mrs.
See Craik, Dinah Maria (Mulock)
Craik, Dinah Maria (Mulock) 1826-1887 ... 34
Crandall, Court 1965- 175
Crandell, Rachel 1943- 152
Crane, Barbara (Joyce) 1934- 31
Crane, Caroline 1930- 11
Crane, Jordan 1973- 174
Crane, M. A.
See Wartski, Maureen (Ann Crane)
Crane, Royston Campbell 1901-1977
Obituary 22
Crane, Stephen 1871-1900
See YABC 2
See also CLR 132
Crane, Stephen Townley
See Crane, Stephen
Crane, Walter 1845-1915 100
Earlier sketch in SATA 18
See also CLR 56
Crane, William D(wight) 1892-1976 1
Cranfield, Ingrid 1945- 74
Cranshaw, Stanley
See Fisher, Dorothy (Frances) Canfield
Crary, Elizabeth (Ann) 1942- 99
Brief entry 43
Crary, Margaret (Coleman) 1906-1986 9
Craste, Marc 201
Cravath, Lynne Avril
See Cravath, Lynne W.
Cravath, Lynne W. 1951- 182
Earlier sketches in SATA 98, 148
Craven, Thomas 1889-1969 22
Crawford, Charles P. 1945- 28
Crawford, Deborah 1922- 6
Crawford, John E(dmund) 1904-1971 3
Crawford, K(aren) Michael 1959- 155
Crawford, Mel 1925- 44
Brief entry 33
Crawford, Phyllis 1899- 3
Crawley, Dave 177
Cray, Roberta
See Emerson, Ru
Crayder, Dorothy 7
Crayder, Teresa
See Colman, Hila
Crayon, Geoffrey
See Irving, Washington
Craz, Albert G. 1926- 24
Crebbin, June 1938- 169
Earlier sketch in SATA 80
Crecy, Jeanne
See Williams, Jeanne
Credle, Ellis 1902-1998 1
Creech, Sharon 1945- 172
Earlier sketches in SATA 94, 139
See also CLR 89
Creeden, Sharon 1938- 91

Creel, Ann Howard 1953- *187*
Creighton, (Mary) Helen 1899-1989
  Obituary *64*
Creighton, Jill 1949- *96*
Crenson, Victoria 1952- *159*
  Earlier sketch in SATA *88*
Cresp, Gael 1954- *119*
Crespo, George 1962- *82*
Cresswell, Helen 1934-2005 .... *79*
  Obituary *168*
  Earlier sketches in SATA *1, 48*
  See also CLR *18*
  See also SAAS *20*
Cressy, Michael 1955- *124*
Cressy, Mike
  See Cressy, Michael
Cretan, Gladys (Yessayan) 1921- *2*
Cretzmeyer, Stacy (Megan) 1959- *124*
Crew, Gary 1947- *163*
  Earlier sketches in SATA *75, 110*
  See also CLR *42*
Crew, Helen (Cecilia) Coale 1866-1941
  See YABC *2*
Crew, Linda (Jean) 1951- *137*
  Earlier sketch in SATA *71*
Crews, Donald 1938- *76*
  Brief entry *30*
  Earlier sketch in SATA *32*
  See also CLR *7*
Crews, Nina 1963- *158*
  Earlier sketch in SATA *97*
Crichton, John Michael
  See Crichton, Michael
Crichton, Michael 1942-2008 .... *88*
  Obituary *199*
  Earlier sketch in SATA *9*
Crider, Allen Billy
  See Crider, Bill
Crider, Bill 1941- *99*
Crilley, Mark 1966- *210*
  Autobiography Feature *148*
  Earlier sketches in SATA *120, 148*
Crimi, Carolyn 1959- *176*
Cripps, Enid Margaret
  See Appiah, Peggy
Crisler, Curtis L. *188*
Crisman, Ruth 1914- *73*
Crisp, Marta Marie
  See Crisp, Marty
Crisp, Marty 1947- *128*
Crispin, A(nn) C(arol) 1950- *86*
Crist, James J. 1961- *168*
Cristall, Barbara *79*
Crist-Evans, Craig 1954- *153*
Crocker, Carter *193*
Crocker, Nancy 1956- *185*
Crofford, Emily (Ardell) 1927- *61*
Crofut, William E. III 1934- *23*
Croggon, Alison 1962- *194*
Croll, Carolyn 1945- *102*
  Brief entry *52*
  Earlier sketch in SATA *56*
Croman, Dorothy Young
  See Rosenberg, Dorothy
Cromie, Alice Hamilton 1914-2000 .... *24*
Cromie, William J(oseph) 1930- *4*
Crompton, Anne Eliot 1930- *73*
  Earlier sketch in SATA *23*
Crompton, Richmal
  See Lamburn, Richmal Crompton
Cronbach, Abraham 1882-1965 .... *11*
Crone, Ruth 1919-2003 .... *4*
Cronin, A(rchibald) J(oseph) 1896-1981 ..... *47*
  Obituary *25*
Cronin, Doreen (A.) *125*
Cronin, Doreen 1966(?)- *178*
  See also CLR *136*
Cronin, Doreen A.
  See Cronin, Doreen
Crook, Beverly Courtney *38*
  Brief entry *35*

Crook, Connie Brummel 1930- *168*
  Earlier sketch in SATA *98*
Crook, Constance
  See Crook, Connie Brummel
Crosby, Alexander L. 1906-1980 .... *2*
  Obituary *23*
Crosby, Harry C.
  See Anvil, Christopher
Crosby, Margaret
  See Rathmann, Peggy
Crosher, G. R. *14*
Cross, Gilbert B. 1939- *60*
  Brief entry *51*
Cross, Gillian 1945- *178*
  Autobiography Feature *178*
  Earlier sketches in SATA *38, 71, 110, 165*
  See also CLR *28*
Cross, Gillian Clare
  See Cross, Gillian
Cross, Helen Reeder
  See Broadhead, Helen Cross
Cross, Peter 1951- *95*
Cross, Shauna 1976(?)- *196*
Cross, Tom 1954- *146*
Cross, Verda 1914- *75*
Cross, Wilbur Lucius III 1918- *2*
Crossland, Caroline 1964- *83*
Crossley-Holland, Kevin 1941- *165*
  Earlier sketches in SATA *5, 74, 120*
  See also CLR *84*
  See also SAAS *20*
Crossley-Holland, Kevin John William
  See Crossley-Holland, Kevin
Crouch, Marcus 1913-1996 .... *4*
Crout, George C(lement) 1917- *11*
Crow, Donna Fletcher 1941- *40*
Crow, Francis Luther
  See Luther, Frank
Crow, Kristyn *208*
Crowe, Andrew *111*
Crowe, Carole 1943- *204*
Crowe, Chris *206*
Crowe, Ellie *203*
Crowe, John
  See Lynds, Dennis
Crowe, (Bettina) Peter Lum 1911- *6*
Crowell, Grace Noll 1877-1969 .... *34*
Crowell, Pers 1910-1990 .... *2*
Crowell, Robert Leland 1909-2001 .... *63*
Crowfield, Christopher
  See Stowe, Harriet Beecher
Crowley, Arthur McBlair 1945- *38*
Crowley, John 1942- *140*
  Earlier sketch in SATA *65*
Crowley, Suzanne 1963- *196*
Crowley, Suzanne Carlisle
  See Crowley, Suzanne
Crownfield, Gertrude 1867-1945
  See YABC *1*
Crowther, James Gerald 1899-1983 .... *14*
Crowther, Robert 1948- *163*
Cruikshank, George 1792-1878 .... *22*
  See also CLR *63*
Cruise, Robin 1951- *179*
Crum, Shutta *192*
  Earlier sketch in SATA *134*
Crummel, Susan Stevens 1949- *176*
  Earlier sketch in SATA *130*
Crump, Fred H., Jr. 1931- *76*
  Earlier sketch in SATA *11*
Crump, J(ames) Irving 1887-1979 .... *57*
  Obituary *21*
Crump, William D(rake) 1949- *138*
Crunden, Reginald
  See Cleaver, Hylton Reginald
Crunk, T.
  See Crunk, Tony
Crunk, Tony 1956- *130*
Crutcher, Chris 1946- *196*
  Earlier sketches in SATA *52, 99, 153*
  See also CLR *28*

Crutcher, Christopher C.
  See Crutcher, Chris
Cruz, Ray(mond) 1933- *6*
Cruz Martinez, Alejandro (?)-1987 .... *74*
Crystal, Billy 1947- *154*
Crystal, William
  See Crystal, Billy
Ctvrtek, Vaclav 1911-1976
  Obituary *27*
Cuetara, Mittie 1957- *158*
  Earlier sketch in SATA *106*
Cuffari, Richard 1925-1978 .... *66*
  Obituary *25*
  Earlier sketch in SATA *6*
Cuffe-Perez, Mary 1946- *199*
Cullen, Countee 1903-1946 .... *18*
Cullen, Lynn *190*
Culliford, Pierre 1928-1992 .... *40*
  Obituary *74*
Cullinan, Bernice E(llinger) 1926- *135*
Culp, Louanna McNary 1901-1965 .... *2*
Culper, Felix
  See McCaughrean, Geraldine
Cumbaa, Stephen 1947- *72*
Cumming, Peter 1951- *168*
Cumming, Primrose Amy 1915- *24*
Cumming, Robert 1945- *65*
Cummings, Betty Sue 1918- *15*
  See also SAAS *9*
Cummings, Mary 1951- *185*
Cummings, Parke 1902-1987 .... *2*
  Obituary *53*
Cummings, Pat 1950- *203*
  Earlier sketches in SATA *42, 71, 107*
  See also CLR *48*
  See also SAAS *13*
Cummings, Phil 1957- *123*
  Earlier sketch in SATA *74*
Cummings, Priscilla 1951- *170*
  Earlier sketch in SATA *129*
Cummings, Richard
  See Gardner, Richard (M.)
Cummins, Julie *200*
Cummins, Maria Susanna 1827-1866
  See YABC *1*
Cumpliano, Ina *207*
Cuneo, Mary Louise -2001 .... *85*
Cunliffe, John Arthur 1933- *86*
  Earlier sketch in SATA *11*
Cunliffe, Marcus (Falkner) 1922-1990 .... *37*
  Obituary *66*
Cunnane, Kelly *175*
Cunningham, Bob
  See May, Julian
Cunningham, Captain Frank
  See Glick, Carl (Cannon)
Cunningham, Cathy
  See Cunningham, Chet
Cunningham, Chet 1928- *23*
Cunningham, Dale S(peers) 1932- *11*
Cunningham, Dru *91*
Cunningham, E. V.
  See Fast, Howard
Cunningham, Julia (Woolfolk) 1916- *132*
  Earlier sketches in SATA *1, 26*
  See also SAAS *2*
Cunningham, Lawrence J. 1943- *125*
Cunningham, Virginia
  See Holmgren, Virginia C(unningham)
Curiae, Amicus
  See Fuller, Edmund (Maybank)
Curie, Eve 1904-2007 .... *1*
  Obituary *188*
Curlee, Lynn 1947- *190*
  Earlier sketches in SATA *98, 141*
Curley, Daniel 1918-1988 .... *23*
  Obituary *61*
Curley, Marianne 1959- *175*
  Earlier sketch in SATA *131*
Currey, Anna *194*
Currie, Robin 1948- *120*

Currie, Stephen 1960- *132*
　Earlier sketch in SATA *82*
Curry, Ann (Gabrielle) 1934- *72*
Curry, Jane L(ouise) 1932- *138*
　Autobiography Feature *138*
　Earlier sketches in SATA *1, 52, 90*
　See also CLR *31*
　See also SAAS *6*
Curry, Peggy Simson 1911-1987 .... *8*
　Obituary *50*
Curry, Tom *185*
Curtis, Bruce (Richard) 1944- *30*
Curtis, Chara M(ahar) 1950- *78*
Curtis, Christopher Paul 1954(?)- *187*
　Earlier sketches in SATA *93, 140*
　See also CLR *68*
Curtis, Gavin 1965- *107*
Curtis, Jamie Lee 1958- *144*
　Earlier sketch in SATA *95*
　See also CLR *88*
Curtis, Jennifer Keats *185*
Curtis, Marci *160*
Curtis, Munzee
　See Caseley, Judith
Curtis, Neil 1950-2006 .... *202*
Curtis, Patricia 1921- *101*
　Earlier sketch in SATA *23*
Curtis, Peter
　See Lofts, Norah (Robinson)
Curtis, Philip (Delacourt) 1920- *62*
Curtis, Richard 1937- *29*
Curtis, Richard Alan
　See Curtis, Richard
Curtis, Richard Hale
　See Deming, Richard
　and Levinson, Leonard
　and Rothweiler, Paul Roger
Curtis, Stacy *205*
Curtis, Wade
　See Pournelle, Jerry (Eugene)
Curtiss, A(rlene) B. 1934- *90*
Cusack, Margaret 1945- *58*
Cushman, Doug 1953- *210*
　Earlier sketches in SATA *65, 101, 157*
Cushman, Jerome *2*
Cushman, Karen 1941- *147*
　Earlier sketch in SATA *89*
　See also CLR *55*
Cusick, Richie Tankersley 1952- *140*
　Earlier sketch in SATA *67*
Cutbill, Andy 1972- *201*
Cutchen, Billye Walker 1930- *15*
Cutchins, Judy 1947- *59*
Cutler, Daniel S(olomon) 1951- *78*
Cutler, Ebbitt 1923- *9*
Cutler, Ivor 1923-2006 .... *24*
　Obituary *174*
Cutler, Jane 1936- *162*
　Earlier sketches in SATA *75, 118*
Cutler, May Ebbitt
　See Cutler, Ebbitt
Cutler, Samuel
　See Folsom, Franklin (Brewster)
Cutlip, Kimbra L(eigh-Ann) 1964- *128*
Cutrate, Joe
　See Spiegelman, Art
Cutt, W(illiam) Towrie 1898-1981 .... *16*
　Obituary *85*
Cuyler, Margery 1948- *195*
　Earlier sketches in SATA *39, 99, 156*
Cuyler, Margery Stuyvesant
　See Cuyler, Margery
Cuyler, Stephen
　See Bates, Barbara S(nedeker)
Cyrus, Kurt 1954- *179*
　Earlier sketch in SATA *132*
Czernecki, Stefan 1946- *178*

D

Dabba Smith, Frank *174*
Dabcovich, Lydia *99*
　Brief entry *47*
　Earlier sketch in SATA *58*
Dace, Dolores B(oelens) 1929- *89*
Da Costa, Deborah *193*
Daddo, Andrew 1967- *198*
Dadey, Debbie 1959- *136*
　Earlier sketch in SATA *73*
Dahl, Borghild (Margarethe) 1890-1984 .... *7*
　Obituary *37*
Dahl, Roald 1916-1990 .... *73*
　Obituary *65*
　Earlier sketches in SATA *1, 26*
　See also CLR *111*
Dahlberg, Maurine F. 1951- *171*
Dahlstedt, Marden (Stewart) 1921-1983 .... *8*
　Obituary *110*
Dahme, Joanne *206*
Dain, Martin J. 1924-2000 .... *35*
Dakos, Kalli 1950- *115*
　Earlier sketch in SATA *80*
Dale, Anna 1971- *170*
Dale, Gary
　See Reece, Colleen L.
Dale, George E.
　See Asimov, Isaac
Dale, Jack
　See Holliday, Joseph
Dale, Kim 1957- *123*
Dale, Margaret J(essy) Miller 1911- *39*
Dale, Mitzi
　See Hemstock, Gillian
Dale, Norman
　See Denny, Norman (George)
Dale, Penny 1954- *151*
　Earlier sketch in SATA *70*
Daley, Michael J. *170*
Dalgliesh, Alice 1893-1979 .... *17*
　Obituary *21*
　See also CLR *62*
Dalkey, Kara 1953- *132*
Dalkey, Kara Mia
　See Dalkey, Kara
Dallas, Ruth 1919- *86*
Dalmas, John
　See Jones, John R(obert)
Dalton, Alene
　See Chapin, Alene Olsen Dalton
Dalton, Annie 1948- *140*
　Earlier sketch in SATA *40*
Dalton, Kit
　See Cunningham, Chet
Dalton, Pamela
　See Johnson, Pamela
Dalton, Sean
　See Chester, Deborah
Dalton, Sheila 1949- *108*
D'Aluisio, Faith 1957- *205*
Daly, Jim
　See Stratemeyer, Edward L.
Daly, Jude 1951- *177*
Daly, Kathleen N(orah) *124*
　Brief entry *37*
Daly, Maureen 1921-2006 .... *129*
　Obituary *176*
　Earlier sketch in SATA *2*
　See also CLR *96*
　See also SAAS *1*
Daly, Nicholas 1946- *164*
　Earlier sketches in SATA *37, 76, 114*
　See also CLR *41*
　See also SAAS *21*
　See Daly, Niki
Daly, Niki *198*
　See Daly, Nicholas
D'Amato, Alex 1919- *20*
D'Amato, Janet (Potter) 1925- *9*
Damerow, Gail 1944- *83*

Damerow, Gail Jane
　See Damerow, Gail
D'Amico, Carmela *170*
D'Amico, Steve *170*
Damrell, Liz 1956- *77*
Damrosch, Helen
　See Tee-Van, Helen Damrosch
Dana, Barbara 1940- *22*
Dana, Richard Henry, Jr. 1815-1882 .... *26*
Danachair, Caoimhin O
　See Danaher, Kevin
Danaher, Kevin 1913-2002 .... *22*
Danakas, John 1963- *94*
Dandi
　See Mackall, Dandi Daley
D'Andrea, Kate
　See Steiner, Barbara A(nnette)
Dangerfield, Balfour
　See McCloskey, (John) Robert
Daniel, Alan 1939- *76*
　Brief entry *53*
Daniel, Anita 1893(?)-1978 .... *23*
　Obituary *24*
Daniel, Anne
　See Steiner, Barbara A(nnette)
Daniel, Becky 1947- *56*
Daniel, Claire 1949- *164*
Daniel, Colin
　See Windsor, Patricia
Daniel, Hawthorne 1890- *8*
Daniel, (Donna) Lee 1944- *76*
Daniel, Rebecca
　See Daniel, Becky
Daniels, Guy 1919-1989 .... *11*
　Obituary *62*
Daniels, Lucy
　See Oldfield, Jenny
Daniels, Max
　See Gellis, Roberta
Daniels, Olga
　See Sinclair, Olga
Daniels, Patricia 1955- *93*
Daniels, Zoe
　See Laux, Constance
Dank, Gloria Rand 1955- *56*
　Brief entry *46*
Dank, Leonard D(ewey) 1929- *44*
Dank, Milton 1920- *31*
Dann, Max 1955- *62*
Danneberg, Julie 1958- *173*
Dantz, William R.
　See Philbrick, Rodman
Danziger, Paula 1944-2004 .... *149*
　Brief entry *30*
　Obituary *155*
　Earlier sketches in SATA *36, 63, 102*
　See also CLR *20*
Darby, Gene Kegley
　See Darby, Jean (Kegley)
Darby, J. N.
　See Govan, (Mary) Christine Noble
Darby, Jean (Kegley) 1921- *68*
Darby, Patricia (Paulsen) *14*
Darby, Ray(mond) 1912-1982 .... *7*
d'Arcy, Willard
　See Cox, William R(obert)
Dare, Geena
　See McNicoll, Sylvia (Marilyn)
Darian, Shea 1959- *97*
Daringer, Helen Fern 1892-1986 .... *1*
Darke, Marjorie 1929- *87*
　Earlier sketch in SATA *16*
Darley, F(elix) O(ctavius) C(arr)
　1822-1888 .... *35*
Darling, David J. 1953- *60*
　Brief entry *44*
Darling, Kathy
　See Darling, Mary Kathleen
Darling, Lois (MacIntyre) 1917-1989 .... *3*
　Obituary *64*

Author Index

Darling, Louis, (Jr.) 1916-1970 3
    Obituary 23
Darling, Mary Kathleen 1943- 124
    Earlier sketches in SATA 9, 79
Darling, Sandra Louise Woodward
    See Day, Alexandra
Darnell, K(athryn) L(ynne) 1955- 150
Darroll, Sally
    See Odgers, Sally Farrell
Darrow, Sharon 181
Darrow, Whitney, (Jr.) 1909-1999 13
    Obituary 115
Darwin, Len
    See Darwin, Leonard
Darwin, Leonard 1916- 24
Dasent, Sir George Webbe 1817-1896 62
    Brief entry 29
Dash, Joan 1925- 142
Daskam, Josephine Dodge
    See Bacon, Josephine Dodge (Daskam)
D'ath, Justin 1953- 174
    Earlier sketch in SATA 106
Dauer, Rosamond 1934- 23
Daugherty, Charles Michael 1914- 16
Daugherty, James (Henry) 1889-1974 13
    See also CLR 78
Daugherty, Richard D(eo) 1922- 35
Daugherty, Sonia Medwedeff (?)-1971
    Obituary 27
d'Aulaire, Edgar Parin 1898-1986 66
    Obituary 47
    Earlier sketch in SATA 5
    See also CLR 21
d'Aulaire, Ingri 1904-1980 66
    Obituary 24
    Earlier sketch in SATA 5
    See also CLR 21
d'Aulaire, Ingri Mortenson Parin
    See d'Aulaire, Ingri
Dave, Dave
    See Berg, David
Daveluy, Paule Cloutier 1919- 11
Davenier, Christine 1961- 179
    Earlier sketch in SATA 127
Davenport, John 1960- 156
Daves, Michael 1938- 40
David, A. R.
    See David, A(nn) Rosalie
David, A(nn) Rosalie 1946- 103
David, Jonathan
    See Ames, Lee J(udah)
David, Lawrence 1963- 165
    Earlier sketch in SATA 111
David, Peter 1956- 72
David, Peter Allen
    See David, Peter
David, Rosalie
    See David, A(nn) Rosalie
Davidson, Alice Joyce 1932- 54
    Brief entry 45
Davidson, Basil 1914- 13
Davidson, (Marie) Diane 1924- 91
Davidson, Hugh
    See Hamilton, Edmond
Davidson, Jessica 1915-1986 5
Davidson, Judith 1953- 40
Davidson, Lionel 1922-2009 87
Davidson, Margaret 1936- 5
Davidson, Marion
    See Garis, Howard R.
Davidson, Mary R. 1885-1973 9
Davidson, Mary S. 1940- 61
Davidson, Mickie
    See Davidson, Margaret
Davidson, Nicole
    See Jensen, Kathryn
Davidson, R.
    See Davidson, Raymond
Davidson, Raymond 1926- 32
Davidson, Rosalie 1921- 23

Davie, Helen K(ay) 1952- 148
    Earlier sketch in SATA 77
Davies, Andrew (Wynford) 1936- 27
Davies, Andy Robert 200
Davies, Bettilu D(onna) 1942- 33
Davies, Hunter 1936- 55
    Brief entry 45
Davies, Jacqueline 1962- 186
    Earlier sketch in SATA 155
Davies, Joan 1934- 50
    Brief entry 47
Davies, Nicola 1958- 182
    Earlier sketches in SATA 99, 150
Davies, Peter J(oseph) 1937- 52
Davies, Sumiko 1942- 46
Davis, (A.) Aubrey 1949- 153
Davis, Barbara Steincrohn
    See Davis, Maggie S.
Davis, Bette J. 1923- 15
Davis, Burke 1913- 4
Davis, Christopher 1928- 6
Davis, D(elbert) Dwight 1908-1965 33
Davis, Daniel S(heldon) 1936- 12
Davis, David R. 1948- 106
Davis, Donald 1944- 169
    Earlier sketch in SATA 93
Davis, Donald D.
    See Davis, Donald
Davis, Eleanor 1983(?)- 209
Davis, Emma
    See Davis, Maggie S.
Davis, Gibbs 1953- 102
    Brief entry 41
    Earlier sketch in SATA 46
Davis, Grania 1943- 88
    Brief entry 50
Davis, H(arold) L(enoir) 1896-1960 114
Davis, Hubert J(ackson) 1904-1997 31
Davis, Jack E. 210
Davis, Jacky 204
Davis, James Robert 1945- 32
Davis, Jenny 1953- 74
Davis, Jim
    See Davis, James Robert
Davis, Julia 1900(?)-1993 6
    Obituary 75
Davis, Karen (Elizabeth) 1944- 109
Davis, Katie 1959(?)- 208
    Earlier sketch in SATA 152
Davis, Lambert 176
Davis, Leslie
    See Guccione, Leslie Davis
Davis, Louise Littleton 1921- 25
Davis, Maggie S. 1943- 57
Davis, Marguerite 1889- 34
Davis, Mary L(ee) 1935- 9
Davis, Mary Octavia 1901-1976 6
Davis, Nelle 1958- 73
Davis, Ossie 1917-2005 81
    See also CLR 56
Davis, Paxton 1925-1994 16
Davis, Rich 1958- 206
Davis, Robert 1881-1949
    See YABC 1
Davis, Robin W(orks) 1962- 87
Davis, Russell Gerard 1922- 3
Davis, Tim(othy N.) 1957- 94
Davis, Verne Theodore 1889-1973 6
Davis, Yvonne 1927- 115
Davol, Marguerite W. 1928- 146
    Earlier sketch in SATA 82
DaVolls, Andy (P.) 1967- 85
DaVolls, Linda 1966- 85
Davys, Sarah
    See Manning, Rosemary
Dawes, Claiborne 1935- 111
Dawson, Arthur L. 207
Dawson, Elmer A. 67
    Earlier sketch in SATA 1
Dawson, Imogen (Zoe) 1948- 126
    Earlier sketch in SATA 90

Dawson, Janine 1957- 196
Dawson, Mary 1919- 11
Dawson, Willow 1975- 208
Day, A(rthur) Grove 1904-1994 59
Day, Alexandra 1941- 197
    Autobiography Feature 197
    Earlier sketches in SATA 67, 97, 169
    See also CLR 22
    See also SAAS 19
Day, Beth (Feagles) 1924- 33
Day, Donna
    See Asay, Donna Day
Day, Edward C. 1932- 72
Day, Jon 1936(?)- 79
Day, Karen 187
Day, Larry 1956- 181
Day, Nancy 1953- 140
Day, Nancy Raines 1951- 148
    Earlier sketch in SATA 93
Day, Shirley 1962- 94
Day, Thomas 1748-1789
    See YABC 1
Day, Trevor 1955- 124
Dazey, Agnes J(ohnston) 2
Dazey, Frank M. 2
Deacon, Alexis 1978- 139
Deacon, Eileen
    See Geipel, Eileen
Deacon, Richard
    See McCormick, (George) Donald (King)
Deadman, Ronald 1919-1988(?)
    Obituary 56
Deak, Erzsi 1959- 152
Dean, Anabel 1915- 12
Dean, Carolee 1962- 148
Dean, David 1976- 192
Dean, Karen Strickler 1923- 49
Dean, Ruth (Brigham) 1947- 145
Dean, Zoey
    See Bennett, Cherie
de Angeli, Marguerite (Lofft) 1889-1987 .. 100
    Obituary 51
    Earlier sketches in SATA 1, 27
    See also CLR 1
Deans, Karen 195
Deans, Sis Boulos 1955- 136
    Earlier sketch in SATA 78
DeArmand, Frances Ullmann
    1904(?)-1984 10
    Obituary 38
DeArmond, Dale 1914- 70
DeArmond, Dale Burlison
    See DeArmond, Dale
Deary, Terry 1946- 171
    Brief entry 41
    Earlier sketches in SATA 51, 101
Deaver, Julie Reece 1953- 68
de Banke, Cecile 1889-1965 11
De Bello, Rosario 1923- 89
Debon, Nicolas 186
    Earlier sketch in SATA 151
de Bono, Edward 1933- 66
de Brissac, Malcolm
    See Dickinson, Peter
de Brunhoff, Jean
    See Brunhoff, Jean de
De Brunhoff, Laurent
    See Brunhoff, Laurent de
De Bruyn, Monica G. 1952- 13
De Bruyn, Monica Jean Grembowicz
    See De Bruyn, Monica G.
DeBry, Roger K. 1942- 91
de Camp, Catherine Crook 1907-2000 83
    Earlier sketch in SATA 12
de Camp, L. Sprague 1907-2000 83
    Earlier sketch in SATA 9
de Camp, Lyon Sprague
    See de Camp, L. Sprague
DeCandido, Keith R.A. 112
Dechausay, Sonia E. 94
Decker, C.B. 172

Decker, Cynthia B.
　See Decker, C.B.
Decker, Duane 1910-1964 5
Decker, Timothy 1974- 197
DeClements, Barthe (Faith) 1920- 131
　Earlier sketches in SATA *35, 71*
　See also CLR *23*
de Clercq Zubli, Rita la Fontaine 1929- ... *199*
de Conte, Sieur Louis
　See Twain, Mark
Dedman, Stephen *108*
Dee, Catherine 1964- *138*
Dee, Ruby
　See Wallace, Ruby Ann
Deedy, Carmen Agra 1960- *196*
Deedy, John 1923- *24*
Deegan, Paul Joseph 1937- *48*
　Brief entry *38*
Deem, James M. 1950- *191*
　Autobiography Feature *191*
　Earlier sketches in SATA *75, 134*
Deem, James Morgan
　See Deem, James M.
Deeter, Catherine 1947- *137*
DeFelice, Cynthia 1951- *165*
　Earlier sketches in SATA *79, 121*
DeFelice, Cynthia C.
　See DeFelice, Cynthia
Defoe, Daniel 1660(?)-1731 .... *22*
　See also CLR *61*
DeFord, Deborah H. *123*
deFrance, Anthony
　See DiFranco, Anthony (Mario)
Degen, Bruce 1945- *205*
　Brief entry *47*
　Earlier sketches in SATA *57, 97, 147*
DeGering, Etta (Belle) Fowler 1898-1996 .... *7*
De Goldi, Kate
　See De Goldi, Kathleen Domenica
De Goldi, Kathleen Domenica 1959- *123*
de Goursac, Olivier 1959- *184*
De Grazia, Ettore 1909-1982 .... *39*
De Grazia, Ted
　See De Grazia, Ettore
deGroat, Diane 1947- *169*
　Earlier sketches in SATA *31, 90*
deGros, J. H.
　See Villiard, Paul
de Grummond, Lena Young *62*
　Earlier sketch in SATA *6*
de Hamel, Joan Littledale 1924- *86*
De Haven, Tom 1949- *72*
de Hugo, Pierre
　See Brackers de Hugo, Pierre
Deiss, Joseph Jay 1915- *12*
de Jenkins, Lyll Becerra 1925-1997 .... *102*
DeJong, David C(ornel) 1905-1967 .... *10*
de Jong, Dola
　See de Jong, Dorothea Rosalie
de Jong, Dorothea Rosalie 1911-2003 .... *7*
　Obituary *149*
DeJong, Meindert 1906-1991 .... *2*
　Obituary *68*
　See also CLR *73*
DeJonge, Joanne E. 1943- *56*
Deka, Connie
　See Laux, Constance
de Kay, Ormonde (Jr.) 1923-1998 .... *7*
　Obituary *106*
de Kiriline, Louise
　See Lawrence, Louise de Kiriline
Dekker, Carl
　See Laffin, John (Alfred Charles)
　and Lynds, Dennis
deKruif, Paul (Henry) 1890-1971 .... *50*
　Earlier sketch in SATA *5*
Delacre, Lulu 1957- *209*
　Earlier sketches in SATA *36, 156*
DeLaCroix, Alice 1940- *195*
　Earlier sketch in SATA *75*
de la Cruz, Melissa 1971- *179*

De la Garza, Phyllis 1942- *169*
De Lage, Ida 1918- *11*
de la Mare, Walter (John) 1873-1956 .... *16*
　See also CLR *148*
Delaney, Harry 1932- *3*
Delaney, Joseph 1945- *172*
Delaney, M.C.
　See Delaney, Michael
Delaney, Michael 1955- *180*
　Earlier sketch in SATA *96*
Delaney, Michael Clark
　See Delaney, Michael
Delaney, Ned
　See Delaney, Thomas Nicholas III
Delaney, Thomas Nicholas III 1951- *28*
DeLange, Alex Pardo
　See Pardo DeLange, Alex
Delano, Hugh 1933- *20*
Delany, Samuel R., Jr. 1942- *92*
Delany, Samuel Ray
　See Delany, Samuel R., Jr.
de la Pena, Matt *205*
De La Ramee, Marie Louise 1839-1908 ..... *20*
de la Roche, Mazo 1879-1961 .... *64*
De La Roche Saint Andre, Anne 1950- *75*
Delaune, (Jewel) Lynn (de Grummond) *7*
DeLaurentis, Louise Budde 1920- *12*
del Barco, Lucy Salamanca 1900(?)-1989
　Obituary *64*
Delderfield, Eric R(aymond) 1909-1995 .... *14*
Delderfield, Ronald Frederick 1912-1972 .... *20*
DeLeeuw, Adele (Louise) 1899-1988 .... *30*
　Obituary *56*
　Earlier sketch in SATA *1*
De Leon, Nephtali 1945- *97*
Delessert, Etienne 1941- *179*
　Brief entry *27*
　Earlier sketches in SATA *46, 130*
　See also CLR *81*
Delgado, James P. 1958- *122*
de Lint, Charles 1951- *207*
　Earlier sketches in SATA *115, 157*
de Lint, Charles Henri Diederick Hofsmit
　See de Lint, Charles
Delmar, Roy
　See Wexler, Jerome (LeRoy)
Del Negro, Janice M. *197*
Deloria, Vine, Jr. 1933-2005 .... *21*
　Obituary *171*
Deloria, Vine Victor, Jr.
　See Deloria, Vine, Jr.
del Rey, Lester 1915-1993 .... *22*
　Obituary *76*
Delrio, Martin
　See Doyle, Debra
　and Macdonald, James D.
Delton, Judy 1931-2001 .... *77*
　Obituary *130*
　Earlier sketch in SATA *14*
　See also SAAS *9*
Delulio, John 1938- *15*
Delving, Michael
　See Williams, Jay
de Marcken, Gail *186*
Demarest, Chris L. 1951- *175*
　Brief entry *44*
　Earlier sketches in SATA *45, 82, 128*
Demarest, Christopher Lynn
　See Demarest, Chris L.
Demarest, Doug
　See Barker, Will
De Mari, Silvana 1953- *193*
Demas, Corinne *203*
　See Bliss, Corinne Demas
Demas, Vida 1927- *9*
Dematons, Charlotte 1957- *203*
DeMatteis, J.M. 1953- *180*
DeMatteis, John Marc
　See DeMatteis, J.M.
De Mejo, Oscar 1911-1992 .... *40*
Demers, Dominique 1956- *177*

de Messieres, Nicole 1930- *39*
Demi 1942- *210*
　Earlier sketches in SATA *11, 66, 102, 152*
　See also CLR *58*
Demijohn, Thom
　See Disch, Thomas M.
　and Sladek, John
Deming, Richard 1915-1983 .... *24*
Deming, Sarah *191*
de Monfreid, Dorothee 1973- *189*
Demuth, Patricia Brennan 1948- *84*
　Brief entry *51*
Dendinger, Roger E. 1952- *158*
Denenberg, Barry 1940- *175*
Dengler, Marianna (Herron) 1935- *103*
Dengler, Sandy 1939- *54*
　Brief entry *40*
Denim, Sue
　See Pilkey, Dav
Denise, Anika *210*
Denise, Christopher 1968- *193*
　Earlier sketch in SATA *147*
Denman, K.L. 1957- *186*
Denmark, Harrison
　See Zelazny, Roger
Dennard, Deborah 1953- *136*
　Earlier sketch in SATA *78*
Denney, Diana 1910-2000 .... *25*
　Obituary *120*
Dennis, Morgan 1891(?)-1960 .... *18*
Dennis, Wesley 1903-1966 .... *18*
Denniston, Elinore 1900-1978
　Obituary *24*
Denny, Norman (George) 1901-1982 .... *43*
Denos, Julia *202*
Denslow, Sharon Phillips 1947- *142*
　Earlier sketch in SATA *68*
Denslow, W(illiam) W(allace) 1856-1915 .. *16*
　See also CLR *15*
Dent, Grace 1973- *187*
Denton, Kady MacDonald *181*
　Earlier sketches in SATA *66, 110*
　See also CLR *71*
Denton, Terry 1950- *186*
Denver, Walt
　See Redding, Robert Hull
　and Sherman, Jory (Tecumseh)
Denzel, Justin F(rancis) 1917-1999 .... *46*
　Brief entry *38*
Denzer, Ann Wiseman
　See Wiseman, Ann (Sayre)
DePalma, Mary Newell 1961- *185*
　Earlier sketch in SATA *139*
De Palma, Toni *199*
dePaola, Thomas Anthony 1934- *155*
　Earlier sketches in SATA *11, 59, 108*
　See also CLR *81*
　See also SAAS *15*
　See dePaola, Tomie
dePaola, Tomie *200*
　See dePaola, Thomas Anthony
deParrie, Paul 1949- *74*
DePauw, Linda Grant 1940- *24*
DeRan, David 1946- *76*
Derby, Ken 1956- *181*
Derby, Kenneth R.
　See Derby, Ken
Derby, Pat 1942- *172*
Derby, Sally 1934- *189*
　Earlier sketches in SATA *89, 132*
de Regniers, Beatrice Schenk (Freedman)
　1914-2000 .... *68*
　Obituary *123*
　Earlier sketch in SATA *2*
　See also SAAS *6*
Dereske, Jo 1947- *72*
Deriso, Christine Hurley 1961- *210*
Derleth, August (William) 1909-1971 .... *5*
Derman, Martha (Winn) *74*
Derman, Sarah Audrey 1915- *11*

DeRoberts, Lyndon
  See Silverstein, Robert Alan
de Roo, Anne Louise 1931-1997 .... *84*
  Earlier sketch in SATA *25*
  See also CLR *63*
deRosa, Dee *70*
Derrick, Lionel
  See Cunningham, Chet
Derrickson, Jim 1959- *141*
Derry Down Derry
  See Lear, Edward
Dervaux, Isabelle 1961- *106*
Derwent, Lavinia *14*
Desai, Anita 1937- *126*
  Earlier sketch in SATA *63*
DeSaix, Deborah Durland *188*
De Saulles, Tony 1958- *119*
Desbarats, Peter 1933- *39*
de Selincourt, Aubrey 1894-1962 .... *14*
de Seve, Randall *198*
Deshpande, Chris 1950- *69*
Desimini, Lisa 1964- *148*
  Earlier sketch in SATA *86*
Desjarlais, John 1953- *71*
Desjarlais, John J.
  See Desjarlais, John
Desmoinaux, Christel 1967- *149*
  Earlier sketch in SATA *103*
Desmond, Adrian J(ohn) 1947- *51*
Desmond, Alice Curtis 1897-1990 .... *8*
Desnoettes, Caroline *183*
DeSpain, Pleasant 1943- *87*
Desputeaux, Helene 1959- *95*
Dessen, Sarah 1970- *172*
  Earlier sketch in SATA *120*
Detine, Padre
  See Olsen, Ib Spang
de Trevino, Elizabeth B.
  See Trevino, Elizabeth B(orton) de
de Trevino, Elizabeth Borton
  See Trevino, Elizabeth B(orton) de
Detwiler, Susan Dill 1956- *58*
Deuker, Carl 1950- *196*
  Earlier sketches in SATA *82, 150*
Deutsch, Babette 1895-1982 .... *1*
  Obituary *33*
Deutsch, Eva Costabel
  See Costabel, Eva Deutsch
Deutsch, Helen 1906-1992 .... *76*
Deutsch, Kurt
  See Singer, Kurt D.
De Valera, Sinead 1879(?)-1975
  Obituary *30*
Devaney, John 1926-1994 .... *12*
de Varennes, Monique 1947- *168*
de Varona, Frank J. 1943- *83*
Devereux, Frederick L(eonard), Jr.
  1914-1993 .... *9*
Devi, Nila
  See Woody, Regina Jones
deVinck, Christopher 1951- *85*
DeVita, James *195*
DeVito, Cara 1956- *80*
Devlin, Dorothy Wende
  See Devlin, Wende
Devlin, Harry 1918-2001 .... *136*
  Earlier sketches in SATA *11, 74*
Devlin, Wende 1918-2002 .... *74*
  Earlier sketch in SATA *11*
Devon, Paddie 1953- *92*
Devons, Sonia 1974- *72*
Devorah-Leah *111*
de Vos, Gail 1949- *122*
DeVries, Douglas 1933- *122*
De Waard, E(lliott) John 1935- *7*
Dewan, Ted 1961- *157*
  Earlier sketch in SATA *108*
Dewdney, Anna *184*
Dewdney, Selwyn (Hanington) 1909-1979 . *64*
DeWeese, Gene
  See DeWeese, Thomas Eugene

DeWeese, Jean
  See DeWeese, Thomas Eugene
DeWeese, Thomas Eugene 1934- *46*
  Brief entry *45*
Dewey, Ariane 1937- *178*
  Earlier sketches in SATA *7, 109*
Dewey, Jennifer (Owings) 1941- *103*
  Brief entry *48*
  Earlier sketch in SATA *58*
Dewey, Kenneth Francis 1940- *39*
De Wire, Elinor 1953- *180*
deWit, Dorothy (May Knowles)
  1916-1980 .... *39*
  Obituary *28*
Dexter, Alison 1966- *125*
Dexter, John
  See Bradley, Marion Zimmer
Deyneka, Anita 1943- *24*
Deyrup, Astrith Johnson 1923- *24*
Dezern, Chad *201*
Dhami, Narinder 1958- *152*
Dhondy, Farrukh 1944- *152*
  Earlier sketch in SATA *65*
  See also CLR *41*
Diakite, Baba Wague 1961- *174*
Diakite, Penda 1993(?)- *174*
Diamond, Arthur 1957- *76*
Diamond, Donna 1950- *69*
  Brief entry *30*
  Earlier sketch in SATA *35*
Diamond, Petra
  See Sachs, Judith
Diamond, Rebecca
  See Sachs, Judith
Dias, Earl Joseph 1916- *41*
Dias, Ron 1937- *71*
Diaz, David 1959(?)- *189*
  Earlier sketches in SATA *96, 150*
  See also CLR *65*
Dibley, Glin *188*
DiCamillo, Kate 1964- *202*
  Earlier sketches in SATA *121, 163*
  See also CLR *117*
Di Certo, J(oseph) J(ohn) 1933- *60*
DiCianni, Ron 1952- *107*
Dick, Trella Lamson 1889-1974 .... *9*
Dickens, Charles 1812-1870 .... *15*
  See also CLR *95*
Dickens, Charles John Huffam
  See Dickens, Charles
Dickens, Frank
  See Huline-Dickens, Frank William
Dickens, Monica (Enid) 1915-1992 .... *4*
  Obituary *74*
Dickerson, Roy Ernest 1886-1965
  Obituary *26*
Dickinson, Emily 1830-1886 .... *29*
Dickinson, Emily Elizabeth
  See Dickinson, Emily
Dickinson, Mary 1949- *48*
  Brief entry *41*
Dickinson, Mary-Anne
  See Rodda, Emily
Dickinson, Peter 1927- *150*
  Earlier sketches in SATA *5, 62, 95*
  See also CLR *125*
Dickinson, Peter Malcolm de Brissac
  See Dickinson, Peter
Dickinson, Susan 1931- *8*
Dickinson, Terence 1943- *102*
Dickinson, W(illiam) Croft 1897-1963 .... *13*
Dickson, Gordon R. 1923-2001 .... *77*
Dickson, Gordon Rupert
  See Dickson, Gordon R.
Dickson, Helen
  See Reynolds, Helen Mary Greenwood Campbell
Dickson, Naida 1916- *8*
Diehn, Gwen 1943- *80*
Dierssen, Andreas 1962- *190*
Diesen, Deborah 1967- *200*

Dieterich, Michele M. 1962- *78*
Dietz, David H(enry) 1897-1984 .... *10*
  Obituary *41*
Dietz, Lew 1907-1997 .... *11*
  Obituary *95*
Diffily, Deborah *159*
Di Fiori, Larry
  See Di Fiori, Lawrence
Di Fiori, Lawrence 1934- *130*
DiFranco, Anthony (Mario) 1945- *42*
Digby, Anne 1935- *72*
Digges, Jeremiah
  See Berger, Josef
Digman, Kristina 1959- *176*
D'Ignazio, Fred(erick) 1949- *39*
  Brief entry *35*
Di Grazia, Thomas (?)-1983 .... *32*
Dijkstra, Lida 1961- *195*
Dikty, Julian May
  See May, Julian
Dillard, Annie 1945- *140*
  Earlier sketch in SATA *10*
Dillard, Kristine 1964- *113*
Dillard, Polly Hargis 1916- *24*
Diller, Harriett 1953- *78*
Dillon, Anna
  See Scott, Michael
Dillon, Barbara 1927- *44*
  Brief entry *39*
Dillon, Diane 1933- *194*
  Earlier sketches in SATA *15, 51, 106*
  See also CLR *44*
Dillon, Diane Claire
  See Dillon, Diane
Dillon, Eilis 1920-1994 .... *74*
  Autobiography Feature *105*
  Obituary *83*
  Earlier sketch in SATA *2*
  See also CLR *26*
Dillon, Jana (a pseudonym) 1952- *117*
Dillon, Leo 1933- *194*
  Earlier sketches in SATA *15, 51, 106*
  See also CLR *44*
Dillon, Sharon Saseen
  See Saseen, Sharon (Dillon)
Dils, Tracey E. 1958- *83*
Dilson, Jesse 1914-1988 .... *24*
Dinan, Carolyn *59*
  Brief entry *47*
Dines, Carol 1956- *175*
Dines, (Harry) Glen 1925-1996 .... *7*
Dinesen, Isak
  See Blixen, Karen
Dinessi, Alex
  See Schembri, Jim
Dinneen, Betty 1929- *61*
Dinnerstein, Harvey 1928- *42*
Dinsdale, Tim(othy Kay) 1924-1987 .... *11*
Diop, Birago (Ismael) 1906-1989
  Obituary *64*
Diouf, Sylviane A. *168*
Diouf, Sylviane Anna
  See Diouf, Sylviane A.
DiPucchio, Kelly *204*
  Earlier sketch in SATA *159*
Dirk
  See Gringhuis, Richard H.
Dirks, Wilhelmina 1916- *59*
Dirks, Willy
  See Dirks, Wilhelmina
Dirtmeister
  See Tomecek, Steve
DiSalvo, DyAnne 1960- *144*
  Earlier sketch in SATA *59*
DiSalvo-Ryan, DyAnne
  See DiSalvo, DyAnne
Disch, Thomas M. 1940-2008 .... *92*
  Obituary *195*
  See also CLR *18*
  See also SAAS *15*

Disch, Thomas Michael
　See Disch, Thomas M.
Disch, Tom
　See Disch, Thomas M.
Disher, Garry 1949- 125
　Earlier sketch in SATA *81*
Disney, Walt(er Elias) 1901-1966 28
　Brief entry 27
Ditchfield, Christin 1973- 189
DiTerlizzi, Tony 1969- 154
Divakaruni, Chitra Banerjee 1956- 160
Di Valentin, Maria (Amelia) Messuri
　1911-1985 7
Divine, Arthur Durham 1904-1987
　Obituary 52
Divine, David
　See Divine, Arthur Durham
Dixon, Ann R. 1954- 127
　Earlier sketch in SATA *77*
Dixon, Ann Renee
　See Dixon, Ann R.
Dixon, Dougal 1947- 190
　Earlier sketches in SATA *45, 127*
Dixon, Franklin W.
　See Barrett, Neal, Jr.
　and Goulart, Ron
　and Lantz, Francess L(in)
　and Lerangis, Peter
　and McFarlane, Leslie
　and Stanley, George Edward
　and Stratemeyer, Edward L.
Dixon, Jeanne 1936- 31
Dixon, Paige
　See Corcoran, Barbara (Asenath)
Dixon, Peter L(ee) 1931- 6
Dixon, Rachel 1952- 74
Djoleto, (Solomon Alexander) Amu 1929- . 80
d'lacey, Chris 1949- 165
Doak, Annie
　See Dillard, Annie
Doane, Pelagie 1906-1966 7
Dob, Bob 207
Dobell, I(sabel) M(arian) B(arclay)
　1909-1998 11
Dobie, J(ames) Frank 1888-1964 43
Dobkin, Alexander 1908-1975
　Obituary 30
Dobler, Lavinia G. 1910- 6
Dobrin, Arnold 1928- 4
Dobson, Jill 1969- 140
Dobson, Julia 1941- 48
Dobson, Mary 1954- 117
Docherty, James
　See Docherty, Jimmy
Docherty, Jimmy 1976- 204
Dockery, Wallene T. 1941- 27
Dockray, Tracy 1962- 139
Dockrey, Karen 1955- 103
Doctor, Bernard
　See Doctor, Bernard Aquina
Doctor, Bernard Aquina 1950- 81
Doctor X
　See Nourse, Alan E(dward)
Dodd, Ed(ward Benton) 1902-1991 4
　Obituary 68
Dodd, Emma 1969- 203
Dodd, Lynley (Stuart) 1941- 132
　Earlier sketches in SATA *35, 86*
　See also CLR *62*
Dodd, Marty 1921- 142
Dodd, Quentin 1972- 137
Dodds, Bill 1952- 78
Dodds, Dayle Ann 1952- 201
　Earlier sketches in SATA *75, 150*
Doder, Josh 1968- 187
Dodge, Bertha S(anford) 1902-1995 8
Dodge, Fremont
　See Grimes, Lee
Dodge, Gil
　See Hano, Arnold

Dodge, Mary (Elizabeth) Mapes
　1831(?)-1905 100
　Earlier sketch in SATA *21*
　See also CLR *62*
Dodgson, Charles Lutwidge
　See Carroll, Lewis
Dodson, Kenneth MacKenzie 1907-1999 11
Dodson, Susan 1941- 50
　Brief entry 40
Dogar, Sharon 1962- 211
Dogyear, Drew
　See Gorey, Edward (St. John)
Doherty, Berlie 1943- 111
　Earlier sketch in SATA *72*
　See also CLR *21*
　See also SAAS *16*
Doherty, Charles Hugh 1913- 6
Doherty, Craig A. 1951- 169
　Earlier sketch in SATA *83*
Doherty, Katherine M(ann) 1951- 83
Doherty, Kieran 1945- 164
Dokey, Cameron 1956- 97
Dolan, Edward F(rancis), Jr. 1924- 94
　Brief entry 31
　Earlier sketch in SATA *45*
Dolan, Ellen M(eara) 1929-1998 88
Dolan, Sean J. 1958- 74
Dolce, J. Ellen 1948- 75
Dolch, Edward William 1889-1961 50
Dolch, Marguerite Pierce 1891-1978 50
Dollar, Diane (Hills) 1933- 57
Dolson, Hildegarde
　See Lockridge, Hildegarde (Dolson)
Domanska, Janina 1913(?)-1995 68
　Obituary 84
　Earlier sketch in SATA *6*
　See also CLR *40*
　See also SAAS *18*
Dominguez, Angel 1953- 76
Domino, John
　See Averill, Esther (Holden)
Domjan, Joseph (Spiri) 1907-1992 25
Domm, Jeffrey C. 1958- 84
Donahue, Dorothy 178
Donald, Rhonda Lucas 1962- 147
Donalds, Gordon
　See Shirreffs, Gordon D(onald)
Donaldson, Bryna
　See Stevens, Bryna
Donaldson, Gordon 1913-1993 64
　Obituary 76
Donaldson, Joan 1953- 78
Donaldson, Julia 1948- 180
　Earlier sketches in SATA *82, 132*
Donaldson, Stephen R. 1947- 121
Donaldson, Stephen Reeder
　See Donaldson, Stephen R.
Doner, Kim 1955- 208
　Earlier sketch in SATA *91*
Doney, Todd L. W. 1959- 104
Dong-Sung, Kim 1970- 195
Dong-Sung Kim
　See Dong-Sung, Kim
Donkin, Nance (Clare) 1915- 95
Donna, Natalie 1934-1979 9
Donnelly, Elfie 1950-
　See CLR *104*
Donnelly, Jennifer 1963- 154
Donnelly, Matt 1972- 148
Donnio, Sylviane 188
Donofrio, Beverly 1950- 209
Donoghue, Emma 1969- 101
Donohue, Moira Rose 1954- 201
Donoughue, Carol 1935- 139
Donovan, Frank (Robert) 1906-1975
　Obituary 30
Donovan, John 1928-1992 72
　Brief entry 29
　See also CLR *3*
Donovan, Mary Lee 1961- 86

Donovan, William
　See Berkebile, Fred D(onovan)
Donze, Mary Terese 1911- 89
Doob, Leonard W(illiam) 1909-2000 8
Dooley, Norah 1953- 74
Dooling, Michael 1958- 105
Dor, Ana
　See Ceder, Georgiana Dorcas
Doran, Colleen 1963- 211
Dore, (Louis Christophe Paul) Gustave
　1832-1883 19
Doremus, Robert 1913- 30
Doren, Marion (Walker) 1928- 57
Dorenkamp, Michelle 1957- 89
Dorflinger, Carolyn 1953- 91
Dorfman, Joaquin 1979- 180
Dorfman, Joaquin Emiliano
　See Dorfman, Joaquin
Dorian, Edith M(cEwen) 1900-1983 5
Dorian, Harry
　See Hamilton, Charles (Harold St. John)
Dorian, Marguerite 7
Dorin, Patrick C(arberry) 1939- 59
　Brief entry 52
Dorman, Brandon 194
Dorman, Michael 1932- 7
Dorman, N. B. 1927- 39
Dormer, Frank W. 200
Dorris, Michael 1945-1997 75
　Obituary 94
　See also CLR *58*
Dorris, Michael A.
　See Dorris, Michael
Dorris, Michael Anthony
　See Dorris, Michael
Dorritt, Susan
　See Schlein, Miriam
Dorros, Alex 1991- 194
Dorros, Arthur 1950- 168
　Earlier sketches in SATA *78, 122*
　See also CLR *42*
　See also SAAS *20*
Dorros, Arthur M.
　See Dorros, Arthur
Dorson, Richard M(ercer) 1916-1981 30
Doss, Helen (Grigsby) 1918- 20
Doss, Margot Patterson 6
dos Santos, Joyce Audy 1949- 57
　Brief entry 42
Dothers, Anne
　See Chess, Victoria (Dickerson)
Dotlich, Rebecca Kai 1951- 182
Dottig
　See Grider, Dorothy
Dotts, Maryann J. 1933- 35
Doty, Jean Slaughter 1929- 28
Doty, Roy 1922- 28
Doubtfire, Dianne (Abrams) 1918- 29
Doucet, Sharon Arms 1951- 144
　Autobiography Feature 144
　Earlier sketch in SATA *125*
Dougherty, Charles 1922- 18
Dougherty, Terri (L.) 1964- 146
Doughty, Rebecca 1955- 174
Douglas, Blaise 1960- 101
Douglas, Carole Nelson 1944- 73
Douglas, Garry
　See Kilworth, Garry
Douglas, James McM.
　See Griffin, W.E.B.
Douglas, Kathryn
　See Ewing, Kathryn
Douglas, Leonard
　See Bradbury, Ray
Douglas, Lola
　See Zeises, Lara M.
Douglas, Marjory Stoneman 1890-1998 10
Douglas, Michael
　See Bright, Robert Sr.)
Douglas, Michael
　See Crichton, Michael

Douglas, Shirley Stewart
See Tepper, Sheri S.
Douglass, Barbara 1930- 40
Douglass, Frederick 1817(?)-1895 29
Douglass, Keith
See Cunningham, Chet
Douty, Esther M(orris) 1909-1978 8
Obituary 23
Dow, Emily R. 1904-1987 10
Dow, Vicki
See McVey, Vicki
Dowd, John David 1945- 78
Dowd, Siobhan 1960-2007 204
Dowdell, Dorothy (Florence) Karns 1910- . 12
Dowden, Anne Ophelia Todd 1907-2007 7
Obituary 180
See also SAAS 10
Dowdey, Landon Gerald 1923- 11
Dowdy, Mrs. Regera
See Gorey, Edward (St. John)
Dowell, Frances O'Roark 205
Earlier sketch in SATA 157
Dower, Laura 1967- 185
Dowling, Terry 1947- 101
Downard, Barry 1956- 202
Downer, Ann 1960- 155
Downer, Marion 1892(?)-1971 25
Downes, Belinda 1962- 180
Downey, Fairfax D(avis) 1893-1990 3
Obituary 66
Downey, Lynn 1961- 185
Downham, Jenny 1964- 192
Downie, John 1931- 87
Downie, Mary Alice 1934- 171
Earlier sketches in SATA 13, 87
Downie, Mary Alice Dawe
See Downie, Mary Alice
Downing, David A(lmon) 1958- 84
Downing, Johnette 184
Downing, Julie 1956- 148
Earlier sketch in SATA 81
Downing, Paula E. 1951- 80
Downing, Warwick
See Downing, Wick
Downing, Wick 1931- 138
Dowswell, Paul 1957- 184
Doyle, A. Conan
See Doyle, Sir Arthur Conan
Doyle, Sir Arthur Conan 1859-1930 24
See also CLR 106
Doyle, Brian 1935- 156
Earlier sketches in SATA 67, 104
See also CLR 22
See also SAAS 16
Doyle, Charlotte 1937- 178
Earlier sketch in SATA 94
Doyle, Charlotte Lackner
See Doyle, Charlotte
Doyle, Conan
See Doyle, Sir Arthur Conan
Doyle, Debra 1952- 165
Earlier sketch in SATA 105
Doyle, Donovan
See Boegehold, Betty (Doyle)
Doyle, John
See Graves, Robert
Doyle, Malachy 1954- 165
Earlier sketch in SATA 120
See also CLR 83
Doyle, Richard 1824-1883 21
Doyle, Sir A. Conan
See Doyle, Sir Arthur Conan
Dr. A
See Asimov, Isaac
and Silverstein, Alvin
and Silverstein, Virginia B.
Dr. Alphabet
See Morice, Dave
Dr. Fred
See Bortz, Alfred B(enjamin)

Dr. Laura
See Schlessinger, Laura (Catherine)
Dr. Seuss 1904-1991 100
Obituary 67
Earlier sketches in SATA 1, 28, 75
See also CLR 100
Dr. Zed
See Penrose, Gordon
Drabble, Margaret 1939- 48
Drackett, Phil(ip Arthur) 1922- 53
Draco, F.
See Davis, Julia
Dracup, Angela 1943- 74
Dragisic, Patricia 116
Dragonwagon, Crescent 1952- 186
Autobiography Feature 186
Earlier sketches in SATA 11, 41, 75, 133
See also SAAS 14
Drake, David 1945- 85
Drake, David Allen
See Drake, David
Drake, Frank
See Hamilton, Charles (Harold St. John)
Drake, Jane 1954- 82
Drake, Salamanda
See Barlow, Steve
Drakeford, Dale B 1952- 113
Drakeford, Dale Benjamin
See Drakeford, Dale B
Draper, Hastings
See Jeffries, Roderic
Draper, Sharon
See Draper, Sharon M.
Draper, Sharon M. 1948- 195
Autobiography Feature 146
Earlier sketches in SATA 98, 146
See also CLR 57
Draper, Sharon Mills
See Draper, Sharon M.
Drapier, M. B.
See Swift, Jonathan
Drawson, Blair 1943- 126
Earlier sketch in SATA 17
Dray, Matt 1967- 177
Dray, Matthew Frederick
See Dray, Matt
Dresang, Eliza (Carolyn Timberlake)
1941- 19
Drescher, Henrik 1955- 172
Earlier sketches in SATA 67, 105
See also CLR 20
Drescher, Joan E(lizabeth) 1939- 137
Earlier sketch in SATA 30
Dressen-McQueen, Stacey 191
Dreves, Veronica R. 1927-1986
Obituary 50
Drew, Patricia (Mary) 1938- 15
Drewery, Mary 1918- 6
Drewery, Melanie 1970- 165
Drewry, Henry N(athaniel) 1924- 138
Dreyer, Ellen 177
Drial, J. E.
See Laird, Jean E(louise)
Drimmer, Frederick 1916-2000 60
Obituary 124
Driskill, J. Lawrence 1920- 90
Driskill, Larry
See Driskill, J. Lawrence
Driving Hawk, Virginia
See Sneve, Virginia Driving Hawk
Dron, Laura
See Matthews, L.S.
Dronzek, Laura 199
Drucker, Malka 1945- 111
Brief entry 29
Earlier sketch in SATA 39
Drucker, Olga Levy 1927- 79
Druitt, Tobias
See Purkiss, Diane
Drummond, Allan 1957- 209
Drummond, V(iolet) H(ilda) 1911-2000 6

Drummond, Walter
See Silverberg, Robert
Drury, Clare Marie
See Hoskyns-Abrahall, Clare (Constance Drury)
Drury, Roger W(olcott) 1914-1996 15
Druse, Eleanor
See King, Stephen
Dryden, Pamela
See St. John, Nicole
D.T., Hughes
See Hughes, Dean
Duane, Diane (Elizabeth) 1952- 145
Brief entry 46
Earlier sketches in SATA 58, 95
Dubanevich, Arlene 1950- 56
Dubelaar, Thea 1947- 60
Dubin, Jill 205
du Blane, Daphne
See Groom, Arthur William
Duble, Kathleen Benner 1958- 164
Dubois, Claude K. 1960- 196
DuBois, Rochelle Holt 1946- 41
Du Bois, Shirley Graham 1907(?)-1977 24
See Graham, Shirley
Du Bois, W. E. B. 1868-1963 42
Du Bois, William Edward Burghardt
See Du Bois, W. E. B.
du Bois, William Pene
See Pene du Bois, William (Sherman)
Duboise, Novella 1911-1999 88
Dubosarsky, Ursula 1961- 193
Earlier sketches in SATA 107, 147
DuBose, LaRocque (Russ) 1926- 2
Dubrovin, Vivian 1931- 139
Earlier sketch in SATA 65
DuBurke, Randy 172
Ducey, Jean Sparks 1915- 93
Duchacek, Ivo D(uka) 1913-1988
Obituary 55
Du Chaillu, Paul (Belloni) 1835(?)-1903 26
Ducharme, Dede Fox
See Ducharme, Lilian Fox
Ducharme, Lilian Fox 1950- 122
Ducornet, Erica 1943- 7
Ducornet, Rikki
See Ducornet, Erica
Duden, Jane 1947- 136
Duder, Tessa 1940- 117
Earlier sketch in SATA 80
See also CLR 43
See also SAAS 23
Dudley, Helen
See Hope Simpson, Jacynth
Dudley, Martha Ward 1909(?)-1985
Obituary 45
Dudley, Nancy
See Cole, Lois Dwight
Dudley, Robert
See Baldwin, James
Dudley, Ruth H(ubbell) 1905-2001 11
Dudley-Smith, T.
See Trevor, Elleston
Due, Linnea A. 1948- 64
Dueck, Adele 1955- 97
Dueland, Joy V(ivian) 27
Duerr, Gisela 1968- 89
Duey, Kathleen 1950- 199
Earlier sketch in SATA 132
Dufault, Joseph Ernest Nephtali
See James, Will(iam Roderick)
Duff, Annis (James) 1904(?)-1986
Obituary 49
Duff, Maggie
See Duff, Margaret K(app)
Duff, Margaret K(app) 1916-2003 37
Obituary 144
Duffey, Betsy (Byars) 1953- 131
Earlier sketch in SATA 80
Duffie, Charles 1960- 144
Duffield, Katy S. 1961- 147

Duffy, Carol Ann 1955- 165
  Earlier sketch in SATA 95
Dugan, Jack
  See Griffin, W.E.B.
Dugan, John Kevin
  See Griffin, W.E.B.
Dugan, Karen 202
Dugan, Karen M.
  See Dugan, Karen
Dugan, Michael (Gray) 1947- 15
Duggan, Alfred Leo 1903-1964 25
Duggan, Maurice 1922-1974 40
  Obituary 30
Duggan, Maurice Noel
  See Duggan, Maurice
Duggleby, John 1952- 94
Dugin, Andrej 1955- 77
Dugina, Olga 1964- 77
du Jardin, Rosamond Neal 1902-1963 2
Duka, Ivo
  See Duchacek, Ivo D(uka)
Duke, Kate 1956- 192
  Earlier sketches in SATA 90, 148
  See also CLR 51
Duke, Will
  See Gault, William Campbell
Dulac, Edmund 1882-1953 19
Dumas, Alexandre (pere) 1802-1870 18
  See also CLR 134
Dumas, Jacqueline 1946- 55
Dumas, Philippe 1940- 119
  Earlier sketch in SATA 52
du Maurier, Daphne 1907-1989 27
  Obituary 60
Dumbleton, Mike 1948- 206
  Earlier sketches in SATA 73, 124
Dunbar, Fiona 1961- 167
Dunbar, Joyce 1944- 162
  Earlier sketches in SATA 76, 112
Dunbar, Paul Laurence 1872-1906 34
Dunbar, Polly 1980(?)- 211
  Earlier sketch in SATA 181
Dunbar, Robert E(verett) 1926- 32
Duncan, Alexandra
  See Moore, Ishbel (Lindsay)
Duncan, Alice Faye 1967- 168
  Earlier sketch in SATA 95
Duncan, Gregory
  See McClintock, Marshall
Duncan, Jane
  See Cameron, Elizabeth Jane
Duncan, Julia K.
  See Benson, Mildred
Duncan, Lois 1934- 141
  Autobiography Feature 141
  Earlier sketches in SATA 1, 36, 75, 133
  See also CLR 129
  See also SAAS 2
Duncan, Norman 1871-1916
  See YABC 1
Duncan, Terence
  See Nolan, William F.
Duncombe, Frances (Riker) 1900-1994 25
  Obituary 82
Dungy, Anthony
  See Dungy, Tony
Dungy, Tony 1955- 206
Dunham, Montrew 1919- 162
Dunham, Montrew Goetz
  See Dunham, Montrew
Dunkle, Clare B. 1964- 155
Dunlap, Julie 1958- 84
Dunleavy, Deborah 1951- 133
Dunlop, Agnes M. R. (?)-1982 87
Dunlop, Eileen (Rhona) 1938- 76
  Earlier sketch in SATA 24
  See also SAAS 12
Dunmore, Helen 1952- 201
Dunn, Anne M. 1940- 107
Dunn, Carolyn 1965- 208
Dunn, Harvey T(homas) 1884-1952 34

Dunn, Herb
  See Gutman, Dan
Dunn, John M. (III) 1949- 93
Dunn, Judy
  See Spangenberg, Judith Dunn
Dunn, Mary Lois 1930- 6
Dunnahoo, Terry Janson 1927- 7
Dunne, Jeanette 1952- 72
Dunne, Kathleen 1933- 126
Dunne, Marie
  See Clark, Ann Nolan
Dunne, Mary Collins 1914- 11
Dunne, Mary Jo
  See Dunne, Mary Collins
Dunnett, Kaitlyn
  See Emerson, Kathy Lynn
Dunnett, Margaret (Rosalind) 1909-1977 ... 42
Dunnick, Regan 178
Dunrea, Olivier 1953- 160
  Brief entry 46
  Earlier sketches in SATA 59, 118
Dunrea, Olivier Jean-Paul Dominique
  See Dunrea, Olivier
Dunton, Dorothy 1912- 92
Dupasquier, Philippe 1955- 151
  Earlier sketch in SATA 86
duPont, Lindsay 207
duPont, Lindsay Harper
  See duPont, Lindsay
DuPrau, Jeanne 1944- 144
Dupuy, T(revor) N(evitt) 1916-1995 4
  Obituary 86
DuQuette, Keith 1960- 155
  Earlier sketch in SATA 90
Duran, Gloria 1924- 171
Duran, Gloria Bradley
  See Duran, Gloria
Duranceau, Suzanne 1952- 162
Durand, Delphine 1971- 200
Durango, Julia 1967- 173
Durant, Alan 1958- 165
  Earlier sketch in SATA 121
Durant, John 1902- 27
Durbin, William 1951- 174
  Earlier sketch in SATA 143
Durell, Ann 1930- 66
Durkee, Sarah 173
Durney, Ryan 205
Durrant, Lynda 1954- 148
  Earlier sketch in SATA 96
Durrant, Sabine 210
Durrell, Gerald (Malcolm) 1925-1995 8
  Obituary 84
Durrell, Julie 1955- 94
Durrett, Deanne 1940- 144
  Earlier sketch in SATA 92
Durst, Sarah Beth 1974- 203
Du Soe, Robert C. 1892-1958
  See YABC 2
Dussling, Jennifer 1970- 143
  Earlier sketch in SATA 96
DuTemple, Lesley A. 1952- 113
Dutton, Sandra 191
Dutz
  See Davis, Mary Octavia
Duval, Katherine
  See James, Elizabeth
Duval, Kathy 1946- 181
Duvall, Aimee
  See Thurlo, Aimee
  and Thurlo, David
Duvall, Evelyn Millis 1906- 9
Duvall, Jill D(onovan) 1932- 102
Duvoisin, Roger (Antoine) 1904-1980 30
  Obituary 23
  Earlier sketch in SATA 2
  See also CLR 23
Dwiggins, Don(ald J.) 1913-1988 4
  Obituary 60
Dwight, Allan
  See Cole, Lois Dwight

Dwyer, Deanna
  See Koontz, Dean
Dwyer, K.R.
  See Koontz, Dean
Dyck, Peter J. 1914- 75
Dyer, James (Frederick) 1934- 37
Dyer, Jane 191
  Earlier sketch in SATA 147
Dyess, John (Foster) 1939- 76
Dygard, Thomas J. 1931-1996 97
  Obituary 92
  Earlier sketch in SATA 24
  See also SAAS 15
Dyke, John 1935- 35

E

E. V. L.
  See Lucas, E(dward) V(errall)
Eagar, Frances (Elisabeth Stuart)
  1940-1978 11
  Obituary 55
Eager, Edward (McMaken) 1911-1964 17
  See also CLR 43
Eager, George 1921- 56
Eager, George B.
  See Eager, George
Eagle, Ellen 1953- 61
Eagle, Kin
  See Adlerman, Daniel (Ezra)
  and Adlerman, Kimberly M(arie)
Eagle, Mike 1942- 11
Earle, Olive L(ydia) 1888-1982 7
Earle, William
  See Johns, W(illiam) E(arle)
Earls, Nick 1963- 156
  Earlier sketch in SATA 95
Early, Jack
  See Scoppettone, Sandra
Early, Jon
  See Johns, W(illiam) E(arle)
Early, Margaret 1951- 72
Earnshaw, Brian 1929- 17
Earnshaw, Micky
  See Earnshaw, Spencer Wright
Earnshaw, Spencer Wright 1939- 88
Easley, MaryAnn 94
Eason, Alethea 1957- 197
Eastman, Charles A(lexander) 1858-1939
  See YABC 1
Eastman, P(hilip) D(ey) 1909-1986 33
  Obituary 46
Easton, Kelly 1960- 192
  Earlier sketch in SATA 141
Eastwick, Ivy (Ethel) O(live) 3
Eaton, Anne T(haxter) 1881-1971 32
Eaton, Anthony 1971- 167
Eaton, George L.
  See Verral, Charles Spain
Eaton, Janet
  See Givens, Janet E(aton)
Eaton, Jeanette 1886-1968 24
Eaton, Maxwell III 1981- 199
Eaton, Tom 1940- 22
Ebbeler, Jeff
  See Ebbeler, Jeffrey
Ebbeler, Jeffrey 1974- 206
Ebel, Alex 1927- 11
Eber, Dorothy (Margaret) Harley 1930- 27
Eberhart, Sheri S.
  See Tepper, Sheri S.
Eberle, Irmengarde 1898-1979 2
  Obituary 23
Eble, Diane 1956- 74
Eboch, Chris 113
Eccles Williams, Ferelith 1920- 22
Echlin, Kim 1955- 166
Eckblad, Edith Berven 1923- 23

Ecke, Wolfgang 1927-1983
  Obituary 37
Eckert, Allan W. 1931- 91
  Brief entry 27
  Earlier sketch in SATA 29
  See also SAAS 21
Eckert, Horst 1931- 72
  Earlier sketch in SATA 8
  See also CLR 26
Ecklar, Julia (Marie) 1964- 112
Eddings, David 1931-2009 91
Eddings, David Carroll
  See Eddings, David
Ede, Janina 1937- 33
Edell, Celeste 12
Edelman, Lily (Judith) 1915-1981 22
Edelson, Edward 1932- 51
Edens, Cooper 1945- 166
  Earlier sketches in SATA 49, 112
Edens, (Bishop) David 1926- 39
Edey, Maitland A(rmstrong) 1910-1992 25
  Obituary 71
Edgerton, Perky 196
Edgeworth, Maria 1768-1849 21
Edgson, Alison 211
Edgy, Wardore
  See Gorey, Edward (St. John)
Edison, Theodore
  See Stratemeyer, Edward L.
Edler, Tim(othy) 1948- 56
Edmiston, Jim 1948- 80
Edmonds, I(vy) G(ordon) 1917- 8
Edmonds, Walter D(umaux) 1903-1998 27
  Obituary 99
  Earlier sketch in SATA 1
  See also SAAS 4
Edmund, Sean
  See Pringle, Laurence
Edsall, Marian (Stickney) 1920- 8
Edwards, Al
  See Nourse, Alan E(dward)
Edwards, Anne 1927- 35
Edwards, Audrey 1947- 52
  Brief entry 31
Edwards, Becky (Jane) 1966- 125
Edwards, Bertram
  See Edwards, Herbert Charles
Edwards, Bronwen Elizabeth
  See Rose, Wendy
Edwards, Cecile Pepin 1916- 25
Edwards, David 1962- 198
Edwards, Dorothy 1914-1982 88
  Obituary 31
  Earlier sketch in SATA 4
Edwards, F. E.
  See Nolan, William F.
Edwards, Frank B. 1952- 93
Edwards, Gunvor 32
Edwards, Harvey 1929- 5
Edwards, Hazel (Eileen) 1945- 135
Edwards, Herbert Charles 1912- 12
Edwards, Jane Campbell 1932- 10
Edwards, Julia
  See Stratemeyer, Edward L.
Edwards, Julie
  See Andrews, Julie
Edwards, Julie Andrews
  See Andrews, Julie
Edwards, June
  See Bhatia, Jamunadevi
Edwards, Linda Strauss 1948- 49
  Brief entry 42
Edwards, Margaret (Alexander) 1902-1988
  Obituary 56
Edwards, Michelle 1955- 152
  Earlier sketch in SATA 70
Edwards, Monica le Doux Newton
  1912-1998 12
Edwards, Olwen
  See Gater, Dilys
Edwards, Page (Lawrence, Jr.) 1941-1999 .. 59

Edwards, Pamela Duncan 189
Edwards, R. T.
  See Goulart, Ron
Edwards, Sally (Cary) 1929- 7
Edwards, Samuel
  See Gerson, Noel Bertram
Edwards, Wallace 1957(?)- 170
Eeckhout, Emmanuelle 1976- 208
Egan, E(dward) W(elstead) 1922- 35
Egan, Kerry 175
Egan, Lorraine Hopping 1960- 134
  Earlier sketch in SATA 91
Egan, Tim 1957- 191
  Earlier sketches in SATA 89, 155
Egermeier, Elsie E(milie) 1890-1986 65
Eggenberger, David 1918- 6
Eggleston, Edward 1837-1902 27
Egielski, Richard 1952- 163
  Earlier sketches in SATA 11, 49, 106
Egypt, Ophelia Settle 1903-1984 16
  Obituary 38
Ehlert, Lois 1934- 172
  Earlier sketches in SATA 35, 69, 128
  See also CLR 28
Ehlert, Lois Jane
  See Ehlert, Lois
Ehling, Katalin Olah 1941- 93
Ehrenfreund, Norbert 1921- 86
Ehrenhaft, Daniel 1970- 185
Ehrhardt, Karen 1963- 184
Ehrlich, Amy 1942- 132
  Earlier sketches in SATA 25, 65, 96
Ehrlich, Bettina Bauer 1903-1985 1
Ehrlich, Fred 205
Ehrlich, Fred M.D.
  See Ehrlich, Fred
Ehrlich, H. M.
  See Ziefert, Harriet
Eichenberg, Fritz 1901-1990 50
  Earlier sketch in SATA 9
Eichler, Margrit 1942- 35
Eichner, James A. 1927- 4
Eidson, Thomas 1944- 112
Eifert, Virginia (Louise) S(nider) 1911-1966
  2
Eige, (Elizabeth) Lillian 1915- 65
Eiken, J. Melia 1967- 125
Einhorn, Edward 1970- 204
Einsel, Naiad 10
Einsel, Walter 1926- 10
Einzig, Susan 1922- 43
Eiseman, Alberta 1925- 15
Eisenberg, Azriel (Louis) 1903-1985 12
Eisenberg, Lisa 1949- 155
  Brief entry 50
  Earlier sketch in SATA 57
Eisenberg, Phyllis Rose 1924- 41
Eisner, Vivienne
  See Margolis, Vivienne
Eisner, Will 1917-2005 165
  Earlier sketch in SATA 31
Eisner, William Erwin
  See Eisner, Will
Eitzen, Allan 1928- 9
Eitzen, Ruth (Carper) 1924- 9
Ekwensi, C. O. D.
  See Ekwensi, Cyprian
Ekwensi, Cyprian 1921-2007 66
Ekwensi, Cyprian Odiatu Duaka
  See Ekwensi, Cyprian
Elam, Richard M(ace, Jr.) 1920- 9
Elborn, Andrew
  See Clements, Andrew
  and Clements, Andrew
Elboz, Stephen 1956- 152
Eldin, Peter 1939- 154
Eldon, Kathy 1946- 107
Eldridge, Marion 199
Elfman, Blossom 1925- 8
Elgin, Kathleen 1923- 39

Elia
  See Lamb, Charles
Eliot, A. D.
  See Jewett, Sarah Orne
Eliot, Alice
  See Jewett, Sarah Orne
Eliot, Anne
  See Cole, Lois Dwight
Eliot, Dan
  See Silverberg, Robert
Elish, Dan 1960- 204
  Earlier sketches in SATA 68, 129
Elisha, Ron 1951- 104
Elisofon, Eliot 1911-1973
  Obituary 21
Elkeles, Simone 1970- 187
Elkin, Benjamin 1911-1995 3
Elkins, Dov Peretz 1937- 5
Ellacott, S(amuel) E(rnest) 1911- 19
Elleman, Barbara 1934- 147
Ellen, Jaye
  See Nixon, Joan Lowery
Eller, Scott
  See Holinger, William (Jacques)
  and Shepard, Jim
Ellestad, Myrvin
  See Ellestad, Myrvin H.
Ellestad, Myrvin H. 1921- 120
Elliot, Bruce
  See Field, Edward
Elliot, David 1952- 208
  Earlier sketch in SATA 122
Elliott, Bruce
  See Field, Edward
Elliott, David 1947- 201
  Earlier sketch in SATA 163
Elliott, Don
  See Silverberg, Robert
Elliott, Elizabeth Shippen Green
  See Green, Elizabeth Shippen
Elliott, Janice 1931-1995 119
Elliott, Joey
  See Houk, Randy
Elliott, Laura Malone 1957- 197
Elliott, L.M.
  See Elliott, Laura Malone
Elliott, Louise 111
Elliott, Mark 1949- 210
Elliott, Odette 1939- 75
Elliott, Patricia 1946- 176
Elliott, Sarah M(cCarn) 1930- 14
Elliott, (Robert) Scott 1970- 153
Elliott, William
  See Bradbury, Ray
Elliott, Zetta 206
Ellis, (Mary) Amabel (Nassau Strachey)
  Williams
  See Williams-Ellis, (Mary) Amabel (Nassau
  Strachey)
Ellis, Ann Dee 210
Ellis, Anyon
  See Rowland-Entwistle, (Arthur) Theodore
  (Henry)
Ellis, Carson 1975- 190
Ellis, Carson Friedman
  See Ellis, Carson
Ellis, Deborah 1960- 187
  Earlier sketch in SATA 129
Ellis, E. S.
  See Ellis, Edward S.
Ellis, Edward S. 1840-1916
  See YABC 1
Ellis, Edward Sylvester
  See Ellis, Edward S.
Ellis, Ella Thorp 1928- 127
  Earlier sketch in SATA 7
  See also SAAS 9
Ellis, Harry Bearse 1921-2004 9
Ellis, Herbert
  See Wilson, Lionel

Ellis, Mel(vin Richard) 1912-1984 7
　Obituary 39
Ellis, Richard 1938- 130
Ellis, Sarah 1952- 179
　Earlier sketches in SATA 68, 131
　See also CLR 42
Ellison, Chris 196
Ellison, Elizabeth Stow 1970- 209
Ellison, Emily 114
Ellison, Lucile Watkins 1907(?)-1979 50
　Obituary 22
Ellison, Virginia H(owell) 1910- 4
Ellsberg, Edward 1891-1983 7
Ellsworth, Loretta 1954- 199
Ellsworth, Mary Ellen (Tressel) 1940- 146
Elmer, Robert 1958- 154
　Earlier sketch in SATA 99
Elmore, (Carolyn) Patricia 1933- 38
　Brief entry 35
El-Moslimany, Ann P(axton) 1937- 90
Elschner, Geraldine 1954- 183
Elspeth
　See Bragdon, Elspeth MacDuffie
Elster, Jean Alicia 1953- 150
Elting, Mary 1906- 88
　Earlier sketch in SATA 2
　See also SAAS 20
Elvgren, Jennifer Riesmeyer 179
Elwart, Joan Potter 1927- 2
Elwood, Ann 1931- 55
　Brief entry 52
Elwood, Roger 1943-2007 58
Elya, Susan Middleton 1955- 202
　Earlier sketches in SATA 106, 159
Elzbieta 88
Ember, Kathi 190
Emberley, Barbara A. 1932- 146
　Earlier sketches in SATA 8, 70
　See also CLR 5
Emberley, Barbara Anne
　See Emberley, Barbara A.
Emberley, Ed 1931- 146
　Earlier sketches in SATA 8, 70
　See also CLR 81
Emberley, Edward Randolph
　See Emberley, Ed
Emberley, Michael 1960- 189
　Earlier sketches in SATA 34, 80, 119
Embry, Margaret Jacob 1919-1975 5
Emecheta, Buchi 1944- 66
Emecheta, Florence Onye Buchi
　See Emecheta, Buchi
Emerson, Alice B.
　See Benson, Mildred
Emerson, Kathy Lynn 1947- 63
Emerson, Kevin 209
Emerson, Ru 1944- 107
　Earlier sketch in SATA 70
Emerson, Sally 1952- 111
Emerson, William K(eith) 1925- 25
Emert, Phyllis R(aybin) 1947- 93
Emery, Anne (McGuigan) 1907- 33
　Earlier sketch in SATA 1
Emmens, Carol Ann 1944- 39
Emmett, Jonathan 1965- 188
　Earlier sketch in SATA 138
Emmons, Della (Florence) Gould 1890-1983
　Obituary 39
Emory, Jerry 1957- 96
Emrich, Duncan (Black Macdonald)
　1908-1970(?) 11
Emshwiller, Carol 1921- 174
　Autobiography Feature 174
Emshwiller, Carol Fries
　See Emshwiller, Carol
Emslie, M. L.
　See Simpson, Myrtle L(illias)

Ende, Michael (Andreas Helmuth)
　1929-1995 130
　Brief entry 42
　Obituary 86
　Earlier sketch in SATA 61
　See also CLR 138
Enderle, Dotti 1954- 203
　Earlier sketch in SATA 145
Enderle, Judith (Ann) Ross 1941- 89
　Autobiography Feature 114
　Earlier sketch in SATA 38
　See also SAAS 26
Endle, Kate 207
Enell, Trinka (Gochenour) 1951- 79
Enfield, Carrie
　See Smith, Susan Vernon
Engdahl, Sylvia Louise 1933- 4
　Autobiography Feature 122
　See also CLR 2
　See also SAAS 5
Engel, Diana 1947- 70
Engelbreit, Mary 1952- 169
Engelhart, Margaret S. 1924- 59
Engelmann, Kim (V.) 1959- 87
England, George Allan 1877-1936 102
Englart, Mindi Rose 1965- 146
Engle, Eloise
　See Paananen, Eloise (Katherine)
Engle, Margarita 1951- 193
Englebert, Victor 1933- 8
English, James W(ilson) 1915- 37
English, Karen 202
Engstrom, Elizabeth 1951- 110
Enright, D(ennis) J(oseph) 1920-2002 25
　Obituary 140
Enright, Dominique 194
Enright, Elizabeth (Wright) 1909-1968 9
　See also CLR 4
Ensor, Barbara 180
Ensor, Robert (T.) 1922- 93
Enthoven, Sam 1974- 187
Entwistle, (Arthur) Theodore (Henry) Rowland
　See Rowland-Entwistle, (Arthur) Theodore
　(Henry)
Enys, Sarah L.
　See Sloggett, Nellie
Epanya, Christian A(rthur Kingue) 1956- ... 91
Ephraim, Shelly S(chonebaum) 1952- 97
Ephron, Delia 1944- 197
　Brief entry 50
　Earlier sketch in SATA 65
Epler, Doris M. 1928- 73
Epp, Margaret A(gnes) 1913- 20
Eppenstein, Louise (Kohn) 1892-1987
　Obituary 54
Epple, Anne Orth 1927- 20
Epstein, Anne Merrick 1931- 20
Epstein, Beryl 1910- 31
　Earlier sketch in SATA 1
　See also CLR 26
　See also SAAS 17
Epstein, Beryl M. Williams
　See Epstein, Beryl
Epstein, Perle S(herry) 1938- 27
Epstein, Rachel S. 1941- 102
Epstein, Samuel 1909-2000 31
　Earlier sketch in SATA 1
　See also CLR 26
　See also SAAS 17
Erdman, Loula Grace 1905(?)-1976 1
Erdoes, Richard 1912- 33
　Brief entry 28
Erdogan, Buket 187
Erdrich, Karen Louise
　See Erdrich, Louise
Erdrich, Louise 1954- 141
　Earlier sketch in SATA 94
Erickson, Betty J. 1923- 97
Erickson, Betty Jean
　See Erickson, Betty J.

Erickson, John R. 1943- 136
　Earlier sketch in SATA 70
Erickson, Jon 1948- 141
Erickson, Phoebe 59
Erickson, Russell E(verett) 1932- 27
Erickson, Sabra Rollins 1912-1995 35
Erickson, Walter
　See Fast, Howard
Ericson, Walter
　See Fast, Howard
Ericsson, Jennifer A. 170
Erikson, Mel 1937- 31
Eriksson, Eva 1949- 207
Ering, Timothy Basil 176
Erlanger, Baba
　See Trahey, Jane
Erlbach, Arlene 1948- 160
　Earlier sketches in SATA 78, 115
Erlbruch, Wolf 1948- 181
Erlich, Lillian (Feldman) 1910-1983 10
Erlings, Fridrik 1962- 196
Erlingsson, Fridrik
　See Erlings, Fridrik
Ermatinger, James W. 1959- 170
Ernest, William
　See Berkebile, Fred D(onovan)
Ernst, (Lyman) John 1940- 39
Ernst, Kathleen
　See Ernst, Kathleen A.
Ernst, Kathleen A. 1959- 162
Ernst, Kathryn (Fitzgerald) 1942- 25
Ernst, Lisa Campbell 1957- 154
　Brief entry 44
　Earlier sketches in SATA 55, 95
Erskine, Kathryn 193
Ervin, Janet Halliday 1923- 4
Erwin, Will
　See Eisner, Will
Esbaum, Jill 174
Esbensen, Barbara J(uster) 1925-1996 97
　Brief entry 53
　Earlier sketch in SATA 62
Eschbacher, Roger 160
Eschmeyer, R. E. 1898-1989 29
Escriva, Vivi 182
Eseki, Bruno
　See Mphahlele, Es'kia
Esekie, Bruno
　See Mphahlele, Es'kia
Eshmeyer, Reinhart Ernst
　See Eschmeyer, R. E.
Eskridge, Ann E. 1949- 84
Espeland, Pamela (Lee) 1951- 128
　Brief entry 38
　Earlier sketch in SATA 52
Espinosa, Laura 203
Espinosa, Leo 203
Espriella, Don Manuel Alvarez
　See Southey, Robert
Espy, Willard R(ichardson) 1910-1999 38
　Obituary 113
Essakalli, Julie Klear 200
Essrig, Harry 1912- 66
Estep, Irene Compton 5
Esterl, Arnica 1933- 77
Estes, Eleanor (Ruth) 1906-1988 91
　Obituary 56
　Earlier sketch in SATA 7
　See also CLR 70
Estoril, Jean
　See Allan, Mabel Esther
Estrada, Pau 1961- 200
　Earlier sketch in SATA 74
Etchemendy, Nancy 1952- 166
　Earlier sketch in SATA 38
Etchemendy, Nancy Elise Howell
　See Etchemendy, Nancy
Etchison, Birdie L(ee) 1937- 38
Etchison, Craig 1945- 133
Etherington, Frank 1945- 58

Eton, Robert
  See Meynell, Laurence Walter
Ets, Marie Hall 1893-1984 2
  See also CLR *33*
Ettlinger, Doris 1950- *173*
Eunson, (John) Dale 1904-2002 .... *5*
  Obituary *132*
Evan, Frances Y. 1951- *167*
Evanoff, Vlad 1916- *59*
Evans, Cambria 1981- *178*
Evans, Douglas 1953- *144*
  Earlier sketch in SATA *93*
Evans, Eva (Knox) 1905-1998 .... *27*
Evans, Freddi Williams 1957- *211*
  Earlier sketch in SATA *134*
Evans, Greg 1947- *143*
  Earlier sketch in SATA *73*
Evans, Hubert Reginald 1892-1986 .... *118*
  Obituary *48*
Evans, Katherine (Floyd) 1901-1964 .... *5*
Evans, Larry
  See Evans, Laurence Chubb
Evans, Laurence Chubb 1939- *88*
Evans, Lawrence Watt
  See Watt-Evans, Lawrence
Evans, Lezlie *180*
Evans, Mari 1923- *10*
Evans, Mark *19*
Evans, Nancy 1950- *65*
Evans, Nate *201*
Evans, Patricia Healy
  See Carpenter, Patricia (Healy Evans)
Evans, (Alice) Pearl 1927- *83*
Evans, Shane W. *189*
Evans, Shirlee 1931- *58*
Evans, Tabor
  See Cameron, Lou
  and Knott, William C(ecil, Jr.)
  and Wallmann, Jeffrey M(iner)
  and Whittington, Harry (Benjamin)
Evarts, Esther
  See Benson, Sally
Evarts, Hal G., (Jr.) 1915-1989 .... *6*
Everett, Gail
  See Hale, Arlene
Evernden, Margery 1916- *5*
Eversole, Robyn 1971- *74*
Eversole, Robyn H.
  See Eversole, Robyn
Eversole, Robyn Harbert
  See Eversole, Robyn
Evslin, Bernard 1922-1993 .... *83*
  Brief entry *28*
  Obituary *77*
  Earlier sketch in SATA *45*
Ewart, Claire 1958- *145*
  Earlier sketch in SATA *76*
Ewart, Franzeska G. 1950- *205*
Ewen, David 1907-1985 .... *4*
  Obituary *47*
Ewing, Juliana (Horatia Gatty) 1841-1885 . *16*
  See also CLR *78*
Ewing, Kathryn 1921- *20*
Eyerly, Jeannette 1908-2008 .... *86*
  Obituary *196*
  Earlier sketch in SATA *4*
  See also SAAS *10*
Eyerly, Jeannette Hyde
  See Eyerly, Jeannette
Eyre, Dorothy
  See McGuire, Leslie (Sarah)
Eyre, Frank 1910-1988
  Obituary *62*
Eyre, Katherine Wigmore 1901-1970 .... *26*
Ezzell, Marilyn 1937- *42*
  Brief entry *38*

F

Fabe, Maxene 1943- *15*
Faber, Doris (Greenberg) 1924- *78*
  Earlier sketch in SATA *3*
Faber, Harold 1919-2010 .... *5*
Fabre, Jean Henri (Casimir) 1823-1915 ..... *22*
Fabry, Glenn 1961- *205*
Facklam, Margaret
  See Thomas, Peggy
Facklam, Margery (Metz) 1927- *132*
  Earlier sketches in SATA *20, 85*
Fadden, David Kanietakeron *196*
Fadiman, Clifton (Paul) 1904-1999 .... *11*
  Obituary *115*
Fagan, Cary 1957- *186*
Fahs, Sophia Blanche Lyon 1876-1978 .... *102*
Failing, Barbara Larmon *182*
Fain, Sarah 1971- *204*
Fair, David 1952- *96*
Fair, Sylvia 1933- *13*
Fairfax-Lucy, Brian (Fulke Cameron-Ramsay)
  1898-1974 .... *6*
  Obituary *26*
Fairfield, Flora
  See Alcott, Louisa May
Fairlie, Gerard 1899-1983
  Obituary *34*
Fairman, Joan A(lexandra) 1935- *10*
Faithfull, Gail 1936- *8*
Falcone, L(ucy) M. 1951- *155*
Falconer, Ian 1959- *179*
  Earlier sketch in SATA *125*
  See also CLR *146*
Falconer, James
  See Kirkup, James
Falconer, Lee N.
  See May, Julian
Falkner, Brian 1962- *206*
Falkner, Leonard 1900-1977 .... *12*
Fall, Andrew
  See Arthur, Robert, (Jr.)
Fall, Thomas
  See Snow, Donald Clifford
Faller, Regis 1968- *187*
Falls, C(harles) B(uckles) 1874-1960 .... *38*
  Brief entry *27*
Falstein, Louis 1909-1995 .... *37*
Falwell, Cathryn 1952- *196*
Fancher, Lou 1960- *177*
Fanelli, Sara 1969- *126*
  Earlier sketch in SATA *89*
Fanning, Leonard M(ulliken) 1888-1967 .... *5*
Faralla, Dana 1909- *9*
Faralla, Dorothy W.
  See Faralla, Dana
Farb, Peter 1929-1980 .... *12*
  Obituary *22*
Farber, Norma 1909-1984 .... *75*
  Obituary *38*
  Earlier sketch in SATA *25*
Fardell, John 1967- *195*
Farish, Terry 1947- *146*
  Earlier sketch in SATA *82*
Farjeon, (Eve) Annabel 1919-2004 .... *11*
  Obituary *153*
Farjeon, Eleanor 1881-1965 .... *2*
  See also CLR *34*
Farley, Carol (J.) 1936- *137*
  Earlier sketch in SATA *4*
Farley, Terri *165*
Farley, Walter (Lorimer) 1915-1989 .... *132*
  Earlier sketches in SATA *2, 43*
Farlow, James O(rville, Jr.) 1951- *75*
Farmer, Jacqueline *210*
Farmer, Nancy 1941- *161*
  Earlier sketches in SATA *79, 117*
Farmer, Patti 1948- *79*

Farmer, Penelope (Jane) 1939- *105*
  Brief entry *39*
  Earlier sketch in SATA *40*
  See also CLR *8*
  See also SAAS *22*
Farmer, Peter 1950- *38*
Farmer, Philip Jose
  See Farmer, Philip Jose
Farmer, Philip Jose 1918-2009 .... *93*
  Obituary *201*
Farmer, Philipe Jos
  See Farmer, Philip Jose
Farnham, Burt
  See Clifford, Harold B(urton)
Farnsworth, Bill 1958- *186*
  Earlier sketches in SATA *84, 135*
Farooqi, Musharraf Ali 1968- *207*
Farquhar, Margaret C(utting) 1905-1988 .... *13*
Farquharson, Alexander 1944- *46*
Farquharson, Martha
  See Finley, Martha
Farr, Diana *82*
  Earlier sketch in SATA *3*
Farr, Finis (King) 1904-1982 .... *10*
Farr, Richard 1960- *209*
Farrar, Jill
  See Morris, Jill
Farrar, Susan Clement 1917- *33*
Farrell, Ben
  See Cebulash, Mel
Farrell, John 1951- *204*
Farrell, Patrick
  See Odgers, Sally Farrell
Farrell, Sally
  See Odgers, Sally Farrell
Farrer, Vashti *167*
Farrington, Benjamin 1891-1974
  Obituary *20*
Farrington, S(elwyn) Kip, Jr. 1904-1983 .... *20*
Farris, Christine King 1927- *206*
Farshtey, Greg(ory T.) 1965- *148*
Farthing, Alison 1936- *45*
  Brief entry *36*
Farthing-Knight, Catherine 1933- *92*
Fassler, Joan (Grace) 1931- *11*
Fast, Howard 1914-2003 .... *7*
  Autobiography Feature *107*
Fast, Howard Melvin
  See Fast, Howard
Fasulo, Michael 1963- *83*
Fatchen, Max 1920- *84*
  Earlier sketch in SATA *20*
  See also SAAS *20*
Fate, Marilyn
  See Collins, Paul
Father Goose
  See Ghigna, Charles
Fatigati, (Frances) Evelyn 1948- *24*
Fatio, Louise 1904-1993 .... *6*
Fatus, Sophie 1957- *182*
Faulhaber, Martha 1926- *7*
Faulkner, Anne Irvin 1906- *23*
Faulkner, Frank
  See Ellis, Edward S.
Faulkner, Nancy
  See Faulkner, Anne Irvin
Faulknor, Cliff(ord Vernon) 1913- *86*
Favole, Robert J(ames) 1950- *125*
Fax, Elton Clay 1909-1993 .... *25*
Faxon, Lavinia
  See Russ, Lavinia (Faxon)
Feagles, Anita M(acRae) 1927- *9*
Feagles, Elizabeth
  See Day, Beth (Feagles)
Feague, Mildred H. 1915- *14*
Fearnley, Jan 1965- *205*
  Earlier sketch in SATA *153*
Fearrington, Ann (Peyton) 1945- *146*
Fecher, Constance
  See Heaven, Constance (Christina)
Feder, Chris Welles 1938- *81*

Feder, Harriet K. 1928- 73
Feder, Paula (Kurzband) 1935- 26
Federici, Debbie 1965- 175
Federici, Debbie Tanner
   See Federici, Debbie
Feelings, Muriel 1938- 16
   See also CLR 5
   See also SAAS 8
Feelings, Muriel Lavita Grey
   See Feelings, Muriel
Feelings, Thomas 1933-2003 69
   Obituary 148
   Earlier sketch in SATA 8
   See also CLR 58
   See also SAAS 19
Feelings, Tom
   See Feelings, Thomas
Fehler, Gene 1940- 201
   Earlier sketch in SATA 74
Fehrenbach, T(heodore) R(eed, Jr.) 1925- .. 33
Feiffer, Jules 1929- 201
   Earlier sketches in SATA 8, 61, 111, 157
Feiffer, Jules Ralph
   See Feiffer, Jules
Feiffer, Kate 1964- 206
   Earlier sketch in SATA 170
Feig, Barbara Krane 1937- 34
Feikema, Feike
   See Manfred, Frederick (Feikema)
Feil, Hila 1942- 12
Feilen, John
   See May, Julian
Feinberg, Barbara Jane 1938- 123
   Earlier sketch in SATA 58
Feinberg, Barbara Silberdick
   See Feinberg, Barbara Jane
Feinstein, John 1956- 195
   Earlier sketch in SATA 163
Feldman, Anne (Rodgers) 1939- 19
Feldman, Elane 79
Feldman, Jody 200
Felin, M. Sindy 194
Felix
   See Vincent, Felix
Fell, Derek 1939- 167
Fell, Derek John
   See Fell, Derek
Fellowes, Julian 1950- 198
Fellows, Muriel H. 10
Fellows, Stan 1957- 177
Fellows, Stanley
   See Fellows, Stan
Felsen, Henry Gregor 1916-1995 1
   See also SAAS 2
Felstead, Cathie 1954- 192
Feltenstein, Arlene (H.) 1934- 119
Felton, Harold William 1902-1991 1
Felton, Ronald Oliver 1909- 3
Felts, Shirley 1934- 33
Fenderson, Lewis H., Jr. 1907-1983 47
   Obituary 37
Fenner, Carol (Elizabeth) 1929-2002 89
   Obituary 132
   Earlier sketch in SATA 7
   See also SAAS 24
Fenner, Phyllis R(eid) 1899-1982 1
   Obituary 29
Fensham, Elizabeth 169
Fenten, Barbara D(oris) 1935- 26
Fenten, D(onald) X. 1932- 4
Fenton, Carroll Lane 1900-1969 5
Fenton, Edward 1917-1995 7
   Obituary 89
Fenton, Mildred Adams 1899-1995 21
Fenwick, Patti
   See Grider, Dorothy
Feravolo, Rocco Vincent 1922- 10
Ferber, Brenda A. 1967- 184
Ferber, Edna 1887-1968 7
Fergus, Charles 114

Ferguson, Alane 1957- 182
   Earlier sketch in SATA 85
Ferguson, Bob
   See Ferguson, Robert Bruce
Ferguson, Cecil 1931- 45
Ferguson, Peter 1968- 199
Ferguson, Robert Bruce 1927-2001 13
Ferguson, Sarah 1959- 180
   Earlier sketches in SATA 66, 110
Ferguson, Sarah Margaret
   See Ferguson, Sarah
Ferguson, Walter (W.) 1930- 34
Fergusson, Erna 1888-1964 5
Fermi, Laura 1907-1977 6
   Obituary 28
Fern, Eugene A. 1919-1987 10
   Obituary 54
Fern, Tracey E. 202
Fernandes, Eugenie 1943- 205
   Earlier sketches in SATA 77, 139
Fernandez, Laura 1960- 171
Ferraiolo, Jack D. 208
Ferrari, Maria 123
Ferreiro, Carmen 1958- 158
Ferrell, Nancy Warren 1932- 70
Ferri, Giuliano 1965- 197
Ferrier, Lucy
   See Penzler, Otto
Ferris, Helen Josephine 1890-1969 21
Ferris, James Cody
   See McFarlane, Leslie
Ferris, Jean 1939- 202
   Brief entry 50
   Earlier sketches in SATA 56, 105, 149
Ferris, Jeri Chase 1937- 84
Ferry, Charles 1927- 92
   Earlier sketch in SATA 43
   See also CLR 34
   See also SAAS 20
Fetz, Ingrid 1915- 30
Feydy, Anne Lindbergh
   See Sapieyevski, Anne Lindbergh
Fiammenghi, Gioia 1929- 66
   Earlier sketch in SATA 9
Fiarotta, Noel
   See Ficarotta, Noel
Fiarotta, Phyllis
   See Ficarotta, Phyllis
Ficarotta, Noel 1944- 15
Ficarotta, Phyllis 1942- 15
Fichter, George S. 1922-1993 7
Ficocelli, Elizabeth 189
Fidler, Kathleen (Annie) 1899-1980 87
   Obituary 45
   Earlier sketch in SATA 3
Fiedler, Jean(nette Feldman) 4
Fiedler, Joseph Daniel 159
Fiedler, Lisa 185
Field, Dorothy 1944- 97
Field, Edward 1924- 109
   Earlier sketch in SATA 8
Field, Elinor Whitney 1889-1980
   Obituary 28
Field, Eugene 1850-1895 16
Field, Gans T.
   See Wellman, Manly Wade
Field, James 1959- 113
Field, Peter
   See Drago, Harry Sinclair
   and Dresser, Davis
   and Mann, E(dward) B(everly)
Field, Rachel (Lyman) 1894-1942 15
   See also CLR 21
Fielding, Kate
   See Oldfield, Jenny
Fields, Bryan W. 1958(?)- 188
Fields, Terri 1948- 191
Fields, T.S.
   See Fields, Terri
Fienberg, Anna 1956- 183
   Earlier sketch in SATA 112

Fiery, Ann
   See Barrows, Annie
Fife, Dale (Odile Hollerbach) 1901- 18
Fighter Pilot, A
   See Johnston, H(ugh) A(nthony) S(tephen)
Figler, Jeanie 1949- 123
Figley, Marty Rhodes 1948- 158
   Earlier sketch in SATA 88
Figueredo, D(anilo) H. 1951- 155
Figueroa, Pablo 1938- 9
Fijan, Carol 1918- 12
Filderman, Diane E(lizabeth) 1959- 87
Files, Meg 1946- 107
Fillmore, Parker H(oysted) 1878-1944
   See YABC 1
Filstrup, Chris
   See Filstrup, E(dward) Christian
Filstrup, E(dward) Christian 1942- 43
Filstrup, Janie
   See Merrill, Jane
Finchler, Judy 1943- 93
Finder, Martin
   See Salzmann, Siegmund
Findlay, Jamieson 1958- 169
Findon, Joanne 1957- 161
Fine, Anne 1947- 197
   Earlier sketches in SATA 29, 72, 111, 160
   See also CLR 25
   See also SAAS 15
Fine, Edith Hope 169
Fine, Howard 1961- 181
Fine, Jane
   See Ziefert, Harriet
Finger, Charles J(oseph) 1869(?)-1941 42
Fink, William B(ertrand) 1916- 22
Finke, Blythe Foote 1922- 26
Finkel, George (Irvine) 1909-1975 8
Finkelstein, Norman H. 1941- 137
   Earlier sketch in SATA 73
Finkelstein, Norman Henry
   See Finkelstein, Norman H.
Finlay, Alice Sullivan 1946- 82
Finlay, Winifred Lindsay Crawford
   (McKissack) 1910-1989 23
Finlayson, Ann 1925- 8
Finley, Martha 1828-1909 43
   See also CLR 148
Finley, Mary Peace 1942- 83
Finn, Mary 208
Finney, Jack 1911-1995 109
Finney, Patricia 1958- 163
Finney, Shan 1944- 65
Finney, Walter Braden
   See Finney, Jack
Firer, Ben Zion
   See Firer, Benzion
Firer, Benzion 1914- 64
Fireside, Bryna J. 1932- 73
Firmin, Charlotte 1954- 29
Firmin, Peter 1928- 58
   Earlier sketch in SATA 15
Firth, Barbara 179
Fischbach, Julius 1894-1988 10
Fischer, John
   See Fluke, Joanne
Fischer, R.J.
   See Fluke, Joanne
Fischer, Scott M. 1971- 195
Fischer-Nagel, Andreas 1951- 56
Fischer-Nagel, Heiderose 1956- 56
Fischler, Shirley (Walton) 66
Fischler, Stan(ley I.) 66
   Brief entry 36
Fischtrom, Harvey 1933-1974 3
Fishback, Margaret
   See Antolini, Margaret Fishback
Fishbone, Greg R. 195
Fisher, Aileen (Lucia) 1906-2002 73
   Obituary 143
   Earlier sketches in SATA 1, 25
   See also CLR 49

Fisher, Barbara 1940- *44*
  Brief entry *34*
Fisher, Carolyn 1968- *154*
Fisher, Catherine 1957- *155*
Fisher, Chris 1958- *80*
Fisher, Clavin C(argill) 1912- *24*
Fisher, Cynthia *195*
Fisher, Dorothy (Frances) Canfield 1879-1958
  See YABC *1*
  See also CLR *71*
Fisher, Gary L. 1949- *86*
Fisher, John 1909-1996 .... *15*
Fisher, John Oswald Hamilton
  See Fisher, John
Fisher, Laura Harrison 1934- *5*
Fisher, Leonard Everett 1924- *176*
  Autobiography Feature *122*
  Earlier sketches in SATA *4, 34, 73, 120*
  See also CLR *18*
  See also SAAS *1*
Fisher, Lois I. 1948- *38*
  Brief entry *35*
Fisher, Margery (Turner) 1913-1992 .... *20*
  Obituary *74*
Fisher, Marshall Jon 1963- *113*
Fisher, Nikki
  See Strachan, Ian
Fisher, Robert (Tempest) 1943- *47*
Fisher, Suzanne
  See Staples, Suzanne Fisher
Fisher, Valorie *177*
Fishman, Cathy Goldberg 1951- *106*
Fisk, Nicholas
  See Higginbottom, David
Fisk, Pauline 1948- *160*
  Earlier sketch in SATA *66*
Fiske, Tarleton
  See Bloch, Robert (Albert)
Fisscher, Catharina G. M. 1958- *142*
Fisscher, Tiny
  See Fisscher, Catharina G. M.
Fitch, Clarke
  See Sinclair, Upton
Fitch, John IV
  See Cormier, Robert
Fitch, Sheree 1956- *178*
  Earlier sketch in SATA *108*
Fitschen, Dale 1937- *20*
Fitzalan, Roger
  See Trevor, Elleston
Fitzgerald, Captain Hugh
  See Baum, L. Frank
FitzGerald, Cathleen 1932-1987
  Obituary *50*
Fitzgerald, Dawn *175*
Fitzgerald, Edward Earl 1919-2001 .... *20*
Fitzgerald, F(rancis) A(nthony) 1940- *15*
Fitzgerald, Joanne 1956- *198*
Fitzgerald, John D(ennis) 1907(?)-1988 ...... *20*
  Obituary *56*
  See also CLR *1*
Fitzgerald, Merni Ingrassia 1955- *53*
Fitzgibbon, Terry 1948- *121*
Fitzhardinge, Joan Margaret 1912- *73*
  Earlier sketch in SATA *2*
  See also CLR *5*
  See also SAAS *3*
Fitzhugh, Louise (Perkins) 1928-1974 .... *45*
  Obituary *24*
  Earlier sketch in SATA *1*
  See also CLR *72*
Fitzhugh, Percy Keese 1876-1950 .... *65*
Fitzpatrick, Marie-Louise 1962- *189*
  Earlier sketch in SATA *125*
FitzRalph, Matthew
  See McInerny, Ralph
Fitz-Randolph, Jane (Currens) 1915- *51*
Fitzsimons, Cecilia 1952- *97*
Fitzsimons, Cecilia A.L.
  See Fitzsimons, Cecilia

Flack, Marjorie 1897-1958 .... *100*
  See also YABC *2*
  See also CLR *28*
Flack, Naomi John White -1999 .... *40*
  Brief entry *35*
Flake, Sharon G. *166*
Flanagan, John 1944- *180*
Flanagan, John Anthony
  See Flanagan, John
Flannery, Kate
  See De Goldi, Kathleen Domenica
Flatt, Lizann 1966- *88*
Fleagle, Gail S(hatto) 1940- *117*
Fleetwood, Jenni 1947- *80*
Fleischer, Jane
  See Oppenheim, Joanne
Fleischhauer-Hardt, Helga 1936- *30*
Fleischman, Albert Sidney
  See Fleischman, Sid
Fleischman, John 1948- *145*
Fleischman, Paul 1952- *156*
  Brief entry *32*
  Earlier sketches in SATA *39, 72, 110*
  See also CLR *66*
  See also SAAS *20*
Fleischman, Sid 1920- *185*
  Earlier sketches in SATA *8, 59, 96, 148*
  See also CLR *15*
Fleischner, Jennifer 1956- *188*
  Earlier sketch in SATA *93*
Fleisher, Paul 1948- *132*
  Earlier sketch in SATA *81*
Fleisher, Robbin 1951-1977 .... *52*
  Brief entry *49*
Fleishman, Seymour 1918- *66*
  Brief entry *32*
Fleming, A. A.
  See Arthur, Robert, (Jr.)
Fleming, Alice Mulcahey 1928- *9*
Fleming, Candace 1962- *190*
  Earlier sketches in SATA *94, 143*
Fleming, Denise 1950- *173*
  Earlier sketches in SATA *81, 126*
Fleming, Elizabeth P. 1888-1985
  Obituary *48*
Fleming, Ian 1908-1964 .... *9*
Fleming, Ian Lancaster
  See Fleming, Ian
Fleming, Ronald Lee 1941- *56*
Fleming, Sally
  See Walker, Sally M(acArt)
Fleming, Stuart
  See Knight, Damon (Francis)
Fleming, Susan 1932- *32*
Fleming, Thomas 1927- *8*
Fleming, Thomas James
  See Fleming, Thomas
Fleming, Virginia (Edwards) 1923- *84*
Flesch, Y.
  See Flesch, Yolande (Catarina)
Flesch, Yolande (Catarina) 1950- *55*
Fletcher, Charlie May Hogue 1897-1977 ...... *3*
Fletcher, Colin 1922-2007 .... *28*
Fletcher, Dirk
  See Cunningham, Chet
Fletcher, George U.
  See Pratt, (Murray) Fletcher
Fletcher, Helen Jill 1910- *13*
Fletcher, Ralph 1953- *195*
  Earlier sketches in SATA *105, 149*
  See also CLR *104*
Fletcher, Ralph J.
  See Fletcher, Ralph
Fletcher, Richard E. 1917(?)-1983
  Obituary *34*
Fletcher, Rick
  See Fletcher, Richard E.
Fletcher, Susan 1951- *181*
  Earlier sketches in SATA *70, 110*
Fletcher, Susan Clemens
  See Fletcher, Susan

Fleur, Paul
  See Pohl, Frederik
Flexner, James Thomas 1908-2003 .... *9*
Flinn, Alex 1966- *198*
  Earlier sketch in SATA *159*
Flint, Helen 1952- *102*
Flint, Russ 1944- *74*
Flitner, David P(erkins), Jr. 1949- *7*
Floca, Brian *190*
  Earlier sketch in SATA *155*
Floethe, Louise Lee 1913-1988 .... *4*
Floethe, Richard 1901-1998 .... *4*
Floherty, John Joseph 1882-1964 .... *25*
Flood, Bo
  See Flood, Nancy Bo
Flood, Nancy Bo 1945- *130*
Flood, Pansie Hart 1964- *140*
Flood, William 1942- *129*
Flooglebuckle, Al
  See Spiegelman, Art
Flora, James (Royer) 1914-1998 .... *30*
  Obituary *103*
  Earlier sketch in SATA *1*
  See also SAAS *6*
Flores-Galbis, Enrique 1952- *186*
Florian, Douglas 1950- *177*
  Earlier sketches in SATA *19, 83, 125*
Flory, Jane Trescott 1917- *22*
Flournoy, Valerie 1952- *95*
Flournoy, Valerie Rose
  See Flournoy, Valerie
Flowerdew, Phyllis -1994 .... *33*
Flowers, Pam 1946- *136*
Flowers, Sarah 1952- *98*
Floyd, Gareth 1940- *62*
  Brief entry *31*
Fluchere, Henri 1914-1991 .... *40*
Fluke, Joanne 1943- *88*
Flutsztejn-Gruda, Ilona 1930- *170*
Flynn, Barbara 1928- *9*
Flynn, Jackson
  See Bensen, Donald R.
  and Shirreffs, Gordon D(onald)
Flynn, Nicholas
  See Odgers, Sally Farrell
Flynn, Rachel 1953- *171*
  Earlier sketch in SATA *109*
Flynn, Warren (G.) 1950- *154*
Fodor, R(onald) V(ictor) 1944- *25*
Fogelin, Adrian 1951- *175*
  Earlier sketch in SATA *129*
Foley, (Anna) Bernice Williams
  1902-1987 .... *28*
Foley, Greg E. 1969- *190*
Foley, June 1944- *44*
Foley, (Mary) Louise Munro 1933- *106*
  Brief entry *40*
  Earlier sketch in SATA *54*
Foley, Rae
  See Denniston, Elinore
Folke, Will
  See Bloch, Robert (Albert)
Follett, Helen Thomas 1884(?)-1970
  Obituary *27*
Folsom, Franklin (Brewster) 1907-1995 .... *5*
  Obituary *88*
Folsom, Michael (Brewster) 1938-1990 ...... *40*
  Obituary *88*
Fontenot, Mary Alice 1910-2003 .... *91*
  Obituary *209*
  Earlier sketch in SATA *34*
Fontes, Justine *172*
Fontes, Ron 1952- *183*
Foon, Dennis 1951- *119*
Fooner, Michael *22*
Foote, Timothy (Gilson) 1926- *52*
Forberg, Ati
  See Forberg, Beate Gropius
Forberg, Beate Gropius 1925- *22*
Forbes, Anna 1954- *101*
Forbes, Bryan 1926- *37*

Forbes, Cabot L.
  See Hoyt, Edwin P(almer), Jr.
Forbes, Esther 1891-1967 .... *100*
  Earlier sketch in SATA *2*
  See also CLR *147*
Forbes, Graham B. *1*
Forbes, Kathryn
  See McLean, Kathryn (Anderson)
Forbes, Robert
  See Arthur, Robert, (Jr.)
Ford, Albert Lee
  See Stratemeyer, Edward L.
Ford, Barbara *56*
  Brief entry *34*
Ford, Brian J(ohn) 1939- *49*
Ford, Carolyn (Mott) 1938- *98*
Ford, Christine 1953- *176*
Ford, David
  See Baldacci, David
  and Baldacci, David
Ford, David B.
  See Baldacci, David
Ford, David Baldacci
  See Baldacci, David
Ford, Elbur
  See Hibbert, Eleanor Alice Burford
Ford, Ellen 1949- *89*
Ford, George (Jr.) *31*
Ford, Hilary
  See Youd, Samuel
Ford, Hildegarde
  See Morrison, Velma Ford
Ford, Jerome W. 1949- *78*
Ford, Jerry
  See Ford, Jerome W.
Ford, Juwanda G(ertrude) 1967- *102*
Ford, Marcia
  See Radford, Ruby L(orraine)
Ford, Nancy K(effer) 1906-1961
  Obituary *29*
Ford, Peter 1936- *59*
Ford, S. M.
  See Uhlig, Susan
Forde, Catherine 1961- *170*
Foreman, Mark *199*
Foreman, Michael 1938- *184*
  Earlier sketches in SATA *2, 73, 129, 135*
  See also CLR *32*
  See also SAAS *21*
Foreman, Wilmoth 1939- *153*
Forest, Antonia 1915-2003 .... *29*
  Obituary *149*
Forest, Dial
  See Gault, William Campbell
Forest, Heather 1948- *185*
  Earlier sketch in SATA *120*
Forester, C. S. 1899-1966 .... *13*
Forester, Cecil Scott
  See Forester, C. S.
Forman, Brenda 1936- *4*
Forman, James
  See Forman, James D.
Forman, James D. 1932- *70*
  Earlier sketch in SATA *8*
Forman, James Douglas
  See Forman, James D.
Forman, Ruth 1970- *186*
Forrest, Elizabeth
  See Salsitz, Rhondi Vilott
Forrest, Mary
  See Pausacker, Jenny
Forrest, Sybil
  See Markun, Patricia Maloney
Forrestal, Elaine 1941- *165*
  Earlier sketch in SATA *117*
Forrester, Frank H. 1919(?)-1986
  Obituary *52*
Forrester, Helen
  See Bhatia, Jamunadevi
Forrester, Jade
  See Pausacker, Jenny

Forrester, Marian
  See Schachtel, Roger
Forrester, Sandra 1949- *166*
  Earlier sketch in SATA *90*
Forrester, Victoria 1940- *40*
  Brief entry *35*
Forsee, (Frances) Aylesa -1986 .... *1*
Forsey, Chris 1950- *59*
Forshay-Lunsford, Cin 1965- *60*
Forster, E. M. 1879-1970 .... *57*
Forster, Edward Morgan
  See Forster, E. M.
Forsyth, Kate 1966- *154*
Fort, Paul
  See Stockton, Francis Richard
Forte, Maurizio 1961- *110*
Fortey, Richard 1946- *109*
Fortey, Richard A.
  See Fortey, Richard
Fortey, Richard Alan
  See Fortey, Richard
Forth, Melissa D(eal) *96*
Fortnum, Peggy
  See Nuttall-Smith, Margaret Emily Noel
Fortune, Eric *182*
Forward, Robert L(ull) 1932-2002 .... *82*
Foster, Alan Dean 1946- *70*
Foster, Brad W. 1955- *34*
Foster, Doris Van Liew 1899-1993 .... *10*
Foster, E(lizabeth) C(onnell) 1902- *9*
Foster, Elizabeth 1902- *12*
Foster, Elizabeth 1905-1963 .... *10*
Foster, F. Blanche 1919- *11*
Foster, G(eorge) Allen 1907-1969 .... *26*
Foster, Genevieve (Stump) 1893-1979 .... *2*
  Obituary *23*
  See also CLR *7*
Foster, Gerald L. *198*
Foster, Hal
  See Foster, Harold
Foster, Harold 1892-1982 .... *31*
Foster, Jeanne
  See Williams, Jeanne
Foster, John
  See Foster, John L(ouis)
  and Furcolo, Foster
Foster, John (Thomas) 1925- *8*
Foster, John L(ouis) 1941- *102*
Foster, Juliana *196*
Foster, Laura Louise (James) 1918- *6*
Foster, Leila Merrell 1929- *73*
Foster, Lynne 1937- *74*
Foster, Margaret Lesser 1899(?)-1979
  Obituary *21*
Foster, Marian Curtis 1909-1978 .... *23*
Foster, Mark 1961- *197*
Foster, Sally *58*
Fotheringham, Edwin *201*
Foulds, E. V.
  See Foulds, Elfrida Vipont
Foulds, Elfrida Vipont 1902-1992 .... *52*
Fountas, Angela Jane *180*
Fourie, Corlia 1944- *91*
Fourth Brother, The
  See Aung, (Maung) Htin
Fowke, Edith (Margaret) 1913-1996 .... *14*
Fowles, John 1926-2005 .... *22*
  Obituary *171*
Fowles, John Robert
  See Fowles, John
Fowles, Shelley 1956- *205*
Fox, Aileen 1907-2005 .... *58*
  Obituary *170*
Fox, Aileen Mary
  See Fox, Aileen
Fox, Annie 1950- *175*
Fox, Charles Philip 1913-2003 .... *12*
  Obituary *150*
Fox, Christyan *188*
Fox, Diane *188*

Fox, Eleanor
  See St. John, Wylly Folk
Fox, Fontaine Talbot, Jr. 1884-1964
  Obituary *23*
Fox, Fred 1903(?)-1981
  Obituary *27*
Fox, Freeman
  See Hamilton, Charles (Harold St. John)
Fox, Geoffrey 1941- *73*
Fox, Grace
  See Anderson, Grace Fox
Fox, Helen 1962- *181*
Fox, Larry *30*
Fox, Lorraine 1922-1976 .... *27*
  Earlier sketch in SATA *11*
Fox, Louisa
  See Kroll, Virginia L.
Fox, Mary Virginia 1919- *152*
  Brief entry *39*
  Earlier sketches in SATA *44, 88*
Fox, Mem *211*
  See Fox, Merrion Frances
Fox, Merrion Frances 1946- *155*
  Earlier sketches in SATA *51, 103*
  See also CLR *80*
  See Fox, Mem
Fox, Michael W(ilson) 1937- *15*
Fox, Norma Diane
  See Mazer, Norma Fox
Fox, Paula 1923- *167*
  Earlier sketches in SATA *17, 60, 120*
  See also CLR *96*
Fox, Robert J. 1927- *33*
Fox-Davies, Sarah 1956- *199*
Foyt, Victoria .... *187.*
Fradin, Dennis
  See Fradin, Dennis Brindell
Fradin, Dennis Brindell 1945- *185*
  Earlier sketches in SATA *29, 90, 135*
Fradin, Judith Bloom 1945- *185*
  Earlier sketches in SATA *90, 152*
Frailey, Paige (Menefee) 1965- *82*
Frame, Janet 1924-2004 .... *119*
Frame, Paul 1913-1994 .... *60*
  Brief entry *33*
  Obituary *83*
Frances, Miss
  See Horwich, Frances R(appaport)
Franchere, Ruth *18*
Francis, Charles
  See Holme, Bryan
Francis, Dee
  See Haas, Dorothy F.
Francis, Dorothy 1926- *127*
  Earlier sketch in SATA *10*
Francis, Dorothy B.
  See Francis, Dorothy
Francis, Dorothy Brenner
  See Francis, Dorothy
Francis, Jaye
  See Pausacker, Jenny
Francis, Pamela (Mary) 1926- *11*
Franck, Eddie
  See Cooke, Frank E.
Franco, Betsy *188*
  Earlier sketch in SATA *150*
Franco, Eloise (Bauder) 1910- *62*
Franco, Johan (Henri Gustave) 1908-1988 . *62*
Franco, Marjorie *38*
Francois, Andre 1915-2005 .... *25*
Francoise
  See Seignobosc, Francoise
Frank, Anne 1929-1945 .... *87*
  Brief entry *42*
  See also CLR *101*
Frank, Annelies Marie
  See Frank, Anne
Frank, Daniel B. 1956- *55*
Frank, E. R. 1967- *157*
Frank, Emily R.
  See Frank, E. R.

Frank, Helene
  See Vautier, Ghislaine
Frank, Hillary 1976- 148
Frank, John 199
Frank, Josette 1893-1989 10
  Obituary 63
Frank, Lucy 1947- 166
  Earlier sketch in SATA 94
Frank, Mary 1933- 34
Frank, R., Jr.
  See Ross, Frank (Xavier), Jr.
Frankau, Mary Evelyn Atkinson 1899-1974 . 4
Frankel, Alona 1937- 66
Frankel, Bernice 9
Frankel, Edward 1910- 44
Frankel, Ellen 1951- 78
Frankel, Julie 1947- 40
  Brief entry 34
Frankenberg, Robert 1911- 22
Frankland, David 207
Franklin, Cheryl J. 1955- 70
Franklin, Harold 1926- 13
Franklin, Kristine L. 1958- 124
  Earlier sketch in SATA 80
Franklin, Lance
  See Lantz, Francess L(in)
Franklin, Madeleine
  See L'Engle, Madeleine
Franklin, Madeleine L'Engle
  See L'Engle, Madeleine
Franklin, Madeleine L'Engle Camp
  See L'Engle, Madeleine
Franklin, Max
  See Deming, Richard
Franklin, Steve
  See Stevens, Franklin
Franson, Leanne R. 1963- 111
Franson, Scott E. 1966- 192
Franzen, Nils-Olof 1916- 10
Frascino, Edward 48
  Brief entry 33
  See also SAAS 9
Frasconi, Antonio 1919- 131
  Earlier sketches in SATA 6, 53
  See also SAAS 11
Fraser, Betty
  See Fraser, Elizabeth Marr
Fraser, Elizabeth Marr 1928- 31
Fraser, Eric (George) 1902-1983 38
Fraser, Mary Ann 1959- 137
  Earlier sketch in SATA 76
  See also SAAS 23
Fraser, Wynnette (McFaddin) 1925- 90
Frasier, Debra 1953- 182
  Earlier sketches in SATA 69, 112
Fraustino, Lisa Rowe 1961- 146
  Autobiography Feature 146
  Earlier sketch in SATA 84
Frazee, Marla 1958- 187
  Earlier sketches in SATA 105, 151
Frazetta, Frank 1928- 58
Frazier, Craig 1955- 177
Frazier, Neta (Osborn) Lohnes 1890-1990 7
Frazier, Sundee T. 1968- 198
Frazier, Sundee Tucker
  See Frazier, Sundee T.
Frederic, Mike
  See Cox, William R(obert)
Frederick, Heather Vogel 207
Fredericks, Anthony D. 1947- 113
Freed, Alvyn M. 1913-1993 22
Freedman, Benedict 1919- 27
Freedman, Claire 185
Freedman, Deborah 1960- 191
Freedman, Jeff 1953- 90
Freedman, Nancy 1920- 27
Freedman, Russell 1929- 175
  Earlier sketches in SATA 16, 71, 123
  See also CLR 71
Freedman, Russell Bruce
  See Freedman, Russell

Freeman, Barbara C. 1906-1999 28
Freeman, Barbara Constance
  See Freeman, Barbara C.
Freeman, Bill
  See Freeman, William Bradford
Freeman, Don 1908-1978 17
  See also CLR 90
Freeman, Ira Maximilian 1905-1987 21
Freeman, Kimberley
  See Wilkins, Kim
Freeman, Laura 200
Freeman, Lucy (Greenbaum) 1916-2004 24
Freeman, Mae 1907-1985 25
Freeman, Mae Blacker
  See Freeman, Mae
Freeman, Marcia S. 1937- 102
Freeman, Martha 1956- 201
  Earlier sketches in SATA 101, 152
Freeman, Nancy 1932- 61
Freeman, Peter J.
  See Calvert, Patricia
Freeman, Sarah (Caroline) 1940- 66
Freeman, Tor 1977- 164
Freeman, VicToria
  See Freeman, Tor
Freeman, William Bradford 1938- 58
  Brief entry 48
Fregosi, Claudia (Anne Marie) 1946- 24
Freitas, Donna 1972- 205
French, Allen 1870-1946
  See YABC 1
French, Dorothy Kayser 1926- 5
French, Fiona 1944- 132
  Earlier sketches in SATA 6, 75
  See also CLR 37
  See also SAAS 21
French, Jackie 186
  Autobiography Feature 139
  Earlier sketches in SATA 108, 139
  See French, Jackie Anne
  and French, Jacqueline Anne
French, Kathryn
  See Mosesson, Gloria R(ubin)
French, Martin 176
French, Michael 1944- 49
  Brief entry 38
French, Paul
  See Asimov, Isaac
French, Simon 1957- 147
  Earlier sketch in SATA 86
French, Vivian 209
  Earlier sketch in SATA 165
Frenette, Liza 126
Freschet, Gina 1960- 175
  Earlier sketch in SATA 139
Frewer, Glyn (M.) 1931- 11
Frey, Darcy 98
Freymann, Saxton 1958(?)- 178
Freymann-Weyr, (Rhoda) Garret (Michaela)
  1965- 145
Frick, C. H.
  See Irwin, Constance (H.) Frick
Frick, Constance
  See Irwin, Constance (H.) Frick
Fricke, Aaron 1962- 89
Fridell, Ron 1943- 124
Fried, Janice 197
Friedlander, Joanne K(ohn) 1930- 9
Friedman, Aimee 1979- 189
Friedman, D. Dina 1957- 180
Friedman, Debra 1955- 150
Friedman, Estelle (Ehrenwald) 1920- 7
Friedman, Frieda 1905- 43
Friedman, Ina R(osen) 1926- 136
  Brief entry 41
  Earlier sketch in SATA 49
Friedman, Jerrold David
  See Gerrold, David
Friedman, Judi 1935- 59
Friedman, Laurie 1964- 179
  Earlier sketch in SATA 138

Friedman, Marvin 1930- 42
  Brief entry 33
Friedman, Robin 1968- 162
Friedmann, Stan 1953- 80
Friedrich, Otto (Alva) 1929-1995 33
Friedrich, Priscilla 1927- 39
Friend, Catherine 1957(?)- 194
Friend, David Michael 1975- 195
Friend, Natasha 1972- 184
Friendlich, Dick
  See Friendlich, Richard J.
Friendlich, Richard J. 1909- 11
Friermood, Elisabeth Hamilton 1903-1992 ... 5
Friesen, Bernice (Sarah Anne) 1966- 105
Friesen, Gayle 1960- 200
  Earlier sketch in SATA 109
Friesen, Jonathan 1967(?)- 206
Friesner, Esther 1951- 207
  Earlier sketches in SATA 71, 168
Friesner, Esther M.
  See Friesner, Esther
Friis-Baastad, Babbis Ellinor 1921-1970 7
Frimmer, Steven 1928- 31
Frischmuth, Barbara 1941- 114
Friskey, Margaret (Richards) 1901-1995 5
Fritts, Mary Bahr
  See Bahr, Mary (Madelyn)
Fritz, Jean (Guttery) 1915- 163
  Autobiography Feature 122
  Earlier sketches in SATA 1, 29, 72, 119
  See also CLR 96
  See also SAAS 2
Froehlich, Margaret W(alden) 1930- 56
Frois, Jeanne 1953- 73
Froissart, Jean 1338(?)-1410(?) 28
Froman, Elizabeth Hull 1920-1975 10
Froman, Robert (Winslow) 1917- 8
Fromm, Lilo 1928- 29
Frommer, Harvey 1937- 41
Frost, A(rthur) B(urdett) 1851-1928 19
Frost, Elizabeth
  See Frost-Knappman, Elizabeth
Frost, Erica
  See Supraner, Robyn
Frost, Helen 1949- 194
  Autobiography Feature 194
  Earlier sketches in SATA 157, 183
Frost, Helen Marie
  See Frost, Helen
Frost, Lesley 1899-1983 14
  Obituary 34
Frost, Robert 1874-1963 14
  See also CLR 67
Frost, Robert Lee
  See Frost, Robert
Frost, Shelley 1960- 138
Frost-Knappman, Elizabeth 1943- 179
Froud, Brian 1947- 150
Fry, Annette R(iley) 89
Fry, Christopher 1907-2005 66
Fry, Edward Bernard 1925- 35
Fry, Rosalie Kingsmill 1911-1992 3
  See also SAAS 11
Fry, Virginia Lynn 1952- 95
Frye, Sally
  See Moore, Elaine
Fuchs, Bernie 1932- 162
  Earlier sketch in SATA 95
Fuchs, Erich 1916- 6
Fuchshuber, Annegert 1940- 43
Fuerst, Jeffrey B. 1956- 143
Fuertes, Gloria 1918-1998 115
Fuge, Charles 1966- 144
  Earlier sketch in SATA 74
Fujikawa, Gyo 1908-1998 76
  Brief entry 30
  Obituary 110
  Earlier sketch in SATA 39
  See also CLR 25
  See also SAAS 16
Fujita, Tamao 1905-1999 7

Fujiwara, Kim 1957- *81*
Fujiwara, Michiko 1946- *15*
Fuka, Vladimir 1926-1977
  Obituary *27*
Fulcher, Jennifer
  See Westwood, Jennifer
Fuller, Catherine Leuthold 1916- *9*
Fuller, Edmund (Maybank) 1914- *21*
Fuller, Iola
  See McCoy, Iola Fuller
Fuller, John G(rant, Jr.) 1913-1990 .... *65*
Fuller, Kathleen
  See Gottfried, Theodore Mark
Fuller, Lois Hamilton 1915- *11*
Fuller, Margaret 1810-1850 .... *25*
Fuller, Maud
  See Petersham, Maud
Fuller, Roy (Broadbent) 1912-1991 .... *87*
Fuller, Sarah Margaret
  See Fuller, Margaret
Fults, John Lee 1932- *33*
Funk, Thompson 1911- *7*
Funk, Tom
  See Funk, Thompson
Funke, Cornelia 1958- *209*
  Earlier sketches in SATA *154, 174*
  See also CLR *145*
Funke, Cornelia Caroline
  See Funke, Cornelia
Funke, Lewis 1912-1992 .... *11*
Fuqua, Jonathon Scott 1966- *141*
Furbee, Mary R.
  See Furbee, Mary Rodd
Furbee, Mary Rodd 1954- *138*
Furchgott, Terry 1948- *29*
Furlong, Monica (Mavis) 1930-2003 .... *86*
  Obituary *142*
Furman, Gertrude Lerner Kerman 1909- *21*
Furniss, Tim 1948- *49*
Furrow, Robert 1985- *172*
Furukawa, Toshi 1924- *24*
Fusillo, Archimede 1962- *137*
Futcher, Jane P. 1947- *76*
Futehali, Zahida
  See Whitaker, Zai
Fyleman, Rose (Amy) 1877-1957 .... *21*
Fyson, Jenny Grace
  See Fyson, J.G.
Fyson, J.G. 1904-1998 .... *42*

G

Gaan, Margaret 1914- *65*
Gaber, Susan 1956- *169*
  Earlier sketch in SATA *115*
Gaberman, Judie Angell
  See Angell, Judie
Gabhart, Ann
  See Gabhart, Ann H.
Gabhart, Ann H. 1947- *75*
Gable, Brian 1949- *195*
Gabler, Mirko 1951- *77*
Gabriel, Adriana
  See Rojany, Lisa
Gabrys, Ingrid Schubert
  See Schubert-Gabrys, Ingrid
Gackenbach, Dick 1927- *79*
  Brief entry *30*
  Earlier sketch in SATA *48*
Gadd, Jeremy 1949- *116*
Gaddis, Vincent H. 1913-1997 .... *35*
Gadler, Steve J. 1905-1985 .... *36*
Gaeddert, Lou Ann (Bigge) 1931- *103*
  Earlier sketch in SATA *20*
Gaeddert, Louann
  See Gaeddert, Lou Ann (Bigge)
Gaer, Joseph 1897-1969 .... *118*
Gaer, Yossef
  See Gaer, Joseph

Gaetz, Dayle Campbell 1947- *138*
Gaffney, Timothy R. 1951- *170*
  Earlier sketch in SATA *69*
Gaffron, Norma (Bondeson) 1931- *97*
Gag, Flavia 1907-1979
  Obituary *24*
Gag, Wanda (Hazel) 1893-1946 .... *100*
  See also YABC *1*
  See also CLR *150*
Gage, Brian *162*
Gage, Wilson
  See Steele, Mary Q(uintard Govan)
Gagliano, Eugene M. 1946- *150*
Gagliardo, Ruth Garver 1895(?)-1980
  Obituary *22*
Gagnon, Cecile 1936- *58*
Gaillard, Jason 1965- *200*
Gaiman, Neil 1960- *197*
  Earlier sketches in SATA *85, 146*
  See also CLR *109*
Gaiman, Neil Richard
  See Gaiman, Neil
Gainer, Cindy 1962- *74*
Gaines, Ernest J. 1933- *86*
  See also CLR *62*
Gaines, Ernest James
  See Gaines, Ernest J.
Gaither, Gloria 1942- *127*
Gal, Laszlo 1933- *96*
  Brief entry *32*
  Earlier sketch in SATA *52*
  See also CLR *61*
Galbraith, Ben 1980- *200*
Galbraith, Kathryn O(sebold) 1945- *85*
Galdone, Paul 1907(?)-1986 .... *66*
  Obituary *49*
  Earlier sketch in SATA *17*
  See also CLR *16*
Galindo, Claudia 1979- *203*
Galinsky, Ellen 1942- *23*
Gall, Chris 1961- *176*
Gallagher, Diana G. 1946- *153*
Gallagher, Lurlene Nora
  See McDaniel, Lurlene
Gallagher-Cole, Mernie 1958- *206*
Gallant, Roy A(rthur) 1924- *110*
  Earlier sketches in SATA *4, 68*
  See also CLR *30*
Gallardo, Evelyn 1948- *78*
Gallaz, Christophe 1948- *162*
  See also CLR *126*
Gallego Garcia, Laura 1977- *173*
Gallico, Paul (William) 1897-1976 .... *13*
Gallo, Donald R. 1938- *112*
  Autobiography Feature *104*
Gallo, Donald Robert
  See Gallo, Donald R.
Galloway, Owateka (S.) 1981- *121*
Galloway, Priscilla 1930- *112*
  Earlier sketch in SATA *66*
Gallup, Joan 1957- *128*
Galouchko, Annouchka Gravel 1960- *95*
Galt, Thomas Franklin, Jr. 1908-1989 .... *5*
Galt, Tom
  See Galt, Thomas Franklin, Jr.
Galvin, Matthew R. 1950- *93*
Galvin, Matthew Reppert
  See Galvin, Matthew R.
Gamble, Kim 1952- *183*
  Earlier sketches in SATA *81, 124*
Gambrell, Jamey *82*
Gamerman, Martha 1941- *15*
Gammell, Stephen 1943- *128*
  Earlier sketches in SATA *53, 81*
  See also CLR *83*
Ganly, Helen (Mary) 1940- *56*
Gannett, Ruth Chrisman (Arens)
  1896-1979 .... *33*
Gannett, Ruth Stiles 1923- *3*
Gannij, Joan *208*

Gannij, Joan Levine
  See Gannij, Joan
Gannon, Ned 1974- *205*
Gannon, Robert Haines 1931- *8*
Gano, Lila 1949- *76*
Gans, Roma 1894-1996 .... *45*
  Obituary *93*
Gant, Matthew
  See Hano, Arnold
Gantner, Susan (Verble) 1939- *63*
Gantos, Jack 1951- *169*
  Earlier sketches in SATA *20, 81, 119*
  See also CLR *85*
Gantos, John Bryan, Jr.
  See Gantos, Jack
Ganz, Yaffa 1938- *61*
  Brief entry *52*
Garafano, Marie 1942- *84*
Garant, Andre J. 1968- *123*
Garbe, Ruth Moore
  See Moore, Ruth (Ellen)
Garber, Esther
  See Lee, Tanith
Garcia, Cristina 1958- *208*
Garcia, Emma 1969- *198*
Garcia, Yolanda P. 1952- *113*
Garcia, Yolanda Pacheco
  See Garcia, Yolanda P.
Gard, Janice
  See Latham, Jean Lee
Gard, Joyce
  See Reeves, Joyce
Gard, Robert Edward 1910-1992 .... *18*
  Obituary *74*
Gard, (Sanford) Wayne 1899-1986
  Obituary *49*
Gardam, Jane 1928- *130*
  Brief entry *28*
  Earlier sketches in SATA *39, 76*
  See also CLR *12*
  See also SAAS *9*
Gardam, Jane Mary
  See Gardam, Jane
Gardella, Tricia 1944- *96*
Garden, Nancy 1938- *147*
  Autobiography Feature *147*
  Earlier sketches in SATA *12, 77, 114*
  See also CLR *51*
  See also SAAS *8*
Gardiner, John Reynolds 1944-2006 .... *64*
  Obituary *174*
Gardiner, Lindsey 1971- *144*
Gardner, Craig Shaw 1949- *99*
Gardner, Dic
  See Gardner, Richard (M.)
Gardner, Graham *159*
Gardner, Hugh 1910-1986
  Obituary *49*
Gardner, Jane Mylum 1946- *83*
Gardner, Jeanne LeMonnier 1925- *5*
Gardner, John, Jr. 1933-1982 .... *40*
  Obituary *31*
Gardner, John Champlin, Jr.
  See Gardner, John, Jr.
Gardner, John E(dward) 1917- *192*
Gardner, Lyn *192*
Gardner, Martin 1914- *142*
  Earlier sketch in SATA *16*
Gardner, Miriam
  See Bradley, Marion Zimmer
Gardner, Richard (M.) 1931- *24*
Gardner, Richard A(lan) 1931-2003 .... *13*
  Obituary *144*
Gardner, Sally *177*
Gardner, Sandra 1940- *70*
Gardner, Scot 1968- *143*
Gardner, Sheldon 1934- *33*
Gardner, Ted
  See Gardner, Theodore Roosevelt II
Gardner, Theodore Roosevelt
  See Gardner, Theodore Roosevelt II

Gardner, Theodore Roosevelt II 1934- 84
Garelick, May 1910-1989 19
Garfield, James B. 1881-1984 6
    Obituary 38
Garfield, Leon 1921-1996 76
    Obituary 90
    Earlier sketches in SATA 1, 32
    See also CLR 21
Garfinkle, Debra L.
    See Garfinkle, D.L.
Garfinkle, D.L. 187
Garis, Howard R. 1873-1962 13
Garis, Howard Roger
    See Garis, Howard R.
Garland, Mark 1953- 79
Garland, Mark A.
    See Garland, Mark
Garland, Michael 1952- 208
    Earlier sketch in SATA 168
Garland, Sarah 1944- 135
    Earlier sketch in SATA 62
Garland, Sherry 1948- 145
    Autobiography Feature 145
    Earlier sketches in SATA 73, 114
Garner, Alan 1934- 69
    Autobiography Feature 108
    Earlier sketch in SATA 18
    See also CLR 130
Garner, David 1958- 78
Garner, Eleanor Ramrath 1930- 122
Garner, James Finn 1960(?)- 92
Garnet, A. H.
    See Slote, Alfred
Garnett, Eve C. R. 1900-1991 3
    Obituary 70
Garofoli, Viviana 1970- 186
Garou, Louis P.
    See Bowkett, Stephen
Garraty, John A. 1920-2007 23
    Obituary 189
Garraty, John Arthur
    See Garraty, John A.
Garren, Devorah-Leah
    See Devorah-Leah
Garret, Maxwell R. 1917- 39
Garretson, Victoria Diane 1945- 44
Garrett, Helen 1895- 21
Garrett, Randall 1927-1987 180
Garrett, Richard 1920- 82
Garrigue, Sheila 1931- 21
Garrison, Barbara 1931- 163
    Earlier sketch in SATA 19
Garrison, Frederick
    See Sinclair, Upton
Garrison, Mary 1952- 146
Garrison, Peter
    See Gardner, Craig Shaw
Garrison, Webb B(lack) 1919-2000 25
Garrity, Jennifer Johnson 1961- 124
Garrity, Linda K. 1947- 128
Garsee, Jeannine 199
Garst, Doris Shannon 1894-1981 1
Garst, Shannon
    See Garst, Doris Shannon
Garth, Will
    See Hamilton, Edmond
    and Kuttner, Henry
Garthwaite, Marion H(ook) 1893-1981 7
Garton, Malinda D(ean) (?)-1976
    Obituary 26
Garvie, Maureen 1944- 175
Garvie, Maureen McCallum
    See Garvie, Maureen
Garza, Carmen Lomas 1948- 182
Garza, Xavier 184
Gascoigne, Bamber 1935- 62
Gaskins, Pearl Fuyo 1957- 134
Gasperini, Jim 1952- 54
    Brief entry 49
Gater, Dilys 1944- 41

Gates, Doris 1901-1987 34
    Obituary 54
    Earlier sketch in SATA 1
    See also SAAS 1
Gates, Frieda 1933- 26
Gates, Susan 1950- 153
Gates, Viola R. 1931- 101
Gathorne-Hardy, Jonathan G. 1933- 124
    Earlier sketch in SATA 26
Gatti, Anne 1952- 103
Gatty, Juliana Horatia
    See Ewing, Juliana (Horatia Gatty)
Gauch, Patricia Lee 1934- 80
    Earlier sketch in SATA 26
    See also CLR 56
    See also SAAS 21
Gaudasinska, Elzbieta 1943- 190
Gaul, Randy 1959- 63
Gault, Clare 1925- 36
Gault, Frank 1926-1982 36
    Brief entry 30
Gault, William Campbell 1910-1995 8
Gauthier, Gail 1953- 203
    Earlier sketches in SATA 118, 160
Gaver, Becky
    See Gaver, Rebecca
Gaver, Rebecca 1952- 20
Gavin, Jamila 1941- 125
    Earlier sketch in SATA 96
Gay, Amelia
    See Hogarth, Grace (Weston Allen)
Gay, Francis
    See Gee, H(erbert) L(eslie)
Gay, Kathlyn 1930- 144
    Earlier sketch in SATA 9
Gay, Marie-Louise 1952- 179
    Earlier sketches in SATA 68, 126
    See also CLR 27
    See also SAAS 21
Gay, Michel 1947- 162
Gay, Zhenya 1906-1978 19
Gaze, Gillian
    See Barklem, Jill
Gear, Kathleen M. O'Neal
    See Gear, Kathleen O'Neal
Gear, Kathleen O'Neal 1954- 166
    Earlier sketch in SATA 71
Gear, W. Michael 1955- 166
    Earlier sketch in SATA 71
Geary, Rick 1946- 142
Geason, Susan 1946- 122
Gedalof, Robin
    See McGrath, Robin
Gedge, Pauline (Alice) 1945- 101
Gee, H(erbert) L(eslie) 1901-1977
    Obituary 26
Gee, Maurice 1931- 101
    Earlier sketch in SATA 46
    See also CLR 56
Gee, Maurice Gough
    See Gee, Maurice
Geehan, Wayne (E.) 1947- 107
Geer, Charles 1922- 42
    Brief entry 32
Geeslin, Campbell 1925- 163
    Earlier sketch in SATA 107
Gehman, Mary W. 1923- 86
Gehr, Mary 1910(?)-1997 32
    Obituary 99
Geipel, Eileen 1932- 30
Geis, Alissa Imre 1976- 189
Geis, Darlene Stern 1918(?)-1999 7
    Obituary 111
Geisel, Helen 1898-1967 26
Geisel, Theodor Seuss
    See Dr. Seuss
Geisert, Arthur 1941- 171
    Brief entry 52
    Earlier sketches in SATA 56, 92, 133
    See also CLR 87
    See also SAAS 23

Geisert, Arthur Frederick
    See Geisert, Arthur
Geisert, Bonnie 1942- 165
    Earlier sketch in SATA 92
Geist, Ken 191
Gelber, Lisa 210
Geldart, William 1936- 15
Gelinas, Paul J. 1904-1996 10
Gellis, Roberta 1927- 128
Gellis, Roberta Leah Jacobs
    See Gellis, Roberta
Gellman, Marc 112
Gelman, Amy 1961- 72
Gelman, Jan 1963- 58
Gelman, Rita Golden 1937- 131
    Brief entry 51
    Earlier sketch in SATA 84
Gelman, Steve 1934- 3
Gemming, Elizabeth 1932- 11
Gendel, Evelyn W. 1916(?)-1977
    Obituary 27
Gennaro, Joseph F(rancis), Jr. 1924- 53
Gentieu, Penny 204
Gentile, Petrina 1969- 91
Gentle, Mary 1956- 48
Gentleman, David (William) 1930- 7
Geoghegan, Adrienne 1962- 143
George, Barbara
    See Katz, Bobbi
George, Emily
    See Katz, Bobbi
George, Gail
    See Katz, Bobbi
George, Jean
    See George, Jean Craighead
George, Jean C.
    See George, Jean Craighead
George, Jean Craighead 1919- 170
    Earlier sketches in SATA 2, 68, 124
    See also CLR 136
George, Jessica Day 1976- 210
George, John L(othar) 1916- 2
George, Kristine O'Connell 1954- 156
    Earlier sketch in SATA 110
George, Lindsay Barrett 1952- 206
    Earlier sketches in SATA 95, 155
George, S(idney) C(harles) 1898- 11
George, Sally
    See Orr, Wendy
George, Twig C. 1950- 114
George, W(illiam) Lloyd 1900(?)-1975
    Obituary 30
Georgiou, Constantine 1927- 7
Georgiou, Theo
    See Odgers, Sally Farrell
Geraghty, Paul 1959- 130
Gerard, Jean Ignace Isidore 1803-1847 45
Geras, Adele 1944- 180
    Autobiography Feature 180
    Earlier sketches in SATA 23, 87, 129, 173
    See also SAAS 21
Geras, Adele Daphne Weston
    See Geras, Adele
Gerber, Carole 1947- 207
Gerber, Merrill Joan 1938- 170
    Autobiography Feature 170
    Earlier sketches in SATA 64, 127
Gerber, Perren 1933- 104
Gerberg, Mort 1931- 64
Gergely, Tibor 1900-1978 54
    Obituary 20
Geringer, Laura 1948- 164
    Earlier sketches in SATA 29, 94
Gerler, William R(obert) 1917-1996 47
Gerrard, Jean 1933- 51
Gerrard, Roy 1935-1997 90
    Brief entry 45
    Obituary 99
    Earlier sketch in SATA 47
    See also CLR 23
Gerritsen, Paula 1956- 177

Gerrold, David 1944- *144*
  Earlier sketch in SATA *66*
Gershator, David 1937- *180*
Gershator, Phillis 1942- *188*
  Earlier sketches in SATA *90, 158*
Gershon, Dann 1955- *187*
Gershon, Gina 1962- *187*
Gerson, Corinne 1927- *37*
Gerson, Mary-Joan *136*
  Earlier sketch in SATA *79*
Gerson, Noel Bertram 1914-1988 .... *22*
  Obituary *60*
Gerstein, Mordicai 1935- *178*
  Brief entry *36*
  Earlier sketches in SATA *47, 81, 142*
  See also CLR *102*
Gertridge, Allison 1967- *132*
Gervais, Bernadette 1959- *80*
Gervay, Susanne *183*
Gesner, Clark 1938-2002 .... *40*
  Obituary *143*
Gessner, Lynne 1919- *16*
Geter, Tyrone *150*
Getz, David 1957- *91*
Getzinger, Donna 1968- *128*
Geus, Mireille 1964- *207*
Gevirtz, Eliezer 1950- *49*
Gevry, Claudine *188*
Gewe, Raddory
  See Gorey, Edward (St. John)
Ghan, Linda (R.) 1947- *77*
Ghent, Natale 1962- *148*
Gherman, Beverly 1934- *123*
  Earlier sketch in SATA *68*
Ghigna, Charles 1946- *153*
  Earlier sketch in SATA *108*
Giacobbe, Beppe 1953- *174*
Giambastiani, Kurt R. A. 1958- *141*
Giannini, Enzo 1946- *68*
Gibala-Broxholm, Scott 1959(?)- *205*
Gibbons, Alan 1953- *198*
  Earlier sketch in SATA *124*
Gibbons, Faye 1938- *103*
  Earlier sketch in SATA *65*
Gibbons, Gail 1944- *201*
  Earlier sketches in SATA *23, 72, 104, 160*
  See also CLR *8*
  See also SAAS *12*
Gibbons, Gail Gretchen
  See Gibbons, Gail
Gibbons, Kaye 1960- *117*
Gibbs, Adrea 1960- *126*
Gibbs, Alonzo (Lawrence) 1915-1992 .... *5*
Gibbs, (Cecilia) May 1877-1969
  Obituary *27*
Gibbs, Tony
  See Gibbs, Wolcott, Jr.
Gibbs, Wolcott, Jr. 1935- *40*
Giblin, James Cross 1933- *197*
  Earlier sketches in SATA *33, 75, 122*
  See also CLR *29*
  See also SAAS *12*
Gibson, Andrew (William) 1949- *72*
Gibson, Barbara L. *205*
Gibson, Barbara Leonard
  See Gibson, Barbara L.
Gibson, Betty 1911- *75*
Gibson, Jo
  See Fluke, Joanne
Gibson, Josephine
  See Hine, Sesyle Joslin
  and Hine, Al(fred Blakelee)
Gibson, Sarah P. 1962- *211*
Gibson, William 1914-2008 .... *66*
  Obituary *199*
Gibson, William Ford
  See Gibson, William
Gidal, Nachum
  See Gidal, Tim Nachum
Gidal, Sonia (Epstein) 1922- *2*
Gidal, Tim Nachum 1909-1996 .... *2*

Gidalewitsch, Nachum
  See Gidal, Tim Nachum
Gideon, Melanie 1963- *175*
Giegling, John A(llan) 1935- *17*
Gifaldi, David 1950- *209*
  Earlier sketch in SATA *76*
Giff, Patricia Reilly 1935- *203*
  Earlier sketches in SATA *33, 70, 121, 160*
Giffard, Hannah 1962- *83*
Gifford, Clive 1966- *198*
Gifford, Griselda 1931- *171*
  Earlier sketch in SATA *42*
Gifford, Kerri 1961- *91*
Gifford, Peggy 1952- *191*
Gilbert, Ann
  See Taylor, Ann
Gilbert, Anne Yvonne 1951- *185*
Gilbert, Barbara Snow 1954- *97*
Gilbert, Catherine
  See Murdock, Catherine Gilbert
Gilbert, Frances
  See Collings, Gillian
Gilbert, Harriett 1948- *30*
Gilbert, (Agnes) Joan (Sewell) 1931- *10*
Gilbert, John (Raphael) 1926- *36*
Gilbert, Nan
  See Gilbertson, Mildred Geiger
Gilbert, Roby Goodale 1966- *90*
Gilbert, Ruth Gallard Ainsworth
  See Ainsworth, Ruth (Gallard)
Gilbert, Sara (Dulaney) 1943- *82*
  Earlier sketch in SATA *11*
Gilbert, Sheri L. *157*
Gilbert, Suzie 1956- *97*
Gilbert, W(illiam) S(chwenck) 1836-1911 .. *36*
Gilbert, Yvonne
  See Gilbert, Anne Yvonne
Gilbertson, Mildred Geiger 1908-1988 .... *2*
Gilbreath, Alice 1921- *12*
Gilbreth, Frank B., Jr. 1911-2001 .... *2*
Gilbreth, Frank Bunker
  See Gilbreth, Frank B., Jr.
Gilchrist, Jan Spivey 1949- *130*
  Earlier sketch in SATA *72*
Gilden, Mel 1947- *97*
Giles, Gail *196*
  Earlier sketch in SATA *152*
Gilfond, Henry *2*
Gilge, Jeanette 1924- *22*
Gili, Phillida 1944- *70*
Gill, Derek (Lewis Theodore) 1919-1997 ..... *9*
Gill, Margery Jean 1925- *22*
Gill, Shelley *176*
Gill, Stephen 1932- *63*
Gillespie, Carol Ann 1951- *158*
Gillett, Mary (Bledsoe) *7*
Gillette, Henry Sampson 1915- *14*
Gillette, J(an) Lynett 1946- *103*
Gilley, Jeremy 1969- *174*
Gillham, Bill
  See Gillham, W(illiam) E(dwin) C(harles)
Gillham, W(illiam) E(dwin)
  C(harles) 1936- *42*
Gilliam, Stan 1946- *39*
  Brief entry *35*
Gilliland, Alexis A(rnaldus) 1931- *72*
Gilliland, (Cleburne) Hap 1918- *92*
Gilliland, Judith Heide *180*
Gillmor, Don 1954- *127*
Gilman, Dorothy 1923- *5*
Gilman, Esther 1925- *15*
Gilman, Laura Anne *178*
Gilman, Phoebe 1940-2002 .... *104*
  Obituary *141*
  Earlier sketch in SATA *58*
Gilmore, Iris 1900-1982 .... *22*
Gilmore, Kate 1931- *87*
Gilmore, Mary (Jean Cameron) 1865-1962
  .... *49*
Gilmore, Rachna 1953- *209*
Gilmore, Susan 1954- *59*

Gilpin, Stephen *177*
Gilroy, Beryl (Agatha) 1924- *80*
Gilson, Barbara
  See Gilson, Charles James Louis
Gilson, Charles James Louis 1878-1943
  See YABC *2*
Gilson, Jamie 1933- *176*
  Brief entry *34*
  Earlier sketches in SATA *37, 91*
Gimpel, Carolyn
  See Hart, Carolyn
Ginsburg, Mirra 1909-2000 .... *92*
  Earlier sketch in SATA *6*
  See also CLR *45*
Giovanni, Nikki 1943- *208*
  Earlier sketches in SATA *24, 107*
  See also CLR *73*
Giovanni, Yolanda Cornelia
  See Giovanni, Nikki
Giovanni, Yolande Cornelia
  See Giovanni, Nikki
Giovanni, Yolande Cornelia, Jr.
  See Giovanni, Nikki
Giovanopoulos, Paul (Arthur) 1939- *7*
Gipson, Billie
  See Letts, Billie
Gipson, Fred(erick Benjamin) 1908-1973 ..... *2*
  Obituary *24*
Girard, Linda (Walvoord) 1942- *41*
Girion, Barbara 1937- *78*
  Earlier sketch in SATA *26*
  See also SAAS *14*
Girl, Nerdy
  See Castellucci, Cecil
Girouard, Patrick 1957- *155*
Girzone, Joseph F. 1930- *76*
Girzone, Joseph Francis
  See Girzone, Joseph F.
Gise, Joanne
  See Mattern, Joanne
Gist, E.M. *206*
Gittings, Jo (Grenville) Manton 1919- *3*
Gittings, Robert (William Victor)
  1911-1992 .... *6*
  Obituary *70*
Givens, Janet E(aton) 1932- *60*
Givner, Joan 1936- *171*
Givner, Joan Mary
  See Givner, Joan
Gladstone, Eve
  See Werner, Herma
Gladstone, Gary 1935- *12*
Gladstone, M(yron) J. 1923- *37*
Glanville, Brian (Lester) 1931- *42*
Glanzman, Louis S. 1922- *36*
Glaser, Byron 1954- *154*
Glaser, Dianne E(lizabeth) 1937- *50*
  Brief entry *31*
Glaser, Isabel Joshlin 1929- *94*
Glaser, Milton 1929- *151*
  Earlier sketch in SATA *11*
Glaser, Shirley *151*
Glaspell, Susan 1882(?)-1948
  See YABC *2*
Glass, Andrew 1949- *150*
  Brief entry *46*
  Earlier sketch in SATA *90*
Glass, Linzi *175*
Glass, Linzi Alex
  See Glass, Linzi
Glasscock, Amnesia
  See Steinbeck, John
Glassman, Bruce 1961- *76*
Glauber, Uta (Heil) 1936- *17*
Glazer, Thomas (Zachariah) 1914-2003 .... *9*
Glazer, Tom
  See Glazer, Thomas (Zachariah)
Gleasner, Diana (Cottle) 1936- *29*
Gleason, Judith 1929- *24*
Gleason, Katherine (A.) 1960- *104*

Gleeson, Libby 1950- *142*
   Autobiography Feature *142*
   Earlier sketches in SATA *82, 118*
Gleiter, Jan 1947- *111*
Gleitzman, Morris 1953- *156*
   Earlier sketch in SATA *88*
   See also CLR *88*
Glen, Maggie 1944- *88*
Glendinning, Richard 1917-1988 .... *24*
Glendinning, Sally
   See Glendinning, Sara W(ilson)
Glendinning, Sara W(ilson) 1913-1993 .... *24*
Glenn, John W. *195*
Glenn, Mel 1943- *93*
   Brief entry *45*
   Earlier sketch in SATA *51*
   See also CLR *51*
Glenn, Patricia Brown 1953- *86*
Glenn, Sharlee *159*
Glenn, Sharlee Mullins
   See Glenn, Sharlee
Glennon, Karen M. 1946- *85*
Gles, Margaret Breitmaier 1940- *22*
Glick, Carl (Cannon) 1890-1971 .... *14*
Glick, Ruth (Burtnick) 1942- *125*
Glick, Virginia Kirkus 1893-1980
   Obituary *23*
Gliewe, Unada (Grace) 1927- *3*
Glimmerveen, Ulco 1958- *85*
Glines, Carroll V(ane), Jr. 1920- *19*
Gliori, Debi 1959- *189*
   Earlier sketches in SATA *72, 138*
Globe, Leah Ain 1900- *41*
Glori Ann
   See Blakely, Gloria
Glovach, Linda 1947- *105*
   Earlier sketch in SATA *7*
Glover, Denis (James Matthews)
   1912-1980 .... *7*
Glubok, Shirley (Astor) *146*
   Autobiography Feature *146*
   Earlier sketches in SATA *6, 68*
   See also CLR *1*
   See also SAAS *7*
Gluck, Felix 1923-1981
   Obituary *25*
Glyman, Caroline A. 1967- *103*
Glynne-Jones, William 1907-1977 .... *11*
Gobbato, Imero 1923- *39*
Gobbletree, Richard
   See Quackenbush, Robert M(ead)
Goble, Dorothy *26*
Goble, Paul 1933- *131*
   Earlier sketches in SATA *25, 69*
   See also CLR *21*
Goble, Warwick (?)-1943 .... *46*
Godden, (Margaret) Rumer 1907-1998 .... *36*
   Obituary *109*
   Earlier sketch in SATA *3*
   See also CLR *20*
   See also SAAS *12*
Gode, Alexander
   See Gode von Aesch, Alexander (Gottfried
   Friedrich)
Gode von Aesch, Alexander (Gottfried
   Friedrich) 1906-1970 .... *14*
Godfrey, Jane
   See Bowden, Joan Chase
Godfrey, Martyn
   See Godfrey, Martyn N.
   and Godfrey, Martyn N.
Godfrey, Martyn N. 1949-2000 .... *95*
   See also CLR *57*
Godfrey, William
   See Youd, Samuel
Godkin, Celia (Marilyn) 1948- *145*
   Earlier sketch in SATA *66*
Godon, Ingrid 1958- *186*
Godwin, Laura 1956- *179*
Godwin, Sam
   See Pirotta, Saviour

Goede, Irene 1966- *208*
Goedecke, Christopher (John) 1951- *81*
Goekler, Susan
   See Wooley, Susan Frelick
Goembel, Ponder *204*
Goertzen, Glenda *172*
Goettel, Elinor 1930- *12*
Goetz, Delia 1898-1996 .... *22*
   Obituary *91*
Goffe, Toni 1936- *61*
Goffstein, Brooke
   See Goffstein, M(arilyn) B(rooke)
Goffstein, M(arilyn) B(rooke) 1940- *70*
   Earlier sketch in SATA *8*
   See also CLR *3*
Goforth, Ellen
   See Francis, Dorothy
Gogol, Sara 1948-2004 .... *80*
Goh, Chan Hon 1969- *145*
Going, Kelly L.
   See Going, K.L.
Going, Kelly Louise
   See Going, K.L.
Going, K.L. *199*
   Earlier sketch in SATA *156*
Golann, Cecil Paige 1921-1995 .... *11*
Golbin, Andree 1923- *15*
Gold, Alison Leslie 1945- *104*
Gold, Bernice *150*
Gold, Phyllis
   See Goldberg, Phyllis
Gold, Robert S(tanley) 1924- *63*
Gold, Sharlya *9*
Gold, Susan
   See Gold, Susan Dudley
Gold, Susan Dudley 1949- *147*
Goldberg, Grace 1956- *78*
Goldberg, Herbert S. 1926- *25*
Goldberg, Jacob 1943- *94*
Goldberg, Jake
   See Goldberg, Jacob
Goldberg, Myla 1972(?)- *210*
Goldberg, Phyllis 1941- *21*
Goldberg, Stan J. 1939- *26*
Goldberg, Susan 1948- *71*
Goldberg, Whoopi 1955- *119*
Goldberger, Judith M. 1948- *80*
Goldblatt, Stacey 1969(?)- *191*
Golden, Christie 1963- *167*
   Earlier sketch in SATA *116*
Goldentyer, Debra 1960- *84*
Goldfeder, Cheryl
   See Pahz, Cheryl Suzanne
Goldfeder, James
   See Pahz, James Alon
Goldfeder, Jim
   See Pahz, James Alon
Goldfinger, Jennifer P. 1963- *185*
Goldfrank, Helen Colodny 1912- *6*
Goldin, Augusta 1906-1999 .... *13*
Goldin, Barbara Diamond 1946- *129*
   Autobiography Feature *129*
   Earlier sketch in SATA *92*
   See also SAAS *26*
Goldin, David 1963- *101*
Golding, Julia 1969- *188*
Golding, Theresa Martin 1960- *150*
Golding, William 1911-1993
   See CLR *130*
Golding, William Gerald
   See Golding, William
Goldman, Alex J. 1917- *65*
Goldman, Arthur Steven
   See Goldman, Steven
Goldman, E(leanor) M(aureen) 1943- *103*
Goldman, Elizabeth 1949- *90*
Goldman, Steven 1964- *207*
Goldring, Ann 1937- *149*
Goldsborough, June 1923- *19*
Goldschmidt, Judy *202*
Goldsmith, Connie 1945- *147*

Goldsmith, Howard 1943- *108*
   Earlier sketch in SATA *24*
Goldsmith, John Herman Thorburn 1903-1987
   Obituary *52*
Goldsmith, Oliver 1730(?)-1774 .... *26*
Goldsmith, Ruth M. 1919- *62*
Goldstein, Nathan 1927- *47*
Goldstein, Philip 1910-1997 .... *23*
Goldston, Robert (Conroy) 1927- *6*
Goldstone, Bruce *183*
Goldstone, Lawrence A.
   See Treat, Lawrence
Goldszmit, Henryk 1878-1942 .... *65*
   See also CLR *152*
Golembe, Carla 1951- *79*
Golenbock, Peter 1946- *99*
Goll, Reinhold W(eimar) 1897-1993 .... *26*
Gollub, Matthew 1960- *134*
   Earlier sketch in SATA *83*
Gomes, Filomena 1965- *183*
Gomez, Elena *191*
Gomez, Elizabeth *133*
Gomez-Freer, Elizabeth
   See Gomez, Elizabeth
Gomi, Taro 1945- *103*
   Earlier sketch in SATA *64*
   See also CLR *57*
Gondosch, Linda 1944- *58*
Gonsalves, Rob 1959- *209*
Gonyea, Mark *194*
Gonzalez, Catherine Troxell 1917-2000 .... *87*
Gonzalez, Christina
   See Gonzalez, Maya Christina
Gonzalez, Gloria 1940- *23*
Gonzalez, Julie 1958- *174*
Gonzalez, Julie Sehers
   See Gonzalez, Julie
Gonzalez, Lucia M. 1957- *202*
Gonzalez, Maya
   See Gonzalez, Maya Christina
Gonzalez, Maya Christina 1964- *175*
   Earlier sketch in SATA *115*
Gonzalez, Rigoberto 1970- *147*
Goobie, Beth 1959- *128*
Good, Alice 1950- *73*
Good, Clare
   See Romano, Clare
Goodall, Daphne Machin
   See Machin Goodall, Daphne (Edith)
Goodall, Jane 1934- *111*
Goodall, John S(trickland) 1908-1996 .... *66*
   Obituary *91*
   Earlier sketch in SATA *4*
   See also CLR *25*
Goodbody, Slim
   See Burstein, John
Goode, Diane 1949- *170*
   Earlier sketches in SATA *15, 84, 114*
Goode, Diane Capuozzo
   See Goode, Diane
Goode, Stephen Ray 1943- *55*
   Brief entry *40*
Goodenow, Earle 1913- *40*
Goodhart, Pippa 1958- *196*
   Earlier sketch in SATA *153*
Goodhue, Thomas W. 1949- *143*
Goodin, Sallie (Brown) 1953- *74*
Goodman, Alison 1966- *111*
Goodman, Deborah Lerme 1956- *50*
   Brief entry *49*
Goodman, Elaine 1930- *9*
Goodman, Joan Elizabeth 1950- *162*
   Earlier sketches in SATA *50, 94*
Goodman, Susan E. 1952- *181*
Goodman, Walter 1927-2002 .... *9*
Goodman Koz, Paula *211*
Goodrich, Samuel Griswold 1793-1860 ...... *23*
Goodsell, Jane Neuberger 1921(?)-1988
   Obituary *56*
Goodweather, Hartley
   See King, Thomas

GoodWeather, Hartley
  See King, Thomas
Goodwin, Hal
  See Goodwin, Harold L(eland)
Goodwin, Harold L(eland) 1914-1990 51
  Obituary 65
  Earlier sketch in SATA *13*
Goodwin, William 1943- 117
Goor, Nancy (Ruth Miller) 1944- 39
  Brief entry 34
Goor, Ron(ald Stephen) 1940- 39
  Brief entry 34
Goossen, Agnes
  See Epp, Margaret A(gnes)
Goossens, Philippe 1963- 195
Gootman, Marilyn E. 1944- 179
Gopnik, Adam 1956- 171
Gorbachev, Valeri 1944- 184
  Autobiography Feature 143
  Earlier sketches in SATA *98, 143*
Gordion, Mark
  See Turtledove, Harry
Gordon, Ad
  See Hano, Arnold
Gordon, Amy 1949- 197
  Earlier sketches in SATA *115, 156*
Gordon, Bernard Ludwig 1931- 27
Gordon, Colonel H. R.
  See Ellis, Edward S.
Gordon, David
  See Garrett, Randall
Gordon, Donald
  See Payne, Donald Gordon
Gordon, Dorothy 1893-1970 20
Gordon, Esther S(aranga) 1935- 10
Gordon, Frederick 1
Gordon, Gaelyn 1939-1997
  See CLR *75*
Gordon, Garrett
  See Garrett, Randall
Gordon, Gary
  See Edmonds, I(vy) G(ordon)
Gordon, Hal
  See Goodwin, Harold L(eland)
Gordon, Jeffie Ross
  See Enderle, Judith (Ann) Ross
  and Gordon, Stephanie Jacob
Gordon, John
  See Gesner, Clark
Gordon, John (William) 1925- 84
Gordon, Lew
  See Baldwin, Gordon C(ortis)
Gordon, Margaret (Anna) 1939- 9
Gordon, Mike 1948- 101
Gordon, Mildred 1912-1979
  Obituary 24
Gordon, Selma
  See Lanes, Selma Gordon
Gordon, Sheila 1927- 88
  See also CLR *27*
Gordon, Shirley 1921- 48
  Brief entry 41
Gordon, Sol 1923- 11
Gordon, Stephanie Jacob 1940- 89
  Autobiography Feature 114
  Earlier sketch in SATA *64*
  See also SAAS *26*
Gordon, Stewart
  See Shirreffs, Gordon D(onald)
Gordons, The
  See Gordon, Mildred
  and Gordon, Gordon
Gore, Leonid 185
Gorelick, Molly C(hernow) 1920-2003 9
  Obituary 153
Gorey, Edward (St. John) 1925-2000 70
  Brief entry 27
  Obituary 118
  Earlier sketch in SATA *29*
  See also CLR *36*
Gorham, Charles Orson 1868-1936 36

Gorham, Michael
  See Folsom, Franklin (Brewster)
Gorman, Carol 187
  Earlier sketch in SATA *150*
Gorman, Jacqueline Laks 1955- 148
Gorman, Mike 206
Gormley, Beatrice 1942- 202
  Brief entry 35
  Earlier sketches in SATA *39, 127*
Gorog, Judith (Katharine Allen) 1938- 75
  Earlier sketch in SATA *39*
Gorrell, Gena K. 1946- 170
Gorsline, Douglas (Warner) 1913-1985 11
  Obituary 43
Gorsline, (Sally) Marie 1928- 28
Gorsline, S. M.
  See Gorsline, (Sally) Marie
Gorton, Kaitlyn
  See Emerson, Kathy Lynn
Gorton, Kathy Lynn
  See Emerson, Kathy Lynn
Goryan, Sirak
  See Saroyan, William
Goschke, Julia 1973- 208
Goscinny, Rene 1926-1977 47
  Brief entry 39
  See also CLR *37*
Goss, Clay(ton E.) 1946- 82
Goss, Gary 1947- 124
Goss, Mini 1963- 186
Goto, Scott 203
Gott, Barry 197
Gottesman, S. D.
  See Kornbluth, C(yril) M.
  and Lowndes, Robert A(ugustine) W(ard)
  and Pohl, Frederik
Gottfried, Ted
  See Gottfried, Theodore Mark
Gottfried, Theodore Mark 1928- 150
  Earlier sketch in SATA *85*
Gottlieb, Gerald 1923- 7
Gottlieb, William P. 1917-2006 24
Gottlieb, William Paul
  See Gottlieb, William P.
Goudey, Alice E(dwards) 1898-1993 20
Goudge, Eileen 1950- 88
Goudge, Elizabeth (de Beauchamp)
  1900-1984 2
  Obituary 38
  See also CLR *94*
Gough, Catherine
  See Mulgan, Catherine
Gough, Philip 1908-1986 45
Gough, Sue 1940- 106
Goulart, Ron 1933- 67
  Earlier sketch in SATA *1*
Goulart, Ronald Joseph
  See Goulart, Ron
Gould, Alberta 1945- 96
Gould, Chester 1900-1985 49
  Obituary 43
Gould, Jean R(osalind) 1909-1993 11
  Obituary 77
Gould, Lilian 6
Gould, Marilyn 1928- 76
  Earlier sketch in SATA *15*
Gould, Robert 154
Gould, Steven 1955- 95
Gould, Steven Charles
  See Gould, Steven
Gourley, Catherine 1950- 190
  Earlier sketch in SATA *95*
Gourse, Leslie 1939-2004 89
Govan, (Mary) Christine Noble 1898-1985 .. 9
Gove, Doris 1944- 72
Govenar, Alan 1952- 189
Govenar, Alan Bruce
  See Govenar, Alan
Govern, Elaine 1939- 26
Gowen, L. Kris 1968- 156

Graaf, Peter
  See Youd, Samuel
Graber, Alexander 1914-1997 98
  Earlier sketch in SATA *7*
Graber, George Alexander
  See Graber, Alexander
Graber, Janet 1942- 170
Graber, Richard (Fredrick) 1927- 26
Grabianski, Janusz 1928-1976 39
  Obituary 30
Graboff, Abner 1919-1986 35
Grace, Fran(ces Jane) 45
Grace, N.B.
  See Harper, Suzanne
Grace, Theresa
  See Mattern, Joanne
Gracza, Margaret Young 1928- 56
Graduate of Oxford, A
  See Ruskin, John
Grady, Denise 1952- 189
Graeber, Charlotte Towner 106
  Brief entry 44
  Earlier sketch in SATA *56*
Graef, Renee 1956- 204
Graeme, Roderic
  See Jeffries, Roderic
Graf, Michael
  See Graf, Mike
Graf, Mike 1960- 164
Grafe, Max 198
Graff, Lisa 1981- 188
Graff, Polly Anne Colver
  See Colver, Anne
Graff, (S.) Stewart 1908- 9
Graham, Ada 1931- 11
Graham, Alastair 1945- 74
Graham, Arthur Kennon
  See Harrison, David L.
Graham, Bob 1942- 187
  Earlier sketches in SATA *63, 101, 151*
  See also CLR *31*
Graham, Brenda Knight 1942- 32
Graham, Charlotte
  See Bowden, Joan Chase
Graham, Eleanor 1896-1984 18
  Obituary 38
Graham, Ennis
  See Molesworth, Mary Louisa
Graham, Frank, Jr. 1925- 11
Graham, Georgia 1959- 190
Graham, Ian 1953- 112
Graham, John 1926-2007 11
Graham, Kennon
  See Harrison, David L.
Graham, Larry
  See Graham, Lawrence
Graham, Lawrence 1962- 63
Graham, Lawrence Otis
  See Graham, Lawrence
Graham, Linda
  See Graham-Barber, Lynda
Graham, Lorenz (Bell) 1902-1989 74
  Obituary 63
  Earlier sketch in SATA *2*
  See also CLR *10*
  See also SAAS *5*
Graham, Margaret Bloy 1920- 11
Graham, Robin Lee 1949- 7
Graham, Shirley 1896(?)-1977
  See Du Bois, Shirley Graham
Graham-Barber, Lynda 1944- 159
  Earlier sketch in SATA *42*
Graham-Cameron, M.
  See Graham-Cameron, M(alcolm) G(ordon)
Graham-Cameron, M(alcolm) G(ordon)
  1931- 53
  Brief entry 45
Graham-Cameron, Mike
  See Graham-Cameron, M(alcolm) G(ordon)

Grahame, Kenneth 1859-1932 .... *100*
  See also YABC *1*
  See also CLR *135*
Gralley, Jean *166*
Gramatky, Hardie 1907-1979 .... *30*
  Obituary *23*
  Earlier sketch in SATA *1*
  See also CLR *22*
Grambling, Lois G. 1927- *206*
  Earlier sketches in SATA *71, 148*
Grambo, Rebecca L(ynn) 1963- *109*
Grammer, June Amos 1927- *58*
Grand, Samuel 1912-1988 .... *42*
Grandits, John 1949- *192*
GrandPre, Mary 1954- *184*
Grandville, J. J.
  See Gerard, Jean Ignace Isidore
Grandville, Jean Ignace Isidore Gerard
  See Gerard, Jean Ignace Isidore
Granfield, Linda 1950- *160*
  Earlier sketch in SATA *96*
Grange, Peter
  See Nicole, Christopher (Robin)
Granger, Margaret Jane 1925(?)-1977
  Obituary *27*
Granger, Michele 1949- *88*
Granger, Peggy
  See Granger, Margaret Jane
Granowsky, Alvin 1936- *101*
Granstaff, Bill 1925- *10*
Granstrom, Brita 1969- *167*
  Earlier sketch in SATA *111*
Grant, Bruce 1893-1977 .... *5*
  Obituary *25*
Grant, Cynthia D. 1950- *147*
  Earlier sketches in SATA *33, 77*
Grant, Eva 1907-1996 .... *7*
Grant, Evva H. 1913-1977
  Obituary *27*
Grant, Gordon 1875-1962 .... *25*
Grant, Gwen(doline Ellen) 1940- *47*
Grant, Judyann Ackerman *211*
Grant, Katie M.
  See Grant, K.M.
Grant, K.M. *175*
Grant, (Alice) Leigh 1947- *10*
Grant, Matthew G.
  See May, Julian
Grant, Maxwell
  See Gibson, Walter B(rown)
  and Lynds, Dennis
Grant, Melvyn *183*
Grant, Myrna (Lois) 1934- *21*
Grant, Neil 1938- *154*
  Earlier sketch in SATA *14*
Grant, Nicholas
  See Nicole, Christopher (Robin)
Grant, Richard 1948- *80*
Grant, Skeeter
  See Spiegelman, Art
Grater, Michael 1923- *57*
Gravel, Fern
  See Hall, James Norman
Gravelle, Karen 1942- *166*
  Earlier sketch in SATA *78*
Graves, Charles Parlin 1911-1972 .... *4*
Graves, Keith *191*
  Earlier sketch in SATA *156*
Graves, Robert 1895-1985 .... *45*
Graves, Robert von Ranke
  See Graves, Robert
Graves, Valerie
  See Bradley, Marion Zimmer
Gravett, Emily 1972(?)- *189*
Gray, Betsy
  See Poole, Gray Johnson
Gray, Caroline
  See Nicole, Christopher (Robin)
Gray, Dianne E. *183*
Gray, Elizabeth Janet
  See Vining, Elizabeth Gray

Gray, Genevieve S(tuck) 1920-1995 .... *4*
Gray, Harold (Lincoln) 1894-1968 .... *33*
  Brief entry *32*
Gray, Jenny
  See Gray, Genevieve S(tuck)
Gray, John Lee
  See Jakes, John
Gray, Judith A. 1949- *93*
Gray, Judith Anne
  See Gray, Judith A.
Gray, Keith *151*
Gray, Kes 1960- *153*
Gray, Les 1929- *82*
Gray, Libba Moore 1937- *83*
Gray, Luli 1945- *149*
  Earlier sketch in SATA *90*
Gray, Marian
  See Pierce, Edith Gray
Gray, Nicholas Stuart 1922-1981 .... *4*
  Obituary *27*
Gray, Nigel 1941- *104*
  Earlier sketch in SATA *33*
Gray, (Lucy) Noel (Clervaux) 1898-1983 ... *47*
Gray, Patricia (Clark) *7*
Gray, Patsey
  See Gray, Patricia (Clark)
Gray, Rita *184*
Graydon, Shari 1958- *158*
Grayland, V. Merle
  See Grayland, Valerie (Merle Spanner)
Grayland, Valerie (Merle Spanner) *7*
Grayson, Devin (Kalile) 1970- *119*
Grayson, Kristine
  See Rusch, Kristine Kathryn
Grayson, Paul 1946- *79*
Graystone, Lynn
  See Brennan, Joseph Lomas
Great Comte, The
  See Hawkesworth, Eric
Greaves, Margaret 1914-1995 .... *87*
  Earlier sketch in SATA *7*
Greaves, Nick 1955- *77*
Gree, Alain 1936- *28*
Green, Adam
  See Weisgard, Leonard (Joseph)
Green, Anne Canevari 1943- *62*
Green, Brian
  See Card, Orson Scott
Green, Cliff(ord) 1934- *126*
Green, Connie Jordan 1938- *80*
Green, D.
  See Casewit, Curtis W(erner)
Green, Elizabeth Shippen 1871-1954 .... *139*
Green, Hannah
  See Greenberg, Joanne (Goldenberg)
Green, Jane 1937- *9*
Green, Jessica *211*
Green, John 1977(?)- *170*
Green, Mary Moore 1906- *11*
Green, Morton 1937- *8*
Green, Norma B(erger) 1925- *11*
Green, Phyllis 1932- *20*
Green, Roger (Gilbert) Lancelyn
  1918-1987 .... *2*
  Obituary *53*
Green, (James Le)Roy 1948- *89*
Green, Sheila Ellen 1934- *148*
  Earlier sketches in SATA *8, 87*
Green, Timothy 1953- *91*
Greenaway, Kate 1846-1901 .... *100*
  See also YABC *2*
  See also CLR *111*
Greenbank, Anthony Hunt 1933- *39*
Greenberg, David 1954- *171*
Greenberg, David T.
  See Greenberg, David
Greenberg, Harvey R. 1935- *5*
Greenberg, Jan 1942- *211*
  Earlier sketches in SATA *61, 125*
Greenberg, Joanne (Goldenberg) 1932- *25*
Greenberg, Melanie Hope 1954- *72*

Greenberg, Polly 1932- *52*
  Brief entry *43*
Greenblat, Rodney Alan 1960- *106*
Greenburg, Dan 1936- *175*
  Earlier sketch in SATA *102*
Greene, Bette 1934- *161*
  Earlier sketches in SATA *8, 102*
  See also CLR *140*
  See also SAAS *16*
Greene, Carla 1916- *67*
  Earlier sketch in SATA *1*
Greene, Carol *102*
  Brief entry *44*
  Earlier sketch in SATA *66*
Greene, Constance C(larke) 1924- *72*
  Earlier sketch in SATA *11*
  See also CLR *62*
  See also SAAS *11*
Greene, Edgar
  See Papademetriou, Lisa
Greene, Ellin 1927- *23*
Greene, Graham 1904-1991 .... *20*
Greene, Graham Henry
  See Greene, Graham
Greene, Jacqueline Dembar 1946- *131*
  Earlier sketch in SATA *76*
Greene, Laura Offenhartz 1935- *38*
Greene, Meg
  See Malvasi, Meg Greene
Greene, Michele 1962- *178*
Greene, Michele Dominguez
  See Greene, Michele
Greene, Rhonda Gowler 1955- *160*
  Earlier sketch in SATA *101*
Greene, Stephanie 1953- *173*
  Earlier sketch in SATA *127*
Greene, Wade 1933- *11*
Greene, Yvonne
  See Flesch, Yolande (Catarina)
Greenfeld, Howard (Scheinman) 1928- *140*
  Earlier sketch in SATA *19*
Greenfeld, Josh(ua Joseph) 1928- *62*
Greenfield, Eloise 1929- *155*
  Earlier sketches in SATA *19, 61, 105*
  See also CLR *38*
  See also SAAS *16*
Greenhaus, Thelma Nurenberg 1903-1984
  Obituary *45*
Greenhut, Josh
  See Mercer, Sienna
Greening, Hamilton
  See Hamilton, Charles (Harold St. John)
Greenlaw, M. Jean 1941- *107*
Greenleaf, Barbara Kaye 1942- *6*
Greenleaf, Peter 1910-1997 .... *33*
Greenlee, Sharon 1935- *77*
Greeno, Gayle 1949- *81*
Greenseid, Diane 1948- *178*
  Earlier sketch in SATA *93*
Greenspun, Adele Aron 1938- *142*
  Earlier sketch in SATA *76*
Greenstein, Elaine 1959- *150*
  Earlier sketch in SATA *82*
Greenwald, Sheila
  See Green, Sheila Ellen
Greenwood, Barbara 1940- *129*
  Earlier sketch in SATA *90*
Greenwood, Mark 1958- *202*
Greenwood, Pamela D. 1944- *115*
Greer, Richard
  See Garrett, Randall
  and Silverberg, Robert
Gregg, Andrew K. 1929- *81*
Gregg, Charles T(hornton) 1927- *65*
Gregg, Walter H(arold) 1919- *20*
Gregor, Arthur 1923- *36*
Gregor, Lee
  See Pohl, Frederik
Gregori, Leon 1919- *15*
Gregorian, Joyce Ballou 1946-1991 .... *30*
  Obituary *83*

Gregorich, Barbara 1943- 184
 Earlier sketch in SATA 66
Gregorowski, Christopher 1940- 30
Gregory, Diana (Jean) 1933- 49
 Brief entry 42
Gregory, Harry
 See Gottfried, Theodore Mark
Gregory, Jean
 See Ure, Jean
Gregory, Kristiana 1951- 136
 Earlier sketch in SATA 74
Gregory, Nan 1944- 192
 Earlier sketch in SATA 148
Gregory, Philippa 1954- 122
Gregory, Stephen
 See Penzler, Otto
Gregory, Valiska 1940- 82
Greif, Jean-Jacques 1944- 195
Greisman, Joan Ruth 1937- 31
Grendon, Stephen
 See Derleth, August (William)
Grenville, Pelham
 See Wodehouse, P. G.
Gretz, Susanna 1937- 7
Gretzer, John 18
Grewdead, Roy
 See Gorey, Edward (St. John)
Grey, Carol
 See Lowndes, Robert A(ugustine) W(ard)
Grey, Christopher 191
Grey, Christopher Peter
 See Grey, Christopher
Grey, Jerry 1926- 11
Grey, Mini 205
 Earlier sketch in SATA 166
Greybeard the Pirate
 See Macintosh, Brownie
Grey Owl
 See Belaney, Archibald Stansfeld
Gri
 See Denney, Diana
Gribbin, John 1946- 159
Gribbin, John R.
 See Gribbin, John
Grice, Frederick 1910-1983 6
Grider, Dorothy 1915- 31
Gridley, Marion E(leanor) 1906-1974 35
 Obituary 26
Grieco-Tiso, Pina 1954- 108
Grieder, Walter 1924- 9
Griego, Tony A. 1955- 77
Griese, Arnold A(lfred) 1921- 9
Griessman, Annette 1962- 170
 Earlier sketch in SATA 116
Grieve, James 1934- 146
Grifalconi, Ann 1929- 210
 Earlier sketches in SATA 2, 66, 133
 See also CLR 35
 See also SAAS 16
Griffin, Adele 1970- 195
 Earlier sketches in SATA 105, 153
Griffin, Elizabeth May 1985- 89
Griffin, Gillett Good 1928- 26
Griffin, Judith Berry 34
Griffin, Kitty 1951- 137
Griffin, Peni R. 1961- 193
 Earlier sketches in SATA 67, 99
Griffin, Steven A. 1953- 89
Griffin, Steven Arthur
 See Griffin, Steven A.
Griffin, W.E.B. 1929- 5
Griffith, Connie 1946- 89
Griffith, Gershom 1960- 85
Griffith, Helen V(irginia) 1934- 87
 Autobiography Feature 107
 Earlier sketch in SATA 39
Griffith, Jeannette
 See Eyerly, Jeannette
Griffith, Saul 1974- 200
Griffiths, Andy 1961- 196
 Earlier sketch in SATA 152

Griffiths, G(ordon) D(ouglas) 1910-1973
 Obituary 20
Griffiths, Helen 1939- 86
 Earlier sketch in SATA 5
 See also CLR 75
 See also SAAS 5
Grigson, Jane (McIntire) 1928-1990 63
Grimes, Lee 1920- 68
Grimes, Nikki 1950- 174
 Earlier sketches in SATA 93, 136
 See also CLR 42
Grimly, Gris 186
Grimm, Jacob Ludwig Karl 1785-1863 22
 See also CLR 112
Grimm, Wilhelm Karl 1786-1859 22
 See also CLR 112
Grimm, William C(arey) 1907-1992 14
Grimm and Grim
 See Grimm, Jacob Ludwig Karl
 and Grimm, Wilhelm Karl
Grimm Brothers
 See Grimm, Jacob Ludwig Karl
 and Grimm, Wilhelm Karl
Grimsdell, Jeremy 1942- 83
Grimshaw, Nigel (Gilroy) 1925- 23
Grimsley, Gordon
 See Groom, Arthur William
Grindley, Jane Sally
 See Grindley, Sally
Grindley, Sally 1953- 148
Gringhuis, Dirk
 See Gringhuis, Richard H.
Gringhuis, Richard H. 1918-1974 6
 Obituary 25
Grinnell, David
 See Wollheim, Donald A(llen)
Grinnell, George Bird 1849-1938 16
Grinspoon, David
 See Grinspoon, David H.
Grinspoon, David H. 1959- 156
Grinspoon, David Harry
 See Grinspoon, David H.
Gripe, Maria 1923- 74
 Earlier sketch in SATA 2
 See also CLR 5
Gripe, Maria Kristina
 See Gripe, Maria
Grobler, Piet 1959- 201
Groch, Judith (Goldstein) 1929- 25
Grode, Redway
 See Gorey, Edward (St. John)
Groener, Carl
 See Lowndes, Robert A(ugustine) W(ard)
Groening, Matt 1954- 116
 Earlier sketch in SATA 81
Grohmann, Susan 1948- 84
Grohskopf, Bernice 7
Grol, Lini R(icharda) 1913- 9
Grollman, Earl A. 1925- 22
Groom, Arthur William 1898-1964 10
Grooms, Duffy 1964- 169
Gross, Alan 1947- 54
 Brief entry 43
Gross, Ernie 1913- 67
Gross, Philip 1952- 164
 Earlier sketch in SATA 84
Gross, Philip John
 See Gross, Philip
Gross, Ruth Belov 1929- 33
Gross, Sarah Chokla 1906-1976 9
 Obituary 26
Grosser, Morton 1931- 74
Grosser, Vicky 1958- 83
Grossman, Bill 1948- 126
 Earlier sketch in SATA 72
Grossman, Nancy 1940- 29
Grossman, Patricia 1951- 73
Grossman, Robert 1940- 11
Grote, JoAnn A. 1951- 113
Groten, Dallas 1951- 64

Groth, John (August) 1908-1988 21
 Obituary 56
Groth-Fleming, Candace
 See Fleming, Candace
Grove, Vicki 1948- 151
 Autobiography Feature 151
 Earlier sketch in SATA 122
Grover, Lorie Ann 1964- 168
Grover, Wayne 1934- 69
Groves, Georgina
 See Symons, (Dorothy) Geraldine
Groves, Maketa 1950- 107
Groves, Seli 77
Grubb, Lisa 160
Gruber, Michael 1940- 173
Gruber, Terry (deRoy) 1953- 66
Gruelle, John 1880-1938 35
 Brief entry 32
 See also CLR 34
Gruelle, Johnny
 See Gruelle, John
Gruenberg, Sidonie Matsner 1881-1974 2
 Obituary 27
Gruhzit-Hoyt, Olga (Margaret) 1922- 127
 Earlier sketch in SATA 16
Grummer, Arnold E(dward) 1923- 49
Grunewalt, Pine
 See Kunhardt, Edith
Grunwell, Jeanne Marie 1971- 147
Grupper, Jonathan 137
Gryski, Camilla 1948- 72
Guarino, Dagmar
 See Guarino, Deborah
Guarino, Deborah 1954- 68
Guay, Georgette (Marie Jeanne) 1952- 54
Guay, Rebecca 209
Guay-Mitchell, Rebecca
 See Guay, Rebecca
Guback, Georgia 88
Guccione, Leslie Davis 1946- 111
 Earlier sketch in SATA 72
Guck, Dorothy 1913-2002 27
Guerny, Gene
 See Gurney, Gene
Guest, Elissa Haden 1953- 125
Guest, Jacqueline 1952- 135
Guevara, Susan 167
 Earlier sketch in SATA 97
Gugler, Laurel Dee 95
Gugliotta, Bobette 1918-1994 7
Guianan, Eve 1965- 102
Guiberson, Brenda Z. 1946- 211
 Earlier sketches in SATA 71, 124
Guibert, Emmanuel 1964- 181
Guile, Melanie 1949- 152
 Earlier sketch in SATA 104
Guillaume, Jeanette G. Flierl 1899-1990 8
Guillot, Rene 1900-1969 7
 See also CLR 22
Guisewite, Cathy (Lee) 1950- 57
Gulbis, Stephen 1959- 142
Gulley, Judie 1942- 58
Gump, P. Q.
 See Card, Orson Scott
Gundrey, Elizabeth 1924- 23
Gunn, James E. 1923- 35
Gunn, James Edwin
 See Gunn, James E.
Gunn, Robin Jones 1955- 84
Gunnella 1956- 197
Gunning, Monica Olwen 1930- 161
Gunston, Bill
 See Gunston, William Tudor
Gunston, William Tudor 1927- 9
Gunterman, Bertha Lisette 1886(?)-1975
 Obituary 27
Gunther, John 1901-1970
Guravich, Dan 1918- 74
Gurko, Leo 1914- 9
Gurko, Miriam 1910(?)-1988 9
 Obituary 58

Gurney, Gene 1924- *65*
Gurney, James 1958- *120*
  Earlier sketch in SATA *76*
Gurney, John Steven 1962- *143*
  Earlier sketch in SATA *75*
Gustafson, Sarah R.
  See Riedman, Sarah R(egal)
Gustafson, Scott 1956- *34*
Gustavson, Adam *176*
Guthrie, A(lfred) B(ertram), Jr. 1901-1991 . *62*
  Obituary *67*
Guthrie, Anne 1890-1979 .... *28*
Guthrie, Donna W. 1946- *105*
  Earlier sketch in SATA *63*
Gutierrez, Akemi *172*
Gutierrez, Rudy *203*
Gutman, Bill *128*
  Brief entry *43*
  Earlier sketch in SATA *67*
Gutman, Dan 1955- *188*
  Earlier sketches in SATA *77, 139*
Gutman, Naham 1899(?)-1981
  Obituary *25*
Gutmann, Bessie Pease 1876-1960 .... *73*
Guy, Geoffrey 1942- *153*
Guy, Ginger Foglesong 1954- *171*
Guy, Rosa 1925- *122*
  Earlier sketches in SATA *14, 62*
  See also CLR *137*
Guy, Rosa Cuthbert
  See Guy, Rosa
Guy, Susan 1948- *149*
Guymer, (Wilhelmina) Mary 1909- *50*
Guzman, Lila 1952- *168*
Guzman, Rick 1957- *168*
Gwaltney, Doris 1932- *181*
Gwynne, Fred(erick Hubbard) 1926-1993 .. *41*
  Brief entry *27*
  Obituary *75*
Gwynne, Oscar A.
  See Ellis, Edward S.
Gwynne, Oswald A.
  See Ellis, Edward S.

H

Haab, Sherri 1964- *169*
  Earlier sketch in SATA *91*
Haar, Jaap ter
  See ter Haar, Jaap
Haarsma, P.J. *183*
Haas, Carolyn Buhai 1926- *43*
Haas, Dan 1957- *105*
Haas, Dorothy F. *46*
  Brief entry *43*
  See also SAAS *17*
Haas, Irene 1929- *96*
  Earlier sketch in SATA *17*
Haas, James E(dward) 1943- *40*
Haas, (Katherine) Jessie 1959- *135*
  Autobiography Feature *135*
  Earlier sketch in SATA *98*
Haas, Merle S. 1896(?)-1985
  Obituary *41*
Habenstreit, Barbara 1937- *5*
Haber, Karen 1955- *78*
Haber, Louis 1910-1988 .... *12*
Hacker, Randi 1951- *185*
Hacker, Randi Dawn
  See Hacker, Randi
Hackett, John Winthrop 1910-1997 .... *65*
Hacks, Peter 1928-2003
  Obituary *151*
Haddix, Margaret Peterson 1964- *187*
  Earlier sketches in SATA *94, 125*
Haddon, Mark 1962- *155*
Hader, Berta (Hoerner) 1891(?)-1976 .... *16*
Hader, Elmer (Stanley) 1889-1973 .... *16*

Hadithi, Mwenye
  See Hobson, Bruce
Hadley, Franklin
  See Winterbotham, R(ussell) R(obert)
Hadley, Lee 1934-1995 .... *89*
  Brief entry *38*
  Obituary *86*
  Earlier sketch in SATA *47*
  See also CLR *40*
  See also SAAS *14*
Haeffele, Deborah 1954- *76*
Haenel, Wolfram 1956- *89*
  See also CLR *64*
Hafner, Marylin 1925- *179*
  Earlier sketches in SATA *7, 121*
Haft, Erin
  See Ehrenhaft, Daniel
Hager, Alan 1940- *176*
Hager, Alice Rogers 1894-1969
  Obituary *26*
Hager, Betty 1923- *89*
Hager, Jenna Bush
  See Bush, Jenna
Hager, Sarah *171*
Hager, Thomas 1953- *119*
Hager, Tom
  See Hager, Thomas
Hagerup, Klaus 1946- *186*
Haggard, H(enry) Rider 1856-1925 .... *16*
Haggerty, James J(oseph) 1920- *5*
Hagon, Priscilla
  See Allan, Mabel Esther
Hague, (Susan) Kathleen 1949- *49*
  Brief entry *45*
Hague, Michael 1948- *185*
  Brief entry *32*
  Earlier sketches in SATA *48, 80, 129*
Hague, Michael R.
  See Hague, Michael
Hahn, Emily 1905-1997 .... *3*
  Obituary *96*
Hahn, Hannelore *8*
Hahn, James (Sage) 1947- *9*
Hahn, (Mona) Lynn 1949- *9*
Hahn, Mary Downing 1937- *208*
  Autobiography Feature *157*
  Brief entry *44*
  Earlier sketches in SATA *50, 81, 138, 157*
  See also SAAS *12*
Hahn, Michael T. 1953- *92*
Haig-Brown, Roderick (Langmere)
  1908-1976 .... *12*
  See also CLR *31*
Haight, Anne Lyon 1895-1977
  Obituary *30*
Haight, Rip
  See Carpenter, John
Haight, Sandy 1949- *79*
Haij, Vera
  See Jansson, Tove (Marika)
Haines, Gail Kay 1943- *11*
Haines, Margaret Ann Beck
  See Beck, Peggy
Haining, Peter 1940-2007 .... *14*
  Obituary *188*
Haining, Peter Alexander
  See Haining, Peter
Hains, Harriet
  See Watson, Carol
Hajdusiewicz, Babs Bell *163*
Hakim, Joy 1931- *173*
  Earlier sketch in SATA *83*
Halacy, D. S., Jr. 1919-2002 .... *36*
  See also SAAS *8*
Halacy, Dan
  See Halacy, D. S., Jr.
Halam, Ann
  See Jones, Gwyneth A(nn)
Haldane, Roger John 1945- *13*
Hale, Arlene 1924-1982 .... *49*

Hale, Bruce 1957- *203*
  Earlier sketch in SATA *123*
Hale, Christy
  See Apostolou, Christine Hale
Hale, Edward Everett 1822-1909 .... *16*
Hale, Glenn
  See Walker, Robert W.
Hale, Helen
  See Mulcahy, Lucille Burnett
Hale, Irina 1932- *26*
Hale, Kathleen 1898-2000 .... *66*
  Obituary *121*
  Earlier sketch in SATA *17*
Hale, Linda (Howe) 1929- *6*
Hale, Lucretia P.
  See Hale, Lucretia Peabody
Hale, Lucretia Peabody 1820-1900 .... *26*
  See also CLR *105*
Hale, Marian *194*
Hale, Nancy 1908-1988 .... *31*
  Obituary *57*
Hale, Nathan 1976- *210*
Hale, Shannon *200*
  Earlier sketch in SATA *158*
Haley, Amanda *205*
Haley, Gail E(inhart) 1939- *161*
  Autobiography Feature *161*
  Brief entry *28*
  Earlier sketches in SATA *43, 78, 136*
  See also CLR *21*
  See also SAAS *13*
Haley, Neale *52*
Halfmann, Janet 1944- *208*
Hall, Adam
  See Trevor, Elleston
Hall, Adele 1910- *7*
Hall, Anna Gertrude 1882-1967 .... *8*
Hall, August *207*
Hall, Barbara 1961- *68*
Hall, Becky 1950- *186*
Hall, Beverly B. 1918- *95*
Hall, Borden
  See Yates, Raymond F(rancis)
Hall, Brian P(atrick) 1935- *31*
Hall, Cameron
  See del Rey, Lester
Hall, Caryl
  See Hansen, Caryl (Hall)
Hall, Donald 1928- *97*
  Earlier sketch in SATA *23*
Hall, Donald Andrew, Jr.
  See Hall, Donald
Hall, Douglas 1931- *43*
Hall, Elizabeth 1929- *77*
Hall, Elvajean 1910-1984 .... *6*
Hall, Francie 1940- *166*
Hall, James Norman 1887-1951 .... *21*
Hall, Jesse
  See Boesen, Victor
Hall, Katy
  See McMullan, Kate
Hall, Kirsten Marie 1974- *67*
Hall, Lynn 1937- *79*
  Earlier sketches in SATA *2, 47*
  See also SAAS *4*
Hall, Malcolm 1945- *7*
Hall, Marcellus *203*
Hall, Marjory
  See Yeakley, Marjory Hall
Hall, Melanie W. 1949- *169*
  Earlier sketches in SATA *78, 116*
Hall, Patricia 1940- *136*
Hall, Rosalys Haskell 1914- *7*
Hall, Willis 1929-2005 .... *66*
Hallard, Peter
  See Catherall, Arthur
Hallas, Richard
  See Knight, Eric
Hall-Clarke, James
  See Rowland-Entwistle, (Arthur) Theodore
  (Henry)

Hallensleben, Georg 1958- *173*
Haller, Dorcas Woodbury 1946- *46*
Hallett, Mark 1947- *83*
Halliburton, Richard 1900-1939(?) *81*
Halliburton, Warren J. 1924- *19*
Halliday, Brett
   See Dresser, Davis
   and Johnson, (Walter) Ryerson
   and Terrall, Robert
Halliday, William R(oss) 1926- *52*
Hallin, Emily Watson 1916-1995 .... *6*
Hallinan, P(atrick) K(enneth) 1944- *39*
   Brief entry *37*
Hallman, Ruth 1929- *43*
   Brief entry *28*
Hallowell, Tommy
   See Hill, Thomas
Hall-Quest, (Edna) Olga W(ilbourne)
   1899-1986 .... *11*
   Obituary *47*
Halls, Kelly Milner 1957- *131*
Hallstead, William F(inn III) 1924- *11*
Hallward, Michael 1889-1982 .... *12*
Halperin, Michael *156*
Halperin, Wendy Anderson 1952- *200*
   Earlier sketches in SATA *80, 125*
Halpern, Julie 1975- *198*
Halpin, Brendan 1968- *193*
Halpin, Marlene 1927- *88*
Halsell, Grace (Eleanor) 1923-2000 .... *13*
Halsey, Megan *185*
Halsted, Anna Roosevelt 1906-1975
   Obituary *30*
Halter, Jon C(harles) 1941- *22*
Halverson, Deborah *202*
Halvorson, Marilyn 1948- *123*
Hamalian, Leo 1920- *41*
Hamberger, John 1934- *14*
Hamblin, Dora Jane 1920- *36*
Hambly, Barbara 1951- *108*
Hambly, Barbara Joan
   See Hambly, Barbara
Hamer, Martyn
   See Eldin, Peter
Hamerstrom, Frances 1907-1998 .... *24*
Hamil, Thomas Arthur 1928- *14*
Hamill, Ethel
   See Webb, Jean Francis (III)
Hamilton, (John) Alan 1943- *66*
Hamilton, Alice
   See Cromie, Alice Hamilton
Hamilton, Anita 1919- *92*
Hamilton, Buzz
   See Hemming, Roy G.
Hamilton, Carol (Jean Barber) 1935- *94*
Hamilton, Charles (Harold St. John)
   1876-1961 .... *13*
Hamilton, Charles 1913-1996 .... *65*
   Obituary *93*
Hamilton, Clive
   See Lewis, C. S.
Hamilton, Dorothy (Drumm) 1906-1983 .... *12*
   Obituary *35*
Hamilton, Edith 1867-1963 .... *20*
Hamilton, Edmond 1904-1977 .... *118*
Hamilton, (Muriel) Elizabeth (Mollie)
   1906- *23*
Hamilton, Emma Walton 1962- *177*
Hamilton, Franklin
   See Silverberg, Robert
Hamilton, Gail
   See Corcoran, Barbara (Asenath)
   and Dodge, Mary Abigail
Hamilton, Kersten 1958- *204*
   Earlier sketch in SATA *134*
Hamilton, K.R.
   See Hamilton, Kersten
Hamilton, Martha 1953- *183*
   Earlier sketch in SATA *123*
Hamilton, Mary (E.) 1927- *55*

Hamilton, Mollie
   See Kaye, M.M.
Hamilton, Morse 1943-1998 .... *101*
   Earlier sketch in SATA *35*
Hamilton, Peter F. 1960- *109*
Hamilton, Priscilla
   See Gellis, Roberta
Hamilton, Ralph
   See Stratemeyer, Edward L.
Hamilton, Virginia 1936-2002 .... *123*
   Obituary *132*
   Earlier sketches in SATA *4, 56, 79*
   See also CLR *127*
Hamilton, Virginia Esther
   See Hamilton, Virginia
Hamilton-Paterson, James 1941- *82*
Hamlet, Ova
   See Lupoff, Richard A(llen)
Hamley, D. C.
   See Hamley, Dennis
Hamley, Dennis 1935- *69*
   Earlier sketch in SATA *39*
   See also CLR *47*
   See also SAAS *22*
Hamley, Dennis C.
   See Hamley, Dennis
Hamlin, Peter J. 1970- *84*
Hamm, Diane Johnston 1949- *78*
Hammer, Charles 1934- *58*
Hammer, Richard 1928- *6*
Hammerman, Gay M(orenus) 1926- *9*
Hammill, Matt 1982- *206*
Hammond, Andrew 1970- *181*
Hammond, Ralph
   See Hammond Innes, Ralph
Hammond, Winifred G(raham) 1899-1992 . *29*
   Obituary *107*
Hammond Innes, Ralph 1913-1998 .... *116*
Hammontree, Marie (Gertrude) 1913- *13*
Hample, Zack 1977- *161*
Hampshire, Joyce Gregorian
   See Gregorian, Joyce Ballou
Hampshire, Susan 1942- *98*
Hampson, (Richard) Denman 1929- *15*
Hampson, Frank 1918(?)-1985
   Obituary *46*
Hampton, Wilborn 1940- *196*
   Earlier sketch in SATA *156*
Hamre, Leif 1914- *5*
Hamsa, Bobbie 1944- *52*
   Brief entry *38*
Han, Jenny 1981- *175*
Han, Lu
   See Stickler, Soma Han
Han, Soma
   See Stickler, Soma Han
Han, Suzanne Crowder 1953- *89*
Hancock, Mary A. 1923- *31*
Hancock, Sibyl 1940- *9*
Hand, Elizabeth 1957- *167*
   Earlier sketch in SATA *118*
Handford, Martin (John) 1956- *64*
   See also CLR *22*
Handforth, Thomas (Schofield) 1897-1948 . *42*
Handler, Daniel
   See Snicket, Lemony
Handville, Robert (Tompkins) 1924- *45*
Hane, Roger 1940-1974
   Obituary *20*
Hanel, Wolfram
   See Haenel, Wolfram
Haney, Lynn 1941- *23*
Hanff, Helene 1916-1997 .... *97*
   Earlier sketch in SATA *11*
Hanft, Josh 1956- *197*
Hanft, Joshua E.
   See Hanft, Josh
Hanley, Boniface Francis 1924- *65*
Hanlon, Emily 1945- *15*
Hann, Jacquie 1951- *19*
Hann, Judith 1942- *77*

Hanna, Bill
   See Hanna, William (Denby)
Hanna, Cheryl 1951- *84*
Hanna, Dan *200*
Hanna, Jack (Bushnell) 1947- *74*
Hanna, Nell(ie L.) 1908- *55*
Hanna, Paul R(obert) 1902-1988 .... *9*
Hanna, William (Denby) 1910-2001 .... *51*
   Obituary *126*
Hannam, Charles 1925- *50*
Hannan, Peter 1954- *187*
Hannigan, Katherine *170*
Hannon, Ezra
   See Hunter, Evan
Hann-Syme, Marguerite *127*
Hano, Arnold 1922- *12*
Hano, Renee Roth
   See Roth-Hano, Renee
Hanover, Terri
   See Huff, Tanya
Hansen, Ann Larkin 1958- *96*
Hansen, Brooks 1965- *104*
Hansen, Caryl (Hall) 1929- *39*
Hansen, Ian V. 1929- *113*
Hansen, Jennifer 1972- *156*
Hansen, Joyce 1942- *172*
   Autobiography Feature *172*
   Brief entry *39*
   Earlier sketches in SATA *46, 101*
   See also CLR *21*
   See also SAAS *15*
Hansen, Joyce Viola
   See Hansen, Joyce
Hansen, Mark Victor *112*
Hansen, Ron 1947- *56*
Hansen, Ronald Thomas
   See Hansen, Ron
Hanser, Richard (Frederick) 1909-1981 ...... *13*
Hanson, Joan 1938- *8*
Hanson, Joseph E. 1894(?)-1971
   Obituary *27*
Hanson, Mary Elizabeth *188*
Hanson, Warren 1949- *155*
Hansson, Gunilla 1939- *64*
Hantman, Clea *200*
Harald, Eric
   See Boesen, Victor
Harazin, S.A. *210*
Harcourt, Ellen Knowles 1890(?)-1984
   Obituary *36*
Hard, Charlotte (Ann) 1969- *98*
Hardcastle, Michael 1933- *47*
   Brief entry *38*
Harding, Lee 1937- *32*
   Brief entry *31*
Hardinge, Frances 1973- *210*
Hardt, Helga Fleischhauer
   See Fleischhauer-Hardt, Helga
Hardwick, Richard Holmes, Jr. 1923- *12*
Hardy, Alice Dale *67*
   Earlier sketch in SATA *1*
Hardy, David A(ndrews) 1936- *9*
Hardy, Jon 1958- *53*
Hardy, LeAnne 1951- *154*
Hardy, Stuart
   See Schisgall, Oscar
Hare, Norma Q(uarles) 1924- *46*
   Brief entry *41*
Harel, Nira 1936- *154*
Harford, Henry
   See Hudson, W(illiam) H(enry)
Hargrave, Leonie
   See Disch, Thomas M.
Hargreaves, (Charles) Roger 1935-1988
   Obituary *56*
Hargrove, James 1947- *57*
   Brief entry *50*
Hargrove, Jim
   See Hargrove, James
Harik, Elsa
   See Marston, Elsa

Harik, Elsa M.
See Marston, Elsa
Harik, Elsa Marston
See Marston, Elsa
Hariton, Anca I. 1955- *79*
Hark, Mildred
See McQueen, Mildred Hark
Harkaway, Hal
See Stratemeyer, Edward L.
Harkins, Philip 1912-1997 .... *6*
Obituary *129*
Harlan, Elizabeth 1945- *41*
Brief entry *35*
Harlan, Glen
See Cebulash, Mel
Harlan, Judith 1949- *135*
Earlier sketch in SATA *74*
See also CLR *81*
Harland, Richard 1947- *152*
Harlee, J. V.
See Leese, Jennifer L.B.
Harler, Ann
See Van Steenwyk, Elizabeth (Ann)
Harley, Avis *183*
Harley, Bill 1954- *208*
Earlier sketch in SATA *87*
Harlow, Joan Hiatt 1932- *157*
Harman, Fred 1902(?)-1982
Obituary *30*
Harman, Hugh 1903-1982
Obituary *33*
Harmelink, Barbara (Mary) *9*
Harmer, Mabel 1894-1992 .... *45*
Harmon, Dan
See Harmon, Daniel E(lton)
Harmon, Daniel E(lton) 1949- *157*
Harmon, Margaret 1906- *20*
Harmon, Michael 1969- *189*
Harmon, Michael B.
See Harmon, Michael
Harmon, William (Ruth) 1938- *65*
Harnan, Terry 1920- *12*
Harness, Cheryl 1951- *178*
Earlier sketch in SATA *131*
Harnett, Cynthia (Mary) 1893-1981 .... *5*
Obituary *32*
Harper, Anita 1943- *41*
Harper, Betty 1946- *126*
Harper, Charise
See Harper, Charise Mericle
Harper, Charise Mericle *179*
Harper, Elaine
See Hallin, Emily Watson
Harper, Ellen
See Noble, Marty
Harper, Jamie *174*
Harper, Jessica 1949- *148*
Harper, Jo 1932- *169*
Earlier sketch in SATA *97*
Harper, Lee *201*
Harper, Mary Wood
See Dixon, Jeanne
Harper, Piers 1966- *161*
Earlier sketch in SATA *105*
Harper, Suzanne *194*
Harper, Wilhelmina 1884-1973 .... *4*
Obituary *26*
Harrah, Madge 1931- *154*
Harrah, Michael 1940- *41*
Harrah, Monique
See Harrah, Madge
Harrar, George E. 1949- *124*
Harrell, Beatrice Orcutt 1943- *93*
Harrell, Janice 1945- *70*
Harries, Joan 1922- *39*
Harrill, Ronald 1950- *90*
Harrington, Denis J(ames) 1932- *88*
Harrington, Evelyn Davis 1911- *5*
Harrington, Janice N. 1956- *187*
Harrington, Lyn
See Harrington, Evelyn Davis

Harris, Alan 1944- *71*
Harris, Aurand 1915-1996 .... *37*
Obituary *91*
Harris, Bob
See Harris, Robert J.
Harris, Carol Flynn 1933- *135*
Harris, Catherine
See Ainsworth, Catherine Harris
Harris, Christie
See Harris, Christie (Lucy) Irwin
Harris, Christie (Lucy) Irwin 1907-2002 .... *74*
Autobiography Feature *116*
Earlier sketch in SATA *6*
See also CLR *47*
See also SAAS *10*
Harris, Christine 1955- *105*
Harris, Colver
See Colver, Anne
Harris, David 1942- *118*
Harris, David William
See Harris, David
Harris, Dorothy Joan 1931- *153*
Earlier sketch in SATA *13*
Harris, Geraldine (Rachel) 1951- *54*
Harris, Jacqueline L. 1929- *62*
Harris, Janet 1932-1979 .... *4*
Obituary *23*
Harris, Jesse
See Standiford, Natalie
Harris, Joan 1946- *146*
Harris, Joe 1928- *201*
Harris, Joel Chandler 1848-1908 .... *100*
See also YABC *1*
See also CLR *128*
Harris, John (Wyndham Parkes Lucas) Beynon
1903-1969 .... *118*
Harris, Johnson
See Harris, John (Wyndham Parkes Lucas)
Beynon
Harris, Jonathan 1921-1997 .... *52*
Harris, Larry Vincent 1939- *59*
Harris, Lavinia
See St. John, Nicole
Harris, Leon A., Jr. 1926-2000 .... *4*
Harris, Lois V. *199*
Harris, Lorle K(empe) 1912-2001 .... *22*
Harris, Marilyn
See Springer, Marilyn Harris
Harris, Mark Jonathan 1941- *84*
Earlier sketch in SATA *32*
Harris, Mary K(athleen) 1905-1966 .... *119*
Harris, Robert J. 1955- *195*
Harris, Robie H. 1940- *203*
Brief entry *53*
Earlier sketches in SATA *90, 147*
Harris, Robin
See Shine, Deborah
Harris, Rosemary (Jeanne) *82*
Earlier sketch in SATA *4*
See also CLR *30*
See also SAAS *7*
Harris, Ruth Elwin 1935- *164*
Harris, Sherwood 1932-2009 .... *25*
Harris, Steven Michael 1957- *55*
Harris, Trudy 1949- *191*
Earlier sketch in SATA *128*
Harris-Filderman, Diane
See Filderman, Diane E(lizabeth)
Harrison, C(hester) William 1913-1994 ...... *35*
Harrison, Carol
See Harrison, Carol Thompson
Harrison, Carol Thompson *113*
Harrison, David L. 1937- *186*
Earlier sketches in SATA *26, 92, 150*
Harrison, Deloris 1938- *9*
Harrison, Edward Hardy 1926- *56*
Harrison, Elizabeth (Allen) Cavanna
1909-2001 .... *30*
Earlier sketch in SATA *1*
See also SAAS *4*
Harrison, Harry 1925- *4*

Harrison, Harry Max
See Harrison, Harry
Harrison, Mette Ivie 1970- *202*
Earlier sketch in SATA *149*
Harrison, Michael 1939- *106*
Harrison, Molly (Hodgett) 1909-2002 .... *41*
Harrison, Sarah 1946- *63*
Harrison, Ted
See Harrison, Edward Hardy
Harsh, Fred (T.) 1925- *72*
Harshaw, Ruth H(etzel) 1890-1968 .... *27*
Harshman, Marc 1950- *109*
Earlier sketch in SATA *71*
Hart, Alexandra 1939- *14*
Hart, Alison
See Leonhardt, Alice
Hart, Bruce 1938-2006 .... *57*
Brief entry *39*
Hart, Carole 1943- *57*
Brief entry *39*
Hart, Carolyn 1936- *74*
Hart, Carolyn G.
See Hart, Carolyn
Hart, Carolyn Gimpel
See Hart, Carolyn
Hart, Jan Siegel 1940- *79*
Hart, Joyce 1954- *148*
Hart, Karen *185*
Hart, Lenore *171*
Hart, Philip S. 1944- *180*
Hart, Virginia 1949- *83*
Harte, Bret 1836(?)-1902 .... *26*
Harte, Francis Brett
See Harte, Bret
Harter, Debbie 1963- *107*
Hartfield, Claire 1957- *147*
Hartinger, Brent 1964- *174*
Earlier sketch in SATA *145*
Hartland, Jessie *171*
Hartley, Ellen (Raphael) 1915-1980 .... *23*
Hartley, Fred Allan III 1953- *41*
Hartley, William B(rown) 1913-1980 .... *23*
Hartling, Peter
See Hartling, Peter
Hartling, Peter 1933- *66*
See also CLR *29*
Hartman, Cassie *202*
Hartman, Dan 1955- *202*
Hartman, Evert 1937- *38*
Brief entry *35*
Hartman, Jane E(vangeline) 1928- *47*
Hartman, Louis F(rancis) 1901-1970 .... *22*
Hartman, Rachel *174*
Hartman, Victoria 1942- *91*
Hartnett, Sonya 1968- *176*
Earlier sketches in SATA *93, 130*
Hartshorn, Ruth M. 1928- *11*
Hartung, Susan Kathleen *192*
Earlier sketch in SATA *150*
Hartwig, Manfred 1950- *81*
Harvey, Brett 1936- *61*
Harvey, Edith 1908(?)-1972
Obituary *27*
Harvey, Gill *189*
Harvey, Karen D. 1935- *88*
Harvey, Roland 1945- *179*
Earlier sketches in SATA *71, 123*
Harvey-Fitzhenry, Alyxandra 1974- *189*
Harwick, B. L.
See Keller, Beverly L(ou)
Harwin, Brian
See Henderson, LeGrand
Harwood, Pearl Augusta (Bragdon)
1903-1998 .... *9*
Haseley, Dennis 1950- *157*
Brief entry *44*
Earlier sketches in SATA *57, 105*
Hashmi, Kerri 1955- *108*
Haskell, Arnold L(ionel) 1903-1981(?) *6*
Haskins, James
See Haskins, James S.

Haskins, James S. 1941-2005 .... *132*
  Autobiography Feature *132*
  Earlier sketches in SATA *9, 69, 105*
  See also CLR *39*
  See also SAAS *4*
Haskins, Jim
  See Haskins, James S.
Hasler, Eveline 1933- *181*
Hasler, Joan 1931- *28*
Hass, Robert 1941- *94*
Hassall, Joan 1906-1988 .... *43*
  Obituary *56*
Hassett, Ann 1958- *162*
Hassett, John *162*
Hassler, Jon 1933-2008 .... *19*
  Obituary *191*
Hassler, Jon Francis
  See Hassler, Jon
Hastings, Beverly
  See Barkin, Carol
  and James, Elizabeth
Hastings, Graham
  See Jeffries, Roderic
Hastings, Ian 1912- *62*
Hastings, Victor
  See Disch, Thomas M.
Haszard, Patricia Moyes 1923-2000 .... *63*
Hatch, Lynda S. 1950- *90*
Hathaway, Barbara *164*
Hathorn, Elizabeth
  See Hathorn, Elizabeth Helen
Hathorn, Elizabeth Helen 1943- *156*
  Autobiography Feature *156*
  Earlier sketches in SATA *74, 120*
Hathorn, Libby 1943-
  See Hathorn, Elizabeth Helen
Hatkoff, Craig 1954- *192*
Hatlo, Jimmy 1898-1963
  Obituary *23*
Hatton, Caroline 1957- *205*
Haugaard, Erik Christian 1923- *68*
  Earlier sketch in SATA *4*
  See also CLR *11*
  See also SAAS *12*
Haugaard, Kay *117*
Haugen, Hayley Mitchell 1968- *172*
Haugen, Tormod 1945- *66*
Hauman, Doris 1898-1984 .... *32*
Hauman, George 1890-1961 .... *32*
Hauptly, Denis J(ames) 1945- *57*
Hauser, Jill Frankel 1950- *127*
Hauser, Margaret L(ouise) 1909- *10*
Hausherr, Rosmarie 1943- *86*
Hausman, Gerald 1945- *180*
  Earlier sketches in SATA *13, 90, 132*
  See also CLR *89*
Hausman, Gerry
  See Hausman, Gerald
Hauth, Katherine B. 1940- *99*
Hautman, Pete 1952- *173*
  Earlier sketches in SATA *82, 128*
Hautman, Peter Murray
  See Hautman, Pete
Hautzig, Deborah 1956- *106*
  Earlier sketch in SATA *31*
Hautzig, Esther Rudomin 1930-2009 .... *148*
  Earlier sketches in SATA *4, 68*
  See also CLR *22*
  See also SAAS *15*
Havel, Geoff 1955- *152*
Havel, Jennifer
  See Havill, Juanita
Havelin, Kate 1961- *143*
Havighurst, Walter (Edwin) 1901-1994 .... *1*
  Obituary *79*
Haviland, Virginia 1911-1988 .... *6*
  Obituary *54*
Havill, Juanita 1949- *155*
  Earlier sketch in SATA *74*
Hawes, Judy 1913- *4*

Hawes, Louise 1943- *180*
  Earlier sketch in SATA *60*
Hawke, Rosanne 1953- *165*
  Earlier sketch in SATA *124*
Hawke, Rosanne Joy
  See Hawke, Rosanne
Hawkes, Kevin 1959- *201*
  Earlier sketches in SATA *78, 150*
Hawkes, Nigel 1943- *119*
Hawkesworth, Eric 1921- *13*
Hawking, Lucy 1969- *197*
Hawkins, Arthur 1903-1985 .... *19*
Hawkins, Colin 1945- *162*
  Earlier sketch in SATA *112*
Hawkins, Jacqui *162*
  Earlier sketch in SATA *112*
Hawkins, Jimmy 1941- *188*
Hawkins, Laura 1951- *74*
Hawkins, (Helena Ann) Quail 1905-2002 ..... *6*
  Obituary *141*
Hawkinson, John (Samuel) 1912-1994 .... *4*
Hawkinson, Lucy (Ozone) 1924-1971 .... *21*
Hawks, Robert 1961- *85*
Hawley, Mabel C. *67*
  Earlier sketch in SATA *1*
Haworth, Danette *207*
Hawthorne, Captain R. M.
  See Ellis, Edward S.
Hawthorne, Nathaniel 1804-1864
  See YABC *2*
  See also CLR *103*
Hay, Jeff T. *154*
Hay, John 1915- *13*
Hay, Timothy
  See Brown, Margaret Wise
Hayashi, Leslie Ann 1954- *115*
Hayashi, Nancy 1939- *186*
  Earlier sketch in SATA *80*
Haycak, Cara 1961- *180*
Haycock, Kate 1962- *77*
Haycraft, Howard 1905-1991 .... *6*
  Obituary *70*
Haycraft, Molly Costain 1911- *6*
Hayden, Gwendolen Lampshire 1904- *35*
Hayden, Robert
  See Hayden, Robert Earl
Hayden, Robert C(arter), Jr. 1937- *47*
  Brief entry *28*
Hayden, Robert E.
  See Hayden, Robert Earl
Hayden, Robert Earl 1913-1980 .... *19*
  Obituary *26*
Hayden, Torey L. 1951- *163*
  Earlier sketch in SATA *65*
Hayden, Torey Lynn
  See Hayden, Torey L.
Hayes, Carlton J(oseph) H(untley)
  1882-1964 .... *11*
Hayes, Daniel 1952- *109*
  Earlier sketch in SATA *73*
Hayes, Geoffrey 1947- *207*
  Earlier sketches in SATA *26, 91*
Hayes, Joe 1945- *131*
  Earlier sketch in SATA *88*
Hayes, John F. 1904-1980 .... *11*
Hayes, Karel 1949- *207*
Hayes, Rosemary *158*
Hayes, Sarah 1945- *208*
Hayes, Sheila 1937- *51*
  Brief entry *50*
Hayes, Will *7*
Hayes, William D(imitt) 1913-1976 .... *8*
Haynes, Betsy 1937- *94*
  Brief entry *37*
  Earlier sketch in SATA *48*
  See also CLR *90*
Haynes, David 1955- *97*
Haynes, Linda
  See Swinford, Betty (June Wells)
Haynes, Mary 1938- *65*
Haynes, Max 1956- *72*

Hays, H(offmann) R(eynolds) 1904-1980 ... *26*
Hays, Thomas Anthony 1957- *84*
Hays, Tony
  See Hays, Thomas Anthony
Hays, Wilma Pitchford 1909- *28*
  Earlier sketch in SATA *1*
  See also CLR *59*
  See also SAAS *3*
Hayward, Linda 1943- *185*
  Brief entry *39*
  Earlier sketch in SATA *101*
Haywood, Carolyn 1898-1990 .... *75*
  Obituary *64*
  Earlier sketches in SATA *1, 29*
  See also CLR *22*
Hazell, Rebecca (Eileen) 1947- *141*
Hazen, Barbara Shook 1930- *178*
  Earlier sketches in SATA *27, 90*
Hazen, Lynn E. *202*
Head, Gay
  See Hauser, Margaret L(ouise)
Head, Tom 1978- *167*
Headley, Elizabeth
  See Harrison, Elizabeth (Allen) Cavanna
Headley, Justina Chen 1968- *176*
Headstrom, (Birger) Richard 1902-1985 .... *8*
Heady, Eleanor B(utler) 1917-1979 .... *8*
Heagy, William D. 1964- *76*
Heal, Edith 1903-1995 .... *7*
Heal, Gillian 1934- *89*
Heale, Jay (Jeremy Peter Wingfield)
  1937- *84*
Healey, Brooks
  See Albert, Burton
Healey, Larry 1927- *44*
  Brief entry *42*
Heap, Sue 1954- *187*
  Earlier sketch in SATA *150*
Heaps, Willard A(llison) 1908-1987 .... *26*
Hearn, Diane Dawson 1952- *209*
  Earlier sketch in SATA *79*
Hearn, Emily
  See Valleau, Emily
Hearn, Julie 1958- *152*
Hearn, Lian
  See Rubinstein, Gillian
Hearn, Sneed
  See Gregg, Andrew K.
Hearne, Betsy 1942- *146*
  Earlier sketches in SATA *38, 95*
Heath, Charles D(ickinson) 1941- *46*
Heath, Veronica
  See Blackett, Veronica Heath
Heaven, Constance (Christina) 1911- *7*
Hebert-Collins, Sheila 1948- *111*
Hecht, George J(oseph) 1895-1980
  Obituary *22*
Hecht, Henri Joseph 1922- *9*
Hechtkopf, Henryk 1910- *17*
Heck, Bessie (Mildred) Holland
  1911-1995 .... *26*
Heck, Ed 1963- *173*
Heckert, Connie K(aye Delp) 1948- *82*
Hector, Julian *205*
Hedderwick, Mairi 1939- *145*
  Earlier sketches in SATA *30, 77*
Hedges, Sid(ney) G(eorge) 1897-1974 .... *28*
Hedrick, Irene Hope 1920- *175*
Heelan, Jamee Riggio 1965- *146*
Heerboth, Sharon
  See Leon, Sharon
Heffernan, John 1949- *168*
  Earlier sketch in SATA *121*
Heffron, Dorris 1944- *68*
Hefter, Richard 1942- *31*
Hegamin, Tonya C. 1975- *209*
Hegarty, Reginald Beaton 1906-1973 .... *10*
Hehenberger, Shelly 1968- *126*
Heidbreder, Robert 1947- *196*
  Earlier sketch in SATA *130*

Heidbreder, Robert K.
See Heidbreder, Robert
Heide, Florence Parry 1919- *192*
Earlier sketches in SATA *32, 69, 118*
See also CLR *60*
See also SAAS *6*
Heiderstadt, Dorothy 1907-2001 .... *6*
Heidi Louise
See Erdrich, Louise
Heidler, David S(tephen) 1955- *132*
Heidler, Jeanne T. 1956- *132*
Heilbroner, Joan Knapp 1922- *63*
Heilbrun, Lois Hussey 1922(?)-1987
Obituary *54*
Heiligman, Deborah 1958- *193*
Earlier sketches in SATA *90, 144*
Heilman, Joan Rattner *50*
Heimann, Rolf 1940- *164*
Earlier sketch in SATA *120*
Hein, Lucille Eleanor 1915-1994 .... *20*
Heine, Helme 1941- *135*
Earlier sketch in SATA *67*
See also CLR *18*
Heinlein, Robert A. 1907-1988 .... *69*
Obituary *56*
Earlier sketch in SATA *9*
See also CLR *75*
Heinlein, Robert Anson
See Heinlein, Robert A.
Heins, Ethel L(eah) 1918-1997 .... *101*
Heins, Paul 1909- *13*
Heintze, Carl 1922- *26*
Heinz, Bill
See Heinz, W. C.
Heinz, Brian J. 1946- *181*
Earlier sketch in SATA *95*
Heinz, Brian James
See Heinz, Brian J.
Heinz, W. C. 1915-2008 .... *26*
Heinz, Wilfred Charles
See Heinz, W. C.
Heinzen, Mildred
See Masters, Mildred
Heisel, Sharon E(laine) 1941- *125*
Earlier sketch in SATA *84*
Heitzmann, William Ray 1948- *73*
Heitzmann, Wm. Ray
See Heitzmann, William Ray
Helakoski, Leslie *178*
Helberg, Shirley Adelaide Holden 1919- .. *138*
Helfer, Andrew *187*
Helfer, Ralph 1937- *177*
Helfman, Elizabeth S(eaver) 1911-2001 .... *3*
Helfman, Harry Carmozin 1910-1995 .... *3*
Helgerson, Joseph 1950- *181*
Hellard, Susan *182*
Hellberg, Hans-Eric 1927- *38*
Heller, Linda 1944- *46*
Brief entry *40*
Heller, Mike
See Hano, Arnold
Heller, Ruth M. 1924- *112*
Earlier sketch in SATA *66*
Hellman, Hal
See Hellman, Harold
Hellman, Harold 1927- *4*
Helman, Andrea (Jean) 1946- *160*
Earlier sketch in SATA *107*
Helmer, Diana Star 1962- *86*
Helmer, Marilyn *160*
Earlier sketch in SATA *112*
Helps, Racey 1913-1971 .... *2*
Obituary *25*
Helquist, Brett *187*
Earlier sketch in SATA *146*
Helweg, Hans H. 1917- *50*
Brief entry *33*
Helyar, Jane Penelope Josephine 1933- *5*
Autobiography Feature *138*
See also SAAS *2*
Hemmant, Lynette 1938- *69*

Hemming, Roy G. 1928-1995 .... *11*
Obituary *86*
Hemphill, Helen 1955- *179*
Hemphill, Kris (Harrison) 1963- *118*
Hemphill, Martha Locke 1904-1973 .... *37*
Hemphill, Stephanie *190*
Hemstock, Gillian 1956- *173*
Henba, Bobbie 1926- *87*
Henbest, Nigel 1951- *55*
Brief entry *52*
Henderley, Brooks *1*
Henderson, Aileen Kilgore 1921- *178*
Henderson, Aileen Mary
See Fox, Aileen
Henderson, Gordon 1950- *53*
Henderson, Kathy 1949- *155*
Brief entry *53*
Earlier sketches in SATA *55, 95*
Henderson, Lauren 1966- *201*
Henderson, LeGrand 1901-1965 .... *9*
Henderson, Nancy Wallace 1916- *22*
Henderson, Zenna (Chlarson) 1917-1983 ..... *5*
Hendrickson, Walter Brookfield, Jr. 1936- *9*
Hendrix, John 1976- *208*
Hendry, Diana 1941- *106*
Earlier sketch in SATA *68*
Hendry, Frances Mary 1941- *171*
Earlier sketch in SATA *110*
Hendry, Linda (Gail) 1961- *83*
Heneghan, James 1930- *160*
Earlier sketches in SATA *53, 97*
Henkes, Kevin 1960- *207*
Earlier sketches in SATA *43, 76, 108, 154*
See also CLR *108*
Hennessy, Barbara G.
See Hennessy, B.G.
Hennessy, Barbara Gulbrandsen
See Hennessy, B.G.
Hennessy, B.G. 1951- *175*
Henney, Carolee Wells 1928- *102*
Henriod, Lorraine 1925- *26*
Henriquez, Emile F. 1937- *170*
Earlier sketch in SATA *89*
Henry, April 1959- *174*
Henry, Ernest 1948- *107*
Henry, Joanne Landers 1927- *6*
Henry, Maeve 1960- *75*
Henry, Marguerite 1902-1997 .... *100*
Obituary *99*
See also CLR *4*
See also SAAS *7*
Henry, Marie H. 1935- *65*
Henry, Marilyn 1939- *117*
Henry, Marion
See del Rey, Lester
Henry, O. 1862-1910
See YABC *2*
Henry, Oliver
See Henry, O.
Henry, T. E.
See Rowland-Entwistle, (Arthur) Theodore
(Henry)
Henschel, Elizabeth Georgie *56*
Henson, Heather *206*
Henson, James Maury
See Henson, Jim
Henson, Jim 1936-1990 .... *43*
Obituary *65*
Henstra, Friso 1928- *73*
Earlier sketch in SATA *8*
See also SAAS *14*
Hentoff, Nat(han Irving) 1925- *133*
Brief entry *27*
Earlier sketches in SATA *42, 69*
See also CLR *52*
Henty, G(eorge) A(lfred) 1832-1902 .... *64*
See also CLR *76*
Heo, Yumi 1964- *206*
Earlier sketches in SATA *94, 146*
Hepler, Heather *177*

Herald, Kathleen
See Peyton, Kathleen Wendy
Herb, Angela M. 1970- *92*
Herbert, Cecil
See Hamilton, Charles (Harold St. John)
Herbert, Don 1917-2007 .... *2*
Obituary *184*
Herbert, Donald Jeffrey
See Herbert, Don
Herbert, Frank 1920-1986 .... *37*
Obituary *47*
Earlier sketch in SATA *9*
Herbert, Frank Patrick
See Herbert, Frank
Herbert, Helen (Jean) 1947- *57*
Herbert, Janis 1956- *139*
Herbert, Wally 1934-2007 .... *23*
Herbert, Walter William
See Herbert, Wally
Herbst, Judith 1947- *74*
Herda, D.J. 1948- *80*
Herge
See Remi, Georges
Heritage, Martin
See Horler, Sydney
Herkimer, L(awrence) R(ussell) 1925(?)- ... *42*
Herlihy, Dirlie Anne 1935- *73*
Herlong, Madaline
See Herlong, M.H.
Herlong, M.H. *211*
Herman, Charlotte 1937- *203*
Earlier sketches in SATA *20, 99*
Hermanson, Dennis (Everett) 1947- *10*
Hermes, Jules 1962- *92*
Hermes, Patricia 1936- *191*
Earlier sketches in SATA *31, 78, 141*
Hermes, Patricia Mary
See Hermes, Patricia
Hernandez, Natalie Nelson 1929- *123*
Herndon, Ernest *91*
Herold, Ann Bixby 1937- *72*
Herrera, Juan Felipe 1948- *127*
Herrick, Steven 1958- *209*
Earlier sketches in SATA *103, 156*
Herriman, George (Joseph) 1880-1944 ..... *140*
Herriot, James 1916-1995 .... *135*
Brief entry *44*
Earlier sketch in SATA *86*
See also CLR *80*
Herrmanns, Ralph 1933- *11*
Herrold, Tracey
See Dils, Tracey E.
Herron, Carolivia 1947- *203*
Herron, Edward A(lbert) 1912- *4*
Herschler, Mildred Barger *130*
Hersey, John 1914-1993 .... *25*
Obituary *76*
Hersey, John Richard
See Hersey, John
Hershberger, Priscilla (Gorman) 1951- *81*
Hershenhorn, Esther 1945- *151*
Hershey, Kathleen M. 1934- *80*
Hershey, Mary *173*
Hersom, Kathleen 1911- *73*
Hertz, Grete Janus 1915- *23*
Herzig, Alison Cragin 1935- *87*
Herzog, Brad 1968- *131*
Heslewood, Juliet 1951- *82*
Hess, Lilo 1916- *4*
Hess, Paul 1961- *134*
Hesse, Hermann 1877-1962 .... *50*
Hesse, Karen 1952- *158*
Autobiography Feature *113*
Earlier sketches in SATA *74, 103*
See also CLR *141*
See also SAAS *25*
Hest, Amy 1950- *193*
Earlier sketches in SATA *55, 82, 129*
Heuer, Karsten 1968(?)- *202*
Heuer, Kenneth John 1927- *44*
Heuman, William 1912-1971 .... *21*

Heuston, Kimberley 1960- 167
Heuston, Kimberley Burton
  See Heuston, Kimberley
Hewes, Agnes Danforth 1874-1963 35
Hewett, Anita 1918-1989 13
Hewett, Joan 1930- 140
  Earlier sketch in SATA 81
Hewett, Richard 1929- 81
Hewitson, Jennifer 1961- 97
Hewitt, Margaret 1961- 84
Hewitt, Sally 1949- 127
Hext, Harrington
  See Phillpotts, Eden
Hey, Nigel S(tewart) 1936- 20
Heyduck-Huth, Hilde 1929- 8
Heyer, Carol 1950- 130
  Earlier sketch in SATA 74
Heyer, Marilee 1942- 102
  Earlier sketch in SATA 64
Heyerdahl, Thor 1914-2002 52
  Earlier sketch in SATA 2
Heyes, (Nancy) Eileen 1956- 150
  Earlier sketch in SATA 80
Heyliger, William 1884-1955
  See YABC 1
Heyman, Ken(neth Louis) 1930- 114
  Earlier sketch in SATA 34
Heyward, (Edwin) DuBose 1885-1940 21
Heywood, Karen 1946- 48
Hezlep, William (Earl) 1936- 88
Hiaasen, Carl 1953- 208
Hibbert, Arthur Raymond
  See Hibbert, Christopher
Hibbert, Christopher 1924-2008 4
  Obituary 201
Hibbert, Eleanor Alice Burford 1906-1993 ... 2
  Obituary 74
Hickman, Estella (Lee) 1942- 111
Hickman, Janet 1940- 127
  Earlier sketch in SATA 12
Hickman, Martha Whitmore 1925- 26
Hickman, Pamela 1958- 186
  Earlier sketch in SATA 128
Hickock, Will
  See Harrison, C(hester) William
Hickok, Lorena A. 1893-1968 20
Hickox, Rebecca (Ayres) 116
Hicks, Barbara Jean 1953- 165
Hicks, Betty 191
Hicks, Clifford B. 1920- 50
Hicks, Eleanor B.
  See Coerr, Eleanor (Beatrice)
Hicks, Harvey
  See Stratemeyer, Edward L.
Hicks, Peter 1952- 111
Hicyilmaz, Gaye 1947- 157
  Earlier sketch in SATA 77
Hieatt, Constance B(artlett) 1928- 4
Hiebert, Ray Eldon 1932- 13
Higdon, Hal 1931- 4
Higginbottom, David 1923- 87
  Earlier sketch in SATA 25
Higginbottom, J(effrey) Winslow 1945- 29
Higgins, Joanna 1945- 125
Higgins, Simon (Richard) 1958- 105
Higginsen, Vy 79
High, Linda Oatman 1958- 188
  Autobiography Feature 188
  Earlier sketches in SATA 94, 145
High, Philip E. 1914- 119
High, Philip Empson
  See High, Philip E.
Higham, David (Michael) 1949- 50
Higham, Jon Atlas
  See Higham, Jonathan Huw
Higham, Jonathan Huw 1960- 59
Highet, Helen
  See MacInnes, Helen (Clark)
Hightman, Jason 1971(?)- 189
Hightman, J.P.
  See Hightman, Jason

Hightower, Florence Cole 1916-1981 4
  Obituary 27
Highwater, Jamake (Mamake)
  1942(?)-2001 69
  Brief entry 30
  Earlier sketch in SATA 32
  See also CLR 17
Hilb, Nora 1953- 178
Hildebrandt, Greg 1939- 172
  Brief entry 33
  Earlier sketch in SATA 55
Hildebrandt, Tim 1939-2006 55
  Brief entry 33
Hildebrandt, Timothy
  See Hildebrandt, Tim
Hildebrandts, The
  See Hildebrandt, Greg
  and Hildebrandt, Tim
Hilder, Rowland 1905-1993 36
  Obituary 77
Hildick, E. W.
  See Hildick, Wallace
Hildick, Wallace 1925-2001 68
  Earlier sketch in SATA 2
  See also SAAS 6
Hilgartner, Beth 1957- 58
Hill, Alexis
  See Craig, Mary (Francis) Shura
  and Glick, Ruth (Burtnick)
Hill, Anthony R. 1942- 164
  Earlier sketch in SATA 91
Hill, Anthony Robert
  See Hill, Anthony R.
Hill, David 1942- 152
  Earlier sketch in SATA 103
Hill, Donna (Marie) 1921- 124
  Earlier sketch in SATA 24
Hill, Douglas 1935-2007 78
  Earlier sketch in SATA 39
Hill, Douglas Arthur
  See Hill, Douglas
Hill, Elizabeth Starr 1925- 143
  Earlier sketch in SATA 24
Hill, Eric 1927- 133
  Brief entry 53
  Earlier sketch in SATA 66
  See also CLR 13
Hill, Gordon
  See Eldin, Peter
Hill, Grace Brooks 67
  Earlier sketch in SATA 1
Hill, Grace Livingston 1865-1947
  See YABC 2
Hill, Helen M(orey) 1915- 27
Hill, John
  See Koontz, Dean
Hill, Johnson
  See Kunhardt, Edith
Hill, Judy I. R.
  See Roberts, Judy I.
Hill, Kathleen Louise 1917- 4
Hill, Kay
  See Hill, Kathleen Louise
Hill, Kirkpatrick 1938- 188
  Earlier sketches in SATA 72, 126
Hill, Laban
  See Hill, Laban Carrick
Hill, Laban Carrick 170
Hill, Lee Sullivan 1958- 96
Hill, Lorna 1902-1991 12
Hill, Margaret (Ohler) 1915- 36
Hill, Meg
  See Hill, Margaret (Ohler)
Hill, Meredith
  See Craig, Mary (Francis) Shura
Hill, Monica
  See Watson, Jane Werner
Hill, Pamela Smith 1954- 112
Hill, Ralph Nading 1917-1987 65
Hill, Robert W(hite) 1919-1982 12
  Obituary 31

Hill, Ruth A.
  See Viguers, Ruth Hill
Hill, Ruth Livingston
  See Munce, Ruth Hill
Hill, Stuart 1958- 186
Hill, Susan 1942- 183
Hill, Susan Elizabeth
  See Hill, Susan
Hill, Susanna Leonard 1965- 193
Hill, Thomas 1960- 82
Hillcourt, William 1900-1992 27
Hillenbrand, Will 1960- 210
  Earlier sketches in SATA 84, 147
Hiller, Ilo (Ann) 1938- 59
Hillerman, Anthony Grove
  See Hillerman, Tony
Hillerman, Tony 1925-2008 6
  Obituary 198
Hillert, Margaret 1920- 91
  Earlier sketch in SATA 8
Hilliard, Richard 183
Hillman, Ben 1957- 202
Hillman, Elizabeth 1942- 75
Hillman, John 1952- 120
Hillman, Martin
  See Hill, Douglas
Hillman, Priscilla 1940- 48
  Brief entry 39
Hillman, Shane 200
Hills, C.A.R. 1955- 39
Hills, Charles Albert Reis
  See Hills, C.A.R.
Hills, Tad 173
Hilton, Irene Pothus -1979 7
Hilton, James 1900-1954 34
Hilton, Margaret Lynette 1946- 105
  Earlier sketch in SATA 68
  See also CLR 25
  See also SAAS 21
Hilton, Nette
  See Hilton, Margaret Lynette
Hilton, Ralph 1907-1982 8
Hilton, Suzanne 1922- 4
Hilton-Bruce, Anne
  See Hilton, Margaret Lynette
Him, George 1937-1982
  Obituary 30
Himelblau, Linda -2005 179
Himelstein, Shmuel 1940- 83
Himler, Ann 1946- 8
Himler, Ronald 1937- 183
  Earlier sketches in SATA 6, 92, 137
Himler, Ronald Norbert
  See Himler, Ronald
Himmelman, John C(arl) 1959- 159
  Earlier sketches in SATA 47, 94
Hinckley, Helen
  See Jones, Helen Hinckley
Hind, Dolores (Ellen) 1931- 53
  Brief entry 49
Hindin, Nathan
  See Bloch, Robert (Albert)
Hindley, Judy 1940- 179
  Earlier sketch in SATA 120
Hinds, P(atricia) Mignon 98
Hine, Sesyle Joslin 1929- 2
Hines, Anna Grossnickle 1946- 209
  Brief entry 45
  Earlier sketches in SATA 51, 95, 141
  See also SAAS 16
Hines, Gary (Roger) 1944- 136
  Earlier sketch in SATA 74
Hinojosa, Maria (de Lourdes) 1961- 88
Hinton, Nigel 1941- 166
Hinton, S. E. 1950- 160
  Earlier sketches in SATA 19, 58, 115
  See also CLR 23
Hinton, Sam 1917-2009 43
Hinton, Susan Eloise
  See Hinton, S. E.

Hintz, Martin 1945- *128*
  Brief entry *39*
  Earlier sketch in SATA *47*
Hintz, Stephen V. 1975- *129*
Hippopotamus, Eugene H.
  See Kraus, (Herman) Robert
Hirano, Cathy 1957- *68*
Hirao, Amiko *203*
Hirsch, Karen 1941- *61*
Hirsch, Odo *157*
  Earlier sketch in SATA *111*
Hirsch, Phil 1926- *35*
Hirsch, S. Carl 1913-1990 .... *2*
  See also SAAS *7*
Hirschfelder, Arlene B. 1943- *138*
  Earlier sketch in SATA *80*
Hirschi, Ron 1948- *192*
  Earlier sketches in SATA *56, 95*
Hirschmann, Linda (Ann) 1941- *40*
Hirsh, Marilyn 1944-1988 .... *7*
  Obituary *58*
Hirshberg, Al(bert Simon) 1909-1973 .... *38*
Hiscock, Bruce 1940- *204*
  Earlier sketches in SATA *57, 137*
Hiser, Constance 1950- *71*
Hiser, Iona Seibert -1998 .... *4*
Hislop, Julia Rose Catherine 1962- *74*
Hissey, Jane 1952- *130*
  Autobiography Feature *130*
  Earlier sketches in SATA *58, 103*
Hissey, Jane Elizabeth
  See Hissey, Jane
Hitchcock, Alfred (Joseph) 1899-1980 .... *27*
  Obituary *24*
Hite, Sid 1954- *175*
  Earlier sketches in SATA *75, 136*
Hitte, Kathryn 1919- *16*
Hitz, Demi
  See Demi
Hitzeroth, Deborah L. 1961- *78*
Hnizdovsky, Jacques 1915- *32*
Ho, Louise *185*
Ho, Minfong 1951- *151*
  Earlier sketches in SATA *15, 94*
  See also CLR *28*
Hoagland, Edward (Morley) 1932- *51*
Hoare, Robert J(ohn) 1921-1975 .... *38*
Hoban, Lillian 1925-1998 .... *69*
  Obituary *104*
  Earlier sketch in SATA *22*
  See also CLR *67*
Hoban, Russell 1925- *136*
  Earlier sketches in SATA *1, 40, 78*
  See also CLR *139*
Hoban, Russell Conwell
  See Hoban, Russell
Hoban, Tana 1917(?)-2006 .... *104*
  Obituary *173*
  Earlier sketches in SATA *22, 70*
  See also CLR *76*
  See also SAAS *12*
Hobart, Lois (Elaine) *7*
Hobbie, Holly 1944- *178*
  See also CLR *88*
Hobbie, Jocelyn *190*
Hobbie, Nathaniel *196*
Hobbs, Leigh 1953- *166*
Hobbs, Valerie 1941- *193*
  Autobiography Feature *145*
  Earlier sketches in SATA *93, 145*
  See also CLR *148*
Hobbs, Will 1947- *177*
  Autobiography Feature *127*
  Earlier sketches in SATA *72, 110*
  See also CLR *59*
Hobbs, William Carl
  See Hobbs, Will
Hoberman, Mary Ann 1930- *158*
  Earlier sketches in SATA *5, 72, 111*
  See also CLR *22*
  See also SAAS *18*

Hobson, Bruce 1950- *62*
Hobson, Burton (Harold) 1933- *28*
Hobson, Laura Z(ametkin) 1900-1986 .... *52*
Hobson, Sally 1967- *172*
  Earlier sketch in SATA *84*
Hoce, Charley E. *174*
Hochman, David *202*
Hochschild, Arlie Russell 1940- *11*
Hockaby, Stephen
  See Mitchell, Gladys (Maude Winifred)
Hockenberry, Hope
  See Newell, Hope Hockenberry
Hodge, Deborah 1954- *163*
  Earlier sketch in SATA *122*
Hodge, P. W.
  See Hodge, Paul W(illiam)
Hodge, Paul W(illiam) 1934- *12*
Hodgell, P(atricia) C(hristine) 1951- *42*
Hodges, C. Walter 1909-2004 .... *2*
  Obituary *158*
Hodges, Carl G. 1902-1964 .... *10*
Hodges, Cyril Walter
  See Hodges, C. Walter
Hodges, Elizabeth Jamison *1*
Hodges, Margaret 1911-2005 .... *167*
  Obituary *172*
  Earlier sketches in SATA *1, 33, 75, 117*
  See also SAAS *9*
Hodges, Margaret Moore
  See Hodges, Margaret
Hodgetts, Blake Christopher 1967- *43*
Hodgkins, Fran 1964- *199*
Hodgkinson, Leigh 1975- *202*
Hodgman, Ann 1956- *198*
Hodgson, Harriet (W.) 1935- *84*
Hoehne, Marcia 1951- *89*
Hoellwarth, Cathryn Clinton
  See Clinton, Cathryn
Hoestlandt, Jo 1948- *94*
Hoestlandt, Jocelyne
  See Hoestlandt, Jo
Hoexter, Corinne K. 1927- *6*
Hoeye, Michael 1947- *136*
Hoff, Carol 1900-1979 .... *11*
Hoff, Mary (King) 1956- *157*
  Earlier sketch in SATA *74*
Hoff, Syd(ney) 1912-2004 .... *138*
  Obituary *154*
  Earlier sketches in SATA *9, 72*
  See also CLR *83*
  See also SAAS *4*
Hoffman, Edwin D. *49*
Hoffman, Elizabeth P(arkinson) 1921-2003
  Obituary *153*
Hoffman, Mary 1945- *211*
  Earlier sketches in SATA *59, 97, 144*
  See also SAAS *24*
Hoffman, Mat 1972- *150*
Hoffman, Nina Kiriki 1955- *160*
Hoffman, Phyllis M(iriam) 1944- *4*
Hoffman, Rosekrans 1926- *15*
Hoffmann, E(rnst) T(heodor) A(madeus)
  1776-1822 .... *27*
  See also CLR *133*
Hoffmann, Felix 1911-1975 .... *9*
Hoffmann, Heinrich 1809-1894
  See CLR *122*
Hoffmann, Margaret Jones 1910- *48*
Hoffmann, Peggy
  See Hoffmann, Margaret Jones
Hofher, Catherine Baxley 1954- *130*
Hofher, Cathy
  See Hofher, Catherine Baxley
Hofmeyr, Dianne (Louise) *138*
Hofsepian, Sylvia A. 1932- *74*
Hofsinde, Robert 1902-1973 .... *21*
Hogan, Bernice Harris 1929- *12*
Hogan, Inez 1895-1973 .... *2*
Hogan, James P(atrick) 1941- *81*
Hogan, Jamie *192*
Hogan, Linda 1947- *132*

Hogan, Mary 1957- *210*
Hogarth, Burne 1911-1996 .... *89*
  Earlier sketch in SATA *63*
Hogarth, Grace (Weston Allen) 1905-1995 . *91*
Hogarth, Jr.
  See Kent, Rockwell
Hogarth, (Arthur) Paul 1917-2001 .... *41*
Hogg, Garry 1902-1976 .... *2*
Hogg, Gary 1957- *172*
  Earlier sketch in SATA *105*
Hogner, Dorothy Childs *4*
Hogner, Nils 1893-1970 .... *25*
Hogrogian, Nonny 1932- *74*
  Autobiography Feature *127*
  Earlier sketch in SATA *7*
  See also CLR *95*
  See also SAAS *1*
Hoh, Diane 1937- *102*
  Brief entry *48*
  Earlier sketch in SATA *52*
Hoke, Helen
  See Watts, Helen L. Hoke
Hoke, Helen L.
  See Watts, Helen L. Hoke
Hoke, John (Lindsay) 1925- *7*
Hokenson, Terry 1948- *193*
Hol, Coby 1943- *126*
Holabird, Katharine 1948- *135*
  Earlier sketch in SATA *62*
Holaday, Bobbie 1922- *153*
Holbeach, Henry
  See Rands, William Brighty
Holberg, Ruth L(angland) 1889-1984 .... *1*
Holbrook, Kathy 1963- *107*
Holbrook, Peter
  See Glick, Carl (Cannon)
Holbrook, Sabra
  See Erickson, Sabra Rollins
Holbrook, Sara *131*
Holbrook, Stewart Hall 1893-1964 .... *2*
Holcomb, Jerry (Leona) Kimble 1927- *113*
Holcomb, Nan
  See McPhee, Norma H.
Holden, Elizabeth Rhoda
  See Lawrence, Louise
Holding, James (Clark Carlisle, Jr.)
  1907-1997 .... *3*
Hole, Stian 1969- *204*
Holeman, Linda 1949- *136*
  Autobiography Feature *136*
  Earlier sketch in SATA *102*
Holinger, William (Jacques) 1944- *90*
Holisher, Desider 1901-1972 .... *6*
Holl, Adelaide Hinkle 1910- *8*
Holl, Kristi D(iane) 1951- *51*
Holland, Gay W. 1941- *128*
Holland, Isabelle (Christian) 1920-2002 ..... *70*
  Autobiography Feature *103*
  Obituary *132*
  Earlier sketch in SATA *8*
  See also CLR *57*
Holland, Janice 1913-1962 .... *18*
Holland, John L(ewis) 1919- *20*
Holland, Joyce
  See Morice, Dave
Holland, Julia 1954- *106*
Holland, Lynda (H.) 1959- *77*
Holland, Lys
  See Gater, Dilys
Holland, Marion 1908-1989 .... *6*
  Obituary *61*
Hollander, John 1929- *13*
Hollander, Nicole 1940(?)- *101*
Hollander, Paul
  See Silverberg, Robert
Hollander, Phyllis 1928- *39*
Hollander, Zander 1923- *63*
Holldobler, Turid 1939- *26*
Holliday, Joe
  See Holliday, Joseph
Holliday, Joseph 1910- *11*

Holling, Holling C(lancy) 1900-1973 .... *15*
  Obituary *26*
  See also CLR *50*
Hollingsworth, Alvin C(arl) 1930- *39*
Hollingsworth, Mary 1947- *166*
  Earlier sketch in SATA *91*
Holloway, Teresa (Bragunier) 1906- *26*
Hollyer, Belinda *204*
Holm, (Else) Anne (Lise) 1922-1998 .... *1*
  See also CLR *75*
  See also SAAS *7*
Holm, Jennifer L. 1968(?)- *183*
  Earlier sketches in SATA *120, 163*
Holm, Matthew 1974- *174*
Holm, Sharon Lane 1955- *114*
  Earlier sketch in SATA *78*
Holman, Felice 1919- *82*
  Earlier sketch in SATA *7*
  See also SAAS *17*
Holm and Hamel
  See Holm, Jennifer L.
Holmberg, Bo R. 1945- *203*
Holme, Bryan 1913-1990 .... *26*
  Obituary *66*
Holmes, Barbara Ware 1945- *127*
  Earlier sketch in SATA *65*
Holmes, Elizabeth 1957- *191*
Holmes, Elizabeth Ann
  See Holmes, Elizabeth
Holmes, John
  See Souster, (Holmes) Raymond
Holmes, Marjorie (Rose) 1910-2002 .... *43*
Holmes, Martha 1961- *72*
Holmes, Mary Tavener 1954- *199*
Holmes, Mary Z(astrow) 1943- *80*
Holmes, Oliver Wendell 1809-1894 .... *34*
Holmes, Peggy 1898- *60*
Holmes, Raymond
  See Souster, (Holmes) Raymond
Holmes, Rick
  See Hardwick, Richard Holmes, Jr.
Holmes, Sara Lewis *186*
Holmgren, Helen Jean 1930- *45*
Holmgren, Sister George Ellen
  See Holmgren, Helen Jean
Holmgren, Virginia C(unningham) 1909- ... *26*
Holmquist, Eve 1921- *11*
Holt, Kimberly Willis 1960- *179*
  Earlier sketch in SATA *122*
Holt, Margaret 1937- *4*
Holt, Margaret Van Vechten (Saunders)
  1899-1963 .... *32*
Holt, Michael (Paul) 1929- *13*
Holt, Rackham
  See Holt, Margaret Van Vechten (Saunders)
Holt, Rochelle L.
  See DuBois, Rochelle Holt
Holt, Stephen
  See Thompson, Harlan
Holt, Victoria
  See Hibbert, Eleanor Alice Burford
Holton, Leonard
  See Wibberley, Leonard
Holtz, Thomas R., Jr. 1965- *203*
Holtze, Sally Holmes 1952- *64*
Holtzman, Jerome 1926-2008 .... *57*
  Obituary *194*
Holub, Joan 1956- *149*
  Earlier sketch in SATA *99*
Holub, Josef 1926- *175*
Holubitsky, Katherine 1955- *165*
  Earlier sketch in SATA *121*
Holyer, Erna Maria 1925- *22*
Holyer, Ernie
  See Holyer, Erna Maria
Holz, Loretta (Marie) 1943- *17*
Homel, David 1952- *97*
Homze, Alma C. 1932- *17*
Honey, Elizabeth 1947- *137*
  Autobiography Feature *137*
  Earlier sketch in SATA *112*

Honeycutt, Natalie 1945- *97*
Hong, Lily Toy 1958- *76*
Hong, Maxine Ting Ting
  See Kingston, Maxine Hong
Honig, Donald 1931- *18*
Honness, Elizabeth H. 1904- *2*
Hoobler, Dorothy 1941- *161*
  Earlier sketches in SATA *28, 109*
Hoobler, Thomas *161*
  Earlier sketches in SATA *28, 109*
Hood, Joseph F. 1925- *4*
Hood, Robert E. 1926- *21*
Hood, Sarah
  See Killough, (Karen) Lee
Hook, Brendan 1963- *105*
Hook, Frances 1912-1983 .... *27*
Hook, Geoffrey R(aynor) 1928- *103*
Hook, Jeff
  See Hook, Geoffrey R(aynor)
Hook, Martha 1936- *27*
Hooker, Richard
  See Heinz, W. C.
Hooker, Ruth 1920-1998 .... *21*
hooks, bell 1952(?)- *170*
  Earlier sketch in SATA *115*
Hooks, William H(arris) 1921- *94*
  Earlier sketch in SATA *16*
Hoon, Patricia Easterly 1954- *90*
Hooper, Byrd
  See St. Clair, Byrd Hooper
Hooper, Mary 1948- *205*
  Earlier sketch in SATA *160*
Hooper, Maureen Brett 1927- *76*
Hooper, Meredith 1939- *159*
  Earlier sketches in SATA *28, 101*
Hooper, Meredith Jean
  See Hooper, Meredith
Hooper, Patricia 1941- *95*
Hoopes, Lyn Littlefield 1953- *49*
  Brief entry *44*
Hoopes, Ned E(dward) 1932- *21*
Hoopes, Roy 1922-2009 .... *11*
Hoose, Phillip M. 1947- *137*
Hoover, H(elen) M(ary) 1935- *132*
  Brief entry *33*
  Earlier sketches in SATA *44, 83*
  See also SAAS *8*
Hoover, Helen (Drusilla Blackburn)
  1910-1984 .... *12*
  Obituary *39*
Hope, Christopher 1944- *62*
Hope, Christopher David Tully
  See Hope, Christopher
Hope, Laura Lee
  See Goulart, Ron
  and Stanley, George Edward
Hope Simpson, Jacynth 1930- *12*
Hopf, Alice (Martha) L(ightner) 1904-1988 . *5*
  Obituary *55*
Hopkins, A. T.
  See Turngren, Annette
Hopkins, C. M.
  See Hopkins, Cathy
Hopkins, Cathy 1953- *165*
Hopkins, Cathy M.
  See Hopkins, Cathy
Hopkins, Clark 1895-1976
  Obituary *34*
Hopkins, Ellen 1955- *128*
  See Hopkins, Ellen L.
Hopkins, Ellen L.
  See Hopkins, Ellen
Hopkins, Jackie
  See Hopkins, Jackie Mims
Hopkins, Jackie Mims 1952- *178*
  Earlier sketch in SATA *92*
Hopkins, Joseph G(erard) E(dward) 1909- .. *11*
Hopkins, (Hector) Kenneth 1914-1988
  Obituary *58*

Hopkins, Lee Bennett 1938- *168*
  Earlier sketches in SATA *3, 68, 125*
  See also CLR *44*
  See also SAAS *4*
Hopkins, Lyman
  See Folsom, Franklin (Brewster)
Hopkins, Marjorie 1911-1999 .... *9*
Hopkins, Mary R(ice) 1956- *97*
Hopkinson, Amanda 1948- *84*
Hopkinson, Deborah 1952- *180*
  Autobiography Feature *180*
  Earlier sketches in SATA *76, 108, 159*
  See also CLR *118*
Hopman, Philip 1961- *177*
Hoppe, Joanne 1932- *42*
Hoppe, Matthias 1952- *76*
Hoppe, Paul *209*
Hopper, Nancy J. 1937- *38*
  Brief entry *35*
Hopping, Lorraine Jean
  See Egan, Lorraine Hopping
Horacek, Judy 1961- *211*
Horacek, Petr *163*
Horenstein, Henry 1947- *108*
Horgan, Paul (George Vincent O'Shaughnessy)
  1903-1995 .... *13*
  Obituary *84*
Horlak, E.E.
  See Tepper, Sheri S.
Horler, Sydney 1888-1954 .... *102*
Horn, Sandra Ann 1944- *154*
Hornblow, Arthur, Jr. 1893-1976 .... *15*
Hornblow, Leonora 1920-2005 .... *18*
  Obituary *171*
Hornblow, Leonora Schinasi
  See Hornblow, Leonora
Horne, Constance 1927- *149*
Horne, Richard 1960-2007 .... *169*
  Obituary *180*
  Earlier sketch in SATA *111*
Horne, Richard Henry Hengist
  1802(?)-1884 .... *29*
Horner, Althea (Jane) 1926- *36*
Horner, Dave 1934- *12*
Horner, Jack
  See Horner, John R(obert)
Horner, John R(obert) 1946- *106*
Hornik, Laurie Miller *159*
Horniman, Joanne 1951- *167*
  Earlier sketch in SATA *98*
Hornos, Axel 1907-1994 .... *20*
Hornstein, Reuben Aaron 1912- *64*
Horowitz, Anthony 1955- *195*
  Earlier sketch in SATA *137*
Horowitz, Dave 1970- *204*
  Earlier sketch in SATA *172*
Horowitz, Ruth 1957- *136*
Horrocks, Anita 1958- *169*
Horse, Harry
  See Horne, Richard
Horsfield, Alan 1939- *153*
Hort, Lenny *179*
Horton, James O. 1943- *173*
Horton, James Oliver
  See Horton, James O.
Horton, Madelyn (Stacey) 1962- *77*
Horvath, Betty 1927- *4*
Horvath, David 1972(?)- *192*
Horvath, Polly 1957- *194*
  Earlier sketches in SATA *85, 140*
  See also CLR *90*
Horwich, Frances R(appaport) 1908-2001 .. *11*
  Obituary *130*
Horwitz, Elinor Lander *45*
  Brief entry *33*
Horwood, William 1944- *85*
Hosford, Dorothy (Grant) 1900-1952 .... *22*
Hosford, Jessie 1892-1990 .... *5*
Hoshi, Shin'ichi 1926- *101*
Hoshino, Felicia 1968- *189*

Hoskyns-Abrahall, Clare (Constance
Drury) *13*
Hosler, Danamarie 1978- *184*
Hossack, Sylvia 1939- *83*
Hossack, Sylvie Adams
See Hossack, Sylvia
Hosseini, Khaled 1965- *156*
Hossell, Karen Price
See Price, Karen
Hosta, Dar *192*
Hostetler, Marian 1932- *91*
Houck, Carter 1924- *22*
Hough, Charlotte 1924-2008 .... *9*
Obituary *202*
Hough, Helen Charlotte
See Hough, Charlotte
Hough, Judy Taylor 1932- *63*
Brief entry *51*
Earlier sketch in SATA *56*
Hough, Richard (Alexander) 1922-1999 ..... *17*
Houghton, Eric 1930- *7*
Houk, Randy 1944- *97*
Houlehen, Robert J. 1918- *18*
Houlton, Peggy Mann 1925(?)-1990 .... *6*
Household, Geoffrey (Edward West)
1900-1988 .... *14*
Obituary *59*
Housman, Laurence 1865-1959 .... *25*
Houston, Dick 1943- *74*
Houston, Gloria *138*
Autobiography Feature *138*
Earlier sketch in SATA *81*
Houston, James A(rchibald) 1921-2005 ...... *74*
Obituary *163*
Earlier sketch in SATA *13*
See also CLR *3*
See also SAAS *17*
Houston, James D. 1933-2009 .... *78*
Obituary *203*
Houston, James Dudley
See Houston, James D.
Houston, James Dudley
See Houston, James D.
Houston, Jeanne Toyo Wakatsuki
See Houston, Jeanne Wakatsuki
Houston, Jeanne Wakatsuki 1934- *168*
Autobiography Feature *168*
Earlier sketch in SATA *78*
Houston, Juanita C. 1921- *129*
Houton, Kathleen
See Kilgore, Kathleen
Houts, Amy F. *164*
Hovey, Kate *158*
Howard, Alan 1922- *45*
Howard, Alyssa
See Buckholtz, Eileen (Garber)
and Glick, Ruth (Burtnick)
and Titchener, Louise
Howard, Arthur 1948- *165*
Howard, Arthur Charles
See Howard, Arthur
Howard, Elizabeth Fitzgerald 1927- *119*
Earlier sketch in SATA *74*
Howard, Ellen 1943- *184*
Earlier sketches in SATA *67, 99*
Howard, Jane R(uble) 1924- *87*
Howard, Norman Barry 1949- *90*
Howard, P. M.
See Howard, Pauline Rodriguez
Howard, Paul 1967- *190*
Earlier sketch in SATA *118*
Howard, Pauline Rodriguez 1951- *124*
Howard, Prosper
See Hamilton, Charles (Harold St. John)
Howard, Robert West 1908-1988 .... *5*
Howard, Todd 1964- *135*
Howard, Tristan
See Currie, Stephen
Howard, Vernon (Linwood) 1918-1992 ...... *40*
Obituary *73*

Howard, Warren F.
See Pohl, Frederik
Howarth, Daniel *188*
Howarth, David (Armine) 1912-1991 .... *6*
Obituary *68*
Howarth, Lesley 1952- *94*
Howe, Deborah 1946-1978 .... *29*
Howe, James 1946- *161*
Earlier sketches in SATA *29, 71, 111*
See also CLR *9*
Howe, John F. 1957- *79*
Howe, Norma 1930- *126*
Howell, Pat 1947- *15*
Howell, S.
See Styles, (Frank) Showell
Howell, Virginia
See Ellison, Virginia H(owell)
Howes, Barbara 1914-1996 .... *5*
Howie, Diana 1945- *122*
Howie, Diana Melson
See Howie, Diana
Howker, Janni 1957- *72*
Brief entry *46*
See also CLR *14*
See also SAAS *13*
Howland, Ethan 1963- *131*
Hoy, Linda 1946- *65*
Hoy, Nina
See Roth, Arthur J(oseph)
Hoyle, Geoffrey 1942- *18*
Hoyt, Ard *190*
Hoyt, Edwin P(almer), Jr. 1923- *28*
Hoyt, Erich 1950- *140*
Earlier sketch in SATA *65*
Hoyt, Olga
See Gruhzit-Hoyt, Olga (Margaret)
Hrdlitschka, Shelley 1956- *167*
Earlier sketch in SATA *111*
Hrdlitschka, Shelley Joanne
See Hrdlitschka, Shelley
Htin Aung, U.
See Aung, (Maung) Htin
Hu, Ying-Hwa *173*
Huang, Benrei 1959- *86*
Hubalek, Linda K. 1954- *111*
Hubbard, Crystal *209*
Hubbard, Margaret Ann
See Priley, Margaret (Ann) Hubbard
Hubbard, Michelle Calabro 1953- *122*
Hubbard, Patricia 1945- *124*
Hubbard, Woodleigh Marx *160*
Earlier sketch in SATA *98*
Hubbell, Patricia 1928- *186*
Earlier sketches in SATA *8, 132*
Hubery, Julia *195*
Hubley, Faith Elliot 1924-2001 .... *48*
Obituary *133*
Hubley, John 1914-1977 .... *48*
Obituary *24*
Huck, Charlotte S. 1922- *136*
Earlier sketch in SATA *82*
Hudak, Michal 1956- *143*
Hudson, Cheryl Willis 1948- *160*
Earlier sketch in SATA *81*
Hudson, Jan 1954-1990 .... *77*
See also CLR *40*
Hudson, Jeffery
See Crichton, Michael
Hudson, Jeffrey
See Crichton, Michael
Hudson, (Margaret) Kirsty 1947- *32*
Hudson, Margaret
See Shuter, Jane (Margaret)
Hudson, W(illiam) H(enry) 1841-1922 .... *35*
Hudson, Wade 1946- *162*
Earlier sketch in SATA *74*
Huelsmann, Eva 1928- *16*
Huerlimann, Bettina 1909-1983 .... *39*
Obituary *34*
Huerlimann, Ruth 1939- *32*
Brief entry *31*

Huff, Barbara A. 1929- *67*
Huff, Tanya 1957- *171*
Earlier sketch in SATA *85*
Huff, Tanya Sue
See Huff, Tanya
Huff, T.S.
See Huff, Tanya
Huff, Vivian 1948- *59*
Huffaker, Sandy 1943- *10*
Huffman, Tom *24*
Huggins, Nathan Irvin 1927-1989 .... *63*
Huggins, Peter 1951- *178*
Hughes, Carol 1955- *108*
Hughes, Dean 1943- *139*
Earlier sketches in SATA *33, 77*
See also CLR *76*
Hughes, Eden
See Griffin, W.E.B.
Hughes, Edward James
See Hughes, Ted
Hughes, James Langston
See Hughes, Langston
Hughes, Langston 1902-1967 .... *33*
Earlier sketch in SATA *4*
See also CLR *17*
Hughes, Libby *71*
Hughes, Matilda
See MacLeod, Charlotte (Matilda)
Hughes, Monica 1925-2003 .... *162*
Earlier sketches in SATA *15, 70, 119*
See also CLR *60*
See also SAAS *11*
Hughes, Monica Ince
See Hughes, Monica
Hughes, Pat *197*
Hughes, Richard (Arthur Warren)
1900-1976 .... *8*
Obituary *25*
Hughes, Sara
See Saunders, Susan
Hughes, Shirley 1927- *159*
Earlier sketches in SATA *16, 70, 110*
See also CLR *15*
Hughes, Ted 1930-1998 .... *49*
Brief entry *27*
Obituary *107*
See also CLR *131*
Hughes, Thomas 1822-1896 .... *31*
Hughes, Virginia
See Campbell, Hope
Hughes, Walter (Llewellyn) 1910-1993 ...... *26*
Hughey, Roberta 1942- *61*
Hugo, Pierre Brackers de
See Brackers de Hugo, Pierre
Hugo, Victor 1802-1885 .... *47*
Hugo, Victor Marie
See Hugo, Victor
Huline-Dickens, Frank William 1931- *34*
Huling, Jan *172*
Huliska-Beith, Laura *175*
Hull, Eleanor (Means) 1913- *21*
Hull, Eric Traviss
See Harnan, Terry
Hull, H. Braxton
See Jacobs, Helen Hull
Hull, Jesse Redding
See Hull, Jessie Redding
Hull, Jessie Redding 1932- *51*
Hull, Katharine 1921-1977 .... *23*
Hull, Lise (E.) 1954- *148*
Hull, Maureen 1949- *142*
Hulme, Joy N. 1922- *161*
Earlier sketches in SATA *74, 112*
Hults, Dorothy Niebrugge 1898-2000 .... *6*
Humble, Richard 1945- *60*
Hume, Lachie *189*
Hume, Lotta Carswell *7*
Hume, Ruth Fox 1922-1980 .... *26*
Obituary *22*
Hume, Stephen Eaton 1947- *136*
Hummel, Berta 1909-1946 .... *43*

Hummel, Sister Maria Innocentia
  See Hummel, Berta
Humphrey, Carol Sue 1956- *167*
Humphrey, Henry (III) 1930- *16*
Humphrey, Kate
  See Forsyth, Kate
Humphrey, Sandra McLeod 1936- *95*
Humphreys, Martha 1943- *71*
Humphreys, Susan L.
  See Lowell, Susan
Hundal, Nancy 1957- *128*
Huneck, Stephen 1949- *183*
  Earlier sketch in SATA *129*
Hungerford, Hesba Fay
  See Brinsmead, H(esba) F(ay)
Hungerford, Pixie
  See Brinsmead, H(esba) F(ay)
Hunkin, Timothy Mark Trelawney 1950- ... *53*
Hunt, Angela Elwell 1957- *159*
  Earlier sketch in SATA *75*
Hunt, Bernice 1920- *4*
Hunt, Charlotte Dumaresq
  See Demi
Hunt, Francesca
  See Holland, Isabelle (Christian)
Hunt, Irene 1907-2001 .... *91*
  Earlier sketch in SATA *2*
  See also CLR *1*
Hunt, Janie Louise 1963- *102*
Hunt, Jonathan 1966- *84*
Hunt, Joyce 1927- *31*
Hunt, Linda 1940- *39*
Hunt, Lisa B(ehnke) 1967- *84*
Hunt, Mabel Leigh 1892-1971 .... *1*
  Obituary *26*
Hunt, Morton M(agill) 1920- *22*
Hunt, Nigel
  See Greenbank, Anthony Hunt
Hunt, Peter (Leonard) 1945- *76*
Hunter, Anne B. 1966- *118*
Hunter, Bernice Thurman 1922-2002 .... *85*
  Brief entry *45*
Hunter, Bobbi Dooley 1945- *89*
Hunter, Captain Marcy
  See Ellis, Edward S.
Hunter, Chris
  See Fluke, Joanne
Hunter, Clingham M.D.
  See Adams, William Taylor
Hunter, Edith Fisher 1919- *31*
Hunter, Erin
  See Cary, Kate
Hunter, Evan 1926-2005 .... *25*
  Obituary *167*
Hunter, George E.
  See Ellis, Edward S.
Hunter, Hilda 1921- *7*
Hunter, Jana
  See Hunter, Jana Novotny
Hunter, Jana Novotny *190*
Hunter, Jim 1939- *65*
Hunter, Kristin
  See Lattany, Kristin Hunter
Hunter, Leigh
  See Etchison, Birdie L(ee)
Hunter, Lieutenant Ned
  See Ellis, Edward S.
Hunter, Mel 1927-2004 .... *39*
Hunter, Mollie 1922- *139*
  Autobiography Feature *139*
  Earlier sketches in SATA *2, 54, 106*
  See also CLR *25*
  See also SAAS *7*
Hunter, Ned
  See Ellis, Edward S.
Hunter, Norman (George Lorimer)
  1899-1995 .... *84*
  Earlier sketch in SATA *26*
Hunter, Ryan Ann
  See Greenwood, Pamela D.
  and Macalaster, Elizabeth G.

Hunter, Sara Hoagland 1954- *98*
Hunter Blair, Pauline
  See Clarke, Pauline
Huntington, Amy 1956- *180*
  Earlier sketch in SATA *138*
Huntington, Geoffrey *145*
Huntington, Harriet E(lizabeth) 1909- *1*
Huntsberry, William E(mery) 1916- *5*
Hurd, Clement (G.) 1908-1988 .... *64*
  Obituary *54*
  Earlier sketch in SATA *2*
  See also CLR *49*
Hurd, Edith Thacher 1910-1997 .... *64*
  Obituary *95*
  Earlier sketch in SATA *2*
  See also CLR *49*
  See also SAAS *13*
Hurd, (John) Thacher 1949- *94*
  Autobiography Feature *123*
  Brief entry *45*
  Earlier sketch in SATA *46*
Hurley, Jo
  See Dower, Laura
Hurley, Tonya *207*
Hurlimann, Bettina
  See Huerlimann, Bettina
Hurlimann, Ruth
  See Huerlimann, Ruth
Hurmence, Belinda 1921- *77*
  See also CLR *25*
  See also SAAS *20*
Hurst, Carol Otis 1933-2007 .... *185*
  Earlier sketch in SATA *130*
Hurt-Newton, Tania 1968- *84*
Hurwin, Davida Wills 1950- *180*
Hurwitz, Johanna 1937- *175*
  Earlier sketches in SATA *20, 71, 113*
  See also SAAS *18*
Hurwood, Bernhardt J. 1926-1987 .... *12*
  Obituary *50*
Husain, Shahrukh 1950- *108*
Huser, Glen 1943- *151*
Hutchens, Paul 1902-1977 .... *31*
Hutchins, Carleen M.
  See Hutchins, Carleen Maley
Hutchins, Carleen Maley 1911-2009 .... *9*
  Obituary *206*
Hutchins, Hazel J. 1952- *175*
  Brief entry *51*
  Earlier sketches in SATA *81, 135*
  See also SAAS *24*
Hutchins, Pat 1942- *178*
  Earlier sketches in SATA *15, 70, 111*
  See also CLR *20*
  See also SAAS *16*
Hutchins, Ross Elliott 1906- *4*
Hutchison, Linda 1942- *152*
Huthmacher, J. Joseph 1929- *5*
Hutto, Nelson (Allen) 1904-1985 .... *20*
Hutton, Kathryn 1915- *89*
Hutton, Sam
  See Jones, Allan Frewin
Hutton, Warwick 1939-1994 .... *20*
  Obituary *83*
  See also SAAS *17*
Huxley, Aldous 1894-1963 .... *63*
  See also CLR *151*
Huxley, Aldous Leonard
  See Huxley, Aldous
Huxley, Elspeth (Josceline Grant)
  1907-1997 .... *62*
  Obituary *95*
Hyde, Catherine R.
  See Hyde, Catherine Ryan
Hyde, Catherine Ryan 1955- *141*
Hyde, Dayton O(gden) *9*
Hyde, Hawk
  See Hyde, Dayton O(gden)
Hyde, Jeannette
  See Eyerly, Jeannette

Hyde, Margaret O. 1917- *139*
  Earlier sketches in SATA *1, 42, 76*
  See also CLR *23*
  See also SAAS *8*
Hyde, Margaret Oldroyd
  See Hyde, Margaret O.
Hyde, Shelley
  See Reed, Kit
Hyde, Wayne Frederick 1922- *7*
Hylander, Clarence J(ohn) 1897-1964 .... *7*
Hyman, Miles 1962- *210*
Hyman, Robin P(hilip) 1931- *12*
Hyman, Trina Schart 1939-2004 .... *95*
  Obituary *158*
  Earlier sketches in SATA *7, 46*
  See also CLR *50*
Hymes, Lucia M(anley) 1907-1998 .... *7*
Hyndman, Jane Andrews Lee 1912-1978 ... *46*
  Obituary *23*
  Earlier sketch in SATA *1*
Hyndman, Robert Utley 1906-1973 .... *18*
Hynes, Pat *98*

I

Iannone, Jeanne
  See Balzano, Jeanne (Koppel)
Ibatoulline, Bagram 1965(?)- *174*
Ibbitson, John Perrie 1955- *102*
Ibbotson, Eva 1925- *156*
  Earlier sketches in SATA *13, 103*
Ibbotson, M. C(hristine) 1930- *5*
Icenoggle, Jodi 1967- *168*
Icenoggle, Jodi O.
  See Icenoggle, Jodi
Ichikawa, Satomi 1949- *208*
  Brief entry *36*
  Earlier sketches in SATA *47, 78, 146*
  See also CLR *62*
Iggulden, Hal 1972- *196*
Ignoffo, Matthew 1945- *92*
Igus, Toyomi 1953- *112*
  Earlier sketch in SATA *76*
Ihimaera, Witi (Tame) 1944- *148*
Ikeda, Daisaku 1928- *77*
Ilowite, Sheldon A. 1931- *27*
Ilsey, Dent
  See Chapman, John Stanton Higham
Ilsley, Dent
  See Chapman, John Stanton Higham
Ilsley, Velma (Elizabeth) 1918- *12*
Imai, Ayano 1980- *190*
Imai, Miko 1963- *90*
Imershein, Betsy 1953- *62*
Immel, Mary Blair 1930- *28*
Immell, Myra H. 1941- *92*
Impey, Rose 1947- *152*
  Earlier sketch in SATA *69*
Ingelow, Jean 1820-1897 .... *33*
Ingermanson, Randall 1958- *134*
Ingermanson, Randy
  See Ingermanson, Randall
Ingersoll, Norman 1928- *79*
Ingham, Colonel Frederic
  See Hale, Edward Everett
Ingman, Bruce 1963- *182*
  Earlier sketch in SATA *134*
Ingman, Nicholas 1948- *52*
Ingold, Jeanette *128*
Ingpen, Robert 1936- *166*
  Earlier sketch in SATA *109*
Ingpen, Robert Roger
  See Ingpen, Robert
Ingraham, Erick 1950- *145*
Ingraham, Leonard W(illiam) 1913-2003 ..... *4*
Ingram, Scott 1948- *167*
  Earlier sketch in SATA *92*
Ingram, W. Scott
  See Ingram, Scott

Ingrams, Doreen 1906-1997 97
  Earlier sketch in SATA 20
Ingrid, Charles
  See Salsitz, Rhondi Vilott
Ingves, Gunilla (Anna Maria Folkesdotter)
  1939- 101
Inkpen, Mick 1952- 154
  Earlier sketch in SATA 99
Innes, (Ralph) Hammond
  See Hammond Innes, Ralph
Innes, Ralph Hammond
  See Hammond Innes, Ralph
Innocenti, Roberto 1940- 159
  Earlier sketch in SATA 96
  See also CLR 126
Innocenti and Gallaz
  See Gallaz, Christophe
  and Innocenti, Roberto
Inyart, Gene
  See Namovicz, Gene Inyart
Ionesco, Eugene 1909-1994 7
  Obituary 79
Ipcar, Dahlov (Zorach) 1917- 147
  Autobiography Feature 147
  Earlier sketches in SATA 1, 49
  See also SAAS 8
Ireland, Karin 151
  Earlier sketch in SATA 101
Ironside, Jetske 1940- 60
Irvin, Fred 1914- 15
Irvine, Georgeanne 1955- 72
Irvine, Joan 1951- 80
Irving, Alexander
  See Hume, Ruth Fox
Irving, Robert
  See Adler, Irving
Irving, Washington 1783-1859
  See YABC 2
  See also CLR 97
Irwin, Ann(abelle Bowen) 1915-1998 89
  Brief entry 38
  Obituary 106
  Earlier sketch in SATA 44
  See also CLR 40
  See also SAAS 14
Irwin, Constance (H.) Frick 1913-1995 6
Irwin, Hadley
  See Hadley, Lee
  and Irwin, Ann(abelle Bowen)
Irwin, Keith Gordon 1885-1964 11
Isaac, Joanne 1934- 21
Isaacs, Anne 1949- 185
  Earlier sketch in SATA 90
Isaacs, Jacob
  See Kranzler, George G(ershon)
Isaacson, Philip M(arshal) 1924- 87
Isadora, Rachel 1953(?)- 204
  Brief entry 32
  Earlier sketches in SATA 54, 79, 121, 165
  See also CLR 7
Isbell, Rebecca T(emple) 1942- 125
Isham, Charlotte H(ickock) 1912- 21
Ishida, Jui 176
Ish-Kishor, Judith 1892-1972 11
Ish-Kishor, Sulamith 1896-1977 17
Ishmael, Woodi 1914-1995 31
  Obituary 109
Isle, Sue 1963- 105
Israel, Elaine 1945- 12
Israel, Marion Louise 1882-1973
  Obituary 26
Iterson, S(iny) R(ose) Van
  See Van Iterson, S(iny) R(ose)
Ivanko, John D. 1966- 111
Ivanko, John Duane
  See Ivanko, John D.
Iversen, Jeremy 1980(?)- 174
Iversen, Jeremy Watt
  See Iversen, Jeremy
Iverson, Carol (L.) 1941- 145
Iverson, Diane 1950- 122

Iverson, Eric G.
  See Turtledove, Harry
Ivery, Martha M. 1948- 124
Ives, David 1951- 173
Ives, Morgan
  See Bradley, Marion Zimmer
Iwai, Melissa 183
Iwamatsu, Jun Atsushi 1908-1994 81
  Earlier sketch in SATA 14
  See also CLR 4
Iwasaki (Matsumoto), Chihiro 1918-1974
  See CLR 18

J

Jabar, Cynthia 210
Jablonski, Carla 184
Jac, Lee
  See Morton, Lee Jack, Jr.
Jacka, Martin 1943- 72
Jackson, Alison 1953- 160
  Earlier sketches in SATA 73, 108
Jackson, Anne 1896(?)-1984
  Obituary 37
Jackson, Barry
  See Jackson, Barry E.
Jackson, Barry E. 200
Jackson, C(aary) Paul 1902-1991 6
Jackson, Caary
  See Jackson, C(aary) Paul
Jackson, Charlotte E. (Cobden) 1903(?)-1989
  Obituary 62
Jackson, Dave
  See Jackson, J. David
Jackson, Donna M. 1959- 206
Jackson, Ellen B. 1943- 167
  Earlier sketches in SATA 75, 115
Jackson, Garnet Nelson 1944- 87
Jackson, Geoffrey (Holt Seymour) 1915-1987
  Obituary 53
Jackson, Gina
  See Fluke, Joanne
Jackson, Guida M. 1930- 71
Jackson, J. David 1944- 91
Jackson, Jacqueline 1928- 65
Jackson, Jacqueline Dougan
  See Jackson, Jacqueline
Jackson, Jesse 1908-1983 29
  Obituary 48
  Earlier sketch in SATA 2
  See also CLR 28
Jackson, Marjorie 1928- 127
Jackson, Melanie 1956- 141
Jackson, Mike 1946- 91
Jackson, Neta J. 1944- 91
Jackson, O. B.
  See Jackson, C(aary) Paul
Jackson, Rob 1961- 176
Jackson, Robert B(lake) 1926- 8
Jackson, Robert Bradley
  See Jackson, Rob
Jackson, Sally
  See Kellogg, Jean (Defrees)
Jackson, Shirley 1919-1965 2
Jackson, Woody 1948- 92
Jackson Issa, Kai 205
Jacob, Helen Pierce 1927- 21
Jacobin
  See Bisson, Terry
Jacobs, Deborah Lynn 187
Jacobs, Flora Gill 1918-2006 5
  Obituary 178
Jacobs, Francine 1935- 150
  Brief entry 42
  Earlier sketch in SATA 43
Jacobs, Frank 1929- 30
Jacobs, Helen Hull 1908-1997 12
Jacobs, Joseph 1854-1916 25
Jacobs, Judy 1952- 69

Jacobs, Laurie A. 1956- 89
Jacobs, Leah
  See Gellis, Roberta
Jacobs, Leland Blair 1907-1992 20
  Obituary 71
Jacobs, Linda
  See Altman, Linda Jacobs
Jacobs, Lou(is), Jr. 1921- 2
Jacobs, Shannon K. 1947- 77
Jacobs, Susan
  See Quinn, Susan
Jacobs, William Jay 1933- 89
  Earlier sketch in SATA 28
Jacobsen, Laura 177
Jacobson, Daniel 1923- 12
Jacobson, Jennifer
  See Jacobson, Jennifer Richard
Jacobson, Jennifer Richard 1958- 170
Jacobson, Morris K(arl) 1906- 21
Jacobson, Rick 170
Jacopetti, Alexandra
  See Hart, Alexandra
Jacques, Brian 1939- 176
  Earlier sketches in SATA 62, 95, 138
  See also CLR 21
Jacques, Robin 1920-1995 32
  Brief entry 30
  Obituary 86
  See also SAAS 5
Jaekel, Susan M. 1948- 89
Jaffe, Michele 179
Jaffe, Michele Sharon
  See Jaffe, Michele
Jaffee, Al(lan) 1921- 66
  Earlier sketch in SATA 37
Jagendorf, Moritz (Adolf) 1888-1981 2
  Obituary 24
Jahn, Joseph Michael
  See Jahn, Michael
Jahn, Michael 1943- 28
Jahn, Mike
  See Jahn, Michael
Jahn-Clough, Lisa 1967- 193
  Earlier sketches in SATA 88, 152
Jahsmann, Allan Hart 1916- 28
Jakes, John 1932- 62
Jakes, John William
  See Jakes, John
James, Andrew
  See Kirkup, James
James, Ann 1952- 168
  Earlier sketches in SATA 82, 117
James, Betsy 183
James, Brian 1976- 140
James, Bronte
  See Nash, Renea Denise
James, Captain Lew
  See Stratemeyer, Edward L.
James, Charlie 1961- 185
James, Curtis E. 182
James, Dynely
  See Mayne, William (James Carter)
James, Edwin
  See Gunn, James E.
James, Elizabeth 1942- 97
  Earlier sketches in SATA 39, 45, 52
James, Emily
  See Standiford, Natalie
James, Gordon C. 1973- 195
James, Harry Clebourne 1896-1978 11
James, J. Alison 1962- 146
  Earlier sketch in SATA 83
James, Josephine
  See Sterne, Emma Gelders
James, Mary
  See Meaker, Marijane
James, Matt 201
James, Philip
  See del Rey, Lester
  and Moorcock, Michael
James, Robin 1953- 50

James, Robin Irene
   See James, Robin
James, Simon 202
   See Kunen, James Simon
James, T. F.
   See Fleming, Thomas
James, Tegan
   See Odgers, Sally Farrell
James, Will(iam Roderick) 1892-1942 19
Jameson, W. C. 1942- 93
Jamieson, Ian R.
   See Goulart, Ron
Jamiolkowski, Raymond M. 1953- 81
Jane, Mary Childs 1909- 6
Jane, Pamela 158
Janeczko, Paul B(ryan) 1945- 155
   Earlier sketches in SATA 53, 98
   See also CLR 47
   See also SAAS 18
Janes, Edward C. 1908-1984 25
Janes, J(oseph) Robert 1935- 148
   Brief entry 50
   Earlier sketch in SATA 101
Janeway, Elizabeth (Hall) 1913-2005 19
Janger, Kathleen N. 1940- 66
Jango-Cohen, Judith 1955- 208
Janice
   See Brustlein, Janice Tworkov
Janisch, Heinz 1960- 181
Janosch
   See Eckert, Horst
Janover, Caroline (Davis) 1943- 141
   Earlier sketch in SATA 89
Janovitz, Marilyn 194
Jansen, Jared
   See Cebulash, Mel
Janson, Dora Jane (Heineberg) 1916- 31
Janson, H(orst) W(oldemar) 1913-1982 9
Jansson, Tove (Marika) 1914-2001 41
   Earlier sketch in SATA 3
   See also CLR 125
Janus, Grete
   See Hertz, Grete Janus
Jaques, Faith 1923-1997 97
   Earlier sketches in SATA 21, 69
Jaquith, Priscilla 1908- 51
Jaramillo, Mari-Luci 1928- 139
Jarman, Julia 1946- 198
   Earlier sketch in SATA 133
Jarman, Rosemary Hawley 1935- 7
Jarrell, Mary Von Schrader 1914- 35
Jarrell, Randall 1914-1965 7
   See also CLR 111
Jarrett, Clare 1952- 201
Jarrett, Roxanne
   See Werner, Herma
Jarrow, Gail 1952- 185
   Earlier sketch in SATA 84
Jarvis, E.K.
   See Ellison, Harlan
   and Silverberg, Robert
Jarvis, Robin 1963- 181
Jaskol, Julie 1958- 127
Jasner, W. K.
   See Watson, Jane Werner
Jassem, Kate
   See Oppenheim, Joanne
Jauss, Anne Marie 1902(?)-1991 10
   Obituary 69
Javernick, Ellen 1938- 89
Jay, Alison 196
Jayne, Lieutenant R. H.
   See Ellis, Edward S.
Jaynes, Clare
   See Mayer, Jane Rothschild
Jeake, Samuel, Jr.
   See Aiken, Conrad
Jean-Bart, Leslie 1954- 121
Jeapes, Ben 1965- 174
Jecan, Gavriel 1962- 200

Jefferds, Vincent H(arris) 1916- 59
   Brief entry 49
Jefferies, (John) Richard 1848-1887 16
Jeffers, Dawn 189
Jeffers, Oliver 1977- 175
Jeffers, Susan 1942- 202
   Earlier sketches in SATA 17, 70, 129, 137
   See also CLR 30
Jefferson, Sarah
   See Farjeon, (Eve) Annabel
Jeffries, Roderic 1926- 4
Jeffries, Roderic Graeme
   See Jeffries, Roderic
Jenkin-Pearce, Susie 1943- 80
Jenkins, A. M. 1961- 174
Jenkins, Amanda McRaney
   See Jenkins, A. M.
Jenkins, Debra Reid
   See Reid Jenkins, Debra
Jenkins, Emily 1967- 174
   Earlier sketch in SATA 144
Jenkins, Jean 98
Jenkins, Jerry B. 1949- 149
Jenkins, Jerry Bruce
   See Jenkins, Jerry B.
Jenkins, Leonard 189
Jenkins, Marie M(agdalen) 1909- 7
Jenkins, Patrick 1955- 72
Jenkins, Steve 1952- 188
   Earlier sketch in SATA 154
Jenkins, William A(twell) 1922-1998 9
Jenkyns, Chris 1924- 51
Jennings, Christopher S. 1971(?)- 201
Jennings, Coleman A(lonzo) 1933- 64
Jennings, C.S.
   See Jennings, Christopher S.
Jennings, Dana Andrew 1957- 93
Jennings, Elizabeth (Joan) 1926-2001 66
Jennings, Gary 1928-1999 9
   Obituary 117
Jennings, Gary Gayne
   See Jennings, Gary
Jennings, Linda 1937- 211
Jennings, Linda M.
   See Jennings, Linda
Jennings, Patrick 1962- 205
   Earlier sketches in SATA 96, 160
Jennings, Paul 1943- 165
   Earlier sketch in SATA 88
   See also CLR 40
Jennings, Richard W. 1945- 185
   Earlier sketch in SATA 136
Jennings, Robert
   See Hamilton, Charles (Harold St. John)
Jennings, S. M.
   See Meyer, Jerome Sydney
Jennings, Sharon 1954- 95
Jennings, Sharon Elizabeth
   See Jennings, Sharon
Jennison, C. S.
   See Starbird, Kaye
Jennison, Keith Warren 1911-1995 14
Jensen, Kathryn 1949- 81
Jensen, Kristine Mary 1961- 78
Jensen, Niels 1927- 25
Jensen, Vickie (Dee) 1946- 81
Jensen, Virginia Allen 1927- 8
Jenson-Elliott, Cynthia L(ouise) 1962- 143
Jeram, Anita 1965- 154
   Earlier sketches in SATA 71, 102
Jerman, Jerry 1949- 89
Jernigan, E. Wesley 1940- 85
Jernigan, Gisela (Evelyn) 1948- 85
Jeschke, Susan 1942- 42
   Brief entry 27
Jessel, Camilla (Ruth) 1937- 143
   Earlier sketch in SATA 29
Jessell, Tim 177
Jessey, Cornelia
   See Sussman, Cornelia Silver

Jewel
   See Kilcher, Jewel
Jewell, Nancy 1940- 109
   Brief entry 41
Jewett, Eleanore Myers 1890-1967 5
Jewett, Sarah Orne 1849-1909 15
Jewett, Theodora Sarah Orne
   See Jewett, Sarah Orne
Jezard, Alison 1919- 57
   Brief entry 34
Jiang, Cheng An 1943- 109
Jiang, Ji-li 1954- 101
Jiang, Zheng An
   See Jiang, Cheng An
Jiler, John 1946- 42
   Brief entry 35
Jimenez, Francisco 1943- 108
Jinks, Catherine 1963- 207
   Earlier sketches in SATA 94, 155
Jobb, Jamie 1945- 29
Jobling, Curtis 131
Jocelyn, Ann Henning 1948- 92
Jocelyn, Marthe 1956- 198
   Earlier sketches in SATA 118, 163
Joerns, Consuelo 44
   Brief entry 33
Joey D
   See Macaulay, Teresa (E.)
Johansen, Krista V.
   See Johansen, K.V.
Johansen, K.V 1968- 186
Johansen, K.V. 1968- 186
   Earlier sketch in SATA 129
Johansson, Philip 163
John, Antony 1972- 206
John, Joyce 59
Johns, Avery
   See Cousins, Margaret
Johns, Elizabeth 1943- 88
Johns, Janetta
   See Quin-Harkin, Janet
Johns, Linda 1945- 173
Johns, W(illiam) E(arle) 1893-1968 55
Johns, Captain W. E.
   See Johns, W(illiam) E(arle)
Johnson, A.
   See Johnson, Annabell
Johnson, A. E.
   See Johnson, Annabell
   and Johnson, Edgar (Raymond)
Johnson, Angela 1961- 188
   Earlier sketches in SATA 69, 102, 150
   See also CLR 33
Johnson, Annabel
   See Johnson, Annabell
Johnson, Annabell 1921- 72
   Earlier sketch in SATA 2
Johnson, Art 1946- 123
Johnson, B. F. 1920- 1
Johnson, Benjamin F., of Boone
   See Riley, James Whitcomb
Johnson, Bettye 1858-1919
   See Rogers, Bettye
Johnson, Caryn
   See Goldberg, Whoopi
Johnson, Caryn E.
   See Goldberg, Whoopi
Johnson, Caryn Elaine
   See Goldberg, Whoopi
Johnson, Charles R. 1925- 11
Johnson, Charlotte Buel
   See von Wodtke, Charlotte Buel Johnson
Johnson, Chuck
   See Johnson, Charles R.
Johnson, Crockett
   See Leisk, David (Johnson)
Johnson, D(ana) William 1945- 23
Johnson, Daniel Shahid 1954- 73
Johnson, David
   See Johnson, David A.
Johnson, David A. 1951- 191

Johnson, D.B. 1944- *183*
  Earlier sketch in SATA *146*
Johnson, Dianne 1960- *130*
Johnson, Dinah
  See Johnson, Dianne
Johnson, Dolores 1949- *69*
Johnson, Donald B.
  See Johnson, D.B.
Johnson, Dorothy M(arie) 1905-1984 .... *6*
  Obituary *40*
Johnson, E(ugene) Harper *44*
Johnson, Edgar (Raymond) 1912-1990 .... *72*
  Earlier sketch in SATA *2*
Johnson, Eleanor Murdock 1892-1987
  Obituary *54*
Johnson, Elizabeth 1911-1984 .... *7*
  Obituary *39*
Johnson, Eric W(arner) 1918-1994 ....
  Obituary *82*
  Earlier sketch in SATA *8*
Johnson, Evelyne 1922- *20*
Johnson, Fred 19(?)-1982 .... *63*
Johnson, Gaylord 1884-1972 .... *7*
Johnson, Gerald White 1890-1980 .... *19*
  Obituary *28*
Johnson, Harper
  See Johnson, E(ugene) Harper
Johnson, Harriett 1908-1987
  Obituary *53*
Johnson, James Ralph 1922- *1*
Johnson, James Weldon 1871-1938 .... *31*
  See also CLR *32*
Johnson, Jane 1951- *48*
Johnson, Joan J. 1942- *59*
Johnson, John E(mil) 1929- *34*
Johnson, Johnny 1901-1995
  See Johnson, (Walter) Ryerson
Johnson, Kathleen Jeffrie 1950- *186*
Johnson, La Verne B(ravo) 1925- *13*
Johnson, Layne *187*
Johnson, Lee Kaiser 1962- *78*
Johnson, Lissa H(alls) 1955- *65*
Johnson, Lois Smith 1894-1993 .... *6*
Johnson, Lois Walfrid 1936- *130*
  Earlier sketches in SATA *22, 91*
Johnson, Margaret S(weet) 1893-1964 .... *35*
Johnson, Marguerite Annie
  See Angelou, Maya
Johnson, Mary Frances K. 1929(?)-1979
  Obituary *27*
Johnson, Maud Battle 1918(?)-1985
  Obituary *46*
Johnson, Maureen 1973- *200*
Johnson, Meredith Merrell 1952- *104*
Johnson, Milton 1932- *31*
Johnson, Neil 1954- *135*
  Earlier sketch in SATA *73*
Johnson, Pamela 1949- *71*
Johnson, Patricia Polin 1956- *84*
Johnson, Paul Brett 1947- *132*
  Earlier sketch in SATA *83*
Johnson, Rebecca L. 1956- *147*
  Earlier sketch in SATA *67*
Johnson, Rick L. 1954- *79*
Johnson, (Walter) Ryerson 1901-1995 .... *10*
  Obituary *106*
Johnson, Scott 1952- *119*
  Earlier sketch in SATA *76*
Johnson, Sherrie 1948- *87*
Johnson, Shirley K(ing) 1927- *10*
Johnson, Siddie Joe 1905-1977
  Obituary *20*
Johnson, Spencer 1938- *145*
  Brief entry *38*
Johnson, Stacie
  See Myers, Walter Dean
Johnson, Stephen T. 1964- *189*
  Earlier sketches in SATA *84, 141*
Johnson, Steve 1960- *177*
Johnson, Sue Kaiser 1963- *78*

Johnson, Sylvia A. *166*
  Brief entry *52*
  Earlier sketch in SATA *104*
Johnson, William R. *38*
Johnson, William Weber 1909-1992 .... *7*
Johnson-Feelings, Dianne
  See Johnson, Dianne
Johnston, Agnes Christine
  See Dazey, Agnes J(ohnston)
Johnston, Annie Fellows 1863-1931 .... *37*
Johnston, Dorothy Grunbock 1915-1979 .... *54*
Johnston, Ginny 1946- *60*
Johnston, H(ugh) A(nthony) S(tephen)
  1913-1967 .... *14*
Johnston, Janet 1944- *71*
Johnston, Jeffry W. *188*
Johnston, Johanna 1914(?)-1982 .... *12*
  Obituary *33*
Johnston, Julie 1941- *110*
  Autobiography Feature *128*
  Earlier sketch in SATA *78*
  See also CLR *41*
  See also SAAS *24*
Johnston, Lynn 1947- *118*
Johnston, Lynn Beverley
  See Johnston, Lynn
Johnston, Mark *194*
Johnston, Norma
  See St. John, Nicole
Johnston, Portia
  See Takakjian, Portia
Johnston, Susan Taylor 1942- *180*
  Earlier sketches in SATA *8, 83, 128*
Johnston, Tim(othy Patrick) 1962- *146*
Johnston, Tony
  See Johnston, Susan Taylor
Joinson, Carla *160*
Jolin, Paula *186*
Jonas, Ann 1932- *135*
  Brief entry *42*
  Earlier sketch in SATA *50*
  See also CLR *74*
Jonell, Lynne 1956- *196*
  Earlier sketch in SATA *109*
Jones, Adrienne 1915-2000 .... *82*
  Earlier sketch in SATA *7*
  See also SAAS *10*
Jones, Allan Frewin 1954- *204*
Jones, Annabel
  See Lewis, Mary
Jones, Betty Millsaps 1940- *54*
Jones, Carol 1942- *153*
  Earlier sketch in SATA *79*
Jones, Carrie 1971- *191*
Jones, Charles M. 1912-2002 .... *53*
  Obituary *133*
Jones, Charlotte Foltz 1945- *122*
  Earlier sketch in SATA *77*
Jones, Chuck
  See Jones, Charles M.
Jones, Constance *112*
Jones, Constance A.
  See Jones, Constance
Jones, David 1956- *202*
Jones, Diana Wynne 1934- *160*
  Earlier sketches in SATA *9, 70, 108*
  See also CLR *120*
  See also SAAS *7*
Jones, Douglas B. *202*
Jones, Douglas C(lyde) 1924-1998 .... *52*
Jones, Elizabeth McDavid *155*
Jones, Elizabeth Orton 1910-2005 .... *18*
  Obituary *164*
Jones, Evan 1915-1996 .... *3*
Jones, Frewin
  See Jones, Allan Frewin
Jones, Geraldine
  See McCaughrean, Geraldine
Jones, Gillingham
  See Hamilton, Charles (Harold St. John)
Jones, Gwyneth A(nn) 1952- *159*

Jones, Harold 1904-1992 .... *14*
  Obituary *72*
Jones, Helen Hinckley 1903-1991 .... *26*
Jones, Helen L(ouise) 1903-1973
  Obituary *22*
Jones, Hettie 1934- *42*
  Brief entry *27*
Jones, Hortense P. 1918- *9*
Jones, J. Sydney 1948- *101*
Jones, Jasmine
  See Papademetriou, Lisa
Jones, Jennifer (Berry) 1947- *90*
Jones, Jessie Mae Orton 1887(?)-1983
  Obituary *37*
Jones, John R(obert) 1926- *76*
Jones, Jon Sydney
  See Jones, J. Sydney
Jones, Kimberly K. 1957- *187*
Jones, Marcia Thornton 1958- *115*
  Earlier sketch in SATA *73*
Jones, Martha T(annery) 1931- *130*
Jones, Mary Alice 1898(?)-1980 .... *6*
Jones, McClure *34*
Jones, Noah Z. *182*
Jones, Patrick 1961- *210*
  Earlier sketch in SATA *136*
Jones, Penelope 1938- *31*
Jones, Rebecca C(astaldi) 1947- *99*
  Earlier sketch in SATA *33*
Jones, Robin D(orothy) 1959- *80*
Jones, Sanford W.
  See Thorn, John
Jones, Sylvie *185*
Jones, Sylvie Michelle
  See Jones, Sylvie
Jones, Terence Graham Parry 1942- *127*
  Brief entry *51*
  Earlier sketch in SATA *67*
Jones, Terry
  See Jones, Terence Graham Parry
Jones, Tim Wynne
  See Wynne-Jones, Tim
Jones, Traci L. *186*
Jones, V. M. 1958- *147*
Jones, Veda Boyd 1948- *119*
Jones, Victoria Mary
  See Jones, V. M.
Jones, Volcano
  See Mitchell, Adrian
Jones, Weyman (B.) 1928- *4*
  See also SAAS *11*
Jones, William Glynne
  See Glynne-Jones, William
Jonk, Clarence 1906-1987 .... *10*
Jonsberg, Barry 1951- *168*
Joos, Francoise 1956- *78*
Joos, Frederic 1953- *78*
Joosse, Barbara M. 1949- *164*
  Earlier sketches in SATA *52, 96*
Joosse, Barbara Monnot
  See Joosse, Barbara M.
Jordan, Alexis Hill
  See Glick, Ruth (Burtnick)
  and Titchener, Louise
Jordan, Anne Devereaux 1943- *80*
Jordan, Chris
  See Philbrick, Rodman
Jordan, Deloris *191*
Jordan, Don
  See Howard, Vernon (Linwood)
Jordan, Hope Dahle 1905-1995 .... *15*
Jordan, Jael (Michal) 1949- *30*
Jordan, June 1936-2002 .... *136*
  Earlier sketch in SATA *4*
  See also CLR *10*
Jordan, June Meyer
  See Jordan, June
Jordan, Lee
  See Scholefield, Alan
Jordan, Martin George 1944- *84*
Jordan, Robert 1948-2007 .... *95*

Jordan, Robert K.
See Jordan, Robert
Jordan, Rosa 1939- 191
Jordan, Roslyn M. 189
Jordan, Sherryl 1949- 122
Earlier sketch in SATA 71
See also SAAS 23
Jordan, Shirley 1930- 154
Jordan, Tanis 1946- 84
Jorgensen, Ivar
See Ellison, Harlan
and Garrett, Randall
Jorgensen, Mary Venn -1995 36
Jorgensen, Norman 1954- 157
Jorgenson, Ivar
See Silverberg, Robert
Jorisch, Stephane 178
Joseph, Anne
See Coates, Anna
Joseph, James (Herz) 1924- 53
Joseph, Joan 1939- 34
Joseph, Joseph M(aron) 1903-1979 22
Joseph, Patrick
See O'Malley, Kevin
Josephs, Rebecca
See Talbot, Toby
Josephson, Judith Pinkerton 1943- 198
Josh
See Twain, Mark
Joshua, Peter
See Stone, Peter
Joslin, Mary 1953- 176
Joslin, Sesyle
See Hine, Sesyle Joslin
Joubert, Beverly 1957- 204
Joubert, Dereck 204
Journet, Mireille
See Marokvia, Mireille
Joyce, Bill
See Joyce, William
Joyce, J(ames) Avery 1902-1987 11
Obituary 50
Joyce, Peter 1937- 127
Joyce, William 1957- 118
Brief entry 46
Earlier sketch in SATA 72
See also CLR 26
Joyner, Jerry 1938- 34
Juan, Ana 1961- 179
Jubb, Sophie 210
Jubert, Herve 185
Juby, Susan 1969- 202
Earlier sketch in SATA 156
Jucker, Sita 1921- 5
Judah, Aaron 1923- 118
Judd, Cyril
See Kornbluth, C(yril) M.
and Merril, Judith
and Pohl, Frederik
Judd, Denis (O'Nan) 1938- 33
Judd, Frances K.
See Benson, Mildred
Jude, Conny 81
Judge, Lita 192
Judson, Clara Ingram 1879-1960 38
Brief entry 27
Judy, Stephen
See Tchudi, Stephen N.
Judy, Stephen N.
See Tchudi, Stephen N.
Juhasz, Victor 1954- 177
Jukes, Mavis 1947- 111
Brief entry 43
Earlier sketch in SATA 72
See also SAAS 12
Jules, Jacqueline 1956- 183
Earlier sketch in SATA 148
Julesberg, Elizabeth Rider Montgomery
1902-1985 34
Obituary 41
Earlier sketch in SATA 3

Julian, Jane
See Wiseman, David
Jumpp, Hugo
See MacPeek, Walter G.
Jungman, Ann 165
Jupo, Frank J. 1904-1981 7
Jurmain, Suzanne 1945- 169
Earlier sketch in SATA 72
Jurmain, Suzanne Tripp
See Jurmain, Suzanne
Juster, Norton 1929- 132
Earlier sketch in SATA 3
See also CLR 112
Justus, May 1898-1989 1
Obituary 106
Juvenilia
See Taylor, Ann

K

Kaaberbol, Lene
See Kaaberbol, Lene
Kaaberbol, Lene 1960- 159
Kabdebo, Tamas
See Kabdebo, Thomas
Kabdebo, Thomas 1934- 10
Kabibble, Osh
See Jobb, Jamie
Kacer, Kathy 1954- 184
Earlier sketch in SATA 142
Kaczman, James 156
Kadair, Deborah Ousley 184
Kadesch, Robert R(udstone) 1922- 31
Kadohata, Cynthia 1956(?)- 180
Earlier sketch in SATA 155
See also CLR 121
Kaempfert, Wade
See del Rey, Lester
Kaestner, Erich 1899-1974 14
See also CLR 4
Kahl, Jonathan (D.) 1959- 77
Kahl, M(arvin) P(hilip) 1934- 37
Kahl, Virginia (Caroline) 1919-2004 48
Brief entry 38
Obituary 158
Kahn, Joan 1914-1994 48
Obituary 82
Kahn, Katherine Janus 1942- 167
Earlier sketch in SATA 90
Kahn, Peggy
See Katz, Bobbi
Kahn, Roger 1927- 37
Kahukiwa, Robyn 1940- 134
Kains, Josephine
See Goulart, Ron
Kaizuki, Kiyonori 1950- 72
Kakimoto, Kozo 1915- 11
Kalashnikoff, Nicholas 1888-1961 16
Kalb, Jonah 1926- 23
Kalbacken, Joan 1925- 96
Kalechofsky, Roberta 1931- 92
Kaler, James Otis 1848-1912 15
Kalis, Jennifer 207
Kalish, Claire M. 1947- 92
Kallen, Stuart A(rnold) 1955- 126
Earlier sketch in SATA 86
Kallevig, Christine Petrell 1955- 164
Kalman, Bobbie 1947- 63
Kalman, Maira 1949- 137
Earlier sketch in SATA 96
See also CLR 32
Kalnay, Francis 1899-1992 7
Kaloustian, Rosanne 1955- 93
Kalow, Gisela 1946- 32
Kalstein, Dave 175
Kamen, Gloria 1923- 98
Earlier sketch in SATA 9
Kamerman, Sylvia E.
See Burack, Sylvia K.

Kamm, Josephine (Hart) 1905-1989 24
Kammerman, Sylvia K.
See Burack, Sylvia K.
Kandel, Michael 1941- 93
Kandell, Alice S. 1938- 35
Kane, Bob 1916-1998 120
Kane, Henry Bugbee 1902-1971 14
Kane, L. A.
See Mannetti, Lisa
Kane, Robert W. 1910- 18
Kane, Wilson
See Bloch, Robert (Albert)
Kanefield, Teri 1960- 135
Kaner, Etta 1947- 198
Earlier sketch in SATA 126
Kanetzke, Howard W(illiam) 1932- 38
Kangas, Juli 1958- 200
Kann, Elizabeth 180
Kann, Victoria 180
Kanninen, Barbara 196
Kanninen, Barbara J.
See Kanninen, Barbara
Kanoza, Muriel Canfield
See Canfield, Muriel
Kantner, Seth 1965- 179
Kanzawa, Toshiko
See Furukawa, Toshi
Kanzler, John 1963- 188
Kaplan, Andrew 1960- 78
Kaplan, Anne Bernays
See Bernays, Anne
Kaplan, Bess 1927- 22
Kaplan, Boche 1926- 24
Kaplan, Elizabeth 1956- 83
Kaplan, Elizabeth A.
See Kaplan, Elizabeth
Kaplan, Irma 1900- 10
Kaplan, Jean Caryl Korn 1926- 10
Kaplow, Robert 1954- 70
Karageorge, Michael
See Anderson, Poul
Karas, G. Brian 1957- 178
Karas, George Brian
See Karas, G. Brian
Karasz, Ilonka 1896-1981
Obituary 29
Karen, Ruth 1922-1987 9
Obituary 54
Kark, Nina Mary
See Bawden, Nina
Karl, Herb 1938- 73
Karl, Jean E(dna) 1927-2000 122
Earlier sketch in SATA 34
See also SAAS 10
Karlin, Bernie 1927- 68
Karlin, Eugene 1918- 10
Karlin, Nurit 103
Earlier sketch in SATA 63
Karnes, Frances A. 1937- 110
Karp, Naomi J. 1926- 16
Karpinski, J. Rick
See Karpinski, John Eric
Karpinski, John Eric 1952- 81
Karpinski, Rick
See Karpinski, John Eric
Karr, Kathleen 1946- 127
Earlier sketch in SATA 82
Karr, Phyllis Ann 1944- 119
Karwoski, Gail 1949- 127
Karwoski, Gail Langer
See Karwoski, Gail
Kashiwagi, Isami 1925- 10
Kaslik, Ibi
See Kaslik, Ibolya Emma
Kaslik, Ibolya Emma 1973- 185
Kassem, Lou 1931- 62
Brief entry 51
Kastel, Warren
See Silverberg, Robert
Kastner, Erich
See Kaestner, Erich

Kastner, Jill (Marie) 1964- 117
  Earlier sketch in SATA 70
Kasuya, Masahiro 1937- 51
Kasza, Keiko 1951- 191
  Earlier sketch in SATA 124
Kataphusin
  See Ruskin, John
Katchen, Carole 1944- 9
Katcher, Brian 1975- 203
Kathryn
  See Searle, Kathryn Adrienne
Kato, Aya 1982- 202
Katona, Robert 1949- 21
Katsarakis, Joan Harries
  See Harries, Joan
Katz, Alan 185
Katz, Avi 1949- 199
Katz, Avner 1939- 103
Katz, Bobbi 1933- 179
  Earlier sketch in SATA 12
Katz, Fred(eric Phillip) 1938- 6
Katz, Jane B(resler) 1934- 33
Katz, Karen 1947- 195
  Earlier sketch in SATA 158
Katz, Marjorie P.
  See Weiser, Marjorie P(hillis) K(atz)
Katz, Susan 1945- 156
Katz, Welwyn Wilton 1948- 96
  Autobiography Feature 118
  Earlier sketch in SATA 62
  See also CLR 45
Katz, William 1940- 98
Katz, William Loren 1927- 13
Kaufman, Bel 57
Kaufman, Jeff 1955- 84
Kaufman, Joe 1911-2001 33
Kaufman, Joseph
  See Kaufman, Joe
Kaufman, Mervyn D. 1932- 4
Kaufmann, Angelika 1935- 15
Kaufmann, John 1931- 18
Kaula, Edna Mason 1906-1987 13
Kaur Khalsa, Dayal
  See Khalsa, Dayal Kaur
Kavaler, Lucy 1930- 23
Kavanagh, Jack 1920- 85
Kavanagh, P(atrick) J(oseph Gregory)
  1931- 122
Kavanaugh, Ian
  See Webb, Jean Francis (III)
Kay, Alan N. 1965- 144
Kay, Elizabeth 1949- 165
Kay, Guy Gavriel 1954- 167
  Earlier sketch in SATA 121
Kay, Helen
  See Goldfrank, Helen Colodny
Kay, Jackie 1961- 165
  Earlier sketch in SATA 97
Kay, Jacqueline Margaret
  See Kay, Jackie
Kay, Julia 205
Kay, Mara 13
Kay, Verla 1946- 210
  Earlier sketch in SATA 120
Kaye, Danny 1913-1987
  Obituary 50
Kaye, Geraldine (Hughesdon) 1925- 85
  Earlier sketch in SATA 10
Kaye, Judy
  See Baer, Judy
Kaye, Marilyn 1949- 110
  Earlier sketch in SATA 56
Kaye, Mary Margaret
  See Kaye, M.M.
Kaye, M.M. 1908-2004 62
  Obituary 152
Kaye, Mollie
  See Kaye, M.M.
Kaye, Peggy 1948- 143
Keach, James P. 1950- 125
Keams, Geri 1951- 117

Keane, Bil 1922- 4
Keaney, Brian 1954- 188
  Earlier sketch in SATA 106
Kearney, Meg 1964- 178
Kearny, Jillian
  See Goulart, Ron
Keating, Bern
  See Keating, Leo Bernard
Keating, Frank 1944- 143
Keating, Lawrence A. 1903-1966 23
Keating, Leo Bernard 1915- 10
Keats, Emma 1899(?)-1979(?) 68
Keats, Ezra Jack 1916-1983 57
  Obituary 34
  Earlier sketch in SATA 14
  See also CLR 35
Keefer, Catherine
  See Ogan, George F.
  and Ogan, Margaret E. (Nettles)
Keefer, Janice Kulyk
  See Kulyk Keefer, Janice
Keegan, Marcia 1943- 104
  Earlier sketch in SATA 9
Keehn, Sally M. 1947- 165
  Earlier sketch in SATA 87
Keel, Frank
  See Keeler, Ronald F(ranklin)
Keeler, Patricia 183
Keeler, Patricia A.
  See Keeler, Patricia
Keeler, Ronald F(ranklin) 1913-1983 47
Keely, Jack 1951- 119
Keen, Martin L. 1913-1992 4
Keenan, Sheila 1953- 95
Keene, Ann T(odd) 1940- 86
Keene, Carolyn
  See Benson, Mildred
  and Goulart, Ron
  and Lerangis, Peter
  and McFarlane, Leslie
  and Stanley, George Edward
  and Stratemeyer, Edward L.
Keens-Douglas, Richardo 1953- 154
  Earlier sketch in SATA 95
Keep, Linda Lowery
  See Lowery, Linda
Keep, Richard 1949- 170
Keep, Richard Cleminson
  See Keep, Richard
Keeping, Charles (William James)
  1924-1988 69
  Obituary 56
  Earlier sketch in SATA 9
  See also CLR 34
Keeshan, Robert J. 1927-2004 32
  Obituary 151
Kehlenbeck, Angela 1959- 186
Kehret, Peg 1936- 149
  Autobiography Feature 149
  Earlier sketches in SATA 73, 108
Keillor, Garrison 1942- 58
Keillor, Gary Edward
  See Keillor, Garrison
Keir, Christine
  See Pullein-Thompson, Christine
Keister, Douglas 1948- 88
Keith, Doug 1952- 81
Keith, Eros 1942- 52
Keith, Hal 1934- 36
Keith, Harold (Verne) 1903-1998 74
  Earlier sketch in SATA 2
Keith, Robert
  See Applebaum, Stan
Keleinikov, Andrei 1924- 65
Kelemen, Julie 1959- 78
Kelen, Emery 1896-1978 13
  Obituary 26
Kelleam, Joseph E(veridge) 1913-1975 31
Kelleher, Anne 1959- 97
Kelleher, Annette 1950- 122
Kelleher, Daria Valerian 1955- 79

Kelleher, Victor (Michael Kitchener)
  1939- 129
  Brief entry 52
  Earlier sketch in SATA 75
  See also CLR 36
Keller, Beverly L(ou) 91
  Earlier sketch in SATA 13
Keller, Charles 1942- 82
  Earlier sketch in SATA 8
Keller, Debra 1958- 94
Keller, Dick 1923- 36
Keller, Emily 96
Keller, Gail Faithfull
  See Faithfull, Gail
Keller, Holly 1942- 157
  Brief entry 42
  Earlier sketches in SATA 76, 108
  See also CLR 45
Keller, Irene (Barron) 1927-2002 36
  Obituary 139
Keller, Laurie 1961(?)- 196
Kelley, Ellen A. 185
Kelley, Ellen Chavez
  See Kelley, Ellen A.
Kelley, Gary 1945- 183
Kelley, Leo P(atrick) 1928- 32
  Brief entry 31
Kelley, Marty 1971- 211
Kelley, Patrick (G.) 1963- 129
Kelley, Patte 1947- 93
Kelley, True 1946- 179
Kelley, True (Adelaide) 1946- 130
  Brief entry 39
  Earlier sketches in SATA 41, 92
Kelley, True Adelaide
  See Kelley, True
Kellin, Sally Moffet 1932- 9
Kelling, Furn L. 1914-2000 37
Kellogg, Gene
  See Kellogg, Jean (Defrees)
Kellogg, Jean (Defrees) 1916-1978 10
Kellogg, Steven 1941- 177
  Earlier sketches in SATA 8, 57, 130
  See also CLR 6
Kellogg, Steven Castle
  See Kellogg, Steven
Kellow, Kathleen
  See Hibbert, Eleanor Alice Burford
Kelly, C. M. O.
  See Gibbs, (Cecilia) May
Kelly, Clint 1950- 140
Kelly, Eric P(hilbrook) 1884-1960
  See YABC 1
Kelly, Fiona
  See Coleman, Michael
  and Hendry, Frances Mary
  and Jones, Allan Frewin
  and Oldfield, Jenny
  and Welford, Sue
Kelly, Irene 1957- 210
  Earlier sketch in SATA 147
Kelly, Jeff
  See Kelly, Jeffrey
Kelly, Jeffrey 1946- 65
Kelly, Joanne (W.) 1934- 87
Kelly, Kate 1958- 91
Kelly, Kathleen M. 1964- 71
Kelly, Katy 1955- 169
Kelly, Lauren
  See Oates, Joyce Carol
Kelly, Laurene 1954- 123
Kelly, Martha Rose 1914-1983 37
Kelly, Marty
  See Kelly, Martha Rose
Kelly, Mij 166
Kelly, Ralph
  See Geis, Darlene Stern
Kelly, Regina Z(immerman) 1898-1986 5
Kelly, Rosalie (Ruth) 43
Kelly, Tom 1961- 191
Kelly, Walt(er Crawford) 1913-1973 18

Kelsey, Alice Geer 1896-1982 .... *1*
Kelsey, Elin 1961- *159*
Kemly, Kathleen 1958- *197*
Kemnitz, Thomas Milton, Jr. 1984- *152*
Kemnitz, Tom, Jr.
  See Kemnitz, Thomas Milton, Jr.
Kemp, Gene 1926- *75*
  Earlier sketch in SATA *25*
  See also CLR *29*
Kempner, Mary Jean 1913-1969 .... *10*
Kempter, Christa 1945- *187*
Kempton, Jean Welch 1914- *10*
Kenah, Katharine 1949- *182*
Kenda, Margaret 1942- *71*
Kendall, Carol (Seeger) 1917- *74*
  Earlier sketch in SATA *11*
  See also SAAS *7*
Kendall, Katherine
  See Applegate, Katherine
Kendall, Lace
  See Stoutenburg, Adrien (Pearl)
Kendall, Martha E. *87*
Kendall, Russ 1957- *83*
Kenealy, James P. 1927- *52*
  Brief entry *29*
Kenealy, Jim
  See Kenealy, James P.
Kennaway, Adrienne 1945- *171*
  Earlier sketch in SATA *60*
Kennedy, Anne 1955- *198*
Kennedy, Anne Vittur
  See Kennedy, Anne
Kennedy, Brendan 1970- *57*
Kennedy, Dana Forrest 1917- *74*
Kennedy, Dorothy M(intzlaff) 1931- *53*
Kennedy, Doug 1963- *189*
  Earlier sketch in SATA *122*
Kennedy, Frances 1937- *192*
Kennedy, John F. 1917-1963 .... *11*
Kennedy, John Fitzgerald
  See Kennedy, John F.
Kennedy, Joseph Charles 1929- *130*
  Autobiography Feature *130*
  Earlier sketches in SATA *14, 86*
  See also CLR *27*
  See also SAAS *22*
  See Kennedy, X. J.
Kennedy, Kim *189*
Kennedy, Marlane 1962- *210*
Kennedy, Pamela (J.) 1946- *87*
Kennedy, Paul E(dward) 1929- *113*
  Earlier sketch in SATA *33*
Kennedy, Richard (Pitt) 1910-1989
  Obituary *60*
Kennedy, (Jerome) Richard 1932- *22*
Kennedy, Robert 1938- *63*
Kennedy, T.A. 1953- *42*
  Brief entry *35*
Kennedy, Teresa
  See Kennedy, T.A.
Kennedy, Teresa A.
  See Kennedy, T.A.
Kennedy, William 1928- *57*
Kennedy, William Joseph
  See Kennedy, William
Kennedy, X. J.
  See CLR *27*
  See also SAAS *22*
  See Kennedy, Joseph Charles
Kennell, Ruth Epperson 1893-1977 .... *6*
  Obituary *25*
Kennemore, Tim 1957- *133*
Kennen, Ally *190*
Kennett, David 1959- *206*
  Earlier sketch in SATA *121*
Kennison, Ruth *202*
Kenny, Ellsworth Newcomb 1909-1971
  Obituary *26*
Kenny, Herbert Andrew 1912-2002 .... *13*
Kenny, Jude
  See Daly, Jude

Kenny, Kathryn
  See Bowden, Joan Chase
  and Krull, Kathleen
  and Sanderlin, Owenita (Harrah)
  and Stack, Nicolete Meredith
Kenny, Kevin
  See Krull, Kathleen
Kensinger, George
  See Fichter, George S.
Kensington, Kathryn Wesley
  See Rusch, Kristine Kathryn
Kent, Alexander
  See Reeman, Douglas Edward
Kent, David
  See Lambert, David
Kent, Deborah Ann 1948- *155*
  Brief entry *41*
  Earlier sketches in SATA *47, 104*
Kent, Jack
  See Kent, John Wellington
Kent, John Wellington 1920-1985 .... *24*
  Obituary *45*
Kent, Lisa 1942- *90*
Kent, Mallory
  See Lowndes, Robert A(ugustine) W(ard)
Kent, Margaret 1894- *2*
Kent, Rockwell 1882-1971 .... *6*
Kent, Rose *188*
Kent, Sherman 1903-1986 .... *20*
  Obituary *47*
Kenward, Jean 1920- *42*
Kenworthy, Leonard S. 1912-1991 .... *6*
Kenyon, Karen (Smith) 1938- *145*
Kenyon, Kate
  See Adorjan, Carol (Madden)
  and Ransom, Candice F.
Kenyon, Ley 1913-1990 .... *6*
Keown, Elizabeth *78*
Kepes, Juliet A(ppleby) 1919-1999 .... *13*
Kephart, Beth 1960- *196*
Kerby, Mona 1951- *202*
  Earlier sketch in SATA *75*
Kerigan, Florence 1896-1984 .... *12*
Kerley, Barbara 1960- *191*
  Earlier sketch in SATA *138*
Kerman, Gertrude
  See Furman, Gertrude Lerner Kerman
Kerns, Thelma 1929- *116*
Kerr, Anne Louise
  See Mackey, Weezie Kerr
Kerr, Bob 1951- *120*
Kerr, Jessica 1901-1991 .... *13*
Kerr, (Anne-)Judith 1923-1970 .... *24*
Kerr, M. E.
  See Meaker, Marijane
Kerr, P.B.
  See Kerr, Philip
Kerr, Philip 1956- *168*
Kerr, Phyllis Forbes 1942- *72*
Kerr, Tom 1950- *77*
Kerrin, Jessica Scott *174*
Kerry, Frances
  See Kerigan, Florence
Kerry, Lois
  See Duncan, Lois
Kershen, (L.) Michael 1982- *82*
Kerven, Rosalind 1954- *83*
Ker Wilson, Barbara 1929- *121*
  Earlier sketches in SATA *20, 70*
  See also SAAS *18*
Keselman, Gabriela 1953- *128*
Kesey, Ken 1935-2001 .... *66*
  Obituary *131*
Kesey, Ken Elton
  See Kesey, Ken
Kesler, Jay 1935- *65*
Kessel, Joyce Karen 1937- *41*
Kessler, Cristina *190*
Kessler, Ethel 1922- *44*
  Brief entry *37*
Kessler, Leonard P. 1921- *14*

Kessler, Liz 1966- *206*
Kest, Kristin 1967- *168*
  Earlier sketch in SATA *118*
Kesteven, G. R.
  See Crosher, G. R.
Ketcham, Hank
  See Ketcham, Henry King
Ketcham, Henry King 1920-2001 .... *28*
  Brief entry *27*
  Obituary *128*
Ketcham, Sallie 1963- *124*
Ketchum, Liza 1946- *132*
  Earlier sketch in SATA *78*
Ketner, Mary Grace 1946- *75*
Kettelkamp, Larry (Dale) 1933- *2*
  See also SAAS *3*
Ketteman, Helen 1945- *167*
  Earlier sketches in SATA *73, 115*
Kettle, Peter
  See Glover, Denis (James Matthews)
Kevles, Bettyann Holtzmann 1938- *23*
Key, Alexander (Hill) 1904-1979 .... *8*
  Obituary *23*
Key, Samuel M.
  See de Lint, Charles
Key, Watt 1970- *189*
Keyes, Daniel 1927- *37*
Keyes, Diane *207*
Keyes, Fenton 1915-1999 .... *34*
Keyes, Greg 1963- *116*
Keyes, J. Gregory
  See Keyes, Greg
Keyser, Marcia 1933- *42*
Keyser, Sarah
  See McGuire, Leslie (Sarah)
Khalid, Mohamed Nor
  See Lat
Khalsa, Dayal Kaur 1943-1989 .... *62*
  See also CLR *30*
Khan, Rukhsana 1962- *165*
  Earlier sketch in SATA *118*
Khanshendel, Chiron
  See Rose, Wendy
Kheirabadi, Masoud 1951- *158*
Khemir, Sabiha *87*
Kherdian, David 1931- *74*
  Autobiography Feature *125*
  Earlier sketch in SATA *16*
  See also CLR *24*
Khing, T.T. 1933- *192*
Kibbe, Pat (Hosley) *60*
Kidd, Diana 1933-2000 .... *150*
Kidd, Richard 1952-2008 .... *152*
  Obituary *194*
Kidd, Ronald 1948- *173*
  Earlier sketches in SATA *42, 92*
Kiddell, John 1922- *3*
Kiddell-Monroe, Joan 1908-1972 .... *55*
Kidwell, Carl 1910- *43*
Kiefer, Irene 1926- *21*
Kiefer, Kathleen Balmes 1957- *142*
Kiepper, Shirley Morgan 1933- *10*
Kierstead, Vera M.
  See Kierstead-Farber, Vera M.
Kierstead-Farber, Vera M. 1913- *121*
Kierstead-Farber, Vera May
  See Kierstead-Farber, Vera M.
Kiesel, Stanley 1925- *35*
Kiesler, Kate (A.) 1971- *152*
  Earlier sketch in SATA *90*
Kihn, Greg 1952- *110*
Kikukawa, Cecily H(arder) 1919- *44*
  Brief entry *35*
Kilcher, Jewel 1974- *109*
Kile, Joan 1940- *78*
Kilgore, Kathleen 1946- *42*
Kilian, Crawford 1941- *35*
Killdeer, John
  See Mayhar, Ardath
Killien, Christi 1956- *73*
Killilea, Marie (Lyons) 1913-1991 .... *2*

Killingback, Julia 1944- 63
Killough, (Karen) Lee 1942- 64
Kilpatrick, Don 206
Kilreon, Beth
   See Walker, Barbara (Jeanne) K(erlin)
Kilworth, Garry 1941- 94
Kilworth, Garry D.
   See Kilworth, Garry
Kilworth, Garry Douglas
   See Kilworth, Garry
Kim, David 1977- 201
Kim, Helen 1899-1970 98
Kim, Joung Un 1970- 205
Kimball, Gayle 1943- 90
Kimball, Violet T(ew) 1932- 126
Kimball, Yeffe 1914-1978 37
Kimber, Murray 1964- 171
Kimble, Warren 176
Kimbrough, Emily 1899-1989 2
   Obituary 59
Kimeldorf, Martin 1948- 121
Kimeldorf, Martin R.
   See Kimeldorf, Martin
Kimenye, Barbara 1940(?)- 121
Kimmel, Elizabeth Cody 209
   Earlier sketch in SATA *170*
Kimmel, Eric A. 1946- 208
   Earlier sketches in SATA *13, 80, 125, 176*
Kimmel, Margaret Mary 1938- 43
   Brief entry 33
Kimmelman, Burt 1947- 180
Kimmelman, Leslie 1958- 211
   Earlier sketches in SATA *85, 156*
Kincaid, Jamaica 1949-
   See CLR *63*
Kincher, Jonni 1949- 79
Kindl, Patrice 1951- 128
   Earlier sketch in SATA *82*
   See also CLR *132*
Kindred, Wendy (Good) 1937- 7
Kinerk, Robert 199
Kines, Pat Decker 1937- 12
King, Adam
   See Hoare, Robert J(ohn)
King, Alison
   See Martini, Teri
King, (Maria) Anna 1964- 72
King, Billie Jean 1943- 12
King, Christopher (L.) 1945- 84
King, (David) Clive 1924- 144
   Earlier sketch in SATA *28*
King, Colin 1943- 76
King, Cynthia 1925- 7
King, Daniel (John) 1963- 130
King, Daren 1972- 197
King, Elizabeth 1953- 83
King, Frank O. 1883-1969
   Obituary 22
King, Frank R. 1904-1999 127
King, Jane
   See Currie, Stephen
King, Jeanette (Margaret) 1959- 105
King, Larry L. 1929- 66
King, Laurie R. 1952- 88
King, Marian 1900(?)-1986 23
   Obituary 47
King, Martin Luther, Jr. 1929-1968 14
King, Mary Ellen 1958- 93
King, Paul
   See Drackett, Phil(ip Arthur)
King, Paula
   See Downing, Paula E.
King, Stephen 1947- 161
   Earlier sketches in SATA *9, 55*
   See also CLR *124*
King, Stephen Edwin
   See King, Stephen
King, Stephen Michael 157
King, Steve
   See King, Stephen
King, Thomas 1943- 96

King, Thomas Hunt
   See King, Thomas
King, Tony 1947- 39
King, Willie Christine
   See Farris, Christine King
Kingfisher, Rupert 209
Kingman, Dong (Moy Shu) 1911-2000 44
Kingman, Lee
   See Natti, Lee
Kingsland, Leslie William 1912- 13
Kingsley, Charles 1819-1875
   See YABC *2*
   See also CLR *77*
Kingsley, Emily Perl 1940- 33
Kingsley, Kaza 193
King-Smith, Dick 1922- 192
   Brief entry 38
   Earlier sketches in SATA *47, 80, 135*
   See also CLR *40*
Kingston, Maxine Hong 1940- 53
Kingston, Maxine Ting Ting Hong
   See Kingston, Maxine Hong
Kinney, C. Cle(land) 1915- 6
Kinney, Harrison 1921- 13
Kinney, Jean Stout 1912- 12
Kinney, Jeff 1971- 187
Kinsey, Elizabeth
   See Clymer, Eleanor
Kinsey, Helen 1948- 82
Kinsey-Warnock, Natalie 1956- 167
   Earlier sketches in SATA *71, 116*
Kinzel, Dorothy 1950- 57
Kinzel, Dottie
   See Kinzel, Dorothy
Kipling, Joseph Rudyard
   See Kipling, Rudyard
Kipling, Rudyard 1865-1936 100
   See also YABC *2*
   See also CLR *65*
Kippax, Frank
   See Needle, Jan
Kirby, David 1944- 78
Kirby, David K.
   See Kirby, David
Kirby, David Kirk
   See Kirby, David
Kirby, Margaret
   See Bingley, Margaret (Jane Kirby)
Kirby, Susan E. 1949- 62
Kirk, Connie Ann 1957- 167
Kirk, Daniel 1952- 196
   Earlier sketches in SATA *107, 153*
Kirk, David 1955- 161
   Earlier sketch in SATA *117*
Kirk, Heather 1949- 166
Kirk, Ruth (Kratz) 1925- 5
Kirkham, Dinah
   See Card, Orson Scott
Kirkland, Will
   See Hale, Arlene
Kirkpatrick, Katherine (Anne) 1964- 113
Kirkup, James 1918-2009 12
Kirkus, Virginia
   See Glick, Virginia Kirkus
Kirkwood, Kathryn
   See Fluke, Joanne
Kirsch, Vincent X. 211
Kirshenbaum, Binnie 79
Kirshner, David S. 1958- 123
Kirtland, G. B.
   See Hine, Sesyle Joslin
   and Hine, Al(fred Blakelee)
Kirwan, Wednesday 198
Kish, Eleanor M(ary) 1924- 73
Kish, Ely
   See Kish, Eleanor M(ary)
Kishida, Eriko 1929- 12
Kisinger, Grace Gelvin (Maze) 1913-1965 . 10
Kissel, Richard 209
Kissin, Eva H. 1923- 10

Kissinger, Rosemary K.
   See Updyke, Rosemary K.
Kistler, John M. 1967- 160
Kitamura, Satoshi 1956- 201
   Earlier sketches in SATA *62, 98, 143*
   See also CLR *60*
Kitchen, Bert
   See Kitchen, Herbert Thomas
Kitchen, Herbert Thomas 1940- 70
Kite, L. Patricia
   See Kite, Pat
Kite, Pat 1940- 78
Kitt, Tamara
   See de Regniers, Beatrice Schenk (Freedman)
Kittinger, Jo S(usenbach) 1955- 148
   Earlier sketch in SATA *96*
Kituomba
   See Odaga, Asenath (Bole)
Kitzinger, Sheila 1929- 57
Kiwak, Barbara 1966- 103
Kjelgaard, James Arthur 1910-1959 17
   See also CLR *81*
   See Kjelgaard, Jim
Kjelgaard, Jim
   See Kjelgaard, James Arthur
Kjelle, Marylou Morano 1954- 146
Klages, Ellen 1954- 196
Klagsbrun, Francine (Lifton) 36
Klaits, Barrie 1944- 52
Klam, Cheryl 191
Klaperman, Gilbert 1921- 33
Klaperman, Libby Mindlin 1921-1982 33
   Obituary 31
Klass, David 1960- 207
   Earlier sketches in SATA *88, 142*
Klass, Morton 1927-2001 11
Klass, Sheila Solomon 1927- 99
   Autobiography Feature 126
   Earlier sketch in SATA *45*
   See also SAAS *26*
Klause, Annette Curtis 1953- 175
   Earlier sketch in SATA *79*
   See also CLR *104*
Klaveness, Jan O'Donnell 1939- 86
Kleberger, Ilse 1921- 5
Kleeberg, Irene (Flitner) Cumming 1932- .. 65
Klein, Aaron E. 1930-1998 45
   Brief entry 28
Klein, Bill 1945- 89
Klein, David 1919-2001 59
Klein, Frederick C. 1938- 154
Klein, Gerda Weissmann 1924- 44
Klein, H(erbert) Arthur 8
Klein, James 1932- 115
Klein, Leonore (Glotzer) 1916- 6
Klein, Lisa 1958- 211
Klein, Lisa M.
   See Klein, Lisa
Klein, Mina C(ooper) 1906-1979 8
Klein, Norma 1938-1989 57
   Earlier sketch in SATA *7*
   See also CLR *19*
   See also SAAS *1*
Klein, Rachel S. 1953- 105
Klein, Robin 1936- 164
   Brief entry 45
   Earlier sketches in SATA *55, 80*
   See also CLR *21*
Klemin, Diana 65
Klemm, Barry 1945- 104
Klemm, Edward G., Jr. 1910-2001 30
Klemm, Roberta K(ohnhorst) 1884-1975 30
Kleven, Elisa 1958- 173
   Earlier sketch in SATA *76*
   See also CLR *85*
Klevin, Jill Ross 1935- 39
   Brief entry 38
Kliban, B(ernard) 1935-1990 35
   Obituary 66
Klier, Kimberly Wagner 208
Klimowicz, Barbara 1927- 10

Kline, Christina Baker 1964- *101*
Kline, James
  See Klein, James
Kline, Jim
  See Kline, Jim
Kline, Lisa Williams 1954- *143*
Kline, Suzy 1943- *193*
  Autobiography Feature *193*
  Brief entry *48*
  Earlier sketches in SATA *67, 99, 152*
Kliros, Thea 1935- *106*
Klise, Kate *181*
Klise, M. Sarah 1961- *180*
  Earlier sketch in SATA *128*
Klots, Alexander Barrett 1903-1989
  Obituary *62*
Klug, Ron(ald) 1939- *31*
Knaak, Richard A. 1961- *166*
  Earlier sketch in SATA *86*
Knaak, Richard Allen
  See Knaak, Richard A.
Knapman, Timothy *200*
Knapp, Edward
  See Kunhardt, Edith
Knapp, Ron 1952- *34*
Knebel, Fletcher 1911-1993 .... *36*
  Obituary *75*
Kneeland, Linda Clarke 1947- *94*
Knickerbocker, Diedrich
  See Irving, Washington
Knifesmith
  See Cutler, Ivor
Knigge, Robert (R.) 1921(?)-1987 .... *50*
Knight, Anne (Katherine) 1946- *34*
Knight, Brenda *112*
Knight, Christopher G. 1943- *96*
Knight, Damon (Francis) 1922-2002 .... *9*
  Obituary *139*
Knight, David C(arpenter) 1925-1984 .... *14*
  See also CLR *38*
Knight, Eric 1897-1943 .... *18*
Knight, Eric Mowbray
  See Knight, Eric
Knight, Francis Edgar 1905- *14*
Knight, Frank
  See Knight, Francis Edgar
Knight, Hilary 1926- *132*
  Earlier sketches in SATA *15, 69*
Knight, Joan (MacPhail) *159*
  Earlier sketch in SATA *82*
Knight, Joan
  See Knight, Joan (MacPhail)
Knight, Kathryn Lasky
  See Lasky, Kathryn
Knight, Mallory T.
  See Hurwood, Bernhardt J.
Knight, Ruth Adams 1898-1974
  Obituary *20*
Knight, Theodore O. 1946- *77*
Knobloch, Dorothea 1951- *88*
Knoepfle, John (Ignatius) 1923- *66*
Knorr, Laura 1971- *200*
Knott, Bill
  See Knott, William C(ecil, Jr.)
Knott, William C(ecil, Jr.) 1927- *3*
Knotts, Howard (Clayton, Jr.) 1922- *25*
Knowles, Anne 1933- *37*
Knowles, Jo 1970- *197*
Knowles, Johanna Beth
  See Knowles, Jo
Knowles, John 1926-2001 .... *89*
  Obituary *134*
  Earlier sketch in SATA *8*
  See also CLR *98*
Knox, Calvin M.
  See Silverberg, Robert
Knox, (Mary) Eleanor Jessie 1909-2000 .... *59*
  Earlier sketch in SATA *30*
Knox, Elizabeth 1959- *176*
Knox, Elizabeth Fiona
  See Knox, Elizabeth

Knox, James
  See Brittain, William
Knox, Jolyne 1937- *76*
Knudsen, James 1950- *42*
Knudsen, Michelle 1974- *171*
Knudson, Mike 1965- *209*
Knudson, R. R.
  See Knudson, Rozanne
Knudson, Richard L(ewis) 1930- *34*
Knudson, Rozanne 1932-2008 .... *79*
  Earlier sketch in SATA *7*
  See also SAAS *18*
Knutson, Barbara 1959-2005 .... *166*
Knutson, Kimberley *115*
Knye, Cassandra
  See Disch, Thomas M.
Kobayashi, Masako Matsuno 1935- *6*
Koch, Dorothy Clarke 1924- *6*
Koch, Kenneth 1925-2002 .... *65*
Koch, Kenneth Jay
  See Koch, Kenneth
Koch, Phyllis (Mae) McCallum 1911- *10*
Kochalka, James 1967- *196*
Kocsis, J. C.
  See Paul, James
Koda-Callan, Elizabeth 1944- *140*
  Earlier sketch in SATA *67*
Kodman, Stanislawa *201*
Koehler, Phoebe 1955- *85*
Koehler-Pentacoff, Elizabeth 1957- *160*
  Earlier sketch in SATA *96*
Koehn, Ilse
  See Van Zwienen, Ilse Charlotte Koehn
Koeller, Carol *192*
Koenig, Viviane 1950- *80*
Koering, Ursula 1921-1976 .... *64*
Koerner, W(illiam) H(enry) D(avid)
  1878-1938 .... *21*
Koertge, Ron 1940- *209*
  Earlier sketches in SATA *53, 92, 131*
Koestler-Grack, Rachel A. 1973- *156*
Koff, Richard Myram 1926- *62*
Koffinke, Carol 1949- *82*
Kogan, Deborah
  See Kogan Ray, Deborah
Kogan Ray, Deborah 1940- *203*
  Earlier sketches in SATA *8, 50, 161*
Kogawa, Joy 1935- *99*
Kogawa, Joy Nozomi
  See Kogawa, Joy
Kogler, Jennifer Anne 1982(?)- *174*
Kohara, Kazuno *207*
Kohl, Herbert 1937- *47*
Kohl, Herbert R.
  See Kohl, Herbert
Kohl, MaryAnn F(aubion) 1947- *144*
  Earlier sketch in SATA *74*
Kohler, Julilly H(ouse) 1908-1976
  Obituary *20*
Kohn, Bernice
  See Hunt, Bernice
Kohn, Rita (T.) 1933- *89*
Kohner, Frederick 1905-1986 .... *10*
  Obituary *48*
Koide, Tan 1938-1986 .... *50*
Koike, Kay 1940- *72*
Koja, Kathe 1960- *199*
  Earlier sketch in SATA *155*
Koja, Stephan *198*
Kolar, Bob 1960(?)- *206*
Kolb, Larry J. 1953- *175*
Kolba, St. Tamara *22*
Kolibalova, Marketa
  See Kolibalova, Marketa
Kolibalova, Marketa 1953- *126*
Koller, Jackie French 1948- *157*
  Earlier sketch in SATA *72, 109*
  See also CLR *68*
Kolodny, Nancy J. 1946- *76*
Kolosov, Jacqueline 1967- *199*

Komaiko, Leah 1954- *164*
  Earlier sketch in SATA *97*
Komisar, Lucy 1942- *9*
Komoda, Beverly 1939- *25*
Komoda, Kiyo 1937- *9*
Kompaneyets, Marc 1974- *169*
Komroff, Manuel 1890-1974 .... *2*
  Obituary *20*
Konigsberg, Bill 1970- *207*
Konigsburg, E.L. 1930- *194*
  Earlier sketches in SATA *4, 48, 94, 126*
  See also CLR *81*
Konigsburg, Elaine Lobl
  See Konigsburg, E.L.
Koning, Hans 1921-2007 .... *5*
  Obituary *182*
Koningsberger, Hans
  See Koning, Hans
Konkle, Janet Everest 1917- *12*
Kono, Erin Eitter 1973- *177*
Konzak, Burt 1946- *151*
Koob, Theodora (J. Foth) 1918- *23*
Kooiker, Leonie
  See Kooyker-Romijn, Johanna Maria
Koons, James
  See Pernu, Dennis
Koontz, Dean 1945- *165*
  Earlier sketch in SATA *92*
Koontz, Dean R.
  See Koontz, Dean
Koontz, Dean Ray
  See Koontz, Dean
Koontz, Robin Michal 1954- *136*
  Earlier sketch in SATA *70*
Kooyker, Leonie
  See Kooyker-Romijn, Johanna Maria
Kooyker-Romijn, Johanna Maria 1927- *48*
Kooyker-Romyn, Johanna Maria
  See Kooyker-Romijn, Johanna Maria
Kopelke, Lisa 1963- *154*
Kopper, Lisa (Esther) 1950- *105*
  Brief entry *51*
Koppes, Steven N. 1957- *169*
Koppes, Steven Nelson
  See Koppes, Steven N.
Korach, Mimi 1922- *9*
Koralek, Jenny 1934- *140*
  Earlier sketch in SATA *71*
Korczak, Janusz
  See Goldszmit, Henryk
Koren, Edward (Benjamin) 1935- *148*
  Earlier sketch in SATA *5*
Koren, Edward 1935- *206*
Korinets, Iurii Iosifovich
  See Korinetz, Yuri (Iosifovich)
Korinetz, Yuri (Iosifovich) 1923- *9*
  See also CLR *4*
Korman, Bernice 1937- *78*
Korman, Gordon 1963- *167*
  Brief entry *41*
  Earlier sketches in SATA *49, 81, 119*
  See also CLR *25*
Korman, Gordon Richard
  See Korman, Gordon
Korman, Justine 1958- *70*
Kornblatt, Marc 1954- *147*
  Earlier sketch in SATA *84*
Kornprobst, Jacques 1937- *177*
Korte, Gene J. 1950- *74*
Korthues, Barbara 1971- *203*
Korty, Carol 1937- *15*
Koscielniak, Bruce 1947- *153*
  Earlier sketches in SATA *67, 99*
Koshin, Alexander (A.) 1952- *86*
Kositsky, Lynne 1947- *158*
Koskenmaki, Rosalie
  See Maggio, Rosalie
Koss, Amy Goldman 1954- *158*
  Earlier sketch in SATA *115*
Kossin, Sandy (Sanford) 1926- *10*
Kossman, Nina 1959- *84*

Kostecki-Shaw, Jenny Sue 203
Kostick, Conor 1964- 186
Kotzwinkle, William 1938- 146
  Earlier sketches in SATA 24, 70
  See also CLR 6
Kouhi, Elizabeth 1917- 54
  Brief entry 49
Kouts, Anne 1945- 8
Koutsky, Jan Dale 1955- 146
Kovacs, Deborah 1954- 132
  Earlier sketch in SATA 79
Kovalski, Maryann 1951- 175
  Earlier sketches in SATA 58, 97
  See also CLR 34
  See also SAAS 21
Kowalski, Kathiann M. 1955- 151
  Earlier sketch in SATA 96
Koz, Paula G.
  See Goodman Koz, Paula
Kozjan, Drazen 209
Kraft, Betsy Harvey 1937- 157
Kraft, Erik P. 193
Krahn, Fernando 1935- 49
  Brief entry 31
  See also CLR 3
Krakauer, Hoong Yee Lee 1955- 86
Krakauer, Jon 1954- 108
Kramer, George
  See Heuman, William
Kramer, Nora 1896(?)-1984 26
  Obituary 39
Kramer, Remi (Thomas) 1935- 90
Krantz, Hazel (Newman) 12
Kranzler, George G(ershon) 1916- 28
Kranzler, Gershon
  See Kranzler, George G(ershon)
Krasilovsky, Phyllis 1926- 38
  Earlier sketch in SATA 1
  See also CLR 83
  See also SAAS 5
Krasne, Betty
  See Levine, Betty K(rasne)
Krasner, Steven 1953- 154
Krasno, Rena 1923- 104
Kratman, Tom 175
Kraus, Joanna Halpert 1937- 87
Kraus, (Herman) Robert 1925-2001 93
  Obituary 130
  Earlier sketches in SATA 4, 65
  See also SAAS 11
Krauss, Ruth (Ida) 1911-1993 30
  Obituary 75
  Earlier sketch in SATA 1
  See also CLR 42
Krautter, Elisa (Bialk) 1912(?)-1990 1
  Obituary 65
Krautwurst, Terry 1946- 79
Kray, Robert Clement 1930- 82
Krech, Bob 1956- 185
Krech, Robert
  See Krech, Bob
Kredel, Fritz 1900-1973 17
Kreikemeier, Gregory Scott 1965- 85
Kreloff, Elliot 189
Krementz, Jill 1940- 134
  Earlier sketches in SATA 17, 71
  See also CLR 5
  See also SAAS 8
Kremer, Marcie
  See Sorenson, Margo
Krenina, Katya 1968- 101
Krensky, Stephen 1953- 188
  Brief entry 41
  Earlier sketches in SATA 47, 93, 136
Krensky, Stephen Alan
  See Krensky, Stephen
Kresh, Paul 1919-1997 61
  Obituary 94
Kress, Nancy 1948- 147
  Autobiography Feature 147
  Earlier sketch in SATA 85

Kricher, John C. 1944- 113
Krieger, Melanie 96
Krinitz, Esther Nisenthal 1927-2001 194
Kripke, Dorothy Karp 30
Krisher, Trudy 1946- 160
  Earlier sketch in SATA 86
Krisher, Trudy B.
  See Krisher, Trudy
Krishnaswami, Uma 1956- 182
  Earlier sketch in SATA 144
Kristiansen, Teddy 1964- 210
Kristiansen, Teddy H.
  See Kristiansen, Teddy
Kristof, Jane 1932- 8
Kroeber, Theodora (Kracaw) 1897-1979 1
Kroeger, Mary Kay 1950- 92
Krohn, Katherine E(lizabeth) 1961- 125
  Earlier sketch in SATA 84
Kroll, Francis Lynde 1904-1973 10
Kroll, Steven 1941- 135
  Autobiography Feature 135
  Earlier sketches in SATA 19, 66, 125
  See also SAAS 7
Kroll, Virginia L. 1948- 168
  Earlier sketches in SATA 76, 114
Kroll, Virginia Louisa
  See Kroll, Virginia L.
Kromhout, Rindert 1958- 189
Krommes, Beth 1956- 208
  Earlier sketches in SATA 128, 181
Kronenwetter, Michael 1943- 62
Kroniuk, Lisa
  See Berton, Pierre (Francis de Marigny)
Kropp, Paul 1948- 38
  Brief entry 34
  See also CLR 96
Kropp, Paul Stephan
  See Kropp, Paul
Krosoczka, Jarrett J. 1977- 200
  Earlier sketch in SATA 155
Krovatin, Christopher 1985- 171
Krudop, Walter
  See Krudop, Walter Lyon
Krudop, Walter Lyon 1966- 210
Kruess, James
  See Kruss, James
Kruglik, Gerald 187
Krull, Kathleen 1952- 184
  Autobiography Feature 106
  Brief entry 39
  Earlier sketches in SATA 52, 80, 149
  See also CLR 44
Krumgold, Joseph (Quincy) 1908-1980 48
  Obituary 23
  Earlier sketch in SATA 1
Krupinski, Loretta 1940- 161
  Earlier sketches in SATA 67, 102
Krupnick, Karen 1947- 89
Krupp, E(dwin) C(harles) 1944- 123
  Earlier sketch in SATA 53
Krupp, Robin Rector 1946- 53
Krush, Beth 1918- 18
Krush, Joe 1918-
  See Krush, Joseph P.
Krush, Joseph P. 1918- 18
Kruss, James 1926-1997 8
  See also CLR 9
Kruusval, Catarina 1951- 201
Krykorka, Vladyana 1945- 96
Krystoforski, Andrej 1943- 196
Kubie, Eleanor Gottheil
  See Kubie, Nora Gottheil Benjamin
Kubie, Nora Benjamin
  See Kubie, Nora Gottheil Benjamin
Kubie, Nora Gottheil Benjamin
  1899-1988 39
  Obituary 59
Kubinyi, Laszlo 1937- 94
  Earlier sketch in SATA 17
Kudlinski, Kathleen V. 1950- 150
Kuehnert, Stephanie 1979- 205

Kuenstler, Morton 1927- 10
Kuh, Charlotte 1892(?)-1985
  Obituary 43
Kuharski, Janice 1947- 128
Kuhn, Dwight 199
Kuijer, Guus 1942- 179
Kujoth, Jean Spealman 1935-1975
  Obituary 30
Kuklin, Susan 1941- 163
  Earlier sketches in SATA 63, 95
  See also CLR 51
Kulikov, Boris 1966- 205
  Earlier sketch in SATA 170
Kulka, Joe 188
Kulling, Monica 1952- 89
Kullman, Harry 1919-1982 35
Kulyk Keefer, Janice 1952- 132
Kumin, Maxine 1925- 12
Kumin, Maxine Winokur
  See Kumin, Maxine
Kunhardt, Dorothy (Meserve) 1901-1979 ... 53
  Obituary 22
Kunhardt, Edith 1937- 67
Kunjufu, Jawanza 1953- 73
Kunstler, Morton
  See Kuenstler, Morton
Kuntz, J(ohn) L. 1947- 91
Kuntz, Jerry 1956- 133
Kupferberg, Herbert 1918-2001 19
Kuratomi, Chizuko 1939- 12
  See also CLR 32
Kurczok, Belinda 1978- 121
Kurelek, William 1927-1977 8
  Obituary 27
  See also CLR 2
Kurian, George 1928- 65
Kurjian, Judi(th M.) 1944- 127
Kurland, Gerald 1942- 13
Kurland, Michael 1938- 118
  Earlier sketch in SATA 48
Kurland, Michael Joseph
  See Kurland, Michael
Kuroi, Ken 1947- 120
Kurokawa, Mitsuhiro 1954- 88
Kurten, Bjorn (Olof) 1924-1988 64
Kurtz, Jane 1952- 139
  Earlier sketch in SATA 91
  See also CLR 123
Kurtz, Katherine 1944- 182
  Earlier sketches in SATA 76, 126
Kurtz, Katherine Irene
  See Kurtz, Katherine
Kurz, Rudolf 1952- 95
Kushner, Donn (J.) 1927- 52
  See also CLR 55
Kushner, Ellen 1955- 202
  Earlier sketch in SATA 98
Kushner, Ellen Ruth
  See Kushner, Ellen
Kushner, Jill Menkes 1951- 62
Kushner, Lawrence 1943- 169
  Earlier sketch in SATA 83
Kushner, Tony 1956- 160
Kuskin, Karla 1932-2009 164
  Obituary 206
  Earlier sketches in SATA 2, 68, 111
  See also CLR 4
  See also SAAS 3
Kuskin, Karla Seidman
  See Kuskin, Karla
Kusugak, Michael 1948- 143
Kusugak, Michael Arvaarluk
  See Kusugak, Michael
Kutner, Merrily 1948- 196
Kuttner, Paul 1922- 18
Kuyper, Sjoerd 1952- 177
Kuzma, Kay 1941- 39
Kvale, Velma R(uth) 1898-1979 8
Kvasnosky, Laura McGee 1951- 182
  Earlier sketches in SATA 93, 142
Kwasney, Michelle D. 1960- 162

Kyle, Benjamin
  See Gottfried, Theodore Mark
Kyle, Elisabeth
  See Dunlop, Agnes M. R.
Kyte, Kathy S. 1946- 50
  Brief entry 44

L

L., Barry
  See Longyear, Barry B(rookes)
L., Tommy
  See Lorkowski, Thomas V(incent)
Labouisse, Eve Curie
  See Curie, Eve
Labouisse, Eve Denise
  See Curie, Eve
Lace, William W. 1942- 126
Lacey, Joshua
  See Doder, Josh
Lachner, Dorothea
  See Knobloch, Dorothea
Lachtman, Ofelia Dumas 1919- 179
Lackey, Mercedes R. 1950- 127
  Earlier sketch in SATA *81*
Lackey, Mercedes Ritchie
  See Lackey, Mercedes R.
Lacoe, Addie 78
Lacombe, Benjamin 1982- 198
Lacome, Julie 1961- 174
  Earlier sketch in SATA *80*
Lacy, Leslie Alexander 1937- 6
Ladd, Cheryl (Jean) 1951- 113
Ladd, London 1972(?)- 206
Ladd, Louise 1943- 97
Ladd, Veronica
  See Miner, Jane Claypool
Laden, Nina 1962- 148
  Earlier sketch in SATA *85*
Lader, Lawrence 1919-2006 6
  Obituary 178
LaDoux, Rita C. 1951- 74
Lady, A
  See Taylor, Ann
Lady Mears
  See Tempest, Margaret Mary
Lady of Quality, A
  See Bagnold, Enid
La Farge, Oliver 1901-1963 19
La Farge, Oliver Hazard Perry
  See La Farge, Oliver
La Farge, Phyllis 14
LaFave, Kim 196
LaFaye, A. 1970- 156
  Earlier sketch in SATA *105*
LaFaye, Alexandria R.T.
  See LaFaye, A.
LaFevers, R.L. 191
LaFevers, Robin L.
  See LaFevers, R.L.
Laffin, John (Alfred Charles) 1922- 31
LaFontaine, Bruce 1948- 176
  Earlier sketch in SATA *114*
La Fontaine, Jean de 1621-1695 18
Lafrance, Marie 1955- 197
Lager, Claude
  See Lapp, Christiane (Germain)
Lager, Marilyn 1939- 52
Lagercrantz, Rose (Elsa) 1947- 39
Lagerloef, Selma
  See Lagerlof, Selma
Lagerlof, Selma 1858-1940 15
  See also CLR *7*
Laguna, Sofie 1968- 158
LaHaye, Tim F. 1926- 149
LaHaye, Timothy F.
  See LaHaye, Tim F.
Laidlaw, Rob 205

Laiken, Deirdre S(usan) 1948- 48
  Brief entry 40
Laimgruber, Monika 1946- 11
Lain, Anna
  See Lamb, Nancy
Laing, Alexander (Kinnan) 1903-1976 117
Laing, Martha 1951- 39
Laird, Christa 1944- 108
  Autobiography Feature 120
  See also SAAS *26*
Laird, Elizabeth (Mary Risk) 1943- 159
  Earlier sketches in SATA *77, 114*
  See also CLR *65*
Laird, Jean E(louise) 1930- 38
Laite, Gordon 1925- 31
Lake, Harriet
  See Taylor, Paula (Wright)
Lakin, Patricia 1944- 190
Laklan, Carli 1907-1988 5
Laliberte, Louise-Andree 1958- 169
Lalicki, Barbara 61
Lalicki, Tom 1949- 186
Lally, Soinbhe 1945- 119
LaMarche, Jim 162
Lamb, Albert 187
Lamb, Beatrice Pitney 1904-1997 21
Lamb, Charles 1775-1834 17
Lamb, Elizabeth Searle 1917- 31
Lamb, G(eoffrey) F(rederick) 10
Lamb, Harold (Albert) 1892-1962 53
Lamb, Lynton (Harold) 1907-1977 10
Lamb, Mary Ann 1764-1847 17
Lamb, Nancy 1939- 80
Lamb, Robert (Boyden) 1941- 13
Lamba, Marie 195
Lambert, David 1932- 84
  Brief entry 49
Lambert, David Compton
  See Lambert, David
Lambert, Janet 1895(?)-1973 25
Lambert, Martha L. 113
Lambert, Saul 1928- 23
Lambert, Stephen 174
Lamburn, Richmal Crompton 1890-1969 5
Lamensdorf, Len 1930- 120
Lamensdorf, Leonard
  See Lamensdorf, Len
Laminack, Lester L. 1956- 163
  Earlier sketch in SATA *120*
Lamont, Priscilla 200
Lamorisse, Albert (Emmanuel) 1922-1970 . 23
Lampert, Emily 1951- 52
  Brief entry 49
Lamplugh, Lois 1921- 17
Lampman, Evelyn Sibley 1907-1980 87
  Obituary 23
  Earlier sketch in SATA *4*
Lamprey, Louise 1869-1951
  See YABC *2*
Lampton, Chris
  See Lampton, Christopher F.
Lampton, Christopher
  See Lampton, Christopher F.
Lampton, Christopher F. 67
  Brief entry 47
Lamstein, Sarah 1943- 174
  Earlier sketch in SATA *126*
Lamstein, Sarah Marwil
  See Lamstein, Sarah
Lanagan, Margo 1960- 201
  Earlier sketch in SATA *163*
Lancaster, Bruce 1896-1963 9
Lancaster, Matthew 1973(?)-1983
  Obituary 45
Lance, Kathryn 1943- 76
Land, Barbara (Neblett) 1923- 16
Land, Jane
  See Borland, Kathryn Kilby
  and Speicher, Helen Ross S(mith)
Land, Myrick (Ebben) 1922-1998 15

Land, Ross
  See Borland, Kathryn Kilby
  and Speicher, Helen Ross S(mith)
Landau, Elaine 1948- 141
  Earlier sketches in SATA *10, 94*
Landau, Jacob 1917- 38
Landeck, Beatrice 1904-1978 15
Landin, Les 1923- 2
Landis, J(ames) D(avid) 1942- 60
  Brief entry 52
Landis, James D.
  See Landis, J(ames) D(avid)
Landis, Jill Marie 1948- 101
Landman, Tanya 207
Landmann, Bimba 1968- 176
Landon, Dena 1978(?)- 168
Landon, Lucinda 1950- 56
  Brief entry 51
Landon, Margaret (Dorothea Mortenson)
  1903-1993 50
Landowne, Youme 1970- 211
Landry, Leo 202
Landshoff, Ursula 1908-1989 13
Landstrom, Lena 1943- 206
  Earlier sketch in SATA *146*
Landstrom, Olof 1943- 146
Landy, Derek 1974- 210
Lane, Carolyn 1926-1993 10
Lane, Connie
  See Laux, Constance
Lane, Dakota 1959- 166
  Earlier sketch in SATA *105*
Lane, Jerry
  See Martin, Patricia Miles
Lane, John (Richard) 1932- 15
Lane, Leena 199
Lane, Margaret 1907-1994 65
  Brief entry 38
  Obituary 79
Lane, Rose Wilder 1887-1968 29
  Brief entry 28
Lanes, Selma Gordon 1929- 3
Lanfredi, Judy 1964- 83
Lang, Andrew 1844-1912 16
  See also CLR *101*
Lang, Aubrey 169
Lang, Lang 1982- 208
Lang, Paul 1948- 83
Lang, Susan S. 1950- 68
Lang, T.T.
  See Taylor, Theodore
Langart, Darrell T.
  See Garrett, Randall
Langdo, Bryan 1973- 191
  Earlier sketch in SATA *138*
Lange, John
  See Crichton, Michael
Lange, Karen E. 190
Lange, Suzanne 1945- 5
Langley, Andrew 1949- 166
  Earlier sketch in SATA *104*
Langley, Charles P(itman) III 1949- 103
Langley, Jonathan 1952- 122
Langley, Noel 1911-1980
  Obituary 25
Langley, Wanda 173
Langner, Nola
  See Malone, Nola Langner
Langone, John (Michael) 1929- 46
  Brief entry 38
Langreuter, Jutta 1944- 122
Langrish, Katherine 177
Langsen, Richard C. 1953- 95
Langstaff, John 1920-2005 68
  Obituary 172
  Earlier sketch in SATA *6*
  See also CLR *3*
Langstaff, John Meredith
  See Langstaff, John
Langstaff, Launcelot
  See Irving, Washington

Langston, Laura 1958- 186
Langton, Jane 1922- 200
  Autobiography Feature 140
  Earlier sketches in SATA 3, 68, 129, 140
  See also CLR 33
  See also SAAS 5
Lanier, Sidney 1842-1881 18
Lanier, Sterling E. 1927-2007 109
Lanier, Sterling Edmund
  See Lanier, Sterling E.
Lanino, Deborah 1964- 123
Lankford, Mary D. 1932- 112
  Earlier sketch in SATA 77
Lannin, Joanne 1951- 121
Lannin, Joanne A.
  See Lannin, Joanne
Lansdale, Joe R. 1951- 116
Lansdale, Joe Richard
  See Lansdale, Joe R.
Lansing, Alfred 1921-1975 35
Lansing, Karen E. 1954- 71
Lansky, Vicki 1942- 177
Lanthier, Jennifer 1964- 204
Lantier-Sampon, Patricia 1952- 92
Lantz, Fran
  See Lantz, Francess L(in)
Lantz, Francess L(in) 1952-2004 153
  Autobiography Feature 153
  Obituary 159
  Earlier sketches in SATA 63, 109
Lantz, Paul 1908- 45
Lantz, Walter 1900-1994 37
  Obituary 79
Lanza, Barbara 1945- 101
Lapp, Christiane (Germain) 1948- 74
Lappin, Peter 1911-1999 32
Larbalestier, Justine 178
Lardy, Philippe 1963- 168
LaReau, Jenna 181
LaReau, Kara 181
Larios, Julie 1949- 178
Larios, Julie Hofstrand
  See Larios, Julie
Larkin, Amy
  See Burns, Olive Ann
Larkin, Maia
  See Wojciechowska, Maia (Teresa)
Larkspur, Penelope
  See Wyatt, Valerie
Laroche, Giles 1956- 126
  Earlier sketch in SATA 71
LaRochelle, David 1960- 171
  Earlier sketch in SATA 115
Larom, Henry V. 1903(?)-1975
  Obituary 30
LaRose, Linda 125
Larrabee, Lisa 1947- 84
Larrecq, John M(aurice) 1926-1980 44
  Obituary 25
Larrick (Crosby), Nancy 1910-2004 4
Larsen, Anita 1942- 78
Larsen, Egon 1904- 14
Larsen, Rebecca 1944- 54
Larson, Eve
  See St. John, Wylly Folk
Larson, Gary 1950- 57
Larson, Hope 1982- 205
Larson, Ingrid D(ana) 1965- 92
Larson, Jean Russell 1930- 121
Larson, Kirby 1954- 181
  Earlier sketch in SATA 96
Larson, Norita D(ittberner) 1944- 29
Larson, William H. 1938- 10
Larsson, Carl (Olof) 1853-1919 35
LaSalle, Charles A.
  See Ellis, Edward S.
LaSalle, Charles E.
  See Ellis, Edward S.
Lasell, Elinor H. 1929- 19
Lasell, Fen H.
  See Lasell, Elinor H.

Lasenby, Jack 1931- 172
  Earlier sketches in SATA 65, 103
Laser, Michael 1954- 117
Lash, Joseph P. 1909-1987 43
Lasher, Faith B. 1921- 12
Lasker, David 1950- 38
Lasker, Joe
  See Lasker, Joseph Leon
Lasker, Joseph Leon 1919- 83
  Earlier sketch in SATA 9
  See also SAAS 17
Laski, Marghanita 1915-1988 55
Laskin, Pamela L. 1954- 75
Lasky, Kathryn 1944- 210
  Earlier sketches in SATA 13, 69, 112, 157
  See also CLR 140
Lasky Knight, Kathryn
  See Lasky, Kathryn
Lass, Bonnie 131
Lassalle, C. E.
  See Ellis, Edward S.
Lassiter, Mary
  See Hoffman, Mary
Lassiter, Rhiannon 1977- 157
Lat 1951- 196
Latham, Barbara 1896- 16
Latham, Frank B(rown) 1910-2000 6
Latham, Jean Lee 1902-1995 68
  Earlier sketch in SATA 2
  See also CLR 50
Latham, Mavis
  See Clark, Mavis Thorpe
Latham, Philip
  See Richardson, Robert S(hirley)
Lathrop, Dorothy P(ulis) 1891-1980 14
  Obituary 24
Lathrop, Francis
  See Leiber, Fritz (Reuter, Jr.)
Latimer, Jim 1943- 80
Latta, Rich
  See Latta, Richard
Latta, Richard 1946- 113
Latta, Sara L. 1960- 174
Lattany, Kristin
  See Lattany, Kristin Hunter
Lattany, Kristin (Eggleston)
  Hunter 1931- 154
  Autobiography Feature 154
  Earlier sketch in SATA 132
Lattany, Kristin Hunter 1931- 132
  Earlier sketch in SATA 12
  See also CLR 3
  See also SAAS 10
Lattimore, Eleanor Frances 1904-1986 7
  Obituary 48
Lattin, Ann
  See Cole, Lois Dwight
Lauber, Patricia (Grace) 1924- 138
  Earlier sketches in SATA 1, 33, 75
  See also CLR 16
Laugesen, Malene 207
Laugesen, Malene Reynolds
  See Laugesen, Malene
Laugesen, Mary E(akin) 1906-1995 5
Laughbaum, Steve 1945- 12
Laughlin, Florence Young 1910-2001 3
Laughlin, Rosemary 1941- 123
Launder, Sally 206
Laure, Ettagale
  See Blauer, Ettagale
Laure, Jason 1940- 50
  Brief entry 44
Laurence, Ester Hauser 1935- 7
Laurence, Jean Margaret Wemyss
  See Laurence, Margaret
Laurence, Margaret 1926-1987
  Obituary 50
Laurie, Rona 1916- 55
Laurin, Anne
  See McLaurin, Anne
Lauritzen, Jonreed 1902-1979 13

Lauscher, Hermann
  See Hesse, Hermann
Lauture, Denize 1946- 86
Laux, Connie
  See Laux, Constance
Laux, Constance 1952- 97
Laux, Dorothy 1920- 49
Lavallee, Barbara 1941- 166
  Earlier sketch in SATA 74
Lavender, David (Sievert) 1910-2003 97
  Obituary 145
  Earlier sketch in SATA 64
Lavender, William D. 1921- 143
Laverne, Christine 175
Lavert, Gwendolyn Battle 1951-
  See Battle-Lavert, Gwendolyn
Laverty, Donald
  See Blish, James
  and Knight, Damon (Francis)
Lavigne, Louis-Dominique 107
Lavine, David 1928- 31
Lavine, Sigmund Arnold 1908-1986 82
  Earlier sketch in SATA 3
  See also CLR 35
Lavond, Paul Dennis
  See Kornbluth, C(yril) M.
  and Lowndes, Robert A(ugustine) W(ard)
  and Pohl, Frederik
Lawford, Paula Jane 1960- 57
  Brief entry 53
Lawhead, Stephen R. 1950- 109
Lawhead, Steve
  See Lawhead, Stephen R.
Lawlor, Laurie 1953- 137
  Earlier sketch in SATA 80
Lawlor, William
  See Lawlor, William T.
Lawlor, William T. 1951- 183
Lawrence, Ann (Margaret) 1942-1987 41
  Obituary 54
Lawrence, Caroline 1954- 203
Lawrence, Iain 1955- 183
  Earlier sketch in SATA 135
Lawrence, J. T.
  See Rowland-Entwistle, (Arthur) Theodore
  (Henry)
Lawrence, Jerome 1915-2004 65
Lawrence, John 1933- 30
Lawrence, Josephine 1890(?)-1978
  Obituary 24
Lawrence, Louise 1943- 119
  Earlier sketches in SATA 38, 78
Lawrence, Louise de Kiriline 1894-1992 13
Lawrence, Lynn
  See Garland, Sherry
Lawrence, Margery H. 1889-1969 120
Lawrence, Michael 1943- 132
Lawrence, Mildred Elwood 1907-1997 3
Lawrence, R(onald) D(ouglas) 1921- 55
Lawrinson, Julia 1969- 141
Lawson, Amy
  See Gordon, Amy
Lawson, Carol (Antell) 1946- 42
Lawson, Don(ald Elmer) 1917-1990 9
Lawson, Joan 1906- 55
Lawson, Julie 1947- 126
  Earlier sketch in SATA 79
  See also CLR 89
Lawson, Marion Tubbs 1896-1994 22
Lawson, Robert 1892-1957 100
  See also YABC 2
  See also CLR 73
Lawton, Clive A. 1951- 145
Laxdal, Vivienne 1962- 112
Laybourn, Emma 193
Laycock, George (Edwin) 1921- 5
Layne, Laura
  See Knott, William C(ecil, Jr.)
Layne, Steven L. 171
Layson, Annelex Hofstra 1938(?)- 211

Layton, Neal 1971- *187*
  Earlier sketch in SATA *152*
Layton, Neal Andrew
  See Layton, Neal
Lazare, Gerald John 1927- *44*
Lazare, Jerry
  See Lazare, Gerald John
Lazarevich, Mila 1942- *17*
Lazarus, Keo Felker 1913-1993 .... *21*
  Obituary *129*
Lea, Alec 1907- *19*
Lea, Bob 1952- *203*
Lea, Joan
  See Neufeld, John (Arthur)
Leach, Maria 1892-1977 .... *39*
  Brief entry *28*
Leacock, Elspeth 1946- *131*
Leacroft, Helen (Mabel Beal) 1919- *6*
Leacroft, Richard (Vallance Becher) 1914- ... *6*
Leaf, Margaret P. 1909(?)-1988
  Obituary *55*
Leaf, (Wilbur) Munro 1905-1976 .... *20*
  See also CLR *25*
Leaf, VaDonna Jean 1929- *26*
Leah, Devorah
  See Devorah-Leah
Leakey, Richard E(rskine Frere) 1944- *42*
Leander, Ed
  See Richelson, Geraldine
Lear, Edward 1812-1888 .... *100*
  Earlier sketch in SATA *18*
  See also CLR *75*
Lears, Laurie 1955- *127*
Leasor, James 1923-2007 .... *54*
Leasor, Thomas James
  See Leasor, James
Leavitt, Jerome E(dward) 1916- *23*
Leavitt, Martine 1953- *170*
LeBar, Mary E(velyn) 1910-1982 .... *35*
LeBlanc, Annette M. 1965- *68*
LeBlanc, L(ee) 1913- *54*
LeBox, Annette 1943- *145*
Lebrun, Claude 1929- *66*
Le Cain, Errol (John) 1941-1989 .... *68*
  Obituary *60*
  Earlier sketch in SATA *6*
Lechner, Jack *201*
Lechner, John 1966- *200*
Lecourt, Nancy (Hoyt) 1951- *73*
Ledbetter, Suzann 1953- *119*
Leder, Jane Mersky 1945- *61*
  Brief entry *51*
Lederer, Muriel 1929- *48*
Lederer, William J. 1912-2009 .... *62*
Lederer, William Julius
  See Lederer, William J.
Lee, Amanda
  See Baggett, Nancy
  and Buckholtz, Eileen (Garber)
  and Glick, Ruth (Burtnick)
Lee, Benjamin 1921- *27*
Lee, Betsy 1949- *37*
Lee, Carol
  See Fletcher, Helen Jill
Lee, Carol Ann 1969- *185*
Lee, Chinlun *182*
Lee, Cora
  See Anderson, Catherine Corley
Lee, Dennis (Beynon) 1939- *102*
  Earlier sketch in SATA *14*
  See also CLR *3*
Lee, Dom 1959- *146*
  Autobiography Feature *121*
  Earlier sketch in SATA *83*
  See also SAAS *26*
Lee, Doris Emrick 1905-1983 .... *44*
  Obituary *35*
Lee, Edward
  See Lee, J. Edward
Lee, Elizabeth Rogers 1940- *90*
Lee, Harper 1926- *11*

Lee, Hector Viveros 1962- *115*
Lee, Howard N.
  See Goulart, Ron
Lee, Huy Voun 1969- *129*
Lee, J. Edward 1953- *130*
Lee, Jeanne M. 1943- *138*
Lee, John R(obert) 1923-1976 .... *27*
Lee, Jordan
  See Scholefield, Alan
Lee, Joseph Edward
  See Lee, J. Edward
Lee, Julian
  See Latham, Jean Lee
Lee, Linda
  See Eyerly, Jeannette
Lee, Liz
  See Lee, Elizabeth Rogers
Lee, Lucy
  See Talbot, Charlene Joy
Lee, Lyn 1953- *128*
Lee, Manning de Villeneuve 1894-1980 ..... *37*
  Obituary *22*
Lee, Marian
  See Clish, (Lee) Marian
Lee, Marie G. 1964- *178*
  Earlier sketches in SATA *81, 130*
Lee, Marie Myung-Ok
  See Lee, Marie G.
Lee, Mary Price 1934- *82*
  Earlier sketch in SATA *8*
Lee, Mildred
  See Scudder, Mildred Lee
Lee, Nelle Harper
  See Lee, Harper
Lee, Richard S. 1927- *82*
Lee, Robert C. 1931- *20*
Lee, Robert Edwin 1918-1994 .... *65*
  Obituary *82*
Lee, Robert J. 1921- *10*
Lee, Roy
  See Hopkins, Clark
Lee, Sally 1943- *67*
Lee, Suzy *193*
Lee, Tammie
  See Townsend, Thomas L.
Lee, Tanith 1947- *185*
  Earlier sketches in SATA *8, 88, 134*
Lee, Virginia 1976- *208*
Leech, Ben
  See Bowkett, Stephen
Leeds, Contance *188*
Leedy, Loreen 1959- *175*
  Brief entry *50*
  Earlier sketches in SATA *54, 84, 128*
Leedy, Loreen Janelle
  See Leedy, Loreen
Lee-Hostetler, Jeri 1940- *63*
Leekley, Thomas B(riggs) 1910-2001 .... *23*
Leeming, Jo Ann
  See Leeming, Joseph
Leeming, Joseph 1897-1968 .... *26*
Leemis, Ralph B. 1954- *72*
Leese, Jennifer L.B. 1970- *163*
Leeson, Muriel 1920- *54*
Leeson, R. A.
  See Leeson, Robert (Arthur)
Leeson, Robert (Arthur) 1928- *76*
  Earlier sketch in SATA *42*
Lee Tae-Jun 1904-1956(?) *194*
Lee-Tai, Amy 1964- *189*
Leffland, Ella 1931- *65*
Leffler, Silke *197*
Lefler, Irene (Whitney) 1917- *12*
LeFrak, Karen *182*
Le Gallienne, Eva 1899-1991 .... *9*
  Obituary *68*
Legg, Gerald 1947- *143*
Legg, Sarah Martha Ross Bruggeman (?)-1982
  Obituary *40*
LeGrand
  See Henderson, LeGrand

Le Guin, Ursula K. 1929- *194*
  Earlier sketches in SATA *4, 52, 99, 149*
  See also CLR *91*
Le Guin, Ursula Kroeber
  See Le Guin, Ursula K.
Legum, Colin 1919-2003 .... *10*
Lehman, Barbara 1963- *170*
  Earlier sketch in SATA *115*
Lehman, Bob *91*
Lehman, Elaine *91*
Lehmann, Debra Lynn
  See Vanasse, Deb
Lehn, Cornelia 1920- *46*
Lehne, Judith Logan 1947- *93*
Lehr, Delores 1920- *10*
Lehr, Norma 1930- *71*
Leiber, Fritz (Reuter, Jr.) 1910-1992 .... *45*
  Obituary *73*
Leibold, Jay 1957- *57*
  Brief entry *52*
Leichman, Seymour 1933- *5*
Leick, Bonnie *205*
Leigh, Nila K. 1981- *81*
Leigh, Tom 1947- *46*
Leigh-Pemberton, John 1911-1997 .... *35*
Leighton, Clare (Veronica Hope)
  1899-1989 .... *37*
Leighton, Margaret (Carver) 1896-1987 .... *1*
  Obituary *52*
Leiner, Al(an) 1938- *83*
Leiner, Katherine 1949- *93*
Leipold, L. Edmond 1902-1983 .... *16*
Leisk, David (Johnson) 1906-1975 .... *30*
  Obituary *26*
  Earlier sketch in SATA *1*
  See also CLR *98*
Leister, Mary 1917- *29*
Leitch, Patricia 1933- *98*
  Earlier sketch in SATA *11*
Leitner, Isabella 1924- *86*
Lekich, John *202*
Leland, Bob 1956- *92*
Leland, Robert E.
  See Leland, Bob
Lematre, Pascal 1967- *176*
Lember, Barbara Hirsch 1941- *92*
LeMieux, A.C. 1954- *125*
  Earlier sketch in SATA *90*
LeMieux, Anne
  See LeMieux, A.C.
LeMieux, Anne Connelly
  See LeMieux, A.C.
Lemieux, Michele 1955- *139*
Lemke, Horst 1922- *38*
Lenain, Thierry 1959- *201*
Lenanton, Carola Mary Anima Oman
  See Oman, Carola (Mary Anima)
Lenard, Alexander 1910-1972
  Obituary *21*
Lendroth, Susan *207*
L'Engle, Madeleine 1918-2007 .... *128*
  Obituary *186*
  Earlier sketches in SATA *1, 27, 75*
  See also CLR *57*
  See also SAAS *15*
L'Engle, Madeleine Camp Franklin
  See L'Engle, Madeleine
Lengyel, Cornel Adam 1915- *27*
Lengyel, Emil 1895-1985 .... *3*
  Obituary *42*
Lennon, John 1940-1980 .... *114*
Lennon, John Ono
  See Lennon, John
Leno, Jay 1950- *154*
LeNoir, Janice 1941- *89*
Lens, Sidney 1912-1986 .... *13*
  Obituary *48*
Lenski, Lois 1893-1974 .... *100*
  Earlier sketches in SATA *1, 26*
  See also CLR *26*

Lent, Blair 1930-2009 .... *133*
  Obituary *200*
  Earlier sketch in SATA *2*
Lent, Henry Bolles 1901-1973 .... *17*
Lent, John 1948- *108*
Leodhas, Sorche Nic
  See Alger, Leclaire (Gowans)
Leokum, Arkady 1916(?)- *45*
Leon, Sharon 1959- *79*
Leonard, Alison 1944- *70*
Leonard, Anna
  See Gilman, Laura Anne
Leonard, Constance (Brink) 1923- *42*
  Brief entry *40*
Leonard, Dutch
  See Leonard, Elmore
Leonard, Elmore 1925- *163*
Leonard, Elmore John, Jr.
  See Leonard, Elmore
Leonard, Jonathan N(orton) 1903-1975 ...... *36*
Leonard, Laura 1923- *75*
Leonard, Tom 1955- *207*
Leonetti, Mike 1958- *202*
Leong, Gor Yun
  See Ellison, Virginia H(owell)
Leonhardt, Alice 1950- *152*
Lerangis, Peter 1955- *171*
  Earlier sketch in SATA *72*
Lerner, Aaron 1920-2007 .... *35*
  Obituary *179*
Lerner, Aaron Bunsen
  See Lerner, Aaron
Lerner, Carol 1927- *86*
  Earlier sketch in SATA *33*
  See also CLR *34*
  See also SAAS *12*
Lerner, Gerda 1920- *65*
Lerner, Harriet 1944- *101*
Lerner, Marguerite Rush 1924-1987 .... *11*
  Obituary *51*
Lerner, Sharon (Ruth) 1938-1982 .... *11*
  Obituary *29*
Leroe, Ellen W(hitney) 1949- *99*
  Brief entry *51*
  Earlier sketch in SATA *61*
Leroux, Gaston 1868-1927 .... *65*
Leroux-Hugon, Helene 1955- *132*
LeRoy, Gen *52*
  Brief entry *36*
Lerrigo, Marion Olive 1898-1968
  Obituary *29*
LeShan, Eda J(oan) 1922-2002 .... *21*
  See also CLR *6*
LeSieg, Theo.
  See Dr. Seuss
Lesinski, Jeanne M. 1960- *120*
Leslie, Robert Franklin 1911-1990 .... *7*
Leslie, Roger 1961- *168*
Leslie, Roger James
  See Leslie, Roger
Leslie, Sarah
  See McGuire, Leslie (Sarah)
LeSourd, Catherine
  See Marshall, (Sarah) Catherine (Wood)
Lessac, Frane
  See Lessac, Frane
Lessac, Frane 1954- *209*
  Earlier sketches in SATA *61, 148*
Lessem, Dino Don
  See Lessem, Don
Lessem, Don 1951- *182*
  Earlier sketches in SATA *97, 155*
Lesser, Margaret 1899(?)-1979
  Obituary *22*
Lesser, Rika 1953- *53*
Lester, Alison 1952- *129*
  Earlier sketches in SATA *50, 90*
Lester, Helen 1936- *189*
  Earlier sketches in SATA *46, 92, 145*

Lester, Julius 1939- *157*
  Earlier sketches in SATA *12, 74, 112*
  See also CLR *143*
Lester, Julius Bernard
  See Lester, Julius
Lester, Mike 1955- *206*
  Earlier sketch in SATA *131*
Le Sueur, Meridel 1900-1996 .... *6*
Leszczynski, Diana *211*
Lethcoe, Jason *191*
Le Tord, Bijou 1945- *95*
  Earlier sketch in SATA *49*
Letts, Billie 1938- *121*
Letts, Elizabeth
  See Alalou, Elizabeth
Leuck, Laura 1962- *192*
  Earlier sketches in SATA *85, 146*
Leutscher, Alfred (George) 1913- *23*
Levai, Blaise 1919- *39*
Levenkron, Steven 1941- *86*
Leverich, Kathleen 1948- *103*
LeVert, (William) John 1946- *55*
Levert, Mireille 1956- *211*
Levete, Sarah 1961- *153*
Levin, Betty 1927- *201*
  Earlier sketches in SATA *19, 84, 137*
  See also SAAS *11*
Levin, Ira 1929-2007 .... *66*
  Obituary *187*
Levin, Ira Marvin
  See Levin, Ira
Levin, Marcia Obrasky 1918- *13*
Levin, Meyer 1905-1981 .... *21*
  Obituary *27*
Levin, Miriam (Ramsfelder) 1962- *97*
Levine, Abby 1943- *54*
  Brief entry *52*
Levine, Betty K(rasne) 1933- *66*
Levine, David 1926-2009 .... *43*
  Brief entry *35*
Levine, Edna S(imon) *35*
Levine, Ellen 1939- *190*
Levine, Evan 1962- *77*
  Earlier sketch in SATA *74*
Levine, Gail Carson 1947- *195*
  Earlier sketches in SATA *98, 161*
  See also CLR *85*
Levine, I(srael) E. 1923-2003 .... *12*
  Obituary *146*
Levine, Joan Goldman *11*
Levine, Joseph 1910- *33*
Levine, Marge 1934- *81*
Levine, Rhoda *14*
Levine, Sarah 1970- *57*
Levine, Shar 1953- *131*
Levine-Freidus, Gail
  See Provost, Gail Levine
Levinson, Nancy Smiler 1938- *211*
  Earlier sketches in SATA *33, 80, 140*
Levinson, Riki *99*
  Brief entry *49*
  Earlier sketch in SATA *52*
Levithan, David 1972- *166*
Levitin, Sonia 1934- *192*
  Autobiography Feature *131*
  Earlier sketches in SATA *4, 68, 119, 131*
  See also CLR *53*
  See also SAAS *2*
Levitt, Sidney (Mark) 1947- *68*
Levon, O. U.
  See Kesey, Ken
Levoy, Myron *49*
  Brief entry *37*
Levy, Barrie *112*
Levy, Constance 1931- *140*
  Earlier sketch in SATA *73*
  See also SAAS *22*
Levy, Elizabeth 1942- *169*
  Earlier sketches in SATA *31, 69, 107*
  See also SAAS *18*
Levy, Janice *172*

Levy, Marilyn 1937- *67*
Levy, Nathan 1945- *63*
Levy, Robert 1945- *82*
Lewees, John
  See Stockton, Francis Richard
Lewin, Betsy 1937- *169*
  Autobiography Feature *115*
  Earlier sketches in SATA *32, 90*
Lewin, Hugh 1939- *72*
  Brief entry *40*
  See also CLR *9*
Lewin, Ted 1935- *195*
  Autobiography Feature *115*
  Earlier sketches in SATA *21, 76, 119, 165*
Lewis, Alice C. 1936- *46*
Lewis, Alice Hudson 1895(?)-1971
  Obituary *29*
Lewis, Amanda 1955- *80*
Lewis, Anthony 1927- *27*
Lewis, Anthony 1966- *120*
Lewis, Barbara A. 1943- *73*
Lewis, Beverly 1949- *80*
Lewis, Brenda Ralph 1932- *72*
Lewis, Brian 1963- *128*
Lewis, C. S. 1898-1963 .... *100*
  Earlier sketch in SATA *13*
  See also CLR *109*
Lewis, Claudia (Louise) 1907-2001 .... *5*
Lewis, Clive Staples
  See Lewis, C. S.
Lewis, Cynthia Copeland 1960- *111*
Lewis, E. M. *123*
  Earlier sketch in SATA *20*
Lewis, Earl Bradley
  See Lewis, E.B.
Lewis, E.B. 1956- *211*
  Earlier sketches in SATA *93, 124, 168*
Lewis, Elizabeth Foreman 1892-1958 .... *121*
  See also YABC *2*
Lewis, Francine
  See Wells, Helen
Lewis, Harry Sinclair
  See Lewis, Sinclair
Lewis, Hilda (Winifred) 1896-1974
  Obituary *20*
Lewis, J. Patrick 1942- *205*
  Earlier sketches in SATA *69, 104, 162*
Lewis, Jack P(earl) 1919- *65*
Lewis, Jean 1924- *61*
Lewis, Jon Samuel
  See Lewis, J.S.
Lewis, Joseph Anthony
  See Lewis, Anthony
Lewis, J.S. 1972- *203*
Lewis, Julinda
  See Lewis-Ferguson, Julinda
Lewis, Kevin *173*
Lewis, Kim 1951- *136*
  Earlier sketch in SATA *84*
Lewis, Linda (Joy) 1946- *67*
Lewis, Lucia Z.
  See Anderson, Lucia (Lewis)
Lewis, Marjorie 1929- *40*
  Brief entry *35*
Lewis, Mary 1907(?)-1988 .... *64*
  Obituary *56*
Lewis, Mervyn
  See Frewer, Glyn (M.)
Lewis, Michael
  See Untermeyer, Louis
Lewis, Naomi 1911-2009 .... *144*
  Earlier sketch in SATA *76*
Lewis, Paeony 1960- *173*
Lewis, Paul
  See Gerson, Noel Bertram
Lewis, Richard 1935- *3*
Lewis, Richard 1956- *209*
Lewis, Rob 1962- *72*
Lewis, Roger
  See Zarchy, Harry
Lewis, Rose *209*

Lewis, Rose A.
  See Lewis, Rose
Lewis, Shannon
  See Llywelyn, Morgan
Lewis, Shari 1934-1998 35
  Brief entry 30
  Obituary 104
Lewis, Sylvan R.
  See Aronson, Virginia
Lewis, Thomas P(arker) 1936- 27
Lewis, Wendy A. 1966- 150
Lewis-Ferguson, Julinda 1955- 85
Lewison, Wendy Cheyette 177
Lewiton, Mina 1904-1970 2
Lew-Vriethoff, Joanne 186
Lexau, Joan M. 130
  Earlier sketches in SATA *1, 36*
Ley, Willy 1906-1969 2
Leydon, Rita (Floden) 1949- 21
Leyland, Eric (Arthur) 1911- 37
L'Hommedieu, Dorothy Keasley 1885-1961
  Obituary 29
Li, Xiao Jun 1952- 86
Liao, Jimmy 1958- 202
Liatsos, Sandra Olson 1942- 103
Libby, Alisa M. 189
Libby, Barbara M. 153
Libby, Bill
  See Libby, William M.
Libby, William M. 1927-1984 5
  Obituary 39
Liberty, Gene 1924- 3
Lichtenheld, Tom 208
  Earlier sketch in SATA *152*
Lichtman, Wendy 1946- 193
Liddell, Kenneth 1912-1975 63
Lidz, Jane 120
Lieberman, E(dwin) James 1934- 62
Liebers, Arthur 1913-1984 12
Lieblich, Irene 1923- 22
Liers, Emil E(rnest) 1890-1975 37
Lies, Brian 1963- 190
  Earlier sketch in SATA *131*
Liestman, Vicki 1961- 72
Lietz, Gerald S. 1918- 11
Life, Kay (Guinn) 1930- 83
Lifton, Betty Jean 118
  Earlier sketch in SATA *6*
Lifton, Robert Jay 1926- 66
Lightburn, Ron 1954- 91
Lightburn, Sandra 1955- 91
Lightner, A. M.
  See Hopf, Alice (Martha) L(ightner)
Lightner, Alice
  See Hopf, Alice (Martha) L(ightner)
Lignell, Lois 1911- 37
Liles, Maurine Walpole 1935- 81
Lillegard, Dee 184
Lilley, Stephen R. 1950- 97
Lilley, Stephen Ray
  See Lilley, Stephen R.
Lillington, Kenneth (James) 1916-1998 39
Lilly, Nate 182
Lilly, Ray
  See Curtis, Richard
Lim, John 1932- 43
Liman, Ellen (Fogelson) 1936- 22
Limb, Sue 1946- 203
  Earlier sketch in SATA *158*
Limburg, Peter R(ichard) 1929- 13
Lin, Grace 1974- 198
  Earlier sketches in SATA *111, 162*
Lincoln, C(harles) Eric 1924-2000 5
Lincoln, Christopher 1952- 208
Lincoln, Hazel 187
Lincoln, James
  See Bates, Katharine Lee
Lindbergh, Anne
  See Sapieyevski, Anne Lindbergh
Lindbergh, Anne Morrow 1906-2001 33
  Obituary 125

Lindbergh, Anne Spencer Morrow
  See Lindbergh, Anne Morrow
Lindbergh, Charles A(ugustus, Jr.)
  1902-1974 33
Lindbergh, Reeve 1945- 163
  Earlier sketch in SATA *116*
Lindblom, Steven (Winther) 1946- 94
  Brief entry 39
  Earlier sketch in SATA *42*
Linde, Gunnel 1924- 5
Lindenbaum, Pija 1955- 183
  Earlier sketches in SATA *77, 144*
Lindgren, Astrid (Anna Emilia Ericsson)
  1907-2002 38
  Obituary 128
  Earlier sketch in SATA *2*
  See also CLR *119*
Lindgren, Barbro 1937- 207
  Brief entry 46
  Earlier sketches in SATA *63, 120*
  See also CLR *86*
Lindman, Maj (Jan) 1886-1972 43
Lindop, Edmund 1925- 5
Lindquist, Jennie Dorothea 1899-1977 13
Lindquist, Rowena Cory 1958- 98
Lindquist, Willis 1908-1988 20
Lindsay, Nicholas Vachel
  See Lindsay, Vachel
Lindsay, Norman Alfred William
  1879-1969 67
  See also CLR *8*
Lindsay, Vachel 1879-1931 40
Lindsey, Kathleen D(orothy) 1949- 153
Line, David
  See Davidson, Lionel
Line, Les 1935- 27
Lines, Kathleen Mary 1902-1988
  Obituary 61
Linfield, Esther 40
Lingard, Joan (Amelia) 1932- 130
  Autobiography Feature 130
  Earlier sketches in SATA *8, 74, 114*
  See also CLR *89*
  See also SAAS *5*
Link, Martin 1934- 28
Linn, Margot
  See Ziefert, Harriet
Linnea, Sharon 1956- 82
Lion, Melissa 1976- 176
Lionni, Leo(nard) 1910-1999 72
  Obituary 118
  Earlier sketch in SATA *8*
  See also CLR *71*
Lipinsky de Orlov, Lino S. 1908- 22
Lipkind, William 1904-1974 15
Lipman, David 1931-2008 21
Lipman, Matthew 1923- 14
Lipp, Frederick 204
Lippincott, Bertram 1898(?)-1985
  Obituary 42
Lippincott, Gary A. 1953- 119
  Earlier sketch in SATA *73*
Lippincott, Joseph W(harton) 1887-1976 17
Lippincott, Sarah Lee 1920- 22
Lippman, Peter J. 1936- 31
Lipsyte, Robert 1938- 198
  Earlier sketches in SATA *5, 68, 113, 161*
  See also CLR *76*
Lipsyte, Robert Michael
  See Lipsyte, Robert
Lisandrelli, Elaine Slivinski 1951- 94
Lisker, Sonia O. 1933- 44
Lisle, Holly 1960- 208
  Earlier sketch in SATA *98*
Lisle, Janet Taylor 1947- 150
  Brief entry 47
  Earlier sketches in SATA *59, 96*
  See also SAAS *14*
Lisle, Rebecca 162
Lisle, Seward D.
  See Ellis, Edward S.

Lisowski, Gabriel 1946- 47
  Brief entry 31
Liss, Howard 1922-1995 4
  Obituary 84
Lissiat, Amy
  See Thompson, Colin
Lisson, Deborah 1941- 110
  Earlier sketch in SATA *71*
List, Ilka Katherine 1935- 6
Liston, Robert A. 1927- 5
Litchfield, Ada B(assett) 1916-1999 5
Litchfield, Jo 1973- 116
Lithgow, John 1945- 145
Lithgow, John Arthur
  See Lithgow, John
Litowinsky, Olga (Jean) 1936- 26
Littke, Lael J. 1929- 140
  Earlier sketches in SATA *51, 83*
Little, A. Edward
  See Klein, Aaron E.
Little, Douglas 1942- 96
Little, (Flora) Jean 1932- 149
  Earlier sketches in SATA *2, 68, 106*
  See also CLR *4*
  See also SAAS *17*
Little, Lessie Jones 1906-1986 60
  Obituary 50
Little, Mary E. 1912-1999 28
Littlechild, George 1958- 85
Littledale, Freya (Lota) 1929-1992 74
  Earlier sketch in SATA *2*
Littlefield, Bill 1948- 83
Littlefield, Holly 1963- 97
Littlesugar, Amy 1953- 176
  Earlier sketch in SATA *122*
Littleton, Mark R. 1950- 142
  Earlier sketch in SATA *89*
Littlewood, Karin 211
Littman, Sarah Darer 175
Litty, Julie 1971- 181
Litzinger, Rosanne 1948- 196
Lively, Penelope 1933- 164
  Earlier sketches in SATA *7, 60, 101*
  See also CLR *7*
Lively, Penelope Margaret
  See Lively, Penelope
Liverakos, L. A.
  See Gilman, Laura Anne
Liversidge, (Henry) Douglas 1913- 8
Livesey, Claire (Warner) 1927- 127
Livingston, Carole 1941- 42
Livingston, (M.) Irene 1932- 150
Livingston, Myra Cohn 1926-1996 68
  Obituary 92
  Earlier sketch in SATA *5*
  See also CLR *7*
  See also SAAS *1*
Livingston, Richard R(oland) 1922- 8
Livo, Norma J. 1929- 76
Liwska, Renata 199
Ljungkvist, Laura 180
Llerena Aguirre, Carlos 1952- 19
Llerena Aguirre, Carlos Antonio
  See Llerena Aguirre, Carlos
Llewellyn, Claire 1954- 196
  Earlier sketches in SATA *77, 143*
Llewellyn, Grace 1964- 110
Llewellyn, Richard
  See Llewellyn Lloyd, Richard Dafydd Vivian
Llewellyn, Sam 1948- 185
  Earlier sketch in SATA *95*
Llewellyn Lloyd, Richard Dafydd Vivian
  1906-1983 11
  Obituary 37
Llewelyn, T. Harcourt
  See Hamilton, Charles (Harold St. John)
Lloyd, Alan
  See Lloyd, A.R.
Lloyd, Alan Richard
  See Lloyd, A.R.

Lloyd, A.R. 1927- 168
    Earlier sketch in SATA 97
Lloyd, David
    See Lloyd, David T.
Lloyd, David T. 1954- 167
Lloyd, E. James
    See James, Elizabeth
Lloyd, Errol 1943- 22
Lloyd, Hugh
    See Fitzhugh, Percy Keese
Lloyd, James
    See James, Elizabeth
Lloyd, Megan 1958- 189
    Earlier sketches in SATA 77, 117
Lloyd, Norman 1909-1980
    Obituary 23
Lloyd, (Mary) Norris 1908-1993 10
    Obituary 75
Lloyd, Sam 183
Lloyd-Jones, Sally 1960- 179
Lloyd Webber, Andrew 1948- 56
Llywelyn, Morgan 1937- 109
Lo, Ginnie 165
Lo, Virginia M.
    See Lo, Ginnie
Lobato, Jose Bento Monteiro 1882-1948 .. 114
Lobel, Anita (Kempler) 1934- 162
    Earlier sketches in SATA 6, 55, 96
Lobel, Arnold (Stark) 1933-1987 55
    Obituary 54
    Earlier sketch in SATA 6
    See also CLR 5
Lobel, Gillian 181
Lobsenz, Amelia 12
Lobsenz, Norman M(itchell) 1919- 6
Lochak, Michele 1936- 39
Lochlons, Colin
    See Jackson, C(aary) Paul
Locke, Clinton W. 1
Locke, Elsie (Violet) 1912-2001 87
Locke, Gary 1963- 197
Locke, Lucie 1904-1989 10
Locke, Robert 1944- 63
    See also CLR 39
Locker, Thomas 1937- 109
    Earlier sketch in SATA 59
    See also CLR 14
Lockhart, E.
    See Jenkins, Emily
Lockridge, Hildegarde (Dolson)
    1908-1981 121
    Earlier sketch in SATA 5
Lockwood, Mary
    See Spelman, Mary
Lodge, Bernard 1933- 107
    Earlier sketch in SATA 33
Lodge, Jo 1966- 173
    Earlier sketch in SATA 112
Loeb, Jeffrey 1946- 57
Loeb, Robert H., Jr. 1917- 21
Loefgren, Ulf 1931- 3
Loehfelm, Bill 1969- 153
Loehr, Mallory 184
Loehr, Patrick 1968(?)- 194
Loeper, John J(oseph) 1929- 118
    Earlier sketch in SATA 10
Loescher, Ann Dull 1942- 20
Loescher, Gil(burt Damian) 1945- 20
Loewer, Jean Jenkins
    See Jenkins, Jean
Loewer, (Henry) Peter 1934- 98
LoFaro, Jerry 1959- 77
Lofo
    See Heimann, Rolf
Lofthouse, Liz 199
Lofting, Hugh (John) 1886-1947 100
    Earlier sketch in SATA 15
    See also CLR 143
Lofts, Norah (Robinson) 1904-1983 8
    Obituary 36

Logan, Jake
    See Knott, William C(ecil, Jr.)
    and Krepps, Robert W(ilson)
    and Pearl, Jacques Bain
    and Riefe, Alan
    and Rifkin, Shepard
    and Smith, Martin Cruz
Logan, Mark
    See Nicole, Christopher (Robin)
Logan, Rochelle 1954- 169
Logston, Anne 1962- 112
Logue, Christopher 1926- 23
Logue, Mary 1952- 161
    Earlier sketch in SATA 112
Logue, Mary Louise
    See Logue, Mary
Loh, Morag 1935- 73
Lohans, Alison 1949- 101
Loizeaux, William 185
Loken, Newton Clayton 1919- 26
Lomas, Steve
    See Brennan, Joseph Lomas
Lomask, Milton (Nachman) 1909-1991 20
Lombard, Jenny 178
Lombino, Salvatore
    See Hunter, Evan
LoMonaco, Palmyra 1932- 102
London, Jack 1876-1916 18
    See also CLR 108
London, Jane
    See Geis, Darlene Stern
London, John Griffith
    See London, Jack
London, Jonathan (Paul) 1947- 157
    Earlier sketches in SATA 74, 113
Lonergan, (Pauline) Joy (MacLean) 1909- . 10
Lonette, Reisie (Dominee) 1924- 43
Long, Cathryn J. 1946- 89
Long, Earlene (Roberta) 1938- 50
Long, Emmett
    See Leonard, Elmore
Long, Ethan 1968(?)- 182
Long, Helen Beecher 1
Long, Judith Elaine 1953- 20
Long, Judy
    See Long, Judith Elaine
Long, Kim 1949- 69
Long, Laura Mooney 1892-1967
    Obituary 29
Long, Laurel 203
Long, Loren 1966(?)- 188
    Earlier sketch in SATA 151
Long, Melinda 1960- 152
Long, Sylvia 1948- 179
    Earlier sketch in SATA 120
Longbeard, Frederick
    See Longyear, Barry B(rookes)
Longfellow, Henry Wadsworth 1807-1882 . 19
    See also CLR 99
Longfellow, Layne (A.) 1937- 102
Longman, Harold S. 1919- 5
Longsworth, Polly 1933- 28
Longtemps, Kenneth 1933- 17
Longway, A. Hugh
    See Lang, Andrew
Longyear, Barry B(rookes) 1942- 117
Look, Lenore 180
Loomans, Diane 1955- 90
Loomis, Christine 160
    Earlier sketch in SATA 113
Loomis, Jennifer A. 1942- 101
Loomis, Robert D. 5
Lopez, Angelo (Cayas) 1967- 83
Lopez, Barry 1945- 67
Lopez, Barry Holstun
    See Lopez, Barry
Lopez, Jack 1950- 178
Lopez, Loretta 1963- 190
Lopez, Lorraine 1956- 181
Lopez, Lorraine M.
    See Lopez, Lorraine

Lopez, Rafael 1961(?)- 198
Lopshire, Robert M(artin) 1927- 6
Loraine, Connie
    See Reece, Colleen L.
Lorbiecki, Marybeth 1959- 172
    Earlier sketch in SATA 121
Lord, Athena V. 1932- 39
Lord, Beman 1924-1991 5
    Obituary 69
Lord, Bette Bao 1938- 58
    See also CLR 151
Lord, Cynthia 182
Lord, Doreen Mildred Douglas
    See Lord, Douglas
Lord, Douglas 1904-1992 12
Lord, Janet 204
Lord, John Vernon 1939- 21
Lord, Michele 201
Lord, Nancy
    See Titus, Eve
Lord, Patricia C. 1927-1988
    Obituary 58
Lord, Walter 1917-2002 3
Lorde, Diana
    See Reno, Dawn E(laine)
Lorenz, Albert 1941- 115
Lorenzini, Carlo
    See Collodi, Carlo
Lorey, Dean 1967- 193
Lorimer, Janet 1941- 60
Loring, Emilie (Baker) 1864(?)-1951 51
Lorkowski, Thomas V(incent) 1950- 92
Lorkowski, Tom
    See Lorkowski, Thomas V(incent)
Lorraine, Walter (Henry) 1929- 16
Lorrimer, Claire
    See Clark, Patricia Denise
Loss, Joan 1933- 11
Lothrop, Harriet Mulford Stone
    1844-1924 20
Lottridge, Celia Barker 1936- 157
    Earlier sketch in SATA 112
LoTurco, Laura 1963- 84
Lotz, Wolfgang 1912-1981 65
Louie, Ai-Ling 1949- 40
    Brief entry 34
Louis, Catherine 1963- 186
Louis, Pat
    See Francis, Dorothy
Louisburgh, Sheila Burnford
    See Burnford, Sheila (Philip Cochrane Every)
Louise, Anita
    See Riggio, Anita
Louise, Tina 1934- 191
Lourie, Helen
    See Storr, Catherine (Cole)
Lourie, Peter 1952- 183
    Earlier sketches in SATA 82, 142
Lourie, Peter King
    See Lourie, Peter
Love, Ann 1947- 168
    Earlier sketch in SATA 79
Love, D. Anne 1949- 180
    Earlier sketches in SATA 96, 145
Love, Douglas 1967- 92
Love, Judith Dufour
    See Love, Judy
Love, Judy 188
Love, Katherine (Isabel) 1907- 3
Love, Kathleen Ann
    See Love, Ann
Love, Sandra (Weller) 1940- 26
Lovejoy, Jack 1937- 116
Lovelace, Delos Wheeler 1894-1967 7
Lovelace, Maud Hart 1892-1980 2
    Obituary 23
Lovell, Ingraham
    See Bacon, Josephine Dodge (Daskam)
Loverseed, Amanda (Jane) 1965- 75
Lovett, Margaret (Rose) 1915- 22

Low, Alice 1926- *156*
Earlier sketches in SATA *11, 76*
Low, Elizabeth Hammond 1898-1991 .... *5*
Low, Joseph 1911-2007 .... *14*
Low, Penelope Margaret
See Lively, Penelope
Low, William *177*
Lowe, Helen 1961- *206*
Lowe, Jay, Jr.
See Loeper, John J(oseph)
Lowell, Pamela *187*
Lowell, Susan 1950- *206*
Earlier sketches in SATA *81, 127*
Lowenstein, Dyno 1914-1996 .... *6*
Lowenstein, Sallie 1949- *116*
Lowery, Linda 1949- *151*
Earlier sketch in SATA *74*
Lowitz, Anson C. 1901(?)-1978 .... *18*
Lowitz, Sadyebeth Heath 1901-1969 .... *17*
Lowndes, Robert A(ugustine) W(ard)
1916-1998 .... *117*
Lowrey, Janette Sebring 1892-1986 .... *43*
Lowry, Lois 1937- *177*
Autobiography Feature *127*
Earlier sketches in SATA *23, 70, 111*
See also CLR *72*
See also SAAS *3*
Lowry, Lois Hammersberg
See Lowry, Lois
Lowry, Peter 1953- *7*
Lowther, George F. 1913-1975
Obituary *30*
Loyie, Larry 1933- *150*
Lozansky, Edward D. 1941- *62*
Lozier, Herbert 1915- *26*
Lubar, David 1954- *190*
Earlier sketch in SATA *133*
Lubell, Cecil 1912-2000 .... *6*
Lubell, Winifred (A. Milius) 1914- *6*
Lubin, Leonard
See Lubin, Leonard B.
Lubin, Leonard B. 1943-1994 .... *45*
Brief entry *37*
Lubka, S. Ruth 1948- *154*
Lubner, Susan *185*
Luby, Thia 1954- *124*
Lucado, Max (Lee) 1955- *104*
Lucas, Cedric 1962- *101*
Lucas, David 1966- *208*
Lucas, E(dward) V(errall) 1868-1938 .... *20*
Lucas, Eileen 1956- *113*
Earlier sketch in SATA *76*
Lucas, George 1944- *56*
Lucas, Jerry 1940- *33*
Lucas, Margeaux *186*
Lucas, Victoria
See Plath, Sylvia
Lucashenko, Melissa 1967- *104*
Luccarelli, Vincent 1923- *90*
Luce, Celia (Geneva Larsen) 1914- *38*
Luce, Willard (Ray) 1914-1990 .... *38*
Lucht, Irmgard 1937- *82*
Lucke, Deb *202*
Luckett, Dave 1951- *167*
Earlier sketch in SATA *106*
Luckhardt, Mildred Corell 1898-1990 .... *5*
Ludden, Allen (Ellsworth) 1918(?)-1981
Obituary *27*
Ludel, Jacqueline 1945- *64*
Ludlow, Geoffrey
See Meynell, Laurence Walter
Ludlum, Mabel Cleland
See Widdemer, Mabel Cleland
Ludwig, Helen *33*
Ludwig, Lyndell 1923- *63*
Ludwig, Trudy 1959- *209*
Earlier sketch in SATA *166*
Lueders, Edward (George) 1923- *14*
Luenn, Nancy 1954- *79*
Earlier sketch in SATA *51*
Lufkin, Raymond H. 1897- *38*

Lugard, Flora Louisa Shaw 1852-1929 .... *21*
Luger, Harriett Mandelay 1914- *23*
Luhrmann, Winifred B(ruce) 1934- *11*
Luis, Earlene W. 1929- *11*
Lujan, Jorge *201*
Luke, Pauline *178*
Luke, Pauline R.
See Luke, Pauline
Lum, Peter
See Crowe, (Bettina) Peter Lum
Lumry, Amanda (R.) *159*
Lund, Deb *157*
Lund, Doris Herold 1919- *12*
Lunde, Darrin *202*
Lung, Chang
See Jordan, Robert
Lunge-Larsen, Lise 1955- *184*
Earlier sketch in SATA *138*
Lunn, Carolyn (Kowalczyk) 1960- *67*
Lunn, Janet (Louise Swoboda) 1928- *110*
Earlier sketches in SATA *4, 68*
See also CLR *18*
See also SAAS *12*
Lunsford, Cin Forshay
See Forshay-Lunsford, Cin
Lupica, Michael
See Lupica, Mike
Lupica, Michael Thomas
See Lupica, Mike
Lupica, Mike 1952- *177*
Lupoff, Dick
See Lupoff, Richard A(llen)
Lupoff, Richard A(llen) 1935- *60*
Lurie, Alison 1926- *112*
Earlier sketch in SATA *46*
Lurie, Morris 1938- *72*
Lussert, Anneliese 1929- *101*
Lusted, Marcia Amidon 1962- *143*
Lustig, Arnost 1926- *56*
Lustig, Loretta 1944- *46*
Lutes, Jason 1967- *210*
Luthardt, Kevin 1973- *172*
Luther, Frank 1905-1980
Obituary *25*
Luther, Rebekah (Lyn) S(tiles) 1960- *90*
Luttmann, Gail
See Damerow, Gail
Luttrell, Guy L. 1938- *22*
Luttrell, Ida (Alleene) 1934- *91*
Brief entry *35*
Earlier sketch in SATA *40*
Luttrell, William (J. III) 1954- *149*
Lutz, John 1939- *180*
Lutz, John Thomas
See Lutz, John
Lutz, Norma Jean 1943- *122*
Lutzeier, Elizabeth 1952- *72*
Lutzker, Edythe 1904-1991 .... *5*
Luxbacher, Irene M. 1970- *153*
Luzadder, Patrick 1954- *89*
Luzzati, Emanuele 1921-2007 .... *7*
Luzzatto, Paola Caboara 1938- *38*
Ly, Many 1977- *208*
Lybbert, Tyler 1970- *88*
Lydon, Michael 1942- *11*
Lyfick, Warren
See Reeves, Lawrence F.
Lyle, Katie Letcher 1938- *8*
Lynch, Chris 1962- *209*
Earlier sketches in SATA *95, 131, 171*
See also CLR *58*
Lynch, Jay 1945- *204*
Lynch, Lorenzo 1932- *7*
Lynch, Marietta 1947- *29*
Lynch, P(atrick) J(ames) 1962- *122*
Earlier sketch in SATA *79*
Lynch, Patricia (Nora) 1898-1972 .... *9*
Lynds, Dennis 1924-2005 .... *47*
Brief entry *37*
Lyne, Alison Davis *188*

Lyngseth, Joan
See Davies, Joan
Lynn, Elizabeth A(nne) 1946- *99*
Lynn, Mary
See Brokamp, Marilyn
Lynn, Patricia
See Watts, Mabel Pizzey
Lynn, Tracy *175*
Lyon, Elinor 1921-2008 .... *6*
Obituary *192*
Lyon, Elinor Bruce
See Lyon, Elinor
Lyon, George Ella 1949- *207*
Autobiography Feature *148*
Earlier sketches in SATA *68, 119, 148*
Lyon, Lyman R.
See de Camp, L. Sprague
Lyons, Dorothy M(arawee) 1907-1997 .... *3*
Lyons, Grant 1941- *30*
Lyons, Marcus
See Blish, James
Lyons, Mary E. 1947- *195*
Autobiography Feature *195*
Earlier sketches in SATA *93, 142*
Lyons, Mary Evelyn
See Lyons, Mary E.
Lystad, Mary (Hanemann) 1928- *11*
Lytle, Elizabeth Stewart 1949- *79*
Lytle, Robert A. 1944- *119*
Lyttle, Richard B(ard) 1927- *23*
Lytton of Knebworth, Baron
See Bulwer-Lytton, Edward

M

Ma, Wenhai 1954- *84*
Maar, Leonard (Frank, Jr.) 1927- *30*
Maartens, Maretha 1945- *73*
Maas, Selve -1997 .... *14*
Maass, Robert *195*
Mabie, Grace
See Mattern, Joanne
Mac
See MacManus, Seumas
and Maccari, Ruggero
Macalaster, Elizabeth G. 1951- *115*
MacAlister, Katie *159*
MacAllan, Andrew
See Leasor, James
MacAodhagain, Eamon
See Egan, E(dward) W(elstead)
MacArthur-Onslow, Annette Rosemary
1933- *26*
Macaulay, David (Alexander) 1946- *137*
Brief entry *27*
Earlier sketches in SATA *46, 72*
See also CLR *14*
Macaulay, Teresa (E.) 1947- *95*
Macavinta, Courtney *176*
MacBeth, George (Mann) 1932-1992 .... *4*
Obituary *70*
MacBride, Roger Lea 1929-1995 .... *85*
MacCarter, Don 1944- *91*
MacClintock, Dorcas 1932- *8*
MacCready, Robin Merrow 1959(?)- *190*
MacCullough, Carolyn *174*
MacDonald, Alan 1958- *192*
MacDonald, Amy 1951- *156*
Autobiography Feature *156*
Earlier sketches in SATA *76, 136*
MacDonald, Anne Elizabeth Campbell Bard
-1958
See MacDonald, Betty
MacDonald, Anson
See Heinlein, Robert A.
MacDonald, Betty 1908-1958
See YABC *1*
Macdonald, Blackie
See Emrich, Duncan (Black Macdonald)

Macdonald, Caroline 1948- 86
    Obituary 111
    See also CLR 60
Macdonald, Dwight 1906-1982 29
    Obituary 33
MacDonald, George 1824-1905 100
    Earlier sketch in SATA 33
    See also CLR 67
MacDonald, Golden
    See Brown, Margaret Wise
Macdonald, Guy 195
Macdonald, James D. 1954- 67
    Earlier sketches in SATA 81, 114, 165, 1
Macdonald, Marcia
    See Hill, Grace Livingston
MacDonald, Margaret Read 1940- 194
    Earlier sketches in SATA 94, 164
Macdonald, Marianne 1934- 113
Macdonald, Mary
    See Gifford, Griselda
Macdonald, Maryann 1947- 189
    Earlier sketch in SATA 72
MacDonald, Ross 1957- 201
Macdonald, Shelagh 1937- 25
MacDonald, Suse 1940- 193
    Brief entry 52
    Earlier sketches in SATA 54, 109
Macdonald, Zillah K(atherine) 1885-1979 .. 11
MacDonnell, Megan
    See Stevens, Serita
MacDougal, John
    See Blish, James
Mace, Elisabeth 1933- 27
Mace, Varian 1938- 49
MacEachern, Stephen 206
MacEwen, Gwendolyn (Margaret)
    1941-1987 50
    Obituary 55
Macfarlan, Allan A. 1892-1982 35
MacFarlane, Iris 1922- 11
MacGill-Callahan, Sheila 1926-2000 78
MacGregor, Carol Lynn 153
MacGregor, Ellen 1906-1954 39
    Brief entry 27
MacGregor-Hastie, Roy (Alasdhair Niall)
    1929- 3
MacGrory, Yvonne 1948- 142
Machado, Ana Maria 1941- 150
MacHale, D.J. 1956- 175
MacHale, Donald James
    See MacHale, D.J.
Machetanz, Frederick 1908- 34
Machin, Sue
    See Williams, Sue
Machin Goodall, Daphne (Edith) 37
Macht, Norm
    See Macht, Norman L.
Macht, Norman L. 1929- 122
Macht, Norman Lee
    See Macht, Norman L.
MacInnes, Helen (Clark) 1907-1985 22
    Obituary 44
Macintosh, Brownie 1950- 98
MacIntyre, Elisabeth 1916- 17
MacIntyre, Rod
    See MacIntyre, R.P.
MacIntyre, R.P. 1947- 203
MacIntyre, R.P. 1947- 203
MacIntyre, Wendy 1947- 196
Mack, Jeff 194
Mack, L.V.
    See Kimmelman, Burt
Mack, Stan(ley) 17
Mack, Todd 168
Mack, Tracy 1968- 183
    Earlier sketch in SATA 128
Mackall, Dandi D.
    See Mackall, Dandi Daley
Mackall, Dandi Daley 1949- 182
    Earlier sketches in SATA 118, 177

Mackay, Claire 1930- 97
    Autobiography Feature 124
    Earlier sketch in SATA 40
    See also CLR 43
Mackay, Constance D'Arcy (?)-1966 125
Mackay, Donald 1914-2005 81
    Obituary 173
Mackay, Donald Alexander
    See Mackay, Donald
MacKaye, Percy (Wallace) 1875-1956 32
Mackel, Kathryn 1950- 162
Mackel, Kathy
    See Mackel, Kathryn
MacKellar, William 1914- 4
Macken, JoAnn Early 1953- 201
Macken, Walter 1915-1967 36
MacKenzie, Jill (Kelly) 1947- 75
Mackenzie, Robert 1974- 204
Mackey, Ernan
    See McInerny, Ralph
Mackey, Weezie Kerr 188
Mackie, Maron
    See McNeely, Jeannette
Mackin, Edward
    See McInerny, Ralph
MacKinnon, Bernie 1957- 69
MacKinnon Groomer, Vera 1915- 57
MacKinstry, Elizabeth 1879-1956 42
Mackler, Carolyn 1973- 156
MacLachlan, Emily
    See Charest, Emily MacLachlan
MacLachlan, Patricia 1938- 168
    Brief entry 42
    Earlier sketches in SATA 62, 107
    See also CLR 14
MacLane, Jack
    See Crider, Bill
MacLean, Alistair 1922(?)-1987 23
    Obituary 50
MacLean, Alistair Stuart
    See MacLean, Alistair
Maclean, Art
    See Shirreffs, Gordon D(onald)
MacLean, Christine Kole 1962- 177
MacLean, Glynne 1964- 150
MacLean, Jill 1941- 211
MacLeod, Beatrice 1910- 162
    Earlier sketch in SATA 10
MacLeod, Beatrice Beach
    See MacLeod, Beatrice
MacLeod, Charlotte (Matilda) 1922-2005 ... 28
    Obituary 160
MacLeod, Doug 1959- 201
    Earlier sketch in SATA 60
MacLeod, Elizabeth 184
    Earlier sketch in SATA 158
MacLeod, Ellen Jane (Anderson) 1916- 14
MacManus, James
    See MacManus, Seumas
MacManus, Seumas 1869-1960 25
MacMaster, Eve (Ruth) B(owers) 1942- 46
MacMillan, Annabelle
    See Quick, Annabelle
MacMillan, Dianne M(arie) 1943- 125
    Earlier sketch in SATA 84
Macnaughton, Tina 182
Macneill, Janet
    See McNeely, Jeannette
MacPeek, Walter G. 1902-1973 4
    Obituary 25
MacPhail, Catherine 1946- 197
    Earlier sketch in SATA 130
MacPherson, Margaret 1908-2001 9
    See also SAAS 4
MacPherson, Thomas George 1915-1976
    Obituary 30
MacPherson, Winnie 1930- 107
MacRae, Tom 1980- 181
Macrae, Travis
    See Feagles, Anita M(acRae)
MacRaois, Cormac 1944- 72

Macumber, Mari
    See Sandoz, Mari(e Susette)
Macy, Sue 1954- 134
    Earlier sketch in SATA 88
Madaras, Lynda 1947- 151
Madden, Don 1927- 3
Madden, Kerry 1961- 168
Madden-Lunsford, Kerry
    See Madden, Kerry
Maddern, Eric 1950- 166
Maddigan, Beth 1967- 174
Maddison, Angela Mary 1923- 10
    See also CLR 24
Maddock, Reginald (Bertram) 1912-1994 ... 15
Madenski, Melissa (Ann) 1949- 77
Madian, Jon 1941- 9
Madison, Alan 182
Madison, Arnold 1937- 6
Madison, Winifred 5
Madonna 1958- 149
Madsen, Gunnar 171
Madsen, Jim 1964- 202
Madsen, Ross Martin 1946- 82
Madsen, Susan A. 1954- 90
Madsen, Susan Arrington
    See Madsen, Susan A.
Maehlqvist, Stefan 1943- 30
Maestro, Betsy (Crippen) 1944- 106
    Brief entry 30
    Earlier sketch in SATA 59
    See also CLR 45
Maestro, Giulio 1942- 106
    Earlier sketches in SATA 8, 59
    See also CLR 45
Maeterlinck, Maurice 1862-1949 66
Magee, Doug 1947- 78
Magee, Wes 1939- 64
Maggio, Rosalie 1943- 69
Magid, Ken(neth Marshall) 65
Magnus, Erica 1946- 77
Magoon, Scott 182
Magorian, James 1942- 92
    Earlier sketch in SATA 32
Magorian, Michelle 1947- 128
    Earlier sketch in SATA 67
Magorian, Michelle Jane
    See Magorian, Michelle
Magovern, Peg 103
Maguire, Anne
    See Nearing, Penny
Maguire, Gregory 1954- 200
    Autobiography Feature 200
    Earlier sketches in SATA 28, 84, 129
    See also SAAS 22
Maguire, Gregory Peter
    See Maguire, Gregory
Maguire, Jack 1920-2000 74
Maguire, Jesse
    See Smith, Sherwood
Maguire, Jessie
    See Smith, Sherwood
Maher, Ramona 1934- 13
Mahlqvist, Stefan
    See Maehlqvist, Stefan
Mahon, Julia C(unha) 1916- 11
Mahony, Elizabeth Winthrop
    See Winthrop, Elizabeth
Mahood, Kenneth 1930- 24
Mahy, Margaret 1936- 171
    Earlier sketches in SATA 14, 69, 119
    See also CLR 78
Mahy, Margaret May
    See Mahy, Margaret
Maiden, Cecil (Edward) 1902-1981 52
Maidoff, Ilka
    See List, Ilka Katherine
Maifair, Linda Lee 1947- 83
Maik, Henri
    See Hecht, Henri Joseph
Maillu, David G(ian) 1939- 111

Maine, Trevor
  See Catherall, Arthur
Mains, Randolph P. 1946- 80
Maione, Heather 189
Maiorano, Robert 1946- 43
Maisner, Heather 1947- 89
Maison, Della
  See Katz, Bobbi
Maitland, Antony Jasper 1935- 25
Maitland, Barbara 102
Mai-Wyss, Tatjana 1972- 187
Maizels, Jennie 210
Major, Kevin (Gerald) 1949- 134
  Earlier sketches in SATA *32, 82*
  See also CLR *11*
Majure, Janet 1954- 96
Makhijani, Pooja 188
Makie, Pam 1943- 37
Makowski, Silk
  See Makowski, Silvia Ann
Makowski, Silvia Ann 1940- 101
Malam, John 1957- 152
  Earlier sketch in SATA *89*
Maland, Nick 195
Malcolm, Dan
  See Silverberg, Robert
Malcolm, Jahnna N.
  See Beecham, Jahnna
Malcolmson, Anne
  See von Storch, Anne B.
Malcolmson, David 1899-1978 6
Maletta, Dr. Arlene
  See Feltenstein, Arlene (H.)
Maley, Carleen
  See Hutchins, Carleen Maley
Mali, Jane Lawrence 1937-1995 51
  Brief entry 44
  Obituary 86
Malkin, Nina 1959(?)- 179
Mallett, Jerry J. 1939- 76
Malley, Gemma 198
Malley, G.R.
  See Malley, Gemma
Mallory, Kenneth 1945- 185
  Earlier sketch in SATA *128*
Mallowan, Agatha Christie
  See Christie, Agatha
Malmberg, Carl 1904-1979 9
Malmgren, Dallin 1949- 65
Malo, John W. 1911-2000 4
Malone, James Hiram 1930- 84
Malone, Nola Langner 1930-2003 8
  Obituary 151
Malone, Patricia 1932- 155
Malone, Peter 1953- 191
Maloney, Pat
  See Markun, Patricia Maloney
Malory, Sir Thomas 1410(?)-1471(?) 59
  Brief entry 33
Maltese, Michael 1909(?)-1981
  Obituary 24
Malvasi, Meg Greene 143
Malvern, Corinne 1905-1956 34
Malvern, Gladys (?)-1962 23
Mama G.
  See Davis, Grania
Mammano, Julie 1962- 202
  Earlier sketch in SATA *107*
Mamonova, Tatyana 1943- 93
Manchel, Frank 1935- 10
Manchess, Gregory 1955- 203
Manchester, William (Raymond)
  1922-2004 65
Mandabach, Brian 1962(?)- 197
Mandel, Brett H. 1969- 108
Mandel, Peter 1957- 87
Mandel, Sally (Elizabeth) 1944- 64
Mandell, Muriel (Hortense Levin) 1921- 63
Manders, John 1957- 175

Manes, Stephen 1949- 99
  Brief entry 40
  Earlier sketch in SATA *42*
Manfred, Frederick (Feikema) 1912-1994 .. 30
Mangin, Marie France 1940- 59
Mangione, Gerlando 1909-1998 6
  Obituary 104
Mangione, Jerre
  See Mangione, Gerlando
Mango, Karin N. 1936- 52
Mangurian, David 1938- 14
Mania, Cathy 1950- 102
Mania, Robert 1952- 102
Mania, Robert C., Jr.
  See Mania, Robert
Maniatty, Taramesha 1978- 92
Maniscalco, Joseph 1926- 10
Manley, Deborah 1932- 28
Manley, Seon 1921- 15
  See also CLR *3*
  See also SAAS *2*
Mann, Elizabeth 1948- 153
Mann, Josephine
  See Pullein-Thompson, Josephine (Mary
    Wedderburn)
Mann, Kenny 1946- 91
Mann, Pamela 1946- 91
Mann, Patrick
  See Waller, Leslie
Mann, Peggy
  See Houlton, Peggy Mann
Mannetti, Lisa 1953- 57
  Brief entry 51
Mannheim, Grete (Salomon) 1909-1986 10
Manniche, Lise 1943- 31
Manning, Jane K. 185
Manning, Maurie
  See Manning, Maurie J.
Manning, Maurie J. 211
Manning, Maurie Jo
  See Manning, Maurie J.
Manning, Mick 1959- 176
Manning, Rosemary 1911-1988 10
Manning, Sarra 162
Manning-Sanders, Ruth (Vernon)
  1895(?)-1988 73
  Obituary 57
  Earlier sketch in SATA *15*
Mannion, Diane
  See Paterson, Diane
Mannis, Celeste Davidson 173
Mannon, Warwick
  See Hopkins, (Hector) Kenneth
Manos, Helen 199
Mansir, A. Richard 1932- 170
Manson, Ainslie Kertland 1938- 115
Manson, Beverlie 1945- 57
  Brief entry 44
Manthorpe, Helen 1958- 122
Mantinband, Gerda (B.) 1917- 74
Manton, Jo
  See Gittings, Jo (Grenville) Manton
Manuel, Lynn 1948- 179
  Earlier sketch in SATA *99*
Manushkin, Fran 1942- 205
  Earlier sketches in SATA *7, 54, 93, 166*
Manushkin, Frances
  See Manushkin, Fran
Man Without a Spleen, A
  See Chekhov, Anton
Many, Paul 1947- 210
Many, Paul A.
  See Many, Paul
Manzano, Sonia 1950- 167
Mapes, Mary A.
  See Ellison, Virginia H(owell)
Maple, Marilyn 1931- 80
Mappin, Strephyn 1956- 109
Mara, Barney
  See Roth, Arthur J(oseph)

Mara, Jeanette
  See Cebulash, Mel
Mara, Rachna
  See Gilmore, Rachna
Marais, Josef 1905-1978
  Obituary 24
Marasmus, Seymour
  See Rivoli, Mario
Marbach, Ethel
  See Pochocki, Ethel (Frances)
Marcal, Annette B.
  See Callaway, Bernice (Anne)
Marcelino
  See Agnew, Edith J(osephine)
Marcellino, Fred 1939-2001 118
  Obituary 127
  Earlier sketch in SATA *68*
March, Carl
  See Fleischman, Sid
Marchant, Bessie 1862-1941
  See YABC *2*
Marchant, Catherine
  See Cookson, Catherine (McMullen)
Marcher, Marion Walden 1890-1987 10
Marchesi, Stephen 1951- 114
Marchesi, Steve
  See Marchesi, Stephen
  and Older, Effin
  and Older, Jules
Marchetta, Melina 1965- 170
Marciano, John Bemelmans 1970- 167
  Earlier sketch in SATA *118*
  See also CLR *93*
Marco, Lou
  See Gottfried, Theodore Mark
Marcus, Leonard S. 1950- 187
  Earlier sketch in SATA *133*
Marcus, Paul 1953- 82
Marcus, Rebecca B(rian) 1907- 9
Marcuse, Aida E. 1934- 89
Marek, Margot L. 1934(?)-1987
  Obituary 54
Maren, Julie 1970- 199
Margaret, Karla
  See Andersdatter, Karla M(argaret)
Margolin, Harriet
  See Ziefert, Harriet
Margolis, Jeffrey A. 1948- 108
Margolis, Leslie 187
Margolis, Richard J(ules) 1929-1991 86
  Obituary 67
  Earlier sketch in SATA *4*
Margolis, Vivienne 1922- 46
Mariana
  See Foster, Marian Curtis
Marie, Geraldine 1949- 61
Mariner, Scott
  See Pohl, Frederik
Marino, Dorothy Bronson 1912- 14
Marino, Jan 1936- 114
Marino, Nick
  See Deming, Richard
Marino, Peter 1960- 179
Mario, Anna
  See Odgers, Sally Farrell
Marion, Henry
  See del Rey, Lester
Maris, Ron 71
  Brief entry 45
Mark, Jan 1943-2006 164
  Obituary 173
  Earlier sketches in SATA *22, 69, 114*
  See also CLR *11*
Mark, Janet Marjorie
  See Mark, Jan
Mark, Joan T. 1937- 122
Mark, Pauline (Dahlin) 1913-1997 14
Mark, Polly
  See Mark, Pauline (Dahlin)
Mark, Ted
  See Gottfried, Theodore Mark

Markel, Michelle *169*
Marker, Sherry 1941- *76*
Markert, Jennifer 1965- *83*
Markert, Jenny
   See Markert, Jennifer
Markham, Lynne 1947- *102*
Markham, Marion M. 1929- *60*
Markham, Wendy
   See Staub, Wendy Corsi
Markins, W. S.
   See Jenkins, Marie M(agdalen)
Markle, Sandra L. 1946- *185*
   Brief entry *41*
   Earlier sketches in SATA *57, 92, 148*
Markle, Sandra Lee
   See Markle, Sandra L.
Marklew, Gilly *211*
Marko, Katherine D(olores) *28*
Markoosie
   See Patsauq, Markoosie
Marks, Alan 1957- *187*
   Earlier sketches in SATA *77, 151*
Marks, Burton 1930- *47*
   Brief entry *43*
Marks, Graham *158*
Marks, Hannah K.
   See Trivelpiece, Laurel
Marks, J.
   See Highwater, Jamake (Mamake)
Marks, J(ames) M(acdonald) 1921- *13*
Marks, Laurie J. 1957- *68*
Marks, Margaret L. 1911(?)-1980
   Obituary *23*
Marks, Mickey Klar -1986 .... *12*
Marks, Peter
   See Smith, Robert Kimmel
Marks, Rita 1938- *47*
Marks, Stan(ley) *14*
Marks-Highwater, J.
   See Highwater, Jamake (Mamake)
Markun, Patricia Maloney 1924- *15*
Markusen, Bruce (Stanley Rodriguez)
   1965- *141*
Marley, Louise 1952- *173*
   Earlier sketch in SATA *120*
Marlin, Hilda
   See Van Stockum, Hilda
Marlow, Layne *204*
Marlow, Max
   See Nicole, Christopher (Robin)
Marlow, Susan K. 1953- *178*
Marlowe, Amy Bell *67*
   Earlier sketch in SATA *1*
Marlowe, Jack
   See Deary, Terry
Marney, Dean 1952- *90*
Marokvia, Artur 1909- *31*
Marokvia, Mireille 1908-2008 .... *5*
   Obituary *197*
Marokvia, Mireille Journet
   See Marokvia, Mireille
Marol, Jean-Claude 1946- *125*
Marr, John S(tuart) 1940- *48*
Marr, Melissa 1972- *189*
Marric, J. J.
   See Butler, William Vivian
   and Creasey, John
Marrin, Albert 1936- *193*
   Brief entry *43*
   Earlier sketches in SATA *53, 90, 126*
   See also CLR *53*
Marriott, Alice Lee 1910-1992 .... *31*
   Obituary *71*
Marriott, Janice 1946- *134*
Marriott, Pat(ricia) 1920- *35*
Marroquin, Patricio
   See Markun, Patricia Maloney
Mars, W. T.
   See Mars, Witold Tadeusz J.
Mars, Witold Tadeusz J. 1912-1985 .... *3*

Marsden, Carolyn 1950- *175*
   Earlier sketch in SATA *140*
Marsden, John 1950- *146*
   Earlier sketches in SATA *66, 97*
   See also CLR *34*
   See also SAAS *22*
Marsh, Carole 1946- *127*
Marsh, Dave 1950- *66*
Marsh, J. E.
   See Marshall, Evelyn
Marsh, James 1946- *73*
Marsh, Jean
   See Marshall, Evelyn
Marsh, Joan F. 1923- *83*
Marsh, Paul
   See Hopkins, (Hector) Kenneth
Marsh, Valerie 1954- *89*
Marshall, Anthony D(ryden) 1924- *18*
Marshall, Bonnie C. 1941- *141*
   Earlier sketch in SATA *18*
Marshall, Bridget M(ary) 1974- *103*
Marshall, (Sarah) Catherine (Wood)
   1914-1983 .... *2*
   Obituary *34*
Marshall, Douglas
   See McClintock, Marshall
Marshall, Edmund
   See Hopkins, (Hector) Kenneth
Marshall, Edward
   See Marshall, James
Marshall, Evelyn 1897-1991 .... *11*
Marshall, Felicity 1950- *116*
Marshall, Garry 1934- *60*
Marshall, H. H.
   See Jahn, Michael
Marshall, James 1942-1992 .... *75*
   Earlier sketches in SATA *6, 51*
   See also CLR *21*
Marshall, James Edward
   See Marshall, James
Marshall, James Vance
   See Payne, Donald Gordon
Marshall, Janet (Perry) 1938- *97*
Marshall, Jeff
   See Laycock, George (Edwin)
Marshall, Kim
   See Marshall, Michael (Kimbrough)
Marshall, Michael (Kimbrough) 1948- *37*
Marshall, Percy
   See Young, Percy M(arshall)
Marshall, S(amuel) L(yman) A(twood)
   1900-1977 .... *21*
Marsoli, Lisa Ann 1958- *101*
   Brief entry *53*
Marsten, Richard
   See Hunter, Evan
Marston, Elsa 1933- *156*
Marston, Hope Irvin 1935- *127*
   Earlier sketch in SATA *31*
Marszalek, John F. 1939- *167*
Marszalek, John Francis, Jr.
   See Marszalek, John F.
Marszalek, John Francis 1939-
   See Marszalek, John F.
Martchenko, Michael 1942- *154*
   Earlier sketches in SATA *50, 95*
Martel, Aimee
   See Thurlo, Aimee
   and Thurlo, David
Martel, Suzanne 1924- *99*
Martignoni, Margaret E. 1908(?)-1974
   Obituary *27*
Martin, Ann M. 1955- *192*
   Brief entry *41*
   Earlier sketches in SATA *44, 70, 126*
   See also CLR *32*
Martin, Bill, Jr. 1916-2004 .... *145*
   Brief entry *40*
   Earlier sketches in SATA *40, 67*
   See also CLR *97*

Martin, Charles E(lmer)
   See Mastrangelo, Charles E(lmer)
Martin, Christopher
   See Hoyt, Edwin P(almer), Jr.
Martin, C.K. Kelly *207*
Martin, Claire 1933- *76*
Martin, Courtney Autumn 1984- *205*
Martin, David Stone 1913-1992 .... *39*
Martin, Del 1921-2008 .... *47*
Martin, Donald
   See Honig, Donald
Martin, Dorothy
   See Martin, Del
Martin, Dorothy L.
   See Martin, Del
Martin, Eugene *1*
Martin, Eva M. 1939- *65*
Martin, Frances M(cEntee) 1906-1998 .... *36*
Martin, Francesca 1947- *101*
Martin, Fred 1948- *119*
Martin, Fredric
   See Christopher, Matt(hew Frederick)
Martin, George Raymond Richard
   See Martin, George R.R.
Martin, George R.R. 1948- *118*
Martin, J(ohn) P(ercival) 1880(?)-1966 ...... *15*
Martin, Jacqueline Briggs 1945- *188*
   Earlier sketches in SATA *98, 149*
Martin, Jane Read 1957- *84*
Martin, Jeremy
   See Levin, Marcia Obrasky
Martin, Les
   See Schulman, L(ester) M(artin)
Martin, Linda 1961- *82*
Martin, Lynne 1923- *21*
Martin, Marcia
   See Levin, Marcia Obrasky
Martin, Marvin 1926- *126*
Martin, Melanie
   See Pellowski, Michael (Joseph)
Martin, Nancy
   See Salmon, Annie Elizabeth
Martin, Patricia *200*
Martin, Patricia A.
   See Martin, Patricia
Martin, Patricia Miles 1899-1986 .... *43*
   Obituary *48*
   Earlier sketch in SATA *1*
Martin, Peter
   See Chaundler, Christine
Martin, Rafe 1946- *175*
Martin, Rene 1891-1977 .... *42*
   Obituary *20*
Martin, Rupert (Claude) 1905- *31*
Martin, S. R.
   See Mappin, Strephyn
Martin, Stefan 1936- *32*
Martin, Vicky
   See Storey, Victoria Carolyn
Martin, Webber
   See Silverberg, Robert
Martin, Wendy
   See Martini, Teri
Martin, William Ivan, Jr.
   See Martin, Bill, Jr.
Martineau, Diane 1940- *178*
Martineau, Harriet 1802-1876
   See YABC *2*
Martinet, Jeanne 1958- *80*
Martinez, Agnes *167*
Martinez, Arturo O. 1933- *192*
Martinez, Ed(ward) 1954- *98*
Martinez, Elizabeth Coonrod 1954- *85*
Martinez, Victor 1954- *95*
Martini, Teri 1930- *3*
Martini, Therese
   See Martini, Teri
Martino, Alfred C. 1964- *174*
Martinson, Janis
   See Herbert, Janis

Marton, Jirina 1946- 144
　Earlier sketch in SATA 95
Marton, Pierre
　See Stone, Peter
Martson, Del
　See Lupoff, Richard A(llen)
Martyr, Paula (Jane)
　See Lawford, Paula Jane
Maruki, Toshi 1912-2000 112
　See also CLR 19
Marvin, Isabel R(idout) 1924- 84
Marx, Patricia Windschill
　See Marx, Trish
Marx, Robert F(rank) 1936- 24
Marx, Trish 1948- 202
　Earlier sketches in SATA 112, 160
Marzani, Carl (Aldo) 1912-1994 12
Marzollo, Jean 1942- 190
　Autobiography Feature 190
　Earlier sketches in SATA 29, 77, 130
　See also SAAS 15
Masefield, John (Edward) 1878-1967 19
Masoff, Joy 1951- 118
Mason, Adrienne 1962- 163
Mason, Cherie 170
Mason, Edwin A. 1905-1979
　Obituary 32
Mason, Ernst
　See Pohl, Frederik
Mason, F(rancis) van Wyck 1901-1978 3
　Obituary 26
Mason, Frank W.
　See Mason, F(rancis) van Wyck
Mason, George Frederick 1904-2000 14
Mason, Miriam E(vangeline) 1900-1973 2
　Obituary 26
Mason, Prue 195
Mason, Simon 1962- 178
Mason, Tally
　See Derleth, August (William)
Mason, Van Wyck
　See Mason, F(rancis) van Wyck
Mass, Wendy 1967- 196
　Earlier sketch in SATA 158
Mass, William
　See Gibson, William
Masselman, George 1897-1971 19
Massie, Dianne Redfield 1938- 125
　Earlier sketch in SATA 16
Massie, Elizabeth 108
Masson, Sophie 1959- 179
　Earlier sketch in SATA 133
Masters, Anthony (Richard) 1940-2003 112
　Obituary 145
Masters, Kelly R(ay) 1897-1987 3
Masters, Mildred 1932- 42
Masters, William
　See Cousins, Margaret
Masters, Zeke
　See Bensen, Donald R.
　and Goulart, Ron
Mastrangelo, Charles E(lmer) 1910-1995 ... 70
　Earlier sketch in SATA 69
Masuda, Takeshi 1944- 56
Matas, Carol 1949- 194
　Autobiography Feature 112
　Earlier sketch in SATA 93
　See also CLR 52
Matchette, Katharine E. 1941- 38
Math, Irwin 1940- 42
Mathabane, Mark 1960- 123
Mather, Kirtley F(letcher) 1888-1978 65
Mathers, Petra 1945- 176
　Earlier sketch in SATA 119
　See also CLR 76
Matheson, Richard (Christian) 1953- 119
Matheson, Shirlee Smith 1942- 155
Mathews, Eleanor
　See Mathews, Ellie
Mathews, Ellie 1946(?)- 193
Mathews, Janet 1914-1992 41

Mathews, Judith
　See Goldberger, Judith M.
Mathews, Louise
　See Tooke, Louise Mathews
Mathiesen, Egon 1907-1976
　Obituary 28
Mathieu, Joe 1949- 185
　Brief entry 36
　Earlier sketches in SATA 43, 94
Mathieu, Joseph P.
　See Mathieu, Joe
Mathis, Sharon Bell 1937- 58
　Earlier sketch in SATA 7
　See also CLR 147
　See also SAAS 3
Matlin, Marlee 1965- 181
Matlin, Marlee Beth
　See Matlin, Marlee
Matloff, Gregory 1945- 73
Matott, Justin 1961- 109
Matranga, Frances Carfi 1922- 78
Matray, James I. 1948- 161
Matray, James Irving
　See Matray, James I.
Matson, Emerson N(els) 1926- 12
Matsui, Tadashi 1926- 8
Matsuno, Masako
　See Kobayashi, Masako Matsuno
Matsuoka, Mei 1981- 192
Matte, (Encarnacion) L'Enc 1936- 22
Mattern, Joanne 1963- 122
Mattheson, Jenny 180
Matthew, James
　See Barrie, J. M.
Matthews, Aline
　See De Wire, Elinor
Matthews, Andrew 1948- 138
Matthews, Caitlin 1952- 122
Matthews, Downs 1925- 71
Matthews, Elizabeth 1978- 194
Matthews, Ellen
　See Bache, Ellyn
Matthews, Ellen 1950- 28
Matthews, Harold Downs
　See Matthews, Downs
Matthews, Jacklyn Meek
　See Meek, Jacklyn O'Hanlon
Matthews, John (Kentigern) 1948- 116
Matthews, Laura S.
　See Matthews, L.S.
Matthews, Liz
　See Pellowski, Michael (Joseph)
Matthews, L.S. 183
Matthews, Morgan
　See Pellowski, Michael (Joseph)
Matthews, Nicola
　See Browne, N.M.
Matthews, Patricia 1927-2006 28
Matthews, Patricia Anne
　See Matthews, Patricia
Matthews, Tina 1961- 190
Matthews, Tom L.
　See Lalicki, Tom
Matthews, William Henry III 1919- 45
　Brief entry 28
Matthiessen, Peter 1927- 27
Mattingley, Christobel (Rosemary) 1931- ... 85
　Earlier sketch in SATA 37
　See also CLR 24
　See also SAAS 18
Matulay, Laszlo 1912- 43
Matus, Greta 1938- 12
Maugham, W. S.
　See Maugham, W. Somerset
Maugham, W. Somerset 1874-1965 54
Maugham, William S.
　See Maugham, W. Somerset
Maugham, William Somerset
　See Maugham, W. Somerset
Maurer, Diane Philippoff
　See Maurer-Mathison, Diane V(ogel)

Maurer, Diane Vogel
　See Maurer-Mathison, Diane V(ogel)
Maurer-Mathison, Diane V(ogel) 1944- 89
Mauser, Pat Rhoads
　See McCord, Patricia
Mauser, Patricia Rhoads
　See McCord, Patricia
Maves, Mary Carolyn 1916- 10
Maves, Paul B(enjamin) 1913-1994 10
Mavor, Salley 1955- 125
Mawicke, Tran 1911- 15
Max 1906-1989
　See Diop, Birago (Ismael)
Max, Peter 1939- 45
Maxon, Anne
　See Best, (Evangel) Allena Champlin
Maxwell, Arthur S. 1896-1970 11
Maxwell, B.E. 1957- 211
Maxwell, Bruce E.
　See Maxwell, B.E.
Maxwell, Edith 1923- 7
Maxwell, Gavin 1914-1969 65
Maxwell, Katie
　See MacAlister, Katie
Maxwell, William (Keepers, Jr.) 1908-2000
　Obituary 128
Maxwell-Hyslop, Miranda 1968- 154
May, Charles Paul 1920- 4
May, Elaine Tyler 1947- 120
May, J. C.
　See May, Julian
May, Julian 1931- 11
May, Robert Lewis 1905-1976
　Obituary 27
May, Robert Stephen 1929-1996 46
May, Robin
　See May, Robert Stephen
Mayall, Beth 171
Mayberry, Florence V(irginia) Wilson 10
Maybury, Richard J. 1946- 72
Maybury, Rick
　See Maybury, Richard J.
Mayer, Agatha
　See Maher, Ramona
Mayer, Albert Ignatius, Jr. 1906-1994
　Obituary 29
Mayer, Ann M(argaret) 1938- 14
Mayer, Bill 200
Mayer, Danuta 1958- 117
Mayer, Hannelore Valencak 1929- 42
Mayer, Jane Rothschild 1903-2001 38
Mayer, Marianna 1945- 132
　Earlier sketches in SATA 32, 83
Mayer, Mercer 1943- 137
　Earlier sketches in SATA 16, 32, 73, 129
　See also CLR 11
Mayerson, Charlotte Leon 36
Mayerson, Evelyn Wilde 1935- 55
Mayfield, Katherine 1958- 118
Mayfield, Sue 1963- 146
　Earlier sketch in SATA 72
Mayhar, Ardath 1930- 38
Mayhew, James 1964- 204
　Earlier sketches in SATA 85, 149
Maynard, Olga 1920- 40
Mayne, William (James Carter) 1928- 122
　Earlier sketches in SATA 6, 68
　See also CLR 123
　See also SAAS 11
Maynes, J. O. Rocky, Jr.
　See Maynes, J. Oscar, Jr.
Maynes, J. Oscar, Jr. 1929- 38
Mayo, Gretchen Will 1936- 163
　Earlier sketch in SATA 84
Mayo, Margaret 1935- 165
　Earlier sketches in SATA 38, 96
Mayo, Margaret Mary
　See Mayo, Margaret
Mayr, Diane 1949- 197
Mays, Lucinda L(a Bella) 1924- 49
Mays, (Lewis) Victor (Jr.) 1927- 5

Mazellan, Ron *210*
Mazer, Anne 1953- *192*
  Earlier sketches in SATA *67, 105*
Mazer, Harry 1925- *167*
  Earlier sketches in SATA *31, 67, 105*
  See also CLR *16*
  See also SAAS *11*
Mazer, Norma Fox 1931-2009 .... *198*
  Earlier sketches in SATA *24, 67, 105, 168*
  See also CLR *23*
  See also SAAS *1*
Mazille, Capucine 1953- *96*
Mazza, Adriana 1928- *19*
Mazzio, Joann 1926- *74*
Mbugua, Kioi Wa 1962- *83*
McAfee, Carol 1955- *81*
McAllister, Amanda
  See Dowdell, Dorothy (Florence) Karns
  and Hager, Jean
  and Meaker, Eloise
McAllister, Angela *182*
McAllister, Margaret I. 1956- *169*
  Earlier sketch in SATA *117*
McAllister, M.I.
  See McAllister, Margaret I.
McArdle, Paula 1971- *198*
McArthur, Nancy *96*
McAvoy, Jim 1972- *142*
McBain, Ed
  See Hunter, Evan
McBain, Georgina *189*
McBratney, Sam 1943- *203*
  Earlier sketches in SATA *89, 164*
  See also CLR *44*
McBrier, Michael
  See Older, Effin
  and Older, Jules
McCafferty, Jim 1954- *84*
McCaffery, Janet 1936- *38*
McCaffrey, Anne 1926- *152*
  Autobiography Feature *152*
  Earlier sketches in SATA *8, 70, 116*
  See also CLR *130*
  See also SAAS *11*
McCaffrey, Anne Inez
  See McCaffrey, Anne
McCaffrey, Mary
  See Szudek, Agnes S(usan) P(hilomena)
McCain, Becky Ray 1954- *138*
McCain, Murray (David, Jr.) 1926-1981 .... *7*
  Obituary *29*
McCall, Bruce 1935(?)- *209*
McCall, Edith (Sansom) 1911- *6*
McCall, Virginia Nielsen 1909-2000 .... *13*
McCall, Wendell
  See Pearson, Ridley
McCall Smith, Alexander
  See Smith, Alexander McCall
McCallum, Phyllis
  See Koch, Phyllis (Mae) McCallum
McCallum, Stephen 1960- *91*
McCampbell, Darlene Z. 1942- *83*
McCann, Edson
  See del Rey, Lester
  and Pohl, Frederik
McCann, Gerald 1916- *41*
McCann, Helen 1948- *75*
McCannon, Dindga *41*
McCants, William D. 1961- *82*
McCarter, Neely Dixon 1929- *47*
McCarthy, Agnes 1933- *4*
McCarthy, Colin (John) 1951- *77*
McCarthy, Mary 1951- *203*
McCarthy, Meghan *199*
  Earlier sketch in SATA *168*
McCarthy, Ralph F. 1950- *139*
McCarthy-Tucker, Sherri N. 1958- *83*
McCarty, Peter 1966- *182*
McCarty, Rega Kramer 1904-1986 .... *10*
McCaslin, Nellie 1914-2005 .... *12*

McCaughrean, Geraldine 1951- *173*
  Earlier sketches in SATA *87, 139*
  See also CLR *38*
McCaughren, Tom 1936- *75*
McCauley, Adam 1965- *209*
  Earlier sketch in SATA *128*
McCay, (Zenas) Winsor 1869-1934 .... *134*
  Earlier sketch in SATA *41*
McClafferty, Carla Killough 1958- *137*
McClary, Jane Stevenson 1919-1990
  Obituary *64*
McCleery, Patsy R. 1925- *133*
  Earlier sketch in SATA *88*
McClements, George *196*
McClintock, Barbara 1955- *146*
  Earlier sketches in SATA *57, 95*
McClintock, Marshall 1906-1967 .... *3*
McClintock, May Garelick
  See Garelick, May
McClintock, Mike
  See McClintock, Marshall
McClintock, Norah *178*
McClintock, Theodore 1902-1971 .... *14*
McClinton, Leon 1933- *11*
McCloskey, Kevin 1951- *79*
McCloskey, (John) Robert 1914-2003 .... *100*
  Obituary *146*
  Earlier sketches in SATA *2, 39*
  See also CLR *7*
McCloy, James F(loyd) 1941- *59*
McClung, Robert M(arshall) 1916- *135*
  Earlier sketches in SATA *2, 68*
  See also CLR *11*
  See also SAAS *15*
McClure, Gillian Mary 1948- *31*
McColley, Kevin 1961- *80*
  See also SAAS *23*
McConduit, Denise Walter 1950- *89*
McConnell, James Douglas Rutherford
  1915-1988 .... *40*
  Obituary *56*
McCord, Anne 1942- *41*
McCord, David (Thompson Watson)
  1897-1997 .... *18*
  Obituary *96*
  See also CLR *9*
McCord, Jean 1924- *34*
McCord, Pat Mauser
  See McCord, Patricia
McCord, Patricia 1943- *159*
  Earlier sketch in SATA *37*
McCord, Patricia Sue Rhoads Mauser
  See McCord, Patricia
McCormick, Brooks
  See Adams, William Taylor
McCormick, Dell J. 1892-1949 .... *19*
McCormick, (George) Donald (King)
  1911-1998 .... *14*
McCormick, Edith (Joan) 1934- *30*
McCormick, Kimberly A. 1960- *153*
McCormick, Patricia 1956- *181*
  Earlier sketch in SATA *128*
McCourt, Edward (Alexander) 1907-1972
  Obituary *28*
McCourt, Lisa 1964- *159*
  Earlier sketch in SATA *117*
McCourt, Malachy 1931- *126*
McCoy, Iola Fuller *3*
McCoy, J(oseph) J(erome) 1917- *8*
McCoy, Karen Kawamoto 1953- *82*
McCoy, Lois (Rich) 1941- *38*
McCrady, Lady 1951- *16*
McCrea, James (Craig, Jr.) 1920- *3*
McCrea, Ruth (Pirman) 1921- *3*
McCreigh, James
  See Pohl, Frederik
McCrumb, Sharyn 1948- *109*
McCue, Lisa 1959- *177*
  Earlier sketch in SATA *65*
McCue, Lisa Emiline
  See McCue, Lisa

McCullen, Andrew
  See Arthur, Robert, (Jr.)
McCullers, Carson 1917-1967 .... *27*
McCullers, Lula Carson Smith
  See McCullers, Carson
McCulloch, Derek (Ivor Breashur) 1897-1967
  Obituary *29*
McCulloch, John Tyler
  See Burroughs, Edgar Rice
McCulloch, Sarah
  See Ure, Jean
McCullough, David 1933- *62*
McCullough, David Gaub
  See McCullough, David
McCullough, Frances Monson 1938- *8*
McCullough, Sharon Pierce 1943- *131*
McCully, Emily Arnold *210*
  See Arnold, Emily
McCune, Dan
  See Haas, Dorothy F.
McCunn, Ruthanne Lum 1946- *63*
McCurdy, Michael (Charles) 1942- *147*
  Earlier sketches in SATA *13, 82*
McCutcheon, Elsie (Mary Jackson) 1937- .. *60*
McCutcheon, John 1952- *97*
McDaniel, Becky Bring 1953- *61*
McDaniel, Lurlene 1944- *146*
  Earlier sketch in SATA *71*
McDaniels, Pellom III 1968- *121*
McDaniels, Preston 1952- *192*
McDearmon, Kay *20*
McDermott, Beverly Brodsky 1941- *11*
McDermott, Eleni *156*
McDermott, Gerald (Edward) 1941- *163*
  Earlier sketches in SATA *16, 74*
  See also CLR *9*
McDermott, Michael 1962- *76*
McDevitt, Jack 1935- *155*
  Earlier sketch in SATA *94*
McDevitt, John Charles
  See McDevitt, Jack
McDole, Carol
  See Farley, Carol (J.)
McDonald, Collin 1943- *79*
McDonald, Gerald D(oan) 1905-1970 .... *3*
McDonald, Jamie
  See Heide, Florence Parry
McDonald, Janet 1953-2007 .... *204*
  Earlier sketch in SATA *148*
McDonald, Jill (Masefield) 1927-1982 .... *13*
  Obituary *29*
McDonald, Joyce 1946- *164*
  Earlier sketch in SATA *101*
McDonald, Lucile Saunders 1898-1992 ...... *10*
McDonald, Mary Ann 1956- *84*
McDonald, Megan 1958- *202*
  Autobiography Feature *151*
  Earlier sketches in SATA *67, 99, 148, 151*
  See also CLR *94*
McDonald, Meme 1954- *112*
McDonald, Mercedes 1956- *169*
  Earlier sketch in SATA *97*
McDonald, Rae A. 1952- *201*
McDonell, Chris 1960- *138*
McDonnell, Christine 1949- *115*
  Earlier sketch in SATA *34*
McDonnell, Flora (Mary) 1963- *146*
  Earlier sketch in SATA *90*
McDonnell, Kathleen 1947- *186*
McDonnell, Lois Eddy 1914-2001 .... *10*
McDonnell, Patrick 1956- *179*
McDonough, Yona Zeldis 1957- *73*
McElligott, Matt 1968- *196*
  Earlier sketch in SATA *135*
McElligott, Matthew
  See McElligott, Matt
McElmeel, Sharron L. 1942- *128*
McElmurry, Jill *198*
  Earlier sketch in SATA *159*
McElrath, William N. 1932- *65*

McElrath-Eslick, Lori 1960- 204
  Earlier sketch in SATA 96
McEntee, Dorothy (Layng) 1902- 37
McEwen, Katherine 183
McEwen, Robert (Lindley) 1926-1980
  Obituary 23
McFadden, Kevin Christopher
  See Pike, Christopher
McFall, Christie 1918- 12
McFall, Gardner 1952- 183
McFarlan, Donald M(aitland) 1915- 59
McFarland, Henry "Hammer"
  See McFarland, Henry O.
McFarland, Henry O. 1934- 143
McFarland, Kenton D(ean) 1920- 11
McFarland, Martha
  See Smith-Ankrom, M. E.
McFarlane, Leslie 1902-1977 100
  Earlier sketches in SATA 31, 1, 65, 67
  See also CLR 118
McFarlane, Leslie Charles
  See McFarlane, Leslie
McFarlane, Peter (William) 1940- 95
McFarlane, Sheryl P. 1954- 86
McFarlane, Todd 1961- 117
McGaw, Jessie Brewer 1913-1997 10
McGee, Barbara 1943- 6
McGee, Marni 163
McGhee, Alison 1960- 196
McGiffin, (Lewis) Lee (Shaffer) 1908-1978 . 1
McGill, Alice 159
McGill, Ormond 1913- 92
McGinley, Jerry 1948- 116
McGinley, Phyllis 1905-1978 44
  Obituary 24
  Earlier sketch in SATA 2
McGinnis, Lila S(prague) 1924- 44
McGinty, Alice B. 1963- 202
  Earlier sketch in SATA 134
McGivern, Justin 1985- 129
McGivern, Maureen Daly
  See Daly, Maureen
McGivern, Maureen Patricia Daly
  See Daly, Maureen
McGough, Elizabeth (Hemmes) 1934- 33
McGovern, Ann 1930- 132
  Earlier sketches in SATA 8, 69, 70
  See also CLR 50
  See also SAAS 17
McGowen, Thomas E. 1927- 109
  Earlier sketch in SATA 2
McGowen, Tom
  See McGowen, Thomas E.
McGrady, Mike 1933- 6
McGrath, Barbara Barbieri 1953- 169
  Earlier sketch in SATA 108
McGrath, Robin 1949- 121
McGrath, Thomas (Matthew) 1916-1990 41
  Obituary 66
McGraw, Eloise Jarvis 1915-2000 67
  Obituary 123
  Earlier sketch in SATA 1
  See also SAAS 6
McGraw, William Corbin 1916-1999 3
McGreal, Elizabeth
  See Yates, Elizabeth
McGregor, Barbara 1959- 82
McGregor, Craig 1933- 8
McGregor, Iona 1929- 25
McGrory, Anik 193
McGuffey, Alexander Hamilton
  1816-1896 60
McGuigan, Mary Ann 1949- 106
McGuire, Edna 1899- 13
McGuire, Leslie (Sarah) 1945- 94
  Brief entry 45
  Earlier sketch in SATA 52
McGuire, Robert 187
McGuirk, Leslie (A.) 1960- 152
McGurk, Slater
  See Roth, Arthur J(oseph)

McHargue, Georgess 1941- 77
  Earlier sketch in SATA 4
  See also CLR 2
  See also SAAS 5
McHenry, E.B. 1963(?)- 193
McHugh, (Berit) Elisabet 1941- 55
  Brief entry 44
McIlvaine, Jane
  See McClary, Jane Stevenson
McIlwraith, Maureen Mollie Hunter
  See Hunter, Mollie
McInerney, Judith W(hitelock) 1945- 49
  Brief entry 46
McInerny, Ralph 1929-2010 93
McInerny, Ralph Matthew
  See McInerny, Ralph
McKaughan, Larry (Scott) 1941- 75
McKay, Donald 1895- 45
McKay, Hilary 1959- 208
  Earlier sketches in SATA 92, 145
  See also SAAS 23
McKay, Hilary Jane
  See McKay, Hilary
McKay, Lawrence, Jr. 1948- 114
McKay, Robert W. 1921- 15
McKay, Sharon E. 1954- 165
McKay, Simon
  See Nicole, Christopher (Robin)
McKean, Dave 1963- 197
McKean, David Jeff
  See McKean, Dave
McKeating, Eileen 1957- 81
McKee, David (John) 1935- 158
  Earlier sketches in SATA 70, 107
  See also CLR 38
McKee, Tim 1970- 111
McKeever, Marcia
  See Laird, Jean E(louise)
McKelvey, Carole A. 1942- 78
McKelvy, Charles 1950- 124
McKendrick, Melveena (Christine) 1941- ... 55
McKendry, Joe 1972- 170
McKenna, Colleen O'Shaughnessy 1948- . 136
  Earlier sketch in SATA 76
McKenzie, Dorothy Clayton 1910-1981
  Obituary 28
McKenzie, Ellen Kindt 1928- 80
McKernan, Victoria 1957- 171
McKie, Robin 112
McKillip, Patricia A. 1948- 174
  Earlier sketches in SATA 30, 80, 126
McKillip, Patricia Anne
  See McKillip, Patricia A.
McKim, Audrey Margaret 1909-1999 47
McKimmie, Chris 194
McKinley, Jennifer Carolyn Robin
  See McKinley, Robin
McKinley, Robin 1952- 195
  Brief entry 32
  Earlier sketches in SATA 50, 89, 130
  See also CLR 127
McKinney, Barbara Shaw 1951- 116
McKinney, Nadine 1938- 91
McKinty, Adrian 186
McKissack, Fredrick L. 1939- 162
  Brief entry 53
  Earlier sketches in SATA 73, 117
  See also CLR 55
McKissack, Fredrick Lemuel
  See McKissack, Fredrick L.
McKissack, Patricia C. 1944- 195
  Earlier sketches in SATA 51, 73, 117, 162
  See also CLR 129
McKissack, Patricia L'Ann Carwell
  See McKissack, Patricia C.
McKissack and McKissack
  See McKissack, Fredrick L.
  and McKissack, Patricia C.
McKown, Robin (?)-1976 6
McKy, Katie 1956- 184

McLaren, Clemence 1938- 158
  Earlier sketch in SATA 105
McLaughlin, Frank 1934- 73
McLaughlin, Lauren 209
McLaurin, Anne 1953- 27
McLean, Andrew 1946- 172
  Earlier sketch in SATA 113
McLean, J. Sloan
  See Gillette, Virginia M(ary)
  and Wunsch, Josephine (McLean)
McLean, Jacqueline
  See Kolosov, Jacqueline
McLean, Janet 1946- 113
McLean, Kathryn (Anderson) 1909-1966 9
McLean, Virginia Overton 1946- 90
McLean-Carr, Carol 1948- 122
McLeish, Kenneth 1940-1997 35
McLenighan, Valjean 1947- 46
  Brief entry 40
McLennan, Connie 171
McLennan, Will
  See Wisler, G(ary) Clifton
McLeod, Bob 1951- 173
McLeod, Chum 1955- 95
McLeod, Emilie Warren 1926-1982 23
  Obituary 31
McLeod, Kirsty
  See Hudson, (Margaret) Kirsty
McLeod, Margaret Vail
  See Holloway, Teresa (Bragunier)
McLerran, Alice 1933- 137
  Earlier sketch in SATA 68
McLimans, David 1949- 182
McLoughlin, John C. 1949- 47
McMahon, Bob 1956- 208
McManus, Patrick F. 1933- 46
McManus, Patrick Francis
  See McManus, Patrick F.
McMeekin, Clark
  See McMeekin, Isabel McLennan
McMeekin, Isabel McLennan 1895-1973 3
McMenemy, Sarah 1965- 156
McMillan, Bruce 1947- 192
  Earlier sketches in SATA 22, 70, 129
  See also CLR 47
McMillan, Naomi
  See Grimes, Nikki
McMorey, James L.
  See Moyer, Terry J.
McMorrow, Annalisa 1969- 104
McMullan, Jim 1934- 150
  Earlier sketch in SATA 87
McMullan, K. H.
  See McMullan, Kate
McMullan, Kate 1947- 189
  Brief entry 48
  Earlier sketches in SATA 52, 87, 132
McMullan, Kate Hall
  See McMullan, Kate
McMullan, Margaret 1960- 203
McMurtrey, Martin A(loysias) 1921- 21
McNabb, Linda 1963- 147
McNair, Kate 3
McNair, Sylvia 1924-2002 74
McNamara, Margaret C(raig) 1915-1981
  Obituary 24
McNaught, Harry 32
McNaughton, Colin 1951- 211
  Earlier sketches in SATA 39, 92, 134
  See also CLR 54
McNaughton, Janet 1953- 162
  Earlier sketch in SATA 110
McNeal, Laura 194
McNeal, Tom 194
McNeely, Jeannette 1918- 25
McNeer, May (Yonge) 1902-1994 81
  Earlier sketch in SATA 1
McNeese, Tim 1953- 139
McNeill, Janet
  See Alexander, Janet
McNicholas, Shelagh 191

McNickle, D'Arcy 1904-1977
   Obituary 22
McNickle, William D'Arcy
   See McNickle, D'Arcy
McNicoll, Sylvia (Marilyn) 1954- *113*
   See also CLR 99
McNulty, Faith 1918-2005 .... *168*
   Earlier sketches in SATA *12, 84, 139*
McPhail, David 1940- *183*
   Brief entry 32
   Earlier sketches in SATA *47, 81, 140*
McPhail, David M.
   See McPhail, David
McPhail, David Michael
   See McPhail, David
McPhee, Norma H. 1928- 95
McPhee, Richard B(yron) 1934- *41*
McPherson, James M. 1936- *141*
   Earlier sketch in SATA *16*
McPherson, James Munro
   See McPherson, James M.
McQueen, Lucinda 1950- 58
   Brief entry 48
McQueen, Mildred Hark 1908-1978 12
McQuillan, Mary 200
McRae, Russell (William) 1934- 63
McShean, Gordon 1936- 41
Mc Swigan, Marie 1907-1962 24
McTavish, Sandy
   See Eyerly, Jeannette
McVeity, Jen 148
McVey, Vicki 1946- 80
McVicker, Charles (Taggart) 1930- 39
McVicker, Chuck
   See McVicker, Charles (Taggart)
McWhirter, A(lan) Ross 1925-1975 37
   Obituary 31
McWhirter, Norris (Dewar) 1925-2004 37
McWilliams, Karen 1943- 65
Mdurvwa, Hajara E. 1962- 92
Meacham, Margaret 1952- 203
   Earlier sketch in SATA 95
Meachum, Virginia 1918- 133
   Earlier sketch in SATA 87
Mead, Alice 1952- 146
   Earlier sketch in SATA 94
Mead, Margaret 1901-1978
   Obituary 20
Mead, Russell (M., Jr.) 1935- 10
Mead, Stella (?)-1981
   Obituary 27
Meade, Ellen
   See Roddick, Ellen
Meade, Holly 207
Meade, Marion 1934- 127
   Earlier sketch in SATA 23
Meader, Stephen W(arren) 1892-1977 1
Meadmore, Susan
   See Sallis, Susan (Diana)
Meadow, Charles T(roub) 1929- 23
Meadowcroft, Enid LaMonte
   See Wright, Enid Meadowcroft (LaMonte)
Meadows, Graham (W.) 1934- *161*
Meadows, Michelle 202
Meaker, M. J.
   See Meaker, Marijane
Meaker, Marijane 1927- *160*
   Autobiography Feature *111*
   Earlier sketches in SATA *20, 61, 99*
   See also CLR 29
   See also SAAS 1
Meaker, Marijane Agnes
   See Meaker, Marijane
Means, Florence Crannell 1891-1980 1
   Obituary 25
   See also CLR 56
Mearian, Judy Frank 1936- 49
Mecca, Judy Truesdell 1955- 127
Mechling, Lauren 1978(?)- 194
Mechling, Lauren 1978(?)- 194
Mechner, Jordan 1964- 205

Medary, Marjorie 1890-1980 .... *14*
Meddaugh, Susan 1944- *176*
   Earlier sketches in SATA *29, 84, 125*
Medearis, Angela Shelf 1956- *123*
   Earlier sketch in SATA *72*
Medearis, Mary 1915- 5
Medina, Jane 1953- *167*
   Earlier sketch in SATA *122*
Medina, Nico 1982- *193*
Medlicott, Mary 1946- 88
Mee, Charles L., Jr. 1938- 72
   Earlier sketch in SATA *8*
Meehl, Brian 204
Meek, Jacklyn O'Hanlon 1933- 51
   Brief entry 34
Meek, S(terner St.) P(aul) 1894-1972
   Obituary 28
Meeker, Clare Hodgson 1952- 96
Meeker, Oden 1919(?)-1976 .... *14*
Meeker, Richard
   See Brown, Fornan
Meeks, Esther MacBain *1*
Meggs, Libby Phillips 1943- *130*
Mehdevi, Alexander (Sinclair) 1947- 7
Mehdevi, Anne (Marie) Sinclair 1947- 8
Meidell, Sherry 1951- 73
Meier, Minta 1906- 55
Meighan, Donald Charles 1929- 30
Meigs, Cornelia Lynde 1884-1973 6
   See also CLR 55
Meilach, Dona Z(weigoron) 1926- 34
Meilman, Philip W(arren) 1951- 79
Meinstereifel, Ronald L. 1960- *134*
Meisel, Paul *184*
Meister, Cari 204
Melanson, Luc 198
Melcher, Daniel 1912-1985
   Obituary 43
Melcher, Frederic Gershom 1879-1963
   Obituary 22
Melcher, Marguerite Fellows 1879-1969 .... *10*
Meldrum, Christina 206
Melendez, Francisco 1964- 72
Melhuish, Eva 199
Melin, Grace Hathaway 1892-1973 .... *10*
Mellersh, H(arold) E(dward) L(eslie)
   1897- *10*
Melling, David *186*
Melmoth, Sebastian
   See Wilde, Oscar
Melnikoff, Pamela (Rita) 97
Meltzer, Amy 1968- 202
Meltzer, Milton 1915-2009 201
   Autobiography Feature *124*
   Earlier sketches in SATA *1, 50, 80, 128*
   See also CLR 13
   See also SAAS 1
Melville, Anne
   See Potter, Margaret
Melville, Herman 1819-1891 59
Melwood, Mary
   See Lewis, E. M.
Melzack, Ronald 1929- 5
Memling, Carl 1918-1969 6
Menchin, Scott *188*
Mendel, Jo
   See Bond, Gladys Baker
   and Gilbertson, Mildred Geiger
Mendelson, Steven T. 1958-1995 86
Mendelson-Stevens, Serita Deborah
   See Stevens, Serita
Mendes, Valerie 1939- *157*
Mendez, Raymond A. 1947- 66
Mendonca, Susan
   See Smith, Susan Vernon
Mendoza, George 1934- 41
   Brief entry 39
   See also SAAS 7
Menendez, Shirley (C.) 1937- 146
Meng, Cece 194
Meng, Heinz (Karl) 1924- *13*

Mennen, Ingrid 1954- 85
Menotti, Gian Carlo 1911-2007 29
   Obituary *180*
Menuhin, Sir Yehudi 1916-1999 .... *40*
   Obituary *113*
Menville, Douglas 1935- 64
Menzel, Barbara Jean 1946- 63
Menzel, Peter 1948- 207
Mercati, Cynthia *164*
Mercati, Cynthia J.
   See Mercati, Cynthia
Mercer, Charles (Edward) 1917-1988 .... *16*
   Obituary *61*
Mercer, Jessie 21
Mercer, Sienna *192*
Meredith, Arnold
   See Hopkins, (Hector) Kenneth
Meredith, David William
   See Miers, Earl Schenck
Meringoff, Laurene Krasny
   See Brown, Laurene Krasny
Meriwether, Louise 1923- 52
   Brief entry 31
Merlin, Arthur
   See Blish, James
Merlin, Christina
   See Heaven, Constance (Christina)
Merriam, Eve 1916-1992 73
   Earlier sketches in SATA *3, 40*
   See also CLR 14
Merrill, Jane 1946- *42*
Merrill, Jane Merrill
   See Merrill, Jane
Merrill, Jean (Fairbanks) 1923- 82
   Earlier sketch in SATA *1*
   See also CLR 52
Merrill, Phil
   See Merrill, Jane
Merriman, Alex
   See Silverberg, Robert
Merriman, Rachel 1971- *149*
   Earlier sketch in SATA *98*
Merrit, Elizabeth
   See Goudge, Eileen
Merski, Patricia K.
   See Merski, P.K.
Merski, P.K. *172*
Mertz, Barbara
   See Peters, Elizabeth
Mertz, Barbara Gross
   See Peters, Elizabeth
Merveille, David 200
Merz, Jennifer J. *196*
Meschel, Susan V. 1936- 83
Meserve, Jessica 211
Messenger, Charles (Rynd Milles) 1942- 59
Messick, Dale 1906-2005 64
   Brief entry 48
Messier, Claire 1956- *103*
Messieres, Nicole de
   See de Messieres, Nicole
Messinger, Carla 198
Messmer, Otto 1892(?)-1983 37
Mesta, Gabriel
   See Moesta, Rebecca
Metaxas, Eric 1963- 211
Metcalf, Doris H(unter) 91
Metcalf, Suzanne
   See Baum, L. Frank
Metos, Thomas H(arry) 1932- *37*
Metter, Bert(ram Milton) 1927- 56
Metzenthen, David 1958- *167*
   Earlier sketch in SATA *106*
Meunier, Brian 1954- 195
Meyer, Barbara 1939- 77
Meyer, Carolyn 1935- *142*
   Autobiography Feature *142*
   Earlier sketches in SATA *9, 70, 118*
   See also SAAS 9
Meyer, Carolyn Mae
   See Meyer, Carolyn

Meyer, Edith Patterson 1895-1993 5
Meyer, F(ranklyn) E(dward) 1932- 9
Meyer, Jean Shepherd 11
Meyer, Jerome Sydney 1895-1975 3
　Obituary 25
Meyer, June
　See Jordan, June
Meyer, Kerstin 1966- 190
Meyer, L. A.
　See Meyer, Louis A(lbert), Jr.
Meyer, Louis A(lbert), Jr. 1942- 144
　Earlier sketch in SATA 12
Meyer, Renate 1930- 6
Meyer, Stephenie 1973- 193
　See also CLR 142
Meyer, Susan E. 1940- 64
Meyerhoff, Jenny 1972- 208
Meyers, Susan 1942- 164
　Earlier sketches in SATA 19, 108
Meynell, Laurence Walter 1899-1989
　Obituary 61
Meynier, Yvonne (Pollet) 1908- 14
Mezey, Robert 1935- 33
Micale, Albert 1913- 22
Michael, James
　See Scagnetti, Jack
Michael, Livi 1960- 172
Michael, Manfred
　See Winterfeld, Henry
Michael, Olivia
　See Michael, Livi
Michaels, Barbara
　See Peters, Elizabeth
Michaels, Jamie 195
Michaels, Joanne Louise
　See Teitelbaum, Michael
Michaels, Kristin
　See Williams, Jeanne
Michaels, Molly
　See Untermeyer, Louis
Michaels, Neal
　See Teitelbaum, Michael
Michaels, Rune 194
Michaels, Ski
　See Pellowski, Michael (Joseph)
Michaels, Steve 1955- 71
Michaels, William M. 1917- 77
Michel, Anna 1943- 49
　Brief entry 40
Michel, Francois 1948- 82
Michelin, Linda 183
Michelson, Richard 198
　Earlier sketch in SATA 173
Micich, Paul 74
Micklish, Rita 1931- 12
Micklos, John, Jr. 1956- 173
　Earlier sketch in SATA 129
Micklos J., John, Jr. 1956-
　See Micklos, John, Jr.
Micucci, Charles (Patrick, Jr.) 1959- 144
　Earlier sketch in SATA 82
Middleton, Haydn 1955- 152
　Earlier sketch in SATA 85
Miers, Earl Schenck 1910-1972 1
　Obituary 26
Migdale, Lawrence 1951- 89
Miglio, Paige 1966- 201
Mikaelsen, Ben 1952- 173
　Earlier sketches in SATA 73, 107
Mikaelsen, Benjamin John
　See Mikaelsen, Ben
Miklowitz, Gloria D. 1927- 129
　Earlier sketches in SATA 4, 68
　See also SAAS 17
Mikolaycak, Charles 1937-1993 78
　Obituary 75
　Earlier sketch in SATA 9
　See also SAAS 4
Mild, Warren (Paul) 1922- 41
Milelli, Pascal 1965- 135

Miles, Betty 1928- 78
　Earlier sketch in SATA 8
　See also SAAS 9
Miles, Miska
　See Martin, Patricia Miles
Miles, (Mary) Patricia 1930- 29
Miles, Patricia A.
　See Martin, Patricia Miles
Miles, Victoria 1966- 188
Milgrim, David 187
　Earlier sketch in SATA 158
Milgrom, Harry 1912-1978 25
Milhous, Katherine 1894-1977 15
Milich, Zoran 174
Milios, Rita 1949- 79
Militant
　See Sandburg, Carl
Millais, Raoul 1901- 77
Millar, Barbara F. 1924- 12
Millar, Margaret (Ellis Sturm) 1915-1994 .. 61
　Obituary 79
Millard, Glenda 203
Millard, Kerry 204
Millbank, Captain H. R.
　See Ellis, Edward S.
Millen, C(ynthia) M. 1955- 114
Miller, Albert G(riffith) 1905-1982 12
　Obituary 31
Miller, Alice Ann 1958- 150
Miller, Alice P(atricia McCarthy) 22
Miller, Debbie 1951- 160
　Earlier sketch in SATA 103
Miller, Debbie S.
　See Miller, Debbie
Miller, Deborah Uchill 1944- 61
Miller, Don 1923- 15
Miller, Doris R.
　See Mosesson, Gloria R(ubin)
Miller, Eddie
　See Miller, Edward
Miller, Edna Anita 1920- 29
Miller, Edward 1905-1974 8
Miller, Edward 1964- 183
Miller, Elizabeth 1933- 41
Miller, Ellanita 1957- 87
Miller, Eugene 1925- 33
Miller, Frances A. 1937- 52
　Brief entry 46
Miller, Helen M(arkley) -1984 5
Miller, Helen Topping 1884-1960
　Obituary 29
Miller, Jane (Judith) 1925-1989 15
Miller, Jewel 1956- 73
Miller, John
　See Samachson, Joseph
Miller, Judi 117
Miller, Karen 1949- 210
Miller, Karen Hokanson
　See Miller, Karen
Miller, Kate 1948- 193
Miller, Kirsten 1973- 185
Miller, Louise (Rolfe) 1940- 76
Miller, M. L. 85
Miller, Madge 1918- 63
Miller, Margaret J.
　See Dale, Margaret J(essy) Miller
Miller, Marilyn (Jean) 1925- 33
Miller, Marvin 65
Miller, Mary
　See Northcott, (William) Cecil
Miller, Mary Beth 1942- 9
Miller, Mary Beth 1964- 185
Miller, Maryann 1943- 73
Miller, Natalie 1917-1976 35
Miller, Robert H. 1944- 91
Miller, Ron 1947- 185
Miller, Ruth White
　See White, Ruth C.
Miller, Sandra
　See Miller, Sandy

Miller, Sandra Peden
　See Miller, Sandy
Miller, Sandy 1948- 41
　Brief entry 35
Miller, Sarah 1969- 175
Miller, Virginia
　See Austin, Virginia
Miller, William R. 1959- 116
Milligan, Bryce 1953- 170
Milligan, Spike
　See Milligan, Terence Alan
Milligan, Terence Alan 1918-2002 29
　Obituary 134
　See also CLR 92
Millington, Ada
　See Deyneka, Anita
Millman, Isaac 1933- 140
Mills, Adam
　See Stanley, George Edward
Mills, Claudia 1954- 191
　Brief entry 41
　Earlier sketches in SATA 44, 89, 145
Mills, Elaine (Rosemary) 1941- 72
Mills, G. Riley 196
Mills, Joyce C. 1944- 102
Mills, Judith Christine 1956- 130
Mills, Yaroslava Surmach 1925- 35
Millspaugh, Ben P. 1936- 77
Millstead, Thomas E. 30
Millward, Gwen 202
Milne, A. A. 1882-1956 100
　See also YABC 1
　See also CLR 108
Milne, Alan Alexander
　See Milne, A. A.
Milne, Lorus J. 5
　See also CLR 22
　See also SAAS 18
Milne, Margery 5
　See also CLR 22
　See also SAAS 18
Milne, Terry
　See Milne, Theresa Ann
Milne, Theresa Ann 1964- 84
Milnes, Irma McDonough 1924- 101
Milonas, Rolf
　See Myller, Rolf
Milone, Karen
　See Dugan, Karen
Milone-Dugan, Karen
　See Dugan, Karen
Milord, Susan 1954- 200
　Earlier sketches in SATA 74, 147
Milotte, Alfred G(eorge) 1904-1989 11
　Obituary 62
Milstein, Linda 1954- 80
Milton, Ann 134
Milton, Hilary (Herbert) 1920- 23
Milton, John R(onald) 1924- 24
Milton, Joyce 1946- 101
　Brief entry 41
　Earlier sketch in SATA 52
Milverton, Charles A.
　See Penzler, Otto
Milway, Katie Smith 1960- 203
Minahan, John A. 1956- 92
Minar, Barbra (Goodyear) 1940- 79
Minard, Rosemary 1939- 63
Minarik, Else Holmelund 1920- 127
　Earlier sketch in SATA 15
　See also CLR 33
Miner, Jane Claypool 1933- 103
　Brief entry 37
　Earlier sketch in SATA 38
Miner, Lewis S. 1909-1971 11
Mines, Jeanette 1948- 61
Mines, Jeanette Marie
　See Mines, Jeanette
Minier, Nelson
　See Stoutenburg, Adrien (Pearl)

Minnitt, Ronda Jacqueline
　See Armitage, David
Minor, Wendell 1944- 199
　Earlier sketches in SATA 78, 109, 164
Minter, Daniel 1961- 176
Mintonye, Grace 4
Miranda, Anne 1954- 109
　Earlier sketch in SATA 71
Miranda, Inaki 1983(?)- 207
Mirocha, Paul 192
Mirsky, Jeannette 1903-1987 8
　Obituary 51
Mirsky, Reba Paeff 1902-1966 1
Misako Rocks! 192
Mishica, Clare 1960- 91
Miskovits, Christine 1939- 10
Miss Frances
　See Horwich, Frances R(appaport)
Miss Read
　See Saint, Dora Jessie
Mister Rogers
　See Rogers, Fred McFeely
Mitchard, Jacquelyn 1956- 168
　Earlier sketch in SATA 98
Mitchell, Adrian 1932-2008 166
　Obituary 200
　Earlier sketch in SATA 104
Mitchell, Allison
　See Griffin, W.E.B.
Mitchell, Betty Jo
　See Mitchell, B.J.
Mitchell, B.J. 1931- 120
Mitchell, Clyde
　See Ellison, Harlan
　and Silverberg, Robert
Mitchell, Cynthia 1922- 29
Mitchell, (Sibyl) Elyne (Keith) 1913- 10
Mitchell, Gladys (Maude Winifred)
　1901-1983 46
　Obituary 35
Mitchell, Jay
　See Roberson, Jennifer
Mitchell, Joyce Slayton 1933- 142
　Brief entry 43
　Earlier sketch in SATA 46
Mitchell, K. L.
　See Lamb, Elizabeth Searle
Mitchell, Kathy 1948- 59
Mitchell, Lori 1961- 128
Mitchell, Margaree King 1953- 84
Mitchell, Marianne 1947- 145
Mitchell, Rhonda 89
Mitchell, Stephen 1943- 199
Mitchell, Susan
　See Mitchell, Susan K.
Mitchell, Susan K. 1972- 210
Mitchell, Todd 1974- 191
Mitchell, Yvonne 1925-1979
　Obituary 24
Mitchelson, Mitch
　See Mitchelson, Peter Richard
Mitchelson, Peter Richard 1950- 104
Mitchison, Naomi (Margaret Haldane)
　1897-1999 24
　Obituary 112
Mitchnik, Helen 1901-1982 41
　Brief entry 35
Mitchum, Hank
　See Knott, William C(ecil, Jr.)
　and Murray, Stuart A. P.
　and Newton, D(wight) B(ennett)
　and Sherman, Jory (Tecumseh)
Mitgutsch, Ali 1935- 76
Mitsuhashi, Yoko 45
　Brief entry 33
Mitton, Jacqueline 1948- 162
　Earlier sketches in SATA 66, 115
Mitton, Simon 1946- 66
Mitton, Tony 1951- 203
　Earlier sketches in SATA 104, 149
Miura, Taro 1968- 181

Mizner, Elizabeth Howard 1907- 27
Mizumura, Kazue 18
Mlynowski, Sarah 1977(?)- 180
Mobin-Uddin, Asma 172
Mobley, Joe A. 1945- 91
Moche, Dinah (Rachel) L(evine) 1936- 44
　Brief entry 40
Mochi, Ugo (A.) 1889-1977 38
Mochizuki, Ken 1954- 146
　Earlier sketch in SATA 81
　See also SAAS 22
Modarressi, Mitra 1967- 200
　Earlier sketch in SATA 126
Modell, Frank B. 1917- 39
　Brief entry 36
Modesitt, Jeanne 1953- 143
　Earlier sketch in SATA 92
Modesitt, L.E., Jr. 1943- 164
　Earlier sketch in SATA 91
Modesitt, Leland Exton, Jr.
　See Modesitt, L.E., Jr.
Modrell, Dolores 1933- 72
Moe, Barbara 1937- 20
Moe, Jorgen (Ingebretsen) 1813-1882
　See CLR 104
Moed-Kass, Pnina 169
Moerbeek, Kees 1955- 98
Moeri, Louise 1924- 93
　Earlier sketch in SATA 24
　See also SAAS 10
Moesta, Rebecca 1956- 182
Moffett, Jami 1952- 84
Moffett, Mark W. 1957(?)- 203
Moffett, Martha (Leatherwood) 1934- 8
Mogensen, Suzanne A(ncher) 1946- 129
Mohammed, Khadra 197
Mohn, Peter B(urnet) 1934- 28
Mohn, Viola Kohl 1914- 8
Mohr, Nicholasa 1938- 97
　Autobiography Feature 113
　Earlier sketch in SATA 8
　See also CLR 22
　See also SAAS 8
Mok, Esther 1953- 93
Molan, Christine 1943- 84
Molarsky, Osmond 1909- 16
Moldon, Peter L(eonard) 1937- 49
Mole, John 1941- 103
　Earlier sketch in SATA 36
　See also CLR 61
Molesworth, Mary Louisa 1839-1921 98
Molin, Charles
　See Mayne, William (James Carter)
Molina, Silvia 1946- 97
Molk, Laurel 1957- 162
　Earlier sketch in SATA 92
Mollel, Tololwa M. 1952- 88
Molloy, Anne Baker 1907-1999 32
Molloy, Michael (John) 1940- 162
Molloy, Paul (George) 1924- 5
Moloney, James 1954- 202
　Autobiography Feature 144
　Earlier sketches in SATA 94, 144
Momaday, N. Scott 1934- 48
　Brief entry 30
Momaday, Navarre Scott
　See Momaday, N. Scott
Monaco, Octavia 1963- 169
Monagle, Bernie 1957- 121
Moncure, Jane Belk 1926- 23
Monjo, F(erdinand) N(icholas III)
　1924-1978 16
　See also CLR 2
Monk, Isabell 1952- 136
Monks, Lydia 189
Monroe, Lyle
　See Heinlein, Robert A.
Monroe, Marion
　See Cox, Marion Monroe
Monroy, Manuel 1970- 196
Monsell, Helen Albee 1895-1971 24

Monson-Burton, Marianne 1975- 139
Montana, Bob 1920-1975
　Obituary 21
Montanari, Eva 1977- 209
Montecalvo, Janet 177
Montenegro, Laura Nyman 1953- 95
Montero, Gloria 1933- 109
Montes, Marisa 1951- 144
Montgomerie, Norah (Mary) 1913- 26
Montgomery, Constance
　See Cappel, Constance
Montgomery, Elizabeth
　See Julesberg, Elizabeth Rider Montgomery
Montgomery, Elizabeth Rider
　See Julesberg, Elizabeth Rider Montgomery
Montgomery, Hugh (Edward) 1962- 146
Montgomery, L. M. 1874-1942 100
　See also YABC 1
　See also CLR 145
Montgomery, Lucy Maud
　See Montgomery, L. M.
Montgomery, Michael G. 1952- 208
Montgomery, Raymond A. (Jr.) 1936- 39
Montgomery, Rutherford George
　1894-1985 3
Montgomery, Sy 1958- 184
　Autobiography Feature 132
　Earlier sketches in SATA 114, 132
Montgomery, Vivian 36
Monthei, Betty 179
Montijo, Rhode 179
Montileaux, Donald F. 1948- 183
Montpetit, Charles 1958- 101
Montresor, Beni 1926-2001 38
　Earlier sketch in SATA 3
　See also SAAS 4
Montserrat, Pep 181
Monty Python
　See Chapman, Graham
　and Cleese, John (Marwood)
　and Gilliam, Terry
　and Idle, Eric
　and Jones, Terence Graham Parry
　and Palin, Michael
Moodie, Craig 1956- 172
Moodie, Fiona 1952- 133
Moody, Minerva
　See Alcott, Louisa May
Moody, Ralph Owen 1898-1982 1
Moon, Carl 1879(?)-1948 25
Moon, Grace (Purdie) 1877(?)-1947 25
Moon, Lily
　See Warnes, Tim
Moon, Nicola 1952- 147
　Earlier sketch in SATA 96
Moon, Pat 1946- 113
Moon, Sheila 1910-1991 5
　Obituary 114
Moon, Sheila Elizabeth
　See Moon, Sheila
Mooney, Bel 1946- 95
Mooney, Bill 1936- 122
Mooney, Elizabeth C(omstock) 1918-1986
　Obituary 48
Mooney, William
　See Mooney, Bill
Moor, Emily
　See Deming, Richard
Moorcock, Michael 1939- 166
　Earlier sketch in SATA 93
Moorcock, Michael John
　See Moorcock, Michael
Moorcock, Michael John
　See Moorcock, Michael
Moore, Anne Carroll 1871-1961 13
Moore, Cheri
　See Ladd, Cheryl (Jean)
Moore, Clement Clarke 1779-1863 18
Moore, Cyd 1957- 186
　Earlier sketches in SATA 83, 133

Moore, Don W. 1905(?)-1986
  Obituary 48
Moore, Elaine 1944- 86
Moore, Eva 1942- 103
  Earlier sketch in SATA 20
Moore, Ishbel (Lindsay) 1954- 140
Moore, Jack (William) 1941- 46
  Brief entry 32
Moore, Janet Gaylord 1905-1992 18
Moore, Jim 1946- 42
Moore, John Travers 1908- 12
Moore, Lilian 1909-2004 137
  Obituary 155
  Earlier sketch in SATA 52
  See also CLR 15
Moore, Liz
  See Moore, M. Elizabeth
Moore, M. Elizabeth 1959- 156
Moore, Margaret R(umberger) 1903- 12
Moore, Margie 176
Moore, Marianne 1887-1972 20
Moore, Marianne Craig
  See Moore, Marianne
Moore, Patrick (Alfred Caldwell) 1923- 49
  Brief entry 39
  See also SAAS 8
Moore, Patrick 1959- 184
Moore, Perry 193
Moore, Peter 1963- 175
Moore, Peter G.
  See Moore, Peter
Moore, Ray (S.) 1905(?)-1984
  Obituary 37
Moore, Regina
  See Dunne, Mary Collins
Moore, Rosalie (Gertrude) 1910-2001 9
Moore, Ruth (Ellen) 1908-1989 23
Moore, Ruth Nulton 1923- 38
Moore, S(arah) E. 23
Moore, Sarah Margaret
  See Hodges, Margaret
Moore, Tara 1950- 61
Moore, Yvette 1958- 154
  Earlier sketches in SATA 69, 70
Moores, Dick
  See Moores, Richard (Arnold)
Moores, Richard (Arnold) 1909-1986
  Obituary 48
Mooser, Stephen 1941- 75
  Earlier sketch in SATA 28
Mora, Francisco X(avier) 1952- 90
Mora, Pat 1942- 186
  Earlier sketches in SATA 92, 134
  See also CLR 58
Mora, Patricia
  See Mora, Pat
Morais, Flavio 207
Morales, Yuyi 180
  Earlier sketch in SATA 154
Moran, Tom 1943- 60
Moranville, Sharelle Byars 196
  Earlier sketch in SATA 152
Moray Williams, Ursula 1911-2006 3
  Obituary 177
  See also SAAS 9
Morden, Simon 1966(?)- 211
Mordvinoff, Nicolas 1911-1973 17
More, Caroline
  See Cone, Molly (Lamken)
  and Strachan, Margaret Pitcairn
Moreno, Rene King 190
Moreton, Andrew Esq.
  See Defoe, Daniel
Morey, Charles
  See Fletcher, Helen Jill
Morey, Walt(er Nelson) 1907-1992 51
  Obituary 70
  Earlier sketch in SATA 3
  See also SAAS 9
Morgan, Alfred P(owell) 1889-1972 33

Morgan, Alison (Mary) 1930- 85
  Earlier sketch in SATA 30
Morgan, Anne 1954- 121
Morgan, Christopher 1956- 199
Morgan, Clay 1950- 198
Morgan, Douglas
  See Macdonald, James D.
Morgan, Ellen
  See Bumstead, Kathleen Mary
Morgan, Geoffrey 1916- 46
Morgan, Helen (Gertrude Louise)
  1921-1990 29
Morgan, Jane
  See Cooper, James Fenimore
  and Franklin, Jane (Morgan)
  and Moren, Sally M(oore)
Morgan, Lenore H. 1908-1976 8
Morgan, Mary 1957- 114
  Earlier sketch in SATA 81
Morgan, McKayla
  See Basile, Gloria Vitanza
Morgan, Michaela
  See Basile, Gloria Vitanza
Morgan, Nicola 1961- 161
Morgan, Nina 1953- 110
Morgan, Pierr 1952- 122
  Earlier sketch in SATA 77
Morgan, Robin (Evonne) 1941- 80
Morgan, Roxanne
  See Gentle, Mary
Morgan, Sarah (Nicola) 1959- 68
Morgan, Shirley
  See Kiepper, Shirley Morgan
Morgan, Stacy T(owle) 1959- 104
Morgan, Stevie
  See Davies, Nicola
Morgan, Tom 1942- 42
Morgan, Wendy
  See Staub, Wendy Corsi
Morgan-Vanroyen, Mary
  See Morgan, Mary
Morgenstern, Susie Hoch 1945- 133
Mori, Hana 1909-1990(?) 88
Mori, Kyoko 1957- 122
  Autobiography Feature 126
  See also CLR 64
  See also SAAS 26
Moriarty, Jaclyn 162
Moriarty, William J. 1930- 127
Morice, Dave 1946- 93
Morin, Isobel V. 1928- 110
Morine, Hoder
  See Conroy, John Wesley
Morley, Taia 199
Morley, Wilfred Owen
  See Lowndes, Robert A(ugustine) W(ard)
Morningstar, Mildred (Whaley)
  1912-1997 61
  Obituary 114
Morozumi, Atsuko 110
Morpurgo, Michael 1943- 184
  Earlier sketches in SATA 93, 143
  See also CLR 51
Morrah, Dave
  See Morrah, David Wardlaw, Jr.
Morrah, David Wardlaw, Jr. 1914-1991 10
Morreale-de la Garza, Phyllis
  See De la Garza, Phyllis
Morressy, John 1930-2006 23
Morrill, Leslie H(olt) 1934-2003 48
  Brief entry 33
  Obituary 148
  See also SAAS 22
Morris, Carla 210
Morris, Carla D.
  See Morris, Carla
Morris, Chris(topher Crosby) 1946- 66
Morris, Deborah 1956- 91
Morris, Desmond 1928- 14
Morris, Desmond John
  See Morris, Desmond

Morris, Don 1954- 83
Morris, Gerald 1963- 207
  Earlier sketches in SATA 107, 150
Morris, Gerald Paul
  See Morris, Gerald
Morris, Gilbert (Leslie) 1929- 104
Morris, Jackie 202
  Earlier sketch in SATA 151
Morris, Janet (Ellen) 1946- 66
Morris, Jay
  See Tatham, Julie Campbell
Morris, (Margaret) Jean 1924- 98
Morris, Jeffrey B(randon) 1941- 92
Morris, Jennifer E. 1969- 179
Morris, Jill 1936- 165
  Earlier sketch in SATA 119
Morris, Juddi 85
Morris, Judy K. 1936- 61
Morris, Oradel Nolen 128
Morris, Robert A(da) 1933- 7
Morris, William 1913-1994 29
Morrison, Bill 1935- 66
  Brief entry 37
Morrison, Chloe Anthony Wofford
  See Morrison, Toni
Morrison, Dorothy Nafus 29
Morrison, Frank 1971- 185
Morrison, Gordon 1944- 183
  Earlier sketches in SATA 87, 128
Morrison, Joan 1922- 65
Morrison, Lillian 1917- 108
  Earlier sketch in SATA 3
Morrison, Lucile Phillips 1896- 17
Morrison, Martha A. 1948- 77
Morrison, Meighan 1966- 90
Morrison, P.R. 196
Morrison, Richard
  See Lowndes, Robert A(ugustine) W(ard)
Morrison, Robert
  See Lowndes, Robert A(ugustine) W(ard)
Morrison, Roberta
  See Webb, Jean Francis (III)
Morrison, Susan Dudley
  See Gold, Susan Dudley
Morrison, Taylor 1971- 187
  Earlier sketches in SATA 95, 159
Morrison, Toni 1931- 144
  Earlier sketch in SATA 57
  See also CLR 99
Morrison, Velma Ford 1909- 21
Morrison, Wilbur Howard 1915- 64
Morrison, William
  See Samachson, Joseph
Morriss, James E(dward) 1932- 8
Morrissey, Dean 183
Morrow, Barbara Olenyik 1952- 167
Morrow, Betty
  See Bacon, Elizabeth
Morse, C. Scott
  See Morse, Scott
Morse, Carol
  See Yeakley, Marjory Hall
Morse, C.S.
  See Morse, Scott
Morse, Dorothy B(ayley) 1906-1979
  Obituary 24
Morse, Flo 1921- 30
Morse, Scott 1973- 200
Morse, Tony 1953- 129
Mort, Vivian
  See Cromie, Alice Hamilton
Mortensen, Denise Dowling 179
Mortimer, Anne 1958- 206
  Earlier sketch in SATA 116
Mortimer, Mary H.
  See Coury, Louise Andree
Morton, Alexandra (Hubbard) 1957- 144
Morton, Anthony
  See Arthur, Robert, (Jr.)
Morton, Christine
  See Morton-Shaw, Christine

Morton, Jane 1931- 50
Morton, Joseph C. 1932- 156
Morton, Lee Jack, Jr. 1928- 32
Morton, Miriam 1918(?)-1985 9
    Obituary 46
Morton-Shaw, Christine 1957- 211
Mosatche, Harriet
    See Mosatche, Harriet
Mosatche, Harriet 1949- 122
Moscow, Alvin 1925- 3
Mosel, Arlene (Tichy) 1921-1996 7
Moseley, James W(illett) 1931- 139
Moseng, Elisabeth 1967- 90
Moser, Barry 1940- 185
    Earlier sketches in SATA *56, 79, 138*
    See also CLR *49*
    See also SAAS *15*
Moser, Don(ald Bruce) 1932- 31
Moser, Laura 194
Moser, Lisa 192
Moses, Sheila P. 1961- 168
Moses, Will 1956- 178
    Earlier sketch in SATA *120*
Mosesson, Gloria R(ubin) 24
Mosher, Richard 1949- 120
Moskin, Marietta D(unston) 1928- 23
Moskof, Martin Stephen 1930- 27
Mosley, Francis 1957- 57
Moss, Don(ald) 1920- 11
Moss, Elaine (Dora) 1924- 57
    Brief entry 31
Moss, Jeff(rey) 1942-1998 73
    Obituary 106
Moss, Marissa 1959- 163
    Earlier sketches in SATA *71, 104*
    See also CLR *134*
Moss, Miriam 1955- 202
    Earlier sketches in SATA *76, 140*
Moss, Thylias 1954- 108
Moss, Thylias Rebecca Brasier
    See Moss, Thylias
Most, Bernard 1937- 134
    Brief entry 40
    Earlier sketches in SATA *48, 91*
Mosz, Gosia 1972- 194
Mott, Evelyn Clarke 1962- 133
    Earlier sketch in SATA *75*
Motz, Lloyd 1909-2004 20
Mould, Chris 205
Mould, Edwin
    See Whitlock, Ralph
Mouly, Francoise 155
Mountain, Robert
    See Montgomery, Raymond A. (Jr.)
Mountfield, David
    See Grant, Neil
Mourlevat, Jean-Claude 1952- 187
Mourning, Tuesday 206
Moussard, Jacqueline 1924- 24
Mowat, Claire 1933- 123
Mowat, Claire Angel Wheeler
    See Mowat, Claire
Mowat, Farley 1921- 55
    Earlier sketch in SATA *3*
    See also CLR *20*
Mowat, Farley McGill
    See Mowat, Farley
Mowll, Joshua 1970(?)- 188
Mowry, Jess 1960- 131
    Autobiography Feature 131
    Earlier sketch in SATA *109*
    See also CLR *65*
Moxley, Sheila 1966- 96
Moyer, Terry J. 1937- 94
Moyes, Patricia
    See Haszard, Patricia Moyes
Moyler, Alan (Frank Powell) 1926- 36
Mozelle, Shirley 179
Mozley, Charles 1915- 43
    Brief entry 32

Mphahlele, Es'kia 1919-2008 119
    Obituary 198
Mphahlele, Ezekiel
    See Mphahlele, Es'kia
Mphahlele, Zeke
    See Mphahlele, Es'kia
Mr. McGillicuddy
    See Abisch, Roslyn Kroop
Mr. Sniff
    See Abisch, Roslyn Kroop
Mr. Tivil
    See Lorkowski, Thomas V(incent)
Mr. Wizard
    See Herbert, Don
Mrs. Fairstar
    See Horne, Richard Henry Hengist
Muchamore, Robert 1972- 175
Muchmore, Jo Ann 1937- 103
Mude, O.
    See Gorey, Edward (St. John)
Mudgeon, Apeman
    See Mitchell, Adrian
Mueller, Jorg 1942- 67
    See also CLR *43*
Mueller, Miranda R. 201
Mueller, Virginia 1924- 28
Muggs
    See Watkins, Lois
Muir, Diana
    See Appelbaum, Diana Muir Karter
Muir, Frank (Herbert) 1920-1998 30
Muir, Helen 1937- 65
Mukerji, Dhan Gopal 1890-1936 40
    See also CLR *10*
Mulcahy, Lucille Burnett 12
Mulford, Philippa G. 1948- 112
    Earlier sketch in SATA *43*
Mulford, Philippa Greene
    See Mulford, Philippa G.
Mulgan, Catherine 1931- 24
Mulila, Vigad G.
    See Maillu, David G(ian)
Mull, Brandon 1974- 190
Mullen, Michael 1937- 122
Muller, Billex
    See Ellis, Edward S.
Muller, Jorg
    See Mueller, Jorg
Muller, (Lester) Robin 1953- 86
Mullin, Caryl Cude 1969- 130
Mullins, Edward S(wift) 1922- 10
Mullins, Hilary 1962- 84
Mulock, Dinah Maria
    See Craik, Dinah Maria (Mulock)
Mulvihill, William Patrick 1923- 8
Mumford, Ruth
    See Dallas, Ruth
Mumy, Bill 1954- 112
Mun
    See Leaf, (Wilbur) Munro
Munari, Bruno 1907-1998 15
    See also CLR *9*
Munce, Ruth Hill 1898- 12
Mundy, Simon 1954- 64
Mundy, Simon Andrew James Hainault
    See Mundy, Simon
Munger, Nancy 170
Munowitz, Ken 1935-1977 14
Munoz, Claudio 208
Munoz, William 1949- 92
    Earlier sketch in SATA *42*
Munro, Alice 1931- 29
Munro, Alice Anne
    See Munro, Alice
Munro, Eleanor 1928- 37
Munro, Roxie 1945- 184
    Earlier sketches in SATA *58, 136*
Munsch, Bob
    See Munsch, Robert (Norman)

Munsch, Robert (Norman) 1945- 120
    Brief entry 48
    Earlier sketches in SATA *50, 83*
    See also CLR *19*
Munsinger, Lynn 1951- 177
    Earlier sketches in SATA *33, 94*
Munson, Derek 1970- 139
Munson, R. W.
    See Karl, Jean E(dna)
Munson-Benson, Tunie 1946- 15
Munsterberg, Peggy 1921- 102
Muntean, Michaela 182
Munthe, Nelly 1947- 53
Munves, James (Albert) 1922- 30
Munzer, Martha E. 1899-1999 4
Murawski, Darlyne A. 193
Murch, Mel
    See Manes, Stephen
Murdoch, David H(amilton) 1937- 96
Murdoch, Patricia 1957- 192
Murdock, Catherine Gilbert 185
Murhall, J(acqueline) J(ane) 1964- 143
Murphy, Barbara Beasley 1933- 130
    Earlier sketch in SATA *5*
Murphy, Claire Rudolf 1951- 137
    Earlier sketch in SATA *76*
Murphy, E(mmett) Jefferson 1926- 4
Murphy, Elizabeth Ann Maureen
    See Murphy, Liz
Murphy, Jill (Frances) 1949- 142
    Earlier sketches in SATA *37, 70*
    See also CLR *39*
Murphy, Jim 1947- 185
    Brief entry 32
    Earlier sketches in SATA *37, 77, 124*
    See also CLR *53*
Murphy, Joseph E., Jr. 1930- 65
Murphy, Kelly 1977- 190
    Earlier sketch in SATA *143*
Murphy, Liz 1964- 210
Murphy, Louise 1943- 155
Murphy, Mary 1961- 196
Murphy, Pat
    See Murphy, E(mmett) Jefferson
Murphy, Patricia J. 1963- 132
Murphy, Rita 180
Murphy, Robert (William) 1902-1971 10
Murphy, Shirley Rousseau 1928- 126
    Earlier sketches in SATA *36, 71*
    See also SAAS *18*
Murphy, Stuart J. 1942- 157
    Earlier sketch in SATA *115*
Murphy, Thomas Basil, Jr. 1935- 191
Murphy, Tim
    See Murphy, Jim
Murphy, Tom
    See Murphy, Thomas Basil, Jr.
Murray, John 1923- 39
Murray, Kirsty 1960- 165
    Earlier sketch in SATA *108*
Murray, Marguerite 1917- 63
Murray, Marian 5
Murray, Martine 1965- 125
Murray, (Judith) Michele (Freedman)
    1933-1974 7
Murray, Ossie 1938- 43
Murray, Peter
    See Hautman, Pete
Murrow, Liza Ketchum
    See Ketchum, Liza
Musgrave, Florence 1902-1999 3
Musgrove, Margaret W(ynkoop) 1943- 124
    Earlier sketch in SATA *26*
Musgrove, Marianne 207
Mussey, Virginia Howell
    See Ellison, Virginia H(owell)
Mussey, Virginia T.H.
    See Ellison, Virginia H(owell)
Mussi, Sarah 206
Mutel, Cornelia F. 1947- 74

Muth, Jon J. 206
Earlier sketch in SATA 165
Mutz
See Kuenstler, Morton
Mwangi, Meja 1948- 174
My Brother's Brother
See Chekhov, Anton
Myers, Anna 160
Myers, Arthur 1917- 91
Earlier sketch in SATA 35
Myers, Bernice 81
Earlier sketch in SATA 9
Myers, Caroline Elizabeth Clark 1887-1980
.... 28
Myers, Christopher 1975- 183
See also CLR 97
Myers, Edward 1950- 172
Earlier sketch in SATA 96
Myers, Elisabeth P(erkins) 1918- 36
Myers, (Mary) Hortense (Powner)
1913-1987 10
Myers, Jack 1913-2006 83
Obituary 178
Myers, Jack Edgar
See Myers, Jack
Myers, Lou 1915-2005 81
Obituary 171
Myers, Louis
See Myers, Lou
Myers, R.E. 1924- 119
Myers, Robert Eugene
See Myers, R.E.
Myers, Tim 1953- 176
Earlier sketch in SATA 147
Myers, Timothy Joseph
See Myers, Tim
Myers, Walter Dean 1937- 193
Brief entry 27
Earlier sketches in SATA 41, 71, 109, 157
See also CLR 110
See also SAAS 2
Myers, Walter M.
See Myers, Walter Dean
Myller, Rolf 1926-2006 27
Obituary 175
Myra, Harold L(awrence) 1939- 46
Brief entry 42
Myracle, Lauren 1969- 204
Earlier sketch in SATA 162
Myrus, Donald (Richard) 1927- 23
Mysterious Traveler, The
See Arthur, Robert, (Jr.)

N

Na, An 149
Naaslund, Goorel Kristina 1940- 170
Nadel, Laurie 1948- 74
Naden, Corinne J. 1930- 166
Earlier sketch in SATA 79
Nadimi, Suzan 188
Nagda, Ann Whitehead 199
Nagel, Andreas Fischer
See Fischer-Nagel, Andreas
Nagel, Heiderose Fischer
See Fischer-Nagel, Heiderose
Nagle, Shane 176
Naidoo, Beverley 1943- 180
Earlier sketches in SATA 63, 135
See also CLR 29
Nakae, Noriko 1940- 59
Nakata, Hiroe 205
Nakatani, Chiyoko 1930-1981 55
Brief entry 40
See also CLR 30
Nally, Susan W. 1947- 90

Namioka, Lensey 1929- 157
Autobiography Feature 116
Earlier sketches in SATA 27, 89
See also CLR 48
See also SAAS 24
Namovicz, Gene Inyart 1927- 6
Nance, Andrew 210
Nanji, Shenaaz 1954- 204
Earlier sketch in SATA 131
Nanogak Agnes 1925- 61
Napier, Mark
See Laffin, John (Alfred Charles)
Napoli, Donna Jo 1948- 190
Earlier sketches in SATA 92, 137
See also CLR 51
See also SAAS 23
Napp, Daniel 1974- 204
Narahashi, Keiko 1959- 115
Earlier sketch in SATA 79
Narayan, R. K. 1906-2001 62
Narayan, Rasipuram Krishnaswami
See Narayan, R. K.
Nascimbene, Yan 1949- 173
Earlier sketch in SATA 133
Nash, Bruce M(itchell) 1947- 34
Nash, Fredric Ogden
See Nash, Ogden
Nash, Linell
See Smith, Linell Nash
Nash, Mary (Hughes) 1925- 41
Nash, Ogden 1902-1971 46
Earlier sketch in SATA 2
Nash, Renea Denise 1963- 81
Nast, Elsa Ruth
See Watson, Jane Werner
Nast, Thomas 1840-1902 51
Brief entry 33
Nastick, Sharon 1954- 41
Natale, Vince 196
Natarajan, Srividya 187
Nathan, Adele (Gutman) 1900(?)-1986
Obituary 48
Nathan, Amy 155
Earlier sketch in SATA 104
Nathan, Dorothy (Goldeen) (?)-1966 15
Nathan, Robert (Gruntal) 1894-1985 6
Obituary 43
Nathanson, Laura Walther 1941- 57
Natti, Lee 1919- 67
Earlier sketch in SATA 1
See also SAAS 3
Natti, Susanna 1948- 125
Earlier sketch in SATA 32
Nau, Thomas 186
Naughtie, Eleanor
See Updale, Eleanor
Naughton, Bill
See Naughton, William John (Francis)
Naughton, James Franklin 1957- 85
Naughton, Jim
See Naughton, James Franklin
Naughton, William John (Francis)
1910-1992 86
Navarra, John Gabriel 1927- 8
Naylor, Penelope 1941- 10
Naylor, Phyllis 1933- 152
Autobiography Feature 152
Earlier sketches in SATA 12, 66, 102
See also CLR 135
See also SAAS 10
See Naylor, Phyllis Reynolds
Naylor, Phyllis Reynolds 1933- 209
See Naylor, Phyllis
Nazarian, Nikki
See Nichols, Cecilia Fawn
Nazaroff, Alexander I(vanovich) 1898-1981 . 4
Nazoa, Aquiles 1920-1976 198
Neal, Harry Edward 1906-1993 5
Obituary 76
Neal, Michael
See Teitelbaum, Michael

Nearing, Penny 1916- 47
Brief entry 42
Nebel, Gustave E. 45
Brief entry 33
Nebel, Mimouca
See Nebel, Gustave E.
Nee, Kay Bonner 10
Needham, Kate 1962- 95
Needle, Jan 1943- 98
Earlier sketch in SATA 30
See also CLR 43
See also SAAS 23
Needleman, Jacob 1934- 6
Neel, David 1960- 82
Neel, Preston 1959- 93
Negri, Rocco 1932- 12
Negrin, Fabian 1963- 189
Neidigh, Sherry 1956- 204
Neier, Aryeh 1937- 59
Neigoff, Anne 13
Neigoff, Mike 1920- 13
Neilan, Eujin Kim 1969- 200
Neilson, Frances Fullerton (Jones)
1910-2001 14
Neimark, Anne E. 1935- 145
Earlier sketch in SATA 4
Neimark, Paul G. 1934- 80
Brief entry 37
Neitzel, Shirley 1941- 134
Earlier sketch in SATA 77
Nell
See Hanna, Nell(ie L.)
Nelscott, Kris
See Rusch, Kristine Kathryn
Nelson, Blake 1960- 177
Nelson, Catherine Chadwick 1926- 87
Nelson, Cordner 1918-2009 54
Brief entry 29
Nelson, Cordner Bruce
See Nelson, Cordner
Nelson, Drew 1952- 77
Nelson, Esther L. 1928- 13
Nelson, Jim A.
See Stotter, Mike
Nelson, Julie L. 1970- 117
Nelson, Kadir 181
Earlier sketch in SATA 154
Nelson, Kris
See Rusch, Kristine Kathryn
Nelson, Lawrence E(rnest) 1928-1977
Obituary 28
Nelson, Marilyn 1946- 60
Autobiography Feature 180
Nelson, Mary Carroll 1929- 23
Nelson, O. Terry 1941- 62
Nelson, Peter N. 1953- 73
Nelson, R. A. 197
Nelson, Richard K(ing) 1941- 65
Nelson, Robin Laura 1971- 141
Nelson, Roy Paul 1923- 59
Nelson, S.D. 181
Nelson, Sharlene (P.) 1933- 96
Nelson, Suzanne 1976- 184
Nelson, Ted (W.) 1931- 96
Nelson, Theresa 1948- 143
Autobiography Feature 143
Earlier sketch in SATA 79
Nemeth, Sally 187
Neri, G. 197
Neri, Greg
See Neri, G.
Neri, Gregory
See Neri, G.
Nerlove, Miriam 1959- 53
Brief entry 49
Nesbit, E. 1858-1924 100
See also YABC 1
See also CLR 70
Nesbit, Edith
See Nesbit, E.

Nesbit, Troy
    See Folsom, Franklin (Brewster)
Nespojohn, Katherine V(eronica)
    1912-1975 7
Ness, Evaline (Michelow) 1911-1986 26
    Obituary 49
    Earlier sketch in SATA *1*
    See also CLR *6*
    See also SAAS *1*
Ness, Patrick 1971- 207
Nestor, Larry 1940- 149
Nestor, William P(rodromos) 1947- 49
Nethery, Mary 93
Neubecker, Robert 170
Neuberger, Julia (Babette Sarah) 1950- ... 142
    Earlier sketch in SATA *78*
Neufeld, John (Arthur) 1938- 131
    Autobiography Feature 131
    Earlier sketches in SATA *6, 81*
    See also CLR *52*
    See also SAAS *3*
Neuhaus, David 1958- 83
Neumeyer, Peter F(lorian) 1929- 13
Neurath, Marie (Reidemeister) 1898-1986 1
Neuschwander, Cindy 1953- 157
    Earlier sketch in SATA *107*
Neusner, Jacob 1932- 38
Neville, Charles
    See Bodsworth, (Charles) Fred(erick)
Neville, Emily Cheney 1919- 1
    See also SAAS *2*
Neville, Mary
    See Woodrich, Mary Neville
Nevins, Albert (Francis) J(erome)
    1915-1997 20
Nevius, Carol 1955- 186
Newberger, Devra
    See Speregen, Devra Newberger
Newberry, Clare Turlay 1903-1970 1
    Obituary 26
Newbery, John 1713-1767 20
    See also CLR *147*
Newbery, Linda 1952- 184
    Earlier sketch in SATA *142*
Newbigging, Martha 198
Newbold, Greg 199
Newcomb, Ellsworth
    See Kenny, Ellsworth Newcomb
Newcombe, Eugene A. 1923-1990 45
    Brief entry 33
Newcombe, Jack
    See Newcombe, Eugene A.
Newcome, Robert 1955- 91
Newcome, Zita 1959- 88
Newell, Crosby
    See Bonsall, Crosby Barbara (Newell)
Newell, Edythe W(eatherford) 1910-1989 .. 11
Newell, Hope Hockenberry 1896-1965 24
Newfeld, Frank 1928- 26
Newgarden, Mark 1959- 194
Newlon, (Frank) Clarke 1905(?)-1982 6
    Obituary 33
Newman, Barbara Johansen 191
Newman, C.J.
    See Newman, Coleman J.
Newman, Coleman J. 1935- 82
Newman, Daisy 1904-1994 27
    Obituary 78
Newman, Gerald 1939- 46
    Brief entry 42
Newman, Jerry
    See Newman, Coleman J.
Newman, Leslea 1955- 134
    Earlier sketches in SATA *71, 128*
Newman, Margaret
    See Potter, Margaret
Newman, Marjorie 146
Newman, Matthew (Harrison) 1955- 56
Newman, Nanette 1934- 162

Newman, Robert (Howard) 1909-1988 87
    Obituary 60
    Earlier sketch in SATA *4*
Newman, Shirlee P(etkin) 144
    Earlier sketches in SATA *10, 90*
Newsom, Carol 1948- 92
    Earlier sketch in SATA *40*
Newsom, Tom 1944- 80
Newth, Mette 1942- 140
Newton, David E(dward) 1933- 67
Newton, James R(obert) 1935- 23
Newton, Jill 1964- 200
Newton, Robert 1965- 191
Newton, Suzanne 1936- 77
    Earlier sketch in SATA *5*
Newton, Vanessa
    See Newton, Vanessa Brantley
Newton, Vanessa Brantley 1962(?)- 206
Ney, John 1923- 43
    Brief entry 33
Nez, John 155
Ng, Franklin 82
Nguyen, Vincent 187
Nichol, B(arrie) P(hillip) 1944-1988 66
Nicholas, Louise D.
    See Watkins, Dawn L.
Nicholls, Judith (Ann) 1941- 61
Nicholls, Sally 1983- 209
Nichols, Cecilia Fawn 1906-1987 12
Nichols, Grace 1950- 164
    Earlier sketch in SATA *98*
Nichols, Janet (Louise) 1952- 67
Nichols, Judy 1947- 124
Nichols, Leigh
    See Koontz, Dean
Nichols, Paul
    See Hawks, Robert
Nichols, Peter
    See Youd, Samuel
Nichols, (Joanna) Ruth 1948- 15
    See also CLR *149*
Nichols, Travis 206
Nicholson, C. R.
    See Nicole, Christopher (Robin)
Nicholson, Christina
    See Nicole, Christopher (Robin)
Nicholson, Joyce Thorpe 1919- 35
Nicholson, Lois P. 1949- 88
Nicholson, Robin
    See Nicole, Christopher (Robin)
Nicholson, William 180
Nicholson, William 1872-1949
    See CLR *76*
Nickel, Barbara 1966- 188
Nickell, Joe 1944- 167
    Earlier sketch in SATA *73*
Nickelsburg, Janet 1893-1983 11
Nickerson, Betty 1922- 14
Nickerson, Elizabeth
    See Nickerson, Betty
Nickl, Barbara (Elisabeth) 1939- 56
Nicklaus, Carol 62
    Brief entry 33
Nickle, John 181
Nickless, Will 1902-1979(?) 66
Nic Leodhas, Sorche
    See Alger, Leclaire (Gowans)
Nicol, Ann
    See Turnbull, Ann
Nicolas
    See Mordvinoff, Nicolas
Nicolay, Helen 1866-1954
    See YABC *1*
Nicole, Christopher (Robin) 1930- 5
Nicoll, Helen 1937- 87
Nicolson, Cynthia Pratt 1949- 141
Ni Dhuibhne, Eilis 1954- 91
Niehaus, Paddy Bouma
    See Bouma, Paddy
Nields, Nerissa 1967- 166

Nielsen, Kay (Rasmus) 1886-1957 16
    See also CLR *16*
Nielsen, Laura F. 1960- 93
Nielsen, Laura Farnsworth
    See Nielsen, Laura F.
Nielsen, Nancy J. 1951- 77
Nielsen, Susin 1964- 195
Nielsen, Virginia
    See McCall, Virginia Nielsen
Nielsen-Fernlund, Susin
    See Nielsen, Susin
Niemann, Christoph 1970- 191
Nieuwsma, Milton J(ohn) 1941- 142
Nightingale, Sandy 1953- 76
Nikolajeva, Maria 1952- 127
Nikola-Lisa, W. 1951- 180
    Earlier sketch in SATA *71*
Niland, Deborah 1951- 172
    Earlier sketch in SATA *27*
Niland, Kilmeny 75
Nilsen, Anna 1948- 174
    Earlier sketch in SATA *96*
Nilsson, Eleanor 1939- 117
    Earlier sketch in SATA *81*
    See also SAAS *23*
Nilsson, Per 1954- 159
Nimmo, Jenny 1944- 144
    Earlier sketch in SATA *87*
    See also CLR *44*
Nishimura, Kae 196
Niven, Larry 1938- 171
    Earlier sketch in SATA *95*
Niven, Laurence VanCott
    See Niven, Larry
Nivola, Claire A. 1947- 208
    Earlier sketches in SATA *84, 140*
Nix, Garth 1963- 210
    Earlier sketches in SATA *97, 143*
    See also CLR *68*
Nixon, Hershell Howard 1923- 42
Nixon, Joan Lowery 1927-2003 115
    Obituary 146
    Earlier sketches in SATA *8, 44, 78*
    See also CLR *24*
    See also SAAS *9*
Nixon, K.
    See Nixon, Kathleen Irene (Blundell)
Nixon, Kathleen Irene (Blundell)
    1894-1988(?) 14
    Obituary 59
Nobati, Eugenia 1968- 201
Nobisso, Josephine 1953- 121
    Earlier sketch in SATA *78*
Noble, Iris (Davis) 1922-1986 5
    Obituary 49
Noble, Marty 1947- 125
    Earlier sketch in SATA *97*
Noble, Trinka Hakes 1944- 197
    Brief entry 37
    Earlier sketch in SATA *123*
Nobleman, Marc Tyler 1972- 203
Noda, Takayo 1961- 168
Nodelman, Perry 1942- 101
Nodset, Joan L.
    See Lexau, Joan M.
Noel Hume, Ivor 1927- 65
Noestlinger, Christine
    See Nostlinger, Christine
Noguere, Suzanne 1947- 34
Nolan, Dennis 1945- 166
    Brief entry 34
    Earlier sketches in SATA *42, 92*
Nolan, Han 1956- 157
    Earlier sketch in SATA *109*
Nolan, Janet 1956- 191
    Earlier sketch in SATA *145*
Nolan, Jeannette Covert 1897-1974 2
    Obituary 27
Nolan, Paul T(homas) 1919- 48
Nolan, William F. 1928- 88
    Brief entry 28

Nolan, William Francis
  See Nolan, William F.
Nolen, Jerdine 1953- *157*
  Earlier sketch in SATA *105*
Noll, Sally 1946- *82*
Noonan, Brandon 1979- *184*
Noonan, Diana 1960- *146*
Noonan, Julia 1946- *148*
  Earlier sketches in SATA *4, 95*
Norac, Carl 1960- *166*
Norcross, John
  See Conroy, John Wesley
Nordan, Robert W(arren) 1934-2004 .... *133*
Nordhoff, Charles Bernard 1887-1947 .... *23*
Nordlicht, Lillian *29*
Nordstrom, Ursula 1910-1988 .... *3*
  Obituary *57*
Nordtvedt, Matilda 1926- *67*
Norling, Beth 1969- *149*
Norman, Charles 1904-1996 .... *38*
  Obituary *92*
Norman, Howard
  See Norman, Howard A.
Norman, Howard A. 1949- *81*
Norman, James
  See Schmidt, James Norman
Norman, Jay
  See Arthur, Robert, (Jr.)
Norman, Lilith 1927- *120*
  Earlier sketch in SATA *86*
Norman, Mary 1931- *36*
Norman, Steve
  See Pashko, Stanley
Norment, Lisa 1966- *91*
Norris, Gunilla Brodde 1939- *20*
North, Andrew
  See Norton, Andre
North, Anthony
  See Koontz, Dean
North, Captain George
  See Stevenson, Robert Louis
North, Captain George
  See Stevenson, Robert Louis
North, Howard
  See Trevor, Elleston
North, Joan 1920- *16*
North, Milou
  See Erdrich, Louise
North, Robert
  See Withers, Carl A.
North, Sara
  See Bonham, Barbara Thomas
  and Hager, Jean
North, Sherry *201*
North, Sterling 1906-1974 .... *45*
  Obituary *26*
  Earlier sketch in SATA *1*
Northcott, (William) Cecil 1902-1987
  Obituary *55*
Northeast, Brenda V(ictoria) 1948- *106*
Northmore, Elizabeth Florence
  1906-1974 .... *122*
Norton, Alice Mary
  See Norton, Andre
Norton, Andre 1912-2005 .... *91*
  Earlier sketches in SATA *1, 43*
  See also CLR *50*
Norton, Browning
  See Norton, Frank R. B(rowning)
Norton, Frank R. B(rowning) 1909-1989 .... *10*
Norton, Mary 1903-1992 .... *60*
  Obituary *72*
  Earlier sketch in SATA *18*
  See also CLR *140*
Nosredna, Trebor
  See Anderson, Bob
Nostlinger, Christine 1936- *162*
  Brief entry *37*
  Earlier sketch in SATA *64*
  See also CLR *12*

Nourse, Alan E(dward) 1928-1992 .... *48*
  See also CLR *33*
Novak, Matt 1962- *204*
  Brief entry *52*
  Earlier sketches in SATA *60, 104, 165*
Novelli, Luca 1947- *61*
Nowell, Elizabeth Cameron *12*
Noyes, Deborah 1965- *194*
  Earlier sketch in SATA *145*
Nugent, Cynthia 1954- *205*
Nugent, Nicholas 1949- *73*
Numeroff, Laura 1953- *206*
  Earlier sketches in SATA *28, 90, 142*
  See also CLR *85*
Numeroff Joffe, Laura
  See Numeroff, Laura
Nunes, Lygia Bojunga 1932- *154*
  Earlier sketch in SATA *75*
Nunn, Laura (Donna) Silverstein 1968- *124*
Nurenberg, Thelma
  See Greenhaus, Thelma Nurenberg
Nurnberg, Maxwell 1897-1984 .... *27*
  Obituary *41*
Nussbaumer, Paul (Edmund) 1934- *16*
Nutt, Ken 1951- *163*
  Earlier sketch in SATA *97*
Nuttall-Smith, Margaret Emily Noel
  1919- *26*
Nuygen, Mathieu 1967- *80*
Nuzum, K. A. *195*
Nuzum, Kathy A.
  See Nuzum, K. A.
Nyberg, (Everett Wayne) Morgan 1944- *87*
Nyce, (Nellie) Helene von Strecker
  1885-1969 .... *19*
Nyce, Vera 1862-1925 .... *19*
Nye, Naomi Shihab 1952- *198*
  Earlier sketches in SATA *86, 147*
  See also CLR *59*
Nye, Robert 1939- *6*
Nyeu, Tao *206*
Nyikos, Stacy A. 1969- *164*
Nystrom, Carolyn 1940- *130*
  Earlier sketch in SATA *67*

O

O. Henry
  See Henry, O.
Oakes, Elizabeth H. 1964- *132*
Oakes, Vanya 1909-1983 .... *6*
  Obituary *37*
Oakley, Don(ald G.) 1927- *8*
Oakley, Graham 1929- *84*
  Earlier sketch in SATA *30*
  See also CLR *7*
Oakley, Helen (McKelvey) 1906- *10*
Oana, Katherine 1929- *53*
  Brief entry *37*
Oates, Eddie H. 1943- *88*
Oates, Joyce Carol 1938- *159*
Oates, Stephen B(aery) 1936- *59*
Obed, Ellen Bryan 1944- *74*
Oberle, Joseph 1958- *69*
Oberman, Sheldon 1949-2004 .... *85*
  Autobiography Feature *114*
  Obituary *153*
  See also CLR *54*
  See also SAAS *26*
Obligado, Lilian (Isabel) 1931- *61*
  Brief entry *45*
Obrant, Susan 1946- *11*
O'Brian, E.G.
  See Clarke, Arthur C.
O'Brien, Anne Sibley 1952- *80*
  Brief entry *48*
  Earlier sketch in SATA *53*
O'Brien, E.G.
  See Clarke, Arthur C.

O'Brien, Esse Forrester 1895(?)-1975
  Obituary *30*
O'Brien, Patrick 1960- *193*
O'Brien, Robert C.
  See Conly, Robert Leslie
O'Brien, Thomas C(lement) 1938- *29*
O'Callaghan, Julie 1954- *113*
O'Callahan, Jay 1938- *88*
O'Carroll, Ryan
  See Markun, Patricia Maloney
Ochiltree, Dianne 1953- *117*
Ockham, Joan Price
  See Price, Joan
O'Connell, Margaret F(orster) 1935-1977 .. *30*
  Obituary *30*
O'Connell, Peg
  See Ahern, Margaret McCrohan
O'Connell, Rebecca 1968- *130*
O'Connor, Barbara 1950- *193*
  Earlier sketch in SATA *154*
O'Connor, Francine M(arie) 1930- *90*
O'Connor, Genevieve A. 1914- *75*
O'Connor, George *183*
O'Connor, Ian 1965- *188*
O'Connor, Jane 1947- *186*
  Brief entry *47*
  Earlier sketches in SATA *59, 103, 150*
O'Connor, Karen 1938- *89*
  Earlier sketch in SATA *34*
O'Connor, Patrick
  See Wibberley, Leonard
O'Connor, Richard 1915-1975
  Obituary *21*
O'Conor, Jane 1958- *78*
Odaga, Asenath (Bole) 1937- *130*
  Earlier sketch in SATA *67*
  See also SAAS *19*
O Danachair, Caoimhin
  See Danaher, Kevin
Odanaka, Barbara *159*
O'Daniel, Janet 1921- *24*
O'Day, Cathy
  See Crane, Barbara (Joyce)
O'Dell, Scott 1898-1989 .... *134*
  Earlier sketches in SATA *12, 60*
  See also CLR *126*
Odenwald, Robert P(aul) 1899-1965 .... *11*
Odgers, Sally
  See Odgers, Sally Farrell
Odgers, Sally Farrell 1957- *139*
  Earlier sketch in SATA *72*
Odone, Jamison 1980- *209*
O'Donnell, Dick
  See Lupoff, Richard A(llen)
  and Thompson, Don(ald Arthur)
O'Donnell, Liam 1970- *209*
Odriozola, Elena *186*
Oechsli, Kelly 1918-1999 .... *5*
Oesterle, Virginia Rorby
  See Rorby, Ginny
Ofek, Uriel 1926- *36*
  See also CLR *28*
Ofer, Avi 1975- *207*
Offenbacher, Ami 1958- *91*
Offill, Jenny 1968- *211*
Offit, Sidney 1928- *10*
Ofosu-Appiah, L(awrence) H(enry) 1920- .. *13*
Ogan, George F. 1912-1983 .... *13*
Ogan, M. G.
  See Ogan, George F.
  and Ogan, Margaret E. (Nettles)
Ogan, Margaret E. (Nettles) 1923-1979 ...... *13*
Ogburn, Charlton (Jr.) 1911-1998 .... *3*
  Obituary *109*
Ogburn, Jacqueline K. *162*
Ogilvie, Elisabeth May 1917-2006 .... *40*
  Brief entry *29*
  Obituary *176*
Ogilvy, Gavin
  See Barrie, J. M.
Ogilvy, Ian 1943- *177*

Ogilvy, Ian Raymond
    See Ogilvy, Ian
Ogle, Lucille Edith 1904-1988
    Obituary 59
Ogletree, Charles J. 1952- 175
O'Green, Jennifer
    See Roberson, Jennifer
O'Green, Jennifer Roberson
    See Roberson, Jennifer
O'Hagan, Caroline 1946- 38
O'Hanlon, Jacklyn
    See Meek, Jacklyn O'Hanlon
O'Hara, Elizabeth
    See Ni Dhuibhne, Eilis
O'Hara, Kenneth
    See Morris, (Margaret) Jean
O'Hara, Mary
    See Alsop, Mary O'Hara
O'Hara (Alsop), Mary
    See Alsop, Mary O'Hara
O'Hare, Jeff(rey A.) 1958- 105
Ohi, Ruth 1964- 95
Ohiyesa
    See Eastman, Charles A(lexander)
Ohlsson, Ib 1935- 7
Ohmi, Ayano 1959- 115
Ohtomo, Yasuo 1946- 37
o huigin, sean 1942- 138
    See also CLR 75
Oiseau
    See Moseley, James W(illett)
Oke, Janette 1935- 97
O'Keefe, Susan Heyboer 176
    Earlier sketch in SATA 133
O'Keeffe, Frank 1938- 99
O'Kelley, Mattie Lou 1908-1997 97
    Earlier sketch in SATA 36
Okimoto, Jean Davies 1942- 103
    Earlier sketch in SATA 34
Okomfo, Amasewa
    See Cousins, Linda
olafsdottir, Gudrun Elin
    See Gunnella
Olaleye, Isaac O. 1941- 96
    See also SAAS 23
Olcott, Frances Jenkins 1872(?)-1963 19
Old, Wendie C(orbin) 1943- 154
Old Boy
    See Hughes, Thomas
Oldenburg, E(gbert) William 1936-1974 35
Older, Effin 1942- 114
Older, Jules 1940- 156
    Earlier sketch in SATA 114
Oldfield, Jenny 1949- 140
Oldfield, Margaret J(ean) 1932- 56
Oldfield, Pamela 1931- 86
Oldham, June 70
Oldham, Mary 1944- 65
Olds, Elizabeth 1896-1991 3
    Obituary 66
Olds, Helen Diehl 1895-1981 9
    Obituary 25
Oldstyle, Jonathan
    See Irving, Washington
O'Leary, Brian (Todd) 1940- 6
O'Leary, Chris 208
O'Leary, Patsy B(aker) 1937- 97
Oleynikov, Igor 1953- 202
Oliphant, B.J.
    See Tepper, Sheri S.
Oliver, Burton
    See Burt, Olive Woolley
Oliver, Chad
    See Oliver, Symmes C.
Oliver, John Edward 1933- 21
Oliver, Lin 202
Oliver, Marilyn Tower 1935- 89
Oliver, Narelle 1960- 197
    Earlier sketch in SATA 152
Oliver, Shirley (Louise Dawkins) 1958- 74
Oliver, Symmes C. 1928-1993 101

Oliviero, Jamie 1950- 84
Olmsted, Lorena Ann 1890-1989 13
Olney, Ross R. 1929- 13
Olschewski, Alfred (Erich) 1920- 7
Olsen, Barbara 148
Olsen, Carol 1945- 89
Olsen, Ib Spang 1921- 81
    Earlier sketch in SATA 6
Olsen, Violet (Mae) 1922-1991 58
Olson, Arielle North 1932- 67
Olson, David J. 1974- 198
Olson, Gene 1922- 32
Olson, Gretchen 187
Olson, Helen Kronberg 48
Olson, Kay Melchisedech 1948- 175
Olson, Marianne
    See Mitchell, Marianne
Olson-Brown, Ellen 1967- 183
Olten, Manuela 1970- 197
Olugebefola, Ademole 1941- 15
Oluonye, Mary N(kechi) 1955- 111
Om
    See Gorey, Edward (St. John)
O'Malley, Donough 208
O'Malley, Kevin 1961- 191
    Earlier sketch in SATA 157
Oman, Carola (Mary Anima) 1897-1978 35
O'Mara, Carmel 1965- 166
O'Mara-Horwitz, Carmel
    See O'Mara, Carmel
O'Meara, Walter (Andrew) 1897-1989 65
Ommanney, F(rancis) D(ownes)
    1903-1980 23
O Mude
    See Gorey, Edward (St. John)
Oneal, Elizabeth 1934- 82
    Earlier sketch in SATA 30
    See also CLR 13
O'Neal, Katherine Pebley 1957- 204
O'Neal, Reagan
    See Jordan, Robert
O'Neal, Regan
    See Jordan, Robert
Oneal, Zibby
    See Oneal, Elizabeth
O'Neill, Amanda 1951- 111
O'Neill, Catharine 203
O'Neill, Gerard K(itchen) 1927-1992 65
O'Neill, Judith (Beatrice) 1930- 34
O'Neill, Mary L(e Duc) 1908(?)-1990 2
    Obituary 64
O'Neill, Reagan
    See Jordan, Robert
Onslow, Annette Rosemary MacArthur
    See MacArthur-Onslow, Annette Rosemary
Onslow, John 1906-1985
    Obituary 47
Onyefulu, Ifeoma 1959- 157
    Earlier sketches in SATA 81, 115
Opie, Iona (Margaret Balfour) 1923- 118
    Earlier sketches in SATA 3, 63
    See also SAAS 6
Opie, Peter (Mason) 1918-1982 118
    Obituary 28
    Earlier sketches in SATA 3, 63
Oppel, Kenneth 1967- 199
    Earlier sketches in SATA 99, 153
Oppel, Kenneth Kerry
    See Oppel, Kenneth
Oppenheim, Joanne 1934- 174
    Earlier sketches in SATA 5, 82, 136
Oppenheim, Shulamith Levey 1928- 177
Oppenheimer, Joan L(etson) 1925- 28
Oppong, Joseph Ransford 1953- 160
Optic, Oliver
    See Adams, William Taylor
    and Stratemeyer, Edward L.
Oram, Hiawyn 1946- 101
    Earlier sketch in SATA 56
Orbach, Ruth Gary 1941- 21
Orback, Craig 197

Orczy, Emma
    See Orczy, Baroness Emmuska
Orczy, Emma Magdalena Rosalia Maria Josefa
    See Orczy, Baroness Emmuska
Orczy, Emmuska
    See Orczy, Baroness Emmuska
Orczy, Baroness Emmuska 1865-1947 40
Orde, A.J.
    See Tepper, Sheri S.
O'Reilly, Jackson
    See Jordan, Robert
Orenstein, Denise Gosliner 1950- 157
Orgad, Dorit 1936- 199
Orgel, Doris 1929- 148
    Earlier sketches in SATA 7, 85
    See also CLR 48
    See also SAAS 19
Orgill, Roxane 198
Oriolo, Joe
    See Oriolo, Joseph D.
Oriolo, Joseph D. 1913-1985
    Obituary 46
Orlean, Susan 1955- 209
Orleans, Ilo 1897-1962 10
Orlev, Uri 1931- 135
    Earlier sketch in SATA 58
    See also CLR 30
    See also SAAS 19
Ormai, Stella 57
    Brief entry 48
Ormerod, Jan 1946- 210
    Brief entry 44
    Earlier sketches in SATA 55, 70, 132
    See also CLR 20
Ormerod, Janette Louise
    See Ormerod, Jan
Ormes, Jackie
    See Ormes, Zelda J.
Ormes, Zelda J. 1914-1986
    Obituary 47
Ormondroyd, Edward 1925- 14
Ormsby, Virginia H(aire) 1906-1990 11
Orona-Ramirez, Kristy 1964- 189
Orozco, Jose-Luis 1948- 179
Orr, Katherine S(helley) 1950- 72
Orr, Wendy 1953- 206
    Earlier sketches in SATA 90, 141
Orris
    See Ingelow, Jean
Orth, Richard
    See Gardner, Richard (M.)
Ortiz Cofer, Judith
    See Cofer, Judith Ortiz
Orwell, George 1903-1950 29
    See also CLR 68
Orwin, Joanna 1944- 141
Osborn, Elinor 1939- 145
Osborn, Kathy 1955(?)- 199
Osborn, Lois D(orothy) 1915- 61
Osborne, Charles 1927- 59
Osborne, Chester G(orham) 1915-1987 11
Osborne, David
    See Silverberg, Robert
Osborne, George
    See Silverberg, Robert
Osborne, Leone Neal 1914-1996 2
Osborne, Mary Pope 1949- 144
    Earlier sketches in SATA 41, 55, 98
    See also CLR 88
Osceola
    See Blixen, Karen
Osgood, William E(dward) 1926- 37
O'Shaughnessy, Darren
    See Shan, Darren
O'Shaughnessy, Ellen Cassels 1937- 78
O'Shea, Catherine Patricia Shiels
    See O'Shea, Pat
O'Shea, Pat 1931-2007 87
    See also CLR 18
Osmond, Edward 1900- 10

Ossoli, Sarah Margaret
See Fuller, Margaret
Ostendorf, (Arthur) Lloyd, (Jr.)
1921-2000 65
Obituary 125
Ostow, Micol 1976- 170
Otfinoski, Steven 1949- 116
Earlier sketch in SATA 56
Otis, James
See Kaler, James Otis
O'Toole, Thomas 1941- 71
O'Trigger, Sir Lucius
See Horne, Richard Henry Hengist
Otten, Charlotte
See Otten, Charlotte F.
Otten, Charlotte F. 1926- 98
Otten, Charlotte Fennema
See Otten, Charlotte F.
Ottley, Matt 1962- 171
Earlier sketch in SATA 102
Ottley, Reginald Leslie 1909-1985 26
See also CLR 16
Otto, Margaret Glover 1909-1976
Obituary 30
Otto, Svend
See Soerensen, Svend Otto
Oughton, Jerrie (Preston) 1937- 131
Earlier sketch in SATA 76
Oughton, (William) Taylor 1925- 104
Ouida
See De La Ramee, Marie Louise
Ousley, Odille 1896-1976 10
Outcalt, Todd 1960- 123
Overmyer, James E. 1946- 88
Overton, Jenny (Margaret Mary) 1942- 52
Brief entry 36
Owen, Ann
See Qualey, Marsha
Owen, Annie 1949- 75
Owen, Caroline Dale
See Snedeker, Caroline Dale (Parke)
Owen, Clifford
See Hamilton, Charles (Harold St. John)
Owen, Dilys
See Gater, Dilys
Owen, (Benjamin) Evan 1918-1984 38
Owen, (John) Gareth 1936-2002 162
Earlier sketch in SATA 83
See also CLR 31
See also SAAS 14
Owen, James A. 185
Owens, Bryant 1968- 116
Owens, Dana Elaine
See Queen Latifah
Owens, Gail 1939- 54
Owens, Mary Beth 191
Owens, Thomas S(heldon) 1960- 86
Owens, Tom
See Owens, Thomas S(heldon)
Oxenbury, Helen 1938- 149
Earlier sketches in SATA 3, 68
See also CLR 70
Oxendine, Bess Holland 1933- 90
Oz, Frank (Richard) 1944- 60
Ozer, Jerome S. 1927- 59

P

Paananen, Eloise (Katherine) 1923-1993 9
Pace, Lorenzo 1943- 131
Pace, Mildred Mastin 1907- 46
Brief entry 29
Pachter, Hedwig (?)-1988 63
Pack, Janet 1952- 77
Pack, Robert 1929- 118
Packard, Edward 1931- 148
Earlier sketches in SATA 47, 90
Packer, Kenneth L. 1946- 116

Packer, Vin
See Meaker, Marijane
Pad, Peter
See Stratemeyer, Edward L.
Page, Eileen
See Heal, Edith
Page, Eleanor
See Coerr, Eleanor (Beatrice)
Page, Gail 1950- 205
Page, Jake 1936- 81
Page, James Keena, Jr.
See Page, Jake
Page, Lou Williams 1912-1997 38
Page, Mary
See Heal, Edith
Page, Robin 1943- 154
Pagnucci, Susan 1944- 90
Pahlen, Kurt 1907-2003
Obituary 147
Pahz, Cheryl
See Pahz, Cheryl Suzanne
Pahz, Cheryl Suzanne 1949- 11
Pahz, James Alon 1943- 11
Paice, Margaret 1920- 10
Paige, Harry W(orthington) 1922- 41
Brief entry 35
Paige, Richard
See Koontz, Dean
Paige, Robin
See Albert, Susan Wittig
Paine, Penelope Colville 1946- 87
Paine, Roberta M. 1925- 13
Paisley, Tom 1932- 11
See also CLR 3
Palatini, Margie 207
Earlier sketches in SATA 134, 174
Palazzo, Anthony D.
See Palazzo, Tony
Palazzo, Tony 1905-1970 3
Palder, Edward L. 1922- 5
Palecek, Josef 1932- 56
Palecek, Libuse 1937- 89
Palen, Debbie 195
Palin, Michael 1943- 67
Palin, Michael Edward
See Palin, Michael
Palladini, David (Mario) 1946- 40
Brief entry 32
Pallas, Norvin 1918-1983 23
Pallister, John C(lare) 1891-1980
Obituary 26
Pallotta, Gerard Larry
See Pallotta, Jerry
Pallotta, Jerry 1953- 186
Pallotta-Chiarolli, Maria 1960- 117
Palmer, Bernard (Alvin) 1914-1998 26
Palmer, C. Everard 1930- 14
Palmer, (Ruth) Candida 1926- 11
Palmer, Cyril Everard
See Palmer, C. Everard
Palmer, Don
See Benson, Mildred
Palmer, Hap 1942- 68
Palmer, Heidi 1948- 15
Palmer, Helen Marion
See Geisel, Helen
Palmer, Jessica 1953- 120
Palmer, Judd 1972- 153
Palmer, Juliette 1930- 15
Palmer, Kate Salley 1946- 97
Palmer, Maria
See Strachan, Ian
Palmer, Maria
See Brennan, Herbie
Palmer, Robin 1909-2000 43
Palmero Caceres, Ana 198
Palmisciano, Diane 202
Paltrowitz, Donna 1950- 61
Brief entry 50
Paltrowitz, Donna Milman
See Paltrowitz, Donna

Paltrowitz, Stuart 1946- 61
Brief entry 50
Pamela, Todd 1950- 124
Pamintuan, Macky 178
Panagopoulos, Janie Lynn 149
Panati, Charles 1943- 65
Panchyk, Richard 1970- 138
Panetta, George 1915-1969 15
Panetta, Joseph N. 1953- 96
Pang, YaWen Ariel 206
Panik, Sharon 1952- 82
Panowski, Eileen Thompson 1920- 49
Pansy
See Alden, Isabella (Macdonald)
Pantell, Dora (Fuchs) 39
Panter, Carol 1936- 9
Paolini, Christopher 1983- 157
See also CLR 102
Papademetriou, Lisa 175
Paparone, Pam 185
Paparone, Pamela
See Paparone, Pam
Papas, Bill
See Papas, William
Papas, William 1927-2000 50
Papashvily, George 1898-1978 17
Papashvily, Helen (Waite) 1906-1996 17
Pape, D. L.
See Pape, Donna (Lugg)
Pape, Donna (Lugg) 1930- 82
Earlier sketch in SATA 2
Paperny, Myra (Green) 1932- 51
Brief entry 33
Papp, Robert 1967- 205
Paradis, Adrian A(lexis) 1912- 67
Earlier sketch in SATA 1
See also SAAS 8
Paradis, Marjorie Bartholomew
1886(?)-1970 17
Paradiz, Valerie 1963- 176
Paratore, Coleen
See Paratore, Coleen Murtagh
Paratore, Coleen Murtagh 1958- 200
Pardo DeLange, Alex 211
Parenteau, Shirley 1935- 199
Brief entry 40
Earlier sketch in SATA 47
Parish, Margaret 1927-1988 73
Obituary 59
Earlier sketch in SATA 17
See also CLR 22
Parish, Margaret Holt
See Holt, Margaret
Parish, Peggy
See Parish, Margaret
Park, Barbara 1947- 123
Brief entry 35
Earlier sketches in SATA 40, 78
See also CLR 34
Park, Bill
See Park, W(illiam) B(ryan)
Park, Frances 1955- 171
Park, Ginger 173
Park, Janie Jaehyun 150
Park, Jordan
See Kornbluth, C(yril) M.
and Pohl, Frederik
Park, Linda Sue 1960- 200
Earlier sketches in SATA 127, 173
See also CLR 84
Park, Nick 1958- 113
Park, (Rosina) Ruth (Lucia) 1923(?)- 93
Earlier sketch in SATA 25
See also CLR 51
Park, W(illiam) B(ryan) 1936- 22
Parke, Marilyn 1928- 82
Parker, Barbara Keevil 1938- 157
Parker, Daniel
See Ehrenhaft, Daniel
Parker, Elinor Milnor 1906- 3
Parker, Julie F. 1961- 92

Parker, Kim 1963- 174
Parker, Kristy 1957- 59
Parker, Lois M(ay) 1912-1996 30
Parker, Margot M. 1937- 52
Parker, Marjorie Blain 1960- 205
    Earlier sketch in SATA 145
Parker, Mary Jessie 1948- 71
Parker, Nancy Winslow 1930- 132
    Earlier sketches in SATA 10, 69
    See also SAAS 20
Parker, Richard 1915-1990 14
Parker, Robert
    See Boyd, Waldo T.
    and Parker, Robert Andrew
Parker, Robert Andrew 1927- 200
Parker, Toni Trent 1947-2005 142
    Obituary 169
Parker-Rees, Guy 193
Parkes, Lucas
    See Harris, John (Wyndham Parkes Lucas)
    Beynon
Parkhill, John
    See Cox, William R(obert)
Parkins, David 1955- 176
Parkinson, Ethelyn M(inerva) 1906-1999 ... 11
Parkinson, Kathryn N. 1954- 71
Parkinson, Kathy
    See Parkinson, Kathryn N.
Parkinson, Siobhan
    See Parkinson, Siobhan
Parkinson, Siobhan 1954- 178
Parks, Deborah A. 1948- 133
    Earlier sketch in SATA 91
Parks, Edd Winfield 1906-1968 10
Parks, Gordon 1912-2006 108
    Obituary 175
    Earlier sketch in SATA 8
Parks, Gordon Roger Alexander
    See Parks, Gordon
Parks, Peggy J. 1951- 143
Parks, PJ
    See Parks, Peggy J.
Parks, Rosa 1913-2005 83
    Obituary 169
Parks, Rosa Louise Lee
    See Parks, Rosa
Parks, Van Dyke 1943- 62
Parley, Peter
    See Goodrich, Samuel Griswold
Parlin, John
    See Graves, Charles Parlin
Parme, Fabrice 1966- 191
Parnall, Peter 1936- 69
    Earlier sketch in SATA 16
    See also SAAS 11
Paros, Jennifer 210
Parotti, Phillip (Elliott) 1941- 109
Parr, Ann 1943- 144
Parr, Danny
    See Parr, Ann
Parr, Letitia (Evelyn) 1906-1985(?) 37
Parr, Lucy 1924- 10
Parr, Todd 179
    Earlier sketch in SATA 134
Parrish, Anne 1888-1957 27
Parrish, Mary
    See Cousins, Margaret
Parrish, Maxfield
    See Parrish, (Frederick) Maxfield
Parrish, (Frederick) Maxfield 1870-1966 14
Parry, Marian 1924- 13
Parson Lot
    See Kingsley, Charles
Parsons, Alexandra 1947- 92
Parsons, Ellen
    See Dragonwagon, Crescent
Parsons, Garry 197
Parsons, Martin 1951- 116
Parsons, Martin Leslie
    See Parsons, Martin

Parsons, Tom
    See MacPherson, Thomas George
Parsons-Yazzi, Evangeline 172
Partch, Virgil Franklin II 1916-1984 39
    Obituary 39
Parton, Dolly 1946- 94
Parton, Dolly Rebecca
    See Parton, Dolly
Partridge, Benjamin W., Jr. 1915-2005 28
    Obituary 163
Partridge, Benjamin Waring, Jr.
    See Partridge, Benjamin W., Jr.
Partridge, Cora Cheney
    See Cheney, Cora
Partridge, Elizabeth 134
Partridge, Jenny (Lilian) 1947- 52
    Brief entry 37
Pasachoff, Naomi 1947- 147
Pascal, David 1918- 14
Pascal, Francine 1938- 143
    Brief entry 37
    Earlier sketches in SATA 51, 80
    See also CLR 25
Paschal, Nancy
    See Trotter, Grace V(iolet)
Paschkis, Julie 1957- 177
Pascudniak, Pascal
    See Lupoff, Richard A(llen)
Pashko, Stanley 1913-1982 29
Passailaigue, Thomas E.
    See Paisley, Tom
Pastel, Elyse 201
Pateman, Robert 1954- 84
Patent, Dorothy Hinshaw 1940- 162
    Autobiography Feature 162
    Earlier sketches in SATA 22, 69, 120
    See also CLR 19
    See also SAAS 13
Paterson, A(ndrew) B(arton) 1864-1941 97
Paterson, Banjo
    See Paterson, A(ndrew) B(arton)
Paterson, Diane 1946- 177
    Brief entry 33
    Earlier sketch in SATA 59
Paterson, John (Barstow) 1932- 114
Paterson, Katherine 1932- 204
    Earlier sketches in SATA 13, 53, 92, 133
    See also CLR 127
Paterson, Katherine Womeldorf
    See Paterson, Katherine
Patience, John 1949- 90
Patneaude, David 1944- 159
    Earlier sketch in SATA 85
Paton, Alan 1903-1988 11
    Obituary 56
Paton, Alan Stewart
    See Paton, Alan
Paton, Jane (Elizabeth) 1934- 35
Paton, Priscilla 1952- 98
Paton Walsh, Gillian
    See Paton Walsh, Jill
Paton Walsh, Jill 1937- 190
    Autobiography Feature 190
    Earlier sketches in SATA 4, 72, 109
    See also CLR 128
    See also SAAS 3
Patricelli, Leslie 207
Patrick, Susan
    See Clark, Patricia Denise
Patron, Susan 1948- 182
    Earlier sketch in SATA 76
Patsauq, Markoosie 1942-
    See CLR 23
Patschke, Steve 1955- 125
Patten, Brian 1946- 152
    Earlier sketch in SATA 29
Patterson, Charles 1935- 59
Patterson, Geoffrey 1943- 54
    Brief entry 44
Patterson, James 1947- 197
    Earlier sketch in SATA 164

Patterson, James B.
    See Patterson, James
Patterson, Lillie G. -1999 88
    Earlier sketch in SATA 14
Patterson, Nancy Ruth 1944- 148
    Earlier sketch in SATA 72
Pattison, Darcy (S.) 1954- 126
    Earlier sketch in SATA 72
Pattou, Edith 164
Patz (Blaustein), Nancy 154
Paul, Aileen 1917- 12
Paul, Alison 196
Paul, Ann Whitford 1941- 209
    Earlier sketches in SATA 76, 110, 168
Paul, David (Tyler) 1934-1988
    Obituary 56
Paul, Dominique 1973- 184
Paul, Elizabeth
    See Crow, Donna Fletcher
Paul, Hamish Vigne Christie 1951- 151
    See also CLR 87
Paul, James 1936- 23
Paul, Korky
    See Paul, Hamish Vigne Christie
Paul, Robert
    See Roberts, John G(aither)
Paul, Tessa 1944- 103
Pauley, Kimberly 1973- 208
Pauli, Hertha (Ernestine) 1909-1973 3
    Obituary 26
Paull, Grace A. 1898- 24
Paulsen, Gary 1939- 189
    Earlier sketches in SATA 22, 50, 54, 79, 111,
    158
    See also CLR 82
Paulson, Jack
    See Jackson, C(aary) Paul
Pauquet, Gina Ruck
    See Ruck-Pauquet, Gina
Pausacker, Jenny 1948- 72
    See also SAAS 23
Pausewang, Gudrun 1928- 165
    Earlier sketch in SATA 104
Pavel, Frances 1907- 10
Paver, Michelle 170
Paxton, Thomas R. 1937- 70
Paxton, Tom
    See Paxton, Thomas R.
Paye, Won-Ldy 185
Payne, Alan
    See Jakes, John
Payne, Bernal C., Jr. 1941- 60
Payne, C. Douglas
    See Payne, C.D.
Payne, C.D. 1949- 133
Payne, C.F. 1956- 179
Payne, Chris Fox
    See Payne, C.F.
Payne, Donald Gordon 1924- 37
Payne, Emmy
    See West, Emily Govan
Payne, Nina 135
Payne, Rachel Ann
    See Jakes, John
Payson, Dale 1943- 9
Payzant, Charles 18
Paz, A.
    See Pahz, James Alon
Paz, Natalia Toledo
    See Toledo, Natalia
Paz, Zan
    See Pahz, Cheryl Suzanne
Peace, Mary
    See Finley, Mary Peace
Peacock, Louise 210
Peacock, Shane 1957- 192
Peake, Mervyn 1911-1968 23
Peale, Norman Vincent 1898-1993 20
    Obituary 78
Pearce, Ann Philippa
    See Pearce, Philippa

Pearce, Emily Smith 1975- 199
Pearce, Jacqueline 1962- 146
Pearce, Margaret 104
Pearce, Philippa 1920-2006 129
   Obituary 179
   Earlier sketches in SATA 1, 67
   See also CLR 9
Peare, Catherine Owens 1911- 9
Pearle, Ida 207
Pearsall, Shelley 1966- 190
Pearson, Gayle 1947- 119
   Earlier sketch in SATA 53
Pearson, Jean Mary
   See Gardam, Jane
Pearson, Kit 1947- 77
   Autobiography Feature 117
   See also CLR 26
Pearson, Mary E. 1955- 211
   Earlier sketch in SATA 134
Pearson, Ridley 1953- 182
Pearson, Susan 1946- 166
   Brief entry 27
   Earlier sketches in SATA 39, 91
Pearson, Tracey Campbell 1956- 155
   Earlier sketch in SATA 64
Pease, (Clarence) Howard 1894-1974 2
   Obituary 25
Peavy, Linda 1943- 54
Peck, Anne Merriman 1884-1976 18
Peck, Beth 1957- 190
   Earlier sketch in SATA 79
Peck, Jan 159
Peck, Jeanie J. 1967- 147
Peck, Marshall III 1951- 92
Peck, Richard 1934- 190
   Autobiography Feature 110
   Earlier sketches in SATA 18, 55, 97, 110, 158
   See also CLR 142
   See also SAAS 2
Peck, Richard Wayne
   See Peck, Richard
Peck, Robert Newton 1928- 156
   Autobiography Feature 108
   Earlier sketches in SATA 21, 62, 111
   See also CLR 45
   See also SAAS 1
Peck, Sylvia 1953- 133
Peck-Whiting, Jeanie J.
   See Peck, Jeanie J.
Peddicord, Jane Ann 199
Pedersen, Janet 193
Pederson, Sharleen
   See Collicott, Sharleen
Pedler, Caroline 197
Peebles, Anne
   See Galloway, Priscilla
Peek, Merle 1938- 39
Peel, John 1954- 79
Peel, Norman Lemon
   See Hirsch, Phil
Peeples, Edwin A(ugustus, Jr.) 1915-1994 6
Peers, Judi 1956- 119
Peers, Judith May West
   See Peers, Judi
Peet, Bill
   See Peet, William Bartlett
Peet, Creighton B. 1899-1977 30
Peet, Mal 171
Peet, Malcolm
   See Peet, Mal
Peet, William Bartlett 1915-2002 78
   Obituary 137
   Earlier sketches in SATA 2, 41
   See also CLR 12
Peguero, Leone 116
Pelaez, Jill 1924- 12
Pelham, David 1938- 70
Pell, Ed(ward) 1950- 157
Pelletier, Andrew T. 195
Pelletier, Andrew Thomas
   See Pelletier, Andrew T.

Pellowski, Anne 1933- 20
Pellowski, Michael (Joseph) 1949- 151
   Brief entry 48
   Earlier sketch in SATA 88
Pellowski, Michael Morgan
   See Pellowski, Michael (Joseph)
Pelta, Kathy 1928- 18
Peltier, Leslie C(opus) 1900-1980 13
Pemberton, Bonnie 191
Pemberton, John Leigh
   See Leigh-Pemberton, John
Pembury, Bill
   See Groom, Arthur William
Pemsteen, Hans
   See Manes, Stephen
Pendennis, Arthur Esquir
   See Thackeray, William Makepeace
Pender, Lydia Podger 1907- 61
Pendery, Rosemary (Schmitz) 7
Pendle, Alexy 1943- 29
Pendle, George 1906-1977
   Obituary 28
Pendleton, Don
   See Cunningham, Chet
   and Garside, Jack
   and Jagninski, Tom
   and Krauzer, Steven M(ark)
   and Obstfeld, Raymond
Pendleton, Thomas 1965- 206
Pendziwol, Jean E. 1965- 177
Pene du Bois, William (Sherman)
   1916-1993 68
   Obituary 74
   Earlier sketch in SATA 4
   See also CLR 1
Penn, Audrey 1950- 22
Penn, Ruth Bonn
   See Rosenberg, Eth Clifford
Pennac, Daniel 1944- 155
Pennage, E. M.
   See Finkel, George (Irvine)
Penner, Fred 1946- 169
   Earlier sketch in SATA 67
Penner, Frederick Ralph Cornelius
   See Penner, Fred
Penney, Grace Jackson 1904-2000 35
Penney, Ian 1960- 76
Penney, Sue 1957- 152
   Earlier sketch in SATA 102
Pennington, Eunice 1923- 27
Pennington, Lillian Boyer 1904-2003 45
Pennypacker, Sara 1951- 187
Penrose, Gordon 1925- 66
Penson, Mary E. 1917- 78
Penzler, Otto 1942- 38
Pepe, Phil 1935- 20
Pepe, Philip
   See Pepe, Phil
Peppe, Rodney (Darrell) 1934- 74
   Earlier sketch in SATA 4
   See also SAAS 10
Pepper, Frank S. 1910-1988
   Obituary 61
Percy, Charles Henry
   See Smith, Dorothy Gladys
Percy, Rachel 1930- 63
Perdrizet, Marie-Pierre 1952- 79
Perenyi, Constance 1954- 93
Perenyi, Constance Marie
   See Perenyi, Constance
Perera, Hilda 1926- 105
Perera, Thomas Biddle 1938- 13
Peretti, Frank E. 1951- 141
   Earlier sketch in SATA 80
Perez, L. King 1940- 199
Perez, Lana
   See Perez, Marlene
Perez, Lucia Angela 1973- 182
Perez, Marlene 170
Pericoli, Matteo 1968- 178
Perkins, Al(bert Rogers) 1904-1975 30

Perkins, Lucy Fitch 1865-1937 72
Perkins, Lynne Rae 1956- 172
   Earlier sketch in SATA 131
Perkins, (Richard) Marlin 1905-1986 21
   Obituary 48
Perkins, Mitali 1963- 188
   Earlier sketch in SATA 88
Perks, Anne-Marie 1955- 122
Perl, Erica S. 188
Perl, Lila 72
   Earlier sketch in SATA 6
Perl, Susan 1922-1983 22
   Obituary 34
Perlman, Rhea 1948- 183
Perlmutter, O(scar) William 1920-1975 8
Pernu, Dennis 1970- 87
Perrault, Charles 1628-1703 25
   See also CLR 134
Perret, Delphine 1980- 190
Perret, Gene (Richard) 1937- 76
Perrine, Mary 1913-1976 2
Perrins, Lesley 1953- 56
Perrow, Angeli 1954- 121
Perry, Andrea 1956- 190
   Earlier sketch in SATA 148
Perry, Barbara Fisher
   See Fisher, Barbara
Perry, Elizabeth 1959- 174
Perry, Elizabeth Goodwin
   See Perry, Elizabeth
Perry, Marie Fritz 165
Perry, Patricia 1949- 30
Perry, Phyllis J(ean) 1933- 152
   Earlier sketches in SATA 60, 101
Perry, Ritchie (John Allen) 1942- 105
Perry, Roger 1933- 27
Perry, Steve(n Carl) 1947- 76
Pershall, Mary K. 1951- 172
   Earlier sketch in SATA 70
Pershing, Marie
   See Schultz, Pearle Henriksen
Perske, Robert 1927- 57
Persun, Morgan Reed
   See Watkins, Dawn L.
Petach, Heidi 149
Peter
   See Stratemeyer, Edward L.
Peters, Alexander
   See Hollander, Zander
Peters, Andrew Fusek 1965- 169
   Earlier sketch in SATA 107
Peters, Caroline
   See Betz, Eva Kelly
Peters, David
   See David, Peter
Peters, Elizabeth 1927- 49
Peters, Emma
   See Price, Karen
Peters, Gabriel
   See Matott, Justin
Peters, Julie Anne 1952- 197
   Earlier sketches in SATA 82, 128
Peters, Linda
   See Catherall, Arthur
Peters, Lisa Westberg 1951- 161
   Earlier sketches in SATA 74, 115
Peters, Patricia 1953- 84
Peters, Russell M. 1929- 78
Peters, S. H.
   See Henry, O.
   and Proffitt, Nicholas
Petersen, David 1946- 109
   Earlier sketch in SATA 62
Petersen, Gwenn Boardman 1924- 12
Petersen, P(eter) J(ames) 1941- 118
   Brief entry 43
   Earlier sketches in SATA 48, 83
Petersen, Palle 1943- 85
Petersham, Maud 1890-1971 17
   See also CLR 24

Petersham, Maud Sylvia Fuller
    See Petersham, Maud
Petersham, Miska 1888-1960 17
    See also CLR 24
Peterson, Cris 1952- 174
    Earlier sketches in SATA 84, 145
Peterson, Dawn 1934- 86
Peterson, Esther (Allen) 1934- 35
Peterson, Hans 1922- 8
Peterson, Harold L(eslie) 1922-1978 8
Peterson, Helen Stone 1910- 8
Peterson, Jean Sunde 1941- 108
Peterson, Jeanne Whitehouse 1939- 159
    Earlier sketch in SATA 29
Peterson, Kathleen B. 1951- 119
Peterson, Lorraine 1940- 56
    Brief entry 44
Peterson, Shelley 1952- 146
Peterson, Will
    See Cocks, Peter
Petie, Haris
    See Petty, Roberta
Petricic, Dusan 1946- 176
Petrides, Heidrun 1944- 19
Petrie, Catherine 1947- 52
    Brief entry 41
Petrone, Valeria 186
Petrosino, Tamara 193
Petroski, Catherine (Ann Groom) 1939- 48
Petrovich, Michael B(oro) 1922- 40
Petrovskaya, Kyra
    See Wayne, Kyra Petrovskaya
Petruccio, Steven James 1961- 67
Petry, Ann 1908-1997 5
    Obituary 94
    See also CLR 12
Petry, Ann Lane
    See Petry, Ann
Pettit, Jayne 1932- 108
Petty, J.T. 1977- 189
Petty, Kate 1951-2007 204
Petty, Roberta 1915- 10
Pevsner, Stella 131
    Earlier sketches in SATA 8, 77
    See also SAAS 14
Peyo
    See Culliford, Pierre
Peyton, K. M.
    See Peyton, Kathleen Wendy
Peyton, Kathleen Wendy 1929- 157
    Earlier sketches in SATA 15, 62
    See also CLR 3
    See also SAAS 17
Pfanner, (Anne) Louise 1955- 68
Pfeffer, Susan Beth 1948- 180
    Earlier sketches in SATA 4, 83
    See also CLR 11
    See also SAAS 17
Pfeffer, Wendy 1929- 204
    Earlier sketches in SATA 78, 142
Pfeiffer, Janet (B.) 1949- 96
Pfister, Marcus 207
    Earlier sketches in SATA 83, 150
    See also CLR 42
Pfitsch, Patricia Curtis 1948- 148
Pflieger, Pat 1955- 84
Pham, LeUyen 1973- 201
    Earlier sketch in SATA 175
Phelan, Mary Kay 1914- 3
Phelan, Matt 1970- 172
Phelan, Terry Wolfe 1941- 56
Phelps, Ethel Johnston 1914-1984 35
Philbrick, Rodman 1951- 163
Philbrick, W. R.
    See Philbrick, Rodman
Philbrick, W. Rodman
    See Philbrick, Rodman
Philbrook, Clem(ent E.) 1917- 24
Phillips, Aileen Paul
    See Paul, Aileen

Phillips, Betty Lou
    See Phillips, Elizabeth Louise
Phillips, Bob 1940- 95
Phillips, Douglas A. 1949- 161
Phillips, Elizabeth Louise 58
    Brief entry 48
Phillips, Irv(ing W.) 1905-2000 11
    Obituary 125
Phillips, Jack
    See Sandburg, Carl
Phillips, Leon
    See Gerson, Noel Bertram
Phillips, Loretta (Hosey) 1893-1987 10
Phillips, Louis 1942- 102
    Earlier sketch in SATA 8
Phillips, Mark
    See Garrett, Randall
    and Janifer, Laurence M(ark)
Phillips, Mary Geisler 1881-1964 10
Phillips, Michael
    See Nolan, William F.
Phillips, (Woodward) Prentice 1894-1981 .. 10
Phillpotts, Eden 1862-1960 24
Phin
    See Thayer, Ernest Lawrence
Phipson, Joan
    See Fitzhardinge, Joan Margaret
Phiz
    See Browne, Hablot Knight
Phleger, Fred B. 1909-1993 34
Phleger, Marjorie Temple 1908(?)-1986 1
    Obituary 47
Piaget, Jean 1896-1980
    Obituary 23
Piatti, Celestino 1922- 16
Picard, Barbara Leonie 1917- 89
    Earlier sketch in SATA 2
    See also SAAS 10
Pichon, Liz 174
Pickard, Charles 1932- 36
Pickering, James Sayre 1897-1969 36
    Obituary 28
Pickering, Jimmy 195
Pickering, Robert B. 1950- 93
Pielichaty, Helena 1955- 142
Pienkowski, Jan (Michal) 1936- 131
    Earlier sketches in SATA 6, 58
    See also CLR 6
Pierce, Edith Gray 1893-1977 45
Pierce, Katherine
    See St. John, Wylly Folk
Pierce, Meredith Ann 1958- 127
    Brief entry 48
    Earlier sketch in SATA 67
    See also CLR 20
Pierce, Ruth (Ireland) 1936- 5
Pierce, Sharon
    See McCullough, Sharon Pierce
Pierce, Tamora 1954- 187
    Brief entry 49
    Earlier sketches in SATA 51, 96, 153
Pierce, Terry 178
Pierik, Robert 1921- 13
Piernas-Davenport, Gail 199
Piers, Robert
    See Anthony, Piers
Pig, Edward
    See Gorey, Edward (St. John)
Pike, Bob
    See Pike, Robert W(ilson)
Pike, Christopher 1954(?)- 156
    Earlier sketch in SATA 68
    See also CLR 29
Pike, Deborah 1951- 89
Pike, E(dgar) Royston 1896-1980 22
    Obituary 56
Pike, R. William 1956- 92
Pike, Robert W(ilson) 1931- 102
Pilarski, Laura 1926- 13
Pilgrim, Anne
    See Allan, Mabel Esther

Pilkey, Dav 1966- 166
    Earlier sketches in SATA 68, 115
    See also CLR 48
Pilkey, David Murray, Jr.
    See Pilkey, Dav
Pilkington, Francis Meredyth 1907-1993 4
Pilkington, Roger (Windle) 1915-2003 10
    Obituary 144
Pilutti, Deb 208
Pin, Isabel 1975- 183
Pinchot, David 1914(?)-1983
    Obituary 34
Pincus, Harriet 1938- 27
Pinczes, Elinor J(ane) 1940- 81
Pine, Nicholas 1951- 91
Pine, Tillie S(chloss) 1896-1999 13
Pini, Richard (Alan) 1950- 89
Pini, Wendy 1951- 89
Pinkerton, Kathrene Sutherland (Gedney)
    1887-1967
    Obituary 26
Pinkett, Jada
    See Smith, Jada Pinkett
Pinkney, Andrea Davis 1963- 160
    Earlier sketch in SATA 113
Pinkney, Brian 1961- 206
    Earlier sketches in SATA 74, 148
    See also CLR 54
Pinkney, Gloria Jean 1941- 85
Pinkney, J. Brian
    See Pinkney, Brian
Pinkney, Jerry 1939- 198
    Autobiography Feature 198
    Brief entry 32
    Earlier sketches in SATA 41, 71, 107, 151
    See also CLR 43
    See also SAAS 12
Pinkney, John 97
Pinkney, Sandra L. 193
    Earlier sketch in SATA 128
Pinkwater, D. Manus
    See Pinkwater, Daniel
Pinkwater, Daniel 1941- 210
    Earlier sketches in SATA 8, 46, 76, 114, 158
    See also CLR 4
    See also SAAS 3
Pinkwater, Daniel M.
    See Pinkwater, Daniel
Pinkwater, Daniel Manus
    See Pinkwater, Daniel
Pinkwater, Jill 188
Pinkwater, Manus
    See Pinkwater, Daniel
Pinner, Joma
    See Werner, Herma
Pinto, Sara 200
Pioneer
    See Yates, Raymond F(rancis)
Piowaty, Kim Kennelly 1957- 49
Piper, Roger
    See Fisher, John
Pirner, Connie White 1955- 72
Piro, Richard 1934- 7
Pirot, Alison Lohans
    See Lohans, Alison
Pirotta, Saviour 184
Pirsig, Robert M(aynard) 1928- 39
Pita
    See Rendon, Maria
Pitcher, C.
    See Pitcher, Caroline
Pitcher, Caroline 1948- 128
Pitcher, Caroline Nell
    See Pitcher, Caroline
Pitman, (Isaac) James 1901-1985
    Obituary 46
Pitre, Felix 1949- 84
Pitrone, Jean Maddern 1920- 4
Pittman, Helena Clare 1945- 71
Pitz, Henry C(larence) 1895-1976 4
    Obituary 24

Pitzer, Susanna 1958- *181*
Piven, Hanoch 1963- *173*
Pixley, Marcella *194*
Pizer, Vernon 1918- 21
Place, Marian T(empleton) 1910- *3*
Place, Robin (Mary) 1926- *71*
Plaidy, Jean
    See Hibbert, Eleanor Alice Burford
Plain, Belva 1919- 62
Plaine, Alfred R. 1898(?)-1981
    Obituary 29
Plath, Sylvia 1932-1963 96
Platt, Chris 1959- *185*
Platt, Kin 1911- 86
    Earlier sketch in SATA *21*
    See also SAAS *17*
Platt, Randall 1948- 95
Platt, Randall Beth
    See Platt, Randall
Platt, Richard 1953- *166*
    Earlier sketch in SATA *120*
Playfellow, Robin
    See Ellis, Edward S.
Playsted, James
    See Wood, James Playsted
Plecas, Jennifer 1966- *149*
    Earlier sketch in SATA *84*
Plimpton, George 1927-2003 .... *10*
    Obituary *150*
Plimpton, George Ames
    See Plimpton, George
Plomer, William Charles Franklin
    1903-1973 24
Plotz, Helen Ratnoff 1913-2000 38
Plourde, Lynn 1955- *168*
    Earlier sketch in SATA *122*
Plowden, David 1932- 52
Plowden, Martha Ward 1948- 98
Plowhead, Ruth Gipson 1877-1967 43
Plowman, Stephanie 1922- 6
Pluckrose, Henry (Arthur) 1931- *141*
    Earlier sketch in SATA *13*
Plum, J.
    See Wodehouse, P. G.
Plum, Jennifer
    See Kurland, Michael
Plumb, Charles P. 1900(?)-1982
    Obituary 29
Plume, Ilse *170*
    Brief entry 43
Plumme, Don E.
    See Katz, Bobbi
Plummer, Margaret 1911- 2
Plum-Ucci, Carol *184*
Pochocki, Ethel (Frances) 1925- 76
Podendorf, Illa (E.) 1903(?)-1983 18
    Obituary 35
Podwal, Mark 1945- *160*
    Earlier sketch in SATA *101*
Podwal, Mark H.
    See Podwal, Mark
Poe, Edgar Allan 1809-1849 23
Poe, Ty (Christopher) 1975- 94
Pogany, William Andrew 1882-1955 44
    Brief entry 30
Pogany, Willy
    See Pogany, William Andrew
Pohl, Frederik 1919- 24
Pohlmann, Lillian (Grenfell) 1902-1997 11
Pohrt, Tom 1953- *195*
    Earlier sketches in SATA *67, 152*
Pointon, Robert
    See Rooke, Daphne
Points, Larry G. 1945- *177*
    Earlier sketch in SATA *133*
Points, Larry Gene
    See Points, Larry G.
Pokeberry, P.J.
    See Mitchell, B.J.
POLA
    See Watson, Pauline

Polacco, Patricia 1944- *180*
    Earlier sketches in SATA *74, 123*
    See also CLR *40*
Polacco, Patricia Ann
    See Polacco, Patricia
Polak, Monique 1960- *178*
Polatnick, Florence T. 1923- *5*
Polcovar, Jane 1948- *211*
Polder, Markus
    See Kruss, James
Polese, Carolyn 1947- 58
Polese, James 1914- 87
Polette, Nancy (Jane) 1930- 42
Polhamus, Jean Burt 1928- 21
Polhemus, Coleman *210*
Policoff, Stephen Phillip 1948- 77
Polikoff, Barbara G. 1929- *162*
    Earlier sketch in SATA *77*
Polikoff, Barbara Garland
    See Polikoff, Barbara G.
Polisar, Barry Louis 1954- *134*
    Earlier sketch in SATA *77*
Politi, Leo 1908-1996 47
    Obituary 88
    Earlier sketch in SATA *1*
    See also CLR *29*
Polking, Kirk 1925- *5*
Pollack, Jill S. 1963- 88
Pollack, Merrill S. 1924-1988
    Obituary 55
Polland, Barbara K(ay) 1939- 44
Polland, Madeleine A(ngela Cahill) 1918- .. 68
    Earlier sketch in SATA *6*
    See also SAAS *8*
Pollema-Cahill, Phyllis 1958- *123*
Pollock, Bruce 1945- 46
Pollock, Mary
    See Blyton, Enid
Pollock, Penny 1935- *137*
    Brief entry 42
    Earlier sketch in SATA *44*
Pollowitz, Melinda Kilborn 1944- 26
Polner, Murray 1928- 64
Polonsky, Arthur 1925- 34
Polseno, Jo 17
Pomaska, Anna 1946- *117*
Pomerantz, Charlotte 1930- *177*
    Earlier sketches in SATA *20, 80*
Pomeroy, Pete
    See Roth, Arthur J(oseph)
Pond, Alonzo W(illiam) 1894-1986 5
Pontiflet, Ted 1932- 32
Poole, Gray Johnson 1906- *1*
Poole, Josephine
    See Helyar, Jane Penelope Josephine
Poole, (Jane Penelope) Josephine
    See Helyar, Jane Penelope Josephine
Poole, Lynn 1910-1969 .... *1*
Poole, Peggy 1925- 39
Poortvliet, Rien 1932- 65
    Brief entry 37
Pope, Elizabeth Marie 1917-1992 38
    Brief entry 36
Pope, Kevin 1958- *183*
Popescu, Christine
    See Pullein-Thompson, Christine
Poploff, Michelle 1956- 67
Popp, K. Wendy 91
Poppel, Hans 1942- 71
Porfirio, Guy 1958- *197*
Portal, Colette 1936- 6
Porte, Barbara Ann 1943- *152*
    Brief entry 45
    Earlier sketches in SATA *57, 93*
Porter, A(nthony) P(eyton) 1945- 68
Porter, Connie (Rose) 1959(?)- *129*
    Earlier sketch in SATA *81*
Porter, Donald Clayton
    See Gerson, Noel Bertram
Porter, Eleanor H(odgman) 1868-1920
    See CLR *110*

Porter, Gene Stratton
    See Stratton-Porter, Gene
Porter, Janice Lee 1953- *108*
    Earlier sketch in SATA *68*
Porter, Katherine Anne 1890-1980 39
    Obituary 23
Porter, Kathryn
    See Swinford, Betty (June Wells)
Porter, Pamela 1956- *193*
Porter, Sheena 1935- 24
    See also SAAS *10*
Porter, Sue
    See Limb, Sue
Porter, Sue 1951- 76
Porter, Tracey *191*
Porter, William Sydney
    See Henry, O.
Portis, Antoinette *189*
Porto, Tony 1960- *153*
Portteus, Eleanora Marie Manthei (?)-1983
    Obituary 36
Posada, Mia *187*
Posell, Elsa Z(eigerman) -1995 3
Posten, Margaret L(ois) 1915- 10
Posthuma, Sieb 1960- *150*
Postier, Jim 1965- *202*
Potok, Chaim 1929-2002 .... *106*
    Obituary *134*
    Earlier sketch in SATA *33*
    See also CLR *92*
Potok, Herbert Harold
    See Potok, Chaim
Potok, Herman Harold
    See Potok, Chaim
Potter, Beatrix 1866-1943 .... *132*
    Earlier sketch in SATA *100*
    See also YABC *1*
    See also CLR *73*
Potter, Giselle *187*
    Earlier sketch in SATA *150*
Potter, Helen Beatrix
    See Potter, Beatrix
Potter, Margaret 1926-1998 21
    Obituary *104*
Potter, Marian 1915- 9
Potter, Miriam Clark 1886-1965 3
Poulin, Stephane 1961- 98
    See also CLR *28*
Poulton, Kimberly 1957(?)- *136*
Pournelle, Jerry (Eugene) 1933- *161*
    Earlier sketches in SATA *26, 91*
Povelite, Kay 1955- *102*
Pow, Tom 1950- *163*
Powe-Allred, Alexandra
    See Allred, Alexandra Powe
Powell, A. M.
    See Morgan, Alfred P(owell)
Powell, Consie *174*
Powell, E. Sandy 1947- 72
Powell, E.S.
    See Powell, E. Sandy
Powell, Pamela 1960- 78
Powell, Patricia Hruby 1951- *136*
Powell, Randy 1956- *118*
Powell, Richard Stillman
    See Barbour, Ralph Henry
Powell, Robert (Stephenson Smyth) Baden
    See Baden-Powell, Robert (Stephenson
    Smyth)
Powell, Stephanie 1953- 93
Power, Margaret (M.) 1945- *125*
    Earlier sketch in SATA *75*
Powers, Anne
    See Schwartz, Anne Powers
Powers, Bill 1931- 52
    Brief entry 31
Powers, Daniel 1959- *164*
Powers, J. L. *195*
Powers, Jessica
    See Powers, J. L.

Powers, Jessica Lynn
  See Powers, J. L.
Powers, Margaret
  See Heal, Edith
Powers, Tim 1952- *107*
Powers, Timothy Thomas
  See Powers, Tim
Powledge, Fred 1935- *37*
Poydar, Nancy *190*
Poynter, Margaret 1927- *27*
Prachaticka, Marketa
  See Kolibalova, Marketa
Prachatika, Marketa
  See Kolibalova, Marketa
Prager, Arthur *44*
Prager, Ellen J. 1962- *136*
Prange, Beckie *172*
Prap, Lila 1955- *177*
Praprotnik-Zupancic, Lilijana
  See Prap, Lila
Pratchett, Terence David John
  See Pratchett, Terry
Pratchett, Terry 1948- *185*
  Earlier sketches in SATA *82, 139*
  See also CLR *64*
Prater, John 1947- *149*
  Earlier sketches in SATA *72, 103*
Prato, Rodica *184*
Pratt, (Murray) Fletcher 1897-1956 .... *102*
Pratt, Kristin Joy 1976- *87*
Pratt, Pierre 1962- *208*
  Earlier sketches in SATA *95, 166*
Preiss, Byron 1953-2005 .... *166*
  Brief entry *42*
  Earlier sketch in SATA *47*
Preiss, Byron Cary
  See Preiss, Byron
Preller, James 1961- *209*
  Earlier sketch in SATA *88*
Prelutsky, Jack 1940- *171*
  Earlier sketches in SATA *22, 66, 118*
  See also CLR *115*
Prentice, Amy
  See Kaler, James Otis
Prescott, Casey
  See Morris, Chris(topher Crosby)
Presnall, Judith (Ann) Janda 1943- *96*
Pressler, Mirjam 1940- *155*
Preston, Douglas 1956- *113*
Preston, Edna Mitchell *40*
Preston, Lillian Elvira 1918- *47*
Preus, Margi *209*
Preussler, Otfried 1923- *24*
Prevert, Jacques (Henri Marie) 1900-1977
  Obituary *30*
Prevost, Guillaume 1964- *192*
Prevost, Mikela *203*
Price, Beverley Joan 1931- *98*
Price, Charlie *187*
Price, Christine (Hilda) 1928-1980 .... *3*
  Obituary *23*
Price, Garrett 1896-1979
  Obituary *22*
Price, Jennifer
  See Hoover, Helen (Drusilla Blackburn)
Price, Joan 1931- *124*
Price, Jonathan (Reeve) 1941- *46*
Price, Karen 1957- *125*
Price, Kathy Z. 1957- *172*
Price, Lucie Locke
  See Locke, Lucie
Price, Olive 1903-1991 .... *8*
Price, Susan 1955- *128*
  Earlier sketches in SATA *25, 85*
Price, Willard 1887-1983 .... *48*
  Brief entry *38*
Price-Groff, Claire *127*
Priceman, Marjorie 1958- *168*
  Earlier sketches in SATA *81, 120*
Prichard, Katharine Susannah 1883-1969 ... *66*

Prideaux, Tom 1908-1993 .... *37*
  Obituary *76*
Priestley, Alice 1962- *95*
Priestley, Chris 1958- *198*
Priestley, Lee (Shore) 1904-1999 .... *27*
Priestly, Doug 1954- *122*
Priestly, Douglas Michael
  See Priestly, Doug
Prieto, Mariana Beeching 1912-1999 .... *8*
Priley, Margaret (Ann) Hubbard 1909-1992
  Obituary *130*
Primavera, Elise 1954- *185*
  Brief entry *48*
  Earlier sketches in SATA *58, 109*
Prime, Derek (James) 1931- *34*
Prince, Alison (Mary) 1931- *86*
  Earlier sketch in SATA *28*
Prince, April Jones 1975- *180*
Prince, J(ack) H(arvey) 1908- *17*
Prince, Joshua *188*
Prince, Maggie *102*
Prineas, Sarah *204*
Pringle, Eric *138*
Pringle, Laurence 1935- *201*
  Autobiography Feature *201*
  Earlier sketches in SATA *4, 68, 104, 154*
  See also CLR *57*
  See also SAAS *6*
Pringle, Laurence Patrick
  See Pringle, Laurence
Prinz, Yvonne 1960- *175*
Prior, Natalie Jane 1963- *106*
Pritchett, Elaine H(illyer) 1920- *36*
Pritchett, Laura 1971- *178*
Pritchett, Laura Rose
  See Pritchett, Laura
Pritts, Kim Derek 1953- *83*
Prochazkova, Iva 1953- *68*
Proctor, Everitt
  See Montgomery, Rutherford George
Proeysen, Alf 1914-1970 .... *67*
  See also CLR *24*
Professor Scribbler
  See Hollingsworth, Mary
Proimos, James 1955- *173*
Prose, Francine 1947- *198*
  Earlier sketches in SATA *101, 149*
Protopopescu, Orel *186*
Protopopescu, Orel Odinov
  See Protopopescu, Orel
Provensen, Alice 1918- *147*
  Earlier sketches in SATA *9, 70*
  See also CLR *11*
Provensen, Martin 1916-1987 .... *70*
  Obituary *51*
  Earlier sketch in SATA *9*
  See also CLR *11*
Provensen, Martin Elias
  See Provensen, Martin
Provenzo, Eugene (F., Jr.) 1949- *142*
  Earlier sketch in SATA *78*
Provist, d'Alain 1906-1989
  See Diop, Birago (Ismael)
Provost, Gail Levine 1944- *65*
Provost, Gary (Richard) 1944-1995 .... *66*
Proysen, Alf
  See Proeysen, Alf
Pruett, Candace (J.) 1968- *157*
Pryor, Bonnie H. 1942- *69*
Pryor, Boori (Monty) 1950- *112*
Pryor, Helen Brenton 1897-1972 .... *4*
Pryor, Michael 1957- *153*
Pucci, Albert John 1920- *44*
Pudney, John (Sleigh) 1909-1977 .... *24*
Pugh, Ellen (Tiffany) 1920- *7*
Pullein-Thompson, Christine 1925-2005 ..... *82*
  Obituary *172*
  Earlier sketch in SATA *3*
Pullein-Thompson, Diana
  See Farr, Diana

Pullein-Thompson, Joanna Maxwell
  1898-1961 .... *82*
Pullein-Thompson, Josephine (Mary
  Wedderburn) *82*
  Earlier sketch in SATA *3*
Pullen, Zachary *189*
Pullman, Philip 1946- *198*
  Earlier sketches in SATA *65, 103, 150*
  See also CLR *84*
  See also SAAS *17*
Pullman, Philip Nicholas
  See Pullman, Philip
Pulver, Harry, Jr. 1960- *129*
Pulver, Robin 1945- *208*
  Earlier sketches in SATA *76, 133*
Puner, Helen W(alker) 1915-1989 .... *37*
  Obituary *63*
Purdy, Carol 1943- *120*
  Earlier sketch in SATA *66*
Purdy, Susan G(old) 1939- *8*
Purkiss, Diane 1961- *194*
Purmell, Ann 1953- *206*
  Earlier sketch in SATA *147*
Purnell, Idella 1901-1982 .... *120*
Purscell, Phyllis 1934- *7*
Purtill, Richard L. 1931- *53*
Pushker, Gloria 1927- *162*
  Earlier sketch in SATA *75*
Pushker, Gloria Teles
  See Pushker, Gloria
Pushkin, Aleksandr Sergeevich
  See Pushkin, Alexander
Pushkin, Alexander 1799-1837 .... *61*
Putnam, Alice 1916- *61*
Putnam, Arthur Lee
  See Alger, Horatio, Jr.
Putnam, Peter B(rock) 1920-1998 .... *30*
  Obituary *106*
Puttapipat, Niroot *199*
Puttock, Simon *178*
Puvilland, Alex *205*
Puvilland, Alexandre
  See Puvilland, Alex
Puybaret, Eric 1976- *195*
Pyle, Howard 1853-1911 .... *100*
  Earlier sketch in SATA *16*
  See also CLR *117*
Pyle, Katharine 1863-1938 .... *66*
Pyne, Mable Mandeville 1903-1969 .... *9*
Pyrnelle, Louise-Clarke 1850-1907 .... *114*

Q

Quackenbush, Robert M(ead) 1929- *133*
  Autobiography Feature *133*
  Earlier sketches in SATA *7, 70*
  See also CLR *122*
  See also SAAS *7*
Qualey, Marsha 1953- *124*
  Earlier sketch in SATA *79*
Qualls, Sean *177*
Quammen, David 1948- *7*
Quark, Jason
  See Eldin, Peter
Quarles, Benjamin 1904-1996 .... *12*
Quarles, Benjamin Arthur
  See Quarles, Benjamin
Quatermass, Martin
  See Carpenter, John
Quattlebaum, Mary 1958- *185*
  Earlier sketches in SATA *88, 134*
Quay, Emma *173*
  Earlier sketch in SATA *119*

Queen, Ellery
　See Deming, Richard
　and Dannay, Frederic
　and Davidson, Avram (James)
　and Fairman, Paul W.
　and Flora, Fletcher
　and Holding, James (Clark Carlisle, Jr.)
　and Hoch, Edward D.
　and Kane, Henry
　and Lee, Manfred B.
　and Marlowe, Stephen
　and Powell, (Oval) Talmage
　and Sheldon, Walter J(ames)
　and Sturgeon, Theodore (Hamilton)
　and Tracy, Don(ald Fiske)
　and Vance, Jack
Queen Latifah 1970- *185*
Quennell, Marjorie Courtney 1884-1972 .... *29*
Quentin
　See Sheldon, David
Quentin, Brad
　See Bisson, Terry
Quest, (Edna) Olga W(ilbourne) Hall
　See Hall-Quest, (Edna) Olga W(ilbourne)
Quick, Annabelle 1922-1986 .... *2*
Quigg, Jane (Hulda) (?)-1986
　Obituary *49*
Quill, Monica
　See McInerny, Ralph
Quin-Harkin, Janet 1941- *165*
　Earlier sketches in SATA *18, 90, 119*
Quin-Harkin, Janet Elizabeth
　See Quin-Harkin, Janet
Quinlan, Susan E. 1954- *88*
Quinlan, Susan Elizabeth
　See Quinlan, Susan E.
Quinn, Elisabeth 1881-1962 .... *22*
Quinn, Pat 1947- *130*
Quinn, Patrick 1950- *73*
Quinn, Rob 1972- *138*
Quinn, Susan 1940- *30*
Quinn, Susan Taft
　See Quinn, Susan
Quinn, Theodora K.
　See Kroeber, Theodora (Kracaw)
Quinn, Vernon
　See Quinn, Elisabeth
Quirk, Anne (E.) 1956- *99*
Quixley, Jim 1931- *56*
Quyth, Gabriel
　See Jennings, Gary

R

Ra, Carol F. 1939- *76*
Raab, Evelyn 1951- *129*
Rabb, Margo 1972- *188*
Rabb, M.E.
　See Rabb, Margo
Rabe, Berniece (Louise) 1928- *148*
　Autobiography Feature *148*
　Earlier sketches in SATA *7, 77*
　See also SAAS *10*
Rabe, Olive H(anson) (?)-1968 .... *13*
Rabin, Staton 1958- *162*
　Earlier sketch in SATA *84*
Rabinowich, Ellen 1946- *29*
Rabinowitz, Sandy 1954- *52*
　Brief entry *39*
Rachlin, Carol K(ing) 1919- *64*
Rachlin, Harvey 1951- *47*
Rachlin, Harvey Brant
　See Rachlin, Harvey
Rachlin, Nahid *64*
Rachlis, Eugene (Jacob) 1920-1986
　Obituary *50*
Rackham, Arthur 1867-1939 .... *100*
　Earlier sketch in SATA *15*
　See also CLR *57*

Racoma, Robin Yoko 1953- *207*
Raczka, Bob 1963- *191*
　Earlier sketch in SATA *163*
Radencich, Marguerite C. 1952-1998 .... *79*
Rader, Laura *197*
Radford, Ruby L(orraine) 1891-1971 .... *6*
Radin, Ruth Yaffe 1938- *107*
　Brief entry *52*
　Earlier sketch in SATA *56*
Radlauer, David 1952- *28*
Radlauer, Edward 1921- *15*
Radlauer, Ruth Shaw 1926- *98*
　Earlier sketch in SATA *15*
Radley, Gail 1951- *112*
　Earlier sketch in SATA *25*
Radunsky, Vladimir *177*
Rae, Gwynedd 1892-1977 .... *37*
Raebeck, Lois 1921- *5*
Rael, Elsa Okon 1927-
　See CLR *84*
Raffi
　See Cavoukian, Raffi
Raftery, Gerald (Bransfield) 1905-1986 ...... *11*
Ragan-Reid, Gale 1956- *90*
Rahaman, Vashanti 1953- *98*
Rahn, Joan Elma 1929- *27*
Rai, Bali 1971- *152*
Raible, Alton (Robert) 1918- *35*
Raiff, Stan 1930- *11*
Raines, Shirley C(arol) 1945- *128*
Rainey, W. B.
　See Blassingame, Wyatt Rainey
Rake, Jody 1961- *157*
Rallison, Janette 1966- *183*
Ralston, Jan
　See Dunlop, Agnes M. R.
Rama, Sue *190*
Ramal, Walter
　See de la Mare, Walter (John)
Ramanujan, A(ttipat) K(rishnaswami)
　1929-1993 .... *86*
Rame, David
　See Divine, Arthur Durham
Ramirez, Jose 1967- *198*
Ramirez, Orlando L. 1972- *194*
Ramos, Jorge 1958- *205*
Ramstad, Ralph L. 1919- *115*
Rana, Indi
　See Rana, Indira Higham
Rana, Indira Higham 1944- *82*
Rana, J.
　See Bhatia, Jamunadevi
Ranadive, Gail 1944- *10*
Rand, Ann (Binkley) *30*
Rand, Gloria 1925- *156*
　Earlier sketch in SATA *101*
Rand, Paul 1914-1996 .... *6*
Randall, Carrie
　See Ransom, Candice F.
Randall, David 1972- *167*
Randall, Florence Engel 1917-1997 .... *5*
Randall, Janet
　See Young, Janet Randall
　and Young, Robert W(illiam)
Randall, Robert
　See Garrett, Randall
　and Silverberg, Robert
Randall, Ruth (Elaine) Painter 1892-1971 .... *3*
Randell, Beverley
　See Price, Beverley Joan
Randle, Kristen D. 1952- *92*
　Autobiography Feature *119*
　See also SAAS *24*
Randle, Kristen Downey
　See Randle, Kristen D.
Randolph, Boynton M.D.
　See Ellis, Edward S.
Randolph, Ellen
　See Rawn, Melanie
Randolph, Geoffrey
　See Ellis, Edward S.

Randolph, J. H.
　See Ellis, Edward S.
Randolph, Lieutenant J. H.
　See Ellis, Edward S.
Rands, William Brighty 1823-1882 .... *17*
Raney, Ken 1953- *74*
Rankin, Joan 1940- *148*
　Earlier sketch in SATA *88*
Rankin, Laura 1953(?)- *176*
Ranney, Agnes V. 1916-1985 .... *6*
Ransom, Candice F. 1952- *183*
　Brief entry *49*
　Earlier sketches in SATA *52, 89, 135*
Ransom, Jeanie Franz 1957- *187*
Ransome, Arthur (Michell) 1884-1967 .... *22*
　See also CLR *8*
Ransome, James E. 1961- *178*
　Earlier sketches in SATA *76, 123*
　See also CLR *86*
Rant, Tol E.
　See Longyear, Barry B(rookes)
Raphael, Elaine
　See Bolognese, Elaine
Raposo, Joseph Guilherme 1938-1989
　Obituary *61*
Rapp, Adam 1968- *148*
Rappaport, Doreen *211*
　Earlier sketch in SATA *151*
Rappaport, Eva 1924- *6*
Rappoport, Ken 1935- *167*
　Earlier sketch in SATA *89*
Rarick, Carrie 1911-2002 .... *41*
Raschka, Chris 1959- *207*
　Earlier sketches in SATA *80, 117, 166*
Raschka, Christopher
　See Raschka, Chris
Rascol, Sabina I. *159*
Rash, Andy *162*
Raskin, Edith Lefkowitz 1908-1987 .... *9*
Raskin, Ellen 1928-1984 .... *139*
　Earlier sketches in SATA *2, 38*
　See also CLR *12*
Raskin, Joseph 1897-1982 .... *12*
　Obituary *29*
Rathjen, Carl Henry 1909-1984 .... *11*
Rathmann, Peggy 1953- *157*
　Earlier sketch in SATA *94*
　See also CLR *77*
Ratliff, Thomas M. 1948- *118*
Ratner, Sue Lynn
　See Alexander, Sue
Rattigan, Jama Kim 1951- *99*
Ratto, Linda Lee 1952- *79*
Rattray, Simon
　See Trevor, Elleston
Ratz de Tagyos, Paul 1958- *198*
　Earlier sketch in SATA *76*
Rau, Dana Meachen 1971- *167*
　Earlier sketch in SATA *94*
Rau, Margaret 1913- *168*
　Earlier sketch in SATA *9*
　See also CLR *8*
Rauch, Mabel Thompson 1888-1972
　Obituary *26*
Raucher, Herman 1928- *8*
Raude, Karina *199*
Rauh, Sherry
　See North, Sherry
Raum, Elizabeth 1949- *155*
Raven, Margot Theis *184*
RavenWolf, Silver 1956- *155*
Ravielli, Anthony 1916-1997 .... *3*
　Obituary *95*
Ravilious, Robin 1944- *77*
Ravishankar, Anushka 1961- *200*
Rawding, F(rederick) W(illiam) 1930- *55*
Rawlings, Marjorie Kinnan 1896-1953 ..... *100*
　See also YABC *1*
　See also CLR *63*
Rawlins, Donna 1956- *206*
Rawlinson, Julia *175*

Rawls, (Woodrow) Wilson 1913-1984 22
   See also CLR 81
Rawlyk, George Alexander 1935- 64
Rawn, Melanie 1954- 98
Rawn, Melanie Robin
   See Rawn, Melanie
Rawson, Katherine 1955- 190
Ray, Carl 1943-1978 63
Ray, Deborah
   See Kogan Ray, Deborah
Ray, Delia 1963- 179
   Earlier sketch in SATA 70
Ray, Irene
   See Sutton, Margaret Beebe
Ray, Jane 1960- 196
   Earlier sketches in SATA 72, 152
Ray, JoAnne 1935- 9
Ray, Mary (Eva Pedder) 1932- 127
   Earlier sketch in SATA 2
Ray, Mary Lyn 1946- 154
   Earlier sketch in SATA 90
Rayban, Chloe 1944- 167
Rayevsky, Robert 1955- 190
   Earlier sketch in SATA 81
Raymond, James Crossley 1917-1981
   Obituary 29
Raymond, Robert
   See Alter, Robert Edmond
Rayner, Catherine 204
Rayner, Hugh 151
Rayner, Mary 1933- 87
   Earlier sketch in SATA 22
   See also CLR 41
Rayner, Shoo
   See Rayner, Hugh
Rayner, William 1929- 55
   Brief entry 36
Raynor, Dorka 28
Rayson, Steven 1932- 30
Razzell, Arthur (George) 1925- 11
Razzell, Mary (Catherine) 1930- 102
Razzi, James 1931- 10
Read, Elfreida 1920- 2
Read, Nicholas 1956- 146
Read, Piers Paul 1941- 21
Reade, Deborah 1949- 69
Reader, Dennis 1929- 71
Reading, Richard P(atrick) 1962- 161
Readman, Jo 1958- 89
Ready, Kirk L(ewis) 1943- 39
Reaney, James 1926-2008 43
Reaney, James Crerar
   See Reaney, James
Reardon, Joyce
   See Pearson, Ridley
Reaver, Chap 1935-1993 69
   Obituary 77
Reaver, Herbert R.
   See Reaver, Chap
Reaves, J. Michael
   See Reaves, (James) Michael
Reaves, (James) Michael 1950- 99
Reber, Deborah 189
Recorvits, Helen 191
Redding, Robert Hull 1919- 2
Redekopp, Elsa 61
Redlich, Ben 1977- 181
Redsand, Anna 1948- 184
Redway, Ralph
   See Hamilton, Charles (Harold St. John)
Redway, Ridley
   See Hamilton, Charles (Harold St. John)
Reece, Colleen L. 1935- 116
Reece, Gabrielle 1970- 108
Reed, Betty Jane 1921- 4
Reed, Dallas
   See Pendleton, Thomas
Reed, E.
   See Evans, Mari
Reed, Gwendolyn E(lizabeth) 1932- 21

Reed, Kit 1932- 184
   Autobiography Feature 184
   Earlier sketches in SATA 34, 116
Reed, Lynn Rowe 171
Reed, Mike 1951- 211
Reed, Neil 1961- 99
Reed, Talbot Baines 1852-1893
   See CLR 76
Reed, Thomas (James) 1947- 34
Reed, William Maxwell 1871-1962 15
Reeder, Carolyn 1937- 97
   Earlier sketch in SATA 66
   See also CLR 69
Reeder, Colin (Dawson) 1938- 74
Reeder, Colonel Red
   See Reeder, Russell P(otter), Jr.
Reeder, Russell P(otter), Jr. 1902-1998 4
   Obituary 101
Reeder, Stephanie Owen 1951- 102
Reed-Jones, Carol 1955- 112
Reef, Catherine 1951- 189
   Earlier sketches in SATA 73, 128
Reekie, Jocelyn (Margaret) 1947- 145
Reeman, Douglas Edward 1924- 63
   Brief entry 28
Rees, Celia 1949- 124
Rees, David (Bartlett) 1936-1993 69
   Obituary 76
   Earlier sketch in SATA 36
   See also SAAS 5
Rees, Douglas 1947- 169
Rees, Ennis (Samuel, Jr.) 1925- 3
Rees, (George) Leslie (Clarence)
   1905-2000 105
   Obituary 135
Reese, Bob
   See Reese, Robert A.
Reese, Carolyn Johnson 1938- 64
Reese, Della 1931(?)- 114
Reese, Lyn
   See Reese, Carolyn Johnson
Reese, Robert A. 1938- 60
   Brief entry 53
Reese, (John) Terence 1913-1996 59
Reeve, Joel
   See Cox, William R(obert)
Reeve, Kirk 1934- 117
Reeve, Philip 201
   Earlier sketch in SATA 170
Reeve, Rosie 188
   Earlier sketch in SATA 186
Reeves, Faye Couch 1953- 76
Reeves, James
   See Reeves, John Morris
Reeves, Jeni 1947- 111
Reeves, John Morris 1909-1978 87
   Earlier sketch in SATA 15
Reeves, Joyce 1911- 17
Reeves, Lawrence F. 1926- 29
Reeves, Ruth Ellen
   See Ranney, Agnes V.
Regan, Dian Curtis 1950- 149
   Autobiography Feature 149
   Earlier sketches in SATA 75, 133
Regehr, Lydia 1903-1991 37
Reger, James P. 1952- 106
Reggiani, Renee 1925- 18
Rehm, Karl M. 1935- 72
Reibstein, Mark 211
Reich, Ali
   See Katz, Bobbi
Reich, Susanna 1954- 113
Reiche, Dietlof 1941- 159
Reichert, Edwin C(lark) 1909-1988
   Obituary 57
Reichert, Mickey Zucker
   See Reichert, Miriam Zucker
Reichert, Miriam Zucker 1962- 85
Reichert, Renee 172
Reichhold, Jane(t E.) 1937- 147
Reid, Alastair 1926- 46

Reid, Barbara 1922- 21
Reid, Barbara (Jane) 1957- 93
   See also CLR 64
Reid, Desmond
   See Moorcock, Michael
   and McNeilly, Wilfred (Glassford)
Reid, Eugenie Chazal 1924- 12
Reid, John Calvin 21
Reid, (Thomas) Mayne 1818-1883 24
Reid, Meta Mayne 1905-1991 58
   Brief entry 36
Reid, Robin (Nicole) 1969- 145
Reid Banks, Lynne 1929- 165
   Earlier sketches in SATA 22, 75, 111
   See also CLR 86
Reider, Katja 1960- 126
Reid Jenkins, Debra 1955- 87
Reiff, Stephanie Ann 1948- 47
   Brief entry 28
Reig, June 1933- 30
Reigot, Betty Polisar 1924- 55
   Brief entry 41
Reilly, Joan 195
Reim, Melanie (K.) 1956- 104
Reinach, Jacquelyn (Krasne) 1930-2000 28
Reiner, Carl 1922- 151
Reiner, William B(uck) 1910-1976 46
   Obituary 30
Reinfeld, Fred 1910-1964 3
Reinhardt, Dana 1971- 175
Reinhart, Matthew 1971- 197
   Earlier sketch in SATA 161
Reiniger, Lotte 1899-1981 40
   Obituary 33
Reinsma, Carol 1949- 91
Reinstedt, Randall A. 1935- 101
Reinstedt, Randy
   See Reinstedt, Randall A.
Reisberg, Mira 1955- 82
Reisberg, Veg
   See Reisberg, Mira
Reiser, Lynn 1944- 180
   Earlier sketches in SATA 81, 138
Reiser, Lynn Whisnant
   See Reiser, Lynn
Reisgies, Teresa (Maria) 1966- 74
Reiss, Johanna (de Leeuw) 1929(?)- 18
   See also CLR 19
Reiss, John J. 23
Reiss, Kathryn 1957- 144
   Earlier sketch in SATA 76
Reit, Seymour Victory 1918-2001 21
   Obituary 133
Reit, Sy
   See Reit, Seymour Victory
Relf, Patricia 1954- 134
   Earlier sketch in SATA 71
Remi, Georges 1907-1983 13
   Obituary 32
   See also CLR 114
Remington, Frederic S(ackrider)
   1861-1909 41
Remkiewicz, Frank 1939- 152
   Earlier sketch in SATA 77
Rempt, Fiona 1973- 198
Remy, Georges
   See Remi, Georges
Renaud, Anne 1957- 211
Renaud, Bernadette 1945- 66
Renault, Mary 1905-1983 23
   Obituary 36
Rendell, Joan 28
Rendina, Laura (Jones) Cooper 1902- 10
Rendon, Marcie R. 1952- 97
Rendon, Maria 1965- 116
Renee, Janina 1956- 140
Renfro, Ed 1924- 79
Renick, Marion (Lewis) 1905-1983 23
Renier, Aaron 1977- 202
Renken, Aleda 1907- 27
Renlie, Frank H. 1936- 11

Rennert, Richard Scott 1956- *67*
Rennison, Louise 1951- *149*
Reno, Dawn E(laine) 1953- *130*
Rensie, Willis
  See Eisner, Will
Renton, Cam
  See Armstrong, Richard
Renvoize, Jean *5*
Resau, Laura 1973- *190*
Resciniti, Angelo G. 1952- *75*
Resnick, Michael David
  See Resnick, Mike
Resnick, Mike 1942- *159*
  Earlier sketches in SATA *38, 106*
Resnick, Seymour 1920- *23*
Retla, Robert
  See Alter, Robert Edmond
Rettig, Liz *199*
Rettstatt, Chris
  See Ashland, Monk
Reuter, Bjarne (B.) 1950- *142*
  Earlier sketch in SATA *68*
Reuter, Carol (Joan) 1931- *2*
Revena
  See Wright, Betty Ren
Revsbech, Vicki
  See Liestman, Vicki
Rex, Adam *186*
Rex, Michael *191*
Rey, H. A. 1898-1977 .... *100*
  Earlier sketches in SATA *1, 26, 69*
  See also CLR *93*
Rey, Hans Augusto
  See Rey, H. A.
Rey, Luis V. 1955- *201*
Rey, Margret 1906-1996 .... *86*
  Obituary *93*
  Earlier sketch in SATA *26*
  See also CLR *93*
Rey, Margret Elisabeth
  See Rey, Margret
Reyher, Becky
  See Reyher, Rebecca Hourwich
Reyher, Rebecca Hourwich 1897-1987 .... *18*
  Obituary *50*
Reynold, Ann
  See Bernardo, Anilu
Reynolds, Aaron 1970- *197*
Reynolds, Adrian 1963- *192*
Reynolds, C. Buck 1957- *107*
Reynolds, Dickson
  See Reynolds, Helen Mary Greenwood Camp-
  bell
Reynolds, Helen Mary Greenwood Campbell
  1884-1969
  Obituary *26*
Reynolds, Jan 1956- *180*
Reynolds, John
  See Whitlock, Ralph
Reynolds, Madge
  See Whitlock, Ralph
Reynolds, Malvina 1900-1978 .... *44*
  Obituary *24*
Reynolds, Marilyn 1935- *121*
  See also SAAS *23*
Reynolds, Marilyn M.
  See Reynolds, Marilyn
Reynolds, Marilynn 1940- *141*
  Earlier sketch in SATA *80*
Reynolds, Pamela 1923- *34*
Reynolds, Peter H. 1961- *128*
Reynolds, Peter J. 1961- *179*
Reynolds, Susan *179*
Rhine, Richard
  See Silverstein, Alvin
  and Silverstein, Virginia B.
Rhoades, Diane 1952- *90*
Rhodes, Bennie (Loran) 1927- *35*
Rhodes, Donna McKee 1962- *87*
Rhodes, Frank Harold Trevor 1926- *37*

Rhue, Morton
  See Strasser, Todd
Rhyne, Nancy 1926- *66*
Rhynes, Martha E. 1939- *141*
Ribbons, Ian 1924- *37*
  Brief entry *30*
  See also SAAS *3*
Ricciuti, Edward R(aphael) 1938- *10*
Rice, Alice (Caldwell) Hegan 1870-1942 ... *63*
Rice, Bebe Faas 1932- *89*
Rice, Charles D(uane) 1910-1971
  Obituary *27*
Rice, Dale R. 1948- *42*
Rice, Dale Richard
  See Rice, Dale R.
Rice, Dick
  See Rice, R. Hugh
Rice, Earle (Wilmont), Jr. 1928- *151*
  Earlier sketch in SATA *92*
Rice, Edward 1918-2001 .... *47*
  Brief entry *42*
Rice, Elizabeth 1913-1976 .... *2*
Rice, Eve 1951- *91*
  Earlier sketch in SATA *34*
Rice, Eve Hart
  See Rice, Eve
Rice, Inez 1907- *13*
Rice, James 1934- *93*
  Earlier sketch in SATA *22*
Rice, John F. 1958- *82*
Rice, R. Hugh 1929- *115*
Rice, Richard H.
  See Rice, R. Hugh
Rich, Barbara
  See Graves, Robert
Rich, Elaine Sommers 1926- *6*
Rich, Josephine Bouchard 1912- *10*
Rich, Louise Dickinson 1903-1991 .... *54*
  Obituary *67*
Richard, Adrienne 1921- *5*
  See also SAAS *9*
Richard, James Robert
  See Bowen, Robert Sydney
Richards, Chuck 1957- *170*
Richards, Frank
  See Hamilton, Charles (Harold St. John)
Richards, Hilda
  See Hamilton, Charles (Harold St. John)
Richards, Jackie 1925- *102*
Richards, Jean 1940- *135*
Richards, Justin *169*
Richards, Kay
  See Baker, Susan (Catherine)
Richards, Laura E(lizabeth Howe) 1850-1943
  See YABC *1*
  See also CLR *54*
Richards, Leigh
  See King, Laurie R.
Richards, Marlee
  See Brill, Marlene Targ
Richards, Norman 1932- *48*
Richards, R(onald) C(harles)
  W(illiam) 1923- *59*
  Brief entry *43*
Richards, Walter Alden (Jr.) 1907-1988
  Obituary *56*
Richardson, Andrew (William) 1986- *120*
Richardson, Carol 1932- *58*
Richardson, Frank Howard 1882-1970
  Obituary *27*
Richardson, Grace Lee
  See Dickson, Naida
Richardson, Jean (Mary) *59*
Richardson, Judith Benet 1941- *77*
Richardson, Nigel 1957- *187*
Richardson, Robert S(hirley) 1902-1981 .... *8*
Richardson, Sandy 1949- *116*
Richardson, V.A. *189*
Richardson, Willis 1889-1977 .... *60*
Richelson, Geraldine 1922- *29*
Richemont, Enid 1940- *82*

Richler, Mordecai 1931-2001 .... *98*
  Brief entry *27*
  Earlier sketch in SATA *44*
  See also CLR *17*
Richman, Sophia 1941- *142*
Rich-McCoy, Lois
  See McCoy, Lois (Rich)
Richmond, Robin 1951- *75*
Richoux, Pat(ricia) 1927- *7*
Richter, Alice 1941- *30*
Richter, Conrad (Michael) 1890-1968 .... *3*
Richter, Hans Peter 1925-1993 .... *6*
  See also CLR *21*
  See also SAAS *11*
Richter, Jutta 1955- *184*
Rickard, Graham 1949- *71*
Rico, Don(ato) 1917-1985
  Obituary *43*
Riddell, Chris 1962- *166*
  Earlier sketch in SATA *114*
Riddell, Christopher Barry
  See Riddell, Chris
Riddell, Edwina 1955- *82*
Ridden, Brian (John) 1934- *123*
Riddle, Tohby 1965- *151*
  Earlier sketch in SATA *74*
Riddleburger, Sam *202*
Riddles, Libby 1956- *140*
Rideout, Sandy *194*
Ridge, Antonia (Florence) (?)-1981 .... *7*
  Obituary *27*
Ridge, Martin 1923-2003 .... *43*
Ridley, Philip *171*
  Earlier sketch in SATA *88*
Ridlon, Marci
  See Balterman, Marcia Ridlon
Riedman, Sarah R(egal) 1902-1995 .... *1*
Riehecky, Janet 1953- *164*
Ries, Lori *185*
Riesenberg, Felix, Jr. 1913-1962 .... *23*
Rieu, E(mile) V(ictor) 1887-1972 .... *46*
  Obituary *26*
Riffenburgh, Beau 1955- *175*
Rigg, Sharon
  See Creech, Sharon
Riggenbach, Holly
  See Black, Holly
Riggio, Anita 1952- *148*
  Earlier sketch in SATA *73*
Riggs, Shannon *190*
Riggs, Sidney Noyes 1892-1975
  Obituary *28*
Riggs, Stephanie 1964- *138*
Riglietti, Serena 1969- *189*
Rigney, James Oliver, Jr.
  See Jordan, Robert
Rikhoff, Jean 1928- *9*
Rikki
  See Ducornet, Erica
Riley, James A. 1939- *97*
Riley, James Whitcomb 1849-1916 .... *17*
Riley, Jocelyn 1949- *60*
  Brief entry *50*
Riley, Jocelyn Carol
  See Riley, Jocelyn
Riley, Linda Capus 1950- *85*
Riley, Martin 1948- *81*
Rimbauer, Steven
  See Pearson, Ridley
Rimes, (Margaret) LeAnn 1982- *154*
Rinaldi, Ann 1934- *202*
  Brief entry *50*
  Earlier sketches in SATA *51, 78, 117, 161*
  See also CLR *46*
Rinard, Judith E(llen) 1947- *140*
  Earlier sketch in SATA *44*
Rinder, Lenore 1949- *92*
Ring, Elizabeth 1920- *79*
Ringdahl, Mark
  See Longyear, Barry B(rookes)

Ringgold, Faith 1930- 187
    Earlier sketches in SATA *71, 114*
    See also CLR *30*
Ringi, Kjell (Arne Soerensen) 1939- 12
Rinkoff, Barbara Jean (Rich) 1923-1975 4
    Obituary 27
Rinn, Miriam 1946- 127
Riordan, James 1936- 95
Riordan, Rick 208
    Earlier sketch in SATA *174*
Rios, Tere
    See Versace, Marie Teresa Rios
Ripken, Cal, Jr. 1960- 114
Ripken, Calvin Edward, Jr.
    See Ripken, Cal, Jr.
Ripley, Catherine 1957- 82
Ripley, Elizabeth Blake 1906-1969 5
Ripper, Charles L(ewis) 1929- 3
Ripper, Chuck
    See Ripper, Charles L(ewis)
Riq
    See Atwater, Richard (Tupper)
Rish, David 1955- 110
Riskind, Mary 1944- 60
Rissinger, Matt 1956- 93
Rissman, Art
    See Sussman, Susan
Rissman, Susan
    See Sussman, Susan
Ritchie, Barbara Gibbons 14
Ritter, Felix
    See Kruss, James
Ritter, John H. 1951- 137
    Earlier sketch in SATA *129*
Ritter, Lawrence S(tanley) 1922-2004 58
    Obituary 152
Ritthaler, Shelly 1955- 91
Ritts, Paul 1920(?)-1980
    Obituary 25
Ritz, Karen 1957- 202
    Earlier sketch in SATA *80*
Rivera, Geraldo (Miguel) 1943- 54
    Brief entry 28
Rivers, Elfrida
    See Bradley, Marion Zimmer
Rivers, Karen 1970- 131
Riverside, John
    See Heinlein, Robert A.
Rivkin, Ann 1920- 41
Rivoli, Mario 1943- 10
Roach, Marilynne K. 1946- 9
Roach, Marilynne Kathleen
    See Roach, Marilynne K.
Roach, Portia
    See Takakjian, Portia
Robb, Don 1937- 194
Robb, Laura 1937- 95
Robberecht, Thierry 1960- 182
Robbins, Frank 1917-1994(?) 42
    Brief entry 32
Robbins, Ken 1945- 147
    Brief entry 53
    Earlier sketch in SATA *94*
Robbins, Raleigh
    See Hamilton, Charles (Harold St. John)
Robbins, Ruth 1917(?)- 14
Robbins, Tony
    See Pashko, Stanley
Robbins, Wayne
    See Cox, William R(obert)
Robel, S. L.
    See Fraustino, Lisa Rowe
Roberson, Jennifer 1953- 72
Roberson, John R(oyster) 1930- 53
Robert, Adrian
    See St. John, Nicole
Roberts, Bethany 202
    Earlier sketch in SATA *133*
Roberts, Bruce (Stuart) 1930- 47
    Brief entry 39

Roberts, Charles G(eorge) D(ouglas)
    1860-1943 88
    Brief entry 29
    See also CLR *33*
Roberts, David
    See Cox, John Roberts
Roberts, David 1970- 191
Roberts, Diane 1937- 184
Roberts, Elizabeth 1944- 80
Roberts, Elizabeth Madox 1886-1941 33
    Brief entry 27
    See also CLR *100*
Roberts, Jim
    See Bates, Barbara S(nedeker)
Roberts, John G(aither) 1913-1993 27
Roberts, Judy I. 1957- 93
Roberts, Katherine 1962- 152
Roberts, M. L.
    See Mattern, Joanne
Roberts, Nancy Correll 1924- 52
    Brief entry 28
Roberts, Priscilla 1955- 184
Roberts, Terence
    See Sanderson, Ivan T(erence)
Roberts, Willo Davis 1928-2004 150
    Autobiography Feature 150
    Obituary 160
    Earlier sketches in SATA *21, 70, 133*
    See also CLR *95*
    See also SAAS *8*
Robertson, Barbara (Anne) 1931- 12
Robertson, Don 1929-1999 8
    Obituary 113
Robertson, Dorothy Lewis 1912- 12
Robertson, Ellis
    See Ellison, Harlan
    and Silverberg, Robert
Robertson, James I., Jr. 1930- 182
Robertson, James Irvin
    See Robertson, James I., Jr.
Robertson, Janet (E.) 1935- 68
Robertson, Jennifer Sinclair 1942-1998 12
Robertson, Jenny
    See Robertson, Jennifer Sinclair
Robertson, Keith (Carlton) 1914-1991 85
    Obituary 69
    Earlier sketch in SATA *1*
    See also SAAS *15*
Robertson, Mark
    See Robertson, M.P.
Robertson, M.P. 1965- 197
Robertson, Stephen
    See Walker, Robert W.
Robertus, Polly M. 1948- 73
Robeson, Kenneth
    See Dent, Lester
    and Goulart, Ron
Robeson, Kenneth
    See Johnson, (Walter) Ryerson
Robinet, Harriette Gillem 1931- 104
    Earlier sketch in SATA *27*
    See also CLR *64*
Robins, Deri 1958- 166
    Earlier sketch in SATA *117*
Robins, Patricia
    See Clark, Patricia Denise
Robins, Rollo, Jr.
    See Ellis, Edward S.
Robins, Seelin
    See Ellis, Edward S.
Robinson, Adjai 1932- 8
Robinson, Aminah Brenda Lynn 1940- 159
    Earlier sketch in SATA *77*
Robinson, Barbara (Webb) 1927- 84
    Earlier sketch in SATA *8*
Robinson, C(harles) A(lexander), Jr.
    1900-1965 36
Robinson, Charles 1870-1937 17
Robinson, Charles 1931- 6
Robinson, Dorothy W. 1929- 54
Robinson, Elizabeth Keeler 1959- 204

Robinson, Eve
    See Tanselle, Eve
Robinson, Glen 1953- 92
Robinson, Glendal P.
    See Robinson, Glen
Robinson, Jan M. 1933- 6
Robinson, Jean O. 1934- 7
Robinson, Joan (Mary) G(ale Thomas)
    1910-1988 7
Robinson, Kim Stanley 1952- 109
Robinson, Lee 1948- 110
Robinson, Lloyd
    See Silverberg, Robert
Robinson, Lynda S(uzanne) 1951- 107
Robinson, Marileta 1942- 32
Robinson, Maudie Millian Oller 1914- 11
Robinson, Maurice R(ichard) 1895-1982
    Obituary 29
Robinson, Nancy K(onheim) 1942-1994 91
    Brief entry 31
    Obituary 79
    Earlier sketch in SATA *32*
Robinson, Ray 1920- 23
Robinson, Raymond Kenneth
    See Robinson, Ray
Robinson, Shari
    See McGuire, Leslie (Sarah)
Robinson, Sharon 1950- 197
    Earlier sketch in SATA *162*
Robinson, Spider 1948- 118
Robinson, Sue
    See Robinson, Susan Maria
Robinson, Susan Maria 1955- 105
Robinson, Susan Patricia
    See Gates, Susan
Robinson, Suzanne
    See Robinson, Lynda S(uzanne)
Robinson, T(homas) H(eath) 1869-1950 17
Robinson, Tim 1963- 205
Robinson, (Wanda) Veronica 1926- 30
Robinson, W(illiam) Heath 1872-1944 17
Robison, Bonnie 1924- 12
Robison, Nancy L(ouise) 1934- 32
Robles, Harold E. 1948- 87
Robottom, John 1934- 7
Robson, Eric 1939- 82
Roca, Francois 1971- 200
Rocco, John 1967- 188
Roche, A. K.
    See Abisch, Roslyn Kroop
    and Kaplan, Boche
Roche, Denis 1967- 196
    Earlier sketch in SATA *99*
Roche, Denis Mary
    See Roche, Denis
Roche, Luane 1937- 170
Roche, P(atricia) K. 1935- 57
    Brief entry 34
Roche, Terry
    See Poole, Peggy
Rochman, Hazel 1938- 105
Rock, Lois
    See Joslin, Mary
Rock, Maxine 1940- 108
Rocker, Fermin 1907- 40
Rocklin, Joanne 1946- 134
    Earlier sketch in SATA *86*
Rockwell, Anne F. 1934- 194
    Earlier sketches in SATA *33, 71, 114, 162*
    See also SAAS *19*
Rockwell, Anne Foote
    See Rockwell, Anne F.
Rockwell, Bart
    See Pellowski, Michael (Joseph)
Rockwell, Harlow 1910-1988 33
    Obituary 56
Rockwell, Lizzy 1961- 185
Rockwell, Norman (Percevel) 1894-1978 ... 23
Rockwell, Thomas 1933- 70
    Earlier sketch in SATA *7*
    See also CLR *6*

Rockwood, Joyce 1947- 39
Rockwood, Roy
  See McFarlane, Leslie
  and Stratemeyer, Edward L.
Rodanas, Kristina 1952- 155
Rodari, Gianni 1920-1980
  See CLR 24
Rodd, Kathleen Tennant
  See Rodd, Kylie Tennant
Rodd, Kylie Tennant 1912-1988 57
  Obituary 55
  Earlier sketch in SATA 6
Rodda, Emily 1948- 146
  Earlier sketch in SATA 97
  See also CLR 32
Roddenberry, Eugene Wesley 1921-1991 45
  Obituary 69
Roddenberry, Gene
  See Roddenberry, Eugene Wesley
Roddick, Ellen 1936- 5
Roddie, Shen 153
Roddy, Lee 1921- 57
Rodenas, Paula 73
Rodgers, Frank 1944- 69
Rodgers, Mary 1931- 130
  Earlier sketch in SATA 8
  See also CLR 20
Rodman, Emerson
  See Ellis, Edward S.
Rodman, Eric
  See Silverberg, Robert
Rodman, Maia
  See Wojciechowska, Maia (Teresa)
Rodman, Mary Ann 185
Rodman, (Cary) Selden 1909-2002 9
Rodowsky, Colby 1932- 164
  Earlier sketches in SATA 21, 77, 120
  See also SAAS 22
Rodowsky, Colby F.
  See Rodowsky, Colby
Rodriguez, Alejo 1941- 83
Rodriguez, Alex 1975- 189
Rodriguez, Christina 1981- 177
Rodriguez, Edel 1971- 196
Rodriguez, Luis J. 1954- 125
Rodriguez, Rachel 180
Rodriguez, Rachel Victoria
  See Rodriguez, Rachel
Roeder, Virginia Marsh 1926- 98
Roehrig, Catharine H. 1949- 67
Roennfeldt, Robert 1953- 78
Roessel-Waugh, C. C.
  See Waugh, Carol-Lynn Rossel
  and Waugh, Charles G(ordon)
Roets, Lois F. 1937- 91
Roever, J(oan) M(arilyn) 1935- 26
Rofes, Eric 1954-2006 52
Rofes, Eric Edward 1954-2006
  See Rofes, Eric
Roffey, Maureen 1936- 33
Rogak, Lisa 1962- 80
Rogak, Lisa Angowski
  See Rogak, Lisa
Rogan, S. Jones 199
Rogan, Sally Jones
  See Rogan, S. Jones
Rogasky, Barbara 1933- 144
  Earlier sketch in SATA 86
Rogers, (Thomas) Alan (Stinchcombe)
  1937- 81
  Earlier sketch in SATA 2
Rogers, Bettye 1858-1919 103
Rogers, Cindy 1950- 89
Rogers, Emma 1951- 74
Rogers, Frances 1888-1974 10
Rogers, Fred McFeely 1928-2003 33
  Obituary 138
Rogers, Gregory 1957- 211
Rogers, Hal
  See Sirimarco, Elizabeth

Rogers, Jean 1919- 55
  Brief entry 47
Rogers, Matilda 1894-1976 5
  Obituary 34
Rogers, Pamela 1927- 9
Rogers, Paul 1950- 98
  Earlier sketch in SATA 54
Rogers, Robert
  See Hamilton, Charles (Harold St. John)
Rogers, Sherry 193
Rogers, W(illiam) G(arland) 1896-1978 23
Rohan, M. S.
  See Rohan, Michael Scott
Rohan, Michael Scott 1951- 98
Rohan, Mike Scott
  See Rohan, Michael Scott
Rohmann, Eric 1957- 171
  See also CLR 100
Rohmer, Harriet 1938- 56
Rohrer, Doug 1962- 89
Rojan
  See Rojankovsky, Feodor (Stepanovich)
Rojankovsky, Feodor (Stepanovich)
  1891-1970 21
Rojany, Lisa 94
Rokeby-Thomas, Anna E(lma) 1911- 15
Roland, Albert 1925-2002 11
Roland, Mary
  See Lewis, Mary
Roleff, Tamara L. 1959- 143
Rolerson, Darrell A(llen) 1946- 8
Roll, Winifred 1909-1998 6
Rollins, Charlemae Hill 1897-1979 3
  Obituary 26
Rollock, Barbara T(herese) 1924- 64
Rolston, Steve 1978- 209
Romack, Janice Reed
  See LeNoir, Janice
Romain, Trevor 134
Romanenko, Vitaliy 1962- 101
Romano, Christy
  See Romano, Christy Carlson
Romano, Christy Carlson 1984- 210
Romano, Clare 1922- 111
  Earlier sketch in SATA 48
Romano, Louis G. 1921- 35
Romano, Melora A. 1966- 118
Romano, Ray 1957- 170
Romano, Raymond
  See Romano, Ray
Romijn, Johanna Maria Kooyker
  See Kooyker-Romijn, Johanna Maria
Romyn, Johanna Maria Kooyker
  See Kooyker-Romijn, Johanna Maria
Rong, Yu 1970- 174
Rongen, Bjoern 1906- 10
Rongen, Bjorn
  See Rongen, Bjoern
Ronson, Mark
  See Alexander, Marc
Rood, Ronald (N.) 1920- 12
Rook, Sebastian
  See Jeapes, Ben
Rooke, Daphne 1914-2009 12
Rooke, Daphne Marie
  See Rooke, Daphne
Roop, Connie 1951- 167
  Brief entry 49
  Earlier sketches in SATA 54, 116
Roop, Constance Betzer
  See Roop, Connie
Roop, Peter 1951- 167
  Brief entry 49
  Earlier sketches in SATA 54, 116
Roop, Peter G.
  See Roop, Peter
Roop, Peter Geiger
  See Roop, Peter
Roos, Stephen 1945- 128
  Brief entry 41
  Earlier sketches in SATA 47, 77

Roose-Evans, James 1927- 65
Roosevelt, Eleanor 1884-1962 50
Root, Barry 182
Root, Betty 84
Root, Kimberly Bulcken 192
Root, Phyllis 1949- 184
  Brief entry 48
  Earlier sketches in SATA 55, 94, 145
Root, Shelton L., Jr. 1923-1986
  Obituary 51
Roper, Laura (Newbold) Wood 1911-2003 . 34
  Obituary 150
Roper, Robert 1946- 142
  Earlier sketch in SATA 78
Roraback, Robin (Ellan) 1964- 111
Rorby, Ginny 1944- 94
Rorer, Abigail 1949- 85
Rosaler, Maxine 208
Rosamel, Godeleine de 1968- 151
Roscoe, D(onald) T(homas) 1934- 42
Rose, Anne 8
Rose, Deborah Lee 1955- 185
  Earlier sketches in SATA 71, 124
Rose, Elizabeth (Jane Pretty) 1933- 68
  Brief entry 28
Rose, Florella
  See Carlson, Vada F.
Rose, Gerald (Hembdon Seymour) 1935- ... 68
  Brief entry 30
Rose, Malcolm 1953- 168
  Earlier sketch in SATA 107
Rose, Nancy A.
  See Sweetland, Nancy A(nn)
Rose, Ted 1940- 93
Rose, Wendy 1948- 12
Rosen, Elizabeth 1961- 205
Rosen, Lillian (Diamond) 1928- 63
Rosen, Marvin 1933- 161
Rosen, Michael 1946- 181
  Brief entry 40
  Earlier sketches in SATA 48, 84, 137
  See also CLR 45
Rosen, Michael J. 1954- 199
  Earlier sketch in SATA 86
Rosen, Michael Wayne
  See Rosen, Michael
Rosen, Sidney 1916- 1
Rosen, Winifred 1943- 8
Rosenbaum, Maurice 1907-1987 6
Rosenberg, Amye 1950- 74
Rosenberg, Dorothy 1906- 40
Rosenberg, Eth Clifford 1915- 92
  See also SAAS 22
Rosenberg, Jane 1949- 58
Rosenberg, Liz 1958- 129
  Earlier sketch in SATA 75
Rosenberg, Maxine B(erta) 1939- 93
  Brief entry 47
  Earlier sketch in SATA 55
Rosenberg, Nancy (Sherman) 1931- 4
Rosenberg, Sharon 1942- 8
Rosenberry, Vera 1948- 144
  Earlier sketch in SATA 83
Rosenblatt, Arthur
  See Rosenblatt, Arthur S.
Rosenblatt, Arthur S. 1938- 68
  Brief entry 45
Rosenblatt, Lily 1956- 90
Rosenbloom, Joseph 1928- 21
Rosenblum, Richard 1928- 11
Rosenburg, John M. 1918- 6
Rosenfeld, Dina 1962- 99
Rosenstiehl, Agnes 1941- 203
Rosenthal, Amy Krouse 1965- 177
Rosenthal, Betsy R. 1957- 178
Rosenthal, Harold 1914-1999 35
Rosenthal, M(acha) L(ouis) 1917-1996 59
Rosenthal, Marc 1949- 193
Rosenthal, Mark A(lan) 1946- 64
Rosing, Norbert 1953- 196
Rosman, Steven M 1956- 81

Rosman, Steven Michael
  See Rosman, Steven M
Rosoff, Meg 1956- 209
  Earlier sketch in SATA 160
Ross, Alan
  See Warwick, Alan R(oss)
Ross, Christine 1950- 172
  Earlier sketch in SATA 83
Ross, Clare
  See Romano, Clare
Ross, Dana Fuller
  See Cockrell, Amanda
  and Gerson, Noel Bertram
Ross, Dave
  See Ross, David
Ross, David 1896-1975 49
  Obituary 20
Ross, David 1949- 133
  Earlier sketch in SATA 32
Ross, Deborah J.
  See Wheeler, Deborah
Ross, Diana
  See Denney, Diana
Ross, Edward S(hearman) 1915- 85
Ross, Eileen 1950- 115
Ross, Frank (Xavier), Jr. 1914- 28
Ross, Jane 1961- 79
Ross, John 1921- 45
Ross, Judy 1942- 54
Ross, Katharine Reynolds
  See Ross, Kathy
Ross, Kathy 1948- 169
  Earlier sketch in SATA 89
Ross, Kent 1956- 91
Ross, Lillian Hammer 1925- 72
Ross, Michael Elsohn 1952- 170
  Earlier sketches in SATA 80, 127
Ross, Pat(ricia Kienzle) 1943- 53
  Brief entry 48
Ross, Ramon R(oyal) 1930- 62
Ross, Stewart 1947- 134
  Earlier sketch in SATA 92
  See also SAAS 23
Ross, Tom 1958- 84
Ross, Tony 1938- 176
  Earlier sketches in SATA 17, 65, 130
Ross, Wilda 1915- 51
  Brief entry 39
Rossel, Seymour 1945- 28
Rossell, Judith 1953- 187
Rossel-Waugh, C. C.
  See Waugh, Carol-Lynn Rossel
Rossetti, Christina 1830-1894 20
  See also CLR 115
Rossetti, Christina Georgina
  See Rossetti, Christina
Rossi, Joyce 1943- 116
Rossotti, Hazel Swaine 1930- 95
Rostkowski, Margaret I. 1945- 59
Roth, Arnold 1929- 21
Roth, Arthur J(oseph) 1925-1993 43
  Brief entry 28
  Obituary 75
  See also SAAS 11
Roth, David 1940- 36
Roth, Julie Jersild 180
Roth, Matthue 1978(?)- 174
Roth, Roger 190
Roth, Stephanie 202
Roth, Susan L. 181
  Earlier sketch in SATA 134
Rothberg, Abraham 1922- 59
Roth-Hano, Renee 1931- 85
Rothkopf, Carol Z. 1929- 4
Rothman, Joel 1938- 7
Rotner, Shelley 1951- 169
  Earlier sketch in SATA 76
Rottman, S.L. 1970- 157
  Earlier sketch in SATA 106
Rottman, Susan Lynn
  See Rottman, S.L.

Roueche, Berton 1911-1994 28
Roughsey, Dick 1921(?)-1985 35
  See also CLR 41
Roughsey, Goobalathaldin
  See Roughsey, Dick
Rounds, Glen (Harold) 1906-2002 112
  Obituary 141
  Earlier sketches in SATA 8, 70
Rourke, Constance Mayfield 1885-1941
  See YABC 1
Rouss, Sylvia 211
Rovetch, Gerda 1925(?)- 202
Rovetch, L. Bob
  See Rovetch, Lissa
Rovetch, Lissa 201
Rowan, Deirdre
  See Williams, Jeanne
Rowe, Jennifer
  See Rodda, Emily
Rowe, John A. 1949- 198
  Earlier sketch in SATA 146
Rowe, Viola Carson 1903-1969
  Obituary 26
Rowh, Mark 1952- 90
Rowland, Florence Wightman 1900-1997 8
  Obituary 108
Rowland-Entwistle, (Arthur) Theodore (Henry)
  1925- 94
  Earlier sketch in SATA 31
Rowling, J. K. 1965- 174
  Earlier sketch in SATA 109
  See also CLR 112
Rowling, Joanne Kathleen
  See Rowling, J. K.
Rowsome, Frank (Howard), Jr. 1914-1983 . 36
Roy, Gabrielle 1909-1983 104
Roy, Jacqueline 1954- 74
Roy, Jennifer
  See Roy, Jennifer Rozines
Roy, Jennifer Rozines 1967- 178
Roy, Jessie Hailstalk 1895-1986
  Obituary 51
Roy, Liam
  See Scarry, Patricia (Murphy)
Roy, Ron(ald) 1940- 110
  Brief entry 35
  Earlier sketch in SATA 40
Roybal, Laura 1956- 85
Roybal, Laura Husby
  See Roybal, Laura
Royds, Caroline 1953- 55
Royston, Angela 1945- 169
  Earlier sketch in SATA 120
Rozakis, Laurie E. 1952- 84
Rozen, Anna 1960- 206
Rubel, Nicole 1953- 181
  Earlier sketches in SATA 18, 95, 135
Rubin, Eva Johanna 1925- 38
Rubin, Susan Goldman 1939- 182
  Earlier sketches in SATA 84, 132
Rubin, Vicky 1964- 193
Rubinetti, Donald 1947- 92
Rubinstein, Gillian 1942- 158
  Autobiography Feature 116
  Earlier sketches in SATA 68, 105
  See also CLR 35
  See also SAAS 25
Rubinstein, Gillian Margaret
  See Rubinstein, Gillian
Rubinstein, Patricia -2003
  See Forest, Antonia
Rubinstein, Patricia Giulia Caulfield Kate
  See Forest, Antonia
Rubinstein, Robert E(dward) 1943- 49
Rublowsky, John M(artin) 1928- 62
Rubright, Lynn 1936- 171
Ruby, Laura 181
  Earlier sketch in SATA 155

Ruby, Lois 1942- 184
  Autobiography Feature 105
  Brief entry 34
  Earlier sketches in SATA 35, 95
Ruby, Lois F.
  See Ruby, Lois
Ruchlis, Hy(man) 1913-1992 3
  Obituary 72
Rucker, Mike 1940- 91
Ruckman, Ivy 1931- 93
  Earlier sketch in SATA 37
Ruck-Pauquet, Gina 1931- 40
  Brief entry 37
Ruddell, Deborah 1949- 210
Ruditis, Paul 190
Rudley, Stephen 1946- 30
Rudolph, Marguerita 1908- 21
Rudomin, Esther
  See Hautzig, Esther Rudomin
Rue, Leonard Lee III 1926- 142
  Earlier sketch in SATA 37
Rueda, Claudia 183
Ruedi, Norma Paul
  See Ainsworth, Norma
Ruelle, Karen Gray 1957- 209
  Earlier sketches in SATA 84, 126
Ruemmler, John D(avid) 1948- 78
Ruepp, Krista 1947- 143
Ruffell, Ann 1941- 30
Ruffins, Reynold 1930- 125
  Earlier sketch in SATA 41
Rugg, Jim 206
Rugoff, Milton 1913- 30
Ruhen, Olaf 1911-1989 17
Rukeyser, Muriel 1913-1980
  Obituary 22
Rumbaut, Hendle 1949- 84
Rumford, James 1948- 193
  Earlier sketch in SATA 116
Rumsey, Marian (Barritt) 1928- 16
Rumstuckle, Cornelius
  See Brennan, Herbie
Runnerstroem, Bengt Arne 1944- 75
Runyan, John
  See Palmer, Bernard (Alvin)
Runyon, Catherine 1947- 62
Ruoff, A. LaVonne Brown 1930- 76
Rupp, Rebecca 185
Rusch, Elizabeth 1966- 198
Rusch, Kris
  See Rusch, Kristine Kathryn
Rusch, Kristine Kathryn 1960- 113
Rush, Alison 1951- 41
Rush, Peter 1937- 32
Rushdie, Ahmed Salman
  See Rushdie, Salman
Rushdie, Salman 1947-
  See CLR 125
Rushford, Patricia H(elen) 1943- 134
Rushmore, Helen 1898-1994 3
Rushmore, Robert (William) 1926-1986 8
  Obituary 49
Ruskin, Ariane
  See Batterberry, Ariane Ruskin
Ruskin, John 1819-1900 24
Russ, Lavinia (Faxon) 1904-1992 74
Russell, Charlotte
  See Rathjen, Carl Henry
Russell, Ching Yeung 1946- 107
Russell, Don(ald Bert) 1899-1986
  Obituary 47
Russell, Franklin (Alexander) 1926- 11
Russell, Gertrude Barrer
  See Barrer-Russell, Gertrude
Russell, Helen Ross 1915- 8
Russell, James 1933- 53
Russell, Jim
  See Russell, James
Russell, Joan Plummer 1930- 139
Russell, P(hilip) Craig 1951- 162
  Earlier sketch in SATA 80

Russell, Patrick
    See Sammis, John
Russell, Paul (Gary) 1942- 57
Russell, Sarah
    See Laski, Marghanita
Russell, Sharman Apt 1954- 123
Russell, Solveig Paulson 1904-1985 3
Russo, Marisabina 1950- 188
    Earlier sketches in SATA *106, 151*
Russo, Monica J. 1950- 83
Russo, Susan 1947- 30
Russon, Penni 1974- 179
Rutgers van der Loeff, An
    See Rutgers van der Loeff-Basenau, An(na)
    Maria Margaretha
Rutgers van der Loeff-Basenau, An(na) Maria
    Margaretha 1910- 22
Ruth, Rod 1912-1987 9
Rutherford, Douglas
    See McConnell, James Douglas Rutherford
Rutherford, Meg 1932- 34
Ruthin, Margaret
    See Catherall, Arthur
Rutledge, Jill Zimmerman 1951- 155
Rutz, Viola Larkin 1932- 12
Ruurs, Margriet 1952- 147
    Earlier sketch in SATA *97*
Ruzicka, Rudolph 1883-1978
    Obituary 24
Ruzzier, Sergio 1966- 210
    Earlier sketch in SATA *159*
, Ryan
    See Ryan, John
Ryan, Betsy
    See Ryan, Elizabeth (Anne)
Ryan, Cheli Duran 20
Ryan, Darlene 1958- 176
Ryan, Elizabeth (Anne) 1943- 30
Ryan, Jeanette
    See Mines, Jeanette
Ryan, John 1921-2009 22
Ryan, Margaret 1950- 166
    Earlier sketch in SATA *78*
Ryan, Mary E. 1953- 61
Ryan, Mary Elizabeth
    See Ryan, Mary E.
Ryan, Pam Munoz 1951- 197
    Earlier sketch in SATA *134*
Ryan, Patrick 1957- 138
Ryan, Peter (Charles) 1939- 15
Ryan-Lush, Geraldine 1949- 89
Rybakov, Anatoli (Naumovich) 1911-1998 . 79
    Obituary 108
Rybakov, Anatolii (Naumovich)
    See Rybakov, Anatoli (Naumovich)
Rybolt, Thomas R. 1954- 62
Rybolt, Thomas Roy
    See Rybolt, Thomas R.
Rybolt, Tom
    See Rybolt, Thomas R.
Rydberg, Ernest E(mil) 1901-1993 21
Rydberg, Lou(isa Hampton) 1908- 27
Rydell, Katy 1942- 91
Rydell, Wendell
    See Rydell, Wendy
Rydell, Wendy 4
Ryden, Hope 91
    Earlier sketch in SATA *8*
Ryder, Joanne (Rose) 1946- 163
    Brief entry 34
    Earlier sketches in SATA *65, 122*
    See also CLR *37*
Ryder, Pamela
    See Lamb, Nancy
Rye, Anthony
    See Youd, Samuel
Rylant, Cynthia 1954- 195
    Brief entry 44
    Earlier sketches in SATA *50, 76, 112, 160*
    See also CLR *86*
    See also SAAS *13*

Rymer, Alta May 1925- 34
Rymond, Lynda Gene 199

S

S. L. C.
    See Twain, Mark
S., Svend Otto
    See Soerensen, Svend Otto
Saaf, Donald W(illiam) 1961- 124
Saal, Jocelyn
    See Sachs, Judith
Sabbeth, Carol (Landstrom) 1957- 125
Saberhagen, Fred 1930-2007 89
    Obituary 184
    Earlier sketch in SATA *37*
Saberhagen, Fred T.
    See Saberhagen, Fred
Saberhagen, Fred Thomas
    See Saberhagen, Fred
Saberhagen, Frederick Thomas
    See Saberhagen, Fred
Sabin, Edwin L(egrand) 1870-1952
    See YABC *2*
Sabin, Francene 27
Sabin, Lou
    See Sabin, Louis
Sabin, Louis 1930- 27
Sabre, Dirk
    See Laffin, John (Alfred Charles)
Sabuda, Robert (James) 1965- 120
    Earlier sketch in SATA *81*
Sabuda, Robert 1965- 170
Sabuda, Robert James
    See Sabuda, Robert
Sachar, Louis 1954- 154
    Brief entry 50
    Earlier sketches in SATA *63, 104*
    See also CLR *79*
Sachs, Elizabeth-Ann 1946- 48
Sachs, Judith 1947- 52
    Brief entry 51
Sachs, Marilyn 1927- 164
    Autobiography Feature 110
    Earlier sketches in SATA *3, 68*
    See also CLR *2*
    See also SAAS *2*
Sachs, Marilyn Stickle
    See Sachs, Marilyn
Sackett, S(amuel) J(ohn) 1928- 12
Sackson, Sid 1920- 16
Sacre, Antonio 1968- 152
Saddler, Allen
    See Richards, R(onald) C(harles) W(illiam)
Saddler, K. Allen
    See Richards, R(onald) C(harles) W(illiam)
Sadie, Stanley 1930-2005 14
Sadie, Stanley John
    See Sadie, Stanley
Sadiq, Nazneen 1944- 101
Sadler, Catherine Edwards 1952- 60
    Brief entry 45
Sadler, Marilyn (June) 1950- 79
Sadler, Mark
    See Lynds, Dennis
Saffer, Barbara 144
Sagan, Carl 1934-1996 58
    Obituary 94
Sagan, Carl Edward
    See Sagan, Carl
Sage, Angie 1952- 197
Sage, Juniper
    See Brown, Margaret Wise
    and Hurd, Edith Thacher
Sagsoorian, Paul 1923- 12
Said, S.F. 1967- 174
Saidman, Anne 1952- 75
Saint, Dora Jessie 1913- 10
St. Anthony, Jane 175

St. Antoine, Sara L. 1966- 84
St. Clair, Byrd Hooper 1905-1976
    Obituary 28
Saint-Exupery, Antoine de 1900-1944 20
    See also CLR *142*
Saint-Exupery, Antoine Jean Baptiste Marie
    Roger de
    See Saint-Exupery, Antoine de
St. George, Judith 1931- 161
    Earlier sketches in SATA *13, 99*
    See also CLR *57*
    See also SAAS *12*
St. George, Judith Alexander
    See St. George, Judith
St. James, Blakely
    See Gottfried, Theodore Mark
    and Platt, Charles
St. James, Blakely
    See Griffin, W.E.B.
St. James, Sierra
    See Rallison, Janette
Saint James, Synthia 1949- 152
    Earlier sketch in SATA *84*
St. John, Nicole 143
    Autobiography Feature 143
    Earlier sketches in SATA *29, 89*
    See also CLR *46*
    See also SAAS *7*
St. John, Patricia Mary 1919-1993
    Obituary 79
St. John, Philip
    See del Rey, Lester
St. John, Wylly Folk 1908-1985 10
    Obituary 45
St. Max, E. S.
    See Ellis, Edward S.
St. Meyer, Ned
    See Stratemeyer, Edward L.
St. Mox, E. A.
    See Ellis, Edward S.
St. Myer, Ned
    See Stratemeyer, Edward L.
St. Tamara
    See Kolba, St. Tamara
Saito, Michiko
    See Fujiwara, Michiko
Sakaki, Ichiro 1969- 192
Sakamoto, Miki 198
Sakers, Don 1958- 72
Sakharnov, S.
    See Sakharnov, Svyatoslav
Sakharnov, Svyatoslav 1923- 65
Sakharnov, Svyatoslav Vladimirovich
    See Sakharnov, Svyatoslav
Saksena, Kate 148
Sakurai, Gail 1952- 153
    Earlier sketch in SATA *87*
Salamanca, Lucy
    See del Barco, Lucy Salamanca
Salassi, Otto R(ussell) 1939-1993 38
    Obituary 77
Salat, Cristina 82
Saldana, Rene, Jr. 186
Saldutti, Denise 1953- 39
Sale, Tim 1956- 153
Salem, Kay 1952- 92
Salerno, Steven 176
Salinger, J.D. 1919-2010 67
    See also CLR *18*
Salinger, Jerome David
    See Salinger, J.D.
Salisbury, Graham 1944- 195
    Earlier sketches in SATA *76, 108, 161*
Salisbury, Joyce E(llen) 1944- 138
Salkey, (Felix) Andrew (Alexander)
    1928-1995 118
    Earlier sketch in SATA *35*
Salley, Coleen 166
Sallis, Susan (Diana) 1929- 55
Salmieri, Daniel 1983- 208
Salmon, Annie Elizabeth 1899- 13

Salonen, Roxane Beauclair 1968- *184*
Salsi, Lynn 1947- *130*
Salsitz, R. A. V.
  See Salsitz, Rhondi Vilott
Salsitz, Rhondi Vilott *115*
Salten, Felix
  See Salzmann, Siegmund
Salter, Cedric
  See Knight, Francis Edgar
Saltman, Judith 1947- *64*
Saltzberg, Barney 1955- *194*
  Earlier sketch in SATA *135*
Saltzman, David (Charles Laertes)
  1967-1990 .... *86*
Salvadori, Mario (George) 1907-1997 .... *97*
  Earlier sketch in SATA *40*
Salwood, F.K.
  See Kilworth, Garry
Salzer, L. E.
  See Wilson, Lionel
Salzman, Marian 1959- *77*
Salzmann, Siegmund 1869-1945 .... *25*
Samachson, Dorothy (Mirkin) 1914-1997 ..... *3*
Samachson, Joseph 1906-1980 .... *3*
  Obituary *52*
Sammis, John 1942- *4*
Sampson, Emma (Keats) Speed
  1868-1947 .... *68*
Sampson, Fay (Elizabeth) 1935- *151*
  Brief entry *40*
  Earlier sketch in SATA *42*
Sampson, Michael 1952- *143*
  Earlier sketch in SATA *95*
Samson, Anne S(tringer) 1933- *2*
Samson, Joan 1937-1976 .... *13*
Samson, Suzanne M. 1959- *91*
Samuels, Barbara *199*
Samuels, Charles 1902-1982 .... *12*
Samuels, Cynthia K(alish) 1946- *79*
Samuels, Gertrude 1910(?)-2003 .... *17*
  Obituary *147*
Sanborn, Duane 1914-1996 .... *38*
Sancha, Sheila 1924- *38*
Sanchez, Alex 1957- *151*
Sanchez, Anita 1956- *209*
Sanchez, Sonia 1934- *136*
  Earlier sketch in SATA *22*
  See also CLR *18*
Sanchez-Silva, Jose Maria 1911- *132*
  Earlier sketch in SATA *16*
  See also CLR *12*
Sand, George X. *45*
Sandak, Cass R(obert) 1950-2001 .... *51*
  Brief entry *37*
Sandberg, (Karin) Inger 1930- *15*
Sandberg, Karl C. 1931- *35*
Sandberg, Lasse (E. M.) 1924- *15*
Sandburg, Carl 1878-1967 .... *8*
  See also CLR *67*
Sandburg, Carl August
  See Sandburg, Carl
Sandburg, Charles
  See Sandburg, Carl
Sandburg, Charles A.
  See Sandburg, Carl
Sandburg, Helga 1918- *3*
  See also SAAS *10*
Sandell, Lisa Ann 1977- *175*
Sandemose, Iben 1950- *211*
Sander, Heather L. 1947- *157*
Sanderlin, George 1915- *4*
Sanderlin, Owenita (Harrah) 1916- *11*
Sanders, Betty Jane
  See Monthei, Betty
Sanders, Nancy I. 1960- *141*
  Earlier sketch in SATA *90*
Sanders, Scott Russell 1945- *109*
  Earlier sketch in SATA *56*
Sanders, Winston P.
  See Anderson, Poul
Sanderson, Irma 1912- *66*

Sanderson, Ivan T(erence) 1911-1973 .... *6*
Sanderson, Margaret Love
  See Keats, Emma
  and Sampson, Emma (Keats) Speed
Sanderson, Ruth 1951- *172*
  Earlier sketches in SATA *41, 109*
Sanderson, Ruth L.
  See Sanderson, Ruth
Sand-Eveland, Cyndi *211*
Sandin, Joan 1942- *197*
  Earlier sketches in SATA *12, 94, 153*
Sandison, Janet
  See Cameron, Elizabeth Jane
Sandler, Martin W. *160*
Sandom, J. Gregory
  See Welsh, T.K.
Sandom, J.G.
  See Welsh, T.K.
Sandoz, Mari(e Susette) 1900-1966 .... *5*
Sanford, Agnes (White) 1897-1976 .... *61*
Sanford, Doris 1937- *69*
Sanford, Rose
  See Simmonds, Posy
Sanger, Amy Wilson 1967- *205*
Sanger, Marjory Bartlett 1920- *8*
San Jose, Christine 1929- *167*
Sankey, Alice (Ann-Susan) 1910- *27*
San Souci, Daniel *192*
  Earlier sketch in SATA *96*
San Souci, Robert D. 1946- *158*
  Earlier sketches in SATA *40, 81, 117*
  See also CLR *43*
Santamaria, Benjamin 1955- *184*
Santat, Dan *188*
Santesson, Hans Stefan 1914(?)-1975
  Obituary *30*
Santiago, Esmeralda 1948- *129*
Santore, Charles 1935- *200*
Santos, Helen
  See Griffiths, Helen
Santrey, Louis
  See Sabin, Louis
Santucci, Barbara 1948- *130*
Sapergia, Barbara 1943- *181*
Sapieyevski, Anne Lindbergh 1940-1993 ... *81*
  Brief entry *32*
  Earlier sketches in SATA *35, 78*
Saport, Linda 1954- *123*
Sapp, Allen 1929- *151*
Sarac, Roger
  See Caras, Roger A(ndrew)
Sarah, Duchess of York
  See Ferguson, Sarah
Sarasin, Jennifer
  See Sachs, Judith
Sardinha, Rick *192*
Sarg, Anthony Frederick
  See Sarg, Tony
Sarg, Tony 1882-1942
  See YABC *1*
Sargent, Pamela 1948- *78*
  Earlier sketch in SATA *29*
Sargent, Robert 1933- *2*
Sargent, Sarah 1937- *44*
  Brief entry *41*
Sargent, Shirley 1927-2004 .... *11*
Sarnoff, Jane 1937- *10*
Saroff, Phyllis V. *202*
Saroyan, William 1908-1981 .... *23*
  Obituary *24*
Sarton, Eleanor May
  See Sarton, May
Sarton, May 1912-1995 .... *36*
  Obituary *86*
Sasaki, Chris *182*
Sasaki, Ellen Joy *206*
Saseen, Sharon (Dillon) 1949- *59*
Sasek, Miroslav 1916-1980 .... *16*
  Obituary *23*
  See also CLR *4*

Sasso, Sandy Eisenberg 1947- *162*
  Earlier sketches in SATA *86, 116*
Sathre, Vivian 1952- *133*
  Earlier sketch in SATA *79*
Satterfield, Charles
  See del Rey, Lester
  and Pohl, Frederik
Sattgast, L. J.
  See Sattgast, Linda J.
Sattgast, Linda J. 1953- *91*
Sattler, Helen Roney 1921-1992 .... *74*
  Earlier sketch in SATA *4*
  See also CLR *24*
Sauer, Julia Lina 1891-1983 .... *32*
  Obituary *36*
Sauerwein, Leigh 1944- *155*
Saul, Carol P. 1947- *117*
  Earlier sketch in SATA *78*
Saul, John III
  See Saul, John
Saul, John 1942- *98*
Saul, John W.
  See Saul, John
Saul, John W. III
  See Saul, John
Saul, John Woodruff III
  See Saul, John
Saul, (Ellen) Wendy 1946- *42*
Saulnier, Karen Luczak 1940- *80*
Saunders, Caleb
  See Heinlein, Robert A.
Saunders, Dave 1939- *85*
Saunders, Julie 1939- *85*
Saunders, (William) Keith 1910-1994 .... *12*
Saunders, Rubie (Agnes) 1929- *21*
Saunders, Steven
  See Jones, Allan Frewin
Saunders, Susan 1945- *96*
  Brief entry *41*
  Earlier sketch in SATA *46*
Saunders-Smith, Gail 1952- *169*
Sauvain, Philip Arthur 1933- *111*
Savadier, Elivia 1950- *164*
  Earlier sketch in SATA *79*
Savage, Alan
  See Nicole, Christopher (Robin)
Savage, Blake
  See Goodwin, Harold L(eland)
Savage, Candace 1949- *142*
Savage, Deborah 1955- *76*
Savage, Jeff 1961- *97*
Savage, Katharine James 1905-1989
  Obituary *61*
Savage, Stephen 1965- *194*
Savage, Thomas 1915-2003
  Obituary *147*
Savageau, Cheryl 1950- *96*
Savery, Constance (Winifred) 1897-1999 ..... *1*
Saville, Andrew
  See Taylor, Andrew
Saville, (Leonard) Malcolm 1901-1982 ...... *23*
  Obituary *31*
Saviozzi, Adriana
  See Mazza, Adriana
Savitt, Sam 1917-2000 .... *8*
  Obituary *126*
Savitz, Harriet May 1933- *72*
  Earlier sketch in SATA *5*
  See also SAAS *26*
Sawicki, Mary 1950- *90*
Sawyer, (Frederick) Don(ald) 1947- *72*
Sawyer, Kem Knapp 1953- *84*
Sawyer, Robert J. 1960- *149*
  Earlier sketch in SATA *81*
Sawyer, Robert James
  See Sawyer, Robert J.
Sawyer, Ruth 1880-1970 .... *17*
  See also CLR *36*
Saxby, H.M.
  See Saxby, (Henry) Maurice
Saxby, (Henry) Maurice 1924- *71*

Saxon, Andrew
　　See Arthur, Robert, (Jr.)
Saxon, Antonia
　　See Sachs, Judith
Say, Allen 1937- 161
　　Earlier sketches in SATA 28, 69, 110
　　See also CLR 135
Sayers, Frances Clarke 1897-1989 3
　　Obituary 62
Sayles, Elizabeth 1956- 163
　　Earlier sketch in SATA 108
Saylor-Marchant, Linda 1963- 82
Sayre, April Pulley 1966- 191
　　Earlier sketches in SATA 88, 131
Sazer, Nina 1949- 13
Scabrini, Janet 1953- 13
Scagell, Robin 1946- 107
Scagnetti, Jack 1924- 7
Scamander, Newt
　　See Rowling, J. K.
Scamell, Ragnhild 1940- 180
　　Earlier sketch in SATA 77
Scanlon, Marion Stephany 11
Scannel, John Vernon
　　See Scannell, Vernon
Scannell, Vernon 1922-2007 59
　　Obituary 188
Scarborough, Elizabeth
　　See Scarborough, Elizabeth Ann
Scarborough, Elizabeth Ann 1947- 171
　　Earlier sketch in SATA 98
Scarf, Maggi
　　See Scarf, Maggie
Scarf, Maggie 1932- 5
Scariano, Margaret M. 1924- 86
Scarlett, Susan
　　See Streatfeild, Noel
Scarry, Huck
　　See Scarry, Richard McClure, Jr.
Scarry, Patricia (Murphy) 1924- 2
Scarry, Patsy
　　See Scarry, Patricia (Murphy)
Scarry, Richard (McClure) 1919-1994 75
　　Obituary 90
　　Earlier sketches in SATA 2, 35
　　See also CLR 41
Scarry, Richard McClure, Jr. 1953- 35
Schachner, Judith Byron 1951- 178
　　Earlier sketch in SATA 88
Schachner, Judy
　　See Schachner, Judith Byron
Schachtel, Roger 1949- 38
Schachtel, Roger Bernard
　　See Schachtel, Roger
Schade, Susan 189
Schaedler, Sally 116
Schaefer, Carole Lexa 173
Schaefer, Jack (Warner) 1907-1991 66
　　Obituary 65
　　Earlier sketch in SATA 3
Schaefer, Lola M. 1950- 183
　　Earlier sketches in SATA 91, 144
Schaeffer, Mead 1898- 21
Schaeffer, Susan Fromberg 1941- 22
Schaer, Brigitte 1958- 112
Schaller, George
　　See Schaller, George B.
Schaller, George B. 1933- 30
Schaller, George Beals
　　See Schaller, George B.
Schanzer, Rosalyn (Good) 1942- 138
　　Earlier sketch in SATA 77
Schatell, Brian 66
　　Brief entry 47
Schechter, Betty (Goodstein) 1921- 5
Schechter, Simone
　　See Elkeles, Simone
Schecter, Ellen 1944- 85
Scheeder, Louis 1946- 141
Scheer, Julian (Weisel) 1926-2001 8
Scheffer, Victor B(lanchard) 1906- 6

Scheffler, Axel 1957- 180
Scheffler, Ursel 1938- 81
Scheffrin-Falk, Gladys 1928- 76
Scheidl, Gerda Marie 1913- 85
Scheier, Michael 1943- 40
　　Brief entry 36
Schell, Mildred 1922- 41
Schell, Orville (Hickok) 1940- 10
Scheller, Melanie 1953- 77
Schellie, Don 1932- 29
Schembri, Jim 1962- 124
Schembri, Pamela 1969- 195
Schemm, Mildred Walker 1905-1998 21
　　Obituary 103
Schenker, Dona 1947- 133
　　Earlier sketch in SATA 68
Scher, Paula 1948- 47
Scherer, Jeffrey 194
Scherf, Margaret 1908-1979 10
Schermer, Judith (Denise) 1941- 30
Schertle, Alice 1941- 192
　　Earlier sketches in SATA 36, 90, 145
Schick, Alice 1946- 27
Schick, Eleanor 1942- 144
　　Earlier sketch in SATA 9, 82
Schick, Joel 1945- 31
　　Brief entry 30
Schields, Gretchen 1948- 75
Schiff, Ken(neth Roy) 1942- 7
Schiller, Andrew 1919- 21
Schiller, Barbara (Heyman) 1928- 21
Schiller, Pamela (Byrne) 127
Schindel, John 1955- 115
　　Earlier sketch in SATA 77
Schindelman, Joseph 1923- 67
　　Brief entry 32
Schindler, S.D. 1952- 198
　　Brief entry 50
　　Earlier sketches in SATA 75, 118, 171
Schindler, Steven D.
　　See Schindler, S.D.
Schinto, Jeanne 1951- 93
Schisgall, Oscar 1901-1984 12
　　Obituary 38
Schlaepfer, Gloria G. 1931- 154
Schlee, Ann 1934- 44
　　Brief entry 36
Schleichert, Elizabeth 1945- 77
Schlein, Miriam 1926-2004 130
　　Obituary 159
　　Earlier sketches in SATA 2, 87
　　See also CLR 41
Schlesinger, Arthur M., Jr. 1917-2007 61
　　Obituary 181
　　See Schlesinger, Arthur Meier
Schlesinger, Arthur Meier 1888-1965
Schlessinger, Laura (Catherine) 1947- 160
　　Earlier sketch in SATA 110
Schlitz, Laura Amy 184
Schloat, G. Warren, Jr. 1914-2000 4
Schmatz, Pat 197
Schmid, Eleonore 1939- 126
　　Earlier sketches in SATA 12, 84
Schmid, Susan Maupin 208
Schmiderer, Dorothy 1940- 19
Schmidt, Annie M. G. 1911-1995 67
　　Obituary 91
　　See also CLR 22
Schmidt, C.A. 196
Schmidt, Diane 1953- 70
Schmidt, Elizabeth 1915- 15
Schmidt, Gary D. 1957- 193
　　Earlier sketches in SATA 93, 135
Schmidt, James Norman 1912-1983 21
Schmidt, Karen Lee 1953- 185
　　Earlier sketch in SATA 94
Schmidt, Lynette 1952- 76
Schmitz, Tamara 207
Schneider, Antonie 1954- 167
　　Earlier sketch in SATA 89

Schneider, Christine M. 1972(?)- 171
　　Earlier sketch in SATA 120
Schneider, Dick
　　See Schneider, Richard H.
Schneider, Elisa
　　See Kleven, Elisa
Schneider, Herman 1905-2003 7
　　Obituary 148
Schneider, Howie -2007 181
Schneider, Josh 1980- 196
Schneider, Laurie
　　See Adams, Laurie
Schneider, Nina 1913-2007 2
　　Obituary 186
Schneider, Nina Zimet
　　See Schneider, Nina
Schneider, Rex 1937- 44
Schneider, Richard H. 1922- 171
Schneider, Richard Henry
　　See Schneider, Richard H.
Schneider, Robyn 1986- 187
Schnirel, James R. 1931- 14
Schnitter, Jane T. 1958- 88
Schnitzlein, Danny 134
Schnur, Steven 1952- 144
　　Earlier sketch in SATA 95
Schnurre, Wolfdietrich 1920-1989
　　Obituary 63
Schoberle, Cecile 1949- 80
Schock, Pauline 1928- 45
Schoell, William 1951- 160
Schoen, Barbara (Taylor) 1924-1993 13
Schoenherr, Ian 177
Schoenherr, John (Carl) 1935- 66
　　Earlier sketch in SATA 37
　　See also SAAS 13
Schofield, Sandy
　　See Rusch, Kristine Kathryn
Scholastica, Sister Mary
　　See Jenkins, Marie M(agdalen)
Scholefield, A. T.
　　See Scholefield, Alan
Scholefield, Alan 1931- 66
Scholefield, Edmund O.
　　See Griffin, W.E.B.
Scholey, Arthur 1932- 28
Scholz, Jackson Volney 1897-1986
　　Obituary 49
Schone, Virginia 22
Schongut, Emanuel 1936- 184
　　Brief entry 36
　　Earlier sketch in SATA 52
Schoonover, Frank (Earle) 1877-1972 24
Schoor, Gene 1921- 3
Schories, Pat 1952- 164
　　Earlier sketch in SATA 116
Schorr, Melissa 1972- 194
Schorr, Melissa Robin
　　See Schorr, Melissa
Schott, Jane A. 1946- 172
Schotter, Roni 190
　　Earlier sketches in SATA 105, 149
Schraff, Anne E(laine) 1939- 92
　　Earlier sketch in SATA 27
Schram, Peninnah 1934- 119
Schrank, Joseph 1900-1984
　　Obituary 38
Schrecengost, Maity 1938- 118
Schrecengost, S. Maitland
　　See Schrecengost, Maity
Schreck, Karen
　　See Schreck, Karen Halvorsen
Schreck, Karen Halvorsen 1962- 185
Schrecker, Judie 1954- 90
Schreiber, Elizabeth Anne (Ferguson)
　　1947- 13
Schreiber, Ralph W(alter) 1942- 13
Schreiner, Samuel A(gnew), Jr. 1921- 70
Schroeder, Alan 1961- 98
　　Earlier sketch in SATA 66

Schroeder, Binette
See Nickl, Barbara (Elisabeth)
Schroeder, Russell (K.) 1943- 146
Schroeder, Ted 1931(?)-1973
Obituary 20
Schubert, Dieter 1947- 101
Earlier sketch in SATA 62
Schubert, Leda 1950(?)- 181
Schubert-Gabrys, Ingrid 1953- 101
Earlier sketch in SATA 62
Schuelein-Steel, Danielle
See Steel, Danielle
Schuelein-Steel, Danielle Fernande
See Steel, Danielle
Schuerger, Michele R. 110
Schuett, Stacey 1960- 168
Earlier sketch in SATA 75
Schulke, Flip Phelps Graeme 1930- 57
Schulman, Arlene 1961- 105
Schulman, Janet 1933- 208
Earlier sketches in SATA 22, 137
Schulman, L(ester) M(artin) 1934- 13
Schulte, Elaine L(ouise) 1934- 36
Schultz, Betty K(epka) 1932- 125
Schultz, Gwendolyn 21
Schultz, James Willard 1859-1947
See YABC 1
Schultz, Pearle Henriksen 1918- 21
Schulz, Charles M. 1922-2000 10
Obituary 118
Schulz, Charles Monroe
See Schulz, Charles M.
Schumacher, Julie 1958- 191
Schumaker, Ward 1943- 96
Schuman, Michael A. 1953- 134
Earlier sketch in SATA 85
Schur, Maxine
See Schur, Maxine Rose
Schur, Maxine Rose 1948- 135
Autobiography Feature 135
Brief entry 49
Earlier sketches in SATA 53, 98
Schurfranz, Vivian 1925- 13
Schutzer, A. I. 1922- 13
Schuyler, Pamela R. 1948- 30
Schwabach, Karen 185
Schwager, Tina 1964- 110
Schwandt, Stephen (William) 1947- 61
Schwark, Mary Beth 1954- 51
Schwartz, Alvin 1927-1992 56
Obituary 71
Earlier sketch in SATA 4
See also CLR 89
Schwartz, Amy 1954- 189
Brief entry 41
Earlier sketches in SATA 47, 83, 131
See also CLR 25
See also SAAS 18
Schwartz, Anne Powers 1913-1987 10
Schwartz, Carol 1954- 77
Schwartz, Charles W(alsh) 1914- 8
Schwartz, David M. 1951- 110
Earlier sketch in SATA 59
Schwartz, David Martin
See Schwartz, David M.
Schwartz, Elizabeth Reeder 1912- 8
Schwartz, Ellen 1949- 117
Schwartz, Jerome L.
See Lawrence, Jerome
Schwartz, Joel L. 1940- 54
Brief entry 51
Schwartz, Joyce R. 1950- 93
Schwartz, Julius 1907-2004 45
Schwartz, Perry 1942- 75
Schwartz, Sheila (Ruth) 1929- 27
Schwartz, Stephen (Lawrence) 1948- 19
Schwartz, Virginia Frances 1950- 184
Earlier sketch in SATA 131
Schwarz, Silvia Tessa Viviane
See Schwarz, Viviane
Schwarz, Viviane 1977- 204

Schwarz, (Silvia Tessa) Viviane 1977- 141
Schweitzer, Byrd Baylor
See Baylor, Byrd
Schweitzer, Iris 59
Brief entry 36
Schweninger, Ann 1951- 168
Earlier sketches in SATA 29, 98
Schwerin, Doris H(alpern) 1922- 64
Schy, Yael 197
Scieszka, Jon 1954- 199
Earlier sketches in SATA 68, 105, 160
See also CLR 107
Scillian, Devin 199
Earlier sketch in SATA 128
Scioscia, Mary (Hershey) 1926- 63
Sciurba, Katie 1957- 196
Scofield, Penrod 1933- 62
Obituary 78
Scoggin, Margaret C(lara) 1905-1968 47
Brief entry 28
Scoltock, Jack 1942- 141
Earlier sketch in SATA 72
Scoppettone, Sandra 1936- 92
Earlier sketch in SATA 9
Scot, Michael
See Rohan, Michael Scott
Scot-Bernard, P.
See Bernard, Patricia
Scotland, Jay
See Jakes, John
Scott, Alastair
See Allen, Kenneth S.
Scott, Ann Herbert 1926- 140
Autobiography Feature 140
Brief entry 29
Earlier sketches in SATA 56, 94
Scott, Bill
See Scott, William N(eville)
Scott, Bill 1920(?)-1985
Obituary 46
Scott, Cora Annett (Pipitone) 1931- 11
Scott, Dan
See Barker, S. Omar
Scott, Elaine 1940- 198
Earlier sketches in SATA 36, 90, 164
Scott, Elizabeth 1972- 194
Scott, Jack Denton 1915-1995 83
Earlier sketch in SATA 31
See also CLR 20
See also SAAS 14
Scott, Jane (Harrington) 1931- 55
Scott, Jessica
See De Wire, Elinor
Scott, John 1912-1976 14
Scott, John Anthony 1916- 23
Scott, John M(artin) 1913- 12
Scott, Mary
See Mattern, Joanne
Scott, Melissa 1960- 109
Scott, Michael 1959- 211
Scott, Mike
See Scott, Michael
Scott, Richard
See Rennert, Richard Scott
Scott, Roney
See Gault, William Campbell
Scott, Sally 1909-1978 43
Scott, Sally 1948- 44
Scott, Sally Elisabeth
See Scott, Sally
Scott, W. N.
See Scott, William N(eville)
Scott, Sir Walter 1771-1832
See YABC 2
Scott, Warwick
See Trevor, Elleston
Scott, William N(eville) 1923- 87
Scotti, Anna
See Coates, Anna
Scotton, Rob 1960- 177

Scribner, Charles, Jr. 1921-1995 13
Obituary 87
Scribner, Joanne L. 1949- 33
Scribner, Kimball 1917- 63
Scrimger, Richard 1957- 164
Earlier sketch in SATA 119
Scrimsher, Lila Gravatt 1897-1974
Obituary 28
Scroder, Walter K. 1928- 82
Scroggs, Kirk 187
Scruggs, Sandy 1961- 89
Scudder, Brooke 1959- 154
Scudder, Mildred Lee 1908- 6
See also SAAS 12
Scull, Marie-Louise 1943-1993 77
Scuro, Vincent 1951- 21
Seabrooke, Brenda 1941- 148
Earlier sketches in SATA 30, 88
Seaman, Augusta Huiell 1879-1950 31
Seamands, Ruth 1916- 9
Searcy, Margaret Zehmer 1926- 54
Brief entry 39
Searight, Mary W(illiams) 1918- 17
Searle, Kathryn Adrienne 1942- 10
Searle, Ronald (William Fordham) 1920- ... 70
Earlier sketch in SATA 42
Sears, Stephen W. 1932- 4
Seaskull, Cecil
See Castellucci, Cecil
Sebastian, Lee
See Silverberg, Robert
Sebestyen, Igen
See Sebestyen, Ouida
Sebestyen, Ouida 1924- 140
Earlier sketch in SATA 39
See also CLR 17
See also SAAS 10
Sebrey, Mary Ann 1951- 62
Sechrist, Elizabeth Hough 1903-1991 2
Sederman, Marty 211
Sedges, John
See Buck, Pearl S.
Sedgwick, Marcus 1968- 197
Earlier sketch in SATA 160
Seed, Cecile Eugenie 1930- 86
Earlier sketch in SATA 8
See also CLR 76
Seed, Jenny
See Seed, Cecile Eugenie
Seed, Sheila Turner 1937(?)-1979
Obituary 23
Seeger, Elizabeth 1889-1973
Obituary 20
Seeger, Laura Vaccaro 200
Earlier sketch in SATA 172
Seeger, Pete 1919- 139
Earlier sketch in SATA 13
Seeger, Peter R.
See Seeger, Pete
Seeley, Laura L. 1958- 71
Seever, R.
See Reeves, Lawrence F.
Sefozo, Mary 1925- 82
Sefton, Catherine
See Waddell, Martin
Segal, John 178
Segal, Joyce 1940- 35
Segal, Lore 1928- 163
Earlier sketches in SATA 4, 66
See also SAAS 11
Segal, Lore Groszmann
See Segal, Lore
Segar, E(lzie) C(risler) 1894-1938 61
Segovia, Andres 1893(?)-1987
Obituary 52
Seguin, Marilyn W(eymouth) 1951- 91
Seguin-Fontes, Marthe 1924- 109
Seibold, J. Otto 1960- 196
Earlier sketches in SATA 83, 149
See also SAAS 22
Seidel, Ross 95

Seidelman, James Edward 1926- 6
Seiden, Art(hur) 107
  Brief entry 42
Seidensticker, John 1944- 200
Seidler, Ann (G.) 1925- 131
Seidler, Tor 1952- 149
  Brief entry 46
  Earlier sketches in SATA 52, 98
Seidman, Karla
  See Kuskin, Karla
Seidman, Laurence Ivan 1925- 15
Seigel, Kalman 1917-1998 12
  Obituary 103
Seignobosc, Françoise 1897-1961 21
Seinfeld, Jerry 1954- 146
Seitz, Jacqueline 1931- 50
Seixas, Judith S. 1922- 17
Sejima, Yoshimasa 1913- 8
Selberg, Ingrid (Maria) 1950- 68
Selden, George
  See Thompson, George Selden
Selden, Neil R(oy) 1931- 61
Self, Margaret Cabell 1902-1996 24
Selfors, Suzanne 1963- 193
Selick, Henry 1952- 183
Selig, Sylvie 1942- 13
Selkirk, Jane
  See Chapman, John Stanton Higham
Sellers, Naomi
  See Flack, Naomi John White
Selman, LaRue W. 1927- 55
Selsam, Millicent E(llis) 1912-1996 29
  Obituary 92
  Earlier sketch in SATA 1
  See also CLR 1
Seltzer, Meyer 1932- 17
Seltzer, Richard 1946- 41
Seltzer, Richard Warren, Jr.
  See Seltzer, Richard
Selvadurai, Shyam 1965(?)- 171
Selway, Martina 1940- 169
  Earlier sketch in SATA 74
Selzer, Adam 1980- 192
Selznick, Brian 1966- 210
  Earlier sketches in SATA 79, 117, 171
Semel, Nava 1954- 107
Semloh
  See Holmes, Peggy
Sendak, Jack 1924(?)-1995 28
Sendak, Maurice 1928- 165
  Earlier sketches in SATA 1, 27, 113
  See also CLR 131
Sendak, Maurice Bernard
  See Sendak, Maurice
Sender, Ruth M(insky) 1926- 62
Sengler, Johanna 1924- 18
Senisi, Ellen B. 1951- 116
Senisi, Ellen Babinec
  See Senisi, Ellen B.
Senn, J(oyce) A(nn) 1941- 115
Senn, Steve 1950- 60
  Brief entry 48
Sensel, Joni 1962- 204
Serafini, Frank 201
Serage, Nancy 1924- 10
Seredy, Kate 1899-1975 1
  Obituary 24
  See also CLR 10
Serfozo, Mary 1925- 194
Seroff, Victor I(ilyitch) 1902-1979 12
  Obituary 26
Serra, Sebastia 1966- 202
Serraillier, Ian (Lucien) 1912-1994 73
  Obituary 83
  Earlier sketch in SATA 1
  See also CLR 2
  See also SAAS 3
Serros, Michele 175
Serros, Michele M.
  See Serros, Michele
Servello, Joe 1932- 10

Service, Pamela F. 1945- 64
Service, Robert
  See Service, Robert W.
Service, Robert W. 1874(?)-1958 20
Serwadda, W(illiam) Moses 1931- 27
Serwer-Bernstein, Blanche L(uria)
  1910-1997 10
Sescoe, Vincent E. 1938- 123
Seskin, Steve 1953- 211
Seth, Mary
  See Lexau, Joan M.
Seton, Anya 1904(?)-1990 3
  Obituary 66
Seton, Ernest (Evan) Thompson
  1860-1946 18
  See also CLR 59
Seton-Thompson, Ernest
  See Seton, Ernest (Evan) Thompson
Seuling, Barbara 1937- 193
  Earlier sketches in SATA 10, 98, 145
  See also SAAS 24
Seuss, Dr.
  See Dr. Seuss
Severn, Bill
  See Severn, William Irving
Severn, David
  See Unwin, David S.
Severn, William Irving 1914- 1
Sewall, Marcia 1935- 119
  Earlier sketches in SATA 37, 69
Seward, Prudence 1926- 16
Sewell, Anna 1820-1878 100
  Earlier sketch in SATA 24
  See also CLR 17
Sewell, Helen (Moore) 1896-1957 38
Sexton, Anne 1928-1974 10
Sexton, Anne Harvey
  See Sexton, Anne
Seymour, Alta Halverson 10
Seymour, Jane 1951- 139
Seymour, Tres 1966- 164
  Earlier sketch in SATA 82
Sfar, Joann 1971- 182
Shachtman, Tom 1942- 49
Shackleton, C.C.
  See Aldiss, Brian W.
Shader, Rachel
  See Sofer, Barbara
Shadow, Jak
  See Sutherland, Jon
Shadyland, Sal
  See Cooper, Louise
Shafer, Audrey 183
Shafer, Robert E(ugene) 1925- 9
Shaffer, Terea 1968- 79
Shahan, Sherry 1949- 134
  Earlier sketch in SATA 92
Shahn, Ben(jamin) 1898-1969
  Obituary 21
Shahn, Bernarda Bryson
  See Bryson, Bernarda
Shaik, Fatima 114
Shalant, Phyllis 1949- 150
Shan, Darren 1972- 199
  Earlier sketches in SATA 129, 168
Shan, D.B.
  See Shan, Darren
Shanahan, Lisa 199
Shanberg, Karen
  See Shragg, Karen (I.)
Shane, Harold Gray 1914-1993 36
  Obituary 76
Shange, Ntozake 1948- 157
Shanks, Ann Zane (Kushner) 10
Shannon, David 1959- 152
  Earlier sketch in SATA 107
  See also CLR 87
Shannon, George 1952- 202
  Earlier sketches in SATA 35, 94, 143
Shannon, George William Bones
  See Shannon, George

Shannon, Jacqueline 63
Shannon, Margaret
  See Silverwood, Margaret Shannon
Shannon, Monica 1905(?)-1965 28
Shannon, Terry
  See Mercer, Jessie
Shannon, Terry Miller 1951- 148
Shapiro, Irwin 1911-1981 32
Shapiro, Jody Fickes 1940- 193
Shapiro, Karen Jo 1964- 186
Shapiro, Michelle 1961- 196
Shapiro, Milton J. 1926- 32
Shapiro, Tricia
  See Andryszewski, Tricia
Shapp, Charles M(orris) 1906-1989
  Obituary 61
Shapp, Martha Glauber 1910- 3
Sharenow, Robert 193
Sharfman, Amalie 14
Sharma, Partap 1939- 15
Sharma, Rashmi
  See Singh, Rashmi Sharma
Sharman, Alison
  See Leonard, Alison
Sharmat, Marjorie Weinman 1928- 133
  Earlier sketches in SATA 4, 33, 74
Sharmat, Mitchell 1927- 127
  Earlier sketch in SATA 33
Sharp, Anne Wallace 1947- 144
Sharp, Luke
  See Alkiviades, Alkis
Sharp, Margery 1905-1991 29
  Obituary 67
  Earlier sketch in SATA 1
  See also CLR 27
Sharp, Zerna A. 1889-1981
  Obituary 27
Sharpe, Jon
  See Duncan, Alice
  and Knott, William C(ecil, Jr.)
  and Messman, Jon
Sharpe, Mitchell R(aymond) 1924- 12
Sharpe, Susan 1946- 71
Sharratt, Nick 1962- 199
  Earlier sketches in SATA 104, 153
Shasha, Mark 1961- 80
Shattuck, Roger 1923-2005 64
  Obituary 174
Shattuck, Roger Whitney
  See Shattuck, Roger
Shaw, Arnold 1909-1989 4
  Obituary 63
Shaw, Carolyn V. 1934- 91
Shaw, Charles (Green) 1892-1974 13
Shaw, Evelyn S. 1927- 28
Shaw, Flora Louisa
  See Lugard, Flora Louisa Shaw
Shaw, Janet 1937- 146
  Earlier sketch in SATA 61
  See also CLR 96
Shaw, Janet Beeler
  See Shaw, Janet
Shaw, Lisa
  See Rogak, Lisa
Shaw, Margret 1940- 68
Shaw, Mary 1965- 180
Shaw, Nancy 1946- 162
  Earlier sketch in SATA 71
Shaw, Ray 7
Shaw, Richard 1923- 12
Shawn, Frank S.
  See Goulart, Ron
Shay, Art
  See Shay, Arthur
Shay, Arthur 1922- 4
Shay, Lacey
  See Shebar, Sharon Sigmond
Shea, Bob 188
Shea, George 1940- 54
  Brief entry 42

Shea, Pegi Deitz 1960- *172*
  Earlier sketches in SATA *77, 137*
Shearer, Alex 1949- *204*
Shearer, John 1947- *43*
  Brief entry *27*
  See also CLR *34*
Shearer, Ted 1919- *43*
Shearing, Leonie 1972- *184*
Sheban, Chris *182*
Shebar, Sharon Sigmond 1945- *36*
Shecter, Ben 1935- *16*
Shedd, Warner 1934- *147*
  Earlier sketch in SATA *87*
Sheedy, Alexandra Elizabeth 1962- *39*
  Earlier sketch in SATA *19*
Sheehan, Ethna 1908-2000 .... *9*
Sheehan, Patty 1945- *77*
Sheehan, Sean 1951- *154*
  Earlier sketch in SATA *86*
Sheen, Barbara 1949- *143*
Shefelman, Janice 1930- *205*
  Earlier sketches in SATA *58, 129*
Shefelman, Janice Jordan
  See Shefelman, Janice
Shefelman, Tom 1927- *204*
  Earlier sketch in SATA *58*
Sheffer, H. R.
  See Abels, Harriette S(heffer)
Sheffield, Charles 1935-2002 .... *109*
Sheffield, Janet N. 1926- *26*
Sheikh, Nazneen
  See Sadiq, Nazneen
Sheinkin, Steve 1968- *204*
Sheinmel, Courtney 1977- *211*
Shekerjian, Regina Tor *16*
Shelby, Anne 1948- *85*
  Autobiography Feature *121*
  See also SAAS *26*
Sheldon, Ann
  See Antle, Nancy
Sheldon, Ann *67*
  Earlier sketch in SATA *1*
Sheldon, Aure 1917-1976 .... *12*
Sheldon, David *185*
Sheldon, Deyan *181*
Sheldon, John
  See Bloch, Robert (Albert)
Sheldon, Muriel 1926- *45*
  Brief entry *39*
Shell, Barry 1951- *176*
Shelley, Frances
  See Wees, Frances Shelley
Shelley, John 1959- *202*
Shelley, Mary
  See Shelley, Mary Wollstonecraft
Shelley, Mary Wollstonecraft 1797-1851 .... *29*
  See also CLR *133*
Shelton, William Roy 1919-1995 .... *5*
  Obituary *129*
Shemie, Bonnie (Jean Brenner) 1949- *96*
Shemin, Margaretha (Hoeneveld) 1928- *4*
Shen, Michele 1953- *173*
Shenker, Michele
  See Shen, Michele
Shenton, Edward 1895-1977 .... *45*
Shepard, Aaron 1950- *187*
  Earlier sketches in SATA *75, 113*
Shepard, Ernest Howard 1879-1976 .... *100*
  Obituary *24*
  Earlier sketches in SATA *3, 33*
  See also CLR *27*
Shepard, James R.
  See Shepard, Jim
Shepard, Jim 1956- *164*
  Earlier sketch in SATA *90*
Shepard, Mary
  See Knox, (Mary) Eleanor Jessie
Shephard, Esther 1891-1975 .... *5*
  Obituary *26*
Shepherd, Amanda *201*

Shepherd, Donna Walsh
  See Walsh Shepherd, Donna
Shepherd, Elizabeth *4*
Shepherd, Irana *173*
Shepherd, Roni
  See Shepherd, Irana
Sheppard, Kate *195*
Shepperson, Rob *178*
Sherburne, Zoa (Lillian Morin) 1912-1995 ... *3*
  See also SAAS *18*
Sherk-Savage, Candace
  See Savage, Candace
Sherlock, Patti *71*
Sherman, D(enis) R(onald) 1934- *48*
  Brief entry *29*
Sherman, Diane (Finn) 1928- *12*
Sherman, Elizabeth
  See Friskey, Margaret (Richards)
Sherman, Harold (Morrow) 1898-1987 .... *37*
  Obituary *137*
Sherman, Josepha *163*
  Earlier sketch in SATA *75*
Sherman, Michael
  See Lowndes, Robert A(ugustine) W(ard)
Sherman, Nancy
  See Rosenberg, Nancy (Sherman)
Sherman, Pat *174*
Sherman, Peter Michael
  See Lowndes, Robert A(ugustine) W(ard)
Sherrard, Valerie (Anne) 1957- *141*
Sherrod, Jane
  See Singer, Jane Sherrod
Sherry, Clifford J. 1943- *84*
Sherry, (Dulcie) Sylvia 1932- *122*
  Earlier sketch in SATA *8*
Sherwan, Earl 1917- *3*
Sherwood, Jonathan
  See London, Jonathan (Paul)
Sheth, Kashmira *186*
Shetterly, Will 1955- *78*
  Autobiography Feature *106*
Shetterly, William Howard
  See Shetterly, Will
Shiefman, Vicky 1942- *22*
Shields, Brenda Desmond (Armstrong)
  1914- *37*
Shields, Carol Diggory *174*
Shields, Charles 1944- *10*
Shields, Gillian *203*
Shiels, Barbara
  See Adams, Barbara Johnston
Shiffman, Lena 1957- *101*
Shiina, Makoto 1944- *83*
Shimin, Symeon 1902-1984 .... *13*
Shimko, Bonnie 1941- *191*
Shine, Andrea 1955- *104*
Shine, Deborah 1932- *71*
Shinn, Everett 1876-1953 .... *21*
Shinn, Sharon 1957- *164*
  Earlier sketch in SATA *110*
Shippen, Katherine B(inney) 1892-1980 .... *1*
  Obituary *23*
  See also CLR *36*
Shippey, T. A. 1943- *143*
Shippey, Thomas Alan
  See Shippey, T. A.
Shipton, Eric Earle 1907-1977 .... *10*
Shipton, Paul 1963- *196*
Shiraz, Yasmin *173*
Shirer, William L(awrence) 1904-1993 .... *45*
  Obituary *78*
Shirley, Debra *203*
Shirley, Gayle C 1955- *96*
Shirley, Gayle Corbett
  See Shirley, Gayle C
Shirley, Jean 1919- *70*
Shirreffs, Gordon D(onald) 1914-1996 .... *11*
Shirts, Morris A(lpine) 1922- *63*
Shlichta, Joe 1968- *84*
Shmurak, Carole B. 1944- *118*

Sholokhov, Mikhail 1905-1984
  Obituary *36*
Sholokhov, Mikhail Aleksandrovich
  See Sholokhov, Mikhail
Shore, Diane Z. *179*
Shore, Diane ZuHone
  See Shore, Diane Z.
Shore, June Lewis *30*
Shore, Nancy 1960- *124*
Shore, Robert 1924- *39*
Short, Michael 1937- *65*
Short, Roger
  See Arkin, Alan
Shortall, Leonard W. *19*
Shortt, Tim(othy Donald) 1961- *96*
Shotwell, Louisa Rossiter 1902-1993 .... *3*
Shoup, Barbara 1947- *156*
  Earlier sketch in SATA *86*
  See also SAAS *24*
Shoveller, Herb *184*
Showalter, Jean B(reckinridge) *12*
Showell, Ellen Harvey 1934- *33*
Showers, Paul C. 1910-1999 .... *92*
  Obituary *114*
  Earlier sketch in SATA *21*
  See also CLR *6*
  See also SAAS *7*
Shpakow, Tanya 1959(?)- *94*
Shpitalnik, Vladimir 1964- *83*
Shragg, Karen (I.) 1954- *142*
Shreeve, Elizabeth 1956- *156*
Shreve, Susan
  See Shreve, Susan Richards
Shreve, Susan Richards 1939- *152*
  Brief entry *41*
  Earlier sketches in SATA *46, 95*
Shriver, Jean Adair 1932- *75*
Shriver, Maria 1955- *134*
Shriver, Maria Owings
  See Shriver, Maria
Shrode, Mary
  See Hollingsworth, Mary
Shtainmets, Leon *32*
Shub, Elizabeth 1915(?)-2004 .... *5*
Shuken, Julia 1948- *84*
Shulevitz, Uri 1935- *165*
  Earlier sketches in SATA *3, 50, 106*
  See also CLR *61*
Shulman, Alix Kates 1932- *7*
Shulman, Dee 1957- *146*
Shulman, Irving 1913-1995 .... *13*
Shulman, Lisa *202*
Shulman, Mark 1962- *184*
Shulman, Max 1919-1988
  Obituary *59*
Shulman, Milton 1913-2004
  Obituary *154*
Shulman, Neil B(arnett) 1945- *89*
Shumsky, Zena
  See Collier, Zena
Shura, Mary Francis
  See Craig, Mary (Francis) Shura
Shusterman, Neal 1962- *201*
  Autobiography Feature *140*
  Earlier sketches in SATA *85, 121, 140*
Shuter, Jane (Margaret) 1955- *151*
  Earlier sketch in SATA *90*
Shuttlesworth, Dorothy Edwards *3*
Shwartz, Susan (Martha) 1949- *94*
Shyer, Christopher 1961- *98*
Shyer, Marlene Fanta *13*
Siberell, Anne *29*
Sibley, Don 1922- *12*
Siburt, Ruth 1951- *121*
Siculan, Daniel 1922- *12*
Siddon, Barbara
  See Bradford, Barbara Taylor
Sidgwick, Ethel 1877-1970 .... *116*
Sidjakov, Nicolas 1924- *18*
Sidman, Joyce 1956- *181*
  Earlier sketch in SATA *145*

Sidney, Frank
    See Warwick, Alan R(oss)
Sidney, Margaret
    See Lothrop, Harriet Mulford Stone
Siebert, Diane 1948- 189
Siegal, Aranka 1930- 88
    Brief entry 37
Siegel, Beatrice 36
Siegel, Helen
    See Siegl, Helen
Siegel, Robert 1939- 39
Siegel, Robert Harold
    See Siegel, Robert
Siegel, Siena Cherson 1967(?)- 185
Siegelson, Kim L. 1962- 114
Sieger, Ted 1958- 189
Siegl, Helen 1924- 34
Siepmann, Mary Aline
    See Wesley, Mary (Aline)
Sierra, Judy 1945- 195
    Earlier sketches in SATA *104, 162*
Sieswerda, Paul L. 1942- 147
Sievert, Terri
    See Dougherty, Terri (L.)
Sigsawa, Keiichi 1972- 211
Silas
    See McCay, (Zenas) Winsor
Silcock, Sara Lesley 1947- 12
Silin-Palmer, Pamela 184
Sill, Cathryn 1953- 141
    Earlier sketch in SATA *74*
Sill, John 1947- 140
    Earlier sketch in SATA *74*
Sillitoe, Alan 1928- 61
Sills, Leslie (Elka) 1948- 129
Silly, E. S.
    See Kraus, (Herman) Robert
Silsbe, Brenda 1953- 73
Silva, Joseph
    See Goulart, Ron
Silver, Ruth
    See Chew, Ruth
Silverberg, Robert 1935- 91
    Autobiography Feature 104
    Earlier sketch in SATA *13*
    See also CLR *59*
Silverman, Erica 1955- 165
    Earlier sketches in SATA *78, 112*
Silverman, Janis L. 1946- 127
Silverman, Mel(vin Frank) 1931-1966 9
Silverman, Robin L. 1954- 96
Silverman, Robin Landew
    See Silverman, Robin L.
Silverstein, Alvin 1933- 124
    Earlier sketches in SATA *8, 69*
    See also CLR *25*
Silverstein, Herma 1945- 106
Silverstein, Robert Alan 1959- 124
    Earlier sketch in SATA *77*
Silverstein, Shel 1932-1999 92
    Brief entry 27
    Obituary 116
    Earlier sketch in SATA *33*
    See also CLR *96*
Silverstein, Sheldon Allan
    See Silverstein, Shel
Silverstein, Virginia B. 1937- 124
    Earlier sketches in SATA *8, 69*
    See also CLR *25*
Silverstein, Virginia Barbara Opshelor
    See Silverstein, Virginia B.
Silverthorne, Elizabeth 1930- 35
Silverwood, Margaret Shannon 1966- 137
    Earlier sketch in SATA *83*
Silvey, Diane F. 1946- 135
Sim, David 1953- 162
Sim, Dorrith M. 1931- 96
Simak, Clifford D(onald) 1904-1988
    Obituary 56
Simard, Remy 1959- 168
Simmie, Lois (Ann) 1932- 106

Simmonds, Posy 1945- 130
    See also CLR *23*
Simmonds, Rosemary Elizabeth
    See Simmonds, Posy
Simmons, Andra 1939- 141
Simmons, Elly 1955- 134
Simmons, Michael 1970- 185
Simms, Laura 1947- 117
Simner, Janni Lee 113
Simon, Charlie May
    See Fletcher, Charlie May Hogue
Simon, Francesca 1955- 111
Simon, Gabriel 1972- 118
Simon, Hilda Rita 1921- 28
    See also CLR *39*
Simon, Howard 1903-1979 32
    Obituary 21
Simon, Joe
    See Simon, Joseph H.
Simon, Joseph H. 1913- 7
Simon, Martin P(aul William) 1903-1969 ... 12
Simon, Mina Lewiton
    See Lewiton, Mina
Simon, Norma (Feldstein) 1927- 129
    Earlier sketches in SATA *3, 68*
Simon, Seymour 1931- 202
    Earlier sketches in SATA *4, 73, 138*
    See also CLR *63*
Simon, Shirley (Schwartz) 1921- 11
Simon, Solomon 1895-1970 40
Simonetta, Linda 1948- 14
Simonetta, Sam 1936- 14
Simons, Barbara B(rooks) 1934- 41
Simont, Marc 1915- 126
    Earlier sketches in SATA *9, 73*
Simpson, Colin 1908-1983 14
Simpson, Harriette
    See Arnow, Harriette (Louisa) Simpson
Simpson, Jacynth Hope
    See Hope Simpson, Jacynth
Simpson, Lesley 1963- 150
Simpson, Margaret 1943- 128
Simpson, Myrtle L(illias) 1931- 14
Sims, Blanche 168
    Earlier sketch in SATA *75*
Sims, Blanche L.
    See Sims, Blanche
Simundsson, Elva 1950- 63
Sinclair, Clover
    See Gater, Dilys
Sinclair, Emil
    See Hesse, Hermann
Sinclair, Jeff 1958- 77
Sinclair, Olga 1923- 121
Sinclair, Rose
    See Smith, Susan Vernon
Sinclair, Upton 1878-1968 9
Sinclair, Upton Beall
    See Sinclair, Upton
Singer, A.L.
    See Lerangis, Peter
Singer, Arthur 1917-1990 64
Singer, Isaac
    See Singer, Isaac Bashevis
Singer, Isaac Bashevis 1904-1991 27
    Obituary 68
    Earlier sketch in SATA *3*
    See also CLR *1*
Singer, Jane Sherrod 1917-1985 4
    Obituary 42
Singer, Julia 1917- 28
Singer, Kurt D. 1911-2005 38
    Obituary 172
Singer, Marilyn 1948- 201
    Autobiography Feature 158
    Brief entry 38
    Earlier sketches in SATA *48, 80, 125, 158*
    See also CLR *48*
    See also SAAS *13*
Singer, Muff 1942-2005 104
    Obituary 160

Singer, Nicky 1956- 194
Singer, Susan (Mahler) 1941- 9
Singh, Rashmi Sharma 1952- 90
Singleton, Linda Joy 1957- 166
    Earlier sketch in SATA *88*
Singleton, L.J.
    See Singleton, Linda Joy
Sinykin, Sheri
    See Sinykin, Sheri Cooper
Sinykin, Sheri Cooper 1950- 142
    Autobiography Feature 142
    Earlier sketches in SATA *72, 133*
Sinykin, Sheril Terri Cooper
    See Sinykin, Sheri Cooper
Sipiera, Paul P., (Jr.) 1948- 144
    Earlier sketch in SATA *89*
Siracusa, Catherine (Jane) 1947- 82
Sirett, Dawn (Karen) 1966- 88
Sirimarco, Elizabeth 1966- 158
Sirof, Harriet 1930- 94
    Earlier sketch in SATA *37*
Sirois, Allen L. 1950- 76
Sirvaitis (Chernyaev), Karen (Ann) 1961- .. 79
Sis, Peter 1949- 192
    Earlier sketch in SATA *149*
    See also CLR *110*
Sisson, Rosemary Anne 1923- 11
Sister Mary Terese
    See Donze, Mary Terese
Sita, Lisa 1962- 87
Sitarski, Anita 200
Sitomer, Alan Lawrence 174
Sitomer, Harry 1903-1985 31
Sitomer, Mindel 1903-1987 31
Sittenfeld, Curtis 1975(?)- 164
Sive, Helen R(obinson) 1951- 30
Sivulich, Sandra (Jeanne) Stroner 1941- 9
Siy, Alexandra 193
Skarmeta, Antonio 1940- 57
Skeers, Linda 1958- 207
Skelly, James R(ichard) 1927- 17
Skelton, Matthew 1971- 185
Skinner, Constance Lindsay 1877-1939
    See YABC *1*
Skinner, Cornelia Otis 1901-1979 2
Skipper, G. C. 1939- 46
    Brief entry 38
Sklansky, Amy E. 1971- 204
Sklansky, Amy E(dgar) 1971- 145
Skofield, James 95
    Brief entry 44
Skold, Betty Westrom 1923- 41
Skorpen, Liesel Moak 1935- 3
Skott, Maria
    See Nikolajeva, Maria
Skrypuch, Marsha Forchuk 1954- 134
Skultety, Nancy Laney 1960- 175
Skurzynski, Gloria 1930- 145
    Autobiography Feature 145
    Earlier sketches in SATA *8, 74, 122*
    See also SAAS *9*
Skurzynski, Gloria Joan
    See Skurzynski, Gloria
Skutch, Robert 1925- 89
Skye, Maggie
    See Werner, Herma
Skye, Obert 200
    Earlier sketch in SATA *170*
Slack, Michael 1969- 189
Slackman, Charles B. 1934- 12
Slade, Arthur G. 1967- 149
    Earlier sketch in SATA *106*
Slade, Arthur Gregory
    See Slade, Arthur G.
Slade, Christian 1974- 193
Slade, Richard 1910-1971 9
Slangerup, Erik Jon 1969- 130
Slate, Joseph 1928- 174
    Earlier sketches in SATA *38, 122*
Slate, Joseph Frank
    See Slate, Joseph

Slater, Dashka 1963- *179*
Slater, Ray
    See Lansdale, Joe R.
Slaughter, Hope 1940- *84*
Slaughter, Jean
    See Doty, Jean Slaughter
Slaughter, Tom 1955- *152*
Slavicek, Louise Chipley 1956- *144*
Slavin, Bill 1959- *199*
    Earlier sketches in SATA *76, 148*
Slaymaker, Melissa Eskridge 1958- *158*
Sleator, William 1945- *208*
    Earlier sketches in SATA *3, 68, 118, 161*
    See also CLR *128*
Sleator, William Warner III
    See Sleator, William
Slegers, Liesbet 1975- *154*
Sleigh, Barbara 1906-1982 .... *86*
    Obituary *30*
    Earlier sketch in SATA *3*
Slepian, Jan 1921- *85*
    Brief entry *45*
    Earlier sketch in SATA *51*
    See also SAAS *8*
Slepian, Janice B.
    See Slepian, Jan
Slicer, Margaret O. 1920- *4*
Slier, Debby
    See Shine, Deborah
Sloan, Brian 1966- *172*
Sloan, Carolyn 1937- *116*
    Earlier sketch in SATA *58*
Sloan, Glenna (Davis) 1930- *120*
Sloane, Eric 1910(?)-1985 .... *52*
    Obituary *42*
Sloane, Todd 1955- *88*
Sloat, Teri 1948- *164*
    Earlier sketches in SATA *70, 106*
Slobodkin, Florence Gersh 1905-1994 .... *5*
    Obituary *107*
Slobodkin, Louis 1903-1975 .... *26*
    Earlier sketch in SATA *1*
Slobodkina, Esphyr 1908-2002 .... *1*
    Obituary *135*
    See also SAAS *8*
Sloggett, Nellie 1851-1923 .... *44*
Slonim, David 1966- *207*
Sloss, Lesley Lord 1965- *72*
Slote, Alfred 1926- *72*
    Earlier sketch in SATA *8*
    See also CLR *4*
    See also SAAS *21*
Slote, Elizabeth 1956- *80*
Small, Charlie
    See Ward, Nick
Small, David 1945- *183*
    Brief entry *46*
    Earlier sketches in SATA *50, 95, 126*
    See also CLR *53*
Small, Ernest
    See Lent, Blair
Small, Mary 1932- *165*
Small, Terry 1942- *75*
Smallcomb, Pam 1954- *159*
Smallman, Steve *197*
Smalls, Irene
    See Smalls-Hector, Irene
Smalls-Hector, Irene 1950- *146*
    Earlier sketch in SATA *73*
    See also CLR *103*
Smallwood, Norah (Evelyn) 1910(?)-1984
    Obituary *41*
Smaridge, Norah (Antoinette) 1903-1994 ..... *6*
Smath, Jerry 1933- *198*
Smee, Nicola 1948- *167*
    Earlier sketch in SATA *76*
Smiley, Virginia Kester 1923- *2*
Smit, Noelle 1972- *199*
Smith, Alexander McCall 1948- *179*
    Earlier sketch in SATA *73*
Smith, Andrew 1959- *209*

Smith, Andrew Anselmo
    See Smith, Andrew
Smith, Andy J. 1975- *207*
Smith, Anne Warren 1938- *41*
    Brief entry *34*
Smith, Barry (Edward Jervis) 1943- *75*
Smith, Beatrice S(chillinger) *12*
Smith, Betsy Covington 1937- *55*
    Earlier sketch in SATA *43*
Smith, Betty (Wehner) 1904-1972 .... *6*
Smith, Bradford 1909-1964 .... *5*
Smith, Brenda 1946- *82*
Smith, C. Pritchard
    See Hoyt, Edwin P(almer), Jr.
Smith, Caesar
    See Trevor, Elleston
Smith, Cat Bowman 1939- *201*
Smith, Charles R., Jr. 1969- *203*
    Earlier sketch in SATA *159*
Smith, Craig 1955- *172*
    Earlier sketches in SATA *81, 117*
Smith, Cynthia Leitich 1967- *152*
Smith, Datus C(lifford), Jr. 1907-1999 .... *13*
    Obituary *116*
Smith, Debra 1955- *89*
Smith, Derek 1943- *141*
Smith, Dick King
    See King-Smith, Dick
Smith, Dodie
    See Smith, Dorothy Gladys
Smith, Doris Buchanan 1934-2002 .... *75*
    Obituary *140*
    Earlier sketch in SATA *28*
    See also SAAS *10*
Smith, Dorothy Gladys 1896-1990 .... *82*
    Obituary *65*
Smith, Dorothy Stafford 1905- *6*
Smith, Duane 1974- *202*
Smith, E(lmer) Boyd 1860-1943
    See YABC *1*
Smith, E(dric) Brooks 1917- *40*
Smith, Elwood H. 1941- *203*
Smith, Emma 1923- *52*
    Brief entry *36*
Smith, (Katherine) Eunice (Young)
    1902-1993 .... *5*
Smith, Frances C(hristine) 1904-1986 .... *3*
Smith, Gary R. 1932- *14*
Smith, Geof 1969- *102*
Smith, George Harmon 1920- *5*
Smith, Gordon 1951- *184*
Smith, Greg Leitich *152*
Smith, H(arry) Allen 1907-1976
    Obituary *20*
Smith, Helene 1937- *142*
Smith, Hope Anita *202*
Smith, Howard E(verett), Jr. 1927- *12*
Smith, Hugh L(etcher) 1921-1968 .... *5*
Smith, Imogene Henderson 1922- *12*
Smith, Jacqueline B. 1937- *39*
Smith, Jada Pinkett 1971- *161*
Smith, James D. 1955- *176*
Smith, James Noel 1950- *193*
Smith, Janet (Buchanan) Adam
    See Adam Smith, Janet (Buchanan)
Smith, Janice Lee 1949- *155*
    Earlier sketch in SATA *54*
Smith, Jean
    See Smith, Frances C(hristine)
Smith, Jean Pajot 1945- *10*
Smith, Jeff 1958- *161*
    Earlier sketch in SATA *93*
Smith, Jeff Allen
    See Smith, Jeff
Smith, Jenny 1963- *90*
Smith, Jessie
    See Kunhardt, Edith
Smith, Jessie Willcox 1863-1935 .... *21*
    See also CLR *59*
Smith, Joan (Mary) 1933- *54*
    Brief entry *46*

Smith, Johnston
    See Crane, Stephen
Smith, Jos A. 1936- *181*
    Earlier sketches in SATA *73, 120*
Smith, Joseph Arthur
    See Smith, Jos A.
Smith, Judie R. 1936- *80*
Smith, Kirsten 1970- *210*
Smith, Lafayette
    See Higdon, Hal
Smith, Lane 1959- *179*
    Earlier sketches in SATA *76, 131*
    See also CLR *47*
Smith, Lee
    See Albion, Lee Smith
Smith, Lendon H(oward) 1921- *64*
Smith, Lillian H(elena) 1887-1983
    Obituary *32*
Smith, Linda 1949- *177*
Smith, Linell Nash 1932- *2*
Smith, Lucia B. 1943- *30*
Smith, Maggie 1965- *190*
Smith, Margaret Emily Noel Nuttall
    See Nuttall-Smith, Margaret Emily Noel
Smith, Marion Hagens 1913- *12*
Smith, Marion Jaques 1899-1987 .... *13*
Smith, Mary Ellen *10*
Smith, Marya 1945- *78*
Smith, Mike
    See Smith, Mary Ellen
Smith, Nancy Covert 1935- *12*
Smith, Norman F. 1920- *70*
    Earlier sketch in SATA *5*
Smith, Patricia Clark 1943- *96*
Smith, Pauline C.
    See Arthur, Robert, (Jr.)
Smith, Pauline C(oggeshall) 1908-1994 ...... *27*
Smith, Philip Warren 1936- *46*
Smith, R. Alexander McCall
    See Smith, Alexander McCall
Smith, Rebecca 1946- *123*
Smith, Robert Kimmel 1930- *77*
    Earlier sketch in SATA *12*
Smith, Robert Paul 1915-1977 .... *52*
    Obituary *30*
Smith, Roland 1951- *193*
    Earlier sketches in SATA *115, 161*
Smith, Rosamond
    See Oates, Joyce Carol
Smith, Ruth Leslie 1902- *2*
Smith, Samantha 1972-1985
    Obituary *45*
Smith, Sandra Lee 1945- *75*
Smith, Sarah Stafford
    See Smith, Dorothy Stafford
Smith, Sharon 1947- *82*
Smith, Sherri L. 1971- *156*
Smith, Sherwood 1951- *206*
    Autobiography Feature *206*
    Earlier sketches in SATA *82, 140*
Smith, Shirley Raines
    See Raines, Shirley C(arol)
Smith, Susan Carlton 1923- *12*
Smith, Susan Mathias 1950- *43*
    Brief entry *35*
Smith, Susan Vernon 1950- *48*
    Brief entry *45*
Smith, Tim(othy R.) 1945- *151*
Smith, Ursula 1934- *54*
Smith, Vian (Crocker) 1920-1969 .... *11*
Smith, Wanda VanHoy 1926- *65*
Smith, Ward
    See Goldsmith, Howard
Smith, William A. 1918- *10*
Smith, William Jay 1918- *154*
    Autobiography Feature *154*
    Earlier sketches in SATA *2, 68*
    See also SAAS *22*
Smith, Winsome 1935- *45*
Smith, Z.Z.
    See Westheimer, David

Smith-Ankrom, M. E. 1942- *130*
Smith-Griswold, Wendy 1955- *88*
Smith-Rex, Susan J. 1950- *94*
Smithsen, Richard
  See Pellowski, Michael (Joseph)
Smits, Teo
  See Smits, Theodore R(ichard)
Smits, Theodore R(ichard) 1905-1996 .... *45*
  Brief entry *28*
Smolinski, Dick 1932- *86*
Smothers, Ethel Footman 1944- *149*
  Earlier sketch in SATA *76*
Smucker, Anna Egan 1948- *209*
Smucker, Barbara 1915-2003 .... *130*
  Earlier sketches in SATA *29, 76*
  See also CLR *10*
  See also SAAS *11*
Smucker, Barbara Claassen
  See Smucker, Barbara
Smyth, Iain 1959- *105*
Snedeker, Caroline Dale (Parke) 1871-1956
  See YABC *2*
Sneed, Brad *191*
Sneider, Marian 1932-2005 .... *197*
Snell, Nigel (Edward Creagh) 1936- *57*
  Brief entry *40*
Snellgrove, L(aurence) E(rnest) 1928- *53*
Snelling, Dennis (Wayne) 1958- *84*
Sneve, Virginia Driving Hawk 1933- *95*
  Earlier sketch in SATA *8*
  See also CLR *2*
Snicket, Lemony 1970- *187*
  Earlier sketch in SATA *126*
  See also CLR *79*
Sniegoski, Thomas E. *195*
Sniegoski, Tom
  See Sniegoski, Thomas E.
Snodgrass, Mary Ellen 1944- *75*
Snodgrass, Quentin Curtius
  See Twain, Mark
Snodgrass, Thomas Jefferson
  See Twain, Mark
Snook, Barbara (Lillian) 1913-1976 .... *34*
Snow, Alan 1959- *190*
Snow, Carol 1965- *208*
Snow, Donald Clifford 1917-1979 .... *16*
Snow, Dorothea J(ohnston) 1909- *9*
Snow, Richard F(olger) 1947- *52*
  Brief entry *37*
Snyder, Anne 1922-2001 .... *4*
  Obituary *125*
Snyder, Bernadette McCarver 1930- *97*
Snyder, Carol 1941- *35*
Snyder, Gerald S(eymour) 1933- *48*
  Brief entry *34*
Snyder, Jerome 1916-1976
  Obituary *20*
Snyder, Laurel 1974- *209*
Snyder, Midori 1954- *106*
Snyder, Paul A. 1946- *125*
Snyder, Zilpha Keatley 1927- *163*
  Autobiography Feature *163*
  Earlier sketches in SATA *1, 28, 75, 110*
  See also CLR *121*
  See also SAAS *2*
Snyderman, Reuven K. 1922- *5*
So, Meilo *162*
Sobel, June 1950- *149*
Soble, Jennie
  See Cavin, Ruth (Brodie)
Sobol, Donald J. 1924- *132*
  Earlier sketches in SATA *1, 31, 73*
  See also CLR *4*
Sobol, Harriet Langsam 1936- *47*
  Brief entry *34*
Sobol, Richard *211*
Sobol, Rose 1931- *76*
Sobott-Mogwe, Gaele 1956- *97*
Soderlind, Arthur E(dwin) 1920- *14*
Soentpiet, Chris K. 1970- *159*
  Earlier sketch in SATA *97*

Soerensen, Svend Otto 1916- *67*
Sofer, Barbara 1949- *109*
Sofer, Rachel
  See Sofer, Barbara
Softly, Barbara Frewin 1924- *12*
Sogabe, Aki *207*
Soglow, Otto 1900-1975
  Obituary *30*
Sohl, Frederic J(ohn) 1916- *10*
Sohr, Daniel 1973- *190*
Sokol, Bill
  See Sokol, William
Sokol, William 1923- *37*
Sokolov, Kirill 1930- *34*
Solbert, Romaine G. 1925- *2*
Solbert, Ronni
  See Solbert, Romaine G.
Solheim, James *133*
Solomon, Heather M. *188*
Solomon, Joan 1930- *51*
  Brief entry *40*
Solomons, Ikey Esquir
  See Thackeray, William Makepeace
Solonevich, George 1915-2003 .... *15*
Solot, Mary Lynn 1939- *12*
Soman, David 1965- *200*
Somerlott, Robert 1928-2001 .... *62*
Somers, Kevin *205*
Somervill, Barbara A(nn) 1948- *140*
Sommer, Angela
  See Sommer-Bodenburg, Angela
Sommer, Carl 1930- *175*
  Earlier sketch in SATA *126*
Sommer, Elyse 1929- *7*
Sommer, Robert 1929- *12*
Sommer-Bodenburg, Angela 1948- *113*
  Earlier sketch in SATA *63*
Sommerdorf, Norma 1926- *131*
Sommerdorf, Norma Jean
  See Sommerdorf, Norma
Sommerfelt, Aimee 1892-1975 .... *5*
Son, John *160*
Sones, Sonya *131*
Sonneborn, Ruth (Cantor) 1899-1974 .... *4*
  Obituary *27*
Sonnenblick, Jordan 1969- *185*
  See also CLR *144*
Sonnenmark, Laura A. 1958- *73*
Soo, Kean *201*
Sopko, Eugen 1949- *58*
Sorel, Edward 1929- *126*
  Brief entry *37*
  Earlier sketch in SATA *65*
Sorensen, Henri 1950- *115*
  Earlier sketch in SATA *77*
Sorensen, Svend Otto
  See Soerensen, Svend Otto
Sorensen, Virginia 1912-1991 .... *2*
  Obituary *72*
  See also SAAS *15*
Sorenson, Jane 1926- *63*
Sorenson, Margo 1946- *96*
Sorley Walker, Kathrine *41*
Sorra, Kristin *185*
Sorrells, Walter *177*
Sorrentino, Joseph N. 1937- *6*
Sortor, June Elizabeth 1939- *12*
Sortor, Toni
  See Sortor, June Elizabeth
Sosa, Hernan 1977- *203*
Soskin, V. H.
  See Ellison, Virginia H(owell)
Soto, Gary 1952- *174*
  Earlier sketches in SATA *80, 120*
  See also CLR *38*
Sotomayor, Antonio 1902-1985 .... *11*
Souci, Robert D. San
  See San Souci, Robert D.
Soudley, Henry
  See Wood, James Playsted
Souhami, Jessica *176*

Soule, Gardner (Bosworth) 1913-2000 .... *14*
Soule, Jean Conder 1919- *10*
Souster, (Holmes) Raymond 1921- *63*
South, Sheri Cobb 1959- *82*
Southall, Ivan 1921-2008 .... *134*
  Autobiography Feature *134*
  Earlier sketches in SATA *3, 68*
  See also CLR *2*
  See also SAAS *3*
Southall, Ivan Francis
  See Southall, Ivan
Southey, Robert 1774-1843 .... *54*
Southgate, Vera *54*
Souza, Janet
  See Tashjian, Janet
Sovak, Jan 1953- *115*
Sowden, Celeste
  See Walters, Celeste
Sowter, Nita *69*
Spafford, Suzy 1945- *160*
Spagnoli, Cathy 1950- *134*
  Earlier sketch in SATA *79*
Spain, Sahara Sunday 1991- *133*
Spain, Susan Rosson *185*
Spalding, Andrea 1944- *150*
  Earlier sketch in SATA *101*
Spalenka, Greg 1958- *198*
Spanfeller, James J. 1930- *19*
  See also SAAS *8*
Spanfeller, Jim
  See Spanfeller, James J.
Spangenberg, Judith Dunn 1942- *5*
Spanyol, Jessica 1965- *206*
  Earlier sketch in SATA *137*
Spar, Jerome 1918- *10*
Sparks, Barbara 1942- *78*
Sparks, Beatrice (Mathews) 1918- *44*
  Brief entry *28*
  See also CLR *139*
Sparks, Mary W. 1920- *15*
Spaulding, Douglas
  See Bradbury, Ray
Spaulding, Leonard
  See Bradbury, Ray
Spaulding, Norma *107*
Speare, Elizabeth George 1908-1994 .... *62*
  Obituary *83*
  Earlier sketch in SATA *5*
  See also CLR *8*
Spearing, Judith (Mary Harlow) 1922- *9*
Spears, Rick *182*
Speck, Katie *196*
Speck, Nancy 1959- *104*
Specking, Inez 1890-1960(?) *11*
Speed, Nell
  See Keats, Emma
  and Sampson, Emma (Keats) Speed
Speed, Nell (Ewing) 1878-1913 .... *68*
Speer, Bonnie Stahlman 1929- *113*
Speer-Lyon, Tammie L. 1965- *89*
Speicher, Helen Ross S(mith) 1915- *8*
Speir, Nancy 1958- *210*
  Earlier sketch in SATA *81*
Spellman, John W(illard) 1934- *14*
Spellman, Roger G.
  See Cox, William R(obert)
Spelman, Cornelia Maude 1946- *144*
  Earlier sketch in SATA *96*
Spelman, Mary 1934- *28*
Spelvin, George
  See Lerangis, Peter
  and Phillips, David Atlee
Spence, Cynthia
  See Eble, Diane
Spence, Eleanor (Rachel) 1928- *21*
  See also CLR *26*
Spence, Geraldine 1931- *47*
Spencer, Ann 1918- *10*
Spencer, Britt *206*
Spencer, Cornelia
  See Yaukey, Grace S(ydenstricker)

Spencer, Donald D(ean) 1931- *41*
Spencer, Elizabeth 1921- *14*
Spencer, Leonard G.
   See Garrett, Randall
   and Silverberg, Robert
Spencer, William 1922- *9*
Spencer, Zane A(nn) 1935- *35*
Sper, Emily 1957- *142*
Speregen, Devra Newberger 1964- *84*
Sperling, Dan(iel Lee) 1949- *65*
Sperry, Armstrong W. 1897-1976 .... *1*
   Obituary *27*
Sperry, Raymond
   See Garis, Howard R.
Sperry, Raymond, Jr. *1*
Spetter, Jung-Hee 1969- *134*
Spicer, Dorothy Gladys -1975 .... *32*
Spiegel, Beth *184*
Spiegelman, Art 1948- *158*
   Earlier sketch in SATA *109*
Spiegelman, Judith M. *5*
Spielberg, Steven 1947- *32*
Spier, Peter (Edward) 1927- *54*
   Earlier sketch in SATA *4*
   See also CLR *5*
Spilhaus, Athelstan (Frederick) 1911-1998 . *13*
   Obituary *102*
Spilka, Arnold 1917- *6*
Spillane, Frank Morrison
   See Spillane, Mickey
Spillane, Mickey 1918-2006 .... *66*
   Obituary *176*
Spinelli, Eileen 1942- *186*
   Earlier sketches in SATA *38, 101, 150*
Spinelli, Jerry 1941- *195*
   Earlier sketches in SATA *39, 71, 110, 158*
   See also CLR *82*
Spink, Reginald (William) 1905-1994 .... *11*
Spinka, Penina Keen 1945- *72*
Spinner, Stephanie 1943- *132*
   Earlier sketches in SATA *38, 91*
Spinossimus
   See White, William, Jr.
Spiotta-DiMare, Loren *173*
Spires, Ashley 1978- *183*
Spires, Elizabeth 1952- *111*
   Earlier sketch in SATA *71*
Spiridellis, Gregg 1971(?)- *199*
Spirin, Gennadii
   See Spirin, Gennady
Spirin, Gennadij
   See Spirin, Gennady
Spirin, Gennady 1948- *204*
   Earlier sketches in SATA *95, 134*
   See also CLR *88*
Spiro, Ruth *208*
Spivak, Dawnine *101*
Spizman, Robyn Freedman *194*
Spohn, David 1948- *72*
Spohn, Kate 1962- *147*
   Earlier sketch in SATA *87*
Spollen, Christopher 1952- *12*
Spooner, Michael (Tim) 1954- *92*
Spowart, Robin 1947- *177*
   Earlier sketch in SATA *82*
Spradlin, Michael P. *204*
Sprague, Gretchen 1926-2003 .... *27*
Spranger, Nina 1969- *203*
Sprengel, Artie
   See Lerangis, Peter
Sprigge, Elizabeth (Miriam Squire)
   1900-1974 .... *10*
Spring, (Robert) Howard 1889-1965 .... *28*
Springer, Margaret 1941- *78*
Springer, Marilyn Harris 1931- *47*
Springer, Nancy 1948- *172*
   Earlier sketches in SATA *65, 110*
Springstubb, Tricia 1950- *78*
   Brief entry *40*
   Earlier sketch in SATA *46*

Spudvilas, Anne 1951- *199*
   Earlier sketch in SATA *94*
Spurll, Barbara 1952- *78*
Spurr, Elizabeth *172*
Spykman, E(lizabeth) C(hoate) 1896-1965 . *10*
   See also CLR *35*
Spyri, Johanna (Heusser) 1827-1901 .... *100*
   Earlier sketch in SATA *19*
   See also CLR *115*
Squires, Phil
   See Barker, S. Omar
Srba, Lynne *98*
Sreenivasan, Jyotsna 1964- *101*
S-Ringi, Kjell
   See Ringi, Kjell (Arne Soerensen)
Staake, Bob 1957- *209*
Stacey, Cherylyn 1945- *96*
Stacy, Donald
   See Pohl, Frederik
Stadler, John *204*
Stadtler, Bea 1921- *17*
Stafford, Jean 1915-1979
   Obituary *22*
Stafford, Liliana 1950- *141*
Stafford, Paul 1966- *116*
Stahl, Ben(jamin) 1910-1987 .... *5*
   Obituary *54*
Stahl, Hilda 1938-1993 .... *48*
   Obituary *77*
Stahler, David, Jr. *162*
Stainton, Sue *187*
Stair, Gobin (John) 1912- *35*
Stalder, Valerie *27*
Stamaty, Mark Alan 1947- *12*
Stambler, Irwin 1924- *5*
Stampler, Ann Redisch *209*
Standiford, Natalie 1961- *169*
   Earlier sketch in SATA *81*
Stanek, Lou Willett 1931- *63*
Stang, Judit 1921-1977 .... *29*
Stang, Judy
   See Stang, Judit
Stangl, (Mary) Jean 1928- *67*
Stanhope, Eric
   See Hamilton, Charles (Harold St. John)
Stankevich, Boris 1928- *2*
Stanley, Diane 1943- *164*
   Brief entry *32*
   Earlier sketches in SATA *37, 80, 115*
   See also CLR *46*
   See also SAAS *15*
Stanley, Elizabeth 1947- *206*
Stanley, George Edward 1942- *67*
   Earlier sketches in SATA *53, 111, 157, 1*
Stanley, Jerry 1941- *127*
   Earlier sketch in SATA *79*
Stanley, Mandy *165*
Stanley, Robert
   See Hamilton, Charles (Harold St. John)
Stanley, Sanna 1962- *145*
Stanli, Sue
   See Meilach, Dona Z(weigoron)
Stanstead, John
   See Groom, Arthur William
Stanton, Karen 1960- *190*
Stanton, Schuyler
   See Baum, L. Frank
Staples, Suzanne Fisher 1945- *207*
   Earlier sketches in SATA *70, 105, 151*
   See also CLR *137*
Stapleton, Marjorie (Winifred) 1932- *28*
Stapp, Arthur D(onald) 1906-1972 .... *4*
Starbird, Kaye 1916- *6*
   See also CLR *60*
Stark, Evan 1942- *78*
Stark, James
   See Goldston, Robert (Conroy)
Stark, Ken 1943- *199*
Stark, Ulf 1944- *124*
Starke, Ruth (Elaine) 1946- *129*
Starkey, Marion L(ena) 1901-1991 .... *13*

Starr, Ward
   See Manes, Stephen
Starret, William
   See McClintock, Marshall
Starr Taylor, Bridget 1959- *99*
Stasiak, Krystyna *49*
Staub, Frank 1949- *116*
Staub, Frank Jacob
   See Staub, Frank
Staub, Wendy Corsi 1964- *114*
Stauffacher, Sue 1961- *199*
   Earlier sketch in SATA *155*
Stauffer, Don
   See Berkebile, Fred D(onovan)
Staunton, Schuyler
   See Baum, L. Frank
Staunton, Ted 1956- *167*
   Earlier sketch in SATA *112*
Stead, Judy *210*
Stead, Rebecca 1968(?)- *188*
Steadman, Ralph 1936- *123*
   Earlier sketch in SATA *32*
Steadman, Ralph Idris
   See Steadman, Ralph
Stearman, Kaye 1951- *118*
Stearns, Monroe (Mather) 1913-1987 .... *5*
   Obituary *55*
Steckler, Arthur 1921-1985 .... *65*
Steding, Laurie 1953- *119*
Steel, Danielle 1947- *66*
Steel, Danielle Fernande
   See Steel, Danielle
Steele, Addison II
   See Lupoff, Richard A(llen)
Steele, Alexander 1958- *116*
Steele, Henry Maxwell
   See Steele, Max
Steele, Mary 1930- *94*
Steele, Mary Q(uintard Govan) 1922-1992 . *51*
   Obituary *72*
   Earlier sketch in SATA *3*
Steele, Max 1922-2005 .... *168*
   Earlier sketch in SATA *10*
Steele, Philip 1948- *140*
   Earlier sketch in SATA *81*
Steele, William O(wen) 1917-1979 .... *51*
   Obituary *27*
   Earlier sketch in SATA *1*
Steelhammer, Ilona 1952- *98*
Steelsmith, Shari 1962- *72*
Stefanik, Alfred T. 1939- *55*
Steffanson, Con
   See Cassiday, Bruce (Bingham)
   and Goulart, Ron
Steffens, Bradley 1955- *166*
   Earlier sketch in SATA *77*
Steffensmeier, Alexander 1977- *195*
Stegeman, Janet Allais 1923- *49*
   Brief entry *49*
Steggall, Susan 1967- *182*
Steig, William 1907-2003 .... *111*
   Obituary *149*
   Earlier sketches in SATA *18, 70*
   See also CLR *103*
Steig, William H.
   See Steig, William
Stein, David Ezra *211*
   Earlier sketch in SATA *180*
Stein, M(eyer) L(ewis) 1920- *6*
Stein, Mathilde 1969- *195*
Stein, Mini *2*
Stein, R(ichard) Conrad 1937- *154*
   Earlier sketches in SATA *31, 82*
Stein, Wendy 1951- *77*
Steinbeck, John 1902-1968 .... *9*
Steinbeck, John Ernst
   See Steinbeck, John
Steinberg, Alfred 1917-1995 .... *9*
Steinberg, David 1962- *200*
Steinberg, D.J.
   See Steinberg, David

Author Index

Steinberg, Fannie 1899-1990 .... *43*
Steinberg, Fred J. 1933- *4*
Steinberg, Phillip Orso 1921- *34*
Steinberg, Rafael (Mark) 1927- *45*
Steinberg, Saul 1914-1999 .... *67*
Steincrohn, Maggie
   See Davis, Maggie S.
Steiner, Barbara A(nnette) 1934- *83*
   Earlier sketch in SATA *13*
   See also SAAS *13*
Steiner, Charlotte 1900-1981 .... *45*
Steiner, George 1929- *62*
Steiner, Joan *199*
   Earlier sketch in SATA *110*
Steiner, Jorg
   See Steiner, Jorg
Steiner, Jorg 1930- *35*
Steiner, K. Leslie
   See Delany, Samuel R., Jr.
Steiner, Stan(ley) 1925-1987 .... *14*
   Obituary *50*
Steins, Richard 1942- *79*
Stem, Jacqueline 1931- *110*
Stemple, Jason *179*
Steneman, Shep 1945- *132*
Stengel, Joyce A. 1938- *158*
Stephanie, Gordon
   See Gordon, Stephanie Jacob
Stephens, Alice Barber 1858-1932 .... *66*
Stephens, Casey
   See Wagner, Sharon B.
Stephens, Henrietta Henkle 1909-1993 .... *6*
Stephens, J.B.
   See Lynn, Tracy
Stephens, Mary Jo 1935- *8*
Stephens, Rebecca 1961- *141*
Stephens, Reed
   See Donaldson, Stephen R.
Stephens, Suzanne
   See Kirby, Susan E.
Stephens, William M(cLain) 1925- *21*
Stephensen, A. M.
   See Manes, Stephen
Stephenson, Lynda 1941- *179*
Stephenson, Lynda A.
   See Stephenson, Lynda
Stepp, Ann 1935- *29*
Stepto, Michele 1946- *61*
Steptoe, Javaka 1971- *151*
Steptoe, John (Lewis) 1950-1989 .... *63*
   Earlier sketch in SATA *8*
   See also CLR *12*
Sterling, Brett
   See Bradbury, Ray
   and Hamilton, Edmond
   and Samachson, Joseph
Sterling, Dorothy 1913-2008 .... *83*
   Autobiography Feature *127*
   Obituary *200*
   Earlier sketch in SATA *1*
   See also CLR *1*
   See also SAAS *2*
Sterling, Helen
   See Watts, Helen L. Hoke
Sterling, Philip 1907-1989 .... *8*
   Obituary *63*
Sterling, Shirley (Anne) 1948- *101*
Stern, Ellen Norman 1927- *26*
Stern, Judith M. 1951- *75*
Stern, Madeleine
   See Stern, Madeleine B.
Stern, Madeleine B. 1912-2007 .... *14*
Stern, Madeleine Bettina
   See Stern, Madeleine B.
Stern, Maggie 1953- *156*
Stern, Philip Van Doren 1900-1984 .... *13*
   Obituary *39*
Stern, Simon 1943- *15*
Sterne, Emma Gelders 1894- *6*
Steurt, Marjorie Rankin 1888-1978 .... *10*
Stevens, April 1963- *208*

Stevens, Bryna 1924- *65*
Stevens, Carla M(cBride) 1928- *13*
Stevens, Chambers 1968- *128*
Stevens, Diane 1939- *94*
Stevens, Franklin 1933- *6*
Stevens, Greg
   See Cook, Glen
Stevens, Gwendolyn 1944- *33*
Stevens, Helen *209*
Stevens, Jan Romero 1953- *95*
Stevens, Janet 1953- *193*
   Earlier sketches in SATA *90, 148*
Stevens, Kathleen 1936- *49*
Stevens, Leonard A. 1920- *67*
Stevens, Lucile Vernon 1899-1994 .... *59*
Stevens, Margaret Dean
   See Aldrich, Bess Streeter
Stevens, Patricia Bunning 1931- *27*
Stevens, Peter
   See Geis, Darlene Stern
Stevens, Serita 1949- *70*
Stevens, Serita Deborah
   See Stevens, Serita
Stevens, Serita Mendelson
   See Stevens, Serita
Stevens, Shira
   See Stevens, Serita
Stevenson, Anna (M.) 1905- *12*
Stevenson, Augusta 1869(?)-1976 .... *2*
   Obituary *26*
Stevenson, Burton Egbert 1872-1962 .... *25*
Stevenson, Drew 1947- *60*
Stevenson, Emma *207*
Stevenson, Harvey 1960- *148*
   Earlier sketch in SATA *80*
Stevenson, James 1929- *195*
   Brief entry *34*
   Earlier sketches in SATA *42, 71, 113, 161*
   See also CLR *17*
Stevenson, Janet 1913- *8*
Stevenson, Robert Louis 1850-1894 .... *100*
   See also YABC *2*
   See also CLR *107*
Stevenson, Robert Louis Balfour
   See Stevenson, Robert Louis
Stevenson, Sucie
   See Stevenson, Sucie
Stevenson, Sucie 1956- *194*
   Earlier sketch in SATA *104*
Stewart, A(gnes) C(harlotte) *15*
Stewart, Amber *181*
Stewart, Chantal 1945- *173*
   Earlier sketch in SATA *121*
Stewart, Charles
   See Zurhorst, Charles (Stewart, Jr.)
Stewart, Eleanor
   See Porter, Eleanor H(odgman)
Stewart, Elisabeth J(ane) 1927- *93*
Stewart, Elizabeth Laing 1907- *6*
Stewart, Gail B. 1949- *141*
Stewart, George Rippey 1895-1980 .... *3*
   Obituary *23*
Stewart, Jennifer J(enkins) 1960- *128*
Stewart, Joel *211*
   Earlier sketch in SATA *151*
Stewart, John 1920- *14*
Stewart, Mary (Florence Elinor) 1916- *12*
Stewart, Mary Rainbow
   See Stewart, Mary (Florence Elinor)
Stewart, Melissa 1968- *209*
   Earlier sketches in SATA *111, 167*
Stewart, Paul 1955- *199*
   Earlier sketches in SATA *114, 163*
Stewart, Robert Neil 1891-1972 .... *7*
Stewart, Sarah *143*
Stewart, Scott
   See Zaffo, George J.
Stewart, W(alter) P. 1924- *53*
Stewart, Whitney 1959- *167*
   Earlier sketch in SATA *92*

Stewig, John Warren 1937- *162*
   Earlier sketches in SATA *26, 110*
Stickler, Soma Han 1942- *128*
Stidworthy, John 1943- *63*
Stiegemeyer, Julie *180*
Stier, Catherine *198*
Stiles, Martha Bennett *108*
   Earlier sketch in SATA *6*
Still, James 1906-2001 .... *29*
   Obituary *127*
Stille, Darlene R. 1942- *170*
   Earlier sketch in SATA *126*
Stille, Darlene Ruth
   See Stille, Darlene R.
Stillerman, Marci *104*
Stillerman, Robbie 1947- *12*
Stilley, Frank 1918- *29*
Stilton, Geronimo *158*
Stimpson, Gerald
   See Mitchell, Adrian
Stine, Catherine *165*
Stine, G(eorge) Harry 1928-1997 .... *136*
   Earlier sketch in SATA *10*
Stine, Jovial Bob
   See Stine, R.L.
Stine, R.L. 1943- *194*
   Earlier sketches in SATA *31, 76, 129*
   See also CLR *111*
Stine, Robert Lawrence
   See Stine, R.L.
Stinetorf, Louise (Allender) 1900-1992 ...... *10*
Stinson, Kathy 1952- *98*
Stirling, Arthur
   See Sinclair, Upton
Stirling, Ian 1941- *77*
Stirling, Nora B(romley) 1900-1997 .... *3*
Stirnweis, Shannon 1931- *10*
Stobbs, William 1914-2000 .... *17*
   Obituary *120*
Stock, Carolmarie 1951- *75*
Stock, Catherine 1952- *158*
   Earlier sketches in SATA *65, 114*
Stockdale, Susan 1954- *206*
   Earlier sketch in SATA *98*
Stockham, Peter (Alan) 1928- *57*
Stockton, Francis Richard 1834-1902 .... *44*
   Brief entry *32*
Stockton, Frank R.
   See Stockton, Francis Richard
Stockwell-Moniz, Marc J. 1954- *164*
Stoddard, Edward G. 1923- *10*
Stoddard, Hope 1900-1987 .... *6*
Stoddard, Sandol 1927- *98*
   Earlier sketch in SATA *14*
Stoehr, Shelley 1969- *107*
Stoeke, Janet Morgan 1957- *202*
   Earlier sketches in SATA *90, 136*
Stohner, Anu 1952- *179*
Stoiko, Michael 1919- *14*
Stojic, Manya 1967- *156*
Stoker, Abraham
   See Stoker, Bram
Stoker, Bram 1847-1912 .... *29*
Stokes, Cedric
   See Beardmore, George
Stokes, Jack (Tilden) 1923- *13*
Stokes, Olivia Pearl 1916- *32*
Stolarz, Laurie Faria *203*
Stolz, Mary 1920-2006 .... *133*
   Obituary *180*
   Earlier sketches in SATA *10, 71*
   See also SAAS *3*
Stolz, Mary Slattery
   See Stolz, Mary
Stone, Alan
   See Svenson, Andrew E(dward)
Stone, David K(arl) 1922- *9*
Stone, David Lee 1978- *166*
Stone, Eugenia 1879-1971 .... *7*
Stone, Gene
   See Stone, Eugenia

Stone, Helen V(irginia) 6
Stone, Idella Purnell
  See Purnell, Idella
Stone, Ikey
  See Purnell, Idella
Stone, Irving 1903-1989 3
  Obituary 64
Stone, Jeff 178
Stone, Jon 1931-1997 39
  Obituary 95
Stone, Josephine Rector
  See Dixon, Jeanne
Stone, Kyle M. 1972- 202
Stone, Lesley
  See Trevor, Elleston
Stone, Peter 1930-2003 65
  Obituary 143
Stone, Phoebe 205
  Earlier sketch in SATA *134*
Stone, Raymond 1
Stone, Rosetta
  See Dr. Seuss
Stone, Tanya Lee 1965- 182
Stonehouse, Bernard 1926- 140
  Earlier sketches in SATA *13, 80*
Stones, (Cyril) Anthony 1934- 72
Stong, Phil(ip Duffield) 1899-1957 32
Stoops, Erik D(aniel) 1966- 142
  Earlier sketch in SATA *78*
Stoppelmoore, Cheryl Jean
  See Ladd, Cheryl (Jean)
Stops, Sue 1936- 86
Storace, Patricia 193
Storad, Conrad J. 1957- 119
Storey, Margaret 1926- 9
Storey, Victoria Carolyn 1945- 16
Stork, Francisco
  See Stork, Francisco X.
Stork, Francisco X. 1953- 210
Storme, Peter
  See Stern, Philip Van Doren
Storr, Catherine (Cole) 1913-2001 87
  Obituary 122
  Earlier sketch in SATA *9*
Story, Josephine
  See Loring, Emilie (Baker)
Stotko, Mary-Ann 1960- 154
Stott, Dorothy (M.) 1958- 99
  Earlier sketch in SATA *67*
Stott, Dot
  See Stott, Dorothy (M.)
Stotter, Mike 1957- 108
Stout, William 1949- 132
Stoutenburg, Adrien (Pearl) 1916-1982 3
Stoutland, Allison 1963- 130
Stover, Allan C(arl) 1938- 14
Stover, Jill (Griffin) 1958- 82
Stover, Marjorie Filley 1914- 9
Stowe, Harriet Beecher 1811-1896
  See YABC *1*
  See also CLR *131*
Stowe, Harriet Elizabeth Beecher
  See Stowe, Harriet Beecher
Stowe, Leland 1899-1994 60
  Obituary 78
Stowe, Rosetta
  See Ogan, George F.
  and Ogan, Margaret E. (Nettles)
Stower, Adam 195
Strachan, Bruce 1959- 205
Strachan, Ian 1938- 85
Strachan, Linda 167
Strachan, Margaret Pitcairn 1908-1998 14
Strahinich, H. C.
  See Strahinich, Helen C.
Strahinich, Helen C. 1949- 78
Strait, Treva Adams 1909-2002 35
Strand, Mark 1934- 41
Strange, Philippa
  See Coury, Louise Andree

Stranger, Joyce
  See Wilson, Joyce M.
Strangis, Joel 1948- 124
Strannigan, Shawn 1956- 93
Strannigan, Shawn Alyne
  See Strannigan, Shawn
Strasser, Todd 1950- 153
  Earlier sketches in SATA *41, 45, 71, 107*
  See also CLR *11*
Stratemeyer, Edward L. 1862-1930 100
  Earlier sketches in SATA *1, 67*
  See Adams, Harrison
Stratford, Philip 1927- 47
Stratton, Allan 1951- 178
Stratton, J. M.
  See Whitlock, Ralph
Stratton, Thomas
  See Coulson, Robert S(tratton)
  and DeWeese, Thomas Eugene
Stratton-Porter, Gene 1863-1924 15
  See also CLR *87*
Strauss, Gwen 1963- 77
Strauss, Joyce 1936- 53
Strauss, Linda Leopold 1942- 127
Strauss, Susan (Elizabeth) 1954- 75
Strayer, E. Ward
  See Stratemeyer, Edward L.
Streano, Vince(nt Catello) 1945- 20
Streatfeild, Mary Noel
  See Streatfeild, Noel
Streatfeild, Noel 1897(?)-1986 20
  Obituary 48
  See also CLR *83*
Street, Janet Travell 1959- 84
Street, Julia Montgomery 1898-1993 11
Streissguth, Thomas 1958- 116
Strelkoff, Tatiana 1957- 89
Stren, Patti 1949- 88
  Brief entry 41
  See also CLR *5*
Strete, Craig Kee 1950- 96
  Earlier sketch in SATA *44*
Stretton, Barbara (Humphrey) 1936- 43
  Brief entry 35
Strickland, Brad 1947- 200
  Earlier sketches in SATA *83, 137, 142*
Strickland, Craig (A.) 1956- 102
Strickland, Dorothy S(alley) 1933- 89
Strickland, Michael R. 1965- 144
  Earlier sketch in SATA *83*
Strickland, Shadra 209
Strickland, Tessa 173
Strickland, William Bradley
  See Strickland, Brad
Striegel, Jana 1955- 140
Striegel-Wilson, Jana
  See Striegel, Jana
Striker, Lee
  See Clark, Margaret (D.)
Striker, Susan 1942- 63
Stringer, Lauren 1957- 183
  Earlier sketch in SATA *129*
Stroeyer, Poul 1923- 13
Stromoski, Rick 1958- 111
Strong, Charles
  See Epstein, Beryl
  and Epstein, Samuel
Strong, David
  See McGuire, Leslie (Sarah)
Strong, Jeremy 1949- 175
  Earlier sketches in SATA *36, 105*
Strong, J.J.
  See Strong, Jeremy
Strong, Pat
  See Hough, Richard (Alexander)
Strong, Stacie 1965- 74
Stroud, Bettye 1939- 165
  Earlier sketch in SATA *96*
Stroud, Jonathan 1970- 159
  Earlier sketch in SATA *102*
  See also CLR *134*

Stroyer, Poul
  See Stroeyer, Poul
Strug, Kerri 1977- 108
Stryer, Andrea Stenn 1938- 192
Stryker, Daniel
  See Morris, Chris(topher Crosby)
  and Stump, Jane Barr
Stuart, David
  See Hoyt, Edwin P(almer), Jr.
Stuart, Derek
  See Foster, John L(ouis)
Stuart, Forbes 1924- 13
Stuart, Ian
  See MacLean, Alistair
Stuart, Jesse (Hilton) 1906-1984 2
  Obituary 36
Stuart, Ruth McEnery 1849(?)-1917 116
Stuart, Sheila
  See Baker, Mary Gladys Steel
Stuart-Clark, Christopher (Anthony) 1940- . 32
Stubis, Talivaldis 1926- 5
Stubley, Trevor (Hugh) 1932- 22
Stuchner, Joan Betty 209
Stucky, Naomi R. 1922- 72
Stucley, Elizabeth
  See Northmore, Elizabeth Florence
Stultifer, Morton
  See Curtis, Richard
Sture-Vasa, Mary
  See Alsop, Mary O'Hara
Sturges, Philemon 174
Sturtevant, Katherine 1950- 180
  Earlier sketch in SATA *130*
Sturton, Hugh
  See Johnston, H(ugh) A(nthony) S(tephen)
Sturtzel, Howard A(llison) 1894-1985 1
Sturtzel, Jane Levington 1903-1996 1
Stutley, D(oris) J(ean) 1959- 142
Stutson, Caroline 1940- 104
Stuve-Bodeen, Stephanie
  See Bodeen, S. A.
Stux, Erica 1929- 140
Styles, (Frank) Showell 1908- 10
Stynes, Barbara White 133
Suarez, Maribel 1952- 201
Suba, Susanne 4
Subond, Valerie
  See Grayland, Valerie (Merle Spanner)
Sudbery, Rodie 1943- 42
Sudyka, Diana 208
Sue, Majella Lue 209
Suen, Anastasia 1956(?)- 157
Sufrin, Mark 1925- 76
Sugarman, Joan G. 1917- 64
Sugarman, Tracy 1921- 37
Sugita, Yutaka 1930- 36
Suhl, Yuri (Menachem) 1908-1986 8
  Obituary 50
  See also CLR *2*
  See also SAAS *1*
Suhr, Joanne 129
Suid, Murray 1942- 27
Sullivan, Edward T. 206
Sullivan, George (Edward) 1927- 147
  Earlier sketches in SATA *4, 89*
Sullivan, Jacqueline Levering 203
Sullivan, Jody
  See Rake, Jody
Sullivan, Kathryn A. 1954- 141
Sullivan, Mary Ann 1954- 63
Sullivan, Mary W(ilson) 1907- 13
Sullivan, Pat
  See Messmer, Otto
Sullivan, Paul 1939- 106
Sullivan, Sarah G. 1953- 179
Sullivan, Silky
  See Makowski, Silvia Ann
Sullivan, Sue
  See Sullivan, Susan E.
Sullivan, Susan E. 1962- 123
Sullivan, Thomas Joseph, Jr. 1947- 16

Sullivan, Tom
  See Sullivan, Thomas Joseph, Jr.
Sully, Tom 1959- 104
Sumichrast, Jozef 1948- 29
Sumiko
  See Davies, Sumiko
Summerforest, Ivy B.
  See Kirkup, James
Summers, Barbara 1944- 182
Summers, Cassia Joy
  See Cowley, Joy
Summers, James L(evingston) 1910-1973 .. 57
  Brief entry 28
Summertree, Katonah
  See Windsor, Patricia
Summy, Barrie 208
Sun, Chyng Feng 1959- 90
Sunderlin, Sylvia (S.) 1911-1997 28
  Obituary 99
Sung, Betty Lee 26
Supeene, Shelagh Lynne 1952- 153
Supplee, Suzanne 204
Supraner, Robyn 1930- 101
  Earlier sketch in SATA 20
Supree, Burt(on) 1941-1992 73
Surface, Mary Hall 1958- 126
Surge, Frank 1931- 13
Susac, Andrew 1929- 5
Susi, Geraldine Lee 1942- 98
Sussman, Cornelia Silver 1914-1999 59
Sussman, Irving 1908-1996 59
Sussman, Susan 1942- 48
Sutcliff, Rosemary 1920-1992 78
  Obituary 73
  Earlier sketches in SATA 6, 44
  See also CLR 138
Sutcliffe, Jane 1957- 138
Sutherland, Colleen 1944- 79
Sutherland, Efua (Theodora Morgue)
  1924-1996 25
Sutherland, Jon 1958- 167
Sutherland, Jonathan D.
  See Sutherland, Jon
Sutherland, Jonathan David
  See Sutherland, Jon
Sutherland, Margaret 1941- 15
Sutherland, Zena Bailey 1915-2002 37
  Obituary 137
Suttles, Shirley (Smith) 1922- 21
Sutton, Ann (Livesay) 1923- 31
Sutton, Eve(lyn Mary) 1906-1992 26
Sutton, Felix 1910(?)-1973 31
Sutton, Jane 1950- 52
  Brief entry 43
Sutton, Larry M(atthew) 1931- 29
Sutton, Margaret Beebe 1903-2001 1
  Obituary 131
Sutton, Myron Daniel 1925- 31
Sutton, Roger 1956- 93
Suzanne, Jamie
  See Hawes, Louise
  and Lantz, Francess L(in)
  and Singleton, Linda Joy
  and Zach, Cheryl (Byrd)
Suzuki, David 1936- 138
Suzuki, David Takayoshi
  See Suzuki, David
Svendsen, Mark 1962- 181
  Earlier sketch in SATA 120
Svendsen, Mark Nestor
  See Svendsen, Mark
Svenson, Andrew E(dward) 1910-1975 2
  Obituary 26
Swaab, Neil 1978- 191
Swaim, Jessica 1950- 202
Swain, Carol 1962- 172
Swain, Gwyneth 1961- 134
  Earlier sketch in SATA 84
Swain, Ruth
  See Swain, Ruth Freeman

Swain, Ruth Freeman 1951- 161
  Earlier sketch in SATA 119
Swain, Su Zan (Noguchi) 1916- 21
Swallow, Pamela Curtis 178
Swamp, Jake 1941- 98
Swan, Susan 1944- 108
  Earlier sketch in SATA 22
Swann, Brian (Stanley Frank) 1940- 116
Swann, E.L.
  See Lasky, Kathryn
Swann, Ruth Rice 1920- 84
Swanson, Diane 1944- 203
Swanson, Helen M(cKendry) 1919- 94
Swanson, June 1931- 76
Swanson, Susan Marie 209
Swanson, Wayne 1942- 167
Swarthout, Glendon (Fred) 1918-1992 26
Swarthout, Kathryn 1919- 7
Swayne, Sam(uel F.) 1907- 53
Swayne, Zoa (Lourana) 1905- 53
Sweat, Lynn 1934- 168
  Earlier sketch in SATA 57
Swede, George 1940- 67
Sweeney, James B(artholomew)
  1910-1999 21
Sweeney, Joyce 1955- 167
  Earlier sketches in SATA 65, 68, 108
Sweeney, Joyce Kay
  See Sweeney, Joyce
Sweeney, Karen O'Connor
  See O'Connor, Karen
Sweeney, Matthew (Gerard) 1952- 156
Sweet, Melissa 1956- 211
  Earlier sketch in SATA 172
Sweet, Sarah C.
  See Jewett, Sarah Orne
Sweetland, Nancy A(nn) 1934- 48
Swenson, Allan A(rmstrong) 1933- 21
Swenson, May 1919-1989 15
Swentzell, Rina 1939- 79
Swiatkowska, Gabi 1971(?)- 180
Swift, Bryan
  See Knott, William C(ecil, Jr.)
Swift, David
  See Kaufmann, John
Swift, Hildegarde Hoyt 1890(?)-1977
  Obituary 20
Swift, Jonathan 1667-1745 19
  See also CLR 53
Swift, Merlin
  See Leeming, Joseph
Swiger, Elinor Porter 1927- 8
Swinburne, Laurence (Joseph) 1924- 9
Swinburne, Stephen R. 1952- 188
  Earlier sketch in SATA 150
Swinburne, Steve
  See Swinburne, Stephen R.
Swindells, Robert (Edward) 1939- 150
  Brief entry 34
  Earlier sketches in SATA 50, 80
  See also SAAS 14
Swinford, Betty (June Wells) 1927- 58
Swinford, Bob
  See Swinford, Betty (June Wells)
Swithen, John
  See King, Stephen
Switzer, Ellen 1923- 48
Swope, Sam 156
Swope, Samuel
  See Swope, Sam
Sybesma, Jetske
  See Ironside, Jetske
Sydney, Frank
  See Warwick, Alan R(oss)
Sydor, Colleen 1960- 207
Sykes, Julie 1963- 202
Sylvada, Peter 1964- 202
Sylvester, Natalie G(abry) 1922- 22
Syme, (Neville) Ronald 1913-1992 87
  Earlier sketch in SATA 2
Symes, R. F. 77

Symes, Ruth Louise 1962- 179
Symons, (Dorothy) Geraldine 1909- 33
Symons, Stuart
  See Stanley, George Edward
Symynkywicz, Jeffrey B. 1954- 87
Symynkywicz, Jeffrey Bruce
  See Symynkywicz, Jeffrey B.
Synge, (Phyllis) Ursula 1930- 9
Sypher, Lucy Johnston 1907- 7
Szasz, Suzanne (Shorr) 1915-1997 13
  Obituary 99
Szekeres, Cyndy 1933- 157
  Autobiography Feature 157
  Earlier sketches in SATA 5, 60, 131
  See also SAAS 13
Szekessy, Tanja 98
Szpura, Beata 1961- 93
Szudek, Agnes S(usan) P(hilomena) 57
  Brief entry 49
Szulc, Tad 1926-2001 26
Szydlow, Jarl
  See Szydlowski, Mary Vigliante
Szydlowski, Mary Vigliante 1946- 94
Szymanski, Lois 1957- 91

                                   T

Taback, Simms 1932- 170
  Brief entry 36
  Earlier sketches in SATA 40, 104
  See also CLR 100
Taber, Gladys (Bagg) 1899-1980
  Obituary 22
Tabor, Nancy Maria Grande 1949- 161
  Earlier sketch in SATA 89
Tabrah, Ruth Milander 1921- 14
Tackach, James 1953- 123
Tackach, James M.
  See Tackach, James
Tadgell, Nicole 1969- 177
Tafuri, Nancy 1946- 192
  Autobiography Feature 192
  Earlier sketches in SATA 39, 75, 130
  See also CLR 74
  See also SAAS 14
Tagg, Christine Elizabeth 1962- 138
Tagliaferro, Linda 173
Taha, Karen T(erry) 1942- 156
  Earlier sketch in SATA 71
Tai, Sharon O. 1963- 153
Tait, Douglas 1944- 12
Takabayashi, Mari 1960- 156
  Earlier sketch in SATA 115
Takahashi, Hideko 209
Takahashi, Rumiko 1957- 163
Takakjian, Portia 1930- 15
Takashima, Misako
  See Misako Rocks!
Takashima, Shizuye 1928- 13
Takayama, Sandi 1962- 106
Takeda, Pete(r M.) 1964- 148
Tal, Eve 1947- 176
Talbert, Marc (Alan) 1953- 154
  Autobiography Feature 154
  Earlier sketches in SATA 68, 99
Talbot, Charlene Joy 1928- 10
Talbot, Toby 1928- 14
Talbott, Hudson 1949- 131
  Earlier sketch in SATA 84
Taliaferro, Dorothy L.
  See Martin, Del
Talifero, Gerald 1950- 75
Talker, T.
  See Rands, William Brighty
Tallarico, Tony 1933- 116
Tallcott, Emogene 10
Tallec, Olivier 1970- 197
Tallis, Robyn
  See Smith, Sherwood

Tallon, Robert 1939- *43*
  Brief entry *28*
Talmadge, Marian *14*
Tamaki, Jillian 1980- *201*
Tamar, Erika 1934- *150*
  Earlier sketches in SATA *62, 101*
Tamarin, Alfred H. 1913-1980 .... *13*
Tamburine, Jean 1930- *12*
Tames, Richard (Lawrence) 1946- *102*
  Earlier sketch in SATA *67*
Tamminga, Frederick W(illiam) 1934- *66*
Tammuz, Benjamin 1919-1989
  Obituary *63*
Tan, Amy 1952- *75*
Tan, Amy Ruth
  See Tan, Amy
Tan, Shaun 1974- *198*
Tanaka, Beatrice 1932- *76*
Tanaka, Shelley *136*
Tang, Charles 1948- *81*
Tang, Greg *172*
Tang, You-Shan 1946- *53*
Tania B.
  See Blixen, Karen
Tankard, Jeremy 1973- *191*
Tannen, Mary 1943- *37*
Tannenbaum, Beulah Goldstein 1916- *3*
Tannenbaum, D(onald) Leb 1948- *42*
Tanner, Jane 1946- *74*
Tanner, Louise S(tickney) 1922-2000 ...... *9*
Tanobe, Miyuki 1937- *23*
Tanselle, Eve 1933- *125*
Tapio, Pat Decker
  See Kines, Pat Decker
Tapp, Kathy Kennedy 1949- *88*
  Brief entry *50*
Tarbescu, Edith 1939- *107*
Tarkington, (Newton) Booth 1869-1946 ..... *17*
Tarpley, Natasha A(nastasia) 1971- *147*
Tarr, Judith 1955- *149*
  Earlier sketch in SATA *64*
Tarry, Ellen 1906- *16*
  See also CLR *26*
  See also SAAS *16*
Tarshis, Jerome 1936- *9*
Tarshis, Lauren *187*
Tarsky, Sue 1946- *41*
Taschek, Karen 1956- *185*
Tashjian, Janet 1956- *151*
  Earlier sketch in SATA *102*
Tashjian, Virginia A. 1921-2008 .... *3*
Tasker, James 1908- *9*
Tate, Don(ald E.) *159*
Tate, Eleanora E. 1948- *191*
  Earlier sketches in SATA *38, 94*
  See also CLR *37*
Tate, Eleanora Elaine
  See Tate, Eleanora E.
Tate, Ellalice
  See Hibbert, Eleanor Alice Burford
Tate, Joan 1922- *86*
  Earlier sketch in SATA *9*
  See also SAAS *20*
Tate, Mary Anne
  See Hale, Arlene
Tate, Nikki *134*
Tate, Richard
  See Masters, Anthony (Richard)
Tate, Suzanne 1930- *91*
Tatham, Betty *142*
Tatham, Campbell
  See Elting, Mary
Tatham, Julie
  See Tatham, Julie Campbell
Tatham, Julie Campbell 1908-1999 .... *80*
Tavares, Matt *198*
  Earlier sketch in SATA *159*
Tavares, Victor 1971- *176*
Taves, Isabella 1915- *27*
Taylor, Alastair 1959- *130*
Taylor, Andrew 1951- *70*

Taylor, Andrew John Robert
  See Taylor, Andrew
Taylor, Ann 1782-1866 .... *41*
  Brief entry *35*
Taylor, Audilee Boyd 1931- *59*
Taylor, Barbara J. 1927- *10*
Taylor, Ben
  See Strachan, Ian
Taylor, Brooke *205*
Taylor, Carl 1937- *14*
Taylor, Cheryl Munro 1957- *96*
Taylor, Cora (Lorraine) 1936- *103*
  Earlier sketch in SATA *64*
  See also CLR *63*
Taylor, Dave 1948- *78*
Taylor, David
  See Taylor, Dave
Taylor, David 1900-1965 .... *10*
Taylor, Debbie A. 1955- *169*
Taylor, Eleanor 1969- *206*
Taylor, Elizabeth 1912-1975 .... *13*
Taylor, Florance Walton *9*
Taylor, Florence M(arian Tompkins)
  1892-1983 .... *9*
Taylor, Gage 1942-2000 .... *87*
Taylor, Geoff 1946- *204*
Taylor, G.P. 1958(?)- *156*
Taylor, Graham Peter
  See Taylor, G.P.
Taylor, Herb(ert Norman, Jr.) 1942-1987 .... *22*
  Obituary *54*
Taylor, J. David
  See Taylor, Dave
Taylor, Jane 1783-1824 .... *41*
  Brief entry *35*
Taylor, Jerry D(uncan) 1938- *47*
Taylor, John Robert
  See Taylor, Andrew
Taylor, Judy
  See Hough, Judy Taylor
Taylor, Kenneth N. 1917-2005 .... *26*
Taylor, Kenneth Nathaniel
  See Taylor, Kenneth N.
Taylor, Kim *180*
Taylor, L(ester) B(arbour), Jr. 1932- *27*
Taylor, Lois Dwight Cole
  See Cole, Lois Dwight
Taylor, Louise Todd 1939- *47*
Taylor, Margaret 1950- *106*
Taylor, Mark 1927- *32*
  Brief entry *28*
Taylor, Mildred D. 1943- *135*
  See also CLR *144*
  See also SAAS *5*
Taylor, Mildred Delois
  See Taylor, Mildred D.
Taylor, Paula (Wright) 1942- *48*
  Brief entry *33*
Taylor, Peter Lane *210*
Taylor, Robert Lewis 1912-1998 .... *10*
Taylor, Sean 1965- *192*
Taylor, Sydney (Brenner) 1904(?)-1978 ..... *28*
  Obituary *26*
  Earlier sketch in SATA *1*
Taylor, Theodore 1921-2006 .... *128*
  Obituary *177*
  Earlier sketches in SATA *5, 54, 83*
  See also CLR *30*
  See also SAAS *4*
Taylor, William 1938- *164*
  Earlier sketches in SATA *78, 113*
  See also CLR *63*
Tazewell, Charles 1900-1972 .... *74*
Tchana, Katrin
  See Tchana, Katrin Hyman
Tchana, Katrin H.
  See Tchana, Katrin Hyman
Tchana, Katrin Hyman 1963- *177*
  Earlier sketch in SATA *125*
Tchekhov, Anton
  See Chekhov, Anton

Tchen, Richard *120*
Tchudi, Stephen N. 1942- *55*
Teague, Bob
  See Teague, Robert
Teague, Mark 1963- *205*
  Earlier sketches in SATA *68, 99, 170*
Teague, Mark Christopher
  See Teague, Mark
Teague, Robert 1929- *32*
  Brief entry *31*
Teal, Val 1902-1997 .... *10*
  Obituary *114*
Teal, Valentine M.
  See Teal, Val
Teale, Edwin Way 1899-1980 .... *7*
  Obituary *25*
Teasdale, Sara 1884-1933 .... *32*
Tebbel, John (William) 1912-2004 .... *26*
Teckentrup, Britta 1969- *200*
Tedesco, P.R.
  See Naylor, Phyllis Reynolds
Teensma, Lynne Bertrand
  See Bertrand, Lynne
Tee-Van, Helen Damrosch 1893-1976 ...... *10*
  Obituary *27*
Tegner, Bruce 1928- *62*
Teitelbaum, Michael 1953- *116*
  Earlier sketch in SATA *59*
Tejima
  See Tejima, Keizaburo
Tejima, Keizaburo 1931- *139*
  See also CLR *20*
Telander, Todd (G.) 1967- *88*
Teleki, Geza 1943- *45*
Telemaque, Eleanor Wong 1934- *43*
Telescope, Tom
  See Newbery, John
Tellis, Annabel 1967- *191*
Temkin, Sara Anne Schlossberg
  1913-1996 .... *26*
Temko, Florence *13*
Tempest, Margaret Mary 1892-1982
  Obituary *33*
Templar, Maurice
  See Groom, Arthur William
Temple, Arthur
  See Northcott, (William) Cecil
Temple, Charles 1947- *79*
Temple, Frances (Nolting) 1945-1995 ...... *85*
Temple, Herbert 1919- *45*
Temple, Paul
  See McConnell, James Douglas Rutherford
Temple, William F(rederick) 1914-1989 ... *107*
Tenggren, Gustaf 1896-1970 .... *18*
  Obituary *26*
Tennant, Kylie
  See Rodd, Kylie Tennant
Tennant, Veronica 1947- *36*
Tenneshaw, S.M.
  See Beaumont, Charles
  and Garrett, Randall
  and Silverberg, Robert
Tenniel, John 1820-1914 .... *74*
  Brief entry *27*
  See also CLR *146*
Tepper, Sheri S. 1929- *113*
Terada, Alice M. 1928- *90*
Terban, Marvin 1940- *54*
  Brief entry *45*
Teresi, Judith M.
  See Goldberger, Judith M.
ter Haar, Jaap 1922- *6*
  See also CLR *15*
Terhune, Albert Payson 1872-1942 .... *15*
Terkel, Susan N(eiburg) 1948- *103*
  Earlier sketch in SATA *59*
Terlouw, Jan (Cornelis) 1931- *30*
Terrell, John Upton 1900-1988
  Obituary *60*
Terrill, Beth *198*

Terrill, Elizabeth
  See Terrill, Beth
Terris, Susan 1937- 77
  Earlier sketch in SATA *3*
Terry, Luther L(eonidas) 1911-1985 .... *11*
  Obituary *42*
Terry, Margaret
  See Dunnahoo, Terry Janson
Terry, Walter 1913-1982 .... *14*
Terry, Will 1966- *205*
Terzian, James P. 1915- *14*
Tessendorf, K(enneth) C(harles)
  1925-2003 .... *75*
  Obituary *142*
Tessler, Manya *200*
Tessler, Stephanie Gordon
  See Gordon, Stephanie Jacob
Testa, Dom *208*
Tester, Sylvia Root 1939- *64*
  Brief entry *37*
Tether, (Cynthia) Graham 1950- *46*
  Brief entry *36*
Tetzner, Lisa 1894-1963 .... *169*
Thach, James Otis 1969- *195*
Thacher, Mary McGrath 1933- *9*
Thackeray, William Makepeace
  1811-1863 .... *23*
Thaler, Michael C.
  See Thaler, Mike
Thaler, Mike 1936- *93*
  Brief entry *47*
  Earlier sketch in SATA *56*
Thaler, Shmuel 1958- *126*
  Earlier sketch in SATA *72*
Thamer, Katie 1955- *42*
Thane, Elswyth 1900-1984(?) *32*
Tharp, Louise (Marshall) Hall 1898-1992 .... *3*
  Obituary *129*
Tharp, Tim 1957- *189*
Thayer, Ernest Lawrence 1863-1940 .... *60*
Thayer, Jane
  See Woolley, Catherine
Thayer, Marjorie 1908-1992 .... *74*
  Brief entry *37*
Thayer, Peter
  See Wyler, Rose
Thelwell, Norman 1923-2004 .... *14*
Themerson, Stefan 1910-1988 .... *65*
Thermes, Jennifer 1966- *155*
Theroux, Paul 1941- *109*
  Earlier sketch in SATA *44*
Theroux, Paul Edward
  See Theroux, Paul
Thesman, Jean *124*
  Earlier sketch in SATA *74*
The Tjong-Khing
  See Khing, T.T.
Thieda, Shirley Ann 1943- *13*
Thiele, Colin 1920-2006 .... *125*
  Earlier sketches in SATA *14, 72*
  See also CLR 27
  See also SAAS 2
Thiele, Colin Milton
  See Thiele, Colin
Thiesing, Lisa 1958- *159*
  Earlier sketch in SATA *95*
Thimmesh, Catherine *189*
Thiry, Joan (Marie) 1926- *45*
Thistlethwaite, Miles 1945- *12*
Thollander, Earl 1922- *22*
Thomas, Abigail 1941- *112*
Thomas, Andrea
  See Hill, Margaret (Ohler)
Thomas, Art(hur Lawrence) 1952- *48*
  Brief entry *38*
Thomas, Carroll
  See Ratliff, Thomas M.
  and Shmurak, Carole B.
Thomas, Dylan 1914-1953 .... *60*
Thomas, Dylan Marlais
  See Thomas, Dylan

Thomas, Egbert S.
  See Ellis, Edward S.
Thomas, Estelle Webb 1899-1982 .... *26*
Thomas, Frances 1943- *171*
  Earlier sketch in SATA *92*
Thomas, H. C.
  See Keating, Lawrence A.
Thomas, Ianthe 1951- *139*
  Brief entry *42*
  See also CLR 8
Thomas, J. F.
  See Fleming, Thomas
Thomas, Jan 1958- *197*
Thomas, Jane Resh 1936- *171*
  Earlier sketches in SATA *38, 90*
Thomas, Jerry D. 1959- *91*
Thomas, Joan Gale
  See Robinson, Joan (Mary) G(ale Thomas)
Thomas, Joyce Carol 1938- *210*
  Autobiography Feature *137*
  Earlier sketches in SATA *40, 78, 123, 137*
  See also CLR 19
  See also SAAS 7
Thomas, Lee
  See Floren, Lee
  and Pendleton, Thomas
Thomas, Lowell Jackson, Jr. 1923- *15*
Thomas, Margaret
  See Thomas, Peggy
Thomas, Meredith 1963- *119*
Thomas, Michael
  See Wilks, Michael Thomas
Thomas, Middy 1931- *191*
Thomas, Patricia 1934- *199*
  Earlier sketch in SATA *51*
Thomas, Peggy *174*
Thomas, Rob 1965- *97*
Thomas, Scott 1959- *147*
Thomas, Velma Maia 1955- *171*
Thomas, Vernon (Arthur) 1934- *56*
Thomas, Victoria
  See DeWeese, Thomas Eugene
  and Kugi, Constance Todd
Thomasma, Kenneth R. 1930- *90*
Thomassie, Tynia 1959- *92*
Thompson, Brenda 1935- *34*
Thompson, Carol 1951- *189*
  Earlier sketch in SATA *85*
Thompson, China
  See Lewis, Mary
Thompson, Colin 1942- *198*
  Earlier sketches in SATA *95, 163*
Thompson, David H(ugh) 1941- *17*
Thompson, Eileen
  See Panowski, Eileen Thompson
Thompson, George Selden 1929-1989 .... *73*
  Obituary *63*
  Earlier sketch in SATA *4*
  See also CLR 8
Thompson, Harlan 1894-1987 .... *10*
  Obituary *53*
Thompson, Hilary 1943- *56*
  Brief entry *49*
Thompson, Joanna Maxwell Pullein
  See Pullein-Thompson, Joanna Maxwell
Thompson, Julian F(rancis) 1927- *155*
  Brief entry *40*
  Earlier sketches in SATA *55, 99*
  See also CLR 24
  See also SAAS 13
Thompson, K(athryn Carolyn)
  Dyble 1952- *82*
Thompson, Kate 1956- *204*
Thompson, Kay 1912(?)-1998 .... *16*
  See also CLR 22
Thompson, Lauren 1962- *200*
  Earlier sketches in SATA *132, 174*
Thompson, Lauren Stevens
  See Thompson, Lauren
Thompson, Megan Lloyd
  See Lloyd, Megan

Thompson, Richard 1951- *184*
Thompson, Ruth Plumly 1891-1976 .... *66*
Thompson, Sharon 1952- *119*
Thompson, Sharon Elaine
  See Thompson, Sharon
Thompson, Stith 1885-1976 .... *57*
  Obituary *20*
Thompson, Vivian L(aubach) 1911- *3*
Thomson, Bill 1963- *187*
Thomson, Celia
  See Lynn, Tracy
Thomson, David (Robert Alexander)
  1914-1988 .... *40*
  Obituary *55*
Thomson, Melissa 1979- *205*
Thomson, Pat 1939- *122*
  Earlier sketch in SATA *77*
Thomson, Peggy 1922- *31*
Thomson, Sarah L. *178*
Thon, Melanie Rae 1957- *132*
Thong, Roseanne *174*
Thorburn, John
  See Goldsmith, John Herman Thorburn
Thorn, John 1947- *59*
Thorndyke, Helen Louise
  See Benson, Mildred
Thorne, Ian
  See May, Julian
Thorne, Jean Wright
  See May, Julian
Thornhill, Jan 1955- *148*
  Earlier sketch in SATA *77*
Thornton, Hall
  See Silverberg, Robert
Thornton, W. B.
  See Burgess, Thornton Waldo
Thornton, Yvonne S(hirley) 1947- *96*
Thorpe, E(ustace) G(eorge) 1916- *21*
Thorpe, J. K.
  See Nathanson, Laura Walther
Thorvall, Kerstin 1925- *13*
Thorvall-Falk, Kerstin
  See Thorvall, Kerstin
Thrasher, Crystal (Faye) 1921- *27*
Threadgall, Colin 1941- *77*
Three Little Pigs
  See Lantz, Francess L(in)
Thum, Gladys 1920- *26*
Thum, Marcella *28*
  Earlier sketch in SATA *3*
Thundercloud, Katherine
  See Witt, Shirley Hill
Thurber, James 1894-1961 .... *13*
Thurber, James Grover
  See Thurber, James
Thurlo, Aimee *161*
Thurlo, David *161*
Thurman, Judith 1946- *33*
Thurman, Mark (Gordon Ian) 1948- *63*
Thwaite, Ann (Barbara Harrop) 1932- *14*
Tibbetts, Peggy *127*
Tibbles, Jean-Paul 1958- *115*
Tibo, Gilles 1951- *107*
  Earlier sketch in SATA *67*
Tiburzi, Bonnie 1948- *65*
Ticheburn, Cheviot
  See Ainsworth, William Harrison
Tichenor, Tom 1923-1992 .... *14*
Tichnor, Richard 1959- *90*
Tichy, William 1924- *31*
Tickle, Jack
  See Chapman, Jane
Tiegreen, Alan F. 1935- *94*
  Brief entry *36*
Tierney, Frank M. 1930- *54*
Tierney, Tom 1928- *113*
Tiffault, Benette W. 1955- *77*
Tildes, Phyllis Limbacher 1945- *210*
Tiller, Ruth L. 1949- *83*
Tilley, Debbie *190*
Tillman, Nancy *211*

Tilly, Nancy 1935- 62
Tilton, Madonna Elaine 1929- 41
Tilton, Rafael
    See Tilton, Madonna Elaine
Timberlake, Amy 156
Timberlake, Carolyn
    See Dresang, Eliza (Carolyn Timberlake)
Timmers, Leo 1970- 190
Timmins, William F(rederick) 10
Tinbergen, Niko(laas) 1907-1988
    Obituary 60
Tincknell, Cathy 194
Tiner, John Hudson 1944- 32
Tingle, Dolli (?)-
    See Brackett, Dolli Tingle
Tingle, Rebecca 174
Tingle, Tim 208
Tingum, Janice 1958- 91
Tinkelman, Murray 1933- 12
Tinkham, Kelly A. 188
Tinkle, (Julien) Lon 1906-1980 36
Tinling, Marion (Rose) 1904- 140
Tipene, Tim 1972- 141
Tippett, James S(terling) 1885-1958 66
Tirone Smith, Mary-Ann 1944- 143
Titlebaum, Ellen 195
Titler, Dale M(ilton) 1926- 35
    Brief entry 28
Titmarsh, Michael Angelo
    See Thackeray, William Makepeace
Titus, Eve 1922- 2
Tjia, Sherwin 1975- 204
Tjong Khing, The 1933- 76
Tobias, Katherine
    See Gottfried, Theodore Mark
Tobias, Tobi 1938- 82
    Earlier sketch in SATA 5
    See also CLR 4
Todd, Anne Ophelia
    See Dowden, Anne Ophelia Todd
Todd, Barbara 1961- 173
Todd, Barbara K(eith) 1917- 10
Todd, Chuck 195
Todd, H(erbert) E(atton) 1908-1988 84
    Earlier sketch in SATA 11
Todd, Loreto 1942- 30
Todd, Peter
    See Hamilton, Charles (Harold St. John)
Toews, Miriam 1964- 165
Tofel, Richard J. 1957- 140
Toft, Kim Michelle 1960- 170
Tokunbo, Dimitrea 187
Tolan, Stephanie S. 1942- 142
    Earlier sketches in SATA 38, 78
Toland, John (Willard) 1912-2004 38
Tolbert, Steve 1944- 143
Toledo, Francisco 1940- 198
Toledo, Natalia 1967- 197
Tolkien, J. R. R. 1892-1973 100
    Obituary 24
    Earlier sketches in SATA 2, 32
    See also CLR 152
Tolkien, John Ronald Reuel
    See Tolkien, J. R. R.
Toll, Emily
    See Cannon, Eileen E(mily)
Toll, Nelly S. 1935- 78
Tolland, W. R.
    See Heitzmann, William Ray
Tolles, Martha 1921- 76
    Earlier sketch in SATA 8
Tolliver, Ruby C(hangos) 1922- 110
    Brief entry 41
    Earlier sketch in SATA 55
Tolmie, Kenneth Donald 1941- 15
Tolstoi, Lev
    See Tolstoy, Leo
Tolstoy, Leo 1828-1910 26
Tolstoy, Count Leo
    See Tolstoy, Leo

Tolstoy, Leo Nikolaevich
    See Tolstoy, Leo
Tomalin, Ruth 29
Tomaselli, Rosa
    See Pausacker, Jenny
Tomecek, Steve 172
Tomes, Margot (Ladd) 1917-1991 70
    Brief entry 27
    Obituary 69
    Earlier sketch in SATA 36
Tomey, Ingrid 1943- 77
Tomfool
    See Farjeon, Eleanor
Tomic, Tomislav 1977- 202
Tomkins, Jasper
    See Batey, Tom
Tomline, F. Latour
    See Gilbert, W(illiam) S(chwenck)
Tomlinson, Heather 192
Tomlinson, Jill 1931-1976 3
    Obituary 24
Tomlinson, Reginald R(obert) 1885-1979(?)
    Obituary 27
Tomlinson, Theresa 1946- 165
    Earlier sketch in SATA 103
    See also CLR 60
Tommaso, Rich 1970(?)- 200
Tompert, Ann 1918- 139
    Earlier sketches in SATA 14, 89
Tompkins, Troy
    See Cle, Troy
Toner, Raymond John 1908-1986 10
Tong, Gary S. 1942- 66
Tong, Paul 188
Took, Belladonna
    See Chapman, Vera (Ivy May)
Tooke, Louise Mathews 1950- 38
Tooke, Susan 173
Toonder, Martin
    See Groom, Arthur William
Toothaker, Roy Eugene 1928- 18
Tooze, Ruth (Anderson) 1892-1972 4
Topek, Susan Remick 1955- 78
Topping, Audrey R(onning) 1928- 14
Tor, Regina
    See Shekerjian, Regina Tor
Torbert, Floyd James 1922- 22
Torgersen, Don Arthur 1934- 55
    Brief entry 41
Torley, Luke
    See Blish, James
Torrecilla, Pablo 1967- 206
Torres, Andres Segovia
    See Segovia, Andres
Torres, Daniel 1958- 102
Torres, John A. 1965- 163
    Earlier sketch in SATA 94
Torres, John Albert
    See Torres, John A.
Torres, Laura 1967- 146
    Earlier sketch in SATA 87
Torres, Leyla 1960- 155
Torrey, Rich
    See Torrey, Richard
Torrey, Richard 189
Torrie, Malcolm
    See Mitchell, Gladys (Maude Winifred)
Toten, Teresa 1955- 99
Totham, Mary
    See Breinburg, Petronella
Touponce, William F. 1948- 114
Tournier, Michel 1924- 23
Tournier, Michel Edouard
    See Tournier, Michel
Towle, Wendy 1963- 79
Towne, Mary
    See Spelman, Mary
Towney, Rod
    See Townley, Roderick
Townley, Roderick 1942- 177
Townsend, Brad W. 1962- 91

Townsend, John Rowe 1922- 132
    Autobiography Feature 132
    Earlier sketches in SATA 4, 68
    See also CLR 2
    See also SAAS 2
Townsend, Michael 1981- 194
Townsend, Sue 1946- 93
    Brief entry 48
    Earlier sketch in SATA 55
Townsend, Susan Lilian
    See Townsend, Sue
Townsend, Thomas L. 1944- 59
Townsend, Tom
    See Townsend, Thomas L.
Townsend, Wendy 1962- 201
Townson, Hazel 134
Toye, William Eldred 1926- 8
Traherne, Michael
    See Watkins-Pitchford, Denys James
Trahey, Jane 1923-2000 36
    Obituary 120
Trapani, Iza 1954- 116
    Earlier sketch in SATA 80
Trapp, Maria Augusta von
    See von Trapp, Maria Augusta
Travers, P(amela) L(yndon) 1899-1996 100
    Obituary 90
    Earlier sketches in SATA 4, 54
    See also CLR 93
    See also SAAS 2
Travis, Lucille 133
    Earlier sketch in SATA 88
Treadgold, Mary 1910- 49
Trease, (Robert) Geoffrey 1909-1998 60
    Obituary 101
    Earlier sketch in SATA 2
    See also CLR 42
    See also SAAS 6
Treat, Lawrence 1903-1998 59
Tredez, Alain 1926- 17
Tredez, Denise 1930- 50
Treece, Henry 1912-1966 2
    See also CLR 2
Tregarthen, Enys
    See Sloggett, Nellie
Tregaskis, Richard 1916-1973 3
    Obituary 26
Treherne, Katie Thamer 1955- 76
Trell, Max 1900-1996 14
    Obituary 108
Tremain, Ruthven 1922- 17
Trembath, Don 1963- 168
    Earlier sketch in SATA 96
Tremens, Del
    See MacDonald, Amy
Trent, Robbie 1894-1988 26
Trent, Timothy
    See Malmberg, Carl
Treseder, Terry Walton 1956- 68
Tresilian, (Cecil) Stuart 1891-(?) 40
Tresselt, Alvin 1916-2000 7
    See also CLR 30
Trevino, Elizabeth B(orton) de 1904- 29
    Earlier sketch in SATA 1
    See also SAAS 5
Trevor, Elleston 1920-1995 28
Trevor, Frances
    See Teasdale, Sara
Trevor, Glen
    See Hilton, James
Trevor, (Lucy) Meriol 1919-2000 113
    Obituary 122
    Earlier sketch in SATA 10
Trewellard, J.M. 195
Trewellard, Juliet
    See Trewellard, J.M.
Trez, Alain
    See Tredez, Alain
Trez, Denise
    See Tredez, Denise

Trezise, Percy 1923-
See CLR *41*
Trezise, Percy James
See Trezise, Percy
Triggs, Tony D. 1946- *70*
Trimble, Marshall I(ra) 1939- *93*
Trimby, Elisa 1948- *47*
Brief entry *40*
Tring, A. Stephen
See Meynell, Laurence Walter
Tripp, Eleanor B(aldwin) 1936- *4*
Tripp, Janet 1942- *108*
Tripp, Jenny *188*
Tripp, John
See Moore, John Travers
Tripp, Nathaniel 1944- *101*
Tripp, Paul 1916-2002 .... *8*
Obituary *139*
Tripp, Valerie 1951- *168*
Earlier sketch in SATA *78*
Tripp, Wallace (Whitney) 1940- *31*
Trivelpiece, Laurel 1926- *56*
Brief entry *46*
Trivett, Daphne Harwood 1940- *22*
Trivizas, Eugene 1946- *84*
Trnka, Jiri 1912-1969 .... *43*
Brief entry *32*
Trollope, Anthony 1815-1882 .... *22*
Trost, Lucille W(ood) 1938- *149*
Earlier sketch in SATA *12*
Trott, Betty 1933- *91*
Trotter, Deborah W. *184*
Trotter, Grace V(iolet) 1900-1991 .... *10*
Trottier, Maxine 1950- *175*
Earlier sketch in SATA *131*
Troughton, Joanna (Margaret) 1947- *37*
Trout, Kilgore
See Farmer, Philip Jose
Trout, Richard E. *123*
Trudeau, Garretson Beekman
See Trudeau, G.B.
Trudeau, Garry
See Trudeau, G.B.
Trudeau, Garry B.
See Trudeau, G.B.
Trudeau, G.B. 1948- *168*
Earlier sketch in SATA *35*
Trueit, Trudi
See Trueit, Trudi Strain
Trueit, Trudi Strain 1963- *179*
Trueman, Matthew *183*
Trueman, Terry 1947- *178*
Earlier sketch in SATA *132*
Truesdell, Judy
See Mecca, Judy Truesdell
Truesdell, Sue
See Truesdell, Susan G.
Truesdell, Susan G. *108*
Brief entry *45*
Trumbauer, Lisa (Trutkoff) 1963- *149*
Truss, Jan 1925- *35*
Truss, Lynne 1955(?)- *194*
Tryon, Leslie *194*
Earlier sketch in SATA *139*
Tubb, Jonathan N. 1951- *78*
Tubb, Kristin O'Donnell 1971- *209*
Tubby, I. M.
See Kraus, (Herman) Robert
Tucker, Caroline
See Nolan, Jeannette Covert
Tudor, Edward
See Browne, Anthony
Tudor, Tasha 1915-2008 .... *160*
Obituary *205*
Earlier sketches in SATA *20, 69*
See also CLR *13*
Tuerk, Hanne 1951- *71*
Tugeau, Jeremy *199*
Tulloch, Richard 1949- *180*
Earlier sketch in SATA *76*

Tulloch, Richard George
See Tulloch, Richard
Tulloch, Shirley *169*
Tully, John (Kimberley) 1923- *14*
Tumanov, Vladimir A. 1961- *138*
Tung, Angela 1972- *109*
Tunis, Edwin (Burdett) 1897-1973 .... *28*
Obituary *24*
Earlier sketch in SATA *1*
See also CLR *2*
Tunis, John R(oberts) 1889-1975 .... *37*
Brief entry *30*
Tunnell, Michael
See Tunnell, Michael O.
Tunnell, Michael O. 1950- *157*
Earlier sketch in SATA *103*
Tunnell, Michael O'Grady
See Tunnell, Michael O.
Tunnicliffe, C(harles) F(rederick)
1901-1979 .... *62*
Turck, Mary C. 1950- *144*
Turk, Hanne
See Tuerk, Hanne
Turk, Ruth 1917- *82*
Turkle, Brinton 1915- *79*
Earlier sketch in SATA *2*
Turlington, Bayly 1919-1977 .... *5*
Obituary *52*
Turnbull, Agnes Sligh 1888-1982 .... *14*
Turnbull, Ann 1943- *160*
Earlier sketch in SATA *18*
Turnbull, Ann Christine
See Turnbull, Ann
Turner, Alice K. 1940- *10*
Turner, Ann 1945- *188*
Autobiography Feature *188*
Earlier sketches in SATA *14, 77, 113, 178*
Turner, Ann Warren
See Turner, Ann
Turner, Bonnie 1932- *75*
Turner, Elizabeth 1774-1846
See YABC *2*
Turner, Glennette Tilley 1933- *183*
Earlier sketch in SATA *71*
Turner, Josie
See Crawford, Phyllis
Turner, Megan Whalen 1965- *174*
Earlier sketch in SATA *94*
Turner, Pamela S. 1957- *211*
Turner, Philip (William) 1925- *83*
Earlier sketch in SATA *11*
See also CLR *89*
See also SAAS *6*
Turner, Robyn 1947- *77*
Turner, Sheila R.
See Seed, Sheila Turner
Turngren, Annette 1902(?)-1980
Obituary *23*
Turngren, Ellen (?)-1964 .... *3*
Turska, Krystyna (Zofia) 1933- *31*
Brief entry *27*
Turteltaub, H.N.
See Turtledove, Harry
Turtledove, Harry 1949- *166*
Earlier sketch in SATA *116*
Turtledove, Harry Norman
See Turtledove, Harry
Tusa, Tricia 1960- *207*
Earlier sketches in SATA *72, 111*
Tusiani, Joseph 1924- *45*
Twain, Mark 1835-1910 .... *100*
See also YABC *2*
See also CLR *66*
Tweit, Susan J 1956- *94*
Tweit, Susan Joan
See Tweit, Susan J
Tweton, D. Jerome 1933- *48*
Twinem, Neecy 1958- *92*
Twohill, Maggie
See Angell, Judie

Tworkov, Jack 1900-1982 .... *47*
Obituary *31*
Tyche
See Papademetriou, Lisa
Tyers, Jenny 1969- *89*
Tyers, Kathy 1952- *82*
Tyler, Anne 1941- *173*
Earlier sketches in SATA *7, 90*
Tyler, Linda
See Tyler, Linda W(agner)
Tyler, Linda W(agner) 1952- *65*
Tyler, Vicki 1952- *64*
Tyne, Joel
See Schembri, Jim
Tyrrell, Frances 1959- *107*

U

Ubell, Earl 1926-2007 .... *4*
Obituary *182*
Uchida, Yoshiko 1921-1992 .... *53*
Obituary *72*
Earlier sketch in SATA *1*
See also CLR *56*
See also SAAS *1*
Udall, Jan Beaney 1938- *10*
Uden, (Bernard Gilbert) Grant 1910- *26*
Uderzo, Albert 1927-
See CLR *37*
Udovic, David 1950- *189*
Udry, Janice May 1928- *152*
Earlier sketch in SATA *4*
Uegaki, Chieri 1969- *211*
Earlier sketch in SATA *153*
Ueno, Noriko
See Nakae, Noriko
Ugliano, Natascia *196*
Uhlberg, Myron *174*
Uhlig, Richard 1970- *195*
Uhlig, Susan 1955- *129*
Ulam, S(tanislaw) M(arcin) 1909-1984 .... *51*
Ullman, Barb Bentler *210*
Ullman, James Ramsey 1907-1971 .... *7*
Ulm, Robert 1934-1977 .... *17*
Ulmer, Louise 1943- *53*
Ulmer, Wendy K. 1950- *201*
Ulrich, Maureen 1958- *206*
Ulriksen, Mark 1957- *210*
Ulyatt, Kenneth 1920- *14*
Umansky, Kaye 1946- *188*
Earlier sketch in SATA *158*
Unada
See Gliewe, Unada (Grace)
Uncle Carter
See Boucher, (Clarence) Carter
Uncle Eric
See Maybury, Richard J.
Uncle Gus
See Rey, H. A.
Uncle Mac
See McCulloch, Derek (Ivor Breashur)
Uncle Ray
See Coffman, Ramon Peyton
Uncle Shelby
See Silverstein, Shel
Underhill, Alice Mertie (Waterman)
1900-1971 .... *10*
Underhill, Liz 1948- *53*
Brief entry *49*
Underwood, Deborah 1962- *206*
Unger, Harlow G. 1931- *75*
Unger, Harlow Giles
See Unger, Harlow G.
Unger, Jim 1937- *67*
Ungerer, (Jean) Thomas 1931- *106*
Earlier sketches in SATA *5, 33*
See also CLR *77*
Ungerer, Tomi 1931-
See Ungerer, (Jean) Thomas

Unkelbach, Kurt 1913-1992 4
Unnerstad, Edith (Totterman) 1900-1982 3
  See also CLR 36
Unobagha, Uzo 139
Unrau, Ruth 1922- 9
Unstead, R(obert) J(ohn) 1915-1988 12
  Obituary 56
Unsworth, Walt(er) 1928- 4
Untermeyer, Bryna Ivens 1909-1985 61
Untermeyer, Louis 1885-1977 37
  Obituary 26
  Earlier sketch in SATA 2
Unwin, David S. 1918- 14
Unwin, David Storr
  See Unwin, David S.
Unwin, Nora S(picer) 1907-1982 3
  Obituary 49
Unzner, Christa 1958- 141
  Earlier sketch in SATA 80
Unzner-Fischer, Christa
  See Unzner, Christa
Updale, Eleanor 1953- 175
Updyke, Rosemary K. 1924- 103
Upitis, Alvis 109
Urbain, Cat 1956- 211
Urbain, Catherine
  See Urbain, Cat
Urban, Helle (Denise) 1957- 149
Urban, Linda 199
Urbanovic, Jackie 189
Urbigkit, Cat 1965- 196
Ure, Jean 1943- 192
  Autobiography Feature 192
  Earlier sketches in SATA 48, 78, 129
  See also CLR 34
  See also SAAS 14
U'Ren, Andrea 1968- 142
Uris, Leon 1924-2003 49
  Obituary 146
Uris, Leon Marcus
  See Uris, Leon
Ursu, Anne 177
Ury, Allen B. 1954- 98
Uschan, Michael V. 1948- 129
Usher, Margo Scegge
  See McHargue, Georgess
Uslan, Michael E. 1951- 169
Uston, Ken(neth Senzo) 1935-1987 65
Uttley, Alice Jane 1884-1976 88
  Obituary 26
  Earlier sketch in SATA 3
Uttley, Alison
  See Uttley, Alice Jane
Utz, Lois (Marie) 1932-1986 5
  Obituary 50

V

Vaeth, J. Gordon 1921- 17
Vaeth, Joseph Gordon
  See Vaeth, J. Gordon
Vagin, Vladimir (Vasilevich) 1937- 142
Vail, Rachel 1966- 201
  Earlier sketches in SATA 94, 163
Vainio, Pirkko 1957- 123
  Earlier sketch in SATA 76
Valen, Nanine 1950- 21
Valencak, Hannelore
  See Mayer, Hannelore Valencak
Valens, Amy 1946- 70
Valens, E(vans) G(ladstone), Jr. 1920-1992 .. 1
Valentine, Johnny 72
Valerio, Geraldo 1970- 180
Valgardson, W. D. 1939- 151
  Earlier sketch in SATA 101
Valgardson, William Dempsey
  See Valgardson, W. D.
Valleau, Emily 1925- 51
Van Abbe, Salaman 1883-1955 18

Van Allsburg, Chris 1949- 156
  Earlier sketches in SATA 37, 53, 105
  See also CLR 113
Van Anrooy, Francine 1924- 2
Van Anrooy, Frans
  See Van Anrooy, Francine
Vanasse, Deb 1957- 170
Van Buren, David 203
Vance, Cynthia 207
Vance, Eleanor Graham 1908-1985 11
Vance, Gerald
  See Garrett, Randall
  and Silverberg, Robert
Vance, Marguerite 1889-1965 29
Vance-Abrams, Cynthia
  See Vance, Cynthia
VanCleave, Janice 1942- 116
  Autobiography Feature 123
  Earlier sketch in SATA 75
Vandenburg, Mary Lou 1943- 17
Vander Boom, Mae M. 14
Vander-Els, Betty 1936- 63
van der Heide, Iris 1970- 183
van der Linde, Laurel 1952- 78
van der Meer, Ron 1945- 98
van de Ruit, John 1975- 199
Van der Veer, Judy 1912-1982 4
  Obituary 33
Vanderwerff, Corrine 1939- 117
Vander Zee, Ruth 199
  Earlier sketch in SATA 159
Vande Velde, Vivian 1951- 211
  Earlier sketches in SATA 62, 95, 141
  See also CLR 145
Vandivert, Rita (Andre) 1905-1986 21
Van Draanen, Wendelin 207
  Earlier sketch in SATA 122
Van Dusen, Chris 173
Van Duyn, Janet 1910- 18
Van Dyne, Edith
  See Baum, L. Frank
  and Sampson, Emma (Keats) Speed
  and van Zantwijk, Rudolf (Alexander
  Marinus)
Vane, Mitch
  See Vane, Mitchelle
Vane, Mitchelle 176
van Frankenhuyzen, Gijsbert 1951- 132
Van Genechten, Guido 1957- 165
van Haeringen, Annemarie 193
Van Hook, Beverly H. 1941- 99
Van Horn, William 1939- 43
van Hout, Mies 1962- 178
Van Iterson, S(iny) R(ose) 26
Van Kampen, Vlasta 1943- 163
  Earlier sketch in SATA 54
Van Laan, Nancy 1939- 105
van Lawick-Goodall, Jane
  See Goodall, Jane
Van Leeuwen, Jean 1937- 211
  Autobiography Feature 141
  Earlier sketches in SATA 6, 82, 132, 141
  See also SAAS 8
van Lhin, Erik
  See del Rey, Lester
van Lieshout, Maria 201
Van Loon, Hendrik Willem 1882-1944 18
van Ommen, Sylvia 1978- 186
VanOosting, James 1951- 170
Van Orden, M(erton) D(ick) 1921- 4
Van Patter, Bruce 183
Van Reek, Wouter 204
Van Rensselaer, Alexander (Taylor Mason)
  1892-1962 14
Van Riper, Guernsey, Jr. 1909-1995 3
van Rossum, Heleen 1962- 174
Van Rynbach, Iris 1952- 102
Vansant, Rhonda Joy Edwards 1950- 92
Van Steenwyk, Elizabeth (Ann) 1928- 89
  Earlier sketch in SATA 34

Van Stockum, Hilda 1908-2006 5
  Obituary 179
van Straaten, Harmen 1961- 195
Van Tuyl, Barbara 1940- 11
van Vogt, A(lfred) E(lton) 1912-2000 14
  Obituary 124
Van Wassenhove, Sue 1951- 202
Van Woerkom, Dorothy (O'Brien)
  1924-1996 21
Van Wormer, Joe
  See Van Wormer, Joseph Edward
Van Wormer, Joseph Edward 1913-1998 35
Van Wright, Cornelius 173
Van Zwienen, Ilse Charlotte Koehn 1929-1991
  34
  Brief entry 28
  Obituary 67
Van Zyle, Jon 1942- 176
  Earlier sketch in SATA 84
Varela, Barry 180
Varga, Judy
  See Stang, Judit
Varley, Dimitry V. 1906-1984 10
Varley, Susan 1961- 134
  Earlier sketch in SATA 63
Varon, Sara 195
Vasileva, Tatiana
  See Wassiljewa, Tatjana
Vasiliev, Valery 1949- 80
Vasilieva, Tatiana
  See Wassiljewa, Tatjana
Vasiliu, Mircea 1920- 2
Vass, George 1927- 57
  Brief entry 31
Vaughan, Carter A.
  See Gerson, Noel Bertram
Vaughan, Harold Cecil 1923- 14
Vaughan, Marcia (K.) 1951- 159
  Earlier sketches in SATA 60, 95
Vaughan, Richard 1947- 87
Vaughan, Sam(uel) 1928- 14
Vaughn, Ruth 1935- 14
Vaught, Susan 1965- 195
Vaupel, Robin 198
Vautier, Ghislaine 1932- 53
Vavra, Robert James 1935- 8
Vecsey, George Spencer 1939- 9
Vedral, Joyce L(auretta) 1943- 65
Vega, Denise 174
Vega, Denise B.
  See Vega, Denise
Vega, Diego
  See Adkins, Jan
Veglahn, Nancy (Crary) 1937- 5
Vejjajiva, Jane 1963- 189
Velasquez, Eric 192
Velasquez, Gloria 1949- 113
Velasquez, Gloria 1949-
  See Velasquez, Gloria
Velthuijs, Max 1923-2005 110
  Obituary 160
  Earlier sketch in SATA 53
Venable, Alan (Hudson) 1944- 8
Venezia, Mike 1945- 150
Ventura, Anthony
  See Pellowski, Michael (Joseph)
Ventura, Piero (Luigi) 1937- 61
  Brief entry 43
  See also CLR 16
Vequin, Capini
  See Quinn, Elisabeth
Verba, Joan Marie 1953- 78
Verboven, Agnes 1951- 103
verDorn, Bethea (Stewart) 1952- 76
Vere, Ed 197
Verissimo, Erico (Lopes) 1905-1975 113
Verne, Jules 1828-1905 21
  See also CLR 88
Verne, Jules Gabriel
  See Verne, Jules

Verner, Gerald 1897(?)-1980
  Obituary 25
Verney, John 1913-1993 14
  Obituary 75
Verniero, Joan C. 1949- 181
Vernon, (Elda) Louise A(nderson) 1914- 14
Vernon, Rosemary
  See Smith, Susan Vernon
Vernon, Ursula 204
Vernor, D.
  See Casewit, Curtis W(erner)
Verr, Harry Coe
  See Kunhardt, Edith
Verral, Charles Spain 1904-1990 11
  Obituary 65
Verrillo, Erica 1953- 199
Verrillo, Erica F.
  See Verrillo, Erica
Verrone, Robert J. 1935(?)-1984
  Obituary 39
Versace, Marie Teresa Rios 1917- 2
Vertreace, Martha M(odena) 1945- 78
Vesey, A(manda) 1939- 62
Vesey, Mark (David) 1958- 123
Vesey, Paul
  See Allen, Samuel W(ashington)
Vestergaard, Hope 178
Vestly, Anne-Cath(arina) 1920- 14
  See also CLR 99
Vevers, (Henry) Gwynne 1916-1988 45
  Obituary 57
Viator, Vacuus
  See Hughes, Thomas
Viau, Nancy 208
Vicar, Henry
  See Felsen, Henry Gregor
Vick, Helen Hughes 1950- 88
Vicker, Angus
  See Felsen, Henry Gregor
Vickers, Sheena 1960- 94
Vickery, Kate
  See Kennedy, T.A.
Victor, Edward 1914- 3
Victor, Joan Berg 1942- 30
Vidrine, Beverly Barras 1938- 188
  Earlier sketch in SATA 103
Vieceli, Emma 1979- 210
Viereck, Ellen K. 1928- 14
Viereck, Phillip 1925- 3
Viertel, Janet 1915- 10
Vigliante, Mary
  See Szydlowski, Mary Vigliante
Vigna, Judith 1936- 102
  Earlier sketch in SATA 15
Viguers, Ruth Hill 1903-1971 6
Vila, Laura 207
Villareal, Ray 187
Villasenor, Edmund
  See Villasenor, Victor E.
Villasenor, Edmundo
  See Villasenor, Victor E.
Villasenor, Victor
  See Villasenor, Victor E.
Villasenor, Victor E. 1940- 171
Villasenor, Victor Edmundo
  See Villasenor, Victor E.
Villiard, Paul 1910-1974 51
  Obituary 20
Villiers, Alan (John) 1903-1982 10
Vilott, Rhondi
  See Salsitz, Rhondi Vilott
Vincent, Eric Douglas 1953- 40
Vincent, Erin 1969- 188
Vincent, Felix 1946- 41
Vincent, Gabrielle 1928-2000 121
  Earlier sketch in SATA 61
  See also CLR 13
Vincent, Mary Keith
  See St. John, Wylly Folk
Vincent, William R.
  See Heitzmann, William Ray

Vinegar, Tom
  See Gregg, Andrew K.
Vinest, Shaw
  See Longyear, Barry B(rookes)
Vinge, Joan (Carol) D(ennison) 1948- 113
  Earlier sketch in SATA 36
Vining, Elizabeth Gray 1902-1999 6
  Obituary 117
Vinson, Kathryn 1911-1995 21
Vinton, Iris 1906(?)-1988 24
  Obituary 55
Viola, Herman J(oseph) 1938- 126
Viorst, Judith 1931- 172
  Earlier sketches in SATA 7, 70, 123
  See also CLR 90
Vip
  See Partch, Virgil Franklin II
Vipont, Charles
  See Foulds, Elfrida Vipont
Vipont, Elfrida
  See Foulds, Elfrida Vipont
Viramontes, Helena Maria 1954-
  See CLR 285
Viscott, David S(teven) 1938-1996 65
Visser, W(illem) F(rederik) H(endrik)
  1900-1968 10
Vitale, Stefano 1958- 180
  Earlier sketch in SATA 114
Vivas, Julie 1947- 96
Vivelo, Jackie 1943- 63
Vivelo, Jacqueline J.
  See Vivelo, Jackie
Vivelo, Jacqueline Jean
  See Vivelo, Jackie
Vizzini, Ned 1981- 179
  Earlier sketch in SATA 125
Vlahos, Olivia 1924- 31
Vlasic, Bob
  See Hirsch, Phil
Voake, Charlotte 180
  Earlier sketch in SATA 114
Voake, Steve 1961- 178
Vo-Dinh, Mai 1933- 16
Vogel, Carole Garbuny 1951- 105
  Earlier sketch in SATA 70
Vogel, Ilse-Margret 1918- 14
Vogel, John H., Jr. 1950- 18
Vogt, Esther Loewen 1915-1999 14
Vogt, Gregory L. 94
Vogt, Marie Bollinger 1921- 45
Vohwinkel, Astrid 1969- 207
Voight, Virginia Frances 1909-1989 8
Voigt, Cynthia 1942- 160
  Brief entry 33
  Earlier sketches in SATA 48, 79, 116
  See also CLR 141
Voigt, Erna 1925- 35
Voigt-Rother, Erna
  See Voigt, Erna
Vojtech, Anna 1946- 108
  Earlier sketch in SATA 42
Vollstadt, Elizabeth Weiss 1942- 121
Volponi, Paul 175
Volting, Dr. R.E.
  See Lerangis, Peter
Von Ahnen, Katherine 1922- 93
von Buhler, Cynthia 185
Vondra, J. Gert
  See Vondra, Josef
Vondra, Josef 1941- 121
Vondra, Josef Gert
  See Vondra, Josef
Von Gunden, Kenneth 1946- 113
Von Hagen, Victor Wolfgang 1908-1985 29
von Klopp, Vahrah
  See Malvern, Gladys
von Schmidt, Eric 1931-2007 50
  Brief entry 36
  Obituary 181
von Storch, Anne B. 1910- 1
von Trapp, Maria Augusta 1905-1987 16

von Wodtke, Charlotte Buel Johnson
  1918-1982 46
von Ziegesar, Cecily 1970- 161
Vos, Ida 1931-2006 121
  Earlier sketch in SATA 69
  See also CLR 85
Vosburgh, Leonard (W.) 1912- 15
Votaw, Carol 1961- 201
Voyle, Mary
  See Manning, Rosemary
Vrettos, Adrienne Maria 187
Vriens, Jacques 1946- 151
Vugteveen, Verna Aardema
  See Aardema, Verna
Vulture, Elizabeth T.
  See Gilbert, Suzie
Vuong, Lynette Dyer 1938- 110
  Earlier sketch in SATA 60

W

Waas, Uli
  See Waas-Pommer, Ulrike
Waas-Pommer, Ulrike 1949- 85
Waber, Bernard 1924- 155
  Brief entry 40
  Earlier sketches in SATA 47, 95
  See also CLR 55
Wachtel, Shirley Russak 1951- 88
Wachter, Oralee (Roberts) 1935- 61
  Brief entry 51
Waddell, Evelyn Margaret 1918- 10
Waddell, Martin 1941- 129
  Autobiography Feature 129
  Earlier sketches in SATA 43, 81, 127
  See also CLR 31
  See also SAAS 15
Waddy, Lawrence (Heber) 1914- 91
Wade, Mary Dodson 1930- 151
  Earlier sketch in SATA 79
Wade, Suzanne
  See Kirby, Susan E.
Wade, Theodore E., Jr. 1936- 37
Wademan, Peter John 1946- 122
Wademan, Spike
  See Wademan, Peter John
Wadsworth, Ginger 1945- 157
  Earlier sketch in SATA 103
Wagenheim, Kal 1935- 21
Wagner, Michele R. 1975- 157
Wagner, Sharon B. 1936- 4
Wagoner, David (Russell) 1926- 14
Wahl, Jan (Boyer) 1933- 132
  Earlier sketches in SATA 2, 34, 73
  See also SAAS 3
Wahl, Mats 1945- 186
Waide, Jan 1952- 29
Wainscott, John Milton 1910-1981 53
Wainwright, Richard M. 1935- 91
Wainwright, Ruth
  See Symes, Ruth Louise
Wait, Lea 1946- 137
Waite, Judy 174
Waite, Judy Bernard
  See Bernard, Patricia
Waite, Michael
  See Waite, Michael P.
Waite, Michael P. 1960- 101
Waite, P(eter) B(usby) 1922- 64
Waites, Joan C. 187
Waitley, Douglas 1927- 30
Wakefield, Jean L.
  See Laird, Jean E(louise)
Wakin, Daniel (Joseph) 1961- 84
Wakin, Edward 1927- 37
Wakiyama, Hanako 1966- 192
Walck, Henry Z. 1908(?)-1984
  Obituary 40
Walden, Amelia Elizabeth 3

Walden, Mark *188*
Waldherr, Kris 1963- *76*
Waldman, Bruce 1949- *15*
Waldman, Neil 1947- *203*
  Earlier sketches in SATA *51, 94, 142*
Waldrep, Richard *198*
Waldron, Ann Wood 1924- *16*
Waldron, Kathleen Cook *176*
Wales, Dirk 1931- *205*
Walgren, Judy 1963- *118*
Walker, Addison
  See Walker, (Addison) Mort
Walker, Alice 1944- *31*
Walker, Alice Malsenior
  See Walker, Alice
Walker, Barbara (Jeanne) K(erlin) 1921- *80*
  Earlier sketch in SATA *4*
Walker, Barbara M(uhs) 1928- *57*
Walker, (James) Braz(elton) 1934-1983 ...... *45*
Walker, David 1965- *197*
Walker, David G(ordon) 1926- *60*
Walker, David Harry 1911-1992 .... *8*
  Obituary *71*
Walker, Diana 1925- *9*
Walker, Diane Marie Catherine
  See Walker, Kate
Walker, Dick
  See Pellowski, Michael (Joseph)
Walker, Frank 1931-2000 .... *36*
Walker, Holly Beth
  See Bond, Gladys Baker
Walker, Kate 1950- *165*
  Earlier sketch in SATA *82*
Walker, Kathrine Sorley
  See Sorley Walker, Kathrine
Walker, Lou Ann 1952- *66*
  Brief entry *53*
Walker, Louise Jean 1891-1976
  Obituary *35*
Walker, Mary Alexander 1927- *61*
Walker, Mildred
  See Schemm, Mildred Walker
Walker, (Addison) Mort 1923- *8*
Walker, Pamela 1948- *142*
  Earlier sketch in SATA *24*
Walker, Paul Robert 1953- *154*
Walker, Robert W. 1948- *66*
Walker, Sally M(acArt) 1954- *135*
Walker, Stephen J. 1951- *12*
Walker-Blondell, Becky 1951- *89*
Wallace, Barbara Brooks 1922- *136*
  Earlier sketches in SATA *4, 78*
  See also CLR *150*
  See also SAAS *17*
Wallace, Beverly Dobrin 1921- *19*
Wallace, Bill 1947- *169*
  Brief entry *47*
  Earlier sketches in SATA *53, 101*
Wallace, Daisy
  See Cuyler, Margery
Wallace, Ian 1950- *141*
  Earlier sketches in SATA *53, 56*
  See also CLR *37*
Wallace, John 1966- *155*
  Earlier sketch in SATA *105*
Wallace, John A(dam) 1915-2004 .... *3*
  Obituary *155*
Wallace, Karen 1951- *188*
  Earlier sketches in SATA *83, 139*
Wallace, Nancy Elizabeth 1948- *186*
  Earlier sketch in SATA *141*
Wallace, Nigel
  See Hamilton, Charles (Harold St. John)
Wallace, Paula S. *153*
Wallace, Rich 1957- *196*
  Earlier sketches in SATA *117, 158*
Wallace, Robert 1932-1999 .... *47*
  Brief entry *37*
Wallace, Ruby Ann 1923(?)- *77*
Wallace, William Keith
  See Wallace, Bill

Wallace-Brodeur, Ruth 1941- *169*
  Brief entry *41*
  Earlier sketches in SATA *51, 88*
Wallenta, Adam 1974- *123*
Waller, Leslie 1923-2007 .... *20*
Walley, Byron
  See Card, Orson Scott
Wallis, Diz 1949- *77*
Wallis, G. McDonald
  See Campbell, Hope
Wallner, Alexandra 1946- *156*
  Brief entry *41*
  Earlier sketches in SATA *51, 98*
Wallner, John C. 1945- *133*
  Earlier sketches in SATA *10, 51*
Wallower, Lucille *11*
Walrod, Amy 1973(?)- *182*
Walsh, Ann 1942- *176*
  Earlier sketch in SATA *62*
Walsh, Ellen Stoll 1942- *194*
  Earlier sketches in SATA *49, 99, 147*
Walsh, George Johnston 1889-1981 .... *53*
Walsh, Gillian Paton
  See Paton Walsh, Jill
Walsh, Jill Paton
  See Paton Walsh, Jill
Walsh, Joanna 1970- *182*
Walsh, Lawrence 1942- *170*
Walsh, Marissa 1972- *195*
Walsh, Mary Caswell 1949- *118*
Walsh, Mitzy
  See Walsh, Marissa
Walsh, Suella *170*
Walsh, V. L.
  See Walsh, Vivian
Walsh, Vivian 1960- *120*
Walsh Shepherd, Donna 1948- *78*
Walter, Frances V. 1923- *71*
Walter, Mildred Pitts 1922- *133*
  Brief entry *45*
  Earlier sketch in SATA *69*
  See also CLR *61*
  See also SAAS *12*
Walter, Villiam Christian
  See Andersen, Hans Christian
Walter, Virginia
  See Walter, Virginia A.
Walter, Virginia A. *134*
Walters, Audrey 1929- *18*
Walters, Celeste 1938- *126*
Walters, Eric 1957- *205*
  Earlier sketches in SATA *99, 155*
Walters, Eric Robert
  See Walters, Eric
Walters, Helen B. (?)-1987
  Obituary *50*
Walters, Hugh
  See Hughes, Walter (Llewellyn)
Walther, Thomas A. 1950- *31*
Walther, Tom
  See Walther, Thomas A.
Waltner, Elma 1912-1987 .... *40*
Waltner, Willard H. 1909- *40*
Walton, Darwin McBeth 1926- *119*
Walton, Fiona L. M. 1959- *89*
Walton, Richard J. 1928- *4*
Walton, Rick 1957- *204*
  Earlier sketches in SATA *101, 151*
Waltrip, Lela (Kingston) 1904-1995 .... *9*
Waltrip, Mildred 1911- *37*
Waltrip, Rufus (Charles) 1898-1988 .... *9*
Walworth, Nancy Zinsser 1917- *14*
Wangerin, Walter, Jr. 1944- *98*
  Brief entry *37*
  Earlier sketch in SATA *45*
Waniek, Marilyn Nelson 1946-
  See Nelson, Marilyn
Wannamaker, Bruce
  See Moncure, Jane Belk
Warbler, J. M.
  See Cocagnac, Augustin Maurice(-Jean)

Warburg, Sandol Stoddard
  See Stoddard, Sandol
Ward, E. D.
  See Gorey, Edward (St. John)
  and Lucas, E(dward) V(errall)
Ward, Ed
  See Stratemeyer, Edward L.
Ward, Helen 1962- *206*
  Earlier sketches in SATA *72, 144*
Ward, Jay 1920-1989
  Obituary *63*
Ward, Jennifer 1963- *146*
Ward, John (Stanton) 1917- *42*
Ward, Jonas
  See Ard, William
  and Cox, William R(obert)
  and Garfield, Brian (Francis Wynne)
Ward, Lynd (Kendall) 1905-1985 .... *36*
  Obituary *42*
  Earlier sketch in SATA *2*
Ward, Martha (Eads) *5*
Ward, Melanie
  See Curtis, Richard
  and Lynch, Marilyn
Ward, Nicholas John
  See Ward, Nick
Ward, Nick 1955- *190*
Ward, Tom
  See Stratemeyer, Edward L.
Wardell, Dean
  See Prince, J(ack) H(arvey)
Wardlaw, Lee 1955- *115*
  Earlier sketch in SATA *79*
Ware, Cheryl 1963- *101*
Ware, Chris 1967- *140*
Ware, Leon (Vernon) 1909-1976 .... *4*
Wargin, Kathy-jo 1964- *210*
  Earlier sketch in SATA *145*
Warhola, James 1955- *187*
Warner, Frank A. *67*
  Earlier sketch in SATA *1*
Warner, Gertrude Chandler 1890-1979 .... *9*
  Obituary *73*
Warner, J(ohn) F. 1929- *75*
Warner, Lucille Schulberg *30*
Warner, Matt
  See Fichter, George S.
Warner, Oliver (Martin Wilson)
  1903-1976 .... *29*
Warner, Sally 1946- *131*
Warner, Sunny (B.) 1931- *108*
Warnes, Tim 1971- *166*
  Earlier sketch in SATA *116*
Warnes, Timothy
  See Warnes, Tim
Warnick, Elsa 1942- *113*
Warren, Andrea 1946- *98*
Warren, Betsy
  See Warren, Elizabeth Avery
Warren, Billy
  See Warren, William Stephen
Warren, Cathy 1951- *62*
  Brief entry *46*
Warren, Elizabeth
  See Supraner, Robyn
Warren, Elizabeth Avery 1916- *46*
  Brief entry *38*
Warren, Jackie M. 1953- *135*
Warren, Joshua P(aul) 1976- *107*
Warren, Joyce W(illiams) 1935- *18*
Warren, Mary Phraner 1929- *10*
Warren, Robert Penn 1905-1989 .... *46*
  Obituary *63*
Warren, Scott S. 1957- *79*
Warren, William Stephen 1882-1968 .... *9*
Warrick, Patricia Scott 1925- *35*
Warriner, John 1907(?)-1987
  Obituary *53*
Warsh
  See Warshaw, Jerry
Warshaw, Jerry 1929- *30*

Warshaw, Mary 1931- 89
Warshofsky, Fred 1931- 24
Warshofsky, Isaac
    See Singer, Isaac Bashevis
Wartski, Maureen (Ann Crane) 1940- 50
    Brief entry 37
Warwick, Alan R(oss) 1900-1973 42
Wa-Sha-Quon-Asin
    See Belaney, Archibald Stansfeld
Wa-sha-quon-asin
    See Belaney, Archibald Stansfeld
Washburn, Bradford 1910-2007 38
    Obituary 181
Washburn, Henry Bradford, Jr.
    See Washburn, Bradford
Washburn, Jan(ice) 1926- 63
Washburn, Lucia 193
Washburne, Carolyn Kott 1944- 86
Washburne, Heluiz Chandler 1892-1970 10
    Obituary 26
Washington, Booker T. 1856-1915 28
Washington, Donna L. 1967- 159
    Earlier sketch in SATA 98
Wasserman, Robin 1978- 207
Wasserstein, Wendy 1950-2006 94
    Obituary 174
Wassiljewa, Tatjana 1928- 106
Watanabe, Shigeo 1928- 131
    Brief entry 32
    Earlier sketch in SATA 39
    See also CLR 8
Waters, John F(rederick) 1930- 4
Waters, Summer
    See Sykes, Julie
Waters, Tony 1958- 75
Waterton, Betty 1923- 99
    Brief entry 34
    Earlier sketch in SATA 37
Waterton, Betty Marie
    See Waterton, Betty
Watkins, Dawn L. 126
Watkins, Gloria Jean
    See hooks, bell
Watkins, Lois 1930- 88
Watkins, Peter 1934- 66
Watkins, Yoko Kawashima 1933- 93
Watkins-Pitchford, Denys James
    1905-1990 87
    Obituary 66
    Earlier sketch in SATA 6
    See also SAAS 4
Watling, James 1933- 117
    Earlier sketch in SATA 67
Watson, Aldren A(uld) 1917- 42
    Brief entry 36
Watson, Amy Zakrzewski 1965- 76
Watson, B. S.
    See Teitelbaum, Michael
Watson, Carol 1949- 78
Watson, C.G. 193
Watson, Clyde 1947- 68
    Earlier sketch in SATA 5
    See also CLR 3
Watson, Helen Orr 1892-1978
    Obituary 24
Watson, James 1936- 106
    Earlier sketch in SATA 10
Watson, Jane Werner 1915- 54
    Earlier sketch in SATA 3
Watson, Jesse Joshua 199
Watson, John H.
    See Farmer, Philip Jose
Watson, Mary 1953- 117
Watson, N. Cameron 1955- 81
Watson, Nancy Dingman 32
Watson, Pauline 1925- 14
Watson, Richard F.
    See Silverberg, Robert
Watson, Richard Jesse 1951- 211
    Earlier sketch in SATA 62
Watson, Sally (Lou) 1924- 3

Watson, Sasha 211
Watson, Wendy (McLeod) 1942- 142
    Earlier sketches in SATA 5, 74
Watson Taylor, Elizabeth 1915- 41
Watt, Melanie 1975- 193
    Earlier sketch in SATA 136
Watt, Thomas 1935- 4
Wattenberg, Jane 174
Watterson, Bill 1958- 66
Watt-Evans, Lawrence 1954- 121
Watts, (Anna) Bernadette 1942- 103
    Earlier sketch in SATA 4
Watts, Ephraim
    See Horne, Richard Henry Hengist
Watts, Franklin (Mowry) 1904-1978 46
    Obituary 21
Watts, Helen L. Hoke 1903-1990
    Obituary 65
Watts, Irene N(aemi) 1931- 111
    Earlier sketch in SATA 56
Watts, Isaac 1674-1748 52
Watts, James K(ennedy) M(offitt) 1955- 59
Watts, Jeri Hanel 1957- 170
Watts, Julia 1969- 103
Watts, Leander 1956- 146
Watts, Leslie Elizabeth 1961- 168
Watts, Mabel Pizzey 1906-1994 11
Watts, Nigel 1957-1999 121
Waugh, C. C. Roessel
    See Waugh, Carol-Lynn Rossel
    and Waugh, Charles G(ordon)
Waugh, Carol-Lynn Rossel 1947- 41
Waugh, Dorothy -1996 11
Waugh, Sylvia 1935- 169
Waugh, Virginia
    See Sorensen, Virginia
Wax, Wendy A. 1963- 163
    Earlier sketch in SATA 73
Wayland, April Halprin 1954- 143
    Earlier sketch in SATA 78
    See also SAAS 26
Wayland, Patrick
    See O'Connor, Richard
Wayne, (Anne) Jenifer 1917-1982 32
Wayne, Kyra Petrovskaya 1918- 8
Wayne, Richard
    See Decker, Duane
Wayshak, Deborah Noyes
    See Noyes, Deborah
Waystaff, Simon
    See Swift, Jonathan
Weales, Gerald (Clifford) 1925- 11
Weary, Ogdred
    See Gorey, Edward (St. John)
Weatherford, Carole Boston 1956- 181
    Earlier sketch in SATA 138
Weatherill, Cat 203
Weatherly, Lee 1967- 192
Weatherly, Myra 1926- 130
Weatherly, Myra S.
    See Weatherly, Myra
Weaver, Harriett E. 1908-1993 65
Weaver, John L. 1949- 42
Weaver, Robyn
    See Conley, Robyn
Weaver, Robyn M.
    See Conley, Robyn
Weaver, Tess 197
Weaver, Ward
    See Mason, F(rancis) van Wyck
Weaver, Will 1950- 161
    Earlier sketches in SATA 88, 109
Weaver, William Weller
    See Weaver, Will
Weaver-Gelzer, Charlotte 1950- 79
Webb, Christopher
    See Wibberley, Leonard
Webb, Jacqueline
    See Pearce, Margaret

Webb, Jacquelyn
    See Pearce, Margaret
    and Pearce, Margaret
Webb, Jean Francis (III) 1910-1991 35
Webb, Kaye 1914- 60
Webb, Lois Sinaiko 1922- 82
Webb, Margot 1934- 67
Webb, Sharon 1936- 41
Webb, Sophie 1958- 135
Webber, Andrew Lloyd
    See Lloyd Webber, Andrew
Webber, Desiree Morrison 1956- 170
Webber, Irma E(leanor Schmidt)
    1904-1995 14
Weber, Alfons 1921- 8
Weber, Bruce 1942- 120
    Earlier sketch in SATA 73
Weber, Debora 1955- 58
Weber, EdNah New Rider 1919(?)- 168
Weber, Jill 1950- 209
    Earlier sketch in SATA 127
Weber, Judith E(ichler) 1938- 64
Weber, Ken(neth J.) 1940- 90
Weber, Lenora Mattingly 1895-1971 2
    Obituary 26
Weber, Michael 1945- 87
Weber, Sandra 1961- 158
Weber, William J(ohn) 1927- 14
Webster, Alice Jane Chandler 1876-1916 ... 17
Webster, David 1930- 11
Webster, Frank V. 67
    Earlier sketch in SATA 1
Webster, Gary
    See Garrison, Webb B(lack)
Webster, James 1925-1981 17
    Obituary 27
Webster, Jean
    See Webster, Alice Jane Chandler
Wechsler, Doug 189
Wechsler, Herman J. 1904-1976
    Obituary 20
Wechter, Nell (Carolyn) Wise 1913-1989 . 127
    Earlier sketch in SATA 60
Weck, Thomas L. 1942- 62
Wedd, Kate
    See Gregory, Philippa
Weddle, Ethel Harshbarger 1897-1996 11
Wedekind, Annie 204
Weeks, Sarah 194
    Earlier sketch in SATA 158
Weems, David B(urnola) 1922- 80
Wees, Frances Shelley 1902-1982 58
Weevers, Peter 1944- 59
Wegen, Ronald 1946-1985 99
Wegman, William (George) 1943- 135
    Earlier sketches in SATA 78, 129
Wegner, Fritz 1924- 20
Weidhorn, Manfred 1931- 60
Weidt, Maryann N. 1944- 85
Weigel, Jeff 1958- 170
Weigelt, Udo 1960- 201
    Earlier sketch in SATA 168
Weihs, Erika 1917- 107
    Earlier sketch in SATA 15
Weik, Mary Hays 1898(?)-1979 3
    Obituary 23
Weil, Ann Yezner 1908-1969 9
Weil, Lisl 1910- 7
Weilerstein, Sadie Rose 1894-1993 3
    Obituary 75
Weill, Cynthia 1959- 167
Wein, Elizabeth E. 1964- 151
    Earlier sketch in SATA 82
Wein, Elizabeth Eve
    See Wein, Elizabeth E.
Weinberg, Larry
    See Weinberg, Lawrence (E.)
Weinberg, Lawrence (E.) 92
    Brief entry 48
Weinberger, Tanya 1939- 84
Weiner, Sandra 1922- 14

Weingarten, Violet (Brown) 1915-1976 .... *3*
   Obituary *27*
Weingartner, Charles 1922- *5*
Weinheimer, Beckie 1958- *186*
Weinstein, Ellen Slusky 1959- *200*
Weinstein, Nina 1951- *73*
Weinstock, Robert 1967- *204*
Weir, Bob 1947- *76*
Weir, Diana (R.) Loiewski 1958- *111*
Weir, Joan S(herman) 1928- *99*
Weir, LaVada *2*
Weir, Rosemary (Green) 1905-1994 .... *21*
Weir, Wendy 1949- *76*
Weis, Margaret 1948- *164*
   Earlier sketches in SATA *38, 92*
Weisberger, Bernard A(llen) 1922- *21*
Weisburd, Stefi 1957- *202*
Weiser, Marjorie P(hillis) K(atz) 1934- *33*
Weisgard, Leonard (Joseph) 1916-2000 ...... *85*
   Obituary *122*
   Earlier sketches in SATA *2, 30*
   See also SAAS *19*
Weiss, Adelle 1920- *18*
Weiss, Ann E(dwards) 1943- *69*
   Earlier sketch in SATA *30*
   See also SAAS *13*
Weiss, Edna
   See Barth, Edna
Weiss, Ellen 1953- *44*
Weiss, Harvey 1922- *76*
   Earlier sketches in SATA *1, 27*
   See also CLR *4*
   See also SAAS *19*
Weiss, Jaqueline Shachter 1926- *65*
Weiss, Malcolm E. 1928- *3*
Weiss, Margaret Edith
   See Weis, Margaret
Weiss, Miriam
   See Schlein, Miriam
Weiss, Mitch 1951- *183*
   Earlier sketch in SATA *123*
Weiss, Nicki 1954- *86*
   Earlier sketch in SATA *33*
Weiss, Renee Karol 1923- *5*
Weissberger, Ela 1930- *181*
Weissberger, Ela Stein
   See Weissberger, Ela
Weissenborn, Hellmuth 1898-1982
   Obituary *31*
Weitzman, David L. 1936- *172*
   Earlier sketch in SATA *122*
Wekesser, Carol A. 1963- *76*
Welber, Robert *26*
Welch, Amanda (Jane) 1945- *75*
Welch, D'Alte Aldridge 1907-1970
   Obituary *27*
Welch, Holly *206*
Welch, Jean-Louise
   See Kempton, Jean Welch
Welch, Pauline
   See Bodenham, Hilda Morris
Welch, Ronald
   See Felton, Ronald Oliver
Welch, Sheila Kelly 1945- *130*
Welch, Willy 1952- *93*
Weldin, Frauke 1969- *188*
Welford, Sue 1942- *75*
Weller, George 1907-2002 .... *31*
   Obituary *140*
Weller, George Anthony
   See Weller, George
Welling, Peter J. 1947- *135*
Wellington, Monica 1957- *157*
   Earlier sketches in SATA *67, 99*
Wellman, Alice 1900-1984 .... *51*
   Brief entry *36*
Wellman, Manly Wade 1903-1986 .... *6*
   Obituary *47*
Wellman, Paul I. 1898-1966 .... *3*
Wellman, Paul Iselin
   See Wellman, Paul I.

Wellman, Sam(uel) 1939- *122*
Wells, H. G. 1866-1946 .... *20*
   See also CLR *133*
Wells, Helen
   See Campbell, Hope
Wells, Helen 1910-1986 .... *49*
   Earlier sketch in SATA *2*
Wells, Herbert George
   See Wells, H. G.
Wells, J. Wellington
   See de Camp, L. Sprague
Wells, June
   See Swinford, Betty (June Wells)
Wells, Robert
   See Welsch, Roger L(ee)
Wells, Robert E. *184*
Wells, Rosemary 1943- *207*
   Earlier sketches in SATA *18, 69, 114, 156*
   See also CLR *69*
   See also SAAS *1*
Wells, Susan (Mary) 1951- *78*
Wels, Byron G(erald) 1924-1993 .... *9*
Welsbacher, Anne 1955- *89*
Welsch, Roger L(ee) 1936- *82*
Welsh, David
   See Hills, C.A.R.
Welsh, Mary Flynn 1910(?)-1984
   Obituary *38*
Welsh, T.K. 1956- *184*
Weltner, Linda R(iverly) 1938- *38*
Welton, Jude 1955- *143*
   Earlier sketch in SATA *79*
Welty, S. F.
   See Welty, Susan F.
Welty, Susan F. 1905- *9*
Wemmlinger, Raymond *190*
Wendelin, Rudolph 1910-2000 .... *23*
Weninger, Brigitte 1960- *189*
Wentworth, Robert
   See Hamilton, Edmond
Werlin, Nancy 1961- *161*
   Earlier sketches in SATA *87, 119*
Werner, Elsa Jane
   See Watson, Jane Werner
Werner, Herma 1926- *47*
   Brief entry *41*
Werner, Jane
   See Watson, Jane Werner
Werner, K.
   See Casewit, Curtis W(erner)
Wersba, Barbara 1932- *58*
   Autobiography Feature *103*
   Earlier sketch in SATA *1*
   See also CLR *78*
   See also SAAS *2*
Werstein, Irving 1914(?)-1971 .... *14*
Werth, Kurt 1896-1983 .... *20*
Wesley, Alison
   See Barnes, Michael
Wesley, Kathryn
   See Rusch, Kristine Kathryn
Wesley, Mary (Aline) 1912-2002 .... *66*
Wesley, Valerie Wilson 1947- *168*
   Earlier sketch in SATA *106*
West, Andrew
   See Arthur, Robert, (Jr.)
West, Anna 1938- *40*
West, Barbara
   See Price, Olive
West, Betty 1921- *11*
West, Bruce 1951- *63*
West, C. P.
   See Wodehouse, P. G.
West, Dorothy
   See Benson, Mildred
West, Emily Govan 1919- *38*
West, Emmy
   See West, Emily Govan
West, James
   See Withers, Carl A.

West, Jerry
   See Svenson, Andrew E(dward)
West, (Mary) Jessamyn 1902-1984
   Obituary *37*
West, John
   See Arthur, Robert, (Jr.)
West, Owen
   See Koontz, Dean
West, Ward
   See Borland, Harold Glen
Westall, Robert (Atkinson) 1929-1993 .... *69*
   Obituary *75*
   Earlier sketch in SATA *23*
   See also CLR *13*
   See also SAAS *2*
Westaway, Jane 1948- *121*
Westcott, Nadine Bernard 1949- *130*
Westera, Marleen 1962- *187*
Westerberg, Christine 1950- *29*
Westerduin, Anne 1945- *105*
Westerfeld, Scott 1963- *161*
Westervelt, Virginia Veeder 1914-2005 ...... *10*
Westheimer, David 1917-2005 .... *14*
   Obituary *170*
Westheimer, David Kaplan
   See Westheimer, David
Westmacott, Mary
   See Christie, Agatha
Westman, Barbara *70*
Westman, Paul (Wendell) 1956- *39*
Westmoreland, William C. 1914-2005 .... *63*
Westmoreland, William Childs
   See Westmoreland, William C.
Weston, Allen
   See Hogarth, Grace (Weston Allen)
   and Norton, Andre
Weston, Carol 1956- *135*
Weston, Carrie *190*
Weston, John (Harrison) 1932- *21*
Weston, Martha 1947- *119*
   Earlier sketch in SATA *53*
Weston, Robert Paul *209*
Westphal, Arnold Carl 1897- *57*
Westrup, Hugh *102*
Westwood, Jennifer 1940-2008 .... *10*
   Obituary *192*
Wexler, Jerome (LeRoy) 1923- *14*
Weyland, Jack 1940- *81*
Weyn, Suzanne 1955- *164*
   Earlier sketches in SATA *63, 101*
Weyr, Garret
   See Freymann-Weyr, (Rhoda) Garret
   (Michaela)
Wezyk, Joanna 1966- *82*
Whaley, Joyce Irene 1923- *61*
Whalin, W. Terry 1953- *93*
Wharf, Michael
   See Weller, George
Wharmby, Margot *63*
Wharton, Edith 1862-1937
   See CLR *136*
Wharton, Edith Newbold Jones
   See Wharton, Edith
Whatley, Bruce 1954- *177*
Wheatley, Arabelle 1921- *16*
Wheatley, Nadia 1949- *147*
Wheeler, Cindy 1955- *49*
   Brief entry *40*
Wheeler, Deborah 1947- *83*
Wheeler, Janet D. *1*
Wheeler, Jill C. 1964- *136*
   Earlier sketch in SATA *86*
Wheeler, Jody 1952- *148*
   Earlier sketch in SATA *84*
Wheeler, Lisa 1963- *200*
   Earlier sketch in SATA *162*
Wheeler, Opal 1898- *23*
Whelan, Elizabeth M(urphy) 1943- *14*
Whelan, Gloria 1923- *178*
   Earlier sketches in SATA *85, 128*
   See also CLR *90*

Whelan, Gloria Ann
  See Whelan, Gloria
Whipple, A(ddison) B(eecher) C(olvin)
  1918- 64
Whipple, Cal
  See Whipple, A(ddison) B(eecher) C(olvin)
Whisp, Kennilworthy
  See Rowling, J. K.
Whistler, Reginald John 1905-1944 30
Whistler, Rex
  See Whistler, Reginald John
Whitaker, Zai 183
Whitcher, Susan (Godsil) 1952- 96
Whitcomb, Jon 1906-1988 10
  Obituary 56
Whitcomb, Laura 1958- 171
White, Anne Terry 1896-1980 2
White, Bessie (Felstiner) 1892(?)-1986
  Obituary 50
White, Carolyn 1948- 130
White, Dale
  See Place, Marian T(empleton)
White, Dori 1919- 10
White, E. B. 1899-1985 100
  Obituary 44
  Earlier sketches in SATA 2, 29
  See also CLR 107
White, Eliza Orne 1856-1947
  See YABC 2
White, Elwyn Brooks
  See White, E. B.
White, Florence M(eiman) 1910- 14
White, Laurence B(arton), Jr. 1935- 10
White, Lee 176
White, Martin 1943- 51
White, Nancy 1942- 126
White, Ramy Allison 67
  Earlier sketch in SATA 1
White, Robb 1909-1990 83
  Earlier sketch in SATA 1
  See also CLR 3
  See also SAAS 1
White, Ruth C. 1942- 186
  Autobiography Feature 186
  Earlier sketches in SATA 39, 117, 165
White, T(erence) H(anbury) 1906-1964 12
  See also CLR 139
White, Tekla N. 1934- 115
White, Timothy (Thomas Anthony)
  1952-2002 60
White, Tom 1923- 148
White, William, Jr. 1934- 16
Whitehead, Don(ald) F. 1908-1981 4
Whitehead, Jenny 1964- 191
Whitehead, Kathy 1957- 176
Whitehouse, Arch
  See Whitehouse, Arthur George Joseph
Whitehouse, Arthur George Joseph
  1895-1979 14
  Obituary 23
Whitehouse, Elizabeth S(cott) 1893-1968 ... 35
Whitehouse, Jeanne
  See Peterson, Jeanne Whitehouse
Whitelaw, Nancy 1933- 166
  Earlier sketch in SATA 76
Whitesel, Cheryl Aylward 162
Whiting, Sue 1960- 205
Whiting, Susan Allana
  See Whiting, Sue
Whitinger, R. D.
  See Place, Marian T(empleton)
Whitley, Mary Ann
  See Sebrey, Mary Ann
Whitley, Peggy 1938- 140
Whitlock, Pamela 1921(?)-1982
  Obituary 31
Whitlock, Ralph 1914-1995 35
Whitman, Alice
  See Marker, Sherry
Whitman, Candace 1958- 208

Whitman, Sylvia (Choate) 1961- 135
  Earlier sketch in SATA 85
Whitman, Walt 1819-1892 20
Whitman, Walter
  See Whitman, Walt
Whitmore, Arvella 1922- 125
Whitmore, Benette 1955- 203
Whitney, Alex(andra) 1922- 14
Whitney, David C(harles) 1921- 48
  Brief entry 29
Whitney, Kim Ablon 162
Whitney, Phyllis A. 1903-2008 30
  Obituary 189
  Earlier sketch in SATA 1
  See also CLR 59
Whitney, Phyllis Ayame
  See Whitney, Phyllis A.
Whitney, Sharon 1937- 63
Whitney, Thomas P. 1917-2007 25
  Obituary 189
Whitney, Thomas Porter
  See Whitney, Thomas P.
Whittington, Mary K(athrine) 1941- 75
Whitworth, John 1945- 123
Whybrow, Ian 202
  Earlier sketch in SATA 132
Whyte, Mal(colm Kenneth, Jr.) 1933- 62
Whyte, Mary 1953- 148
  Earlier sketch in SATA 94
Whyte, Ron 1942(?)-1989
  Obituary 63
Whytock, Cherry 177
Wiater, Stanley 1953- 84
Wibbelsman, Charles J(oseph) 1945- 59
Wibberley, Leonard 1915-1983 45
  Obituary 36
  Earlier sketch in SATA 2
  See also CLR 3
Wibberley, Leonard Patrick O'Connor
  See Wibberley, Leonard
Wiberg, Harald (Albin) 1908- 93
  Brief entry 40
Wick, Walter 1953- 148
Wickberg, Susan
  See Rottman, S.L.
Wickens, Elaine 86
Wicker, Ireene 1905(?)-1987
  Obituary 55
Wickstrom, Sylvie 1960- 169
Wickstrom, Thor 1960- 200
Widdemer, Mabel Cleland 1902-1964 5
Widener, Terry 1950- 209
  Earlier sketch in SATA 105
Widerberg, Siv 1931- 10
Wiebe, Rudy 1934- 156
Wiebe, Rudy Henry
  See Wiebe, Rudy
Wieler, Diana (Jean) 1961- 109
Wiener, Lori 1956- 84
Wier, Ester (Alberti) 1910-2000 3
Wiese, Kurt 1887-1974 36
  Obituary 24
  Earlier sketch in SATA 3
  See also CLR 86
Wiesel, Elie 1928- 56
Wiesel, Eliezer
  See Wiesel, Elie
Wiesner, David 1956- 181
  Earlier sketches in SATA 72, 117, 139
  See also CLR 84
Wiesner, Portia
  See Takakjian, Portia
Wiesner, William 1899-1984 5
Wiggers, Raymond 1952- 82
Wiggin, Eric E. 1939- 167
  Earlier sketch in SATA 88
Wiggin, Eric Ellsworth 1939-
  See Wiggin, Eric E.

Wiggin (Riggs), Kate Douglas (Smith)
  1856-1923
  See YABC 1
  See also CLR 52
Wiggins, VeraLee (Chesnut) 1928-1995 89
Wight, James Alfred
  See Herriot, James
Wignell, Edel 1936- 69
Wijnberg, Ellen 85
Wikland, Ilon 1930- 93
  Brief entry 32
Wikler, Madeline 1943- 114
Wilber, Donald N(ewton) 1907-1997 35
Wilbur, C. Keith 1923- 27
Wilbur, Frances 1921- 107
Wilbur, Helen L. 1948- 204
Wilbur, Richard 1921- 108
  Earlier sketch in SATA 9
Wilbur, Richard Purdy
  See Wilbur, Richard
Wilburn, Kathy 1948- 68
Wilcox, Charlotte 1948- 72
Wilcox, Leah 1975(?)- 207
Wilcox, R(uth) Turner 1888-1970 36
Wilcox, Roger
  See Collins, Paul
Wild, Jocelyn 1941- 46
Wild, Kate 1954- 192
Wild, Margaret 1948- 197
  Earlier sketch in SATA 151
Wild, Robin (Evans) 1936- 46
Wild, Robyn 1947- 117
Wilde, D. Gunther
  See Hurwood, Bernhardt J.
Wilde, Oscar 1854(?)-1900 24
  See also CLR 114
Wilde, Oscar Fingal O'Flahertie Willis
  See Wilde, Oscar
Wilder, Buck
  See Smith, Tim(othy R.)
Wilder, Laura Elizabeth Ingalls
  See Wilder, Laura Ingalls
Wilder, Laura Ingalls 1867-1957 100
  Earlier sketches in SATA 15, 29
  See also CLR 111
Wildsmith, Brian 1930- 124
  Earlier sketches in SATA 16, 69
  See also CLR 52
  See also SAAS 5
Wiles, Deborah 171
Wilhelm, Doug 1952- 190
Wilhelm, Hans 1945- 196
  Autobiography Feature 196
  Earlier sketches in SATA 58, 135
  See also CLR 46
  See also SAAS 21
Wilkie, Katharine E(lliott) 1904-1980 31
Wilkin, Eloise 1904-1987 49
  Obituary 54
Wilkins, Frances 1923- 14
Wilkins, Kim 147
Wilkins, Marilyn (Ruth) 1926- 30
Wilkins, Marne
  See Wilkins, Marilyn (Ruth)
Wilkins, Mary Huiskamp 1926- 2
  See also CLR 42
Wilkins, Mary Huiskamp Calhoun
  See Wilkins, Mary Huiskamp
Wilkins, Rose 180
Wilkinson, (Thomas) Barry 1923- 50
  Brief entry 32
Wilkinson, Beth 1925- 80
Wilkinson, Brenda 1946- 91
  Earlier sketch in SATA 14
  See also CLR 20
Wilkinson, (John) Burke 1913-2000 4
Wilkinson, Carole 1950- 210
Wilkinson, Sylvia 1940- 56
  Brief entry 39
Wilkon, Jozef 1930- 133
  Earlier sketches in SATA 31, 71

Wilkowski, Sue *193*
Wilks, Michael Thomas 1947- *44*
Wilks, Mike
    See Wilks, Michael Thomas
Will
    See Lipkind, William
Willard, Barbara (Mary) 1909-1994 .... *74*
    Earlier sketch in SATA *17*
    See also CLR *2*
    See also SAAS *5*
Willard, Elizabeth Kimmel
    See Kimmel, Elizabeth Cody
Willard, Mildred Wilds 1911-1978 .... *14*
Willard, Nancy 1936- *191*
    Brief entry *30*
    Earlier sketches in SATA *37, 71, 127*
    See also CLR *5*
Willcox, Isobel 1907-1996 .... *42*
Willems, Mo *180*
    Earlier sketch in SATA *154*
    See also CLR *114*
Willett, Edward 1959- *115*
Willett, Edward C.
    See Willett, Edward
Willey, Bee *184*
Willey, Margaret 1950- *86*
Willey, Robert
    See Ley, Willy
Willhoite, Michael A. 1946- *71*
William, Kate
    See Armstrong, Jennifer
Williams, Alex 1969- *209*
Williams, Arlene *171*
Williams, Barbara 1925- *107*
    Earlier sketch in SATA *11*
    See also CLR *48*
    See also SAAS *16*
Williams, Barbara 1937- *62*
Williams, Beryl
    See Epstein, Beryl
Williams, Brian (Peter) 1943- *54*
Williams, Carol Lynch 1959- *110*
Williams, Charles
    See Collier, James Lincoln
Williams, Clyde C. 1881-1974 .... *8*
    Obituary *27*
Williams, Coe
    See Harrison, C(hester) William
Williams, Colleen Madonna Flood 1963- . *156*
Williams, Cynthia G. 1958- *123*
Williams, Dar 1967- *168*
Williams, Donna Reilly 1945- *83*
Williams, Dorothy
    See Williams, Marcia
Williams, Dorothy Snowden
    See Williams, Dar
Williams, Eric (Ernest) 1911-1983 .... *14*
    Obituary *38*
Williams, Ferelith Eccles
    See Eccles Williams, Ferelith
Williams, Frances B.
    See Browin, Frances Williams
Williams, Garth (Montgomery) 1912-1996 . *66*
    Obituary *90*
    Earlier sketch in SATA *18*
    See also CLR *57*
    See also SAAS *7*
Williams, Guy R(ichard) 1920- *11*
Williams, Hawley
    See Heyliger, William
Williams, Helen 1948- *77*
Williams, J. R.
    See Williams, Jeanne
Williams, J. Walker
    See Wodehouse, P. G.
Williams, Jay 1914-1978 .... *41*
    Obituary *24*
    Earlier sketch in SATA *3*
    See also CLR *8*
Williams, Jeanne 1930- *5*
Williams, Jenny 1939- *60*

Williams, Karen Lynn 1952- *99*
    Earlier sketch in SATA *66*
Williams, Kit 1946(?)- *44*
    See also CLR *4*
Williams, L. E.
    See Williams, Laura E.
Williams, Laura E.
    See Williams, Laura Ellen
Williams, Laura Ellen *180*
Williams, Leslie 1941- *42*
Williams, Linda 1948- *59*
Williams, Louise Bonino 1904(?)-1984
    Obituary *39*
Williams, Lynn
    See Hale, Arlene
Williams, Marcia 1945- *159*
    Earlier sketches in SATA *71, 97*
Williams, Marcia Dorothy
    See Williams, Marcia
Williams, Margery
    See Bianco, Margery Williams
Williams, Mark
    See Arthur, Robert, (Jr.)
Williams, Mark London 1959- *140*
Williams, Maureen 1951- *12*
Williams, Michael
    See St. John, Wylly Folk
Williams, Patrick J.
    See Griffin, W.E.B.
Williams, Pete
    See Faulknor, Cliff(ord Vernon)
Williams, S. P.
    See Hart, Virginia
Williams, Sam *177*
    Earlier sketch in SATA *124*
Williams, Selma R(uth) 1925- *14*
Williams, Sherley Anne 1944-1999 .... *78*
    Obituary *116*
Williams, Sheron 1955- *77*
Williams, Shirley
    See Williams, Sherley Anne
Williams, Slim
    See Williams, Clyde C.
Williams, Sophy 1965- *135*
Williams, Sue 1948-2007 .... *208*
Williams, Susan
    See Beckhorn, Susan Williams
Williams, Suzanne
    See Williams, Suzanne Morgan
Williams, Suzanne 1953- *202*
    Earlier sketch in SATA *71*
Williams, Suzanne M.
    See Williams, Suzanne Morgan
Williams, Suzanne Morgan 1949- *207*
Williams, Ursula Moray
    See Moray Williams, Ursula
Williams, Vera B(aker) 1927- *102*
    Brief entry *33*
    Earlier sketch in SATA *53*
    See also CLR *9*
Williams-Andriani, Renee 1963- *98*
Williams-Ellis, (Mary) Amabel (Nassau
    Strachey) 1894-1984 .... *29*
    Obituary *41*
Williams-Garcia, Rita 1957- *160*
    Earlier sketch in SATA *98*
    See also CLR *36*
Williamson, Gwyneth 1965- *109*
Williamson, Henry (William) 1895-1977 .... *37*
    Obituary *30*
Williamson, Joanne S(mall) 1926- *122*
    Earlier sketch in SATA *3*
Williamson, Melanie *196*
Willis, Charles
    See Clarke, Arthur C.
Willis, Connie 1945- *110*
    See also CLR *66*
Willis, Jeanne 1959- *195*
    Earlier sketches in SATA *61, 123*
Willis, Jeanne Mary
    See Willis, Jeanne

Willis, Meredith Sue 1946- *101*
Willis, Nancy Carol 1952- *139*
    Earlier sketch in SATA *93*
Willis, Paul J. 1955- *113*
Willms, Russ *95*
Willoughby, Lee Davis
    See Avallone, Michael (Angelo, Jr.)
    and Brandner, Gary (Phil)
    and Deming, Richard
    and DeAndrea, William L(ouis)
    and Laymon, Richard (Carl)
    and Streib, Dan(iel Thomas)
    and Toombs, John
    and Webb, Jean Francis (III)
Willson, Robina Beckles
    See Beckles Willson, Robina
Wilma, Dana
    See Faralla, Dana
Wilsdorf, Anne 1954- *191*
Wilson, April *80*
Wilson, Barbara Ker
    See Ker Wilson, Barbara
Wilson, Beth P(ierre) *8*
Wilson, Budge 1927- *55*
    Brief entry *51*
Wilson, Carletta 1951- *81*
Wilson, Carter 1941- *6*
Wilson, Charles Morrow 1905-1977 .... *30*
Wilson, Christopher B. 1910(?)-1985
    Obituary *46*
Wilson, Darryl B(abe) 1939- *90*
Wilson, Diane Lee *172*
Wilson, Dirk
    See Pohl, Frederik
Wilson, Dorothy Clarke 1904-2003 .... *16*
Wilson, Edward A(rthur) 1886-1970 .... *38*
Wilson, Ellen (Janet Cameron) (?)-1976 .... *9*
    Obituary *26*
Wilson, Eric (H.) 1940- *34*
    Brief entry *32*
Wilson, Erica *51*
Wilson, Forrest 1918- *27*
Wilson, Gahan 1930- *35*
    Brief entry *27*
Wilson, Gina 1943- *85*
    Brief entry *34*
    Earlier sketch in SATA *36*
Wilson, (Leslie) Granville 1912- *14*
Wilson, Hazel (Hutchins) 1898-1992 .... *3*
    Obituary *73*
Wilson, J(erry) M. 1964- *121*
Wilson, Jacqueline 1945- *199*
    Brief entry *52*
    Earlier sketches in SATA *61, 102, 153*
Wilson, John 1922- *22*
Wilson, John 1951- *182*
Wilson, John Alexander
    See Wilson, John
Wilson, Johnniece Marshall 1944- *75*
Wilson, Jonathan 1950- *181*
Wilson, Joyce M. *84*
    Earlier sketch in SATA *21*
    See also SAAS *24*
Wilson, Karma *174*
Wilson, Leslie 1952- *166*
Wilson, Linda Miller 1936- *116*
Wilson, Lionel 1924-2003 .... *33*
    Brief entry *31*
    Obituary *144*
Wilson, Marjorie
    See Wilson, Budge
Wilson, Martin 1973- *205*
Wilson, Maurice (Charles John) 1914- *46*
Wilson, Nancy Hope 1947- *138*
    Earlier sketch in SATA *81*
Wilson, Nathan D.
    See Wilson, N.D.
Wilson, N.D. 1978- *194*
Wilson, Nick
    See Ellis, Edward S.
Wilson, Phil 1948- *181*

Wilson, Ron(ald William) 1941- *38*
Wilson, Sarah 1934- *208*
  Earlier sketches in SATA *50, 142*
Wilson, Tom 1931- *33*
  Brief entry *30*
Wilson, Troy 1970- *169*
Wilson, Walt(er N.) 1939- *14*
Wilson-Max, Ken 1965- *170*
  Earlier sketch in SATA *93*
Wilton, Elizabeth 1937- *14*
Wilton, Hal
  See Pepper, Frank S.
Wilwerding, Walter Joseph 1891-1966 .... *9*
Wimmer, Mike 1961- *194*
  Earlier sketch in SATA *70*
Winborn, Marsha (Lynn) 1947- *75*
Winch, John 1944- *165*
  Earlier sketch in SATA *117*
Winchester, James H(ugh) 1917-1985 .... *30*
  Obituary *45*
Winchester, Stanley
  See Youd, Samuel
Windawi, Thura al- 1983(?)- *165*
Winders, Gertrude Hecker -1987 .... *3*
Windham, Basil
  See Wodehouse, P. G.
Windham, Kathryn T(ucker) 1918- *14*
Windham, Sophie *184*
Windling, Terri 1958- *151*
Windrow, Martin
  See Windrow, Martin Clive
Windrow, Martin C.
  See Windrow, Martin Clive
Windrow, Martin Clive 1944- *68*
Windsor, Claire
  See Hamerstrom, Frances
Windsor, Linda 1950- *124*
Windsor, Patricia 1938- *78*
  Earlier sketch in SATA *30*
  See also SAAS *19*
Wineman-Marcus, Irene 1952- *81*
Winer, Yvonne 1934- *120*
Winerip, Michael *175*
Winfield, Arthur M.
  See Stratemeyer, Edward L.
Winfield, Edna
  See Stratemeyer, Edward L.
Winfield, Julia
  See Armstrong, Jennifer
Wing, Natasha 1960- *200*
  Earlier sketch in SATA *82*
Wingerter, Linda S. 1973(?)- *207*
Winget, Susan *211*
Winick, Judd 1970- *124*
Winks, Robin William 1930-2003 .... *61*
Winn, Alison
  See Wharmby, Margot
Winn, Chris 1952- *42*
Winn, Janet Bruce 1928- *43*
Winn, Marie 1936(?)- *38*
Winnick, Karen B. 1946- *211*
Winnick, Karen B(eth) B(inkoff) 1946- *51*
Winn-Lederer, Ilene *198*
Winslow, Barbara 1947- *91*
Winstead, Rosie *180*
Winston, Clara 1921-1983 .... *54*
  Obituary *39*
Winston, Richard 1917-1979 .... *54*
Winston, Sherri 1964(?)- *201*
Winter, Janet 1926- *126*
Winter, Jeanette 1939- *184*
  Earlier sketch in SATA *151*
Winter, Jonah 1962- *179*
Winter, Milo (Kendall) 1888-1956 .... *21*
Winter, Paula Cecelia 1929- *48*
Winter, R. R.
  See Winterbotham, R(ussell) R(obert)
Winter, Susan *182*
Winterbotham, R(ussell) R(obert)
  1904-1971 .... *10*

Winterbotham, Russ
  See Winterbotham, R(ussell) R(obert)
Winterfeld, Henry 1901-1990 .... *55*
Winters, J. C.
  See Cross, Gilbert B.
Winters, Jon
  See Cross, Gilbert B.
Winters, Katherine
  See Winters, Kay
Winters, Kay 1936- *153*
  Earlier sketch in SATA *103*
Winters, Nina 1944- *62*
Winters, Paul A. 1965- *106*
Winterson, Jeanette 1959- *190*
Winterton, Gayle
  See Adams, William Taylor
Winthrop, Elizabeth 1948- *164*
  Autobiography Feature *116*
  Earlier sketches in SATA *8, 76*
  See also CLR *89*
Winton, Ian (Kenneth) 1960- *76*
Winton, Tim 1960- *98*
Wintz-Litty, Julie
  See Litty, Julie
Wirt, Ann
  See Benson, Mildred
Wirt, Mildred A.
  See Benson, Mildred
Wirtenberg, Patricia Z. 1932-2007 .... *10*
Wirtenberg, Patricia Zarrella
  See Wirtenberg, Patricia Z.
Wirth, Beverly 1938- *63*
Wirths, Claudine (Turner) G(ibson)
  1926-2000 .... *104*
  Earlier sketch in SATA *64*
Wise, Bill 1958- *191*
Wise, Lenny
  See Wise, Leonard
Wise, Leonard 1940- *167*
Wise, Leonard A.
  See Wise, Leonard
Wise, Leonard Allan
  See Wise, Leonard
Wise, William 1923- *163*
  Earlier sketch in SATA *4*
Wise, Winifred E. *2*
Wiseman, Ann (Sayre) 1926- *31*
Wiseman, B(ernard) 1922-1995 .... *4*
Wiseman, David 1916- *43*
  Brief entry *40*
Wiseman, Eva 1947- *210*
Wishinsky, Frieda 1948- *166*
  Earlier sketches in SATA *70, 112*
Wisler, G(ary) Clifton 1950- *103*
  Brief entry *46*
  Earlier sketch in SATA *58*
Wismer, Donald (Richard) 1946- *59*
Wisner, Bill
  See Wisner, William L.
Wisner, William L. 1914(?)-1983 .... *42*
Wisnewski, David 1953-2002
  See Wisniewski, David
Wisniewski, David 1953-2002 .... *95*
  Obituary *139*
  See also CLR *51*
Wister, Owen 1860-1938 .... *62*
Witham, (Phillip) Ross 1917- *37*
Withers, Carl A. 1900-1970 .... *14*
Withers, Pam 1956- *182*
Withrow, Sarah 1966- *199*
  Earlier sketch in SATA *124*
Witt, Dick 1948- *80*
Witt, Shirley Hill 1934- *17*
Wittanen, Etolin 1907- *55*
Wittels, Harriet Joan 1938- *31*
Wittig, Susan
  See Albert, Susan Wittig
Wittlinger, Ellen 1948- *189*
  Autobiography Feature *128*
  Earlier sketches in SATA *83, 122*
Wittman, Sally (Anne Christensen) 1941- .. *30*

Witty, Paul 1898-1976 .... *50*
  Obituary *30*
Wodehouse, P. G. 1881-1975 .... *22*
Wodehouse, Pelham Grenville
  See Wodehouse, P. G.
Wodge, Dreary
  See Gorey, Edward (St. John)
Woelfle, Gretchen 1945- *145*
Wohlberg, Meg 1905-1990 .... *41*
  Obituary *66*
Wohlrabe, Raymond A. 1900-1977 .... *4*
Wohnoutka, Mike *195*
Wojciechowska, Maia (Teresa) 1927-2002 . *83*
  Autobiography Feature *104*
  Obituary *134*
  Earlier sketches in SATA *1, 28*
  See also CLR *1*
  See also SAAS *1*
Wojciechowski, Susan *126*
  Earlier sketch in SATA *78*
Wojnarowski, Adrian 1970- *190*
Wojtusik, Elizabeth *208*
Wolcott, Patty 1929- *14*
Wold, Allen L. 1943- *64*
Wold, Jo Anne 1938- *30*
Woldin, Beth Weiner 1955- *34*
Wolf, Allan 1963- *192*
Wolf, Bernard 1930- *102*
  Brief entry *37*
Wolf, Erica (Van Varick) 1978- *156*
Wolf, Gita 1956- *101*
Wolf, J. M.
  See Wolf, Joan M.
Wolf, Janet 1957- *78*
Wolf, Joan M. 1966- *193*
Wolf, Sallie 1950- *205*
  Earlier sketch in SATA *80*
Wolfe, Art 1952- *76*
Wolfe, Burton H. 1932- *5*
Wolfe, Gene 1931- *165*
  Earlier sketch in SATA *118*
Wolfe, Gene Rodman
  See Wolfe, Gene
Wolfe, Gillian *199*
Wolfe, Louis 1905-1985 .... *8*
  Obituary *133*
Wolfe, Rinna (Evelyn) 1925- *38*
Wolfenden, George
  See Beardmore, George
Wolfer, Dianne 1961- *167*
  Autobiography Feature *117*
  Earlier sketch in SATA *104*
Wolff, Alexander (Nikolaus) 1957- *137*
  Earlier sketch in SATA *63*
Wolff, Ashley 1956- *203*
  Earlier sketches in SATA *50, 81, 155*
Wolff, Diane 1945- *27*
Wolff, Ferida 1946- *164*
  Earlier sketch in SATA *79*
Wolff, Jennifer Ashley
  See Wolff, Ashley
Wolff, Nancy *202*
Wolff, Robert Jay 1905-1977 .... *10*
Wolff, Sonia
  See Levitin, Sonia
Wolff, Virginia Euwer 1937- *137*
  Earlier sketch in SATA *78*
  See also CLR *62*
Wolfman, Judy 1933- *138*
Wolfson, Evelyn 1937- *62*
Wolitzer, Hilma 1930- *31*
Wolkoff, Judie (Edwards) *93*
  Brief entry *37*
Wolkstein, Diane 1942- *138*
  Earlier sketches in SATA *7, 82*
Wollheim, Donald A(llen) 1914-1990
  Obituary *69*
Wolny, P.
  See Janeczko, Paul B(ryan)
Wolters, Richard A. 1920-1993 .... *35*
Wondriska, William 1931- *6*

Wong, Jade Snow 1922-2006 .... *112*
   Obituary *175*
Wong, Janet S. 1962- *210*
   Earlier sketches in SATA *98, 148*
   See also CLR *94*
Woo, Howie 1974- *207*
Wood, Anne (Savage) 1937- *64*
Wood, Audrey *198*
   Brief entry *44*
   Earlier sketches in SATA *50, 81, 139*
   See also CLR *26*
Wood, Catherine
   See Etchison, Birdie L(ee)
Wood, David 1944- *87*
Wood, Don 1945- *50*
   Brief entry *44*
   See also CLR *26*
Wood, Douglas 1951- *180*
   Earlier sketches in SATA *81, 132*
Wood, Douglas Eric
   See Wood, Douglas
Wood, Edgar A(llardyce) 1907-1998 .... *14*
Wood, Esther
   See Brady, Esther Wood
Wood, Frances Elizabeth *34*
Wood, Frances M. 1951- *97*
Wood, Jacqueline
   See Wood, Jakki
Wood, Jakki 1957- *211*
Wood, James Playsted 1905- *1*
Wood, Jenny 1955- *88*
Wood, John Norris 1930- *85*
Wood, June Rae 1946- *120*
   Earlier sketch in SATA *79*
   See also CLR *82*
Wood, Kerry
   See Wood, Edgar A(llardyce)
Wood, Kim Marie *134*
Wood, Laura N.
   See Roper, Laura (Newbold) Wood
Wood, Linda C(arol) 1945- *59*
Wood, Marcia 1956- *80*
Wood, Marcia Mae
   See Wood, Marcia
Wood, Nancy
   See Wood, Nancy C.
Wood, Nancy C. 1936- *178*
   Earlier sketch in SATA *6*
Wood, Nuria
   See Nobisso, Josephine
Wood, Owen 1929- *64*
Wood, Phyllis Anderson 1923- *33*
   Brief entry *30*
Wood, Richard 1949- *110*
Wood, Tim(othy William Russell) 1946- *88*
Wood, Wallace 1927-1981
   Obituary *33*
Woodard, Carol 1929- *14*
Woodburn, John Henry 1914- *11*
Woodbury, David Oakes 1896-1981 .... *62*
Woodford, Peggy 1937- *25*
Woodhouse, Barbara (Blackburn)
   1910-1988 .... *63*
Woodhull, Ann Love *194*
Wooding, Chris 1977- *166*
Wooding, Sharon
   See Wooding, Sharon L(ouise)
Wooding, Sharon L(ouise) 1943- *66*
Woodman, Allen 1954- *76*
Woodrich, Mary Neville 1915- *2*
Woodruff, Elvira 1951- *211*
   Earlier sketches in SATA *70, 106, 162*
Woodruff, Joan Leslie 1953- *104*
Woodruff, Liza 1971(?)- *182*
Woodruff, Marian
   See Goudge, Eileen
Woodruff, Noah 1977- *86*
Woods, George A(llan) 1926-1988 .... *30*
   Obituary *57*

Woods, Geraldine 1948- *111*
   Brief entry *42*
   Earlier sketch in SATA *56*
Woods, Harold 1945- *56*
   Brief entry *42*
Woods, Lawrence
   See Lowndes, Robert A(ugustine) W(ard)
Woods, Margaret 1921- *2*
Woods, Nat
   See Stratemeyer, Edward L.
Woods, Titania
   See Weatherly, Lee
Woodson, Jack
   See Woodson, John Waddie Jr.
Woodson, Jacqueline 1964- *189*
   Earlier sketches in SATA *94, 139*
   See also CLR *49*
Woodson, Jacqueline Amanda
   See Woodson, Jacqueline
Woodson, John Waddie Jr. 1913- *10*
Woodtor, Dee
   See Woodtor, Delores Parmer
Woodtor, Dee Parmer 1945(?)-2002
   See Woodtor, Delores Parmer
Woodtor, Delores Parmer 1945-2002 .... *93*
Wood-Trost, Lucille
   See Trost, Lucille W(ood)
Woodward, (Landon) Cleveland
   1900-1986 .... *10*
   Obituary *48*
Woodworth, Chris 1957- *168*
Woodworth, Viki 1952- *127*
Woody, Regina Jones 1894-1983 .... *3*
Woodyadd, Charlotte
   See Hough, Charlotte
Woog, Adam 1953- *125*
   Earlier sketch in SATA *84*
Wooldridge, Connie Nordhielm 1950- *143*
   Earlier sketch in SATA *92*
Wooldridge, Frosty 1947- *140*
Wooldridge, Rhoda 1906-1988 .... *22*
Wooley, Susan Frelick 1945- *113*
Woolf, Paula 1950- *104*
Woolfe, Angela 1976- *169*
Woolley, Catherine 1904-2005 .... *3*
   Obituary *166*
Woolman, Steven 1969-2004 .... *163*
   Earlier sketch in SATA *90*
Woolsey, Janette 1904-1989 .... *3*
   Obituary *131*
Worcester, Donald E(mmet) 1915- *18*
Word, Reagan 1944- *103*
Work, Virginia 1946- *57*
   Brief entry *45*
Worline, Bonnie Bess 1914- *14*
Wormell, Christopher 1955- *154*
   Earlier sketch in SATA *103*
Wormell, Mary 1959- *96*
Wormser, Richard 1933- *106*
   Autobiography Feature *118*
   See also SAAS *26*
Wormser, Sophie 1897-1979 .... *22*
Worth, Richard 1945- *59*
   Brief entry *46*
Worth, Valerie 1933-1994 .... *81*
   Earlier sketches in SATA *8, 70*
   See also CLR *21*
Worthington, Leonie 1956- *200*
Wortis, Avi
   See Avi
Wortis, Edward Irving
   See Avi
Wosmek, Frances 1917- *29*
Woychuk, Denis 1953- *71*
Wrede, Patricia C(ollins) 1953- *146*
   Earlier sketch in SATA *67*
Wriggins, Sally Hovey 1922- *17*
Wright, Alexandra 1979- *103*
Wright, Betty Ren 1927- *109*
   Brief entry *48*
   Earlier sketch in SATA *63*

Wright, Cliff 1963- *168*
   Earlier sketch in SATA *76*
Wright, Courtni
   See Wright, Courtni C(rump)
Wright, Courtni C(rump) 1950- *84*
Wright, Courtni Crump
   See Wright, Courtni C(rump)
Wright, Dare 1914(?)-2001 .... *21*
   Obituary *124*
Wright, David K. 1943- *112*
   Earlier sketch in SATA *73*
Wright, Elinor
   See Lyon, Elinor
Wright, Enid Meadowcroft (LaMonte)
   1898-1966 .... *3*
Wright, Esmond 1915-2003 .... *10*
Wright, Frances Fitzpatrick 1897-1982 .... *10*
Wright, J. B.
   See Barkan, Joanne
Wright, Judith 1915-2000 .... *14*
   Obituary *121*
Wright, Judith Arundell
   See Wright, Judith
Wright, Katrina
   See Gater, Dilys
Wright, Kenneth
   See del Rey, Lester
Wright, Kit 1944- *87*
Wright, Leslie B(ailey) 1959- *91*
Wright, Michael 1954- *198*
Wright, Nancy Means *38*
Wright, R(obert) H(amilton) 1906- *6*
Wright, Rachel *134*
Wright, Susan Kimmel 1950- *97*
Wrightfrierson
   See Wright-Frierson, Virginia (Marguerite)
Wright-Frierson, Virginia (Marguerite)
   1949- *110*
   Earlier sketch in SATA *58*
Wrightson, (Alice) Patricia 1921- *112*
   Earlier sketches in SATA *8, 66*
   See also CLR *14*
   See also SAAS *4*
Wroble, Lisa A. 1963- *134*
Wrongo, I.B.
   See Katz, Alan
Wronker, Lili
   See Wronker, Lili Cassel
Wronker, Lili Cassel 1924- *10*
Wryde, Dogear
   See Gorey, Edward (St. John)
Wu, Elizabeth
   See Wu, Liz
Wu, Liz *184*
Wu, Norbert 1961- *155*
   Earlier sketch in SATA *101*
Wulf, Linda Press *205*
Wulffson, Don 1943- *155*
   Earlier sketches in SATA *32, 88*
Wulffson, Don L.
   See Wulffson, Don
Wummer, Amy 1955- *201*
Wunderli, Stephen 1958- *79*
Wunsch, Josephine (McLean) 1914- *64*
Wunsch, Marjory 1942- *82*
Wuorio, Eva-Lis 1918- *34*
   Brief entry *28*
Wurts, Janny 1953- *98*
Wyatt, B. D.
   See Robinson, Spider
Wyatt, David 1968- *185*
Wyatt, Jane
   See Bradbury, Bianca (Ryley)
Wyatt, Melissa 1963- *177*
Wyatt, Valerie *209*
Wyeth, Betsy James 1921- *41*
Wyeth, N(ewell) C(onvers) 1882-1945 .... *17*
   See also CLR *106*
Wyler, Rose 1909-2000 .... *18*
   Obituary *121*
Wylie, Betty Jane *48*

Wylie, Laura
 See Matthews, Patricia
Wylie, Laurie
 See Matthews, Patricia
Wyllie, Stephen 86
Wyman, Andrea 75
Wyman, Carolyn 1956- 83
Wymer, Norman (George) 1911- 25
Wynard, Talbot
 See Hamilton, Charles (Harold St. John)
Wyndham, John
 See Harris, John (Wyndham Parkes Lucas)
 Beynon
Wyndham, Lee
 See Hyndman, Jane Andrews Lee
Wyndham, Robert
 See Hyndman, Robert Utley
Wynne, Patricia J. 210
Wynne-Jones, Tim 1948- 186
 Autobiography Feature 136
 Earlier sketches in SATA *67, 96, 136*
 See also CLR *58*
Wynne-Jones, Timothy
 See Wynne-Jones, Tim
Wynter, Edward (John) 1914- 14
Wynyard, Talbot
 See Hamilton, Charles (Harold St. John)
Wyss, Johann David Von 1743-1818 29
 Brief entry 27
 See also CLR *92*
Wyss, Thelma Hatch 1934- 202
 Earlier sketches in SATA *10, 140*

X

Xavier, Father
 See Hurwood, Bernhardt J.
Xuan, YongSheng 1952- 116
 Autobiography Feature 119

Y

Yaccarino, Dan 192
 Earlier sketch in SATA *141*
Yadin, (Rav-Aloof) Yigael 1917-1984 55
Yaffe, Alan
 See Yorinks, Arthur
Yagher, Kevin 1962- 143
Yakovetic, (Joseph Sandy) 1952- 59
Yakovetic, Joe
 See Yakovetic, (Joseph Sandy)
Yamada, Utako 1963- 188
Yamaguchi, Marianne (Illenberger) 1936- 7
Yamaka, Sara 1978- 92
Yamanaka, Lois-Ann 1961- 166
Yamasaki, Katie 206
Yancey, Diane 1951- 138
 Earlier sketch in SATA *81*
Yancey, Richard 193
Yancey, Rick
 See Yancey, Richard
Yang, Belle 1960- 170
Yang, James 1960- 190
Yang, Jay 1941- 12
Yang, Mingyi 1943- 72
Yarbrough, Camille 1938- 79
 See also CLR *29*
Yarbrough, Ira 1910(?)-1983
 Obituary 35
Yaroslava
 See Mills, Yaroslava Surmach
Yarrow, Peter 1938- 195
Yashima, Taro
 See Iwamatsu, Jun Atsushi
Yates, Elizabeth 1905-2001 68
 Obituary 128
 Earlier sketch in SATA *4*
 See also SAAS *6*

Yates, Janelle K(aye) 1957- 77
Yates, John 1939- 74
Yates, Kelly 1971- 208
Yates, Philip 1958- 149
 Earlier sketch in SATA *92*
Yates, Raymond F(rancis) 1895-1966 31
Yaukey, Grace S(ydenstricker) 1899-1994 .. 80
 Earlier sketch in SATA *5*
Yazzie, Johnson 1946- 205
Ye, Ting-xing 1952- 106
Yeahpau, Thomas M. 1975- 187
Yeakley, Marjory Hall 1908- 21
Yeatman, Linda 1938- 42
Yee, Brenda Shannon 133
Yee, Lisa 1959- 160
Yee, Paul 1956- 211
 Earlier sketches in SATA *67, 96, 143*
 See also CLR *44*
Yee, Tammy 206
Yee, Wong Herbert 1953- 172
 Earlier sketches in SATA *78, 115*
Yeh, Chun-Chan 1914- 79
Ye Junjian
 See Yeh, Chun-Chan
Yelchin, Eugene 1956- 196
Yenawine, Philip 1942- 85
Yensid, Retlaw
 See Disney, Walt(er Elias)
Yeo, Wilma (Lethem) 1918-1994 81
 Earlier sketch in SATA *24*
Yeoman, John 1934- 80
 Earlier sketch in SATA *28*
 See also CLR *46*
Yep, Kathleen S. 203
Yep, Laurence 1948- 176
 Earlier sketches in SATA *7, 69, 123*
 See also CLR *132*
Yep, Laurence Michael
 See Yep, Laurence
Yepsen, Roger B(ennet), Jr. 1947- 59
Yerian, Cameron John 21
Yerian, Margaret A. 21
Yerxa, Leo 1947- 181
Yetska
 See Ironside, Jetske
Yezerski, Thomas F. 1969- 190
Yin 194
Ylvisaker, Anne 1965(?)- 172
Yoder, Carolyn P. 1953- 149
Yoder, Carolyn Patricia
 See Yoder, Carolyn P.
Yoder, Dorothy Meenen 1921- 96
Yoder, Dot
 See Yoder, Dorothy Meenen
Yoder, Walter D. 1933- 88
Yolen, Jane 1939- 194
 Autobiography Feature 111
 Earlier sketches in SATA *4, 40, 75, 112, 158*
 See also CLR *149*
 See also SAAS *1*
Yolen, Jane Hyatt
 See Yolen, Jane
Yonezu, Yusuke 196
Yonge, Charlotte 1823-1901 17
Yonge, Charlotte Mary
 See Yonge, Charlotte
Yoo, Paula 1969(?)- 174
Yoo, Taeeun 191
Yoon, Salina 1972- 204
Yorinks, Adrienne 1956- 171
Yorinks, Arthur 1953- 200
 Earlier sketches in SATA *33, 49, 85, 144*
 See also CLR *20*
York, Alison
 See Nicole, Christopher (Robin)
York, Andrew
 See Nicole, Christopher (Robin)
York, Carol Beach 1928- 77
 Earlier sketch in SATA *6*

York, Rebecca
 See Buckholtz, Eileen (Garber)
 and Glick, Ruth (Burtnick)
York, Simon
 See Heinlein, Robert A.
Yoshida, Toshi 1911- 77
Yoshikawa, Sachiko 181
Yost, Edna 1889-1971
 Obituary 26
Youd, C. S.
 See Youd, Samuel
Youd, Samuel 1922- 135
 Brief entry 30
 Earlier sketch in SATA *47*
 See also CLR *2*
 See also SAAS *6*
Youme
 See Landowne, Youme
Young, Amy L. 185
Young, Anne Mortimer
 See Mortimer, Anne
Young, Bob
 See Young, Robert W(illiam)
 and Young, James Robert
Young, Carol 1945- 102
Young, Catherine
 See Olds, Helen Diehl
Young, Clarence
 See Garis, Howard R.
 and Stratemeyer, Edward L.
Young, Collier
 See Bloch, Robert (Albert)
Young, Dan 1952- 126
Young, Dianne 1959- 88
Young, Dorothea Bennett 1924- 31
Young, Ed 1931- 211
 Earlier sketches in SATA *10, 74, 122, 173*
 See also CLR *27*
Young, Ed Tse-chun
 See Young, Ed
Young, Edward
 See Reinfeld, Fred
Young, Elaine L.
 See Schulte, Elaine L(ouise)
Young, James
 See Graham, Ian
Young, Jan
 See Young, Janet Randall
Young, Janet 1957- 188
Young, Janet Randall 1919-1994 3
Young, Janet Ruth
 See Young, Janet
Young, Jeff C. 1948- 132
Young, John
 See Macintosh, Brownie
Young, Judy 1956- 207
 Earlier sketch in SATA *155*
Young, Judy (Elaine) Dockrey 1949- 72
Young, Karen Romano 1959- 168
 Earlier sketch in SATA *116*
Young, Ken 1956- 86
Young, Lois Horton 1911-1981 26
Young, Louisa 161
Young, Louise B. 1919- 64
Young, Margaret B. 1922-2009 2
Young, Margaret Buckner
 See Young, Margaret B.
Young, Mary 1940- 89
Young, Miriam 1913-1974 7
Young, Noela 1930- 89
Young, (Rodney Lee) Patrick (Jr.) 1937- 22
Young, Percy M(arshall) 1912-2004 31
 Obituary 154
Young, Richard Alan 1946- 72
Young, Robert W(illiam) 1916-1969 3
Young, Ross B. 1955- 150
Young, Ruth 1946- 67
Young, Sara
 See Pennypacker, Sara
Young, Scott A. 1918-2005 5

Young, Scott Alexander
  See Young, Scott A.
Young, Selina 1971-2006 .... *201*
Young, Vivien
  See Gater, Dilys
Younger, Barbara 1954- *108*
Youngs, Betty 1934-1985 .... *53*
  Obituary *42*
Younkin, Paula 1942- *77*
Yount, Lisa (Ann) 1944- *124*
  Earlier sketch in SATA *74*
Yourgrau, Barry *179*
Yuditskaya, Tatyana 1964- *75*
Yum, Hyewon *211*
Yumoto, Kazumi 1959- *153*

Z

Zach, Cheryl (Byrd) 1947- *98*
  Brief entry *51*
  Earlier sketch in SATA *58*
  See also SAAS *24*
Zacharias, Gary L. 1946- *153*
Zaffo, George J. (?)-1984 .... *42*
Zagarenski, Pamela 1969(?)- *183*
Zagwyn, Deborah Turney 1953- *138*
  Earlier sketch in SATA *78*
Zahares, Wade *193*
Zahn, Timothy 1951- *156*
  Earlier sketch in SATA *91*
Zaid, Barry 1938- *51*
Zaidenberg, Arthur 1908(?)-1990 .... *34*
  Obituary *66*
Zalben, Jane Breskin 1950- *170*
  Earlier sketches in SATA *7, 79, 120*
  See also CLR *84*
Zallinger, Jean (Day) 1918- *115*
  Earlier sketches in SATA *14, 80*
Zallinger, Peter Franz 1943- *49*
Zambreno, Mary Frances 1954- *140*
  Earlier sketch in SATA *75*
Zanderbergen, George
  See May, Julian
Zappa, Ahmet 1974- *180*
Zappa, Ahmet Emuukha Rodan
  See Zappa, Ahmet
Zappler, Lisbeth 1930- *10*
Zarchy, Harry 1912-1987 .... *34*
Zarin, Cynthia 1959- *192*
  Earlier sketch in SATA *108*
Zaring, Jane (Thomas) 1936- *40*
Zarins, Joyce Audy
  See dos Santos, Joyce Audy
Zaslavsky, Claudia 1917- *36*
Zaugg, Sandra L. 1938- *118*
Zaugg, Sandy
  See Zaugg, Sandra L.
Zaunders, Bo 1939- *137*
Zawadzki, Marek 1958- *97*
Zebra, A.
  See Scoltock, Jack
Zebrowski, George 1945- *67*
Zebrowski, George T.
  See Zebrowski, George
Zecca, Katherine *207*
Zeck, Gerald Anthony 1939- *40*
Zeck, Gerry
  See Zeck, Gerald Anthony
Zed, Dr.
  See Penrose, Gordon

Zei, Alki 1925- *24*
  See also CLR *6*
Zeier, Joan T(heresa) 1931- *81*
Zeinert, Karen 1942-2002 .... *137*
  Earlier sketch in SATA *79*
Zeises, Lara M. 1976- *184*
  Earlier sketch in SATA *145*
Zelazny, Roger 1937-1995 .... *57*
  Brief entry *39*
Zelazny, Roger Joseph
  See Zelazny, Roger
Zeldis, Malcah 1931- *146*
  Earlier sketch in SATA *86*
Zelinsky, Paul O. 1953- *154*
  Brief entry *33*
  Earlier sketches in SATA *49, 102*
  See also CLR *55*
Zellan, Audrey Penn
  See Penn, Audrey
Zemach, Harve
  See Fischtrom, Harvey
Zemach, Kaethe 1958- *149*
  Brief entry *39*
  Earlier sketch in SATA *49*
Zemach, Margot 1931-1989 .... *70*
  Obituary *59*
  Earlier sketch in SATA *21*
Zemach-Bersin, Kaethe
  See Zemach, Kaethe
Zeman, Ludmila 1947- *153*
Zepeda, Gwendolyn 1971- *206*
Zephaniah, Benjamin 1958- *189*
  Earlier sketches in SATA *86, 140*
Zephaniah, Benjamin Obadiah Iqbal
  See Zephaniah, Benjamin
Zephaniah, Benjamin Pbadiah Iqubal
  See Zephaniah, Benjamin
Zerman, Melvyn Bernard 1930- *46*
Zettner, Pat 1940- *70*
Zevin, Gabrielle *176*
Zhang, Christopher Zhong-Yuan 1954- *91*
Zhang, Song Nan 1942- *170*
  Earlier sketch in SATA *85*
Ziefert, Harriet 1941- *205*
  Earlier sketches in SATA *101, 154*
Ziegler, Jack (Denmore) 1942- *60*
Ziemienski, Dennis (Theodore) 1947- *10*
Ziliox, Marc
  See Fichter, George S.
Zillah
  See Macdonald, Zillah K(atherine)
Zim, Herbert S(pencer) 1909-1994 .... *30*
  Obituary *85*
  Earlier sketch in SATA *1*
  See also CLR *2*
  See also SAAS *2*
Zim, Sonia Bleeker 1909-1971 .... *2*
  Obituary *26*
Zima, Gordon 1920- *90*
Zimelman, Nathan 1921- *65*
  Brief entry *37*
Zimmer, Dirk 1943- *147*
  Earlier sketch in SATA *65*
Zimmer, Tracie Vaughn *169*
Zimmerman, Andrea 1950- *192*
  Earlier sketch in SATA *123*
Zimmerman, Andrea Griffing
  See Zimmerman, Andrea
Zimmerman, H. Werner 1951- *101*
Zimmerman, Heinz Werner
  See Zimmerman, H. Werner
Zimmerman, Naoma 1914-2004 .... *10*

Zimmermann, Arnold E. 1909- *58*
Zimmermann, Karl 1943- *211*
Zimmermann, Karl R.
  See Zimmermann, Karl
Zimmett, Debbie
  See Becker, Deborah Zimmett
Zimmy
  See Stratemeyer, Edward L.
Zimnik, Reiner 1930- *36*
  See also CLR *3*
Zindel, Bonnie 1943- *34*
Zindel, Lizabeth *187*
Zindel, Paul 1936-2003 .... *102*
  Obituary *142*
  Earlier sketches in SATA *16, 58*
  See also CLR *85*
Ziner, Feenie
  See Ziner, Florence
Ziner, Florence 1921- *5*
Zingara, Professor
  See Leeming, Joseph
Zinger, Yitskhok
  See Singer, Isaac Bashevis
Zion, Eugene 1913-1975 .... *18*
Zion, Gene
  See Zion, Eugene
Zoehfeld, Kathleen Weidner 1954- *193*
Zohorsky, Janet R. 1958- *148*
Zolkower, Edie Stoltz *171*
Zolkowski, Cathy (A.) 1969- *121*
Zollars, Jaime *191*
Zolotow, Charlotte 1915- *138*
  Earlier sketches in SATA *1, 35, 78*
  See also CLR *77*
Zolotow, Charlotte Gertrude Shapiro
  See Zolotow, Charlotte
Zolotow, Ellen
  See Dragonwagon, Crescent
Zonderman, Jon 1957- *92*
Zonia, Dhimitri 1921- *20*
Zonta, Pat 1951- *143*
Zubrowski, Bernard 1939- *90*
  Earlier sketch in SATA *35*
Zubrowski, Bernie
  See Zubrowski, Bernard
Zucker, Miriam S.
  See Reichert, Miriam Zucker
Zuckerman, Linda *190*
Zudeck, Darryl 1961- *61*
Zug, Mark *204*
Zupa, G. Anthony
  See Zeck, Gerald Anthony
Zupancic, Lilijana Praprotnik
  See Prap, Lila
Zurbo, Matt(hew) 1967- *98*
Zurhorst, Charles (Stewart, Jr.) 1913-1989 . *12*
Zurlo, Tony 1941- *145*
Zuromskis, Diane
  See Stanley, Diane
Zuromskis, Diane Stanley
  See Stanley, Diane
Zusak, Markus 1975- *149*
Zwahlen, Diana 1947- *88*
Zweifel, Frances W. 1931- *14*
Zwerger, Lisbeth 1954- *194*
  Earlier sketches in SATA *66, 130*
  See also CLR *46*
  See also SAAS *13*
Zwinger, Ann (H.) 1925- *46*
Zymet, Cathy Alter 1965- *121*